INTRODUCTION
TO SOCIAL
WORK AND
SOCIAL
WELFARE

INTRODUCTION

TO SOCIAL

WORK

AND SOCIAL

WELFARE

Sixth Edition

Charles Zastrow

University of Wisconsin—Whitewater

Brooks/Cole Publishing Company

I(T)P™ An International
Thomson Publishing Company

Pacific Grove • Albany • Bonn • Boston
• Cincinnati • Detroit • London • Madrid • Melbourne
• Mexico City • New York • Paris • San Francisco
• Singapore • Tokyo • Toronto • Washington

Sponsoring Editor: *Lisa Gebo*
Marketing Team: *Nancy Kernal, Margaret Parks*
Editorial Assistants: *Dorothy Kormos, Patsy Vienneau*
Production Editor: *Nancy L. Shammas*
Manuscript Editor: *Micky Lawler*
Permissions Editor: *Elaine Jones*
Interior Design: *Wendy LaChance*
Cover Design: *Laurie Albrecht, E. Kelly Shoemaker*

Cover Photo: *Ed Young*
Art Editor: *Lisa Torri*
Photo Editor: *Robert Western*
Indexer: *Do Mi Stauber*
Typesetting: *Weimer Graphics*
Cover Printing: *Color Dot Graphics, Inc.*
Printing and Binding: *R. R. Donnelley & Sons*

For more information, contact:

BROOKS/COLE PUBLISHING COMPANY
511 Forest Lodge Road
Pacific Grove, CA 93950
USA

International Thomson Editores
Campos Eliseos 385, Piso 7
Col. Polanco
11560 México D.F. México

International Thomson Publishing Europe
Berkshire House 168-173
High Holborn
London WC1V 7AA
England

International Thomson Publishing GmbH
Königswinterer Strasse 418
53227 Bonn
Germany

Thomas Nelson Australia
102 Dodds Street
South Melbourne, 3205
Victoria, Australia

International Thomson Publishing Asia
221 Henderson Road
#05-10 Henderson Building
Singapore 0315

Nelson Canada
1120 Birchmount Road
Scarborough, Ontario
Canada M1K 5G4

International Thomson Publishing Japan
Hirakawacho Kyowa Building, 3F
2-2-1 Hirakawacho
Chiyoda-ku, Tokyo 102
Japan

Printed in the United States of America

10   9   8   7   6   5   4   3   2   1

Library of Congress Cataloging-in-Publication Data

Zastrow, Charles.
    Introduction to social work and social welfare / Charles Zastrow.
— 6th ed.
        p.   cm.
    Includes bibliographical references (p.   ) and index.
    ISBN 0-534-33852-6
    1. Social service—United States.   2. Social service—Vocational
guidance—United States.   3. Public welfare—United States.
I. Title.
HV91.Z37   1996
362—dc20   95-12701
                                                  CIP

To Ginny

About the Author

CHARLES ZASTROW, MSW and PhD, is Professor in the Social Work Department, University of Wisconsin—Whitewater. He has worked as a practitioner in a variety of public and private social welfare agencies and has chaired 11 social work accreditation site visit teams for the Council on Social Work Education. He is a member of the National Association of Social Workers, the Council on Social Work Education, and NASW Register of Clinical Social Workers. In addition to *Introduction to Social Work and Social Welfare,* Dr. Zastrow has written four other textbooks: *The Practice of Social Work, Social Work with Groups, Social Problems,* and *Understanding Human Behavior and the Social Environment* (with Dr. Karen Kirst-Ashman).

Contributing Authors

DON NOLAN
Social Worker
Jefferson County Public School System
Wisconsin

LLOYD G. SINCLAIR
Psychotherapist
Midwest Center for Psychotherapy and Sex
    Therapy
Madison, Wisconsin

CONTENTS

PART III   SOCIAL WORK PRACTICE   577

PREFACE

This book is designed to stimulate student interest in social work and to provide an experiential "flavor" of what the fields of social welfare and social work are really like. Using a social problems approach, the book describes how people are affected by poverty, child abuse, emotional difficulties, sexism, alcoholism, crime, AIDS, physical and mental disabilities, racism, overpopulation, sexual dysfunctions, and other problems. Information on the nature, extent, and causes of such problems is also presented. In teaching introductory courses in social work, a number of my colleagues and I have found that students tend to be more interested when they come face-to-face with the tragic social conditions that people experience. This book also includes case examples through which the reader is able to identify with people in need of help.

Knowledge about social problems prepares and motivates the student to read the sections of the text that cover current services, merits and shortcomings of those services, and new programs that are needed to fill service gaps.

In addition, *Introduction to Social Work and Social Welfare* is designed to:

■ Provoke the reader's thinking about some of the controversial, contemporary issues in social welfare. I believe developing the student's reasoning capacities is much more important than teaching unimportant facts to be recited on exams.

■ Convey material on counseling techniques and on the analysis of policy issues that the reader can use in working with people and in arriving at policy decisions.

■ Provide case examples of the functions, roles, responsibilities, gratifications, and frustrations of social workers that will help the student who is considering a social work major to make an informed career decision.

■ Provide a brief historical review of the development of social welfare, social work, and various social services.

■ Help the reader "sort out" his or her value structure in relation to welfare recipients, single parents, ex-convicts, the mentally ill, the divorced, persons with AIDS, abusive parents, minority groups, those who are prejudiced, and so on. The aim is not to sell any particular set of values but to help the reader arrive at a value system that she or he will be comfortable with and find functional in interacting with others.

Plan of the Book

Part I introduces the student to the fields of social welfare, social work, and human services. These terms are defined, and their relationships to sociology, psychology, and other disciplines are described. A brief history of social welfare and social work is provided, and the future is examined. A discussion of social work as a career and as a profession is included, and this gives the reader a basis for deciding whether to pursue a career in social work.

Part II focuses on the most common social problems served by the field of social welfare. This part constitutes the main emphasis of the text and describes:

- Contemporary social problems in our society.
- Current social services for meeting these problems.
- Gaps in current services.
- Controversial issues in each service area.
- Proposed new programs to meet current gaps in services.

Numerous case examples provide the reader with a "feeling" awareness of how the problems affect people and convey what it is really like to be a social worker.

Part III focuses on generalist social work practice with systems of all sizes, including individuals, groups, families, organizations, and communities. This part presents a conceptualization of generalist social work practice and summarizes the change process in social work practice. The knowledge, skills, and values needed for effective social work practice are summarized.

This sixth edition updates information in all of the chapters. Several chapters have been extensively revised in accordance with suggestions from a number of faculty members who reviewed and commented on the fifth edition. New topics include health care reform, recent welfare reform proposals, illegal immigration issues, physician-assisted suicide, DSM-IV categories of mental illness, feminist perspectives on therapy, codependency, crack babies, anabolic steroids, recent research on sexual orientation, and types of sexual harassment.

The Council on Social Work Education (CSWE) is the national organization that accredits baccalaureate and master's-degree programs in social work education in the United States. In 1992 CSWE adopted revisions in its Curriculum Policy Statements for undergraduate and graduate programs. A major thrust of this edition of *Introduction to Social Work and Social Welfare* is to present material that is consistent with the revisions of these policy statements. Material has been added in this sixth edition on social work values and ethics, diversity, promotion of social and economic justice, populations at risk, social work practice with organizations, the change process in social work, and feminist perspectives on intervention.

The book is intended for use in introductory social work and social welfare courses. It introduces prospective social work majors to the field of social welfare and will help them arrive at career decisions and prepare for future social work courses. For nonmajors, the book provides information about current social problems and social services; the text also gives a framework for analyzing policy issues and for making citizenship decisions.

Acknowledgments

I wish to express my deep appreciation to the various people who made this book possible. Special thanks to the contributing authors, to the artist (Don Baumgart) for the line drawings, and to the photo researcher, Bob Western. I would like to thank the following colleagues who provided comments on the manuscript for this edition:

Mich Barbezat, Elgin Community College; Gloria Carpenter, University of Texas; Bruce Friedman, Wayne State University; Mary Hart, University of Wyoming; Ken Herrmann, State University of New York at Brockport; Janine Mariscotti, LaSalle University; Ann Boydston Park, Cabrini College; William Roberts; David Storm, Central Missouri State University; and Carolyn Tice, Ohio University at Athens. A sincere thank you to Linda Brown, Ralph Navarre, Nancy Sienko, Mace J. Delorme, and Vicki Vogel, who were "alter egos" for conceptualizing various chapters and helped in a number of ways with the writing of this text.

Charles Zastrow

INTRODUCTION: SOCIAL WELFARE AND SOCIAL WORK

1

SOCIAL
WELFARE:
ITS BUSINESS,
HISTORY,
AND FUTURE

In our industrialized, complex, and rapidly changing society, social welfare activities have become important functions in terms of the money spent, the human misery treated, and the number of people served.[1] This chapter will:

- Define social welfare and describe its goals.
- Describe the relationship between social welfare and the following disciplines: sociology, social work, and human services.
- Provide a history of social welfare.
- Describe how the future of social welfare will be affected by technological advances.
- Illustrate that the future of social welfare will also be partially affected by changes in the American family system. A summary of many of the changes that are occurring in the American family is provided.

GOAL OF SOCIAL WELFARE

The goal of social welfare is to fulfill the social, financial, health, and recreational requirements of all individuals in a society. Social welfare seeks to enhance the social functioning of all age groups, both rich and poor. When other institutions in our society, such as the market economy and the family, fail at times to meet the basic needs of individuals or groups of people, then social services are needed and demanded.

In more primitive societies, people's basic needs have been fulfilled in more direct and informal ways. Even in this country, less than 150 years ago most Americans lived on farms or in small towns, with extended families and relatives close by. If financial or other needs arose, relatives, the church, and neighbors were there to "lend a helping hand." Problems were visible and personal; everyone knew everyone else in the community. When a need arose, it was taken for granted that those with resources would do whatever they could to alleviate the difficulty. If, for example, the need was financial, personal acquaintance with the storekeeper or banker usu-

ally was sufficient to obtain needed goods or money.

Clearly, we are now living in a different era. Our technology, economic base, social patterns, and living styles have changed dramatically. Our commercial, industrial, political, educational, and religious institutions are considerably larger and more impersonal. We tend to live in large urban communities, away from families or relatives—frequently without even establishing acquaintances with neighbors. We have become much more mobile, often having few roots and limited knowledge of the community in which we live. Vocationally, we have specialized and become more interdependent on others, and as a result we have diminishing control over large aspects of our lives. Our rapidly changing society is a breeding ground for exacerbating former social ills and creating new problems, such as the expanding number of homeless people, higher crime rates, recurring energy crises, terrorism, and the destruction of our environment. Obviously, the old rural-frontier methods of meeting social welfare needs are no longer viable.

It is the business of social welfare:

- To find homes for parentless children.
- To rehabilitate people who are addicted to alcohol or drugs.
- To treat those with emotional difficulties.
- To make life more meaningful for the elderly.
- To provide vocational rehabilitation services to persons with a physical or mental disability.
- To meet the financial needs of the poor.
- To rehabilitate juveniles and adults who have committed criminal offenses.
- To end all types of discrimination and oppression.
- To provide child-care services for parents who work outside the home.
- To counteract violence in families, including child abuse and spouse abuse.
- To fulfill the health and legal exigencies of those in financial need.

One of the basic functions of social welfare is to aid those struck by natural disasters. Here a rescue worker gives water to a man trapped in the rubble of his home after a volcanic landslide swept through Armero, Colombia in 1985.

- To counsel individuals and groups experiencing a wide variety of personal and social difficulties.
- To provide services to persons with AIDS and to their families and friends.
- To provide recreational and leisure-time services to all age groups.
- To educate and provide socialization experiences to children who have a cognitive disability* or an emotional disorder.
- To serve families struck by such physical disasters as fires and tornadoes.
- To provide adequate housing for the homeless.

- To provide programs that support and enhance the normal growth and development of all children and adults.
- To provide vocational training and employment opportunities to the unskilled and unemployed.
- To meet the special needs of people of color, migrant workers, and other minority groups.

SOCIAL WELFARE AS AN INSTITUTION AND AS A DISCIPLINE

The term *social welfare* has different meanings, as it is both an *institution* and an *academic discipline*. The National Association of Social Workers

---

*The term *cognitive disability* is used in this text in lieu of *mental retardation,* which has negative connotations.

Social welfare institutions attempt to improve the well-being of individuals, families, groups, organizations, and communities. They offer a wide range of services, involving both professionals and volunteers, such as these Meals on Wheels volunteers.

(the primary professional organization for social workers) gives the following definition of social welfare as an institution.

A nation's system of programs, benefits, and services that help people meet those social, economic, educational, and health needs that are fundamental to the maintenance of society.[2]

Examples of social welfare programs and services are foster care, adoption, day care, Head Start, probation and parole, public assistance programs such as Aid to Families with Dependent Children, public health nursing, sex therapy, suicide counseling, recreational services such as Boy Scouts and YWCA programs, services to minority groups, services to veterans, school social services, medical and legal services to the poor, family planning services, Meals on Wheels, nursing-home services, shelters for battered spouses, protective services for child abuse and neglect, assertiveness-training programs, encounter groups and sensitivity training, public housing projects, family counseling, Alcoholics Anonymous, runaway services, services to persons with a developmental disability, and sheltered workshops.

Social welfare programs and social service organizations are sometimes referred to as "social welfare institutions." The purposes of social welfare institutions are to prevent, alleviate, or contribute to the solution of recognized social problems in order to directly improve the well-being of individuals, groups, families, organizations, and communities. Social welfare institutions are established by policies and laws, with the programs and services being provided by voluntary (private) and governmental (public) agencies.

The term *social welfare institution* is applied to various levels of complexity and abstraction. It may be applied to a single program or organization—for example, foster care or Planned Parenthood. Or, the term may be applied to a group of services or programs. For example, child welfare services is a social welfare institution that includes such services as adoption, foster care, juvenile probation, protective services, runaway services, day care, school social services, and residential treatment. The highest aggregate level to which the term *social welfare institution* is applied includes *all* of the social programs and organizations in a country that are designed to prevent, alleviate, or contribute to the solution of recognized social problems.

Another meaning of social welfare derives from its role as an academic discipline. In this context social welfare is "the study of agencies, programs, personnel, and policies which focus on the delivery of social services to individuals, groups, and communities."[3] One of the functions of the social welfare discipline is to educate and train social workers. (Some colleges and universities call their professional preparation programs for social work practice "social work," and others call their programs "social welfare.")

SOCIAL WELFARE'S RELATIONSHIP TO SOCIOLOGY AND TO OTHER ACADEMIC DISCIPLINES

Social welfare has often been confused with "sociology," "social work," and "human services." In addition, many people are confused about how social welfare and social work relate to psychology, psychiatry, and other related disciplines. The next few sections will seek to clarify the relationships between social welfare and these other disciplines.

Several academic disciplines seek to obtain knowledge about social problems, their causes, and their alleviation. The most common disciplines are social welfare, sociology, psychology, political science, economics, psychiatry, and cultural anthropology. Figure 1.1 shows the relationship of these disciplines to social welfare.

Each of these disciplines has a distinct focus. The following definitions highlight the similarities and differences among these disciplines.

Sociology: The study of human social behavior, especially the study of the origins, organizations, institutions, and development of human society.

Psychology: The study of mental processes and behavior.

Psychiatry: The study of the diagnosis, treatment, and prevention of mental illness.

Political science: The study of the processes, principles, and structure of government and of political institutions.

Economics: The study of the production, distribution, and consumption of commodities.

FIGURE 1.1

Overlap of Knowledge Base of Social Welfare with Other Disciplines

Cultural anthropology: The study of human culture based on archeological, ethnographic, linguistic, social, and psychological data and methods of analysis.[4]

Theories and research in these disciplines may or may not, depending on the nature of the content, be considered part of the knowledge base of social welfare. When the theories and research have direct application to the social welfare goal of enhancing the social functioning of people, such knowledge can also be considered to be part of the knowledge base of social welfare. In the past, social welfare has been more of an applied science than a pure science; that is, it has formed its knowledge base primarily from the theories and research of other disciplines and has focused on applying such knowledge through social programs. In recent years the academic discipline

**CASE
EXAMPLE 1.1   What It's All About**

S hortly after their marriage in the fall of 1962, Frank Lund, age 24, and his wife, Jean, age 22, moved from their rural farm area in northern Wisconsin to a large midwestern city. They had bright hopes for their future. Frank obtained a well-paying job on the assembly line of an auto manufacturing company. Jean worked part-time as a file clerk until her first pregnancy in the spring of 1964. In the next four years they had three children and also purchased a three-bedroom home in a suburb. Then, in 1969, while on a hunting trip, Frank was accidentally killed. Ms. Lund was never quite the same. She suffered periodic bouts of depression and had considerable difficulty in finding the energy to care for her three young children.

By 1970 the Lunds' financial resources were depleted. Unable to make the payments on the house, they were forced to move to a rundown two-bedroom apartment closer to the center of the city. In the winter of 1970, Ms. Lund applied for financial assistance under the Aid to Families with Dependent Children program. The state in which the Lunds lived had negative attitudes toward welfare, and consequently the monthly payments the Lunds received were barely sufficient to meet their basic needs. In addition, the neighbors never attempted to understand the Lunds' plight. They were more concerned about their tax dollars being spent for "such people." Ms. Lund felt she was a second-class citizen, stigmatized because she was a "welfare" case. She also soon became aware that some of her neighbors would not permit their children to play with hers. When her children entered school, they began to feel different from other youngsters; they were poorly dressed, the lunches they brought from home usually consisted of cheese sandwiches, and they had no father. A few years later Ms. Lund dated a salesman for a while; being lonely, she permitted him to stay over some evenings at the apartment. The neighbors frowned upon this behavior and made moral accusations. Several months later Ms. Lund ended the relationship, after she realized she would be unable to change the man's drinking problem. (When intoxicated, he was sometimes abusive to Ms. Lund and the children.)

When the oldest child, Tom, was 15, he was arrested for starting three fires in the neighborhood. Perhaps he just wanted attention, or maybe it was his way of demonstrating that he needed help. Anyway, he was judged to have emotional difficulties and was sent to a residential treatment center. At the age of 20 he was released. He applied for several semiskilled jobs, but, partly because of potential employers' concerns about his past, someone else was always hired. He therefore obtained a series of odd jobs as a maintenance man, dishwasher, store clerk, and so forth. Not finding more stimulating work, he began drinking, sometimes to excess. At 25 he married and within the next few years fathered four children. Because of his family responsibilities, low-paying job, and drinking problem, he and his family are now locked into poverty.

The second child, Corine, wanted to escape from her home and from school when she became a teenager. She ran away several times but was always returned by the police. At 16 she became involved with Mike, a high school dropout, and became pregnant. Mike's parents would not give their consent to a marriage. Corine dropped out of school, delivered the baby, and decided to keep it. For the next six years she continued to live with her mother, even though there were frequent arguments. At 22 she met and within a year married Bill Loomans, a seasonal construction worker and a widower with three children. Already Bill and Corine were close to being locked into poverty for the rest of their lives due to their large family and limited incomes. The two additional children they had after marriage did not help.

Ms. Lund's youngest child, Dave, was also a problem for her. In the early years of school he had considerable difficulty learning to read. He soon fell behind the rest of his classmates. By the fourth grade he felt self-conscious about being unable to read. In class he no longer would put forth much effort to do academic work and instead spent most of his time clowning around. Psychological testing indicated Dave had average mental ability and suggested he had developed an "emotional block" to academic work that appeared to be related to his home environment. On entering the fifth grade, he was placed in a special class for children with cognitive disabilities. Dave was very sensitive about this and became involved in several fights when referred to as a "dummy" by his peers. At age 16 he dropped out of school and was fortunate to obtain a job pumping gas. Two years later he was "forced" to marry Terri Fernandez after she became pregnant. Terri and Dave had a stormy marriage, with frequent disputes. Within a year and a half they had two children. Six months later they separated, and Dave was ordered by the court to pay child support until the children were 18. Two years later, on being named as the father of another child borne by a different woman, Dave was ordered to make monthly support payments for this child as well. He tried to meet these responsibilities, but his income would not stretch; he therefore wrote some checks that "bounced." Recently he was arrested and placed on probation for two years. He now appears to be solidly locked into poverty for the remainder of his life. His chances of securing a better-paying job are slight because of his past, his lack of training for a skilled job, his inability to read, and his financial obligations.

The story of the Lund family raises a number of questions for social welfare. Who is to "blame" for the difficulties of this family—or is no one at fault? Are this cycle of poverty (which has been transmitted from one generation to the next) and the social difficulties associated with it likely to be continued among the grandchildren of Frank and Jean Lund? What should be done now to help the members of the Lund family? Who should pay for the help provided? What kind of help (both services and money), if provided to Jean Lund when her husband was accidentally killed, would probably have prevented the social difficulties experienced by her children and likely to be faced by her grandchildren?

of social welfare (called social work at many campuses) has been active in research projects and in theory development. This increased research and theory development activity is an indication that social welfare is a discipline that is maturing, as it is now developing much of its own knowledge base.

A few examples may be useful in illustrating how the knowledge base of other disciplines overlaps with social welfare. Sociological research on and conceptualization of the causes of social problems (for example, juvenile delinquency, mental illness, poverty, and racial discrimination) may be considered part of the knowledge base of social welfare. Only through an understanding of such problems can social welfare effectively prevent and control such problems. Sociological studies on the effects of institutions (for example, mental hospitals and prisons) on individuals are currently of considerable interest to and have important application in social welfare. Sociological investigations of other subjects, such as mobility, urbanization, secularization, formation of groups, race relations, prejudice, and the process of acculturation, have also become part of social welfare's knowledge base because such investigations are directly applicable to enhancing people's social well-being. However, research in other sociological areas, such as studies of social organizations among primitive tribes, is usually considered outside the knowledge base of social welfare because such research usually does not have direct applications to the goal of social welfare.

Comparable overlap occurs between social welfare and the other previously mentioned disciplines. Using psychology as an example, studies and theory development in such areas as personality growth and therapeutic techniques can be considered part of the knowledge base of social welfare because they have direct social welfare applications. On the other hand, experimental investigations of, for example, the perceptions and thinking processes of animals do not, at least at the present time, have such applications and would not therefore be considered part of the social welfare knowledge base.

SOCIAL WELFARE'S RELATIONSHIP TO SOCIAL WORK

The institutional definition (previously given) of social welfare is applicable when the relationship between social welfare and social work is examined. *Social welfare* is a more comprehensive term than *social work*; social welfare encompasses social work. Social welfare and social work are primarily related at the level of practice. *Social work* has been defined by the National Association of Social Workers as follows:

> *Social work is the professional activity of helping individuals, groups, or communities to enhance or restore their capacity for social functioning and to create societal conditions favorable to their goals.*
>
> *Social work practice consists of the professional application of social work values, principles, and techniques to one or more of the following ends: helping people obtain tangible services; providing counseling and psychotherapy for individuals, families, and groups; helping communities or groups provide or improve social and health services; and participating in relevant legislative processes.*
>
> *The practice of social work requires knowledge of human development and behavior; of social, economic, and cultural institutions; and of the interaction of all these factors.*[5]

The term *social worker* has been defined by the National Association of Social Workers as follows:

> *Graduates of schools of social work (with either bachelor's or master's degrees), who use their knowledge and skills to provide social services for clients (who may be individuals, families, groups, communities, organizations, or society in general). Social workers help people increase their capacities for problem solving and coping and help them obtain needed resources, facilitate interactions between individuals and between people and their environments, make organizations responsible to people, and influence social policies.*[6]

FIGURE 1.2

Examples of Professional Groups within the Field of Social Welfare

Almost all social workers are working in the field of social welfare. There are, however, many other professional and occupational groups that may be working in the field of social welfare, as illustrated in Figure 1.2. Professional people providing social welfare services include attorneys who offer legal services to the poor; urban planners in social-planning agencies; physicians in public health agencies; teachers in residential treatment facilities for the emotionally disturbed; psychologists, nurses, and recreational therapists in mental hospitals; and psychiatrists in mental health clinics.

SOCIAL WELFARE'S RELATIONSHIP TO OTHER INSTITUTIONS

Social welfare overlaps with such institutions as the family, education, religion, and politics. One of the functions of the family is raising and caring for children. Social welfare assists families by providing such services as counseling, day care, foster care, and adoption. Certain educational courses have both educational and social welfare aspects; for example, social science and physical education courses provide socialization experiences and are important in the social development of youth. Structured religion has long been interested in people's social well-being and has provided such social welfare services as counseling, financial assistance, day care, and recreation. The overlap between politics and social welfare primarily involves the political processes that occur in regard to the funding of social service programs. Some social welfare programs (for example, public assistance) are controversial political topics. Securing the necessary funding for essential social welfare programs is a crucial component of the social welfare system in any country.

SOCIAL WELFARE'S RELATIONSHIP TO HUMAN SERVICES

Human services may be defined as those systems of services and allied occupations and professions that concentrate on improving or maintaining the physical and mental health and general well-being of individuals, groups, or communities in our society. Alfred Kahn has conceptualized human services as being composed of the following four service categories:[7]

1. Personal services (casework, counseling, recreation, rehabilitation, religion, therapy).
2. Protection services (consumer protection, corrections, courts, fire prevention/firefighting, housing-code enforcement, law enforcement, public health services).
3. Information/advising services (consulting, consumer information, education, financial counseling, hotlines, and library services).

Blaming the Victim

J erry Jorgenson and Joyce Mantha decided to get married after dating for three years. Both looked forward to a big wedding and a happy future. They had met in college, and now both were working in Mayville, a small town that Jerry had grown up in. Joyce was a kindergarten teacher, and Jerry was manager of an A&P grocery store. Against Jerry's wishes, Joyce drove one weekend to a nearby city to attend a bridal shower with some of her women college friends. The party was still going strong at 2:00 A.M., when Joyce thought it was time to go back to her motel in order to return to Mayville early on Sunday. In the parking lot Joyce was sexually assaulted. She tried to fight off the assailant and suffered a number of bruises and abrasions. After the assault, a passerby called the police and an ambulance. Joyce called Jerry the next day. At first he was angry at the rapist. But the more he thought about it, the more he assigned blame to Joyce: She went to the party against his wishes, and she had probably dressed and acted in such a way as to interest the rapist (especially since Jerry further assumed that she had been intoxicated).

The weeks that followed became increasingly difficult for Jerry and Joyce. Joyce sensed that Jerry was blaming her for being raped. She tried to talk it out with Jerry, but it did not help. Their sexual relationship became practically nil, as Jerry felt his "sexual rights" had been violated, and the few times he made sexual advances he had images of Joyce being attacked by a stranger. They postponed the marriage.

When they first heard about the rape, many townspeople also thought that Joyce had "asked for it" while partying in the big city. Postponement of the marriage was interpreted by the townspeople as evidence for this belief, and they began shunning Joyce. After several months of such treatment, Joyce began to believe that she was at fault and increasingly blamed herself for her predicament. She became despondent and moved back with her parents for refuge.

---

4. Maintenance services (child care, unemployment assistance, institutional services, public welfare programs, retirement plans, and Social Security programs).

Kahn indicates that there is a tendency to use the term *human services* for what in the past has been called social welfare.[8] Actually, *human services* is a broader term because it includes services (such as library services, law enforcement, housing-code enforcement, consumer protection, and fire prevention and firefighting) that are usually not considered social welfare services. The term *social welfare* is thus more limited because it focuses on conceptualizing and resolving social problems. *Human services* is a broader term that encompasses social welfare programs. The two terms relate at a *program* level.

RESIDUAL VIEW VERSUS INSTITUTIONAL VIEW OF SOCIAL WELFARE

The present social welfare scene is being substantially influenced by the past. Currently, there are two conflicting views of the role of social welfare in our society.[9] One of these roles has been termed *residual*—a gap-filling or first-aid role. This view holds that social welfare services should be pro-

This story is only one illustration of the tendency in American culture to blame the victim. Others abound. If an adult is unemployed for a long time, often that person is believed to be "lazy" or "unmotivated." AFDC mothers (mothers receiving Aid to Families with Dependent Children) are erroneously stereotyped as being promiscuous, irresponsible, lazy, and desirous of having more children in order to increase their monthly grant. When a marriage breaks up, either the husband or the wife or both are blamed, rather than the relationship viewed as having deteriorated. When unfortunate circumstances occur (for example, lightning striking someone's home), some people believe it is a punishment for sinful activity. Slapping one's wife is justified by some segments of the population as being a way to "keep her in line" and to "show her who's boss." People living in poverty are often erroneously viewed as being personally inadequate, incompetent, or lazy or as having a culture that holds them in poverty. The problems of slum housing in inner cities are sometimes traced to the characteristics of "southern rural migrants" not yet "acculturated" to life in the big city. Such blaming of the victim sometimes sadly leads to acceptance by the general public of the victimization, with few efforts then being made to assist current victims or to prevent similar victimizations in the future.

But perhaps the saddest feature of victim blaming is that the erroneous explanation often becomes a self-fulfilling prophecy. If a teacher is told that a child is a poor learner, that teacher will interact with the child as if he or she were a slow learner. Unfortunately, the child will eventually come to believe the teacher is correct and learn little. Labeling people as lazy, criminal, immoral, or mentally ill strongly influences the expectations others hold for them and simultaneously influences the victims themselves in their expectations and self-definition.

vided only when an individual's needs are not properly met through other societal institutions, primarily the family and the market economy. According to the residual view, social services and financial aid should not be provided until all other measures or efforts have been exhausted, including the individual's and his or her family's resources. In addition, this view asserts that funds and services should be provided on a short-term basis (primarily during emergencies) and should be withdrawn when the individual or the family again becomes capable of being self-sufficient.

The residual view has been characterized as "charity for unfortunates."[10] Funds and services are seen not as a right (something that one is entitled to) but as a gift, with the receiver having certain obligations; for example, in order to receive financial aid, recipients may be required to perform certain low-grade work assignments. Associated with the residual view is the belief that the causes of clients' difficulties are rooted in their own malfunctioning—that is, that clients are to blame for their predicaments because of personal inadequacies or ill-advised activities or sins.

Under the residual view there is usually a stigma attached to receiving services or funds. The prevalence of the residual stigma can be shown by asking "Have you ever in the past felt a reluctance to seek counseling for a personal or emotional situation you faced because you were wary of what others might think of you?" For almost everyone the answer is yes. An example of this stigma in American society was evidenced in 1968, when Senator Thomas Eagleton was dropped as a vice-presidential candidate on the Democratic ticket after it became known that he had once received psychiatric counseling.

The opposing point of view, which has been coined the *institutional view,** holds that social welfare programs are to be "accepted as a proper, legitimate function of modern industrial society in helping individuals achieve self-fulfillment."[11] Under this view there is no stigma attached to receiving funds or services; recipients are viewed as being entitled to such help. Associated with this view is the belief that an individual's difficulties are due to causes largely beyond his or her control (for example, a person may be unemployed because of a lack of employment opportunities). When difficulties arise, causes are sought in the environment (society), and efforts are focused on improving the social institutions within which the individual functions.

The residual approach characterized social welfare programs from our early history to the depression of the 1930s. Since the Great Depression, both approaches have been applied to social welfare programs, with some programs being largely residual in nature and others being more institutional in design and implementation. Social insurance programs, such as Old-Age, Survivors, Health, and Disability Insurance (described in Chapter 3), are examples of "institutional" programs. Public assistance programs (also described in Chapter 3) are examples of residual programs.

LIBERALISM VERSUS CONSERVATISM

The two prominent political philosophies in the United States are liberalism and conservatism. The Republican party is considered to be relatively conservative, and the Democratic party is considered to be relatively liberal. (It should be noted, however, that there are some Democrats who are primarily conservative in ideology and some Republicans who are primarily liberal in ideology.)

Conservatives (derived from the verb "to conserve") tend to resist change. They emphasize tradition and believe that rapid change usually results in more negative than positive consequences. In economic matters, conservatives feel that government should not interfere with the workings of the marketplace. They encourage the government to support (for example, through tax incentives), rather than regulate, business and industry in society. A free-market economy is thought to be the best way to ensure prosperity and fulfillment of individual needs. Conservatives embrace the old adage that "government governs best which governs least." They believe that most government activities constitute grave threats to individual liberty and to the smooth functioning of the free market.

Conservatives generally advocate a residual approach to social welfare programs. They believe that dependency is a result of personal failure and that it is natural for inequality to exist among humans. They assert that the family, the church, and gainful employment should be the primary defenses against dependency. Social welfare should be only a temporary function that is used sparingly; prolonged social welfare assistance will lead recipients to become permanently dependent. Conservatives also believe that charity is a moral virtue and that the "fortunate" are obligated to help the "less fortunate" become productive, contributing citizens in a society. If government funds are provided for health and social welfare services, conservatives advocate that such funding should go to private organizations, which are thought to be more effective and efficient than public agencies in providing services.

In contrast, liberals believe that change is generally good, as it usually brings progress. Moderate change is best. They view society as needing regulation to ensure fair competition among various interests. In particular, a free-market economy is viewed as needing regulation to ensure fairness. Government programs, including social

---

*The term *institutional view of social welfare* is distinctly different from, and not to be confused with, the term *social welfare institutions.*

welfare programs, are necessary to help meet basic human needs. Liberals advocate government action to remedy social deficiencies and to improve human welfare. They feel that government regulation and intervention are often required to safeguard human rights, to control the excesses of capitalism, and to provide equal chances for success. They emphasize egalitarianism and the rights of minorities.

Liberals generally adhere to an institutional view of social welfare. They assert that, because modern society has become so fragmented and complex and because traditional institutions (such as the family) have been unable to meet emerging human needs, few individuals can now function without the help of social services (including work training, job placement services, child care, health care, and counseling).

HISTORY OF SOCIAL WELFARE

Early European History

All societies must develop ways to meet the needs of those who are unable to be self-sufficient—the orphaned, the blind, persons with a physical or mental disability, the poor, and the sick. Before the Industrial Revolution, this responsibility was met largely by the family, by the church, and by neighbors. An important value of the Judeo-Christian tradition throughout history—and one that has considerable relevance for social welfare—is humanitarianism: ascribing a high value to human life and benevolently helping those in need.

With the development of the feudal system in Europe, when a tenant family was unable to meet a relative's basic needs, the feudal lord usually provided whatever was necessary.

The Elizabethan Poor Law

In the Middle Ages, famines, wars, crop failures, pestilence, and the breakdown in the feudal system all contributed to substantial increases in the number of people in need. Former approaches, primarily through the church and the family, were unsuccessful at meeting the needs of many who were unable to be self-sufficient. As a result, many of these individuals were forced to resort to begging. To attempt to solve this social problem, England passed several Poor Laws between the mid-1300s and the mid-1800s. The most significant of these was the Elizabethan Poor Law of 1601, enacted during the reign of Queen Elizabeth I. The fundamental provisions of this Poor Law were incorporated into the laws of the American colonies and have had an important influence on our current approaches to public assistance and other social legislation. (It is interesting to observe that the social problem that these Poor Laws were designed to alleviate was conceptualized not as poverty but, rather, as the ruling class's annoyance with begging.)

The Elizabethan Poor Law established three categories of relief recipients:

1. The able-bodied poor. This group was given low-grade employment, and citizens were prohibited from offering them financial help. Anyone who refused to work was placed in stocks or in jail.

2. The impotent poor. People unable to work composed this group—the elderly, the blind, the deaf, mothers with young children, and those with a physical or mental disability. They were usually placed together in an almshouse (institution). If the impotent poor had a place to live and if it appeared less expensive to maintain them there, they were permitted to live outside the almshouse, where they were granted "outdoor relief," usually "in kind" (food, clothing, and fuel).

3. Dependent children. Children whose parents or grandparents were unable to support them were apprenticed out to other citizens. Boys were taught the trade of their master and had to serve until their 24th birthday. Girls were brought up as domestic servants and were required to remain until they were 21 or married.

This Poor Law did not permit the registration of a person as being in need of charity if his or her parents, spouse, children, or other relatives were

When Paul Strand photographed a blind newspaper dealer in 1916, "charity for unfortunates" was still the widely held view of social welfare. Those who were unable to be self-sufficient were treated—at best—with condescension. As a licensed New York City peddler, this woman's lot may have been only marginally better than other "unfortunates" of her day.

able to provide support. Although the law was passed by the English Parliament, the parish (town or local community) was assigned the responsibility of implementing its provisions, with the program expenses to be met by charitable donations and a tax in the parish on lands, houses, and tithes. The Poor Law also stated that the parish's responsibility extended only to those who had legal residence in the parish, which was variously defined as having been born in the parish or having lived in the parish for three years. (Residence requirements are still part of current public assistance programs.) The Poor Law of 1601 set the pattern of public relief under governmental responsibility in both Great Britain and this country for the next 300 years.

Most of the provisions of the Elizabethan Poor Law were incorporated into the social welfare policies of colonial America. Towns were assigned the responsibility of providing for the needy, almshouses were built to house the unemployable, orphaned children were apprenticed out, and a system of legal residency was established to make it clear that towns were not responsible for meeting the needs of destitute strangers. Conditions in almshouses, it should be noted, were unbelievably deplorable. Into almshouses were packed not only the poor but also the sick, the emotionally disturbed, the blind, the alcoholic, and dependent children. Straw and old cots served for beds, there were no sanitary facilities, and the dilapidated buildings were barely heated in winter.

The Industrial Revolution

In the 17th, 18th, and 19th centuries the Industrial Revolution flourished in Europe and America. A major reason for its growth was technological advances, such as the development of the steam engine. But the revolution was also made possible by the *Protestant ethic* and the *laissez-faire economic view*. These two themes also had important effects on social welfare. The Protestant ethic emphasized *individualism*, the view that one is master of one's own fate. Hard work and self-ambition were highly valued. An overriding goal for human beings set by the Protestant ethic was to acquire material goods. People were largely judged not on the basis of their personalities and other attributes but on how much wealth they had acquired. To be poor was thought to be one's own moral fault.

The laissez-faire economic theory asserted that the economy and society in general would best prosper if businesses and industries were permitted to do whatever they desired to make a profit. Any regulation by the government of business practices (for example, setting safety standards, passing minimum-wage laws, prohibiting child labor) was discouraged. The Protestant ethic and laissez-faire economics, together, justified such business practices as cutthroat competition, formation of monopolies, deplorable safety and working conditions, and exploitation of the working class through low pay, long hours, and child labor.

The social welfare implications of the Protestant ethic reached their most inhumane level in the theory of *social Darwinism*, which was based on Charles Darwin's theory of evolution. Darwin theorized that higher forms of life evolved from lower forms by the process of survival of the fittest; he had seen in the animal world a fierce struggle for survival that destroyed the weak, rewarded the strong, and produced evolutionary change. Herbert Spencer extended this theory to humanity: Struggle, destruction, and survival of the fit were thought to be essential to progress in human society as well. The theory stated in its most inhumane form that the strong (the wealthy) survived because they were superior, whereas the weak (the needy) deserved to perish; it would be a mistake to help the weak survive. Although leaving the weak to perish was never advocated on a wide scale, the theory did have a substantial influence in curbing the development of innovative and more humane social welfare programs.

Prior to the Industrial Revolution there were few communities in Europe or America with a population larger than few thousand. One of the consequences of the Industrial Revolution was the development of large urban areas close to where factories were located. Because employment opportunities were limited in rural areas, many workers moved to cities. With such movement, family and kinship ties were broken, and those who were unable to adapt faced a loss of community identity, alienation, and social breakdown. To attempt to meet the needs of people living in urban areas, private social welfare services began to spring up in the 1800s—primarily at the initiation of the clergy and religious groups. (A public social welfare agency receives its funds through tax dollars, whereas a private or voluntary agency generally receives a large part of its funds from charitable contributions.*) Because of the lack of development of public social services, private agencies provided most of the funds and services to the needy until the 1930s. In the 1800s social services and funds were usually provided by upper-middle-class volunteers who combined "charity" with religious admonitions.

Turn of the 20th Century

Around 1880 various segments of the population became aware of the evils of unlimited competition and of abuses by those with economic power. It became clear that a few captains of industry were becoming very wealthy, whereas the standard of living for the bulk of the population was remaining static and only slightly above the subsistence level. One of the theorists who objected to social Darwinism was Lester Ward, who in *Dynamic Sociology* (1883) drew a sharp distinction between purposeless animal evolution and human evolution.[12] Ward asserted that humans, unlike animals, could and should provide social welfare programs to help the needy and that humans have the capacity for regulation through social and economic controls. Ward declared that such programs and controls would be beneficial to everyone. This new thinking was in direct opposition to social Darwinism and laissez-faire economics. It called on the federal government to take on new functions, to establish legislation to regulate business practices, and to provide social welfare programs. As a result, around 1900 there was an awakening to social needs, with the federal government beginning to place some (although limited) funds into such programs as health, housing, and slum clearance.

In the early 1900s, social welfare became more professionalized. Prior to this time such

---

*Some private agencies are now contracting with public agencies to receive public funds to provide services to certain clients. Public agencies are established and administered by governmental units, whereas private agencies are established and administered by nongovernmental groups or private citizens.

services were generally provided by well-meaning but untrained volunteers (do-gooders) from the middle and upper socioeconomic groups. At this time people with more formalized training were employed in some positions, and there was an increased interest in developing therapeutic skills and methods in counseling clients. In this era some of our present patterns of specialization in social welfare programs also developed, such as family services and probation and parole. It was also at this time that the first schools of social work and social welfare were founded in universities.

The Great Depression and the Social Security Act

Before 1930 social services were provided primarily by churches and voluntary organizations, as was financial assistance for people in need. Some cities and some counties had local relief directors who distributed public tax money financed by local governments. In those days poverty was associated with laziness and immorality. Public relief money was viewed as "pauper aid," and receiving it was a huge social disgrace.

The Roaring Twenties were largely a time of prosperity and festivities. Then, in October 1929, the New York Stock Exchange crashed. Many investors lost their businesses, homes, and life savings. The crash of the stock market was a significant sign that our economy (along with the whole world's economy) was heading for a severe depression.

The number of people who were unemployed rose from 3 million in the spring of 1929 to 15 million in January 1933.[13] More than 20% of workers were jobless in 1933.[14] Many banks closed. Many farmers and business owners went bankrupt.

In 1931 some states began providing unemployment relief to prevent starvation among the jobless and their families. Herbert Hoover, who was president at the time, believed that only private charity should meet the needs of the unemployed. He thought public relief (state and federal money) would demoralize people and make them

Nearly 15 million people were unemployed at the height of the Great Depression. These formerly unemployed workers are selling apples as part of a plan devised by the International Apple Association to help meet the demand for jobs.

permanently dependent on the state and federal governments. His attitude was graphically illustrated in December 1930, when he approved a $45 million bill to feed starving livestock in Arkansas but opposed a $25 million bill to feed starving farmers and their families in the same state.[15]

Chapters of the Community Chest and the Red Cross, as well as other voluntary organizations, were unable to meet the demand for financial assistance in the early 1930s. Because people were unemployed, private charity also had trouble raising the funds necessary to maintain the jobless.

Local and state funds proved inadequate to protect the growing millions of unemployed against hunger, cold, and despair. Many sick people could not pay for, and therefore did not receive, medical care. Children were passed around among neighbors because their parents had no food or were out looking for jobs. The number of suicides increased, as did the incidence of tuberculosis and malnutrition in children. Many middle-class people became penniless, factories lay idle, and stores had few customers.

In 1933, when President Franklin D. Roosevelt took office, 40% of the population in some states was receiving local and state public relief money.[16] Pressure grew for the federal government to bail out the states and counties by helping finance public relief for those living in poverty. Conditions were so desperate that our political leaders became concerned that there might be a Socialist or Communist revolution in this country.

President Roosevelt immediately proposed, and Congress passed, temporary emergency programs to provide paid work for some unemployed workers. For those unable to obtain a job, the federal government provided financial assistance.

The depression of the 1930s brought about profound changes in social welfare. Until that time the belief in individualism was still widely held—that is, the belief that one is master of one's fate. The depression shattered this myth. It became clear that situations and events beyond individual control can cause deprivation, misery, and poverty. It also became clear that the federal government must play a role in providing financial assistance and social services.

The experience with emergency relief and work programs during the Great Depression demonstrated the need for more permanent federal efforts in dealing with some of the critical problems of unemployment, aging, disability, illness, and dependent children. As a result, in 1935 the Social Security Act was passed, which formed the basis of most of our current public social welfare programs, and federal legislation for the following three major categories of programs was enacted.

SOCIAL INSURANCE

This category was set up with an "institutional" orientation and provided insurance for unemployment, retirement, or death. It has two main programs: (a) Unemployment Compensation, which provides weekly benefits for a limited time for workers who lose their jobs, and (b) Old-Age, Survivors, Health, and Disability Insurance, which provides monthly payments to individuals and their families when a worker retires, becomes disabled, or dies. In everyday conversation this program is generally referred to as *Social Security.*

PUBLIC ASSISTANCE

This category has many residual aspects. To receive benefits, an individual must undergo a "means test" in which one's assets and expenses are reviewed to determine if there is a financial need. There were four programs under this category, with the titles indicating eligible groups: Aid to the Blind (people of any age whose vision is 20/200 or less with correction), Aid to the Disabled (people between the ages of 18 and 65 who are permanently disabled), Old Age Assistance* (people 65 and older), and Aid to Families with Dependent Children (AFDC) (primarily mothers with children under age 18 and no father in the home). Public assistance programs incorporated several features of the English Poor Laws: there were residence requirements and a means test, some of the aid "in kind" such as food, and the benefits were viewed as "charity" rather than aid to which recipients are entitled. Public assistance, particularly the AFDC program, is frequently criticized and stigmatized by politicians and the general public. An inaccurate public perception is that "welfare" means public assistance *only.* In actuality, public assistance is only one of several hundred social welfare programs. A frequent complaint is that too much money is being spent on public assistance, yet it is generally unknown that five to six times more money is spent annually on social insurance programs than on public assistance![17]

PUBLIC HEALTH AND WELFARE SERVICES

Whereas the first two categories provided financial benefits, this category established the role of

---

*In January 1974 three programs, Aid to the Blind, Aid to the Disabled, and Old Age Assistance, were combined into one program, Supplemental Security Income (see Chapter 3).

EXHIBIT 1.1

How Welfare Became a Dirty Word

Linda Gordon notes:

> *In the last half-century, the American definition*
> *of "welfare" has been reversed. A term that once*
> *meant prosperity, good health, good spirits, and*
> *social respect now implies poverty, bad health,*
> *despondency, and social disrespect. A word used*
> *to describe the health of the body politic now*
> *evokes images of its disease—slums, depressed*
> *single mothers, neglected children, crime,*
> *despair.*[a]

How did this reversal of the concept of welfare occur? The term *welfare* could logically apply to hundreds of society's programs that enhance citizens' well-being: pollution control, schools, parks, counseling, recreational programs, regulation of food and drugs, and so on. Yet the general public today views "welfare" as Aid to Families with Dependent Children (AFDC) and this program and its recipients are now negatively stigmatized.

AFDC was one of the programs enacted by the 1935 Social Security Act. The program was not intended by the writers of that act to be inferior to the other Social Security programs that were created. AFDC was intended to be small-scale and temporary, because the framers believed that the model of the family in which the male was the breadwinner and the female the homemaker would be the standard. AFDC was intended to serve the most deserving of all needy groups— namely, helpless mothers left alone with children by heartless men. In 1935 it was believed that mothers should stay home to raise their children; the vast majority of women were married, and it

was considered the obligation of the husband to support the family. Unmarried or abandoned mothers, it was thought, should be helped by the government to stay at home for the *welfare* (well-being) of their children.

Linda Gordon notes that the stigmatization of the AFDC program first began on a large scale in the 1950s and 1960s. There were three main reasons.

The role of women began to be redefined in the 1950s and 1960s. More women were entering the work force, and it began to be expected that women would work outside the home. As a consequence, single mothers on AFDC began to be shamed for being on the welfare rolls. Negative terms such as "lazy," "undeserving," and "charity cases" were hurled at them.

Another development that contributed to the stigmatization was the increasing divorce rate, which left more women alone to raise their children. With AFDC rolls expanding, the general public became more critical of using taxpayers' money to support single mothers and their children.

A third development in the 1950s that contributed to the stigmatization was that African American women began to assert that AFDC was a right they were entitled to as citizens, just like the right to vote. The success of this claim increased not only the number of AFDC recipients but also the proportion of African Americans among the recipients. As a consequence, the stigma attached to welfare intensified, strengthened now by racist animosity toward the growing number of welfare recipients among minority groups.

[a] Linda Gordon, "How 'Welfare' Became a Dirty Word," *The Chronicle of Higher Education,* July 20, 1994, p. B1.

the federal government in providing social services (for example, adoption, foster care, services to children with a disability, protective services, and services to single parents).

Following the enactment of the Social Security Act, public social welfare services became dominant in terms of expenditures, people served, and personnel. The private role shifted from financial aid to certain specialized service areas. One of the roles of private agencies has been to test the value of new services and approaches. If such new services are found to be cost effective and successful in alleviating human problems, public funds are sometimes requested to provide them on a large-scale basis.

The programs established by the Social Security Act have been controversial. Some authorities credit the act with bringing economic stability to our country and helping to bring us out of the worst depression we have ever seen. Other authorities, including fiscal conservatives, view Social Security expenditures as perpetuating poverty by making people dependent on government for their livelihood. It has been claimed for many years that people would rather live it up on welfare than work. It is also claimed that the expenditures are highly inflationary, as they represent a sizable portion of our federal government's budget.

The basic intent of the Social Security Act was to provide a decent standard of living to every American. President Roosevelt believed that financial security (including public assistance) should not be a matter of charity, but a matter of justice. He asserted that every individual has a right to a minimum standard of living in a civilized society. He believed that liberty and security are synonymous; without financial security, people will eventually despair and revolt. Therefore, Roosevelt held the conviction that the very existence of a democratic society depended on the health and welfare of its citizens.[18]

From the 1930s to the 1980s the federal government gradually expanded its role in providing financial assistance and social programs to Americans suffering from social problems.

The Great Society and War on Poverty

A major push for expansion of social welfare programs came in the 1960s, when President Lyndon Johnson declared a War on Poverty and sought to create what he called a "Great Society." In 1964 Johnson noted in his State of the Union address that one-fifth of our population was living in poverty and that nearly half of all African Americans were poor. Funding for existing social welfare programs was sharply increased, and many new programs were created (such as Head Start, Medicare, and Medicaid*).

The early 1960s were characterized by optimism; there was a feeling that we were on our way to a golden era in which poverty would gradually disappear, racial integration would occur, and other social problems would be smoothly and painlessly solved. The late 1960s were therefore a shock: Martin Luther King, Jr., and Robert Kennedy were assassinated; many of our inner cities were torched and burned to the ground during protests against racial discrimination; there were substantial increases in crime; there were student protests and riots on campuses over the Vietnam War and other issues; racial minorities and poor people organized to demand their piece of the national financial pie; there was a revolution in sexual values and behaviors; and there was a recognition of other social ills such as the drug problem and the need to preserve the environment.

In the social welfare field the late 1960s brought a renewed interest in changing the environment, or "the system," to better meet the needs of clients (sociological approach), rather than enabling clients to better adapt and adjust to their life situations (the psychological approach). Social action again became an important part of social work, with some social workers becoming active as advocates of clients, community organizers, and political organizers for social reform.

Conservatism in the 1970s and 1980s

In the 1970s, after the end of the Vietnam War, the turmoil of the late 1960s was replaced for several years with an atmosphere of relative calm on both the foreign and domestic fronts. In contrast to the hope of the 1960s that government programs

---

*Medicare and Medicaid are described in Chapter 14.

Members of Women's Strike for Peace rally in opposition to the Vietnam War outside the Pentagon in 1967. The Great Society programs and the Vietnam War protests of the late 1960s helped mobilize public sentiment toward an entire range of social issues.

could cure our social ills, the opposing philosophy emerged that many problems were beyond the capacity of the government to alleviate. Hence the liberalism of the 1960s, which resulted in the expansion and development of new social programs, was replaced by a more conservative approach in the 1970s and the 1980s. Practically no new, large-scale social welfare programs were initiated in the 1970s, the 1980s, or the early 1990s. Unfortunately, other crises (including Vietnam, Watergate, inflation, recession, the Israeli-Arab conflict, energy crises, political turmoil in Iran, the Iran-Contra affair, the 1991 war against Iraq, political turmoil in Haiti, and the large federal budget deficit) have received more attention in the last 25 years than our ongoing social problems. These latter problems include dismal living conditions in the inner cities, the AIDS crisis, homelessness, racial discrimination, increasing crime rates, prison conditions, family violence,

the high divorce rate, overpopulation, the financial crisis among farmers, and the increasing number of people living in poverty.

During President Jimmy Carter's administration (1976 to 1980), there was increased recognition that the federal government simply did not have the power—no matter how much money it spent—to cure *all* the country's social ills. But, instead of a desire for the government to partially allay *many* of these problems, there appears to have been a complete turnaround in philosophy: Many citizens began despairing and demanding that government sharply reduce the amount of tax money it was spending on social welfare programs.

In 1980 our domestic economy was in a mess. The rates of both unemployment and inflation were high, and the country had been in a recession for several years. Ronald Reagan was elected president that year and proceeded, as he had promised during his campaign, to make a number of changes to revitalize the economy and to strengthen the military. The following changes were implemented:

- Taxes were sharply cut for both individuals and corporations. These tax cuts resulted in business and consumers having more money to spend, which stimulated the economy and led to a reduction in the unemployment rate.

- Military expenditures were sharply increased, which resulted in a strengthening of our armed forces.

- Expenditures for social programs were sharply cut. This massive cutback was the first large-scale federal reduction in social welfare expenditures in our country's history.

In 1988 George Bush was elected president on a conservative platform, and he continued the social welfare policies of the Reagan administration. Bush believed (as did Reagan) that the federal government is not a solution to social problems but in fact is part of the problem. Reagan and Bush held that federally funded social welfare programs make recipients dependent on the government, rather than industrious and productive. The Reagan and Bush administrations endorsed an economic program that cut taxes and government spending, eliminated cumbersome federal regulations and red tape that restricted the growth of business and industry, and provided incentives to the private sector for expansion and greater employment. The stated objective was to create a period of prosperity that would "trickle down" to the lowest stratum so that everyone would benefit. The result, however, was that the gap between the rich and the poor widened, with the poor failing to benefit from the improved financial circumstances of the rich.[19] The people who were hurt the most by cutbacks in federally financed social welfare programs were current and former recipients.

What have been the longer-term effects of these cutbacks? Many of our present social problems intensified: The proportion of people living in poverty increased,[20] the income gap between the rich and the poor widened, efforts to reduce

racial discrimination slowed, prisons became overcrowded, many of the chronically mentally ill were released from mental hospitals and became homeless without receiving supportive services, the plight of people living in our inner cities worsened, there was an increase in single-parent families, environmental problems (such as acid rain and chemical waste hazards) increased in severity, and the overall number of homeless and hungry skyrocketed.

A Move toward Liberalism— and Back—in the 1990s

Throughout history the predominant philosophy in our society has swung back and forth like a pendulum between the two poles of liberalism and conservatism. Bill Clinton was elected president in 1992. His views on resolving social problems are consistent with a moderate (middle-of-the-road) to liberal orientation. His liberal proposals have included a universal health insurance program for all Americans, significantly expanded educational and training programs for individuals on welfare in order to help them become self-supporting, an effort to prevent discrimination against gays and lesbians, an increase in funding for AIDS research, and efforts to enact legislation on handgun control. Clinton also has taken a pro-choice stance on the abortion issue.

The move toward liberalism in the early 1990s may, however, have been short-lived. In the congressional elections of 1994, the Republicans (most with a conservative orientation) won majority control of both the Senate and the House of Representatives. (This was the first time in 40 years that Republicans held a majority in the House.) These Republicans have a conservative political agenda that includes such components as shifting spending from crime prevention to prison construction, eliminating welfare benefits for unmarried teens who have children, reducing spending for many social welfare programs, and cutting the capital gains tax by 50% (a tax cut that primarily benefits the rich).

Although many people's perception is that the United States spends more on social welfare than

With the election of President Bill Clinton in 1992, the nation looked toward a moderate to liberal leadership. However, this orientation may have been short-lived as the elections of 1994 gave the mostly conservative Republicans control of Congress.

any other country in the world, this is far from accurate. As Figure 1.3 shows, among industrialized nations we rank very low in our proportionate expenditures for social welfare programs.

Where Do We Stand Today?

The status of social welfare today offers more questions than answers. Here are some of the issues that need to be addressed at all levels of society:

Should some of the cutbacks in federal support for social welfare programs that occurred in the 1980s be restored? What services and programs should be developed to combat the AIDS crisis? How can drug abuse (such as alcohol and cocaine abuse) be more effectively controlled?

What new programs should be developed for the homeless? What new services should be provided to the chronically mentally ill, especially those living on the streets of our cities? How can crime be curbed more effectively and the correctional system be made more rehabilitative? What measures should be taken to eliminate racial discrimination? How can we meet the problems of our inner cities?

Should transracial adoptions be encouraged? How should we remedy broken treaties to Native Americans, and what kinds of services need to be developed for Native Americans to alleviate the wide range of social problems they face? Should abortion laws be made more or less restrictive? Should a national health insurance program be established? How can child pornography be prevented? How can we prevent the Social Security

FIGURE 1.3

Social Welfare Spending

This figure illustrates the percentage of gross national product (GNP) that industrialized countries spend on social welfare programs. Contrary to popular belief, the United States tends to spend proportionately less on social welfare programs than do most other industrialized countries.

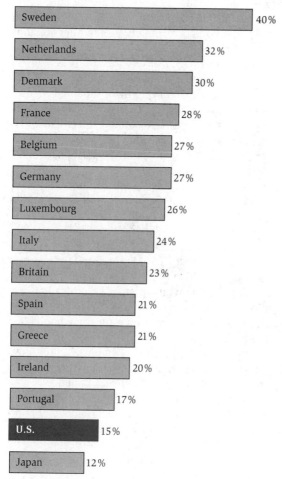

Sweden	40%
Netherlands	32%
Denmark	30%
France	28%
Belgium	27%
Germany	27%
Luxembourg	26%
Italy	24%
Britain	23%
Spain	21%
Greece	21%
Ireland	20%
Portugal	17%
U.S.	15%
Japan	12%

Source: Dick Polman, "Swedes Shaken as the Welfare State Shrinks," *Wisconsin State Journal,* July 3, 1994, p. 1B.

system from going bankrupt? How can we curb fraud in Medicaid, AFDC, and other social welfare programs? How can child abuse, sexual abuse, and spousal abuse be curbed? How can we prevent suicides, especially the increasing number among teenagers? Should prostitution be legalized? What should be done about the teenage runaway problem?

Should busing to achieve racial integration be expanded or cut back? Do some affirmative action programs involve reverse discrimination against white males? What programs are needed to prevent rape? How can retirement living be made more meaningful? What measures should be taken to protect the civil rights of gays and lesbians? Should legislation be enacted to curb the sale of handguns? What changes are needed to improve the welfare system? Do we really want to provide the funds and services that are necessary to break the cycle of poverty, or do we still believe that many poor people are undeserving in the sense that they would rather be on welfare than working?

THE FUTURE

The future direction and nature of social services will be determined largely by technological advances. In the past 50 years the following advances have resulted in dramatic changes in our lifestyles[21]: auto and air travel, nuclear power, television, birth control devices, automation, new electrical appliances, shopping centers, the discovery of penicillin and other wonder drugs, and computers.

The relationship between technological breakthroughs and changes in social welfare programs generally follows this format: Technological advances foster changes in our lifestyles; lifestyle changes affect changes in our future social, financial, health, and recreational needs; and the latter changes largely determine what changes will be demanded in social service programs.

Predicting what technological breakthroughs will occur and how these advances will affect our lifestyles is highly speculative. A number of advances are being predicted: robots that talk and act like humans; space travel; computers capable of thinking, as well as diagnosing medical illnesses and recommending treatments; vaccines that will prevent most forms of cancer; artificial hearts and kidneys; home shopping via two-way cable television; vaccines to prevent HIV infection; weather and climate control; minicomputers in autos that tell the driver how each part of the car is working; and lawn mowers and vacuum cleaners with a memory, programmed to follow a route of mowing or cleaning. Because there are more scientists involved in technological research and development now than at any other time in the history of civilization, future technological breakthroughs are likely to occur even more rapidly than in the past.[22] In fact, Alvin Toffler, in *Future Shock,* asserts that adjusting psychologically to rapid lifestyle changes is currently a major problem and will become the most difficult adjustment people will have to make in future years.[23]

At the same time, environmentalists are predicting that our civilization is in serious danger due to overpopulation, depletion of energy resources, excessive use of toxic chemicals, likelihood of mass famines and starvation, and dramatic declines in the quality of life.

What the future will hold is difficult to predict accurately. The worst mistake, however, it to take the ''ostrich head in the sand'' approach, in which no effort is made to plan and control the future.

A key concern for social welfare in the future is changes in the American family. When there is family breakdown, social services are generally needed; as the needs of families change, there is a corresponding demand to change social services.

DRAMATIC CHANGES FORESEEN IN THE AMERICAN FAMILY

In viewing the future of the American family, it is helpful to gain a perspective by taking a quick glance at some of the changes that have occurred in the past. Two hundred years ago marriages were primarily arranged by parents, with economic considerations being the most important determinant of who married whom. Divorce was practically unheard of; now one out of two marriages ends in divorce or annulment.[24] Two hundred years ago women did not work outside the home, and children were an economic asset; now over 50% of married women work outside the home, and children are a financial liability.[25] Since colonial days the family has lost (or there has been a sharp decline in) a number of functions: educational, economic production, religious, protective, and recreational.[26] Today the two main functions that remain are the affectional or companionship and the child-rearing functions.

In our fast-paced society the family is likely to change even more dramatically in the future. As in the past, the family will be affected significantly by technological changes.[27] Labor-saving devices in the home (for example, electrical appliances) have in the past been and currently are an important factor in making it possible for both spouses to work outside the home. Birth control devices have undoubtedly been an important factor in leading to an increase in premarital sexual relationships and in extramarital affairs.

The increased use of abortions has been a factor in sharply reducing the number of children available for adoption. Many adoption agencies have suspended taking applications from couples desiring healthy white infants. An ethically questionable business has developed in which women are paid to deliver and give up their babies for adoption in order to meet the demands of infertile couples who want a child. Women willing to bypass the normal adoption channels may sell an unwanted infant for as much as $20,000.[28]

In the future the American family is likely to be substantially affected by technological breakthroughs in biology and medicine. Let's look at a few developments in these areas—developments that are as alarming as they intriguing.

Biomedical Technology

ARTIFICIAL INSEMINATION
Thousands of babies are born annually in the United States through the process of artificial insemination, with the usage expected to continue to increase in the future.[29] The process of artificial

Unethical Use of Technology

Dr. Cecil Jacobson was well known for having introduced amniocentesis in the United States for diagnosing defects in unborn babies. For many years he operated an infertility clinic in Virginia. In March 1992 a federal jury found him guilty of 52 counts of fraud and perjury. He was charged with defrauding patients by artificially inseminating them with his own sperm while claiming to use other donors. He also was charged with tricking patients into believing they were pregnant when they were not. The prosecution alleged that Jacobson may have fathered as many as 75 children through artificial insemination. He was sentenced to five years in prison, ordered to pay $116,805 in fines and restitution, and required to serve three years' probation after release from prison. This case example illustrates that the new biomedical reproductive technology can be used unscrupulously.

Dr. Cecil Jacobson

insemination has long been used in livestock breeding because it eliminates all the problems that can be associated with breeding. A breeder can transport a prized animal's frozen sperm across the world and raise a whole new herd of animals almost effortlessly.

Human sperm can be frozen for long periods of time (the length of time has not been determined; it is generally acknowledged that five years would be safe with close to 100% assurance). The sperm can then be thawed and used to impregnate a female. This new technology has led to the development of a unique new institution, the sperm bank. Sperm banks are usually private institutions. They collect and maintain sperm, which is withdrawn at some later date to impregnate (with a physician's assistance) a woman.

The sperm used in artificial insemination may be the husband's (called AIH, for artificial insemination—husband). There may be several reasons for using AIH. It is possible to pool several ejacu-

lations from a man with a low sperm count and to inject them simultaneously into the vaginal canal of his spouse, thus vastly increasing the chance of pregnancy. AIH may also be used for family planning purposes; for example, a man might deposit his sperm in the bank, then undergo a vasectomy, and then later withdraw the sperm to have children. High-risk jobs (such as a danger of being exposed to radioactive material) might prompt a man to make a deposit in case of sterility or untimely death.

A second type of artificial insemination is called AID (artificial insemination—donor), in which the donor of the sperm is someone other than the husband. AID has been used for several decades to circumvent male infertility. It is also used when it is known that the husband is a carrier of a genetic disease (such as hemophilia). In recent years, an increasing number of single women who want a child but do not (at least for the near future) want a husband are requesting the services of a sperm bank. The woman specifies the general genetic characteristics she wants from the father, and the bank then tries to match those requests from the information known about donors.

A third type of artificial insemination is of recent origin and has received considerable publicity. Some married couples, in which the wife is infertile, have contracted for another woman to be artificially inseminated with the husband's sperm. Under the terms of the contract this "surrogate mother" is paid and is expected to give the infant to the married couple shortly after birth. (Surrogate motherhood is discussed in greater detail in the next section.)

A number of ethical, social, and legal questions have been raised about artificial insemination. There are the objections from religious leaders that this practice is wrong—that God did not mean for people to reproduce in this way. In the case of AID, there are certain psychological stresses placed on husbands and on marriages; the procedure emphasizes the husband's infertility and involves having a baby that he has not fathered. On a broader scale, artificial insemination raises other questions: What are the purposes of marriage and of sex? What will happen to male/female relationships if we do not even have to see each other to reproduce?

Some unusual court cases point to the need for new laws to resolve the questions that are arising. For instance, consider the case of Mr. and Mrs. John M. Prutting. Mr. Prutting was medically determined to be sterile as a result of radiation exposure received at work. Without her husband's knowledge, Mrs. Prutting was inseminated. After the birth of the baby, he sued her for divorce on the grounds of adultery.[30]

In another case, a wife was artificially inseminated with the husband's consent by AID. The couple later divorced. When the husband requested child visitation privileges, his wife took him to court on the grounds that he was not the father and thus had no such right. In New York, he won; but she moved to Oklahoma, where the decision was reversed.[31]

Finally, there was a reported case of an engaged couple whose mothers were discovered to have had the same artificial insemination donor.

The couple were thus biologically half-brother and -sister. The marriage would have been incestuous and was therefore canceled.[32]

There are other possible legal implications. What happens if the AIH sperm at a bank is not paid for? Would it become the property of the bank? Could it be auctioned off? If a woman was artificially inseminated by a donor and the child was later found to have genetic defects, could the parents bring suit against the physician, the donor, or the bank? Does the child have a right to know the identity of the donor father?

Sperm banks can also be used in genetic engineering. In the spring of 1980, it was disclosed that Robert Graham had set up an exclusive sperm bank to produce exceptionally bright children. Graham stated that at least five Nobel Prize winners had donated sperm. A number of women had already given birth through the services of this bank.[33] This approach raises questions about whether reproductive technology should be used to produce "superior" children and what characteristics should be defined as superior.

SURROGATE MOTHERHOOD

Thousands of married couples who want children but are unable to reproduce because the wife is infertile have turned to surrogate motherhood. With this type of motherhood, a surrogate gives birth to a baby conceived by artificial insemination, using the husband's sperm. (Often the surrogate mother is paid a fee for her services.) At birth the surrogate mother terminates her parental rights, and the child is then legally adopted by the sperm donor and his wife.

Couples using the services of a surrogate mother are generally delighted with this medical technique and believe it is a highly desirable solution to their personal difficulty of being unable to bear children. However, other groups assert that surrogate motherhood raises a number of moral, legal, and personal issues.

Many theologians and religious leaders firmly believe that God intended conception to occur only among married couples through sexual intercourse. These religious leaders view surrogate motherhood as ethically wrong because the surrogate mother is not married to the sperm donor and because artificial insemination is viewed as "unnatural." Some religious leaders also assert that it is morally despicable for a surrogate mother to accept a fee (often between $5000 and $10,000). They maintain that procreation is a blessing from God and should not be commercialized.

Surrogate motherhood also raises complicated legal questions that have considerable social consequences. For example, surrogate mothers usually sign a nonbinding contract stipulating that the mother will give up the child for adoption at birth. What if the surrogate mother changes her mind shortly before birth and decides to keep the baby? Women who have been surrogate mothers usually report that they become emotionally attached to the child during pregnancy.[34]

Most surrogate mothers to date are married and already have children. A number of issues are likely to arise. How does the husband of a surrogate mother feel about his wife being pregnant by another man's sperm? How does such a married couple explain to their children that their half-brother or half-sister will be given up for adoption to another family? How does such a married couple explain what they are doing to relatives, neighbors, and the surrounding community? If the child is born with severe mental or physical handicaps, who will care for the child and pay for the expenses? Will it be the surrogate mother and her husband, the contracting adoptive couple, or society?

In 1983 a surrogate mother gave birth in Michigan to a baby who was born with microcephaly, a condition in which the head is smaller than normal and mental retardation is likely. At first, neither the surrogate mother nor the contacting adoptive couple wanted to care for the child. The adoptive couple refused to pay the $10,000 fee to the surrogate mother. A legal battle ensued. Blood tests were eventually taken that indicated the probable father was not the contracting adoptive father but rather the husband of the surrogate mother. Following the blood tests, the surrogate mother and her husband assumed the care of the child. (This example illustrates another problem with the surrogate motherhood approach: If the surrogate mother engages in sexual intercourse with her partner/husband at about the same time that artificial insemination occurs, it becomes difficult to determine who is actually the genetic father of the child that is conceived.)

In 1986 Mary Beth Whitehead was a surrogate mother who gave birth to a child. She refused to give up the baby for adoption by the genetic father and his wife, even though she had signed a $10,000 contract in which she agreed to give up the child. The genetic father, William Stern, took the case to court, demanding that Whitehead honor the contract she had signed. Whitehead claimed she was the mother of the child and therefore had maternal rights to the child. The case received national attention. In April 1987, in the nation's first judicial ruling on a disputed surrogate contract, the judge ruled that the contract was valid. Just as men have a constitutional right to sell their sperm, women can decide what to do with their wombs.[35] Whitehead appealed this decision to the New Jersey State Supreme Court. In 1988 this court ruled that the contract between Whitehead and the Sterns was invalid because it involved the sale of a mother's right to her child, which violates state laws prohibiting child selling. This decision voided the adoption of the baby by Mrs. Stern; Mr. Stern was given custody, and Whitehead was granted visitation rights. Whether this decision will become the legal guideline for disputed surrogate contracts will be determined by future court decisions about surrogate contracts.

TEST-TUBE BABIES

In England, on July 24, 1978, Mrs. Lesley Brown gave birth to the first "test-tube baby." An egg taken from her reproductive system had been externally artificially impregnated using AIH and then implanted in her uterus to complete the normal process of pregnancy. The technique, called embryo transfer, was developed for women whose fallopian tubes are so damaged that the fertilized egg cannot pass through the tubes to the womb as is necessary for it to develop and grow until birth. Following the announcement of this birth, there was a surge of applications from thousands of childless couples asking fertility experts for similar implants.[36]

CASE EXAMPLE 1.4   Embryo Case Gains International Attention

A South American-born couple, Elsa and Mario Rios, amassed a fortune (several million dollars) in real estate in Los Angeles. In 1981 they enrolled in a "test-tube baby" program at Queen Victoria Medical Center in Melbourne, Australia, after their young daughter died. Several eggs were removed from Mrs. Rios and fertilized by her husband's sperm, which had been collected in a laboratory container. One of the fertilized eggs was implanted in Mrs. Rios's womb, but she had a miscarriage ten days later. The two remaining embryos were frozen so that doctors could try implantation at a later time.

On April 2, 1983, the couple was killed in the crash of a private plane in Chile. Because doctors have successfully thawed and implanted frozen embryos (which have resulted in births), a number of social and legal questions arise:

■ Should the embryos be implanted in the womb of a surrogate mother in the hope that they will develop to delivery?

■ Are the embryos legal heirs to the multimillion-dollar estate?

■ Does life legally begin at conception? If a surrogate mother carries the embryo to birth, is she legally the mother, and is she entitled to some of the inheritance?

■ Do embryos conceived outside the womb have rights? If so, what rights? Should these rights be the same as those accorded humans? (An Australian court ruled in 1987 that the embryos must be thawed and carried to term if a volunteer surrogate could be found. However, the offspring will not be viewed as legally entitled to inherit their biological parents' estate.)

This case highlights how the rapid advanced of *in vitro* fertilization (fertilization outside the human body) has outstripped attitudes and laws.

Sources: "Embryo Case Opens New Debate," *Wisconsin State Journal,* June 19, 1984, pp. 1–2; Stephen Budiansky, "The New Rules of Reproduction," *U.S. News & World Report,* April 18, 1988, pp. 66–67.

Another breakthrough in this area occurred in 1984, when an egg donated by one woman was fertilized and then implanted in another woman. Australian researchers in January 1984 reported the first successful birth resulting from a procedure in which an embryo was externally conceived and then implanted in the uterus of a surrogate.[37] This type of surrogate motherhood is a modern-day twist on the wet nurse (a woman who cares for and breast-feeds a child not her own) of earlier times. An unusual application of this new technology occurred in South Africa in 1987, when a grandmother, Pat Anthony, gave birth to her own grandchildren. The daughter was infertile, so her eggs (which had been fertilized in the lab) were implanted into Ms. Anthony. Several months later Ms. Anthony gave birth to triplets.[38]

This type of surrogate motherhood differs from the earlier version in which the surrogate mother contributes half of the genetic characteristics through the use of her egg. Here the surrogate contributes neither her own egg nor any of the genetic characteristics of the child.

Surrogate pregnancies can, in one respect, be seen as the final step in the biological liberation

CASE EXAMPLE 1.5 Redefining Motherhood

I n August 1990 surrogate mother Anna Johnson filed legal papers seeking parental rights to a child created from the sperm and egg of Mark and Crispina Calvert in California. Ms. Johnson gave birth to the child under a $10,000 surrogacy contract. She was the first surrogate mother to seek custody of a child not genetically related to her. In October 1990 the judge handling the case ruled that Ms. Johnson had no parental rights under California law. The judge assigned permanent custody of the child to the genetic parents. If the judge's ruling stands, it could lead to a new definition of motherhood—one in which genetics is the primary criterion for determining parentage when a surrogate carries a child genetically unrelated to her.

Anna Johnson

Source: From Susan Peterson and Susan Kelleher, "Surrogate's Loss Could Redefine Motherhood," *Wisconsin State Journal,* Oct. 23, 1990, p. 4A.

---

of women. Like men, women can "sire" children without the responsibility of pregnancy and childbirth.

However, surrogate pregnancies promise to create a legal nightmare. Do the genetic mother and father have any binding legal rights? Can the genetic parents place reasonable restrictions on health, medical care, and diet during the pregnancy? Can the genetic parents require the surrogate mother not to smoke or drink? Could the genetic parents require the surrogate to abort? Could the surrogate abort without the genetic parents' consent? Whose child is it if both the genetic mother and the surrogate mother want to be recognized as the legal mother after the child is born? Will the lower class and minorities come to serve as "holding tanks" for upper-class women's children? Legal experts see far-reaching changes in family law, inheritance, and the concept of legitimacy if laboratory fertilization and child rearing by surrogate mothers become accepted practices.

Human embryo transplants, when combined with principles of genetic selection, would allow people who want "superhuman" children to select embryos in which the resultant infant would have a high probability of being free of genetic defects. The technology would also allow parents to choose, with a high probability of success, the genetic characteristics they desired—such as the child's sex, color of eyes and hair, skin color, probable height, probable muscular capabilities, and probable IQ. A superhuman embryo would be formed from combining the sperm and egg of a male and female who are thought to have the desired genetic characteristics.

This breakthrough will raise a number of personal and ethical questions. Couples desiring children may be faced with the decision of having a child through natural conception or of preselecting superhuman genetic characteristics through embryo transplants. Another question that will arise is whether our society will attempt to use this new technology to control human evolutionary development. If the answer is affirmative, decisions will need to be made about which genetic characteristics should be considered "desirable," and questions will arise about who should have the authority to make such decisions. Although our country may not want to control human evolutionary development in this manner, will we not feel it necessary to do so if a rival nation begins a massive evolutionary program? In addition, will parents have the same or somewhat different feelings toward children who result from embryo transplants compared to children who result from natural conception?

GENETIC SCREENING

Practically all states now require mandatory genetic screening programs for various disorders. There are about 2000 human disorders caused by defective genes, and it is estimated that each of us carries two or three of them.[39] Mass genetic screening could eliminate some of these disorders. One screening approach that is increasingly being used with pregnant women is amniocentesis, a technique that can determine chromosomal abnormality. Amniocentesis is the surgical insertion of a hollow needle through the abdominal wall and uterus of a pregnant female to obtain amniotic fluid for the determination of chromosomal abnormality. More and more pregnant women are being pressured to terminate the pregnancy of a high-risk or proven genetically inferior fetus. Also, some genetic disorders can be corrected if diagnosed in time.

Several years ago *Fortune* magazine carried an article with the heading "How to Save $100 Billion," which urged that genetic screening be used much more extensively to reduce the incidence of genetic diseases: "If we allow our genetic problems to get out of hand by not acting promptly . . . we can run the risk of overcommitting ourselves to the care of and maintenance of a large population of mentally deficient patients at the expense of other urgent social problems."[40] Genetic screening programs raise serious questions: Who shall live? Who shall be allowed to have children?

Who shall make such decisions? Is this a direction our country ought to take?

In the future, genetic screening during pregnancy could be used to detect a wide variety of inherited disorders. For example, Huntington's chorea is an inherited disease whose principal symptoms are involuntary movements—either rapid, forcible, and jerky or smooth and sinuous. This disorder is often associated with loss of intellectual abilities. Its onset is usually evidenced during middle age. If a fetus is diagnosed as having this disorder (which usually results in serious mental and physical deterioration in midlife), the pregnant woman and her partner would then be faced with the heart-wrenching decision of whether it would be best to terminate the pregnancy.

The eugenics (scientific breeding) movement was proposed late in the 19th century and embraced by many scientists and government officials. Similar to today, eugenics was designed to improve humanity or individual races by encouraging procreation by those deemed "most desirable" and discouraging it in those judged "deficient." The movement fell into disfavor for a while when Adolf Hitler used it to justify the Holocaust, in which millions of Jews, Gypsies, homosexuals, persons with a cognitive disability, and others were exterminated. Are we headed in a similar direction again?

CLONING

This term refers to the process whereby a new organism is reproduced from the nucleus of a single cell. The resultant new organism has the same genetic characteristics of the organism that contributes the nucleus. In effect, it probably will be possible to make biological carbon copies of humans from a single cell. Biologically, each cell is a blueprint containing all the genetic code information for the design of the organism. Cloning has already been used to reproduce frogs, mice, cattle, sheep, and other animals.[41]

One type of cloning amounts to a nuclear transplant. The nucleus of an unfertilized egg is destroyed and removed. The egg is then injected with the nucleus of a body cell by one means or another. It should then start to take orders from the new nucleus, begin to reproduce cells, and eventually manufacture a baby with the same genetic features as the donor. The embryo would need a place to develop into a baby—either an artificial womb or a woman willing to supply her own. (The technology for a complete artificial womb is not yet in sight.) The resultant clone would start life with a genetic endowment identical to that of the donor, although learning experiences might alter the physical development or personality. The possibilities are as fantastic as they are repulsive. With a quarter-inch piece of skin, one could produce 1000 genetic copies of any noted scientist or of anyone else! Imagine a professional basketball team that is composed of two Shaquille O'Neals and three Michael Jordans!

In 1993 a university researcher in Washington cloned human embryos, using a technique that already was widely used to clone animal embryos. The process involves taking a single human embryo and splitting it into identical twins.[42] Because human embryos can be frozen and gestated at a later date, it is now possible for parents to have a child and then, years later, use a cloned, frozen embryo to give birth to an identical twin. It is also possible for parents to save identical copies of embryos so that, if a child ever needed an organ transplant, the mother could give birth to the child's identical twin, who would be a perfect match for organ donation.

Cloning could, among other things, be used to resolve the ancient controversy of heredity versus environment. But there are grave dangers and undreamed-of complications. What is to prevent the Adolf Hitlers from making copies of themselves? Will cloning fuel the population explosion? What legal rights will clones be accorded (regarding inheritance, for example)? Will religions recognize clones as having a "soul"? Who will decide which individuals can make clones of themselves? Couples may face the choice of having children naturally or raising children who are copies of themselves.

EXHIBIT 1.2

Mr. Mom: Men Can Give Birth

Scientists say that the technology now exists to enable men to give birth! Male pregnancy would involved fertilizing a donated egg with sperm outside the body. The embryo would then be implanted into the bowel area, where it could attach itself to a major organ, such as a kidney or the wall of the large intestine. In addition, to achieve pregnancy, men would have to receive hormone treatment to stimulate changes that occur naturally in women during pregnancy. Because the embryo creates the placenta, the embryo theoretically would receive sufficient nourishment. The baby would be delivered by cesarean section.

Any attempt at male pregnancy would carry risks (perhaps some as-yet-unknown risks) for both the man and the embryo. Will some men try it? If people risk their lives climbing Mt. Everest, someone is likely to try this.

Source: "Mr. Mom," *Wisconsin State Journal,* May 9, 1986, sec. 1, p. 2.

BREAKING THE GENETIC CODE
Biochemical genetics is the discipline that studies the mechanisms whereby genes control the development and maintenance of the organism. Current research is focused on understanding more precisely the roles of DNA (deoxyribonucleic acid) and messenger RNA (ribonucleic acid) in affecting the growth and maintenance of humans. When genes, DNA, and RNA are more fully understood, it may become possible to keep people alive, young, and healthy almost indefinitely.[43] It is predicted that aging will be controlled, and any medical condition (for example, an allergy, obesity, cancer, arthritic pain) will be relatively easily treated and eradicated. Such possibilities stagger the imagination.

EXHIBIT 1.3

Will Fetal Tissue Be Used for Medical Treatments?

Pioneering surgery has demonstrated that fetal tissue transplants can be used successfully to replace damaged nerve cells in victims of Parkinson's disease. Parkinson's disease is a neurological disorder that causes severe shaking and eventually death. Transplants of insulin-producing cells from fetuses also show promise in treating diabetes as well.

Would some women seek to abort a fetus so that its tissue could be used for such medical purposes? In January 1988 a woman appeared on Ted Koppel's *Nightline* television show and declared that she wanted to get pregnant for the sole purpose of aborting the fetus and using its tissue to treat her Parkinson's disease–stricken father.

Budiansky reported a case of a woman seeking to conceive in order to abort the fetus, whose tissue could then be used to treat her own diabetes.[a]

Many people would find this use of reproductive technology to be horrifying. Yet most states have no legal means to stop such activities—or even to prohibit the sale of fetal tissue.

---

[a] Stephen Budiansky, "The New Rules of Reproduction," *U.S. News & World Report*, April 18, 1988, pp. 66–67.

Scientists have already discovered the genes that cause a variety of illnesses, such as cystic fibrosis, and demonstrated that gene therapy can be used to correct the underlying defect.[44] The approach uses genetically engineered cold viruses to ferry healthy genes into the body. (Cystic fibrosis results from a mutation in the gene that produces a protein called cystic fibrosis transmembrane conductive regulator. When the protein is missing, thick mucus builds up in the lungs, causing lung damage and eventually death, often by age 30.)

With this potential to break the genetic code and to keep people alive and healthy indefinitely, we will be faced with many legal and ethical issues. Perhaps the most crucial issues will be who will live and who will die and who will be permitted to have children. A fountain of youth may occur within our lifetime.

New Family Forms

As we've seen, technology has had profound effects on the family. Now we'll look at some changes in the social structure of our society that also are causing us to redefine our notion of what a family is.

CHILDLESS COUPLES

Traditionally, our society has fostered the perception that there is something wrong with a couple who decides not to have children. Parenthood is regarded legally and religiously as one of the central components of a marriage. In some states, deceiving one's spouse before marriage about the desire to remain childless is grounds for an annulment. Perhaps in the future this myth of procreation will be shattered by the concern about overpopulation, by the high cost of raising children (the average cost of raising a child from birth to age 18 is estimated to be over $140,000),[45] and by a shift in interests among married people away from the domestic tasks related to raising children and toward other types of recreational, cultural, educational, and leisure-time experiences.

POSTPONEMENT OF PARENTHOOD UNTIL MIDDLE AGE OR LATER

Biological innovations, such as embryo transfers, are now making it possible for women in their fifties and even their sixties to give birth. As a result, couples have more leeway in deciding at what age they wish to raise children. Young couples today are often torn in their time commitments between their children and their careers. In our society most couples now have children at the busiest time of their lives. Deferring raising children until later in life provides substantial activity and meaning to old age. A major question, of course, is whether such a family pattern will generate a population of orphans, thus affecting adoption and foster-care services. Another important question is whether such a pattern would lead to even more gaps in values between older parents and their young children.

PROFESSIONAL PARENTS

Alvin Toffler predicts that our society will develop a system of professional, trained, and licensed parents, to whom a number of natural parents (bioparents) will turn to raise their children.[46] The natural parents would of course be permitted frequent visits, telephone contacts, and time to care for the children whenever they desire. Toffler states: "Even now millions of parents, given the opportunity, would happily relinquish their parental responsibilities—and not necessarily through irresponsibility or lack of love. Harried, frenzied, up against the wall, they have come to see themselves as inadequate to the tasks."[47] The high rates of child abuse, child neglect, and teenage runaways seen to bear out the assertion that in a large number of families the parent/child relationship is more dissatisfying than satisfying.[48] Many parents already hire part-time professional parents in the form of nannies and day-care-center workers.

In our society there is currently a belief system that bioparents should care for their children, even if they find the responsibility unrewarding. Only a tiny fraction of bioparents currently terminate their parental rights. Why? Could it be that many parents who have an unsatisfying relationship with their children are reluctant to give up their parenting responsibilities because of the stigma that would be attached? Two hundred years ago divorces were rare, mostly due to a similar stigma. Now, with increased acceptance of divorce, one out of two marriages is being terminated. Is it not also feasible that a number of parents who cannot choose the characteristics of their children may also find the relationships with those children to be more dissatisfying than satisfying? The point is reinforced when it is remembered that a number of pregnancies are unplanned *and* unwanted.

SERIAL AND CONTRACT MARRIAGES

Culturally, religiously, and legally speaking, marriages are still expected to be permanent, for a lifetime. Such a view implies that the two partners made the right decision when they married, that their personalities and abilities complement each other, and that their personalities and interests will develop in tandem for the rest of their lives. All of these suppositions (along with the concept of permanency) are being called into question, however.

With the high rates of divorce and remarriage, a number of sociologists have pointed out that a small proportion of our population is entering (perhaps unintentionally) into serial marriages— that is, a pattern of successive, temporary marriages.[49] Serial marriages among celebrities have been widely publicized for a number of years. Viewing marriage as temporary in nature may help reduce some of the embarrassment and pain still associated with divorce and perhaps result in an increase in the number of unhappily married people who will seek a divorce. Divorce per se is neither good nor bad; if both partners find that their lives are happier and more satisfying following legal termination, the end result may well be viewed as desirable.

The growing divorce rate has resulted in the development of extensive services involving premarital counseling, marriage counseling, divorce counseling, single-parent services and programs, and remarriage counseling for spouses and the children involved. If marriage is increasingly viewed as temporary in nature, divorce may become even more frequent and result in an expansion of related social services.

Several sociologists have proposed that the concept of marriage as temporary be legally institutionalized through contract marriage. For example, a couple would be legally married for a two-year period, and (only in those marriages where there are no children) the marriage would automatically be terminated unless they filed legal papers for a continuation.[50]

Another arrangement embodying the temporary concept is "trial marriage," which is increasingly being tested out by young people. They live on a day-by-day basis and share expenses. Closely related—and perhaps more common—is the arrangement in which the two maintain separate addresses and domiciles but for several days a month actually live together. (Perhaps this latter form is more accurately described as a "serial honeymoon" than a "trial marriage.") Acceptance of trial marriages is currently being advocated by some religious philosophers, and many states no longer define cohabitation as illegal.

Increasingly, courts are ruling that cohabiting couples who dissolve their living arrangements have certain legal obligations to each other quite similar to the obligations of a married couple.

OPEN MARRIAGES

O'Neill and O'Neill contrast traditional marriages with "open marriages," of which they are advocates.[51] A traditional or "closed" marriage, the O'Neills assert, embodies concepts such as (1) possession or ownership of mate; (2) denial or stifling of self; (3) playing of the "couples game" by doing everything together during leisure time; (4) the man's dominating and being out in the world and the woman's being domestic and passive and staying at home with the children; and (5) absolute fidelity. An open marriage, in contrast, offers freedom to pursue individual interests, flexible roles in meeting financial responsibilities, shared domestic tasks, and expansion and growth through openness. Such a marriage is based on communication, trust, and respect, and it is expected that one partner's growth will facilitate the other partner's development.

Marriage counselors increasingly report that couples have serious interaction difficulties because one spouse has a traditional orientation whereas the other has an open-marriage orientation. The feminist movement and the changing roles of women have brought the conflict between open and closed marriages into public awareness. Marriage counselors now see large numbers of couples in which the wife wants a career, her own identity, and a sharing of domestic responsibilities but the husband, traditionally oriented, wants his wife to stay at home and take care of the domestic tasks.

GROUP MARRIAGES

Group marriage provides insurance against isolation. In the 1960s and 1970s, communes of young people flourished. In the later 1970s and in the 1980s most communes disbanded. The goals, as well as the structure, of these communes varied widely, involving diverse social, political, religious, sexual, or recreational objectives.

Interestingly, geriatric communes (which have many of the characteristics and obligations of group marriages) are being advocated by a number of sociologists.[52] Such arrangements may be a solution to a number of social problems of the elderly. They may provide companionship, new meaning, and interest to the participants' lives, as well as an arrangement in which elderly people with reduced functioning capacities can be of mutual assistance to one another. The elderly can thereby band together, pool resources, hire nursing or domestic help if needed, and feel that "life begins at 60." In nursing homes a number of the elderly are presently developing relationships that have similarities to a group marriage.

HOMOSEXUAL MARRIAGES AND ADOPTIONS

Gay liberation groups seek to inform the public about the "naturalness" of homosexual expression and attempt to change current legislation.[53] England has already rewritten its statutes: Homosexual relations between consenting adults in that country are no longer considered a crime. A number of marriages between homosexuals have taken place in churches in the United States, in Europe, and in other countries. (It should be noted, however, that no state in this country yet recognizes homosexual marriages as legal.)

Adoption agencies and the courts are now facing decisions about whether to allow homosexual couples to adopt children. Single people are already being permitted by some agencies and courts to adopt children, so the argument that a child needs both a male and a female figure in the family is diluted.

TRANSRACIAL ADOPTIONS

Oriental and Native American children have been adopted by white parents for more than four decades.[54] About 30 years ago some white couples

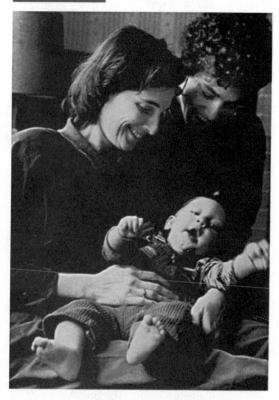

In the last few years gay parenting has led to an unforeseen kind of baby boom. Although some couples still face legal obstacles as adoptive and foster parents, many others, like this lesbian couple, have chosen to have their own babies, often through artificial insemination procedures.

began adopting African American children. A number of questions have arisen about the desirability of black/white placement, which brings together into a family unit the two polar races in our society. To answer some of these questions, I conducted a study comparing the satisfactions derived and problems encountered between transracial adoptive parents and inracial adoptive parents.[55] Transracial adoptions were found to be as satisfying as inracial adoptions. In addition, transracial adoptive children were found to have been accepted by relatives, friends, neighbors, and the general community following placement.

The transracial adoptive parents reported that substantially fewer problems have arisen due to the race of the child than even they anticipated before the adoption. They also indicated that they had parental feelings that the child was really their own. They reported becoming "color-blind" following placement—that is, they came to see the child not as African American, but as a member of their family.

Unfortunately, none of the children in the study were older than 6. Some observers, a number of whom are African American, have raised questions about whether black children reared by white parents will experience serious identity problems as they grow older. For example, will they experience difficulty in deciding which race to identify with, in learning how to cope with racial discrimination due to being raised in a white home, and in interacting with both whites and blacks due to a (speculated) confused sense of who they are? On the other hand, advocates of transracial adoption respond by asserting that the parent/child relationship is more crucial to identity formation than the racial composition of the members of the family. The question of course is critical, especially since there are a large number of homeless African American children and a shortage of black adoptive parents.

One organization that has been strongly opposed to the adoptive placement of black children in white homes is the National Association of Black Social Workers. This group views such placements as "cultural genocide."[56]

In 1971 Rita J. Simon began studying 204 white families who had adopted minority children. Joined later by Howard Altstein and many generations of graduate students, she went back to talk to the families over a period of 20 years.[57] The researchers interviewed the families in 1971, 1979, 1983, and 1991. Most of the children they studied now live away from their parents' homes. The majority of adoptees, despite occasional family conflicts, believe that their parents raised them well. If anything, some felt that the parents had overdone it a bit in trying to educate them about their heritage. African American adoptees, for example, complained that too many dinnertime conversations turned into lectures on black history.

The parents, although also acknowledging occasional conflicts, reported satisfaction with their decisions to adopt across racial lines. Fully 90% said they recommended transracial adoption for families who are planning to adopt. The researchers concluded that minority children who grow up in white families do not become confused about their identities, racial or otherwise.

COMARITAL SEX

The term *comarital sex* refers to mate swapping and other organized extramarital relations in which both spouses agree to participate. Comarital sex is distinctly different from a traditional extramarital affair, which is usually clandestine, with the straying spouse trying to hide the relationship.

Although some couples appear able to integrate comarital agreements into their lives successfully, others find their marriages breaking up as a consequence.[58] According to marriage counselors, a major reason why couples drop out of comarital relationships, and sometimes end their marriage, is because of jealousy, competition, and possessiveness.[59]

The interest in comarital sex and extramarital sex raises the age-old question of whether any *one* individual can satisfy all of the intimate, sexual, and interpersonal needs of another. In the future (and perhaps already now) there may be a decrease in comarital and extramarital relationships due to the increasing fear of AIDS.

SINGLE PARENTHOOD

Although in many people's minds marriage and parenthood "go together," single parenthood is emerging as a prominent form in our society. In many states it is possible for unmarried people to adopt a child. Also, an unmarried pregnant woman can refuse to marry and yet keep her child after it is born. Some unmarried fathers have been successful in obtaining custody of their child. Today, although the stigma attached to being single and pregnant is not as strong as it once was, this situation is still seriously frowned on by some.

Similar to single parenthood is the one-parent family, in which a person divorces or legally separates and assumes custody of one or more children and chooses not to remarry. Although traditionally the mother has been awarded custody of the children, today the courts are granting custody to more fathers. Another arrangement is shared custody, wherein both mother and father have the children part of the time.

Do single parents and one-parent families pose a serious problem for society? Are children adversely affected by being raised in a one-parent family? Papalia and Olds summarize some of the problems children face in growing up in one-parent families:

> Children growing up in one-parent homes undoubtedly have more problems and more adjustments to make than children growing up in homes where there are two adults to share the responsibilities for child rearing, to provide a higher income, to more closely approximate cultural expectations of the "ideal family," and to offer a counterpoint of sex-role models and an interplay of personalities. But the two-parent home is not always ideal, and the one-parent home is not necessarily pathological.[60]

Research indicates that it is better for children to be raised in a non-tension-laden one-parent family than in a tension-laden two-parent family.[61]

BLENDED FAMILIES

Many terms have been used to describe two families joined by the marriage of one parent to another: *stepfamilies, blended families, reconstituted families,* and *nontraditional families.* Here we will use the term *blended families.*

One out of two marriages ends in divorce, and many divorcees have children. Most people who divorce remarry someone else within a few years. Moreover, some individuals who are marrying for the first time may have a child born out of wedlock. Thus a variety of blended families are now being formed in our society.

In blended families one or both spouses have biologically produced one or more children with someone else prior to their current marriage. Often the newly married couple give birth to additional children. In yet other blended families the children are biologically a combination of "his, hers, and theirs."

Blended families are increasing in number and proportion in our society, and the family dynamics and relationships are much more complex than in the traditional nuclear family. Blended families, in short, are burdened by much more "baggage" than are two childless adults marrying for the first time. Blended families must deal with stress that arises from the loss (through divorce or death) experienced by both adults and children, which can make them afraid to love and to trust. Previously established bonds between children and their biological parents, or loyalty to a dead or absent parent, may interfere with the formation of ties to the stepparent. If children go back and forth between two households, conflicts between stepchildren and stepparents may be intensified. Sometimes, divorced spouses continue to feud; in these cases the children are likely to be used as "pawns," thus generating additional strife in the recently formed blended family.

Some difficulties in adjustment for the children are to be expected.[62] Jealousies may arise because the child resents sharing parental attention with the new spouse and with new siblings. Another issue for children is the adjustment to a new parent who may have different ideas, values, rules, and expectations. Sharing space with new people can be a source of stress as well. In addition, if one member of the couple enters the marriage with no child-rearing experience, an adjustment will be necessary by all family members to allow time for the new parent to learn and adapt.

People come into a blended family with ideas and issues based on past experiences. Old relationships and ways of doing things still have their impacts. In discussing blended families, Stuart and Jacobson note that marrying a new partner involves marrying a whole new family.[63] A blended family differs from a traditional family in that more people are involved, including ex-spouses, former in-laws, and an assortment of cousins, uncles, and aunts. The married couple may have both positive and negative interactions with this large supporting cast. If a prior marriage ended bitterly, the unresolved emotions that remain (such as anger and insecurity) will affect the present relationship.

The area of greatest stress for most stepparents is that of child rearing. A stepchild, used to being raised in a certain way, may balk at having to conform to new rules or at accepting the stepparent as a parental figure. Such difficulty is more likely to arise if the stepchild feels remorse over the missing parent. If the husband and wife disagree about how to raise children, the chances of conflict are substantially increased. Stepparents and stepchildren also face the problem of adjusting to each other's habits and personalities. Kompara recommends that stepparents not rush into establishing a relationship with stepchildren; proceeding gradually is more likely to result in a trusting and positive relationship.[64] Kompara also notes that becoming a stepparent is usually more difficult for a woman because children tend to be emotionally closer to their biological mother and have spent more time with her than with the father.

Three myths about blended families need to be addressed.[65] First, there is the myth of the "wicked stepmother"—the idea that the stepmother is not really concerned about what is best for the children but only about her own well-being. A scene from the children's story "Cinderella" might be brought to mind. Here, the "wicked stepmother" cruelly keeps Cinderella from going to the ball in hopes that her own biological daughters will have a better chance at nabbing the handsome prince. In reality, stepmothers have been found to establish positive and caring relationships with their stepchildren, provided that the stepmothers have a strong self-concept and the affirmation of their husband.[66]

A second myth is that "step is less."[67] In other words, stepchildren will never hold the same place in the hearts of parents that biological children do. The fact is that people can learn to love each other and are motivated to bind members of their new family together.

The third myth is that, the moment families are joined, they will have instant love for each other.[68] Relationships take time to develop and grow. The idea of instant strong love bonds is unrealistic. People involved in any relationship need time to get to know each other, test each other out, and grow to feel comfortable with each other.

Stinnet and Walters reviewed the research literature on stepparenthood and came to the following conclusions: (1) integration tends to be easier in families that have been split by divorce rather than by death, perhaps because the children realize the first marriage did not work out; (2) stepparents and stepchildren come to the blended family with· unrealistic expectations that love and togetherness will occur rapidly; (3) children tend to see a stepparent of the opposite sex as playing favorites with their own children; (4) most children continue to miss and admire the absent biological parent; (5) male children tend more readily to accept a stepparent, particularly if the new parent is a male; and (6) adolescents have greater difficulty accepting a stepparent than do young children or adult children.[69]

Berman and Visher and Visher offer the following suggestions to parents in blended families for increasing the chances of positive relationships developing between adults and children:[70]

1. *Maintain a courteous relationship with the former spouse or spouses.* Children adjust best after a divorce when there is a harmonious relationship between former spouses. Problems are intensified when former spouses continue to insult each other and when the children are used as weapons (''pawns'') for angry former spouses to hurt each other.

2. *Understand the emotions of children.* Although the newlyweds in a recently blended family may be fairly euphoric about their relationship, they need to be perceptive and responsive to the fears, concerns, and resentments of their children.

3. *Allow time for loving relationships to develop between stepparents and stepchildren.* Stepparents need to be aware that their stepchildren will probably have emotional ties to their absent biological parent and that the stepchildren may resent the breakup of the marriage between their biological parents. Some children may even feel responsible for their biological parents' separation. Others may try to make life difficult for the stepparent so that he or she will leave, with the hope that the biological parents will then reunite. Stepparents need to be perceptive and understanding of such feelings and patiently allow the stepchildren to work out their concerns and take time in bonding.

4. *New rituals, traditions, and ways of doing things need to be developed that seem right and enjoyable for all members of the blended family.* Sometimes it is helpful to move to a new residence that does not hold memories of the past. Leisure time should be structured so that the children spend time alone with the biological parent, with the stepparent, with both, and with the absent parent or parents. In addition, the new spouses need to spend some time alone with each other. New rituals should be developed for holidays, birthdays, and other special days.

5. *Seek social support.* Parents in blended families should seek to share their concerns, feelings, frustrations, experiences, coping strategies, and triumphs with other stepparents and stepchildren. Such sharing allows them to view their own situations more realistically and to learn from the experiences of others.

THE SINGLE LIFE

In our society, women—and, to a lesser extent, men—are brought up to believe that one of their most important goals is to marry. Women who remain unmarried are labeled ''old maids.'' Elaborate rituals have been developed to romanticize engagement and marriage. Unfortunately, many couples discover after the honeymoon that marriage is not always romantic or exciting. Many people deal with unfulfilled marriages with a series of divorces and remarriages. In the 1970s and early 1980s an increasing number of adults turned away from the responsibilities and restrictions of marriage by choosing to remain single. Temporary and sometimes long-term deep emotional relationships were entered into without the duties and restrictions imposed by a legal arrangement.

At present there appears to be a shift in sexual values. The sexual revolution that began in the 1960s and that glamorized multiple recreational sexual relationships appears to be on the decline. The current renewed interest in sharply limiting the number of sexual partners is largely due to the fear of acquiring AIDS. People are recognizing that, the more sexual partners they have, the greater their chances of being exposed to the AIDS virus.

It is unclear at this point where the threat of AIDS will lead to a decline in the number of people who choose to remain single. It should be noted that increases in the number of people who remain single have significant implications for social welfare: Statistics show higher rates of depression, loneliness, alcoholism, suicide, drug abuse, and alienation among those who are single.

Concluding Comments

To summarize, it appears that the family of tomorrow will face a future shock. Technological developments (particularly in biology and medicine—for example, cloning and human embryo implants) may dramatically affect the family, raising a number of ethical, legal, social, and personal questions. In addition, the family is assuming a number of different forms that may dramatically alter the central characteristics of future families. We are now seeing childless couples, postponement of child rearing until middle age or later, professional parents, serial and contract marriages, one-parent families, blended families, comarital sex, open marriages, group marriages for all age groups, homosexual marriages and adoptions, transracial adoptions, and a growing number of unmarrieds.

Other changes being experimented with are interracial marriages and marriages involving partners of unequal ages. Because of technological advances and the experimentation with new family forms, the style of living for all families may be substantially changed. Some individuals will probably find these changes exciting, personally satisfying, and functional; others may be less adaptable and find such changes extremely difficult and perhaps even overwhelming, resulting in personal disintegration. In any case, changes that are made in the American family will have important implications for the field of social welfare.

SUMMARY

The goal of social welfare is to fulfill the social, financial, health, and recreational needs of everyone in a society. The provision of social services has become one of the most important activities in our society in terms of the money spent, the human misery treated, and the number of people served.

Social welfare overlaps with sociology, psychology, and other disciplines on a knowledge-base level. When theories and research in other academic disciplines have direct applications to the social welfare goal of enhancing the social functioning of people, then this knowledge is also part of the knowledge base of social welfare.

Social welfare overlaps with social work at a practice (service) level. Almost all social workers work in the field of social welfare, but there are also many other professional and occupational groups that work within this field. Social welfare is erroneously conceived at times as synonymous with public assistance, but public assistance is only one of several hundred social welfare programs.

Social welfare institutions are composed of social service programs and social service organizations. The purposes of social welfare institutions are to prevent, alleviate, and contribute to the solution of recognized social problems so as to directly improve the well-being of individuals, groups, families, organizations, and communities.

Currently there are two conflicting views of the role of social welfare in our society: the residual versus the institutional orientation. The residual approach characterized social welfare programs from early history to the depression of the 1930s, at which time programs with an institutional orientation began to be implemented. Social welfare programs have in the past been influenced (and to some extent still are) by the Protestant ethic, the laissez-faire economic view, social Darwinism, individualism, the Industrial Revolution, and humanitarian ideals. The two prominent political philosophies in the United States are liberalism and conservatism. Liberals generally adhere to an institutional orientation, whereas conservatives tend to adhere to a residual orientation.

There are likely to be important changes in the social welfare field in the future, primarily due to anticipated technological advances. In summary form, technological advances largely determine changes in our lifestyles; lifestyle changes largely determine changes in our future social, financial, health, and recreational needs; and the latter changes largely determine changes in needed social service programs.

Dramatic changes are also anticipated in the American family of the future, due to technological advances in biology and medicine and to the current experimentation with new family forms. Some of these new forms will be found dysfunctional and will be discarded, whereas others will be found satisfying and functional and will probably be incorporated into the "typical" family of the future. The anticipated technological advances and the adoption of new family forms will result in the creation of new social service programs and the expansion of certain existing programs. Unless such changes are carefully examined and planned, our society faces a future shock.

NOTES

1. Ralph Dolgoff and Donald Feldstein, *Undergraduate Social Welfare* (New York: Harper & Row, 1980).
2. Robert L. Barker, *The Social Work Dictionary*, 2d ed. (Silver Spring, MD: National Association of Social Workers, 1991), p. 221.
3. *The American Heritage Dictionary*, 2d college ed. (Boston: Houghton Mifflin, 1982), p. 1103.
4. Ibid.
5. National Association of Social Workers, *Standards for Social Service Manpower* (New York: NASW, 1983), pp. 4–5.
6. Barker, *The Social Work Dictionary*, p. 222.
7. Alfred Kahn, *Shaping the New Social Work* (New York: Columbia University Press, 1973), pp. 12–34.
8. Ibid., p. 10.
9. Harold Wilensky and Charles Lebeaux, *Industrial Society & Social Welfare* (New York: Free Press, 1965).
10. Ibid., p. 138.
11. Ibid., p. 139.
12. Lester F. Ward, *Dynamic Sociology*; reprint of 1883 ed. (New York: Johnson Reprint, 1968).
13. Walter Trattner, *From Poor Law to Welfare State: A History of Social Welfare in America* (New York: Free Press, 1974).
14. Beulah Compton, *Introduction to Social Welfare & Social Work* (Homewood, IL: Dorsey Press, 1980).
15. Trattner, *From Poor Law to Welfare State*.
16. J. M. Romanyshyn, *Social Welfare: Charity to Justice* (New York: Random House, 1971).
17. U.S. Bureau of the Census, *Statistical Abstract of the United States, 1994* (Washington D.C.: U.S. Government Printing Office, 1994).
18. Romanyshyn, *Social Welfare: Charity to Justice*.
19. "Poverty Gap Widens, Studies Reveal," *NASW News*, January 1990, p. 19.
20. William Kornblum and Joseph Julian, *Social Problems*, 7th ed. (Englewood Cliffs, NJ: Prentice-Hall, 1992), pp. 221–226.
21. W. F. Ogburn and M. F. Nimkoff, *Technology and the Changing Family* (New York: Houghton Mifflin, 1955).
22. Kornblum and Julian, *Social Problems*, pp. 468–475.
23. Alvin Toffler, *Future Shock* (New York: Bantam Books, 1970).
24. U.S. Bureau of the Census, *Statistical Abstract of the United States, 1994*.
25. Ibid.
26. Ogburn and Nimkoff, *Technology and the Changing Family*.
27. Ibid.
28. Alfred Kadushin and Judith A. Martin, *Child Welfare Services*, 4th ed. (New York: Macmillan, 1988).
29. Janet S. Hyde, *Understanding Human Sexuality*, 4th ed. (New York: McGraw-Hill, 1990), p. 608.
30. L. Rifken, *Who Should Play God?* (New York: Dell, 1977).
31. Ibid.
32. Ibid.
33. Art Caplan, "Superbaby Sperm Bank Morally Bankrupt," *Wisconsin State Journal*, Nov. 28, 1989, p. 9A.
34. Rita Christopher, "Mother's Little Helper," *Maclean's Magazine*, Mar. 10, 1980, p. 10.
35. "Dad Wins Custody of Baby M," *Wisconsin State Journal*, April 1987, p. 1.
36. Hyde, *Understanding Human Sexuality*, pp. 149–150.
37. "Healthy Baby Is Born from Donated Embryo," *Wisconsin State Journal*, Feb. 4, 1984, sec. 1, p. 2.
38. Stephen Budiansky, "The New Rules of Reproduc-

tion," *U.S. News & World Report,* Apr. 18, 1988, pp. 66–69.

39. Philip Reilly, *Genetics, Law, and Social Policy* (Cambridge, MA: Harvard University Press, 1977).

40. G. Bylinsky, "What Science Can Do about Hereditary Disease," *Fortune,* September 1974, pp. 148–160.

41. William R. Wineke, "Calves Cloned Successfully in UW Experiment," *Wisconsin State Journal,* Sept. 9, 1987, p. 1.

42. Gina Kolata, "Human Clones," *Wisconsin State Journal,* Oct. 23, 1993, p. 3A.

43. David M. Rorvik, "Making Men and Women without Men and Women," *Esquire,* April 1969, pp. 110–115.

44. Daniel O. Haney, "Cystic Fibrosis Therapy Promising," *Wisconsin State Journal,* Oct. 29, 1993, p. 7A.

45. Beth Brophy, "Children under Stress," *U.S. News & World Report,* Oct. 27, 1986, p. 59.

46. Toffler, *Future Shock,* p. 27.

47. Ibid., pp. 243–244.

48. Kadushin and Martin, *Child Welfare Services.*

49. Ethel Alpenfels, "Progressive Monogamy: An Alternate Pattern?" in *The Family in Search of a Future,* Herbert Otto, ed. (New York: Appleton-Century-Crofts, 1970), pp. 67–74.

50. Ibid.

51. George O'Neill and Nena O'Neill, *Open Marriage* (New York: M. Evans, 1971).

52. Victor Kassel, "Polygamy after Sixty," *Geriatrics,* 21 (April 1966).

53. Carl Wittman, "A Gay Manifesto," *Liberation,* February 1970, pp. 24–35.

54. David Fanshel, *Far from the Reservation* (Metuchen, NJ: Scarecrow Press, 1972).

55. Charles Zastrow, *Outcome of Black Children–White Parents Transracial Adoptions* (San Francisco: R & E Research Associated, 1977).

56. David L. Wheeler, "Black Children, White Parents:

The Difficult Issue of Transracial Adoption," *Chronicle of Higher Education,* Sept. 15, 1993, p. A16.

57. Ibid., p. A9.

58. Brian Gilmartin and D. V. Kusisto, "Some Personal and Social Characteristics of Mate-Sharing Swingers," in *Renovating Marriage,* R. Libby and R. Whitehurst, eds. (San Francisco: Consensus, 1973), pp. 146–166.

59. Duane Denfeld, "Dropouts from Swinging," *Family Coordinator,* January 1974, pp. 45–49.

60. Diane E. Papalia and Sally W. Olds, *Human Development,* 2d ed. (New York: McGraw-Hill, 1981), p. 326.

61. Kornblum and Julian, *Social Problems,* pp. 348–350.

62. C. Janzen and O. Harris, *Family Treatment in Social Work Practice,* 2d ed. (Itasca, IL: Peacock, 1986), p. 273.

63. R. B. Stuart and B. Jacobson, *Second Marriage: Make It Happy! Make It Last!* (New York: Norton, 1985).

64. D. Kompara, "Difficulties in the Socialization Process of Step-Parenting," *Family Relations,* 29 (1980), pp. 69–73.

65. Janzen and Harris, *Family Treatment,* pp. 275–276.

66. G. L. Shulman, "Myths That Intrude on the Adaptation of the Step-Family," *Social Casework,* 53, no. 3 (1972), pp. 131–139.

67. E. Wald, *The Remarried Family* (New York: Family Service Association of America, 1981).

68. Ibid.

69. N. Stinnet and J. Walters, *Relationships in Marriage and Family* (New York: Macmillan, 1977).

70. C. Berman, *Making It as a Stepparent: New Roles/New Rules* (New York: Bantam, 1981); E. Visher and J. Visher, "Stepparenting: Blending Families," in *Stress and the Family: Vol. I. Coping with Normative Transitions,* H. I. McCubbin and C. R. Figley, eds. (New York: Brunner/Mazel, 1983), pp. 87–98.

2

SOCIAL
WORK AS
A PROFESSION
AND A
CAREER

S ocial work is one of the primary professions that provides social welfare services. This chapter will:

- Define the profession of social work.
- Provide a brief history of social work.
- Describe the following social work activities: casework, case management, group work, group therapy, family therapy, and community organization.
- Describe the person-in-environment conceptualization for social work practice.
- Specify the goals of social work practice.
- Summarize societal stereotypes of social workers.
- Summarize employment settings and career opportunities in social work.
- Briefly describe international social work.

A BRIEF HISTORY OF SOCIAL WORK

Social work as a profession is of relatively recent origin. The first social welfare agencies began to be developed in the early 1800s in an attempt to meet the needs of people living in urban areas. These agencies, or services, were private agencies that were developed primarily at the initiation of the clergy and religious groups. Up until the early 1900s these services were provided exclusively by members of the clergy and wealthy "do-gooders" who had no formal training and little understanding of human behavior. The focus was on meeting such basic physical needs as food and shelter and attempting to "cure" emotional and personal difficulties with religious admonitions.

An illustration of an early social welfare organization was the Society for the Prevention of Pauperism, founded by John Griscom in 1820.[1] This society's goals were to investigate the habits and circumstances of the poor, to suggest plans by which the poor could help themselves, and to encourage the poor to save and economize. Toward these ends, they conducted house-to-house visitation of the poor (a very elementary type of social work).

By the last half of the 1800s a fairly large number of private relief agencies had been established in large cities to help the unemployed, the poor, the ill, persons with a physical or mental disability, and orphans. These agencies' programs were uncoordinated and sometimes overlapped. Therefore, an English innovation—the Charity Organization Society (COS)—caught the interest of a number of American cities.[2] Starting in Buffalo, New York, in 1877, COS was rapidly adopted in many cities. In charity organization societies, private agencies joined together to (1) provide direct services to individuals and families—in this respect they were forerunners of social casework and of family counseling approaches—and (2) plan and coordinate the efforts of private agencies to meet the pressing social problems of cities—in this respect they were precursors of community organization and social planning approaches. Charity organizations conducted a detailed investigation of each applicant for services and financial help, maintained a central system of registration of clients to avoid duplication, and used volunteer "friendly visitors" to work with those in difficulty. The friendly visitors were primarily "doers of good works"; they generally gave sympathy rather than money and encouraged the poor to save and to seek employment. Poverty was looked on as the result of a personal shortcoming. Most of the "friendly visitors" were women.

Concurrent with the COS movement was the establishment of settlement houses in the late 1800s. In 1884 Toynbee Hall became the first settlement house established in London; many others were soon formed in larger U.S. cities. Many of the early settlement house workers were daughters of ministers, usually from the middle and upper classes. In contrast to "friendly visitors," they lived in the impoverished neighborhoods and used the missionary approach of teaching residents how to live moral lives and improve their circumstances. They sought to improve housing, health, and living conditions; find jobs for neighborhood residents; teach English, hygiene, and occupational skills; and change environmental surroundings through cooperative efforts. Settlement houses used change techniques that are now referred to as social group work, social action, and community organization.

Settlement houses emphasized "environmental reform." At the same time "they continued to struggle to teach the poor the prevailing middle-class values of work, thrift, and abstinence as the keys to success."[3] In addition to dealing with local problems by local action, settlement houses played important roles in drafting legislation and in organizing to influence social policy and legislation. The most noted leader in the settlement house movement was Jane Addams of Hull House in Chicago (see Case Example 2.1).

It appears that the first paid social workers were executive secretaries of charity organization societies in the late 1800s.[4] At that time COSs received some contracts from the cities in which they were located to administer relief funds. They then hired people as executive secretaries to organize and train the "friendly visitors" and to establish bookkeeping procedures to show accountability for the funds received. To improve the services of "friendly visitors," executive secretaries established standards and training courses. The first such training course was offered for charity workers in 1898 by the New York Charity Organization Society. By 1904 a one-year program was offered by the New York School of Philanthropy. Soon many colleges and universities were offering training programs in social work.

Richard Cabot introduced medical social work at Massachusetts General Hospital in 1905.[5] Gradually social workers were employed in schools, courts, child guidance clinics, and other settings.

Early training programs in social work focused both on environmental reform efforts and on efforts to help individuals to adjust better to society. In 1917 Mary Richmond published *Social Diagnosis,* a text that presented for the first time a theory and methodology for social work.[6] The book focused on how the worker should intervene with individuals. The process is still used today and involves study (collecting information), diagnosis (stating what is wrong), prognosis (stating the prospect of improvement), and

treatment planning (stating what should be done to help clients improve). This text was important because it formulated a common body of knowledge for casework.

In the 1920s, Sigmund Freud's theories of personality development and therapy became popular. The concepts and explanations of psychiatrists appeared particularly appropriate for social workers, who also worked in one-to-one relationships with clients. The psychiatric approach emphasized intrapsychic processes and focused on enabling clients to adapt and adjust to their social situations. Thus most social workers switched their emphasis from "reform" to "therapy" for the next three decades. (In the 1960s, however, there was a renewed interest in sociological approaches, or reform, by social workers. Several reasons account for this change. Questions arose about the relevance and appropriateness of "talking" approaches with low-income clients, who tend to be nonverbal and who have urgent social and economic pressures. Furthermore, the effectiveness of many psychotherapeutic approaches was questioned.[7] Other reasons for the renewed interest included an increase in the status of sociology and the mood of the 1960s, which raised questions about the relevancy of social institutions in meeting the needs of the population. Social work at present embraces both the reform approach and the therapy approach.)

Not until the end of World War I did social work begin to be recognized as a distinct profession. The depression of the 1930s and the enactment of the Social Security Act in 1935 brought about an extensive expansion of public social services and job opportunities for social workers. Throughout this century there has been a growing awareness by social agency boards and the public that professionally trained social workers are needed to provide social services competently. In 1955 the National Association of Social Workers was formed, which represents the social work profession in this country. The purpose of this association is to improve social conditions in society and promote high quality and effectiveness in social work practice. The association publishes (1) several professional journals, most notably *Social Work;* (2) *The Encyclopedia of Social Work;*

CASE EXAMPLE 2.1   Jane Addams: A Prominent Founder of Social Work

Jane Addams

Jane Addams was born in 1860 in Cedarville, Illinois, the daughter of a successful couple who owned a flour mill and a wood mill. Jane graduated from Rockford Seminary (a college in Rockford, Illinois). She briefly attended medical school but was forced to leave because of illness. She then traveled for a few years in Europe, perplexed about what her life work should be. At the age of 25 she joined the Presbyterian Church, which helped her find a focus for her life: religion and humanitarianism—in particular, serving the poor. (Later in her life she joined the Congregational Church, now known as the United Church of Christ.) Addams heard about the establishment of Toynbee Hall in England and returned to Europe to study this approach. Its staff was composed of college students and graduates, mainly from Oxford, who lived in the slums of London to learn conditions firsthand and to contribute to the improvement of life in the slums with their own financial and personal resources.

Addams returned to the United States and rented a two-story house (later called Hull House) in Chicago. Hull House was located in an impoverished neighborhood. With a few friends, Addams initiated a variety of group and individual activities for the community. She started a literature reading group for young women and a kindergarten. There also were groups focusing on social relationships, sports, music, painting, art, and current affairs. Hull House also provided services to individuals who came asking for immediate help, such as food and shelter and information and referral for other services. A Hull House Social Science Club was formed, which studied social problems in a scientific manner and then became involved in social action efforts to improve living conditions. One of its successful efforts was to work for passage of Illinois legislation to prevent the employment of children in the sweatshops of the area. Addams also became interested in the various ethnic groups in the neighborhood around Hull House. She was fairly successful in bringing the various nationalities together at Hull House, where they could interact and interchange cultural values.

The success of Hull House served as a model for the establishment of settlement houses in other areas of Chicago and in many other large cities in the United States. Settlement house leaders believed that, by improving neighborhoods, they would improve communities; by altering communities, they would develop a better society. For her extraordinary contributions, Jane Addams received the Nobel Prize for Peace in 1931.

Source: Adapted from "Jane Addams," by Herbert Stroup, pp. 1–29, in *Social Welfare Pioneers.* Copyright © 1986 by Nelson-Hall Publishers. Reprinted by permission.

and (3) a monthly newsletter entitled *NASW News*. The newsletter publishes current social work news as well as a list of job vacancies throughout the country.

In recent years there has been considerable activity in developing a system of certification, or licensing of social workers. Such a system both helps assure the public that qualified personnel are providing social work services and advances the recognition of social work as a profession. All states have now passed legislation to license or regulate the practice of social work. Although a young profession, social work is growing and gaining increased respect and recognition.

A MULTISKILLED PROFESSION

Social work is the professional activity of helping individuals, groups, families, organizations, and communities to enhance or restore their capacity for social functioning and to create societal conditions favorable to their goals.[8] The term *social worker* has been defined by the National Association of Social Workers as follows:

> *Graduates of schools of social work (with either bachelor's or master's degrees), who use their knowledge and skills to provide social services for* clients *(who may be individuals, families, groups, communities, organizations, or society in general). Social workers help people increase their capacities for problem solving and coping and help them obtain needed resources, facilitate interactions between individuals and between people and their environments, make organizations responsible to people, and influence social policies.*[9]

Social work is distinct from other professions (such as psychology and psychiatry) by virtue of its responsibility and mandate to provide social services.

A social worker needs training and expertise in a wide range of areas to be able to handle effectively the problems faced by individuals, groups, families, organizations, and the larger commu-

nity. Whereas most professions are becoming more specialized (for example, nearly all medical doctors now specialize in one or two areas), social work continues to emphasize a generic (broad-based) approach. The practice of social work is analogous to the old, now-fading practice of general medicine. A general practitioner in medicine was trained to handle a wide range of common medical problems faced by people; a social worker is trained to handle a wide range of common social and personal problems faced by people. Case Example 2.2 highlights some of the skills needed by social workers. This "success" story (in most cases the outcome is not as promising) documents the range of abilities displayed by Mr. Tounsend: interviewing skills, knowledge of how to counsel people with sexual problems and feelings of depression, ability to work effectively with other agencies, premarital counseling skills, research and grant-writing skills, program development and fund-raising skills, and knowledge of how to handle ethical/legal issues that arise.

Perhaps the most basic skill that a social worker needs is the ability to counsel clients effectively. Anyone who is not able to do this should probably not be in social work—certainly not in direct service. The second most important skill is the ability to interact effectively with other groups and professionals in the area. A social worker, like a general practitioner, requires a wide range of skills that will enable him or her to intervene effectively in (1) the common personal and emotional problems of clients and (2) the common social problems faced by groups, organizations, and the larger community. Social workers also need to have an accurate perception of their professional strengths and weaknesses. If a situation arises that a worker knows she or he does not have the training or expertise to handle, then the worker needs to be a "broker" and link those affected with available services.

A Problem-Solving Approach

In working with individuals, families, groups, organizations, and communities, social workers use a problem-solving approach. Steps in the problem-solving process can be stated in a variety of ways. Here is a simple description of the process:

1. Identify as precisely as possible the problem or problems.
2. Generate possible alternative solutions.
3. Evaluate the alternative solutions.
4. Select a solution or solutions to be used, and set goals.
5. Implement the solution(s).
6. Follow up to evaluate how the solution(s) worked.

(It should be noted that another conceptualization of the problem-solving approach is the change process of social work practice, which is described in Chapter 17.)

Generalist Social Work Practice

The Council on Social Work Education (the national accrediting entity for baccalaureate and master's programs in social work) requires all undergraduate and graduate-level programs to train their students in generalist social work practice. (MSW programs, in addition, usually require their students to select and study in an area of specialization. MSW programs generally offer several specializations, such as family therapy, administration, corrections, and clinical social work.)

A generalist social worker is trained to use the problem-solving process to assess and intervene with the problems confronting individuals, families, groups, organizations, and communities. Because of the importance of generalist practice, a full chapter (Chapter 17 in this text) is devoted to this topic.

MICRO, MEZZO, AND MACRO PRACTICE

Social workers practice at three levels: (1) micro—working on a one-to-one basis with an individual; (2) mezzo—working with families and other small groups; and (3) macro—working with organizations and communities or seeking changes in statutes and social policies.

The specific activities performed by workers include, but are not limited to, the following.

Social Casework

Aimed at helping individuals on a one-to-one basis to meet personal and social problems, casework may be geared to helping the client adjust to his/her environment or to changing certain social and economic pressures that are adversely affecting an individual. Social casework services are provided by nearly every social welfare agency that offers direct services to people.

Social casework encompasses a wide variety of activities, such as counseling runaway youths, helping unemployed people secure training or employment, counseling someone who is suicidal, placing a homeless child in an adoptive or foster home, providing protective services to abused children and their families, finding nursing homes for stroke victims who no longer require hospitalization, counseling individuals with sexual dysfunctions, helping alcoholics to acknowledge that they have a drinking problem, counseling those with a terminal illness; serving as a probation or parole officer, providing services to single parents, and working in medical and mental hospitals as a member of a rehabilitation team.

Case Management

Recently a number of social service agencies have labeled their social workers *case managers*. The tasks performed by case managers are similar to those of caseworkers. The job descriptions of case managers vary from service area to service area. For example, case managers in a juvenile probation setting are highly involved in supervising clients, providing some counseling, monitoring clients to make certain they are following the rules of probation, linking clients and their families with needed services, preparing court reports, and testifying in court. On the other hand, case

A Case Involving Suicide and Sexual Deviancy

D r. John Pritchard referred Dick Cherwenka to the Riverland Counseling Center (a mental health center). Mr. Cherwenka had briefly been hospitalized after slashing his wrists. This case was assigned to Tom Tounsend, MSW (master's degree in social work), who in the recent past had counseled most of the agency's attempted suicide cases. At the first two sessions Mr. Cherwenka presented an unusual account of the events that had led to his slashing his wrists.

His main problem centered around his desire to fondle the genitals of young girls (9 to 12 years old) whenever he felt depressed, tense, or at a "low tide." In the past four years he had been arrested on three occasions for this offense. The last time, 11 months ago, he was placed on probation for two years, and the judge warned that he would be sentenced to prison for an indeterminate sentence as a "sex deviant" if there were a recurrence of the offense. The day he slashed his wrists, he had felt quite depressed. While driving home from work, he stopped at a playground and began talking to a young girl. He offered her a ride home, and she accepted. Instead, he drove out into the country, where he fondled her. The girl was terrified. Mr. Cherwenka then drove her back, dropped her off a few blocks from her home, and informed her that serious harm would come to her if she told anyone. Mr. Cherwenka, after thinking about what he had done, became even more depressed and slashed his wrists a few hours later.

The social worker at this point informed Mr. Cherwenka that he (the social worker) faced an ethical/legal question of whether the police should be informed and that he would have to discuss his obligations with the director of the agency. Mr. Cherwenka indicated that he understood and proceeded to relate the following account of why he believed he had developed the desire to fondle young girls.

He had normal childhood experiences until age 8, when his mother died. After his mother's death, his father continued to raise him and his sister, who was 14 months older. However, his father changed; he became bitter toward life and began drinking heavily. In the evening he was at times in a drunken stupor. During these times he would be abusive, verbally and physically, to his children. Dick and his sister became very fearful of their father when he was drunk and sought ways to hide from him. Gradually, they learned to hide together under a blanket. While fearful and tense under the blanket, they sought ways to occupy their time and reduce their fear. As a result, they began fondling each other. Mr. Cherwenka indicated that this activity of hiding and fondling under a blanket when their father was drunk lasted for nearly three years, until an aunt moved into their home and began raising them.

managers at a sheltered workshop are likely to be involved in providing job training to clients, counseling clients, arranging transportation, disciplining clients for unacceptable behavior, acting as an advocate for clients, and acting as liaison with the people who supervise clients during their non-work hours (such as at a group home, foster home, residential treatment facility, or the parents' home). Hepworth and Larsen describe the role of a case manager as follows:

The social worker agreed with Mr. Cherwenka that his present desires to fondle young girls apparently resulted from his past learning experiences of coping with unwanted emotions. The problems that needed to be dealt with now were: (1) what ethical/legal obligations Mr. Tounsend and the mental health center had in regard to this admitted offense; (2) how to prevent Mr. Cherwenka from fondling young girls in the future; (3) how to help Mr. Cherwenka handle unwanted emotions; and (4) how to prevent Mr. Cherwenka from trying to take his life in the future. Because Mr. Cherwenka was engaged and planning to marry in two months, an additional situation that needed to be handled was his future relationship with his fiancée.

The following treatment plan was developed and then implemented. Mr. Tounsend discussed the ethical/legal obligations of this case with the agency director. It was decided that the probation department needed to be informed. Mr. Tounsend discussed this decision with Mr. Cherwenka. Mr. Tounsend then arranged a meeting with Mr. Cherwenka and his probation officer. Following this meeting it was agreed that the offense would be noted, but proceedings to revoke Mr. Cherwenka's probation would not be initiated as long as Mr. Cherwenka remained in counseling and no other offenses occurred.

The problems of preventing Mr. Cherwenka from fondling young girls and from committing suicide in the future were then addressed. It was agreed that, whenever Mr. Cherwenka had strong desires to fondle young girls or to take his life, he should immediately come to the center and voluntarily admit himself as an inpatient for a few hours or a few days until his desires subsided. (During the next 14 months, Mr. Cherwenka did voluntarily admit himself on three occasions.)

Gradually, by using rational therapy (described in Chapter 4), Mr. Cherwenka gained better control of his feelings of depression and his other unwanted emotions. Several meetings with Mr. Cherwenka and his fiancée were also held. After the initial shock of learning about Mr. Cherwenka's interest in young girls, his fiancée agreed to postpone the marriage for a year, while continuing the engagement.

As indicated earlier, this was only one of several potential suicide cases that Mr. Tounsend was handling. These cases led him to the conclusion that an emergency telephone number was needed that would be widely publicized and staffed 24 hours a day with professional counselors. He gathered data on the number of suicides in the area in the past year and obtained information from hospitals in the community about the number of attempted suicides. These data supported the need for an emergency counseling service. Mr. Tounsend then wrote a grant proposal, and, after ten months of searching for funding, his proposal was funded by a joint grant from the United Way and the Easter Seals Society.

Case managers link clients to needed resources that exist in complex service delivery networks and orchestrate the delivery of services in a timely fashion. Case managers function as brokers, facilitators, linkers, mediators, and advocates. A case manager must have extensive knowledge of community resources, rights of clients, and policies and procedures of various agencies and must be skillful in mediation and advocacy.[10]

Barker defines case management as follows:

A procedure to plan, seek, and monitor services from a variety of agencies and staff on behalf of a client. Usually one agency takes primary responsibility for the client and assigns a case manager, who coordinates services, advocates for the client, and sometimes controls resources and purchases services for the client. The procedure makes it possible for many social workers in the agency, or different agencies, to coordinate their efforts to serve a given client through professional teamwork, thus expanding the range of needed services offered. Case management may involve monitoring the progress of a client whose needs require the services of many different professionals, agencies, health care facilities, and human service programs.[11]

Group Work

The intellectual, emotional, and social development of individuals may be fostered through group activities. In contrast to casework or group therapy, it is not primarily therapeutic, except in a broad sense.

Different groups have different objectives, such as improving socialization, exchanging information, curbing delinquency, providing recreation, changing socially unacceptable values, helping to achieve better relations among cultural and racial groups, or explaining adoption procedures and helping applicants prepare for becoming adoptive parents. Activities and focuses of groups vary: arts and crafts, dancing, games, dramatics, music, photography, sports, nature study, woodworking, first aid, home management, information exchange, and discussion of such topics as politics, sex, marriage, religion, and career choice.

Group Therapy

Group therapy is aimed at facilitating the social, behavioral, and emotional adjustment of individuals through the group process. Participants in

group therapy usually have emotional, interactional, or behavioral difficulties. Group therapy has several advantages over one-to-one counseling, such as the operation of the *helper therapy* principle, which maintains that it is therapeutic for the helper (who can be any member of a group) to feel he or she has been helpful to others.[12] Group pressure is often more effective than one-to-one counseling in changing maladaptive behavior of individuals, and group therapy is a time saver in that it enables the therapist to treat several people at the same time. Group therapy has been especially effective for individuals who are severely depressed, have a drinking problem, are victims of a rape, are psychologically addicted to drugs, have a relative who is terminally ill, are single and pregnant, are recently divorced, or have an eating disorder.

Family Therapy

Family therapy, a type of group therapy aimed at helping families with interactional, behavioral, and emotional problems, can be used with parent/child interaction problems, marital conflicts, and conflicts with grandparents. Some of the problems dealt with in family therapy or family counseling include disagreements between parents and youths on choice of friends, drinking and other drug use, domestic tasks, curfew hours, communication problems, sexual values and behavior, study habits and grades received, and choice of dates.

Community Organization

The aim of community organization is stimulating and assisting the local community to evaluate, plan, and coordinate efforts to provide for the community's health, welfare, and recreation needs. It perhaps is not possible to define precisely the activities of a community organizer, but such activities are likely to include encouraging and fostering citizen participation, coordinating efforts between agencies or between groups, performing public relations, providing public educa-

Group work is utilized by a wide variety of institutions with equally wide-ranging objectives. This community center offers emergency shelter, counseling, support groups, recreational activities, and educational and career guidance to homeless teenagers in the San Francisco Bay Area.

tion, doing research, planning, and being a resource person. A community organizer acts as a catalyst in stimulating and encouraging community action.

Agency settings where such specialists are employed include community welfare councils, social planning agencies, health planning councils, and community action agencies. The term *community organization* is now being replaced in some settings by such labels as *planning, social planning, program development, policy development,* and *macro practice.*

Barker defines community organization as follows:

> *An intervention process used by social workers and other professionals to help individuals, groups, and collectives of people with common*

interests or from the same geographic areas to deal with social problems and to enhance social well-being through planned collective action. Methods include identifying problem areas, analyzing causes, formulating plans, developing strategies, mobilizing necessary resources, identifying and recruiting community leaders, and encouraging interrelationships between them to facilitate their efforts.[13]

Administration

Administration involves directing the overall program of a social service agency. Administrative functions include setting agency and program objectives, analyzing social conditions in the community, making decisions relating to what services will be provided, hiring and supervising staff members, setting up an organizational structure, administering financial affairs, and securing funds for the agency's operations. Administration also involves coordinating efforts to achieve selected goals, monitoring and revising internal procedures in order to improve effectiveness and efficiency, and performing whatever functions are required to transform social policy into social services. In social work the term *administration* is often used synonymously with *management*. In a small agency, administrative functions may be carried out by one person; in a larger agency several people may be involved in administrative affairs.

Other areas of professional activity in social work include research, consulting, supervision, planning, program development, policy development, and teaching (primarily at the college level). Social casework, case management, group work, group therapy, family therapy, and community organization constitute the primary professional activities that beginning-level social workers are likely to provide. All of these activities require counseling skills. (Counseling involves helping individuals or groups resolve social and personal problems through the process of developing a relationship, exploring the problem(s) in depth, and exploring alternative solutions; this process is described in Chapter 4.) Caseworkers, case managers, group workers, group therapists, and family therapists obviously need a high level of counseling skills in working with individuals and groups. Community organizers need to have relationship skills, to be perceptive, and to be able to assess problems and develop resolution strategies—abilities that parallel or are analogous to counseling skills.

Additionally, caseworkers must be able to do social histories and to link clients with other human services. In some agencies they are required to do public speaking, to prepare and present reports to courts and other agencies, to teach parents better parenting techniques, and so forth. Knowledge of evaluative procedures for assessing one's own effectiveness and the effectiveness of social programs is also helpful for the social worker. (Essential skills needed for social work practice are described in more detail in Chapter 17.)

A MEDICAL VERSUS A SYSTEMS MODEL OF HUMAN BEHAVIOR

From the 1920s to the 1960s most social work programs used a medical-model approach to assess and change human behavior. This approach was developed by Sigmund Freud.

The medical-model approach views clients as "patients." The task of the provider of services is first to diagnose the causes of a patient's problems and then provide treatment. The patient's problems are viewed as being inside the patient.

People with emotional or behavioral problems are given medical labels, such as schizophrenic, psychotic, borderline personality, or insane. Adherents of the medical approach believe that the disturbed person's mind is affected by some generally unknown, internal condition. That unknown, internal condition is thought to be due to a variety of possible causative factors: genetic endowment, metabolic disorders, infectious diseases, internal conflicts, unconscious use of defense mechanisms, and traumatic early experiences that cause emotional fixations and prevent future psychological growth.

The medical model provided a humane approach to treating people with emotional and behavioral problems. Prior to Freud, the emotionally disturbed were thought to be possessed by demons, viewed as being "mad," blamed for their disturbances, and often treated by being beaten or locked up. The medical-model approach emphasized intrapsychic processes and focused on enabling patients to adapt and adjust to their social situations.

In the 1960s social work began questioning the usefulness of the medical model. Environmental factors were shown to be at least as important in causing a client's problems as internal factors. Research also demonstrated that psychoanalysis was probably ineffective in treating clients' problems.[14] Social work thus shifted at least some of its emphasis to a reform approach.

A reform approach seeks to change systems to benefit clients. Antipoverty programs such as Head Start and the Job Corps are examples of efforts to change systems to benefit clients.

Since the 1960s social work has primarily used a systems approach to assessing human behavior. Social workers are now trained to have a systems perspective in their work with individuals, groups, families, organizations, and communities. The systems perspective emphasizes looking beyond the client's presenting problems in order to assess the complexities and interrelationships of the client's life situation. This perspective is based on systems theory. Key concepts of general systems theory are *wholeness, relationship,* and *homeostasis.*

The concept of wholeness means that the objects or elements within a system produce an entity that is greater than the additive sums of the separate parts. Systems theory is antireductionistic; it asserts that no system can be adequately understood or totally explained once it has been broken down into its component parts. (For example, the central nervous system is able to carry out thought processes that would not occur if only the parts were observed.)

The concept of relationship asserts that the patterning and structuring among the elements in a system are as important as the elements themselves. For example, Masters and Johnson have found that sexual dysfunctions occur primarily due to the nature of the relationship between husband and wife, rather than the psychological makeup of the partners in a marriage system.[15]

Systems theory opposes simple cause-and-effect explanations. For example, whether a child will be abused in a family is determined by a variety of variables, as well as by patterning of these variables: parents' capacity to control their anger, relationships between child and parents, relationships between parents, degree of psychological

stress, characteristics of the child, and opportunities for socially acceptable ways for parents to vent anger.

The concept of homeostasis suggests that most living systems seek a balance to maintain and preserve the system. Jackson, for example, has noted that families tend to establish a behavioral balance or stability and to resist any change from that predetermined level of stability.[16] Emergence of the state of imbalance (generated either within or outside the marriage) ultimately acts to restore the homeostatic balance of the family. If one child is abused in a family, that abuse often serves a function in the family (as indicated by the act that, if that child is removed, a second child is often selected to be abused). Or, if one family member improves through counseling, that improvement will generally upset the balance within the family; as a result, other family members will have to make changes (adaptive or maladaptive) to adjust to the new behavior of the improved family member.

We turn now to a subcategory of systems theory, ecological theory, which has become prominent in social work practice.

AN ECOLOGICAL MODEL OF HUMAN BEHAVIOR

In recent years social work has focused increasingly on using an ecological approach. This approach integrates both treatment and reform by conceptualizing and emphasizing the dysfunctional transactions between people and their physical and social environments. Human beings are viewed as developing and adapting through transactions with all elements of their environments. An ecological model explores both internal and external factors. It views people not as passive reactors to their environments but rather as dynamic and reciprocal interactors with those environments.

An ecological model tries to improve coping patterns so that a better match can be attained

FIGURE 2.1

Person-in-Environment Conceptualization

People in our society continually interact with many systems, some of which are depicted in this figure.

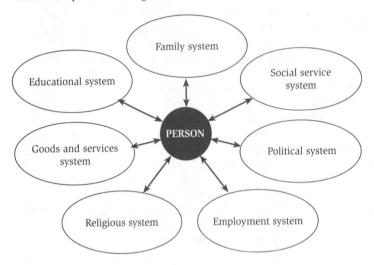

between an individual's needs and the characteristics of his or her environment. One emphasis of an ecological model is on the person-in-environment. This conceptualization is depicted in Figure 2.1, which shows that people interact with many systems. With this conceptualization, social work can focus on three separate areas. First, it can focus on the person and seek to develop his or her problem-solving, coping, and developmental capacities. Second, it can focus on the relationship between a person and the systems he or she interacts with and link the person with needed resources, services, and opportunities. Third, it can focus on the systems and seek to reform them to meet the needs of the individual more effectively.

The ecological model views individuals, families, and small groups as having transitional problems and needs as they move from one life stage to another. Individuals face many changes as they grow older. Examples of some of the transitions are learning to walk, entering first grade, adjust-

ing to puberty, graduating from school, finding a job, getting married, having children, seeing one's children leave home, and retiring.

Families also experience transitions. The following are only a few of the events that require adjustment: engagement, marriage, birth of children, parenting, children's starting school, children's leaving home, and loss of a parent (perhaps through death or divorce).

Small groups also have transitional phases of development. Members of small groups spend time getting acquainted, gradually learn to trust one another, begin to self-disclose more, learn to work together on tasks, develop approaches to handle interpersonal conflict, and face adjustments to the group's eventually terminating or to some members' leaving.

A central concern of an ecological model is to articulate the transitional problems and needs of individuals, families, and small groups. Once these problems and needs are identified, intervention approaches are then selected and applied to help the individuals, families, and small groups resolve the transitional problems and meet their needs.

An ecological model can also focus on maladaptive interpersonal problems and needs. It can seek to articulate the maladaptive communication processes and dysfunctional relationship patterns of families and small groups. These difficulties cover an array of areas, including interpersonal conflicts, power struggles, double binds,* distortions in communicating, scapegoating, and discrimination. An ecological model seeks to identify such interpersonal obstacles and then apply appropriate intervention strategies. For example, some parents set too high a price on honesty for their children. In such families children gradually learn to hide certain behaviors and thoughts and even learn to lie. If the parents discover such dishonesty, an uproar usually occurs. An appropriate intervention in such a family is to open up communication patterns and help the parents to understand that, if they really want honesty from their children, they need to learn to be more accepting of their children's thoughts and actions.

Two centuries ago people interacted primarily within the family system. Families were nearly self-sufficient. In those days the "person-in-family" was a way of conceptualizing the main system that individuals interacted with. Our society has become much more complex. Today a person's life and quality of life are interwoven and interdependent on many systems, as shown in Figure 2.1.

GOALS OF SOCIAL WORK PRACTICE

The National Association of Social Workers (NASW) has conceptualized social work practice

as having four major goals.[17] We'll discuss each of them in turn.

Goal 1: Enhance the Problem-Solving, Coping, and Developmental Capacities of People

Using the person-in-environment concept, the focus of social work practice at this level is on the "person." With this focus a social worker serves primarily as an *enabler*. In this role the worker may take on activities of a counselor, teacher, caregiver (i.e., providing supportive services to those who cannot fully solve their problems and meet their own needs), and behavior changer (i.e., changing specific parts of a client's behavior).

Goal 2: Link People with Systems That Provide Them with Resources, Services, and Opportunities

Using the person-in-environment concept, the focus of social work practice at this level is on the relationships between persons and the systems they interact with. With this focus a social worker serves primarily as a *broker*.

Goal 3: Promote the Effectiveness and Humane Operation of Systems That Provide People with Resources and Services

Using the person-in-environment concept, the focus of social work practice at this level is on the systems people interact with. One role a worker may fill at this level is that of an advocate. Additional roles at this level are the following:

■ *Program developer:* The worker needs to promote or design programs or technologies to meet social needs.

---

*A double bind is a psychological dilemma in which the receiver of a message receives conflicting interpersonal communications from the sender or faces disparagement no matter what her or his response is to a situation.

■ *Supervisor:* The worker seeks to increase the effectiveness and efficiency of the delivery of services through supervising other staff.

■ *Coordinator:* The worker seeks to improve a delivery system through increasing communications and coordination among human service resources.

■ *Consultant:* The worker seeks to provide guidance to agencies and organizations by suggesting ways to increase the effectiveness and efficiency of services.

Goal 4: Develop and Improve Social Policy

As in Goal 3, the focus of social work practice at this level is on the systems people interact with. The distinction between Goal 3 and Goal 4 is that Goal 3 focuses on the available resources for serving people, whereas Goal 4 focuses on the statutes and broader social policies that underlie such resources. Social workers at this level are *planners* and *policy developers.* In these roles, workers develop and seek adoption of new statutes or policies and propose elimination of ineffective or inappropriate statutes and policies. In these planning and policy development processes, social workers may take on an advocate role and, in some instances, an activist role.

A closely related, but somewhat different, conceptualization of the purpose (which incorporates the goals) of social work practice has recently been formulated by the Council on Social Work Education (CSWE), the national accrediting body for social work education in the United States. The CSWE has defined the purpose of social work as follows:

The profession of social work is committed to the enhancement of human well-being and to the alleviation of poverty and oppression. The social work profession receives its sanction from public and private auspices and is the primary profession in the provision of social services.

Within its general scope of concern, professional social work is practiced in a wide variety of settings and has four related purposes:

1. *The promotion, restoration, maintenance, and enhancement of the functioning of individuals, families, groups, organizations, and communities by helping them to accomplish tasks, prevent and alleviate distress, and use resources.*

2. *The planning, formulation, and implementation of social policies, services, resources, and programs needed to meet basic human needs and support the development of human capacities.*

3. *The pursuit of policies, services, resources, and programs through organizational or administrative advocacy and social or political action, so as to empower groups at risk and promote social and economic justice.*

4. *The development and testing of professional knowledge and skills related to these purposes.* *

This definition of the purpose of social work differs from NASW's definition of the goals of social work practice in the following important ways. First, it emphasizes that social work has a commitment to "the enhancement of human well-being and to the alleviation of poverty and oppression." Second, it identifies the client systems of social work practice as "individuals, families, groups, organizations, and communities." This definition, in effect, adds two additional goals to NASW's listing of the goals of social work practice: (1) to empower groups at risk and promote social and economic justice and (2) to develop and test professional knowledge and skills.

The goals (purposes) of social work set forth by NASW and by CSWE should not be viewed as being inconsistent. Each group has identified im-

---

*Reprinted from *Curriculum Policy Statement for Baccalaureate Degree Programs in Social Work Education*, Final Draft July 8, 1992 by permission of the Council on Social Work Education, Alexandria, VA.

portant goals/purposes that all social workers need to attend to.

SOCIAL WORK STEREOTYPES

The image of the social worker has undergone a more rapid change than that of perhaps any other professional. Sixty years ago there was a stereotype of a social worker as a moralistic upper-middle-class older woman who carried a basket of food and had little understanding of the people she tried to help. The image is much more positive today, reflecting the improved professional nature of the training and services provided. The image is also much more varied. Melvin Glasser listed several stereotypes of social workers held by different segments of the population:

- The social worker is a kind, warm, generous, helpful person who makes it possible for people to live richer, more satisfying lives.

- The social worker is a frustrated maiden who meddles in other people's business.

- The social worker is a knowledgeable, dedicated crusader for the needs of all people, particularly the underprivileged.

- The social worker is a radical whose real underlying motive is to bring about a change in the social order.

- The social worker is a hard-hearted, denying administrator of rules and regulations who checks on people to see that they don't cheat the agency.

- The social worker is a professional whose training and experience enable him or her to help with a wide range of problems people have in everyday living.[18]

Ralph Dolgoff and Donald Feldstein summarize some other social work stereotypes:

Depending upon who is doing the "name calling," social workers are referred to in many ways: do-gooders, bleeding hearts, radicals

intent on changing our society, captives of and apologists for "the establishment," organizers of the poor, and servers of the middle class. All these are ways in which people stereotype social workers and the functions they perform in society.[19]

EMPLOYMENT SETTINGS AND OPPORTUNITIES IN SOCIAL WORK

There are currently more employment opportunities available in social work than in many other fields. Social services and their delivery are becoming an integral part of our fast-paced existence, and the demand for qualified personnel is expected to expand. If you are looking for the challenge of working with people to improve social and personal difficulties, then you should seriously consider a career in social work.

From 1960 to 1994 the number of employed social workers grew by 500%—from 95,000 to 484,000.[20] About two out of five social workers are employed by public social welfare agencies.[21] The Bureau of Labor Statistics projects the following job outlook for social work positions:

Employment of social workers is expected to increase faster than the average for all occupations through the year 2005. The number of older people, who are more likely to need social services, is growing rapidly. In addition, requirements for social workers will grow with increases in the need for and concern about services to the mentally ill, the mentally retarded, and individuals and families in crisis. . . .

Employment of social workers in hospitals is projected to grow much faster than the average for the economy as a whole due to greater emphasis on discharge planning, which facilitates early discharge of patients by assuring that the necessary medical services and social supports are in place when individuals leave the hospital. . . .

Social worker employment in home health care services is growing, not only because hospitals are moving to release patients more quickly, but because a large and growing number of people have impairments or disabilities that make it difficult to live at home without some form of assistance.

Opportunities for social workers in private practice will expand because of the anticipated availability of funding from health insurance and from public sector contracts. Also, with increasing affluence, people will be more willing to pay for professional help to deal with personal problems. The growing popularity of employee assistance programs is also expected to spur demand for private practitioners, some of whom provide social work services to corporations on a contract basis.

Employment of school social workers is expected to grow, due to expanded efforts to respond to the adjustment problems of immigrants, children from single-parent families, and others in difficult situations. Moreover, continued emphasis on integrating disabled children into the general school population—a requirement under the Education for All Handicapped Children Act—will probably lead to more jobs. The availability of State and local funding will dictate the actual increase in jobs in this setting, however.[22]

A wide variety of employment settings are available for social workers, including foster care, adoption, probation and parole, public assistance, counseling, services to single parents, day-care services, school social services, services to minority groups and to veterans, recreational services such as Boy Scouts and YWCA programs, social services in a medical or mental hospital, antipoverty programs, social services in nursing homes and other services to the elderly, marital counseling, drug and alcohol counseling, services to the emotionally disturbed, abortion counseling, family planning services, services to persons with a physical disability, sexual counseling, equal rights services, protective services, services in sheltered

workshops, research, social action, and fund raising. (These settings will be described in detail in the chapters that follow.) In addition to these direct services there are employment opportunities for those with experience and advanced professional training in social planning, community organization, consultation, supervision, teaching, and administration.

Social work majors who are most likely to secure employment in social work following graduation are those who are outgoing, dynamic, and able to "sell" themselves during an interview as having the competence, confidence, and skills to perform the job they are applying for. Involvement in groups and extracurricular activities while at college facilitates the development of these capacities, as does volunteer work at one or more social service agencies. A high number of our students secure employment through the relationships they develop with staff during their field placement. If they do well at their field placement and a vacancy occurs, they have an inside track in being hired. Also, through acquaintances with staff at an agency, they hear about employment opportunities at other agencies and frequently also receive a positive letter of reference from their field placement staff.

Students who are considering majoring in social work frequently ask: "Is a graduate degree needed to get a job in social work?" It definitely is not. The vast majority of employed social workers hold only a baccalaureate degree. In fact, some agencies prefer to hire a person with a bachelor's degree because it is less expensive. Of course, as in most fields, a master's degree provides higher status, greater promotion opportunities, and perhaps more gratifying work.

PRIVATE PRACTICE OF SOCIAL WORK

Although the vast majority of social workers are employed by agencies (financed by either public or private funds), a growing number of social workers in the past two decades have opted to provide counseling (also called psychotherapy) and group therapy on a fee basis. This type of *private practice* is similar to the arrangement in which private physicians provide services to patients.

The social worker may conduct a private practice on a part-time basis in addition to working full time for an agency. Or the individual may work full time in private practice. Sometimes social workers form a partnership with psychologists and/or psychiatrists to provide psychotherapy and group therapy through a private, for-profit clinic. In yet another arrangement, social workers may be employed by a private clinic (which may be owned by a psychologist or psychiatrist) to provide therapy to individuals and groups.

Different states have different laws regulating the structure and operation of private clinics and private practice. Such legislation is intended to protect the public. These laws usually require that the social worker in private practice have a master's degree from an accredited school of social work, as well as a few years of supervised practice in counseling individuals and groups.

In most cases, fees for therapy are paid by recipients' health insurance policies. If recipients do not have health insurance coverage, they are expected to pay their own fees for the therapy they receive.

INTERNATIONAL SOCIAL WORK

Social work is a recognized profession in Great Britain, Canada, the United States, India, and numerous other countries. There is a growing recognition that people in all nations are interdependent. In many ways the world has become, as futurist Marshall McLuhan put it, a "global village."[23] The crises and problems experienced by one country often affect other countries. There is a trend in colleges and universities in many countries to "internationalize" the curriculum. Students need to have an understanding and appreciation of the diversity that exists internationally.

Social work educational programs in the United States are increasingly seeking to foster an international perspective for social work majors. Some ways in which this is being done include student exchange programs with other countries, faculty exchange programs with other countries, study-abroad programs (including internship) for social work majors, and new curriculum content on social problems and innovative services in other countries.

The International Federation of Social Workers (IFSW), an organization comprising more than 50 professional membership associations, including the National Association of Social Workers,[24] has devoted considerable effort to identifying values and ethical behaviors appropriate for all social workers. Although social work is significantly affected by the culture in which it is practiced, the IFSW has been successful in developing a code of ethical behavior applicable to the whole of social work practice. The following preamble of that code summarizes the fundamental values of this federation:

> *Social work originates from humanitarian ideals and democratic philosophy and has universal application to meet human needs arising from personal-societal interactions and to develop human potential. Professional social workers are dedicated to service for the welfare and self-realization of human beings; to the disciplined use of scientific knowledge regarding human and societal behavior; to the development of resources to meet individual, group, national and international needs and aspirations; and to the achievement of social justice.*[25]

People of all countries are experiencing many of the social problems described in this text, including poverty, mental illness, crime, divorce, family violence, births outside of marriage, AIDS, rape, incest, drug abuse, worker alienation, international terrorism, unemployment, racism,

The Red Cross is a private agency that coordinates and provides disaster relief on a worldwide basis.

sexism, medical problems, physical and mental disabilities, overpopulation, and misuse of the environment. By studying and analyzing how other countries are combating these problems, social service policymakers and providers in every country can learn to identify more effective programs and service delivery systems. Indeed, some of these problems (such as overpopulation and international terrorism) can be resolved only by coordinated international efforts. Social workers in the future will increasingly need an international perspective in analyzing and combating social problems.

Some international employment opportunities are available for social workers. The United Nations employs some social workers in staff positions for UNESCO (United Nations Educational, Scientific, and Cultural Organization), UNICEF (United Nations Children's Fund), and refugee work. Some units of government in other countries, and some private organizations as well, contract with social workers in the United States to be

consultants. Some private national or international organizations (such as Catholic Charities, Worldwide Adoptions, and the Red Cross) have utilized social workers in their international programs.

SELF-AWARENESS AND IDENTITY DEVELOPMENT

As stated earlier, perhaps the key skill needed to be a competent social worker is the capacity to relate to and counsel individuals.

Increasingly, when training social work students, educators are finding that the students who are best able to counsel others are those who know themselves; that is, they have a high level of self-awareness. A counselor has to be perceptive regarding what clients are thinking and feeling. To be perceptive, the counselor must be able to place himself or herself in the client's situation and determine (with the client's values and pressures) what that person is really feeling and thinking. Unless the counselor has a high level of self-awareness, it is very unlikely that she or he will be able to perceive what others are thinking and feeling.

A variety of approaches have been developed to increase self-awareness, including biofeedback, transcendental meditation, muscle relaxation, Gestalt therapy, identity formation, sensitivity training, and encounter groups.* (Some programs in social work are now offering interpersonal skills courses that are designed to develop self-awareness and interpersonal awareness capacities.)

Identity Formation

One approach to self-awareness—identity formation—will be explored here.† Identity formation is the process of determining who you are and what you want out of life. Arriving at an identity you will be comfortable with is one of the most important tasks you will ever have to face. Whether or not you pursue a social work career, the following information on identity could have considerable importance for your future. As noted, it is especially significant for those considering a social work career because knowing oneself substantially enhances one's ability to counsel others.

Identity development is a lifelong process; there are gradual changes in our identity throughout our lifetime. During the early years our sense of who we are is largely determined by the reactions of others (the looking-glass self-concept). For example, if neighbors, for whatever reason,

perceive a young male to be a "troublemaker" or a "delinquent," they are then likely to accuse the youth of delinquent acts, treat him with suspicion, and label his semidelinquent activities as "delinquent." Although frequently accused and criticized, the youth, to some extent, soon begins to realize that enacting the delinquent role also brings certain rewards; it gives him a type of status and prestige, at least from other youths. In the absence of objective ways to determine whether he is a "delinquent," he relies on the subjective evaluations of others. Gradually, a vicious cycle develops: The more he is related to as a delinquent, the more likely he is to view himself as a delinquent and the more likely he is to enact the delinquent role.

Glasser indicates that a useful perspective for viewing identity is in terms of a success-versus-failure orientation.[26] Those who develop a success identity (view themselves as being generally successful) have two characteristics: (1) they feel they are loved by at least one person, and (2) they feel they are viewed as being a worthy human being by at least one person. People with failure identities are those who feel they are not loved or who do not have a sense of self-worth. People with a failure identity, on the other hand, are likely to be depressed, lonely, anxious, reluctant to face everyday challenges, and indecisive. Escape through drugs or alcohol, withdrawal, criminal behavior, and the development of emotional problems are common.

However, because identity is a lifelong process, significant positive changes can be achieved, even by those with a serious failure identity. An important principle is: *Although we cannot change the past, what we want out of the future, along with our motivation to achieve what we want, is more important (than our past experiences) in determining what our future will be.*

Some of the most important issues you will ever have to face are these:

1. What kind of person do you want to be?

2. What do you want out of life?

3. Who are you?

---

*A review of the specific techniques used in these approaches is contained in Charles Zastrow, *The Practice of Social Work*, 5th ed. (Pacific Grove, CA: Brooks/Cole, 1995).

†This material on identity formation is adapted from an article I wrote entitled "Who Am I: Quest for Identity," in *The Personal Problem Solver*, eds. Charles Zastrow and Dae Chang (Englewood Cliffs, NJ: Prentice-Hall, 1977), pp. 365–370.

Without answers to these questions, you will not be prepared to make such major decisions as selecting a career, choosing where to live and what type of lifestyle you want, and deciding whether to marry and whether to have children. Unfortunately, many people muddle through life without ever arriving at answers to these questions. The answers don't come easy. They require considerable thought and trial and error. During the time you are searching for a sense of who you are, a great deal of anxiety may arise. However, if you are to lead a satisfying, fulfilling life, it is imperative that you know what you want and who you are. Here are some additional questions to aid in identity formations.

Questions for Arriving at a Sense of Identity

To determine who you are, answer the following more specific questions:

1. What do you find satisfying/enjoyable?

2. What are your religious beliefs?

3. What is your moral code? One possible code is to attempt to fulfill your needs and do what you find enjoyable without depriving others of the ability to fulfill their needs.

4. What are your sexual mores? All of us should develop a consistent code that we are comfortable with and that helps us meet our needs without exploiting others. There is no one right code—what works for me may not work for you because of differences in lifestyles, life goals, and personal values.

5. What kind a career do you desire? Ideally, you should seek work that is stimulating and satisfying, that you are skilled at, and that earns you enough money to support the lifestyle you desire.

6. What area of the country or world do you want to live in? Variables to be considered are climate, geography, type of dwelling, rural or urban setting, proximity to relatives or friends, and characteristics of the neighborhood.

7. Do you hope to marry? If yes, to what type of person? When? How consistent are your answers here with your other life goals?

8. Do you want to have children? If yes, how many? When? How consistent are your answers here with your other life goals?

9. What kind of image do you want to project to others? Your image consists of your dressing style and grooming habits, emotions, personality, degree of assertiveness, capacity to communicate, material possessions, moral code, physical features, and voice patterns. You need to honestly assess your strengths and shortcomings in this area and try to make improvements in the latter. Seeking counseling in problem areas may be desirable.

10. What do you enjoy doing in your leisure time?

11. Do you desire to improve the quality of your life and that of others? If yes, in what ways? How do you hope to achieve these goals?

12. What type of people do you enjoy being with? Why?

13. What kind of a relationship do you want to have with your relatives, friends, neighbors, and people you meet for the first time?

14. What are your thoughts about death and dying?

15. What do you hope to be doing in 5 years? In 10 years? In 20 years? What are your plans for achieving these goals in these time periods?

To have a fairly well-developed sense of identity, you need to have answers to most, but not all, of these questions. Very few people are able to arrive at rational, fully consistent answers to all the questions.

Be honest about your strengths and shortcomings. Realize that for practically any shortcoming there are specific intervention strategies to bring about improvement.

In addition, expect some changes in your life goals as time goes on. As you grow as a person, changes will occur in your beliefs, attitudes, and values and in the activities that you find enjoyable.

Your life is shaped by different events that result from the decisions you make and the decisions that are made for you. Without a sense of identity you will not know what decisions are best for you, and your life will be unfulfilled. With a sense of identity, you will be able to direct your life toward goals you select and find personally meaningful.

SUMMARY

A social worker is a multiskilled professional. The social worker needs training and expertise in a wide range of areas in order to be able to deal effectively with problems faced by individuals, groups, families, organizations, and the larger community. Like the general practitioner in medicine, a social worker should acquire a wide range of skills and intervention techniques. Social work is distinct from other careers in that it is the profession that has the responsibility and mandate to provide social services.

The ability to counsel clients effectively is perhaps the most basic skill needed by a social worker. Second in importance is probably the ability to interact effectively with other groups and professionals in the community.

Social work as a profession is of relatively recent origin. Formalized training in social work was first offered at universities in the early 1900s, and individuals were first hired as social workers around 1900.

Social workers work with individuals, groups, families, organizations, and communities. The social worker helps people increase their capacities for problem solving and coping, helps them obtain needed resources, facilitates interactions between individuals and between people and their environments, helps make organizations responsible to people, and influences social policies. There are several types of professional social work activities: casework, case management, group work, group therapy, family therapy, community organization, administration, research, consulting, planning, supervision, and teaching.

The six goals of social work practice are to (1) enhance the problem-solving, coping, and developmental capacities of people, (2) link people with systems that provide them with resources, services, and opportunities; (3) promote the effectiveness and humane operation of systems that provide people with resources and services; (4) develop and improve social policy; (5) empower groups at risk and promote social and economic justice; and (6) develop and test professional knowledge and skills.

Sixty years ago the stereotype of a social worker was that of a moralistic upper-middle-class older woman carrying a basket of food and having little understanding of the people she tried to help. With the rapid development of social work as a profession, there are now many stereotypes (generally more positive) of what a social worker is.

Currently there are more employment opportunities available in social work than in many other fields. A wide variety of employment settings are available for social workers. A majority of people employed as social workers do not have a graduate degree. As in most fields, however, individuals with a master's degree in social work generally have a higher status and greater promotion opportunities.

It is crucial for social workers to have a high level of self-awareness and a sense of who they are and what they want out of life. Arriving at a sense of identity is one of the most important and difficult quests in life—for everyone. With a sense of identity you will be able to direct your life toward goals you select and find personally meaningful.

NOTES

1. Robert M. Bremner, "The Rediscovery of Pauperism," *Current Issues in Social Work Seen in Historical Perspective* (New York: Council on Social Work Education, 1962), p. 13.
2. Nathan E. Cohen, *Social Work in the American Tradition* (Hinsdale, IL: Dryden Press, 1958), p. 66.
3. Dorothy G. Becker, "Social Welfare Leaders as Spokesmen for the Poor," *Social Casework*, 49, no. 2 (February 1968), p. 85.

4. Ralph Dolgoff and Donald Feldstein, *Understanding Social Welfare* (New York: Harper & Row, 1980), pp. 233–234.

5. Ibid., p. 235.

6. Mary E. Richmond, *Social Diagnosis* (New York: Free Press, 1965).

7. H. J. Eysenck, "The Effects of Psychotherapy," in *Handbook of Abnormal Psychology*, ed. H. J. Eysenck (New York: Basic Books, 1961), pp. 697–725.

8. National Association of Social Workers, *Standards for Social Welfare Manpower* (New York: NASW, 1973), pp. 4–5.

9. Robert L. Barker, *The Social Work Dictionary*, 2d ed. (Silver Spring, MD: NASW, 1991), p. 222.

10. Dean H. Hepworth and Jo Ann Larsen, *Direct Social Work Practice: Theory and Skills*, 2d ed. (Chicago: Dorsey Press, 1986), p. 563.

11. Barker, *The Social Work Dictionary*, p. 29.

12. Frank Riessman, "The 'Helper Therapy' Principle," *Journal of Social Work*, 10, no. 2 (April 1965), pp. 27–34.

13. Barker, *The Social Work Dictionary*, p. 43.

14. Richard Stuart, *Trick or Treatment: How and When Psychotherapy Fails* (Champaign, IL: Research Press, 1970).

15. William H. Masters and Virginia E. Johnson, *Human Sexual Inadequacy* (Boston: Little, Brown, 1970).

16. D. D. Jackson, "The Study of the Family," *Family Process*, 4, pp. 1–20.

17. National Association of Social Workers, *Standards for the Classification of Social Work Practice* (Washington, DC: NASW, 1982), p. 17.

18. Melvin A. Glasser, "Public Attitudes toward the Profession: What Shall They Be?" *NASW News*, 3, no. 4 (August 1958), p. 7.

19. Dolgoff and Feldstein, *Understanding Social Welfare*, p. 223.

20. U.S. Department of Labor, *Occupational Outlook Handbook: 1994–95 Edition* (Washington, DC: U.S. Department of Labor, 1994), pp. 136–137.

21. Ibid., pp. 136–137.

22. Ibid., p. 137.

23. See William Kornblum and Joseph Julian, *Social Problems*, 7th ed. (Englewood Cliffs, NJ: Prentice-Hall, 1992), p. 468.

24. Armando Morales and Bradford W. Sheafor, *Social Work, A Profession of Many Faces*, 5th ed. (Boston: Allyn & Bacon, 1989), p. 221.

25. Ibid., p. 222.

26. William Glasser, *The Identity Society* (New York: Harper & Row, 1972).

SOCIAL

PROBLEMS

AND

SOCIAL

SERVICES

3

POVERTY

AND

PUBLIC

WELFARE

P overty has always been one of the most serious social problems in our country. (In most
other countries it is even more severe.) In
our modern, civilized society, one out of seven
Americans is poor.[1] This chapter will:

- Describe the extent of poverty and the effects
  of living in poverty.

- Discuss the income and wealth gaps between
  the rich and the poor in this country.

- Summarize the causes of poverty and identify
  the population groups with the lowest income
  levels.

- Outline current programs to combat poverty
  and discuss their merits and shortcomings.

- Describe and refute some of the myths about
  public welfare.

- Present strategies to reduce poverty in the
  future.

- Describe the role of social work in public
  welfare.

THE PROBLEM

In 1994 over 39 million Americans, or about 15%
of our population, were living below the poverty
line.[2] (The poverty line is the level of income that
the federal government considers sufficient to
meet basic requirements of food, shelter, and
clothing.) A cause for alarm is that the rate of poverty since 1980 has been slowly increasing. The
poverty rate in 1994 was nearly as high as it was
in 1966.[3]

Poverty does not mean simply that poor people in the United States are living less well than
those of average income. It means that the poor
are often hungry. Many are malnourished, with
some turning to dog- or catfood for nourishment.
Poverty may mean not having running water, living in substandard housing, and being exposed to
rats, cockroaches, and other vermin. It means not
having sufficient heat in the winter and being unable to sleep because the walls are too thin to
deaden the sounds from the neighbors living next

*We like to think that we live in a land of equal
opportunity and that upward mobility today is
possible for all those who put forth the effort. But the
reality is otherwise: Poverty is virtually "escape
proof."*

door. It means being embarrassed about the few
ragged clothes that one has to wear. It means great
susceptibility to emotional disturbances, alcoholism, and victimization by criminals, as well as
having a shortened life expectancy. It means lack
of opportunity to advance oneself socially, economically, or educationally. It often means slum
housing, unstable marriages, and few chances to
enjoy the finer things in life—traveling, dining
out, movies, plays, concerts, and sports events.

The infant mortality rate of the poor is almost
double that of the affluent.[4] The poor have less
access to medical services and receive lower-
quality care from health care professionals. The

EXHIBIT 3.1

The Ideology of Individualism

Wealth is generally inherited in this country; few individuals actually move up the social-status ladder on their own. Having wealth opens up many doors (through education and contacts) for children to make large sums of money when they become adults. For children living in poverty there is little chance to escape when they become older. Yet the individualism myth is held by many. It states that the rich are personally responsible for their success and that the poor are to blame for their failure. The main points of this individualism myth are:

1. Each individual should work hard and strive to succeed in competition with others.

2. Those who work hard should be rewarded with success (such as wealth, property, prestige, and power).

3. Because of widespread and equal opportunity, those who work hard will in fact be rewarded with success.

4. Economic failure is an individual's own fault and reveals lack of effort and other character defects.

In our society the poor are blamed for their circumstances. As a result, a stigma has been attached to poverty, particularly to those who receive public assistance (welfare). Although the belief in individualism is less strongly held now than it was prior to the Great Depression in the 1930s, remnants still remain today.

poor are exposed to higher levels of air pollution, water pollution, and unsanitary conditions. They have higher rates of malnutrition and disease. Schools in poor areas are of lower quality and have fewer resources. As a result, the poor achieve less academically and are more likely to drop out of school. They are also more likely to be arrested, indicted, and imprisoned, and they are given longer sentences for the same offenses committed by the nonpoor. They are less likely to receive probation, parole, or suspended sentences.[5]

Poverty also often leads to despair, low self-esteem, and stunted growth—including physical, social, emotional, and intellectual growth. Poverty hurts most when it leads to a view of the self as inferior or second-class.

We like to think that the United States is a land of equal opportunity and that there is considerable upward class mobility for those who put forth effort. The reality is the opposite of the myth. Extensive research has shown that poverty is almost "escape proof." Children raised in poor families are likely to live in poverty in their adult years. Most people have much the same social status their parents had. Movement to a higher social status is an unusual happening in practically all societies—including the United States.[6]

A BRIEF HISTORY OF OUR RESPONSE TO THE POOR

The way a society cares for its needy reflects its values. In primitive societies the needs of those who were not self-sufficient were met by family or other tribal members. During the medieval period in Europe, poor relief was a church responsibility.

The famous Elizabethan Poor Law of 1601 in England combined humanitarianism with the Protestant ethic. This law was enacted because the general public viewed begging (not poverty) as a social problem. The law established three separate programs: (1) The able-bodied poor were offered work. If they refused, they were whipped, imprisoned, or sent back to their birthplace. (2) The impotent poor (the elderly and disabled) were either given public relief or placed in almshouses. (3) Children whose parents could not provide for them were bound out as apprentices to other adults. This Poor Law established the principles of categorical relief by distinguishing between the able-bodied (undeserving) poor and the impotent (deserving) poor. Nearly all the principles contained within this Poor Law became incorporated into the "relief" programs of colonial America.

In the 19th century a controversy raged in both England and the United States between advocates of workhouses and supporters of "outdoor relief" (assistance to people in their own homes). Outdoor relief raised concerns about fraud, and citizens feared cash handouts might destroy moral fiber. On the other hand, workhouses (also called almshouses) were generally overcrowded and unsanitary; contrary to their stated goal, they offered no activity for the able-bodied. Also in the 19th century the first social service organizations sprang up in urban areas to serve the needy. These organizations were private and church sponsored and primarily offered food and shelter. They attempted to solve personal problem with religious admonitions.

As you will recall from the discussions in Chapters 1 and 2, Americans, until the Great Depression, believed in the myth of individualism—that is, the belief that each person is master of his or her own fate. Those in need were viewed as lazy, as unintelligent, or as being justly punished for their sinful ways.

The Great Depression of the 1930s called into question the individualism myth. Nearly one-third of the work force was unemployed.[7] With large numbers of people out of work, including those from the middle class, a new view of relief applicants developed: They were people, not essentially different from others, who were caught up in circumstances beyond their control. Private relief agencies (including private agencies receiving funding support from local governing entities) were unable to meet the financial needs of the unemployed. There was a rapid breakdown in traditional local methods of giving aid to the poor.

Harry Hopkins, a social worker from Iowa, was appointed by President Franklin Roosevelt to oversee national employment programs and emergency assistance. Hopkins became one of Roosevelt's closest advisers and exerted consid-

erable influence in designing and enacting the 1935 Social Security program. As indicated in Chapter 1, this program was of major significance because it initiated the federal government's role in three areas: (1) social insurance programs, (2) public assistance, and (3) social services.

After 1935 the economy of our country slowly began to recover. Some of those who had been living in poverty began to enjoy a more affluent lifestyle—even though many other Americans remained in poverty. The poor were left behind and forgotten. Public concern shifted to World War II in the early 1940s and then to other issues, such as the feared spread of Communism and the Korean War. From the 1940s through the 1950s, poverty was no longer recognized or addressed as a major problem—even though large segments of the population continued to live in abject poverty.

In 1960 John Kennedy saw large numbers of people in many states living in degrading circumstances due to poverty. He made this issue a central one in his national presidential campaign. Hence, poverty was once again defined as a major social problem.

In 1962 Michael Harrington published *The Other America*, which graphically described the plight of the fifth of our population who were living in poverty.[8] The media publicized the poverty issue, and public concern about this problem increased dramatically.

In 1965 President Lyndon Johnson launched his War on Poverty and his plan for creating the "Great Society." Eliminating poverty became one of our nation's highest priorities. A variety of programs were established: Head Start, VISTA, Job Corps, Title I Educational Funding, Community Action Program, Youth Corps, and Neighborhood Legal Services.

Although these programs reduced poverty somewhat, the optimistic hope of the early 1960s that poverty could be eradicated was short-lived. In the late 1960s the Vietnam War drained resources that would otherwise have been spent on domestic programs. It also turned attention away from poverty and finally drove Johnson from office. During periods of economic growth it is eas-

Our response to meeting the needs of the poor is a story of changing values. In the 19th century a bowl of soup was doled out along with prayers or religious admonitions. During the Great Depression the public's attitude toward relief shifted; there was a new belief that financial hardship was often beyond our control. Following a period in the 1950s when the poor were largely ignored, a renewed optimism in the 1960s led to a host of government-sponsored programs designed to eliminate poverty. Today the tide seems to have turned back again: Virtually no large-scale social welfare programs have been initiated in recent years.

ier for a society to allocate resources to the poor in an effort to share the national wealth.

In the mid-1970s, after the end of the Vietnam War, the turmoil of the late 1960s was replaced for several years by an atmosphere of relative calm on both the foreign level and the domestic level. In contrast to the hope of the 1960s that govern-

ment programs could cure our social ills, the opposing philosophy emerged that many problems were beyond the capacity of the government to alleviate. Hence the liberalism of the 1960s, which resulted in the expansion and development of new social programs, was replaced by a more conservative approach in the 1970s and 1980s. Practically no new, large-scale social welfare programs were initiated in those two decades.

It again appears that poverty is taking a back seat to other issues. Government interest in helping the poor has waned considerably. Ronald Reagan was elected in 1980, partly on a program designed to give tax cuts to the rich and to provide decreased funds and services to the poor. Allegations of welfare fraud, high tax rates, and increasing relief roles replaced poverty as a national concern. Welfare again became a political "whipping boy." Since the 1970s there has been a shift away from a liberalized extension of public responsibility to help the poor.

Past history suggests that, as government expenditures to help the poor (and the marginally poor) decrease, the proportion of the population living in poverty increases. There is an adage that history tends to repeat itself. In the early 1930s our country became concerned about the large number of people living in poverty, and the Social Security programs were enacted. Thirty years later, in the early 1960s, our country again became concerned about the large number of people living in poverty, and the War on Poverty programs were initiated. Will this 30-year cycle be repeated in the 1990s? We are now in the mid-1990s, and as yet there has not been a renewed interest in combating poverty.

In 1988 George Bush was elected President on a conservative platform, and he continued the social welfare policies of his predecessor. The Reagan and Bush administrations endorsed an economic program that cut taxes (which primarily benefited the rich) and cut government spending on social welfare programs (which primarily hurt the poor). The result was that the income gap between the rich and the poor widened.[9] The people who were hurt the most were recipients of federally financed social welfare programs who received reduced services and sharp reductions in financial assistance.

Bill Clinton was elected president in 1992. During his campaign Clinton recommended the following changes in the welfare system: increasing funds for educational and training programs for individuals on welfare, strengthening child-support enforcement by establishing a national databank of deadbeat parents, accelerating efforts to establish paternity, and limiting the duration of welfare benefits for families to two years and then requiring recipients to work in private-sector or community-service jobs.

Interestingly, except for the proposal to expand spending on educational and training programs for individuals on welfare, all of the other proposals are consistent with the conservative position on welfare! (See Chapter 1 for a discussion of liberalism and conservatism.) Clinton's views on resolving other social problems are primarily consistent with a liberal orientation. (He has proposed a national health insurance program for all Americans; he has been an advocate for stricter handgun legislation; he has supported the rights of gays and lesbians; and he is pro-choice on the abortion issue.)

THE RICH AND THE POOR

Throughout most countries in the world, wealth is concentrated in the hands of a few individuals and families. Poverty and wealth are closely related in that abundance for a few is often created through deprivation of others.

There are two ways of measuring the extent of economic inequality. *Income* refers to the amount of money a person makes in a given year. *Wealth* refers to a person's total assets—real estate holdings, cash, stocks, bonds, and so forth.

The distribution of wealth and income is highly unequal in our society. Like most countries, the United States is characterized by *social stratification*; that is, it has social classes, with the upper classes having by far the greatest access to the pleasures that money can buy.

Although this chapter focuses on poverty in the United States, it is important to note that there is a growing gap between the rich and the poor everywhere. In the world today there are about 157 billionaires and about 2 million millionaires, but there are approximately 100 million homeless people.[10] Americans spend about $5 billion per year on diets to lower their caloric intake while 400 million people around the world are undernourished to the point of physical deterioration.[11] Kornblum and Julian note:

> These growing disparities between rich and poor throughout the world have a direct bearing on the situation of the poor in the United States because American jobs are being "exported" to areas where extremely poor people are willing to accept work at almost any wage. World poverty also contributes to environmental degradation, political instability, and violence—all problems that drain resources that could be used to meet the nation's domestic needs.[12]

In the United States there are approximately 437,000 people with a net worth of over $1 million and about 38,000 with a net worth of over $5 million.[13] This means that 1% of all households hold about 34% of all personal wealth.[14] (Net worth refers to the value of all assets minus debts; assets include savings and checking accounts, automobiles, real estate, and stocks and bonds.) The distribution of income is also unequal. The wealthiest 20% of households in the United States receive nearly 50% of all income, whereas the poorest 20% receive less than 5% of all income.[15] The average income of the wealthiest 20% of households in 1992 was over $150,000; that of the poorest 20% was around $10,000.[16] The average pay for a chief executive officer of an American corporation in 1990 was $1,952,806; each of the 5 million people earning the minimum wage made only $7670 (if they worked full time for the entire year).[17] In the words of a pastoral letter issued by a committee of Roman Catholic bishops, "The level of inequality in income and wealth in our

EXHIBIT 3.2

Personal Income Disparities Are Astounding

In 1994 Barry Bonds (San Francisco Giants) and Cecil Fielder (Detroit Tigers) were paid more than $7 million a year to play baseball. In 1994 Larry Johnson (Charlotte Hornets) and Chris Webber (Golden State Warriors) were paid more than $7 million a year to play basketball. In 1992 veteran Chicago police officers made $35,814 a year, and schoolteachers in the United States were paid an average of $34,413.

In 1995 Walt Disney Corporation Chairman Michael D. Eisner was paid an astounding $197 million (much of this amount was in stock options that were financed by the corporation). He thus received an average of nearly $4 million per week, or over $750,000 per day of a five-day workweek ($750,000 is more than many U.S. workers earn in their lifetimes). The President of the United States (considered by many people to hold the most important job in the country) is paid less than $300,000 per year.

In 1992 the singer Madonna finalized a deal with a corporation that will pay her $60 million over seven years. Alarmingly, the average *annual* income in the poorest 20% of the nations on this planet is less than $250!

Sources: The statistics cited are from Susan Dentzer, "The Wealth of Nations," *U.S. News & World Report*, May 4, 1992, p. 54; Robert Rankin, "Imbalance of Payments," *Wisconsin State Journal*, May 10, 1992, pp. 1A–2A; and Phil Jasner, "$100,000,000: How Much Is Too Much?" *Wisconsin State Journal*, July 31, 1994, p. 1D.

society . . . must be judged morally unacceptable."[18]

Almost 20% of all American families have a negative net worth, meaning that they have more liabilities than assets.[19] Paul Samuelson, an econ-omist, provides a dramatic metaphor of the disparity between the very rich and most people in the United States:

If we made an income pyramid out of a child's blocks, with each layer portraying $1,000 of income, the peak would be far higher than the Eiffel Tower, but almost all of us would be within a yard of the ground.[20]

Given the enormous wealth of the richest 20%, it is clear that a simple redistribution of some of the wealth from the top one-fifth to the lowest one-fifth could easily wipe out poverty. Of course, that is not politically acceptable to members of the top fifth, who have the greatest control of the government. It should also be noted that many of these rich families avoid paying income taxes by taking advantage of tax loopholes and tax shelters.

An estimated 30 million Americans are hungry, due to lack of financial resources, at least some period of time each month.[21] Millions of those who go hungry in the United States are children.

Hunger can have devastating effects on young children, including causing mental retardation. The brain of an infant grows to 80% of its adult size within the first three years of life. If supplies of protein are inadequate during this period, the brain stops growing, the damage is irreversible, and the child will be permanently retarded.[22]

Coleman and Cressey describe the respective effects of wealth and poverty:

The economic differences between the rich, the poor, and the middle class have profound effects on lifestyles, attitudes toward others, and even attitudes toward oneself. The poor lack the freedom and autonomy so prized in our society. They are trapped by their surroundings, living in run-down, crime-ridden neighborhoods that they cannot afford to leave. They are constantly confronted with things they desire but have little chance to own. On the other hand, wealth provides power, freedom, and the ability to direct

**CASE
EXAMPLE 3.1**

Wealth Perpetuates Wealth, and Poverty Perpetuates Poverty

I n this excerpt, C. Wright Mills describes one way in which living in the world of wealth educates wealthy children to be financially successful:

> *The exclusive schools and clubs and resorts of the upper social classes are not exclusive merely because their members are snobs. Such locales and associations have a real part in building the upper-class character, and more than that, the connections to which they naturally lead help to link one higher circle with another. So the distinguished law student, after prep school and Harvard, is "clerk" to a Supreme Court judge, then a corporation lawyer, then in the diplomatic service, then in the law firm again. In each of these spheres, he meets and knows men of his own kind, and, as a kind of continuum, there are the old family friends and the schoolboy chums, the dinners at the club, and each year of his life the summer resorts. In each of these circles in which he moves, he acquires and exercises a confidence in his own ability to judge, to decide, and in this confidence he is supported by his ready access to the experience and sensibility of those who are his social peers and who act with decision in each of the important institutions and areas of public life. One does not turn one's back on a man whose presence is accepted in such circles, even under most trying circumstances. All over the top of the nation, he is "in," his appearance, a certificate of social position; his voice and manner, a badge of proper training; his associates, proof at once of their acceptance and of his stereotyped discernment.*

In contrast, the following summary of Marcee Calvello's life describes how poverty and dismal living conditions lead to despair, hopelessness, and failure.

Marcee Calvello was born and raised in New York City. Her father had trouble holding a job because he was addicted to cocaine, and her mother was an alcoholic

---

one's own fate. The wealthy live where they choose and do as they please, with few economic constraints. Because the poor lack education and money for travel, their horizons seldom extend beyond the confines of their neighborhood. In contrast, the world of the wealthy offers the best education, together with the opportunity to visit places that the poor haven't even heard of.

The children of the wealthy receive the best that society has to offer, as well as the assurance that they are valuable and important individuals. Because the children of the poor lack so many of the things everyone is "supposed" to have, it is much harder for them to develop the cool confidence of the rich. In our materialistic

society people are judged as much by what they have as by who they are. The poor cannot help but feel inferior and inadequate in such a context.[23]

DEFINING POVERTY IS A POLICY PROBLEM

Despite all the research on poverty, we as yet have not agreed on how to define the condition. A family of four living on a farm that earns $12,000 per year may not view themselves as being "poverty

who divorced her husband when Marcee was 3 years old. Marcee's mother at first sought to provide a better home for Marcee and her three brothers. She worked part-time and also went on AFDC. However, her addiction to alcohol consumed most of her time and money. Neighbors reported the children were living in abject neglect, and Protective Services removed Marcee and her brothers to foster care. Marcee was placed in a series of foster homes—a total of 17 different homes. In one of these homes her foster father sexually assaulted her, and in another a foster brother assaulted her. Being moved from foster home to foster home resulted in frequent school changes. Marcee grew distrustful of the welfare system, schoolteachers and administrators, males, and anyone else who sought to get close to her.

When she turned 18, the state no longer paid for her foster care. She got a small efficiency apartment that cost her several hundred dollars a month. Because she dropped out of school at age 16, she had few marketable job skills. She worked for a while at some fast food restaurants. The minimum wage she received was insufficient to pay her bills. Eight months after she moved into her apartment she was evicted. Unable to afford another place, she started living in the subway system of New York City. She soon lost her job at McDonald's because of poor hygiene and an unkempt appearance.

Unable to shower and improve her appearance, she has not been able to secure another job. For the past two years she has been homeless, living on the street and in the subway. She has given up hope of improving her situation. She now occasionally shares IV needles and has been sexually assaulted periodically at night in the subway by men. She realizes she is at high risk for acquiring the AIDS virus but no longer cares very much. Death appears to be, to her, the final escape from a life filled with victimization and misery.

Sources: C. Wright Mills, *The Power Elite* (New York: Oxford University Press, 1956), pp. 69–70; Ben H. Bagdikian, *In the Midst of Plenty: The Poor in America* (Boston: Beacon Press, 1964), p. 75.

stricken,'' especially if they have no rent to pay, are able to grow much of their own food, and are frugal and creative in securing essential needs. On the other hand, a family of four earning $15,000 per year in a city with a high cost of living may be deeply in debt, especially if they pay high rent and are confronted with unexpected medical bills.

The usual definitions of poverty are based on lack of money, and annual income is the measure most commonly applied. There are two general approaches to defining poverty: the absolute approach and the relative approach.

The *absolute approach* holds that a certain amount of goods and services is essential to an individual's or family's welfare. Those who do not have this minimum amount are viewed as poor. The fundamental problem with this approach is that there is no agreement as to what constitutes "minimum" needs. Depending on the income level selected, the number and percentage of the population who are poor change substantially, along with the characteristics of those defined as poor.

A serious problem with the absolute definition of poverty is that it does not take into account the fact that people are poor not only in terms of their own needs, but also in relation to others who are not poor. That is, poverty is relative to time and

A woman living in a New York City tenement goes to a fire hydrant to get water. She may be considered poor by both the absolute approach and the relative approach to defining poverty.

place. Those Americans labeled poor today would certainly not be poor by the standards of 1850; nor would they be viewed as poor by standards existing in India or in other less developed countries. In the 1890s no one felt particularly poor because of not having electric lights; yet today a family without electricity is usually considered poor. Kenneth Boulding adds:

> In the twentieth century, the per capita income of the richest country is at least forty times that of the poorest . . . and the gulf widens between them all the time. It is this gulf which constitutes the main problem of poverty today. Persons

regarded by a rich society as very poor would be regarded as relatively rich in a poor society. We see this illustrated in the fact that to the American, the migrant laborer is the poorest of the poor and constitutes in his mind a serious problem. To the Mexican villager, joining the ranks of our migrant workers is seen as a road to riches and as a way to lift the grinding burdens of the poverty under which he labors. And yet Mexico is one of the richer of the poor countries. To hundreds of millions of Asians and Africans, the standard of life of the Mexican laborer would seem almost luxurious.[24]

The *relative approach* states, in essence, that a person is poor when his or her income is substantially less than the average income of the population. For example, anyone in the lowest one-fifth (or tenth, or fourth) of the population is regarded as poor. By defining poverty in these terms, we avoid having to define absolute needs, and we also put more emphasis on the inequality of incomes. With a relative approach, poverty will persist as long as income inequality exists. The major weakness with a relative approach is that it tells us nothing about how badly, or how well, the people at the bottom of the income distribution actually live. With poverty measures, ideally, we want to know not only how many people are poor but also how desperate their living conditions are.

The federal government has generally chosen the absolute approach in defining poverty. The poverty line is raised each year to adjust for inflation. In 1993 the government set the poverty line at $14,763 for a family of four.[25]

WHO ARE THE POOR?

An encouraging trend is that the proportion of the population below the poverty line has gradually decreased in the past 100 years. Prior to the 20th century a majority of Americans lived in poverty. In 1937 President Franklin D. Roosevelt stated: "I see one-third of a nation ill-housed, ill-clad, ill-nourished."[26] In 1962 the President's Council of Economic Advisors estimated that one-fifth of the

It is no longer possible to claim that the poor are still "invisible" in our society.

population was living in poverty.[27] In 1993 about 15% of the nation was estimated to be below the poverty line. An alarming concern is that, since 1978, there has been an increase in the proportion of the population that is poor.[28]

Poverty is concentrated in certain population categories, including one-parent families, children, the elderly, large-sized families, and minorities. Educational level, unemployment, and place of residence are also factors related to poverty.

ONE-PARENT FAMILIES

Most one-parent families are headed by a female, and 34% of female-headed families are in poverty, compared to 8% for two-parent families.[29] Single mothers who are members of a racial minority (e.g., African Americans, Latinos, Native Americans) are particularly vulnerable to poverty, as they are subjected to double discrimination (race and sex) in the labor market.

Women who work full time are paid on the average only about two-thirds of what men who work full time are paid.[30] Many single mothers are unable to work due to lack of transportation, the high cost of day-care facilities, and inadequate training. They therefore have to rely on public assistance (benefits that are often below the poverty line) in the form of Aid to Families with Dependent Children (AFDC). Of the families living in poverty, *half* are headed by a single mother.[31] About 1 out of every 5 children in this country is now living apart from one parent, and, because of increasing divorce rates, separations, and births outside marriage, it is estimated that nearly 1 of 2 children born today will spend part of the first 18 years in a family headed by a single mother.[32] Single-parent families now constitute more than 20% of all families in the United States.[33] The increase in one-parent families has led to an increase in the feminization of poverty.

CHILDREN

Nearly 40% of the poor are children under 16.[34] More than one-half of these children live in families with an absentee father,[35] and many rely on AFDC payments for meeting the basic necessities.

THE ELDERLY

Many of the elderly depend on Social Security pensions or public assistance (in the form of Supplemental Security Income) for their basic needs. Since the initiation of the 1964 War on Poverty programs, the population group that has benefited most has been the elderly. Programs such as Medicare and Supplemental Security Income, as well as increases in monthly payments under the Old Age, Survivors, Disability, and Health Insurance Program, have reduced the poverty rate among the elderly from over 25% in 1964 to around 12% at the present time.[36]

LARGE FAMILIES

Large families are more likely than smaller ones to be poor, partly because more income is needed as family size increases. It now costs an estimated $140,000 to raise a child from birth to age 18.[37]

MINORITIES

Contrary to popular stereotypes, most poor people (over 60%) are white.[38] But members of most minority groups are disproportionately likely to be poor. African Americans, for example, constitute about 12% of the total population, but over 25% of all the poor.[39] One out of every 3 African Americans is poor, compared to 1 out of 10 white persons.[40] Approximately one-third of Native American families live below the poverty line, and about 25% of Mexican Americans (or Latinos) live in poverty—particularly migrant agricultural workers.[41] Racial discrimination is a major reason why most racial minorities are disproportionately poor.

EDUCATION

Attainment of less than a ninth-grade education is a good predictor of poverty. A high school diploma, however, is not a guarantee that one will earn wages adequate to avoid poverty, as many of the poor have graduated from high school. A college degree is an excellent predictor of avoiding poverty; only a small proportion of those with a college degree are impoverished.[42]

EMPLOYMENT

Being unemployed is of course associated with being poor. However, being employed is not a guarantee of avoiding poverty; over 1.5 million family heads work full time, but their income is below the poverty level.[43] The general public (and many government officials) wrongly assumes that employment is the key to ending poverty. However, jobs alone cannot end poverty.

PLACE OF RESIDENCE

People who live in rural areas have a higher incidence of poverty than those in urban areas. In rural areas, wages are low, unemployment is high, and work tends to be seasonal. The Ozarks, Appalachia, and the South have pockets of rural poverty with high rates of unemployment.[44]

People who live in urban slums constitute the largest geographical group in terms of numbers of poor people. The decaying cities of the Northeast and Midwest have particularly large urban slums. Poverty is also extensive on Native American reservations and among seasonal migrant workers.

All these factors indicate that some people are more vulnerable to poverty than others. Michael Harrington, who coined the term *other America* for the poor in the United States, notes that the poor made the simple mistake of:

> *being born to the wrong parents, in the wrong section of the country, in the wrong industry, or in the wrong racial or ethnic group. Once that mistake has been made, they could have been paragons of will and morality, but most of them would never even have had a chance to get out of the other America.*[45]

CAUSES OF POVERTY

There are a number of possible causes of poverty:

■ High unemployment
■ Poor physical health
■ Physical disabilities

- Emotional problems
- Extensive medical bills
- Alcoholism
- Drug addiction
- Large families
- Job displacements due to automation
- Lack of an employable skill
- Low educational level
- Households with young children headed by females only
- Lack of cost-of-living increases for people on fixed incomes
- Racial discrimination
- Labels such as "ex-convict" or "crazy"
- Residence in a geographic area where jobs are scarce
- Divorce, desertion, or death of a spouse
- Gambling
- Budgeting problems and mismanagement of resources
- Sex discrimination
- Consequences of being a crime victim
- Anti-work-ethic values
- Underemployment
- Low-paying jobs
- Mental retardation
- Retirement

This list is not exhaustive. However, it shows that there are many causes of poverty, that eliminating the causes of poverty would require a wide range of social programs, and that poverty interacts with almost all other social problems—emotional problems, alcoholism, unemployment, racial and sex discrimination, medical problems, crime, gambling, mental retardation, and so on. The interaction between poverty and these other social problems is complicated. As indicated, these other social problems are contributing causes of poverty. Yet, for some social problems, poverty is also a contributing *cause* of those problems (such as emotional problems, alcoholism, and unem-

ployment). Being poor intensifies the effects (the hurt) of all social problems.

THE CULTURE OF POVERTY

To some extent, poverty is passed on from generation to generation in a cycle (Figure 3.1). Why? Some authorities argue that the explanation is due to a "culture of poverty." Oscar Lewis, an anthropologist, is one of the chief proponents of this cultural explanation.[46]

Lewis examined poor neighborhoods in various parts of the world and concluded that people are poor because they have a distinct culture or lifestyle. The culture of poverty arises after extended periods of economic deprivation in highly stratified capitalistic societies. Such economic deprivation is brought about by high rates of unemployment for unskilled labor and by low wages for those who are employed. Such economic deprivation leads to the development of attitudes and values of despair and hopelessness. Lewis describes these attitudes and values as follows:

> The individual who grows up in this culture has a strong feeling of fatalism, helplessness, dependence, and inferiority, a strong present-time orientation with relatively little disposition to defer gratification and plan for the future, a high tolerance for psychological pathology of all kinds.[47]

Once developed, this culture continues to exist, even when the economic factors that created it (e.g., lack of employment opportunities) no longer exist. The culture's attitudes, norms, and expectations serve to limit opportunities and prevent escape. A major reason why the poor remain locked into their culture is that they are socially isolated. They have few contacts with groups outside their own culture and are hostile toward the social services and educational institutions that might help them escape poverty. They reject such institutions because they perceive them as belonging to the dominant class. Furthermore, because they view their financial circumstances as private and hopeless, and because

FIGURE 3.1

Cycle of Poverty

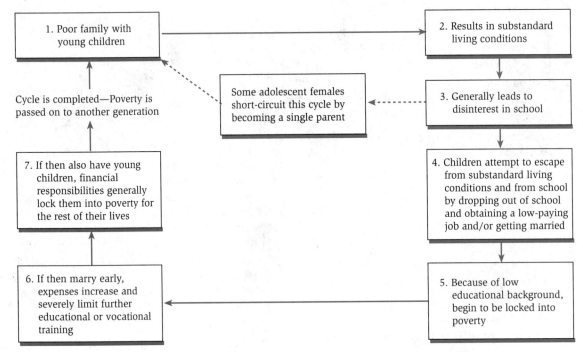

they lack political and organizational skills, they do not take collective action to resolve their problems.

The culture-of-poverty theory has been controversial and widely criticized. Eleanor Leacock argues that the distinctive culture of the poor is not the *cause* but the *result* of their continuing poverty.[48] She agrees that the poor tend to emphasize "instant gratification," which involves spending and enjoying one's money while it lasts. But, she argues, instant gratification is a result of being poor, because it makes no sense to defer gratification when one is pessimistic about the future. Deferred gratification is a rational response only when one is optimistic that postponing pleasures today by saving money will reap greater benefits in the future. (Interestingly, studies have found that, when ghetto residents obtain a stable,

well-paying job, they then display the middle-class value of deferred gratification.[49]) Because of poverty, Leacock argues, the poor are forced to abandon middle-class attitudes and values, which are irrelevant to their circumstances.

In an even stronger indictment, William Ryan criticizes the culture-of-poverty theory as being simply a classic example of "blaming the victim."[50] Blaming the poor for their circumstances is a convenient excuse, according to Ryan, for refusing to endorse the programs and policies thought necessary to eradicate poverty. The real culprit is the social system that allows poverty to exist. Ryan says bluntly that the poor are not poor because of their culture, but because they do not have enough money.

Pro and con arguments for the culture-of-poverty theory persist. There are many reasons, both external and internal, why a person may be poor. External reasons include high rates of unemployment and underemployment; racial discrimination; automation, which throws people out of work; lack of job-training programs; sex discrimination; a shortage of antipoverty programs; and inflation. Internal reasons include physical or mental impairment, alcoholism, obsolete job skills, early parenthood, lack of education, and lack of interest in taking available jobs.

FUNCTIONS OF POVERTY

Obviously, poverty is dysfunctional—mainly to the poor themselves, but also to the affluent. However, the realization that poverty also has some functions in society can help us understand why some decision makers are not actively seeking to eradicate it.

Eleven functions are provided by the poor to affluent groups:

1. They are available to do the unpleasant jobs no one else wants to do.

2. Their activities subsidize the more affluent (for example, domestic service for low pay).

3. They help create jobs (for example, jobs for social workers who provide services to the poor).

4. They purchase poor-quality goods that otherwise could not be sold.

5. They serve as examples of deviance to be frowned on by the majority, thereby supporting dominant norms.

6. They provide an opportunity for others to practice their ''Christian duty'' of helping the less fortunate.

7. They make mobility more likely for others because they are removed from the competition for good education and good jobs.

8. They contribute to cultural activities (for example, by providing cheap labor for the construction of monuments and works of art).

9. They create cultural forms (e.g., jazz and the blues) that are often adopted by the affluent.

10. They serve as symbolic opponents for some political groups and as constituents for others.

11. They often absorb the costs of change (e.g., by being the victims of high levels of unemployment that result from technological advances).[51]

Also, denigrating the poor has the psychological function for some Americans of making them feel better about themselves.

Partly because poverty is functional, our society makes only a halfhearted effort to eliminate—or even reduce—it. To do so would result in a redistribution of income from the rich to the poor, a policy generally seen as undemocratic (sometimes communistic) even by the not-so-affluent. Because the rich control the political power, proposals that would eliminate poverty (such as guaranteed-annual-income programs) have generally met with opposition. Gans emphasizes this point:

> Legislation in America tends to favor the interests of the businessman, not the consumers, even though the latter are a vast majority; of landlords, not tenants; of doctors, not patients. Only organized interest groups have the specific concerns and the time, staff, and money to bring their demands before government officials. . . . The poor are powerless because they are a minority of the population, are not organized politically, are often difficult to organize, and are not even a homogeneous group with similar interests that could be organized into a single pressure group. . . . Given the antagonism toward them on the part of many Americans, any programs that would provide them with significant gains are likely to be voted down by a majority. Legislative proposals for a massive antipoverty effort . . . have always run into concerted and united opposition in Washington.[52]

Our government has the resources to eliminate poverty—but not the will. In the present century our country has been able to find billions of dollars in resources within a few months when we go to war (which has happened several times). But our government has not been willing to allocate similar funds to improve living conditions for the homeless and for millions of other people who are living in poverty in this country.

PROGRAMS TO COMBAT POVERTY

Because poverty relates to nearly every other social problem, almost every existing social service—to some extent—works to combat poverty (including Alcoholics Anonymous, health care programs, vocational rehabilitation, Parents without Partners, foster care, adoption, day care, Head Start, housing programs, urban renewal, and community action programs). Such programs indirectly reduce poverty by alleviating related social problems. These programs are too numerous to describe fully in this text. This section will instead describe income maintenance programs that are directly designed to alleviate poverty. Income maintenance programs include social insurance programs and public assistance programs.

Social Insurance Programs

OLD AGE, SURVIVORS, DISABILITY, AND HEALTH INSURANCE (OASDHI)

This social insurance program was created by the 1935 Social Security Act. Generally, OASDHI is referred to as "Social Security" by the public. It is the largest income insurance program and is designed to partially replace income that is lost when a worker retires or becomes disabled. Cash benefits are also paid to survivors of "insured" workers.

Payments to beneficiaries are based on previous earnings. The rich as well as the poor are eligible if insured. Benefits are provided to fully insured workers at age 65 or older (somewhat smaller benefits can be taken at age 62). Dependent husbands or wives over age 62 and dependent children under age 18 (there is no age limit on disabled children who become disabled be-

fore 18) are also covered under the retirement benefits.

Participation in this insurance program is compulsory for most employees. The program is financed by a payroll tax assessed equally to employer and employee. The rate has gone up gradually. Eligibility for benefits is based on the number of years in which Social Security taxes have been paid.

A major concern has been the financial soundness of OASDHI. Since 1935 the Social Security (FICA) tax has led to a buildup in the trust fund for OASDHI. But the liberalization of benefits and the increase in recipients in recent years have raised concern about the system paying out more than it takes in. In times of high unemployment and recession, the number of workers paying into OASDHI is decreased. The decline in the birthrate, along with a steady increase in the retired population, may jeopardize the financial soundness of the program; the number of recipients is increasing at a faster rate than the number of workers paying into the system. If OASDHI is to remain financially sound, benefits may have to be scaled back, FICA taxes increased, or both.

MEDICARE

In 1965 Congress enacted Title XVIII (Medicare) to the Social Security Act. Medicare has two parts: hospital insurance and medical insurance. Hospital insurance helps pay for inpatient hospital care, inpatient care in a skilled nursing facility, home health care, and hospice care. Medical insurance helps pay for medically necessary doctors' services, outpatient hospital services, and a number of other medical services and supplies that are not covered by the hospital insurance part of Medicare. The hospital insurance part is financed by a surcharge on the Social Security taxes paid by employers and employees. The medical insurance part is a voluntary insurance plan for which enrollees are charged a monthly premium. (More than two-thirds of the costs of the medical insurance premium is paid from general revenues of the federal government.) Medicare, a public health insurance program, is described more fully in Chapter 14.

Despite the existence of unemployment insurance for over 50 years, the suspicion persists that weekly benefits are a disincentive to seeking work.

UNEMPLOYMENT INSURANCE

This program was also created by the 1935 Social Security Act and provides benefits to workers who have been laid off or, in certain cases, fired. Unemployment insurance is financed by a tax on employers. The amount and duration of weekly benefits vary from state to state. In many states the unemployed are eligible for benefits for about a year. To be eligible in most states, a person must (1) have worked a certain number of weeks in covered employment; (2) be ready, willing, and able to work; (3) file a claim for benefits and be registered in a public employment office; and (4) demonstrate that unemployment is due to a lack of work for which she or he is qualified.

Unemployment insurance benefits help individuals and families who become unemployed due to a lack of work. In our society, in which employment is valued highly, being without work can be a demeaning experience. In the past two decades, the unemployment rate has ranged from 4% to 11% of able-bodied workers. High rates clearly indicate a lack of available jobs. Yet the unemployment insurance program has been sharply criticized by claims that some of the unemployed would rather collect insurance benefits than make a concerted effort to obtain employment.[53]

WORKERS' COMPENSATION INSURANCE

This program provides both income and assistance in meeting medical expenses for injuries sustained on a job. The program was enacted after a series of lawsuits by injured employees against employers—the only recourse employees had. The first workers' compensation program was the Federal Employees Compensation Act of 1908. Individual states gradually passed workers' compensation laws modeled after the program for federal employees. By 1920 all but six states had such laws, but it was not until 1948 that all states had adequate coverage.[54] Cash benefits are paid for total or temporary disability or death. Medical benefits cover hospital and doctors' fees. Rehabilitation benefits are also available for those needing aftercare and retraining in order to again become employable. Workers' compensation is financed by a tax on employers.

Public Assistance Programs

Public assistance is sometimes viewed as synonymous with "welfare" by the general public, yet there are hundreds of other social welfare programs. Public assistance has primarily residual aspects, and applicants must undergo a "means test" that reviews their assets and liabilities to determine their eligibility for benefits.

Adherents of the residual view of public assistance generally hold the following opinions:

1. Assistance should be made as unpleasant as possible to discourage its use. This is to be accomplished by giving relief in kind (for example, food or clothes) rather than money, by threatening prosecution, by continually reevaluating need, by making it only temporary, by stopping it if illegitimacy is involved, and by removing children from their own homes when these homes do not come up to standard.

2. Relief should also be made unpleasant by requiring recipients to work for it regardless of what the nature of the work may be, or how depressed the wage, or whether the requirement would be used as means for securing cheap labor; notwithstanding, income from this work is still labeled relief.

3. Assistance should be discouraged by making payments too low for anyone to really want it. It is argued by advocates of this approach that assistance in amounts greater than would be received by the lowest-paid, most menial worker would encourage individuals to seek assistance in lieu of employment.

4. Outsiders should be prevented from seeking help (they may receive only emergency aid and only for short periods).

5. People should be forced to remain on their jobs or to return to employment; this is accomplished by denying assistance to anyone who is guilty of a "voluntary quit."[55]

In contrast, the institutional view of public assistance (generally held by social workers) assumes or advocates the following:

1. Adequate income and the elimination of hunger and destitution should be provided for all citizens as an instrument of social policy.

2. Relief should be extended to applicants who can qualify under eligibility requirements; that is, subjective, biased, and capricious considerations should be removed. Relief should be based on need as it is determined to exist by objective, rather than subjective, criteria and as a legally determined right.

3. It is assumed that workers generally prefer income from employment over public welfare and that motivations to work are built into the economy in the form of social, cultural, and economic advantages to the employed man or woman.

4. Psychological and social barriers sometimes stand in the way of rehabilitation and employment. Counseling and other services may be needed to restore certain individuals to economic and social self-sufficiency.

5. Preservation of the independence and self-respect of the applicant for assistance is a prime consideration in the administration of programs of relief.

6. A punitive approach defeats the purpose for which assistance is used—namely, the restoration of the individual to normal functioning; it deepens feelings of inadequacy and dependency, causes embarrassment and humiliation, and brings destructive psychological defenses into play.

7. There are many pulls in society that make work more appealing than public welfare, such as a higher standard of living and the prestige and sense of importance one receives from gainful employment.[56]

Public assistance programs have several distinguishing features:

■ *Programs have a means test.* Individuals applying for assistance have their income and assets examined in order to determine whether their financial needs meet the eligibility requirements. The means test is designed to ensure that individuals receiving assistance do not already have sufficient resources for a minimum level of subsistence. Resources that are examined include both earned and unearned income. Earned income is money in the form of salary or wages. Unearned income includes benefits from other public and private financial programs, gifts, life insurance annuities, stock dividends, rental income, inheritances, support payments from relatives, and so on.

■ *Eligibility and benefit levels are determined on a case-by-case basis.* All applications for assistance are closely reviewed on an individual basis. Although there are federal, state, and local guidelines on eligibility and on allowable benefits, the staff who administer public assistance have substantial discretion in deciding whether a client will receive special allowances in addition to basic benefits. Staff also have discretion in deciding which social services and other resources might be mobilized on behalf of the client. Eligibility determination, along with benefit-level determination, is a cumbersome, lengthy process involving extensive review of documents.

■ *Benefits are viewed as charity.* In contrast to social insurance benefits, to which recipients are viewed as legally entitled, public assistance benefits are perceived as charity. In this country poor people are not considered to have a constitutionally established right to a minimum income. (In comparison, some foreign countries, such as Great Britain, recognize the right of those in poverty to be maintained and protected by government.)

■ *Program benefits are paid from general government revenues.* Public assistance benefits at the federal, state, and local levels are financed through taxes on personal income and on property.

The main public assistance programs include Supplemental Security Income, General Assistance, Medicaid, food stamps, housing assistance, and Aid to Families with Dependent Children.

SUPPLEMENTAL SECURITY INCOME (SSI)

Under the SSI program, the federal government pays monthly checks to people in financial need who are 65 years of age and older or who are blind or disabled at any age. To qualify for payments, applicants must have no (or very little) regular cash income, own little property, and have little cash or few assets that could be turned into cash (such as stocks, bonds, jewelry, or other valuables).

The SSI program became effective January 1, 1974, and replaces the following programs that were created by the 1935 Social Security Act: Old-Age Assistance, Aid to the Blind, and Aid to the Permanently and Totally Disabled. SSI is the first federally administered assistance program. All other public assistance programs are administered through state and local governments. The word *supplemental* refers to the fact that, in most cases, payments *supplement* whatever income may be available to the claimant. Even OASDHI benefits are supplemented by this program.

SSI provides a guaranteed minimum income (an income floor) for the aged, the blind, and the disabled. Aged, blind, and disabled are defined as follows:

Aged: 65 or over.

Blind: Vision no better than 20/200 (even with glasses) or tunnel vision (limited visual field of 20° or less).

Disabled: A physical or mental disability that prevents a person from doing any substantial, gainful work and is expected to last at least 12 months or result in death.

Administration of SSI has been assigned to the Social Security Administration. Financing of the program is through federal tax dollars, primarily income taxes.

GENERAL ASSISTANCE

The General Assistance (GA) program is supposed to serve those needing temporary, rather than long-term, financial support. It is designed to provide financial help to those in need who are ineligible for any other income-maintenance program. No clearly stated eligibility requirements exist for general assistance. GA is the only public assistance program that receives no federal funds. It is usually funded by property taxes. In large cities, such as New York and Chicago, the state contributes substantially toward meeting the costs of GA. In most localities, however, the program is financed and administered at the local level, through the county or township or by a village or city. In many local governmental units, a political official has arbitrary jurisdiction over whether an applicant receives help. Most expenditures for GA are for medical care. In-kind payments (food, medical care, clothes, and other items other than money) are frequent. Whenever feasible, communities usually attempt to move GA recipients into federally funded public aid programs in order to reduce local expenses.

Payments for GA tend to be minimal and grudgingly made to discourage people from applying and from becoming dependent on welfare. With in-kind and voucher payments, GA conveys to recipients the suspicion that they are incapable of managing their own affairs. Because able-bodied unemployed men and women sometimes find it necessary to seek GA benefits, GA has been viewed as a public assistance program for the "undeserving poor." In some parts of the country, GA has demoralizing effects because many local program directors hold—and convey to recipients—a negative attitude about providing assistance.

MEDICAID

This program provides hospital and medical care to certain poverty-stricken people. Those eligible are individuals who are recipients of Aid to Families with Dependent Children or are SSI recipients. In addition, states have the option to include people who are able to provide for their own daily living but whose income and resources are not sufficient to meet all their medical costs.

Medicaid is administered by the states, with financial participation by the federal government. Direct payments are made to providers of services. As is required for every public assistance program, Medicaid applicants must undergo a means test.

FOOD STAMPS

Tragically, an estimated 30 million people in the United States (the most powerful and one of the richest countries in the world) do not have enough food to eat.[57] Many of those with inadequate diets are poor. Not only does insufficient diet affect the individual, but research suggests that severe nutritional deficits in expectant mothers also may lead to irreversible brain defects in their children.

The food stamp program is designed to combat hunger. Food stamps are available to public assistance recipients and to other low-income families. These stamps are then traded in for groceries. With millions of Americans going hungry, the food stamp program is obviously underfunded.

HOUSING ASSISTANCE

Similar to food stamps and Medicaid, housing assistance is an "in-kind" program, rather than a cash program. Generally, such assistance is provided in the form of public housing, usually large housing projects that are owned and operated by the government. In a public housing project, the tenants have lower, subsidized rents. Because they pay less than the market value of their apartments, they are effectively receiving an income transfer, which, on the average, is approximately $1000 a year.

There are also housing assistance programs for low-income people who are renting and even buying their homes and apartments in the private market. In these programs, the rent or mortgage payment is reduced, with the Department of Housing and Urban Development (HUD) making up the difference.

AID TO FAMILIES WITH DEPENDENT CHILDREN (AFDC)

Originally called Aid to Dependent Children (ADC), AFDC is the most stigmatized public assistance program. The general public's concept of "welfare" is the AFDC program.

Although more money is spent on AFDC than on any other *public assistance* program, several times as much money is spent on *social insurance*

TABLE 3.1

Cash Assistance Programs, 1991

Program	Average Monthly Recipients	Average Monthly Benefit per Recipient	Total Annual Payments (billions)
Aid to Families with Dependent Children (AFDC)	13,489,000	$135	$21.9
Supplemental Security Income (SSI)	5,118,000	$321	$19.7

Source: U.S. Bureau of the Census, *Statistical Abstract of the United States, 1993* (Washington, DC: U.S. Government Printing Office, 1993), p. 381.

Programs.[58] The stigma attached to AFDC is one reason why the average monthly grant per recipient is substantially less than for Supplemental Security Income (see Table 3.1).

In 1991 nearly $30 billion was spent on the AFDC program.[59] The high cost of this program is due to the fact that a majority of all persons receiving public assistance are on AFDC rolls.[60]

The precise parameters of eligibility for AFDC vary from state to state. Payments are made for both the parent (or parents) and the children in eligible families. To be eligible, the children must be deprived of parental support or care because of a parent's death or continued absence from the home (through desertion, divorce, or separation) or because the parent was never married. AFDC payments are also made to low-income two-parent families in which both parents are unemployed. In this situation the breadwinner (or breadwinners) must agree to seek work actively, to register with the state unemployment service, and to participate in job-training programs. Most AFDC families are headed by a single parent, usually the mother and usually because the father is absent from the home.[61]

ADC was renamed AFDC in 1962. When first enacted by the 1935 Social Security Act, one of ADC's objectives was to enable mothers with young children to remain at home. Since 1935 our values surrounding working mothers have changed. There now is substantial effort, for psychological and financial reasons, to help AFDC mothers obtain gainful employment.

Financing and administration of AFDC programs are shared by federal and state governments. In many states, counties also participate in the financing and administration. The federal government, through the Department of Health and Human Services, writes regulations to implement the Social Security laws. States, and often counties, then write their own regulations, within federal guidelines, relating to eligibility criteria, benefit standards, and qualifications of public assistance staff. A state failing to comply with federal guidelines may lose federal financial support.

Decision about AFDC eligibility are made by the executive, legislative, and judicial branches of government and at federal, state, and local levels. As a result, the program is cumbersome, slow to change to meet emerging needs, and heavily bogged down by red tape and bureaucratic processes.

A key question is whether our present punitive, residual approach to AFDC is influencing children born into AFDC families to become recipients when they grow up. Are we training whole generations for a life of dependency? Statistics show that many people on public assistance had parents who were also recipients.[62] Also, it has been found that, the longer a family receives assistance, the higher the rate of social problems their children manifest in their teenage years (births outside marriage, early marriage, emotional problems, truancy, delinquency, and dropping out of school).[63]

The Poverty Trap

E laine Johnson, age 35, has recently become a grandmother. Her oldest daughter, Sylvia, is a 16-year-old unmarried mother. Today, May 13, is a significant day in their lives because Elaine and Sylvia are applying at Chicago's Public Welfare Office to place baby Tony's name on America's welfare rolls. He will represent the third successive generation in the Johnson family to receive AFDC benefits.

Elaine's parents migrated from Mississippi to Chicago in 1952, shortly after Elaine's birth. Her father got a job as a janitor in the school system, and her mother has been a part-time nurse's aide at a hospital. Elaine started high school and received above-average grades. She had hopes of getting a student loan to go to college. She wanted to get out of the ghetto where she was being raised.

At the age of 17, however, Elaine became pregnant. Her parents talked her out of an abortion, and she gave birth to Sylvia. Two months after the birth, she signed up for AFDC at the urging of her parents and friends. It would only be temporary, she thought, until she could get a better handle on her life. She found going to school and caring for a baby to be too much work, so she dropped out of high school in her senior year. She no longer had the same interests as her former friends who did not have children. At times Elaine found it a joy to care for Sylvia, and at other times she found caring for the baby frustrating. Elaine went out as much as she could, when she had a little extra money and when she could find someone to babysit for her. Over the next 15 years, Elaine had three other children. Only one of the four different fathers married her, and that marriage lasted only two and a half years. The husband left home one day, complaining about children and responsibilities. He never returned, and Elaine has never heard from him.

There are some additional serious shortcomings of the AFDC program. Most recipients are kept in poverty by inadequate assistance grants that average well below the poverty level. Moreover, the stigma attached to receiving AFDC keeps many eligible needy people from applying.

WELFARE: MYTHS VERSUS FACTS

When welfare programs are criticized, most of that criticism is leveled at AFDC. However, many of these complaints are unfounded, because they are based on erroneous myths. Let's examine some of these myths.

Myth 1: Most welfare children are "illegitimate."

Fact: A sizable majority of the children receiving AFDC benefits are "legitimate."[64] To help AFDC families avoid unwanted pregnancies, the federal government in recent years has made family planning services available. (I strongly object to labeling any child "illegitimate." The marital status of one's parents has nothing to do with one's value as a human being.)

Myth 2: Welfare makes it profitable for women to have illegitimate babies.

Fact: The size of families on AFDC has actually been declining, particularly since 1967, reflecting a general trend in the birthrate for the population as a whole. Welfare families have an average of 2.2 children.[65] A majority of AFDC families con-

Elaine has tried a variety of jobs while on AFDC—nurse's aide, dishwasher, waitress, and service station attendant. But the costs of transportation, uniforms, and babysitting left her no better off financially than if she stayed home and received her monthly AFDC checks. Life has been hard for Elaine. Because she is on welfare, she feels like a second-class citizen and a "charity" case. She has had to pinch pennies all her life to try to make ends meet. Countless days she has fed her children on beans and rice. She sharply regrets not being able to give her children the material things that many other kids have. While some parents are buying computers for their children, she takes her kids to Goodwill's clothing store to try to find bargains on second-hand sneakers, shirts, jeans, and jackets.

She is living in a ghetto area and is alarmed that her oldest son, Marvin, is experimenting with cocaine and other drugs. The school system is another concern: A high percentage of students drop out, the windows in the buildings are boarded up, vandalism is frequent, physical attacks on teachers sometimes occur, and the educational quality is known to be inferior.

When Elaine discovered that Sylvia was sexually active at 15, she pleaded with her daughter not to make the mistake she had made. Elaine even took her to Planned Parenthood to get birth control pills. Elaine's remaining dream is that her children will have a better life than hers. Tears often come to her eyes when she sees her children getting caught in the same poverty trap that she is in. Sylvia took her pills for several months. When the supply ran out, she never got around to going back to Planned Parenthood to get her prescription refilled.

Yes, today is a significant day for Elaine. As she and Sylvia are walking toward the welfare department, Elaine is solemnly pondering why her life has turned out as it has. She also is wondering what it will take to give at least some of her children a chance for a better life.

---

sist of a mother and one or two children.[66] In the small proportion of AFDC families in which another child is born after the family begins to receive benefits, the main reason may be lack of appropriate family planning resources. Moreover, the average AFDC family would experience a boost of $1600 per year for each additional child.[67] Because it costs over $140,000 to raise a child from birth to age 18, the "profit" a mother might expect to realize from having an additional child is minuscule, even if she minimized all expenditures for the child. In addition, the average per capita amount of a welfare grant decreases as the number of persons in the household increases. Usually, having more babies makes a family poorer.

Myth 3: Give them more money and they'll spend it on alcohol and drugs.

Fact: In 1991 the average monthly grant per recipient in the United States was $135,[68] hardly enough to meet bare essentials. How would you like to live on $135 per month? Furthermore, most AFDC families report that, if they received extra funds, that money would go for essentials.[69]

Myth 4: Most welfare recipients are cheaters and frauds.

Fact: If fraud is defined as a deliberate and knowing attempt by a client to deceive the agency, then the incidence of fraud is remarkably low. A national survey found that 1 out of every 20 AFDC recipients received checks for which he or she was ineligible. Less than half of 1% of welfare cases are referred for prosecution for fraud.[70] Because determining eligibility is a cumbersome, complex process, most of these errors were identified as honest mistakes made by state and local public assistance bureaucrats or by recipients. Simplifying the process for determining eligibility for AFDC, along with reducing the complexities in calculating monthly grants, would undoubtedly reduce such errors. Contrasted with tax fraud, the welfare system is squeaky clean. The Internal Revenue Service estimates a 20–25% error rate in payment of income taxes—most of which is attributable to underreporting of income by taxpayers.[71]

Myth 5: The welfare rolls are soaring out of control.

Fact: Most caseload growth in the AFDC program occurred before 1973, with dramatic increases between 1970 and 1973. Since early 1976 the number of people on AFDC has shown only minimal annual increases.[72] There are many reasons for this recent stabilization, including the declining birthrate and increased use of family planning resources.

Myth 6: Welfare is just a money handout—a dole.

Fact: Most families on AFDC receive one or more social services designed to meet personal and social problems and hopefully to make them self-supportive. Available social services vary widely from area to area and may include health care, financial counseling, counseling on home management, employment counseling, day care, vocational rehabilitation, homemaker services, consumer education, assistance in child rearing, Head Start, job training, and marriage counseling. The provision of social services to low-income families was one of the three programs enacted by the 1935 Social Security Act.

Myth 7: People on welfare are able-bodied loafers.

Fact: Contrary to public opinion, few able-bodied persons receive assistance; the vast majority of AFDC recipients are children. Less than 1% of welfare recipients are able-bodied, unemployed males.[73] The largest group of able-bodied adults is composed of AFDC mothers, most of whom

EXHIBIT 3.3

Women Accused of Welfare Fraud

The merits of AFDC generally go unreported. Welfare fraud, although rare, is big news. Stories like the following help to promote the myth that most welfare recipients are cheaters and frauds.

> CHICAGO (AP)—A woman and her two adult daughters were charged Wednesday with cheating welfare agencies out of $250,000 over the last 11 years, authorities said.
>
> One of the sisters, _____, 32, used eight names for herself and dozens of names for fictitious children in collecting $150,000 in public aid checks, said James G. Piper, an assistant state's attorney. She was charged with 385 counts of theft.
>
> Her sister _____, 26, was charged with 105 counts of theft and the mother, _____, 51, with 59 counts.

Source: Wisconsin State Journal, May 29, 1980, p. 3.

head families in which no able-bodied male is present. Many of these mothers already are working or are actively seeking work, are receiving work training, or are waiting to be called back after a layoff. Other AFDC mothers face serious barriers to obtaining employment: very young children to rear, lack of money for child care, lack of job skills, and lack of extensive medical or rehabilitative services to become employable. Contrary to the stereotype of the "welfare mother" as shiftless, lazy, and unwilling to take a job, even long-term AFDC mothers continue to have a strong work ethic but lack skills and confidence to obtain a job.[74]

Myth 8: Most welfare families are African American.

Fact: The number of white families receiving AFDC is approximately the same as the number of African American families.[75] Because African

Americans constitute about 12% of the U.S. population and over 45% of all AFDC recipients, the stigma attached to AFDC may be partly due to racial prejudice.[76]

Myth 9: "Why work when you can live it up on welfare?"

Fact: As mentioned, the average AFDC monthly payment per recipient in 1991 was $135, hardly enough to "live it up."[77] In most states payments to a welfare family of four with no other income are below the established poverty level.

Myth 10: Once on welfare, always on welfare.

Fact: Only 10% of the households receive AFDC benefits for 10 years or longer. Half the families on welfare have been receiving assistance for 20 months or less and two-thirds for less than three years.[78]

Myth 11: Welfare is eating up tremendous chunks of our tax money, causing inflation, and "bleeding the country dry."

Fact: At the federal level about 1% of the federal budget is allocated to AFDC.[79] The largest single item in the national budget is defense spending.[80]

Myth 12: Welfare is only for the poor.

Fact: The United States pays out much more to the rich than to the poor. These payments are not called welfare but research grants, training grants, tax loopholes, compensation, low-interest loans, and parity. Dale Tussing notes that the United States has two welfare systems:

Two welfare systems exist simultaneously in this country. One is well known. It is explicit, poorly funded, stigmatized and stigmatizing, and is directed at the poor. The other, practically unknown, is implicit, literally invisible, is nonstigmatized and nonstigmatizing, and provides vast but unacknowledged benefits for the nonpoor. . . . Our welfare systems do not distribute benefits on the basis of need. Rather, they distribute benefits on the basis of legitimacy. Poor people are viewed as less legitimate than nonpoor people . . . by and large, welfare programs for the poor are obvious, open and clearly labeled, and those for the nonpoor are either concealed (as in tax laws, for instance) and ill understood, or are clothed in

protective language. . . . Whether or not a person is poor can often be determined by the names of his welfare programs. If his programs are called "relief," "welfare," "assistance," "charity," or the like, he is surely poor; but if they are called "parity," "insurance," "compensation," or "compulsory saving," he is surely a member of the large majority of nonpoor persons who do not even think of themselves as receiving welfare payments.[81]

Eleanor Clift adds:

If one counts a broad range of federal spending and tax programs, an average upper-income person will get more than a typical poor person.

It's no secret that middle- and upper-income families enjoy the benefit of tax breaks and entitlement programs like social security. But such families, many of whom complain bitterly these days that government is ignoring them, may be surprised to learn how much more they get than their poorer counterparts. In some ways, such benefits remain the holiest of sacred cows.[82]

PROPOSED ALTERNATIVES

In the 1960s and 1970s Presidents Kennedy, Johnson, Nixon, Ford, and Carter advanced a number of proposals to alleviate poverty. Johnson, with his War on Poverty programs, was by far the most successful in getting programs passed and implemented. As noted earlier, these programs have had some success in reducing the proportion of people below the poverty line. Yet 15% of our population (39 million people) still remain impoverished. It appears that the efforts of the 1960s and 1970s have dampened, at least temporarily, our country's determination to combat poverty.

Practically everyone agrees that the present welfare system is cumbersome, inefficient, and often unfair. The administrative structure of most public assistance programs is very complicated, with decisions being made at federal, state, and local levels and in the executive, legislative, and judicial branches of government. This section will examine several proposals for changing the welfare system, including eliminating or reducing welfare benefits, replacing welfare with work, offering family allowances, making the government a last-resort employer, guaranteeing a basic annual income, and eliminating or reducing the causes of poverty.

Eliminate or Reduce Welfare Benefits

Author Charles Murray has proposed, in his controversial book *Losing Ground,* that the government should eliminate welfare benefits for all working-age adults.[83] He contends that court decisions, bureaucratic reforms, and antipoverty programs in our society have actually made the poor worse off by creating a dependency. In essence, he asserts, people on welfare decide that being on the government dole is better than working.

Murray is especially critical of the AFDC program. He asserts that it provides an incentive for single women to want to have children in order to receive welfare payments. He also believes that increases in crime and drug abuse, poor educational performance in schools, and deteriorating conditions in inner cities stem largely from the increase in single-parent families, which he attributes to government programs that support such families. His solution to overhauling the AFDC program is simple: "If you want to cut illegitimate births among poor people, . . . I know how to do that. You just rip away every kind of government support there is."[84]

Critics of this approach are horrified. They argue that Murray's plan would make innocent children suffer for their parents' inadequacies, which seems doubly unfair, given that 2 out of 3 AFDC beneficiaries are children.[85] If the AFDC program were eliminated, more families undoubtedly would end up homeless and hungry. Murray's response is that single mothers who are unable to care for their children should place them for adoption. He further asserts that terminating the AFDC program would force single women to think twice about getting pregnant and

would force more low-income males to refrain from fathering children outside of marriage.

Although there is little support for entirely eliminating the AFDC program, political decision makers are becoming increasingly concerned about its leading to long-term dependency for some recipients. For example, in 1993 Wisconsin passed legislation to limit AFDC benefits to two years, with this new program restriction to take effect in 1999. In 1994 Wisconsin Governor Tommy Thompson also proposed that the monthly AFDC benefits no longer be increased in families where the mother gives birth to one or more children while on AFDC.

In the 1994 elections Republicans (mostly conservatives) won a majority of seats in the House of Representatives for the first time in 40 years, and now have control of both houses of Congress. The new House speaker, Newt Gingrich, has proposed there be no AFDC benefits for unmarried teens and their children. In addition, he proposed that AFDC recipients be prohibited from receiving benefits for more than five years, with states having the option of reducing the time limit for welfare benefits to two years. What does he propose happen to the children whose mothers are unable to financially provide for them? The most stunning component of his proposal is to remove these children from their mothers and place them in orphanages. Critics say institutionalizing low-income children is not only highly expensive, but also detrimental to their physical, social, emotional, and intellectual development.

Replace Welfare with Work

When Bill Clinton was campaigning for the presidency in 1992, he promised to "end welfare as we know it." In 1994 he proposed attacking the costly national problem of welfare dependency with a plan that would force growing numbers of young welfare mothers into public or private jobs. The objective of the plan is to make young single mothers self-sufficient by giving them money and child care while they receive job training—but then to cut off their cash benefits after no more than 24 months. Those who are unable to find jobs would be given temporary tax-subsidized work, usually at the minimum wage, either in the private sector or in community service.

The specifics of Clinton's proposal are as follows:

Target welfare mothers born in 1972 or later for education and job training and end welfare benefits to those who skip school, miss training, or turn down a job offer.

Require public service work from welfare recipients born in 1972 or later if they fail to find a job after two years of education and training.

Expand child care to encourage welfare mothers to enroll in education and job training. Child care would continue for up to one year after an adult left welfare for work.

Reward work by continuing medical benefits to families leaving welfare.

Discourage unwed motherhood among teens by refusing to issue separate welfare checks to minors living apart from their parents or a responsible adult.

Launch a publicity campaign against teen pregnancy. A national clearinghouse would provide schools and communities with advice and curricula for teen-pregnancy prevention programs.

Improve child-support enforcement by improving collections and identifying more fathers of out-of-wedlock babies. Each welfare applicant would be required to name her child's father and help find him before getting benefits.

Withhold wages and suspend professional and occupational licenses and drivers' licenses from fathers who fail to pay child support.[86]

Clinton proposed to move slowly with these reforms (largely because the government lacks the money to move more quickly). This is why the new requirements (if enacted) would apply to welfare recipients born in 1972 or later. Even with this moderate pace, however, Clinton's reforms would drive up welfare costs by an estimated $9.3 billion over five years.[87] A major goal of the plan is to stimulate a sense of parental responsibility in the welfare population—responsibility to receive job training and work, to financially provide for one's children, and to delay having children until the adult years.

Offer Family Allowances

The United States is the only Western industrialized country without a family allowance program. Under a family allowance program the government pays each family a set amount based on the number of children in the household. If payments were large enough, a program like this could aid in eliminating poverty, particularly in large families.

There are some strong criticisms of family allowance plans. If payments were made to all children, the program would be very expensive and much of the money would go to nonpoor families. This problem could be solved (as Denmark has done) by varying the family allowance payments with income and terminating payments after a certain income is reached. (However, such an approach would then involve a means test and continue to stigmatize recipients.) A second criticism is that such a program would provide an incentive to increase the birthrate at a time when overpopulation is a major concern. A final criticism is that it would not provide payments to single individuals and childless couples who are poor.

Make the Government a Last-Resort Employer

The unemployment rate among able-bodied workers in recent years has been between 4% and 11%. In addition, over 1.5 million family heads are working full time but earning wages below the poverty line.[88] The government could initiate public works projects (such as building highways and bridges) in which all able-bodied poor could earn a certain minimum amount above the poverty line.

There is doubt about whether such a program is politically feasible. Public works projects are usually viewed by the general public as being expensive, unproductive, and inefficient. Also, employers who pay minimum wages would likely see such a program as competitive; workers could earn more by working for the government than by working for them.

Another criticism is that such a program would serve only a small fraction of AFDC recipients; as indicated earlier, only a small minority of public assistance recipients are able-bodied, unemployed adults. (The proposal by President Clinton to replace welfare with work includes some aspects of government's being a last-resort employer.)

Guarantee a Basic Annual Income

A variety of proposals to guarantee every American a certain annual income have been put forth, including proposals by Presidents Nixon and Carter. The base level could conceivably be set slightly above the poverty line and adjusted each year to account for inflation. Such a proposal, if implemented, would eradicate poverty.

Practically all guaranteed-income proposals are based on the concept of a "negative income tax." That is, persons earning above a certain level would pay income tax, whereas those earning below that level would receive a grant—the negative tax—to bring their income up to the guaranteed level. Most negative-income-tax plans also contain an incentive-to-work provision that allows recipients to keep a proportion of their earnings above the guaranteed base level.

Many variations of the negative income tax are possible, and some have been tested by the federal government. The minimum-income guarantee for a family of four, for example, could be set at the poverty line, and the incentive-to-work factor (the tax-back rate) could range widely. But such plans could be very expensive.

Using a hypothetical example, with a guaranteed base level of $14,000 for a family of four and the tax-back rate at 50%—allowing a family to keep $50 out of every $100 earned—the family would receive subsidies until the break-even point of $28,000. The mathematics of this guaranteed base level and tax-back rate can be illustrated as follows:

If Your Annual Income from a Paying Job is:	Then Your Annual Income from the Government Is:	So Your Total Income Is:
$ 0	$14,000	$14,000
5,000	11,500	16,500
10,000	9000	19,000
15,000	6500	21,500
20,000	4000	24,000
25,000	1500	26,500
28,000	0	28,000

There are a number of advantages to negative-income-tax plans. They would shift the focus of income maintenance programs from "charity" to a "right" of entitlement to a guaranteed income. The stigma of being a recipient would be sharply reduced. Such programs would be relatively simple to administer, as eligibility would be based on income-tax returns. Furthermore, such a program would serve everyone who is poor; if the base level is at the poverty line, poverty would be eradicated. Another advantage would be to reduce equity problems that have occurred under present programs, in which nonworking people are eligible for several types of benefits (for example, food stamps and Medicaid) and may be able to achieve a higher standard of living than a low-income employed person who is eligible for few, if any, benefits. A negative-income-tax plan could also replace practically all other public assistance programs and thereby reduce the expense and complexity of administering a variety of programs.

Several unanswered questions, however, have been raised about a negative-income-tax plan:

■ Such plans are based on the filing of income-tax forms. If a family has little or no income (and no assets), must they wait nearly a year until their tax form is filed before being eligible for benefits?

■ Will a guaranteed income destroy the incentive to work?

■ The cost of living varies greatly between urban and rural areas and among different parts of the country. Should financial adjustments be made for this?

■ Perhaps the biggest problem with a negative-income-tax plan involves what has been called the "unholy triangle"—that is, developing a plan that:

1. Has an adequate guaranteed base level.

2. Allows low-income workers to keep a sufficiently high percentage of their earnings above the guaranteed base level so that the incentive to work is not destroyed.

3. Is not exorbitantly expensive, so that our national economy is not severely affected.

The federal government has shown considerable interest in negative-income-tax programs, as evidenced by the passage in 1973 of the Supplemental Security Income (SSI) program, which has a guaranteed income base. But proposed negative-income-tax plans have been held up in Congress. Liberals argued that the guaranteed base level of payments was too low and would not move families above the poverty line. Conservatives objected that the plans would be too costly and would provide financial payments to many more poor families than do current public assistance programs. Conservatives also opposed the plans because they feared they would destroy the incentive to work and would provide "something for nothing."

Eliminate or Reduce the Causes of Poverty

As noted earlier, a number of factors cause and perpetuate poverty. Another way of combating poverty is to develop and expand programs to alleviate its major causes.

Laws to end racial and sex discrimination can be more vigorously enforced. Programs to curb alcohol and drug abuse can be expanded to reach out and serve more of those who are addicted.

Higher-quality educational programs (and more resources) are needed in pockets of poverty (for example, urban ghettos) to inspire students, to help them stay in school, and to help them achieve higher academic levels. Sex education and family planning services need to be provided to more teenagers and young adults to teach responsible sexuality and prevent unwanted pregnancies, which play a role in locking young people into poverty. Family planning services also need to be expanded to help couples who do not want, and cannot afford, large-sized families. An expanded public housing program is needed to provide adequate living quarters for the poor. A national health insurance program is needed to pay for unusually high medical bills, which at present wipe out the savings of some families and plunge them deep into debt.

Some families need financial counseling to help them more effectively manage and spend within the limits of their financial resources. Many middle-aged adults need educational programs to teach them to plan for their retirement years—what lifestyle they want, how to remain healthy, and how to prepare financially.

Provision of jobs for able-bodied workers is a key to reducing the number of people in poverty. In recent years high unemployment rates have forced many of the unemployed and their families into poverty. A variety of suggestions have been advanced to progress toward a full-employment society.

Able-bodied adults who do not have marketable job skills (perhaps because their skills have become obsolete) need to receive training for jobs that are available. (In Germany adults are paid by the government during the weeks or months they are receiving job training or job retraining.) Our government should have a program to financially assist workers and their families to relocate from areas of high unemployment to booming areas where jobs are readily available. Many areas need more quality day-care centers that charge reasonable rates so that single parents (and also two-parent families) can work. For the unemployed able-bodied, the government could be a "last resort" employer. In many other countries the government offers tax incentives to industries to locate in depressed areas. Another suggestion is to encourage industries to hire workers who have been unemployed for a long time by reimbursing the employers for a portion of the new workers' salaries.

SOCIAL WORK AND PUBLIC WELFARE

Since the enactment of the 1935 Social Security Act, numerous social services have been provided to public assistance recipients. The particular services provided vary widely from area to area (depending on state and county decisions) but include counseling, day care, protective services, foster care, services to people with a physical or mental disability, information and referral, homemaker services, financial counseling, assistance in child rearing, family planning, health services, vocational training, and employment counseling. A large number of social workers are employed to provide such services.

Until 1972 social services and financial assistance were combined, and social workers were involved in financial eligibility determination. The 1972 Amendments to the Social Security Act separated services and assistance. Now, public assistance recipients are informed of available social services and of their right to request such services. Financial eligibility is determined by staff who generally are not social workers.

Social workers find many gratifications in helping people with personal or social problems. Yet social work is frequently frustrating. The sources of these frustrations include:

■ Having extensive paperwork to fill out.

■ Trying to meet the needs of clients when those needs are not served by existing programs.

■ Trying to change the huge public welfare bureaucratic structure to better meet the needs of clients. (The public welfare system is slow to change to meet emerging needs and is filled with extensive "red tape.")

■ Having a larger caseload than one can optimally and effectively serve.

■ Trying to keep informed about the numerous changes (program, organizational, and eligibility determination) that occur on an ongoing basis.

■ Dealing with discouraged clients who lack the necessary motivation to work toward improving their circumstances. Social work "interns" in field placement and new social workers frequently report this as being their greatest frustration and a severe "reality shock." They anticipate that, after carefully working out an "intervention plan" with a client to resolve some problem, the client will follow through. Unfortunately, in many cases this does not happen. Future appointments may be broken by the client, and, even if the client responsibly keeps appointments, she or he is likely to have excuses for not following through on the commitment. These excuses can usually be interpreted to represent a lack of motivation.

Working with Discouraged People

The key variable in determining if clients will make positive changes in their lives is whether they have the motivation to make the efforts necessary to improve their circumstances. Failure in counseling or social work generally occurs when clients do not become motivated.

Many public assistance recipients are discouraged. Continued economic pressures, and generally a long series of past "failure" experiences when they have tried to improve their circumstances, frequently have sapped their motivation. Discouraged people tend to travel through life in an unhappy "rut" that is dull, stagnating, and generally unfulfilling but that is seen by them as normal and predictable. For them, extensive efforts to improve their circumstances are viewed as risky and frightening. Many feel it is safer to remain in their rut than to try something new that might further expose their weaknesses and result in psychological "hurt."

Seeking a job, finding transportation, and making day-care arrangements could be seen as overwhelmingly difficult for an unskilled AFDC mother with young children who has never been employed previously. For a wife with five children who periodically is physically beaten by her husband, seeking counseling or making separation arrangements may be seen as highly risky because the future would be uncertain; she may also fear that such actions would only make her husband more abusive. For a person with a drinking problem who has recently lost his last two jobs, giving up drinking may be seen as giving up his main "crutch."

To motivate a discouraged person, the social worker has to be an "encouraging person." According to Lewis Losoncy, an encouraging person does the following:[89]

Has complete acceptance for the discouraged person and conveys "I accept you exactly as you are, with no conditions attached." (She or he should not, however, convey acceptance of the deviant behavior that needs to be changed.)

Has a nonblaming attitude so that the discouraged person no longer feels a need to lie, pretend, or wear a mask.

Conveys empathy that she or he is aware and can to some extent feel what the discouraged person is feeling.

Conveys to the discouraged person that she or he is genuinely interested in the counselee's progress and conveys that the counselee is an important, worthwhile person. In order for discouraged people to believe in themselves, they generally need an encouraging person who conveys the idea that they are important and worthwhile.

Notices (rewards) every small instance of progress—for example, if the person is wearing something new, the counselor says "That's new, isn't it? It really looks good on you." This is particularly valuable during the beginning of the relationship.

Conveys to the discouraged person that she or he has confidence in that person's capacity to improve.

Conveys sincere enthusiasm about the discouraged person's interests, ideas, and risk-taking actions.

Has the capacity to be a nonjudgmental listener so that the discouraged person's real

thoughts and feelings can be expressed freely, without fear of censure.

Has the time to spend listening and understanding the discouraged person as fully as possible. Motivating a discouraged person takes a long, long time. Discouraged people generally have a long history of failures.

Has a sincere belief in the discouraged person's ability to find a purpose in life.

Allows the person to take risks without judging him or her.

Reinforces efforts made by the discouraged person. The important thing is that one tries and not necessarily whether one succeeds. By making efforts to improve, there is hope.

Helps the discouraged person to see the falsehood and negative consequences of self-defeating statements, such as "I'm a failure." Every person has skills and deficiencies, and every person should be encouraged to improve both strengths and weaknesses.

Recognizes that all that can be done is to give one's best efforts in trying to motivate a discouraged person. Success in motivating a discouraged person is not guaranteed. To give up hope of motivating a discouraged person means one will no longer be effective in working with that person.

Is skilled at looking for uniquenesses and strengths in an individual. These uniquenesses are communicated to the discouraged person so that the person begins to realize she or he is special and worthwhile. This process leads to a sense of improved self-worth and strengthens the courage to take risks and change.

Helps the discouraged person to develop perceptual alternatives (other ways of looking at life). For example, for a woman who is periodically physically beaten by her husband, it is appropriate to point out that other women in similar situations have separated from their husbands, which has led eventually either to an improved marital relationship or to a happier, independent life.

Is aware of the negative consequences of overdependency in a relationship. When the discouraged person is on the way to taking risks and making constructive changes, one should start to help the discouraged person to develop "self-encouragement," in which the client is encouraged to make and trust his or her own decisions and is encouraged to take more risks.

The Future

Programs created by the Social Security Act, along with the War on Poverty programs, have not wiped out poverty as hoped—and such a goal may be unrealistic. But these programs *have* sharply reduced the percentage of Americans who are poor and have helped many of those who remain in poverty. These are significant accomplishments and should be so recognized. If our country continues to retreat by cutting back on social programs, it is likely that the percentage of the population that is poor will increase.

Poverty is interrelated with most other social problems. Therefore, it may well be that, if the poverty problem intensifies, there will be rate increases in crime, emotional disorders, infant mortality, inadequate health care, inner-city problems, substandard housing, alcoholism, the school dropout rate, malnutrition, child neglect, and suicide. Is this what we want?

SUMMARY

About 15% of our population lives below the poverty line. Poverty is relative to time and place. An agreed-on definition of poverty does not exist. The usual definitions are based on a lack of money, with annual income most commonly used to gauge who is poor. Income is defined using either an absolute approach or a relative approach. The pain of poverty involves not only financial hardships but also the psychological implications that being "poverty stricken" has for a person.

Huge income and wealth gaps exist between the highest fifth and lowest fifth in our society. Social mobility (movement up the social status ladder) occurs rarely in our society. Wealth perpetuates wealth, and poverty perpetuates poverty. The ideology of individualism and the Protestant ethic still stigmatize the poor in our society.

Those most likely to be poor include female heads of households, children, people of color, the elderly, large-sized families, those with limited education, the unemployed, and those living in pockets of poverty and high unemployment.

The causes of poverty are numerous. Poverty is interrelated with all other social problems. Therefore almost every social service, to some extent, combats poverty. Some researchers have noted that the poor have a set of values and attitudes that constitute a culture of poverty. There is now considerable controversy about whether this culture *perpetuates* poverty or is simply an *adaptation* to being poor.

Poverty, to some extent, is functional for society. For this and other reasons, some decision makers are not actively seeking to eradicate it.

The major income maintenance programs to combat poverty were created by the 1935 Social Security Act. The federal government's role in providing social insurance programs and public assistance programs was initiated by this act.

Social insurance programs (which are consistent with the institutional view of income transfers) receive less criticism than public assistance programs (which are consistent with the residual view of income transfers). There are many negative myths about public assistance programs, especially the AFDC program. A danger of punitive, stigmatized public assistance programs is that poverty and dependency may be passed on to succeeding generations.

Our society has the resources to eradicate poverty, but it may not currently have the will. Two alternatives for alleviating poverty are (1) enacting a guaranteed annual income plan that would set the base level slightly above the poverty line and (2) providing a variety of programs that would eliminate or reduce the causes of poverty.

Although the profession of social work has gratifications, it also has frustrations, including dealing with mounds of paperwork and red tape, working in a bureaucratic structure that is slow to change in response to emerging needs, and working with discouraged people who do not follow through on "intervention plans" to improve their circumstances.

NOTES

1. U.S. Bureau of the Census, *Statistical Abstract of the United States, 1993* (Washington, DC: U.S. Government Printing Office, 1993), p. 469.
2. "Nation's Poor Top 39 Million," *Wisconsin State Journal*, Oct. 7, 1994, p. 1A.
3. Ibid.
4. William Kornblum and Joseph Julian, *Social Problems*, 7th ed. (Englewood Cliffs, NJ: Prentice-Hall, 1992), p. 234.
5. Ibid., p. 237.
6. Ibid., pp. 224–226.
7. Marilyn Flynn, "Public Assistance," in *Contemporary Social Work*, 2d ed., Donald Brieland, Lela Costin, and Charles Atherton, eds. (New York: McGraw-Hill, 1980), p. 165.
8. Michael Harrington, *The Other America* (New York: Macmillan, 1962).
9. "Poverty Gap Widens, Studies Reveal," *NASW News* (January 1990), p. 19.
10. Kornblum and Julian, *Social Problems*, p. 219.
11. Ibid.
12. Ibid.
13. Ibid., p. 220.
14. Ibid.
15. Ibid.
16. Ibid.
17. James W. Coleman and Donald R. Cressey, *Social Problems*, 5th ed. (New York: HarperCollins, 1993), p. 140.
18. Quoted in Kornblum and Julian, *Social Problems*, pp. 221–222.
19. Coleman and Cressey, *Social Problems*, p. 141.
20. Paul Samuelson, quoted in P. Blumberg, *Inequality in an Age of Decline* (New York: Oxford University Press, 1980), p. 34.
21. Jonathan Yenkin, "Hunger in U.S. Jumps 50% since Mid-80s," *Wisconsin State Journal*, Sept. 10, 1992, p. 1A.
22. Ian Robertson, *Social Problems*, 2d ed. (New York: Random House, 1980), p. 31.
23. James W. Coleman and Donald R. Cressey, *Social Problems*, 4th ed. (New York: Harper & Row, 1990), p. 161.
24. Kenneth E. Boulding, "Reflections on Poverty," in *The Social Welfare Forum: 1961*, National Conference on Social Welfare, ed. (New York: Columbia University Press, 1961), pp. 45–58.
25. "Nation's Poor Top 39 Million," p. 1A.
26. Second inaugural address of President Franklin D. Roosevelt (Jan. 20, 1937).
27. President's Council on Economic Advisors, *Economic Report of the President* (Washington, DC: U.S. Government Printing Office, 1964), pp. 56–57.
28. "Nation's Poor Top 39 Million," p. 1A.
29. *Statistical Abstract of the United States, 1993*, p. 471.
30. John E. Farley, *American Social Problems*, 2d ed. (Englewood Cliffs, NJ: Prentice-Hall, 1992), p. 140.
31. *Statistical Abstract of the United States, 1993*, pp. 469–475.
32. Daniel P. Moynihan, "Our Poorest Citizens—Children," *Focus*, 11, no. 1 (Spring 1988), pp. 5–6.
33. Ibid.
34. *Statistical Abstract of the United States, 1993*, p. 470.
35. Ibid., pp. 469–476.
36. Ibid., p. 470.
37. Beth Brophy, "Children under Stress," *U.S. News & World Report*, Oct. 27, 1986, p. 59.
38. *Statistical Abstract of the United States, 1993*, pp. 469–475.
39. Ibid.
40. Ibid., pp. 469–474.
41. Richard T. Schaefer, *Racial and Ethnic Groups*, 5th ed. (New York: HarperCollins, 1993), pp. 148–298.
42. *Statistical Abstract of the United States, 1993*, pp. 468–447.
43. Ibid., p. 472.
44. Kornblum and Julian, *Social Problems*, p. 231.
45. Harrington, *The Other America*, p. 21.
46. Oscar Lewis, "The Culture of Poverty," *Scientific American*, 215 (October 1966), pp. 19–25.
47. Ibid., p. 23.
48. Eleanor Leacock, ed., *The Culture of Poverty: A Critique* (New York: Simon and Schuster, 1971).
49. Elliott Liebow, *Tally's Corner: A Study of Negro Street-Corner Men* (Boston: Little, Brown, 1967); Ulf Hannertz, *Soulside: An Inquiry into Ghetto Culture and Community* (New York: Columbia University Press, 1969); Leacock, *The Culture of Poverty*.
50. William Ryan, *Blaming the Victim*, rev. ed. (New York: Vintage Books, 1976).
51. Thomas Sullivan, Kendrick Thompson, Richard Wright, George Gross, and Dale Spady, *Social Problems* (New York: Wiley, 1980), p. 390.
52. Herbert J. Gans, *More Equality* (New York: Pantheon, 1968), pp. 133–135.
53. Leila Pine, "Good Life on Unemployment," *Wisconsin State Journal*, Aug. 29, 1976, pp. 1, 8.
54. Helen M. Crampton and Kenneth K. Keiser, *Social Welfare: Institution and Process* (New York: Random House, 1970), p. 73.
55. These conservative views are summarized by Samuel Mencher, "Newburgh: The Recurrent Crisis in

Public Assistance," *Social Work,* 7 (January 1962), pp. 3–4.

56. Rex A. Skidmore and Milton G. Thackeray, *Introduction to Social Work,* 2d ed. (Englewood Cliffs, NJ: Prentice-Hall, 1976), pp. 111–112.

57. Yenkin, "Hunger in U.S. Jumps 50% since Mid-80s," p. 1A.

58. *Statistical Abstract of the United States, 1993,* p. 369.

59. Ibid., p. 381.

60. Ibid.

61. Moynihan, "Our Poorest Citizens—Children," pp. 5–6.

62. Kornblum and Julian, *Social Problems,* pp. 237–244.

63. Ibid.

64. Ibid., pp. 231–232.

65. Ibid., p. 232.

66. Ibid., pp. 231–232.

67. *Statistical Abstract of the United States, 1993,* p. 381.

68. Ibid.

69. Kornblum and Julian, *Social Problems,* p. 232.

70. Ibid., pp. 232–233.

71. Theresa Funiciello, *Tyranny of Kindness* (New York: Atlantic Monthly Press, 1993), p. 60.

72. *Statistical Abstract of the the United States, 1993,* pp. 381–392.

73. Kornblum and Julian, *Social Problems,* p. 233.

74. *Wisconsin Welfare Facts & Figures, 1984* (Madison,

WI: State Dept. of Health & Social Services, 1984), pp. 18–20.

75. Kornblum and Julian, *Social Problems,* p. 230.

76. Schaefer, *Racial and Ethnic Groups,* pp. 224–230.

77. *Statistical Abstract of the United States, 1993,* p. 381.

78. Kornblum and Julian, *Social Problems,* pp. 236–242.

79. *Statistical Abstract of the United States, 1993,* p. 294.

80. Ibid.

81. A. Dale Tussing, "The Dual Welfare System," *Society,* 11 (January–February 1974), pp. 50–57.

82. Eleanor Clift, "Benefits 'R' Us," *Newsweek,* Aug. 10, 1992, p. 56.

83. Charles Murray, *Losing Ground* (New York: Basic Books, 1986).

84. Quoted in David Whitman, "The Next War on Poverty," *U.S. News &World Report,* Oct. 5, 1992, p. 38.

85. *Statistical Abstract of the United States, 1993,* pp. 381–386.

86. "Clinton's Plan," *Wisconsin State Journal,* June 12, 1994, p. 2A.

87. Robert Rankin and David Hess, "Reinventing Welfare," *Wisconsin State Journal,* June 15, 1994, pp. 1A–2A.

88. *Statistical Abstract of the United States, 1993,* p. 472.

89. Lewis Losoncy, *Turning People On* (Englewood Cliffs, NJ: Prentice-Hall, 1977).

4

EMOTIONAL
PROBLEMS
AND
COUNSELING

E veryone, at times, has emotional problems and/or behavioral difficulties. This chapter will:

- Describe the nature and extent of such difficulties.
- Discuss the concept of mental illness.
- Present a theory about the causes of chronic mental illness.
- Present information about the homeless.
- Discuss controversial issues in the mental health field.
- Present research on the relationship between social structure and the rate of mental illness.
- Present a brief history of our society's treatment of the emotionally disturbed.
- Describe treatment approaches for emotional and behavioral problems.
- Describe the role of social work in the mental health field.

A PERSPECTIVE ON EMOTIONAL PROBLEMS

Several years ago I worked as a counselor at a maximum-security hospital for the "criminally insane." A number of the residents at this hospital had committed bizarre crimes due to emotional and behavioral problems. I'll describe a few of these situations to give you an idea of what I encountered.

In one case a 22-year-old male had decapitated his 17-year-old friend. In another a married male with four children had been arrested for the fourth time for exposing himself. In still another a male had dug up several graves and used the corpses to "redecorate" his home. Another married man had been committed after it was discovered that he was involved in incestuous relationships with his 11- and 12-year-old daughters. Another man had been committed after trying to deliver sermons in local taverns and after repeatedly maintaining that clouds followed him

around in whatever direction he was going. Another inmate had brutally killed his father with an ax. Bizarre? Yes, definitely!

Is there a way to explain why these men did what they did? A variety of interpretations have been offered by different authorities—most of whom assert that they acted strangely because they were mentally ill.

Albert Ellis, a prominent psychologist, has advanced a different explanation—one that offers considerable promise for understanding and treating people who commit bizarre offenses. Ellis asserts that, if we look at what the offenders were thinking when they committed unusual offenses, we will be able to gain an understanding of (1) why the bizarre actions occurred, (2) what would have prevented them from happening, and (3) what services are now needed to prevent the offenders from again getting into trouble after their release.[1]

At the maximum-security hospital, Ellis's interpretation was applied to the grave digger's case. Jim Schmidt (the name has been changed) was 46 years old when he began digging up graves and redecorating his home. His mother had died three and a half years earlier. Unfortunately, his mother was the only person who had provided meaning to his life. He was shy and had no other friends, and the two had lived together in a small rural community for the past 22 years. After his mother's death he became even more isolated. Being very lonely, he wished his mother were still alive. As happens with many people who lose someone close, he began dreaming that she was still alive. His dreams appeared so real that, on awakening, he found it difficult to believe his mother was definitely dead. He then began thinking that his mother could in fact be brought back to life and that bringing corpses of females to his home would help bring his mother back. (Now, to us this idea certainly appears irrational. But, being isolated, Jim had no way of checking what was real and what was not.) He decided to give the idea a try.

Jim, of course, needed counseling (then and now). Such services would help him adjust to his mother's death, find new interests in life, become more involved with other people, and exchange thoughts with others to check out what is real and what is not.

NATURE AND EXTENT OF EMOTIONAL AND BEHAVIORAL PROBLEMS

Emotional and behavioral problems are two comprehensive labels covering an array of disturbances: depression, excessive anxiety, feelings of inferiority or isolation, alienation, sadistic or masochistic tendencies, marital difficulties, broken romances, parent/child relationship difficulties, hyperactivity, unusual or bizarre behavior, aggressiveness, phobias, child or spousal abuse, compulsive or obsessive behavior, guilt, shyness, violent displays of temper, vindictiveness, nightmares or insomnia, sexual deviations, eating disorders, and so on.

Each problem has unique and sometimes numerous potential causes. Depression, for example, may stem from loss of a loved one or of something considered highly valuable, from feelings of guilt or shame, from knowledge of an undesirable impending event (for example, discovery of a terminal illness), from aggression turned inward, from certain physical factors such as menopause, from feelings of inadequacy or inferiority, from self-denigrating thoughts, or from feelings of loneliness or isolation. Literally hundreds of thousands of books have been published on the causes and treatments of the wide array of emotional and behavioral problems.

One out of every three Americans experiences a severe emotional or behavioral disorder at some point in his or her life.[2] Such problems may involve suffering a broken romance or marriage, becoming addicted to alcohol or drugs, being a rape or other crime victim, failing to achieve a goal we've set, and so on. Every year more than 6 million people receive mental health care in the United States.[3] At any moment 25% of hospital beds in the United States are filled by mental patients—more than the total for cancer, heart disease, and respiratory illness patients combined.[4]

WHAT IS MENTAL ILLNESS?

Much of the language relating to emotional disturbances has become a part of everyday conversation. We use a number of terms to express a judgment (often unfavorable) about someone's unusual behavior or emotions; for example, we say that he or she is *crazy, weird, psychotic, neurotic, insane, sick, uptight,* or *mad,* or is having a *nervous breakdown* or acting like a *space cadet.* Amazingly, we act as if the label accurately describes the person, and we then relate to that person as if the label were all-encompassing. However, it is impossible to precisely define any of these terms. What, for example, are the specific characteristics that distinguish a "psychotic" or a "space cadet" from other people?

There are two general approaches to viewing and diagnosing people who display emotional disturbances and abnormal behaviors: the medical model and the interactional model (which asserts that mental illness is a myth).

Medical Model

This model views emotional and behavioral problems as mental illness, comparable to physical illness. Medical labels (for example, schizophrenia, paranoia, psychosis, insanity) are thus applied to emotional problems. Adherents of the medical approach believe that the disturbed person's mind is affected by some generally unknown internal condition. That condition, they assert, might be due to genetic endowment, metabolic disorders, infectious diseases, internal conflicts, unconscious use of defense mechanisms, or traumatic early experiences that cause emotional fixations and prevent future psychological growth.

The medical-model approach arose in reaction to the historical notion that emotionally disturbed individuals were possessed by demons, were mad, were to be blamed for their disturbances, and were to be "treated" by being beaten, locked up, or killed. The medical model led to a perception of the disturbed as being in need of help. It also stimulated research into the nature of emotional problems and promoted the development of therapeutic approaches.

The major evidence for the validity of the medical-model approach comes from studies suggesting that some mental disorders, such as schizophrenia, may be influenced by genetics (heredity). The bulk of the evidence for the significance of heredity comes from studies of twins. For instance, in a sample of over 15,000 twins, Hoffer and Polin found a concordance rate (i.e., if one twin has it, both have it) for schizophrenia of 15.5% for identical twins and 4.4% for fraternal twins.[5] Critics of such studies argue that findings may be due to the fact that the physical similarity of identical twins leads family and friends to treat them alike. However, some research indicates a higher concordance rate among identical twins even if they were raised separately.[6]

The medical model has a lengthy classification of mental disorders that are defined by the American Psychiatric Association (see Exhibit 4.2). Several specific mental disorders are discussed in the following material.[7]

SCHIZOPHRENIA

This malady encompasses a large group of disorders, usually of psychotic proportion, manifested by characteristic disturbances of language and communication, thought, perception, affect, and behavior and lasting longer than six months.

DELUSIONAL DISORDER

The essential feature is the presence of one or more delusions that persist for at least one month. A delusion is something that is falsely believed or propagated. An example is the persecutory type, in which an individual erroneously believes that he or she is being conspired against, cheated, spied on, followed, poisoned or drugged, maliciously maligned, harassed, or obstructed in the pursuit of long-term goals.

HYPOCHONDRIASIS

This is a chronic maladaptive style of relating to the environment through preoccupation with shifting somatic concerns and symptoms, a fear or conviction that one has a serious physical illness, the search for medical treatment, inability to accept reassurance, and either hostile or dependent relationships with caregivers and family.

BIPOLAR DISORDER

This is a major affective disorder characterized by episodes of both mania and depression; it was formerly called manic-depressive psychosis. Bipolar disorder may be subdivided into manic, depressed, or mixed types on the basis of currently presenting symptoms.

PHOBIA

A phobia is characterized by an obsessive, persistent, unrealistic, intense fear of an object or situation. A few common phobias are *acrophobia* (fear of heights), *algophobia* (fear of pain), *claustrophobia* (fear of closed spaces), and *erythrophobia* (fear of blushing).

PERSONALITY DISORDERS

Some of the most common personality disorders and their characteristics are as follows:

- *Paranoid.* A pattern of distrust and suspiciousness such that others' motives are interpreted as malevolent.

- *Schizoid.* A pattern of detachment from social relationships and a restricted range of emotional expression.

- *Schizotypal.* A pattern of acute discomfort in close relationships, cognitive or perceptual distortions, and eccentricities of behavior.

- *Antisocial.* A pattern of disregard for, and violation of, the rights of others.

- *Borderline.* A pattern of instability in interpersonal relationships, self-image, and affect; also characterized by marked impulsivity.

- *Histrionic.* A pattern of excessive emotionality and attention seeking.

- *Narcissistic.* A pattern of grandiosity, need for admiration, and lack of empathy.

- *Avoidant.* A pattern of social inhibition, feelings of inadequacy, and hypersensitivity to negative evaluation.

EXHIBIT 4.1

Major Mental Disorders as Defined by the American Psychiatric Association

DISORDERS USUALLY DIAGNOSED IN INFANCY, CHILDHOOD, OR ADOLESCENCE

These include, but are not limited to, mental retardation, learning disorders, communication disorders (such as stuttering), autism, attention-deficit/hyperactivity disorders, and separation-anxiety disorder.

DELIRIUM, DEMENTIA, AND AMNESTIC AND OTHER COGNITIVE DISORDERS

These include delirium due to alcohol and other drug intoxication, dementia due to Alzheimer's disease or Parkinson's disease, dementia due to head trauma, and amnestic disorder.

SUBSTANCE-RELATED DISORDERS

This category includes mental disorders related to abuse of alcohol, caffeine, amphetamines, cocaine, hallucinogens, nicotine, and other mind-altering substances.

SCHIZOPHRENIA AND OTHER PSYCHOTIC DISORDERS

This category includes delusional disorders and all forms of schizophrenia (such as paranoid, disorganized, and catatonic).

MOOD DISORDERS

These include emotional disorders such as depression and bipolar disorders.

ANXIETY DISORDERS

This category includes phobias, posttraumatic stress disorder, and anxiety disorders.

SOMATOFORM DISORDERS

These are psychological problems that manifest themselves as symptoms of physical disease (for example, hypochondria).

DISSOCIATIVE DISORDERS

This category includes problems in which part of the personality is dissociated from the rest, such as dissociative identity disorder (formerly called multiple personality disorder).

SEXUAL AND GENDER IDENTITY DISORDERS

This category includes sexual dysfunctions (such as hypoactive sexual desire, premature ejaculation, male erectile disorder, male and female orgasmic disorders, and vaginismus), exhibitionism, fetishism, pedophilia (child molestation), sexual masochism, sexual sadism, voyeurism, and gender identity disorders (such as cross-gender identification).

EATING DISORDERS

This category includes anorexia nervosa and bulimia nervosa.

SLEEP DISORDERS

This classification includes insomnia and other problems with sleep (such as nightmares and sleepwalking).

IMPULSE-CONTROL DISORDERS

These disorders relate to the inability to control certain undesirable impulses (for example, kleptomania, pyromania, and pathological gambling).

(continued)

EXHIBIT 4.1 *(continued)*

ADJUSTMENT DISORDERS

These involve difficulty in adjusting to the stress created by such common events as unemployment or divorce.

PERSONALITY DISORDERS

This category refers to an enduring pattern of inner experience and behavior that deviates markedly from the expectations of the individual's culture, is pervasive and inflexible, has an onset in adolescence or early adulthood, is stable over time, and leads to distress or impairment. Examples include paranoid personality disorder, antisocial personality disorder, and obsessive-compulsive personality disorder.

OTHER CONDITIONS

This category covers a variety of "other" disorders that may be a focus of clinical attention. The category includes parent/child relational problems; partner relational problems; sibling relational problems; child victimization of physical abuse, sexual abuse, and neglect; adult victimization of physical and sexual abuse; malingering; bereavement; academic problems; occupational problems; identity problems; and religious or spiritual problems.

Source: DSM-IV (The Diagnostic and Statistical Manual of Mental Disorders), 4th ed. (Washington, DC: American Psychiatric Association, 1994).

- *Dependent.* A pattern of submissive and clinging behavior related to an excessive need to be taken care of.
- *Obsessive-Compulsive.* A pattern of preoccupation with orderliness, perfectionism, and control.

Interactional Model

Critics of the mental-illness approach assert that medical labels have no diagnostic or treatment value and frequently have an adverse effect.

Thomas Szasz, in the 1950s, was one of the first authorities to state that mental illness is a myth—that it does not exist.[8] Szasz's theory is interactional; it focuses on the processes of everyday social interaction and the effects of labeling on people. Beginning with the assumption that the term *mental illness* implies a "disease in the mind," Szasz categorizes all of the so-called mental illnesses into three types of emotional disorders and discusses the inappropriateness of calling such human difficulties "mental illnesses":

1. *Personal disabilities,* such as excessive anxiety, depression, fears, and feelings of inadequacy. Another term for personal disabilities is *unwanted emotions.* Szasz says these so-called mental illnesses may appropriately be considered "mental" (in the sense that thinking and feeling are considered "mental" activities), but they are not diseases.

2. *Antisocial acts,* such as bizarre homicides and other social deviations. Homosexuality used to be in this category but was removed from the American Psychiatric Association's list of mental illnesses in 1974. Szasz says such antisocial acts are only social deviations; they are neither "mental" nor "diseases."

3. *Deterioration of the brain with associated personality changes.* This category includes the "mental illnesses" in which personality changes result following brain deterioration from such causes as Alzheimer's disease, arteriosclerosis,

EXHIBIT 4.2

Eating Disorders: An Emerging Problem

In the early 1980s singer Karen Carpenter died of complications resulting from anorexia nervosa. In 1984 actress Jane Fonda acknowledged that for a number of years she had been bulimic. Eating disorders are recognized as very serious afflictions. As many as 20% of college females are estimated to have an eating disorder.

The three primary eating disorders are anorexia nervosa, bulimia nervosa, and compulsive overeating. Both anorexics and bulimics have an excessive concern with food and fatness, but their techniques for staying thin vary greatly. On the one hand, an anorexic eats very little food and is near starvation much of the time. Bulimics, on the other hand, binge and purge themselves.

Although the average American's food intake is around 3000 calories a day, bulimics may devour 40,000 to 60,000 calories a day. They typically binge on high-calorie junk food, such as sweets and fried foods. Because bulimics also want to stay thin, they purge themselves through a variety of tactics, the most common of which is vomiting. Vomiting may be induced initially by putting the fingers down the throat. Some bulimics use cotton swabs or drink copious amounts of fluids. With practice, many bulimics gain control of their esophageal muscles so that they can induce vomiting at will. Other methods of purging include excessive intake of laxatives; fasting; enemas; the spitting out, rather than swallowing, of food after it is chewed; and compulsive exercise, such as swimming, running, and working out with barbells and weights.

Bulimia, although it is much more common than anorexia, went unrecognized for a long time because the binging and purging cycle is almost always done in secret. Bulimics dread being exposed; as a result, very few will report their malady.

Bulimics tend to have few friends, as much of their time is spent on secret binging and purging.

They are often overachievers and in college tend to attain high academic averages. Purging often becomes a purification rite to overcome self-loathing. Through purging, they feel completely fresh and clean again, but these feelings of self-worth are only temporary. They are extremely sensitive to minor insults and frustrations, which are often used as excuses to initiate another food binge.

Anorexia nervosa is a disorder characterized by the relentless pursuit of thinness through voluntary starvation. Anorexics have a distorted body image. They refuse to accept the fact that they are too thin; they will not eat, even when experiencing intense hunger. They stubbornly insist that they need to lose even more weight from their already emaciated bodies. They also erroneously believe that having a perfect body (defined by society as a thin body) will ensure happiness and success. About 95% of all anorexia nervosa cases are females.

Compulsive overeating is the irresistible urge to consume excessive amounts of food; it is eating irrationally, chewing and digesting excessive amounts of food on a long-term basis. Treatment for compulsive overeating is recommended for individuals whose body weight is more than 20% over desirable weight.

Michael O. Koch, Virginia L. Dotson, and Thomas P. Troast describe the relationships among these eating disorders:

Eating disorders seem to exist on a continuum. On one end are the anorexics, who achieve drastic weight loss by severely restricting food intake. In the middle are the anorexic bulimics, who eat and even binge on occasion, but who still maintain a much lower than normal weight by a combination of strict dieting and purging. Also included are normal-weight bulimics who binge and purge but who are not significantly underweight. These bulimics usually diet when

(continued)

EXHIBIT 4.2   *(continued)*

they are not binging and may repeatedly gain and lose ten or more pounds because of their food behaviors. At the other end of the continuum, the compulsive overeater will repeatedly binge, gaining significant amounts of weight without engaging in any of the purging behaviors associated with anorexia or bulimia nervosa. Individuals may move back and forth along this continuum, alternatively restricting or binging, depending on their circumstances.

Anorexics and bulimics have some similarities. For example, both are likely to have been brought up in middle-class, upwardly mobile families in which the mothers were overinvolved in their lives and the fathers were preoccupied with work outside the home. For the most part, bulimics and anorexics were good children, eager to obtain the love and approval of others. Both tend to lack self-esteem, feel ineffective, and have a distorted body image that causes them to view themselves as fatter than others perceive them.

Anorexics and bulimics differ in that anorexics are generally younger, far less socially competent, and much more isolated from and dependent on the family. The anorexic stays away from food. In contrast, bulimics, during times of stress, turn toward food; they binge and then purge. Bulimics are usually able to function in social and work contexts. Their health may be gravely affected by binging and purging, but their lives are not necessarily in imminent danger, as is often the case with anorexics. Anorexics are also *very* thin, whereas bulimics are not as underweight and may even be overweight.

Why are bulimics and anorexics primarily women? One key reason is that our society places more pressure on women than on men to be slender and trim, Our socialization practices also overemphasize the importance of women being slender.

Anorexia, bulimia, and compulsive overeating are dangerous health disorders. Anorexics risk starvation, and both bulimics and anorexics risk serious health problems. Fat synthesis and accumulation are necessary for survival. Fatty acids are a major source of energy. When fat levels are depleted, the body must draw on carbohydrates (sugar). When sugar supplies dwindle, body metabolism decreases, which often leads to drowsiness, inactivity, pessimism, depression, dizziness, and fatigue. For compulsive overeaters, as one's weight increases over that recommended for one's body build, mortality rates increase as well. Obesity is a contributing factor to such health problems as hypertension, heart attacks, and diabetes.

For bulimics and anorexics, psychotropic drugs (tranquilizers and antidepressants) have variable effects on the body due to changes in metabolism. Abnormalities have been found in the electroencephalograms of people with eating disorders. Chronic vomiting may lead to gum disease and cavities, due to the hydrochloric acid content of vomit. Vomiting can also lead to severe tearing and bleeding in the esophagus. Chronic vomiting may result in a potassium deficiency, which then may lead to muscle fatigue, weakness, numbness, erratic heartbeat, kidney damage, and, in severe instances, paralysis.

A variety of treatment programs are available for anorexics, bulimics, and compulsive overeaters. Individual and group therapy programs have been developed to change the psychological thinking patterns that initiated and are sustaining the undesirable eating patterns. For those for whom severe health problems have already developed, medical care is essential. Therapy for eating disorders includes instruction in establishing and maintaining a nutritious diet. Some elementary, secondary, and higher-education school systems are now developing preventive programs that inform students about the risks of eating disorders and identify and provide services for students who have developed an eating disorder.

Sources: Michael O. Koch, Virginia L. Dotson, and Thomas P. Troast, "Treating Eating Disorders," in Charles Zastrow, *Social Work with Groups*, 3rd ed. (Chicago: Nelson-Hall, 1993), pp. 455–478. Quotation from p. 458.

CASE EXAMPLE 4.1	A Case Example Interpreted in Terms of the Mental-Illness Model

CASE EXAMPLE 4.1

A Case Example Interpreted in Terms of the Mental-Illness Model

Dan Vanda was arrested for stabbing his parents to death. He was 22 years old and had always been described as a "loner" by neighbors. In elementary school, junior high, and high school he was frequently absent, had no close friends, and received mostly failing grades. School records showed that teachers had informed protective services on three occasions that they believed his parents were abusing and neglecting him. Protective services' records indicated that his parents were uncooperative but that sufficient evidence could not be found to justify placement in a foster home.

At the time of his arrest, Dan appeared confused. He said he was in communication with King David (the David in the Bible who slew Goliath), who told him to slay his parents because they were out to get him. He tended to ramble on with incoherent statements from the Bible, and he also stated that cosmic rays were in control of people. At his arrest he appeared to be expecting congratulations for what he had done, rather than incarceration.

The court ordered a 90-day observation period in a maximum-security hospital for the mentally ill to determine his sanity.

Neighbors and school officials could add little to explain his actions. He had dropped out of school at age 16. Neighbors felt that he was "weird" and had ordered their children not to associate with him. They reported that they sometimes saw him butchering birds. When they asked him why, he said he was being advised by Alfred Hitchcock (director of the film *The Birds*) to do this in order to prevent an attack.

Psychiatrists concluded that Dan was paranoid schizophrenic. It was felt his insanity was such that he would not be able to understand the nature of court proceedings connected with his offense. With this recommendation the court committed him indefinitely to a maximum-security psychiatric hospital.

chronic alcoholism, general paresis, AIDS, or serious brain damage caused by an accident. Common symptoms are loss of memory, listlessness, apathy, and deterioration of personal grooming habits. Szasz says these disorders can appropriately be considered "diseases," but they are diseases of the brain (that is, brain deterioration that specifies the nature of the problem) rather than diseases of the mind.

According to Szasz, the notion that people with emotional problems are mentally ill is as absurd as the belief that the emotionally disturbed are possessed by demons: "The belief in mental illness as something other than man's trouble in getting along with his fellow man, is the proper heir to the belief in demonology and witchcraft. Mental illness exists or is real in exactly the same sense in which witches existed or were real."[9]

In actuality, there are three steps to becoming labeled mentally ill: (1) The person displays unwanted emotions (such as depression) or some strange, deviant behaviors; (2) the emotions or behaviors are not tolerated by the family or local community; and (3) the professional labeler, usually a psychiatrist, happens to believe in the medical model and assigns a mental-illness label. Thomas Scheff and David Mechanic provide independent evidence that whether the family or community will tolerate the deviant behavior and whether the professional labeler believes in the medical model are more crucial in determining whether someone will be assigned a mentally ill label than are the emotions or behaviors exhibited by the person.[10]

The point that Szasz and many other writers are striving to make is that people *do* have emotional problems, but they *do not* have a mystical mental illness. Terms that describe behavior are very useful—for example, depression, anxiety, obsession, compulsion, excessive fear, hallucinations, feelings of failure. Such terms describe personal problems that people have. But the medical terms are not useful, because there is no distinguishing symptom that would indicate whether a person does or does not have the "illness." In addition, Offer and Sabshin point out that there is considerable variation among cultures regarding what is defined as a mental illness.[11] (Russia, for example, used to define protests against the government as a symptom of mental illness.) The usefulness of the medical model is also questioned because psychiatrists frequently disagree on the medical diagnosis to be assigned to those who are disturbed.[12]

In a dramatic study, psychologist David Rosenhan demonstrated that professional staff in mental hospitals could not distinguish "insane" patients from "sane" patients.[13] Rosenhan and seven "normal" associates went to 12 mental hospitals in five different states claiming they were hearing voices; all eight were admitted. After admission, these pseudopatients stated that the voices had stopped, and they behaved normally. The hospitals, unable to distinguish their "sane" status from the "insane" status of other patients, kept them hospitalized for an average of 19 days. All were then discharged with a diagnosis of "schizophrenia in remission."

The use of medical labels, it has been asserted, has several adverse effects.[14] People labeled "mentally ill" believe that they have a disease for which there may be no known "cure." The label gives people an excuse for not taking responsibility for their actions (for example, pleading innocent by reason of insanity). Because there is no known "cure," the disturbed frequently idle away their time waiting for someone to discover a cure, rather than assuming responsibility for their behavior, examining the reasons why there are problems, and making efforts to improve. Other undesirable consequences of being labeled mentally ill are that the individuals may lose some of their legal rights;[15] may be stigmatized in social interactions as being dangerous, unpredictable, untrustworthy, or of "weak" character;[16] and may find it difficult to secure employment or receive a promotion.[17]

The question of whether mental illness exists is indeed important. The assignment of mental-illness labels to disturbed people has substantial implications for how the disturbed will be treated, for how others will view them, and for how they will view themselves. Cooley's "looking-glass-self" approach crystalizes what is being said here.[18] The "looking glass" means we develop our self-concept in terms of how other people react to us. People are likely to respond to those labeled mentally ill as if they were mentally ill. As a result, those labeled mentally ill may well define themselves as being different or "crazy" and begin playing that role. Authorities who adhere to the interactional model raise a key question: "If we relate to people with emotional problems as if they were mentally ill, how can we expect them to act in emotionally healthy and responsible ways?"

Compared to a physical illness, a diagnosis of a mental illness carries a greater stigma. In 1972 Senator Thomas Eagleton was forced to withdraw his candidacy for vice president on the Democratic ticket after it was revealed that he had received electroshock treatments for depression. The leaders of the Democratic party feared that the public would perceive someone who had once received psychiatric help as too "unstable" and "dangerous" to be in line for the presidency. On the other hand, Franklin Roosevelt had a physical disability resulting from polio, but he was elected president four times.

Szasz also argues that the mental-illness approach is used (perhaps unintentionally) as a means of control over people who do not conform to social expectations.[19] The former Soviet Union had a long history of labeling dissenters (including literary figures and intellectuals who would be respected in this country) as mentally ill and then sending them to concentration camps or to insane asylums. In the past, psychiatrists in Russia often concluded that people who did not accept the Marxist-Leninist philosophy were psychologically impaired.

Are some psychiatrists using mental-illness labels to control the behavior of nonconformists in our country? Szasz asserts that they are and uses the example of homosexuality—listed as a mental disorder by the American Psychiatric Association until 1974. As another example, Szasz cites a quote from Dana L. Farnsworth, a Harvard psychiatrist and an authority on college psychiatric services:

> Library vandalism, cheating and plagiarism, stealing in the college or community stores or in the dormitories, unacceptable or antisocial sexual practices (overt homosexuality, exhibitionism, promiscuity), and the unwise and unregulated use of harmful drugs, are examples of behavior that suggest the presence of emotionally unstable persons. . . .[20]

Mental-illness labels do have a "boundary" effect; they define what behaviors a society defines as "sick," with pressures then being put on citizens to avoid such behaviors. Szasz's point is that a number of nonconformists are adversely affected by the use of the medical model to control their behavior.

LABELING AS THE CAUSE OF CHRONIC "MENTAL ILLNESS"

A question is frequently raised about Szasz's assertion that mental illness is a myth: "If you assert that mental illness doesn't exist, why do some people go through life as if they are mentally ill?" Thomas Scheff has developed a sociological theory that provides an answer.[21] Scheff's main hypothesis is that labeling is the most important

determinant of people's displaying a chronic (long-term) mental illness.

Scheff begins by defining how he determines, for research purposes, who is mentally ill. Before giving his definition, he notes:

> One source of immediate embarrassment to any social theory of "mental illness" is that the terms used in referring to these phenomena in our society prejudge the issue. The medical metaphor "mental illness" suggests a determinate process which occurs within the individual: the unfolding and development of disease. In order to avoid this assumption, we will utilize sociological, rather than medical, concepts to formulate the problem.[22]

He goes on to state that the symptoms of mental illness can be viewed as violations of social norms and that he uses the term *mental illness* only to refer to those assigned such a label by professionals (usually psychiatrists).

Scheff indicates that in recent years literally thousands of studies have been conducted that seek to identify the origins of long-term mental disorders. Practically all of this research has focused on internal causes (for example, metabolic disorders, unconscious conflicts, heredity factors). These research efforts have been based on medical and psychological models of human behavior. Yet, amazingly, in spite of this extensive investigation, the determinants of chronic mental disorders (for example, schizophrenia) are largely unknown.

Scheff suggests that researchers may well be looking in the wrong direction. He asserts that the major determinants are not inside a person but in social processes—that is, in interactions with others. Here's a brief summary of his theory:

Everyone, at times, violates social norms and commits acts that could be labeled as symptoms of mental illness. For example, a person may occasionally get in fights with others, experience intense depression or grief, be highly anxious, use drugs or alcohol to excess, display a fetish, or commit a highly unusual or bizarre act.

Usually the person who has unwanted emotions or who commits deviant acts is not

**CASE
EXAMPLE 4.2**

A Case Example Questioning the Usefulness of the Mental-Illness Concept

While working at a mental hospital, I was assigned the case of George, a 22-year-old male who had decapitated a 17-year-old female friend, Emily (not their real names). Two psychiatrists diagnosed him as schizophrenic, and a court found him "innocent by reason of insanity." He was then committed to a mental hospital.

Why did George do it? Labeling him as insane provides an explanation to the general public: He exhibited this strange behavior because he was "crazy" when he killed her. But does such a label explain why he killed Emily rather than killing someone else or committing some other bizarre act? Does the label explain what would have prevented him from committing this act? Does the label suggest the kind of treatment that will cure him? The answer to all these questions is, of course, no.

WHAT IS SCHIZOPHRENIA?

As noted earlier, schizophrenia is commonly defined as a psychotic condition characterized by disturbances of language and communication, thought, perception, affect, and behavior and lasting longer than six months. People who have Alzheimer's disease exhibit all these symptoms. Are they schizophrenic? No. What about the severely and profoundly mentally retarded who have a mental age of less than 2? They have the above symptoms but are not considered schizophrenic. What about people who go into a coma following a serious accident? They also fit the definition above but are not considered schizophrenic. The 22-year-old male who committed the bizarre homicide knew the act was wrong, was aware of what he was doing, was in contact with reality, and told me his reasons for doing what he did. Then why was *he* labeled schizophrenic?

Many authorities are now asserting that there is no definition of symptoms that separates people who have this "disease" from those who do not. I generally agree with Albert Ellis's assertion that the reasons for the occurrence of any deviant act can be determined by examining what the offender was thinking prior to and during the commission of the act.[a]

THE REASONS UNDERLYING THE SEXUAL ASSAULT AND MURDER

After George described what had happened, it was understandable (even though bizarre) why he had done what he did. His account also identified the specific problems he needed help with. He described himself as a very isolated person who, except for Emily, had no close relatives or friends. He came from a broken home and was raised by a series of relatives and in foster homes. Because of frequent moves, he attended a number of different schools and made no lasting friends. At age 20 George met Emily and dated her periodically for two years. She provided the only real meaning that he had in life. He held the traditional vision of marrying her and living happily ever after. However, a few months before the fatal day, he became very alarmed that he was going to "lose her." She encouraged him to date others, mentioned that she wanted to date others, and suggested that they no longer see as much of each other.

George thought long and hard about how he could preserve the relationship. He also realized he had rather intense sexual tensions for which he had no outlet. Putting the two together, he naively concluded: "If I'm the first person to have sexual relations with her, she will forever feel tied to me." He therefore tried on several occasions to have intercourse, but she always managed to dissuade him. Finally, one afternoon during the summer, when he knew they would be alone together, he arrived at the following decision: "I *will* have sex with her this afternoon, even if I have to knock her unconscious." He stated that he knew such action was wrong but "It was my last hope of saving our relationship. Without her, life would not be worth living."

He again tried to have sexual relations with Emily that afternoon, but she continued to discourage him. George then took a soda bottle and knocked her unconscious. He attempted to have coitus but was unsuccessful for reasons related to her physical structure. In an intense state of emotional and sexual excitement, he was unable to rationally consider the consequences of his actions. (All of us, at times, have done things while angry or in a state of intense emotional excitement that we would not have done in a calmer state.) At this point he felt his whole world was caving in. When asked during an interview what he was thinking at this point, he stated "I felt that if I couldn't have her, no one else would either." He sought and found a knife, became further carried away with emotions, and ended up slaying her. He knew it was wrong, and he was aware of what he was doing.

From talking with George (and identifying his thinking before and during this bizarre murder), I was able to pinpoint certain factors that led to the murder: his loneliness and isolation, his feeling that the romantic relationship was the only source of meaning in his life, his naive thinking that a forced sexual relationship would make Emily feel tied and attracted to him, his having no outlet for his sexual drives, and his jealous and possessive desires to go to extreme lengths to prevent her from developing a romantic relationship with another male. Such reasons help to explain why the bizarre behavior took place, whereas the label *schizophrenia* does not.

If the above problems had been known about prior to the murder, the slaying might have been prevented. What George needed was to find other sources of interest and other meaningful relationships in his life. Joining organizations in the community and developing hobbies may well have helped. An appropriate sexual outlet probably would have also been helpful. Reducing the intensity of his jealous and possessive feelings, along with developing more mature attitudes toward romance and sexuality, might also have been preventive. These specific problems are the ones that will have to be addressed during his hospitalization. In no way do I feel that George should be excused for his actions, as implied by the term "innocent by reason of insanity." But he does need help for these problems. (In 10 or 15 years he will probably be released; if these problems are not rectified, he will be a danger to society upon his release.)

(continued)

**CASE
EXAMPLE 4.2**   *(continued)*

If you are wondering how anyone could reach a point at which he does something as bizarre as slaying someone he loves, remember that it is necessary to attempt to view the situation from the deviant person's perspective. You must try to consider all the circumstances, pressures, values, and belief systems of the deviant person.

Another example highlights the fact that practically anyone will do something bizarre when circumstances become desperate: Several years ago a passenger plane crashed in the Andes Mountains in the wintertime. A number of people were killed, but there were nearly 30 survivors. Rescue efforts initially failed to locate the survivors, who took shelter from the cold in the wreckage of the plane. The survivors were without food for over 40 days before they were finally rescued. During this time they were faced with the choice of dying of starvation or cannibalizing those who had died. It was a desperate, difficult decision. (Psychologically, many people who commit a bizarre act feel they are facing a comparably desperate decision.) In this situation all but one of the initial crash survivors chose cannibalism. The one who refused died of starvation.

[a]Albert Ellis, *Reason and Emotion in Psychotherapy* (New York: Lyle Stuart, 1962).
Source: Adapted from an article written by Charles Zastrow, "When Labeled Mentally Ill," in *The Personal Problem Solver*, eds. Charles Zastrow and Dae H. Chang. © 1977. Used by permission of the publisher, Prentice-Hall/A division of Simon and Schuster, Englewood Cliffs, NJ.

identified (labeled) as mentally ill. His or her emotions and actions are ignored, unrecognized, or rationalized in some other manner.

Occasionally, however, such norm violations are perceived by others as "abnormal." The offenders are then labeled mentally ill and consequently related to as if they were mentally ill. Being highly suggestible to cues from others, they then begin to define and perceive themselves as mentally ill.

Traditional stereotypes define the mentally ill role, both for those who are labeled mentally ill and for the people they interact with. Those labeled mentally ill are often rewarded for enacting that social role. They are given sympathy and attention and are excused from holding a job, fulfilling other role requirements, and being held responsible for their wrongdoings.

In addition, those labeled mentally ill are punished for attempting to return to conventional roles. They are viewed with suspicion and implicitly considered to be still insane. They may have considerable difficulty in obtaining employment or in receiving a job promotion.

Such pressures and interactions with others gradually lead to changes in their self-concept; they begin to view themselves as different, as being insane. Often a vicious circle is created. The more they enact the mentally ill role, the more they are defined and treated as mentally ill; the more explicitly they are defined as mentally ill, the more they are related to as if they are mentally ill, and so on. Unless this vicious circle is interrupted, it will lead to a career of long-term mental illness. Scheff's conclusion is that the labeling is the single most important determinant of chronic mental illness.

Accordingly, significant changes are needed in diagnostic and treatment practices. Mental health personnel are frequently faced with uncertainty in deciding whether a person has a mental disorder. An informal norm has been developed to handle this uncertainty: When in doubt, it is better to judge a well person ill than to judge an ill person well. This norm is based on two assumptions: (1) A diagnosis of illness results in only minimal damage to one's status and reputation. (2) Unless the illness is treated, it will become progressively worse. However, both these assumptions are questionable. Unlike medical treatment, psychiatric treatment can drastically change a person's status in the community; for example, it can remove rights that are difficult to regain. Furthermore, if Scheff is right about the adverse effects of mental-illness labeling, then the exact opposite norm should be established to handle uncertainty (when in doubt, do not label a person mentally ill). This would be in accord with the legal approach "When in doubt, acquit" or "A person is innocent until proved guilty."

If labeling is indeed a major determinant of mental illness, then certain changes are called for in treating violators of social norms. One is to attempt to maintain and treat people with problems in their local community, without labeling them mentally ill or sending them to a mental hospital where their playing the role of the mentally ill is likely to be reinforced. The field of mental health has, in the past several years, been moving in this direction. Another outgrowth of Scheff's theory would be increasing public education efforts to inform the general population of the nature of emotional problems and the adverse effects that result from inappropriate labeling.

OTHER ISSUES

There are other issues at stake in the field of mental health. These include care for the homeless, the civil rights of those labeled mentally ill, the improper use of the insanity plea to excuse criminals from their actions, and the use (or misuse) of drugs in "treating" supposedly mentally ill people.

The Homeless

One of the population groups that has received considerable media attention in recent years is the homeless. Having hundreds of thousands of people homeless in the richest nation in the world is a national disgrace. The number of homeless Americans is large and growing larger. The exact number is unknown, but estimates range from 250,000 to over 3 million people.[23] Many of the homeless are living on the street, in parks, in subways, or in abandoned buildings. Food is often sought from garbage cans.

An estimated 25 to 50% of the homeless are thought to suffer from serious and chronic forms of mental illness.[24] Discharged from institutions without the support they need, tens of thousands of former patients live on the street in abominable conditions. Instead of providing support services for discharged patients, many states have a deinstitutionalization program of simply drugging people and dumping them into the street.

Such an approach is a far cry from what was envisioned 20 years ago when federal authorities embarked on an ambitious program to phase out large state hospitals and move the disturbed to more humane and convenient treatment in communities. This commendable goal has not been fulfilled. Federal, state, and local governments have failed to provide enough housing, transitional care, and job training to integrate patients into society. In many areas of the country, a revolving-door policy prevails: Patients are discharged from state hospitals, only to return again because of a lack of community support.

It is true that institutional care not only is highly expensive (about $50,000 per person per year[25]) but frequently also stifles the intellectual, social, and physical growth of patients. But, tragically, the necessary supportive services have not been developed in most communities to serve discharged patients.

There are a variety of reasons for the large increase in the number of homeless. Deinstitutionalization of state mental hospitals is one cause. Cutbacks in social services by the federal

Although the number of homeless people in America is unknown, estimates range from 250,000 to over 3 million people. Many sleep in streets, subways, parks, abandoned buildings, and cars.

government is another. Urban renewal projects have demolished low-cost housing in many areas. The shift from blue-collar jobs to service and high-tech jobs in our society has sharply reduced the demand for unskilled labor. Another factor has been a recent trend in our society to ignore members of society who are unable to fend for themselves. Most of the homeless are such because they cannot afford the housing that is available; our country does not have a commitment to a social policy of providing affordable housing to the poor. It should be noted that a majority of the homeless are not mentally ill, but simply too poor to afford available housing.

Solutions to the dismal conditions in which the homeless are living include low-cost housing, job-training and placement programs, and community services for those with emotional problems. Is our society willing to provide the necessary resources to meet the needs of the homeless? Deplorably, the answer is "No, not at present."

Civil Rights

State laws have permitted the involuntary confinement of people in mental hospitals, which can be seen as an infringement of their civil right to liberty. Although state laws vary, in some jurisdictions people can be hospitalized without their consent and without due process.[26] Often all that is required for confinement is the statement of a physician.[27]

When I worked at the hospital for the "criminally insane," there was a patient who was originally arrested on a disorderly conduct charge for urinating on a fire hydrant. Some neighbors though he might be mentally ill, so the judge ordered that he be sent to a mental hospital for a 60-day observation period to determine his sanity.

The hospital judged him "insane" and "incompetent to stand trial" on the charge. He was not considered a threat to himself or to others. But, because of the hospital's finding, the judge confined him to a maximum-security hospital for the criminally insane. When I met him there, he had already been hospitalized for nine years—for committing an offense for which, if found guilty, he probably would only have been required to pay a small fine. Involuntary confinement has been a controversial practice for years.

Today, in most jurisdictions, persons cannot be involuntarily confined unless they commit illegal acts (such as aggravated assaults or suicidal attempts) that demonstrate they are a threat either to themselves or to others. Such a policy provides some assurance that emotionally disturbed individuals' right to liberty will be safeguarded. But the policy also has been sharply criticized. Emotionally disturbed persons who provide warning signs of doing bodily harm to others cannot be involuntarily confined unless they actually commit an illegal act. As a result, the civil right of others to safety in our society is sometimes infringed upon.

Striking an acceptable balance between the disturbed person's right to liberty and society's right to safety and protection is a complex issue. Throughout our nation's history, policies on this issue have swung back and forth on the continuum between these two sets of rights.

Another problem in some mental hospitals is that patients do not receive adequate treatment, even after several years of confinement. Lack of treatment became a civil rights violation when, in 1964, Congress established a statutory right to treatment in the Hospitalization of the Mentally Ill Act.[28]

Decisions about providing treatments such as electroconvulsive therapy (which has questionable value and may cause brain damage) also raise civil rights questions. The severely disturbed are often unable to make rational choices about their own welfare. Permission of relatives is sometimes obtained, but this still denies patients their fundamental rights.

The above problems caused the President's Commission on Mental Health to recommend in 1978 that due process be followed in arriving at decisions involving enforced hospitalization and treatment.[29] Federal court decisions have also reflected these concerns; they have held that mental illness is not a sufficient basis for denying liberty and that hospitalized mental patients have a right to either adequate treatment or release.[30]

Plea of Innocent by Reason of Insanity

In 1979 a San Francisco jury found Dan White innocent by reason of insanity on charges of the premeditated murder of Mayor George Moscone and Supervisor Harvey Milk. This verdict was rendered even though testimony clearly showed that the murders had been carefully planned and carried out by White.[31] The general public was as shocked by the jury's decision as it had been by the crime. White was confined in a mental hospital for a few years and then released in 1984. (He subsequently committed suicide.)

In 1982 John Hinckley, Jr., was found innocent by reason of insanity for the attempted assassination of President Reagan a year earlier. Three other people were also injured by Hinckley in the assassination attempt. He is currently receiving treatment in a mental hospital.

In another recent case Kenneth Bianchi (called the Hollywood "Hillside Strangler") was accused of murdering 13 women in the Los Angeles area and 2 more in Washington state. Six different psychiatrists who examined him came to three different conclusions about his mental state: Two judged him sane, two judged him insane, and two were undecided.[32]

Cases such as those of White, Hinckley, and Bianchi have forced the courts and psychiatrists to begin to examine more carefully the plea of innocent by reason of insanity. As indicated earlier, the terms *mental illness* and *mental health* are poorly defined. Mental illness (insanity) may not even exist. In a number of trials involving the insanity plea, it has become routine for the prosecuting attorney to use as witnesses those psychiatrists who are likely to judge the defendant "sane," whereas the defendant's attorney uses as witnesses those psychiatrists who are likely to arrive at an "insane" recommendation. An authority notes:

> Among psychiatrists, there is nothing remotely approaching a consensus on what constitutes insanity. Moreover, psychiatrists themselves concede that they lack reliable means for determining whether a person was insane in any sense at the time of a crime. All too often, they must rely heavily on the accused's behavior and on what he tells them—two types of data that a shrewd defendant can carefully orchestrate.[33]

Defendants are increasingly becoming aware that they can probably get a psychiatrist to label them insane by "acting crazy," such as by openly performing indecent acts or by claiming to hear voices.

The argument for eliminating the insanity plea is that people are literally using it to get away with murder and other serious felonies. Instead of forcing people to take responsibility for their felonies, the insanity plea excuses them for their crimes. The plea enables a clever defendant or attorney to seek refuge from criminal punishment.

When a person is acquitted by reason of insanity, she or he is generally sent to a mental institution. Under the law a person is kept there until doctors determine he or she is no longer dangerous and the judge concurs. Sadly, the measures for determining "no longer dangerous" are as untrustworthy as those used to assign a mental-illness label.

For example, E. E. Kemper III spent five years in a hospital for the criminally insane after murdering his grandparents. Kemper convinced psychiatrists and the judge that he was cured by giving rational answers to a battery of psychological tests. (He had memorized the answers prior to the tests.) Three years after his release he was again arrested for brutally killing eight women—including his mother.[34]

Psychiatrist Lee Coleman urges that the insanity defense be eliminated altogether in order to resolve this dilemma. Doing so would allow courts to deal with the guilt or innocence of an individual without interference from psychiatrists. Coleman states: "Victims are no less injured by one who is mentally sound and violent."[35] Coleman further urges that, if the individual convicted later wishes help for emotional or behavioral problems, he or she can then request it.

Because of the controversy over the insanity plea, a number of states are revising their laws surrounding it. One approach adopted by several states is to have a two-step process in which the jury first determines whether the defendant is innocent or guilty. If the verdict is guilty, the jury then decides if that person is sane or insane. (If found insane, the defendant is usually sent to a maximum-security mental hospital.)

Use of Psychotropic Drugs

Psychotropic drugs include tranquilizers, antipsychotic drugs (such as thorazine), and antidepressants. Since their discovery in 1954, these drugs have been credited with markedly decreasing the number of patients in state and county hospitals, from 550,000 in 1955 to 110,000 in 1990.[36] Psychotropic drugs do not "cure" emotional problems but are useful in reducing high levels of anxiety, depression, and tension.

Americans make extensive use of psychotropic drugs, particularly tranquilizers, like Valium, Librium, and Miltown. Most general practitioners prescribe tranquilizers for the large number of patients who complain of tension and emotional upset. Lithium and Prozac have been found to be fairly effective in reducing depression in a number of clients and are now being widely prescribed by physicians. "Popping pills" (both legal and illegal) has become fashionable. The dangers of excessive drug use include physical and psychological dependence and unwanted side effects. There is also the danger that, because drugs provide temporary symptom relief, users may avoid making the necessary changes in their lives to resolve the problems causing the anxiety, depression, or tension. Physicians face a dilemma in balancing the benefits of psychotropic drugs against the dangers of abuse, particularly when such drugs are sought by patients for extended periods of time. Because psychotropic drugs provide only temporary relief for the *symptoms* (such as anxiety and depression) that patients have, many authorities urge that patients also receive counseling or psychotherapy to help resolve the underlying emotional difficulties.

SOCIAL STRUCTURE AND MENTAL ILLNESS

Sociologists have conducted a number of studies on the relationships between social factors and the rate of mental illness. Questions they have tried to answer include: Is social class status related to the rate of mental illness? Does illness occur more in urban areas, in suburbs, or in rural areas? Which age groups are more prone to be affected? Are men or women more likely to be affected? (As indicated earlier, there is a question as to whether mental illness exists. In this section the term *mental illness* is used to refer to those who are labeled mentally ill.)

SOCIAL CLASS

A classic study was conducted in 1958 by A. B. Hollingshead and F. C. Redlich in New Haven, Connecticut.[37] The study examined the social-class status of patients who were treated for a mental illness in hospitals and in private and public agencies. The researchers used a socio-economic scale ranging from class I (highest) to class V (lowest). The results showed that the rate of mental illness was significantly higher in the lower classes than in the upper classes. Class V had, by far, the highest rate, with schizophrenia being 11 times more prevalent for class V than for class I if measured in terms of hospitalization rates. The study also found that the types of treatment and opportunities for rehabilitation for the lower classes were of lower quality and less satisfactory than those for the upper classes.

A research project by William Rushing studied 4560 males admitted for the first time to mental hospitals in Washington, D.C.[38] As in the Hollingshead and Redlich study, hospitalization rates were found to vary inversely with class. Hospitalization rates were particularly high for the lowest class.

A third study was conducted in midtown Manhattan in the 1950s by Leo Srole and his associates.[39] The study involved conducting extensive interviews with 1660 randomly selected people to find out if they had ever had a nervous breakdown, sought psychotherapy or shown neurotic symptoms. The researchers then gave the information to a team of psychiatrists, who rated each case on degree of psychiatric impairment. Almost 23% of the sample was considered "significantly" impaired in mental functioning, including many people not under treatment. In addition, psychological impairment was found to correlate closely with social class. Nearly one person in every two in the lowest class was considered psychologically impaired, whereas the rate fell to one in eight for the highest class.

These studies clearly suggest that the poor are more likely to be labeled mentally ill. A variety of explanations shed light on these results. Perhaps the poor are less likely to seek treatment when emotional problems first begin to develop; they therefore become mentally ill before receiving help. Perhaps they are under greater psychological stress. Perhaps their attitudes, values, educational histories, and living conditions make them more susceptible to becoming mentally ill. Perhaps mental illness leads to a lower status. Or, there may be *no* actual difference in severity and rate of emotional problems among social classes. It is possible that psychiatrists are less likely to assign a mental-illness label to a person of a higher status because of the stigma associated with the label. In addition, psychiatrists may have less understanding of the value systems of the poor and therefore be more likely to label lower-class behavior as deviant or mentally ill.

A number of studies have also found social-class differences in quality of treatment of those labeled mentally ill.[40] Lower-class patients often receive lower-quality care (often just custodial care when hospitalized) and have lower rates of release when hospitalized in a mental institution.

URBANIZATION

There is some evidence that cities, particularly the inner-city areas, have a higher rate of mental illness than rural areas.[41] This finding may be due to overcrowding and to the deteriorated quality of life—dirt, noise, crime, transportation problems, inadequate housing, unemployment, drugs—which creates a higher level of emotional problems. Also, mental health facilities tend to be located in and around urban areas, which increases the probability that urban dwellers with emotional problems will be identified and treated.

AGE

The elderly are more likely than younger people to have emotional problems, particularly depression (which is partially due to the low status that the elderly have in our society; low status leads to a crushing sense of uselessness and isolation). Additionally, the elderly may experience disturbances associated with degeneration of brain cells from such causes as arteriosclerosis and chronic alcoholism.[42]

MARITAL STATUS

People who are single, divorced, or widowed have higher rates of mental disorder than married people. Unmarried men have somewhat higher rates than unmarried women.[43]

SEX

Men and women are equally likely to be treated, but the nature of the diagnosis varies. Women are more likely to be diagnosed as suffering from anxiety, depression, and phobias and to be hospitalized in a mental institution. Men are more likely to be diagnosed as psychotic.[44] (Why men are more often labeled psychotic but less often hospitalized compared to women is unclear.)

The vast majority of psychiatrists are men, and there is evidence that psychiatrists may consider sexual promiscuity or aggressive behavior in women a mental disorder but overlook such behavior in men.[45]

RACE

Compared with whites, African Americans are more likely to be diagnosed as mentally ill, and their rate of hospitalization is substantially higher.[46] There are several sociological explanations for these trends. African Americans may be under greater psychological pressure due to dis-

crimination. Or, the higher rates may stem from their lower social status, as a greater proportion of people in the lower social classes are diagnosed mentally ill. Or, because most psychiatrists are white, a lack of awareness of the lifestyles of African Americans may lead psychiatrists to more readily assign mentally ill labels to blacks who may differ in class, status, cultural values, and cultural background.

TREATMENT

Brief History

Although the history of treatment for the emotionally disturbed is fascinating, it is also filled with injustices and tragedies. George Rosen explains that most societies have developed unique ways of viewing mental illness and treating those so labeled.[47] In some societies deviants have been highly valued—even treated as prophets with supernatural powers. In others the emotionally disturbed have been viewed as evil and have even been feared as possessing demoniac powers. In medieval times, for example, the emotionally disturbed were viewed as being possessed by demons; they were "treated" by flogging, starving, and dunking them in hot water to drive the devils out. During a brief period in our colonial history, certain of the disturbed were viewed as "witches" and were burned at the stake. Prior to the 19th century the severely disturbed in the United States were confined in "almshouses," received only harsh, custodial care, and often were chained to the walls.[48]

In the 19th century a few mental institutions in France, England, and the United States began to take a more humanitarian approach to treating the disturbed. Although the severely disturbed were still confined in institutions, they began to be viewed either as having an illness or as having an emotional problem. The physical surroundings were improved, and efforts were made to replace the harsh, custodial treatment with a caring approach that recognized each resident as a person deserving of respect and dignity. Unfortunately, these humanitarian efforts were not widely accepted, in part because they were considered too expensive. Most of the severely disturbed continued to be confined in overcrowded, unsanitary dwellings, with inadequate care and diet.

In 1908 Clifford Beers's book *A Mind That Found Itself* was published.[49] Beers had been confined as a patient, and the book recounted the atrocities occurring in this "madhouse." The book reached a wide audience and sensitized the public to the emotional trauma being experienced by those confined. Under Beers's leadership, mental health associations were formed that advocated the need for improved inpatient care and initiated the concept of outpatient treatment.

Between 1900 and 1920, Sigmund Freud developed his psychoanalytic theories about the causes and treatment of emotional problems. According to Freud, emotional problems were mental illnesses that resulted from early traumatic experiences, internal psychological conflicts, fixations at various stages of development, and unconscious psychological processes. Most members of the counseling professions (psychiatry, clinical psychology, social work) accepted, from the 1920s to the 1950s, Freud's and other psychoanalytic theorists' views in regard to diagnosing and treating the disturbed. Due to Freud's influence, the public adopted a more humanitarian approach to treating the disturbed.

However, in the 1950s questions began to arise about the effectiveness of the psychoanalytic method. It was expensive and lengthy (an analysis took four or five years), and research studies began to show that the rate of improvement for those undergoing analysis was no higher than that for people receiving no treatment![50] Since the 1950s a variety of counseling approaches have been developed that reject most or all of the concepts underlying psychoanalysis; these newer approaches include behavior modification, rational therapy, reality therapy, transactional analysis, radical therapy, Gestalt therapy, and client-centered therapy.[51]

It should be mentioned that certain segments of the medical profession have continued to maintain, since the 19th century, that mental illness is akin to other physical illnesses. They assert that

EXHIBIT 4.3

Asylums and Total Institutions

In 1961 Erving Goffman wrote *Asylums*, which described life inside state mental hospitals. Goffman indicates that such mental hospitals are "total institutions." (Other total institutions are prisons, boot camps, monasteries, and convents.) In a total institution a resident is cut off from society for appreciable periods of time and required to lead a regimented life. Inside an asylum residents are stripped of their clothing and deprived of contact with the outside world. Total institutions seek to control residents fully and to resocialize and remake their lives. The fear of expulsion is often a major control mechanism. Long-term confinement in asylums usually causes people to lose their capacities to respond in an independent, rational fashion and undermines their ability to cope with the outside world.

Total institutions teach residents to accept the staff's view of right and wrong, eroding residents' capacities to think independently. Such actions as questioning the therapeutic value of treatment programs are taken not as signs of mental stability but as a symptom of sickness. The "good" patient, from the staff's point of view, is one who is undemanding, docile, and obedient. In general, mental hospitals downgrade patients' feelings of self-esteem and emphasize their failures and inadequacies. Uniform furniture and clothing, a regimented routine, and a custodial atmosphere encourage patients to be docile and unassertive. The use of the medical-model approach to emotional problems encourages patients to view themselves as sick and in need of help. Such "resocialization" actually hinders residents from making a successful return to society. There is a high probability that long-term hospitalization will do more harm than good. The film *One Flew over the Cuckoo's Nest* vividly illustrates the resocialization process described by Goffman.

Source: Erving Goffman, *Asylums: Essays on the Social Situation of Mental Patients and Other Inmates* (New York: Doubleday, 1961).

infectious diseases, genetic endowment, and metabolic imbalances are the causes of mental disorders.[52] However, only a few specific organic causes have been identified. General paresis, for instance, which is a progressive emotional disorder, has been linked to syphilis; pellagra, another disorder, has been found to result from dietary deficiency.

The notion that mental disorders are physiological led to certain medical treatments that now appear to be tragedies. In the 18th century, bloodletting was widely practiced. In the early 20th century, prefrontal lobotomies (surgical slashing of the frontal section of the brain) were performed to "remove" the mental illness. Lobotomies have little therapeutic value, cause lasting brain damage and leave patients docile and retarded.

Current Trends

In the past 30 years there have been two major developments in the treatment of the severely disturbed. The first was the discovery and use of psychoactive drugs, both tranquilizers and antidepressants. The initial hope was that such drugs would cure severe disturbances, but it was soon realized that they provide primarily symptom relief and thereby enable the disturbed person to be more accessible to other therapy programs and approaches.[53] The second development was deinstitutionalization. Mental health practitioners realized that mental hospitals, instead of "curing" the disturbed, were frequently perpetuating disturbed behavior via long-term hospitalization. That is, the disturbed were labeled mentally ill and came to define themselves as "different" and enact the insane role.[54] Also, they became adapted to the relaxed, safe life of a hospital; the longer they stayed, the more they perceived the outside world as threatening.

Mental health professionals now use hospitalization only for those whose emotional problems pose a serious threat to their own well-being or to that of others. Psychotherapy is the main treatment approach used in mental hospitals. In most cases now, hospitalization for an emotional problem is brief.

The concept of deinstitutionalization has brought about a significant expansion of services designed to meet the needs of the disturbed in their home community, including community-based mental health centers, halfway houses, rehabilitation workshops, social therapeutic clubs, and foster-care services for the disturbed.

A criticism of the deinstitutionalization approach has been that some communities have returned long-term hospitalized patients to society *without* developing adequate community-based support services. The result is that many of the patients who have been discharged are living with families, friends, or on the street and are receiving little or no counseling and/or medical services.

Recent investigations have revealed incidents of discharged mental patients living in squalor in unlicensed group homes and low-quality hotels.[55] Many are victims of crime, fire, and medical neglect. Some are fed rancid food and exposed to rats and cockroaches. Sometimes such former patients set fires and abuse others; a few commit homicide or suicide.

TREATMENT FACILITIES: COMMUNITY MENTAL HEALTH CENTERS

Treatment services for emotional problems are provided by nearly every direct-service social welfare agency, including public welfare agencies, probation and parole agencies, penal institutions, school social services, family service agencies, adoption agencies, private psychotherapy clinics, sheltered workshops, social service units in hospitals, and nursing homes. However, in many communities mental health centers are a primary resource for serving those with emotional problems.

Community mental health centers were given their impetus with the passage by the federal government of the Community Mental Health Centers Act of 1963. This act provided for transferring the care and treatment of the majority of "mentally ill" people from state hospitals to their home communities. The emphasis is on local care, with

Many social agencies offer counseling and therapy to people with emotional problems. Art therapy is one activity these professionals use in working with children at a private medical center.

provision of comprehensive services (particularly to underprivileged areas and people).

Other emphases are (1) early diagnosis, treatment, and early return to community; (2) location of centers "near and accessible to" the populations they serve; and (3) the provision of comprehensive care consisting of five basic components: inpatient care, outpatient care, partial hospitalization (that is, day, night, and weekend care), emergency care, and consultation/education. Services provided are expected to relate to a wide range of problem areas and population groups, such as the disturbed, the elderly, minorities, and people with alcohol and other drug-related problems.[56]

Professionals in a community mental health center may include psychiatrists, social workers, psychologists, psychiatric nurses, specialized consultants, occupational and recreational therapists, paraprofessionals, and volunteers. Typical services include outpatient care, inpatient care, alcohol and chemical abuse treatment, work evaluation, occupational therapy, family and group therapy, transportation services, counseling of children and adults, crisis intervention (including 24-hour emergency care), community education, and field training of students in the helping professions.

Community mental health services have in recent years received increasing criticism. Studies have found that some community mental health services are ineffective and inadequate.[57] Patients still have high readmission rates and inadequate levels of adjustment to the community.[58] Many centers have been ineffective in dealing with the personal and societal problems of large numbers of poor people, because many of these so-called comprehensive centers provide little more than traditional inpatient and outpatient care for middle-class patients.[59]

On the other hand, proponents of community mental health centers argue that such centers have shown impressive results. For example, their programs have reduced the number of people in state and county mental hospitals from 550,000 in 1955 to 110,000 in 1990.[60]

SOCIAL WORK AND MENTAL HEALTH

Social workers were first employed in the mental health field in 1906 to take social histories of newly admitted patients to Manhattan State Hospital in New York City.[61] Since then they have been involved in providing a variety of preventive, diagnostic, and treatment services.

Over the years there has been a shift in emphasis from treating the individual to treating the family. Social workers, psychologists, and psychiatrists now function interchangeably as individual, family, and group therapists. All three professional groups are also involved in designing and administering mental health programs. Other professionals involved in working as a team in mental health facilities include psychiatric nurses, occupational therapists, and recreational therapists.

It has been estimated that half the professionals who provide mental health services in the United States today are social workers.[62] Many social agencies, in addition to community mental health centers, provide counseling and psychotherapy to people with emotional problems. Such agencies include schools, family counseling agencies, public welfare departments, hospitals, adoption agencies, and probation and parole departments. An increasing number of clinical social workers are opening private practices to provide individual, family, and group therapy for a variety of emotional problems. Increasingly, payments from public and private insurance programs reimburse social workers for providing therapy on a private basis.

The National Association of Social Workers (NASW) has been promoting state licensing (or registration) requirements to assure the public that social work practitioners, especially those in private practice, meet high standards of competence. All states have now enacted legislation to license social workers.

NASW has also established a national Registry of Clinical Social Workers. Requirements for membership are:

- A master's or doctoral degree in social work from a graduate school accredited by the Council on Social Work Education (CSWE).

- Two years or 3000 hours of postgraduate clinical social work experience, supervised by a clinical social worker with at least two years of experience.

- Active membership in the Academy of Certified Social Workers (ACSW) or a state license that requires an examination.[63]

At one time the social work role in the mental health field was generally considered subordinate to psychiatry. But, with a growing recognition that emotional problems are primarily problems in living rather than organic in nature, social workers are increasingly being employed in agencies to provide counseling and psychotherapy, without being supervised by a psychiatrist.

The primary therapy approach used to treat people with emotional or behavioral problems is psychotherapy or counseling (I use these two terms interchangeably, as there do not appear to be clear-cut distinctions between the two). Counseling is a broad term covering individual, family, and group therapy. A skilled counselor has knowledge of (1) interviewing principles and (2) comprehensive and specific treatment approaches. The next section discusses these two areas and is designed to give you a "flavor" of what counseling is composed of. Additional theoretical material covering these two areas is presented in social work practice and field placement courses. Through role playing of contrived counseling situations and, later, through working with clients, social work students gain skill and confidence in putting this material into practice. Sharpening and further developing one's counseling skills do not end with acquiring a degree in a counseling field; it is an ongoing, lifelong process.

COUNSELING

Counseling services are provided by practically every direct-service social welfare agency. Some agencies, such as welfare departments and mental health centers, provide counseling services covering almost all emotional or interpersonal problems. Other, more specialized agencies provide counseling designed for specific problems that require considerable background knowledge and training in using highly developed treatment techniques. (Such areas include drug abuse counseling, therapy for eating disorders, genetic counseling, and sex therapy.)

The capacity to counsel effectively is one of the key skills needed by social workers; in fact, it may be *the* most important skill. Acquiring in-depth skill at counseling in one area (for example, marriage or adoption counseling) prepares that person for counseling in other areas. Because this skill is transferable, undergraduate and graduate social work programs can take a generic (broad-based) approach to social work training. The emphasis is placed on in-depth training in counseling rather than on training in specialized counseling areas.

How to Counsel*

Counseling someone with personal problems is neither magical nor mystical. Although training and experience in counseling are beneficial, everyone has the potential of helping another by listening and talking through difficulties. Counseling with a successful outcome can be done by a friend, neighbor, relative, hairdresser, banker, or bartender, as well as by social workers, psychiatrists, psychologists, guidance counselors, and the clergy. This is not to say that everyone will be successful at counseling. Professional people, because of their training and experience, have a higher probability of being effective. But competence and empathy, rather than degrees or certificates, are the keys to desirable outcomes.

There are three phases to counseling: (1) building a relationship, (2) exploring problems in depth, and (3) exploring alternative solu-

*This section on "How to Counsel" is reprinted from an article of the same title written by me in *The Personal Problem Solver*, eds. Charles Zastrow and Dae Chang (Englewood Cliffs, NJ: Spectrum Books, 1977). Reprinted by permission of Prentice-Hall, Englewood Cliffs, NJ.

tions. Successful counseling gradually proceeds from one phase to the next, with some overlapping of the stages. For example, in many cases, while exploring problems, the relationship between the counselor and the counselee continues to develop; while exploring alternative solutions, the problems are generally being examined in greater depth.

BUILDING A RELATIONSHIP
The following are guidelines for building a relationship with a client:

1. Seek to establish a nonthreatening atmosphere in which the counselee feels safe to communicate fully his or her troubles while feeling accepted as a person.

2. In initial contacts with the counselee, you need to "sell" yourself—not arrogantly, but as a knowledgeable, understanding person who may be able to help and who wants to try.

3. Be calm. Do not laugh or express shock when the counselee begins to open up about problems. Emotional outbursts, even if subtle, will lead the counselee to believe that you are not going to understand his or her difficulties, and she or he will usually stop discussing them.

4. Generally be nonjudgmental and nonmoralistic. Show respect for the counselee's values, and do not try to sell your values. The values that work for you may not be best for someone else in a different situation. For example, if the counselee is premaritally pregnant, do not attempt to force your values toward adoption or abortion. Let the counselee decide on a course of action after a full examination of the problem and an exploration of the possible solutions.

5. View the counselee as an equal. Rookie counselors sometimes make the mistake of thinking that, because someone is sharing intimate secrets, the counselor must be very important; they then end up creating a superior/inferior relationship. If counselees feel that they are being treated as inferior, they will be less motivated to reveal and discuss personal difficulties.

6. Use "shared vocabulary." This does not mean using the same slang words or the same accent as the counselee. If the counselee sees your speech as artificial, it may seriously offend him

or her. You should use words that the counselee understands and that are not offensive.

7. The tone of your voice should convey the message that you empathetically understand and care about the counselee's feelings.

8. Keep confidential what the counselee has said. All of us by nature have urges to share "juicy secrets" with someone else. But, if the counselee discovers that confidentiality has been violated, a working relationship may be quickly destroyed.

9. If you are counseling a relative or a friend, there is a danger that, because you are emotionally involved, you may get upset or into an argument with the other person. If that happens, it is almost always best to drop the subject immediately, as tactfully as possible. Perhaps, after tempers cool, the subject can be brought up again. Or it may be best to refer the counselee to someone else. Many professionals refuse to counsel friends or relatives because emotional involvement interferes with the calm, detached perspective that is needed to help clients explore problems and alternative solutions.

EXPLORING PROBLEMS IN DEPTH

Following are suggestions to guide counselors in helping clients explore problems in depth:

1. Many rookie counselors make the mistake of suggesting solutions as soon as a problem is identified, without exploring the problem in depth. For example, an advocate of abortions may advise this solution as soon as a single female reveals that she is pregnant. A counselor should take the time to discover whether this person is strongly opposed to abortions, really wants a baby, or intends to marry soon.

2. In exploring problems in depth, the counselor and counselee need to examine such areas as the extent of the problem, its duration, its causes, the counselee's feelings about the problem, and the physical and mental capacities and strengths the counselee has to cope with the problem, before exploring alternative solutions. For example, if a single female is pregnant, the counselor and counselee need to explore the following questions: How does the person feel about being pregnant? Has she seen a doctor? About how long has she been pregnant? Do her parents know? If

so, what are their feelings and concerns? Has the female informed her partner? What are his feelings and concerns? What does she feel is the most urgent situation to deal with first? Answers to such questions will determine the direction of counseling. The most pressing, immediate problem might to be to inform her parents, who may react critically, or it might be to secure medical services.

3. When a problem area is identified, a number of smaller problems may occur (for example, planning how to tell her partner, obtaining medical care, obtaining funds for medical expenses, deciding where to live, deciding whether to leave school or work during the pregnancy, deciding whether to keep the child, and making plans for what to do after the child is delivered or the pregnancy is terminated). Explore all these subproblems.

4. In a multiproblem situation, the best way to decide which problem to handle first is to ask the counselee which one she or he perceives as most pressing. If the problem can be solved, start with exploring that subproblem in depth and developing together a strategy for the solution. Success in solving a subproblem will increase the counselee's confidence in the counselor and thereby will further solidify the relationship.

5. Convey empathy, not sympathy. Empathy is the capacity to show that you are aware of and can to some extent feel what the counselee is saying. Sympathy is also sharing of feelings, but it has the connotation of pity. The difference is subtle, but empathy is oriented toward problem solving, whereas sympathy usually prolongs problems. For example, if you give me sympathy when I'm depressed, I'll keep telling you my sad story over and over, each time having an emotional outpouring supported by your sympathy, without taking any action to improve the situation. This process only reopens old wounds and prolongs my depression.

6. "Trust your guts." The most important tool you have as a counselor is yourself (your feelings and perceptions). You should continually strive to place yourself in the client's situation (with the client's values and pressures). To use the earlier example, if the client is 17 years old, single, and

pregnant, and has parents who are very critical of the situation and want her to have an abortion, a competent counselor would continually strive to feel what she is feeling and to perceive the world from her perspective, with her goals, difficulties, pressures, and values. It probably never happens that a counselor is 100% accurate in placing himself or herself in the counselee's situation, but 70–80% is usually sufficient to gain an awareness of the counselee's pressures, problems, and perspectives. This information helps the counselor to determine what additional areas need to be explored, to decide what to say, and to figure out possible solutions. In other words, a counselor should ask "What is this person trying to tell me, and how can I make it clear that I understand not only intellectually but empathetically?"

7. When you believe that the client has touched on an important area of concern, you can encourage further communication by:

a. Nonverbally showing interest.

b. Pausing. Inexperienced counselors usually become anxious when there is a pause, and they hasten to say something—anything—to have conversation continue. This is usually a mistake, especially when it leads to a change in the topic. Pausing will also make the counselee anxious, give him or her time to think about the important area of concern, and then usually motivate him or her to continue conversation in that area.

c. Using neutral probes. Examples are: "Could you tell me more about it?" "Why do you feel that way?" "I'm not sure I understand what you have in mind."

d. Summarizing what the client is saying. You might offer: "During this past hour you made a number of critical comments about your spouse; it sounds like some things about your marriage are making you unhappy."

e. Reflecting feelings. Examples are "You seem angry" or "You appear to be depressed about that."

8. Approach socially unacceptable issues tactfully. Tact is an essential quality of a competent counselor. Try not to ask a question in such a way that the answer will put the respondent in an embarrassing position. Suppose, for instance, you are counseling a male with poor personal hygiene who has been discharged from a variety of jobs and does not know why. The man explains that employers initially compliment him on his work productivity and then tend, a few weeks later, to discharge him without informing him why. After several possible explanations have been explored and eliminated, you as the counselor may tactfully say "I'm wondering if your personal appearance and hygiene may be a reason for the dismissals. I notice you haven't shaved for a few days, and I sense you may not have bathed for a few days either. Do you think this may be an explanation?" It's very important to confront clients with ineffective actions that are having negative effects on their lives.

9. When pointing out a limitation that a counselee has, also mention and compliment him or her on any assets. Discussion of a limitation will literally make the counselee feel that something is being laid bare or taken away. Complimenting him or her in another area will give something back.

10. Watch for nonverbal cues. A competent counselor will generally use such cues to identify when a sensitive subject is being touched on, as the client will show anxiety by changing tone of voice, fidgeting, yawning, assuming a stiff posture, or appearing flushed.

11. Be honest. An untruth always runs the risk of being discovered. If that happens, the counselee's confidence in you will be seriously damaged and perhaps the relationship seriously jeopardized. But being honest goes beyond not telling lies. The counselor should always point out those shortcomings that are in the counselee's best interest to give attention to. For example, if someone is being fired from jobs because of poor grooming habits, this needs to be brought to his or her attention. Or, if a trainee's relationship skills and personality are not suited for the helping professions, that person needs to be "counseled out" in the interests of clients and in the trainee's own best interests.

12. Listen attentively to what the counselee is saying. Try to hear his or her words not from your perspective but from the counselee's. Unfortunately, many people are caught up in their own interests and concerns, and they do not "tune

out'' their own thoughts while the counselee is speaking. This guideline seems very simple, but it is indeed difficult for many to follow.

EXPLORING ALTERNATIVE SOLUTIONS

The following are guidelines for exploring alternative solutions with a client:

1. After (or sometimes while) a subproblem is explored in depth, the next step is for the counselor and the counselee to consider alternative solutions. In exploring alternative solutions, it is almost always best for the counselor to begin by asking something like "Have you thought about ways to resolve this?" The merits, shortcomings, and consequences of the alternatives thought of by the counselee should then be tactfully and thoroughly examined. If the counselee has not thought of certain viable alternatives, the counselor should mention these, and the merits and shortcomings of these alternatives should also be examined. For example, in the case of the unwed pregnant teenager, if she decides to continue the pregnancy to full term, possible alternatives for the subproblem of making plans for living arrangements include keeping the child, getting married, seeking public assistance, finding foster care after delivery, filing a paternity suit, placing the child for adoption, obtaining the assistance of a close relative to help or care for the child.

2. The counselee usually has the right to self-determination—that is, to choose the course of action among possible alternatives. The counselor's role is to help the counselee clarify and understand the likely consequences of each available alternative but generally not to give advice or choose the alternative for the counselee. If the counselor were to select the alternative, there would be two possible outcomes: (1) The alternative may prove to be undesirable for the counselee, in which case the counselee will probably blame the counselor for the advice, and the future relationship will be seriously hampered. (2) The alternative may prove to be desirable for the counselee. This immediate outcome is advantageous; but the danger is that the counselee will then become overly dependent on the counselor, seeking his or her advice for nearly every decision in the future and generally being reluctant to make de-

cisions independently. In actual practice, most courses of action have desirable and undesirable consequences. For example, if the unmarried mother is advised to keep her child, she may receive considerable gratification from being with and raising the child, but at the same time she may blame the counselor for such possible negative consequences as long-term financial hardships and a restricted social life.

The guideline of not giving advice does *not* mean that a counselor should not suggest alternatives that the client has not considered. On the contrary, it is the counselor's responsibility to suggest and explore all viable alternatives with a client. A good rule to follow is that, when a counselor believes a client should take a certain course of action, this idea should be phrased as a suggestion ("Have you thought about . . . ?") rather than as advice ("I think you should . . . ").

3. Counseling is done *with* the counselee, not *to* or *for* the counselee. In general, the counselee should take responsibility for those tasks that she or he has the capacity to carry out, and the counselor should attempt to do only those that are beyond the capacities of the counselee. As with giving advice, doing things *for* counselees may create a dependency relationship. Furthermore, successful accomplishment of tasks by counselees leads to personal growth and better prepares them for taking on future responsibilities.

4. The counselee's right to self-determination should be taken away only if the selected course or action has a high probability of seriously hurting others or the counselee. For example, if it seems likely that a parent will continue to abuse a child or that a counselee will attempt to take his or her own life, intervention by the counselor is called for. For most situations, however, the counselee should have the right to select his or her alternative, even when the counselor believes that another alternative is a better course of action. Frequently, the counselee is in a better position to know what is best for him or her; if the alternative is not the best, the counselee will probably learn from the mistake.

5. Attempt to form explicit, realistic "contracts" with counselees. When the counselee does select an alternative, he or she should clearly

understand what the goals will be, what tasks need to be carried out, how to do the tasks, and who will carry out each of them. It is often desirable to build into the "contract" a time limit for the accomplishment of each task. For example, if the unmarried mother decides to keep her child and now needs to make long-range financial plans, this goal should be understood and specific courses of action decided on—seeking public assistance, seeking support from the alleged father, securing an apartment within her budget, and so on. Furthermore, who will do what task within a set time limit should be specified.

6. If the counselee fails to meet the terms of the "contract," do not punish, but do not accept excuses. Excuses let people off the hook; they provide temporary relief, but they eventually lead to more failure and to a failure identity. Simply ask "Do you still wish to try to fulfill your commitment?" If the counselee answers affirmatively, another deadline acceptable to the counselee should be set.

7. Perhaps the biggest single factor in determining whether the counselee's situation will improve is the motivation to carry out essential tasks. A counselor should seek to motivate apathetic counselees. One of the biggest reality shocks of inexperienced helping professionals is that many clients, even after making commitments to improve their situation, do not have the motivation to carry out the steps outlined.

8. One way to increase motivation is to clarify what will be gained by meeting the commitment. When counselees fulfill commitments, reward them verbally or in other ways. Avoid punishment if commitments are not met. Punishment usually increases hostility without positive lasting changes. It also serves as only a temporary means of obtaining different behavior; a person who is no longer under surveillance will usually return to the "deviant" behavior.

9. Sometimes the counselee lacks the confidence or experience to carry out certain tasks. In this case it is helpful to "role-play" the tasks. For example, if a pregnant unwed teenager wants help in deciding how to tell her partner about the pregnancy, role playing the situation will assist her in selecting words and developing a strategy for informing him. The counselor can first play her role and model an approach, while she plays her partner's role. Then the roles should be reversed so that the teenager practices telling her partner.

Other helpful hints for counseling could be given here, but the basic format is to develop a relationship, explore problems in depth, and then explore alternative solutions. These guidelines are not to be followed dogmatically; they will probably work 70–80% of the time. Learn to trust your own feelings, perceptions, relationship capacities, and interviewing skills.

One final important guideline is that the counselor should refer the counselee to someone else, or at least seek a professional counselor to discuss the case with, for any of the following situations: if the counselor feels that she or he is unable to empathize with the counselee; if the counselor feels that the counselee is choosing alternatives (such as seeking an abortion) that conflict with the counselor's basic value system; if the counselor feels that the problem is of such a nature that she or he will not be able to help; and if a working relationship is not established. A competent counselor knows that she or he can work with and help some people but not all. If you encounter a client you feel you cannot help, it is in that person's best interests, as well as your own, to refer the client to someone else who can.

Comprehensive and Specialized Counseling Approaches

In addition to having a good grasp of interviewing principles, an effective counselor needs to have a knowledge of comprehensive counseling theories and of specialized treatment techniques to be able to diagnose precisely what problems exist and decide how to intervene effectively. There are a number of contemporary comprehensive counseling approaches: psychoanalysis, rational therapy, client-centered therapy, Adlerian psychotherapy, behavior modification, Gestalt therapy, reality therapy, transactional analysis, neurolinguistic programming, and encounter approaches.* These therapy approaches generally present theoretical material on (1) personality theory, or how normal psychosocial development occurs; (2) behavior pathology, or how emotional problems arise; and (3) therapy, or how to change unwanted emotions and dysfunctional behaviors.

An effective counselor generally has a knowledge of several treatment approaches. Depending on the unique set of problems being presented by the client, the counselor picks and chooses from his or her "bag of tricks" the intervention strategy that is likely to have the highest probability of success. In addition to comprehensive counseling approaches, there are a number of specialized treatment techniques for specific problems, such as assertiveness training for people who are shy or overly aggressive, relaxation techniques for people experiencing high levels of stress, specific sex therapy techniques for such difficulties as premature ejaculation or orgasmic dysfunction, and parent effectiveness training for parent/child relationship difficulties.[†] An effective counselor strives to gain a working knowledge of a wide variety of treatment techniques in order to increase the likelihood of being able to help clients.

For illustrative purposes, one comprehensive therapy approach, rational therapy, will be summarized.

RATIONAL THERAPY

The two main developers of rational therapy are Albert Ellis and Maxie Maultsby.[64] The approach potentially enables those who become skillful in rationally analyzing their self-talk to control or get rid of any undesirable emotion or any dysfunctional behavior.

It is erroneously believed by most people that our emotions and our actions are determined primarily by our experiences (that is, by events that happen to us). On the contrary, rational therapy has demonstrated that the primary cause of all our emotions and actions is what we tell ourselves about what happens to us.

All feelings and actions occur according to the following format:

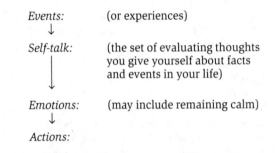

Events:	(or experiences)
↓	
Self-talk:	(the set of evaluating thoughts you give yourself about facts and events in your life)
↓	
Emotions:	(may include remaining calm)
↓	
Actions:	

An example will illustrate this process.

Event:	Cheryl, the 5-year-old daughter of Mr. and Mrs. Shaw, is playing with her brother and knocks over and breaks a lamp.
Mr. Shaw's self-talk:	"That lamp was our favorite. We bought it on our honeymoon— it's irreplaceable. This is awful."
	"Spare the rod and spoil the child. Some stiff discipline will make her shape up."
	"As head of this household it's my duty to make her shape up. I'll teach her a lesson she'll never forget by giving her the spanking of her life."
	"She's always breaking things. I think this might have been intentional! I'll teach her to have respect for me and for our valuable items."
Emotions:	Anger, disappointment, frustration.
Actions:	Spanking and yelling at Cheryl, with the severity of the spanking bordering on abuse.

If, on the other hand, Mr. Shaw gives himself

---

*A good summary of contemporary global counseling approaches is provided in Raymond Corsini, ed., *Current Psychotherapies*, 4th ed. (Itasca, IL: Peacock, 1989); Francis J. Turner, ed., *Social Work Treatment* (New York: Free Press, 1979); and Charles Zastrow, *The Practice of Social Work*, 5th ed. (Pacific Grove, CA: Brooks/Cole, 1995).
[†]A summary of specialized treatment techniques is contained in Charles Zastrow, *The Practice of Social Work*, 5th ed. (Pacific Grove, CA: Brooks/Cole, 1995).

a different set of self-talk, his emotions and actions will be quite different:

Event:	Cheryl, the 5-year-old daughter of Mr. and Mrs. Shaw, is playing with her brother and knocks over and breaks a lamp.
Mr. Shaw's self-talk:	"This was a lamp we cherished, but I know she didn't break it intentionally. It was an accident. My getting angry at this point won't help."
	"I might have prevented this accident by informing Cheryl and our son that they can horse around indoors only in the rec room and in their bedrooms."
	"With young children some accidents are bound to happen."
	"The most constructive thing I can do at this point is to say that I understand that it was an accident, that all of us are disappointed that the lamp broke, and that in the future their horsing around should be limited to the rec room and the bedrooms."
Emotions:	Some disappointment but generally remaining calm.
Actions:	Talking to the children in an understanding fashion and expressing his thoughts in line with his self-talk.

The most important point about the preceding processes is that our self-talk determines how we feel and act; by changing our self-talk, we can change how we feel and act. Generally we cannot control events that happen to us, but we have the power to think rationally and thereby change *all* of our unwanted emotions and ineffective actions.* This is the rehabilitative aspect of the conceptualization.[65]

The self-talk we give ourselves about specific events that happen to us is often based on a variety of factors, including our beliefs, attitudes, values, wants, motives, goals, and desires.[66] For example, the self-talk a married woman might give herself on being informed by her husband that he wants a divorce would be influenced by her desire (or lack of desire) to remain married, by her values and beliefs about being a divorcée, by her attitudes toward her husband, by her present goals (and whether getting a divorce would be consistent or inconsistent with them), and by her beliefs about the reasons why her husband says he wants a divorce.

Another important point about self-talk is that, with repeated occurrences of an event, a person's emotional reaction becomes nearly automatic. That is, the person rapidly gives himself or herself a large set of self-talk gradually acquired through past experiences. For example, a few years ago I counseled a women who became intensely upset and depressed every time her husband came home intoxicated. In examining her emotional reactions, it became clear that, because of the repeated occurrences, she would rapidly tell herself the following on seeing him inebriated:

- "He's making a fool of himself and of me."
- "He's foolishly spending money we desperately need."
- "For the next few hours I'm going to have to put up with his drunken talk and behavior. This is awful."
- "He loves drinking more than he loves me, because he knows I don't want him to get drunk."
- "Woe is me."

The use of rational therapy is demonstrated in Case Example 4.3.

---

*According to Maultsby, rational thinking and rational behavior (1) are consistent with the facts, (2) help you protect your life, (3) help you achieve your short- and long-term goals more quickly, (4) help you get out and stay out of significant trouble with other people, and (5) help you prevent significant unwanted emotions.

**CASE
EXAMPLE 4.3**

A Case Example Using Rational Therapy: Coping with a Sexual Affair

A 21-year-old woman, Cindy, sought counseling after she was informed by her boyfriend, Jim, that a few months earlier he had become sexually involved with another woman, Linda. Jim and Cindy had dated fairly steadily for the past two years. Both were attending the same college. Prior to their summer break they were having frequent arguments and decided not to see each other during the summer. When they returned to college in the fall, they resumed their relationship. A few weeks later Jim (after Cindy questioned him) informed her that on one occasion he had had sex with Linda.

Cindy told the counselor that she wanted to better handle the unwanted emotions she was having about this affair. After discussing her feelings in some depth, the counselor informed her that she could counter her undesirable emotions by doing a rational self-analysis (based on rational therapy). This involves writing down:

A. The facts and events that occurred.

B. The self-talk a person gives himself or herself.

C. The emotions a person experiences.

D. An examination of the statements in section A to determine whether they are factual or whether they belong in section B (a person's self-talk). This section is to be written *only* after sections A, B, and C are written.

E. Positive and rational self-talk challenges to the negative and irrational self-talk in section B (this segment is the main therapeutic part of the process).

F. The emotional and behavioral goals a person has.

For this process to be therapeutic, the person must practice replacing the irrational self-talk with rational self-talk. In writing a rational self-analysis (RSA), the person first writes in the left column the components A, B, and C; then he or she comes back to the beginning to write in the right column the components D, E, and F. The following RSA should be read with this A-B-C-D-E-F format in mind.

A	D
Facts and Events	*Factual Check of A*
My boyfriend, Jim, informed me that he had sexual relations with Linda, after a party at which they had both been drinking.	This is all factual. I know this because Jim told me himself. Jim and I are very close, and I know he would not lie to me.
B	E
My Self-Talk	*My Rational Debates of B*
B-1. It's not fair! How could Jim do such a thing to me? (bad)	E-1. Jim had sex with Linda. I'll just have to accept that. Because people are human and fallible, it's a mistake to expect that I will always be treated with fairness

by others. Besides, Jim and I had broken up, so I'm sure they didn't have me in mind when they did it. At the time they were sexually involved, neither Jim nor I had any commitment to each other. In truth, I also considered getting sexually involved this summer and perhaps would have if I had met the right guy.

B-2. That creep just had sex with Linda because he was horny. (bad)

E-2. Jim probably had sex with Linda for other reasons. I know he's not the type to "use" a woman merely for relief of his sexual tensions. It's also a mistake to label him a creep. No one is a creep. People are humans. If I mislabel him as a creep, it may lead me to view him in terms of an inaccurate label.

B-3. Jim and Linda had no good reasons for doing what they did. They only did it because they were both drunk. What a couple of jerks! (bad)

E-3. I do believe that alcohol had something to do with the fact that Jim and Linda had sex. I know for a fact that Jim becomes much less inhibited when he's had a few drinks. I don't know about Linda, though. The drinking can't be the only reason they had sex. Maybe they felt attracted to each other and wanted to have sex. I've got to remember that this summer Jim and I had no commitments to each other, and therefore I don't have the right to expect that he would be celibate to please me. Also, it's a mistake for me to refer to Jim or Linda as a "jerk." People are people.

B-4. Linda must be some kind of cheap tramp. Only a tramp would have sex with a guy she didn't love. (bad)

E-4. I don't even know Linda, so I shouldn't judge her like this. Furthermore, I have no way of knowing how Linda felt about Jim. Maybe she felt she loved
(continued)

CASE
EXAMPLE 4.3   *(continued)*

him at the time. A woman isn't necessarily loose if she has sex with a guy.

B-5. Jim must think he's some kind of stud now. (bad)

E-5. Jim has told me that he has had sex with only two women. My idea of a "stud" is a guy who thinks he can have sex with any woman who comes along. I know Jim better than that. He doesn't think he could conquer any woman—nor would he try to.

B-6. Jim and I will never again be able to have a good sexual relationship of our own now that he has someone else to compare me to. I just know that he'll be thinking of Linda from now on. (bad)

E-6. Jim and I love each other. Jim told me that he does not love Linda. Just because Jim had sex with Linda does not mean our relationship will always be adversely affected. We can communicate easily during sex, and it has always been satisfying so far. It would be silly for Jim to compare our entire relationship to the one night he spent with Linda.

B-7. This is the worst thing that Jim could have done. (bad)

E-7. This is not the worst thing that Jim could have done. What he did was not a crime, like murder or rape, which would have been worse. The situation would be worse if Jim had slept with Linda while he was still seeing me. I'm glad to know that he would never do that.

B-8. Now that I know Jim had sex with Linda, our whole relationship will be ruined. (bad)

E-8. The fact that Jim had sex with Linda does not have to ruin our relationship. The event occurred

SUMMARY

Emotional and behavioral problems are two comprehensive labels covering an array of problems.

All of us, at times, experience emotional and behavioral problems. Serious or severe emotional problems are sometimes labeled "mental illnesses."

The history of treatment for the emotionally

in the past. It's over. Past sexual experiences should have no bearing on the future of our relationship. I want the relationship to continue, and I don't want to see it ruined.

B-9. I should never have broken up with Jim. Then he would never have slept with Linda. It's all my fault. (bad)

E-9. It's not my fault at all. I broke up with Jim because I felt it was the best thing to do at the time. I know Jim would not have been unfaithful to me had we still been dating, but we weren't dating at the time this happened. I had no way of knowing he would go to bed with Linda, and knowing would not have changed my decision to break up with him. It's not my fault because I wasn't even involved.

B-10. From now on, whenever I hear Linda's name mentioned, I'm going to have a fit! I won't be able to handle it! (bad)

E-10. When I hear Linda's name mentioned, I don't have to respond by having a fit. I can handle my feelings by being calm and not letting the mention of her name bother me.

C

My Emotions

I feel guilty, hurt, angry, upset, and jealous. (very bad)

F

My Emotional and Behavioral Goals

I want to get over my unwanted emoYtions that I have had about this affair. I want to put this affair in our past. At the time it happened, Jim and I had no commitments to each other. What is important to Jim and me is our present and future relationship, not what happened one evening when Jim and I had broken up.

---

disturbed is fascinating but also is filled with injustices and tragedies. In the past the disturbed have been viewed in a variety of ways, ranging from prophets to evil people possessed by demoniac powers. Recent major developments in treat-

ment are the discovery and use of psychoactive drugs and the trend toward deinstitutionalization.

A major controversy is whether mental illness exists. Adherents of the medical approach believe that the disturbed person's mind is affected by some generally unknown, internal condition. Critics of the medical model assert that disturbed people display a social deviation or have an emotional problem but do not have a disease of the mind. Further, the critics assert that mental-illness labels have no diagnostic or treatment value and frequently have an adverse effect.

The large number of homeless people in our nation is a national disgrace. Many of the homeless are thought to suffer from serious and chronic forms of mental illness. Discharged from mental institutions without the support they need, tens of thousands of former mental patients live on the street in abominable conditions.

Another major issue in the mental health field is civil rights concerns over involuntary confinement, inadequate treatment, and enforced use of treatments that have adverse side effects. Other issues include the usefulness of the innocent-by-reason-of-insanity plea, the extent to which psychotropic drugs should be used, and the adequacy of the services provided by local communities to emotionally disturbed individuals who are no longer (because of deinstitutionalization) being sent to state mental hospitals.

Sociologists have found a number of associations between social factors and mental illness. Higher rates of diagnosed mental illness have been found in the lower socioeconomic classes, in inner cities as compared to rural areas, among the elderly, among unmarried people, and among African Americans as compared to whites. Men and women are about equally likely to receive treatment; women are more likely to be diagnosed as suffering from anxiety, depression, and phobias and to be hospitalized. Men are more likely to be labeled psychotic. Lower-class patients often receive lower-quality care.

The main therapy approach used to treat people with emotional and behavioral problems is psychotherapy or counseling. Counseling services are provided by practically every direct-service social welfare agency. The ability to counsel others effectively is perhaps the most important skill needed by social workers. To be a competent counselor, it is essential to have a working knowledge of interviewing principles and of a wide range of treatment approaches. There are three distinct phases to counseling: building a relationship, exploring problems in depth, and exploring alternative solutions.

NOTES

1. Albert Ellis, *Reason and Emotion in Psychotherapy* (New York: Lyle Stuart, 1962).
2. William Kornblum and Joseph Julian, *Social Problems,* 7th ed. (Englewood Cliffs, NJ: Prentice-Hall, 1992), p. 59.
3. Ibid., p. 60.
4. Erica Goode, "When Mental Illness Hits Home," *U.S. News & World Report,* Apr. 24, 1989, pp. 55–65.
5. A. Hoffer and W. Polin, "Schizophrenia in the NAS-NRC Panel of 15,909 Twin Pairs," *Archives of General Psychiatry,* 23 (1970), pp. 469–477.
6. Seymor S. Kety, "The Biological Roots of Schizophrenia," *Harvard Magazine,* 78 (1976), pp. 20–26.
7. *DSM-IV (Diagnostic and Statistical Manual of Mental Disorders),* 4th ed. (Washington, DC: American Psychiatric Association, 1994).
8. Thomas S. Szasz, *The Myth of Mental Illness* (New York: Hoeber-Harper, 1961).
9. Thomas S. Szasz, "The Myth of Mental Illness," in *Clinical Psychology in Transition,* John R. Braun, comp. (Cleveland: Howard Allen, 1961). p. 27.
10. Thomas Scheff, *Being Mentally Ill* (Chicago: Aldine, 1966); David Mechanic, "Some Factors in Identifying and Defining Mental Illness," *Mental Hygiene,* 46, pp. 66–74.
11. Daniel Offer and Melvin Sabshin, *Normality: Theoretical and Clinical Concepts in Mental Health* (New York: Basic Books, 1966), p. 253.
12. Lawrence C. Koll, Viola Bernard, and Bruce P. Dohrenwend, "The Problem of Validity in Field Studies of Psychological Disorder," in *Urban Challenges to Psychiatry,* Bruce P. Dohrenwend and Barbara Snell Dohrenwend, eds. (New York: Wiley, 1969), pp. 429–460.
13. David L. Rosenhan, "On Being Sane in Insane Places," *Science,* 179 (January 1973), pp. 250–257.
14. Scheff, *Being Mentally Ill,* pp. 27–52.
15. Thomas S. Szasz, *Law, Liberty, and Psychiatry* (New York: Macmillan, 1963).
16. Derek L. Phillips, "Rejection: A Possible Consequence of Seeking Help for Mental Disorder," *American Sociological Review,* 28 (1963), pp. 963–973.
17. Edwin M. Lemert, *Social Pathology* (New York: McGraw-Hill, 1951).
18. Charles H. Cooley, *Human Nature and the Social Order* (New York: Scribner, 1902).

19. Thomas S. Szasz, "The Psychiatrist as Double Agent," *Transaction*, 4 (October 1967), p. 16.
20. Ibid., p. 17.
21. Scheff, *Being Mentally Ill.*
22. Ibid., p. 31.
23. Patti Davis, "For an Instant, She Met My Eyes," *Parade*, Sept. 23, 1990, pp. 4–5.
24. Kornblum and Julian, *Social Problems*, pp. 80–84.
25. Ibid., pp. 80–83.
26. Anthony J. Vattano, "Mental Health," in *Contemporary Social Work*, 2d ed., Donald Brieland, Lela B. Costin, and Charles R. Atherton, eds. (New York: McGraw-Hill, 1980), p. 292.
27. Ibid.
28. The President's Commission on Mental Health, *Report to the President from The President's Commission on Mental Health*, vol. 1 (Washington, DC: U.S. Government Printing Office, 1978).
29. Ibid., pp. 69–72.
30. Franklin D. Chu and Sharland Trotter, *The Madness Establishment* (New York: Grossman, 1974), p. 40.
31. "Psychiatric Testimony Clouds Justice in the Courtroom," *Freedom*, February 1980, p. 1.
32. Ibid., p. 4.
33. "Behind Growing Outrage over Insanity Pleas," *U.S. News & World Report*, May 1979, p. 41.
34. Ibid., p. 42.
35. "Psychiatric Testimony Clouds Justice in the Courtroom," p. 4.
36. Kornblum and Julian, *Social Problems*, p. 59.
37. August B. Hollingshead and Frederick C. Redlich, *Social Class and Mental Illness: A Community Study* (New York: Wiley, 1958).
38. William Rushing, "Two Patterns in the Relationship between Social Class and Mental Hospitalization," *American Sociological Review*, 34 (August 1969), pp. 533–541; Leo Srole, T. S. Langer, S. T. Michael, M. K. Opler, and T. A. L. Rennie, *Mental Health in the Metropolis: The Midtown Manhattan Study*, rev. ed. (New York: Harper & Row, 1975).
39. Srole et al.
40. Kornblum and Julian, *Social Problems*, pp. 69–71.
41. Ibid., pp. 71–72.
42. Robert C. Atchley, *The Social Forces in Later Life: An Introduction to Social Gerontology*, 2d ed. (Belmont, CA: Wadsworth, 1977).
43. Daniel J. Curran and Claire M. Renzetti, *Social Problems*, 3rd ed. (Boston: Allyn & Bacon, 1993), p. 484.
44. Kornblum and Julian, *Social Problems*, pp. 73–74.
45. Phyllis Chesler, *Women and Madness* (New York: Avon, 1972).
46. Kornblum and Julian, *Social Problems*, p. 72.
47. George Rosen, *Madness in Society: Chapters in the Historical Sociology of Mental Illness* (New York: Harper & Row, 1969).
48. Ibid., pp. 172–195.
49. Clifford W. Beers, *A Mind That Found Itself* (New York: Longmans, Green, 1908).
50. H. J. Eysenck, "The Effects of Psychotherapy: An Evaluation," *Journal of Consulting Psychology*, 11 (1955), pp. 319–324.
51. A good summary of these therapies is provided in *Current Psychotherapies*, 4th ed., Raymond Corsini, ed. (Itasca, IL: Peacock, 1989).
52. Miriam Siegler and Mumphrey Osmond, *Models of Madness, Models of Medicine* (New York: Harper & Row, 1974).
53. Joseph Mehr, *Human Services* (Boston: Allyn & Bacon, 1980), p. 88.
54. Erving Goffman, *Asylums: Essays on the Social Situation of Mental Patients and Other Inmates* (New York: Doubleday, 1961).
55. Goode, "When Mental Illness Hits Home," pp. 55–65.
56. Kornblum and Julian, *Social Problems*, pp. 78–79.
57. Goode, "When Mental Illness Hits Home," pp. 55–65.
58. Ibid.
59. Kornblum and Julian, *Social Problems*, pp. 78–80.
60. Ibid., p. 59.
61. Vattano, "Mental Health," p. 293.
62. Ibid., p. 294.
63. National Association of Social Workers, *1993 Register of Clinical Social Workers*, 7th ed. (Washington, DC: NASW, 1993), pp. v–vi.
64. Ellis, *Reason and Emotion in Psychotherapy*; Maxie Maultsby, *Help Yourself to Happiness* (Boston: Marborough/Herman, 1975).
65. Maultsby, *Help Yourself to Happiness*, pp. 2–23.
66. Charles Zastrow, *You Are What You Think* (Chicago: Nelson-Hall, 1993).

5

FAMILY PROBLEMS
AND SERVICES
TO FAMILIES

The family is a social institution that is found in every culture. A common definition of a family is "a group of people related by marriage, ancestry, or adoption who live together in a common household."[1] It should be noted that such a definition does not cover a number of living arrangements in which the members consider themselves to be a family, such as:

- A husband and wife raising two foster children who have been in the household for several years.

- Two lesbians in a loving relationship who are raising children born to one of the partners in a previous, heterosexual marriage.

- A family unit in which one of the spouses is living away from home—perhaps because of military service or incarceration.

- A man and woman who have been living together for years in a loving relationship but have never legally married.

Clearly, a definition of the term *family* that encompasses all its diverse forms has not as yet been developed.

Following a short introduction to various family forms throughout the world, this chapter will:

- Present a brief history of changes in the American family since colonial days.

- Describe current problem areas in the American family, including divorce, empty-shell marriages, family violence, and births outside of marriage.

- Describe current social services for family problems.

- Describe current issues involving family problems.

DIVERSE FAMILY FORMS

Families take a variety of forms in different cultures. In some societies husband and wife live in separate buildings. In others they are expected to live apart for several years after the birth of a child. In many societies husbands are permitted to have more than one wife. In a few countries wives are allowed to have more than one husband. Some cultures permit (and even encourage) premarital and extramarital intercourse.

Some societies have large communes where adults and children live together. There are also communes in which the children are raised separately from adults. In some cultures without communes, surrogate parents rather than the genetic parents raise the children. Some societies encourage certain types of homosexual relationships, and a few recognize homosexual as well as heterosexual marriages.

In many cultures marriages are still arranged by the parents. Some societies do not recognize the existence of romantic love. Some cultures expect older men to marry young girls. Others expect older women to marry young boys. Some expect a man to marry his father's brother's daughter; others insist that he marry his mother's sister's daughter. Most societies prohibit the marriage of close relatives, yet a few subcultures encourage marriage between brothers and sisters or between first cousins. In a few societies infants are married before they are born (if the baby is of the wrong sex, the marriage is dissolved). In some societies a man, on marrying, makes a substantial gift to the bride's father; in others the bride's father gives a substantial gift to the new husband.

People in each society generally feel strongly that their particular pattern is normal and proper; many feel the pattern is divinely ordained. Suggested changes in their particular form are usually viewed with suspicion and defensiveness and are often sharply criticized as being unnatural, immoral, and a threat to the survival of the family.

In spite of these variations, practically all family systems can be classified into two basic forms: the extended family and the nuclear family.

An *extended family* consists of a number of relatives living together, such as parents, children, grandparents, great-grandparents, aunts, uncles, in-laws, and cousins. The extended family is the predominant pattern in preindustrial societies. The members share various agricultural, domestic, and other duties.

A *nuclear family* consists of a married couple and their children living together. The nuclear

Extended families, like this one in Bangladesh, are still the predominant pattern in many developing countries.

family emerged from the extended family. Extended families tend to be more functional in agricultural societies in which many "hands" are needed. The nuclear family is more suited to the demands of complex, industrialized societies because its smaller size and potential geographic mobility make it more adaptable to changing conditions—such as the need to relocate to obtain a better job.

It should be noted that in the United States and a number of other countries a third family form is emerging: the single-parent family. Single-parent families are created in a variety of ways, such as by an unmarried person adopting a child, an unmarried woman giving birth to a child, and a married couple divorcing, with one parent (usually the woman) assuming custody of the children. Single-parent families now constitute more than 20% of all families in the United States.[2]

THE AMERICAN FAMILY: PAST AND PRESENT

The Family in Preindustrial Society

We often view the family as being a stable institution in which few changes occur. Surprisingly, a number of changes have taken place since colonial and frontier days.

Prior to the 1800s, the economy in our country was predominantly agricultural. The majority of people lived on small farms in rural areas. In preindustrial society transportation was arduous and travel was constricted. The family was nearly self-sufficient; most of what it consumed was produced on the farm. The house and the farm were the center of production. The most common family type was the extended family, with each member having specific roles and responsibilities. Because there were many tasks to be performed on small farms, the extended family was functional; it contained a number of family members to carry out those tasks.

Economic considerations influenced family patterns. Marriage was highly valued, as was having many children. A large-sized family was needed to do all the tasks involved in planting and harvesting crops and in raising cattle and other animals. With more children a married couple could cultivate more acreage and thereby become more profitable. Children were thus important economic assets. Parent wanted their sons to marry robust, industrious women who could substantially contribute to the work that needed to be done.[3]

John F. Cuber et al. have noted that preindustrial American society developed a *monolithic code* of cultural beliefs that were accepted by most people during this era.[4] A monolithic code permits only one acceptable pattern of behavior. Components of this code were:

1. Adults were expected to be married. Women were expected to marry in their teens or early twenties. Those who delayed marriage or did not ever marry were referred to as "old maids" and "spinsters."

2. Marriage was considered permanent—for life. Divorce was rare and highly disapproved of.

3. An individual was expected to place the welfare of the family unit ahead of his or her individual preferences. For example, an individual's choice about who she or he wanted to marry was considered less important than the parents' notions about what was best for the family as a unit.

4. Sexual relations were to be restricted to marriage. There was a double standard: Women who had premarital or extramarital affairs were more harshly criticized and stigmatized than men who did so.

5. Married couples were expected to have children. Children were not only considered an economic asset but were also viewed as a religious obligation, based on the biblical ethic "Be fruitful and multiply."

6. Parents were expected to take care of their children, whatever the cost. Children were expected to be obedient to their parents and to honor them. When parents became partially disabled (for example, from old age), children were expected to care for them.

7. The father was the head of the family and made the important decisions. Women and children were expected to be subordinate to him. There were numerous advantages to being male. Women left their parents' home upon marriage and moved into the husband's home (usually near or in his parents' home). Male children were more highly valued than female children, partly because males would remain home after marrying. The woman's place was in the home, and she was expected to do the cooking, washing, cleaning, and a variety of other domestic tasks. Thus, American preindustrial society was clearly patriarchal.

These beliefs were so strongly held by most people that they were considered the morally decent way to live. To violate them was viewed as going against nature and against God's will. (As we'll see, remnants of this code still remain in American society.)

The Family in Industrial Society

The Industrial Revolution, which began roughly 200 years ago, greatly changed family life. Factories and large-scale business organizations replaced small family farms as centers of economic production. Urbanization accompanied industrialization, and most people now live in urban or semiurban areas. Products that were mass produced on assembly lines or produced using complex equipment and technology became much cheaper than those produced on small family farms or in small family shops.

As the family gradually began losing its economic-productive function, other changes followed. Fewer people were needed in families to fill essential economic roles. Smaller-sized families became more functional for industrialized societies because they could more readily relocate to fill employment openings that arose.

Gradually, there was a shift toward individualism. A key component of individualism is the belief that the desires of the individual should take precedence over those of the family. As a result, it became increasingly recognized that the choice of a mate should be based on personal preference, not family need.

Also, with the loss of the economic-productive function, children became economic liabilities; that is, they did nothing to increase family income but still had to be clothed, fed, and sheltered. As a response, parents began having fewer children.

There have been numerous other changes. No longer is the wisdom of the elderly as highly valued, partly because children are now trained and educated in institutionalized settings. In a rapidly changing industrial society the job skills of older workers often become obsolete. As a result, the elderly are less esteemed than they once were.

Gradually, women won the right to vote, and in the past three decades the feminist movement has been calling into question the "double standards" of sexual morality. Women are also seeking egalitarian relationships with men. An increasing number of women are entering the labor force and seeking employment in settings (such as police departments) that were once considered appropriate only for men. Sexuality is more openly discussed today, and there has been an increase in the rate of sexual relations outside of marriage.[5] However, recent concern about AIDS has led many adults to reduce their sexual contacts. (The chances of acquiring AIDS increase with the number of sexual partners that one has.)

Still, remnants of the monolithic code remain. Some people continue to find it objectionable if a married couple divorce or choose not to have children or if a single person becomes pregnant or decides never to marry.

In 1934 sociologist William Ogburn summarized changes in function the American family has undergone as a result of industrialization and technological advances.[6]

1. The economic-productive function has been lost. In most families financial resources are now acquired outside the home.

2. The protective function has been lost. The protective function is now being met by such agencies as police departments, hospitals, insurance companies, and nursing homes.

3. The educational function has been sharply reduced. Schools, day-care centers, and Head Start programs have taken on much of this function.

4. The family is less likely to be the center for religious activity.

5. The recreational function has largely been reduced. Each family member is now more likely to join recreational groups outside the home.

6. The status recognition function has been sharply reduced. Individuals now receive recognition through their own achievements in organizations outside the family, such as at school, at work, and in social and religious groups.

7. The family has retained its affectional function. Members receive social and emotional gratification from the family and also have many of their companionship needs met by the family.

Most authorities agree with Ogburn's assessment that many of the functions of the American family have been lost or sharply reduced. It has been noted, however, that the modern family retains certain functions that Ogburn overlooked. Following are five essential functions that families in modern industrial societies perform to help maintain the continuity and stability of society.[7]

1. REPLACEMENT OF THE POPULATION

Every society must have some system for replacing its members. Because practically all societies consider the family as the unit in which children are to be produced, societies have defined the rights and responsibilities of the reproductive partners within the family unit. These rights and responsibilities help maintain the stability of society, although they are defined differently from one society to another.

2. CARE OF THE YOUNG

Children require care and protection until at least the age of puberty. The family is a primary institution for the rearing of children. Modern societies have generally developed supportive institutions to help in caring for the young—for example, medical services, day-care centers, parent training programs, and residential treatment centers.

3. SOCIALIZATION OF NEW MEMBERS

To become productive members of society, children must be socialized into the culture. Children are expected to acquire a language, to learn social values and mores, and to dress and behave within the norms of society. The family plays a major role in this socialization process. In modern societies a number of other groups and resources are involved in this process. Schools, the mass media, peer groups, the police, movies, books, and other written materials are important influences in the socialization process. (Sometimes these different influences clash by advocating opposing values and attitudes.)

4. REGULATION OF SEXUAL BEHAVIOR

Failure to regulate sexual behavior would result in clashes between individuals due to jealousy and exploitation. Unregulated sexual behavior would probably also result in large numbers of births outside of marriage—children for whom no fathers could be held responsible. Every society has rules that regulate sexual behavior within family units. Most cultures, for example, have incest taboos, and most disapprove of extramarital sex.

5. SOURCE OF AFFECTION

Spitz has demonstrated that humans need affection, emotional support, and positive recognition from others (including approval, smiles, encouragement, and reinforcement for accomplishments).[8] Without such affection and recognition, a person's emotional, intellectual, physical, and social growth would be stunted. The family is an important source for obtaining affection and recognition, because members generally regard one another as among the most important people in their lives and gain emotional and social satisfaction from these relationships. (As noted above, Ogburn identified this function as the primary one remaining in modern families.)

This brief sketch of American family history shows that, although a number of changes have occurred, the family retains several important functions. We will now turn to an examination of problem areas for today's American family: divorce, empty-shell marriages, family violence, and births outside of marriage.

PROBLEMS IN THE FAMILY

Divorce

Our society places a higher value on romantic love than do most other societies. In cultures in which marriages are arranged by parents, love generally has no role in mate selection. In the United States, however, romantic love is a key factor in forming a marriage.

American children are socialized from an early age to believe in the glories of romantic love. "Love conquers all," it is asserted. Magazines, films, TV programs, and books continually portray "happy ending" romantic adventures. All of these breathtaking romantic stories suggest that every normal individual falls in love with that one special person, gets married, and lives happily ever after. This ideal rarely happens.

Nearly one out of every two marriages ends in divorce.[9] This high rate has been gradually increasing; before World War I divorce seldom occurred.

Divorce usually leads to a number of difficulties for those involved. First, those who are divorcing face many emotional concerns, such as a feeling that they have failed, doubt over whether they are able to give and receive love, a sense of loneliness, concern over the stigma attached to

EXHIBIT 5.1

Romantic Love versus Rational Love

Achieving a gratifying, long-lasting love relationship is one of our paramount goals. The experience of feeling "in love" is exciting, adds meaning to living, and gives us a good feeling about ourselves.

Unfortunately, few people are able to maintain a long-term love relationship. Most individuals encounter problems, like falling in love with someone who does not love them, falling out of love with someone after an initial stage of infatuation, being highly possessive of someone they love, or having substantial conflicts with the loved one because of differing sets of expectations about the relationship. Failures in love relationships are more often the rule than the exception.

The emotion of love is often viewed (erroneously) as a feeling over which we have no control. A number of common expressions (erroneously) connote or imply that love is a feeling beyond our control: "I *fell* in love." "It was love at first sight." "I just couldn't help it." "He swept me off my feet." It is more useful to think of the emotion of love as being based primarily on our self-talk (that is, what we tell ourselves) about a person we meet. Romantic love can be diagramed as follows:

Event
Meeting or becoming acquainted with a person
who has *some* of the overt characteristics
you seek in a lover.

↓

Self-talk
"This person is attractive and personable and
has *all* of the qualities I admire in a lover/mate."

↓

Emotion
Intense infatuation; a feeling of being
romantically in love; a feeling of being in ecstasy.

Romantic love is often based on self-talk that stems from intense, unsatisfied desires and frustrations rather than on reason or rational thinking. Unsatisfied desires and frustrations include extreme sexual frustration, intense loneliness, parental and personal problems, and extensive desires for security and protection.

A primary characteristic of romantic love is to idealize the person with whom we are infatuated as being "perfect"; that is, we notice that this person has some overt characteristics we desire in a lover and then conclude that this person has *all* the desired characteristics.

A second characteristic is that romantic love thrives on a certain amount of distance. The more forbidden the love, the stronger it becomes. The more social mores are threatened, the stronger the feeling. (For example, couples who live together and later marry often report that living together was more exciting and romantic.) The greater the effort required to be with each other (for example, traveling long distances), the more intense the romance. The greater the frustration (for example, loneliness or sexual needs), the greater the ecstasy.

The irony of romantic love is that, if an ongoing relationship is achieved, the romance usually withers. Through sustained contact, the person in love gradually comes to realize what the idealized loved one is really like—simply another human being with certain strengths and limitations. When this occurs, the romantic love relationship either turns into a rational love relationship or is found to have significant conflicts and dissatisfactions and then is terminated. For people with intense unmet needs, the latter occurs more frequently.

Romantic love thus tends to be of temporary duration and based on make-believe. A person ex-

(continued)

EXHIBIT 5.1   *(continued)*

periencing romantic love never loves the real person—only an idealized imaginary person.

Rational love, in contrast, can be diagrammed in the following way:

Event

While being aware of and comfortable with your own needs, goals, identity, and desires, you become well acquainted with someone who reflects, to a fair extent, the characteristics you desire in a lover or spouse.

↓

Self-talk

"This person has many of the qualities and attributes I seek in a lover or spouse. I admire this person's strengths, and I am aware and accepting of his (her) shortcomings."

↓

Emotion

Rational love.

The following are ingredients of a rational love relationship: (1) You are clear and comfortable about your desires, identity, and goals in life;
(2) you know the other person well; (3) you have accurately and objectively assessed the loved one's strengths and shortcomings and are generally accepting of the shortcomings; (4) your self-talk about this person is consistent with your short- and long-term goals; (5) your self-talk is realistic and rational so that your feelings are not based on fantasy, excessive need, or pity; (6) you and this person are able to communicate openly and honestly so that problems can be dealt with when they arise and so that the relationship can continue to grow and develop; (7) you and the other are able to give and receive, show kindness and affection, and know and do what pleases the other person.

Because love is based on self-talk that causes feelings, it is we who create love. *Theoretically,* it is possible to love anyone by making changes in our self-talk. On the other hand, if we are in love with someone, we can gauge the quality of the relationship by analyzing our self-talk to determine the nature of our attraction and the extent to which our self-talk is rational and in our best interests.

getting a divorce, worry about the reactions of friends and relatives, concern over whether they are doing the right thing by parting, and fear about whether they will be able to make it on their own. Many people who are considering separation feel trapped because they believe they can neither live with their spouse nor live without their spouse. Dividing up the personal property is another matter that frequently leads to bitter differences of opinions. If there are children, there are concerns about how the divorce will affect them.

There are also other issues that need to be decided. Who will get custody of the children? (Joint custody is now an alternative; with joint custody, each parent has the children for part of the time.) If one parent is awarded custody, controversies are likely to arise over visiting rights and child-support payments. Each spouse often faces the difficulties of finding a new place to live, making new friends, doing things alone in a couple-oriented society, trying to make it on one's own financially, and thinking about the hassles connected with dating.

Going through a divorce is very difficult. People are less likely to perform their jobs well and are more likely to be fired during this time period.[10] Divorced people have a shorter life expectancy.[11] Suicide rates are higher for divorced men than for married men.[12]

Divorce per se is no longer automatically assumed to be a social problem, although some of its consequences still are. On the other hand, there is increasing recognition that in some marriages (in which there is considerable tension, bitterness, and dissatisfaction) divorce is sometimes a solution. It may be a concrete step that some people take to end the unhappiness and to begin a more productive and gratifying life. Also, there is increasing awareness that a divorce may be better for the children because they may no longer be subjected to the tension and unhappiness of a marriage that has gone sour.

Mary Jo Bane has noted that the rising divorce rate may not be as serious a threat to the institutions of marriage and family as some people believe.

> It is distressing in and of itself . . . only if staying together at all costs is considered an indicator of healthy marriages or healthy societies. . . . Some things are fairly clear. The majority of marriages do not end in divorce. The vast majority of divorced people remarry. Only a tiny proportion of people marry more than twice. We are thus a long way from a society in which marriage is rejected or replaced by a series of short-term liaisons. . . . Society may be changing its attitudes toward the permanence of marriage and its notions of the roles of husbands and wives. It may simply be recognizing that there is no particular benefit to requiring permanence in unhappy marriages.[13]

The rising divorce rate does not necessarily mean that more marriages are failing. It may simply mean that more people in unhappy marriages are dissolving them rather than continuing to live unhappily.

REASONS FOR MARITAL HAPPINESS

There are many sources of marital breakdown: alcoholism, economic strife caused by unemployment or other financial problems, incompatibility of interests, infidelity, jealousy, verbal or physical abuse of spouse, and interference in the marriage by relatives and friends.

As noted earlier, many people marry because they believe they are romantically in love. If this romantic love does not grow into rational love, the marriage is likely to fail. Unfortunately, young people in our society are socialized to believe that marriage will bring them continual romance, resolve all their problems, and be sexually exciting, thrilling, and full of adventure. (Most young people need only look at their parents' marriage to realize such romantic ideals are seldom attained.) In actuality, living with someone in a marriage involves carrying out the garbage, washing dishes and clothes, being weary from work, putting up with one's partner's distasteful habits (for example, poor hygiene or belching), changing diapers, and dealing with conflicts over such things as finances and differences in sexual interests. *To make a marriage work, each spouse must put considerable effort into that relationship.*

Another factor that is contributing to an increasing divorce rate is the unwillingness of some men to accept the changing status of women. Many men still prefer a traditional marriage in which the husband is dominant and the wife plays a supportive (subordinate) role as child rearer, housekeeper, and the husband's and family's emotional support. Many women are no longer accepting such a status and are demanding egalitarian marriages in which making major decisions, doing the domestic tasks, raising the children, and bringing home paychecks are shared responsibilities.

Over half of today's adult women are now in the labor force.[14] This increase means that women are no longer as heavily reliant financially on their husbands. Women who are able to support themselves financially are more likely to seek a divorce if their marriages go sour.

Another factor contributing to the increasing divorce rate is the growth of individualism. Individualism involves the belief that people should seek to actualize themselves, to be happy, to develop their interests and capacities to the fullest, and to seek to fulfill their own needs and desires. The interests of the individual take precedence over those of the family. People in our society have increasingly come to accept individualism as a way to go through life. In contrast, people in more traditional societies and in extended families are socialized to put the interests of the group first, with their own individual interests being viewed as less important. With America's growing belief in individualism, people who are unhappily married are much more likely to dissolve the marriage and seek a new life.

Yet another reason for the rise in the divorce rate is the growing acceptance of divorce in our society. With less stigma attached to divorce, more people who are unhappily married are now ending those marriages.

An additional factor in the increasing divorce rate is that modern families no longer have as many functions as did traditional families. Education, food, production, entertainment, and other functions once centered in the family are now largely provided by outside agencies. Kenneth Keniston notes:

> In earlier times, the collapse of a marriage was far more likely to deprive both spouses of a great deal more than the pleasure of each other's company. Since family members performed so many functions for one another, divorce in the past meant a farmer without a wife to churn the cream into butter or care for him when he was sick, and a mother without a husband to plow the fields and bring her the food to feed their children. Today, when emotional satisfaction is the bond that holds marriages together, the waning of love or the emergence of real incompatibilities and conflicts between husband and wife leave fewer reasons for a marriage to continue. Schools and doctors and counselors and social workers provide their supports whether the family is intact or not. One loses less by divorce today than in earlier times, because marriage provides fewer kinds of sustenance and satisfaction[15]

Exhibit 5.2 identifies variables that predict whether a marriage will or will not last.

DIVORCE LAWS

In the past, society attempted to make the breakup of marriages almost impossible. One way it did this was through laws that made a divorce difficult to obtain. After one spouse petitioned the

EXHIBIT 5.2

Facts about Divorce

Age of spouses: Divorce is most likely to occur when the partners are in their twenties.

Length of engagement: Divorce rates are higher for those who had a brief engagement.

Age at marriage: People who marry at a very young age (particularly teenagers) are more likely to divorce.

Length of marriage: Most divorces occur within two years after marriage. There is also an increase in divorce shortly after the children are grown. This may be partly because some couples wait until their children leave the nest before dissolving an unhappy marriage.

Social class: Divorce occurs more frequently at the lower socioeconomic levels.

Education: Divorce rates are higher for those with fewer years of schooling. Interestingly, divorce occurs more frequently when the wife's educational level is higher than the husband's.

Residence: Divorce rates are higher in urban areas than in rural areas.

Second marriages: The more often individuals marry, the more likely they are to get divorced again.

Religion: The more religious individuals are, the less likely they are to divorce. Divorce rates are higher for Protestants than for Catholics or Jews. Divorce rates are also higher for interfaith marriages than for intrafaith marriages.

Sources: William J. Goode, "Family Disorganization," in *Contemporary Social Problems,* 4th ed., eds. Robert K. Merton and Robert Nisbet (New York: Harcourt Brace Jovanovich, 1976), pp. 511–556; Goode, *After Divorce* (New York: Free Press, 1956); Paul C. Glick, *American Families* (New York: Wiley, 1957); J. Richard Udrey, *the Social Context of Marriage,* 2d ed. (Philadelphia: Lippincott, 1971); William Kornblum and Joseph Julian, *Social Problems,* 7th ed. (Englewood Cliffs, NJ: Prentice-Hall, 1992), pp. 346–351.

court for a divorce, there were long waiting periods before that divorce could be obtained. Divorce courts also followed the "adversary" judicial procedures in which the spouse seeking the divorce had to document that the other spouse was guilty of some offense, such as adultery, desertion, or cruel and inhuman treatment. In many cases the actual reasons for the divorce (such as no longer finding the relationship satisfying) bore little relationship to the grounds on which the court allowed that divorce. Often the marital partners contrived a story that fit the legal requirements.

In most divorces, both partners contribute to the marital breakdown. Yet traditional divorce laws erroneously assumed that one partner was the guilty party and the other the innocent party. Traditional divorce laws often intensified the trauma that both partners were undergoing and pitted the partners against each other. Moreover, the process was very expensive.

Because of these difficulties, most states have not passed "no fault" divorce laws, which allow the couple to obtain a divorce fairly rapidly by stating to the court that they both agree their marriage has irreparably broken down. (The adversary process is still available for any spouse who chooses to use it.)

Issues that are still often contested between the two partners in divorce proceedings involve the division of property, alimony (a financial allowance paid to one spouse by the other for support after the divorce), child-support payments, and custody of the children. In the past, courts invariably awarded to the woman the custody of the children, child-support payments, and alimony (particularly if she was not employed). A large percentage of the men failed to make some, or all, of their child-support and alimony payments, which left their former wives in dire financial straits.

Changes in sex roles and the increased employment of women have led to changes in divorce settlements. Most states have enacted legislation allowing courts to require that the woman make alimony payments to her former husband (although few courts have as yet issued such orders). Custody of the children is still generally given to the mother, although this assignment is no longer automatic. An increasing number of fathers are requesting custody of their children and are making it known that they resent the sexist bias of many courts, which assumes that a mother is better qualified to raise children.

A critical point about divorce is that, when it occurs, many of the costs are paid by society. In families of average income or less, the burden of divorce-related poverty falls on society as a whole. Examples of such costs include subsidized housing, public sector make-work jobs, and payments to lawyers who are involved in collecting support for women and children.

The recent willingness of courts to award custody to the father is having a hidden cost to society. Fathers often threaten a protracted custody battle. As a result, mothers who want custody of their children without a fight are routinely forced to "barter" custody in exchange for reduced child-support payments. Because such payments are so low, these women and their children then qualify for welfare. Richard Neely, a state supreme court justice, notes:

> Most of us begin with a political conviction that women ought *to be equal to men economically, and then leap to a conclusion that they* are. It then logically follows that women can support children as well as men and that whoever wants the children can pay for them.
>
> The fact is that women are much poorer than men, and this pattern appears highly resistant to change.[16]

Custody battles between fathers and mothers are becoming common in divorce cases. Typical custody battles may take as long as two years and cost thousands of dollars for attorneys, expert witnesses, and court costs. During this process the parents are likely to use the children as "pawns" against each other. They bribe the children with large allowances, relax discipline, and indulge outrageous whims of their children. They may also try to turn their children against the other parent by "badmouthing" him or her. Custody battles are not only costly but also emotionally damaging to all family members.

In many states now, children over age 14 are allowed to select the parent with whom they wish to live if that parent is "fit." As a way of avoiding custody battles and the situation in which women barter reduced child-support payments for custody, Richard Neely recommends that, for children under 14, custody be awarded to the primary caretaker parent, who is defined as:

> . . . the parent who: (1) prepares the food; (2) changes the diapers, dresses, and bathes the child; (3) takes the child to school, church, and other activities; (4) makes appointments with a doctor and generally watches over the child's health; and (5) interacts with the child's friends, the school authorities, and other adults engaged in activities that involve the child. It is not surprising that the "primary caretaker" is usually the mother, but that need not be the case.[17]

In 90% of divorce cases, the mothers are awarded custody of the children.[18] After the divorce, the mother's standard of living sharply declines, whereas the father's standard of living generally increases because he has fewer financial responsibilities.[19] Women are awarded alimony in only 15% of divorce cases.[20] When there are children, the fathers are usually required to pay child support, but the amounts awarded are generally insufficient to meet the financial needs of the children. In addition, many divorced fathers fail to pay the full amount of child-support payments, and some do not make any court-ordered payments.[21] As a result, the income for the divorced mother and her children often plunges below the poverty level. In many cases taxpayers wind up supporting the mother and her children through the welfare system.[22]

In an effort to combat these problems, the state of Wisconsin enacted legislation in 1987 to withhold child support from the paychecks of all noncustodial parents (generally fathers). This has reduced rates of failure to make payments and has increased the chances that the custodial parents (generally mothers) will have a steady income from child support. Wisconsin courts now use fairly generous guidelines in setting child-support awards. For one child the noncustodial parent is expected to pay 17% of his or her gross income for child support—and this guideline gradually rises (based on the number of children)

to 35% for five or more children. Congress has since mandated that all states legislate such guidelines for child-support awards.[23]

Empty-Shell Marriages

In empty-shell marriages the spouses feel no strong attachments to each other. Outside pressures keep the marriage together, rather than feelings of warmth and attraction between the partners. Such outside pressures may include business reasons (for example, an elected official wanting to convey a stable family image), investment reasons (for example, husband and wife may have a luxurious home and other property that they do not want to lose by parting), and outward appearances (for example, a couple living in a small community may remain together to avoid the reactions of relatives and friends to a divorce). In addition, a couple may believe that ending the marriage would harm the children or would be morally wrong.

John F. Cuber and Peggy B. Harroff have identified three types of empty-shell marriages.[24] In a *devitalized relationship* husband and wife lack excitement or any real interest in each other or their marriage. Boredom and apathy characterize this relationship. Serious arguments are rare.

In a *conflict habituated relationship* husband and wife frequently quarrel in private. They may also quarrel in public, or they may put up a facade of being compatible. The relationship is characterized by considerable conflict, tension, and bitterness.

In a *passive-congenial relationship* both partners are not happy but are content with their lives and generally feel adequate. The partners may have some interests in common, but those interests are generally insignificant. The spouses contribute little to each other's real satisfactions. This type of relationship generally has little overt conflict.

The number of empty-shell marriages is unknown: It may be as high as (or even higher than) the number of happy marriages. The atmosphere in empty-shell marriages is usually joyless. Members do not share and discuss their problems or experiences with each other. Communication is kept to a minimum. There is seldom any spontaneous expression of affection. Children in such families are usually starved for love and reluctant to have friends over to visit because they are embarrassed about how their parent interact.

The couples in these marriages engage in few activities together and display no pleasure in being in each other's company. Sexual relations between the partners, as might be expected, are rare and generally unsatisfying. Outsiders may perceive that the partners (and often the children) appear insensitive, cold, and callous to each other. Yet closer observation will reveal that the spouses are highly aware of each other's weaknesses and sensitive areas, and they manage to mention them frequently in order to hurt each other.

William J. Goode compares empty-shell marriages to marriages that end in divorce:

> Most families that divorce pass through a state—
> sometimes after the divorce—in which husband
> and wife no longer feel bound to each other,
> cease to cooperate or share with each other,
> and look on one another as almost a stranger.
> The "empty shell" family is in such a state. Its
> members no longer feel any strong commitment
> to many of the mutual role obligations, but for
> various reasons the husband and wife do not
> separate or divorce.[25]

It is not known how many empty-shell marriages end in divorce. It is likely that a fair number eventually do. Both spouses must put considerable effort into making a marriage work in order to prevent an empty-shell marriage from gradually developing.

MARRIAGE COUNSELING

The primary social service for people who are considering a divorce or who have an empty-shell marriage is marriage counseling. (Those who do obtain a divorce may also need counseling to work out adjustment problems, such as adjusting to single life. Generally such counseling is one-on-one, but at times it may include the ex-spouse and the children, depending on the nature of the problem.)

Marriage counseling is provided by a variety of professionals, including social workers, psychologists, guidance counselors, psychiatrists, and members of the clergy. It is also provided (to a greater or lesser extent) by most direct social service agencies.

Marriage counselors generally use a problem-solving approach in which (1) problems are first identified, (2) alternative solutions are generated, (3) the merits and shortcomings of the alternatives are examined, (4) the clients select one or more alternatives to implement, and (5) the extent to which the problems are being resolved by the alternatives is later assessed. Because the spouses "own" their problems, they are the primary problem solvers.

A wide range of problems may be encountered by married couples. For example, the couple may experience sexual problems, financial problems, communication problems, problems with relatives, conflicts of interest, infidelity, conflicts on how to discipline and raise children, or drug or alcohol problems. Marriage counselors attempt to have spouses precisely identify their problems and then use the problem-solving format to seek to resolve the issues. In some cases couples may rationally decide that a divorce is in their best interest.

In marriage counseling there is considerable effort by the counselor to see both spouses together during sessions. Practically all marital conflicts involve both partners and therefore are best resolved when both partners work together on resolving them. (If the spouses are seen separately, each spouse is likely to become suspicious of what the other is telling the counselor.) By seeing both together, the counselor can facilitate communication between the partners. (When spouses are seen individually, they are also more likely to exaggerate the extent to which their mate is contributing to the disharmony.) Joint sessions allow each partner the opportunity to refute what the other is saying. Only in rare cases is it desirable to hold an individual session with a spouse. For example, if one of the partners wants to work on unwanted emotions concerning a past incestuous relationship, it may be desirable to meet individually with that spouse. (When an individual session is held, the other spouse should be informed of why it is being held and what will be discussed.)

If some of the areas of conflict involve other family members (such as the children), it may be desirable to include these other members in some of the sessions. For example, if a father is irritated that his 14-year-old daughter is often disrespectful to him, the daughter may be invited to the next session to work on this subproblem.

ADDITIONAL MARRIAGE-RELATED SERVICES
Although marriage counseling and divorce counseling are the primary social services for resolving marital conflicts, some other related services are also available:

Premarital counseling services are designed for couples who are considering marriage. Such services help clients assess whether marriage is in their best interest and also help them to prepare for the realities of marriage. Conflicts that people are having while dating are also worked on, and other topics, such as birth control, are explored.

The self-help organization *Parents without Partners (PWP)* serves divorced people, unwed mothers or fathers, and stepparents. It is partially a social group, but it is also an organization to help members with the adjustment problems of raising a family alone.

A recent development in social services is *divorce mediation*, which helps divorcing spouses to resolve (as amicably as possible) such issues as dividing the personal property, deciding custody and child-support issues, and working out possible alimony arrangements.

Some agencies are now offering *relationship workshops* and *encounter couple groups*, which are designed to help those who are dating or married to improve their relationships through sharing concerns and improving communication patterns.

Violence in Families

We tend to view the family as a social institution in which love and gentleness abound. Sadly, the opposite is often true, with violence being pervasive in American families.

Child abuse, spouse abuse, and other physical violence occur in more than half of all U.S. households.[26] An estimated 50 million people fall victim annually to physical harm at the hands of another family member.[27] Studies show that in 20% of child-abuse cases, a spouse is also abused.[28]

Violence in families is not limited to child abuse and spouse abuse. Statistics from a study funded by the National Institute of Mental Health found that the number of children who assault their parents is greater than the number of children who are abused by their parents.[29] *Parent abuse* is increasingly receiving attention. This term refers to abuse of elderly parents by children with whom they live or on whom they depend. The public is virtually unaware of the battered aged, but it is estimated that there may be a million or more people who are abused by their adult children.[30] Lewis and Joanne Koch provide one case example:

> In Chicago, a 19-year-old woman confessed to torturing her 81-year-old father and chaining him to a toilet for seven days. She also hit him with a hammer when he was asleep: "I worked him over real good with it. Then after I made him weak enough, I chained his legs together. After that I left him and rested. I watched TV for a while."[31]

A Cleveland study found the following four types of elder abuse to be the most prevalent:

■ Physical abuse, which included direct beating and the withholding of personal care, food, medicine, and necessary supervision.

■ Psychological abuse—verbal assaults and threats provoking fear.

■ Material abuse or theft of money or personal property.

■ Violation of rights—forcing a parent out of his or her own dwelling, usually into a nursing home.[32]

Violence between children is also common. Some children even use a weapon (such as a knife or a gun) when having conflicts with their siblings.

Patterns of family violence appear to be learned in families. If a child is abused, that child (when he becomes an adult and a parent) is more likely to abuse his children. Also, if an adult was abused as a child by his parents and then becomes the primary caregiver for those parents, he is more likely to abuse his elderly parents.

The victims of family violence—battered children, battered parents, and battered wives—have common disadvantages. They are generally smaller in size, have less physical strength, and usually feel helpless in relation to the aggressors (primarily because they depend on their aggressors for physical, financial, and emotional support).

Before the 1960s little attention was given to violence in families, partly because the family was viewed as a sacred institution and a private domain: What went on within families was viewed as a personal concern and the responsibility of family members alone—not outsiders. Over the past three decades there has been an increasing awareness that violence in families is a major social problem.

Family fights constitute the largest single category of calls to police, and more police fatalities result from trying to handle these situations than from any other.[33] Suzanne Steinmetz and Murray Straus have noted: "It would be hard to find a group or an institution in American society in which violence is more of an everyday occurrence than it is within the family."[34] Violence not only causes physical harm in families; each incident also weakens the loyalty, affection, and trust among members that are basic to positive family functioning.

One explanation of why family violence occurs is based on the theory that frustration often provokes an aggressive response. A husband or wife who is frustrated at work may come home and take out that frustration on the spouse or the children. A young child frustrated by the action of a sibling may take a poke at him or her. Steinmetz and Straus observe: "In a society such as ours, in which aggression is defined as a normal response to frustration, we can expect that the more frus-

trating the familial and occupational roles, the greater the amount of violence."[35]

In another explanation, John O'Brien has noted that family members often use physical force to gain an advantage.[36] A parent spanks a child for disciplinary reasons. A sister may shove her brother out of the way to attempt to obtain something they both want. O'Brien suggests that family members are likely to resort to physical force when other resources are nonexistent, diminished, or exhausted. Thus an alcoholic husband who feels he has lost the respect of his family may resort to physical abuse as a last-ditch effort to assert his authority.

SPOUSE ABUSE

Spouse abuse, particularly wife beating, was, unfortunately, tolerated for many years but has now become an issue of national concern. The problem leaped into the spotlight in 1994 following the death of Nicole Brown Simpson; Nicole was savagely stabbed to death, and her former husband (O. J. Simpson) was charged with the murder. At least eight times prior to her death, police had been called to the Simpson home after Nicole claimed she was being battered by O. J.[37]

It is not just wives who are abused. Husbands are slapped or shoved with about the same frequency as are wives.[38] The greatest physical damage, however, is usually suffered by women. Studies show that men cause more serious injuries, largely because they are physically stronger.[39] Nearly 11% of all murder victims are killed by their spouses.[40] It should be noted that women also tend to endure cruelty and abuse much longer than men, at times because they feel trapped due to unemployment and financial insecurity. Spouse abuse is sometimes precipitated by the victim; that is, the recipient of the abuse may be the first to use verbal or physical violence in the incident.[41] However, the dominant theme in American spouse abuse is the systematic use of violence and the threat of violence by some men to "keep their wives in line." That is to say, there is a traditional belief held by some segments of our society that husbands have a right to control what their wives do and to force them to be submissive.

About 6000 American women are victims of domestic violence each day,[42] which translates into one incident every 15 seconds.[43] Domestic violence from husbands, male partners, or other family members happens so often that violence is the major cause of injury to women.[44] Injuries from woman battering are more common than those from rape, mugging, or even auto accidents.[45]

Incidents of physical abuse between spouses are not widely isolated but tend to recur frequently in a marriage. Moreover, Murray Straus et al. have noted that spouse abuse occurs as often among the well educated as among the less educated.[46]

In 1979 Straus and his associates conducted a survey for the National Commission on the Causes and prevention of Violence. Interviews were held with over 2000 couples who represented a cross-section of American families.[47] The study concluded that wives use knives and other weapons more often than husbands and are as likely to murder their spouses as husbands are. Disturbingly, the study found that one man in four, and one woman in six, approved of a husband slapping his wife under certain conditions. Most wives who are severely beaten by their husbands do not seek to end the marriage. Wives are more likely to remain in the home if (1) the violence is infrequent, (2) they were abused by their parents when they were children, or (3) they believe they are financially dependent on their husbands.

Many authorities believe spouse abuse is related to a norm of tolerating violence in American families. Straus notes:

There seems to be an implicit, taken-for-granted cultural norm which makes it legitimate for family members to hit each other. In respect to husbands and wives, in effect, this means that the marriage license is also a hitting license.[48]

Several studies have found that a sizable number of both men and women believe it is appropriate for a husband to hit his wife "every now and then."[49]

Men batter women for a variety of reasons. Many have a poor self-image; they are insecure about their worth as breadwinners, fathers, and sexual partners. They tend to have a stereotyped view of their wives as playing a submissive role and as needing to be controlled. Many men use alcohol and other drugs to excess and are much more likely to be violent when intoxicated or high.

In battered-spouse families a cycle of violence tends to be continually repeated, as follows: A battering incident occurs, and the wife sustains injuries. The husband feels remorse, but he also fears his wife may leave or may report the abuse to the police, so he tries to "honeymoon" her into thinking he is a good husband who won't abuse her again. (He may even send flowers, buy expensive gifts, or be overly attentive.) Gradually the "honeymoon" efforts on his part cease, and tensions about work or family matters again begin to build inside him. As the tension builds, a minor incident sets him off, often while he's intoxicated, and he again batters his wife. The battering/honeymoon/tension-building/battering cycle tends to be repeated again and again.

Abusive husbands often isolate their spouses and make them dependent. They try to make their wives sever ties with relatives and friends. They ridicule their wives' friends and relatives, and they usually create an embarrassing scene when the wife is with those friends or relatives. The wife then ends contact with them in order to "keep peace." Abusive husbands make their wives dependent on them by continually ridiculing them, which lowers the women's self-esteem and leads them to play a submissive role. Husbands also create financial dependency, such as by creating barriers that prevent their wives from seeking high-paying employment.

A surprising number of battered women do not permanently leave their husbands. There are a variety of reasons for this. Many are socialized to play a subordinate role to their husbands, and the husbands use violence and psychological abuse to make them feel too inadequate to live on their own. Some women believe it is their moral duty to stick it out to the end—that marriage is forever, for better or for worse. Many hope (in spite of the continuing violence) that their husbands will change. Some fear that, if they try to leave, their husbands will retaliate with even more severe beatings. A fair number do not view leaving as a viable alternative because they feel financially dependent. Many have young children and do not believe they have the resources to raise children on their own. Some believe the occasional beatings are better than the loneliness and insecurity connected with leaving. Some dread the stigma associated with separation or divorce. These women are captives in their own homes.

Fortunately, new services in recent years have been developed for battered women. Shelter homes for battered women and their children have been established in many communities. These shelters give abused women an opportunity to flee from their abusive situation. The women also generally receive counseling, assistance in finding a job, and legal help. In some areas programs are also being established for the husbands. These programs include group therapy for batterers, marriage counseling for both spouses, and 24-hour hotlines that encourage potential spouse abusers to call when they are angry. (Unfortunately, many batterers refuse to participate in such programs.) Many communities also have public information programs (for example, short television announcements) to inform battered women that they have a legal right not to be abused and that there are resources to stop the abuse.

In an effort to treat domestic abuse as seriously as crimes between strangers, Wisconsin and some other states have enacted a domestic abuse law. The law requires police to make an arrest (of either spouse, but usually the husband) if physical abuse has occurred and injury or threat of further harm exists. Police face criminal or civil penalties under the law if they do not make a mandated arrest.[50]

As services for battered wives become more widely available, we may expect an increasing number of these women to flee from their homes and to refuse to return until they have some guarantee of their safety.

CHILD ABUSE AND NEGLECT

Although definitions of child abuse and neglect vary somewhat from state to state, Alfred Ka-

dushin and Judith Martin summarize the kinds of situations as including:

■ Physical abuse.

■ Malnourishment; poor clothing; lack of proper shelter, sleeping arrangements, attendance, or supervision. (Includes "failure to thrive" syndrome, which describes infants who fail to grow and develop at a normal rate.)

■ Denial of essential medical care.

■ Failure to attend school regularly.

■ Exploitation, overwork.

■ Exposure to unwholesome or demoralizing circumstances.

■ Sexual abuse.

■ Somewhat less frequently, the definitions include emotional abuse and neglect involving denial of the normal experiences that permit a child to feel loved, wanted, secure, and worthy.[51]

Physical Abuse. In the past 30 years there has been considerable national concern about the "battered-child syndrome." The Children's Division of the American Humane Society conducted a nationwide survey of newspaper reports on child abuse and concluded:

> The forms or types of abuse inflicted on these children are a negative testimony to the ingenuity and inventiveness of man. By far the greater number of injuries resulted from beatings with various kinds of implements and instruments. The hairbrush was a common implement used to beat children. However, the same purpose was accomplished with deadlier impact by the use of bare fists, straps, electric cords, TV aerials, ropes, rubber hoses, fan belts, sticks, wooden shoes, pool cues, bottles, broom handles, baseball bats, chair legs, and, in one case, a sculling oar. Less imaginative, but equally effective, was plain kicking with street shoes or with heavy work shoes.
>
> Children had their extremities—hands, arms, and feet—burned in open flames as from gas burners or cigarette lighters. Others bore burn

wounds inflicted on their bodies with lighted cigarettes, electric irons, or hot pokers, Still others are scalded by hot liquids thrown over them or from being dipped into containers of hot liquids.

Some children were strangled or suffocated by pillows held over their mouths or plastic bags thrown over their heads. A number were drowned in bathtubs, and one child was buried alive.

To complete the list—children were stabbed, bitten, shot, subjected to electric shock, were thrown violently to the floor or against a wall, were stamped on, and one child had pepper forced down his throat.[52]

The survey went on to report that these abused children incurred various kinds of injuries:

The majority had various shapes, sizes, and forms of bruises and contusions. There was a collection of welts, swollen limbs, split lips, black eyes, and lost teeth. One child lost an eye.

Broken bones were common. Some were simple fractures; others compound. There were many broken arms, broken legs, and fractured ribs. Many children had more than one fracture. One five-month-old child was found to have 30 broken bones in his little body.

The grimmest recital of all is the listing of internal injuries and of head injuries. The head injuries particularly were a sizable group. Both the internal injuries and the head injuries were responsible for a great many of the fatalities. In this group, we find damage to internal organs such as ruptured livers, ruptured spleens, and ruptured lungs. Injuries to the head were concussions or skull fractures, with brain hemorrhage and brain damage a frequent diagnosis.

This is indeed a grim, sad, sordid, and horror-filled recital of what happens to children in communities in almost every state of the Union.[53]

Physical abuse involves beating a child to the point at which some physical damage is done. The line between physical abuse and harsh parental discipline is difficult to define. Silver et al. note:

If a parent punishes a child with a belt, is it after the fourth slash with the belt that parental rights end and child abuse begins; is it after the belt raises a welt over two millimeters that it becomes abuse versus parental rights?[54]

Definitions of abuse vary. Some are narrow in scope, restricting abuse to actual serious injury sustained by the child; broader definitions include intent to harm the child and verbal abuse.

In the late 1960s, in response to a growing national concern about child abuse, all states adopted child-abuse and neglect-reporting laws. Such laws are essentially a case-finding device. They require professionals (such as physicians, social workers, counselors, hospital administrators, school administrators, nurses, and dentists) to report suspected cases of child abuse to certain specified agencies, such as the local police department and the county welfare department.

The true extent of child abuse is unknown. Accurate data are difficult to get, for two reasons: the failure of citizens and professionals to report suspected cases and the reluctance of abused children to talk. Many battered children, believing their punishment is deserved, keep mute when interviewed by those who might help, and they develop negative self-images.

A significant result of child abuse is that violence breeds violence. George C. Curtis reports evidence showing that abused children may "become tomorrow's murderers and perpetrators of other crimes of violence."[55] When they become parents, there is also a high probability they will become abusive parents.[56] Theoretically, abuse generates an unusually high degree of hostility, which, in future years, may well be channeled into violence. A disproportionate number of rapists, murderers, robbers, and spouse abusers were child-abuse victims when they were younger. Abused children are high risks to become runaways, which exposes them to other kinds of victimization and sometimes results in their being involved in criminal activity, such as shoplifting, theft, or prostitution.

Although in rare cases abuse is nonrecurrent, generally it is repeated. Nonrecurrent abuse is usually difficult to document, as the abuser can

A Houston police spokesman displays a photo of a 7-year-old boy who was held as a virtual prisoner in a bathroom for years by his family. He escaped from the home and police arrested his parents. Cases like this create a greater public consciousness of family violence but the true extent of child abuse is unknown.

contrive a plausible explanation for the one-time injuries received by the child.

The National Center of Child Abuse and Neglect compiled data on the parents involved in child abuse[57] and found the following:

■ Abuse was more likely to occur among parents with limited education and employment skills, among nonwhite families, and among mother-headed, single-parent families.

■ In many of the families there was evidence of "family discord" and stress due to limited financial resources. (It is possible that the higher incidence of abuse in the lower classes may partly result from the fact that middle- and upper-class parents are in a better position to conceal the abuse.[58]

■ Most abused children (over two-thirds) are permitted to remain in their homes by protective services even after abuse is determined.[59] (Protective services are described later in this section.)

Physical Neglect. In contrast to child abuse, child neglect is more a problem of omission than of commission. Specific types of physical neglect include (1) child abandonment; (2) environmental neglect—letting a child live in filth, without proper clothing, unattended, unsupervised, and without proper nourishment; (3) educational neglect, in which a child is allowed to be excessively absent from school; and (4) medical neglect, in which no effort is made to secure needed medical care for the child. Although child neglect has received less national attention than child abuse, it

CASE
EXAMPLE 5.1   ## A Case of Physical Abuse and Murder

Chicago—Jody Marie Olcott lived only 102 days. She died on November 16, 1988. The coroner's report showed that she had suffered more injuries than most people who live into late adulthood. Charged with second-degree murder in her death was her father, Malcom Olcott, age 34.

Jody Marie was born on August 5, 1988. Her unmarried parents lived together. Her mother, Judy Forbes, worked as a waitress. Her father was unemployed and felt considerable "pressure" over being unemployed and now having parental responsibilities.

Jody's first two months were quite normal. Her pediatrician saw her early in October and reported that she had gained nearly 2 pounds and appeared in good health. Shortly after that, Jody's nightmare began. The pathologist who examined Jody after her death noted that she suffered from at least five broken ribs, caused about a month earlier by kicking or by punching from a fist.

The pathologist noted that about ten days before her death she had received bruises to her head, chest, and left elbow. Also, at about the same time she had received burn marks on her buttocks and her head. The district attorney acknowledged that Mr. Olcott had admitted (at the time of his arrest) to setting Jody on top of a space heater.

The pathologist's report also noted one of Jody's knees was broken, and the other was badly sprained, "possibly resulting from the child being picked up by her legs and then her legs being snapped." At the time of her death Jody's weight had dropped to 6 pounds—1 pound less than when she was born.

The blow that caused Jody's death occurred during the night of November 15. Ms. Forbes was at her waitressing job at a fast-food restaurant. The district attorney stated that Mr. Olcott was feeling on edge with his financial and family responsibilities. He began drinking. Jody was crying, as she had done for the past several days (probably from the pain from all of her injuries). Mr. Olcott stated he just couldn't take the incessant crying. He grabbed Jody and tossed her about 10 feet—hoping she'd land on the sofa. Jody missed the sofa and landed on her head on a hardwood floor. Mr. Olcott told the police that during the next few hours Jody stopped crying but appeared to have trouble breathing and sometimes vomited. When Ms. Forbes came home that evening, she found that Jody did not appear to be breathing. She called for an ambulance. Jody was pronounced dead on arrival, with the cause of death being a blood clot caused by a skull fracture. Ms. Forbes was asked by the police why she did not report the violence occurring to Jody over the past several weeks. Ms. Forbes stated, "Malcom told me if I went to the police, he would leave me and have nothing more to do with me."

is the most common situation in which protective service agencies must intervene.

In rare cases, such as child abandonment, the parent rejects the parental role. In most child-

neglect cases, however, the parent inadequately performs the role. Kadushin and Martin define a typical neglectful mother as being physically exhausted, mentally impoverished, emotionally deprived, and socially isolated.[60] Parental neglect is more likely to be found among those who are poverty stricken or who live on marginal incomes.

Vincent De Francis provides the following description of what a social worker encountered in investigating a neglect complaint:

> What I saw as I entered the room was utter, stark disorganization. The room was a combined kitchen-dining room. At the other end of the room, two scrawny, owl-eyed, frightened children—a girl of about four and a boy of three—stared silently at me. Except for thin cotton undershirts, they were stark naked. They had sore crusts on their legs and arms. They were indescribably dirty, hair matted, body and hands stained and covered with spilled food particles. Sitting on a urine-soaked and soiled mattress in a baby carriage behind them was a younger child—a boy about two.
>
> The floor was ankle-deep in torn newspapers. There were feces in about a half-dozen spots on the floor, and the air was fetid and saturated with urine odor.
>
> There were flies everywhere. What seemed like giant roaches were crawling over the paper-strewn floor. The kitchen sink and gas stove were piled high with greasy and unwashed dishes, pots, and pans.[61]

Emotional Neglect. Meeting a child's affectional needs is as important to normal growth and development as meeting his or her physical needs. Yet emotional neglect is difficult to define and document in the precise terms required by law.

The National Clearinghouse on Child Neglect and Abuse defines emotional neglect as:

> . . . failure to provide the child the emotional nurturing or emotional support necessary for the development of a sound personality, as for example, subjecting the child to rejection or to a home climate charged with tension, hostility, and anxiety-producing occurrences which result in perceivable problems in children.[62]

Interpreted broadly, the problem with this definition is that practically every parent at times is guilty of such neglect. Other definitions of emotional neglect encounter the same problem.

Nevertheless, there is solid agreement that some children do suffer from emotional neglect—even when they are adequately cared for physically.

Emotional neglect is very difficult to document in court. When emotional neglect is accompanied by physical neglect, protective service agencies make a case based on the physical neglect.

Sexual Abuse. Sexual abuse within families has in recent years become an issue of national concern. It is discussed at length in Chapter 6.

Unwholesome or Demoralizing Conditions. Children who are exposed to their parents' continued prostitution, criminal activity, drug addiction, and severe alcoholism are also considered in need of protective services. Such exposure is deemed injurious to the moral development of children.

Exploitation. This category involves forcing a child to work for unreasonably long hours or encouraging a child to beg, steal, or engage in prostitution.

Abusive and Neglectful Parents. No single cause can fully explain why parents abuse or neglect their children. Available research indicates that abusive and neglectful parents may have little in common. The following factors[63] have been found to be associated with parents who abuse their children:

■ Some abusive parents were themselves abused as children. If not abused, they generally had a lack of stable love relationships in their childhood and an inadequate gratification of early emotional needs.

■ Although abuse, like neglect, is more heavily concentrated among the lower classes, it is more randomly distributed through the population than is neglect.

■ Frequently, one child in a family is singled out to be the target of the abuse. Many reasons appear to account for this. The child may be viewed as mentally slow or as a potential delinquent. Where there is marital conflict, one child may be chosen as the victim because of a resemblance to the disliked spouse. One

CASE EXAMPLE 5.2　Is This Emotional Neglect?

The following case example raises a number of as-yet-unanswered questions surrounding emotional neglect.

Gary, age 9, was the only child of Mr. and Mrs. Jim N. The N. family lived in a suburb of a metropolitan area, and Gary's physical needs were adequately met. Yet Gary was not doing well in school. He repeated the first grade and now is repeating the third grade.

Gary was referred for psychological testing and was found to have a very low self-concept. His self-concept was so negative that he refused to study math for fear of failing and would not participate in any competitive games with peers. He instead preferred to play by himself, with toys appropriate to children of an age level of 5.

A home study found that Mr. N. was a stoic, unaffectional person who was seldom at home, as he spent long hours operating a service station he owned. Mrs. N. had such a distasteful personality and disposition that she was unable to hold a job and had no close friends. Below average in intellectual functioning, she completed only the ninth grade. In her interactions with Gary she was observed to have a short tolerance level, would frequently berate and criticize him, and called him "stupid" and "an idiot." Gary appeared somewhat fearful of her and tried to avoid interacting with her. Both parents refused to take parent effectiveness training or to receive counseling.

■ Are Gary's personal problems (negative self-image) a result of interactions with his parents or of some other factors (for example, school environment, a past traumatic experience, or an inherited disposition)?

■ Even if it is assumed that his problems are due to his parental interactions, how can this be proved in court?

■ Would his personal problems be reduced or intensified if he were removed from his home and placed in foster care? For example, would moving him to a foster home lead him to feel rejected by his parents or to blame himself for the move because he erroneously assumed he was "bad"?

---

child may cry more, be more hyperactive, or be more demanding of parental care. The child may be punished because he or she was conceived prior to marriage, is illegitimate, or is the result of an unwanted pregnancy.

■ In some cases the abused child contributes to the process by placing greater-than-normal burdens on parental patience: by having severe temper tantrums; by having feeding, speech, or toilet-training problems; and/or by being restless, negative, unresponsive, listless, whiny, or fussy.

■ The child who is the victim may, in disturbed families, be essential for the psychic stability of the family. It appears that some disturbed families need a "whipping boy" or "scapegoat" to maintain an equilibrium within the family. Sometimes when an abused child is removed, another is selected to be the victim and thereby fulfills the "stability" role.

■ Abusive parents often show an absence of guilt, have a tendency toward social isolation, have a high level of overall aggressiveness, are prone to impulsivity, tend to have emotional problems, have feelings of inadequacy, and have a low tolerance of criticism.

■ Environmental stress factors (for example, marital problems), economic pressures, and social isolation sometimes help trigger abuse.

■ Abusive parents tend to believe in strict discipline and to view misbehavior by their children as willful, deliberate disobedience. Also, they are characterized by a high demand for the child to perform to gratify the parent.

■ Alcohol/drug abuse plays an important contributing role in some cases.

The following factors[64] have been identified as being associated with child neglect:

■ The preponderance of families come from the lower socioeconomic classes. Financial deprivation is a major contributing factor. Many also have inadequate housing.

■ A high percentage (60% in some studies) are one-parent families, generally headed by a female.

■ Neglectful parents frequently have an atypically large number of children.

■ A fair number of neglectful mothers are below normal in intellectual capacity.

■ Neglectful parents (particularly the mothers who have the most contact with children) are physically and emotionally exhausted, have health problems, are socially withdrawn or isolated, are frustrated, are apathetic, and lack hope. Such factors lead them to be "indifferent" toward their children.

■ Neglectful parents tend to have had emotionally deprived early childhood experiences. Similar to abusive parents, they lacked stable affectional relationships when they were young. Such early childhood experiences appear to lead to later emotional inadequacies and then, when combined with severe financial and environmental stress, result in physical and emotional exhaustion.

■ Neglectful parents are not without intrapsychic distress but are generally less emotionally disturbed than abusive parents. Similar to abusive parents, they tend to be socially isolated.

PROTECTIVE SERVICES

Under the concept of *parens patriae,* the state is ultimately a parent to all children. When the natural parents neglect, abuse, or exploit a child, the state has the legal right and responsibility to intervene. Protective services has been defined as "a specialized casework service to neglected, abused, exploited, or rejected children. The focus of the service is preventive and nonpunitive and is geared toward rehabilitation through identification and treatment of the motivating factors which underlie" the problem.[65]

Brief History. In colonial days a child was regarded as chattel (an item of personal property). This gave parents the right to sell the child, exploit his or her labor, offer the child as a sacrifice, or even kill the child at birth. Although most communities regulated and restricted such behaviors, it was not until the era of industrialization that children were considered to have any rights. These rights have gradually been expanded. In the early 20th century, child labor laws were finally enacted, prohibiting parents from exploiting the labor of their children.

Agencies providing protective services in America trace their origin to the case of Mary Ellen in 1875.[66] Mary Ellen was severely beaten and neglected by a couple who had raised her since infancy. Concerned community citizens were unaware of any legal approach to protect her. In desperation, they appealed to the Society for the Prevention of Cruelty to Animals. (It's interesting to note that at this time organizations existed to protect animals, but not children.) Mary Ellen was brought to the court's attention by this society. She was given protection by the court and was placed with another family. The abusive couple were sentenced to prison. Following this dramatic case, the Society for the Prevention of Cruelty to Children was formed in New York. Gradually, other such societies throughout the United States were formed, laws protecting children from abuse and neglect were enacted, and agencies providing protective services were established.

Almost from the start, protective services had two focuses: a law enforcement approach and a rehabilitative approach. The law enforcement focus emphasized punishment for the abusive or neglectful parents, whereas the rehabilitative approach emphasized the importance of helping the parents and keeping the family together rather than disrupting it. Throughout this century, protective services have generally taken the rehabilitative approach.

Since the late 1960s there has been a dramatic growth of interest in services to prevent and treat child abuse. With this interest came, in 1975, passage of Title XX to the Social Security Act, making protective services mandatory for each state and providing federal reimbursement for most costs. A federal Child Abuse Prevention and Treatment Act, passed in January 1974, provides direct assistance to states to help them develop child-abuse and -neglect programs.

Processes in Protective Services. Extensive efforts have been made to encourage parents who have mistreated their children (or feel they may mistreat them) to request agency services voluntarily. Radio and TV announcements, along with posters, announce the availability of stress hotline services that parents may call in many communities.

Parents who mistreat their children, however, do not generally seek help. Currently, initiation of services most often results from the legal requirement of mandatory reporting by professionals of suspected abuse, physical neglect, sexual abuse, and emotional injury. The list of professionals required to report includes, among others, social workers, school personnel, doctors, day-care workers, counselors, legal personnel, nurses, and dentists. The agencies to which reports are made include the local police department, the county welfare department, and the county sheriff. The law grants civil and criminal immunity to the professionals required to make such reports and also specifies penalties for failure to report.

Each state has the legal right and responsibility to intervene when a child is being abused, neglected, or exploited. This right and responsibility are delegated to protective services (in many states protective services are located within public welfare departments).

Case finding is almost always through a complaint referral. Complaints generally are filed by neighbors, relatives, or family friends—in addition to those professionals already mentioned who are required by law to report abuse. A complaint is a report of a possible neglect or abuse situation that needs exploration. The complainant may remain anonymous. Occasionally, unfounded complaints are made to harass a parent.

Some complainants feel guilty about having made a report, and they are given reassurance that they are performing a very useful function that is necessary to protect and safeguard children. They are also informed that their identity (name) will not be revealed to the family against which the report has been made.

All complaints are then investigated by the protective service agency. Some agencies arrange for the initial visit by telephone. Others prefer an unannounced visit. This approach has the advantage of allowing the social worker to view the home environment in its day-to-day appearance. The initial approach is direct and frank. The social worker conveys that a concern about potential danger to a child has been expressed and needs to be explored; if a potential danger does exist, the worker's responsibility and interest are to be helpful to both the parents and their children.

The social worker attempts to obtain an objective and accurate description of the situation. Specific information relevant to the complaint is sought. For example, if the complaint is that a child appears malnourished and is frequently absent from school, specific questions are asked about the daily diet of the child, any illnesses he or she has had, and the specific dates and reasons why the child has been absent from school. Such details are necessary to determine whether the child is in fact in danger and what help (if any) is needed. The information is also essential as evidence if a petition is made to the court to remove the child from the home. Obtaining this information must be done tactfully because it is also important that the social worker try to develop a working relationship with the parents.

During this evaluation process the social worker almost always attempts to see the child who allegedly has been endangered. If abuse or neglect exists, the objective is to convey to the parents that the focus of protective services is to prevent further neglect or abuse and to alleviate the factors that are now a danger to the child. Because many families charged with abuse or neglect have multiple problems, services may be far ranging (involving, for example, services related to health, education, finances, housing, counseling, employment, parent effectiveness training, day care, and so on).

When there is no evidence of neglect or abuse, the case may be closed after the initial interview. For families with serious problems, continued services may be provided for years.

If the child is clearly in danger (for example, is a victim of repeated severe abuse) or if the parents are unable or unwilling to make changes essential for the long-term well-being of the child, the youngster may have to be removed from the home. Protective service agencies view court action as "a means of protecting the child rather than prosecuting the parents."[67]

If the social worker decides it is necessary to remove the child from the home, the parents' voluntary consent is first sought. If it is not received, a petition is made to the court requesting that the child receive protection. (Court action is atypical in protective services; studies suggest that roughly 80% of cases are closed without it.)[68]

After a petition is filed, a preliminary hearing is held within a few weeks. Parents are permitted to be represented by an attorney, and the normal adversarial court procedures are followed. The social worker must support the petition with documented facts. The judge has the responsibility of protecting the rights not only of the child but also of the parents. At the preliminary hearing the parents are asked if they will consent to or contest the petition. If they decide to contest and if evidence of abuse and neglect is substantiated, a trial is held.

In making a disposition, a number of avenues are open to the judge. She or he may decide that there is not sufficient evidence of neglect or abuse to warrant any action. Or, the judge can place the child under supervision of the court while permitting him or her to remain at home. Such supervision puts pressure on the family to make needed changes, with the threat of the child being removed if the changes are not made. The judge also has the option of placing the child under protective legal custody. Under this arrangement, legal custody is assigned to a social agency, which then has the authority to remove the child if essential changes are not made. The judge can also terminate the parents' legal rights and place the child under guardianship of the agency. Under this disposition, the child is automatically removed from the home.

For children who are in imminent danger, many jurisdictions have provisions that allow either the protective service agency or the family court to remove the child immediately. Such children are then usually placed in a temporary foster home. When a child is removed for emergency reasons, a court hearing must be held within 24 hours to determine the appropriateness of the action. Unless the court is satisfied that protection of the child requires removal from the home, the child must be returned to his or her parents.

Involuntary Services. Protective services cannot withdraw from the situation if it finds that the parents are uncooperative or resistant. For most social services, clients are voluntary recipients. Protective services is one of the few services in which participation is involuntary (probation and parole are other examples).

Because protective services are involuntary, and because provision of services is based on an "outside" complaint, the recipients are likely to view the services as an invasion of privacy. The initial contact by the social worker may arouse hostility, be viewed as a threat to the family autonomy, and perhaps raise some guilt about incidents in which the parents have mistreated their children in the past. Having one's functioning as a parent questioned and explored arouses substantial emotional feelings. Although the focus of protective service theoretically is rehabilitative and nonpunitive, Edith Varon found in a study that former protective-service clients generally viewed the service as punitive and investigatory.[69]

Some recipients of protective services remain hostile and resistant throughout the time during which services are provided. Others, in time, form a productive, working relationship with the agency, in which case positive changes are much more likely to occur. A few individuals are cooperative from the beginning, perhaps because they recognize that their family needs help.

In working with parents who neglect or abuse their children, the social worker must show respect for the parents as people while in no way conveying acceptance of their mistreatment. The worker needs to convey empathy with their situation, be warm, and yet be firm about the need for positive changes. This approach is illustrated in the following interview:

The C. family was referred to the child welfare agency by a hospital which treated the 6-year-old boy, Wade, for a broken arm suffered in a beating by his mother.

Both parents said they whipped the children because they believed in firm discipline, and they challenged the worker's right to question this. Mr. C. again attempted to avoid the subject of Wade's beating by describing at length how strict his parents had been with him.

Again the worker brought the conversation back to the C.'s own disciplinary practices by saying that children had to be dealt with firmly, but the injury of a child was a serious matter. He added, "I can understand that one may be so upset he has trouble controlling himself." Mrs. C. hesitatingly said, "I was so upset and too angry," and broke into tears. The worker replied that, if together they could try to understand why Mrs. C. gets so upset, perhaps the behavior would not continue. Mr. C., who had been silent for a while, said he realized it was serious and that he did not approve of Mrs. C. beating the children but did not know what to do. He had told her that this was bad for the youngsters, but she continued. Mrs. C. remarked that looking back on Wade's beating was a terrible experience. She did not realize she had injured him until

his arm became swollen. She supposed it was her anger and her temper that did it. She would like to talk to someone and she does need help.[70]

The protective service worker must be ready to perform a variety of roles: teacher, enabler, adviser, coordinator of treatment, intervener, supporter, confidante, and expediter. The focus must be on constantly identifying concrete needs, selecting intervention approaches, and providing specific services. Workers must also be ready to collaborate with other professional groups: the doctors treating the child, schoolteachers, lawyers, and judges.

A wide variety of treatment resources are used in attempting to make the needed changes. Crisis nurseries, extended day-care centers, and emergency foster homes provide short-term shelter to relieve a potentially damaging crisis situation. Parent effectiveness training programs, group therapy, and family life education programs sometimes are useful in curbing the abuse or neglect. Homemakers relieve the frustrated, overburdened mother of some of the daily load of child care. Emergency relief funds are sometimes provided to meet immediate rent, heat, food, and electricity expenses. Behavior modification programs, such as modeling and role playing, have been used to change the behaviors of parents toward their children. "Emergency parents" have been used in some communities to go into a home and stay with a child who has been left unsupervised and unprotected. Psychotherapy and counseling have also been provided by protective service workers and other professionals. A self-help group, Parents Anonymous, is described in Exhibit 5.3. (It should be noted that very few communities have the resources to provide all of these services. In many cities the primary intervention resources available to protective service workers are their own counseling capacities and their ability to remove from the home children who are in danger.)

Kadushin and Martin have reviewed studies on the effectiveness of protective services and conclude:

In summary, the evaluation studies suggest that the agencies have achieved some modest

EXHIBIT 5.3

Parents Anonymous (PA)

Self-help organizations (such as Alcoholics Anonymous, Parents and Friends of Lesbians and Gays, Overeaters Anonymous, and Weight Watchers) have had considerable rehabilitative success. One such group, Parents Anonymous (PA), has been particularly effective at helping individuals who have abused or neglected their children.

PA was originally established in 1970 in California by Jolly K., who was desperate to find help to meet her needs. For four years she had struggled with an uncontrollable urge to punish her daughter severely. One afternoon she attempted to strangle the child. She sought help from the local child-guidance clinic and was placed in therapy. When asked by her therapist what she could do about this situation, she formed an idea: "If alcoholics can stop drinking by getting together, and gamblers can stop gambling, maybe the same principle would work for abusers, too."[a] With her therapist's encouragement, she formed Mothers Anonymous in 1970 and started a few local chapters in California. Now the organization has chapters in most areas of the United States and Canada, and the name has been changed to Parents Anonymous, because fathers who abuse their children are also eligible to join.

PA uses some of the basic therapeutic concepts of Alcoholics Anonymous. It is a crisis intervention program that offers two main forms of help:

1. Regular group meetings in which members share experiences and feelings and learn to control their emotions better.

2. Personal and telephone contact among members during periods of crisis, particularly when a member feels a nearly uncontrollable desire to take his or her anger or frustration out on a child.

Parents may be referred to PA by a social agency (including protective services) or may be self-referrals who are aware they need help.

Cassie Starkweather and S. Michael Turner describe why some parents who abuse their children would rather participate in a self-help group than receive professional counseling:

It has been our experience that most (abusive) parents judge themselves more harshly than other more objective people tend to judge them. The fear of losing their children frequently diminishes with reassurance from other members that they are not the monsters they think they are.

Generally speaking, PA members are so afraid they are going to be judged by others as harshly as they judge themselves that they are afraid to go out [to] seek help. Frequently, our members express fears of dealing with a professional person, seeing differences in education, sex, or social status as basic differences that would prevent easy communication or mutual understanding.

Members express feelings of gratification at finding that other parents are "in the same boat." They contrast this with their feelings about professionals who, they often assume, have not taken out the time from their training and current job responsibilities to raise families of their own.[b]

PA emphasizes honesty and directness. In the outside world, parents who are prone to abuse their children learn to hide this problem, because society finds it so detestable. In contrast, the goal in PA is to help parents admit and accept the fact that they are abusive. The term *abuse* is used liberally at meetings. PA has found that this insistence on frankness has a healthy effect. Parents are relieved because finally they have found a group of people who are able to accept abusive parents for what they really are. Furthermore, it is

(continued)

EXHIBIT 5.3   *(continued)*

only after they are able to admit they are abusive that they can begin to find ways to cope with this problem.

During PA meetings, parents are expected to say why they believe they are beating their child, and the members challenge one another to find ways to curb the abuse. Members also share constructive approaches that have been successful for them, and efforts are made to help one another develop specific plans for dealing with potentially abusive episodes. Members learn to recognize danger signs and then to take the necessary action to avoid committing abuse.

PA stresses protecting people's anonymity and confidentiality. This protection permits group members to discuss their experiences and asocial thoughts without risk of public disclosure. The fact that they are sharing their experiences with other parents who have abused children assures

their being able to "confess" without danger of humiliation, recrimination, or rejection.

Group members develop a sense of "oneness," and often the group becomes a surrogate family. Each member is given the phone numbers of all others in the group and is urged to reach for the phone instead of the child when feeling distressed. Members are gradually transformed into "lay professionals" who are able to help other abusers and who perceive themselves as skillful at this because they have, at one time, been child abusers.

The group leader or chapter chairperson is always a parent who at one time abused a child. Members can identify more readily with an abuser than they can with a professional therapist. Among the reasons PA is successful is that it diminishes the social isolation of abusive parents and provides them with social supports.

[a]Phyllis Zauner, "Mothers Anonymous: The Last Resort," in Jerome E. Leavitt, *The Battered Child* (Morristown, NJ: General Learning Press, 1974), p. 247.
[b]Cassie L. Starkweather and S. Michael Turner, "Parents Anonymous: Reflections on the Development of a Self-Help Group," in *Child Abuse: Intervention and Treatment*, eds. Nancy C. Ebeling and Deborah A. Hill (Acton, MA: Publishing Sciences Group, 1975), p.151.

measure of success. The amount of change one might reasonably expect the agencies to effect must be assessed against the great social and personal deprivation characteristic of the client families. Even the modest success achieved may have been more than could have been expected initially.

The resources available to treat these families are limited. The technology available to the worker in trying to effect change in such families is blunt and imprecise. . . .

Scarce resources backed by a weak technology applied to a group of involuntary, disturbed clients resistive to change and living in seriously deprived circumstances would seem to guarantee the likelihood of limited success.[71]

Social workers have found protective services to be demanding. "Burnout" occurs at a higher

rate among protective service workers than in many other social welfare areas.

Rights of Children versus Rights of Parents. Earlier in American history the law guarded the rights of parents but gave little attention to the rights of children. In recent years, defining and protecting the rights of children have received national attention, as indicated by a variety of child advocacy efforts and the specification of various "bill of rights for children" proclamations. Protective services, particularly in contested court cases, encounter the problem of defining the respective rights of parents and children. Henry Maas and Richard Engler found that the balance of rights between parents and children varies from community to community.[72]

Some of the situations in which this balance

becomes an issue are the following. If parents, for religious reasons, are opposed to their child's receiving medication for a serious health problem, should the state intervene? Should the state intervene when an unmarried parent is sexually promiscuous yet is meeting his or her children's basic physical and emotional needs? Should the state intervene when a child is being raised in a homosexual environment or in a commune where lifestyles and mores are substantially different? Should the state intervene in families in which a child has serious emotional problems and the parents refuse to seek professional help? Should the state intervene in certain ethnic or minority settings when educational needs are not being met? Should intervention occur when a father uses harsh discipline by whipping a child two or three times a week? Should the state intervene in families in which there is long-term alcoholism and serious marital discord? Should the state intervene when a child is living in filth, has ragged clothing, and seldom bathes, even though his or her emotional and social needs are being met?

Different workers, different judges, and different communities would probably disagree on what should be done. The reluctance to intervene may have tragic consequences, as indicated in the following case:

> In 1953, a boy of 13 was referred to a children's court because of chronic truancy. A psychiatric examination established the fact that the boy was "drawn to violence" and represented "a serious danger to himself and to others." Psychiatric treatment was recommended by the psychiatrist and social workers concerned with the boy's situation. The mother refused to accept the recommendation and refused to bring the boy back for treatment. Should the mother have been forced to accept treatment for the boy? This is a question of limits of protection intervention. Nothing was done. Ten years later the boy, Lee Harvey Oswald, assassinated President Kennedy.[73]

Births outside of Marriage

Women between the ages of 15 and 24 constitute about 40% of the total population of women of child-bearing age—yet they account for roughly 70% of births outside of marriage.[74] More than a million teenage women become pregnant each year. Most of these pregnancies are unplanned and unwanted and result from misinformation or lack of access to birth control. Roughly 60% of these teenagers have babies, with the remainder ending the pregnancy through abortion or miscarriage.[75] Two of every five American women giving birth to their first child were not married when they became pregnant.[76] Four out of five teenage marriages end in divorce; many of these marriages were preceded by a pregnancy.[77] For those who are unmarried when the child is born, over 90% decide to keep the baby rather than give it up for adoption.[78]

Almost 60% of African American babies are born to single women, compared to about 28% for Hispanics and 13% for whites.[79] Coleman and Cressey give the following reasons for the high birthrate among single African American women:

> Although the causes are not entirely clear, several factors stand out. First and foremost, blacks are much more likely to be poor than whites, and the illegitimacy rate is much higher among poor people from all ethnic groups. Second, the prejudice and discrimination that have been aimed at blacks for so many years have hit particularly hard at black males from poor homes. The extremely high rate of unemployment among this group makes it much harder to live up to the expectations of fatherhood, and fathers who feel inadequate to meet the needs of their families are far more likely to withdraw and leave their support to the welfare department. Third, the pattern of early pregnancy and single-parent homes has been passed down from one generation to the next in the black underclass.[80]

The higher birthrates among single nonwhite women do not necessarily mean that unmarried nonwhites are more likely to be promiscuous. It may simply mean that nonwhites have less access to contraceptives, or they may be less likely to seek an abortion, or they may be less likely to marry the father before the birth of the child.

By age 20, nearly 40% of white women and 63% of African American women become pregnant.[81] In the late 1950s only about 5% of all births were to unmarried mothers; by 1993 about 25% were.[82] Although teenage women represent roughly 25% of the population of child-bearing age, they account for over 45% of all births outside of marriage.[83] These statistics emphasize that birth outside of marriage is a problem that is disproportionately faced by adolescents. Teenagers who marry when pregnant are nearly as likely to be single parents sometime in the future (due to divorce) as are those who are unmarried at the time of birth.

Many adolescents are not adequately informed about the reproductive process and tend not to use contraceptives. Some teenage women think that, if they take a birth control pill once a week, they're OK; some believe it's safe to have sex standing up; some are afraid birth control will harm them or their future babies.[84]

Many unmarried mothers are simply not prepared, by education, work experience, or maturity, to undertake the dual responsibility of parenthood and economic support. As a result, society inevitably must contribute to the support of these children through public assistance payments and social welfare services.

Fifty years ago both premarital intercourse and births outside of marriage were considered immoral in our society. (In fact, children born outside of marriage were labeled "illegitimate" and were usually stigmatized as much as the mother. The terms *illegitimate* and *illegitimacy* persist today, even though they stigmatize innocent people.) In the 1940s, Alfred Kinsey found, however, that high percentages of the population had experienced premarital intercourse.[85] Since the Kinsey studies, attitudes toward premarital intercourse have become more tolerant; today, few people are virgins when they marry.

Attitudes toward birth outside of marriage have also become somewhat more tolerant. Few parents now send their pregnant daughter off to a maternity home to avoid "disgracing" the family. However, we sometimes see the unusual situation in which parents tolerate premarital intercourse yet, if their daughter becomes pregnant, they are highly disapproving.

Why are births outside of marriage seen as a social problem by most Americans? There are many answers to this question. Some parents still feel "disgraced" if their daughter becomes pregnant. Some single pregnant women (and their parents) view it as a problem because difficult decisions need to be made about whether to end the pregnancy. If it is decided not to have an abortion, decisions need to be made about adoption, continued education or employment, a possible marriage, living arrangements, and perhaps welfare assistance. The father of the child must make decisions about his role and the extent to which he will seek to provide emotional and financial support.

Some people see birth outside of marriage as a social problem—a sign of a breakdown in the traditional family and a symptom of moral decay. Others assert that it is a problem mainly because the great majority of these children are born to women who are simply not yet prepared—by experience, education, or maturity—to be a parent or to provide for a family financially. Authorities who view birth outside of marriage as a problem for this reason are concerned about the effects on the child of being raised by a mother who is in many ways merely an older child herself. They are also concerned about the effects on the mother of trying to maintain a one-parent family with limited financial and personal resources. Finally, some authorities view birth outside of marriage as a problem because of the high cost to society of having to make welfare payments to large numbers of single-parent families (generally through the Aid to Families with Dependent Children program, which is described in Chapter 3).

Is the social stigma attached to birth outside of marriage functional? Certainly it is not to either the child or the mother. On the other hand, some authorities have argued that the stigma is functional to society because it discourages out-of-wedlock pregnancies and thereby helps perpetuate the nuclear family, which provides a structure for the financial support and socialization of children. In response to this view, it can be argued that this punitive approach may not be the optimal way to reduce the incidence of births outside of marriage. Ursula Myers asserts that a more effective approach would involve quality educational programs about responsible sexuality.

Components of sex education programs for teenagers would include:

1. Basic biological information about reproduction, pregnancy, birth control, venereal disease, childbirth, abortion, and the medical risks of premature pregnancy and parenthood.

2. An examination of some of the consequences of single parenthood, such as economic dependency, turmoil with parents, interruption and/or dropping out of educational programs, inadequate housing, and difficulties in meeting the role requirements of being both a mother and a teenager.

3. Information on alternatives to sexual intercourse—for example, petting.

4. Parenting skills training—that is, training on how to raise a child.

5. Family living training, role expectations of children and of husband and wife, conflict resolution, decision making, financial counseling, and dating and marriage responsibilities.[86]

Even with over one million teenagers becoming pregnant each year, the question of whether to provide sex education is still a controversial issue in many school systems. Apparently, many people believe sex education will lead to promiscuity and to teenage pregnancies. Advocates of sex education argue that such programs reduce the number of teenage pregnancies.

Health clinics located in or near high schools appear to be particularly effective in reducing the number of teenage pregnancies. Such clinics provide birth control information and also prescribe contraceptives for sexually active people. In Baltimore, pregnancy rates dropped 30% in three years at two schools served by health clinics, whereas pregnancy rates in similar schools in Baltimore not served by health clinics shot up 58%.[87] Critics of this approach assert that making birth control information and contraceptives more readily available will simply increase sexual activity. The response of the health clinics to this criticism is that learning accurate information about human reproduction in an educational setting is more desirable than the alternative: receiving largely inaccurate information from peers on the street.

In recent years the peril of AIDS has given sex education in schools a major boost. The best way of stopping the transmission of AIDS is through quality sex education programs that provide accurate information on safe sex practices.[88]

SINGLE-PARENT SERVICES

Services to single women who become pregnant have become known as single-parent services. A high proportion of pregnant single women decide to carry the baby to full term and then keep the child. The scope of single-parent services extends from predelivery to postdelivery. Single-parent services are provided by certain public agencies (generally the public welfare department) and by private agencies (such as Catholic Social Services and Lutheran Social Services).

Typical single-parent services include the following:

■ *Alternatives counseling:* The pregnant single woman is helped to make decisions about carrying the baby to full term, having an abortion, keeping the child, terminating parental rights, deciding on foster placement, and undergoing adoption counseling. (Workers in single-parent services generally refrain from revealing their own values about abortion and the other alternatives to the clients because clients have the legal right to make their own decisions in these matters.)

■ *Physical and mental childbirth preparation:* Clients are informed about the effects of drug and alcohol abuse on the embryo. They are prepared for childbirth, given pre- and postnatal counseling, and provided with information on the effects of venereal diseases. Clients also receive mental and physical health counseling.

■ *Counseling on legal issues:* Areas covered include paternity action, procedures for termination of parental rights, legitimation and/or adoption procedures, rights to attend school, and procedures involved in receiving public assistance.

High schools in several U.S. cities are now freely distributing condoms to teenagers. This program has two objectives: to reduce teen pregnancy and to curb the spread of HIV.

■ *Counseling on interpersonal relationships:* Such counseling focuses on the client's relationships with the alleged father, parents and other relatives, and significant others.

■ *Alternative living arrangements:* Alternatives include a maternity home, the home of parents or other relatives, and foster homes.

■ *Alleged-father counseling:* This involves informing him about his rights and responsibilities, counseling him on his concerns, and providing birth control counseling and perhaps premarital counseling.

■ *Family planning counseling:* Birth control information is provided for both parents, and perhaps referral to a family planning clinic is made.

■ *Educational and employment counseling:* Here, information is provided about remaining in educational programs (including home study programs) or about employment opportunities and work-training programs.

■ *Self-development counseling:* This may include a variety of areas: identity formation, assertiveness training, sexual counseling, rape counseling, and so on.

■ *Financial and money management counseling:* This includes eligibility for AFDC, food stamps, and Medicare.

■ *Child care:* After a baby is born, single-parent services assist the mother in making child-care arrangements (such as day care) when needed. Such assistance may include financial assistance for child care.

■ *Child development counseling:* New parents receive counseling on caring for young children and meeting their physical, social, and emotional needs.

In providing social services to single parents, social workers seek first to establish a helping relationship (see Chapter 4). If the client is single and pregnant, the worker tries to convey that she (not her parents) has the right and responsibility to decide among the alternatives of carrying the child to delivery, having an abortion, keeping the baby after delivery, placing the baby in foster care, or putting the baby up for adoption. To help a client to make such decisions, the worker uses a problem-solving approach. That is, he or she helps the client:

1. Define her problems.
2. Identify the alternatives.
3. Make a pro/con list for each alternative.
4. Evaluate the alternatives.
5. Select one or more alternatives.
6. Implement, and later evaluate, the alternatives that are chosen.

Most single parents decide to keep their baby and the proportion who are making this decision has been increasing. The social stigma of single parenthood has lessened. In addition, unmarried single parents are not as conspicuous as they have been in the past because we now have single foster parents, single adoptive parents, and a large number of one-parent families following a divorce. And, as we've seen, support systems have also become more available to help unmarried mothers who keep their babies.*

Ursula Myers (a former supervisor of a single-parent unit at a social services agency) describes the small minority of single parents who decide to terminate parental rights:

---

*I wish to note that I do not want to take a position on whether, in general, unmarried mothers should keep their babies. Being a parent at a young age has some rewards. But it is certainly an immense responsibility. An unmarried mother often has little time to enjoy young adulthood. Dating, pursuing a career, and having the necessary funds to meet wants and desires are more or less restricted. Most workers in single-parent services feel that it is usually in the long-range best interest of the child and the mother to consider placing the child for adoption. In working with unmarried mothers, however, workers in single-parent services seek to refrain from expressing their views. They instead seek to have the single mother carefully analyze the pros and cons of the available alternatives. Deciding whether to keep the baby is a very difficult, emotionally taxing responsibility.

In our experience, the woman who terminates her parental rights is generally long-range goal, reality oriented. The stigma of single parenthood is for her perceptually more marked. She sees the coming child as an encumbrance or as totally out of place in her present and future world, her immediate culture, and her internal mental health system. She is usually aware that her pregnancy is untimely and that she cannot cope with the vital needs of an infant at this point in her life. The separation process can result in a broad spectrum of responses, all perfectly normal and human. Both or either parent may feel a sense of loss, grief, emptiness, and unreality. There may be a sense of relief and even pleasure at terminating for some, while others may become depressed and withdrawn. Some work through the grief process to a point of rational and emotional acceptance, while others may completely sever themselves from the pregnancy by "cutting out" that part of their lives and/or totally denying its reality.[89]

FOSTER CARE AND ADOPTION

If a single mother relinquishes her parental rights, the child is usually placed temporarily in foster care. Some single parents who are unsure about whether to give up parental rights may also place their child in foster care until they make a decision. (Foster care, as was discussed earlier, is also used for children who are removed from their parents for neglect or abuse.)

The goals of foster care are to protect the children, to rehabilitate the parents, and generally to return the children to their genetic parents as soon as it is feasible to do so. Foster care is the temporary provision of substitute care for children whose parents are unable or unwilling to meet the child's needs in their own home. Except for emergency placement, legal custody of the child is usually transferred, by court action, from the child's parents to the agency responsible for foster placement. (Removal of a child from the parents' legal custody is carefully weighed by the court in an effort to protect the parents' rights while at the same time providing protection to the child.)

An American couple and their adopted 4-year-old son welcome their newly adopted daughter who was born in the Philippines. Many more people have applied for adoptive parenthood in the United States than there are children available for adoption. In recent years, the number of foreign adoptions has risen dramatically as more countries have opened their doors to adoptive parents.

Foster parents face the difficult task of being expected to provide love and affection to foster children, without becoming too emotionally attached. The placement is temporary in nature, and separating is easier when strong emotional bonds have not been established between foster parents and foster children. One of the tragic aspects of some foster placements is that the genetic parents never attain the capacity to care for their children. If they do not relinquish parental rights, the children may end up being raised in a series of foster homes. When this happens, a serious question arises about whether a child's right to be raised in a stable, healthy environment is being preserved. Children who are shuffled among foster homes are likely to experience considerable emotional trauma over relating to and later separating from a variety of parental figures.

Agencies seek to attain quality care in foster placements by studying and selecting applicants for foster parenthood, licensing foster parents, and monitoring each home after a child is placed. While the children are in foster care, the genetic parents have visitation rights. In neglect and abuse cases the hours of visitation are usually arranged through the court and supervised by the foster placement agency. Single parents who decide to relinquish their parental rights often choose not to visit the foster home, because they are in the process of separating emotionally from their child.

If the genetic mother relinquishes her rights, the alleged father does not automatically receive custody of the child. He must first be adjudged the father of the child by a court of law. Then, to obtain custody, he must also convince the court of his fitness and ability to care for the child. (If the mother decides to keep her child, she need not legally demonstrate her fitness.) For a child to be eligible for adoptive placement, both the genetic mother and the alleged father must relinquish their parental rights. In recent years many more people have applied for adoptive parenthood than there are children available for adoption. In particular, there are many more applicants for white, healthy infants than there are available babies.

Adoptive placement agencies carefully study, select, and prepare for parenthood applicants who want a child. After a child is placed, the agency monitors the placement until it is finalized by court action. Courts generally wait several months after a child is placed before finalizing a placement. Only in very rare circumstances is a child removed from an adoptive home. The purpose of this waiting period is to ascertain, as thoroughly as possible, that the placement is working out well.

As fully as possible, the medical histories of both biological parents are compiled to provide physical health and genetic information to the adoptive parents. Efforts are also made by placement agencies to meet the wishes of the biological parents concerning the physical characteristics, religious affiliation, racial characteristics, and geographical location of the adoptive parents.

A recent trend in adoptions is "open adoption," whereby the genetic and adoptive parents are officially known to each other. (In the past, adoptive placement agencies usually did not tell the adoptive parents who the genetic parents were, nor did they tell the genetic parents who the adoptive parents were.) Some adoptive and genetic parents are even maintaining contact with each other. Another trend is for some adoptive children (when they become young adults) to

seek out and make contact with their genetic parents.

It should be noted that not all adoptions are arranged by state-licensed agencies. Although professionally frowned on, some attorneys (for a substantial fee) arrange adoptions for couples seeking a child. These attorneys sometimes pay a fee (which they charge to the adoptive couple) to the birth mother for carrying the pregnancy to term and then relinquishing parental rights.

SUMMARY

The family is a social institution that is found in every culture. Yet there are substantial variations in family patterns and forms. Most families throughout the world can be classified as either extended or nuclear. Our culture has moved from an extended family system (before the Industrial Revolution) to a nuclear family system. In a number of countries a third family form, the single-parent family, is now emerging.

No society has ever existed without the institution of the family. Five essential functions performed by the modern family are replacing the population, caring for the young, socializing new members, regulating sexual behavior, and providing affection.

Four problems in the American family were examined: divorce, empty-shell marriages, family violence, and birth outside of marriage.

One out of two marriages ends in divorce. Divorce per se is not a social problem, but the consequences sometimes are. Reasons for the high divorce rate in our society include the extensive emphasis on romantic love, the changing status of women (who are now increasingly more financially independent), the growth of individualism, the growing acceptance of divorce, and the loss of certain functions in the modern family.

In empty-shell marriages the spouses feel no strong attachments to each other. Three types were described: devitalized relationships, conflict habituated relationships, and passive-congenial relationships. Some empty-shell marriages eventually end in divorce. Marriage counseling is the primary service available to spouses contemplating a divorce or to spouses with an empty-shell marriage.

Spouse abuse, child abuse, and parent abuse occur in more than half of all U.S. households. In the past 20 years family violence has become recognized as one of our major social problems.

With spouse abuse, the greatest physical damage is usually sustained by women. Although husbands are slapped or shoved with about the same frequency as wives, husbands are not controlled through violence to the extent that battered wives are. Spouse abuse appears to be related to a norm of tolerating violence in American families. A sizable number of men and women believe it is acceptable for a husband to occasionally hit his wife. Services (for example, shelter homes) are increasingly being developed in many communities for battered wives.

Large numbers of children are victims of child abuse or neglect. Physical abuse is dramatic and has received considerable national attention. Child neglect has received less national attention, even though it occurs more frequently than physical abuse. *Physical abuse, physical neglect,* and particularly *emotional neglect* are terms that are somewhat ambiguous and difficult to define precisely. The primary service designed to curb child abuse and neglect is protective services.

Premarital intercourse is fairly common and is now often tolerated in our society. If a single woman becomes pregnant, however, there may be considerable turmoil within families. Birth outside of marriage has become somewhat more accepted in our society, yet it is still viewed as a social problem. There is considerable variation in the reasons why it is viewed as a problem—ranging from the assertion that it is a sign of the moral decay and collapse of the family to a concern about the difficulties that the single parent and her child will encounter. A disproportionately high number of births outside of marriage occur among teenagers, suggesting a need for quality educational programs about responsible sexuality. Single-parent services is the primary social service for women who are single and pregnant and for unmarried mothers and fathers.

NOTES

1. James W. Coleman and Donald R. Cressey, *Social Problems*, 5th ed. (New York: HarperCollins, 1993), p. 490.
2. Ibid., p. 113.
3. Philippe Aries, "From the Medieval to the Modern Family," in *Family in Transition*, Arlene S. Skolnick and Jerome H. Skolnick, eds. (Boston: Little, Brown, 1971), pp. 90–104.
4. John F. Cuber, Martha Tyler John, and Kenrick S. Thompson, "Should Traditional Sex Modes and Values Be Changed?" in *Controversial Issues in the Social Studies: A Contemporary Perspective*, Raymond H. Muessig, ed. (Washington, DC: National Council for the Social Studies, 1975), pp. 87–121.
5. Janet S. Hyde, *Understanding Human Sexuality*, 4th ed. (New York: McGraw-Hill, 1990).
6. William F. Ogburn, "The Changing Family," *The Family*, 19 (July 1938), pp. 139–143.
7. George P. Murdock, *Social Structure* (New York: Free Press, 1949); Ogburn, "The Changing Family," pp. 139–143; William J. Goode, "The Sociology of the Family," in *Sociology Today*, Robert K. Merton, Leonard Broom, and Leonard J. Cottrell, eds. (New York: Basic Books, 1959); and Talcott Parsons and Robert F. Bales, *Family, Socialization and Interaction Process* (Glencoe, IL: Free Press, 1955).
8. René Spitz, "Hospitalism: Genesis of Psychiatric Conditions in Early Childhood," *Psychoanalytic Study of the Child* (1945), pp. 53–74.
9. William Kornblum and Joseph Julian, *Social Problems*, 7th ed. (Englewood Cliffs, NJ: Prentice-Hall, 1992), p. 335.
10. Diane E. Papalia and Sally W. Olds, *Human Development*, 5th ed. (New York: McGraw-Hill, 1992) pp. 457–459.
11. Ibid.
12. Ibid., pp. 514–516.
13. Mary Jo Bane, *Here to Stay: American Families in the Twentieth Century* (New York: Basic Books, 1976), pp. 31–33.
14. Kornblum and Julian, *Social Problems*, p. 341.
15. Kenneth Keniston, *All Our Children: The American Family under Pressure* (New York: Harcourt Brace Jovanovich, 1977), p. 21.
16. Richard Neely, "Barter in the Court," *The New Republic*, Feb. 10, 1986, p. 14.

17. Ibid., p. 17.
18. Christopher Scanlan, "Why Deadbeats? No Simple Answers," *Wisconsin State Journal,* Feb. 27, 1994, p. 1B.
19. Ibid.
20. Ibid.
21. Ibid.
22. Ibid.
23. Andrea Saltzman and Kathleen Proch, *Law in Social Work Practice* (Chicago: Nelson, 1990), p. 291.
24. John F. Cuber and Peggy B. Harroff, "Five Types of Marriage," in *Family in Transition,* Arlene S. Skolnick and Jerome H. Skolnick, eds. (Boston: Little, Brown, 1971), pp. 287–299.
25. William J. Goode, "Family Disorganization," in *Contemporary Social Problems,* 4th ed., Robert K. Merton and Robert Nisbet, eds. (New York: Harcourt Brace Jovanovich, 1976), p. 543.
26. Alfred Kadushin and Judith A. Martin, *Child Welfare Services,* 4th ed. (New York: Macmillan, 1988), pp. 218–335.
27. Ibid.
28. Ibid.
29. "Battered Families: A Growing Nightmare," *U.S. News & World Report,* Jan. 15, 1979, p. 60.
30. Coleman and Cressey, *Social Problems,* pp. 121–123.
31. Lewis Koch and Joanne Koch, "Parent Abuse—A New Plague," *Parade,* Jan. 27, 1980, p. 14.
32. Ibid.
33. Federal Bureau of Investigation, *Uniform Crime Reports for the United States,* 1992 (Washington, DC: U.S. Government Printing Office, 1993).
34. Suzanne K. Steinmetz and Murray A. Straus, *Violence in the Family* (New York: Dodd, Mead, 1974), p. 3.
35. Ibid., p. 9.
36. John O'Brien, "Violence in Divorce Prone Families," *Journal of Marriage and the Family,* 33 (November 1971), pp. 692–698.
37. Steven V. Roberts, "Simpson and Sudden Death," *U.S. News & World Report,* June 27, 1994, pp. 26–32.
38. "Battered Families: A Growing Nightmare," p. 62.
39. Ibid.
40. Federal Bureau of Investigation, *Uniform Crime Reports for the United States,* 1992.
41. Richard J. Gelles, *The Violent Home: The Study of Physical Aggression between Husbands and Wives* (Beverly Hills, CA: Sage, 1974).
42. "Facts about Domestic Violence," *Wisconsin State Journal,* Nov. 30, 1989, p. 1D.
43. Ibid.
44. Ibid.
45. Ibid.
46. Murray A. Straus, Richard Gelles, and Suzanne Steinmetz, *Behind Closed Doors: A Survey of Family Violence in America* (Garden City, NY: Doubleday, 1979).
47. Ibid.
48. Murray A. Straus, "Wife Beating: How Common and Why?" *Victimology,* 2, no. 3–4 (Fall–Winter 1977), pp. 443–458.
49. Gelles, *The Violent Home;* Murray A. Straus, "Leveling, Civility, and Violence in the Family," *Journal of Marriage and Family,* 36 (February 1974), pp. 13–30.
50. Saltzman and Proch, *Law in Social Work Practice,* pp. 296–307.
51. Kadushin and Martin, *Child Welfare Services,* pp. 218–327.
52. Vincent De Francis, *Child Abuse—Preview of a Nation-wide Survey* (Denver: American Humane Association, Children's Division, 1963), pp. 5–6.
53. Ibid., p. 6.
54. Larry Silver et al., "Does Violence Breed Violence? Contribution from a Study of the Child-Abuse Syndrome," *American Journal of Psychiatry* (September 1969), pp. 404–407.
55. George C. Curtis, "Violence Breeds Violence—Perhaps?" in Jerome E. Leavitt, *The Battered Child* (Morristown, NJ: General Learning Press, 1974), p. 3.
56. Jerome E. Leavitt, *The Battered Child* (Morristown, NJ: General Learning Press, 1974), p. 183.
57. Kadushin and Martin, *Child Welfare Services,* p. 243.
58. LeRoy Pelton, "Child Abuse and Neglect—The Myth of Classlessness," *American Journal of Orthopsychiatry,* 48, no. 4 (October 1978), pp. 608–616.
59. Kadushin and Martin, *Child Welfare Services,* pp. 277–282.
60. Ibid., pp. 243–244.
61. Vincent De Francis, *Special Skills in Child Protective Services* (Denver: American Humane Association, 1958), p. 11.
62. American Humane Association, *National Analysis of Official Child Neglect and Abuse Reporting* (Denver: Author, 1978). p. 27.
63. C. Henry Kempe and Ray E. Helfer, *Helping the Battered Child and His Family* (Philadelphia: Lippincott, 1972); Kadushin and Martin, *Child Welfare Services;* and Leavitt, *The Battered Child.*
64. Ibid.
65. Kadushin and Martin, *Child Welfare Services,* p. 218.
66. Sallie A. Watkins, "The Mary Ellen Myth: Correcting Child Welfare History," *Social Work,* 35, no. 6 (November 1990), pp. 500–503.

67. Ellen Thomson, *Child Abuse—A Community Challenge* (Buffalo, NY: Henry Stewart, 1971), p. 44.

68. Kadushin and Martin, *Child Welfare Services,* p. 278.

69. Edith Varon, "Communication: Client, Community, and Agency," *Social Work* (April 1964). pp. 36–42.

70. Anna Mae Sandusky, "Services to Neglected Children," *Children* (January–February 1960), p. 24.

71. Kadushin and Martin, *Child Welfare Services,* p. 291.

72. Henry Maas and Richard Engler, *Children in Need of Parents* (New York: Columbia University Press, 1959).

73. Kadushin and Martin, *Child Welfare Services,* p. 315.

74. U.S. Bureau of the Census, *Statistical Abstract of the United States, 1993* (Washington, DC: U.S. Government Printing Office, 1993), pp. 64–70.

75. Jason DeParle, "Unwed Mother Numbers Grow," *Wisconsin State Journal,* July 14, 1993, p. 3A.

76. Ibid.

77. Ibid.

78. Ibid.

79. Ibid.

80. James W. Coleman and Donald R. Cressey, *Social Problems,* 4th ed. (New York: Harper & Row, 1990), p. 136.

81. Art Levine, "Taking on Teen Pregnancy," *U.S. News & World Report,* Mar. 23, 1987, p. 67.

82. Coleman and Cressey, *Social Problems,* 5th ed., p. 118.

83. Kornblum and Julian, *Social Problems,* p. 335.

84. C. P. Green and K. Poteteiger, "Major Problems for Minors," *Society* (1978), pp. 10–13.

85. Alfred C. Kinsey, W. B. Pomeroy, and C. E. Martin, *Sexual Behavior in the Human Male* (Philadelphia: Saunders, 1948); and Alfred C. Kinsey, W. B. Pomeroy, C. E. Martin, and P. H. Gebhard, *Sexual Behavior in the Human Female* (Philadelphia: Saunders, 1953).

86. Ursula S. Myers, "Illegitimacy and Services to Single Parents," in *Introduction to Social Welfare Institutions,* 2d ed., Charles Zastrow, ed. (Homewood, IL: Dorsey Press, 1982), p. 189.

87. Levine, "Taking on Teen Pregnancy," p. 67.

88. Joseph P. Shapiro, "Teenage Sex: Just Say 'Wait,'" *U.S. News & World Report,* July 26, 1993, pp. 56–59.

89. Myers, "Illegitimacy and Services to Single Parents," p. 176.

6

SEXUAL ORIENTATION, SEX VARIANCES, AND SEX THERAPY

I regard sex as the central problem of life. . . .
Sex lies at the root of life, and we can never
learn to reverence life until we know how to
understand sex.

—*Havelock Ellis*[1]

Amazingly, we were able to put a man in space before we learned to understand the physiology of sexual orgasms.[2] This chapter will:

- Present a brief look at sexual expression in history and in other cultures.

- Present a historical review of scientific studies of sexuality.

- Describe three types of sexual variances:
  1. Tolerated sex variances—behaviors such as premarital intercourse and masturbation, which are generally tolerated in our society.
  2. Structural sex variances—sexual actions such as homosexual behavior, which is disapproved of by some persons in our society yet has supportive social structures.
  3. Asocial sex variances—sexual behaviors such as incest and rape, which are highly disapproved of in our society and do not have supportive social structures.

- Discuss personal sexual concerns, including sexual difficulties such as premature ejaculation among males and painful intercourse among females.

- Describe sex counseling and sex therapy.

SEX IN HISTORY AND IN OTHER CULTURES

Practically every conceivable sexual activity and conjugal arrangement, to some degree, has been socially acceptable to at least some people. Intercourse for procreation only, oral-genital relations, premarital sex, adultery, anal intercourse, monogamy, polyandry (more than one husband), polygyny (more than one wife), homosexuality, lifelong celibacy—each has been a method of re-

sponding to sexual desire that has been socially approved by some human community. Not even incest, which is among the most widely prohibited of sexual relationships, has been universally tabooed.[3] Some ancient cultures encouraged incest in royal families as a way to maintain the wealth and power among a small number of people and as a way to ensure the purity of the royal line.

Male and female homosexuality in ancient Greece was not only acceptable but encouraged. Today, homosexual practices are increasingly accepted in Western culture. In northern Sumatra, all youths are taught homosexual techniques from older adolescents of the same gender. Interestingly, most of these young people easily make the transition to heterosexual relationships as they become older and marry.[4]

Only a small minority (the United States is one) of the 190 contemporary societies studied by Clellan Ford and Frank Beach discourage or prohibit sexual expression by children.[5] Inhabitants of the Tobriand Islands encourage premarital sex because it is thought to be an important preparation for marriage. Some societies permit young boys and girls to play husband and wife even before puberty. In Asia the Lepcha society believes that girls need sexual intercourse in order to mature.[6] In contrast, in many Muslim and South American cultures, premarital chastity for women is highly revered: a female who has premarital sex is likely to be shamed and ostracized. However, in some other developing countries, some low-income parents sell their adolescent daughters as prostitutes, particularly to tourists.

There are some cultures in which rape is practically nonexistent, as among the Arapesh of New Guinea. In that society males are socialized to be peaceful and nonaggressive. In contrast, in the Gussi tribe in Kenya the rate of rape is at least five times higher than in the United States. In this tribe

This chapter was coauthored by Lloyd G. Sinclair, MSSW, ACSW. Mr. Sinclair is a psychotherapist at Midwest Center for Psychotherapy and Sex Therapy (Madison, Wisconsin) and is certified as a sex educator, sex therapist, and supervisor by the American Association of Sex Educators, Counselors, and Therapists (AASECT).

EXHIBIT 6.1

Sexuality in Mangaia

Mangaia is an island in the South Pacific. The Mangaians have elaborate rituals that use sex for pleasure and for procreation.

Mangaian boys around the ages of 7 or 8 are instructed on how to masturbate. At about age 13 they have a superincision ritual (in which a slit is made on the full length of the skin on the top part of the penis). This ritual initiates them into manhood. As part of this ritual they are also given instruction in how to kiss, how to bring a female partner to orgasm several times before they have an orgasm themselves, and how to perform cunnilingus. Approximately two weeks later each boy is introduced to sexual intercourse with an experienced woman. She demonstrates intercourse in various positions and further instructs him on how to delay ejaculation in order to have simultaneous orgasms with his partner.

Mangaian girls also receive sexual instruction from adult women. Thereafter, Mangaian boys and girls actively seek each other out, and many have coitus nearly every night. Teenage girls are raised to believe virility in a male is proof of his desire for her. In particular, a male is expected to be able to vigorously continue in-and-out action of intercourse for 15 to 30 minutes or longer while the female moves her hips back and forth in a rhythmic motion. Any male who is unable to perform this act is looked down on.

By age 20 the average male is likely to have had ten or more female partners, and the average "nice" female will have had three or four successive male partners. Mangaian parents encourage such sexual experiences because they want their daughters and sons to find a marriage partner with whom they are sexually compatible. At around age 18 Mangaians typically have sex every night. Men are brought up to believe that bringing their partner to orgasm is one of the chief sources of sexual pleasures for a man.

Source: John C. Messinger, "The Luck of the Irish," and Donald S. Marshall, "Too Much in Mangaia," both in *Human Sexual Behavior,* eds. D. S. Marshall and R. C. Suggs (New York: Basic Books, 1971).

both men and women are socialized to be aggressive and competitive—and women often resist sexual relations, even with their husbands.[7]

It has been fairly common throughout history for soldiers to rape the women of the societies they conquered. In the past some Eskimo husbands offered male guests the privilege of spending the night with their wives, and it was considered a serious insult for guests to refuse. White slave owners in U.S. history often prohibited their slaves from marrying, and some attempted to improve the characteristics of African American children by mating female slaves with an African American male who was considered to have desirable characteristics. Some persons with a cognitive disability in various societies have been sterilized in an effort to prevent them from having children. Hitler, in Nazi Germany in the 1930s and 1940s, mated women with certain soldiers in an effort to "breed" offspring with the characteristics he considered desirable.

Some parents in Europe believe that fathers should have intercourse with their daughters to teach them about sex, although this practice is most often viewed as an excuse for incest or sexual abuse. Although there is a myth in our society that the elderly do not and should not engage in sexual activity, many elderly people are sexually active and may have more than one partner. In many cultures males greet each other with a kiss and a hug.

Sex-change operations have been occurring

since the early 1930s. They became well publicized in 1952, when Christine Jorgensen announced to the world that she had undergone surgery to change her from being biologically male to biologically female. As is often the case with sexual matters that are little understood by the larger society, Jorgensen's surgery met with widespread disapproval. Nonetheless, several thousand people have since undergone such operations.[8]

Clearly, what is defined as acceptable and unacceptable sexual behavior varies from culture to culture and from one time period to another. Let's look briefly at the history of our changing sexual attitudes and mores.

Perhaps the major influence on the current attitudes toward sex in Western culture has been the Judeo-Christian tradition. The Old Testament approved of sexual intercourse only within marriage. The purpose of intercourse, it was asserted, should be only to conceive children. Judaism was somewhat more liberal, stating that heterosexual intercourse for pleasure within a marriage was not sinful. Masturbation, homosexuality, and all other sexual expressions outside of marriage were viewed as sinful.

Early Christianity endorsed the conservative position that sex is evil and degrading and should be indulged in only by married couples and only for the purpose of procreation. This remains the official position of the Roman Catholic church.

The Protestant Reformation, which began in the 16th century, advocated a strict and repressive sexual code. The Protestant ethic that emerged at the time emphasized the importance of hard work and asserted that it was morally wrong to engage in pleasurable activities of any kind. Denying sexual urges and refraining from sexual activities except to procreate were seen as virtues. A major immigrant group that began colonizing America in the 17th century, the Puritans, rigidly adhered to this ascetic (self-denial of pleasurable activities) life.

The views promulgated by the Protestant ethic became incorporated into what has become known as "Victorian morality." The name is derived from the reign of Queen Victoria of England.

EXHIBIT 6.2

Learning Sexual Behavior via Scripts

Sociologists have made a major contribution to our understanding of human sexuality by asserting that sexual behavior (as well as most other human behavior) is developed through learning "scripts." *Scripts* (as in a play) are plans that we learn and then carry around in our heads. These scripts enable us to conceptualize where we are in our activities and provide us with direction for completing those activities and accomplishing our goals. Scripts are also devices for helping us to remember what we have done in the past.

Sexual scripts result from elaborate prior learning in which we acquire an etiquette of sexual behavior. According to this script approach, little in sexual activity is spontaneous. Scripts tell us who appropriate sexual partners are, what sexual activity is expected, where and when the activity should occur, and what the sequence of the different sexual behaviors should be.

Scripts vary greatly from one culture to another. Hortense Powdermaker provides the following description of a script about female masturbation that is generally held by the Lesu of the South Pacific:

> *A woman will masturbate if she is sexually excited and there is no man to satisfy her. A couple may be having intercourse in the same house, or near enough for her to see them, and she may thus become aroused. She then sits down and bends her right leg so that her heel presses against her genitals. Even young girls of about six years may do this quite casually as they sit on the ground. The women and men talk about it freely, and there is no shame attached to it. It is a customary position for women to take, and they learn it in childhood. They never use their hands for manipulation.[a]*

---

[a]Quoted from Hortense Powdermaker, *Life in Lesu* (New York: Norton, 1933), pp. 276–277.

Victorian morality was prominent in the 19th and early 20th centuries. John Gagnon and Bruce Henderson note:

> The Puritan-dominated sex ethic became that of penny-pinching Adam Smith. . . . The moral values of the new middle classes, with their belief in hard work, delayed gratification, and avoidance of pleasure, including the sexual, were to triumph during the Victorian age, not only in England but in most of Western Europe.[9]

Victorian morality all but banished sexuality from discussion in respectable relationships. Modesty was stressed to the point of extreme prudishness. In polite conversations simple anatomical terms such as *legs* or *breasts* were taboo; these body parts instead were referred to as limbs and bosoms. The limbs (legs) of tables were often covered by long tablecloths so that sexual feelings would not be aroused. Women did not get "pregnant"; they were "in a family way" and were expected to remain at home during their "condition." In Philadelphia men and women were not allowed to visit art galleries together for fear their modesty might be offended by the classical statues (on which fig leaves were added to the genital areas to minimize their offensiveness).[10]

Middle- and upper-class women, before marriage, were expected to be virgins. There were considered to be two types of females: The good women were virgins—undamaged property—who were fit to marry. The bad were "fallen women" who were sexually active premaritally. They were pitied but not consoled, because their "fall" was attributed to their own weakness. They were no longer deemed fit to marry but were nevertheless considered available for nonmarital relations with men. A popular myth throughout this period held that men were inherently more sexual than women. This led to the development—still very prevalent today—of two standards of acceptable behavior (the so-called double standard). Although it was hoped that men would remain chaste, because of their "animal natures" they were seldom criticized for having premarital and extramarital relations. Prostitutes and lower-class women were proper outlets for men's excessive sexual urges, which were too beastly to impose on their wives. J. John Palen notes:

> From this division of women—good and bad, mothers and whores—came the double standard that implicitly allowed men to be sexually active but that forbade "nice girls" even to think about such things. Overt sexuality was condemned, while covert premarital or extramarital sex among men was tolerated as a necessary evil, given the male's more pressing sexual urges.[11]

Researchers have since found that the female sex drive is a strong as that of the male. Interestingly, even during the repressive years of the Puritan and Victorian eras there were always certain segments advocating more liberal expressions of sexuality. For example, in the Victorian era there was a profitable trade in erotic drawings and novels.

Since the early 1900s there have been dramatic changes in sexual attitudes and behaviors. For example, in 1974 Morton Hunt reported that most men and women had engaged in premarital sex, and most young women (ages 18 to 24) were not virgins at marriage.[12] Hunt also found that the percentage of those having oral sexual experiences was increasing.

The 1970s in the United States were viewed as a time of sexual permissiveness and experimentation during which many people engaged in sexual behaviors that were previously uncommon. Since then there has been a partial reversal of this permissive trend, with a general movement toward fewer partners, more emphasis on long-term relationships, and a more gradual development of the sexual aspects of a relationship. This reversal has been attributed to a general dissatisfaction with sexual behavior divorced from intimacy, as well as to the very real threat of increased susceptibility to sexually transmitted diseases for persons who have sexual contact with multiple partners.[13]

At present, ambiguity and confusion abound over what ought to be the sexual code and behavior of Americans. On the conservative end of the spectrum are groups such as the Catholic Church and some fundamentalist religious organizations. They advocate that sex be for procreation only and restricted to heterosexual, married people. Such groups express alarm that increased sexual permissiveness will destroy the moral fiber of the family and ultimately result in the destruction of our society.

At the liberal end of the spectrum are groups and individuals holding that sex can legitimately be enjoyed for recreation as well as for procreation. They assert that the ways in which sexuality is expressed should be of no concern except to those consenting adults who participate.

Repercussions of this liberal attitude are visible throughout society. Sexual topics are presented frankly and openly by the mass media, including television, magazines, and newspapers. Nudity is displayed in movies, in magazines, and on television. No longer are women who have premarital sex considered unfit for marriage. One factor that appears to have led to the increases in premarital and extramarital relations is the increased availability of birth control devices, particularly the Pill.[14]

Because of the widely conflicting codes advocated by parents, peers, and other pressure groups in our society, many individuals go through considerable turmoil in arriving at a personal code of sexual behavior—one that they can be comfortable with and seek to live by.

FORMAL STUDY OF SEX

Prior to the 20th century there were practically no scientific studies of sexuality. Since about 1900 the work of four social scientists has had profound effects on our understanding of human sexuality: Sigmund Freud, Alfred Kinsey, and the team of William Masters and Virginia Johnson.

Sigmund Freud

Sigmund Freud was a psychoanalyst who theorized in his writings (from 1895 to 1925) that the sex drive was a fundamental part of human life.

Freud realized that many people had sexual conflicts. He made sexuality a central focus of his theories and defined most emotions and behaviors as being primarily sexual in nature. He interpreted "sexuality" broadly; he thought of it as including physical love, affectional impulses, self-love, love for parents and children, and friendship associations.

Freud advanced a number of controversial theories. He asserted that everyone, from birth on, has sexual interests. He stated that boys at an early age (around age 3) fall sexually in love with their mother and fear their father will discover this interest and then castrate them (a fear referred to as castration anxiety). Girls, on the other hand, at about the same age (age 3) fall sexually in love with their father. They discover that they do not have a penis, and their desire to have one leads to penis envy. Girls conclude that they lost their penis at an earlier age when their mother discovered their sexual interest in their father. That is, they believe their mother castrated them because of their love for their father. Girls also experience castration anxiety, but it stems from their belief that having been castrated makes them inferior to males.

Freud's notion that sexuality was a critical part of human development initially provoked shock and outrage. Before his time it was thought that sexual interests played only a minor role in human development. Gradually, his theories came to have a liberating effect, as sexuality slowly became recognized as playing a key role in personality development. Freud's theories also led to increased communication about sexuality and stimulated scientific investigations of this topic.

Perhaps Freud's greatest contribution was this change he effected on our attitudes toward sexuality. Unfortunately, he developed a number of hypotheses and advanced them as "truths" without scientifically testing their validity. Consequently, some of Freud's specific hypotheses about sexuality have been hotly disputed and widely challenged—for example, his hypotheses involving castration anxiety in boys and castration anxiety and penis envy in girls.

EXHIBIT 6.3

The End of the Sexual Revolution

In the 1960s and 1970s there was a sexual revolution. It featured an increase in premarital and extramarital relationships and a tendency to view sex as relational or recreational rather than procreative. In the 1980s there was substantial publicity about seemingly new epidemics of sexually transmitted diseases, particularly genital herpes and AIDS. The AIDS epidemic has been likened to a modern-day plague. Cures have not yet been found for either genital herpes or AIDS. Publicity about AIDS and the realization that prevention cannot be guaranteed short of sexual abstinence or sexual monogamy with an uninfected partner have led millions of people to shift their patterns of sexual behavior, with some choosing celibacy and others becoming more selective in their choice of sexual partners.[a]

Although some Americans have not changed their sexual practices at all, many others have added precautions to their sexual behaviors (for example, using condoms). Several of the tenets of the sexual revolution, such as the belief that sexual intercourse between relative strangers could be enjoyed purely for recreational pleasure and without consequences, are being rejected in the face of new challenges.

Masters, Johnson, and Kolodny surveyed single adults about changes in their sexual practices with the advent of the AIDS peril. They report as typical the following attitudes expressed by an unmarried woman:

> I used to enjoy the singles bar scene as a way of connecting with men. Now I wouldn't sleep with a guy I met at a bar no matter how terrific he looked or what a great "catch" he might be. You might say I'm getting conservative in my old age, but it's really just a matter of adjusting to the harsh realities out there. Anyone who pretends that isn't so is simply a fool.[b]

[a]William H. Masters, Virginia E. Johnson, and Robert C. Kolodny, *Human Sexuality*, 2d ed. (Boston: Little, Brown, 1988), p. 23.
[b]Ibid., p. 255.

Alfred Kinsey

In 1948 Alfred C. Kinsey, an American zoologist, published *Sexual Behavior in the Human Male*, which was based on interviews with 5300 white American men. This study investigated sexual practices and found that the actual sexual behavior of males differed substantially from the stated moral values of the time. One-third of the respondents had had at least one homosexual experience since puberty; 83% had had premarital relations; half of those who were married had had extramarital affairs; and 92% had masturbated to orgasm.[15]

Five years later, in 1953, Kinsey published *Sexual Behavior in the Human Female*, which was based on interviews with 5940 white American women.[16] This study showed, to some extent, that the double standard was still operating. But it also found that women were not as asexual as was commonly thought. More than half of these respondents had had premarital relations, and one-fourth of those who were married had had extramarital relations. (It should be noted that Kinsey's studies lacked racial diversity in that he studied no people of color. Therefore any conclusions he drew can be applied to white Americans only.)

Kinsey's findings were widely publicized by the mass media. For the first time society was confronted with the wide gaps that existed between sexual mores and sexual practices. Kinsey's studies may have led people to become freer in their sexual behavior, or at least to feel less guilt about sexual behavior that was inconsistent with

Pioneer sexologist Alfred Kinsey's studies revealed the discrepancy between Americans' sexual mores and their sexual practices.

traditional sexual mores. The studies certainly challenged the belief that women were basically uninterested in sex.

William Masters and Virginia Johnson

In 1957 William Masters and Virginia Johnson began their study of the physiology of human sexual response, which culminated in the publication of their classic text *Human Sexual Response*.[17] Their contribution to the scientific understanding of human sexual response has been enormous, and their findings have generally withstood the test of others' replications.

Masters and Johnson were the first to provide accurate information about the physiology of human sexual response based on laboratory observations of people's responses rather than their personal reports. Their findings destroyed a number of myths. Freud, for example, had asserted that vaginal orgasm in women was superior to clitoral orgasm. Masters and Johnson found that the clitoris was the organ having the most nerve endings (and therefore the area of greatest pleasure) in a female's genitals. The clitoris was essentially the main structure being stimulated in both clitoral orgasm and vaginal orgasm, and therefore there were no physiological differences between these orgasms. This finding enhanced the sex lives of many women who were fruitlessly searching for the vaginal orgasm—many of whom felt that they were inadequate or that they were missing out on something. Other important findings were that men and women are able to enjoy sexual activity into advanced age and that some women have numerous orgasms in succession.

On completion of this research, Masters and Johnson began to treat people with sexual dysfunctions, such as premature ejaculation in males and failure to achieve orgasm in females. They departed radically from the prevailing thinking of the day, which viewed sexual dysfunction as a by-product of other individual or relationship problems. Masters and Johnson dealt primarily with the sexual problem and treated people in short-term (two weeks) therapy. Extremely successful results were achieved, and their methods and outcomes were subsequently published in *Human Sexual Inadequacy*.[18] Most contemporary forms of sex therapy are based on Masters and Johnson's original work.

VARIANCES RATHER THAN SEXUAL PROBLEMS

Human beings are capable of expressing their sexuality in an amazing variety of ways, due to both biological determinants and learning. Everyone has some form of a sex drive, but how it is expressed is shaped by biological predispositions, rituals, acceptable role models, trial and error as to what is pleasurable and what is not, and the attitudes of others (parents, peers, teachers, etc.). Gagnon and Henderson note that the learning of ways to express our sexuality is closely related to the process of forming our gender identity (our self-concept of maleness or femaleness):

> We assemble our sexuality beginning with gender identity, and we build upon that the activities we come to think of as fitting to ourselves. Our belief in what is correct and proper results more from our social class, religion, style of family life, and concepts of masculinity and femininity than from the specifically sexual things that we learn.[19]

One approach to studying the wide variety of sexual behaviors is the social problems approach. This approach seeks to classify as social problems all sexual behaviors that differ from a norm to such an extent that a significant number of people (or a number of significant people) feel that something should be done about it. Using this approach requires delineation of the code or norm of acceptability. However, there is no consensus about which sexual expressions are acceptable and which are not. In addition, as the Kinsey study showed, there is a vast difference between the purported sexual norms of society and people's actual sexual behavior.

Another shortcoming in using the social problems approach is that those acts that would be identified as social problems would then be stigmatized as "sick," "degenerate," or "perverted." During the Victorian era our society suffered too much from the efforts of some to make value judgments about what is inappropriate sexual behavior. This text will not attempt to force any specific sexual code onto readers—too many other groups are still trying to do this. Instead of the term *social problems*, the term *sex variances* will be used to refer to sexual expressions that are of concern to certain segments of our society.

Definitions of acceptable and nonacceptable sexual behavior tend to change over time. Some behaviors that were once widely condemned are now generally accepted. Masturbation, for example, used to be viewed as sinful, immoral, and unhealthy but now is widely practiced and is recommended by sex therapists as a way to learn about one's sexuality. Not long ago oral sex was considered immoral or wrong, but today a large majority of young people engage in oral sex.[20]

It may be argued that laws in a society can be used to determine acceptable and unacceptable sexual expressions. Any sexual acts that are legally prohibited could therefore be identified as unacceptable. However, many of our present laws relating to sexual behaviors were enacted during the Victorian era and remain highly conservative. There is a considerable time lag between changes in laws relating to sexuality and changes in attitudes and norms about sexuality. Herant Katchadourian and Donald T. Lunde note: "Almost all sexual activity that may occur between husband and wife, with the exception of kissing, caressing, and vaginal intercourse, is defined as criminal in every state of the union."[21]

Acts that are currently still illegal in at least some states include premarital sex, oral sex, masturbation, extramarital sex, cohabitation, and intercourse in any position other than the missionary position. Historically, severe penalties were imposed for those found guilty of sex "crimes." For example, the 17th-century Puritans made extramarital sex a crime punishable by death.

Laws, to some extent, are an indicator of how societies feel about certain sexual behaviors. For example, the stiff penalties for rape and child molestation suggest strong disapproval. Yet, for the reasons cited above, laws cannot be used as the only measure of prevailing views about acceptable sexual behavior in a society.

TYPES OF SEXUAL VARIANCES

A useful classification of sexual variances is provided by William Kornblum and Joseph Julian, who identify three categories: tolerated sex variance, structural sex variance, and asocial sex variance.[22] Structural sex variances are generally disapproved of by some people in our society, yet have supportive social structures. This category includes homosexuality, prostitution, and pornography. Asocial sex variances are behaviors that our society strongly disapproves of and that do not have supportive social structures. Behaviors in this category include incest and rape.

Tolerated Sex Variance

Behaviors such as masturbation, premarital intercourse, sex between consenting adults in a variety of positions, and heterosexual oral-genital contact may be considered tolerated sex variances. There are a few groups (such as certain fundamentalist religious groups) who assert that such acts are immoral and ought to be prohibited. Laws in some states prohibit such sexual behavior but are seldom enforced. Most segments of our society, however, tolerate these acts. John Gagnon and William Simon note that such acts "are generally disapproved, but . . . either serve a socially useful purpose and/or occur so often among a population with such low social visibility that only a small number are ever actually sanctioned for engaging in [them]."[23] Because these sexual behaviors tend to be tolerated in our society, we will move on to examine structural sexual variances.

Structural Sex Variance: Homosexuality

Sexual behaviors in this category run counter to prevailing norms and legal statutes but have supportive social structures and are participated in by substantial numbers of people. Prostitution and pornography fit this description, but in this section we will focus on homosexuality because in recent years it has generated the greatest interest among social workers.

Kornblum and Julian, who categorize homosexuality together with prostitution and pornography, emphatically state that they are not making a judgment about the desirability or undesirability of homosexuality.[24] Some segments of our society have viewed homosexual behavior as being "deviant," "sick," or "unnatural." As we will see, research is increasingly confirming that sexual orientation is determined very early in life (before age 5) and may be biologically driven. Therefore each person's response to sexual drives is highly individualized in what she or he experiences as "natural" behavior. Homosexuality thus represents a sexual variation, not a social problem.

There is a major difference between homosexuality and the other two structural sex variances (prostitution and pornography). Engaging in prostitution or using pornography appears to have primarily sociological and psychological determinants. In contrast, being gay or lesbian appears to have primarily biological determinants (as described later in this section). Similar to masturbation, homosexuality has been viewed negatively by some segments of our society, yet recent research indicates that both are natural expressions of sexual drives.

HOMOSEXUALITY EXAMINED

A homosexual is a person who has and/or prefers sexual contact with members of the same gender. We use this term to refer to a pervasive pattern that occurs over a long period of time rather than occasional sexual experimentation with someone of the same gender. Teenagers, in experimenting with sexuality, may, for example, have some homosexual experiences. People isolated from the other gender (in prisons, segregated schools, or the military) often have sexual experiences with members of their own sex. On the other hand, it is possible to be a homosexual without practicing homosexual behavior—by ignoring one's homosexuality, denying it, or simply pretending to be heterosexual.

Surveys have found that a majority of Americans regard homosexuality as "very obscene and vulgar" and as being a "curable disease."[25] Homosexuals are also often viewed as being harmful to American life. The negative view of homosexuality in this country is indicated by the array of derogatory slang terms for homosexuals. (It should be noted that similar attitudes and different derogatory terms have been applied in the past to various ethnic minorities, including the Irish, Italians, African Americans, and Latinos.) Homosexuals have frequently been the victims of antigay hate crimes.[26] Many heterosexuals are *homophobic:* They have feelings of personal anxiety and disgust of homosexuals and seek to avoid contact with them.

Such negative attitudes can have considerable psychological impact on gay and lesbian people. It can be devastating to learn that a majority of Americans consider your natural interests and behaviors to be vulgar and obscene. Some homosexuals therefore seek to hide their sexual orientation, and they live in constant fear of being "outed." Some believe (often correctly) that discovery will result in being fired from their job or being ostracized by friends and relatives. Tragically, some gay and lesbian youths become so despondent that they commit suicide. The suicide rate of homosexual adolescents is significantly higher than that of heterosexual teenagers. This is a sad and extreme example of the ultimate costs of bigotry.

There are several erroneous myths about homosexuality:

Myth 1. People are either homosexual or heterosexual.

Fact: Alfred Kinsey found that homosexuality and heterosexuality are not mutually exclusive categories. Most people have had sexual thoughts, feelings, and fantasies about members of the same sex as well as about members of the opposite sex. Kinsey proposed a seven-point rating scale to categorize sexuality, with exclusive heterosexuality at one end and exclusive homosexuality at the other (Exhibit 6.4). Kinsey noted:

> The world is not divided into sheep and goats. . . . Only the human mind invents categories and tries to force facts into pigeonholes. The living world is a continuum in each and every one of its aspects. The sooner we learn this concerning human sexual behavior, the sooner we will reach a sound understanding of the realities of sex.[27]

Myth 2. Homosexuality is universally disapproved of in all cultures.

Fact: Some cultures accept, and even encourage, homosexuality. A young male in ancient Greece was sometimes given a boy slave who served as a sexual partner until the boy was old enough to marry a woman. It was also common for older married men to form a homosexual relationship with a young boy. Today, all males among the Siwans of North Africa are expected to engage in homosexual relationships throughout their lives. Among the Aranda of central Australia there are relationships between young boys and unmarried men, with these liaisons generally ending at marriage.[28]

Myth 3. Male homosexuals are generally "effeminate," and lesbians are generally "masculine." The stereotype is that male homosexuals are limp-wristed, talk with a lisp, and have a "swishy" walk; lesbians are believed to have short hair and to wear clothes that are normally worn by males.

Fact: Most homosexuals are indistinguishable in appearance and mannerisms from heterosexuals.[29] This myth probably comes from confusing homosexuality with transvestism—wearing the clothing of the opposite gender for sexual arousal. Transvestism and homosexuality are in fact quite different: Most transvestites are heterosexual.[30] Interestingly, whereas our culture erroneously associates male homosexuality with effeminacy, the ancient Greeks and Romans associated homosexuality with aggressive masculinity (as among the Spartan warriors).

Brian Garner and Richard Smith found further evidence contradicting the stereotype that male homosexuals are generally effeminate. In a study of male university athletes, they found that 40% had engaged in homosexual behavior to orgasm in the previous two years.[31]

Myth 4. Homosexuals are "sick" and different in personality characteristics from heterosexuals.

Fact: Evelyn Hooker gave a battery of personality and psychological adjustment tests to a homosexual group and to a matched group of heterosexuals. The study found no differences between the two groups in personality traits or in general adjustment. The only difference was their sexual orientation.[32]

Myth 5. One partner in a homosexual liaison generally plays the "active" or masculine role in sexual activity and the other plays the "passive" or feminine role.

EXHIBIT 6.4

The Continuum of Sexuality According to Kinsey

1	2	3	4	5	6	7
Exclusively heterosexual	Heterosexual with incidental homosexual experience	Heterosexual with substantial homosexual experience	Equal heterosexual and homosexual experience	Homosexual with substantial heterosexual experience	Homosexual with incidental heterosexual experience	Exclusively homosexual

Source: Adapted from Alfred C. Kinsey et al., *Sexual Behavior in the Human Male* (Philadelphia: Saunders, 1948), p. 638.

Fact: Most homosexuals play both roles and (similar to heterosexuals) experiment with a variety of arousal techniques. The question is sometimes asked: "What do homosexuals do in bed?" Most of their activities are similar to those in which heterosexuals engage. Foreplay generally includes kissing, hugging, and petting. Male homosexuals may engage in mutual masturbation, oral-genital sex, interfemoral intercourse (in which one man's penis moves between the thighs of the other), and anal intercourse. Lesbians may engage in mutual masturbation, oral-genital sex, and, more infrequently, tribadism (one partner lying on top of the other and making thrusting movements so that both receive genital stimulation); a rarer practice among lesbians is the use of a dildo by one female to stimulate the other.

Myth 6. Male homosexuals primarily seek out young boys.

Fact: Homosexuals are no more attracted to children than are heterosexuals, and homosexual child molesting is less common that its heterosexual counterpart.[33] Charles McCaghy found that 80% of all reported child molesting is done by heterosexual men to young girls.[34] (And there is reason to believe that same-sex child molesting is frequently committed by otherwise-heterosexual men.) Strangely, people who worry that homosexual male teachers will try to seduce young boys in a school do not seem to worry that heterosexual male teachers will try to seduce young

girls—and it is the latter that occurs much more frequently.

Myth 7. Gays and lesbians are to blame for AIDS, which is a punishment from God for their behavior.

Fact: Although gay males are a high-risk group for contracting the AIDS virus in our society, very few cases have been reported among lesbians.[35] (Gay men are at high risk for acquiring AIDS because of the transfer of body fluids that occurs during anal intercourse.) AIDS is a life-threatening disease not only for gay men; it is now a disease whose incidence is increasing rapidly among heterosexuals.[36] In many African countries the majority of people afflicted with AIDS are heterosexuals.[37]

Homosexuals are not the cause of AIDS. Blaming this deadly disease on the group that, in the United States, has suffered and died most disproportionately from it is a classic and regrettable case of blaming the victims. Although it is true that the largest single risk group of people with AIDS is male homosexuals, it is ludicrous to assume this group caused this health crisis. AIDS is caused by a virus. It is even more ludicrous to assert that male homosexuals would want to deliver the disease on the world after first spreading it among themselves. Quite to the contrary, the gay male community in the United States has been in the forefront of educating people about behavior that minimizes the transmission of the disease. Gay men have radically altered their sexual behavior patterns, as evidenced by a substantial drop in the rate of transmission of this disease among this group in the past few years. No group in the United States would benefit more from a cure or treatment for AIDS than would male homosexuals. (Expanded material on AIDS is presented in Chapter 14.)

INCIDENCE OF HOMOSEXUALITY

Determining the extent of homosexuality is difficult. First, there are definitional problems because most people are not exclusively heterosexual or homosexual. Second, because of the stigma attached to homosexuality, some people are reluctant to acknowledge homosexual thoughts, feelings, or acts.

Kinsey found that 4% of white males and 2% of white females were exclusively homosexual— that is, never had sex with someone of the opposite sex. He further estimated that 37% of American males have had one or more homosexual experiences to orgasm and that 10% of American males have long periods of more or less exclusive homosexuality.[38] Other research has resulted in similar estimates.[39] After reviewing several studies, Janet Hyde concludes that the answer to the question "How many people are homosexual and how many are heterosexual?" is complex.

> Probably about 80 percent of men and 90 percent of women are exclusively heterosexual. About 2 percent of men and 1 percent of women are exclusively homosexual. And the remaining [men and women] have had varying amounts of both heterosexual and homosexual experience.[40]

CAUSES OF HOMOSEXUALITY

People are often curious about the causes of homosexuality. Why are some people erotically attracted to members of the same gender and others to members of the other gender? Social, behavioral, and biological scientists have examined and argued this question for decades. Let's see what they have learned.

First, you cannot study the question of why one becomes homosexual without studying the larger question of what determines sexual object choice for anyone, heterosexual or homosexual.

Why do we get aroused by a woman, or a woman with particular attributes, or a man of a certain body type? Is this something we've learned? Are we born with a "script" that determines our sexual object choice?

Many researchers and theoreticians have advanced hypotheses in an effort to explain this complex and important question. Some believe that the biology of an individual determines heterosexuality or homosexuality. Some studies have shown chemical differences between the two groups, but it is impossible to determine causation from the results of these studies. In other words, are the chemical differences between people responsible for this behavior, or does their behavior somehow alter their body chemistry?

Other theorists posit that childhood experiences determine heterosexuality or homosexuality. Here we have the causation question again. If we determined that a certain child had more sex play with a child of the same gender and grew to be a homosexual in adult life, can we say that this sex play led to homosexuality? Perhaps the increased sex play grew out of an inborn desire and erotic potential toward gratification from such play. That is, the behavior grew out of a predisposition toward homosexuality; the predisposition did not grow out of the behavior.

The most comprehensive study of this question to date was undertaken by researchers at the Alfred C. Kinsey Institute for Sex Research.[41] The researchers, Alan P. Bell, Martin S. Weinberg, and Sue Kiefer Hammersmith, studied 979 homosexual and 477 heterosexual men and women, gathering a large amount of information about their lives in an effort to determine critical and statistically significant differences between these two groups. They analyzed their data using a method called "path analysis," which enabled them to examine a large number of independent variables (such as parental traits, parent and sibling relationships, and gender conformity) to determine *causation* of sexual orientation, and not merely association between variables. Their significant findings were as follows: (1) By the time boys and girls reach adolescence, their sexual orientation is likely to be already determined, even though they may not yet have become sexually very active. (2) The homosexual men and women in the study were not particularly lacking in heterosexual experiences during their childhood and adolescent years. They were distinguished from their heterosexual counterparts, however, in finding such experiences ungratifying. (3) Among both the men and women in the study, there was a powerful link between gender nonconformity and the development of homosexuality. (Gender nonconformity refers to children who prefer engaging in activities generally associated in this culture with the other gender—for example, boys playing with dolls.)

What do these findings suggest? First, they show that sexual orientation is established early in life, perhaps long before adolescence. Although every person has the potential to behave sexually in the manner he or she chooses, one's true sexual orientation may be set before birth or at a very early age and then no longer be influenced by the environment. Many homosexually oriented people behave as if they are heterosexual in this society because there are so many sanctions against homosexuality. However, their preferred sexual partner, in the absence of these negative sanctions, would be someone of the same gender. Human beings certainly have the ability to respond sexually to people who are not their most preferred sexual partner, but to do so requires going against the current of their innermost inclinations. We can freely choose various behaviors; we cannot freely choose who or what "turns us on." The question of what causes a person's sexual orientation to be set (either as homosexual or heterosexual) before birth or at a very early age has not as yet been answered. (Some people are naturally left-handed and others are naturally right-handed; it appears that some people are naturally heterosexual in orientation and others are naturally homosexual.)

The possibility that sexual orientation is more a matter of nature than of nurture got a boost in a 1991 study that reported differences in the brain between homosexual and heterosexual men. The research focused on the hypothalamus, the region of the brain thought to control sexual behavior. The results were striking. Certain groups of nerve cells in the hypothalamus were more than two times larger in heterosexual men than in homosexual men. The hypothalamus of a gay man appears to be closer in structure to that of a heterosexual woman than to that of a heterosexual man.[42]

Studies of separated twins were conducted in 1991 and 1993 at the Boston University School of Medicine. It was found that there was greater likelihood of both twins in a pair being homosexual if they were identical (shared the same genes) than if they were fraternal (did not share the same genes).[43] Another study in 1993 found additional evidence that homosexuality is genetically determined. Evidence of a "gay gene" was found when researchers studied the X chromosome in 40 pairs of homosexual brothers. In this group 33 shared identical genetic markers in the tip of the X chromosome, suggesting with more than 99% certainty that the sexual orientation of the men was genetically influenced.[44]

LIFE AS A HOMOSEXUAL

Homosexual behavior between males is illegal in most states. Lesbianism (female homosexuality) is prohibited in fewer states than is male homosexuality. There appear to be several reasons for this: (1) Fewer females than males are homosexual. (2) Lesbians keep their sexual behavior more hidden and are not as likely to form obvious homosexual communities as are males. (3) Most legislators have been males and perhaps see male homosexuality as more of a threat to them than female homosexuality.

The Gay Liberation Movement has been seeking to change negative attitudes and end discriminatory acts toward homosexuals. Yet many people still view homosexuals as psychologically "sick"—as having a form of mental illness. (Until 1974 the American Psychiatric Association defined homosexuality as a mental illness.)

The Gay Liberation Movement is composed of such groups as the Gay Liberation Front, the National Gay Task Force, and the International Union of Gay Athletes. This social movement contends (along with many social scientists) that homosexuality is not a perversion or sickness but is simply a different lifestyle. Their arguments have met with mixed reactions. Some states have repealed antihomosexual legislation, and several cities have passed homosexual civil rights ordinances that prevent discrimination against police officers, teachers, and other city employees who have a homosexual orientation. Other cities and states have rejected bills that sought to ban discrimination against homosexuals.

When Bill Clinton was running for president in 1992, he promised to reverse the 50-year-old policy aimed at keeping homosexuals out of the military. After his election he tried, in 1993, to lift the ban by executive order but encountered strong resistance in the Pentagon and Congress. After months of hearings and negotiations, Congress passed and Clinton signed a bill that has been referred to as "Don't ask, don't tell." New recruits to the military no longer can be asked by military personnel if they are homosexual; however, anyone who openly engages in homosexual conduct can be discharged. As part of the policy, the Pentagon promised to end purges of military personnel who keep their homosexuality private. (Some gay activists consider this new policy to be as onerous as the original prohibition.) The Clinton administration has shown its support for the gay rights movement in another way—by naming more than a dozen openly gay men and women to midlevel government posts.

Courts are increasingly hearing cases involving gay rights issues. Some judges are supportive of gay rights issues, whereas others are not, as illustrated by the following two conflicting decisions (both of which were made in 1993). A federal judge in Virginia denied a lesbian mother custody of her son solely because of her sexuality; he awarded custody to the boy's grandmother. However, in Boston a state supreme court ruling made two lesbians the first gay couple to win approval to adopt a child in Massachusetts.[45]

Because of negative attitudes and discriminatory acts, some homosexuals go to extensive lengths to hide their sexual behavior. They fear discrimination and even loss of employment. They also fear the stigma and embarrassment that they and their families would receive if they "came out" (publicly acknowledged their sexual orientation). Some homosexuals marry someone of the opposite sex and may even hide their

homosexual encounters from their spouses. Leading a double life, with fear of criminal penalties if one's sexual orientation were discovered, is stress producing.

Many larger cities now have homosexual communities that provide an escape from the pressures of leading such a double life. These communities may offer recreational and leisure-time activities and may serve to socialize new entrants into the homosexual subculture. They are often located in a certain geographical area of a city and generally have shops, restaurants, and hotels that are owned and patronized primarily by homosexual customers. The "gay bars" are perhaps the most visible establishments in such communities. Evelyn Hooker describes the social and socialization functions served by gay bars:

> The young man who may have had a few isolated homosexual experiences in adolescence, or indeed none at all . . . may find the excitement and opportunities for sexual gratification appealing and thus begin active participation in the community life. Very often, the debut, referred to by homosexuals as "coming out," of a person who believes himself to be homosexual but who has struggled against it, will occur in a bar when he, for the first time, identifies himself publicly as a homosexual in the presence of other homosexuals. . . . He may be agreeably astonished to discover a large number of men who are physically attractive, personable, and "masculine"-appearing, so that his hesitance in identifying himself as a homosexual is greatly reduced. . . . He becomes convinced that far from being a small minority, the "gay" population is very extensive indeed. Once he has "come out," that is, identified himself as a homosexual to himself and to some others . . . they assist him in providing justifications for the homosexual way of life as legitimate.[46]

Increasingly, homosexuals are "coming out" and acknowledging their sexual orientation. A respondent interviewed by Barry Dank described the functions served by gay bars in this process:

> I knew that there were homosexuals, queers, and whatnot: I had read some books, and I was

Despite the negative and even hostile view many Americans still have of homosexuality, more gay men and women now openly acknowledge their sexual orientation.

resigned to the fact that I was a foul, dirty person, but I wasn't actually calling myself a homosexual yet. . . . The time I really caught myself coming out is the time I walked into this bar and saw a whole crowd of groovy, groovy guys. And I said to myself, there was the realization, that not all gay men are dirty old men or idiots, silly queens, but there are some just normal-looking and acting people, as far as I could see. I saw gay society and I said, "Wow, I'm home."[47]

Unlike other minority-group members, homosexual girls and boys grew up as minorities even within their own families. People of color, for example, are socialized—trained—by their parents, older siblings, and relatives about functioning in a society that is likely to discriminate against them. Gay and lesbian youths have no such training ground, as most young homosexuals are raised in heterosexual families. This makes homosexually identified institutions (the most visible and approachable of which is the gay bar) very important in the life of the homosexual young adult. Most homosexuals patronize these gay bars for only a brief period (primarily while they are formulating their homosexual identity). After this phase, they generally prefer social contact with other homosexuals in environments where the focus is not on alcohol and superficial interactions.

It should be noted that there is a wide variation in homosexual lifestyles, as is true for heterosexuals. Also, lesbians and male homosexuals differ somewhat in their sexual attitudes and practices. Lesbians are more likely to equate sex with love. They tend to engage in sex with fewer partners than do male homosexuals. Their relationships tend to last longer and to be based more on love and affection. Female homosexuals may be less likely to acknowledge their sexual orientation publicly and to participate in a homosexual community.[48]

Lesbians are better able to conceal their sexual orientation because the public is less suspicious of two women living together or otherwise being close to each other. Most female homosexuals have had sexual relationships with men. Jack H. Hedblom notes: "The female homosexual does not prefer sex with a woman because she has had no experience with a man."[49]

The specter of AIDS has had a tremendous impact on homosexual communities, particularly on gay men. Homosexual communities have been active in encouraging federal and state governments to (1) recognize the dangers of AIDS, (2) provide research funds to develop treatments for those who are infected with the AIDS virus, and (3) provide research funds to develop approaches to prevent the spread of AIDS.[50] Homosexual communities have also been advocates of safer sex practices, and many gay men have made responsible and dramatic changes in their sexual practices. Homosexual communities have also developed support systems for people who have

AIDS. (Unfortunately, the larger society has been slow to develop services and programs for people with AIDS, who are often shunned and victimized by discrimination in our society.[51])

CURRENT ISSUES IN HOMOSEXUALITY

As mentioned earlier, a major issue is whether civil rights laws should be enacted to protect homosexuals from discrimination in housing, employment, military service, and other areas. Homosexuals argue that they are refused jobs in teaching, in the military, and in many private corporations. They also are commonly the targets of blackmailers who threaten to reveal their sexual orientation. They assert that legal protection for gay rights will not turn heterosexuals into homosexuals. Having long been the victims of abuse and exploitation, they now want the same protection that other minorities receive.[52]

Those who oppose civil rights laws for homosexuals assert that gays are not like other minority groups who are discriminated against based on physical characteristics (African Americans, women, disabled persons). They believe that homosexuals choose their sexual orientation, which can be changed if they so desire. A number of other objections are also given by opponents: Legislation to protect gay rights would indicate approval of homosexual behavior, which in fact they consider unnatural. Permitting homosexuals to teach in school would unwisely expose children to homosexual attitudes and activities and would probably lead to increased homosexual experimentation. Also, if sanctions were relaxed, homosexuality would flourish, the stability of the family would be threatened, birthrates would drop drastically, and society would be severely damaged. This is, of course, highly unlikely; with or without social sanctions, homosexuals constitute only a small minority of any society. And social support is unlikely to significantly increase behavior so basic to one's being as sexual orientation.

As can be seen, arguments on both sides of this issue are intense. And there are other concerns as well.

Some churches are now marrying homosexual couples who request this ceremony. These marriages are recognized by certain religious groups but not by state laws, which still prohibit homosexuals from marrying. Proponents of gay marriages assert that homosexuals ought to be permitted to receive the same personal gratifications and financial advantages through marriage that are available to heterosexuals. Opponents view these marriages as sacrilegious, as a violation of the purpose of marriage, and as a threat to the stability of the traditional family.

Related issues involve homosexuals' rights to adopt children and to retain custody of their own children after divorce. As we've seen, in some court cases lesbian mothers have won custody of their children; in other cases courts have decreed that lesbian behavior is sufficient evidence that a person is unfit to be a parent. At issue in homosexual adoptions and custody battles is whether homosexuals would pass on their sexual orientation to the child. Initial research findings suggest that this is unlikely to occur.[53] We as a society continue to be confused about how sexual orientation might influence—if at all—other important aspects of life, such as child rearing or work performance.

In the past, psychotherapists who counseled homosexuals generally tried to switch their sexual orientation to heterosexuality.[54] This goal was seldom achieved. Homosexuals often became more anxious and uncomfortable about their sexual orientation but continued to maintain homosexual behavior. The emphasis in counseling has shifted in recent years. Most therapists now help homosexuals to examine their concerns and arrive at a sexual identity they can be comfortable with. The majority of gays choose to continue their homosexual behavior, and counseling is then geared to helping them deal with discrimination and other concerns (such as whether to inform their relatives or employer and whether to "come out" in other ways).

Over time our society has become more tolerant; years ago, efforts to suppress homosexuality were so strong that no newspaper even dared to print the word *homosexual*. Today this orientation is no longer an unmentionable deviancy. It is discussed on the airwaves, in newspapers and magazines, and in political debates. It is depicted in movies and on TV. Openly gay candidates for political office in the United States are increasingly being elected. Officially sanctioned support groups for gays are being established in high schools. Domestic partnerships between gay couples have been officially recognized in dozens of cities, and numerous corporations are granting partners of their homosexual employees the same benefits heterosexual spouses receive. Discrimination on the basis of sexual orientation is now illegal in several states and in nearly 100 cities and counties.

It should be noted that the two most prominent social work organizations in the United States (the Council on Social Work Education and the National Association of Social Workers) have identified gays and lesbians as populations at risk. These organizations also consider it the obligation of all social workers to work toward ending the discrimination and oppression experienced by gays and lesbians in our society.

Asocial Sex Variance

This category of sex variance refers to acts that elicit widespread, strong disapproval and do not have a social structure that supports them. Acts in this category include child molestation, incest, rape, voyeurism, and exhibitionism. People who engage in these behaviors usually act alone; that is, they do not have a social group that encourages and rewards their acts. All of these sex variances are prohibited by laws.

CHILD MOLESTATION

Child molestation is the sexual abuse of a child by an adult. Sexual abuse includes not only sexual intercourse (genital or anal) but also oral-genital contact, fondling, behaviors such as exposing oneself to a child and photographing or viewing a child for the molester's erotic pleasure. Although legal definitions of various forms of sexual contact between older and younger people are clearly delineated in statute books, the central feature that makes the behavior abusive is that the sexual act is designed for the erotic gratification of the older, more powerful person. In child sexual abuse, the child is used as an object for the immediate gratification of another person, generally with no regard for the short- or long-term consequences for the child.

Child molestation is generally regarded as one of the most despicable sexual offenses in our society. The public fears—rightly—that this type of sexual abuse will destroy the innocence of the child and may lead to severe psychological trauma, interrupting the child's (and subsequent adult's) normal sexual development.

How extensive is child molestation? Many studies have been conducted to determine the incidence of child sexual abuse, and they indicate that approximately one in three girls and one in seven boys have experienced sexual abuse.[55]

Over 90% of child molesters are males.[56] A number of factors partially explain this gender imbalance: (1) Men in our culture are socialized toward seeing sexuality as being focused on sexual acts rather than as being a part of an emotional relationship. (2) Men are also socialized to be more aggressive and to believe that appropriate sexual partners are smaller and younger than themselves. In contrast, women are socialized to think that appropriate partners are larger and older than they are. (3) Finally, women in our culture are much more often caregivers of children and therefore are more attuned than men to children's emotional needs. A person who is closely involved since birth with taking care of a child is far less likely to view that child in sexual ways than is someone who has had more incidental contact.

In the past few decades there have been several well-publicized cases of child molestation. In the 1960s a Houston man was convicted for killing nearly 30 runaway male adolescents after having sex with them. In 1979 John Wayne Gacy was arrested and convicted in Chicago for enticing 33 male adolescents into his home, sexually assaulting them, and then killing and burying them under his home. He was executed for these crimes in 1994. On March 11, 1977, Roman Polanski (a noted film director) was arrested in Los Angeles and charged with unlawful sexual intercourse, child molestation, supplying a minor with the drug Quaalude, oral copulation, sodomy, and rape via the use of drugs. A teenage girl was the alleged victim of these charges. After a plea bargain he confessed to and was found guilty of only the first charge. While awaiting sentencing, he fled the United States and has never returned. In 1991 Jeffrey Dahmer in Milwaukee (who was on probation for molesting a 13-year-old boy in 1988) confessed to sexually assaulting, murdering, and dismembering 17 males, some of whom were teenagers. In 1993 Michael Jackson, the immensely popular singer, was accused of prolonged sexual contact with a 13-year-old boy; in 1994 the boy's parents withdrew a civil lawsuit for damages against Jackson after he paid them several million dollars.

Who are child molesters? The stereotype is that a molester is a stranger who lurks in the dark, waiting to pounce on a child who is walking or playing alone. The fact is that in most cases the offender is an acquaintance, friend, or relative.[57] (If the offender is a relative, the abuse is called incest.) Scores of parents, stepparents, scout leaders, child-care workers, and people from all walks of life have been found to be child molesters. Force is rarely used. The abuser generally gains sexual access to the child by manipulation and enticement rather than by use of a threat of force or harm. Actual intercourse is also rare, with the abuse usually being limited to genital fondling.[58] In a small proportion of cases the child may even initiate the contact. However, such initiation does not justify the adult's becoming an active participant and almost always indicates that the child has been sexually abused previously.

A. Nicholas Groth has identified two categories of child molesters: fixated and regressed.[59] A *fixated* child molester's primary sexual object choice is children; he would always prefer a child as a sexual partner over an adult. These men are also known as pedophiles. Pedophilia is a sexual disorder characterized by recurrent sexual fantasies and urges or behaviors involving sexual activity with children.[60] A *regressed* child molester is a person whose usual sexual interest is in adult partners, but, when faced with massive stress (marital difficulty, loss of job, a death in the family, and so on), he "regresses" emotionally (becomes a psychologically younger person) and acts

out sexually toward children to meet his needs. Regressed child molesters generally seek female children as partners; fixated molesters are generally interested in male children. Most incest perpetrators are of the regressed type; they generally function well in society, are in a stable heterosexual relationship, but manage stress inappropriately by acting out sexually toward children. Some molesters have been found to engage in a variety of other inappropriate sexual behaviors, including voyeurism ("Peeping Toms"), exhibitionism, and even rape of adult women.[61] They apparently exercise little control over their sexual impulses; when a child becomes available, he or she becomes a victim.[62]

Even though the most attention in the media and among protective service workers is given to the sexual assault of girls in families (primarily incestual relationships), recent research indicates that child molesters who abuse boys outside the home victimize children in far larger numbers. In an innovative study, Abel and his colleagues discovered that child molesters of boys reported an average (mean) of 150 victims, whereas child molesters of girls reported an average of 20 victims.[63] So why is less attention given to sexual abuse of boys as compared to abuse of girls? The most significant reason is that girls are far more likely to report sexual victimization, whereas boys often view being molested as reflecting an "unmasculine" weakness in themselves. It is thought by many authorities that child molestation of boys is the most underreported major crime in America.

How traumatic is molestation for the child? The factors that have the most emotional impact on child (and later adult) development seem to include (1) the relationship between the child and the adult (it is more damaging to the further development of trust to be abused by someone you are close to than by a stranger); (2) the frequency and duration of the abuse; (3) the actual sexual behaviors engaged in; (4) the number of perpetrators; (5) the reactions of other people if the abuse becomes revealed; (6) the child's general mental and emotional health and coping strategies; and (7) the availability and use of professional intervention by the victim, the abuser, and others (such as the parents). The most helpful interventions following child sexual abuse occur when all significant parties (professionals, parents, siblings, etc.) believe the child's report, when the perpetrator takes full responsibility for his or her actions, and when the child has forums that promote understanding and healing at various stages in his or her later development.

INCEST

Incest is defined as sexual relations between blood relatives. Typically, the definition is extended to include sex between certain nonblood relatives, such as between a stepparent and a child. In the past, families generally attempted to hide this type of abuse, and it usually was not reported. Now, with an increased openness about human sexuality, there is a greater willingness for family members to seek professional help.

In the largest proportion of incest cases reported to the police, the sexual abuse is between father or stepfather and daughter.[64] However, most incest cases are never reported to the police. Brother/sister incest is actually the most common form.[65] This may or may not constitute sexual abuse. If the children are approximately the same age and the sexual activity is mutual and not coerced, this type of incest may be considered normal sexual experimentation. However, if the children are more than a few years apart in age, the potential exists for the younger child to be coerced into activity she or he is not comfortable with. At that point consent no longer exists, and nonconsenting sex is sexual abuse.

Most often incest occurs in the child's home. The child is usually enticed or pressured, rather than physically forced, to participate. The age range of the abused child is from several months to adulthood, although most reports involve teenagers.[66] Children are unlikely to report the sexual abuse because they often have loyalties toward the abuser and realistically fear the consequences for themselves, for the abuser, and for the family.

Causes of Incest. Why does incest occur? Students of sexology have long known that people frequently use sexual behavior to achieve non-sexual rewards. For example, a teenage boy might wish to have intercourse with his girlfriend (sexual behavior) not primarily because he loves her or because he seeks sexual gratification, but rather to enhance his status with his friends and therefore gratify his ego (nonsexual reward).

Adults who are threatened by and fearful of the rejection of other adults often turn for reassurance to children, who are nonthreatening and generally unconditionally loving. This need for acceptance can lead to the adult's initiating sexual behavior (especially if the adult had been sexually abused as a child, as is often the case), because many people view sexual behavior as the ultimate acceptance and ego validation. Most child molesters intend no harm to their victims; they are psychologically needy people who use children in their own battle for emotional survival.

Effects of Incest. Blair and Rita Justice have studied the consequences of incest at three different points in time: while the incest is going on, when the incest is discovered, and years after its occurrence.[67] It is important to bear in mind that incest is a symptom of a disturbed family system.

First we will look at the effects while the incest is occurring. A daughter who has sex with her father often gains special power over him; she controls a very important secret. The daughter can receive special privileges from the father, which makes the other siblings (and even the mother) jealous. Role confusion often occurs. The daughter is still a child, but at times she is a lover and an equal to her father. Victims are deprived of the opportunity to explore and discover their sexuality by themselves or with a peer partner of their choice. Instead, this normal sexual development is violated by an adult imposing his exploitative behavior. The daughter often does not know if her father is going to act as a parent or as a lover, so she is confused about whether she should respond to him as a child or as a sexual partner. The mother may become both a parent and a rival to her daughter. Siblings may also become confused about who is in charge and how to relate to their sister who is receiving special privileges. Fathers in an incestuous family may become jealous and overpossessive of their daughters.

As the daughter grows older, she wants to be more independent and to spend more time with other teenagers. Often she grows more resentful of her father's possessiveness. To make a break from the father, she may run away or tell someone about the incest. Or, she may passively resist the father's rules by, for example, ignoring curfews.

In a small number of cases the incest is discovered when the daughter becomes pregnant. At times it is discovered by the mother, who then may try to stop it by reporting it to the police. (Sometimes the mother discovers the incest but remains quiet.)

If the incest is reported to the police and criminal charges are filed against the father, the entire family is usually caught up in a traumatic, time-consuming, confusing, and costly legal process. When there is legal involvement, the daughter is often subjected to embarrassing and humiliating interrogation. She may feel, at times, that her account of the incest is not believed. Or, she may feel that blame is being placed on her rather than on her father. Once she is recognized as a victim of incest, she may be approached sexually by other men who now view her as "fair game."[68] Often she is removed from the home to prevent further abuse. In addition, the mother and father suffer considerable embarrassment and humiliation. Their marriage may become so conflictful that it ends in divorce.

The long-term effects of incest vary from child to child. Younger children usually do not fully realize the significance of the sexual behavior and tend to suffer less guilt than adolescent victims. However, with young children there is always the danger that, as they grow older and learn about society's taboos against incest, they may start blaming themselves for having participated. Possible long-term effects on the daughter include low self-esteem, guilt, depression, and fear.[69]

The daughter may also become angry at both parents for not protecting her and at the father for exploiting her. Moreover, she may believe that she is somehow to blame for what happened; she may feel tainted by the experience and see herself as worthless or as "damaged goods." Because of her guilt and anger, she may in future years develop difficulties in expressing her sexuality and relating to men. She may feel unable to trust men because she was betrayed and severely hurt by her father, whom she deeply trusted. Some victims seek to blot out their pain and loneliness through self-destructive behavior such as prostitution, drug abuse, or suicide.

If the incest is ongoing and unreported and the victim is an older child, she may attempt to avoid the abuser by running away from home. If she flees, there is a strong possibility that she will become a prostitute to support herself, in part because she has been taught, dysfunctionally, that her sexuality is valued by men and is her most valuable asset. She is also likely to abuse drugs as a method of escaping the life situation she is trapped in.

Some victims during their childhood years seek to deny or suppress the traumas associated with incest. When they become adults, they may experience difficulties in developing relationships with others. Because relationships are founded on trust, and because the victims' fundamental trust in others (and therefore their ability to trust their own judgment of others) has been violated, they often fear making commitments to others in an attempt to protect themselves from further hurt. Many of these victims finally acknowledge as adults the traumas they experience as children. Therapy is highly recommended for these adult victims to help them come to terms with the pain and suffering of having been violated by someone they trusted.

Treatment of Incest. Because incest is only one symptom of a disturbed family, treating these families is difficult and complex. In the past when incest was reported, the victim (usually a teenage girl) was generally placed in a foster home, further victimizing her. Such action was likely to reveal the sexual abuse to the local community. Often, neighbors, relatives, and friends expressed shock and began shunning all members of the family. The disruption usually intensified the marital conflict between husband and wife and generally led to permanent dissolution of the family. In some instances the husband was also prosecuted, which even further intensified the family conflicts.

In recent years a number of social service agencies have been seeking to keep the family intact, particularly when all three of the members involved (husband, wife, and victim) express a desire to maintain the family. A typical intervention requires the father's removal from the home for a period of six months to a year, during which time all family members are involved in individual and group treatment. The incest perpetrator must acknowledge to his wife and daughter that he was entirely responsible for the sexual abuse, that he is sorry it happened, and that he will make the necessary lifestyle and value changes to ensure that the abuse will not recur. The nonabusing parent (typically the mother) is taught assertiveness. Intervention with the mother and daughter is geared toward improving their relationship, which is usually very damaged. The victim (typically the daughter) is helped to process her anger, guilt, and confusion. Eventually all family members are seen in therapy together to help them build, perhaps for the first time, a healthy, functional family system.

RAPE

Forced intercourse is a commonly committed violent crime in the United States.[70] More than 90,000 cases are reported annually, and many more instances go unreported. Victims of rape are hesitant to report the crime, for a variety of reasons. They may feel that reporting the case will do them no good because they have already been victimized. They sometimes fear that they may be humiliated by the questions the police will ask. They are reluctant to press charges because they fear the reactions of the general public and of people close to them, including their boyfriends or husbands. Many fear that, if they report the offense, the rapist will try to attack them again. Some victims just want to try to forget about it. Others fail to report it because they do not want to testify in court. But perhaps the most common reason why women fail to report sexual assault is that they feel—usually wrongly—that they somehow contributed to the rape's occurrence. This

is especially true in the most frequent type of rape—that by an acquaintance.

(In many states rape is defined as a crime that only males can commit. Several years ago there was a former beauty pageant winner who kidnapped a Mormon minister with whom she was infatuated. She tied him up, held him for a few days, and forced him to have sexual relations.[71] More cases in which the woman is the attacker are now being reported, but they are still exceedingly rare.)

There is no profile that fits all rapists. They vary considerably in terms of motivation for committing the rape, prior criminal record, education, occupation, marital status, and so on. In a majority of cases the rapist and his (or her) victim know each other on a first-name basis. A significant proportion of rapes are date rapes.

Rape is primarily an aggressive act and secondarily a sexual act. That is, it is a sexual expression of aggression, not an aggressive expression of sexuality. Many people wrongly believe that rape occurs because the rapist cannot control his sexual arousal or because he is "oversexed." Rape is, instead, the mismanagement of aggression; the rapist's gratification (if any) comes not from the sexual act but rather from the expression of anger or control through the extreme violation of another's body.

There are a number of typologies for classifying rapists, depending on numerous variables. One straightforward model was developed by A. Nicholas Groth,[72] who describes rapists as falling into one of three categories: the anger rapist, the power rapist, and the sadistic rapist.

The *anger rapist* performs his act to discharge feelings of pent-up anger and rage. He is brutal in the commission of his assault, using far more force than is necessary to gain sexual access to his victim. His aim is to hurt and debase his victim; forced sex is his ultimate weapon.

The *power rapist* is interested in possessing his victim sexually, not harming her. He acts out of underlying feelings of inadequacy and is interested in controlling his victim. He uses only the amount of force necessary to gain her compliance. Sometimes he will kidnap his victim and hold her under his control for a long period of time, perhaps engaging in sexual intercourse with her numerous times.

The *sadistic rapist* eroticizes aggression; that is, aggressive force creates sexual arousal in him. He is enormously gratified by his victim's torment, pain, and suffering. His offenses often are ritualistic and involve bondage and torture, particularly to the sexual organs.

We live in a society that promotes aggression and represses sexuality. In the United States males are socialized to be aggressive, even in seeking sexual gratification. For example, men are often expected to play the "aggressive" role in sex. In our culture sex and aggression are frequently confused and combined. In Swedish culture, where sexual information is readily available in the media but depictions of aggression are not, the incidence of rape is low. According to Janet Hyde, the confusion of sex and aggression in socialization practices may lead males to commit rape:

> It may be, then, that rape is a means of proving masculinity for the male who is insecure in his role. For this reason, the statistics on the youthfulness of rapists make sense; youthful rapists may simply be young men who are trying to adopt the adult male role, who feel insecure about doing this, and who commit a rape as proof of their manhood. Further, heterosexuality is an important part of manliness. Raping a woman is a flagrant way to prove that one is a heterosexual.[73]

Date Rape. In a study by Struckman-Johnson of female college students, 22% stated that they had been victimized by at least one incident of forced sexual intercourse on a date.[74] The study demonstrates that date rape is not a rare occurrence.

In some cases date rape seems to result from the mistaken belief on the part of the man that, if he spends money on the woman, he is entitled to (or she is implicitly giving consent to) sexual rewards. The traditional view in dating relationship has been that, when the woman ways "no," she really means "yes." Unfortunately, media depictions of this misinformation abound, from

John Wayne movies to such classics as *Last Tango in Paris* and *Gone with the Wind.* For example, in the movie *The Quiet Man,* John Wayne plays a macho, quiet Irishman. He courts a feisty woman played by Maureen O'Hara, but to no avail. Only after beating up a mean rival, spanking the woman in front of the townspeople, and literally dragging her home does he win her compliance and cooperation. The underlying message seems to be that "real men" obtain power, status, and sexual gratification by violating women sexually—a very dangerous message indeed!

Leon, a college student, described his thinking processes prior to a date rape:

> It's time for me to make my move. Tonight her every dream will come true when I show her what it's like to be with a real man. It'll be the perfect ending to an evening she'll never forget. I knew that she was after more than dinner and dancing from the moment that I picked her up. I mean, check out that dress she's wearing, those fancy jewels, that sexy perfume, and those looks she has been giving me—they're unmistakable. Now that she has agreed to a nightcap at my place, we can end the evening in style. I'll just slide a little closer to her on the couch, slip my arm around her shoulder, and kiss her neck . . . Does she really think that moving away and saying "No!" will stop me? I guess all women play that game. I dropped a bundle on this date and now it's time for her to pay up. Boy, the guys will be impressed to know that I scored with such a classy number. Even if she wanted to, she couldn't stop someone as powerful as me. Besides, everyone knows that when a woman says "No!" she really means "Yes!"

The vast majority of date rapes go unreported. In fact, many of the female victims of sexual assault do not interpret the assault as such.[75] When the victims view themselves as being "in love" with the perpetrator, there is a tendency to see the rape as being within the realm of acceptable behavior.

Kanin studied 71 unmarried college men who were self-disclosed date rapists and compared them to a control group of unmarried college men.[76] The date rapists tended to be sexually predatory. When asked how frequently they attempt to seduce a new date, 62% of the date rapists said "most of the time," compared with 19% of the controls. The date rapists also were much more likely to report using a variety of manipulative techniques on their dates, including falsely professing love, getting the dates high on alcohol or other drugs, and falsely promising to go steady or get engaged.

Men need to learn that "no" means "no." Date-rape educational programs are needed in elementary, secondary, and college settings. Laws against date rape should be more vigorously enforced. And society (including the mass media) must stop glamorizing rape and instead convey that it is a serious crime that takes a devastating toll on its victims.

Effects on Victims. Ann Burgess and Lynda Holmstrom have found that rape generally constitutes a severe crisis for the victims and that aftereffects often persist for six months or longer.[77] They analyzed the reactions of 92 victims of forcible rape and labeled the series of emotional changes experienced by the victims the "rape trauma syndrome."[78]

This syndrome occurs in two phases: an acute phase and a long-term reorganization phase. The *acute phase* begins immediately after the rape (or attempted rape) and may last for several weeks. Victims have an expressive reaction in which they are likely to cry and have feelings of anger, fear, humiliation, tension, anxiety, and a desire for revenge. During this phase victims also usually have periods of controlled reaction in which they mask or deny their feelings and appear calm, composed, or subdued. Victims also undergo many physical reactions during this phase, such as stomach pains, nausea, headaches, insomnia, and jumpiness. In addition, some women who had been forced to have oral sex reported irritation or damage to the throat. Some who had been forced to have anal intercourse reported rectal pain and bleeding. Two feelings were especially common: fear and self-blame. Many women feared future physical violence or continued to suffer from the fear of being murdered during the attack. The self-blame is related to the tendency on the part of the victim and others to "blame the victim." The women often spent hours agonizing over what they thought they had done to bring on the attack or over what they could have done to fight off the attacker. Common self-criticisms are "If only I hadn't walked alone," "If only I had bolt-locked the door," "If only I hadn't worn that tight sweater," and "If only I hadn't been dumb enough to trust that guy."

The *long-term reorganization phase* follows the acute phase. At this point victims may experience a variety of major disruptions. Some women who have been raped outdoors may develop a fear of going outdoors; others who have been raped indoors may develop a fear of being indoors. Some are unable to return to work, particularly if the rape occurred there. Some quit their job and remain unemployed for a long time. Many fear the rapist will find them and assault them again. To attempt to avoid this recurrence, they may move (sometimes several times), change their telephone number, or get an unlisted number. Some develop sexual phobias and have severe difficulties in returning to their regular sexual behaviors. In some cases it takes several years before the victim returns to her previous lifestyle.

In addition, if the victim reports the rape, the police investigation and the trial (if it occurs) are further crises that are experienced. Police and the courts have a history of abusive and callous treatment of rape victims. The police have, at times, conveyed the idea that the victim was fabricating the assault or had willingly agreed to have sex but then changed her mind. The police often ask embarrassing questions about the details of the rape, without showing much understanding or sympathy. In court it is common for the defense attorney to imply that the victim provoked the defendant. Victims are sometimes made to feel as if they are the ones who are on trial.

Of late, fortunately, many police departments have developed sensitive crime units with specially trained officers to intervene in cases of rape and child sexual assault. With such units, victims

EXHIBIT 6.5

How to Attempt to Prevent Rape

There have been a number of suggestions to help women prevent rape and fight off an attacker. These suggestions include having and using secure locks on doors, not walking alone at night, and learning self-defense measures such as judo, aikido, tae kwon do (Korean karate), or jujitsu. Being assertive when saying "no" to unwanted sexual advanced is particularly useful in preventing acquaintance rape.[a] Exercising regularly and keeping in shape are also recommended to give the potential victim the strength to fight back and the speed to run fast. Some experts recommend poking an attacker in the eyes or kneeing him in the groin. Other experts recommend that every women have a psychological strategy to use if attacked, such as telling the rapist that she has cancer of the cervix or a sexually transmittable condition (such as being HIV-positive). If other preventive measures fail, some experts urge dissuading the attacker by regurgitating on him, which can be accomplished by sticking one's finger down one's throat. Another last-ditch strategy is to urinate on him. *It is important that each woman have a strategy, or set of defensive measures, she would seek to use if an attack occurred.* No one type of advice can apply to all situations, because the rapist may respond quite differently to the victim's fighting back, depending on whether he is primarily a power, anger, or sadistic rapist. Therefore, any woman who physically survives a rape should be viewed as having utilized a successful strategy.

On a broader, sociological level, feminists urge a revision in our sex-role socialization practices. Margaret Mead has noted that rape does not occur in societies in which males are socialized to be nurturant rather than aggressive.[b] To reduce rape sharply, Janet S. Hyde recommends the following changes in socialization practices:

If little boys were not so pressed to be aggressive and tough, perhaps rapists would never develop. If adolescent boys did not have to demonstrate that they are hypersexual, perhaps there would be no rapists. . . .

Changes would also need to be made in the way females are socialized, particularly if women are to become good at self-defense. Weakness is not considered a desirable human characteristic, and so it should not be considered a desirable feminine characteristic, especially because it makes women vulnerable to rape. . . . While some people think that it is silly for the federal government to rule that girls must have athletic teams equal to boys' teams, it seems quite possible that the absence of athletic training for girls has contributed to making them rape victims. . . .

Finally, for both males and females, we need a radical restructuring of ideas about sexuality. As long as females are expected to pretend to be uninterested in sex and as long as males and females play games on dates, rape will persist.[c]

[a]Janet S. Hyde, *Understanding Human Sexuality,* 4th ed. (New York: McGraw-Hill, 1990), pp. 484–486.
[b]Margaret Mead, *Sex and Temperament in Three Primitive Societies* (New York: Morrow, 1935).
[c]Hyde, *Understanding Human Sexuality,* pp. 484–486.

are less likely to be further victimized by authorities. Also, a number of states have enacted "shield" evidence laws, which prohibit defense attorneys from asking questions about the victim's previous sexual experiences (except with the alleged rapist) during a rape trial. (In the past, defense attorneys sought to imply that the victim was promiscuous and therefore probably seduced the defendant.)

Because rape and its aftereffects are extremely

Many communities now have rape crisis centers that offer counseling and medical and legal services to rape victims.

traumatic, Burgess and Holmstrom urge counseling for victims in order to (1) provide support and allow the victims to vent their feelings, (2) lend support and guidance during the medical tests and police interrogation, (3) provide similar support during the trial, and (4) provide follow-up counseling for emotional reactions to the rape.

Burgess and Holmstrom also note that, because a majority of rapes are not reported, many of the victims have a *silent rape reaction.* Nonreporters not only fail to report the rape to the police, but many tell no one about it. They are likely to experience the same adjustment problems as victims who report the rape experience. However, the trauma for nonreporters is often intensified because they have no way of expressing or venting their feelings. Some nonreporters eventually seek professional counseling for other problems, such as depression, anxiety, or inability to have orgasms. Often such problems are then found to stem from the rape. Women who have had secret rape experiences should be helped to

talk about them so they can gradually learn to deal with the trauma. A number of communities now have rape crisis centers that provide counseling, medical services, and legal services to victims.

EXHIBITIONISM AND VOYEURISM

Exhibitionists and voyeurs are frequently referred to as "flashers" and "Peeping Toms." They are often considered nuisances rather than serious threats to society or to individuals. There is, of course, more alarm and disdain when exhibitionists disrobe in front of children. Having someone peek into our homes is also alarming. Of greater concern is the recent research finding that exhibitionists and voyeurs are also likely to engage in more assaultive sex offenses, such as sexual abuse of children and even rape.[79] This finding contradicts the traditional view that exhibitionists and voyeurs usually don't commit more harmful sexual acts.

To some extent all of us have probably displayed our bodies to others, perhaps during nude swimming (skinny-dipping) or sunbathing. A number of years ago streaking (running nude on college campuses and other places) was popular. "Mooning" (displaying one's buttocks in public) has been a common fad among high school and college students. However, the exhibitionist obtains a great deal of sexual arousal by exposing his genitals to unwitting strangers. The exhibitionist may be unable to become aroused by more normal expressions of sexuality and is often quite compulsive in his exposure behaviors. For him, exposure is not an occasional lark with the guys but a planned, frequently repeated activity.

Voyeurism is defined as watching people undress, viewing them in the nude, or observing them performing sexual acts without their knowledge or consent. Everyone has probably found enjoyment at times in looking at pictures of people who are nude or seminude, going to nightclubs featuring nude dancers, going to X-rated movies, watching our sex partner undress, or observing the attractive physiques of others out in public. Again, it should be noted that invasion-of-privacy voyeurism is demeaning and threatening to an unwilling victim.

Exhibitionism and voyeurism involve behaviors that differ in degree from the kinds of showing and looking that are considered "normal" in our society.

PERSONAL SEXUAL CONCERNS

All of us at one time or another have had sexual concerns. These concerns can take an infinite variety of forms. A 17-year-old male may feel anxious about becoming sexually involved with someone he is dating. A man who has had sex with a prostitute may be worried that he has acquired AIDS. Adolescents may feel guilty about masturbating. A wife may feel guilty about an extramarital affair. Men may worry about premature ejaculation, failure to have an erection, or failure to become sexually aroused. Some women are concerned because they seldom achieve orgasm. Some married people become alarmed because their sex life seems boring and routine. Some people may be unhappy with various sexual techniques and approaches used by their partners. A rape or incest victim may still be suffering the trauma of the experience. Some people may strongly admire someone of their own sex and wonder if this attraction means they are a homosexual. Middle-aged people may fear losing their sexual capacities in the future. Some may find intercourse painful. A husband may know his wife has had previous sexual experiences with others and feel angry, hurt, or threatened. Sex counseling and sex therapy are directly designed to resolve personal sexual problems.

Sex counseling is short-term, often crisis-oriented, counseling directed toward the alleviation of some immediate sexual concern. Sex therapy, on the other hand, tends to be somewhat more comprehensive and longer in duration and focuses on resolving specific sexual dysfunctions (such as premature ejaculation or erectile difficulties in men and failure to achieve orgasm or painful intercourse in women). Sex therapy involves several stages: problem identification, history gathering, physical examination, information giv-

ing, assignment of sexual experiences designed to resolve the dysfunction, and ongoing evaluation.[80] In actual counseling, the distinctions between sex counseling and sex therapy are not clear-cut. Sex counseling and sex therapy treatment programs are available in many communities. Counselors and psychotherapists at most social service agencies occasionally counsel clients with sexual concerns. Private sex therapy centers, often based on the treatment programs pioneered by Masters and Johnson, provide services in many larger communities.

SEX COUNSELING*

Social workers have long been recognized as resources for people suffering from problems related to sex. Alfred Kinsey observed that social workers were sought out more often than any other professional group by people with sexual concerns.[81] Further, most sex counseling done by social workers is performed by people whose primary professional role is not that of sex counselor. Probation and parole officers, group home supervisors, and school, medical, and psychiatric social workers are frequently sought out for counseling by people with problems related to sex.

Prerequisites to Effective Counseling

In addition to the requirements of the specific professional position, there are two basic prerequisites to becoming an effective sex counselor: comfort and knowledge.

To be effective as a social worker, one must be professionally comfortable with the subject matter. This is absolutely essential in the matter of sex, about which most people tend to be anxious and embarrassed. This certainly doesn't mean that the counselor would feel comfortable *experiencing* all the various sexual behaviors her or his

---

*The remainder of this chapter was written entirely by Lloyd G. Sinclair.

clients might report. Rather, it means the counselor should be comfortable enough with her or his own sexuality that the behaviors reported by clients, however aberrant, don't threaten the worker's personal sexuality or identity. Further, as in all helping relationships, when the counselor is confronted with a situation that demands additional expertise or comfort, ethics dictate that he or she identify the situation honestly and make an appropriate referral. Social workers can be effective as role models to their clients, demonstrating that sex can be discussed directly, clearly, and without embarrassment.

Because social workers aren't inherently more comfortable about sex than anybody else, they need to develop their comfort level. Although there are many ways to do this, some of the most effective include examining one's own sexual history and values, talking frankly with others about sex, gaining some familiarity with sexually explicit material, and gaining as much knowledge— the second prerequisite—as possible.

It is generally assumed that knowledge and training about a subject are necessary if one is to be helpful to others in that area. Surprisingly, many people seem not to apply this premise to sex. They consider themselves to be self-taught "sexperts," believing that their own personal experience provides them with as much knowledge as they need. This assumption is not only incorrect but is downright dangerous and unethical. Particularly in the past three decades, we have learned a great deal about sex; the responsible, competent sex counselor will take it on herself or himself to gain as much of this knowledge as possible.

Case Example 6.1 presents four specific examples of professional sex counseling. As you read them, think about the comfort and knowledge that would be required to effectively resolve the problems presented.

The Choice of Words in Sex Counseling

When talking with clients about sex, careful consideration should be given to the choice of words.

Sex words can be roughly categorized into three groups: slang, colloquial, and scientific. Slang words and expressions, such as *tits* and *getting laid,* are used to describe things vigorously and often demeaningly. Colloquial language, such as *making love* or *coming,* defines things clearly, relatively uneuphemistically, and usually with a positive connotation. Scientific language, like *coitus* and *testicles* connotes precision and a certain value-free detachment.

It is important to realize that most people use slang terms when talking about sex. Warren R. Johnson illustrated this point when he wrote: "Fuck, screw, jack-off, cock, pussy, wet dream, and the like are, perhaps, regrettably vulgar, but they are the dominant linguistic sex vehicles of American English."[82]

This is not to suggest that helping professionals should necessarily use slang terms when talking with clients. Sex counselors must, however, *understand* the meaning of slang terms and be *comfortable* when hearing them. This is particularly critical when working with certain individuals, such as mentally retarded persons, whose language barrier may be severe. The vocabulary that is most comfortable to the counselor may be completely misunderstood by the client. In these cases, the use of slang terms may be essential to communicate effectively.

Most counselors develop a vocabulary that is comfortable for them, somewhere between slang and scientific. When the words used are overly technical, they tend to be misunderstood, or the language may be a mask for the counselor's discomfort. The major problem with slang words is that some clients may interpret them as vulgar.

Emma Lee Doyle, a sex therapist from Dallas, Texas, illustrates the problem of sex words in a colorful case example. When interviewing a woman client, Doyle asked her what her husband did sexually that she really disliked. The woman replied: "He insists on referring to my genital area as my 'pussy.' I hate the word 'pussy.' It's so demeaning and vulgar." When Doyle asked what words she preferred for him to use, she said "I wish he'd call it my 'cunt'; it's so much more refined." The sensitive therapist is cautious in her or his use of words, taking care to listen to

CASE EXAMPLE 6.1   Four Examples of Sex Counseling

BEN, A NURSING-HOME RESIDENT

Fran was a social worker in a nursing home. A nurse who worked nights had become very upset the previous evening because she had walked into the room of an elderly resident, Ben, and found him masturbating. She had scolded him for his behavior and had made the incident known to several other people.

Fran decided that this was something that shouldn't be ignored. She spoke first to the nurse to learn more about the incident. The nurse thought the behavior was abhorrent, using words like "perverted," "juvenile," and "animalistic" in her description. Fran then spoke to Ben. He expressed regret and embarrassment about the incident, felt his privacy had been severely violated, but concluded that he "really should act his age."

Fran knew that masturbation was a healthy, normal sexual outlet for all people, regardless of age. Indeed, for this man, masturbation was perhaps the only attainable means presently available to express his sexuality; his wife of 45 years had died a few years before. Fran was also aware that many people, including older people themselves, believe that sex is for the young and that the only legitimate sexual expression is that which is shared by a heterosexual couple.

Fran convinced Ben of the normalcy of self-stimulation and reassured him that it was not his behavior, but the nurse's, that was the problem. They discussed ways that he could enjoy more privacy, in order to honor his right to personal, solitary space. Ben appeared grateful for the recognition of his personhood. Fran spoke again to the nurse. She obviously had strong ideas about masturbation, and Fran knew she wasn't going to change them. People who have fixed, powerful emotions in response to behavior that is enjoyable to *others* (and that doesn't affect them) are often responding to something in themselves that is threatening.

Fran's goal, instead, was to encourage the nurse to recognize the residents' need for privacy to maintain self-esteem. The nurse agreed that living in a nursing home deprived residents of most of what they had enjoyed throughout their adult lives—self-determination, property, privacy. Because the nursing home was, in part, a medical care facility, there were good reasons why many of the residents' personal needs had to be compromised. But there were also simple ways to respect their rights. Fran and the nurse agreed that residents should not lock themselves into their rooms, but a closed door could be respected by a knock and an invitation to enter, rather than the staff's current habit of merely barging in. They took this idea to the nursing-home director, who agreed to have the staff implement the policy for a trial period.[a]

[a]Two books that address the sexual concerns and habits of older people are Edward M. Brecher, *Love, Sex, and Aging* (Boston: Little, Brown, 1984), and Bernard D. Starr and Marcella Bakur Weiner, *The Starr-Weiner Report on Sex and Sexuality in the Mature Years* (New York: McGraw-Hill, 1981). A film that portrays many issues related to intimacy, sexuality, and loneliness among older people in institutions is *Rose by Any Other Name*, available from Adelphi University Center on Aging, Garden City, NY.

TINA, AN ADOLESCENT GROUP HOME RESIDENT

Pat, a social worker in a group home for adolescent women, became concerned about Tina, a 16-year-old resident. Tina had confided to some of the other girls in the house that she and her friend, Dennis, were having intercourse regularly. Pat was faced with several dilemmas: (1) In wanting to respect their privacy, was it appropriate to confront Tina on the subject? (2) If she did confront her, should Pat try to stop Tina from having intercourse? (3) Should she respect Tina's right to make her own decisions and suggest that they use a contraceptive to reduce the chance of Tina's becoming pregnant or contracting a sexually transmitted disease?

Pat decided that, although ignoring the entire issue would certainly be easiest for *her*, it probably would not be in Tina's best interests. Pat was most concerned that Tina might become pregnant or contract a disease, causing negative consequences for herself, Dennis, the potential child, and others.

Pat examined her values and her knowledge about teenage sexuality. She was aware that Tina might be, among her immediate peer group, in the majority in having intercourse. One recent study had shown that 45% of teenage girls had had intercourse, and the average age of first intercourse for the girls in this study was 16.2 years.[b] Although a 16-year-old might be viewed by Pat as inappropriately young to be sexually active, she realized that Tina's values were different from hers. Besides, practically speaking, there was little that Pat could do to force Tina to stop, even if she wanted to.

Whereas the aspects of Tina's behavior that affected her alone were largely her business, the prospect of a child being born to a 16-year-old was another concern. Pat knew that 1 million teenagers in the United States became pregnant every year and that 13% of all births in this country are to teenage women.[c] She didn't want Tina to be among these statistics. And, although it was admittedly unlikely, the possibility of Tina becoming infected with HIV (the virus that causes AIDS) and passing it on to her child was too horrible to imagine. She decided that it was appropriate to encourage Tina to protect herself from an unwanted pregnancy and disease.

Pat approached Tina to discuss the issue. Although Tina was initially reluctant to talk about it, Pat was able, with some perseverance, to draw her out. Tina confided that she was, indeed, engaging in regular sexual activity with Dennis, that they were not using a contraceptive, and that she certainly did not want to get pregnant. She said they were very much in love with each other and considered their sexual activity to be a testimony of their love. In regard to the possibility of contracting a disease, she thought only gay people got AIDS.

Tina's comments seemed reasonable to Pat—most people believe that sex *is* a statement of love. But Tina was only 16. Could her love be as real as an older

[b]Centers for Disease Control, "Morbidity and Mortality Weekly Report," Jan. 19, 1988, vol. 37, S2.
[c]U.S. Bureau of the Census, *Statistical Abstract of the United States, 1991* (Washington, DC: U.S. Government Printing Office, 1991), pp. 62–73.

(continued)

person's? Pat reflected on her own history, remembering when she was 16 and felt very much in love. She had waited to have intercourse until later—she hadn't even considered it at age 16—but Tina was living in a different environment.

Pat encouraged Tina to talk more about love and sex. Was the sexual aspect of their relationship enhancing other aspects? Did she feel it was good for each of them as individuals?

After considerable discussion, Tina observed that sex really wasn't that important to her. Although it was somewhat pleasurable from an emotional standpoint, it wasn't as physically exciting as it had been early in the relationship. Lately she had felt trapped by the expectation of intercourse whenever she and Dennis were alone together. Sex had, in her mind, taken on entirely too much importance. She feared that their sexual activity was the major reason for Dennis's interest in her.

The more she talked, the clearer it became that Tina wanted permission *not* to have intercourse. Both she and Dennis had been under tremendous peer pressure to "grow up," and she thought they had become involved in intercourse because it was expected behavior. She wondered if Dennis was really that interested in sex, or if perhaps he just needed to act out a role. This uncertainty had allowed her to put off decision making about birth control (she might stop having intercourse, so she wouldn't need it) and confronting Dennis directly (if sex *was* that important to him, maybe he would break up with her if he knew her true feelings).

Pat suggested that Tina discuss her feelings with Dennis and not assume that sex was something too volatile to talk about. She encouraged Tina to be assertive about what was good for her and pointed out that no one should engage in sexual activity primarily for *someone else.* Pat further encouraged Tina to think about possible alternatives to intercourse—sexual and nonsexual—that Tina might feel more comfortable with and Dennis would enjoy. Tina agreed to bring it up with Dennis the next weekend, and she and Pat would talk further after that. In the meantime, Tina agreed that, if intercourse occurred, she should insist they use a condom.

Counselors should be aware that often a sexual problem is really another kind of problem. This is especially the case with children, adolescents, and people who live in institutions, or anyone who may be deprived of adequate attention.

Children learn quite early in life that an effective way to generate attention is to do something that is sexual and inappropriate. Because many adults are anxious about sexual matters, the tendency is to overreact when forced to confront them. When one adds the fact that most people, particularly the young, have very limited access to good information about appropriate sexual behavior, the result is often sexual experimentation, which is seen by society as inappropriate.[d]

[d]For an excellent discussion of adolescent sexuality, see Lorna J. Sarrel and Philip M. Sarrel, *Sexual Unfolding* (Boston: Little, Brown, 1979). A book that is helpful to parents in talking with their adolescent children is Carol Cassell, *Straight from the Heart: How to Talk to Your Teenagers about Love and Sex* (New York: Simon and Schuster, 1987).

JIM, A FOSTER-HOME RESIDENT

Jim was a 14-year-old male who lived in a foster home. His history included many short-term living situations with relatives and in foster and groups homes. Jim's current foster parents became aware, through the parents of 10-year-old Steve, that Jim had repeatedly pressured Steve into exploring and touching each other's genital areas. Jim had also suggested that they experiment with oral sex. Steve was frightened but couldn't seem to say no to Jim.

Jim's social worker intervened in this situation by talking first with Steve's parents to determine what their reaction had been when Steve first reported the incidents to them. They had not, fortunately, reacted with alarm (a not-uncommon response that can be more damaging to the child than the behavior itself). They commended Steve for telling them about it, assured him that he was not at fault, answered his questions, and told him that, although it wasn't that serious, he shouldn't do anything that was being forced on him or otherwise did not seem right. Because Steve's parents responded so appropriately with him, the social worker chose not to meet directly with Steve and encouraged his parents to continue to be *askable* with him. They could, further, suggest ways for Steve to avoid a compromising situation with Jim, should another incident occur.

The social worker then met with Jim's foster parents. When informed of Jim's behavior, they had reacted with alarm, reprimanded him, and confined him to the house afternoons and evenings for several days. The parents remained confused, upset, and angry about Jim's behavior. The social worker acknowledged that forced sexual behavior is clearly inappropriate but conveyed that same-sex behavior is relatively normal for an inquisitive, maturing adolescent. In fact, in boys under the age of 15, homosexual contact is more common than heterosexual contact.[e] The foster parents seemed relieved when the social worker offered to meet with Jim.

When talking to Jim, the social worker informed him of his awareness of the situation and asked him about it. Jim told the worker that he had explored genitals with Steve but initially denied having been the aggressor. When Jim realized that he would not be punished by the social worker for being honest, he conceded that the behavior had been at his initiation.

The social worker pondered the most appropriate method of dealing with the problem. What was Jim's behavior indicating? Was he merely curious? Was he a homosexual? Was he exercising power and dominance over his young friend? Did he not know the behavior was inappropriate? Is this behavior an early indication that Jim might grow into a child molester or even a rapist?

The social worker knew that adult child molesters often began their sexually abusive behaviors as adolescents,[f] and boys who are sexually assaulted sometimes

[e]Ira L. Reiss, *Journey into Sexuality* (Englewood Cliffs, NJ: Prentice-Hall, 1986).
[f]David Finkelhor, *A Sourcebook on Child Sexual Abuse* (Beverly Hills, CA: Sage, 1986).

(continued)

CASE
EXAMPLE 6.1   *(continued)*

become child molesters as adults.[g] So, although it was important not to overreact to this incident, it could not just be ignored as "boys will be boys." If Jim was particularly focused on sex with younger children, professional intervention would be appropriate.

After a lengthy, frank discussion, the social worker concluded that Jim did indeed know that forcing sexual behavior on someone else was wrong. The social worker stressed the importance of consent in sexuality. There did seem to be elements of curiosity operating, but they didn't entirely account for the behavior.

Jim stated that he was as interested sexually in girls as he was in boys, and his preference would be to have a consenting sexual relationship with a teenage girl. His choice of Steve seemed to be more a result of accessibility than anything else. The social worker was aware that a majority of adolescents engage in sex play with members of their own gender and that the label *homosexual* can safely be applied only to adults who have and prefer sexual relationships with members of their own sex.[h]

Jim seemed to have chosen Steve partly because, being older, there was more likelihood of pressuring him to get what he (Jim) wanted. But the most important element seemed to be the attention he was likely to generate in adults—foster parents, social workers, and others—when the behavior was reported.

Had the social worker seen these incidents solely—or indeed primarily—as a sexual problem, he would probably have experienced little success in dealing with Jim. (If attention is the reward, Jim is likely to act out more and more to continue the shower of concern and attention from significant adults. The more therapy the social worker does, the more Jim is likely to continue, even if punishment is involved.)

The social worker was aware that human beings' need for attention and recognition is one of the strongest emotional drives. When people are feeling unnoticed, rejected, or discounted, they may experience huge amounts of pain, to the point of threatening their lives to gain attention.[i] This is a process the person is usually not consciously aware of. Punishment is not necessarily a negative consequence: At least when one is being punished, she or he is being recognized by the punisher.

The treatment plan developed by the social worker was designed to encourage Jim's foster parents to give him attention for appropriate, positive behavior. If inappropriate sexual incidents were to occur, the parents agreed to reprimand Jim briefly but drop further discussion or punishment. The social worker also encouraged the foster parents to talk with Jim about sex, independent of the incidents, to give him information and help him make healthy decisions.[j]

[g]Ann Wolbert Burgess and Christine A. Grant, *Children Traumatized in Sex Rings* (Washington, DC: National Center for Missing and Exploited Children, 1988).

[h]Sol Gordon, "Ten Heavy Facts about Sex" (Syracuse, NY: Ed-U Press, 1975). This exceptionally creative pamphlet designed for adolescents answers frequently asked questions about sex.

[i]A. J. Bachrach, W. J. Erwin, and J. P. Mohr, "The Control of Eating Behavior in an Anorexic by Operant Conditioning Techniques," in *Case Studies in Behavior Modification*, eds. L. P. Ullman and L. Krasner (New York: Holt, Rinehart & Winston, 1965) pp. 153–163.

[j]An excellent book to help young people learn more about sex is Eleanor S. Morrison, Kay Starks, Cynda Hyndman, and Nina Ronzio, *Growing Up Sexual* (New York: Van Nostrand, 1980).

The social worker informed the parents of the possibility of increased attention-getting sexual acts, particularly once the activity following the most recent one died down. A well-known pattern for behavior that gains a reward (in this case, attention) is to undergo a radical increase once the reward is removed.[k] Sometimes people, desperate for attention, escalate their behavior in a vain attempt to force the response they are seeking when they are deprived of it. Usually the behavior will disappear quickly if the previously expected reward is consistently withheld.

In fact, this escalation did not occur. The social worker continued contact with Jim and his foster family, but no further inappropriate sexual acts were reported.

CARRI, SINGLE AND PREGNANT

Carri came to a family planning clinic requesting to speak to someone regarding her pregnancy. She had missed her period and tested positive on a pregnancy test.

Carri told the counselor she had been in a relationship with Bruce for two years, but lately they had been distant and argumentative. She was feeling little support from him in general and had, for that reason, not revealed to him that she was pregnant. It was clear to her that she hadn't wanted to conceive, but they had been irregular users of birth control, assuming a pregnancy wouldn't happen to them.

The counselor asked her to discuss her thoughts about her alternatives. Carri was 19, a sophomore in college, and interested in continuing her studies through a graduate degree in journalism. One of her major concerns was that her pregnancy, if continued, would interrupt her career goals.

She was worried about her relationship with Bruce. They had discussed ending it, but neither seemed to have the courage to do so. Carri felt that, if the relationship had continued as it started—warm, loving, supportive—she would consider getting married to Bruce. But not now. Besides, she felt that a pregnancy was a poor reason to get married.

Carri talked about putting the child up for adoption. Although this would allow her to resume her studies relatively quickly without feeling pressure to get married, she was terrified of her parents' reactions. She felt they might reject her, or influence her to get married, or, at the very least, be extremely disappointed. Carri feared those reactions greatly.

The circumstances seemed to point to abortion as the best alternative. But was abortion murder? She had always abhorred the idea of abortion and never thought she would consider it for herself. Abortion was certainly not an alternative she would feel good about.

The counselor spent a great deal of time simply listening. Carri needed to talk with someone and had not yet trusted her dilemma to a friend. It was also clear that she had spent a lot of time probing her predicament. The counselor helped Carri sort her alternatives. *Would* her parents reject her? *Would* suspending her studies for a semester or two be that serious a problem? What about the option of keeping the child and returning to school once the baby could be taken care of by a sitter?

[k]James Deese and Steward H. Hulse, *The Psychology of Learning* (New York: McGraw-Hill, 1967).

(continued)

CASE
EXAMPLE 6.1   *(continued)*

Carri worried about whether getting an abortion was selfish, or whether it meant she disliked children. They talked about the quality of life as being important. If Carri were to raise the child herself, she might not be as able to give time, love, and energy as fully as if she had planned the pregnancy. Another stark reality was economic: Carri knew that her lack of financial resources would pose an ongoing problem should she decide to keep the child. They agreed it wasn't exactly an act of selflessness to give birth to someone she didn't have time to feed or read to—someone who might grow to feel lonely and resented. The counselor encouraged Carri to recognize her own needs as important and accept the validity of wanting what seemed best for herself.

The counselor raised the question of whether to share the dilemma with Bruce. Although Carri feared rejection from him, they both agreed he had a right to know about the pregnancy. Because Carri was the one who would ultimately be most affected by the pregnancy, the primary decision should rest with her. But a part of her decision might be determined by Bruce's response. Further, Carri felt she needed someone close to talk with about her feelings and to share her burden with. With some encouragement from the counselor, Carri decided to discuss the matter with Bruce. The counselor suggested, further, that it might be helpful to talk with another close friend.

After an intense, 90-minute discussion, the counselor suggested that Carri go home, talk with Bruce, think about it some more, and come back in a couple of days for further discussion. She was early enough in her pregnancy that time was not critical. Although Carri was eager to make her decision, she agreed that additional time would probably help.

As the counselor left the session, she was aware of being emotionally drained. She had talked with many women in a similar predicament before, but she was struck by the pain in each individual. These are almost never simple decisions, and she realized how important it was to present options fairly and accurately, guiding the client but not deciding for her.

---

clients for the connotations they place on the words they use.

Levels of Therapeutic Intervention

Jack S. Annon, a psychologist and sex therapist from Honolulu, Hawaii, has developed an extremely useful conceptual scheme for the treatment of sexual problems.[83] He rejects the notion that the alleviation of sexual dysfunction de-

mands, in every case, intensive therapy. Rather, he suggests a model providing four levels of intervention. It is called the PLISSIT model. The acronym stands for the following:

P   Permission
LI Limited Information
SS Specific Suggestions
IT Intensive Therapy

Annon believes that most sexual problems can be treated effectively by the counselor's simply

Occasionally the decision would seem pretty obvious—the 16-year-old rape victim, the 13-year-old who became pregnant by her father, the women who had been exposed to German measles. But these cases were rare. Most of the people who were coping with an unintended pregnancy would be able to have the child and would probably be at least adequate parents. But should they be forced into parenthood because they had accidentally become pregnant? The courts have said they shouldn't, but each individual needs to decide for herself.

Carri returned one week later. She had talked several times with Bruce and decided to have an abortion. He accompanied her on the day of her appointment. They agreed to postpone any decision about the future of their relationship until the crisis had passed. The counselor explained the medical procedure to them and discussed birth control. Carri had decided to start on oral contraceptives following the abortion.

Although it is a hotly contested issue because of people's deep moral and religious feelings, abortion remains available to people in many areas of the United States. Most abortion counseling is done immediately prior to the medical procedure. Counseling should involve a discussion of at least three matters: the decision to terminate the pregnancy, the medical procedure, and birth control. Prior to the 1973 Supreme Court decision legalizing abortions in all states, the procedures were often performed by unqualified people in unsafe surroundings. As a result, many people have fears and misinformation about the safety of the medical procedure. The abortion counselor can point out that abortion, when performed early in pregnancy by a physician, is considerably safer than carrying the pregnancy to term.[l] She or he should answer whatever questions the patient has about the medical procedure— how she is likely to feel, for what amount of time, what her recovery will involve, what aftercare is required, and so forth.

The decision to terminate a pregnancy is a difficult one for most people, although not for everyone. A sensitive counselor will probe the patient's feelings and thoughts regarding her options. Particularly for the woman who is undecided, it is critical to provide a calm and supportive atmosphere to facilitate her making the best decision.

[l]U.S. Department of Health and Human Services, Center for Disease Control, "Abortion Surveillance Report: 1981," 1985; National Center for Disease Statistics, "Health, United States: 1987," 1988.

---

giving the client well-placed, accurate *permission.* As it is used in this model, permission implies a kind of professional reassurance—letting clients know they are normal, OK, not perverted or deviant. Many people are not bothered by the specific behavior they are engaging in but are concerned that other people may view it as wrong or aberrant. These concerns frequently involve masturbation ("it's only for kids"), fantasies and dreams ("to think about it is equal to doing it"), or behaviors expected by society but not desired by the individual ("anal intercourse is the latest thing"). The case of Tina, discussed in Case Example 6.1, is an illustration of a client seeking permission *not* to engage in a certain sexual activity.

A smaller group of people suffering from sexual problems can be treated by the helping profession's disseminating *limited information.* Limited information, usually expanding on permission, provides the client with "specific factual information directly relevant to the particular sexual concern."[84] An example of this was presented by a 68-year-old client who had believed, for as long as he could remember, that human beings were capable of a certain number of orgasms in life, and no more. So he had *rationed* them, always confining his orgasms to a single intercourse experience each weekend. The therapist informed him that what he had believed was incorrect. In fact, he could enhance his ability to respond sexually by maintaining a frequency and regularity of response. After receiving this information, the client began making up for a great deal of lost time. His need in this area was for a specific piece of accurate information. Because so many people suffer from misinformation about sex, examples of people needing this kind of intervention abound. Often the inaccuracies involve myths about averages (sizes, frequencies), masturbation, menstruation, and aging.

A still smaller number of clients need intervention at Annon's next level, *specific suggestions.* The therapist offers the suggestions only after she or he has taken a *sexual problem history.* The problem history includes (1) description of the current problem, (2) onset and course of the problem, (3) client's concept of the cause and maintenance of the problem, (4) past treatment and outcome, and (5) current expectancies and goals of treatment.[85]

This history is short of a complete sexual history but provides more background than is generally needed for permission or limited information. The history is important to maximize the likelihood that the specific suggestions will be effective in the alleviation of the sexual distress. Specific suggestions are often given to relieve performance problems. For example, the woman who finds intercourse painful due to lack of lubrication might benefit from suggestions to slow down, allowing her adequate time for arousal, and to identify verbally to her partner behaviors that are pleasurable to her.

The final level, *intensive therapy,* is required by a very small number of people with sexual complaints. Their dysfunctions are sufficiently involved and complicated that intervention using permission, limited information, and specific suggestions is not sufficient to alleviate the dysfunction.

SEX THERAPY

Until the late 1960s, most helping professionals assumed that sexual functioning was an entirely natural activity and that any dysfunction was merely a by-product of other individual or relationship problems. Thus the resolution of sexual problems would follow the resolution of other problems. Indeed, if one set out to resolve *only* the sexual problem and was successful, some other problem would surface because the sexual problem was seen as only a symptom of a larger pathology.

Depending on the therapist's theoretical framework and philosophical beliefs, these psychological problems might be the result of unresolved conflicts, incomplete growth in a particular stage, communication problems, or perhaps faulty learning. When a client sought therapeutic help with a sexual problem, the therapist set out to improve functioning in her or his life in general, assuming that sexual functioning would follow suit. Often it did.

But, alarmingly, often it did not. People would undergo psychoanalysis or another form of psychotherapy, would gain insight into themselves and their problems, but would continue to suffer from premature ejaculation, inability to experience orgasm, inhibited sexual desire, or some other sexual problem.

Masters and Johnson

In 1957, William Masters and Virginia Johnson undertook their classic study of the physiology of human sexual response. Their research in this area was the most comprehensive ever performed, either before or since.

On completion of their research on human sexual response, Masters and Johnson began, in 1959, to treat people with sexual dysfunctions. They departed radically from the prevailing thinking of the day, which considered sexual problems merely manifestations of other problems. Masters and Johnson identified the relationship of the two partners as the client, rather than one person or the other; indeed, they *required* both partners to participate in the process of therapy. They did what many others had thought untenable—they isolated the sexual problem, dealt with it directly in short-term therapy, and generated extremely successful results.

Masters and Johnson's methods are reported in *Human Sexual Inadequacy*[86] (a condensation for the layperson is *Understanding Human Sexual Inadequacy*[87]). Virtually all forms of sex therapy developed after Masters and Johnson published their results have been variations on their original approach. Further, there is no evidence that relief of a sexual problem leads to the formation of a replacement problem.

In the 1990s there seems to be another decided trend among sex therapists across the country. It could be described as a pendulum swinging back toward the center. In the past, the pendulum swung one way as therapists sought to treat sexual problems by "traditional" methods (that is, by helping the client gain insight into her or his personality and not by directly talking about sex). Then it swung the other way when counselors attempted to treat sexual problems in a very programmed, behavioral way. The former approach was generally unsuccessful, whereas the latter frequently led to improvement—but sometimes only to a point. Some clients start to get better but then their improvement plateaus, short of their goals. To help clients progress beyond this plateau, sex therapists are now increasingly borrowing other methods of intervention frequently used in relationship therapy.*

Anxiety as a Cause of Sexual Dysfunction

Sexual dysfunctions can be caused by physical difficulties (such as problems with side effects of

---

*Sex therapists have also become much more knowledgeable about diagnosing and treating sexual disorders. Books that describe the present state of this knowledge include: David M. Schnarch, *Constructing the Sexual Crucible* (New York: Norton, 1991); Helen Singer Kaplan, *The Evaluation of Sexual Disorders* (New York: Brunner/Mazel, 1983); and John Money, *Venuses Penises* (Buffalo, N.Y.: Prometheus, 1986).

medication, blood flow, or nervous system transmission), mental difficulties (such as performance fears), or problems in both physical and mental areas. In people under 50 who are generally physically healthy, the most prevalent cause of sexual dysfunction is anxiety. This anxiety can be as straightforward as a fear of a specific sexual failure, such as an inability to reach orgasm. Or it may be much more complex, such as a fear of becoming close to another person, which relates back to negative experiences in early childhood. Or, perhaps most commonly, it may be a combination of anxiety-producing factors exacerbated by physical problems. In any case, anxiety is the common element that, for almost everyone, interrupts the ability to fully function sexually.

Every person defends against anxiety-producing situations differently. Some people are quick to respond; others are slow. Some have physical reactions such as palm sweating or mouth dryness; others want to talk or be quiet. These differences explain why anxiety can result in a problem of erectile difficulty for one person, inability to have orgasm for another, and a lack of sexual interest for a third. We all choose to avoid unsafe situations, so, as we approach danger, we avoid. If you have learned that being sexual with a particular partner is "dangerous," you are likely to feel little desire to be with that person. If you have found that being sexual with all partners is dangerous, you might develop an inhibition of sexual desire for partner sex and instead express your sexuality, anger, and low self-esteem by looking in windows, exposing your genitals to strangers, becoming sexually aroused by certain objects, or engaging in a multitude of other variations.

Helen Singer Kaplan, a noted psychiatrist and sex therapist, has identified three phases of sexual response: desire, excitement, and orgasm.[88] Anxiety can produce dysfunctions in each phase. The principal desire-phase disorder is hypoactive desire—lack of sexual interest. Excitement-phase disorders include erectile difficulty in men and lack of arousal in women, which results in little vaginal lubrication or other normal physical responses to sexual stimulation. (These are discussed later in this chapter). Orgasm-phase dysfunctions include premature ejaculation or retarded ejaculation in men and orgasmic dysfunction in women. Two dysfunctions that are not associated with a particular phase of sexual response are (1) vaginismus in women, a painful, spastic contraction of the pelvic muscles that prohibits vaginal penetration, and (2) the male counterpart to vaginismus, ejaculatory pain due to muscle spasms.

Because some situations may be perceived as safe and others as dangerous, all these dysfunctions can be present in some situations or with some partners and absent at other times or with other partners. And, because sexual problems are almost always relationship problems, the dynamics of the relationship have a profound effect on the success or failure of treatment. This is why treating some sexual problems is straightforward and simple and treating others is extremely complex.

Principles of Sex Therapy

The basic tenets of most common forms of sex therapy are as follows:

1. Sexual behavior, although a natural physiological process, is largely governed by learning. Many people who suffer from sexual dysfunction have experienced inadequate or inaccurate learning. Further, the more information one has (about sex or anything else), the more likely that individual is to make healthy decisions and function in the most satisfying way.

2. Most sexual problems are caused by a combination of psychological and organic factors. They may have physical manifestations (spastic contractions of the pelvic musculature, erectile difficulty), but they originate from mental preoccupations that interrupt sexual response: performance anxiety, fear of failure, unreasonable expectations, focus on a goal, and so on. Some sexual problems are caused, in part, by physical deficits; for example, a man may have difficulty achieving erection *partly* because of performance anxiety and

partly because of poor blood flow to his genitals.

3. People benefit from verbal communication with their partners regarding their sexual behavior preferences.

4. The most effective way to learn about one's own sexual response is through masturbation, an activity that provides immediate, accurate feedback. Only when one is familiar with her or his own response can one accurately communicate it to a partner.

5. In a sexual relationship, both people contribute positively and negatively to the interaction. There is no such thing as an uninvolved partner.[89]

6. Virtually all sexual dysfunctions are either correctable or adaptable; the symptoms can be reversed, or behaviors can be adapted to accommodate performance problems, thereby enabling the people to obtain sexual gratification.

The Sex Therapy Clinic

This section describes the experience a couple might have during the course of sex therapy.*

Bill, age 36, and Mary, age 33, had been married for ten years when they first telephoned a sex therapy clinic. Bill is an attorney; Mary is, at present, primarily responsible for the care of their children, ages 6 and 3, and is active in civic organizations.

Bill and Mary were each aware of sexual problems in their marriage almost from the beginning,

---

*This case history illustrates the method I use when seeing couples in intensive sex therapy. As stated above, virtually all forms of sex therapy currently in practice are based on psychotherapeutic techniques pioneered by William Masters and Virginia Johnson and described in *Human Sexual Inadequacy*. These techniques have been expanded on by many sex therapists, the most notable of whom are Helen Singer Kaplan and David M. Schnarch. Dr. Kaplan's ideas are described in *The New Sex Therapy* and *Disorders of Sexual Desire and Other New Concepts and Techniques in Sex Therapy*. Dr. Schnarch's expansion of previous sex therapy techniques by deeper relationship dynamics is described in *Constructing the Sexual Crucible*.

but for years the difficulties were never discussed, except during arguments. Mary was quite sure she had never experienced orgasm, and Bill had, early in their sexual relationship, been unable to control his ejaculation. His response resulted in his reaching orgasm almost immediately at the commencement of intercourse. More recently, Mary had become turned off to sex, and Bill found he was experiencing increasing difficulty maintaining his erection so that intercourse could occur at all. Both seemed aware, although it had not been stated outright, that the tensions in the sexual area were carrying over into other areas of their relationship. Further, if the sexual problems were not resolved, the relationship would probably continue to deteriorate and eventually end in separation and divorce.

Acknowledging these rather grim realities, Mary finally gathered enough courage to ask her gynecologist for help. He examined her, found no physical problems, reassured her that help was available, and suggested that she call a sex therapy clinic to which he had referred patients before.

Mary and Bill discussed the doctor's advice and agreed that something needed to be done. Because Mary felt that the problem was largely *hers*, she made the telephone call.

Mary's inquiry was referred to a woman therapist. The therapist, realizing the anxiety that almost always accompanies the initial contact, projected a reassuring tone as she briefly explored the problems with Mary. She explained that both of them would be seen by a male/female cotherapy team should they decide to participate in sex therapy. After answering all of Mary's questions, the therapist suggested that she discuss the situation with Bill and, if they desired, set up an evaluation meeting.

THE EVALUATION SESSION

Bill and Mary made a preliminary decision to proceed, so the evaluation session was scheduled. The purposes of this initial meeting were (1) to provide an opportunity for the clients to meet the cotherapists who would be seeing them should they enter therapy; (2) to give the therapists, through discussion with each client, the background and current assessment of the problems necessary to determine whether therapy would likely be helpful, what level might be most appropriate, or whether referral to another agency might be more fruitful; (3) to describe the treatment plan that might be used; and (4) to answer all questions before a decision to proceed further was made. The male therapist suggested a physician for Bill to see to rule out any organic or physiological cause for his erectile difficulty. Although he suspected strongly that the erectile problems were anxiety related and not caused by physical difficulties, he wanted to be sure he wasn't attempting to treat a biological problem with counseling. Bill agreed to see this physician. Bill and Mary left the sex therapy office feeling greatly relieved; they had begun to deal with the situation after ten years of avoidance, and the therapists had reassured them that their problems were neither unique nor hopeless.

THE SEXUAL HISTORY

In the next therapy meeting, the sexual history was gathered. The couple was separated, each meeting with the therapist of his or her own gender. Each therapist explored the client's childhood and adolescent experiences, the goals of therapy, the patterns in the family of origin, the sexual value systems, the history of the sexual problems, the strengths and weaknesses of the marriage, and much more.[90] The purposes of the history-taking session are twofold: (1) for the therapist to understand, as accurately and completely as possible, the client she or he will be principally representing in treatment (the client of the same gender) and (2) for the client to establish "comfort" with that therapist, which will facilitate the entire treatment process.

During the history-taking session, the therapists were particularly careful to ask specific questions and to press for detailed answers. A very important rule for sex counselors and therapists to observe is to avoid *assuming* anything. Because specific, personal sexual experiences are not something people tend to talk about, particularly if there is a sexual problem involved, people often assume their behaviors are similar to everybody else's. The thorough, careful therapist will avoid serious pitfalls that could sabotage the success of therapy if they are not noticed. Two examples, drawn from my clinical experience, illustrate the point.

One couple reported that, when the woman had an orgasm, she "really came." The therapists pressed for more information: The man said she "ejaculated so much it made a puddle on the bed." If the therapists had assumed he was talking about copious lubrication, they might have been pleased to know her body was responding so well. She was, to the couple's shock, suffering from urinary incontinence; her pelvic musculature was so poor that, when she experienced orgasm, she voided her bladder. Although, with the correct diagnosis, this turned out to be a relatively simple problem to treat, the couple would not have known what to do without the therapists' guidance, which begins with specific, accurate information.[91]

Another client who had recently been divorced, in part because of the couple's inability to have children, reported that he could have orgasms through masturbation and intercourse. The therapist asked for more specific information, and learned that what the man was defining as orgasm and ejaculation was, in fact, the secretion of Cowper's gland fluid, a clear substance that drips out of the end of the penis during arousal but *prior to* ejaculation and orgasm. He had developed a lifelong pattern of stimulation to arousal but always stopped prior to orgasm; he didn't realize that there was more he could experience. Previous psychotherapists had taken his report of orgasm at face value. The sex therapist suggested that he continue the stimulation, and he reported a very pleasant surprise with his next sexual experience.

It may be tempting to assume that people who suffer from such gross misinformation might be misinformed in a lot of other areas. Beware—general intelligence is not a measure of sexual knowledge. The couple in the incontinence example were college graduates; the man who was misinformed about his orgasm was a prominent and highly respected professional person.

COUPLE THERAPY

For the next meeting, Bill and Mary met together with the therapists. This session was intended to: (1) review each client's history as it relates to the sexual problem, (2) trace and account for the development of the problem, (3) outline the treatment plan, (4) dispel myths and misinformation that were uncovered in previous meetings, and (5) assign the initial home experiences and communication exercise.

The male therapist, in reviewing Bill's history, discussed how Bill had *learned* a pattern of quick ejaculation from his sexual experiences as a teenager. Because he was fearful at that time that he might be caught masturbating, it was functional for him to come to orgasm quickly. This was long before he learned that prolonging his arousal would be more pleasurable for both his partner and himself. When he entered marriage, he expected his response to slow down as he became more familiar with Mary. But Bill seemed to have learned the pattern of speedy response so thoroughly that he was utterly unable to respond any other way. The more he worried about the problem, the more anxiety he experienced, causing him to have even less control. Eventually he started experiencing difficulty with erection. He had become so preoccupied with his performance that he was blocking all erotic stimulation—a necessary condition for erection to occur in a sexual encounter.

Mary, on the other hand, had learned as a teenager to be *sexy* but not *sexual*. That is, she was expected to attract men but not to "go too far." She became adept at kissing, hugging, and petting—becoming very aroused—but then stopping the sexual encounter. This pattern, arousal followed by turnoff, later victimized her in marriage, long after she had to worry about getting pregnant, contracting sexually transmitted diseases, or ruining her reputation. Not surprisingly, she described her teenage petting experiences as the best sexual encounters of her life.

For the first several years of marriage, Mary remembered experiencing high arousal, but coming short of orgasm, and then "going numb, feeling nothing." In the more recent past, her body felt less and less aroused, as if to say "I'm not going to reach orgasm anyway, so why bother?"

The therapists pointed out these patterns, emphasizing that the sexual problems were neither person's fault. New, more functional patterns could be learned to replace the old, dysfunctional ones.

The woman therapist gave Mary a beginning self-pleasuring assignment. This was to help her learn her own sexual response, so that later she could share it with and teach it to Bill. Both agreed that there was no way Bill could automatically *know* what was pleasurable to Mary, particularly if she didn't know herself. Mary had never masturbated, but with encouragement and specific, graduated instructions, she agreed to try.[92]

The male therapist instructed Bill to continue masturbating, something he had been doing since childhood. He suggested that Bill slow down, however, to learn as much about his various levels of arousal as possible.

TOUCHING

The couple was instructed to abstain from intercourse, in order to eliminate the anxiety that had invariably surrounded that activity. Instead, they were given the following instructions:

To many persons, the idea of touching any part of the body is thought of only as a preliminary to orgasm. Thinking of touching in this way often causes the touching to become less valued in and of itself. Although the entire body may be pleasant to touch and to have touched, emphasis is usually placed on the breasts, vaginal area, penis, and testicles. Touching need not be explicitly genital or goal oriented to be pleasurable. Touching, by yourself or with a partner, can be a joyful expression of discovery and exploration, of giving and getting.

Plan ahead and prepare, together, a quiet, private, warm, and comfortable place. Create an atmosphere that is pleasant for you. It may include soft-colored lights, or candles and music, or other things that help you relax. Make yourselves comfortable by removing your clothing and assuming positions that will permit relaxation during long periods of touching. Give yourselves a lot of time. Slowly become very familiar with your partner's entire body. Remember, this experience is not one of trying to arouse one's partner sexually; it is an experience

that is designed to give you time and space to explore your own feelings about touching and being touched. Touch, stroke, squeeze, and caress your partner for your own pleasure. The feeling you receive need not be an arousing one. You will feel something; get in touch with whatever that feeling is.

You may wish to shower together, using pleasant soaps on each other's body, or try a shower in the dark (you must then really rely on touch). When you do come together for a touching experience, it is suggested that you use a pleasant-tasting, nonalcohol-based lotion or oil, or a baby powder. which is particularly nice in warm weather. These facilitate the movement of skin on skin and reduce friction. Oils or lotions should first be poured in your hands to be warmed, or warmed on a stove or candle stand.

Use your fingers, your fingertips, your palms, and your full hand to touch and caress in different ways. This is not a massage. A massage is designed primarily to give pleasure to the other person. Remember, the major purpose of this touching experience is to discover feelings for yourself through touching your partner. It may be pleasant to close your eyes while touching so you can "get into" your own feelings without observing your partner's response. Try a joyful fantasy, if you like; or pretend you've lost the use of your sight for a while and must rely on touch alone. The person being touched has only to lie there and concentrate on his or her own feelings of being touched. Sometimes, too, you may want to explore your partner's body visually while you are touching and would feel more comfortable if your partner were to close his or her eyes. If so, ask your partner to do so. If it would be pleasant to comb your partner's hair, do so. Because you are touching your partner for yourself, you need not concern yourself with your partner's reaction, unless it is one of discomfort or pain (if so, your partner must tell you). After each touching experience, discuss your feelings with each other, not in a direct or accusatory fashion but with an effort toward understanding each other's feelings about touching and being touched. Do not make assumptions about your partner's feelings. It is important to remember to communicate with each other and not to move faster than your comfort levels.

The first week we ask you to have "touching experiences" a minimum of three times during the week to reinforce comfortable feelings. We will discuss with you which partner should initiate the first touching experience. After the "initiator" has fully explored his or her partner's body for his or her own pleasure, she or he will change off and the person who was touching for his or her own pleasure will then become the one who is touched. During this first week we do not want the man to touch his partner's breasts, nipples, or vaginal area, nor do we want the woman to touch her partner's nipples, penis, or testicles. Touching should be done only with the hands during this week.

VERBAL COMMUNICATIONS

Bill and Mary were also given the following instructions to enhance their verbal communications:[93]

Most sexually intimate couples think they know considerably more about each other's feelings, attitudes, and behaviors than they, in fact, really do know. They take pride in outguessing and in predicting their partner's responses without adequately communicating with each other. They believe "If he or she loved me, he or she would know how I feel."

RESPONSIBILITY FOR SELF
We are each responsible for our own sexuality. We should not wait for someone else to discover it for us. We need to explore, discover, and understand our own sexual responses. We are then free to share or not to share our sexuality with another person. If we decide to share our sexuality, we need to be willing to communicate with our partner what we have learned about ourselves, to be open and vulnerable, to risk. We also need to be willing to learn about our partner's sexuality from our partner. We cannot make assumptions about his or her needs, feelings, or thoughts, without asking. Too often we are wrong. In order to share a sexual experience on an equal basis, we must both have and express knowledge, comfort, and responsibility for our own sexuality. This

responsibility is necessary to take ownership of our own feelings, attitudes, and ideas, as well as our behavior.

REPRESENTATION OF SELF
Once we are responsible for our own sexuality and have made a decision to share our sexuality with another person, we need to learn functional ways to represent ourselves clearly to our partner. Perhaps the simplest and most effective verbal communication method is "I language." The following examples contrast the impacts of "You language" (identified as "a" statements) with "I language" (identified as "b" statements).

I LANGUAGE
a. "You make me so angry when you don't pick up your clothes." (an accusatory statement, which is most likely to place your partner on the defensive)
b. "I'm angry because, in addition to picking up my own clothes, I feel I have to pick your clothes up too." (permits further communication and represents your feelings)
a. "Let's go out to dinner." (a confused message that takes over your partner's response)
b. "I'd like to go out to dinner and wonder if you would like to also." (much clearer)
a. "You're so clumsy when you touch my breasts." (another accusatory message likely to shut down communication—not open it up)
b. "I get turned off when you touch my breasts that way because it hurts; I'd like to show you what kind of touch feels good."
a. "Do you want to go to the movies tonight?" (answer: "I don't know, do you?"—next response: "I don't know. I asked you first."—result: confusion)
b. "I would like to see _____ tonight and wonder if you would also like to see that film." (extremely clear)

The purpose of "I language" is not to promote agreement but rather to promote accurate communication and understanding. Only with accurate understanding can you ever know if you agree or disagree. When you use "I language," you must first be aware of your own feelings, attitudes, ideas, or thoughts, before you can clearly state them to your partner. Thus *the use of "I language" helps you to get in touch with your own feelings first. All feelings are real for you. They exist. They may not always be rational, but you have them. It is your responsibility to represent your feelings. Do not expect your partner to know your feelings clearly unless you represent them. Through the use of "I language" you minimize putting your partner in a defensive position. You also optimize opening further communication. You speak for you, not for someone else. It is hoped that you know yourself better than anyone else because you have given yourself permission to know and to represent yourself. By honestly expressing your feelings, you encourage your partner to do the same. Honesty often seems risky when used with someone you care about; but the alternative may be confusion.*

The therapists asked Bill and Mary about their first week's assignments, focusing on relaxation, learning, and comfort as the goals—not sexual arousal. Both reported feeling awkward during the first touching experiences, but the awkwardness soon passed and both enjoyed the experience of performance-free touching.

Because Bill and Mary seemed comfortable, they were given the next touching assignment. They were instructed to do exactly as they had done the previous week, except now they could include breasts, nipples, and genitals in the touching. These areas were not to become the focus of the sessions, nor was there an expectation of arousal. In fact, if arousal did occur, they were instructed to move the touching to another area. And, of course, they were not to have intercourse.

The therapists asked about "I language." Mary had found it particularly useful in communicating anger to Bill; he had largely forgotten to use it. The therapists reemphasized its importance, particularly following a touching experience.

Bill reported that he was able to slow his arousal in masturbation as much as he wanted. This didn't seem significant to him—his lack of control was associated with intercourse—but he was becoming more aware of his levels of arousal. He was learning to recognize the point of ejacula-

tory inevitability—the few seconds immediately preceding orgasm. The therapist informed him that his efforts at slowing his response needed to be focused prior to ejaculatory inevitability; once he is in that stage, orgasm is, as it states, inevitable.

Mary had spent some private time each day exploring her body. She had many questions for the woman therapist and seemed eager to continue her exploration.

The therapists gave Bill and Mary two additional assignments. They taught the couple the use of the *squeeze technique* for controlling premature ejaculation,[94] and Mary was given exercises designed to strengthen her vaginal muscles, thereby increasing vaginal sensations.[95] They were also asked to read *For Each Other*, by Lonnie Barbach, to learn more about sharing sexual intimacy.[96]

Bill and Mary met with their sex therapists weekly. The purposes of these subsequent meetings were: (1) to review and evaluate the couple's experiences in touching and communication as they worked toward their goals, (2) to make new assignments, and (3) to discuss the physiology of human sexual response.

The therapists presented, using slides, factual information on human sexual response. (This educational experience is used to promote knowledge and understanding of physical changes that occur in the body as a result of sexual arousal. Much of this data was gathered by Masters and Johnson in their studies of the physiology of human sexual response.)

In their discussion of sexual response, the male therapist assumed primary responsibility for presenting male response, the female therapist for presenting female response. They paid particular attention to the physiological components of Bill and Mary's sexual dysfunctions—nonorgasmic response, premature ejaculation, and erectile dysfunction.

Masters and Johnson identified four stages of sexual response in females and males: excitement, plateau, orgasm, and resolution. There are many similarities in the physical responses of men and women. These include the two major body changes that result from sexual stimulation: (1) myotonia, or muscle tension, and (2) vaso-congestion, or blood engorgement.

The male therapist explained the genital response in the male, using slides and models to illustrate the physical changes. In *excitement,* blood flows into the erectile tissue of the penis (vasocongestion), resulting in erection. The scrotum (the sac surrounding the testicles) becomes thicker and more wrinkled, and the testicles move up closer to the body.

Plateau response is characterized by the continuation of erection, although it often waxes and wanes during sex play with a partner. The testicles become fully elevated, rotate toward the front, and become blood-engorged, causing expansion in their size. The Cowper's glad secretes a small amount of clear fluid that comes out of the tip of the penis. The purpose of this fluid is generally thought to be to cleanse the urethra of urine, thereby neutralizing the chemical environment for the passage of sperm.

The *orgasm* stage in men consists of two phases. The first is ejaculatory inevitability, a short period during which stimulation sufficient to trigger orgasm has occurred and the resulting ejaculation becomes inevitable. The second phase, ejaculation, results from rhythmic contractions (myotonia) forcing sperm and semen through the urethra. Simultaneous with this is the very pleasant physical sensation of orgasm.

The final stage, *resolution,* represents a return to the unstimulated state. In resolution, the penis loses its erection, and the testicles lose their engorgement and elevation.

In women, the *excitement* stage of sexual response ushers in many changes. The process of vaginal lubrication begins. This response is analogous to the male erection; it is caused by sexual stimulation and is, physiologically, a blood engorgement response. The uterus and cervix begin to move up and away from the vagina. The clitoris and labia minora (inner lips) enlarge, and the labia majora (outer lips) spread. Breast size increases slightly, and the nipples become erect.

In *plateau,* the uterus continues in its movement up and back, the vagina lengthens and bal-

loons at the rear, and the outer third of the vagina contracts, causing a gripping effect. The clitoris retracts under its hood, making it seem to disappear.

At *orgasm,* the uterus and vagina become involved in wavelike muscular contractions. This response, as well as the subjective pleasure of orgasm, is very similar to the experience of the male.

In *resolution,* the cervix and uterus drop to their normal positions, and the outer third of the vagina returns to normal, followed by the inner two-thirds. The clitoris and the breasts also return to normal.

The therapists also discussed the many involuntary *extragenital* physical responses in men and women. These include muscle tension responses such as facial grimace, spastic contractions of the hands and feet, and pelvic thrusting. Extragenital blood engorgement responses includes sex flush, blood pressure and heart-rate increases, and perspiration on soles of feet and palms of hands.

Finally, the therapists discussed how aging affects sexual response.[97] They emphasized that people are capable of experiencing pleasurable sexual response throughout life; bodies may slow down, but they do not need to stop. The effects of aging on sexual response are summarized in Figures 6.1 and 6.2.

Sex therapy for Bill and Mary continued for eight additional weekly meetings. Mary progressed dramatically in the fourth week; she experienced her first orgasm in self-stimulation, and she continued in her ability to stimulate herself to orgasm.

During one of the couple-touching experiences, Mary stimulated herself to orgasm. Sporadically at first, and then consistently by week six, each was able to bring the other to orgasm through hand stimulation. Touching experiences in the later weeks of therapy emphasized whole-body touching, genital touching, female-active intercourse with simultaneous clitoral stimulation, and lots of verbal feedback.

Bill practiced the penile squeeze (the technique to delay ejaculation) in self-stimulation, and Mary applied it during their couple experi-

FIGURE 6.1

Effects of Aging on Sexual Responses in Men

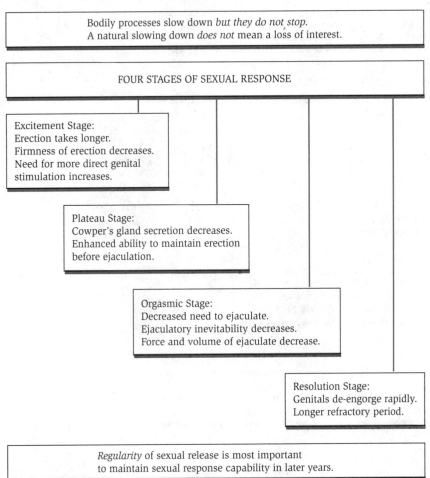

Bodily processes slow down *but they do not stop.*
A natural slowing down *does not* mean a loss of interest.

FOUR STAGES OF SEXUAL RESPONSE

Excitement Stage:
Erection takes longer.
Firmness of erection decreases.
Need for more direct genital
stimulation increases.

Plateau Stage:
Cowper's gland secretion decreases.
Enhanced ability to maintain erection
before ejaculation.

Orgasmic Stage:
Decreased need to ejaculate.
Ejaculatory inevitability decreases.
Force and volume of ejaculate decrease.

Resolution Stage:
Genitals de-engorge rapidly.
Longer refractory period.

Regularity of sexual release is most important
to maintain sexual response capability in later years.

ences. They found he could experience increased stimulation with less need for the squeeze. In the seventh week, Bill was able to control his orgasm—assuming there had not been a period of abstinence from orgasm—as he desired.

Not surprisingly, once Bill understood the mechanisms that had previously precluded his having an erection, and once he and Mary were comfortable in their sexual interactions, erectile

difficulty was seldom a problem. When a problem did occur, Bill was able to identify the cause, take it in stride, and have a better experience the next time.

At the termination of therapy, Mary and Bill reported that they were both enjoying their sexual experiences and that improvement in their sexual intimacy had relieved many other tensions in the relationship. Their communication had also im-

FIGURE 6.2

Effects of Aging on Sexual Response in Women

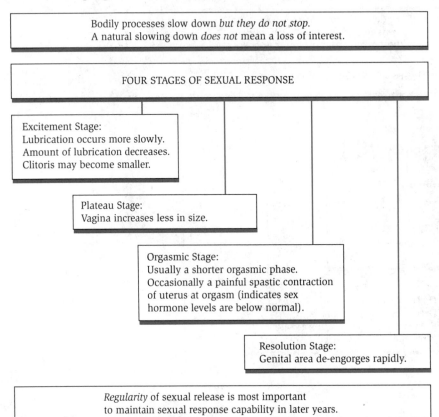

Bodily processes slow down *but they do not stop.*
A natural slowing down *does not* mean a loss of interest.

FOUR STAGES OF SEXUAL RESPONSE

Excitement Stage:
Lubrication occurs more slowly.
Amount of lubrication decreases.
Clitoris may become smaller.

Plateau Stage:
Vagina increases less in size.

Orgasmic Stage:
Usually a shorter orgasmic phase.
Occasionally a painful spastic contraction
of uterus at orgasm (indicates sex
hormone levels are below normal).

Resolution Stage:
Genital area de-engorges rapidly.

Regularity of sexual release is most important
to maintain sexual response capability in later years.

proved greatly. They hoped Mary would come to achieve orgasm in intercourse through penile thrusting alone, but this certainly wasn't an all-important goal. Further, they knew what they could do to work toward that and looked forward to the process.

A major thesis of this chapter is that almost all social workers, regardless of their specific professional responsibilities, are sometimes called on to be sex counselors. Further, the levels of treatment of sexual problems require various degrees of knowledge, comfort, and experience. Because most social workers are not sex therapists, the need for responsible referral arises. To assist people in locating competent, experienced sex therapists, the American Association of Sex Educators, Counselors, and Therapists (AASECT) certifies qualified sex therapists. The association will provide the names of knowledgeable, ethical, and experienced sex therapists to those who contact them at:

435 North Michigan Avenue, Suite 1717
Chicago, IL 60611
(312)644-0828

SUMMARY

Practically every conceivable sexual activity is socially acceptable to some groups of people. What is defined as acceptable and unacceptable sexual behavior varies from culture to culture and from one time period to another. Judeo-Christian values, the Puritan influence, and Victorian morality contributed in our history to repression of sexual expression. At present ambiguity and confusion abound over what ought to be the sexual code and behavior of Americans. For the past several decades our society has been undergoing a revolution in sexual values and mores. The work of four social scientists has had profound effects on our understanding of human sexuality: Sigmund Freud, Alfred Kinsey, and the team of William Masters and Virginia Johnson.

This text uses a social variance approach to examining sexual concerns rather than a social problems approach because there is as yet no general consensus about which sexual acts are acceptable and which are not. Three categories of sexual variances were discussed: tolerated sex variance, structural sex variance, and asocial sex variance. Tolerated sex variance includes masturbation, premarital intercourse, and heterosexual oral-genital contact between consenting adults.

Structural sex variance refers to those acts that run counter to prevailing norms and legal statutes but at the same time have supportive social structures. Homosexuality is in this category and was discussed at some length.

Asocial sex variance includes those acts that elicit strong disapproval and at the same time do not have a social structure that supports them. Acts in this category include incest, child molestation, rape, voyeurism, and exhibitionism.

Almost everyone experiences personal sexual concerns. For example, men may worry about premature ejaculation, and women may experience painful intercourse.

The social worker can be a helping agent to people suffering from sexual problems. The social worker is frequently called on to step out of her or his primary professional role to become a sex counselor. In this role the worker performs short-term, often crisis-oriented counseling directed toward the alleviation of some immediate difficulty related to sex. An important issue specific to effective sex counseling is the counselor's vocabulary.

Sex therapy focuses on the alleviation of sexual dysfunction. It entails a planned change sequence involving several contacts between the client(s) and the therapist(s). The stages of intensive sex therapy are problem definition, history gathering, physical examination, couple therapy, information dissemination, prescribed sexual and communication experiences, and ongoing evaluation. A critical issue in sex therapy is the therapist's need to avoid making assumptions. Intensive sex therapy involves prescribed sexual and communication experiences.

NOTES

1. Havelock Ellis, *Sex and Marriage: Eros in Contemporary Life* (Westport, CT: Greenwood Press, 1977). p. 42.
2. David A. Schulz, *Human Sexuality* (Englewood Cliffs, NJ: Prentice-Hall, 1979), p. 4.
3. Don Grubin, "Sexual Offending: A Cross Cultural Comparison," in *Annual Review of Sex Research*, vol. III, John Bancroft, Clive M. Davis, and Howard J. Ruppel, Jr., eds. (Lake Mills, IO: Society for the Scientific Study of Sex, 1993), pp. 201–217.
4. John Gagnon and Bruce Henderson, *Human Sexuality: The Age of Ambiguity* (Boston: Little, Brown, 1975), p. 10.
5. Clellan S. Ford and Frank A. Beach, *Patterns of Sexual Behavior* (New York: Harper & Row, 1951).
6. Gagnon and Henderson, *Human Sexuality: The Age of Ambiguity*, p. 14.
7. Duncan Chappell, G. Geis, S. Schaefer, and L. Siegel, "Forcible Rape: A Comparative Study of Offenses Known to the Police in Boston and Los Angeles," in *Studies in the Sociology of Sex*, James H. Henslin, ed. (Englewood Cliffs, NJ: Prentice-Hall, 1971), pp. 174–175.
8. Richard A. Maier, *Human Sexuality in Perspective* (Chicago: Nelson-Hall, 1984), pp. 391–393.
9. Gagnon and Henderson, *Human Sexuality: The Age of Ambiguity*, p. 16.
10. J. John Palen, *Social Problems* (New York: McGraw-Hill, 1979), p. 544.

11. Ibid.

12. Morton Hunt, *Sexual Behavior in the 1970s* (Chicago: Playboy Press, 1974).

13. Anke A. Ehrhardt, Sandra Yingling, and Patricia A. Warne, "Sexual Behavior in the Era of AIDS: What Has Changed in the United States?" in *Annual Review of Sex Research*, vol. II, John Bancroft, Clive M. Davis, and Howard J. Ruppel, Jr., eds. (Lake Mills, IO: Society for the Scientific Study of Sex, 1991), pp. 25–47.

14. W. G. Steglich and Margaret K. Snooks, *American Social Problems: An Institutional View* (Santa Monica, CA: Goodyear, 1980).

15. Alfred C. Kinsey, W. B. Pomeroy, and C. E. Martin, *Sexual Behavior in the Human Male* (Philadelphia: Saunders, 1948).

16. Alfred C. Kinsey, W. B. Pomeroy, C. E. Martin, and P. H. Gebhard, *Sexual Behavior in the Human Female* (Philadelphia: Saunders, 1953).

17. William H. Masters and Virginia E. Johnson, *Human Sexual Response* (Boston: Little, Brown, 1966). For a layperson, an excellent summary is Ruth Brecher and Edward Brecher, *An Analysis of Human Sexual Response* (New York: Signet Books, 1966).

18. William H. Masters and Virginia E. Johnson, *Human Sexual Inadequacy* (Boston: Little, Brown, 1970). For a layperson, an excellent summary is Fred Belliveau and Lin Richter, *Understanding Human Sexual Inadequacy* (New York: Bantam Books, 1970).

19. Gagnon and Henderson, *Human Sexuality: The Age of Ambiguity*, p. 14.

20. Maier, *Human Sexuality in Perspective*, pp. 145–147.

21. Herant Katchadourian and Donald T. Lunde, *Fundamentals of Human Sexuality*, 2d ed. (New York: Holt, Rinehart & Winston, 1975). p. 78.

22. William Kornblum and Joseph Julian, *Social Problems*, 6th ed. (Englewood Cliffs, NJ: Prentice-Hall, 1989), pp. 90–102.

23. John H. Gagnon and William Simon, "Introduction: Deviant Behavior and Sexual Deviance," in *Sexual Deviance*, John H. Gagnon and William Simon, eds. (New York: Harper & Row, 1967), p. 8.

24. Kornblum and Julian, *Social Problems*, pp. 90–102.

25. Janet S. Hyde, *Understanding Human Sexuality*, 4th ed. (New York: McGraw-Hill, 1990), pp. 418–423.

26. Kevin T. Berrill, "Anti-Gay Violence and Victimization in the United States," *Journal of Interpersonal Violence*, 5 (1990), pp. 274–294.

27. Kinsey et al., *Sexual Behavior in the Human Male*, p. 639.

28. Thomas Sullivan, Kenrick Thompson, Richard Wright, George Gross, and Dale Spady, *Social Problems* (New York: Wiley, 1980), p. 537.

29. C. A. Tripp, *The Homosexual Matrix* (New York: McGraw-Hill, 1975), p. 99.

30. H. T. Buckner, "The Transvestic Career Path," *Psychiatry*, 33 (1970), pp. 381–389.

31. Brian Garner and Richard W. Smith, "Are There Really Any Gay Male Athletes? An Empirical Survey," *Journal of Sex Research*, 13 (1977), pp. 22–34.

32. Evelyn Hooker, "The Adjustment of the Male Overt Homosexual," *Journal of Projective Techniques*, 21 (1957), pp. 18–31.

33. Ian Robertson, *Social Problems*, 2d ed. (New York: Random House, 1980), p. 414.

34. Charles H. McCaghy, "Child Molesting," *Sexual Behavior*, 1 (1971), pp. 16–24.

35. Hyde, *Understanding Human Sexuality*, pp. 558–568.

36. Ibid.

37. Ibid.

38. Kinsey et al., *Sexual Behavior in the Human Male*; and Kinsey et al., *Sexual Behavior in the Human Female*.

39. Hyde, *Understanding Human Sexuality*, pp. 432–434.

40. Ibid., p. 434.

41. Alan P. Bell, Martin S. Weinberg, and Sue Kiefer Hammersmith, *Sexual Preference* (Bloomington: Indiana University Press, 1981).

42. Charlene Crabb, "Are Some Men Born to Be Homosexual?" *U.S. News & World Report*, Sept. 9, 1991, p. 58.

43. William F. Allman, "The Biology-Behavior Conundrum," *U.S. News & World Report*, July 26, 1993, pp. 6–7.

44. Ibid., pp. 6–9.

45. Kim I. Mills, "Was 1993 'The Year of the Queer'?" *Wisconsin State Journal*, Jan. 1, 1994, p. 4A.

46. Evelyn Hooker, "The Homosexual Community," in *Proceedings of the XIV International Congress of Applied Psychology*, vol. 2, *Personality Research* (Copenhagen: Munksgaard, 1962), pp. 52–53.

47. Barry M. Dank, "Coming Out in the Gay World," *Psychiatry*, 34 (May 1971), p. 186.

48. Karlein M. G. Schrewrs, "Sexuality in Lesbian Couples: The Importance of Gender," in *Annual Review of Sex Research*, vol. IV, John Bancroft, Clive M. Davis, and Howard Ruppel, Jr., eds. (Lake Mills, IO:

Society for the Scientific Study of Sex, 1994), pp. 49–66.

49. Jack H. Hedblom, "The Female Homosexual: Social and Attitudinal Dimensions," in *Deviance: Studies in Definition, Management, and Treatment,* 2d ed., Simon Dinitz, Russell R. Dynes, and Alfred C. Clarke, eds. (New York: Oxford University Press, 1975), p. 246.

50. C. Patton, *Sex and Germs: The Politics of AIDS* (Boston: South End Press, 1985).

51. Kathleen A Rounds, "AIDS in Rural Areas: Challenges to Providing Care," *Social Work,* 33, no. 3 (May–June 1988), pp. 257–261.

52. Aaron S. Greenberg and J. Michael Bailey, "Do Biological Explanations of Homosexuality Have Moral, Legal, or Policy Implications?" *Journal of Sex Research,* 30 (1993), pp. 245–251.

53. Hyde, *Understanding Human Sexuality,* pp. 418–423.

54. Timothy F. Murphy, "Redirecting Sexual Orientation: Techniques and Justifications," *Journal of Sex Research,* 29 (1992), pp. 510–523.

55. Hyde, *Understanding Human Sexuality,* p. 490.

56. Ibid., pp. 486–488.

57. Ibid.

58. Paul H. Gebhard, J. H. Gagnon, W. B. Pomeroy, and Cornelia Christenson, *Sex Offenders: An Analysis of Types* (New York: Harper & Row, 1965).

59. A. Nicholas Groth, "The Incest Offender," in *Intervention in Child Sexual Abuse,* Suzanne M. Sgroi, ed. (Lexington, MA: Lexington Books, 1982), pp. 215–239.

60. *Diagnostic and Statistical Manual of Mental Disorders, Fourth Edition (DSM-IV).* (Washington, DC: American Psychiatric Association, 1994), pp. 527–528.

61. G. G. Abel, J. V. Becker, J. Cunningham-Rathner, M. S. Mittelman, and J. L. Rouleau, "Multiple Paraphilic Diagnoses among Sex Offenders," *Bulletin of the American Academy of Psychiatry and the Law,* 16 (2), (1988), pp. 153–168.

62. R. Karl Hanson, Rocco Gizzarelli, and Heather Scott, "The Attitudes of Incest Offenders," *Criminal Justice and Behavior,* 21, no. 2 (June 1994), pp. 187–202.

63. G. G. Abel, J. V. Becker, M. S. Mittelman, J. Cunningham-Rathner, J. L. Rouleau, and W. D. Murphy, "Self-Reported Sex Crimes of Noncarcerated Parapheliacs," *Journal of Interpersonal Violence,* 2 (1) (1987), pp. 3–25.

64. Hyde, *Understanding Human Sexuality,* p. 488.

65. Ibid.

66. Ibid., pp. 488–490.

67. Blair Justice and Rita Justice, *The Broken Taboo: Sex in the Family* (New York: Human Sciences Press, 1979).

68. Ibid., p. 177.

69. Judith Siegel, Jacqueline M. Golding, Judith A. Stein, M. Audrey Burnam, and Susan B. Sorenson, "Reactions to Sexual Assault," *Journal of Interpersonal Violence,* 5 (1990), pp. 229–246.

70. Hyde, *Understanding Human Sexuality,* p. 474.

71. *Wisconsin State Journal,* Nov. 6, 1982, sec. 1, p. 2.

72. A. Nicholas Groth, *Men Who Rape* (New York: Plenum Press, 1979).

73. Hyde, *Understanding Human Sexuality,* p. 482.

74. Cindy Struckman-Johnson, "Forced Sex on Dates: It Happens to Men, Too," *Journal of Sex Research,* 24 (1988), pp. 234–241.

75. M. P. Koss et al., "Non-stranger Sexual Aggression: A Discriminant Analysis of the Psychological Characteristics of Undetected Offenders," *Sex Roles,* 12 (1985), pp. 981–992.

76. Eugene J. Kanin, "Date Rapists: Differential Sexual Socialization and Relative Deprivation," *Archives of Sexual Behavior,* 14 (1985), pp. 219–232.

77. Ann W. Burgess and Lynda Holmstrom, *Rape: Victims of Crisis* (Bowie, MD: Robert J. Brady, 1974).

78. Ann W. Burgess and Lynda Holmstrom, "Rape Trauma Syndrome," *American Journal of Psychiatry,* 131 (1974), pp. 981–986.

79. Abel et al., "Self-Reported Sex Crimes of Nonincarcerated Paraphiliacs," pp. 3–25.

80. Masters and Johnson, *Human Sexual Inadequacy.*

81. Kinsey et al., *Sexual Behavior in the Human Male*; and Kinsey et al., *Sexual Behavior in the Human Female.*

82. Warren R. Johnson, "Sex Education of the Mentally Retarded," in *Human Sexuality and the Mentally Retarded,* Felix de la Cruz and Gerald D. LaVeck, eds. (New York: Brunner/Mazel, 1973), p. 64.

83. Jack S. Annon, *Behavioral Treatment of Sexual Problems* (Hagerstown, MD: Harper & Row, 1976).

84. Ibid., p. 65.

85. Ibid., p. 77.

86. Masters and Johnson, *Human Sexual Inadequacy.*

87. Belliveau and Richter, *Understanding Human Sexual Inadequacy.*

88. Helen Singer Kaplan, *The New Sex Therapy* (New York: Brunner/Mazel, 1974), p. 290; and Helen Singer Kaplan, *Disorders of Sexual Desire and Other New Concepts and Techniques in Sex Therapy* (New York: Simon and Schuster, 1979).

89. Masters and Johnson, *Human Sexual Inadequacy,* pp. 2–3.

90. An excellent outline for a sexual history can be found in Masters and Johnson, *Human Sexual Inadequacy,* pp. 34–51.

91. Raymond Rosen and J. Gayle Beck, *Patterns of Sexual Arousal* (New York: Guilford, 1987).

92. Lonnie Garfield Barbach, *For Yourself* (Garden City, NY: Doubleday, 1975).

93. ''I language'' is a communication technique suggested by many helping professionals. For a more thorough treatment, see Thomas Gordon, *Parent Effectiveness Training (The Tested New Way to Raise Responsible Children)* (New York: Wyden, 1970).

94. Masters and Johnson, *Human Sexual Inadequacy,* pp. 101–115.

95. Sandra R. Lieblum and Raymond C. Rosen, *Principles and Practice of Sex Therapy* (New York: Guilford, 1989).

96. Lonnie Barbach, *For Each Other* (Garden City, NY: Anchor Press/Doubleday, 1982).

97. Barbara Silverstone and Helen Kandel Hyman, *Growing Older Together: A Couple's Guide to Understanding and Coping with the Challenges of Later Life* (Westminster, MD: Pantheon, 1992).

7

DRUG ABUSE
AND DRUG
TREATMENT
PROGRAMS

P ractically everyone has taken one or more drugs and, on a few occasions, used a drug to excess. A large proportion of our population, as we will see, currently abuses drugs. This chapter will:

- Define drugs and drug abuse.
- Provide a brief history of our drug-taking society.
- Present sociological theories of drug abuse.
- Describe drug subcultures.
- Summarize facts about and effects of commonly used drugs.
- Describe rehabilitation programs for drug abuse.
- Present suggestions for curbing drug abuse in the future.

DRUGS AND DRUG ABUSE

Pharmacologically, a drug is any substance that chemically alters the function or structure of a living organism.[1] This definition would include food, insecticides, air pollutants, water pollutants, acids, vitamins, toxic chemicals, soaps, and soft drinks. Obviously this interpretation is too broad to be useful. For our purposes a definition based on context is more appropriate. In medicine, for example, a drug is any substance that is manufactured specifically to relieve pain or to treat or prevent diseases and other medical conditions.

In a social problems approach, a *drug* is any habit-forming substance that directly affects the brain and nervous system. It is a chemical that affects moods, perceptions, body functions, or consciousness and that has the potential for misuse because it may be harmful to the user.

Drug abuse is the regular or excessive use of a drug when, as defined by a group, the consequences endanger relationships with other people, are detrimental to the user's health, or jeopardize society itself. This definition identifies two key factors that determine what is considered drug abuse in a society: The first is the actual drug

effects, and the second is a group's perception of the effects.

Society's perceptions of the ill effects of a drug are often inconsistent with the actual effects. In our society moderate use of alcohol and tobacco is accepted by many Americans, even though moderate use of both can cause serious health problems. Excessive drinking of coffee (containing caffeine) is accepted in our society but can also lead to health problems. In the 1930s our society was convinced that marijuana was a dangerous drug; it was said to cause insanity, crime, and a host of other ills. Now, available evidence suggests that it may be no more dangerous than alcohol.[2] The occasional use of heroin has been thought for years to be highly dangerous, but evidence now indicates that occasional users suffer few health consequences and can lead productive lives.[3]

The dominant social reaction to a drug is influenced not only by the actual dangers of the drug but also by the social characteristics and motives of the groups that use it. Heroin is considered to be dangerous because its use has been popularly associated with inner-city residents and high crime rates. Society is generally accepting of the use of pills by middle-aged people to reduce stress and anxiety but less accepting of college students using the same pills ''to feel good'' and ''to get high.'' Surprisingly, legal drugs are more often abused and cause more harm in our society than illegal drugs.

One of the most widely used drugs today is aspirin. Millions of Americans use it to relieve pain and other discomforts. Taken in excessive amounts, however, aspirin can be harmful, causing gastrointestinal bleeding, ulcers, and other ailments.

Other over-the-counter drugs (those available without a physician's prescription) can and are being abused. Laxatives, for example, which are taken for constipation, can damage the digestive system. Large doses of vitamins A and D are toxic.

Prescription drugs are also frequently abused. Among the most abused prescription drugs are tranquilizers, pain killers, sedatives, and stimulants. Americans are obsessed with taking pills. More than 1.5 billion drug prescriptions, at a cost of over $30 billion, are filled each year.[4] Many of these prescribed drugs have the potential to be psychologically and physiologically addicting. Drug companies spend millions in advertisements in an effort to convince consumers that there is something wrong with them—that they are too tense, that they are taking too long to fall asleep, that they should lose weight, that they are not "regular" enough—and that their medications will solve these problems. Unfortunately, many Americans accept this easy symptom-relief approach and end up depending on pills rather than making life changes to improve their health (learning stress reduction techniques, changing their diets, deciding to exercise regularly).

Because a drug is legal and readily available does not mean it is harmless. Alcohol and tobacco are legal, but both may seriously damage our health. The rationale determining the acceptability of a drug is often illogical. Drugs favored by the dominant culture (such as alcohol in our society) are generally acceptable, whereas those favored by a small subculture are usually outlawed. It is interesting to note that in many parts of North Africa and the Middle East marijuana is a legal drug and alcohol is outlawed.[5] Our country imposes severe penalties on the use of cocaine, but in certain areas of the Andes Mountains that substance is legal and widely used.[6]

A characteristic of habit-forming drugs is that they lead to a *dependence*, with the user developing a recurring craving for them. This dependence may be physical, psychological, or both. When physical dependence occurs, the user will generally experience bodily withdrawal symptoms, which may take many forms and range in severity from slight tremblings to fatal convulsions. When psychological dependence occurs, the user feels psychological discomfort if use is terminated. Users also generally develop a *tolerance* for the drug, which means that they have to take increasing amounts over time to achieve a given effect. Some drugs (such as aspirin) do not create tolerance.

Drug addiction is somewhat difficult to define. In its broadest usage, the term refers to an intense craving for a particular substance. All of us have intense cravings—such as for ice cream, straw-

berry shortcake, potato chips, or chocolate. To distinguish drug addiction from other intense cravings, some authorities have erroneously defined drug addiction as the physiological dependence that a person develops after heavy use of a particular drug. Most addicts, however, experience periods when they "kick" their physical dependence, yet their psychological craving continues undiminished; as a result, they soon return to using their drug of choice. It is therefore more useful to define drug addiction as the intense craving for a drug that develops after a period of physical dependence from heavy use.[7]

Why are Americans so involved in using and abusing drugs? There are numerous reasons: to feel good, to get high, to escape from reality, to obtain relief from pain or anxiety, and to relax or sleep. Drugs definitely meet a functional need (such as providing temporary relief from unwanted emotions) but can have serious side effects. On a broader level it should be noted that many segments of our society encourage and romanticize the use of drugs. Senator Frank Moss, for example, comments on the role played by advertisements and commercials:

> It is advertising which mounts the message that pills turn rain to sunshine, gloom to joy, depression to euphoria, solve problems, and dispel doubt. Not just pills: cigarette and cigar ads; soft drinks, coffee, tea, and beer ads— all portray the key to happiness as things to swallow, inhale, chew, drink, and eat.[8]

A BRIEF HISTORY OF OUR DRUG-TAKING SOCIETY

When the Pilgrims set sail for America in 1620, they loaded on their ships 14 tons of water—plus 10,000 gallons of wine and 42 tons of beer.[9] Ever since, Americans have been widely using and abusing drugs.

During and after the Civil War thousands of injured soldiers were treated with narcotics to relieve their pain; many became addicted. Narcotics addiction was a serious problem from the 1860s to the first decade of the 20th century. At the turn of the century about 1% of the population was addicted to a narcotic drug—the highest rate in our history.[10] At that time opiates (including heroin and morphine) were readily available for a variety of purposes. They were used to treat such minor ailments as stomach pains and to ease the discomfort of infants during teething. Pharmacies, grocery stores, and mail-order houses did a prosperous business in selling opiates. Such sales were legally stopped in 1914 by the Harrison Narcotics Act, which required that narcotic drugs be dispensed only through prescriptions by licensed physicians.

In colonial times tobacco was a popular substance for chewing, and after 1870 its use for smoking increased greatly. For a brief time shortly after the turn of the century its sale was prohibited in 14 states because it was thought to be a "stepping stone" to alcohol use and to lead to sexual deviance, insanity, and impotence. The laws banning the sale proved ineffective and were repealed after World War I. Today tobacco is one of our most widely used—and abused—drugs, despite what we know about the health hazards of smoking.

Marijuana use has occurred throughout our history. In the mid-19th century it was often smoked by writers and artists in the larger cities. Shortly after the beginning of the 20th century, Latinos and African Americans began smoking it. The drug was then thought to lead to "unruly" behavior, and the first laws prohibiting its use and distribution were passed in the South. The rest of the states soon enacted similar legislation. In 1937 the director of the Federal Bureau of Narcotics labeled marijuana the "assassin of youth." The mass media jumped on this campaign and began publishing stories stereotyping marijuana users as "crazed drug fiends." Later, to continue receiving funds for his bureau, the director asserted that marijuana was dangerous, as it was a "stepping stone" to using narcotic drugs.[11] Marijuana, in the 1960s and 1970s, became increasingly popular among youths, college students, drug subcultures, and the general population. Its use and effects remain a controversial issue.

Alcohol use has continued unabated ever since the Pilgrims landed. The first governor of

Massachusetts complained of excessive drunkenness in his colony, and since that time there have always been some segments of American society that have viewed alcohol use as a social problem. The American Temperance Union was formed in the early 1800s. It was later followed by the Women's Christian Temperance Union, the Anti-Saloon League, and several other temperance organizations. Alcohol was viewed as responsible for many social ills: crime, the collapse of the family, and unemployment. Immigrants, the poor, and certain minority groups were the major consumers of alcohol at this time. Under pressure, several states passed legislation prohibiting the sale and distribution of alcoholic beverages in the latter half of the 19th century. By the start of World War I, nearly half the population resided in "dry" areas.

The Eighteenth Amendment to the Constitution, which prohibited the sale of alcohol, was ratified in 1920. Prohibition had begun. But people continued to drink, and the law was virtually unenforceable. It gave impetus to organized crime. Moonshiners and speakeasies (places where illegal alcoholic beverages were sold) flourished. Prohibition became a political embarrassment and the United States a laughingstock around the world. In 1933 the Eighteenth Amendment was repealed. Following Prohibition the use of alcohol became more widespread.[12] People in the middle and upper-middle classes also began drinking on a rather large scale. As a result, alcohol was no longer viewed as the scourge of society.

It is interesting to note that, whereas narcotics made a transition from respectability to disrepute in the past 100 years, alcohol made exactly the opposite transition.

SOCIOLOGICAL THEORIES OF DRUG ABUSE

A number of biological, psychological, and sociological theories have been advanced to explain drug abuse. Summarizing all of these theories is beyond the scope of this text, but three socio-

In 1920 the Eighteenth Amendment, which prohibited the sale of alcohol, was ratified and thus an era of speakeasies, bootleg liquor, and "bathtub" gin began. Here authorities display a confiscated still in 1925.

logical theories will be presented for illustrative purposes: anomie theory, labeling theory, and differential association.

Anomie Theory

This theory stems largely from the work of Emile Durkheim[13] and Robert Merton.[14] Merton used anomie to explain deviant behavior. Anomie is a condition in which the acceptance of approved standards of conduct is weakened. Every society has both approved goals (such as making a lot of money) and approved means for attaining these goals (such as high-paying jobs). When certain members of society want these goals but have insufficient means for attaining them, a state of anomie results, and these individuals then seek to achieve the desired goals through deviant means. Applied to drug abuse, this theory asserts that, if people are prevented from achieving their goals, they may be "driven to drink" or to use other drugs. The drugs may be used as an escape—to avoid the suffering caused by failure to achieve goals—or they may be used as a substitute for the "highs" that users had originally hoped to experience from successfully accomplishing their goals.

Merton asserts that drug abuse can be reduced if (1) society sets realistic goals that people can attain and then (2) establishes legitimate means, available to everyone, for attaining these goals. It should be noted that anomie theory fails to explain drug abuse by people who appear to be achieving their goals.

Labeling Theory

This theory was developed by a number of researchers.[15] Labeling theorists view drug abuse as largely stemming from occasional users' being labeled "abusers." Initially, occasional users indulge in drug use that is disapproved of by others—such as getting drunk or smoking marijuana. These users do not at this point view themselves as abusers. However, if their use is discovered and made an issue by significant other people (such as parents, police, or teachers), and if they are then publicly labeled as a "drunkard," "pot head," or "dope user," they are more closely watched. Under this closer surveillance, if they continue to occasionally be found using drugs, the label is gradually confirmed. The significant others may begin to relate to them in terms of the label, causing these occasional users to view themselves as people who "are" whatever label is applied. When this happens, the occasional user is likely to embark on a "career" as a habitual drug abuser.

Labeling theory asserts that drug abuse can be reduced by avoiding labeling—that is, by refusing to treat occasional drug users as if they were "abusers." It should be noted that labeling theory fails to explain drug abuse among "secret alcoholics" and others who are already drug abusers before being labeled as such.

Differential Association

This theory, developed by Edwin Sutherland,[16] asserts that behavior is determined primarily by the values and actions that are considered important by the small, intimate groups one interacts with. Applied to drug abuse, differential association theory asserts that people will learn and take on the drug use norms of the small groups they associate with. These groups include family, neighborhood peer groups, and religious and social groups. Differential association has been used to explain differences in alcoholism rates among ethnic and religious groups.

There are, for example, marked differences in alcohol use patterns between the Irish and Italians or Jews in the United States. The Italian subculture (both in Italy and in this country) widely accepts the moderate use of alcohol, particularly at mealtimes. Serving wine with meals is part of the dietary customs, which even the young participate in. Excessive drinking, however, is frowned on. As a result, although alcohol is widely used in the Italian community, drunkenness and alcoholism are relatively rare.[17]

Similarly, the Jewish community uses alcohol widely, including as a component in religious rituals. As with Italian families, the use of alcohol in controlled social settings minimizes its potential negative effects. And, because there are strong norms against drunkenness and abuse, alcoholism among American Jews is rare.[18]

In contrast, the Irish subculture tolerates periodic episodes of excessive drinking, particularly by single males. Such drinking is seen as a way to relieve tension and frustration. With such norms there is a relatively high rate of alcoholism among Irish-American males.[19]

It is, of course, possible for people to be resocialized into the drug use norms of another subculture. For example, a teenager raised in a family opposed to marijuana use may become attracted to a high school group that places a high value on smoking marijuana. This teenager may then, through the principles of differential association, become resocialized by this new group into using marijuana.

As noted, there are many other theories (including psychological and biological ones) concerning the causes of drug abuse.[20] No single theory is sufficient for identifying all causes, and each theory may or may not apply in any given case.

DRUG SUBCULTURES

A person's decision about whether to use a drug depends not only on his or her personality characteristics and family background but also on the attitudes of peers. These views determine which drugs are used, how often they are used, how much is used at any one time, and what other activities will be engaged in when drugs are used.

A group of peers who advocate the use of one or more drugs can be called a *drug subculture*. Most drug taking occurs in a social group that approves the use of the drug. In a classic study, "Becoming a Marijuana User," Howard Becker found that the peer group plays a crucial role in the individual's learning to smoke marijuana.[21] The group introduces the novice to smoking and teaches the new smoker to recognize the pleasant experiences associated with a "high." Membership in this group (drug subculture) also encourages further drug use and instructs the newcomer to reject established norms and instead to accept the norms of the drug subculture.

Drug subcultures appear to function similarly in relation to other drugs. Drug subcultures are more likely to develop around the use of illegal rather than legal drugs. Use of alcohol (among teenagers), marijuana, heroin, LSD, PCP, and cocaine generally occurs in drug subcultures.

In many cities in the United States a number of gangs (composed of juveniles and young adults) have formed and become involved in widespread use and distribution of illegal drugs. Frequently, gang members also engage in other crimes (such as thefts and burglaries) to financially support their drug habits.

Although drug subcultures are often dysfunctional for society, they do serve important functions for the user. They provide instruction in how to use the drug, including guidelines on the safety limits of dosages. They help handle adverse effects, assist in obtaining the drug, and provide protection from arrest when the drug is being used. They also provide a party-type atmosphere to enhance enjoyment of the effects of the drug.

FACTS ABOUT AND EFFECTS OF COMMONLY USED DRUGS

Depressants

In this section we will examine the following drugs, which are classified as depressants: alcohol, barbiturates, tranquilizers, Quaalude, and PCP.

EXHIBIT 7.1

Jokes about Drunks

Jokes about drunks are common, which suggests that our society does not take alcohol abuse seriously. Here are two examples:

A man walked into a pub with a duck under his arm, and a drunk remarked "What are you doing with that pig in here?" The man said "That isn't a pig. It's a duck." The drunk said "I was talking to the duck."

A drunk staggered out of a bar and started to get into her car. An officer stopped her and stated "You don't really intend to drive that car home, do you?" The drunk replied "Of course, officer; I'm in no condition to walk."

ALCOHOL

Alcohol is the most abused drug in American society. Still, its use is so accepted that few Americans view alcohol as a serious social problem. Social drinking is highly integrated into the customs of our society. In many areas of the country the local pub is a center (particularly for men) for meeting and socializing with friends and neighbors. Going out and getting "high" or even "smashed" is a favorite pastime of college students. Taverns and nightclubs are primary sites for meeting and entertaining dates. Businesses frequently use cocktail lounges to wine and dine customers. In some communities it is the custom to have "a second church service" at a local wateringhole after the weekly church service is over. Because of the pervasiveness of alcohol in our society, this chapter will devote considerable attention to its use, abuse, and treatment.

Alcohol is a colorless liquid that is a component of beer, wine, brandy, whiskey, vodka, rum, and other intoxicating beverages. The average American over the age of 21 consumes an average of 34.4 gallons of beer, 3.4 gallons of wine, and 2.3 gallons of hard liquor a year.[22] The vast majority of American teenagers and adults drink alcohol.

Drinking has become so entrenched into our customs that, unfortunately, people who do not drink are sometimes viewed as "weird," "stuck up," or "killjoys" and are often assumed to have something wrong with them. The serving of alcoholic beverages is expected at many rituals and ceremonies for adults: weddings, birthday parties, Christmas parties, graduations, and the like. Some formal religious rites also include alcohol (for example, wine as the blood of Christ during Communion). Many popular songs highlight drinking. But it is not the use of alcohol at rituals and ceremonies that causes most problems. Because most American alcohol use is informal and relatively uncontrolled, it can easily become excessive without the safeguards that are built into the drinking patterns of many ethnic groups.

The type of alcohol found in beverages is ethyl alcohol. (It is also called grain alcohol, because most of it is made from fermenting grain.) Many drinkers believe that alcohol is a stimulant because it relaxes tensions, lessens sexual and aggressive inhibitions, seems to facilitate interpersonal relationships, and usually leads those who have a few drinks to talk more. It is, however, very definitely a depressant to the central nervous system. Its chemical composition and effects are very similar to those of ether (an anesthetic used in medicine to induce unconsciousness).

Alcohol slows mental activity, reasoning ability, speech ability, and muscle reactions. It distorts perceptions, slurs speech, lessens coordination, and slows memory functioning and respiration. In increasing quantities it leads to stupor, sleep, coma, and, finally, death. A hangover (the aftereffects of too much alcohol) may cause headache, thirst, muscle aches, stomach discomfort, and nausea.

The effects of alcohol vary with the percentage of alcohol in the bloodstream as it passes through the brain. Generally, effects are observable when the concentration of alcohol in the blood reaches 1/10 of 1%. Five drinks (with each drink containing 1 ounce of 86-proof alcohol, 12 ounces of beer, or 3 ounces of wine) in two hours

TABLE 7.1

Percent of Alcohol in the Blood and Its Effects

Alcohol	Effects
.05%	Lowered alertness and a "high" feeling
.10	Decreased reactions; reduced coordination (legally drunk in most states)
.20	Massive interference with senses and motor skills
.30	Perceptions nearly gone; understanding nearly gone
.40	Unconsciousness
.50	Potential death

Sources: Adapted from Oakley S. Ray, *Drugs, Society, and Human Behavior* (St. Louis: Mosby, 1972), p. 86; and Erich Goode, *Drugs in American Society* (New York: Knopf, 1972), pp. 142–143.

will result in a blood alcohol concentration of 1/10 of 1% for a 120-pound person. (The heavier the person, the more drinks it takes to increase the level of alcohol in the blood.) Table 7.1 shows the effects of increasing percentages of alcohol in the blood.

In 1990 scientists discovered that women's stomachs are less effective than men's at breaking down alcohol; as a result, women generally become intoxicated more quickly. Men have in their stomachs substantially more dehydrogenase (an enzyme) than do women. This enzyme breaks down much of the alcohol in the stomach—before it reaches the bloodstream. This finding may also help explain why medical complications, including cirrhosis of the liver, anemia, and gastrointestinal bleeding, develop more rapidly in alcoholic women than in alcoholic men.[23]

Who Drinks? The primary factors related to whether an individual will drink and how much alcohol a drinker will use include: socioeconomic factors, gender, age, religion, urban/rural residence, and geographical region.[24]

■ *Socioeconomic factors:* College-educated people are more likely to drink than are those with only a high school education. Young men at the highest socioeconomic level are more likely to drink than young men at lower socioeconomic levels. However, drinkers at the lower socioeconomic levels are more likely to drink excessively than those at higher socioeconomic levels.

■ *Gender:* Men are more likely to use and abuse alcohol than are women. Still, recent decades have seen a dramatic increase in alcoholism among adult women. Why? One explanation is that cultural taboos against heavy drinking among women have weakened. Another explanation is that increased drinking is related to the changing roles of women in our society.

■ *Age:* Older people are less likely to drink than younger people, even if they were drinkers in their youth. Heavy drinking is most common at ages 21 to 30 for men and ages 31 to 50 for women.

■ *Religion:* Nonchurchgoers drink more than regular churchgoers. Heavy drinking is more common among Episcopalians and Catholics, whereas conservative and fundamentalist Protestants are more often nondrinkers or light drinkers.

■ *Urban/rural residence:* Urban residents are more likely to drink than rural residents.

■ *Geographical region:* People who live in the Northeast and along the West Coast are more apt to drink than people who live in the South and Midwest.

In recent years there has been a decline in drinking, especially of hard liquor, in many segments of the American public.[25] For example, some business executives have switched from having martini luncheons to jogging and working out. In recent years the federal government has put considerable financial pressure on states to raise the legal drinking age to 21 or else have federal highway funds withheld. Practically all states have now raised the drinking age to 21. Secondary schools, colleges, and universities have initiated alcohol awareness programs. Many businesses and employers offer Employee Assistance Programs, which are designed to provide treatment services to alcoholics and problem drinkers. Drunk-driving laws have become stricter, and police departments and the courts are more vigorously enforcing such laws. Organizations such as Mothers Against Drunk Driving and Students Against Drunk Driving have been fairly successful in creating greater public awareness of the hazards of drinking and driving. A cultural norm seems to be emerging that it is no longer stylish to have too much to drink. Despite these promising trends, however, rates of alcohol use and abuse in the United States remain extremely high.

Reasons for Drinking. As discussed earlier, social patterns influence people to drink in a wide variety of situations, such as at happy hours, before and after dinner, and at parties.

There are also individual reasons for drinking. Some people drink because alcohol acts as a "social lubricant," relaxing them so that they feel more at ease interacting with others. Some drink simply to relax. Others use alcohol as a kind of anesthetic, to dull the pain of living and to take their minds off their problems. Some excessive drinkers seek a continual "buzz" to avoid facing life. Others drink occasionally to get "high." Some insomniacs drink so that they will sleep (often they pass out). Drinking before a flight is common for persons with a fear of flying, because alcohol has a tranquilizing effect. Also, people often drink to temporarily get rid of unwanted emotions such as loneliness, anxiety, depression, feelings of inadequacy, insecurity, guilt, and resentment.

Alcoholism is a rather imprecise term, because there is no clear-cut distinction between a problem drinker and an alcoholic. Nevertheless, a useful definition of alcoholism is *the repeated and excessive use of alcohol to the extent that it is harmful to interpersonal relations, to job performance, or to the drinker's health.*

Whether a person will be labeled an alcoholic depends to a large extent on the reactions of his or her employers, family, friends, associates, and community. For example, the "drier" the community in which one lives, the less alcohol and the fewer the problem incidents involving alcohol it takes for someone to be defined as an alcoholic.

CASE EXAMPLE 7.1   Courts Are Getting Tougher on Drunk Drivers

L arry Mahoney was a 34-year-old father who was described by a friend as "somebody who wouldn't hurt anybody for the world." On Sunday evening, May 14, 1988, while drunk, Larry climbed into his pickup truck and drove the wrong way down a Kentucky interstate. He had 0.24% alcohol in his blood—more than twice Kentucky's statutory level. He slammed head-on into an old school bus carrying 67 passengers, mainly teenagers, on a church outing from Radcliff, Kentucky. Twenty-four teenagers and three adults were killed in this crash, the worst alcohol-related traffic accident in U.S. history. Larry Mahoney was charged with "capital murder," which carries the death penalty.

In December 1989, Mahoney was found guilty of 27 counts of second-degree manslaughter, 27 counts of first-degree wanton endangerment, 12 counts of first-degree assault, 14 counts of second-degree wanton endangerment, and 1 count of drunken driving. He was sentenced to 16 years in prison. This lengthy sentence is one more indication that the court system is taking a tougher stand on drunk driving. Many states have enacted legislation to immediately suspend the driver's license of offenders and have mandated jail terms for repeat offenders. Also, many states now mandate instant suspension of the driver's license for individuals failing, or refusing to take, a breath test.

Source: "Kentucky's Textbook Case in Drunk Driving," *U.S. News & World Report*, May 30, 1988, pp. 7–8; and "Man Sentenced in Fatal Church Bus Accident," *Wisconsin State Journal*, Feb. 24, 1990, p. 3A.

People's reactions to drinking vary considerably. Some individuals can drink large amounts quite regularly while appearing sober—although their driving is affected, and they may have a high likelihood of becoming alcoholic in the future. Some people drink heavily without experiencing hangovers—although hangovers are functional because they let people know they have ingested too much alcohol and discourage further binges. Generally, as we've seen, the greater the weight of the drinker, the more she or he can consume before becoming intoxicated.

Many alcoholics who stop drinking must abstain *totally*; if they start again, they will have a compulsive, uncontrollable urge to go on a series of binges. Because of this, Alcoholics Anonymous asserts that "Once an alcoholic, always an alcoholic." There is some evidence (highly controversial) that certain alcoholics can, after treatment,

return to social drinking.[26] However, this finding has been highly criticized by a number of treatment organizations because it has led some alcoholics who had quit drinking to try to drink lightly, with the result that they immediately returned to excessive drinking.

There are over 18 million alcoholics in the United States, and each one affects at least four other people close to him or her—including spouse, family, or employer. Approximately two out of three alcoholics are male, but the proportion of female alcoholics has risen in the past 20 years.[27] Contrary to popular stereotypes, only an estimated 5% are "skid-row bums."[28] Most are ordinary people. One out of ten social drinkers becomes an alcoholic.[29]

Some people become alcoholic quite soon after they start drinking. Others may drink for 10, 20, or 30 years before becoming addicted.

An alcoholic may be only psychologically dependent on alcohol, but most are also physically dependent.

Health Problems Caused by Alcohol. The life expectancy of alcoholics is 10 to 12 years lower than that of nonalcoholics.[30] There are several reasons why this is so. Alcohol, over an extended period of time, gradually destroys liver cells, leaving scar tissue in their place. When the scar tissue is extensive, a medical condition called cirrhosis of the liver occurs. This condition is the eighth most frequent cause of death in the United States (over 30,000 per year).[31]

Alcohol has no healthy food value, although it contains a high number of calories. Heavy drinkers, as a result, have a reduced appetite for nutritious food, frequently suffer from vitamin deficiencies, and are highly susceptible to infectious diseases.

Heavy drinking also causes kidney problems, contributes to a variety of heart ailments, is a factor that leads to diabetes, and also appears to contribute to cancer. It is also a contributing cause of ulcers and impotency in males. In addition, heavy drinking is associated with over 10,000 suicides annually.[32] Death can occur from drinking an excessive amount of alcohol—for example, from depression of the respiratory system or from the drinker choking on vomit while unconscious.

Interestingly, for some as-yet-unknown reason, the life expectancy for light to moderate drinkers exceeds that for nondrinkers.[33] Perhaps an occasional drink helps people to relax and thereby reduces the likelihood of life-threatening stress-related illnesses.

Combining alcohol with other drugs can have disastrous and sometimes fatal effects. Sometimes, two drugs taken together have a *synergistic* interaction, meaning that they create an effect much greater than either would produce alone. For example, sedatives like barbiturates (often found in sleeping pills) or Quaaludes, when taken with alcohol, can so depress the central nervous system that a coma or even death may result.

Other drugs tend to have an *antagonistic* response to alcohol, meaning that one drug negates the effects of the other. Many doctors now caution patients not to drink while taking certain prescribed drugs, because the alcohol will reduce, or even totally negate, the beneficial effects of these drugs.

Whether drugs will interact synergistically or antagonistically depends on a wide range of factors: the properties of the drugs, the amounts taken, the user's tolerance to them, the amount of sleep the user has had, the kind and amount of food that has been eaten, and the user's overall health. The interactive effects may be minimal one day and extensive the next.

Withdrawal from alcohol, once the body is physically addicted, may lead to delirium tremens (DTs) and other unpleasant reactions. The DTs are characterized by rapid heartbeat, uncontrollable trembling, severe nausea, and profuse sweating.

Drinking and Driving. Alcohol is a significant contributing factor in approximately half of all automobile fatalities and in many serious automobile injuries. Each year over a million people in the United States are arrested for driving under the influence of alcohol.[34] More people are killed by intoxicated drivers than are killed through violent crimes! Mothers Against Drunk Driving (MADD), an organization that was formed several years ago, is having considerable success in getting states to enact and enforce stricter drunk-driving laws. In addition, the news media (particularly television and radio) in recent years have been airing public service programs and announcements to educate the public about the consequences of drunk driving.

Alcohol and Crime. About one-eighth of all arrests for minor crimes are alcohol related: public drunkenness, violations of liquor laws, disorderly conduct, and vagrancy.[35]

Alcohol is also a contributing factor in many major crimes. In a majority of homicides, aggravated assaults, sexual crimes against children, and sexually aggressive acts against women, the offender had been drinking.[36] This is not to say that alcohol is the main cause of these crimes. However, it appears to be a contributing factor

EXHIBIT 7.2

Polydrug Abuse Is Becoming a Serious Problem

Notables such as Elvis Presley, John Belushi, River Phoenix, and former First Lady Betty Ford were dependent on two or more drugs. Polydrug abuse contributed to the early deaths of Presley, Belushi, and Phoenix. Betty Ford publicly acknowledged that she was dependent on Valium, alcohol, and the medication she was taking for arthritis. She received treatment at the Naval Hospital in Long Beach, California. Later she was instrumental in the founding of the Betty Ford Clinic for treatment of substance abuse problems.

that increases the likelihood of such crimes occurring.

Effects of Alcohol Abuse on the Family. In the past, if there was a problem drinker in the family, it was almost always the husband. Now the likelihood is increasing that it could be the wife or one (or more) of the teenagers.

Heavy drinking is a contributing factor to many family problems: child abuse, child neglect, spouse abuse, parent abuse, financial problems, unemployment of wage earners, violent arguments, and unhappy marriages. Marriage to an alcoholic often ends in divorce, separation, or desertion: Children of an alcoholic parent have higher rates of severe emotional and physical illnesses.[37]

Sharon Wegscheider indicates that family members in alcoholic families tend to assume roles that both protect the chemically dependent person from taking responsibility for his or her behavior and actually serve to maintain the drinking problems. She identifies several roles that are typically played by family members, in addition to the chemically dependent person: the chief enabler, the family hero, the scapegoat, the lost child, and the mascot.[38]

The chief enabler's main purpose is to assume the primary responsibility for the family functioning. The abuser typically continues to lose control and relinquishes responsibility. The chief enabler, on the other hand, takes more and more responsibility and begins making more and more of the family's decisions. A chief enabler is often the parent or spouse of the chemically dependent person.

Conditions in families of chemically dependent people often continue to deteriorate as the dependent person loses control. A positive influence is needed to offset the negative. The family hero fulfills this role. The family hero often is the "perfect" person who does well at everything he or she tries. The hero works very hard at making the family appear to be functioning better than it is. In this way the family hero provides the family with self-worth.

Another typical role played by someone in the chemically dependent family is the scapegoat. Although the alcohol abuse is the real problem, a family rule may mandate that this fact be denied and the blame be placed elsewhere. Frequently, another family member is targeted with the blame. The scapegoat often behaves in negative ways (for example, gets caught for stealing, runs away, becomes extremely withdrawn), which draws the spotlight to him or her. The scapegoat's role is to distract attention away from the dependent person and onto something else. This role helps the family avoid addressing the problem of chemical dependency.

Often there is also a lost child in the family. This is the person who seems rather uninvolved with the rest of the members yet never causes any trouble. The lost child's purpose is to provide relief to the family from some of the pain it is suffering. At least there is someone in the home who neither requires much attention nor causes any stress. The lost child is simply there.

Finally, chemically dependent families often have someone playing the role of mascot. The mascot is the person who probably has a good sense of humor and appears not to take anything seriously. Despite how much the mascot might be suffering inside, he or she provides a little fun for the family.

EXHIBIT 7.3

Fetal Alcohol Syndrome

Prior to the 1940s it was thought that the uterus was a glass bubble that totally separated the fetus from the outside world and fully protected the fetus from whatever drugs the mother happened to be using. Since then, medical science has learned that chemical substances are readily transferred form the mother's uterine arteries, across the placental membrane, into the baby's umbilical vein, and then to the baby's entire body.

When a pregnant woman drinks any alcoholic beverage (including beer and wine), the alcohol easily crosses the placenta, and the fetus attains blood alcohol levels that are similar to those in the mother. Heavy alcohol consumption by pregnant mothers can cause a variety of conditions in the new baby that, taken together, have been labeled fetal alcohol syndrome. These conditions include mental retardation and developmental delays, overall growth retardation before and after birth, and various congenital malformations of the face, head, skeleton, and heart. Such babies also are more likely to be born prematurely, to have a low birth weight, to be hyperirritable, and to have neurological defects and poor muscle tone. They also have a higher infant mortality rate. The chances of microcephaly (a condition in which the baby has a small brain and skull and is mentally retarded) occurring are also increased.

The more alcohol a pregnant woman ingests, the greater the probability that her baby will have fetal alcohol syndrome. Studies suggest that, if a pregnant woman has five or more drinks at any one time, her baby will have a 10% chance of developing fetal alcohol syndrome. Also, if she drinks lightly over a prolonged period, the syndrome may also occur. An average of one ounce per day results in a 10% risk; an average of two ounces per day results in a 20% risk.

The U.S. Public Health Service recommends that pregnant women not drink alcohol. Just as a mother would not give a glass of wine to her newborn, she should not give it to her unborn baby. It is not just alcohol but also other drugs (such as tobacco, marijuana, cocaine, and heroin) during pregnancy that endanger the unborn child.

Source: Mike Samuels and Mary Samuels, "Pregnancy: How Smoking and Drugs Endanger Baby," *Wisconsin State Journal,* July 2, 1986, sec. 2, p. 1.

In summary, alcoholism is a problem affecting the entire family. Each member is suffering over the dependency, yet each assumes a role in order to maintain the family's status quo and to help the family survive. Family members are driven to maintain these roles, no matter what.

Alcohol and Industry. It is estimated that alcoholism costs businesses and industry over $6.5 billion annually.[39] This figure reflects losses in terms of sick leave, absenteeism, missed or late work assignments, and on-the-job accidents. It is further estimated that 6–10% of the work force experience drinking problems to such a degree that job performance is affected.[40]

Alcoholism Gene Theory. Alcoholism has long been assumed to be caused by *both* environmental and genetic factors. There has been considerable controversy in recent years, however, concerning the alcoholism gene theory.

Alcoholism has been found to run in families. In addition, children of alcoholic (biological) parents who are adopted at an early age have a significantly higher chance of becoming alcoholic than do children in the general population.[41]

Researchers in 1990 reported pinpointing a gene in people prone to alcoholism—a finding that adds weight to the argument that alcoholism is a disease and not a moral weakness or willful misconduct.[42] The researchers, Ernest Noble and Kenneth Blum, stated that a particular gene on a chromosome previously linked with alcoholism was far more common in alcoholics than in nonalcoholics. Researchers previously had implicated three chromosomes as possibly having a role in alcoholism, but no one had identified any single gene on these chromosomes as the culprit. (Chromosomes are threadlike structures of thousands of individual genes, the "fingerprints" of DNA that carry each cell's hereditary blueprint. A person's traits are determined by the nearly 100,000 genes in each cell.)

The gene pinpointed by Nobel and Blum has two alternative forms, called "A-1 allele" and "A-2 allele." The researchers looked at both alternative forms of the gene in brain matter from the cadavers of 70 subjects, 35 alcoholics and 35 nonalcoholics. The A-1 allele was found to have a high association with alcoholism, and the A-2 allele was found to be associated with nonalcoholism. The A-1 allele was present in 69% of the alcoholics but in only 20 of the nonalcoholics. (The study suggests, but does not conclusively prove, the existence of an alcoholism gene. Because there is not a 100% association between the A-1 allele and alcoholism, other factors—including the environment—could play a role in causing the problem.) The researchers conclude that the rare form of the gene may make people more prone to alcoholism, but they remain cautious about the implications of these findings.

Previous studies suggesting an association between genes and such diseases as manic depression and schizophrenia have not held up to further scrutiny. If the A-1 allele does turn out to be linked to alcoholism, a test for this allele could identify individuals at high risk before they become addicted to alcohol. The disease may be brought on by a number of genes. Having identified one of the genes would allow scientists to map the chemical pathways to alcoholism and to devise drugs to alter them. Such drugs, for example, could reduce the craving for liquor, giving alcoholics a means of recovery.

Several months after the release of the Noble and Blum study, an investigation by David Goldman cast doubt on the earlier finding linking a particular gene with alcoholism.[43] The Goldman team studied genes from the white blood cells of living people—40 alcoholics compared with a control group of 127 nonalcoholics chosen in a random manner. The A-1 allele was present in 38% of alcoholics and in 30% of the random group—a statistically insignificant difference.

Avoiding Treatment for Alcoholism. Many alcoholics (perhaps the majority) do not seek help because they *deny* they have a drinking problem. In an attempt to prove they can drink like any other person, they wind up sneaking drinks, excusing their drinking behavior, or blaming others ("If you had a job like mine, you'd drink too!"). There are many reasons why alcoholics refuse to admit the severity of their condition. Alcoholism is highly stigmatized. Also, it is viewed as a disease, and they may not want to perceive themselves as "sick." Some see alcohol as essential to their lives. They socialize through drinking and are able to relax, fall asleep, or escape from their problems. Thus they may choose to keep drinking even though they know it is ruining their health, destroying their reputation in the community, getting them fired at a variety of jobs, and breaking up their family. In many ways alcohol becomes their "best friend," which they refuse to abandon—even if it kills them.

If an alcoholic is to be helped, this denial of their problem must be confronted. (We will discuss denial further in the section on rehabilitation programs.)

BARBITURATES

Barbiturates, which are derived from barbituric acid, depress the central nervous system. Barbiturates were first synthesized in the early 1900s, and there are now over 2500 different varieties. They are commonly used to relieve insomnia and anxiety, to treat epilepsy and high blood pressure, and to relax patients before or after surgery. Barbiturates are illegal unless obtained by a physician's prescription.

Taken in sufficient doses, barbiturates have effects similar to strong alcohol. Users experience relief from inhibitions, have a feeling of euphoria, feel "high" or in good humor, and are passively content. However, these moods can change rapidly to gloom, agitation, and aggressiveness. Physiological effects include slurred speech, disorientation, staggering, confusion, drowsiness, and impaired coordination.

Prolonged heavy use of barbiturates can cause physical dependence, with withdrawal symptoms similar to those of heroin addiction. Withdrawal is accompanied by body tremors, cramps, anxiety, fever, nausea, profuse sweating, and hallucinations. Many authorities believe barbiturate addiction is more dangerous than heroin addiction, and it is considered more resistant to treatment than heroin addiction. Abrupt withdrawal can cause fatal convulsions. One forensic pathologist noted: "Show me someone who goes cold turkey (the sudden and complete halting of drug use) on a bad barbiturate habit, and I'll show you a corpse."[44]

Barbiturate overdose can cause convulsions, coma, poisoning, and sometimes death. Barbiturates are particularly dangerous when taken with alcohol because the alcohol acts synergistically to magnify the potency of the barbiturates. Accidental deaths due to excessive doses are frequent. Often the user becomes groggy, forgets how much has been taken, and continues to take more until an overdose level has been reached. Barbiturates are also the most popular suicide drug. A number of famous people, such as Marilyn Monroe, have fatally overdosed on barbiturates.

Generally, barbiturates are taken orally, although some users inject them intravenously. Use of barbiturates, like alcohol, may lead to traffic fatalities.

TRANQUILIZERS
Other depressants are the drugs classified as tranquilizers. Common brand names are Librium, Miltown, Serax, Tranxene, and Valium. They reduce anxiety, relax muscles, and act as sedatives.

Users have moderate potential of becoming physically and psychologically dependent. Tranquilizers are usually taken orally, and the effects last four to eight hours. Side effects include slurred speech, disorientation, and behavior resembling intoxication. Overdoses are possible and result in cold and clammy skin, shallow respiration, dilated pupils, weak and rapid pulse, coma, and possibly death. Withdrawal symptoms are similar to those from alcohol and barbiturates: anxiety, tremors, convulsions, delirium, and sometimes death.

QUAALUDE AND PCP
Both Quaalude and PCP are depressants. (PCP also produces effects similar to those of hallucinogens.)

Methaqualone (better known by its patent name, Quaalude) resembles barbiturates and alcohol in its effects, although it is chemically different. It has the reputation of being a "love drug" because users believe it makes them more eager for sex and enhances sexual pleasure. These effects probably stem from the fact that it lessens inhibitions (similar to alcohol and barbiturates). Quaaludes also reduce anxiety and give a feeling of euphoria. Users can become both physically and psychologically dependent. Overdose can result in convulsions, coma, delirium, and even death. Most deaths occur when the drug is taken together with alcohol, which vastly magnifies its effects. Withdrawal symptoms are severe and unpleasant. Abuse of the drug may also cause hangovers, fatigue, liver damage, and temporary paralysis of the limbs.

The technical name for PCP is phencyclidine, and its street name is "angel dust." PCP was developed in the 1950s as an anesthetic, but this medical use was soon terminated because patients displayed symptoms of severe emotional disturbance after receiving it. PCP is legal today only for tranquilizing elephants and monkeys, which apparently do not experience the adverse side effects.

PCP is used primarily by young people who are unaware of its hazards. It is usually smoked, often after being sprinkled on a marijuana "joint." It may also be sniffed, swallowed, or injected. PCP is a very dangerous drug. It distorts the senses, disrupts balance, and leads to an inability to think clearly. Larger amounts of PCP can cause a person to become paranoid, can lead to aggressive behavior (even violent murder), and can create temporary symptoms of a severe emotional disturbance. Continued use can lead to the development of prolonged emotional disturbance. Overdose may result in coma or even death.

Research has not as yet concluded whether PCP induces physical or psychological dependence. The drug has a potential to be used (and abused) extensively because it is relatively easy to prepare in a home laboratory and because the ingredients and recipes are widely available. An additional danger of PCP is that even one-time users sometimes have flashbacks in which hallucinations are reexperienced, even long after use has ceased. It may be that many accidents and unexplained disasters are caused by someone's previous use of PCP or some other undetectable hallucinogenic substance.

Stimulants

In this section we will examine the following drugs, which are classified as stimulants: caffeine, amphetamines, cocaine and crack, amyl nitrate and butyl nitrate.

CAFFEINE

Caffeine is a stimulant to the central nervous system. It is present in coffee, tea, cocoa, Coca-Cola, and many other soft drinks. It is also available in tablet form (for example, No-Doz). Practically all Americans use caffeine on a daily basis. It reduces hunger, fatigue, and boredom and improves alertness and motor activity. The drug appears to be addictive, because many users develop a tolerance for it. A further sign that it is addictive is that heavy users (for example, habitual coffee drinkers) will experience withdrawal symptoms of mild irritability and depression.

Excessive amounts of caffeine cause insomnia, restlessness, and gastrointestinal irritation and can even, surprisingly, cause death.

Because caffeine has the status of a "non-drug" in our society, users are not labeled criminals, there is no black market for it, and no subculture is formed to give support in obtaining and using the drug. Because caffeine is legal, its price is low compared to that of other drugs. Users are not tempted to resort to crime to support their habit. Some authorities assert that our approach to caffeine should serve as a model for the way we react to other illegal drugs (such as marijuana) that, they feel, are no more harmful than caffeine.[45]

AMPHETAMINES

Amphetamines are called "uppers" because of their stimulating effects. When prescribed by a physician, they are legal. Some truck drivers have obtained prescriptions in order to stay awake and alert during a long haul, with a few becoming addicted. Dieters have received prescriptions to help them lose weight and have also found that the pills tend to give them more self-confidence and buoyance. College students have used them to stay awake and alert while studying. Others who have used amphetamines to increase alertness and performance for relatively short periods of time include athletes, astronauts, and executives. Additional nicknames for these drugs are *speed*, *ups*, *pep pills*, *black beauties*, and *bennies*.

Amphetamines are synthetic drugs. They are similar to adrenalin, a hormone from the adrenal gland that stimulates the central nervous system. The better-known amphetamines include Dexedrine, Benzedrine, and Methedrine. Physical reactions to amphetamines are extensive: Consumption of fat stored in body tissues is accelerated, heartbeat is increased, respiratory processes are stimulated, appetite is reduced, and insomnia is common. Users feel euphoric and stronger and have an increased capacity to concentrate and to express themselves verbally. Prolonged use can lead to irritability, deep anxiety, and an irrational persecution complex that can provoke sudden acts of violence.

Amphetamines are usually taken orally in tablet, powder, or capsule form. They also can be sniffed or injected. "Speeding" (injecting the drug into a vein) produces the most powerful effects but also the greatest harm. An overdose can cause a coma, with possible brain damage, and in rare cases death may occur. Speeders may develop hepatitis, abscesses, convulsions, hallucinations, delusions, and severe emotional disturbances. Another danger is that, when sold on the street, the substance may contain impurities that are additional health hazards.

An amphetamine high is often followed by mental depression and fatigue. Continued amphetamine use leads to psychological dependence. It is unclear whether amphetamines are physically addicting because the withdrawal symptoms are uncharacteristic of withdrawal from other drugs. Amphetamine withdrawal symptoms include sleep disturbances, apathy, decreased activity, disorientation, irritability, exhaustion, and depression. Some authorities see these withdrawal symptoms as indicative of physical addiction.[46]

One of the legal uses of certain amphetamines is in the treatment of hyperactivity in children. Hyperactivity (also called hyperkinesis) is characterized by a short attention span, excessive motor activity, restlessness, and shifts in moods. Little is known about the causes of this condition. As children become older, the symptoms tend to disappear, even without treatment. Interestingly, some amphetamines (Ritalin is a popular one) have a calming and soothing effect on children; the exact opposite effect occurs when Ritalin is taken by adults. It should be noted that treatment of "uncontrollable" children with amphetamines has frequently been abused. Joel Fort and Christopher Cory note:

> Many of the children for whom Ritalin is prescribed are not really hyperactive to begin with. They are normal children who simply refuse to submit to what their teachers and parents consider orderly school and family routines. Categorizing children who are different as hyperactive often is a seductively convenient way to blame the victims of teachers' and parents' own shortcomings. Drugging these children, however, brands them as troublemakers and helps to further institutionalize drug use.[47]

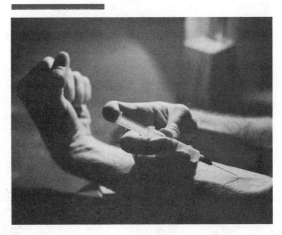

Drug addiction has reached epidemic levels in society, especially in our nation's inner cities.

An amphetamine that has had increasing illegal use in recent years is methamphetamine hydrochloride, known on the street as "meth" or "ice." In liquid form it is often referred to as "speed." Under experimental conditions, cocaine users often have difficulty distinguishing cocaine from methamphetamine hydrochloride. There is a danger this drug may be increasingly abused, as its "high" lasts longer than that from cocaine and the drug can be synthesized relatively easily in laboratories from products that are sold legally in the United States. Methamphetamine hydrochloride (Desoxyn) is legally used to treat obesity as one component of a "last-resort" weight-reduction regimen. There is, however, a serious side effect of this drug when used for weight reduction: The user's appetite returns with greater intensity after withdrawal from the drug.

COCAINE AND CRACK

Cocaine is obtained from the leaves of the South American coca plant. It has a chic status in this country and is rapidly replacing other illegal drugs in popularity. Although legally classified as a narcotic, it is in fact not related to the opiates from which narcotic drugs are derived. It is a powerful stimulant and antifatigue agent.

In the United States, cocaine is generally taken by sniffing and absorbed through the nasal

CASE
EXAMPLE 7.2   **Tragic Cocaine Overdoses**

On June 17, 1986, Len Bias, an All-American forward from the University of
Maryland, was the Boston Celtics' first pick in the National Basketball Association draft. He was the second player chosen overall. The Celtics were his favorite
team, and he looked forward to signing a contract for around $1 million per year. Two
days later he was partying and died of heart failure induced by cocaine intoxication.

Eight days after the death of Len Bias, Don Rogers was celebrating at his bachelor's party. He was to be married the next day. Rogers was a professional football
player for the Cleveland Browns. He had played at UCLA and was the Browns' number-one pick in the 1984 college draft. That year he was selected as the Defensive
Rookie of the Year in the American Football Conference. Rogers died at his bachelor's
party of heart failure induced by cocaine intoxication.

membranes. The most common method is sniffing through a straw or a rolled-up bank note; this
is known as "snorting." It may also be injected
intravenously, and in South America the natives
chew the coca leaf. It may be added in small quantities to a cigarette and smoked. Cocaine has been
used medically in the past as a local anesthetic,
but other drugs have now largely replaced it for
this purpose.

Cocaine constricts the blood vessels and
thereby leads to increased strength and endurance. It also is thought by users to increase creative and intellectual powers. Other effects include
a feeling of euphoria, excitement, restlessness,
and a lessened sense of fatigue. Some users of cocaine claim that it heightens or restores their virility and enables them to prolong intercourse for
long periods.[48]

Larger doses or extended use may result in
hallucinations and delusions. A peculiar effect of
cocaine abuse is *formication*—the illusion that
ants, snakes, or bugs are crawling on or into the
skin. Some abusers have such intense illusions
that they literally scratch, slap, and wound themselves trying to kill these imaginary creatures.

Physical effects of cocaine include increased
blood pressure and pulse rate, insomnia, and loss
of appetite. Heavy users may experience weight

loss or malnutrition due to appetite suppression.
Physical dependence on cocaine is considered to
be a low to medium risk. However, the drug appears to be psychologically habituating; withdrawal usually results in intense depression and
despair, which drive the person back to taking the
drug.[49] Additional effects of withdrawal include
apathy, long periods of sleep, extreme fatigue, irritability, and disorientation. Serious tissue damage to the nose can occur when large quantities of
cocaine are "sniffed" over a prolonged time period. Regular use may result in habitual sniffling
and sometimes leads to an anorexic condition.
High doses can cause agitation, increased body
temperature, and convulsions. A few people who
overdose may die if their breathing and heart
functions become too depressed.

Crack (also called rock) is obtained from cocaine. The inert ingredients are separated from
the cocaine by mixing it with water and ammo-
nium hydroxide. The water is then removed from
the cocaine base by means of a fast-drying solvent, usually ether. The resultant mixture resembles large sugar crystals, similar to rock sugar.
Crack is highly addictive. Some authorities claim
that one use is enough to lead to addiction. Users
generally claim that, after they have finished one
dose, they immediately crave another.

EXHIBIT 7.4

Crack Babies

I n recent years, crack cocaine use by pregnant women has sharply increased. As a result, hundreds of thousands of babies have been born who have been adversely affected by their mother's crack use.

Cocaine causes the blood vessels in a pregnant woman to constrict, thus reducing the vital flow of oxygen and other nutrients to the fetus. Because fetal cells multiply swiftly in the first months, an embryo deprived of a proper blood supply by a mother's early and continuous use of cocaine is likely to suffer an adverse cognitive impact. At birth such babies may look quite normal, but they are likely to be undersized, and the circumference of their heads tends to be unusually small—a trait associated with lower IQ scores. Only the most intensive care after birth will give these babies a fighting chance to have a "normal" life.

In rare cases during the latter months of pregnancy, heavy crack use can lead to an embolism (a clot) that lodges in a fetal vessel and completely disrupts the blood supply to an organ or a limb. The result will be a deformed arm or leg, a missing section of an intestine or kidney, or various other deformities.

Cocaine exposure affects brain chemistry as well. The drug alters the actions of neurotransmitters, the messengers that travel between nerve cells and help control a person's mood and responsiveness. Such changes may explain the behavioral problems, including impulsiveness and moodiness, seen in cocaine-exposed children as they mature.

Some pregnant women repeatedly use crack cocaine in combination with other drugs. This behavior increases the chances that the fetus will be affected, because the other drugs also can damage the baby.

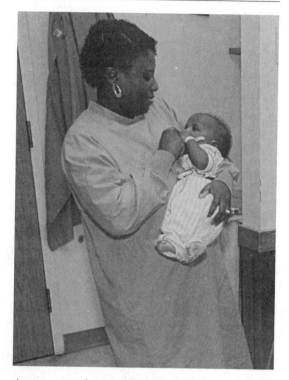

A nurse cares for an infant abandoned by a crack-addicted mother.

The children born to pregnant mothers who used crack cocaine have become known as "crack babies" and "crack kids." A few such children have severe physical deformities from which they will never recover. In others the damage can be more subtle, showing up as behavioral problems that may sabotage the children's schooling and social development. Many of these youngsters look and act like other children, but their early exposure to cocaine makes them less able to over-

(continued)

EXHIBIT 7.4 *(continued)*

come negative influences, such as a disruptive home life.

Crack children often require exhaustive and expensive medical treatment. Some grow up in dysfunctional families and increasingly display behavioral and emotional disorders as they grow older. The injury during gestation is often compounded after birth by an environment of neglect, poverty, and violence. Many crack-addicted mothers continue using the drug, even after giving birth to drug-impaired children.

How can crack babies be helped? What seems to work is a combination of the social services carrot and the legal stick. That is, the best way to rescue a crack child is to rescue the mother as well. Successful programs for the addicted mothers offer a variety of assistance, beginning with detoxification, then extending to pediatric services for the child, psychological and job counseling for the mother, and extensive parenting classes. Crack children often need extensive medical services, social services, and specialized educational services. All of these services need to be backed up with the threat of legal intervention, including the threat of removal of the child to foster care through the protective services system.

Crack is usually smoked, either in a specially made glass pipe or mixed with tobacco or marijuana in a cigarette. The effects are similar to those of cocaine, but the "rush" is more immediate, and the drug gives an intensified high and has an even greater orgasmic effect.

An overdose is more common when crack is injected than when it is smoked. Withdrawal effects include an irresistible compulsion to have the drug, as well as apathy, long periods of sleep, irritability, extreme fatigue, depression, and disorientation.

Communal use of needles spreads AIDS. Cocaine and crack can have serious effects on the heart, straining it with high blood pressure, with interrupted heart rhythm, and with raised pulse rates. Cocaine and crack may also damage the liver. Severe convulsions can cause brain damage, emotional problems, and sometimes death. Smoking crack may also damage the lungs.

AMYL NITRATE AND BUTYL NITRATE

Amyl nitrate ("poppers") is prescribed for patients who risk certain forms of heart failure. It is a volatile liquid that is sold in small bottles. When the container is opened, the chemical begins to evaporate (similar to gasoline). If the vapor is sniffed, the user's blood vessels are immediately dilated, and there is an increase in heart rate. These physical changes create feelings of mental excitation ("head rush") and physical excitation ("body rush"). The drug is legal only by prescription, but (as with many other drugs) illicit dealers readily obtain and distribute it.

Butyl nitrate is legally available in some states without a prescription and has an effect similar to that of amyl nitrate. Trade names under which it is sold are Rush and Locker Room. Similar to amyl nitrate, the vapor is sniffed. It is available at some sexual aid and novelty stores.

Both these drugs have been used as aphrodisiacs and as stimulants while dancing. The drugs have some short-term, unpleasant side effects that may include fainting, headaches, and dizziness. A few deaths have been reported due to overdoses. Both these drugs are classified as stimulants.

Narcotics

The most commonly used narcotic drugs in the United States are the opiates (such as opium, heroin, and morphine). The term *narcotic* means "sleep inducing." In actuality, drugs classified as narcotics are more accurately called analgesics, or painkillers. The principal effect produced by narcotic drugs is a feeling of euphoria.

The opiates are all derived from the opium poppy, which grows in many countries. Turkey, Southeast Asia, and Colombia have in our recent past been major sources of the opiates. The drug opium is the dried form of a milky substance that oozes from the seed pods after the petals fall from the purple or white flower. Opium has been used for centuries.

Morphine is the main active ingredient of opium. It was first identified in the early 1800s and has been used extensively as a painkiller. Heroin was first synthesized from morphine in 1874. It was once thought to be a cure for morphine addiction but later was also found to be addicting. Heroin is a more potent drug than morphine.

Opium is usually smoked, although it can be taken orally. Morphine and heroin are either sniffed (snorted) or injected into a muscle or a vein (called "mainlining"), which maximizes the drugs' effects.

Opiates affect the central nervous system and produce feelings of tranquility, drowsiness, or euphoria. They also generate a sense of well-being, which makes pain, anxiety, or depression seem unimportant. Tony Blaze-Gosden notes:

> It has been described as giving an orgasmlike rush or flash that lasts briefly but memorably. At the peak of the euphoria, the user has a feeling of exaggerated physical and mental comfort and wellbeing; a heightened feeling of buoyancy and bodily health, and a heightened feeling of being competent, in control, capable of any achievement, and being able to cope.[50]

Overdoses can cause convulsions and coma and, in rare cases, death by respiratory failure. All opiates are now recognized as highly addictive.

Heroin is the most widely abused opiate. In addition to the above-mentioned effects, heroin slows the functioning parts of the brain. The user's appetite and sex drive tend to be dulled. After an initial feeling of euphoria, the user generally becomes lethargic and stuporous. Contrary to popular belief, most heroin users take the drug infrequently and do not as a rule become addicted.[51]

Opiate addiction occurs when the user takes the drug regularly for a period of time. Whether addiction will occur depends on the opiate taken, the strength of the dosages, the regularity of use, the characteristics of the user, and the length of time taken. Addiction can occur within a few weeks. Users rapidly develop a tolerance and may eventually need a dose that is up to 100 times stronger than a dose that would have been fatal during the initiation to the drug.[52]

The withdrawal process is very unpleasant. Symptoms include chills, cramps, sweating, nervousness, anxiety, runny eyes and nose, dilated pupils, muscle aches, increased blood pressure, severe cramps, nausea, and fever. Most addicts are obsessed with securing a fix in order to avoid these severe withdrawal symptoms.

Addiction to opiates is extremely difficult to break, partly because intense craving for the drug may recur periodically for several months afterward. Edward Brecher et al. note that the opiate drug

> . . . is one that most users continue to take even though they want to stop, decide to stop, try to stop, and actually succeed in stopping for days, weeks, months, or even years. It is a drug for which men and women will prostitute themselves. It is a drug to which most users return after treatment. . . . It is a drug which most users continue to use despite the threat of long-term imprisonment for its use—and to which they promptly return after experiencing long-term imprisonment.[53]

Most opiate addicts are under age 30, are of low socioeconomic status, and are poorly educated. A disproportionate number are African Americans. Distribution and addiction to narcotic drugs occur primarily in large urban centers.

When heroin was first discovered in the late 1800s, it was initially used as a painkiller, as a substitute for people addicted to morphine, and as a drug taken by many to experience euphoria. A fair number of people became addicted, and in the early 1900s laws were passed to prohibit its sale, possession, and distribution.

Heroin abuse continues to be regarded by many Americans as our most serious drug problem. This stereotype does not appear warranted, because only a tiny fraction of the U.S. population has ever tried heroin. The number of people addicted to heroin is minuscule compared to the number addicted to alcohol or tobacco. In addition, such drugs as alcohol and barbiturates contribute to many more deaths.

One reason why heroin retains its reputation is that users are thought to be "dope fiends" who commit violent crimes and reject the values of contemporary society. Addicts, however, are unlikely to commit such violent crimes as rape or aggravated assault. They are more likely to commit crimes against property (shoplifting, burglary, pickpocketing, larceny, and robbery) in order to support their habit.[54] Prostitution for female addicts is also common. Because the severe withdrawal symptoms begin about 18 hours after the last fix, addicts who have experienced these symptoms will do almost anything to avoid them.

Unsanitary injections of heroin may cause hepatitis and other infections. Communal use of needles can spread AIDS. Also, the high cost of maintaining a heroin habit—often over $100 daily—may create huge financial problems for the user.

Because the price of illicit narcotic drugs is so high, organized crime has made huge profits in the smuggling and distribution of these drugs. Often narcotics are diluted with dangerous impurities, which pose serious health hazards for the users.

Hallucinogens

Hallucinogens were popular as psychedelic drugs in the late 1960s. These drugs distort the user's perceptions, creating hallucinatory impressions of "sights and sounds" that do not exist. The four hallucinogens most commonly used in this country are Mescaline (peyote), psilocybin, psilocin, and LSD. All are taken orally—swallowed in capsule form, eaten on a sugar cube, or licked from the back of a stamp.

Peyote is derived from a cactus plant. Mescaline is the synthetic form of peyote. Psilocybin and psilocin are found in approximately 90 different species of mushrooms (called "magic mushrooms"). Both peyote and psilocybin have had a long history of use among certain Native American tribes. Members of the Native American Church, a religious organization, have won the legal right to use peyote on ceremonial occasions.[55]

The most popular hallucinogen is LSD (lysergic acid diethylamide). LSD is a synthetic material derived from a fungus (ergot) that grows on rye and other plants. It is one of the most potent drugs known; a single ounce will make up to 300,000 doses.

The effects of LSD vary greatly, depending on the expectations and psychological state of the user and on the context in which it is taken. The same person may experience differing reactions on different occasions. Users report "seeing" sounds and "hearing" colors. Colors may seem unusually bright and shift kaleidoscopically, and objects may appear to expand and contract. LSD users become highly suggestible and easily manipulated, including sexually.

Bizarre hallucinations are also common. The experience may be peaceful or may result in panic. Some users have developed severe emotional disturbances that resulted in long-term hospitalization.[56] Usually a "trip" will last 8 to 16 hours. Physical reactions include increased heartbeat, goose bumps, dilated pupils, hyperactivity, tremors, and sweating. Aftereffects include acute anxiety or depression. Flashbacks sometimes occur after the actual drug experience. They may happen at any time and place, with no advance warning. If the user is driving a car when a flashback occurs, the condition could be life threatening for everyone in the vicinity. Users develop tolerance to the drug very rapidly, with larger doses being needed in the future to achieve the desired effects. Cessation of use, even for a few days, will restore sensitivity to the drug, enabling the user to again take smaller quantities to experience the effects.

The effects and dangers of mescaline, psilocybin, and psilocin are similar to those of LSD. LSD is, however, the most potent of the hallucinogens.

The attitudes of Americans toward tobacco use are gradually becoming more negative and have led to various legislation banning smoking.

Tobacco

The use of tobacco has now become recognized as one of the most damaging drug habits in the United States. Smoking can cause emphysema, cancer of the mouth, ulcers, and lung cancer. Users have a reduced life expectancy. Smoking significantly increases the risk of strokes and heart disease, particularly in women who use birth control pills.[57] Smoking by a pregnant woman sometimes leads to miscarriages, premature births, and underweight infants. Yet, in spite of these widely publicized hazards, 27% of Americans continue to smoke.[58]

Tobacco is the number-one drug killer, contributing to far more deaths than all other drugs combined.[59] It is estimated to lead to more than 350,000 deaths per year in the United States.[60] This is more than double the number of deaths caused by alcohol abuse and hundreds of times the number of deaths caused by cocaine.[61] Most of these deaths result from heart disease and lung cancer due to cigarette smoking. However, over 2000 deaths per year result from fires caused by smoking.[62] There is also substantial evidence that "passive smoking" (breathing the smoke from others' cigarettes, cigars, or pipes) is also hazardous to health. One source of such evidence is the finding that young children whose parents smoke have a higher incidence of pneumonia and other respiratory disorders than young children whose parents do not smoke.[63]

The attitudes of Americans toward tobacco use are gradually becoming more negative. Increasingly, we are viewing tobacco as a dangerous drug, and nonsmokers are perceiving smokers as pariahs. Some authorities are now predicting that cigarettes will eventually be outlawed in many countries.

In 1988 the Surgeon General of the United States, C. Everett Koop, declared that tobacco is as addictive as heroin or cocaine.[64] Koop defined people who are addicted to tobacco as drug addicts.

Tobacco is highly habit forming. Nicotine, the primary drug in tobacco, has remarkable capacities; it can act as a depressant, a stimulant, or a tranquilizer. Smokers quickly develop a tolerance for nicotine and gradually increase consumption to one or two packs or more a day.

There are special clinics and a variety of other educational and therapeutic programs to help people quite smoking. Studies show that less than 20% of smokers who make determined efforts to quit actually succeed.[65] Tobacco is indeed a very habit-forming drug. Withdrawal from use leads people to become restless, irritable, and depressed and to have an intense craving to smoke.

At the same time the U.S. Department of Health is widely publicizing the hazards of drugs, the Department of Agriculture is subsidizing tobacco farmers. Educational programs urge people not to smoke, but tobacco companies are permitted to advertise that cigarette smoking is "cool" and "sexy," conveying rugged manliness in men and social sophistication in women.

Marijuana

Marijuana ("grass" or "pot") comes from the hemp plant *Cannabis sativa*. This plant grows throughout the world, and its fibers are legally used to produce rope, twine, paper, and clothing.

The main use of the plant now, however, centers on its dried leaves and flowers—marijuana—and on its dried resin—hashish. Both marijuana and hashish may be taken orally but are usually smoked. Hashish is several times more potent than marijuana.

The effects of marijuana (and hashish) vary, as with any other drug, according to the mood and personality of the user, the circumstances, and the quality of the drug. Marijuana has sedative properties and creates in the user a sense of relaxed well-being and freedom from inhibition. There may also be mild hallucinations that create a dreamy state in which the user experiences fantasies. Smokers become highly suggestible and may engage in actions (such as sexual activities) they might otherwise avoid. The drug may induce feelings of joyousness, hilarity, and sociability. It may lead to talkativeness, disconnected ideas, a feeling of floating, and laughter. Sometimes marijuana intensifies sensory stimulation, creates feelings of enhanced awareness and creativity, and increases self-confidence.

The threat of physical dependence is rated low; the threat of psychological dependence is rated as moderate. Withdrawal, however, may be very unpleasant, with the user suffering from insomnia, hyperactivity, and loss of appetite.

The short-term physical effects of marijuana are minor: a reddening of the eyes, dryness of the throat and mouth, and a slight increase in heart rate. There is some evidence that continued use by young teenagers will result in their becoming apathetic, noncompetitive, and uninterested in school and other activities.

Frequent users may have impairments of short-term memory, concentration, judgment, and coordination. They may find it difficult to read, to understand what they read, or to follow moving objects with their eyes. Users may feel confident that their coordination, reactions, and perceptions are quite normal while they are still experiencing the effects of the drug; under such conditions such activities as driving a vehicle may have tragic consequences to them and to others. Marijuana use by pregnant women may also contribute to malformations in fetuses, much like the effects of alcohol use.

An overdose of the active ingredients of cannabis can lead to panic, fear, confusion, suspiciousness, fatigue, and, sometimes, aggressive acts. One of the most frequently voiced concerns about marijuana is that it will be a "stepping stone" to other drugs. About 60% of marijuana users "progress" to other drugs.[66] However, other factors, such as peer pressure, are probably more crucial determinants of what mind-altering drugs people will "advance" to using.

The attempt to restrict marijuana use through legislation has been described as a "second prohibition,"[67] with similar results: A large number of people are using the drug in disregard of the law. The unfortunate effect of laws that attempt to regulate acts (crimes, as defined by law) without victims is that they criminalize the private acts of many people who are otherwise law abiding. They also foster the development of organized crime and the illicit drug market.

For years, heated debates have raged about the hazards of long-term marijuana use. Some studies claim that it causes brain damage, chromosome damage, irritation of the bronchial tract and lungs, and a reduction in male hormone levels. These findings have not been confirmed by other studies, and the controversy rages on.[68]

In 1982 the National Academy of Science completed an extensive 15-month study on marijuana. The investigation found no evidence that marijuana causes permanent changes in the nervous system and concluded that the drug probably does not break down human chromosomes. It also found that marijuana may be useful in treating glaucoma, asthma, certain seizure disorders, and spastic conditions and in controlling severe nausea caused by cancer chemotherapy.

The study warned, however, that the drug presents a variety of short-term health risks and justifies "serious national concern." One of the reversible, short-term health effects is impairment of motor coordination, which adversely affects driving or machine-operating skills. The drug also impairs short-term memory, slows learning abilities, and may cause periods of confusion and anxiety. There was evidence that smoking marijuana may affect the lungs and respiratory system in much the same way that tobacco smoke does and may be a factor in causing bronchitis and pre-cancerous changes.

Thus the study found some evidence that marijuana may lead to certain adverse, long-term health problems. The major recommendation was that "there be a greatly intensified and more comprehensive program of research into the effects of marijuana on the health of the American people."[69]

Anabolic Steroids

Anabolic steroids are synthetic derivatives of the male hormone testosterone. Although steroids have been banned for use by athletes in sporting competition, they are still being used by some athletes, body builders, and teenagers who want to look more muscular and brawny. From early childhood, many boys have been socialized to believe that the ideal man looks something like Mr. Universe. Such well-known athletes as Olympic sprinter Ben Johnson and Seattle Seahawks linebacker Brian Bosworth are known to have taken the steroid shortcut to muscularity and increased running speed.[70]

An estimated 1 million Americans, half of them adolescents, use black-market steroids. Some young male body builders use steroids to promote tissue growth and to endure arduous workouts, routinely flooding their bodies with 100 times the testosterone they produce naturally.[71] Most steroid users are middle class and white.

Steroid-enhanced physiques are a hazardous prize. Steroids can cause temporary acne and balding, upset hormonal production, and damage the heart and kidneys. Doctors suspect that they may also contribute to liver cancer and athero-sclerosis.[72] For teens the drugs can stunt growth by accelerating bone maturation. Male steroid users have also experienced shrinking of the testicles, impotence, yellowing of the skin and eyes, and development of female-type breasts. In young boys, steroids can have the effect of painfully enlarging the sex organs. In female users the voice deepens permanently, breasts shrink, periods become irregular, the clitoris swells in size, and hair is lost from the head but grows on the face and body.

Steroid drug users are prone to moodiness, depression, and irritability and are likely to experience difficulty in tolerating stress. Some formerly easygoing males display raging hostility after prolonged use, ranging from being obnoxious to continually provoking physical fights. Some users become so depressed that they commit suicide.

Steroid users generally experience considerable difficulty in terminating use of the drugs. One reason is that bulging biceps and ham-hock thighs soon fade when steroid use is discontinued. Concurrent with the decline in muscle mass is the psychological feeling of being less powerful and less "manly." Most users who try to quit wind up back on the drugs. A self-image that relies on a steroid-enhanced physique is difficult to change.

REHABILITATION PROGRAMS

Rehabilitation programs for alcohol abuse are very similar to those for most other drugs. We'll begin by looking closely at the treatment of alcoholism.

Alcohol Treatment Programs

As mentioned earlier, before an alcoholic can be helped, his or her denial of the problem must be confronted. If the alcoholic cannot or does not do so, the confrontation can be arranged by family members, friends, employers, or alcohol counselors—or by all of these together. Tim Bliss briefly describes guidelines for this confrontation:

> *In confronting the alcoholic, documentation of incidents that occurred while drinking becomes extremely important. This is particularly important because the alcoholic may have blackouts. These are periods of amnesia as opposed to passing out or unconsciousness. Both are due to excessive drinking. Many times during confrontation it is important that the entire family be present to reinforce the incident. In documenting the incident, one should be instructed to write down the date and time, and to be as specific as possible in describing the situation. The counselor can be present during this confrontation to act as a facilitator; however, the primary responsibility in breaking through denial is with the spouse, family, or employer.*
>
> *Many times the practicing alcoholic has been threatened with divorce, job discipline, and so on. It is important not to continue these threats; action must occur if the alcoholic continues to drink after confrontation.*[73]

If the alcoholic continues to deny that a problem exists, there are some guidelines for what family members should and should not do. "Nagging" the alcoholic will only increase family arguments and may provoke the alcoholic into verbally or physically abusing someone, particularly when he or she is inebriated. Family members often make the mistake of assuming they are responsible for getting the alcoholic to stop drinking, and they feel guilty or frustrated if the person continues to drink. They, however, do not *own* the drinking problem—the alcoholic is the one responsible for the drinking and is the one who determines whether he or she will stop drinking. When a person is drunk, yelling and screaming at him or her will accomplish nothing (except perhaps to make other family members more upset). What is more productive for the other family members is to isolate themselves from the alcoholic when she or he is drunk—perhaps by going shopping, taking a walk, or, if need be, locking themselves in a room.

There are three self-help groups that family members can attend. Al-Anon is for spouses and other family members of alcoholics. The program reaches out to people affected by another person's drinking regardless of whether the alcoholic recognizes his or her problem. It helps members learn the facts about alcoholism and ways to cope with an alcoholic. Alateen is for teenage children of alcoholics and helps adolescents to understand alcoholism and to learn effective ways to cope with problems. Adult Children of Alcoholics helps adults cope with issues they are still struggling with that largely stem from being raised in an alcoholic family.

If the alcoholic does acknowledge a drinking problem, many treatment programs are available. The best-known and most successful program is Alcoholics Anonymous, which is further described in Exhibit 7.5.

There appear to be several reasons why such self-help groups are successful. The members have an intrinsic understanding of the problem that helps them to help others. Having experienced the misery and consequences of the problem, they are highly motivated and dedicated to find ways to help themselves and others who are fellow sufferers. The participants also benefit from the "helper therapy principle"; that is, the helper gains psychological rewards by helping others.[74] Helping others makes a person feel "good" and worthwhile and also enables the helper to put his or her own problems into perspective by seeing that others have problems that are as serious, or even more serious. From the viewpoint of the new member who is still drinking, having people around who have successfully stopped provides role models of abstinence and gives them reason to believe that they too can break the grip of alcohol abuse.

At one time, intoxicated people were just thrown into jail to sober up. (Unfortunately, this is still happening in some places.) Many communities, however, have now switched to a treatment approach.

Most alcohol treatment facilities offer both inpatient and outpatient programs. Outpatient

EXHIBIT 7.5

Alcoholics Anonymous

In 1929 Bill Wilson was a stock analyst. When the stock market crashed that year, he lost most of his money and turned to alcohol. A few years later his doctor warned him that his continued drinking was jeopardizing his health and his life. Bill W. underwent what he perceived as a spiritual experience, and he made a commitment to stop drinking. He also discovered that, through discussing his drinking problem with other alcoholics, he was helped to remain sober. One of the people he talked with was Robert Smith, an Ohio doctor and also an alcoholic. Together they formed Alcoholics Anonymous (AA), a self-help group composed of recovering alcoholics.

AA stresses the following precepts: (1) confessing to the group that one has a drinking problem, (2) recounting to the group past experiences with the drinking problem and plans for handling the problem in the future, and (3) phoning another member of the group whenever one feels an intense urge to drink. The person called will do whatever can be done to keep the caller "dry," including coming over to stay with the person until the urge subsides.

Today AA has chapters in about 100 countries. Local chapters (around 25 people per chapter) meet once or twice a week for discussions. These sessions resemble traditional group therapy but without the presence of a trained professional leader.

Bill W. and Dr. Bob, as they were known within AA, remained anonymous until their deaths. Local chapters still follow procedures similar to the ones originally initiated—the sharing of similar experiences in order to abstain from taking the first drink (which is "one too many") and the thousandth (which is "not enough").

AA is widely recognized as the treatment approach that has the best chance of helping an alcoholic. Testimony to its value is that hundreds of other self-help groups, having treatment principles based on the AA model, have now been formed to deal with other personal problems—for example, Overeaters Anonymous, Narcotics Anonymous, Prison Families Anonymous, Debtors Anonymous, Gamblers Anonymous, Emotions Anonymous, Emphysema Anonymous, Adult Children of Alcoholics, and many more.

---

treatment usually serves clients who have the potential to stop using alcohol while living at home. If the client is unable to live at home or is still drinking excessively, inpatient treatment will usually be recommended. Those who go through an inpatient program receive subsequent follow-up treatment on an outpatient basis. Inpatient treatment can last anywhere from two weeks to three months, depending on the patient's problems and the treatment program. Inpatient treatment is usually intense, including one-on-one therapy, group therapy, an orientation to Alcoholics Anonymous, and occupational and recreational therapy. Outpatient treatment is not as intense, usually lasts from three to six months, and offers the same forms of treatment.

Outpatient and inpatient services are provided in some medical hospitals, in drug rehabilitation centers, and in community mental health centers. Many communities also have halfway houses that serve the alcoholic who is unable to live with family members but is not yet ready to live alone.

Most larger companies now sponsor alcohol treatment programs (as a component of Employee Assistance Programs, described in Chapter 10) for their employees. These programs seek to identify problem drinkers in their early stages and then to intervene before severe problems arise. The problem drinkers are referred to appropriate community resources. If the employee uses such help, there are no adverse work consequences. Considerable pressure may be placed on the employee to participate, with the threat of eventual discharge if she or he refuses help and continues to display lowered work productivity due to drinking.

Most therapists now believe that alcohol is used to meet some need—the need for socialization, relaxation, escape, and so on. If treatment is to be successful, it must provide alternatives for satisfying these needs: by helping the alcoholic to find a new circle of friends, to learn other ways to relax, to learn to handle life's problems better—whatever may be the unique needs of the drinker. This theory of *functional need equivalents* has been applied to other addictions in addition to alcohol abuse.

Other Drug Treatment Programs

There is a stereotype that "Once an addict, always an addict." This attitude has hampered efforts to rehabilitate those who are chemically dependent. Statistical evidence in the past tended to confirm this myth. More recent evidence, however, suggests that drug addicts *can* successfully kick their habits. Martin Kasindorf found, for example, that American soldiers addicted to heroin in Vietnam could successfully terminate use on returning home.[75]

Physical dependence on practically any drug can be ended with a detoxification program. Generally the user will undergo some intense and highly painful withdrawal symptoms for the first few days, or even for a few weeks. Psychological dependence is more difficult to end. Because drugs meet psychological needs, they are functional. Users receive certain psychic rewards (feelings of relaxation, euphoria, more alertness, less pain, escape from reality and problems). The psychological needs met by taking a drug are often unique to each user. To end the dependence, it is necessary for treatment programs to discover what psychological needs are being met for each user and then to teach the user new (drug-free) ways to meet those needs.

INPATIENT PROGRAMS

Community mental health centers, specialized chemical abuse rehabilitation centers, and some medical hospitals provide inpatient treatment programs. Detoxification lasts from 24 hours to three weeks, depending on the severity of withdrawal. Additional inpatient care lasts two to three more weeks in a chemically free environment. Inpatient care is designed for those chemically dependent individuals who are unable to end the dependence while remaining in the community. Inpatient treatment is highly expensive; it may cost $10,000 or more for a 30-day stay.

OUTPATIENT PROGRAMS

Outpatient care, which is usually less intense than inpatient care, generally lasts three to six months. It is designed for people who no longer need inpatient care, as well as for those who have a good chance of terminating their habit without having to be hospitalized. Outpatient care consists of counseling, medical services, and vocational services. Such services are provided by community mental health centers, specialized rehabilitation centers for treating chemical abuse, medical hospitals, and outpatient clinics for chemical abuse.

SELF-HELP PROGRAMS

Modeled after Alcoholics Anonymous, there are many self-help programs for abusers. They include Narcotics Anonymous, Synanon, Potsmokers Anonymous, Pills Anonymous, Delancey Street Foundation, and Renaissance Project.[76]

THERAPEUTIC COMMUNITIES

These are long-term residential treatment programs, with patients usually staying from 12 to 18 months. Therapeutic communities emphasize making lifestyle changes so that the person will learn to find rewards for staying drug free and to function more appropriately in society. Tim Bliss further describes the focus:

The environment is one of constant confrontation that aims at breaking down walls that cover up the real person. An individual might, for example, come on as a "tough guy" as a result

Methadone is a synthetic narcotic used to treat heroin addiction. At a Manhattan, New York, VA hospital, a group counseling session is a part of their methadone treatment program.

of leading the street life. Actually, this image needs to be broken down. Feelings that are painful (for example, loneliness, fear, depression) are allowed to be expressed, eventually allowing the individual to be honest with himself or herself, and thus not needing to wear a mask.

Many graduates of therapeutic communities remain in close contact for support purposes. It is difficult to measure the success of these programs because there is a high rate of dropouts. However, for those that graduate there is evidence they are successful in obtaining employment and remaining chemically free.[77]

HALFWAY HOUSES

Halfway houses assist those who have been hospitalized (and detoxified) to reenter the community at their own pace. They also serve those who are psychologically dependent and want to kick a habit but do not need to be hospitalized. Halfway houses provide counseling services (both one-to-one and group) to help residents remain drug free and work on resolving other personal problems

they face. Residents also receive vocational training, assistance in finding a job, and room and board. Many halfway houses employ staff who were former addicts. Recovered drug abusers are often more effective than professional staff in relating to the residents and in breaking down the barriers of denial, anger, isolation, and hostility that addicts feel. Former addicts also provide a model, since they are evidence that addiction is a curable disease. Halfway houses emphasize the importance of residents' assuming responsibility for their actions and behaviors.

TREATMENT USING DRUGS

Analogous to the use of Antabuse with alcoholics (see Exhibit 7.6), some chemicals are used in therapeutic programs to treat certain drug addictions.

Methadone, which has received by far the most publicity, is used to treat heroin addiction. Methadone is a synthetic narcotic and is sufficiently similar to heroin to satisfy the addict's physical craving. It prevents the anguish of heroin withdrawal symptoms but does not induce a high.

EXHIBIT 7.6

Antabuse Treatment

Antabuse, developed in Copenhagen in 1947, is a drug that is useful for helping an alcoholic stay sober. When taken, it makes a patient's system react adversely to even small quantities of alcohol. Shortly after a person drinks an alcoholic beverage, Antabuse causes intense flushing, increased pulse rate, and nausea, often to the point of vomiting.

Before beginning treatment, the patient is detoxified. Then the drug is administered for several consecutive days, along with small doses of alcohol. The small amounts of alcohol are used to help the patient recognize the strong and uncomfortable effects that will occur while drinking.

Antabuse is not a cure-all for drinking, because the reasons for drinking still remain. An alcoholic, if she or he chooses, can simply stop taking the drug and resume drinking. However, Antabuse is useful as part of a comprehensive treatment program involving counseling, vocational and social rehabilitation, and AA. By taking Antabuse, a person is forced to remain sober and is thereby more likely to respond to other therapies.

Source: Stanford L. Billet, "Antabuse Therapy," in *Alcoholism: The Total Treatment Approach,* ed. Ronald J. Cantanzaro (Springfield, IL: Charles C Thomas, 1974), pp. 167–174.

Methadone thus allows a heroin addict to function fairly normally in a community. (It is usually not effective for heroin users who are unwilling to give up their "high.")

Methadone itself is addictive. Moreover, it does not cure addicts of their addiction to heroin. It simply *maintains* addicts in their communities without their having to use heroin. Methadone is controversial, and many authorities object to treating heroin addicts by making them dependent on another drug.

Methadone is available (legally) only through approved programs. In the first few weeks of treatment addicts are usually required to report daily to the treatment center to receive their dose. As with any other drug that is in demand, an illicit market has developed in methadone. Some heroin addicts use methadone to tide them over when they cannot obtain heroin; others sometimes seek to treat themselves by taking methadone instead of heroin. As with heroin, an overdose of methadone can result in death.

Scientists have also developed narcotic antagonists that prevent opiate (morphine and heroin) users from experiencing euphoria. Two of the best-known opiate antagonists are Naloxone and Cyclazocine. These drugs prevent addicts from feeling the euphoria they crave and thereby help motivated addicts to kick the habit.

Understanding and Treating Codependency

Codependent people are so trapped by a loved one's addiction that they lose their own identity in the process of obsessively managing the day-to-day trauma created by the addict. Codependency is unhealthy behavior learned amid chaos. Some codependents are as dysfunctional as the addict, if not more so. Living with addiction triggers excessive caretaking, suppression of one's own needs, feelings of low self-worth, and strained relationships.

Many codependents grow up in a dysfunctional family. (Some are adult children of alcoholics.) They marry or become romantically involved with someone who abuses alcohol or some other drug. To some extent the addict fills the need of the codependent—to be a caretaker, to feel inferior, and so on. Codependency can thus be viewed as a normal reaction to abnormal stress.

The addict may terminate the use of his or her drug of choice, but the codependent's dysfunctional behaviors generally continue, unless he or she receives treatment. There are a variety of treatment approaches for codependents: individual psychotherapy, group therapy, and self-help groups (such as Al-Anon, Adult Children of Alcoholics, and Codependents Anonymous). For many codependents, treatment involves recognition that they have a life and an identity separate from the addict, that the addict alone is responsible for his or her substance abuse, and that their life and the addict's will improve by terminating their caretaking and enabling behaviors. Through treatment, many codependents regain (or gain for the first time) their own identity and banish the self-destructive habits that sabotage their happiness.

SUGGESTIONS FOR CURBING DRUG ABUSE IN THE FUTURE

It is, of course, important to treat current drug abusers. But perhaps it is even more important to prevent nonabusers from becoming abusers. This section discusses five preventive approaches: educational programs, prevention of illegal drug trafficking across borders, employee drug-testing programs, stricter laws and enforcement, decriminalization of drug use, and the British approach.

Educational Programs

More programs are appearing that give students as well as the general public a realistic understanding of drug use and abuse. Quality programs teach (1) what effects commonly used drugs produce, (2) how to recognize signs of abuse, (3) how to responsibly decide when and when not to use drugs, (4) how to help someone who overdoses, (5) how to help friends and relatives who are abusing drugs, (6) what treatment resources and programs are available in the community, (7) what to do if you think you may have a drug problem, (8) what to do if a relative or friend refuses to acknowledge his or her drug problem, and (9) how to help abusers learn drug-free ways of meeting their psychological needs.

Educational programs in the past often used scare tactics—showing pictures of fatal automobile crashes after drug use, suggesting that drug users end up on "skid row," and indicating that experimenting with small quantities of drugs

would forever ruin the users' lives. Such tactics are now viewed as ineffective. The young see their parents, other adults, and peers using drugs (particularly alcohol) without dire consequences (generally). These alarmist approaches wound up destroying the credibility of the educators.

Fortunately, books, curriculum guides for teachers, and audiovisual materials now available paint a more realistic picture of drug use and abuse.

In the past decade the mass media and the schools have launched major campaigns to prevent drunk driving, alcohol abuse, smoking, and illegal drug use. Extensive drug abuse prevention programs are now underway in elementary schools, middle schools, high schools, and colleges. These programs, which are tailored to the age level of the students at which they are targeted, include McGruff, the Crime Dog, at the kindergarten level; D.A.R.E. (Drug Abuse Resistance Education), a police-sponsored program, at the elementary school level; and various clubs, retreats, and lock-ins at middle and high school levels. They use a variety of approaches, including pointing out the risks of drug use, providing accurate information on drugs and their effects, offering instructions on how to assertively say "no" to peer pressure to use drugs, providing enjoyable drug-free activities, and enhancing students' self-esteem.

With drug and alcohol abuse increasingly portrayed in the media and in the schools as risky and dangerous rather than glamorous and fashionable, overall drug and alcohol use appears to be declining, among both youngsters and adults.[78] It is highly unlikely that the United States will ever become drug-free. Certain drugs do have valid medical use. But the abuse of drugs can and should be curbed.

One reason why the United States has one of the highest rates of drug abuse in the world is the erroneous view that "there's a pill for everything." Americans tend to believe that medical technology can solve every ill the body encounters, and we use this belief to absolve ourselves of the responsibility of maintaining a healthy lifestyle. At the same time, the tendency to self-medicate is a common response when we feel

Therapy with a Heroin Addict

T im Bliss, a drug counselor, describes the following efforts to treat an addict:

Many times the drug counselor feels he or she isn't making any progress in the recovery process of the heroin addict. Counseling the heroin addict takes a special type of counselor—one who can walk the walk and talk the talk so to speak. To counsel, first off, it takes an extreme amount of dedication, concentration, and effort.

The client I worked with was a 30-year-old black, married male with three children. The history was as follows. The client will be referred to as Bob. Bob was raised in an urban area; he was the middle child and seemingly led a normal childhood. As he reached his early teens, he got more and more involved with drinking and drugs. He graduated from high school and went into the army soon after graduation. This is where many problems arose. Bob had several bouts with the army ranging from insubordination to disorderly conduct. He started chipping [occasionally using] heroin and became quite involved in the drug culture overseas in Germany. He then married a white German girl and brought her back to the United States, where they have lived for the past 10 years. Bob then became involved in an armed robbery and claimed he was innocent; yet he spent three years in prison. After his prison time ended, Bob secured a job at a local factory; this lasted approximately one and one-half years at which time he was fired for excessive absenteeism. The excessive absenteeism was a result of episodic drinking and drug abuse.

Prior to Bob's going to prison, he was involved in the Black Panthers. What was interesting was that he was married to a white, which had to be a conflict with Bob.

In general Bob seemingly had quite a conflict being black. He wanted at times to be white, and yet at other times wanted to be married to a black instead of a white.

Bob became increasingly involved with drugs, and in time developed a habit with heroin. This led to his involvement in both the criminal justice system and treatment.

Fortunately, there was a federal grant at this time that could divert criminal justice clients to alcohol or drug treatment centers. Bob became involved in a local alcohol treatment center while on probation. However, due to the fact that he was a heroin addict, treatment was ineffective. Within a very short period of time after discharge, Bob was back to "junk." He was then involved in another armed robbery and this time was facing 7 to 10 years for several counts of armed robbery and burglary. At this point I became involved with the client. Bob was out on bond and was awaiting his court date. Throughout this time period Bob was seen on an outpatient treatment

worthless, "stressed out," or mistreated by society. In a culture where medication is so much the norm (a view that is boosted by advertising from the massive alcohol, pharmaceutical, and tobacco industries), it is easy to turn to drugs, alcohol, or tobacco as a way of relieving stress or forgetting about one's all-too-real problems. Public education is definitely needed to convey that drug use does not *solve* life's problems—it *intensifies* them.

Prevention of Illegal Drug Trafficking across Borders

Small-time drug dealers often make enormous profits, middle-level dealers frequently become millionaires, and the top drug barons are billionaires. Clearly, illegal drug trade across borders of countries is a big, highly profitable endeavor. One way of combating the illegal drug trade is to take

basis. Urine drug screens were taken, and all turned up negative for opiates for about four weeks. Then Bob started chipping . . . heroin [again]. A therapeutic community which treated heroin addicts had been contacted to arrange an intake interview with Bob. The therapeutic community was a six- to nine-month intensive inpatient treatment program. Their philosophy was that the drug of choice was only a symptom and what needed to be changed was the lifestyle.

The court date was finally reached, and it was time for Bob to "face the music." The therapeutic community had interviewed Bob, and he was accepted into their program. I had arranged for a psychologist to run a series of tests on Bob to determine statistically his chances for succeeding in treatment. The results of this testing were that Bob would have one-third of a chance of succeeding in treatment, one-third not succeeding, and one-third of no change at all. Obviously statistics were against Bob, but in outpatient treatment he had demonstrated that he was sincere and did want to change. So with that, this counselor and Bob's probation officer felt treatment was the best alternative rather than incarceration. The presiding judge was approached with this alternative, and he accepted it. However, Bob was found guilty, so the judge imposed a stayed sentence of seven years to be served if Bob did not successfully complete treatment.

The following week Bob was transferred to the therapeutic community. He stayed there approximately six months, at which time the community voted that he be terminated, unsuccessfully completing treatment. Bob was voted out for a number of reasons: (1) he wasn't following instructions when reprimanded by staff, (2) overall he was an extremely bad influence on the rest of the community as he was always gaming people, not being able to be honest with himself or others, (3) he was breaking cardinal rules, which meant that when he would get angry other members of the community were actually afraid to be around him as they were afraid he might get physically violent. The incident that resulted in Bob's termination was that he was reprimanded for an incident that involved a female client. Supposedly Bob had intercourse with the female, and the female admitted this to staff in one of the community's "cop to" groups. (A "cop to" simply means people in the community who have done something wrong, or are feeling guilty, talk about it in one of these groups.)

The staff told Bob he was on a communication ban (no talking) the following day; they also requested he wear a five-foot sign with some writing on it. This kind of reprimand might seem ineffective or silly to some of us; however, it is quite effective

(continued)

the kind of action that will put drug barons out of business.

The United States and other countries have spent millions of dollars on trying to prevent illegal drugs from being smuggled across borders. A few drug shipments are confiscated, and a few transporters of drugs are arrested. But drug barons are generally successful in finding increasingly creative ways to smuggle drugs across borders. If drug trafficking across borders is to be stopped, more effective steps need to be taken.

One way to combat drug trafficking across borders would be for all the countries of the world to agree among themselves to treat this activity as an international crime, indictable by international law.

An international court to administer this law could be established as a division of the United

**CASE
EXAMPLE 7.3**   *(continued)*

in an atmosphere like a therapeutic community, especially on a long-term basis. Bob didn't follow through the next day, and a vote was taken; he was transferred to the county jail where he would await a decision by the probation officer, the judge, and the original referring agent.

We had decided Bob was still amenable to treatment. However, this would entail a more highly structured treatment environment, a facility that dealt more with the hard-core heroin addict.

Meanwhile Bob was becoming increasingly bitter sitting in jail thinking about what had occurred, and also becoming anxious due to the fact he was facing seven years in prison.

The probation officer and original treatment staff involved with Bob found a treatment facility that would be most favorable to any kind of successful treatment for Bob. The judge also went along with this.

Bob, after about two weeks of sitting in jail, was transferred on a Friday afternoon to this treatment facility. Friday evening he called his wife and absconded from treatment. He has not been heard of since, and consequently his probation has been revoked. When caught, he will be sent to prison.

I have heard unofficial reports that he is still around, back to heroin in his old way of life.

This is not a success story, obviously, but all too often that's all we ever hear. The field is challenging; however, this case history is also a real part of treatment, that oftentimes a therapist has to realize his or her own limitations and accept reality as it is. Not everyone is a success, and no matter what you do, you can't change that. All we can do is seek as much knowledge about the field as possible and utilize every tool available to motivate clients in changing their behavior. Only after this can we say "I gave it my best shot, and that's all there is."

Source: From "Drugs—Use, Abuse, and Treatment," by Tim Bliss in *Introduction to Social Welfare Institutions,* by Charles Zastrow, pp. 315–316. Copyright © 1978 by The Dorsey Press. Reprinted by permission of Brooks/Cole Publishing Company, a division of Thomson Publishing, Pacific Grove, CA 93950.

Nations. This court could have an investigative force with the authority to enter drug-producing countries to gather evidence against the drug barons who are masterminding the production, manufacture, and distribution of illegal drugs across borders. Countries would be expected to arrest and extradite for trial to this international court any individuals indicted for masterminding drug trafficking across borders. Those found guilty could be penalized with a life sentence, with no chance of parole. The United Nations could be empowered to impose trade sanctions against any country that refused to arrest and extradite indicted drug barons. (No country can survive today without international trade and finance.) In addition, armed forces of the United Nations could be made available to those governments that are too weak to combat the private armies employed by some of the notorious drug barons.

The U.S. government appears to be stepping up efforts to put drug barons in foreign countries out of business. In 1989 President George Bush declared a war on international drug trafficking. Manuel Noriega, while President of Panama, is alleged to have personally made between $200 million and $300 million in drug trafficking.[79] In 1989 the U.S. military invaded Panama, arrested Noriega, and brought him to this country to face a variety of drug-trafficking charges. In 1992 he was convicted on several of these charges. The U.S. government has also given financial assistance to the Colombian government to help in arresting and extraditing drug barons to this country to face drug trafficking charges. (Colombia produces much of the cocaine that illegally enters the United States.)

Employee Drug-Testing Programs

In 1986 the President's Commission on Organized Crime recommended that both government and private industry launch drug-testing programs for employees. The Commission asserted that such examinations would help curb a drug abuse epidemic that drains billions of dollars annually from American society and erodes the nation's quality of life.[80]

A number of major U.S. companies require applicants or employees to provide urine for an analysis that can detect the use of such drugs as cocaine, marijuana, heroin, and morphine. The tests are also given in the military, in a few sensitive federal agencies, and in many drug-treatment facilities.[81] Local governments in many communities are now requiring random drug testing of employees in certain job categories, such as bus drivers.

Professional baseball, basketball, and football organizations also have drug-testing programs. For example, the National Football League requires all players to take a mandatory urine test prior to the start of the regular season and two unscheduled tests during the regular season. If a player tests positive, he is first required to receive treatment. If he relapses twice (as identified by three positive tests over a period of time), he is permanently banned from the league. The National Basketball Association and the National Football League have already banned several players for repeated drug violations.

Drug-testing programs are being recommended in the interest of safety, health, and increased productivity. The programs are a clear signal that companies are serious about addressing the hazards caused by drugs. Employees who test positive are generally given an opportunity to enter treatment programs. If further drug tests reveal continued use of illegal drugs, the employee is generally discharged.

Opponents of drug testing assert that such programs violate civil liberties, including the Constitution's ban on unreasonable searches.[82]

Stricter Laws and Enforcement

It is clear from public opinion polls that the most popular approach to curbing drug abuse is enactment of stricter laws and more rigid enforcement of laws involving drug abuse. In recent years a variety of such laws have been passed.

In 1984 federal legislation was enacted that placed considerable pressure on states to raise the minimum drinking age to 21 years; states that do not comply risk losing federal matching funds for highways. Most states have reduced the legal alcohol levels required for conviction of drunken driving and toughened penalties for driving while intoxicated. In regards to tobacco, most states have passed "clean indoor air" laws, requiring nonsmoking areas in restaurants and, in many cases, banning smoking entirely in public places. To combat illegal drugs, various state and local governments established a policy of confiscating property (such as cars or boats) used to carry or store drugs, even small amounts of marijuana for personal use. As we've seen, drug testing in the workplace is becoming more widespread.

Have these efforts worked? Drug, alcohol, and tobacco use appears to be declining in our society. But it's hard to tell how much of the current decline is due to stricter laws and enforcement and how much is due to increased awareness of the risks of drug and alcohol abuse and smoking.

Decriminalization of Drug Use

Over the past century a number of laws have prohibited the use of a variety of drugs. Penalties for violators have become harsher. Yet the proportion of the population using drugs remains high, and jails and prisons are filled with people who have been arrested for drug law violations. Helen Nowlis notes: ''Drug legislation makes possession of a 'potentially dangerous' substance a crime with penalties in some cases equivalent to or in excess of those for such criminal acts as grand larceny and second-degree murder.''[83] In the recent past, states have sentenced people for up to 25 years—and even life—for selling or giving small quantities of marijuana to another person. Such harshness discredits the criminal justice system and contributes to disrespect for the law.

Until recently, drug legislation in this country has been designed to punish users rather than to treat abusers or to prevent use of drugs. Does it really do any good to arrest and jail (sometimes weekly) habitual drunks?

The public's general lack of accurate information about drugs has led to irrational fears about drug use and abuse. For example, there is the fear that use of marijuana will always be a stepping stone to use of narcotic drugs. There are unwarranted fears about the negative effects of such drugs as heroin and opium. These irrational fears have led citizens to demand that harsh legislation be enacted to attempt to curb the use of drugs.

However, it is increasingly recognized that punitive legislation often does not work. Prohibition demonstrated that outlawing alcohol would not end its use. In an analogous vein, laws prohibiting the use of other drugs have been largely responsible for the enormous growth of organized crime and the illicit drug trade. Prison wardens cannot even keep drugs out of their own prisons.

A number of authorities are now urging that drug laws be revised to emphasize treatment

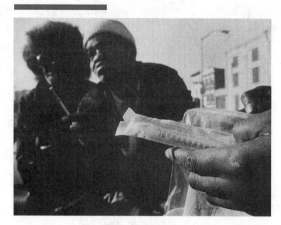

The AIDS crisis has prompted a new look at our drug laws—in particular, the current philosophy that emphasizes punishment over treatment of drug addicts. In an effort to curb the spread of AIDS, New York City launched the first government-sponsored program to give free sterile needles to intravenous drug addicts in 1988. Some critics have argued that needle-exchange programs condone and even encourage further drug abuse.

rather than punishment of addicts and to make the penalties for the possession of drugs more consistent with the actual dangers. It seems irrational to send to prison (at a huge expense to taxpayers) a person who possesses one joint of marijuana (a drug that may be less dangerous than alcohol).

Recent changes in certain drug laws are beginning to emphasize rehabilitation and to reduce harsh penalties for the sale and possession of certain drugs. Many of these revisions have centered on marijuana.

In 1972 the National Commission on Marijuana and Drug Abuse recommended changes in state and federal laws regarding marijuana. The Commission urged that the private possession of marijuana for personal use and the distribution of small amounts without profit to the distributor no longer be considered offenses. Since this 1972 report a number of states have passed laws decriminalizing the use of marijuana.[84]

Laws have also been passed mandating that those arrested for public drunkenness receive treatment rather than simply being thrown into jail. In some areas of the country individuals who acknowledge that they are addicted to a hard drug (such as heroin) are now given treatment without risking arrest or incarceration. Such programs are experimental and often controversial. The British, however, have been successfully using the treatment approach for several decades.

The British Approach

As noted, the United States in the 20th century has primarily used a punitive approach with anyone found guilty of possessing or using prohibited drugs. In contrast, the British for many years have avoided labeling drug users as criminals and have viewed drug use as a disease that should be treated. Because of this rehabilitative emphasis, the British have formulated a very different set of laws and government policies to curb drug abuse. The British regard narcotic addicts as "sick" instead of "criminal." Rather than sending narcotic addicts to prison, they allow them to buy drugs at a low cost. If the addict cannot pay, she or he is given the drug free of charge. The system does not allow the addict to have an unlimited supply of narcotics. Extensive precautions are taken to carefully regulate the distribution of narcotic drugs.

The British program applies to heroin, morphine, and cocaine. (It does not involve marijuana, barbiturates, amphetamines, or hallucinogens.) To qualify, the narcotics user must demonstrate to a physician certified by the government that she or he is an addict. The person is then officially registered as an addict and receives a steady supply of the drug. The dosage is not enough to produce a "high" but is sufficient to prevent withdrawal symptoms. There is a central registry, so it is difficult for addicts to register with more than one clinic to obtain duplicate supplies. If a registered addict is discovered to be receiving a narcotic drug from more than one source, she or he is prosecuted. Also, anyone found possessing a narcotic who is not a registered addict is also prosecuted. Efforts are made to rehabilitate the addicts. For example, with heroin addicts the amount of heroin that is given is gradually decreased or the addicts are switched to methadone.

The British approach appears to be working well for them. The rate of addiction is far lower than in the United States, and the illicit market is far smaller and less profitable. British addicts don't require vast amounts of money to support their habits, and as a result they commit fewer property crimes. Organized crime has little profit incentive to smuggle narcotics into the country, so there are few narcotics available for nonaddicts to experiment with. Because the prescription drug is of uniform strength and is distributed in small dosages, narcotics overdosing is rare. The prescription drug does not contain impurities, thereby minimizing drug fatalities and other health hazards. In addition, a higher percentage of British addicts (compared to American addicts) are able to keep their jobs and be productive.[85]

Whether the British system would work in this country is questionable. The idea of giving heroin and other drugs to addicts runs counter to American values that people should not be drug dependent, that users should be punished to deter others, and that the government should not be involved in distributing potentially harmful drugs. With organized crime's strong position in this country, there is also the danger that it could gain access to the government's supply of drugs and sell them to nonaddicts at inflated prices. However, because the British system is so successful, it certainly warrants careful consideration for adaptation here.

SUMMARY

A drug is any habit-forming substance that directly affects the central nervous system; it affects moods, perceptions, bodily functions, or consciousness. Drug abuse is the regular or excessive use of a drug when, as defined by a group, the consequences endanger relationships with others, are detrimental to a person's health, or jeopardize society itself. The dominant social reaction to a drug is influenced not only by the actual dangers of the drug but also by the social characteristics and motives of the groups that use it. Legal drugs are abused more often and cause more harm in our society than illegal drugs. Many drugs produce psychological or physical dependence (addiction) or both. Often, users develop a tolerance for a drug, which means that they need steadily increasing dosages. Drug addiction is the intense craving for a drug that develops after a period of physical dependency from heavy use.

Social costs of drugs include property crime (generally committed to support a habit), automobile accidents, economic losses, health problems, disrespect for the law, family disruption, spouse and child abuse, financial crises for users, and adverse psychological effects on individuals.

Our society romanticizes and encourages the use of several drugs through commercials, films, books, and TV programs. Widely advertised drugs include alcohol, tobacco, caffeine, and over-the-counter drugs.

The most commonly used drugs include depressants (alcohol, barbiturates, tranquilizers, Quaalude, PCP), stimulants (caffeine, amphetamines, cocaine, crack, amyl nitrate, butyl nitrate), narcotics (opium, heroin, morphine), hallucinogens (peyote, psilocybin, psilocin, LSD), tobacco, marijuana, and anabolic steroids. Alcohol is by far the most widely abused drug in our society.

Treatment programs for drug abuse include inpatient and outpatient services provided by community mental health centers, some medical hospitals, and specialized chemical abuse rehabilitation centers. Additional programs include self-help groups, halfway houses, and therapeutic communities.

Drug abuse will probably never cease in this country, but the extent of the abuse can certainly be reduced. Punitive laws, as Prohibition demonstrated, do not deter drug use for many people and often encourage the development of organized crime and an illicit drug market. Suggestions for curbing abuse include expanding quality educational programs that give accurate information about drugs, indicting drug barons who mastermind the production and distribution of illegal drugs, using employee drug-testing programs, enacting stricter laws and increasing enforcement activity against violations involving drug abuse, and decriminalizing drug use to encourage a treatment approach rather than a punitive approach.

NOTES

1. *Webster's New Collegiate Dictionary* (Springfield, MA: Merriam-Webster, 1990).
2. Bertram S. Brown, "The Decriminalization of Marijuana," *Hearings of the House Select Committee on Narcotic Abuse* (Mar. 14, 1977), First Session, 95th Congress.
3. Howard Abadinsky, *Drug Abuse: An Introduction* (Chicago: Nelson-Hall, 1989), pp. 90–97.
4. U.S. Bureau of the Census, *Statistical Abstract of the United States, 1993* (Washington, DC: U.S. Government Printing Office, 1993).
5. Abadinsky, *Drug Abuse: An Introduction*, pp. 54–58.
6. Richard Ashley, *Cocaine: Its History, Uses, and Effects* (New York: St. Martin's Press, 1975).
7. James W. Coleman and Donald R. Cressey, *Social Problems*, 5th ed. (New York: HarperCollins, 1993), p. 304.
8. Quoted in Earle F. Barcus and Susan M. Jankowski, "Drugs and the Mass Media," *The Annals of the American Academy of Political and Social Science*, 417 (1975), p. 89.
9. Ian Robertson, *Social Problems*, 2d ed. (New York: Random House, 1980), p. 438.
10. Leon G. Hunt and Carl D. Chambers, *the Heroin Epidemics* (New York: Spectrum Books, 1976).
11. Alfred R. Lindesmith, *The Addict and the Law* (Bloomington: Indiana University Press, 1965), p. 228.
12. Joseph Gusfield, *Symbolic Crusade: Status Politics and the American Temperance Movement* (Urbana: University of Illinois Press, 1963).
13. Emile Durkheim, *Suicide: A Study in Sociology*, trans. John Spaulding and George Simpson (New York: Free Press, 1951).
14. Robert Merton, *Social Theory and Social Structure*, 2d ed. (New York: Free Press, 1968).
15. See Charles H. Cooley, *Human Nature and the Social Order* (New York: Scribner, 1902); and Howard S. Becker, *Outsiders: Studies in the Sociology of Deviance* (New York: Free Press, 1963).

16. Edwin H. Sutherland and Donald R. Cressey, *Principles of Criminology*, 7th ed. (Philadelphia: Lippincott, 1966).

17. William Kornblum and Joseph Julian, *Social Problems*, 7th ed. (Englewood Cliffs, NJ: Prentice-Hall, 1992), p. 130.

18. Ibid.

19. Ibid.

20. For a review of these theories, see Abadinsky, *Drug Abuse: An Introduction*, pp. 111–136.

21. Howard S. Becker, "Becoming a Marijuana User," *American Journal of Sociology*, 59 (November 1953), pp. 235–242.

22. Kornblum and Julian, *Social Problems*, p. 128.

23. "Why Liquor is Quicker for Women," *U.S. News & World Report*, Jan. 22, 1990, p. 13.

24. The material in this section is summarized from studies that were reviewed in Kornblum and Julian, *Social Problems*, pp. 129–130.

25. John E. Farley, *American Social Problems*, 2d ed. (Englewood Cliffs, NJ: Prentice-Hall, 1992), pp. 261–262.

26. See David J. Armor, J. Michael Polich, and Harriet G. Stambul, *Alcoholism and Treatment* (New York: Wiley Interscience, 1978).

27. Kornblum and Julian, *Social Problems*, p. 128.

28. Ibid., p. 134.

29. Tim Bliss, "Drugs—Use, Abuse, and Treatment," in *Introduction to Social Welfare Institutions*, Charles Zastrow, ed. (Homewood, IL: Dorsey Press, 1978), p. 29.

30. Kornblum and Julian, *Social Problems*, p. 132.

31. Ibid.

32. Ibid.

33. Farley, *American Social Problems*, p. 237.

34. Kornblum and Julian, *Social Problems*, p. 133.

35. Coleman and Cressey, *Social Problems*, p. 307.

36. Kornblum and Julian, *Social Problems*, p. 133.

37. Ibid.

38. Sharon Wegscheider, *Another Chance: Hope and Health for the Alcoholic Family* (Palo Alto, CA: Science and Behavior Books, 1981).

39. Lewis J. Lord, "Coming to Grips with Alcoholism," *U.S. News & World Report*, Nov. 30, 1987, p. 56.

40. Ibid.

41. Brenda C. Coleman, "Study Adds to Alcoholism Gene Theory," *Wisconsin State Journal*, Apr. 18, 1990, p. 1A.

42. Ibid.

43. Brenda C. Coleman, "Alcoholism Gene May Not Be Key," *Wisconsin State Journal*, Dec. 26, 1990, p. 3A.

44. Wayne W. Dunning and Dae H. Chang, "Drug Facts and Effects," in *The Personal Problem Solver*, Charles Zastrow and Dae H. Chang, eds. (Englewood Cliffs, NJ: Spectrum Books, 1977), p. 177.

45. John Timson, "Is Coffee Safe to Drink?" *Human Nature* (December 1978), pp. 57–59.

46. National Clearinghouse for Drug Abuse Information, *Amphetamine* (Rockville, MD: Alcohol, Drug Abuse, and Mental Health Administration, Report Series 28, no. 1, February 1974), pp. 9–10.

47. Joel Fort and Christopher T. Cory, *American Drug Store* (Boston: Little, Brown, 1975), p. 41.

48. Tony Blaze-Gosden, *Drug Abuse* (Birmingham, Great Britain: David & Charles Publishers, 1987), p. 99.

49. George Andrews and David Solomon, eds., *The Coca Leaf and Cocaine Papers* (New York: Harcourt Brace Jovanovich, 1975).

50. Blaze-Gosden, *Drug Abuse*, p. 95.

51. Abadinsky, *Drug Abuse: An Introduction*, pp. 90–97.

52. Ibid.

53. Edward M. Brecher and the Editors of Consumer Reports, *Licit and Illicit Drugs: The Consumers Union Report on Narcotics, Stimulants, Depressants, Inhalants, Hallucinogens, and Marijuana—Including Coffee, Nicotine, and Alcohol* (Boston: Little, Brown, 1972), p. 84.

54. Abadinsky, *Drug Abuse: An Introduction*, pp. 14–22.

55. Robertson, *Social Problems*, p. 450.

56. "Hallucinogens and Narcotics Alarm Public," *Chemistry and Engineering News*, 48, no. 47 (1976), pp. 44–45.

57. U.S. Department of Health, Education, and Welfare, *Surgeon-General's Report on Smoking and Health* (Washington, DC: U.S. Government Printing Office, 1979).

58. "Anti-Smoking Sentiments Increasing," *Hope Health Letter*, 14, no. 4 (April 1991), p. 6.

59. Farley, *American Social Problems*, p. 249.

60. Ibid.

61. Ibid.

62. Ibid.

63. Ibid.

64. Lynn Rosellini, "Rebel with a Cause: Koop," *U.S. News & World Report*, May 30, 1988, pp. 55–63.

65. William A. Hunt and Joseph D. Matarazzo, "Habit Mechanisms in Smoking," in *Learning Mechanisms of Smoking*, William A. Hunt, ed. (Chicago: Aldine, 1970), p. 76.

66. "About Marijuana," *Hope Health Letter*, 14, no. 4 (April 1991), p. 7.

67. John Kaplan, *Marijuana: A New Prohibition* (New York: World, 1970).

68. National Academy of Sciences, *Marijuana and Health* (Washington, DC: U.S. Government Printing Office, 1982).

69. Ibid.

70. A. Toufexis, "Shortcut to the Rambo Look," *Time,* Jan. 30, 1989, p. 78.

71. Ibid.

72. Ibid.

73. Bliss, "Drugs—Use, Abuse, and Treatment," p. 301.

74. Frank Riessman, "The 'Helper Therapy' Principle," *Journal of Social Work* (April 1965), pp. 27–34.

75. Martin Kasindorf, "By the Time It Gets to Phoenix," *New York Times Magazine,* Oct. 26, 1975, p. 30.

76. For descriptions of these self-help groups, see Alan Gartner and Frank Riessman, *Help: A Working Guide to Self-Help Groups* (New York: New Viewpoints, 1980).

77. Bliss, "Drugs—Use, Abuse, and Treatment," p. 314.

78. Farley, *Social Problems,* p. 260.

79. Brian Duffy, "Now for the Real Drug War," *U.S. News & World Report,* Sept. 11, 1989, pp. 18–20.

80. "A Test-Tube War on Drugs?" *U.S. News & World Report,* Mar. 17, 1986, p. 8.

81. Ibid.

82. Alvin P. Sanoff, "Baseball's Drug Menace," *U.S. News & World Report,* Mar. 17, 1986, p. 57.

83. Helen H. Nowlis, *Drugs on the College Campus* (New York: Doubleday, 1969), p. 51.

84. National Commission on Marihuana and Drug Abuse, *Drug Use in America: Problem in Perspective,* Second Report (Washington, DC: U.S. Government Printing Office, March 1973).

85. Abadinsky, *Drug Abuse: An Introduction,* pp. 264–268.

8

CRIME, JUVENILE DELINQUENCY, AND CORRECTIONAL SERVICES

On August 9, 1969, Sharon Tate was slain in her home, along with four other people. The next night Leno LaBianca (a wealthy president of a grocery chain) and his wife were brutally stabbed to death. In the weeks that followed, Charles Manson and several of his followers were arrested and later convicted for these murders. Manson was head of a commune, "The Family," that lived in Death Valley, California. Why did Manson and his followers commit these bizarre murders? What can be done to prevent such offenses from being committed?

These questions form the focus of this chapter. The main topics to be covered are:

- Nature and extent of crime.
- Crime causation theories.
- Types of crime.
- The criminal justice system (the police, the courts, and the correctional system).
- Ways to reduce crime and delinquency.
- The role of social work in providing correctional services.

NATURE AND EXTENT OF CRIME

What Is Crime?

A *crime* is simply an act committed or omitted in violation of a law. A *law* is a formal social rule that is enforced by a political authority. Usually the state (or the power elite that controls the state) specifies as crimes those acts that violate certain strongly held values and norms. Not all behaviors that violate norms are prohibited by law; in some cases informal processes such as social disapproval regulate norm violations. For example, a swimmer's failure to aid a drowning person is not a criminal act, although it is usually considered morally wrong.

Norms and values change over time, and therefore so do laws. When norms change, there is often a time lag, before laws based on the outdated norms are changed. Some areas still have obsolete laws that prohibit card playing on Sundays and sexual intercourse (even between married couples) in any position other than the missionary position. Certain norms and values differ among cultures and societies; therefore, so do laws. In South Africa it is a serious crime, punishable by whipping and incarceration, for people of different races to have, or even attempt to have, sexual intercourse with each other.[1] In many Arab countries the use of alcohol is illegal but the use of marijuana is acceptable; in the United States the reverse is generally the law.

Everyone, at one time or another, has violated some law. Whether a violator becomes a convicted offender depends on a number of factors, including whether he or she is arrested, how forcefully the prosecuting attorney wants to present the case, how effective the defense attorney is, whether there are witnesses, and how the offender presents himself or herself in court.[2]

With thousands of laws on the books, police, prosecuting attorneys, and judges have considerable discretion over which laws to ignore, which to enforce, and how strongly to enforce them. This discretionary power offers many opportunities for criminal justice officials to choose whom to arrest and whom to release. The act of applying the law often involves issues of political power and favorable treatment for certain groups and classes. Because this power usually resides with the white middle and upper classes, the poor and minority groups are often (intentionally or unintentionally) treated more harshly. For example, authorities are substantially less vigorous in enforcing white-collar crime than they are in enforcing vagrancy laws in middle-class neighborhoods. (The middle-class power structure generally seeks to enforce vagrancy laws in order "to keep bums and other undesirables off the streets, or at least out of respectable neighborhoods."[3])

How Extensive Is Crime?

Crime is one of the most serious problems facing our nation. Former President Richard Nixon on several occasions called crime our "number one enemy" and remarked that "we must declare war against it.'' (Ironically, Nixon and many of his top administrative officials later faced criminal charges—with some being imprisoned—in connection with the Watergate affair.*)

The most comprehensive statistical summary of crime in the United States is the annual publication of the Uniform Crime Reports (UCR) by the FBI. This report lists the crimes and arrests in this country, as reported by law enforcement agencies.

One part of this report is the Serious Crime Index, which is constructed to show the amount of, and trends in, serious crime. The Serious Crime Index is composed of four types of property crimes (burglary, larceny over $50, motor vehicle theft, and arson) and four types of crimes against people (willful homicide, forcible rape, aggravated assault, and robbery). Over 14 million Serious Crime Index offenses are reported to law enforcement agencies in the United States.[4] The Serious Crime Index offenses for 1992 are listed in Table 8.1.

It is generally agreed that serious, violent crime has reached alarming proportions in the United States. Many Americans feel unsafe in their own neighborhood at night, and a high proportion own guns, largely for self-protection.[5] Exhibit 8.1 demonstrates graphically why people are so fearful today.

A report released by the U.S. Senate Judiciary Committee in 1991 noted:

> The United States is the most violent and self-destructive nation on Earth. In 1990, the United States led the world with its murder, rape and robbery rates. When viewed from the national perspective, these crime rates are sobering. When viewed from the international perspective, they are truly embarrassing.[6]

This report also noted that the murder rate in

---

*The Watergate affair involved a break-in in the early 1970s at the Democratic National Committee headquarters (housed in the Watergate building in Washington, D.C.) by persons who were clandestinely employed to help reelect Nixon. Nixon and some of his top aides then committed a variety of offenses in an effort to cover up this break-in. Nixon was eventually forced to resign from the presidency after the coverup was revealed.

TABLE 8.1

Number of Reported Serious Crimes, 1992

Crime	Number
Arson	(Statistics unavailable)
Murder	23,760
Forcible rape	109,060
Robbery	672,480
Aggravated assault	1,126,970
Burglary	2,979,900
Larceny-theft	7,915,200
Motor vehicle theft	1,610,800
Total	14,438,170

Source: Crime in the United States, 1992, FBI Uniform Crime Reports (Washington, DC: U.S. Government Printing Office, 1993), p. 58.

the United States was more than twice that of Northern Ireland (which had a high rate because of a civil war), 4 times that of Italy, 9 times that of England, and 11 times that of Japan. The rape rate was 8 times higher than in France, 15 times higher than in England, 23 times higher than in Italy, and 26 times higher than in Japan. Robbery rates were 6 times higher than in England, 7 times higher than in Italy, and nearly 150 times higher than in Japan.[7]

Who Is Arrested?

Those who are arrested for crimes are disproportionately likely to be males, young, members of a racial minority, and city residents.

Males are arrested about four times as often as females.[8] (Only in juvenile runaway and prostitution cases are females arrested more often.) There are two major reasons why males are more often arrested. One is sex-role stereotyping, which encourages males to be more aggressive and daring, whereas females are encouraged to be more passive and conforming to rules and norms. The second reason is the tendency of police officers and

EXHIBIT 8.1

Crime Clock: Frequency of Reported Crimes in the United States

Murder—one every 22 minutes
Forcible rape—one every 5 minutes
Robbery—one every 47 seconds
Aggravated assault—one every 28 seconds
Violent crime—one every 22 seconds
Motor vehicle theft—one every 20 seconds
Burglary—one every 11 seconds
Larceny-theft—one every 4 seconds
Property crime—one every 3 seconds

Source: *Crime in the United States, 1992, FBI Uniform Crime Reports* (Washington, DC: U.S. Government Printing Office, 1993), p. 4.

the courts to deal more leniently with female offenders.[9] However, it should be noted that in the past two decades crime among females has been increasing faster than that among males,[10] which may be a negative side effect of women's challenging their traditional sex roles.

Young people appear to commit far more than their share of crime, including the crimes that are classified by the FBI as most serious—rape, murder, robbery, arson, burglary, aggravated assault, auto theft, and larceny. In 1992, 29% of all arrests were under age 21 and 45% were under age 25.[11] A partial explanation of the high arrest rate among juveniles and young adults is that they may be less skillful than older adults in avoiding arrest. Also, they tend to commit crimes (such as auto theft) that are highly visible to the police. Even when all these factors are taken into account, it is still the case that the young commit more crimes than the old.

There are differences in arrest rates among various racial and ethnic groups. Chinese Americans and Japanese Americans have the lowest arrest rates in the country.[12] The arrest rate for African Americans is three times higher than for whites.[13] One reason for this higher rate is that a higher proportion of the African American population is poor or unemployed; and there are high correlations between poverty (and unemployment) and the types of crime classified by the FBI as most serious. An additional reason for the higher arrest among certain minority groups may be racial prejudice. A number of studies have shown that the probability of arrest, prosecution, conviction, and incarceration for an offense decreases as the social status of the offender increases. In one study, judges were given fact sheets on a hypothetical case and asked to recommend an appropriate sentence. The fact sheets contained the following information:

"Joe Cut," 27, pleaded guilty to battery. He slashed his common-law wife on the arms with a switchblade. His record showed convictions for disturbing the peace, drunkenness, and hit-run driving. He told a probation officer that he acted in self-defense after his wife attacked him with a broom handle. The prosecutor recommended not more than five days in jail or a $100 fine.[14]

Half the fact sheets identified "Joe Cut" as white, and the other half identified him as African American. The judges who thought he was white recommended a sentence of 3 to 10 days, whereas those who thought he was African American recommended a sentence of from 5 to 30 days.

Kornblum and Julian describe another factor that contributes to higher arrest rates among African Americans:

Still another factor that is thought to contribute to high rates of crime among blacks is family disorganization, especially the rapid increase in the number of female-headed families. Such families lack male role models with legitimate jobs, leaving open the possibility that children will be influenced by others in the community, including individuals who engage in criminal activities.[15]

A majority of reported crimes and reported arrests are in large cities, as compared to suburbs and rural areas.[16] Within large cities crime tends to occur in those sections that are changing rap-

Bond trader Michael Milken enters federal court after pleading guilty to six felony counts related to securities fraud. Miliken, who was sentenced to ten years in prison for illegal trading activities during the corporate takeover boom of the 1980s, owes $900 million in judgments from lawsuits brought against him. The most costly—and perhaps the most frequent—crimes are committed by "respectable" middle- and upper-class citizens.

idly and that have a high concentration of low-income and transient inhabitants. Arrest rates are substantially lower in more stable, higher-income, residential areas.

How Accurate Are Official Crime Statistics?

As described earlier, the Federal Bureau of Investigation annually compiles the Uniform Crime Report (UCR), based on data from law enforcement agencies throughout the country on crimes committed and arrests made. The Serious Crime Index is a part of UCR.

There are a number of problems connected with this index. Actual crime rates are substantially higher than the official rates. Kornblum and Julian estimate that crimes reported to the police account for about 33% of actual offenses and about 50% of violent crimes.[17] Victims often do not report crimes to the police because (among other reasons) they feel that nothing can be done.[18] As indicated in Exhibit 8.2, most crimes go unsolved.

The Serious Crime Index focuses on crimes that are more likely to be committed by people of lower social and economic status. It does not reflect the types of crimes typically committed by higher-income groups: fraud, false advertising,

EXHIBIT 8.2

Disposition of Reported[a] Serious Crimes

For every 100 reported serious crimes:

Only 9 people are arrested.
Only 2 people are convicted.
Less than 2 people go to prison.
Only 1 person serves more than a year.

[a]Less than half of all crimes committed are reported to authorities.

Source: Ted Gest, "Victims of Crime," *U.S. News & World Report,* July 31, 1989, p. 16.

corporate price fixing, bribery, embezzlement, industrial pollution, tax evasion, and so on. If white-collar crimes were included in the Serious Crime Index, and if law enforcement authorities were more vigorous in enforcing such laws, the profile of a typical criminal would very likely be older, wealthier, whiter, and more suburban than suggested by the Serious Crime Index.

Self-report studies, in which respondents are asked anonymously the details of any crimes they may have committed, reveal that "close to 100 percent of all persons have committed some kind of offense, although few have been arrested."[19] In what way, then, do those who are arrested differ from those who are not? For one thing, those who are not caught commit a crime only rarely, whereas those who are arrested break the law more frequently. Perhaps a better explanation, however, lies in the types of crimes committed. Those arrested may be committing the kinds of crimes that are more strictly enforced by law enforcement agencies. The poor, for example, may be more likely to commit high-risk, low-yield crimes such as larceny, burglary, or robbery. In contrast, the wealthier are more likely to commit low-risk, high-yield crimes, such as income-tax evasion and false advertising.

In the past 20 years there have been dramatic increases in the Serious Crime Index. Yet it is un-

certain what this rate increase actually represents. Perhaps crime victims are reporting more offenses. Or perhaps the increase is due to improvements in police-reporting practices; police departments are increasingly using computers, clerical personnel, and statisticians to improve the accuracy of their reports.

Strictly speaking, the Serious Crime Index is not fully comparable among jurisdictions. At times it is even inconsistent from one year to the next within the same reporting unit. A major reason for this difficulty is that each of the 50 states has its own unique criminal code. For example, an offense that is classified as burglary in one state may be classified as larceny or robbery in another; what is classified as sexual assault in one state may be considered a less serious offense in another. Because states occasionally make changes in their criminal codes, inconsistencies may arise from one year to the next within the same reporting unit because of changes in definitions of offenses. Furthermore, individual officers interpret the law differently as they carry out their duties.

Finally, it should be noted that crime statistics are at times manipulated by the police and public officials. Data may be skewed to show higher rates of crime, perhaps to help document the need for a federal or state grant or to politick for a budget increase in personnel or facilities. More often than not, however, police and public officials are under considerable pressure to keep the crime rate low. By manipulating statistics, they can reclassify certain serious crimes into different, less serious categories.

In summary, the Serious Crime Index of the FBI provides an indication of the rates and trends of certain crimes in the United States. Yet these statistics overlook white-collar crime, are affected by police-reporting practices, and must be viewed against the fact that many crimes are unreported. It further appears that the poor, the undereducated, and minorities have been the victims not only of selective law enforcement but also of misleading statistics on crime. Some sociologists have contended that, because higher-income classes are far more involved in white-collar crime (which is often ignored by law enforcement agencies), they may actually have a higher rate of crime than the lower classes.[20]

CRIME CAUSATION THEORIES

A variety of theories about the causes of crime have been advanced by several disciplines. Space limitations permit only a summary of the more prominent theories. Exhibit 8.3 identifies these prominent theories along with their approximate dates of origin. As you read about each of these theories, ask yourself the following questions: Is this theory helpful in explaining why a person committed a rape (or burglary, murder, drug-trafficking offense, aggravated assault, kidnapping, embezzlement, etc.)? Is the theory useful in suggesting a correctional plan to prevent a recurrence of the offense?

Early Theories

Three of the earliest theories on the causes of crime were *demonology,* the *classical/neoclassical theory,* and the *Marxist-Leninist theory.*

DEMONOLOGY

For centuries, many primitive societies conceived of crime as being caused by evil spirits. This belief is commonly referred to as *demonology.* It was thought that those who engaged in deviant behavior were possessed by the devil. The only way to cure the criminal act was to remove the evil spirit through prayer, through a ritual, or by torture (sometimes to the point of death). This theory is no longer prominent, partly because scientific study has found no evidence that law breakers are possessed by evil spirits. Remnants of the theory remain, however, as seen in satanic cults, rock lyrics with satanic themes, and movies (such as *Friday the 13th* and *The Exorcist*) depicting people possessed by demons.

CLASSICAL AND NEOCLASSICAL THEORY

The classical and neoclassical schools were based on hedonistic psychology. Classical theory

EXHIBIT 8.3

Prominent Theories of Crime

Theory	Approximate Date of Origin
Early theories	
Demonology	Primitive societies
Classical/Neoclassical	1775
Marxist-Leninist	1850
Physical and mental trait theories	
Phrenology	1825
Lombrosian	1900
Mental deficiency	1900
Morphological	1920
Psychological theories	
Psychoanalytic	1900
Psychodynamic problem solving	1920
Frustration-aggression	1950
Self-talk	1975
Sociological theories	
Labeling	1900
Differential association	1939
Societal control	1950
Deviant subcultures	1955
Anomie	1957

asserted that a person makes a decision about whether to engage in criminal activity based on the anticipated balance of pleasure and pain. Each individual was assumed to have a free will and to act solely on the basis of the anticipated hedonistic calculations. Advocates of this school considered this to be a full and exhaustive explanation of causality. Applied to corrections, this approach urged that clear-cut punishments be assigned to each offense so the prospective offender could calculate anticipated pleasures and pains. The penalties assigned were to be slightly more severe than anticipated pleasures in order to discourage criminal activity. The neoclassical school accepted the basic notion of hedonistic calculations but urged that children and "lunatics" be exempt from punishment because of their inability to calculate pleasures and pain responsibly. Judicial discretion was also urged for certain mitigating circumstances (for example, an offense now referred to as involuntary manslaughter).

Although correctional systems in the 19th century were based primarily on the neoclassical approach, classical/neoclassical theory has waned in popularity. Some elements of it can still be found in our legal/judicial system—particularly the emphasis on using punishment to deter crime. The theory has been severely criticized because it does not allow for other causes of crime and because the punitive approach it advocates has not been very successful in curbing further criminal activity. In addition, hedonistic psychology ignores the fact that much human behavior is determined by values and morals, rather than by the pleasure-versus-pain calculation.

MARXIST-LENINIST THEORY

Marxist-Leninist theory assumes that all crime results from the exploitation of workers and from intense competition among people. Crime disappears, according to neo-Marxists, when society achieves a "classless" status. The basic tenet of Communism is "From each according to his ability, to each according to his need." Socialist countries (such as Cuba and North Korea) have in the past sought to formulate their societies on the principles advocated by Karl Marx. Class differentials are much less prominent in socialist countries as compared to capitalist nations. Although Marx asserted that crime would be sharply reduced in socialist countries because there would be less class conflict, substantial criminal activity does occur in these countries. (The extensiveness of criminal activity is difficult to determine, because these countries publish almost no crime-rate reports.) The continued existence of crime in socialist countries is not taken by socialists as evidence that the theory is defective; rather, it is explained as being the result of old capitalistic traditions and ideologies and the imperfect application of Marxist theory. (It should be noted that many socialist countries in recent years have been discarding Marxist principles and are moving toward incorporating capitalistic incentives into their economies.)

Physical and Mental Trait Theories

You may have noticed in Exhibit 8.3 that the first "physical and mental trait theory," *phrenology*, actually originated before Marxist-Leninist theory. Although it falls chronologically into the category of "early theories," it is more closely related to "trait theories," and will be discussed in this section along with three other trait theories, the *Lombrosian*, the *mental deficiency*, and the *morphological* theories.

PHRENOLOGY

Phrenology was popular until the turn of the 20th century. Phrenologists maintained that criminal behavior was related to the size and shape of the human skull. They closely scrutinized the grooves, ridges, and number of bumps on a skull. The shape of the brain, which was influenced by the shape of the skull, was thought to be sufficient to predict criminal activity. Although there were isolated incidents in which offenders with "criminal prone" skulls were treated more harshly than other offenders, this approach was not widely incorporated into correctional systems. Scientific studies have found no evidence of correlations between criminal behavior and the shape of the skull.

LOMBROSIAN THEORY

Around the beginning of the 20th century, biological/constitutional theories were popular. The prototype of such theories was Cesare Lombroso's theory of the "born criminal." This school maintained that a criminal inherits certain physical abnormalities or stigmata, such as a scanty beard, low sensitivity to pain, distorted nose, large lips, or long arms. The more such stigmata a person had, the more he or she was thought to be predisposed to a criminal career. People with several stigmata were thought to be unable to refrain from criminal activity unless their social environment was unusually favorable. The theory that criminals have distinct physical characteristics was refuted by Charles Goring, who found no significant physical differences in a study comparing several thousand criminals with several thousand noncriminals.[21]

MENTAL DEFICIENCY THEORY

The mental deficiency theory replaced the Lombrosian school when the latter fell into disrepute. Mental deficiency theory asserted that criminal behavior resulted from "feeblemindedness," which was alleged to impair the capacity to acquire morality and self-control or to appreciate the meaning of laws. As mental tests became standardized and widely used, it was discovered that many criminals achieved average or above-average intelligence scores. The theory waned in popularity in the 1930s. Neither the Lombrosian nor the mental deficiency approach had a lasting, significant effect on corrections.

MORPHOLOGICAL THEORY

Closely related to the mental deficiency and Lombrosian theories is morphological theory, which asserted that there is a fundamental relationship between psychological makeup and physical structure. The most popular variant of this theory was William Sheldon's, developed in the 1940s. Sheldon described three body categories: endomorph (obese), mesomorph (muscular), and ectomorph (lean). To the mesomorph he ascribed an unusual propensity to criminal activity. Sheldon did not assert that mesomorphs were inherently criminally prone. Rather, he asserted that this physique was associated with a distinctive type of temperament, characterized by such traits as love of physical adventure, abundance of restless energy, and enjoyment of exercise. Mesomorphy thus produced energetic, aggressive, and daring types of individuals, such as generals, athletes, and politicians, as well as criminals. Morphological approaches like Sheldon's are still popular in southern European and South American countries. Scientific studies, however, have found little evidence that muscular people are more likely to commit crimes than people who are lean or overweight.

Psychological Theories

Psychological theories about crime attribute its causes to the criminal's thought processes, which are seen as relatively unrelated to overall societal conditions. These theories include the *psychoanalytic, psychodynamic problem-solving, frustration-aggression,* and *self-talk* approaches to understanding criminal behavior.

PSYCHOANALYTIC THEORY

Psychoanalytic theory is not a single coherent theory but a variety of hypotheses developed by psychoanalysts since the turn of the 20th century from the pioneering work of Sigmund Freud. Generally, these theories postulated that delinquent behavior results when the restraining forces in the superego (one's conscience and self-ideal) and the ego (mediator among the superego, the id, and reality) are too weak to curb the instinctual, antisocial pressures from the id (source of psychic energy). Human nature was seen as largely determined by id instincts, which were basically antisocial and immoral in character. This theory postulated that current behavior was largely controlled by early childhood experiences. Deviant behavior was viewed as stemming from unconscious conflicts, fixations, and repressed traumatic experiences.

The psychiatric school, of which psychoanalysis is a large component, has had a significant influence on corrections because it asserts that some offenders commit illegal acts because they are insane. Criminal justice systems frequently call on psychiatrists to determine the "sanity" of accused offenders. If someone is judged by the court to be "innocent by reason of insanity," he or she is sent to a mental hospital, instead of to a jail, to recuperate.

Psychiatry has also classified individuals into numerous categories in terms of their "mental" functioning. One category, *sociopath,* has had considerable relevance for corrections. A sociopath is a person who is thought to have no moral constraints against engaging in criminal activity, doing so whenever it is personally advantageous, even though others may be hurt.

Since 1950, Thomas Szasz and others have

seriously questioned the medical-model approach to emotional problems and have asserted that mental illness is a myth.[22] Szasz believes that people have emotional problems, but not a "disease of the mind," as implied by the medical model (see Chapter 4). Courts, however, continue to use the mental illness model.

Psychoanalytic theory is increasingly falling into disfavor. One reason is the finding that people with emotional problems who undergo psychoanalysis are no more likely to improve than a comparable group who receive no therapy.[23]

PSYCHODYNAMIC PROBLEM-SOLVING THEORY

Psychodynamic problem-solving theory views deviant behavior as being contrived by the personality as a way of dealing with some adjustment problem. The problem is generally perceived as a conflict among various ingredients of the personality: wishes, drives, fears, strivings, loyalties, codes of ethics, and so on. Situational factors are generally deemphasized.

A serious shortcoming of the theory is that it is often extremely difficult (if not impossible) to determine precisely which wishes, drives, fears, or ethics motivated someone to commit a crime. For example, the following internal desires have all been advanced as motivations for committing rape: unfulfilled sexual desires, a desire for violence, and feelings of inferiority; all are theorized to be temporarily alleviated during rape as the offender feels a sense of power and superiority. When a sexual assault occurs, it is nearly impossible to determine the extent to which each of these internal desires contributed to the assault. Frequently, when using this theory, only speculations can be made about why a crime occurred, as few "tools" exist to check out the accuracy of the speculations.

FRUSTRATION-AGGRESSION THEORY

Frustration-aggression theory asserts that frustration often provokes an aggressive response. Thus, violence is seen as a way to release the tension produced by a frustrating situation. An unemployed husband, unable to pay his bills or find a job, for example, may beat his wife. Some authorities saw the burning and rioting in our inner cities in the 1960s as being a reaction by African Americans to the frustration of living in a society that promises equality but does not provide it.

Frustration-aggression theory explains only violent crimes. It does not attempt to explain other kinds of criminal behavior, such as prostitution, fraud, and forgery.

SELF-TALK THEORY

Self-talk theory is a psychological approach for identifying the underlying motives for committing a crime.[24] According to this theory, the reasons for any criminal act can be determined by examining what the offender was thinking prior to and during the time the crime was being committed. A shortcoming of the theory is that, when offenders discuss what they were thinking during a crime, they often seek to slant what they reveal in a socially acceptable way.

Sociological Theories

Sociological theories focus on societal factors that influence people to commit crimes. For ease in understanding these theories, we will examine them out of chronological order (see Exhibit 8.3) as follows: *differential association theory, anomie theory, deviant subcultures theory, societal control theory* and *labeling theory*.

DIFFERENTIAL ASSOCIATION THEORY

Edwin Sutherland, perhaps the best-known criminologist in contemporary sociology, advanced his famous theory of differential association in 1939. The theory asserts that criminal behavior is the result of a learning process that primarily occurs in small, intimate groups—family, neighborhood peer groups, friends, and so on. In essence, "A person becomes delinquent because of the excess of definitions favorable to violation of law over definitions unfavorable to violation of law."[25] Whether a person decides to commit a crime is based on the nature of present and past associations with significant others. People internalize the values of the surrounding culture. When the environment includes frequent contact

CASE
EXAMPLE 8.1 **Self-Talk Theory Explanation of the Manson Murders**

W hy (in August 1969) did Charles Manson and several members of his commune murder Sharon Tate and six other prominent people? Vincent Bugliosi, prosecuting attorney for the state of California, was able to document that the following thought processes led Manson to order the killings.

Manson hoped that brutal murders of the prominent and wealthy would create fear and panic among whites. The whites, unable to determine who actually killed these people, would conclude that the murders were committed by blacks. Then, out of fear, the whites would go into the ghettos and start killing black people, thus causing a race war. Such a war would also lead to a split between white liberals and conservatives, who would then begin killing each other. During this time the "true black race" (at various times identified by Manson as the "Black Panthers" or the "Black Muslims") would go into hiding and would be unaffected. After almost all whites had perished, the "true black race" would come out and kill the remaining whites, except for Manson and his followers, who would be in hiding in Death Valley. The remaining blacks would not have the capacities to govern the nation and, after failing, would then turn to Manson to be the leader of the country.

This strange, unrealistic belief system apparently led Manson and his followers to kill seven people. Having an unrealistic belief system does not in any way make a person "crazy." All of the defendants in this case were judged to be "sane." While living together in isolation in their commune, the members apparently gave mutual support to one another for the correctness of Manson's beliefs, probably partly because objective evidence was not available to refute Manson's interpretations.

Source: Vincent Bugliosi and C. Gentry, *Helter Skelter* (New York: Norton, 1974).

---

with criminal elements and infrequent contact with noncriminal elements, a person is likely to engage in delinquent or criminal activity.

Past and present learning experiences in intimate personal groups thus define whether a person should violate laws; for those deciding to commit crimes, the learning experiences also include choice of which crimes to commit, the techniques of committing these crimes, and the attitudes and rationalizations for committing these crimes. Thus a youth whose most admired person is a member of a gang involved in burglaries or drug trafficking will seek to emulate this model, will receive instruction in committing these crimes from the gang members, and will also receive approval from the gang for successfully committing these crimes.

The theory does little to explain such crimes as arson and embezzlement, in which the offender often has no exposure to others who have committed such crimes.

ANOMIE THEORY

Robert Merton applied anomie theory to crime.[26] This approach views criminal behavior as resulting when an individual is prevented from achieving high-status goals in a society. Merton begins by noting that every society has both approved goals (for example, wealth and material possessions) and approved means for attaining these goals. When certain members of society share these goals but have insufficient access to approved means for attaining them, a state of anomie results. (Anomie is a condition in which acceptance of the approved standards of conduct is weakened.) Unable to achieve the goals through society's legitimately defined channels, they then seek to achieve them through illegal means.

Merton asserts that higher crime rates are likely to occur among groups that are discriminated against (that is, groups that face additional barriers to achieving the high-status goals). These groups include the poor and racial minorities. Societies with high crime rates (such as the United States) differ from those with low crime rates because, according to Merton, they tell all their citizens they can achieve, but in fact they block achievement for some people.

Anomie theory has difficulty explaining why white-collar crime (which is committed primarily by individuals who are seldom discriminated against) is perhaps the most common type of crime committed in this country.[27]

DEVIANT SUBCULTURES THEORY

Deviant subcultures theory is another explanation for crime. This theory asserts that some groups develop their own attitudes, values, and perspectives, which support criminal activity. Walter Miller, for example, argues that American lower-class culture is more conducive to crime than middle-class culture.[28] He asserts that lower-class culture is organized around six values—trouble, toughness, excitement, fate, smartness (ability to con others), and autonomy—and allegiance to these values produces delinquency. Miller concludes the entire lower-class subculture is deviant in the sense that any male growing up in it will accept these values and almost certainly violate the law.

Albert Cohen advanced another subculture theory.[29] He contended that gangs develop a delinquent subculture that offers solutions to the problems of young male gang members. A gang gives them the chance to belong, to amount to something, to develop their masculinity, and to fight middle-class society. In particular, the delinquent subculture, according to Cohen, can effectively solve the status problems of working-class boys, especially those who are rejected by middle-class society. Cohen contends that the main problems of working-class boys revolve around status.

As with the previous theories, deviant subculture theories are unable to explain white-collar crime and other crimes committed by the middle and upper classes.

SOCIETAL CONTROL THEORY

Control theories ask the question "Why do people *not* commit crimes?" Theories in this category assume that all of us would "naturally" commit crimes and therefore must be constrained and controlled by society from breaking the law. Control theorists have identified three factors for preventing crime. One is the internal controls that build up through the process of socialization; a strong conscience and a sense of personal morality will prevent most people from breaking the law. A second factor is a strong attachment to small social groups (for example, the family), which is thought to prevent individuals from breaking the law because they fear rejection and disapproval from the people who are important to them. A third factor (taken from the classical school) is that people do not break the law because they fear arrest and incarceration.

Control theories assume that basic human nature is asocial or evil. Such an assumption has never been proved. Theories that perceive humans as having an evil nature are unable to explain altruistic and other "good" deeds performed by people.

LABELING THEORY

Labeling theorists, similar to differential association theorists, assert that criminals *learn* to break the law. Labeling theory focuses on the process of branding people as criminals and on the effects of such labeling. Contrary to control theory, this theory holds that labeling a person as a delinquent or a criminal encourages rather than discourages criminal behavior.

Charles Cooley developed a labeling theory with his "looking glass self-concept."[30] This theory argues that people develop their self-concept (sense of who and what they are) in terms of how

A new member of a female street gang in East Los Angeles undergoes a violent initiation into the group. According to one theory, gangs develop delinquent subcultures that solve the status problems of working-class adolescents, especially those rejected by middle-class society.

others relate to them, as if others were a looking glass or mirror. For example, if a neighborhood identifies a young boy as being a "troublemaker" or "delinquent," neighbors are likely to relate to the youth as if he were not to be trusted. They may accuse him of delinquent acts, and they will label his semidelinquent and aggressive behavior as being "delinquent." This labeling process also results in a type of prestige and status for the boy, at least from his peers. In the absence of objective ways to gauge whether he is, in fact, a "delinquent," the youth will rely on the subjective evaluations of others. Thus, gradually, as he is related to as being a "delinquent," he begins to perceive himself in that way and to enact the delinquent role.

Labeling theory is unable to explain why some offenders stop committing crimes after being arrested and convicted or why offenders initially begin to break the law.

Usefulness of Theories

One of the most important questions in criminology is "Do our theories identify the reasons why an offender committed a specific crime (for example, an aggravated rape)?" The answer, unfortunately, is that most theories are not very useful in identifying the causes for specific crimes. Also, they are not very useful in explaining why one individual may commit forgery, another may commit rape, and yet another may burglarize someone. Without knowing why a crime occurs, it is extremely difficult to develop an effective rehabilitation approach to curb repeat offenders.

Theories that attempt to explain all types of crime have a built-in limitation. Crime is a comprehensive label covering a wide range of offenses, including purse snatching, auto theft, rape, check forgery, prostitution, drunkenness, possession of narcotics, and sexual exhibition. Obviously, because the natures of these crimes vary widely, the motives or causes underlying each must vary widely. Therefore it is unlikely that any theory can adequately explain the causes of all crimes. It may be more productive to focus on developing more limited theories that attempt to identify the causes of specific offenses (for example, drunkenness, incest, auto theft, rape, or fraud) rather than to develop additional comprehensive theories.

Now let's take a detailed look at specific types of criminal offenses.

TYPES OF CRIME

We tend to think that crime is a well-defined phenomenon and to have stereotyped views about who criminals are. Actually, criminal offenses and the characteristics of lawbreakers are almost as varied as noncriminal offenses and law abiders. Many diverse forms of behaviors are classified as crimes, with the only major common thread being a violation of a criminal statute. Because it is impossible to look at all crimes, we will examine the more important ones. Keep in mind that the following categories are not mutually exclusive; there is overlap among them.

Organized Crime

Organized crime is a large-scale operation. Illegal activities are carried out as part of a well-designed plan developed by a large organization seeking to maximize its overall profit. Activities that lend themselves to organized crime include illegal gambling, drug dealing, fencing (receiving and selling stolen goods), prostitution, bootlegging, and extortion (in the form of selling protection). Large-scale operations are more cost efficient than small-scale operations in certain illegal activities. For example, in drug trafficking, drugs are smuggled into a country and distributed on a large scale, with corrupt officials being paid off to reduce the risks of arrest and prosecution.

It appears the most organized crime efforts start on a small scale, generally with one small organization that carries on a particular crime, such as extortion or gambling. The group then expands to control this activity within a given neighborhood or city, by absorbing or destroying the competition. Eventually the organization expands its activities into other crimes and begins to operate in larger regions or even nationwide.

A major characteristic of organized crime is that many of its activities are not predatory (such as robbery, which takes from its victims). Instead, organized crime generally seeks to provide to the public desired goods and services that cannot be legally obtained (drugs, gambling, prostitution, loan money). For its success, organized crime relies on public demand for illegal services.

Because of the obvious emphasis on secrecy in organized crime, only limited information is available about the extent of offenses, the leaders and members of organized crime, or the nature of the internal organization. In this regard, Thomas Sullivan et al. note:

There is a great deal of myth about the Mafia or Cosa Nostra. Evidence available to social scientists suggests that they are not international syndicates operated by groups outside the United States, nor is there a single syndicate controlling all (or even most) organized crime in this country. American syndicates are very much American in their goals and organization. . . . In addition, just as there is competition between the

	The Saints and the Roughnecks: A Study
CASE	**Showing the Effects of Labeling and of**
EXAMPLE 8.2	**Expectations of Significant Others**

W illiam Chambliss, in a dramatic study, examined factors affecting delinquency within two groups of adolescents at the same high school; one group was composed of middle- and upper-class boys (the Saints), and the other was composed of lower-class boys (the Roughnecks). The Saints were often truant from school, harassed citizens and the police, openly cheated on exams, vandalized homes, drank excessively, and drove recklessly. Teachers, school officials, and the police largely ignored their acts because they were viewed as being basically good boys. They were almost never arrested by the police, and hardly anything negative appeared in their school records. These youths were regarded as harmless pranksters, were allowed to "sow their wild oats," and were expected to succeed in life. Interestingly, the success expectations appeared to be a major factor in determining their futures; practically all of the Saints went on to college and white-collar careers.

On the other hand, the Roughnecks, who committed fewer, although similar, offenses, were labeled "deviants." Because they didn't have cars as the Saints did, the Roughnecks were confined to an area where they were more easily recognized and substantially more often arrested. The police and school officials expected that they would fail—and they did. These "delinquents" did poorly in school and went on to low-status jobs or criminal careers. This study of the Saints and Roughnecks demonstrates that both labeling and the expectations of significant others can have a substantial effect on behavior.

One additional factor that led to fewer arrests for the Saints was their apologetic nature whenever they were stopped by a police officer. They were polite and penitent and pled for mercy when stopped. In contrast, there was a high level of dislike and distrust between the police and the Roughnecks. When stopped by police, they came across as "tough" kids who displayed disdain and hostility—and as a consequence were more frequently arrested.

Source: William Chambliss, "The Saints and the Roughnecks," *Society,* 2, no. 11 (November–December 1973), pp. 24–31.

---

giants in most legitimate business sectors, there is competition in drug dealing, illegal gambling, racketeering, and other financial ventures involving organized crime.[31]

Organized crime is thought to revolve primarily around the Mafia (also called the Cosa Nostra). Its leadership is Italian American, with the lower ranks drawn from a variety of other ethnic groups. The Mafia developed largely during the 1920s and 1930s, when criminal groups organized to supply illegal alcohol during Prohibition. It has grown into a loose network of American regional syndicates or groups. These syndicates coordinate their efforts through a "commission," composed of the heads of the most powerful "families."[32] At the head of each family is a "don," who has absolute authority over the family unless overruled by the commission. Each don is assisted by an underboss and a counselor. Next in the hierarchy are "lieutenants," each of whom supervises a group of "soldiers" who are involved in illegal

Reputed Mafia boss John Gotti (left) was acquitted of assault charges in the shooting of a union leader in 1990. Labor racketeering is one of organized crime's major efforts.

enterprises. Contrary to public opinion, the Mafia is not an international syndicate of Sicilian law breakers; rather, it is a network of syndicates that were developed and organized in this country. The *Godfather* books and films paint a fairly realistic picture of the structure and operations of organized crime.

The costs to society and to our economy from organized crime are enormous. Through gambling and drug traffic, the lives of many individuals and their families are traumatized. Labor racketeering and infiltration of legitimate businesses lead to higher prices for goods, lower-quality products, the forced closing of some businesses, the establishment of monopolies, the unemployment of workers, misuse of pension and welfare benefits, and higher taxes. Through corruption of public officials (a necessary component of many illegal ventures), organized crime leads to public cynicism about the honesty of politicians and the democratic process. It also leads to higher taxes and mismanagement of public funds.

In the 1980s and early 1990s the FBI made immense progress in its battle against organized crime. The heads of 16 of the nation's Mafia families were indicted.[33] In addition, thousands of organized crime members were arrested and convicted of a variety of offenses. Experts credit this breakthrough to a number of factors. The FBI now devotes about one-quarter of its work force to combating organized crime[34] and has been making increased use of electronic eavesdropping. The FBI also is working more closely with state law enforcement authorities and with Italy to curb organized crime. Recently law enforcement agencies have been successful in getting large numbers of gang members to violate the traditional code of *omertà*—conspiracy of silence. Fearing lengthy stays in prison, where they could be vulnerable to mob-ordered murders, many underworld figures are joining a witness-protection effort that provides informants with new identities (including fake biographies) and homes in a different area of the country.

Despite these efforts, no one sees an end to the mob's influence anytime soon. Many of the old leaders are being replaced by a "new breed" of leadership, who have a greater familiarity with the world of high finance and legitimate business. Organized crime is developing new marketplace scams, including counterfeiting consumer credit cards and airline tickets, bootlegging gasoline (thereby avoiding payment of federal and state gasoline taxes), and selling fraudulent tax shelters.[35] In addition, new organizations unassociated with the Mafia are emerging to import and distribute illegal drugs.[36]

Let's examine the major organized crime efforts: gambling, drug trafficking, loan sharking, infiltrating legitimate businesses, labor racketeering, and prostitution.

GAMBLING

Illegal gambling takes place on a wide scale and generates enormous profits. Illegal operations include lotteries, off-track betting, illegal casinos, "numbers," and dice games. Such operations can be located practically anywhere—in a restaurant, garage, tavern, or apartment complex or even on business premises.

DRUG TRAFFICKING

Drug trafficking is an industry that makes billions of dollars annually in the United States. With such profits it is little wonder that organized crime is involved in the importation and distribution of drugs, such as cocaine, heroin, marijuana, crack, amphetamines, and hallucinogens. A recent trend in the illicit drug trade in the United States is the growth of new organizations unassociated with older crime "families." Some of these new organizations have ethnic group identities, such as Colombian, Chinese, Vietnamese, Puerto Rican, or African American.[37]

LOAN SHARKING

This crime involves lending money at interest rates above the legal limit. Interest rates have been reported to go as high as 150% a week.[38] Syndicated crime can ensure repayment by the threat of violence. Major borrowers from loan sharks include gamblers who need to cover losses, drug users, and small business owners who are unable to obtain credit from legitimate sources.

INFILTRATING LEGITIMATE BUSINESSES

The huge profits from illegal activities provide organized crime with the capital to enter into legitimate operations, including the entertainment industry, banking, insurance, restaurants, advertising firms, bars, the automotive industry, and real estate agencies—to name but a few.

Marshall Clinard and Richard Quinney describe the legal and illegal ways in which organized crime infiltrates legitimate businesses:

> *The control of (legitimate) business concerns is secured through (1) investing concealed profits acquired from gambling and other illegal activities, (2) accepting business interests in payment of the owner's gambling debts, (3) foreclosing on usurious loans, and (4) using various forms of extortions. A favorite operation is to place a concern (that organized crime has acquired) into fraudulent bankruptcy after milking its assets.[39]*

Infiltrating legitimate business provides organized crime with tax covers for its members, gives them a certain respectable status in the community, and offers additional profit-making opportunities. With its cash reserves, a syndicate can temporarily lower prices in order to bankrupt competitors. It can also use strong-arm tactics to force customers to buy its goods and services.

LABOR RACKETEERING

This activity involves the systematic extortion of money from labor unions and businesses. Racketeers can extort money from union members by forcing them to pay high union dues and fees in order to obtain and secure employment. Racketeers can short-change employees by paying less than union wages and by misusing the union's pension and welfare funds. Finally, racketeers can extort money from employers by forcing them to make payoffs for union cooperation (for example, to avoid a strike).

PROSTITUTION

Because prostitutes offer a service for which some people are willing to pay high prices, prostitution can be a highly profitable endeavor, which makes it appealing to organized crime. Mobsters serve as brokers for prostitution and customers and also protect them from arrest and prosecution by bribing law enforcement officials. Organized crime has also gotten involved in other sex-related forms of crime, such as the illegal distribution of pornographic films and magazines.

White-Collar Crime

John Johnson and Jack Douglas have noted that the most costly—and perhaps the most frequent—crimes are committed by "respectable" middle-class and upper-class citizens.[40] White-collar crimes are work-related offenses committed by people of high status.[41]

Offenses against customers include false advertising, stock manipulation, violations of food and drug laws, release of industrial waste products into public waterways, illegal emissions from industrial smokestacks, and price-fixing agreements. In 1977, for example, General Motors committed consumer fraud by placing Chevrolet engines in certain Oldsmobiles without informing the public. Their advertisements implicitly indicated that the Oldsmobiles really contained the larger, more expensive, and powerful Oldsmobile engines.

The case of stock speculator Ivan Boesky provides a classic example of white-collar crime. Boesky personally made over $100 million on illegal insider trading (acting on information not available to the public). Brokers who possess inside information (such as knowledge of an impending corporate merger or a change in the financial condition of a company that will affect the price of its stock) are prohibited from profiting from that information themselves or from selling it to others who may be able to profit from it. In 1986 Boesky admitted his illegal activities, paid the Securities and Exchange Commission $100 million in fines and illicit profits, and was later convicted of conspiracy to file false documents with the federal government. Boesky's crimes precipitated a wave of additional allegations of inside trading, which have rocked the financial community in recent years. For these multi-million-dollar offenses, Boesky was imprisoned only two years.

Embezzlement is an offense in which an employee fraudulently converts some of the employer's funds for personal use through altering company records. Embezzlers who take large sums of money are usually thought to be respectable citizens and trusted employees. They are often motivated by financial problems that their regular income is insufficient to handle, such as gambling debts, financial demands of a lover or spouse, and extensive medical bills for a relative.[42] Sullivan et al. note: "Embezzlers rationalize their theft by convincing themselves that they are merely 'borrowing' the money, that their employers are really crooks who deserve to lose the money, or that the employers will not miss the funds."[43]

Embezzlement occurs at all levels of business, from a clerk stealing from petty cash to the president of a company stealing large investment sums. Many cases go undetected or unprosecuted. Often an informal arrangement is worked out whereby the embezzler agrees to pay back the amount stolen and seek employment elsewhere— a solution that is often more effective than prosecution for recovering the stolen funds. Because a scandal involving employee dishonesty threatens the employer's public image and hurts future business, companies often prefer to handle the offense informally and privately.

Other examples of white-collar crime include income-tax evasion, expense-account fraud, misuse of government funds by business organizations, corporate bribes, and computer-related crime. The latter involves illegal use of computer technology. People who have access to a personal computer, a modem, and the correct password can transfer millions of dollars anywhere in the world.

American society, unfortunately, is generally tolerant of white-collar crime. A pickpocket who repeatedly steals small sums of money will likely go to prison, whereas someone who repeatedly fails to report large earnings for income-tax purposes is unlikely to face prosecution. This acceptance of white-collar crime appears to be due largely to the attitude that the victim is a large, impersonal organization (for example, the government) that will be unaffected. People who would never think of taking an item from a private home might feel no qualms about stealing "souvenirs" (towels, sheets, ashtrays) from hotels.

White-collar crime raises serious questions about our conceptions of crime and criminals. It suggests that crime is not necessarily concentrated among the young, the poor, and racial minorities and in our inner cities. Why, in our society, are burglars and pickpockets severely punished and stigmatized, whereas white-collar criminals who commit far more costly offenses are seldom prosecuted or viewed as criminals? Could it be due to the power structure of our society, in which the middle and upper classes define their own offenses as "excusable," but those committed by powerless groups as "intolerable"?

Victimless Crimes

With most crimes there is an identifiable victim, as with embezzlement or robbery. However, there are several crimes in which no one suffers, except perhaps the person who willfully decides to engage in the illegal activity. Victimless crimes include prostitution, vagrancy, pornography, gambling, drunkenness, curfew violations, loitering, drug abuse, fornication, and homosexuality between consenting adults. (Some of these actions are illegal in certain jurisdictions and legal in others.) Laws that make such behaviors criminal are designed to regulate people's private lives rather than to protect some citizens from others. The laws exist because powerful groups within society regard these acts as "undesirable."

The United States invests enormous resources in controlling victimless crime, as evidenced by arrest statistics. Nearly one-fourth of all arrests annually involve victimless crimes.[44] Organized crime makes much of its money from victimless crimes by providing illegal goods and services for which customers willingly pay. Prohibition is the classic example; organized crime supplied illegal alcoholic beverages at wildly inflated prices.

Because victimless crimes are considered less serious (by at least some segments of the population) and because these crimes consume excessive money and time that police and the courts could devote to reducing more serious crime, there have been efforts to decriminalize or repeal some of these laws. Alexander Smith and Harriet Pollack state:

> For every murderer arrested and prosecuted, literally dozens of gamblers, prostitutes, . . . and derelicts crowd our courts' dockets. If we took the numbers runners, the kids smoking pot, and winos out of the criminal justice system, we would substantially reduce the burden on the courts and the police. . . . Moral laws that do not reflect contemporary mores or that cannot be enforced should be removed from the penal code through legislative action because, at best, they undermine respect for the law.[45]

Criminal penalties for such crimes may also do more harm than good. For example, treating someone arrested for homosexual activity as a hardened criminal may well damage the person's self-concept and status in the community. Criminal penalties may also force the offenders to form a subculture in order to continue their illegal activity with greater safety. Such subcultures (for instance, of homosexuals and drug users) serve to separate them even further from the rest of society.

Sex Offenses

Sex offenses include forcible rape, prostitution, soliciting, statutory rape, fornication, sodomy, homosexuality, adultery, and incest.

In most states, only males are legally liable for rape by force. Forcible rape is a highly underreported crime, with less than one-quarter of the victims reporting the assault to the police.[46] Why? In about half of the cases the attacker is a friend or acquaintance of the victim; therefore some victims think police action will only create more interpersonal problems. Many victims are reluctant to report the offense because they believe (perhaps realistically) they have nothing to gain and more to lose by making a report, including social embarrassment, interrogation by sometimes-unsympathetic law enforcement officials, and humiliating public testimony in court about the offense. A danger to society of underreporting of rape is that the rapist is less likely to fear apprehension and thus more likely to seek out other victims.

Statutory rape involves sexual contact between a male who is of a legally responsible age (usually 18) and a female who is a willing participant but is below the legal age of consent (16 in some states and 18 in others). In most states, females are not defined as being liable for committing statutory rape. In some states, a charge of statutory rape can be made on the basis of sexual contact other than sexual intercourse (such as oral-genital contact).

There is considerable variation in homosexuality laws among states. Most states still define male homosexual acts between consenting adults as illegal, although some states have legalized such relations. Some states that prohibit male homosexuality between consenting adults do not prohibit such acts between adult females. (Homosexuality is further discussed in Chapter 6.)

CASE EXAMPLE 8.3   Kepone—A Case Example of Industrial Pollution

In the late 1970s, Life Science Products Company and Allied Chemical Corporation were found guilty of safety violations in producing Kepone and of contaminating the James River in Virginia with Kepone through dumping. Kepone is a chemical pesticide and a hydrocarbon similar to DDT. (DDT has been banned from use because of the adverse side effects it produces in humans and wildlife.)

Life Science was producing Kepone in Hopewell, Virginia, in the mid-1970s, under contract for Allied Chemical. Hopewell is a small town located on the James River. On July 23, 1975, a Virginia health official, Dr. Robert Jackson, inspected the facilities of Life Science. He was appalled at what he found. The "plant" consisted of a metal building and an abandoned service station. Safety precautions were virtually nonexistent. Kepone dust was everywhere in the town—in the air and on the soil. Traffic on streets was slowed by Kepone dust when the wind blew.

Examinations of employees revealed a number of medical problems and the danger that other disorders such as cancer might develop in the future from exposure to the chemical. The most common symptom was called "Kepone shakes," in which the entire body shook. Other symptoms included difficulty in breathing, tension, skin rash, and psychological disorientation. The plant was immediately closed. Yet further examination revealed additional alarming disclosures. Kepone was found to cause

---

Increased attention is now being given to sexual abuse of children. Such abuse includes sexual intercourse (genital or anal), masturbation, oral-genital contact, fondling, and exposure. There is no unambiguous definition of sexual abuse. Sexual intercourse with children is definitely abuse, but other forms of contact are more difficult to judge as being abusive. At some point, hugging, kissing, and fondling become inappropriate. Abusers may be parents, older siblings, extended relatives, friends, acquaintances, or strangers. (Sexual abuse is discussed in greater length in Chapter 6.)

Certain sex offenses (such as incest, rape, and homosexual contact with a minor) incite considerable repugnance among the general public, which results in harsh punishments for offenders. Unfortunately, less attention is given to helping the victims cope with their exploitation or to rehabilitating the offenders.

Homicide and Assault

Criminal homicide involves the unlawful killing of one person by another. Criminal assault is the unlawful application of physical force on another person. Most homicides are unintended outcomes of physical assaults. People get into physical fights because one (or both) is incensed about the other's actions and decides to retaliate. Provoking actions may include ridicule, flirting with the other's spouse or lover, and failure to repay a debt. Fighting is often an attempt by one or both to save face when challenged or degraded. Homicides frequently are "crimes of passion," occurring during a violent argument or other highly charged emotional situation.

Yet, some homicides are carefully planned and premeditated, including most gangland killings, killings to obtain an inheritance, and mercy killings. Homicides are also associated with robber-

cancer in rodents, to cause reproductive problems and infertility in birds, and to have the potential to kill both rodents and birds—and perhaps also humans. It was also discovered that 100,000 pounds of waste products containing Kepone had been dumped into the James River. The James empties into Chesapeake Bay, which has since been found to be contaminated with Kepone.

The Governor of Virginia closed the lower James River to fishing in 1975 after the contamination was revealed. Unfortunately, Kepone accumulates in fish. If the fish are eaten by humans, the chemical can cause cancer, liver problems, and reproductive problems. The Virginia fishing industry lost at least $10 million in 1976 alone. Many businesses associated with the fishing industry have since been forced to close.

A particular difficulty with Kepone is that it is bioaccumulative, which means the body retains all that it consumes rather than passing it off in wastes. Therefore, the greater the exposure, the greater the accumulation in the body and the greater the probability of future disorders, such as cancer. The long-term effects of Kepone contamination are as yet unknown.

A number of criminal and civil suits were filed against Life Science, the city of Hopewell, and Allied. The city of Hopewell was fined $10,000. Life Science was fined $3.8 billion and went bankrupt. Allied Chemical was fined $13.4 million (Allied's fine was reduced to $5 million, with Allied pledging another $8 million for cleanup efforts.) As is often the case with white-collar crime, no one served a prison sentence.

ies, during which the victim, the robber, or a law enforcement official may be shot.

Contrary to public stereotypes, the vast majority of murders occur between relatives, friends, and acquaintances. Statistically, we have more to fear from those we know than from strangers. For example, one study of homicides found that the murderer was a spouse in 8% of the cases, a relative other than a spouse in 9% of the cases, and an acquaintance or friend in 41% of the cases. Only 15% of the homicides were committed by a stranger, and in 27% the relationship between the victim and the murderer was unknown.[47]

Because of the overt physical damage from assault and homicide, these crimes generate the most fear. The police have a higher arrest rate (around 70%) in homicide cases than with any other crime—partly because they devote extensive attention to murders and partly because the questioning of the victim's friends, neighbors, and relatives usually identifies the killer.[48]

Theft

This category of crime refers to illegally taking someone's property without the person's consent. Offenses in this category range from pickpocketing and burglary to sophisticated multimillion-dollar swindles. Thieves range from grocery store clerks who take small amounts of food to people who concoct highly professional confidence schemes to swindle others out of thousands of dollars.

The most successful thieves (labeled professional thieves by the noted criminologist Edwin H. Sutherland[49]) engage in confidence games, forgery, expert safe cracking, counterfeiting, extortion (for example, blackmailing others who are involved in illegal acts), and organized shoplifting. Most such crimes require that professional thieves appear personable and trustworthy and that they be good actors to convince others that they are somebody who they are not. Professional thieves

CASE EXAMPLE 8.4   Murder and the Fall of an American Hero

Orenthal James (O. J.) Simpson was born and raised on Connecticut Street in Potrero Hill, a poor neighborhood in San Francisco, which O. J. once described as "your average black ghetto." His father, Jimmy, a custodian and cook, left home when O. J. was five. Jimmy was a homosexual who died of AIDS in 1985. O. J.'s mother, Eunice, worked long hours as a hospital orderly to support her four children.

As a youth, O. J. joined gangs, picked fights, stole hubcaps, shot craps, and played hookey from school. After a gang fight at age 15 landed O. J. briefly in jail, Lefty Gordon, the supervisor of the local recreational center, arranged for baseball great Willie Mays to meet with the boy. The meeting left a lasting impression on O. J., who stated "He made me realize that we all have it in ourselves to be heroes."

O. J. Simpson

O. J. applied himself to football. He didn't have the grades for a four-year school, so he attended City College of San Francisco, where he set records as a running back. In his junior year he transferred to the University of Southern California. O. J. led USC to two Rose Bowls, and in his senior year he won the Heisman Trophy, given annually to the best player in college football.

use sophisticated, nonviolent techniques. Their crimes are carefully planned, and they tend to steal as a regular business. They define themselves as thieves, have a value system supportive of their career, and often are respected by their colleagues and by law enforcement officials. Because of their cunning and skill, they seldom are arrested. They often justify their activities by claiming that they are simply capitalizing on the fact that all people are dishonest and would probably also be full-time thieves if they had sufficient skills.

Semiprofessional thieves engage in armed robberies, burglaries, holdups, and larcenies that do not involve much detailed planning. Some semiprofessional thieves work alone, holding up service stations, convenience stores, liquor stores,

and the like. Semiprofessionals often wind up spending substantial portions of their lives in prison because they commit the types of crimes that are harshly punished by courts. They also tend to be repeat offenders for similar crimes. Often they define themselves as products and victims of a corrupt and unjust system, having started their careers in low-income and ghetto neighborhoods. They adjust fairly well in prison, because other inmates often have similar backgrounds, lifestyles, and views on life. However, as a group they are poor parole risks.[50]

Amateur thieves are individuals who steal infrequently. In contrast to professional and semiprofessional thieves, these individuals generally define themselves as respectable, law-abiding cit-

After his triumphs at USC, O. J. was drafted by the National Football League. In 1973, while playing halfback for the Buffalo Bills, he broke the single-season rushing record held by Jim Brown.

The world of advertising in the 1970s was searching for a "breakthrough black man" who had the right look, the right smile, and the right nickname. O. J. was it. His magnetic image won him several lucrative advertising contracts.

Even before his retirement from pro football after 11 seasons, he started acting in movies and on TV. He became a sports broadcaster for NBC and ABC. He also was inducted in the football Hall of Fame.

But apparently there was another side to O. J. Simpson. A married man with two children, he met Nicole Brown, a very attractive teenager. Shortly after she turned 19, they began living together. Eventually they married, had two children of their own, and lived a glamorous life in their West Los Angeles mansion. However, on at least eight occasions, police were called to their home to settle domestic fights. In 1989, after one particularly brutal fight, witnesses said O. J. had repeatedly screamed "I'll kill you!" The Los Angeles city attorney filed charges against Simpson for wife beating, and he pleaded no contest.

In 1992 Nicole and O. J. finally divorced. Afterward they continued to see each other, and O. J. hoped for a reconciliation. But, in the spring of 1994, friends say Nicole shattered O. J.'s dreams by telling him she had decided not to reconcile.

During the evening of June 12, 1994, Nicole Simpson was brutally stabbed to death outside her condominium. Also brutally stabbed to death was Ronald Goldman, a friend of hers who reportedly was returning a pair of sunglasses she had left earlier in the evening at the restaurant in which he worked.

A few days later, O. J. was arrested and charged with these murders. If convicted, he could receive a life sentence.

izens. Their criminal acts tend to be crude, unsophisticated, and unplanned, with some offenders being juveniles. Examples of offenses by this group include stealing from employers, shoplifting, stealing an unguarded bicycle, taking an auto for a joyride, taking soda from a truck, and breaking into a home to take CDs or beer. Businesses and industries suffer substantial losses from amateur thieves who are either employees or customers.

Juvenile Delinquency

CRIME AMONG YOUTH

According to official crime statistics, 16% of all people arrested are under age 18.[51] A fair number of these arrests are for crimes that have already been discussed—thefts, robberies, assaults, and rapes. Yet it should be noted that one reason why juveniles have such a high arrest rate is that a majority of the arrests are for status offenses— that is, acts that are defined as illegal if committed by juveniles but not if committed by adults. Status offenses include being truant, having sexual relations, running away from home, being ungovernable, violating curfew, and being beyond the control of parents.

Police arrests of lower-class juveniles are far higher than for middle- and upper-class juveniles.[52] This is partly due to the fact that police are more inclined to arrest lower-class juveniles than middle- and upper-class juveniles.[53] After reviewing a number of studies on the relationships between delinquency and poverty, Kornblum and Julian conclude that these two variables are inter-related in a complex manner. Middle- and upper-class juveniles tend to commit nuisance crimes at about the same rates as lower-class youths, but lower-class youths commit higher rates of serious crimes, such as homicide.[54]

GANGS

Violent delinquent urban gangs have become a major social problem in the United States. It is thought that Los Angeles County currently has the most youth gangs and members in the nation; estimates range from 300 gangs with 30,000 members to 500 gangs with 50,000 members.[55] Morales has categorized youth gangs into the following four types: criminal gangs, conflict gangs, retreatist gangs, and cult/occult gangs.[56]

Criminal gangs have as a primary goal material gain through criminal activities, including theft of property from people or premises, extortion, fencing, and drug trafficking (especially of rock cocaine).

Conflict gangs are turf oriented. They engage in violent conflict with individuals of rival groups that invade their neighborhood or commit acts that they consider degrading or insulting. Respect is highly valued and defended. Latino gangs often fall into this category. Sweeney notes that the Code of the Barrio mandates that gang members watch out for their neighborhood and be willing to die for it.[57]

Retreatist gangs focus on getting "high" or "loaded" on alcohol, cocaine, marijuana, heroin, or other drugs. Individuals tend to join this type of gang in order to secure continued access to drugs. In contrast to criminal gangs that become involved with drugs for financial profit, retreatist gangs become involved with drugs for consumption.

Cult/occult gangs engage in devil or evil worship. *Cult* refers to systematic worshiping of evil or the Devil; *occult* implies keeping something secret or hidden, or a belief in supernatural or mysterious powers. The Charles Manson family (described earlier in this chapter) is one of the better-known cult/occult groups. Some occult groups place extensive emphasis on sexuality and violence, believing that, by sexually violating an innocent child or virgin, they have defiled Christianity. Not all cult/occult gangs are involved in criminal activity. Unlike the other three gang types, which are composed primarily of juveniles, the majority of occult groups are composed of adults.

THE CRIMINAL JUSTICE SYSTEM

The criminal justice system consists of the police, the courts, and the correctional system. It is perceived by many Americans as being cumbersome, ineffective, irrational, and unjust, fostering a perception that "crime does pay." Some segments of the population are suspicious of the police and believe that they abuse their powers. Other segments, particularly the middle and upper classes, see the police as unduly hampered in their work by cumbersome arrest and interrogation procedures designed to protect the civil rights of suspected offenders.

Courts are sharply criticized for their long delays in bringing cases to conclusion and for their sentencing procedures. Opinion polls show that over 80% of the population believes that courts are not harsh enough on offenders. Courts are also criticized for (1) varying widely in the harshness of sentences meted out for apparently similar offenses and (2) giving harsh sentences to "ordinary offenders" but light fines to white-collar offenders.

Prisons, too, have been sharply criticized, as they are viewed as failing to rehabilitate their populations. The rate of recidivism (that is, return to crime) is alarmingly high. Over half of those released from prison later return after being convicted of another crime.[58] Indeed, far from rehabilitating inmates, prisons are accused of being schools for crime.

In all societies criminal justice systems face a conflict between two goals: crime control and due process. The crime-control goal involves the need to curb crime and protect society from law breakers. It emphasizes speedy arrest and punishment for those who commit crimes. The due-process goal involves the need to protect and preserve the rights and liberties of individuals. Some societies are police states that use strong-arm tactics to control their citizens, displaying little concern for individual rights. At the other extreme are societies in which individuals flagrantly break the law, with the government having neither the power nor the respect of its citizens to uphold the law. American society seeks to strike a balance between the conflicting goals of crime control and due process, but the struggle is constant. At times the same individual may seek to have one goal emphasized in one situation but the conflicting goal emphasized in a different setting. For example, a homeowner may want speedy justice when her house is burglarized but may seek to use all the due-process protections when accused of income-tax evasion.

We will now take a closer look at each of these three components of the criminal justice system.

The Police

Police officers are the gatekeepers for the criminal justice system. Whom they arrest determines whom the courts and corrections will have to deal with. As we have seen, nearly everyone commits an occasional crime. Police cannot arrest everyone, or the jails, courts, and prisons would be overloaded and our society would probably collapse. Therefore, police exercise considerable discretion in which laws they vigorously enforce and which types of offenders they arrest. For example, police are more likely to arrest lower-income than middle-income youths.

It should be noted that only a small part of a police department's effort is directly focused on making arrests. Police officers classify as "criminal" only about 10–20% of the calls and incidents they handle on a given day.[59]

David Peterson has noted that the role of a police officer is usually best conceptualized as that of a "peace officer" or even "social worker," rather than as a "law enforcement officer":

A prominent theme in the literature dealing with the work behavior of the police stresses that the role of the uniformed patrol officer is not a strict legalistic one. The patrol officer is routinely involved in tasks that have little relation to police work in terms of controlling crime. His activities on the beat are often centered as much on assisting citizens as upon offenses; he is frequently called upon to perform a "supportive" function as well as an enforcement function. Existing research on the uniformed police officer in field situations indicates that more than half his time is spent as an amateur social worker assisting people in various ways. Moreover, several officers have suggested that the role of the uniformed patrol officer is not sharply defined and that the mixture of enforcement and service functions creates conflict and uncertainties for individual officers.[60]

Service functions of police may include giving first aid to injured people, rescuing trapped animals, and directing traffic. When police do perform law enforcement functions, they squarely face trying to achieve the proper balance between the crime-control model and the due-process model. There is considerable pressure to swiftly apprehend certain law breakers—murderers, rapists, and arsonists. Yet they are expected to perform according to the due-process model so that the legal rights of those arrested are not violated. James Coleman and Donald Cressey note: "Police officers operate more like diplomats than like soldiers engaged in a war on crime."[61]

In many areas of the nation police do not have sufficient resources to do their job effectively. Often there is also considerable hostility toward police officers. Part of this hostility may result from the fact that everyone commits an occasional crime; people may be suspicious of police officers because they fear possible apprehension. In addition, some people (particularly the poor and minority group members) have been harassed by being picked up for crimes they clearly did not commit and by being subjected to long "third-degree" interrogations. Also, some hostility toward the police stems from well-publicized incidents of police corruption (for example, taking bribes), particularly in larger cities.

The Courts

HOW THE COURTS WORK

Criminal justice in the United States is an adversary system. That is, a prosecuting attorney first presents the state's evidence against a defendant, and that defendant, presumed innocent until proved guilty, then has an opportunity to refute the charges with the assistance of a defense attorney.

It should be noted that, contrary to public opinion, over 90% of convictions in the United States are obtained not in court but through plea bargaining between the prosecuting attorney and the defendant, who is often represented by a defense attorney in the plea-bargaining process.[62] For a plea of guilty, a suspect may receive a more lenient sentence, have certain charges dropped, or have the charge reduced to a lesser offense. Plea bargaining is not legally binding in court, but the judge usually goes along with the arrangement. Plea bargaining is highly controversial. It does save taxpayers considerable expense, because court trials are costly. But it may in some cases circumvent due-process protections if an innocent person charged with some serious offense is pressured into pleading guilty to a reduced charge.

There are four key positions in a court: the prosecuting attorney, the defense attorney, the judge, and the jury.

Prosecuting attorneys have considerable discretionary authority in choosing whether to seek a conviction for those arrested and how vigorously to prosecute a defendant. Prosecuting attorneys are either elected or appointed to office and are therefore political figures who must periodically seek reelection or reappointment. Therefore they seek to prosecute most vigorously the cases they perceive the community is most concerned about. Prosecuting attorneys usually focus police departments' attention on which violations will be further processed by the criminal justice system.

Defense attorneys are supposed to represent their clients' interest before the criminal justice system. Impoverished individuals are provided, at the state's expense, a court-appointed attorney.

The skills and competence of the defense attorney are major factors in determining whether a defendant will be found innocent or guilty if there is a trial. The wealthy not only can retain the best attorneys but also can afford additional resources (such as a private investigator) to help to prepare a better defense.

Sometimes the poor are shortchanged by court-appointed defense attorneys, who tend to be young, inexperienced practitioners or less competent older lawyers who resort to this type of practice in order to survive professionally. Because these defense attorneys depend on the good opinion of their legal colleagues (including judges and prosecuting attorneys) to stay in practice, the client's best interest sometimes receives secondary priority.[63]

If a defendant is being prosecuted for a minor offense, the case is generally presented before a lower-court judge, without a jury. For a serious offense the defendant first receives a preliminary hearing, which is solely for the benefit of the suspect. At the hearing the prosecutor presents evidence against the suspect, and the judge decides whether that evidence is sufficient to warrant further legal proceedings. If the evidence is insufficient, the suspect is discharged. If the evidence is judged sufficient, the accused is held over to await a court trial. (Often the held-over cases are then decided by plea bargaining before they go to trial.)

A jury is supposed to be a cross-section of the community. However, there is a tendency for retired persons, housewives with grown children, and the unemployed—those who are not inconvenienced by the duty—to be overrepresented on juries. Juries use the standard of reasonable doubt to decide if the prosecution has provided enough evidence for conviction. In order to obtain the conviction of a defendant charged with a crime, all twelve members of the jury must vote "guilty." A hung jury occurs when a jury is unable to reach a decision. Because of group pressure, only rarely does a lone juror produce a hung jury.

Under the bail system, accused people are allowed to deposit money or credit with the court to obtain a release from jail while awaiting trial. Bail is designed to ensure that the suspect will appear for trial. The amount of bail is set by the court and varies according to the offense and judge's attitudes toward the suspect. The bail system severely discriminates against the poor. Anyone unable to raise enough money must stay in jail while awaiting trial—which may take several months. Those who cannot post bail have less opportunity to prepare a good defense because they are locked up. Also, their case is further prejudiced when they do appear in court because they are brought into the courtroom in handcuffs and often without proper grooming. Being locked up before trial is a form of punishment that runs counter to the notion that the suspect is innocent (and should be treated as such) until proved guilty. In some cases a suspect spends more time in jail awaiting trial than she or he spends in jail if found guilty.

After defendants have been found guilty or have pleaded guilty, they return to the courtroom for sentencing. Judges usually have fairly wide discretion in assigning sentences; for example, they can place one murderer on probation, commit another to prison, and, in those states where capital punishment is legal, order the execution of a third. Judges base their sentences on such factors as the seriousness of the crime, the motives for the crime, the background of the offender, and their attitudes toward the offender.

Judges vary greatly in the extent to which they send convicted offenders to prison, use probation, or assign fines. Concern about disparities in sentences has grown in recent years. Coleman and Cressey note:

> Judges and other sentencing authorities are on the spot. They are supposed to give equal punishments, no matter what the social status of the defendants involved. Yet they are supposed to give individual punishments because the circumstances of each crime and the motivations of each criminal are always different and a just punishment for one burglar or car thief may be completely inappropriate for another. . . . As judges try to satisfy these conflicting demands, they are bound to be denounced as unfair. The judge's task, like the police officer's task, is to walk a thin line between the crime control model

> and the due process model, balancing demands for repressing crime against demands for human rights and freedom.[64]

JUVENILE COURTS

The first juvenile court was established in Cook County, Illinois, in 1899. The philosophy of the juvenile court is that it should act in the best interests of the child, as parents should act. In essence, juvenile courts have a treatment orientation. Adult criminal proceedings focus on charging the defendant with a specific crime, on holding a public trial to determine whether the defendant is guilty as charged, and on sentencing the defendant if he or she is found guilty. In contrast, the focus in juvenile courts is on the current psychological, physical, emotional, and educational needs of children, as opposed to punishment for misdeeds. Reform or treatment of the child is the goal, even though the child or his or her family may not necessarily agree that the court's decision is in the child's best interests. Figure 8.1 presents a model of the operations of a typical juvenile justice system.

Of course, not all juvenile court judges live up to these principles. In practice, some juvenile judges focus more on punishing than on treating juvenile offenders. There is also a danger that court appearances by children can have adverse labeling effects. A Supreme Court decision in the famous Gault case of May 15, 1967, restored to juveniles procedural safeguards that had been ignored—including notification of charges, protection against self-incrimination, confrontation, and cross-examination.[65] There is currently considerable effort to have juvenile probation officers provide informal supervision for youths who commit "minor" violations. With informal supervision, youthful offenders receive counseling and guidance and do not appear in court.

Correctional Systems

Current correctional systems in the United States and throughout the world contain conflicting objectives. Some components are punishment oriented, whereas others are treatment oriented.

FIGURE 8.1

Operations of the Juvenile Justice System

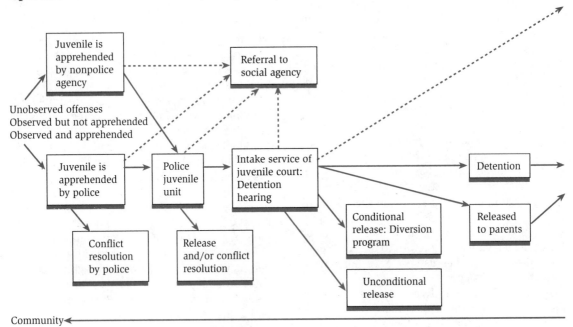

Community◄──

Source: "Youth, Delinquency, and the Juvenile Justice System," by Galan Janeksela, pp. 269–295, in Dae Chang (ed.), *Fundamentals of Criminal Justice.* Copyright © 1977 by Paladin House. Reprinted by permission of Galan Janeksela.

A manifestation of this confusion is the existence, side by side, of correctional programs intended primarily for deterrence and retribution and other programs designed to reform offenders. Only rarely do punitive and treatment components complement each other. Generally, the two components, when combined, result in a system that is ineffective and inefficient in curbing criminal activity. In the past several years correctional systems have moved toward using a more punitive approach.

THE PUNITIVE APPROACH

Throughout history various approaches have been used to punish offenders. These methods include physical torture, social humiliation, financial penalties, exile, the death penalty, and imprisonment.

Physical Torture. Most societies have at one time or another used this method. Specific examples of corporal (bodily) punishment have included stocks, whipping, flogging, branding, hard labor, confinement in irons and cages, arm twisting, and mutilation of body parts. Corporal punishment was particularly popular during the medieval period. Virtually no types of corporal punishment are assigned today by European or U.S. courts.

Social Humiliation. Reducing the social status of an offender is another method of punishment. This approach flourished in the 16th and 17th centuries, and remnants exist today. Specific techniques included some that also had corporal-punishment facets: the stocks, the pillory, the ducking stool, branding, and the brank. (The brank was a small cage that was placed over the offender's head. It had a bar that was inserted

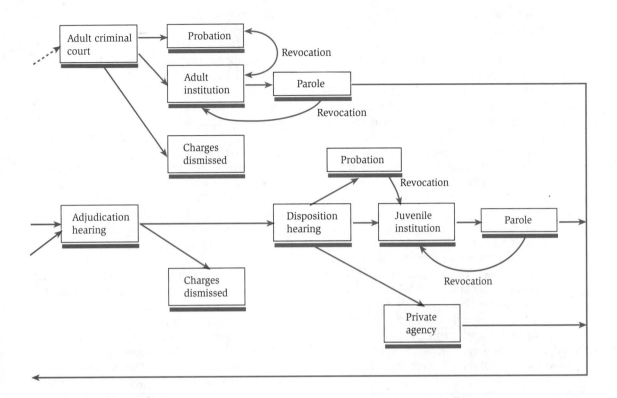

into the mouth of the offender to prevent him or her from talking; occasionally this bar had spikes in it.) Some of these punishments were temporary—for example, the stocks—whereas others had a permanent effect on the offender—for example, branding. One of the objectives of the permanent method was to deter future crime by publicly humiliating offenders. However, the techniques frequently had the opposite effect, as they overtly labeled the offender, thereby making it difficult for him or her to secure employment and earn a living in a law-abiding manner.

Deprivation of civil rights is another approach that has been used for centuries to humiliate the convicted offender socially. The principal rights that are taken away from convicted felons by most states in this country are (1) the right to vote while in prison or while on probation or parole; (2) the right to hold public office; (3) the right to practice certain professions, such as the law; and (4) the right to own or possess firearms.[66]

Financial Penalties. The use of fines in criminal law became widespread in this country about a century ago and is now by far the most frequent court approach to punishing offenders. More than 75% of all penalties imposed at present are fines.[67] The advantages of a fine are: (1) it provides revenue to the state; (2) it costs the state almost nothing to administer, especially in comparison to the cost of imprisonment; (3) the amount of the fine can easily be adjusted to the enormity of the offense, the reaction of the public, and the wealth and character of the offender; (4) it inflicts a material type of suffering; and (5) it can easily be paid back if the alleged offender is later found innocent. A serious disadvantage is that it is highly discriminatory toward the poor, who have less ability to pay. Sweden has found a way to curb this discrimination by the creation of day fines, in which the offender pays the equivalent of the amount earned in a specified number of days of work rather than a flat amount as a fine.

Courts are also increasingly requiring, in their sentencing decisions, that the offender make restitution payments to the victim that are in line with the amount of injury. This kind of reaction to crime is more treatment oriented, as it attempts to give the offender an opportunity to "make good." Restitution is, of course, also advantageous to the victim. Restitution and reparation are used most frequently for minor offenses. Generally, the offender is placed on probation, with restitution being a condition of probation. Some of the work of probation departments now involves acting as a collection agency to obtain restitution payments from probationers.

Exile.   Almost all societies have exiled certain offenders, particularly political criminals. Deportation on a large scale, however, has been used only since about the 16th century. The United States has been deporting alien criminals for decades. In addition, many counties and municipalities in the United States give people accused or convicted of a crime a set number of hours to "get out and stay out" of their jurisdiction.

Death Penalty.   The extent to which the death penalty has been used and the methods for executing offenders have varied considerably in different societies. Criminals have been hanged, electrocuted, shot, burned, gassed, drowned, boiled in oil, broken at the wheel, guillotined, stoned, put in an iron coffin, pierced with a sharp stake, stabbed with a sword, and poisoned. In essence, almost every lethal method has at one time or another been used by some society.

The death penalty has been used in the United States throughout most of our history. In colonial America "witches" in some communities were burned at the stake. While the West was being developed, individuals who stole a horse or committed certain other crimes were sometimes shot or hanged (sometimes by a lynch mob or a "kangaroo court"). From the time of the Civil War until the recent past, African Americans in the South who were thought to have committed a serious crime against whites (for example, rape) were sometimes lynched. Gas chambers, firing squads, lethal injections, hangings, and electric chairs are the current methods of execution used in the United States.

From 1967 to 1977, the death penalty was not used in this country, partly due to U.S. Supreme Court decisions that ruled the penalty unconstitutional. In October 1976, the Supreme Court changed its position on this issue and ruled that states may execute murderers under certain guidelines. On January 17, 1977, Gary Gilmore was the first person in a decade to be executed, and the sensational case attracted national attention. Gilmore was convicted of ruthlessly killing several people. Since 1977 the number of offenders executed annually in the United States has gradually been increasing. The continued use of the death penalty remains a controversial national issue.

The primary argument for using the death penalty for certain crimes is that it is assumed to have a deterrent effect. This assumption is questionable, as statistics generally do *not* show a corresponding decrease in serious crime rates when a country adopts the death penalty.[68] Also, there is no clear-cut evidence that, when a country discontinues use of the death penalty, there will be an increase in serious crimes.[69] Additional arguments for use of the death penalty are that (1) some crimes (such as brutal, premeditated murder) are so abominable that the offender deserves the ultimate punishment, and (2) it is less expensive to society to put hardened criminals to death than to incarcerate them for life.

Arguments against use of the death penalty are as follows: (1) it constitutes cruel and unusual punishment, being the ultimate punishment; (2) if the convicted person is later found innocent, the penalty is irreparable; (3) the "eye for an eye" approach is inconsistent with civilized, humanitarian ideals; (4) the "right to life" is a basic right that should not be infringed on; and (5) the death penalty appears to be assigned in a discriminatory manner (African Americans and Latinos are proportionately much more likely than whites to be sentenced to death).

Imprisonment.   The penal system currently plays an enormous role in our society. Thousands of people are incarcerated each year. As noted, the recidivism rate (return to prison after release) is estimated to be over 50%, which raises questions about the effectiveness of prisons in curbing future criminal activity.[70] Since 1970 several large-scale prison revolts (for example, Attica Prison, in New York, in 1971 and New Mexico State Penitentiary in 1980) have raised the concern of the general public.

Conditions within prisons prior to the 20th century were deplorable. Frequently the young were placed with hardened criminals, and women were not separated from men. Only custodial care was provided, often with "hard-labor" work projects. There were a number of prison reform studies from 1700 to 1850 that criticized within prisons the use of intoxicating liquors, sexual orgies, gambling, and the personal lewdness of security officers. Some prisons kept inmates in solitary confinement for months at a time, and corporal punishment was frequently used.

Since 1800 prisons have become more specialized. Jails are used for shorter sentences and for those awaiting trial. Separate institutions have been built for the young, for women, and for those labeled as criminally insane. Prisons also have various degrees of security: maximum, moderate, and minimum. Special programs have been developed to meet individual needs of inmates (for example, alcohol and drug abuse programs, educational and vocational training, medical and dental programs, and recreational programs).

Prisons are still distasteful and sometimes physically dangerous institutions. There is now the danger of AIDS being transmitted by sexual assaults in prison. However, in the past 100 years the horrors of prison life have been somewhat reduced. In addition to rehabilitative programs, strides have been made in safeguarding civil rights of inmates, abandoning long-term solitary confinement, improving methods of discipline, promoting contact between inmates and the outside world, providing libraries, reducing the monotony of prison life, and improving diet, ventilation, and cleanliness within the facilities. Gone are such humiliating approaches as shaving the head, chaining inmates, issuing striped clothing, and using the ball and chain. Also, corporal-punishment methods, such as whipping, are no

longer officially approved. The most severe punishment that remains for many prisoners is their constant fear of being victimized by their fellow inmates.

Since 1975 there has been a dramatic increase in the number of people sentenced to prison by the courts.[71] Part of this increase is due to the mushrooming of drug-related convictions, including drug trafficking convictions. Another reason is that our society has become more conservative and therefore is demanding a more punitive approach (imprisonment) to handling convicted offenders. As a result of the increased use of imprisonment, many prisons are currently overcrowded. An alternative to imprisonment that is being used for less serious criminal offenders is home confinement with the use of electronic surveillance monitors to ensure that the convicted offenders remain at home.

The first American institution built specifically to house juvenile offenders was opened in New York City in 1825. There are now over 300 state and local training schools for juveniles. It has always been contended that such institutions are not prisons, but schools to educate and reform the young. However, until the recent past most were best described as prisons in terms of functions, methods of discipline, and daily routine. Even today a few are still prison oriented. One of the most significant developments in juvenile institutions was cottage-type architecture, which provides a more homelike setting. The first such juvenile homes were established in Massachusetts and Ohio in 1858. Such settings facilitate, but do not necessarily ensure, a treatment orientation.

Objectives of Incarceration. The conflict between the punitive approach and the treatment approach to corrections is strikingly clear in our penal system. Until a few centuries ago the purpose of incarceration was strictly to punish an offender. In the 20th century there has been an increased emphasis on treatment and a shift away from punishment. There are several reasons for this shift. Practically all prisoners return to society, and it is becoming clear that punitive approaches alone do not produce the desired reformation. Locking a person in an artificial environment, without providing rehabilitative programs, will not sufficiently prepare that person to be a productive citizen on his or her return. Moreover, in this era of accountability, the 50% recidivism rate is unacceptable, especially because the annual cost of incarceration per inmate is more than $25,000.[72]

The most specific objectives for imprisonment are: (1) to reform offenders so they will no longer commit crimes; (2) to incapacitate criminals so they cannot commit crimes for a period of time, thereby protecting society; (3) to achieve retribution for the victim and, to some extent, for the state; and (4) to serve as a warning to the general public, thereby having a deterrent effect. A major problem with these objectives is that some components conflict with others. The infliction of pain and suffering is aimed at meeting the retribution and deterrence objectives, but most punitive approaches are counterproductive in terms of having reformative value.

There are also some dangers with using imprisonment. Association with other offenders may result in inmates learning additional law-breaking techniques. Moreover, incarceration may label the offender as a "law breaker." According to labeling theory, if convicted offenders are related to as "dangerous, second-class citizens who are law violators," they may begin to perceive themselves as being "law violating."[73] They will then play that role upon their release.

In addition, as Sutherland and Cressey note, "Hatred of the criminal by society results in hatred of society by the criminal."[74] Relating to criminals as being dangerous, segregating them, and making them keep their distance (both while they are incarcerated and following their release) may force them into a career of criminal activity.

A third danger of long-term imprisonment is "institutionalization." Some prisoners, especially those who have had problems in adjusting to outside society, may eventually prefer prison life over outside society. After several years they may actually feel more comfortable being confined (with their basic needs being met) than having to return to the world outside, which will have undergone substantial change since their entry into prison. They will also have established a circle of friends

Does imprisonment permanently label individuals as "law breakers"? According to labeling theory, if convicted offenders are treated as "dangerous law violators," the likelihood is great that they will play such a role upon their release.

within the prison from whom they receive respect. If they encounter problems on their return to society (for example, being unemployed and broke), they may yearn at some level to return to prison.

THE TREATMENT APPROACH

There are literally hundreds of treatment programs available in the corrections system. Space limitations prevent an exhaustive discussion of these programs, but a brief summary of major approaches will be covered in this section. It is necessary, however, to remember that the punitive approach has the continuous effect of decreasing the efficiency and effectiveness of treatment programs.

Individualized treatment for offenders has been increasingly popular since the 19th century. It developed as a reaction to the classical school, which advocated uniform penalties for criminals. Throughout history, however, there has been a dual standard of justice, with the rich and politically influential being (1) much less likely to be charged with a crime, (2) much less likely to be found guilty when accused—because of their "character," their position in society, and their better legal representation; and (3) much less likely to receive a severe sentence if found guilty.

Counseling. Both one-to-one counseling and group counseling are used in prisons and by probation and parole officers. The aim is to identify the specific problems of each offender (including the reasons that motivated him or her to become involved in criminal activity) and then to develop programs for solving these problems. The inmate's needs may cover a wide area, including medical, psychological, and financial matters; drug use and abuse patterns; family and peer relationships; housing; education; vocational training; and employment. Attention is also given to the criminal's attitudes, motives, group and peer relationships, and rationalizations regarding criminality.

The effectiveness of counselors (social workers, probation and parole officers, psychologists, vocational rehabilitation counselors) is somewhat mitigated by their "dual" role perception by offenders. Some inmates view them as true helpers, whereas others view them as authority figures in control of rewards and punishments. Offenders with the second perception are reluctant to discuss socially unacceptable needs and motives or to establish a close relationship for fear that information divulged will be used against them.

Prison Education. Education in prison has two objectives: (1) to give inmates formal academic training comparable to schools and (2) to resocialize inmates' attitudes and behaviors. To accomplish these objectives, prisons use TV programs, movies, libraries, lectures, classroom instruction in academic subjects (covering elementary, secondary, and sometimes even college-level material), religious programs, group discussions, and recreational programs. It should be noted, however, that the bitter attitude that most inmates have toward prison and the prison administration often interferes with their accomplishing educational objectives.

Vocational Training. The objective of these programs is to give inmates a job skill suitable to their capacities that will prepare them for employment on release. The quality of such programs in institutions throughout the country varies greatly. In many prisons, vocational training is defined as the maintenance work of the institution: laundry, cooking, custodial work, minor repairs, dishwashing. For a period of time vocational training was considered the main component of rehabilitation, but now rehabilitation is seen as covering many other areas.

Prison Labor. The idea that prisoners should perform work has always existed. Originally, labor in prisons was seen as a method of punishment. England, for example, for a long time had inmates carry a cannonball on treadmills that had a meter measuring the number of units of work produced. For each meal, inmates had to produce a certain number of units. Additional units were assigned for misconduct.

Currently there are two conflicting conceptions of work: (1) it should be productive and train inmates for employment upon their release, and (2) it should be hard, unpleasant, or monotonous for retributive purposes. The second view is still rationalized by some authorities as also having a reformative function; it is said to teach discipline, obedience, and conformity and to develop an appreciation for avoiding criminal activity.

Convict labor has been used for building roads, running agricultural farms, fighting fires, conducting insect control programs, doing lumber-camp work, doing laundry, making state license plates, and performing a wide variety of other tasks. Work and educational release programs in jails and in some prisons allow release of inmates during the day so they may work or attend school while being locked up in the evening.

Good Time. Good-time legislation permits a prison review board to release a prisoner early if she or he has maintained good conduct. Most good-time laws specify that, for every month of acceptable behavior, a certain number of days will be deducted from the sentence. Good-time laws are designed to make inmates responsible for their conduct, to provide an incentive for good conduct and rehabilitation efforts, and to reduce discipline problems within prisons.

Indeterminate sentences, which were first established in the 1800s, have similar objectives. Many sentences are indeterminate, with a minimum and a maximum limit assigned to the amount of time an inmate can be incarcerated. In recent years, however, a movement to return to determinate sentencing has gained considerable support.

Parole and Probation. Parole is the conditional release of a prisoner serving an indeterminate or unexpired sentence. Parole is granted by an administrative board (parole board) or an executive. Parolees are considered "in custody" and are required to maintain acceptable conduct and avoid criminal activity. Parole is designed both to punish (certain behavior is restricted, and there is a threat of return to prison) and to treat the offender (a parole officer generally counsels and helps the parolee meet his or her needs).

Probation is granted by the courts. It involves suspending the sentence of a convicted offender and giving him or her freedom during good behavior under the supervision of a probation officer. Probationers are viewed as undergoing treatment. There is, however, the threat of punishment; if the conditions of probation are violated, the offender will be sent to prison. Similar to parole, probation contains reformation and retribution components.

Probation and parole officers have a dual role responsibility: a police role and a rehabilitative role. The probation and parole officer functions in the "police" or authority role by closely monitoring the activities of probationers and parolees to observe whether they are violating laws or violating the conditions of their parole/probation. Those being supervised are continually aware that the probation/parole officer has the authority to initiate procedures to revoke the probation/parole, which will send them to prison. Many probationers and parolees are distrustful of the criminal justice system and are therefore wary of anyone (including probation and parole officers) who is associated with this system.

This "police" role conflicts at times with the second primary function of probation and parole officers: the rehabilitative role. For rehabilitation to be most effective, the counselee must trust the counselor, must feel free to reveal socially unacceptable attitudes and activities to the counselor, and must form a close working relationship with the counselor. Obviously, those probationers and parolees who view their supervising officer primarily in the "police" role are likely to avoid forming a counseling relationship with that person.

HOW TO REDUCE CRIME AND DELINQUENCY

The heading of this section may be inappropriate. Societies have been trying for centuries to reduce crime through a number of different approaches, yet the rate of crime seems to fluctuate independently of direct crime-suppression efforts. About 25 years ago former President Nixon declared war on crime, and the federal government has since spent billions trying to curb crime. Yet the rate continues to increase. The prospects for reducing crime in the future remain uncertain, because we do not as yet know enough about how to prevent people from committing crimes or how to reform them after they do. Nevertheless, this section will summarize major approaches that have been advanced to improve the situation. (You will note that some of the proposals are contradictory.) We will consider three general areas:

1. Increasing or decreasing sentences.
2. Reforming the correctional system.
3. Preventing crime in the first place.

Increasing or Decreasing Sentences

There are conflicting opinions concerning the appropriateness of various sentences as related to the crime committed. Suggestions to improve the effects of various sentences include shortening the times between arrest, conviction, and punishment; imposing harsher sentences; permanently imprisoning repeat offenders; increasing prosecution of white-collar criminals; creating uniform sentences; decriminalizing victimless offenses; and imposing stricter gun control.

INSTITUTING SWIFT AND CERTAIN PUNISHMENT

It is generally agreed that the deterrent value of punishment decreases as the time lag between the crime and the eventual punishment increases. Only a fraction of those who commit crimes are arrested, and only a fraction of those arrested are ever found guilty. All too often crime does pay—particularly white-collar crime and organized crime. Criminal court proceedings commonly drag on for months and even years: during this time offenders use due-process maneuvers in the hope that public anger over their crimes will dissipate and they will either be found innocent or have the charges reduced. Swifter action in catching, convicting, and punishing a greater percentage of law breakers will, it is argued, lead to greater respect for the law and curb crime. The argument against swifter action is that it would conflict with due-process protections and might result in a higher number of innocent people being arrested, convicted, and incarcerated.

IMPOSING HARSHER SENTENCES

This approach is also based on the assumption that punishment has a deterrent effect. Advocates demand longer prison sentences and increased use of capital punishment. The reasoning is that lengthier sentences will reduce crime because criminals obviously cannot victimize citizens when they are locked up.

Opponents of this approach claim that longer sentences may increase crime rates rather than reduce them; because practically all people sent to prison return to society, lengthier sentences may simply increase the bitterness of those serving time, reduce their respect for our laws and criminal justice system, and give them extended training in breaking the law through association with other hardened criminals. Opponents also note that imprisonment is expensive for society; it costs more per year to send someone to prison than to college.

SEPARATING REPEAT OFFENDERS FROM SOCIETY

Crimes of violence (arson, rape, armed robbery; murder) are of particular concern to society, as are certain other offenses, such as repeated hard-drug trafficking. According to some authorities, repeated arrests and convictions for these offenses demonstrate that the offenders are so dangerous that protection of society must become the primary concern. It is further asserted that, because past efforts at reformation have not been effective, future efforts are not likely to be either. For repeat offenders of serious crimes we should just "throw away the key." Our courts are in fact heading in this direction by locking up "repeaters" for longer periods of time.

A particular problem with this proposal is that serious crimes of violence are often committed by juveniles. As we've seen, juvenile courts use a "child-saving" approach: their main focus is not on the nature of the crime but on treatment or rehabilitation. A number of states now allow juveniles arrested for homicide and other violent crimes to be charged and tried as adults. In adult court, convicted juveniles can then be given sentences commensurate with the seriousness of their offenses.

Advocating that repeat law breakers who commit serious crimes be locked up for long periods is an admission of rehabilitation failure. On the other hand, it is a proclamation that potential victims have rights too and that their rights take priority over the rights of repeaters.

GETTING TOUGHER ON WHITE-COLLAR CRIME

In the early 1970s many high-ranking officials in the Nixon administration (which was pledged to "law and order") were accused of committing such offenses as illegal wiretapping, tax fraud, destruction of evidence, misappropriation of campaign funds, extortion, bribery, conspiracy to pervert the course of justice, and conspiracy to violate civil rights. Many of these officials were convicted but received very light sentences (often in special federal prisons referred to as "resorts") in comparison to the harsher sentences given to ordinary burglars and thieves. Former President Nixon was pardoned by President Gerald Ford prior to facing criminal charges. The Watergate scandal aroused a major discussion of the mild way in which white-collar crime is handled in our society. Yet, today, white-collar crime is still largely ignored or glossed over by the police, the courts, and the correctional system. (It should be noted that organized crime is also increasingly involved in white-collar type offenses.)

It has been argued that more vigorous arrests, prosecution, and sentencing of white-collar crime and organized crime would lead to increased respect for the law by all citizens and would reduce crime. But that would require the white power structure in our society to encourage the police and the courts to arrest and prosecute its own members. In actuality, that power structure is more interested in prosecuting the crimes that are committed by members of the powerless groups in our society.

CREATING UNIFORM SENTENCES

As noted earlier, there are wide variations in sentences imposed on different convicted offenders for the same crime. If justice is to be equal for all, then variables such as the economic status, race, and gender of the offender ought not to influence his or her sentence. Sentencing one murderer to death while putting another on probation undermines respect for the law and the criminal justice system. One way to reduce the disparity in sentences assigned is to make sentences subject to appeal; currently the harshness of a sentence cannot be appealed. A second way is to take legislative action to reduce the latitude that is given to judges in imposing sentences for each type of conviction.

DECRIMINALIZING VICTIMLESS OFFENSES

Prohibition is the classic example of creating problems by outlawing a victimless activity. Prohibition made it a crime to manufacture, distribute, or drink alcohol. Police spent substantial time and resources trying to enforce this law but were largely unsuccessful. Instead, Prohibition led to bootlegging and fostered the rise of organized crime.

Today, victimless crimes are still with us— gambling, marijuana use, fornication, and prostitution, to name just a few. If such actions were decriminalized, immense resources in money and time could be diverted to confronting the crimes that do have victims. There is some movement to decriminalize certain offenses; for example, Nevada now allows prostitution in a few counties. In the past decade, police departments have been less vigorous in making arrests for smoking marijuana, and there are efforts to decriminalize this activity in several states. Gambling laws are beginning to undergo change, as some states have now set up legal gambling activities, such as lotteries, casinos, and parimutuel betting on horse races and dog races.

IMPOSING STRICTER GUN CONTROL

In the past 30 years, John F. Kennedy, Robert Kennedy, Martin Luther King, Jr., Anwar Sadat, and John Lennon were killed by shootings. In 1981 there were assassination attempts on President Ronald Reagan and on the Pope. Over 23,000 homicides and over 600,000 robberies are committed annually in the United States.[75] Many homicides and armed robberies involve the use of a handgun.

There are an estimated 60 million handguns in the United States—one handgun for every two homes and one handgun for every four citizens.[76] More than 300,000 people per year are wounded in the United States by handguns.[77] More Americans have been killed by handguns than in all the wars fought in the 20th century.[78] States that have a higher proportion of guns have higher rates of homicides, suicides, and deaths during domestic disputes.[79] A number of special-interest groups have advocated an end to the sale of handguns except for approved and limited purposes.

It appears that Congress and the federal government are moving in the direction of imposing stricter gun controls. In 1993 the Brady Bill was enacted, which requires that gun buyers wait five business days and undergo a background check by police. (The Brady Bill was named in honor of James Brady, former presidential press secretary who was shot and severely wounded in the 1981 assassination attempt on President Reagan.) Supporters and opponents of the Brady Bill agree that the enactment of this bill will not stop the majority of criminals from obtaining firearms.[80] In 1994 Congress passed, and President Clinton signed, a crime bill banning 19 types of assault-style firearms, which are used primarily to rapidly kill a number of people.

Reforming the Correctional System

Perhaps the first step in improving the correctional system is to clarify its presently conflicting objectives, some of which are punitive in nature and others of which are treatment oriented. When the general public and public officials are confused about what the primary objective for incarceration should be, prison administrators and inmates will also be confused, making rehabilitation difficult to achieve.

If our society decides that retribution, deterrence, and vengeance should be the primary goal, then we can expect a continued high rate of recidivism and continued high crime rates, because those being punished will become increasingly bitter and hostile toward society. However, from a social benefits viewpoint, the primary objective of a correctional system should be to curb future criminal activity of incarcerated offenders in the least expensive way. The current prison system is not only ineffectual in preventing recidivism, but

it is also expensive. The national average per capita cost for institutionalization of adult felons is many times greater than the cost of probation services to adults.

If the correctional system had rehabilitation as its primary objective, a number of changes would occur. For example, sentencing of wrongdoers is now based primarily on the nature of their past deeds. If a convicted person has previously committed serious felonies, a long incarceration is likely. A reformative approach would, instead, focus on identifying ways to curb the supervisee's (or offender's) tendency to break the law. Involved in this identification process would be an assessment of the reasons why the person is committing crimes and a determination of how the offender can legally obtain what he or she wants. Needed services would then be specified, and the responsibilities of the supervisee would be identified—such as maintaining or securing employment, enrolling in an educational or vocational program, receiving counseling or family therapy, undergoing medical or drug treatment, paying debts, and/or making restitution. Removal from society would generally be used only after the supervisee failed to meet requirements of the supervision plan (for example, restitution) or when the supervisee was a definite threat to society.

Let's consider two examples that illustrate this approach.

1. A 17-year-old female runs away from home, has very limited employment and educational skills, and therefore turns to prostitution for financial reasons. Instead of assigning fines after each arrest, would it not make more sense to identify her needs (such as financial needs, educational needs, need for legal employment that pays her more than prostitution, and need to resolve the conflicts with her parents) and then provide her with services to meet these needs?

2. A 32-year-old male is arrested for burglarizing 43 homes in wealthy neighborhoods over a span of four months. The man is unemployed, and he states that he committed the burglaries to support his cocaine habit. Instead of sending him directly to prison at taxpayers' expense, authorities could identify his needs (such as job training,

employment, and drug treatment) and the provide him with services to meet those needs. As part of such a rehabilitative approach, he would be required (over a realistic period of time) to make restitution to the victims. He would be informed that additional convictions or any other failure on his part to fulfill the terms of the rehabilitative plan would result in a lengthy prison sentence.

With this approach, supervisees would become acutely aware that they have the choice and the responsibility to decide which of two avenues to pursue: continuation of criminal activity (resulting in a lengthy prison sentence) or a more law-abiding, productive, and respectable future. If they choose the latter, they would be given access to services (for example, counseling and vocational training) available to assist them, but they would also be made aware of the responsibility and effort required on their part.

With more than one million people behind bars, the United States imprisons a higher proportion of its population than any other nation.[81] Out of every 100,000 U.S. residents, 426 are incarcerated, at an annual cost of $16 billion to taxpayers.[82] Marc Mauer, after reviewing these statistics, notes:

> *The same policies that have helped make us a world leader in incarceration have clearly failed to make us a safer nation. We need a fundamental change of direction, towards proven programs and policies that work to reduce both imprisonment and crime. We've got to stop jailing and start rehabilitating.*[83]

DIVERSION PROGRAMS

Labeling theory suggests that the criminal justice system perpetuates crime by branding offenders and interacting with them as if they were delinquents and criminals. Diversion programs have therefore been developed in a number of communities to divert first-time or minor offenders from entering the criminal justice system; as an alternative, they receive services from community agencies.

One such program is "deferred prosecution," which some communities now provide. Adults who are arrested for the first time for a minor of-

fense (such as shoplifting) are referred by either a judge or a prosecuting attorney to deferred prosecution prior to standing trial. Deferred prosecution programs provide, over a period of several weeks, small-group sessions that are geared to helping the members refrain from committing additional crimes. The case is dismissed if the defendant (1) pays for any damages, (2) is not rearrested while participating in the program, and (3) attends all the group meetings.

Many diversion programs focus on keeping juveniles out of juvenile courts and criminal courts by instead referring them to treatment programs handled by community agencies. Juveniles, for example, may be referred for counseling (from social workers, probation officers, or psychologists); they may receive help for emotional or family problems; or they may receive help with school work.

Many communities have "Scared Straight" programs, which were initially developed at a prison in Rahway, New Jersey. Juveniles who have committed offenses are taken to visit a prison, where inmates harshly describe prison life. Prison conditions are also observed firsthand. The objective is to expose juveniles to the realities of life in prison so that the threat of imprisonment will motivate them to stop breaking the law. It is not yet certain, however, that this exposure has a deterrent effect on juveniles.

TRANSITIONAL PROGRAMS

A variety of transitional programs are now being offered to offenders. While in jail or prison, a person may be allowed to work in the community during the daytime. School-release programs allow inmates to attend college or a technical school during the day. Halfway houses have been used as an alternative to sending a person to prison; they allow residents to work or go to school in their home community. Halfway houses have also been used to help inmates just released from prison to readjust to society. If offenders misbehave while in halfway houses, there is the threat of being sent back to jail or prison.

A goal of transitional programs is for inmates to maintain and develop strong ties to the noncriminal elements in their home community. The programs seek to reduce or alleviate the negative effects of incarceration and provide opportunities and resources for rehabilitation.

Preventing Crime

Theoretically, there are four ways to prevent crime:

1. Make the punishment for violating a law so severe that law breakers will be too terrorized to commit crimes. Studies on the use of capital punishment, however, suggest that even this severest penalty does not deter crime.

2. Keep the convicted law breakers in prison. Such an approach would be very expensive—especially since practically everyone occasionally commits a crime.

3. Change the economic, social, and political conditions that breed crime. Among the numerous proposals that have been advanced are: improve family life; improve the educational system to make education an exciting, growth-producing experience for students; end racial discrimination; provide equal opportunities for achieving success for all citizens, including the poor and minority groups; provide full employment and a decent living wage for all able-bodied people; improve housing conditions and living conditions in our inner cities; and curb alcohol and drug abuse.

4. Educate the general public on how to avoid becoming a victim of crime. This fourth approach will be discussed in some detail and involves reducing opportunities for crime to occur. The approach is being highlighted because it is one everyone should be aware of and participate in.

Dae Chang describes this approach, which developed from victimology, a recent area of study in criminology:

> Research shows that much crime—and by far the greatest portion of street crime and burglary—is the result of opportunity and luck rather than of careful and professional planning.
>
> Someone sees an "opportunity"—in an open window, an empty house, a person alone in a dark alley—and acts on it. Muggers look for likely victims, not specific individuals, burglars,

for a house they can enter, not a particular address. Preselected targets frequently are chosen precisely because they are seen as "easy marks."

> Who is the victim of a crime? What causes crime? Who causes crime? There are some startling answers to these questions. In the majority of cases, the victim contributes, and in some cases is a major cause of a criminal act. All of us are potential victims. We frequently present the criminal or an individual with an invitation to commit a crime. We entice him, advertise to him, coax him, give him the opportunity, and even implant the idea into his head. Through our carelessness, open disregard for our personal possessions, forgetfulness, attitudes, vanity, etc., we frequently invite someone to commit a criminal act either directly at ourselves or to our possessions. We also invite bodily harm upon ourselves by our actions in public and private. Our habits, attitudes, dress, etc. all are signals to the people who would be enticed into crime.[84]

In effect, one must ask oneself "Is this what I'm doing, or failing to do, making me vulnerable to becoming a victim of a crime?" Exhibit 8.4 presents a number of specific precautions to prevent becoming a crime victim.

SOCIAL WORK AND CORRECTIONS

Role of Social Work

The primary role played by social work in the criminal justice system has been confined almost exclusively to the correctional component of the system: social workers in a prison, probation and parole officers, or social workers in a correctional halfway house. There are only a few police departments that employ social workers to provide social services to individuals and families with whom police come in contact.

It should be noted that in treatment programs, individual and group counseling is only one of a variety of rehabilitation services that may be provided. Others include religious programs, vocational training, study release, work release, and educational programs.

EXHIBIT 8.4

Precautions to Prevent Becoming a Crime Victim

AT HOME

- Bolt doors and windows, and use exterior lighting to frustrate burglary techniques.

- Engrave identification numbers on possessions to curb fencing of stolen property.

- If you leave home for part of the evening, make it look as though someone is home. Leave some lights and music on. Or leave the television on, keeping it low so that it sounds as if people are inside talking or the family is home watching TV.

- Double-secure sliding-glass doors by placing lengths of metal rod or wooden dowels in the lower tracks to prevent the doors from being opened.

- Put in exterior lighting over front and back doors. Also, cut back shrubbery that might be used to hide intruders.

- If you hear someone breaking in at night, let the intruder know you have heard the noise, but avoid a confrontation. Chances are the person will leave as fast as possible. If you confront the intruder unexpectedly, you could get hurt. Instead, yell "Get the shotgun!"— even if you are alone. Or yell to the neighbors or call the police. One of the best places to have a strong dead-bolt lock is on the inside of your bedroom door.

- A dog that barks a lot may deter an intruder. The yapping of the dog will make the intruder wary that someone else will hear the barking, so the intruder will probably exit in a hurry.

- Do not leave the key to your home under the doormat, in the mailbox, or on top of the door ledge.

- Be cautious about inviting door-to-door salespeople into your home. Many communities now require salespeople to carry an identification card.

- Do not leave possessions on lawns or in your driveway at night. If left, bicycles, barbecue grills, power tools, and lawn mowers are easily removed.

- Do not leave important papers, expensive jewelry, or large sums of money at home. Rent a bank security deposit box, which protects valuables not only from burglars but also from fires and natural disasters.

- When going on an extended vacation, arrange for a friend to check your home every few days. Do not let newspapers or mail pile up. The post office will hold your mail at no cost while you are away. Inexpensive timers can be purchased to activate lights, radios, or TVs to give the impression you are home.

- When you expect a visitor and are unable to be home, do not leave a telltale note outside: "Welcome—will be back at 8:00 P.M. Walk in and make yourself at home. Door is unlocked." Burglars readily accept such invitations.

- Women are advised to list only their last name and initials on mailboxes and in phone directories.

IN AN AUTOMOBILE

- Flashy equipment on autos will invite theft or break-ins. If you have mag wheels, a stereo tape deck, CB radio, fancy wheel covers, and other expensive gadgets, your car will draw attention. The place where you park your car can be an invitation for it to be stolen or broken into. Always lock your car, put valuables in the trunk, and never leave the key in the ignition.

(continued)

EXHIBIT 8.4   *(continued)*

- If you leave your car someplace for a few days (e.g., at an airport) it will be nearly theft-proof if you pull the center wire out of the distributor in addition to locking the car and taking the keys. (Before pulling the wire, make sure you know how to put it back!)

- Remove identification from key chains so that, if your keys are lost or stolen, no one knows what the keys will open.

- Do not hitchhike or pick up hitchhikers. Hitchhiking has led to a significant number of robberies and assaults. If you cannot avoid hitchhiking, be very selective as to whom you ride with.

IN PUBLIC

- Avoid carrying large sums of money. If forced to do so, take along a second wallet containing three or four bills and some expired credit cards, which you can give a thief if confronted.

- When in a crowd, place your wallet in a safe place—for example, front pocket, a waist pocket, or a buttoned back pocket—to frustrate pickpocketing efforts.

- Never leave a purse unattended.

- Avoid going into a dark parking lot. It may be cheaper to call a taxi than risk being mugged.

- There are a variety of approaches to avoid becoming a victim of rape, including physical techniques of self-defense (for example, the martial arts) and distasteful approaches (for example, vomiting or urinating on the rapist, informing the potential rapist you have tested positive for HIV, sharply squeezing the genitals of the rapist, and poking your fingers into the rapist's eyes). Women should become familiar with these approaches and select a few that they would be comfortable with and prepared to use should an attack occur.

Many probation and parole officers are trained in social work. One of the important responsibilities of a probation and parole officer is to prepare a presentence report. This is a social history of the offender that is prepared to help guide the judge in sentencing. A sample presentence report is presented in Case Example 8.5.

In the field of corrections there are two important factors influencing treatment: custody-treatment conflict and offenders' "con games." Social workers need to understand how these factors operate.

Factors Influencing Treatment

CUSTODY-TREATMENT CONFLICT

In prison settings, administrators emphasize custody. Over 90% of the money spent in such institutions goes for custody.[85] When custody policies clash with treatment programs, treatment almost always comes in second. Prison administrators are primarily concerned with preventing escapes, curbing riots, and calming internal disruptions. New social workers in prison settings soon realize rehabilitation is not the primary focus.

Social workers in prisons, and those who work as probation and parole officers, are often viewed by offenders as part of the larger authoritarian bureaucracy that caught and convicted them. Many offenders are distrustful of social workers because they feel the social workers are "monitoring" or "policing" them.

OFFENDERS' "CON GAME"

Since the 1930s the criminal justice system has promoted both individual and group therapy. Prison administrators and directors of probation

CASE EXAMPLE 8.5   **Presentence Report**

Walworth County Court
June 23, 1994

Name: James LaMartina

Address: 408 Walnut St.
Delavan, WI, 54987

Legal Residence: Same

Age: 34

Date of Birth: 5-8-60

Sex: Male

Race: Caucasian

Citizenship: U.S.A.

Education: 11th grade

Marital Status: Married

Dependents: Two (wife and
a 4-year-old son)

Soc. Sec. No.: 393-42-9067

FBI No.: 287 1237

Detainers or Charges Pending:
None

Offense: Second-degree sexual assault

Penalty: Imprisoned not more than ten years
and/or fined not more than $10,000

Plea: Guilty on 6-10-94

Verdict:

Custody: Posted bail of $5000

Prosecuting Attorney: Richard Jorgenson,
Assistant District Attorney

Defense Counsel: Donald Hauser

OFFENSE: OFFICIAL VERSION

Officers Karen Davenport and David Erdmier stated they arrested Mr. LaMartina in Lakeland County Park at 12:30 P.M. on June 5, 1994, while he was having sexual intercourse with a 17-year-old minor. Mr. LaMartina and the minor were in the back seat of the offender's car and were reported to be unclothed.

Mr. LaMartina stated he had met the woman in Don's Hillside Tavern earlier in the day. He stated that this was the first time he had met her and did not know her age—he assumed she was an adult. A check with Donald Leesburg, owner of the tavern, indicated that Mr. LaMartina was a frequent patron of the tavern but that the woman was not a regular patron. The owner further stated that the night of June 5, 1994, was busy. He noted that Mr. LaMartina was there earlier that evening, but the owner was unaware whether Mr. LaMartina had met this woman at the tavern.

The minor appeared intoxicated at the time of the arrest. Her driver's license the night of the arrest revealed her age to be 17 years and 2 months. She was returned home by the police to her parents, who were very angry; Officers Davenport and Erdmier had to restrain the father from physically hitting her.

DEFENDANT'S VERSION OF OFFENSE

Mr. LaMartina stated that he frequently stopped at Don's Hillside Tavern after work with fellow workers from the construction company he has worked with for the past six years. Mr. LaMartina stated that this evening was the first time he had met this woman. He mentioned he began buying drinks for her and for the two other women friends she was with. He stated that she had drunk considerably more than he had. He emphasized that he assumed she was at least 21 years of age (the legal drinking age in this state).

Around midnight he asked her if she wanted a ride home, which she accepted. He drove instead to Lakeland County Park, where he emphasized she willingly agreed to go to the back seat with him and willingly became sexually involved. When asked whether he had become sexually involved with other women, Mr. LaMartina became defensive and refused to answer.

PRIOR RECORD

Date	Offense	Disposition
9-7-86	Disorderly conduct	$80 fine
10-11-90	Driving motor vehicle while under the influence	$310 fine and group dynamics course

PERSONAL HISTORY

The defendant was born in Fort Atkinson, Wisconsin, on 5-8-69, the older of two children. His parents were dairy farmers. He attended public schools and completed the 11th grade. He received mainly Cs and Ds in school and left school to help on the farm. He had a number of friends in school and was active in several sports, including the high school varsity basketball and baseball teams.

The defendant's father, Leonard, died following a stroke when the defendant was 22 years of age. His mother, Loretta, is still living on the family farm in rural Jefferson County. The defendant ran the farm for six years after his father's death and then sold the cattle in order to work for Johnstone's Road Construction Company. The farm appeared to be only marginally successful when the defendant had dairy cattle. The defendant still plants and harvests crops on the farm.

The defendant's sister, Janine, is 28 years of age and has been married for the past six years to Dennis Richter, a dairy farmer in Dane County.

Mr. LaMartina has been married for the past eight years to Sue Heinz (maiden name). Sue is 32 years of age and graduated from Milton College ten years ago. She taught elementary school for the first four years of their marriage but has not taught school for the past four years—since their son, Tim, was born. She and James LaMartina have lived in the LaMartinas' farm house since their marriage.

Sue LaMartina separated from her husband shortly after she heard he was arrested. She and her son are now staying with her parents. She has ambivalent feelings

(continued)

CASE
EXAMPLE 8.5   *(continued)*

about her husband. She stated that he can be a good father and husband, but she is intensely irritated about his drinking and about his staying out late at night with his "cronies." She stated that she suspected he may occasionally have been having affairs with other women, but this incident is "the last straw." She stated that she is seeing a counselor at the mental health center, has contacted an attorney, and is contemplating a divorce.

Mr. LaMartina stated that he does not want a divorce and appears sincerely remorseful about the family problems he has created. He stated that if he and his wife can reconcile, he will change his ways. He will not stay out late or become involved with other women. Mr. LaMartina has asked his wife to attend marriage counseling with him, but she indicated she is still too emotionally hurt and embarrassed to be able to discuss the incident and their future with him.

There is some evidence that Mr. LaMartina has been drinking to excess for several years. Mr. LaMartina denies this, but his frequent stops after work at a tavern and his past arrest record suggest otherwise. The future of his marriage, however, appears to be a more immediate problem needing attention.

EVALUATIVE SUMMARY

The defendant is a 34-year-old male who entered a plea of guilty to second-degree sexual assault. The defendant was arrested while having sexual intercourse with a 17-year-old woman whom he met, apparently for the first time, earlier that evening at a tavern. The defendant apparently did not know the woman was a minor. The defendant's wife has separated from him following this arrest and is contemplating a divorce. The defendant expressed considerable remorse about the embarrassment and domestic strife he has caused.

Mr. LaMartina has a 4-year-old son and has no prior felony arrest record. He may at times drink to excess. He completed 11 years of schooling and has run a dairy farm. For the past six years he has been a road construction worker. His employer reports that he is dependable and has been a good worker.

RECOMMENDATION

It is recommended that the defendant be fined and placed on probation. If placed on probation, the defendant expresses willingness to seek counseling for his domestic problems. This counseling should also at some future time explore whether he has a drinking problem. The future of his marriage, however, needs first attention.

Respectfully submitted,

Ralph Franzene
Probation and Parole Officer
State of Wisconsin

and parole programs have required offenders to participate in treatment programs. Obviously, compelling clients to submit to treatment interventions can inhibit establishment of rapport with offenders. Yet, enforced treatment is commonplace in corrections.

Offenders are highly skilled at "conning" professional staff through persuasion, deceit, and manipulation. Most convicted offenders disdain correctional staff. This disdain is strengthened when they see therapy being forced on them. Inmates realize that they must participate in such activities as individual and group counseling in order to have a good record. If imprisoned on an indeterminate sentence (as is common in most states), a good record will get them released on parole sooner. If they are on probation or parole, offenders may see their participation in "treatment" programs as a way to get the probation parole officer to do things for them or to overlook minor violations of the rules for probation and parole.

The social worker should be aware that many offenders who request professional assistance have no genuine interest in self-improvement but are seeking to manipulate the worker.

SUMMARY

Crime is one of the most serious problems facing our nation. Serious, violent crime has reached alarming proportions. In addition, the criminal justice system (the police, the courts, and prisons) is perceived as relatively ineffective in curbing crime.

Everyone, at one time or another, has violated some laws. Those arrested for crimes are disproportionately likely to be male, young, a member of a racial minority, and a city resident. If white-collar crime and organized crime were more vigorously prosecuted, the "typical" criminal would more likely be older, white, and a suburban resident.

Official crime statistics are inaccurate for a variety of reasons. Many crimes go unreported. Police and courts vigorously enforce only certain crimes. Police-reporting practices are affected at times by political considerations, such as reclassifying serious offenses as less serious to attempt to make police departments appear more effective in curbing serious crimes. In terms of number of people victimized and financial costs to society, it appears that white-collar crime is our most serious type of crime. Yet this type is less vigorously enforced by the police and the courts.

A variety of theories about the causes of crime have been advanced. These theories identify some of the reasons crime occurs. But we do not have a complete understanding of all the reasons why crime occurs. With the crime rate continuing to increase, it is also clear that we do not as yet know how to reduce crime effectively.

Current correctional systems throughout the world reflect conflicting objectives; some components are punishment oriented, whereas others are treatment oriented. Generally the two components, when combined, result in a system that is confusing and ineffective in curbing criminal activity. There is a danger that prisons may serve as schools for crime and may have a labeling effect that leads to future criminal activity.

A number of proposals have been advanced for reducing crime, including administering swift and certain punishment, imposing harsher sentences, separating repeat offenders from society, getting tougher on white-collar crime, creating uniform sentencing, decriminalizing victimless offenses, imposing stricter gun control, reforming the correctional system to emphasize the treatment approach, increasing use of diversion and transitional programs, and educating citizens on how to avoid becoming crime victims. Some of these proposals contradict others. Although each proposal has some research support, no proposal has conclusively been proved valid in reducing crime.

The ways in which societies have punished convicted offenders are as atrocious as the atrocities offenders have inflicted on victims. The "eye for an eye" retributive approach generally is ineffective in curbing future crime.

NOTES

1. Ian Robertson and Phillip Whitten, "Sexual Politics in South Africa," in *Society As It Is: A Reader,* 2d ed., Glen Gaviglio and David E. Raye, eds. (New York: Macmillan, 1976).

2. Vincent N. Parrillo, John Stimson, and Ardyth Stimson, *Contemporary Social Problems,* 2d ed. (New York: Macmillan, 1989), pp. 127–158.

3. Clayton A. Hartjen, *Crime and Criminalization,* 2d ed. (New York: Praeger, 1978), p. 33.

4. *Crime in the United States, 1992, FBI Uniform Crime Reports* (Washington, DC: U.S. Government Printing Office, 1993), p. 58.

5. Donald Baer, "Guns," *U.S. News & World Report,* May 8, 1989, pp. 20–25.

6. Tim Weiner, "Report: U.S. Leads All in Crime," *Wisconsin State Journal,* Mar. 13, 1991, p. 1A.

7. Ibid.

8. *Crime in the United States, 1992,* p. 226.

9. William Kornblum and Joseph Julian, *Social Problems,* 7th ed. (Englewood Cliffs, NJ: Prentice-Hall, 1992), pp. 166–167.

10. Ibid.

11. *Crime in the United States, 1992,* pp. 227–228.

12. Kornblum and Julian, *Social Problems,* 7th ed., p. 169.

13. Ibid., pp. 169–170.

14. Donald Jackson, "Justice for None," *New Times,* Jan. 11, 1974, p. 51.

15. William Kornblum and Joseph Julian, *Social Problems,* 6th ed. (Englewood Cliffs, NJ: Prentice-Hall, 1989), p. 175.

16. *Crime in the United States, 1992,* pp. 238–281.

17. Kornblum and Julian, *Social Problems,* 7th ed., p. 151.

18. Ibid., p. 152.

19. James W. Coleman and Donald R. Cressey, *Social Problems,* 5th ed. (New York: HarperCollins, 1993), p. 333.

20. Eugene Doleschal and Nora Kapmuts, *Toward a New Criminology* (Hackensack, NJ: National Council on Crime and Delinquency, 1974), p. 4.

21. Charles Goring, *The English Convict* (London, His Majesty's Stationery Office, 1913).

22. Thomas Szasz, *The Myth of Mental Illness* (New York: Hoeber-Harper, 1961).

23. H. J. Eysenck, "The Effects of Psychotherapy," *International Journal of Psychiatry,* 1 (1965), pp. 97–144.

24. Charles Zastrow and Ralph Navarre, "Self-Talk: A New Criminological Theory," *International Journal of Comparative and Applied Criminal Justice* (Fall 1979), pp. 167–176.

25. Edwin H. Sutherland and Donald R. Cressey, *Criminology,* 8th ed. (Philadelphia: Lippincott, 1970), p. 10.

26. Robert K. Merton, *Social Theory and Social Structure* (New York: Free Press, 1968), p. 232.

27. John M. Johnson and Jack Douglas, eds., *Crime at the Top: Deviance in Business and the Professions* (Philadelphia: Lippincott, 1978).

28. Walter B. Miller, "Lower Class Culture as a Generating Milieu of Gang Delinquency," *Journal of Social Issues,* 14 (1958), pp. 5–19.

29. Albert Cohen, *Delinquent Boys: The Culture of the Gang* (New York: Free Press, 1955).

30. Charles Cooley, *Human Nature and the Social Order* (New York: Scribner, 1902).

31. Thomas Sullivan, Kenrick Thompson, Richard Wright, George Gross, and Dale Spady, *Social Problems* (New York: John Wiley, 1980), p. 584.

32. Stewart Powell, Steven Emerson, and Orr Kelly, "Busting the Mob," *U.S. News & World Report,* Feb. 3, 1986, pp. 24–31.

33. Ibid.

34. Ibid.

35. Ibid.

36. Ibid.

37. Coleman and Cressey, *Social Problems,* 5th ed., p. 337.

38. Kornblum and Julian, *Social Problems,* 7th ed., p. 164.

39. Marshall B. Clinard and Richard Quinney, *Criminal Behavior Systems: A Typology,* 2d ed. (New York: Holt, Rinehart & Winston, 1973), p. 227.

40. Johnson and Douglas, *Crime at the Top.*

41. Edwin H. Sutherland, *White Collar Crime* (New York: Dryden Press, 1949), p. 9.

42. Charles H. McCaghy and Stephen A. Cernkovich, *Crime in American Society,* 2d ed. (New York: Macmillan, 1987), pp. 332–335.

43. Sullivan et al., *Social Problems,* p. 586.

44. *Crime in the United States, 1992,* p. 218.

45. Alexander B. Smith and Harriet Pollack, "Crimes without Victims," *Saturday Review,* December 4, 1971, pp. 27–29.

46. Janet S. Hyde, *Understanding Human Sexuality* (New York: McGraw-Hill, 1990), pp. 474–476.

47. McCaghy and Cernkovich, *Crime in American Society,* p. 122.

48. *Crime in the United States, 1992,* p. 207.

49. Edwin H. Sutherland, *The Professional Thief* (Chicago: University of Chicago Press, 1937).

50. McCaghy and Cernkovich, *Crime in American Society,* pp. 245–247.

51. *Crime in the United States, 1992,* p. 227.

52. Kornblum and Julian, *Social Problems,* 7th ed., pp. 165–168.

53. Ibid.
54. Ibid., pp. 167–169.
55. Armando Morales, "Urban Gang Violence," in *Social Work: A Profession of Many Faces*, 5th ed., Armando Morales and Bradford W. Sheafor, eds. (Boston: Allyn & Bacon, 1989), p. 417.
56. Ibid., pp. 419–421.
57. T. A. Sweeney, *Streets of Anger: Streets of Hope* (Glendale, CA: Great Western, 1980), p. 86.
58. Don C. Gibbons, *Society: Crime and Criminal Behavior*, 5th ed. (Englewood Cliffs, NJ: Prentice-Hall, 1987), p. 464.
59. Coleman and Cressey, *Social Problems*, 5th ed., p. 351.
60. David M. Peterson, "The Police Officer's Conception of Proper Police Work," *The Police Journal*, 47 (London: P. Allen, 1974), pp. 102–108.
61. Coleman and Cressey, *Social Problems*, 5th ed., p. 351.
62. Gibbons, *Society, Crime, and Criminal Behavior*, p. 439.
63. Abraham S. Blumberg, *Criminal Justice* (Chicago: Quadrangle Books, 1967).
64. James W. Coleman and Donald R. Cressey, *Social Problems*, 4th ed. (New York: Harper & Row, 1990), p. 418.
65. Alan Neigher, "The Gault Decision: Due Process and the Juvenile Court," *Federal Probation*, 31, no. 4 (December 1967), pp. 8–18.
66. George F. Cole, *The American System of Criminal Justice*, 6th ed. (Pacific Grove, CA: Brooks/Cole, 1992), pp. 506–513.
67. Ibid., pp. 532–537.
68. Kornblum and Julian, *Social Problems*, 7th ed., pp. 176–177.
69. Ibid.
70. Cole, *The American System of Criminal Justice*, p. 663.
71. "Prison Ratio Highest in U.S.," *Wisconsin State Journal*, Jan. 5, 1991, p. 3A.
72. Gordon Witkin and Ted Gest, "Street Crime," *U.S. News & World Report*, Oct. 5, 1992, p. 44.
73. Cooley, *Human Nature and the Social Order*.
74. Sutherland and Cressey, *Criminology*, p. 354.
75. *Crime in the United States, 1992*, p. 58.
76. "Guns, Guns, Guns," NBC News Summer Showcase, July 5, 1988.
77. Ibid.
78. Ibid.
79. Ibid.
80. Ted Gest, "Gun Control's Limits," *U.S. News & World Report*, Dec. 6, 1993, pp. 24–26.
81. "Prison Ratio Highest in U.S.," p. 3A.
82. Ibid.
83. Marc Mauer, quoted in "Prison Ratio Highest in U.S.," p. 3A.
84. Dae H. Chang, "How to Avoid Becoming a Victim of Crime," in *The Personal Problem Solver*, Charles Zastrow and Dae H. Chang, eds. (Englewood Cliffs, NJ: Prentice-Hall, 1977), pp. 348–349.
85. Gibbons, *Society, Crime, and Criminal Behavior*.

9

PROBLEMS
IN EDUCATION
AND SCHOOL
SOCIAL WORK

In 1957 the United States and the Soviet Union were involved in an unofficial race to be first to place a satellite in orbit. The race became a symbol of international honor and prestige. The Soviets won when they successfully launched *Sputnik I* into orbit. Why did the United States lose? There were numerous reasons. However, the general public blamed the American educational system for neglecting subjects that were vital to national survival. For example, one outspoken critic, Max Rafferty, stated "Instead of offering a four-year program of studies in mathematics, history, foreign languages, and other disciplines [high schools] encourage students to divert themselves with ceramics, stagecraft, table decorating, upholstering, and second-year golf."[1] Following these events, the American educational system was called on to emphasize mathematics, natural science, and other courses that would enable our country to successfully compete with the Soviets.

The educational system has frequently been asked to resolve and alleviate social problems. For example, it is currently being called on to help reduce racism and sexism by developing new curriculum designed to change the attitudes of school-age children. (The school setting is one of the few places where real integration of the races is likely to occur.) The educational system is expected to provide students of low-income families with the education and job-training skills that will enable them to escape from a life of poverty. It must identify and refer for treatment those children who have emotional or learning problems and those who abuse alcohol and other drugs. The school system is a mechanism for conveying antidelinquent values. Also, it is required to refer to protective services any children who are suspected of being physically abused, neglected, or sexually abused.

Sometimes the educational system is perceived as being a social problem itself because it is not meeting the expectations of society. Education is in a crisis of controversy and indecision. The self-confidence, morale, and motivation of teachers are often low. Some schools have been accused of perpetuating, rather than alleviating, social inequality for the poor and for minorities. Although recent improvements have occurred, student scores on achievement tests are substantially lower than they were 30 years ago.[2] Some inner-city schools are so victimized by vandalism and violence that students and teachers are as concerned with survival as with education.

This chapter will:

- Summarize problems that school systems currently face.
- Present proposals for improving education.
- Discuss ideas for improving educational opportunities for children of low-income and minority families.
- Summarize the functions of school social workers and describe several role models for school social work practice.

PROBLEMATIC AREAS IN EDUCATION

The educational system in our country faces a number of crises. This section will examine the following problems: the question of the quality of education, the issue of equal access to a quality education, confusion about the goals of education, and intolerable working conditions in some school settings.

The Question of Quality

A number of indicators raise questions about the quality of education in the United States. Mean SAT (Scholastic Aptitude Test) scores of high school students on the verbal-reasoning section and on the mathematics-reasoning section have declined almost steadily over the last three decades. The SAT is taken annually by about 1 million high school students. From the mid-1950s to the mid-1960s the scores were fairly constant, ranging from 472 to 478 on the verbal-reasoning section and from 495 to 502 on the mathematics-reasoning section. In the second half of the 1960s, both scores began to decline and continued to do so until around 1980, when the mean verbal score was 424 and the mean mathematics score was

466. Since 1980 there has been a slight increase, although scores are still significantly below what they were 30 years ago.[3]

The reading and writing skills of American students remained virtually unchanged for many years but now show signs of decline.[4] "Frankly, there has been very little education progress made in the United States," said former U. S. Education Secretary Lauro F. Cavazos, who termed the reading and writing skills of American students "dreadfully inadequate."[5] Studies also indicate that many businesses do not believe that recent graduates possess adequate skills for the workplace.[6]

Boldt examined studies that compared the top 5% and the top 1% of American high school students with their counterparts in Hungary, Scotland, Canada, Finland, Sweden, Japan, New Zealand, Belgium, England, and Israel. He concluded:

> The most able U.S. students scored the lowest of all of these countries in algebra and were among the lowest in calculus. Furthermore, . . . average Japanese students achieved higher than the top 5 percent of the U.S. students in college preparatory mathematics. . . . The results showed that the United States came out as the lowest of any country for which data were available.[7]

The National Commission on Excellence in Education summarized the quality-of-education issue as follows: "For the first time in the history of our country, the educational skills of one generation will not surpass, will not equal, will not even approach, those of their parents."[8]

In 1993 the U.S. Department of Education released the results of a survey showing that nearly half of all adult Americans read and write so poorly that they have trouble holding decent jobs.[9] The survey found that nearly half of all Americans over age 15 cannot write a short letter explaining a billing error or use a calculator to figure out the difference between a sale price and a regular price.

A 1990 study conducted by the National Assessment of Educational Progress showed continuing alarming news about student readiness in mathematics. Only 14% of the eighth-grade students in the sample scored at the seventh-grade level or above. On average, the eighth-graders in the study scored just above the level expected for fifth-grade students.[10]

Two explanations have been offered for the decline in student achievement, neither of which has been proven. One holds the school systems responsible, whereas the other places the cause in societal changes.

The first explanation asserts that school systems responded to the protests of the 1960s by changing their curriculum. At that time there were nationwide protests against racial inequality, the Vietnam War, and the role of traditional institutions (such as education) in our society. In response, many school systems reduced the number of required courses and gave students greater choice in course selections. As a result, for many students there was a decline in the amount of time spent in courses designed to teach basic skills. Such softening of the school curriculum, it has been asserted, led to the decline in achievement scores.

The second explanation focuses on societal changes since the mid-1960s. Students now spend much more time watching television—more time, in fact, than at any other activity except sleeping. Because children watch television more, they spend less time reading books and therefore do not read or write as well. Furthermore, with the advent of the computer age, youngsters are spending much of their time playing computer games and thereby devoting *even less* time to reading and writing. There have also been changes in the family. The proportion of single-parent families has risen dramatically. Also, in two-parent families *both* parents are now more likely to be employed outside the home. Thus parents may be less involved with the school system and may not monitor their children's homework assignments as closely. A similar assertion (not yet proven) is that there has been an increase in the proportion of dysfunctional families. Being raised in a dysfunctional family not only adversely impacts academic performance but also generates personal problems that sometimes lead to anger, violence, or substance abuse.

Doonesbury

BY GARRY TRUDEAU

A recent study reported that Americans between 18 and 24 scored lower in geographic knowledge than similar age groups in eight other industrialized nations. Less than half could identify Great Britain, France, and Japan on a map; one in seven couldn't locate the United States.

Whatever the reason or reasons, there is considerable pressure on school systems to make changes so that students will improve their basic skills of reading, writing, and arithmetic.

Equal Access to Quality Education

An egalitarian society has a responsibility to provide equal opportunity for a high-quality education to all its citizens. Our society has generally failed to meet this responsibility, especially with respect to minority groups and the poor.

A number of studies have found social class to be the single most effective predictor of achievement in school.[11] Students from the middle and upper classes tend to achieve higher grades, stay in school longer, and get higher scores on standardized achievement tests. There are two primary explanations for this relationship; one focuses on family background and the other on school systems.

The family-background explanation ascribes the inequality to the fact that lower-class children live in a very different environment from middle- and upper-class children. The theory asserts that lower-income homes tend to have fewer magazines, newspapers, and books. Parents usually have less education and are less likely to act as role models to encourage reading in their children. Because lower-class families tend to be larger and to be headed by a single parent, it is said, their children receive less guidance and educational encouragement. Because of such factors, poor children may be less likely to view education as a means of achieving in society and less likely to develop educational goals. Also, poor children are more likely to be hungry and undernourished, which also inhibits their motivation to learn. In contrast, middle- and upper-class families tend to place a higher value on education and therefore put more time and effort into helping their children do homework in order to do well in school.

School systems are primarily geared for educating middle- and upper-class students. Youngsters who live in wealthy tax districts benefit from having more money spent on their schools than students who live in poorer districts. Nearly 50%

CASE
EXAMPLE 9.1   **The Pygmalion Effect**

According to Greek mythology, Pygmalion was a king of Cyprus who made a female figure of ivory. Aphrodite, the Greek goddess of love and beauty, brought the statue to life for him. Robert Rosenthal and Lenore Jacobson performed an intriguing experiment to demonstrate that teachers' expectations of students can increase students' IQ scores. They called this self-fulfilling prophecy the Pygmalion Effect.

These experimenters began by giving a standard IQ test to students in 18 classrooms of an elementary school. (The teachers were told that the test was the Harvard Test of Inflected Acquisition—no such test exists.) The researchers then randomly selected 20% of the students and informed their teachers that the test results predicted remarkable progress for these students in the coming school year. When the students were retested eight months later, those who had been expected to be remarkable achievers showed a significantly greater increase in IQ scores than the others. The researchers concluded that this increase was due to the higher expectations of the teachers, who then worked more intensively with these students. If the expectations of teachers do indeed affect student achievement and IQ test scores, lower-class and minority students may be at a disadvantage; most teachers are white, middle-class, and have a tendency to expect less from lower-class and minority students.

Source: Robert Rosenthal and Lenore Jacobson, *Pygmalion in the Classroom* (New York: Harper & Row, 1969).

of the funds for public schools in this country come from local school district taxes.[12] Because most of this money is derived from property taxes, school districts with numerous expensive homes have much more revenue for their schools. (Roughly 40% of public school revenues comes from state taxes, and 10% comes from federal taxes.)[13]

Ironically, those who live in poorer school districts generally pay a higher percentage of the assessed value of their property in taxes than people who live in wealthier districts. One study on education concluded:

It is unconscionable that a poor man in a poor district must often pay local taxes at higher rates for the inferior education of his child than the man of means in a rich district pays for the

superior education of his child. Yet, incredibly, that is the situation today in most of the 50 states.[14]

Most teachers have middle-class backgrounds, which may mean they are better able to establish relationships with middle- and upper-income children, with whom they have more in common. There is also evidence that teachers expect less of poor children academically and behaviorally than they expect of middle- and upper-class children. In turn, low-income students tend to respond to such expectations by underachieving and misbehaving.[15] Thus the expectation becomes a self-fulfilling prophecy.

Many school systems place students in one of several different tracks or ability groups. In high school the so-called most promising are placed in college preparatory courses, whereas others go into "basic" or vocational classes. Lower-class and minority students are much more likely to be placed in the basic or vocational track[16] and are not exposed to college-oriented math, science, and literature.

In addition, because such students have little contact with college-bound students, they are less likely to aspire to a college education. Without a college education they have very limited opportunities to obtain high-paying jobs.

The small proportion of low-income and minority students who do pursue a college education generally do not have the financial resources to attend prestigious colleges and universities. Also, they have more difficulty competing academically with wealthier students, partly because they have to work (at least part time) to offset some of their expenses.

Minority students are particularly likely to have inferior educational opportunities. Until 1954 blacks attended segregated schools in the South that were markedly inferior to those attended by whites. In 1954 the U.S. Supreme Court, in *Brown* v. *Board of Education,* ruled that racial segregation in public schools was unconstitutional. Although *de jure* (legal) segregation ended, *de facto* (actual) segregation remained in many communities with significant proportions of nonwhites.

Schools in such communities tend to remain segregated because housing is segregated. To deal with this problem, the Supreme Court ruled that school districts must seek racial balance in schools. In many districts, school busing is used to attain a racial balance. Studies indicate that segregation has been reduced *within* school districts but has increased *between* districts.[17] This increase is largely due to "white flight"—that is, whites leaving the inner cities and moving to suburbs. In some communities, courts have ordered busing between school districts, and some whites have responded by sending their children to private schools. Chicago's public schools are a classic example of *de facto* segregation. Some authorities have called this the worst school district

in the country. The city's public school system is about 90% nonwhite, whereas the private school system is primarily white.[18]

Ironically, today there is less racial segregation of schools in the South than in other parts of the United States, and the North has become the most heavily segregated region in the country.[19] Much of northern school segregation is due to housing segregation.

Surveys have found that most Americans now favor school integration, but most African Americans and whites are opposed to busing programs to achieve school integration.[20] In many large cities (such as Baltimore, Chicago, Cleveland, and Detroit) public schools are approaching 90% minority enrollment.[21]

Two decades of school busing have failed to deliver all the benefits its boosters hoped for and its critics demanded, but it has produced clear gains for African Americans and whites. Scores of studies generally agree that white students do not suffer academically from school integration via busing, and African American students probably benefit academically; their scores on standardized tests tend to increase after school integration.[22] How much such integration increases scores on standardized tests has not as yet been determined.[23]

There have been other benefits of integration via busing. African Americans who attended elementary and high schools with whites are substantially more likely to attend white-majority colleges, get jobs in desegregated workplaces offering higher pay, and have white friends as adults.[24] Also, African American students who go to integrated suburban schools rather than segregated city ones are less likely to drop out of high school, get in trouble with the police, drop out of college, or bear a child before age 18, and they are more likely to have white friends and live in integrated neighborhoods.[25] Whites also benefit from attending school with African American students, because they learn more about diversity and tend to more thoroughly confront their racial stereotypes.[26] Are the benefits of school busing worth the costs? This is a very complex issue, and we have no definitive answer as yet.

Have desegregation programs decreased racial prejudice? Research shows mixed results. Some studies show a decrease in prejudice, whereas others show that prejudice remains the same or even intensifies.[27] In communities in which desegregation takes place in an atmosphere of cooperation and good will, prejudice tends to be reduced. However, desegregation programs that are court ordered in an atmosphere of antagonism and misunderstanding are unlikely to reduce prejudice. In recent years the Supreme Court appears to be less aggressive in mandating that busing be used to achieve desegregation. For instance, the Court has stated that there must be proof that schools are intentionally discriminating against minority students before busing is ordered.

In 1991 the Supreme Court declared that busing to achieve integration, when ordered, need not continue indefinitely, although the Court did not say precisely how long is enough. The ruling allows communities to end court-ordered busing if they can convince a judge they have done everything "practicable" to eliminate "vestiges of past discrimination" against minorities. In many inner cities, minority students continue to be segregated in dangerous, crowded, and inferior schools.

Urban Latinos and African Americans are not the only ones who have inferior educational opportunities: Native Americans, Alaskan Eskimo, and migrant workers also lack access to high-quality schools. Many Native Americans attend reservation schools, which are inferior in quality.

For Latinos, bilingual/bicultural education is an issue of intense debate. (There is also controversy about whether black English should be taught in inner-city schools that have high proportions of African American students.) With bilingual/bicultural education, students are taught wholly or partly in their native language until they can speak English fairly fluently, and in some cases longer. One side asserts that preserving the culture and language of minorities is a worthwhile (or essential) goal of public education. The opposing side asserts that minority students will be best prepared to compete effectively in American society if they are "immersed" in English-language instruction; moreover, bilingual (using black English or Spanish) education is expensive and reinforces separateness, because it is a factor in keeping minorities in the ghettos.

Given all the above factors, it is not surprising that there are significant differences in educational achievement between whites and minorities. Almost twice as many Latinos and African American students drop out of high school as compared to whites.[28] There are also wide differences between whites and minorities in the proportions estimated to be functionally illiterate—that is, unable to read or write a simple sentence in any language.[29] (There are very few jobs in our society for the functionally illiterate.)

Confusion about the Goals of Education

There is agreement that school systems should teach the basic skills of reading, writing, and arithmetic. However, considerable controversy exists over what other values, knowledge, and skills schools should teach.

- Feminists criticize school systems for teaching and perpetuating sexism—for example, by continuing to use textbooks that show boys and girls in stereotyped sex roles.

- There is controversy over the extent to which school systems should offer educational programs to prevent sexual assaults and date rapes.

- Controversy exists over what roles the schools should play in educating students about sexual harassment and intervening to prevent harassment.

- Schools have been criticized for helping to perpetuate the class system.

- There is considerable disagreement about the extent to which sex education should be taught in the school system.

- There is disagreement on whether prayers should be allowed in public schools, even though the Supreme Court has ruled that prayers in public schools violate the principle of separation of Church and State.

- There is disagreement about the emphasis that should be placed on teaching such subjects as music, sports, and home economics.

- There is disagreement on the extent to which school systems should be used to combat racism, stop drug abuse, prevent unwed pregnancies, help people with a disability, and reduce delinquency.

- There is controversy over whether schools should focus more on developing the creative thinking capacities of students or on teaching academic content.

- Now that the threat of AIDS has arisen, there is controversy over whether school systems should offer information on homosexuality and contraceptive methods that help to prevent AIDS.

In recent years there has been a conservative trend in our society that, in school systems, has been expressed as a "back to basics" movement. Educational conservatives are opposed to schools being experimental, custodial (for the emotionally disturbed), or recreational facilities and to their offering "frill" and elective courses or "social services" such as sex education. This movement is calling for the establishment of clear standards of achievement for students, "criteria mastery" as the basis for grade promotion, participation by students in varsity sports only when certain grade levels are achieved, increased attention to academic subjects and to the teaching of "core values," more testing and homework, longer school hours, and sterner discipline. The movement also urges that teachers receive salary increases based on merit rather than seniority (the underlying assumption is that such a system would motivate teachers to do a better job in the classroom).

There are controversies, however, within the back-to-basics movement. Are goals such as "learning to get along with others" and "communicating effectively" components of a "basic" education? Are "the basics" the same for all students?

A variety of other questions have been raised about education. Should private schooling be financially supported by refunding to those families who send their children to private schools the amounts they spend on public education through taxes? Should public colleges and universities collect more of their funds through higher student tuitions (which makes it more difficult for students of low-income families to attend)? What changes in school curriculum need to be made to train students for the high-technology jobs that are opening up in our society? Clearly there is a need for increased consensus on the priorities and goals in education.

Intolerable Working Conditions for Some Teachers

In surveys, half of all teachers say that, if they had the opportunity to choose careers again, they would not select teaching.[30] Many factors contribute to disenchantment with teaching: low pay, low prestige, inadequate preparation, increased alternative job opportunities for women, and intolerable working conditions. College graduates can earn substantially more money in many other areas: accounting, engineering, computer science, or sales, for example.

Intolerable working conditions in school systems are evidenced by the following examples: A federal study of school violence found that 12% of teachers in secondary schools had been threatened by students, and .05% had been physically attacked.[31] In some schools, teachers spend as much time at trying to keep peace and order (babysitting) as they do at teaching. There are high rates of drug and alcohol abuse among students, and teachers are forced to confront this issue, often without much preparation. Many school districts have insufficient instructional supplies. High student-to-teacher ratios are another concern—the more students, the more difficult it is for teachers to give individualized instruction.

In addition, teachers do not feel adequately prepared to teach protective behavior (such as how to protect oneself against sexual assaults), alcohol and drug abuse education, and similar topics. Teachers are rarely involved in the

Low pay, low prestige, inadequate preparation, and poor working conditions are just a few of the reasons many teachers feel disenchanted with their profession.

decision-making processes in education, which contributes to poor morale and lowers motivation to seek positive changes. Only 12–15% of teachers are still teaching ten years after entering the profession.[32] More than one-fifth of beginning teachers leave the profession after just one year.[33]

STRATEGIES TO IMPROVE EDUCATION

Michael Rutter and his associates evaluated a number of high schools and concluded what most parents already know: "Schools do indeed have important impact on children's development, and it does matter what school a child attends."[34] Rutter found that the best schools required more homework, maintained high academic standards, had well-understood and well-enforced discipline standards, and yet created a comfortable and supportive atmosphere for students.[35] This section

will examine four proposals for improving the school system: increased incentives for teachers, improvement of the curriculum, parental choice of schools, and extension of the school year.

Increase Incentives for Teachers

Perhaps the only way to encourage more high-quality college students to enter the teaching profession, and to raise the morale of existing teachers, is to increase incentives for teaching. Such incentives might include increased pay, expanded in-service training, provision of sufficient school supplies, increased availability for classroom use of high-tech equipment (computers, film and videotape equipment), and improved working conditions.

A controversial recommendation is the creation of a "master teacher" rank that would recognize and reward ability and dedication to teaching. There is growing evidence that superior teaching can have immense positive effects on students. Pedersen and Faucher found evidence of a high correlation between outstanding first-grade teaching and later adult success of students, all of whom came from an inner-city neighborhood.[36] Master teachers would be paid substantially more and have added responsibilities, such as curriculum design and supervision of new teachers. Teachers' unions have generally opposed the concept, fearing that criteria other than ability and dedication (such as favoritism) will be used in making such selections. Unions tend to also be opposed to higher pay and promotion based on merit, because the merit concept conflicts with the preferred union concept of basing pay on seniority.

Improve the Curriculum

If few new resources are required, practically everyone is in favor of this proposal. However, a major question is: In what directions should the curriculum be improved? As noted earlier, considerable confusion exists as to the goals of a quality education. In the 1960s and early 1970s there was criticism of the rigidity and authoritarianism in schools, which led to increases in the number of electives in high schools and colleges and a reduction in the number of basic "academic" classes. Alternative schools were created for students who found traditional schools to be "stifling." History and social studies classes were revised to include content on significant contributions made by Native Americans, African Americans, Latinos, and other minority groups. New courses were developed that attempted to make school work more relevant to the lives of minority students.

In the 1980s and 1990s concern has shifted. There is a focus on the decline in academic achievement, and school systems are returning to stiffer academic programs. In fact, many of the requirements for basic academic courses that were dropped in the 1960s and early 1970s have been reinstated. In the 1980s and 1990s there has been a move toward teaching basic skills (reading, writing, and arithmetic) and away from

teaching electives (sociology, psychology, or specialized areas of literature and history). As part of this movement, children are also taught to respect authority, be patriotic, and lead moral lives. Some schools have reestablished strict dress codes and sought to curb unconventional behavior.

At the same time, a critical-thinking movement is taking place, which focuses on developing the thinking capacities of students. This approach encourages students to make observations and to critically analyze issues. It stresses class discussions and downplays lectures, emphasizes critical analysis over rote learning, and advocates assessing student understanding through use of essay tests rather than objective tests. In some ways the critical-thinking movement conflicts with the back-to-basics movement. The latter places greater emphasis on learning and remembering facts; the former asserts that memorizing is much less important than developing thinking capacities.

In 1994 the Goals 2000 Educate America Act was passed by Congress and signed by President Clinton. The law is a sweeping reform program that establishes the first-ever national goals in the United States for education. The Act is intended to make American students more competitive in the world economy and to give parents a way to define educational excellence and measure their local school systems by it. Participation by states is voluntary, but the Act provides powerful incentives, in the form of educational grants, for school systems to seek to upgrade their classrooms. The eight national goals to be met by the year 2000 are as follows:

1. *All children in America will start school ready to learn.*

2. *The high school graduation rate will increase to at least 90%.*

3. *American students will leave grades 4, 8, and 12 having demonstrated competency in English, math, science, history, and geography. Every school in America will ensure that all students learn to use their minds well so they will be prepared for responsible citizenship, further learning, and productive employment.*

4. *American students will be first in the world in science and math.*

5. *Every adult will be literate.*

6. *Every school in America will be free of drugs and violence and will offer a disciplined environment.*

7. *Schools will encourage parental involvement in education.*

8. *Schools will promote professional training for teachers.*[37]

Allow Parental Choice of Schools

Under a parental choice system, not only are parents entitled to enroll their children in public schools outside their geographical district, but state tax dollars go to the school that wins the enrollment. By creating market incentives, the thinking goes, academically superior schools should thrive, while inferior schools would have to either improve their performance or face bankruptcy.

Parental choice of schools is currently being tried in a number of states, including Minnesota, Iowa, Nebraska, and Arkansas. Initial findings indicate that the reasons parents and students opt out of one school and for another are often unrelated to academics.[38] In some cases the parents select schools with lower educational standards in order to increase the chances that their son or daughter will graduate—or will graduate with higher grades. Other parents pick schools near their work for convenience reasons. Some parents select schools that will increase the chances of their son or daughter playing on a varsity sports team. In many cases transportation problems force parents to select the school located closest to their home.

A major problem with parental choice of schools is that it has the potential to undermine the neighborhood-school concept. This concept asserts that the neighborhood school should be a center of community living, with its facilities being used by both youngsters and adults for a variety of purposes: education, recreation, leisure activities, social gatherings, sporting events, and community meetings. If parents in a neighborhood send their children to a variety of different schools, the neighborhood school will not become a center of community life.

Another drawback of parental choice is that many children are not in a position to travel to faraway schools. Such children (some of whom are already educationally disadvantaged) may then be "left behind" in the worst districts, which become further impoverished as money follows students to better-financed schools.

Extend the School Year

Elementary and secondary schools in the United States are in session an average of 180 days a year. In contrast, Japan's schools are in session an average of 240 days a year. As a result, Japanese students attending 12 years of school receive the equivalent of about 16 years of schooling in the United States.[39] Comparisons with other advanced nations show a similar disparity.[40]

In 1994 the National Education Commission on Time and Learning (NECTL) found that high schools in the United States require students to spend barely 41% of classroom time on academic subjects.[41] As Little notes, "The typical high school student's schedule—1st period: Driver's ed.; 2nd period: AIDS awareness; 3rd period: Counseling—is looking less and less like a classical education."[42] The NECTL found that high school students in the United States spend only three hours a day on English, science, math, civics, languages, or history—half of what is spent on academic courses in Germany, France, and Japan.[43] In 1994 this Commission recommended boosting class time spent on these basic academic subjects to an average of 5½ hours per day; it also strongly recommended extending the nation's school year.[44]

A strong case can be made for extending the school year. In a review of 100 research projects, Toch found that in 9 out of 10 instances student achievement rises with the amount of time in class.[45] Toch notes:

A 1989 study of students taking an international math test found that Japanese students had

EXHIBIT 9.1

Schools without Failure

In 1969 William Glasser wrote *Schools without Failure* (New York: Harper & Row), which has had considerable impact on improving teaching. The major concepts of Glasser's approach can be summarized as follows.

Glasser asserts that a major problem of school systems is that they are organized in such a way that most students experience failure. He is critical of schools for a variety of reasons. Getting an A is considered the paramount goal in schools; because only a few students get a majority of A's, most do not feel successful. Memorizing is more highly valued than developing thinking capacities. (He believes education is the process of developing thinking capacities.) Glasser asserts that thinking and creative, artistic, and fun uses of students' brains are drastically downgraded in schools. Also, schools do not deal with real-life problems faced by children. Relevance is frequently absent from the curriculum; as a result, children do not transfer classroom learning to problem solving outside of school and thus do not gain the motivation to learn.

Glasser notes:

Unless we can provide schools where children, through a reasonable use of their capacities, can succeed, we will do little to solve the major problems of our country. We will have more social disturbances, more people who need to be kept in jails, prisons, and mental hospitals, more people who need social workers to take care of their lives because they feel they cannot succeed in this society and are no longer willing to try [p. 6].

For a child to succeed in this world, she or he has to develop a positive identity (sense of self). Children who develop a failure identity are unlikely to succeed. Instead, they are likely to become angry, depressed, alienated, lonely, or hostile and may express the failure identity through delinquency, withdrawal, or development of emotional disturbances.

Glasser theorizes that there are two needs that must be met for establishment of a positive or success identity: love and self-worth. If these two needs are unmet, then the child will develop a failure identity. If these two needs are met, the child will develop a success identity and will pay off society many times over by being a responsible, contributing citizen.

Because home conditions in many families are less than desirable, many children do not receive the love or the sense of self-worth that they need. When they cannot fulfill their needs at home, Glasser asserts, they must have the opportunity to do so at school, or they will develop a failure identity. Because every child attends school, schools are in a unique position to identify children who are starting to develop a failure identity.

Teachers need to be better trained in identifying children with failure identities. Colleges of education should provide more content on identifying these children and also should put greater emphasis on developing the relationship capacities of education majors.

Glasser asserts that perhaps the greatest strength of a quality teacher is to be able to form positive relationships with students. Teachers need to be able to convey that each student has a sense of self-worth. Teachers must also be able to convey that they sincerely care about the well-being of each student. Those students identified as beginning to develop a failure identity need to be referred to Pupil Services for help, or the teacher needs to find a way to make the classroom a success experience for these (and all other) students.

Glasser recommends that more emphasis be placed on the teaching of personal development: being assertive, learning to solve life's problems,

(continued)

EXHIBIT 9.1 *(continued)*

improving relationships, handling unwanted emotions, learning responsible sexuality, learning to handle stress, and so on.

Group problem-solving meetings could be held daily in classes. Such meetings would focus on identifying alternatives for solving the problems that students are encountering at school and in their lives. The topics to be discussed would often be brought up by the students themselves (for example, relationship difficulties they are having with someone). Such discussions should take place in a supportive, positive atmosphere. Blaming and fault finding should be minimized or eliminated entirely. The atmosphere needs to be one in which everyone's opinion is equally valued.

According to Glasser, students should not be separated into tracts, because those placed in lower-level tracts are likely to view themselves as failures. He also recommends abolishing the current grading system of A-B-C-D-F and replacing it with a system of competence criteria for each course. For example, in a mathematics course, a student would have to be able to perform a predetermined level of mathematical computations in order to pass the course. Students who achieve these standards would receive a P (for pass) on their report card. Students who do superior work and who help other students who are not doing as well may be awarded an S (for superior work). Students who do not achieve the standards would not receive any grade, and no records would be kept of classes that students do not pass. For basic academic courses, students would be required to repeat the classes until they successfully achieve the established competency levels.

---

studied 98 percent of the precalculus and calculus topics on the test, while their U.S. counterparts had been taught only 50 percent. Half of the Japanese performed as well as the top 5 percent of Americans.[46]

Research also reveals that students lose a lot of ground educationally by letting their minds lie fallow during the summer. Teachers spend on average the whole first month of the fall semester reteaching material forgotten over the summer.[47] The problem is particularly acute for students from impoverished families, who often have fewer opportunities to learn during the summer. One study found that affluent students gain an average of one month of knowledge during the summer, whereas disadvantaged students lose three to four months.[48] Extending the school year into the traditional summer break would also assist working parents who have to deal with childcare arrangements during the daytime.

TOWARD EQUAL EDUCATIONAL OPPORTUNITY

As we've seen, educational opportunities are often lacking for minorities and the poor in this country. Nearly everyone agrees that there should be equal educational opportunity for all. But there is considerable disagreement on how this can be achieved. Three proposals for progressing toward equal educational opportunity are:

1. Reforming school financing so that an equal amount of money is spent on each student's education

2. Establishing special compensatory educational programs for disadvantaged students

3. Integrating students from different ethnic backgrounds into the same school

Reform of School Financing

Schools in wealthy districts tend to receive considerably more money per student than schools in poor districts. At the present time, a majority of the revenue for school districts in practically all states comes from local property taxes. Decaying inner cities are especially hard-pressed to finance school systems, and many schools in these areas are inferior.

There is growing opposition in the United States to using property-tax dollars as the primary source of revenue for funding school systems. Taxpayers on fixed incomes (such as the retired elderly) are increasingly unable to pay large annual increases in their property-tax bills. In 1993 taxpayers in Michigan voted to abolish using property-tax revenues to fund the public school system in that state. In 1994 voters in Michigan approved a constitutional amendment to raise the state sales tax and cigarette tax as the primary sources of supporting the state's schools. One result of this action in Michigan is movement toward equalizing among school districts the amount of money spent on each student's education. Will other states follow this approach? Several state legislatures are currently debating similar bills.[49]

Another suggestion for equalizing the amount of money spent on each student's education is for the federal government to pay for all primary and secondary education, giving the same amount of money per student to each school. Critics of this approach assert that schools in this country have excelled because of local control and involvement. If the funding shifted to the federal government, critics say, the result would be greater federal control and increased "red tape," meaning that a huge federal bureaucracy would undoubtedly evolve.

Compensatory Education

Many authorities believe that special programs and extra assistance would improve achievement levels of the poor and minorities. A variety of programs already exist.

EXHIBIT 9.2

Academic Time Requirements

Over four years, the average hours required for academic subjects* in high school classrooms are listed below.

Country	Average Hours
Germany	3528
France	3280
Japan	3170
United States	1460

*The academic subjects were defined to be English, science, mathematics, civics, languages, and history.
Source: Rod Little, "The Endangered Summer Vacation," *U.S. News & World Report*, May 16, 1994, p. 12.

Project Head Start gives preschool instruction to disadvantaged children. Evaluations of the results of Head Start indicate that students who attend are better prepared for starting first grade than disadvantaged students who do not attend Head Start.[50] Recent studies show that Head Start also appears to have long-term benefits for disadvantaged children.[51] For example, an 18-year followup study of 123 children found that, by the age of 15, children who had attended Head Start averaged a full grade higher than children in a control group. Head Start youngsters also displayed significantly less delinquent behavior, were more likely to hold jobs, and were substantially less likely to have been enrolled in special education programs.[52]

Most school districts have Pupil Services departments that seek to assess the academic, social, and emotional needs of children who are not progressing well in school. Once an assessment of a child is completed, programs are developed to meet the unique learning needs of the child. A wide variety of services may be provided, depending on the identified needs. There are special classes for the emotionally disturbed and for those with learning disabilities. Counseling is sometimes provided. Some students are referred for drug abuse and some are for visual or hearing difficulties. Pupil Services departments are staffed by a variety of professionals—school psychologists, social workers, and guidance counselors. In 1975 Congress passed the Education for All Handicapped Children Act, now known as PL 94–142. This law addresses the numerous physical, developmental, learning, and social-emotional problems that hamper the education of children. In sweeping legislation, the law mandated that all school districts identify students with these problems and then develop specialized programs to meet their needs. Unfortunately, many low-income school districts, because of financial constraints, have not been able to meet the objectives of this bill.

In many states programs are being developed to prevent children from dropping out of school. Some school districts have dropout rates approaching 50%, and the national average is over 10%.[53] Dropping out represents an enormous loss to those individuals and to society because of lost potential productivity. The estimated lifetime earnings of high school graduates are $200,000 higher than those of dropouts.[54] Programs for "at-risk" students are a response to the need to help high school students stay in school and learn practical job skills.

Some elementary and secondary school systems now have reading, writing, and arithmetic programs during the summer for students who need assistance in these areas. A variety of compensatory educational programs have been established at the college level as well. These include noncredit courses in English and mathematics, tutoring, and various testing programs. Many colleges have special provisions for the admission of minority students who do not meet standard admission requirements, and such students are encouraged to utilize the educational opportunity programs that are available. (Students who attended inferior elementary and secondary school systems in inner cities are often two to four grade levels behind in reading, writing, and arithmetic and therefore need educational opportunity programs to have a chance to succeed in college.)

Educational opportunity programs have become an accepted part of most colleges and universities. A stickier question involves special admissions of minority students to graduate and professional schools. Supporters assert that these affirmative action admissions are attempts to compensate for the inferior school systems and other discriminations that minorities have been subjected to in the past. On the other hand, because competition is intense for the limited admissions into these schools, white students complain that they are the victims of reverse discrimination—that they are being rejected even though their entrance exam scores are higher than those of some minority students who are accepted. The legal status of this affirmative action policy has not as yet been fully resolved.

Effective Integration

As discussed earlier, school busing has been used to attempt to integrate students within school districts. Many whites in large cities have responded by moving to suburbs or sending their children to private schools. Some big cities, through court orders, are experimenting with merging suburban school districts with inner-city school districts and then busing children within each district. The extent to which such merging will occur is questionable. There is a major problem with distance, as some suburban communities are so far from inner cities that students would have to spend a large part of their day on a bus. Most white parents in suburbs would not raise serious objections to a small number of inner-city children being bused to their schools in the suburbs. However, most suburbanites fearing potential violence and a lower-quality education, would object to their children being bused to inferior school systems in inner cities. Many white parents, if faced with such a court order, would probably respond by placing their children in private schools.

The ideal way to integrate neighborhood schools is through integration of residential areas, so that neighborhood schools are then automati-

A music classroom in New York City reflects current efforts to achieve equal educational opportunity. Children with disabilities in a Brooklyn school have the opportunity to participate in such classes in part because of recent legislation mandating that school districts develop specialized programs to meet their needs.

cally integrated. Such integration would provide ongoing opportunities for interracial cooperation and friendships for children and for adults. The chances of this proposal working, however, are minute. People of different ethnic and racial groups generally are reluctant to live together in the same neighborhood. In addition, many members of minority groups cannot afford to live in affluent neighborhoods, and white residents of such neighborhoods object to having low-cost housing built in their communities.

Another possible avenue toward integration is through the use of "magnet" schools in cities. Magnet schools are ones that offer special courses, programs, or equipment. Examples would be a fine arts middle school or high school and a school emphasizing curriculum in the area of computer science. Proponents of magnet schools hope that placing such schools in inner-city areas would draw students from suburbs because of the excellent educational opportunities they could offer.

The prospects of significant federal help for inner-city schools in the near future are not bright. In this era of trying to reduce the federal deficit through budget cutbacks, the chances of the enactment of a bold new federal program to channel resources to financially distressed school districts are remote.

John E. Farley summarizes the significance to all Americans of providing equal educational opportunities for minorities and the poor:

> If the overall effectiveness of the educational system is poor, American productivity will suffer, and our standard of living will likely fall in our increasingly competitive world. Likewise, if we fail the large and growing proportion of our young people who are African American, Hispanic, or from low-income homes of any race, the result will be the same. Failing to educate those who account for such a large and growing share of the future labor force will have a similar destructive impact on America's productivity and its standard of living.[55]

SCHOOL SOCIAL WORKERS: A RESPONSE TO CRISIS*

Given the problems within the educational system and the societal difficulties that schools have been asked to erase, it is not surprising that specialists, such as school social workers, have become part of the school system. School social work is a relatively new role. Before 1960 there were few school social workers, and they were employed primarily by large, urban school systems (for example, New York City and Chicago). In fact, one of the earliest books on school social workers was first published in 1955.[56] School social work, then, must be discussed within the context of its evolving role.

Before doing this, however, it is necessary to have a method of analyzing behavior so that we have an initial base for understanding the nature of children's problems in schools. It is a practical necessity for any school social worker to understand the dynamics of behavior, because social workers have been and will continue to be closely involved with problematic behavior in children. In 1975 Congress enacted PL94–142 (the Education for All Handicapped Children Act). This statute mandates that each local school district must provide full and appropriate educational opportunities to all children with a disability. Much of the definition of social work services offered in PL94–142 specifies (1) defining the nature of social or behavioral problems, (2) using individual or family counseling skills, and (3) using other resources to make an impact on behavioral, emotional, and social problems.

The Nature of Behavior

We will begin with the premise that behavior is purposeful, that we do things for a reason. We may not always know exactly why we are doing things, in that we don't analyze each of our behaviors. But we always respond to a given situation with a set of beliefs, with a history of past attempts to solve a problem, and within the context of our present environment.[57]

In using his rational-emotive behavior therapy, Albert Ellis looks at behavior within the context of what he calls its ABCs. In essence, he says that B—a belief system composed of attitudes, interpretations, and emotions—is always juxtaposed between an activating situation, A, and a consequence, C.[58] This belief system is based, no matter what our age, on opinions we have about ourselves and others in relation to our perceptions about our place in the larger world. The person, then, can decide on a course of action given certain circumstances. Children, like adults, do not act in a random fashion. They act in relation to a decision they have made about the consistency and stability of their relationships with adults and other children. There are antecedents of behavior that often depend on *decisions* they have made about their abilities, not on their *actual* abilities. Thus, although it may seem that a girl is misbehaving when she approaches new situations, in reality she may have decided from past experience that she will have little success in the task and is thus acting up because she does not want to face the fear of another failure. The child has made a decision, although it may be based on what can be termed a *mistaken belief system*.[59] She wrongly assumes that failure means she is worthless and that trying is not important. To understand how to alter that self-perception, one must look more closely at some primary goals of behavior.

Rudolf Dreikurs postulated that the force behind every human action is a goal. We all know some of what we want, although often we do not consciously act on those goals but rather on unanalyzed means of achieving them. It is possible to understand the psychological motivation of the child if one develops diagnostic skills to analyze four goals of misbehavior: attention getting, power seeking, revenge seeking, and assuming a disability.[60] Some children try to get attention, to always be the focal point for others, because they believe that otherwise they are worthless. Other

---

*This section was written especially for this text by Don Nolan, MSSW, school social worker.

children attempt to prove their power in the belief that only if they can do what they want and defy adult pressure can they be important. Still others may seek revenge: The only means by which they feel significant is to hurt others, just as they feel hurt by them. Others may display actual or imaginary disabilities in order to be left alone so that nothing is demanded of them. The crucial point is that, whatever deviant behaviors children display, there are always reasons for these behaviors.

Anyone who has worked extensively with children, in any situation, can readily remember youngsters who were acting out these goals. For example, Ted, who is constantly in front of the teacher interrupting and is always calling attention to himself by ''forcing'' the teacher to repeatedly reprimand him, is clearly seeking attention. Juan, who is usually confrontational, who is noncompliant to reasonable requests from the teacher, and who rejects praise and social reinforcers from the teacher, is in a power struggle. Noriko, who physically injures others and who usually puts others and herself down, is probably seeking revenge for some perceived wrong. Odell, who is withdrawn, who sinks down in his desk, who is shy with classmates, and who fears new situations, is probably displaying a disability.

We must, of course, be careful not to overgeneralize or analyze too quickly, and we must remember that the child could be displaying these behaviors because of dysfunctional family patterns or because of medical or psychiatric problems. Behavior is complicated and can be deceptive at times. However, if we use the goals-of-behavior construct, with its philosophy of purposeful behavior and actions, we have a starting point for responding to these behaviors. Thus, given a general philosophy of behavior as it applies to the educational system, we can talk about specific ways of intervening to solve problems.

Traditional School Social Work Roles

Because many school systems have never had social workers on their staff, the responsibility for elucidating the many roles of social work and the potential value of these functions often remains with the new school social worker. This will be a long and at times frustrating process, for any fundamental change in basic system services will affect the balance and direction of all services. Consequently, the social worker must be in a position to prove that the change she or he brings will ultimately benefit the system and thus be worth the uneasiness that the other staff will feel in adjusting to a new person in a different and challenging role. Persistence and what Albert Ellis terms self-awareness (being perceptive and accepting of one's strengths and limitations) will be needed initially.[61]

Let's look at some traditional roles for school social work practice: caseworker, group worker, truant officer, counselor, and parent liaison.

CASEWORKER

Intervention has always been the essence of social work. Social workers have responded with a variety of methods to the problems caused by the complexities of modern society. Casework, traditionally, has been one of the first methods used in any given area; it encompasses the more clinical and best-known aspects of social work. Basically, social workers have had to prove their worth; that is, they have had to prove that they do something different from what was already being done. Because social workers have substantial training in family dynamics, they can analyze and diagnose common problems in the dysfunctional family. This is a skill that others in the typical school system do not have, and thus it is viewed as an area of particular expertise for the school social worker.

Consider the case of Mike, age 10, who had a number of problems. He was physically aggressive toward other children and was prone to act with outbursts of emotion and anger when put in new or different situations. He had virtually no coping skills and came to school after weekends or vacations in an angry, violent mood. The family consisted of five children and his mother. His father was no longer living at home but visited on occasion. Mike's emotional problems, and particularly his violent attitudes, were accentuated after these visits. In addition, Mike wore dirty, unkempt clothing, which always seemed either too small or much too big. Mike's behavior in class was, of course, a problem. His goals of misbehavior were a combination of attention seeking and power seeking. In an attempt to change this behavior pattern, the social workers, using a casework strategy, (1) made a referral to the county department of social services to make sure that the family was getting all services that were available—for example, homemaking, medical services, and counseling; (2) modified Mike's behavior at school by devising a system of reinforcers that were important to him; (3) made sure that Mike found success in academic areas in school by helping the teacher to individualize for Mike's needs; (4) tried to help the mother understand that Mike should not be put in situations in which he had to adopt a negative attitude toward adults; and (5) contacted the father about his relationship to his son. All of this takes considerable time and energy. In casework a consistent, organized, step-by-step approach is used. Casework thus becomes a one-to-one involvement with a family in an attempt to solve a problem.

Now let's look at Phyllis, age 6, who was hearing impaired. She was in a special education program four days a week. There were a number of problems: noncompliant behaviors when Phyllis knew what was wanted of her, a difficulty in communicating in any way, and a number of medical problems. The caseworker decided that a home intervention program was necessary. Consistency was needed in the sign language program between home and school. Behavior management was lacking in the home, for Phyllis was not expected to do anything there; the only demands were bathroom skills. The parents needed help in developing reasonable goals and expectations for Phyllis and then following through on a program. Medically, Phyllis needed extensive diagnostic work at a nearby hospital. The caseworker made contact with the hospital, arranged for a meeting, and then made sure that followup came from the hospital. Again, the social worker set specific goals and followed them in an attempt to solve a

multitude of problems. Much of the emphasis in the caseworker model is on doing things that teachers are not prepared for and do not have the time to do. The goals are not strictly educational ones, but have the purpose of enabling children to achieve in school.

GROUP WORKER

As casework came to be considered outmoded in some areas of social work practice,[62] school social workers found another method of intervening in school problems: group work. Essentially, the rationale was that the social worker could influence the lives and educational success of too few people when using the casework approach. A group approach also assumes that, by sharing experiences, students can put their own problems in perspective and can learn new strategies for resolving school-related and personal problems. A few examples of a group approach follow.

Ms. Tanner's fifth-grade class was a problem for her. Specifically, four boys regularly would not listen, clowned around, and did little work in class. In fact, they were doing less well academically than in the past year and were starting to go around as a group, often getting into trouble on the playground. An intervention strategy was designed: the creation of groups as a means of solving these problems. Two groups of five boys were created, with two of the "problem" boys in each group. The groups worked in specific high-interest areas; for example, one group worked on a science project that involved creating a metric unit for the third grade, while the other studied the principles of flight and aerodynamics, making kites, paper airplanes, and wooden models. There were a number of planned goals for each group. First, the social worker wanted to create new friendships and show the disruptive children models of more appropriate behavior, behavior that could be as rewarding as attention-getting behavior. Second, cooperation was fostered in conjunction with the principles of peer pressure. All children worked toward step-by-step, cooperative goals; unless all helped, none could reach their goal. Finally, the social worker wanted everyone—the target boys, their peers in the class, and their teacher—to realize that the boys could be productive and successful so that both teacher's and students' perceptions would be altered. The social worker also discussed with Ms. Tanner how individual programming could be used to provide additional successful educational experiences for these four boys.

In another case, group experience involved high school freshmen who were failing in their initial coursework. Study habits, poor motivation, and a negative attitude toward school success were the main concerns. In this case the social worker organized a group of students who took a special course organized around ways of studying. The course was named "Ten Ways to Beat the System" and was structured in a way that allowed the student to learn enjoyable ways to become successful in school. At the same time a number of older students were organized to meet informally with the freshmen to discuss some positive aspects of high school that the younger students could look forward to. In addition, these upperclassmen offered guidance about which teachers to avoid and which teachers they could expect a fair deal from.

Many school districts are now offering a variety of groups that are often led by social workers. Examples of such groups include *assertiveness training* for students who are shy or nonassertive, *anger control* for students who frequently lose their temper or are aggressive, *relationship building* for students who have love relationship problems, *coping with loss* for students whose parents divorce or who have experienced the death of a loved one, *responsible drug and alcohol use* for students who are using or abusing alcohol or other drugs, and *school-age mothers* for students who are pregnant or are raising a child.

TRUANT OFFICER

Social workers in the school have performed a number of other roles, including that of truant officer. Often the truant officer functions as an advocate for the child. There are times when acting as an agent of social control (the law, the system) need not be looked at negatively. A case in point is a multiproblem family with three boys in high

school. Although none of the boys had reached the legal age after which school was no longer compulsory, the parents decided to keep the boys at home so they could help the father in his job as a farmhand. The boys had mentioned to different teachers that they feared this was about to happen, but they were afraid to tell their father that they wanted to stay in school. The social worker was able to intervene in this case by using the truancy laws to inform the parents that they had no choice but to send their sons to school. In this case the undesirable role of truant officer was transformed into one that was advantageous for the children involved. It was also a means of helping to promote the concept of equal access. Given the high truancy and dropout rates in larger cities, the approach of combining the services of truant officers with creative or alternative approaches to education can be beneficial to children.

COUNSELOR AND PARENT LIAISON

The social worker as a counselor and/or parent liaison or parent trainer is also a fairly common role in school social work. Often, teachers will expect the school social worker to be the liaison between themselves and parents. And it is frequently assumed that the social worker will defend and justify the actions or educational planning of the teacher. This can cause somewhat strained relations between the social worker and the rest of the teaching staff, especially when a worker agrees with a parent that the school system ought to make changes in its educational programs to better serve the children. This role requires a lot of tact and prior planning, as well as a relatively assertive view toward expanding social work services.

In the role of counselor, the social worker also brings a number of skills to the situation. As school social work services have developed, there has been a trend toward perceiving the social worker as a therapist rather than as an academic counselor. This distinction has been more than semantic, because advanced professional (master's degree) training has greatly increased the diagnostic and psychological skills of school social workers relative to other school professionals (such as guidance counselors). Thus, a school social worker can be seen as both a specialist in the diagnosis of emotional difficulties in children and as the support staff person with the most extensive psychiatric and medically based training.

Newer Social Work Roles

In essence, role development and expansion are of critical concern to school social workers. When they join a school system, a number of expectations and specific job-related demands will be placed on them. There are bound to be conflicts because the older roles encompassing casework, group work, counselor, or parent liaison may not provide enough flexibility to meet the demands of the change effort. As a result, school social workers have adapted by developing newer approaches to their role. We'll now look at seven of these newer approaches: advocate, behavioral specialist, mental health consultant, alcohol and other drug abuse specialist, multidisciplinary team member, violence prevention specialist, and systems change specialist.

ADVOCATE

Recently one of the most provocative roles for the social worker has become that of advocate.[63] In the school setting, an advocate is someone who understands and is not intimidated by large complicated systems and can help a family or child in facing the educational bureaucracy of dealing with other social systems.

This can be a particularly useful role when working with families who are not well acquainted with the educational system. For instance, in an early education program that is geared to helping prekindergarten children who show evidence of developmental delay, the social worker can use this role to help the parents understand their rights under the law, including their rights to appeal program decisions if they feel the programs do not fit the needs of their child. The social worker can explain who is teaching what materials and why this should help the child progress. She or he can be the person who follows the child in the program so that the parents can

have a contact who is familiar and with whom they feel comfortable asking questions. The social worker can also be the person who makes them aware of applicable medical or social service agencies that are available to give them a better knowledge of their child or offer supportive services when these are needed. Finally, the social worker can be a person to talk to about the complexities, difficulties, fears, or guilt associated with raising a child who in some way is different from other children. A combination of all of these functions expands the role of home liaison and enables the advocate to meet needs that have not previously been met in the school context.

BEHAVIORAL SPECIALIST

There has been a trend at some major universities toward training school social workers in one discrete, highly recognizable skill. Within this context, emphasis is often put on the social worker's becoming a behavioral specialist, a person who understands and can systematically apply behavior modification. Within the schools a knowledge of how to alter behavior has immediate and long-term applicability. Using behavioral skills, the social worker can provide guidance in general learning principles as applied to overall teaching and can develop specific programs for children who are having difficulty adjusting to normal classroom routine. The following is a case example.

Phillip, age 9, was having difficulty paying attention and was usually noncompliant to directions. His teacher was having trouble understanding his behavior and motivating him to be involved in usual classroom activities—for example, doing independent work in math and reading, participating in small-group activities, and cooperating in play arrangements. A social worker with behavioral training was asked to intervene in the situation. After observing the antecedents of the noncompliant behavior and recording baseline data of on-task or attending behaviors in nonacademic situations,[64] the social worker was able to put together a program. The program included (1) the planned use of social reinforcers (praise from the teacher); (2) a reward system built around interest in science (other work had to be done before the work in science could begin); and (3) a system that involved ignoring Phillip's verbal noncompliance while reinforcing compliance from other students with praise and tangible rewards, such as permitting them to help with a special project and take notes to the office. In this way Phillip's behaviors were changed in a relatively short time.

MENTAL HEALTH CONSULTANT

A school social worker can also function as a mental health consultant to the other staff. Curriculum today is no longer as simple as reading, writing, and arithmetic (if this was ever the case). Although there is currently substantial concern about teaching the "basics" in education, teachers must still seek to improve old curriculum and develop new materials and new teaching styles. Because social workers have training in the social psychology of individual behavior, they can serve as consultants to the mental health and human relations aspects of curriculum and to teaching style. With this focus the social worker plays a preventive role, seeking to help teachers motivate students via stimulating materials. She or he can help create a teaching approach that is not threatening but intriguing, questioning, and supportive of the process of learning. Naturally, the social worker would also be involved in helping teachers to individualize education—to devise materials and teaching styles that meet the needs of all children, no matter what their current academic level.

The social worker can help create a systematized approach to monitoring progress and then create new techniques to facilitate remediation when necessary. To accomplish these goals, it may be necessary to organize brainstorming sessions with all the teachers or to begin an investigation of the materials available on a number of topics.

In this way social workers can help provide guidance in curriculum development, with an overall emphasis on human relations. The inclusion of specific human relations goals in teaching has often been overlooked, even though many problems in the schools (such as trouble on the playground and problems with special and regular education classes) can be seen as directly attributable to a lack of human relations materials. Children need to learn that "different is OK," that cultural or racial differences can be enjoyed rather than feared, that all people deserve respect as human beings; and that values are learned concepts that can be changed.[65] School social workers, because of their training and unique place in the school, can provide the perspective needed to devise such a curriculum and help create systems for implementation.

ALCOHOL AND OTHER DRUG ABUSE SPECIALIST

Drug use and abuse continue to be a major problem in our society. From the days of Prohibition, various segments of society have addressed the "evils" of alcohol and other drug use. Today, with the tragic loss of lives associated with drunk driving and with the much-publicized drug-overdose deaths of sports and entertainment figures, there is a growing realization of the need for drug prevention programs. Programs having a punitive interventive focus have not been successful. Thus there has been a recent emphasis on prevention, and schools have become the mechanism for drug prevention programs.

Because schools generally do not have trained specialists in this area, many school districts have hired school social workers to consult with parents and to refer students who are abusing drugs to appropriate inpatient or outpatient treatment centers. Social workers, because of their knowledge of chemical dependency, their training in interviewing, their skills in interacting with parents, and their knowledge of community resources, have become the logical choice to spearhead the development of prevention programs. They have also been asked to become curriculum specialists in this area. Thus, as part of their overall responsibilities, many school social workers help develop teaching curriculum on drug use and abuse for elementary, middle, and high schools. In this respect, social workers are responding to changes in society and in the family, as education seeks to accomplish more and more societal goals.

Many school districts have developed intervention programs for students who either have become chemically dependent or are concerned about the possibility of this occurring. Student Assistance Programs (SAPs), often led by school social workers, offer a group approach in this area. Groups for students who have returned from alcohol or other drug treatment centers, groups for students who want to know more about the mood-altering effects of alcohol and other drugs, and groups for students who are concerned about others' use of chemicals have become commonplace in many schools. There may also be groups for students affected by others' (such as parents') use of alcohol or other drugs.

MULTIDISCIPLINARY TEAM MEMBER

Another role of the social worker that is gaining increasing popularity involves using his or her skills in conjunction with other members on a team. The school social worker may join with other professionals (psychologist, speech therapist, special education teacher, physical therapist, and regular education teacher) to determine the special educational needs and particular programming appropriate for certain children. This is an area of implementation of PL 94–142, with the group of professionals commonly called an M-Team (multidisciplinary team). In this case the social worker might be involved (1) with an initial assessment of the child and the family, with special emphasis on family functioning and the child's social and adaptive skills; (2) with the parents clinically, either through family counseling and role analysis or through training in special techniques, such as behavior modification or crisis intervention; or (3) in teacher observation, training, and support.

The point here is that the social worker acts as part of a team—as a member with certain discrete skills and knowledge—and in conjunction with the team seeks to alleviate problems. Although this may appear to be a somewhat constricting role, in that other methods may seem to offer more independence, it can be a useful way to find gaps in services and to decrease overlap among individual skills. It has its advantages, especially if one is responsible for a school (or a school system) with a large population. One particular advantage is the learning that takes place for the social worker as she or he interacts with other professionals on the team.

VIOLENCE PREVENTION SPECIALIST

Schools are often said to be a microcosm of the larger society. In many of our cities, violence toward others has become a major problem—a problem that is not limited to adults. Offenses committed by juveniles have become more serious in nature. For example, in 1986 a majority of cases in New York City's juvenile court system were misdemeanors; in 1994 more than 90% were felonies, many of which involved violence.[66] In many inner cities, gangs have become such a destructive force that some school districts now have instituted dress codes in an attempt to counter the influence of gang symbols (the wearing of certain apparel or colors is thought to be a factor in developing and maintaining a "gang identity"). Student violence against teachers has also increased, creating a climate in some schools of fear and intimidation. Police liaison officers are now common in many schools.

Violence prevention is yet another area where schools have traditionally not employed specialists. Some 30 to 40 years ago, in a slower-paced and more stable society, the school principal would usually enforce whatever discipline was necessary. (The principal often solicited parent cooperation in administering strict, often punitive, consequences to students who violated school rules.) Today, gangs have become the "family" of far too many teens. The use of such drugs as crack and cocaine has caused an increase in addictive behaviors and aggression toward others. The methods of maintaining behavioral control in schools have changed, and school social workers are in a unique position to again demonstrate leadership and knowledge of human behavior.

Teachers need to develop more effective ways of working with students who are prone to become violent or aggressive. School social workers can help train teaching staff to become effective in nonviolent intervention techniques. For example, teachers can be instructed in helping students to learn anger-control techniques. Students can be taught how to reframe their angry thought processes so that they express their anger in assertive and nonviolent ways, rather than in aggressive ways. They can also be instructed in how to walk away from a potential fight, and they can learn indirect ways of expressing their anger (such as by hitting a punching bag or by jogging). Teachers who have learned to guide students in anger-control techniques also regain a sense of "being in charge."

Another example of an effective technique for reducing student violence is peer mediation, whereby students mediate their interpersonal conflicts. School social workers develop a training plan to teach a core group of students the skills of active listening, compromising, and problem solving. Through training and supervision this core group can then mediate conflicts that occur in the school, potentially preventing smaller disagreements from becoming violent conflicts. The influence of the social worker is then greatly enhanced, as many more students are ultimately "seen" through the core group of trained students.

Another available approach to minimize school violence is the formation of violence-prevention teams formed from the police department, schools, and youth-serving agencies. Too often, agencies and schools are involved only in intervention efforts. Because of their unique position and skills, and because of the system coordination expectations in their job, school social workers can take a leadership role in developing a team effort for the prevention of violence that uses the resources and energies of professionals from many systems. An example of the team prevention approach is to combine recreational activities and adult mentors for "at risk" children in elementary schools.

SYSTEMS CHANGE SPECIALIST

Allen Pincus and Anne Minahan postulate that the focus of social work practice should be the interaction between people and systems in the social environment.[67] If we look at schools as a natural access point for families (most families must deal with schools at some point in their existence), social workers should be able to

Gangs have become the "family" of far too many teens today. Violence and addictive behavior are part of gangs' destructive force. School social workers can train teachers to effectively intervene with students who are prone to violence or aggression.

perform a unique role in the schools. Given the complex nature of society today, most people need to enhance their problem-solving abilities. Social workers can help in this regard by linking people to systems and improving existing service and delivery mechanisms. This role model can involve situations of equal access or integration, the development of programs to deal with changing family patterns, or issues relating to the quality of education. Schools are a critical link in the total societal resource system. Indeed, the neighborhood school is often the system with which the average citizen feels most comfortable. Thus we must examine our schools and look for the inadequacies in their educational structure. The questions we need to answer are: What do we really need in order to determine success for the student? How can we use the materials and personnel in the most efficient way? Through a system of assessing present data, determining goals, and forming active systems for the purpose of exercising influence, one can answer the above questions and ultimately build a better, more accessible, more demand-based school program.

The social worker has a large role to play in this process, for he or she can become an organizer, a leader, a catalyst toward change, a liaison for the needs and wishes of the families, and a specialist in devising systems to meet change-oriented goals. Typical focuses are on discovering (1) the particular deficiencies in the school and the community, (2) the under- or unserved population, and (3) the programs that are needed to get children back in school and to curb juvenile delinquency. Another focus might be to analyze the interaction among systems components in the schools, or between the schools and the county departments of social services, to see, for example, whether these components are really working together or if they have underlying assumptions that work at cross purposes.

As systems change specialist, a social worker is an institutional change agent, a person analyzing ongoing programs and proposed new programs. The systems change approach seeks to change the goals of the traditional school social worker. The traditional goals were to help the child adapt to the school, to use the learning opportunities available, and to modify student behavior or parent/child relationships to alleviate problems in the school. With the systems approach the goals are to analyze which parts of the system are activating stress in a given situation and then to alter that system so that equilibrium is again maintained. One must find and prioritize targets for change, acknowledging that different approaches must be used to solve different problems.

This approach should become clearer if we analyze a typical problem (see Case Example 9.2) that might be referred to a school social worker. By reevaluating and refocusing the problem, the systems change specialist makes the goals clearer and more meaningful.

SUMMARY

Education, which in the past has been called on to resolve a variety of social problems, is now recognized as a social problem itself. Education is currently facing a variety of crises and problems.

There are a number of indicators that raise questions about the quality of education in this country. For example, scores on the Scholastic Aptitude Test, which is taken annually by high school seniors, are significantly lower than they were 30 years ago.

A second problematic area is that school systems are providing inferior educational opportunities for the poor and for members of minority groups. Less money is spent per student on education in low-income school districts and in school districts in which high proportions of minority students live. In our society, academic achievement is highly correlated with socioeconomic status.

A third problematic area is that there is considerable confusion about the desirable goals of education. There is agreement that schools should teach the basic skills of reading, writing, and arithmetic. However, there is controversy among different interest groups concerning the other learning goals that education should strive to attain.

A fourth problematic area is intolerable working conditions for teachers in some school settings. Intolerable conditions include low pay and low prestige, drug and alcohol abuse among students, physical threats and assaults from some students, insufficient instructional supplies, and high student-to-teacher ratios.

Four proposals for improving education in this country are to increase incentives for teachers, to improve the curriculum, to allow parents to choose the school to which they will send their children, and to extend the school year. One of the controversial proposed incentives for teaching is the creation of master-teacher positions that would reward excellence in teaching. A major problem with seeking to improve the curriculum is a lack of agreement about what the curriculum should teach students. Under the parental-choice-

CASE
EXAMPLE 9.2   ## An Example of the Systems Change Role

John is a 10-year-old boy in a special education class. He is in that class because he is considerably behind the rest of his age group in reading and math. He also demonstrates some behavioral problems, particularly in stressful situations. He has not yet been termed EMR (educable mentally retarded), but, as he gets older and does less well academically, he may ultimately be tested and found to have an IQ in the educable range. He is involved in a specialized program called mainstreaming, whereby he is placed in a regular class for physical education, music, art, and social studies. In the beginning of the year there was hope for further mainstreaming into remedial reading and math, but behavioral problems have interfered. A referral has been sent to the school social worker asking that a behavioral program be started and that mainstreaming be stopped until further reassessment can be done. If the goal is only to put a ''Band-aid'' on the problem, it would be relatively easy to start a behavioral program and withdraw the child from the situation. Seemingly, everyone could accept this ''solution,'' but what would it do for John's learning?

Another way of approaching the problem, using a systems change role, is to form a group composed of the teacher, the support personnel, and the principal to discuss mainstreaming as a general educational goal and to form flexible school policies regarding it. Forming a better mainstreaming program in which John can be successful becomes the main goal, as the assumption is that other students are encountering similar difficulties and will also benefit from any change. At the same time the social worker must provide a support system for the regular education teacher involved with John. This could include (1) giving the teacher some general suggestions regarding behavioral management that are applicable to many children, (2) helping to find curriculum materials that are interesting to John and applicable to the rest of the group, (3) forming a group of students around John who would display good modeling behaviors, (4) writing a contract with John in which he could agree to certain limited goals for himself within the classroom, and (5) making sure through classroom discussion in human relations that John has the potential for friendships in the regular education class. The social worker could also support the special education teacher and continue to give reinforcement for mainstreaming students. Finally, he or she could make John's parents aware of the benefits of mainstreaming so that they could talk about it at home and generally tell John how desirable they thought it was. John's parents could then be more actively involved in his education, which would help to increase John's motivation to learn. Another goal would be to use this (or some other successful) mainstreaming effort to encourage more mainstreaming of additional students with other teachers.

Using this model, the social worker is designing a planned change approach and recognizing motivations for change and problems resulting from change. John is the focus for a much larger problem and is not *the* problem. He is the *access point* for the interconnection among a number of systems: regular education teachers, special education teachers, children with behavioral problems, and children with learning disabilities. As far as the school social worker is concerned, John is a catalyst for the creation of a system that will better serve many children.

of-schools approach, it is theorized that market incentives would be created whereby academically superior schools would thrive and inferior schools would have to improve or face bankruptcy.

Three proposals were presented for seeking to work toward equal education opportunities for low-income and minority students: (1) reform school financing in order to spend an equal amount of money on each student's education, (2) establish special compensatory educational programs for disadvantaged students, and (3) integrate students from different ethnic and racial backgrounds into the same schools.

There are several role models for school social work practice. Traditional roles include those of caseworker, group worker, truant officer, counselor, and parent liaison. Newer roles include advocate, behavioral specialist, mental health consultant, alcohol and other drug abuse specialist, multidisciplinary team member, violence prevention specialist, and systems change specialist.

School social workers cannot solve all of the problems in education. Difficulties with integration, differences over goals, problems with the quality of the teaching staff, and changing roles and expectations in the family are all very complex and demanding problems. However, new ideas and creative approaches can be developed within the role of a systems change specialist, who can help the educational system address the problems of education and ultimately seek solutions.

Notes

1. Quoted in William Kornblum and Joseph Julian, *Social Problems*, 6th ed. (Englewood Cliffs, NJ: Prentice-Hall, 1988), p. 394.
2. James W. Coleman and Donald R. Cressey, *Social Problems*, 5th ed. (New York: HarperCollins, 1993), p. 95.
3. Ibid.
4. "Student Reading, Writing Progress Slows," *Wisconsin State Journal*, Jan. 10, 1990, p. 1A.
5. Ibid.
6. CNN Cable News Report, July 18, 1988.
7. David Boldt, "Schools Failing Even U.S. Elite," *Wisconsin State Journal*, Mar. 4, 1990, p. 18A.
8. Quoted in Lucia Solorzano, "Teaching in Trouble," *U.S. News & World Report*, May 26, 1986, pp. 52–54.
9. "If U Cn Reed Thiz Storie . . . ," *U.S. News & World Report*, Sept. 20, 1993, p. 10.
10. *Newsweek*, June 17, 1991, pp. 64–66.
11. John E. Farley, *American Social Problems*, 2d ed. (Englewood Cliffs, NJ: Prentice-Hall, 1992), pp. 446–451.
12. "Michigan's Model," *U.S. News & World Report*, Mar. 28, 1994, p. 16.
13. Ibid.
14. Manley Fleischman et al., *The Fleischman Report on the Quality, Cost, and Financing of Elementary and Secondary Education in New York State* (New York: Viking, 1974), p. 57.
15. Farley, *American Social Problems*, pp. 448–455.
16. Ibid., pp. 448–464.
17. Coleman and Cressey, *Social Problems*, pp. 89–91.
18. Paul B. Horton, Gerald R. Leslie, and Richard F. Larson, *The Sociology of Social Problems* (Englewood Cliffs, NJ: Prentice-Hall, 1988), pp. 176–191.
19. Ibid.
20. Coleman and Cressey, pp. 89–95.
21. Ibid., pp. 93–95.
22. L. Tye, "Study: U.S. Retreats on Integration," *Wisconsin State Journal*, Jan. 12, 1992, p. 9A.
23. Ibid.
24. Ibid.
25. Ibid.
26. Ibid.
27. Nancy H. St. John, *School Desegregation: Outcomes for Children* (New York: Wiley, 1975), pp. 64–86.
28. William Kornblum and Joseph Julian, *Social Problems*, 7th ed. (Englewood Cliffs, NJ: Prentice-Hall, 1992), pp. 369–372.
29. Ibid.
30. Solorzano, "Teaching in Trouble," p. 52.
31. Ibid., p. 54.
32. Vincent Parrillo, John Stimson, and Ardyth Stimson, *Contemporary Social Problems*, 2d ed. (New York: Macmillan, 1989), p. 384.
33. Ibid.
34. Michael Rutter and associates, quoted in W. William Salgank, "British Study Finds Sharp Differences in Schools," *Los Angeles Times*, Nov. 22, 1979, Part VIII, pp. 1–2.
35. Michael Rutter, *15,000 Hours: Secondary Schools and Their Effects on Children* (Cambridge, MA: Harvard University Press, 1979).

36. Eigil Pederson and Therese Annette Faucher, with William W. Eaton, "A New Perspective on the Effects of First-Grade Teachers on Children's Subsequent Adult Status," *Harvard Educational Review*, 48 (1978), pp. 1–31.

37. "Education Reform Signed," *Wisconsin State Journal*, Apr. 1, 1994, p. 2A.

38. "The Uncertain Benefits of School Choice," *U.S. News & World Report*, Nov. 6, 1989, pp. 79–81.

39. Rod Little, "The Endangered Summer Vacation," *U.S. News & World Report*, May 16, 1994, p. 12.

40. Ibid.

41. Ibid.

42. Ibid.

43. Ibid.

44. Ibid.

45. Thomas Toch, "The Perfect School," *U.S. News & World Report*, Jan. 11, 1993, pp. 60–61.

46. Ibid.

47. Ibid.

48. Ibid.

49. "Michigan's Model," *U.S. News & World Report*, p. 16.

50. Coleman and Cressey, *Social Problems*, p. 98.

51. Ibid., pp. 98–99.

52. "Preschool Training Gets a Better Report Card," *Business Week*, Dec. 29, 1980, pp. 28, 32.

53. U.S. Bureau of the Census, *Statistical Abstract of the United States, 1993* (Washington, D.C.: U.S. Government Printing Office, 1993), pp. 144–149.

54. Kornblum and Julian, *Social Problems*, 7th ed., p. 363.

55. Farley, *American Social Problems*, p. 480.

56. See Mildred Sikkema, "The School Social Worker Serves as a Consultant," *Casework Papers* (New York: Family Service Association of America, 1955), pp. 75–82.

57. Alan Guskin and Samuel Guslan, *A Social Psychology of Education* (Reading, MA: Addison-Wesley, 1970), pp. 1–3.

58. Albert Ellis, *Humanistic Psychotherapy* (New York: McGraw-Hill, 1973), pp. 55–69.

59. Edward Jones and Harold Gerard, *Foundations of Social Psychology* (New York: Wiley, 1967), pp. 83–92.

60. Rudolf Dreikurs, Bernice Grunwald, and Floy Pepper, *Maintaining Sanity in the Classroom* (New York: Harper & Row, 1971), pp. 17–21.

61. Ellis, *Humanistic Psychotherapy*, pp. 129–133.

62. Joel Fisher, "Is Casework Effective?" *Social Work*, 18 (January 1973), pp. 5–21.

63. See Mary J. McCormick, "Social Advocacy: A New Dimension in Social Work," *Social Casework*, 51 (January 1970), pp. 3–11.

64. For a more detailed discussion of behavior modification, see Beth Sulzer and G. Roy Mayer, *Behavior Modification Procedures for School Personnel* (New York: Holt, Rinehart & Winston, 1972).

65. Sidney Simon, *Values Clarification* (New York: Hart, 1972), pp. 20–21.

66. "When Kids Go Bad," *Time*, Sept. 19, 1994, p. 61.

67. Allen Pincus and Anne Minahan, *Social Work Practice: Model and Method* (Itasca, IL: Peacock, 1973), pp. 3–9.

10

WORK-RELATED PROBLEMS AND SOCIAL WORK IN THE WORKPLACE

A question that is commonly asked when two strangers meet is "What do you do for a living?" Work is a central focus of our lives. Work not only enables us to earn money to pay bills, but it can also provide a sense of self-respect, a circle of colleagues and friends, and a source of self-fulfillment. A challenging job can help us to grow intellectually, psychologically, and socially. Work also largely determines our place in the social structure. We are, to a great extent, defined by our work.

In our society we value the "work ethic"; that is, we consider work to be honorable, productive, and useful. Unemployed, able-bodied people are often looked down on. The importance of work is shown in a study by Nancy Morse and Robert Weiss. They asked: "If by some chance you inherited enough money to live comfortably without working, do you think that you would work anyway, or not?" Eighty percent of the respondents stated that they would prefer to keep on working.[1]

This chapter will:

- Present a brief history of work.

- Describe three major problems involving work: alienation, unemployment, and occupational health hazards.

- Summarize current efforts and proposed new approaches to combat these problems.

- Describe social work in the workplace, which is an emerging field of social work practice.

A BRIEF HISTORY OF WORK

Work has not always been so esteemed. The ancient Greeks, for example, viewed work as a curse imposed on humanity by the gods. Work was thought to be an unpleasant and burdensome activity that was incompatible with being a citizen and developing one's mind. The Greeks therefore used slaves and justified slavery on the grounds that it freed citizens to spend their time in philosophic contemplation and cultural enrichment. Aristotle remarked: "No man can practice virtue who is living the life of a mechanic or laborer."[2]

Although the Romans viewed commercial banking as acceptable employment, practically all other occupations were considered vulgar and demeaning.

The ancient Hebrews viewed work ambivalently. On the one hand they regarded it as a drudgery or a grim necessity. On the other hand, they saw it as an expression of love for God.

The early Christians also were ambivalent toward work. They viewed working as doing penance for Original Sin. (The Christian interpretation of the Bible asserts that Original Sin began with Adam and Eve disobeying God in the Garden of Eden.) But they also believed that people needed to work to make their own living and to be able to help those in need.

The Protestant Reformation, which began in the 17th century, brought about profound changes in social values concerning work. Work became highly valued for the first time. One of the Protestant reformers, Martin Luther, asserted that labor was a service to God. Since that time, work has continued to be viewed as honorable and as having religious significance.

Another Protestant reformer, John Calvin, had an even more dramatic effect on changing social views toward work. Calvin preached that work is the will of God. Hard work, good deeds, and success at one's vocation were taken to be signs that one was destined for salvation. God's will was that people should live frugally (that is, spend very little money) and should use profits from work to invest in new ventures, which in turn would bring in more profits for additional investments, and so on. Idleness or laziness came to be viewed as sinful. One religious group that was heavily influenced by Calvin's teachings was the Puritans. The Puritans also developed a strong ascetic lifestyle—that is, the practice of denying worldly pleasures as a demonstration of religious discipline. Calvin's teachings were widely accepted and formed a new cultural value system that became known as the Protestant ethic. This ethic has three core values: hard work, frugality, and asceticism.

The values advanced by the Protestant ethic have continued throughout our history. For example, Benjamin Franklin cleverly praised these values in several axioms.

EXHIBIT 10.1

Max Weber and the Protestant Ethic

In 1904 the German sociologist Max Weber published what has become one of the most provocative theories in sociology. In *The Protestant Ethic and the Spirit of Capitalism,* Weber asserted that the Protestant ethic encouraged and made possible the emergence of capitalism. Weber theorized that the ideas of puritanism (advocated by Martin Luther and John Calvin) provided the value system that led to the transformation from traditional society to the Industrial Revolution.

Weber noted that puritan Protestantism embraced the doctrine that people were divinely selected for either salvation or damnation. There was nothing people could do to alter their fate. No one knew for sure whether she or he was destined for eternal salvation or eternal damnation. However, people looked for signs from God to suggest their fate. Because they also believed that work was a form of service to God, they concluded that success at work (making profits) was a sign of God's favor. They therefore worked very hard to accumulate as much wealth as possible.

Because the Protestant ethic viewed luxury and self-gratification as sinful, the profits acquired were not spent on luxuries. Instead, profits were reinvested into new ventures to increase incomes.

Such new ventures included building factories and developing new machines. Thus, according to Weber, the Industrial Revolution began, and capitalism was born.

Source: Max Weber, *The Protestant Ethic and the Spirit of Capitalism,* rereleased (New York: Scribner's, 1958).

A penny saved is a penny earned.

Time is money.

After industry and frugality, nothing contributes more to the raising of a young man than punctuality.

He who sits idle . . . throws away money.

Waste neither time nor money; an hour lost is money lost.[3]

Former President Nixon, in a speech on welfare reform, declared that labor had intrinsic value, that it had a strong American tradition, and that it was consistent with religious teachings. Nixon added: "Scrubbing floors and emptying bedpans have just as much dignity as there is in any work done in this country—including my own. . . . Most of us consider it immoral to be lazy or slothful."[4]

Although we no longer value the frugal, ascetic lifestyle of puritanism, we still believe strongly in the ethic of hard work. An able-bodied person, to gain approval from others, is expected to be employed (or at least to be receiving job training). People on welfare are often looked down on. There remains a strong link between amount of income and sense of personal worth. The more people are paid, the more highly they are regarded by others and the more highly they regard themselves.

A government report, *Work in America,* found that people in low-status jobs are generally unable to form a satisfying identity from their jobs. Having an assembly-line job, for example, often leads workers to view themselves as being personally insignificant. They routinely perform the same task day in and day out—such as attaching nuts to bolts. Such jobs, *Work in America* noted, lead to a worker's having "an overwhelming sense of inferiority: he cannot talk proudly to his children of his job, and feels he must apologize for his status."[5]

Because our work has immense effects on our self-concept, having a degrading, boring, and dehumanizing job can damage our psychological well-being. We judge ourselves not only by how much we earn but also by whether our job is challenging and satisfying and helps us to grow and develop.

TRENDS IN THE AMERICAN WORK FORCE

Since the turn of the 20th century, unions have generally been growing in power in this country, which has led to significant pay increases and fringe benefits for employees. Since 1980, however, the power balance between unions and management has shifted more toward management. In a number of businesses, management has been asking that employees take zero wage increases (or even pay cuts), with the threat of moving the business elsewhere or closing the doors permanently. Employees have generally chosen, with considerable reluctance, to accept management's offers rather than to strike and risk losing their jobs.

In the 20th century the nature of work and the composition of the work force have changed radically in our society. Six changes seem especially prominent: the increase in white-collar workers, the emergence of an employee society, specialization, changes in the sex and age composition of the work force, the emphasis on intrinsic rewards, and the emphasis on high technology.

Increase in White-Collar Workers

In colonial times most people made a living working on small farms, either their own or someone else's. We have since moved from an agricultural economy to a modern industrial economy.

In 1990, 27% of the labor force were farm workers, and 18% were white-collar workers. In 1992, only 2% were farm workers, and 56% were white-collar workers.[6] The immense productivity of our industrial system has made it possible for 2% of the work force to feed all of us! Farm workers (farmers, farmhands, and farm managers), once the largest occupational group, are now one of the smallest.

White-collar workers (professionals, clerical personnel, sales personnel, managers), once the smallest occupational group, are now the largest. This group surpassed blue-collar workers in terms of numbers in 1956.

Work in industrial societies can be grouped into three categories: primary, secondary, and tertiary.

Primary industry is the gathering or extracting of undeveloped natural resources, such as farming, mining, or fishing. In the early stages of industrialization most workers are employed in this category.

Secondary industry involves turning raw materials into manufactured goods, such as processed food, steel, and automobiles. In the middle stages of industrialization most workers are employed in this category. Most of these workers are blue-collar workers.

Tertiary industry involves service activities of one kind or another, such as dental care, medical services, automobile maintenance, sales, and pest control. In advanced societies such as ours, most workers are employed in service activities, primarily in white-collar jobs. Now, over 60% of our work force is employed in tertiary industry. Work in this category is generally cleaner and more pleasant than work in primary and secondary industries.

Emergence of an Employee Society

No longer are Americans likely to be self-employed, as they generally were in colonial times. Less than 10% of the work force now classify themselves as self-employed.[7] A few small-business owners, small family-owned farms, independent shopkeepers, and independent carpenters and artists still remain. But small, owner-operated businesses increasingly are finding it difficult to compete against well-organized corporations and businesses. The vast majority of workers are employed by someone else: large

Workers assemble a B-1 bomber. Today the vast majority of workers are employed by large corporations, government, or some other organization.

corporations, the government, and so forth. Even physicians, who once were largely self-employed as general practitioners, now generally work for a medical clinic or some other organization.

Specialization

The 1850 census listed a total of only 323 distinct job titles in the United States.[8] There are now over 35,000 job titles—more than 100 times as many different occupations.[9] Some of the unusual jobs one can choose for a career are clock winder, tea taster, and water smeller. With this extensive specialization, production of goods is now fragmented into repetitive and monotonous tasks, with each worker contributing only a small portion of the final product. A worker on an assembly line commented:

The assembly line is no place to work, I can tell you. There is nothing more discouraging than having a barrel beside you with 10,000 bolts in it and using them all up. Then you get a barrel with another 10,000 bolts, and you know every one of those 10,000 bolts has to be picked up and put in exactly the same place as the last 10,000 bolts.[10]

Specialization has contributed substantially to the development and provision of highly sophisticated products and services. But it has also created problems. Workers find it difficult to take pride in their work when they realize they are merely a replaceable adjunct to a machine or a process and when they contribute only a small part to the final product. Such specialization often results in job dissatisfaction. Those who are trained for a single, narrowly defined job that later becomes obsolete are often without marketable skills for other openings. Specialization has also created problems of worker cooperation and co-ordination for managers of organizations. Our society has become highly interdependent because of specialization. With interdependence, disruption in one work area may gravely affect the whole economy. In 1981, for example, 13,000 air traffic controllers went out on strike, seriously disrupting air travel and the entire U.S. economy, which is heavily dependent on air transportation.

Changes in the Sex and Age of the Labor Force

The labor force consists of people 16 years of age and over who are employed or who are actively seeking work (the unemployed). There have been some significant trends in the composition of the labor force.

Older men are becoming less likely to be in the labor force. In 1954, 40% of males over age 65 were in the labor force, but by 1992 only 3% of this category were in the labor force.[11] Employers are reluctant to hire older workers when younger workers with more recent training are available at lower salaries. Job obsolescence and myths about the unproductivity of older workers also make it difficult for unemployed older workers to be hired.

Women are increasingly entering the labor force. In 1900 only 20% of all adult women were in paid employment, compared to over 50% at present.[12] Women, however, still tend to be employed in the less prestigious, lower-paying positions (as will be discussed further in Chapter 12).

Two groups that have historically had high rates of unemployment or received low pay if employed have been minority-group workers and teenage workers. Unemployment rates are particularly high for nonwhite teenagers; in some cities more than 50% of people in this category are unemployed. Women who work full time are paid, on the average, only about two-thirds of what men who work full time are paid. Nonwhite women, subjected to double discrimination, earn even less.

Emphasis on Intrinsic Rewards

Intrinsic rewards are rewards that come from the nature of the work itself. Work that offers intrinsic rewards is fulfilling and challenging, helps one grow socially and emotionally, contributes to physical fitness, promotes a sense of accomplishment through the use of one's talents, generates a feeling of self-respect, provides interest and enjoyment, offers an opportunity to meet new friends, and so on. In the past, people took a job primarily for its extrinsic rewards—a paycheck that would enable them to pay their bills. William Glasser has noted that in the last 30 years workers have become increasingly concerned about the intrinsic rewards prospective jobs will provide.[13]

Emphasis on High Technology

Our society's economy is becoming increasingly based on high technology, such as computers and communication. Automation and robots are now doing more of the work that was previously done by blue-collar workers.

Technology is a double-edged sword. Every major technological innovation has both freed humans from previous hardships and created new, unanticipated problems. For example, the development of nuclear power is an important source of energy, but a nuclear mishap has the potential to kill thousands (and even millions) of people. Technology can be defined as the totality of means used to provide objects necessary for human comfort and sustenance. Daniel Bell defines technological change as "the combination of all methods (apparatus, skills, organization) for increasing the productivity of labor and capital."[14]

Technological innovations are causing major changes in the type of work available to Americans. Blue-collar and agricultural jobs are declining, and jobs in high-technology fields (such as computers and communications) are increasing. People who are laid off or discharged in industries (such as the steel industry) in which jobs are declining face immense obstacles in obtaining employment that pays comparable wages. On the other hand, people who are trained for high-tech positions have excellent career opportunities. In the employment market, technological advances are a boon for some and a disaster for others. Automobile executives welcome the coming of robots to the assembly line because robots are cutting production costs. Unemployed assembly-line workers with home mortgages are cursing the use of robots.

There is a growing concern among many educational, political, and civil rights leaders that, as we come to depend increasingly on computers and other technological innovations, only a select portion of the population will have the skills needed to function well in our society. Those who lack such skills may find themselves trapped in lower social-class positions.

PROBLEMS IN THE WORK SETTING

Alienation

Alienation has a specific sociological meaning: *the sense of meaninglessness and powerlessness that people experience when interacting with social institutions they consider oppressive and beyond their control.* The term *worker alienation* was originally used by Karl Marx. (Perhaps because Marx has been associated with Communism, the subject of worker alienation has tended to be neglected in our country.) Marx suggested that worker alienation occurs largely because workers are separated from ownership of the means of production and from any control over the final product of their labor. They thus feel powerless and view their work as meaningless. Marx described alienation as follows:

> *In what does this alienation consist? First, that work is external to the worker, that it is not part of his nature, that consequently he does not fulfill himself in his work but denies himself, has a feeling of misery, not well-being, does not develop freely a physical and mental energy,*

> *but is physically exhausted and mentally debased. . . . His work is not voluntary but imposed, forced labor. . . . Finally, the alienated character of work for the worker appears in the fact that it is not his work but work for someone else, that in work he does not belong to himself but to another person.*[15]

According to Marx, specialization is a major cause of alienation. With specialization workers are forced to perform an unfulfilling task repeatedly. Because people use only a fraction of their talents, work becomes an enforced, impersonalized activity rather than a creative venture.

Marx believed that worker alienation would eventually lead to such discontent that the workers would band together and revolt against owners. Another reason workers would revolt is that they would realize they were being exploited by the dominant class, who prosper from their toil.

Marx's prediction of a class revolution has not come true in the United States. Marx did not foresee the effectiveness of collective bargaining and new technology in improving the conditions of workers during the 20th century. Interestingly, even workers in such socialist countries as China and Cuba experience considerable alienation. (Marx had predicted that there would be less alienation in socialist countries.)

It may be that much of the alienation that Marx attributed to capitalistic societies was really caused by industrialism. Workers in this country, contrary to what Marx predicted, continue to have basic trust and faith in the American capitalistic system. Many workers have made financial investments in stocks, bonds, real estate, savings, and so forth. To a significant extent, they are also part of the dominant class. Marx saw only a struggle between two classes—owners and workers. He did not foresee considerable overlap occurring between these classes, nor did he foresee the development of a large middle class that tends to include both investors and workers. Because of Americans' faith in our system and their disdain of Communism, it is highly unlikely that there will be a class revolution in our country in the foreseeable future.

In fact, the working class has not successfully

staged a socialist revolution in any industrialized country. The socialist revolutions that have occurred—in the former Soviet Union, China, Cuba, and so forth—have all taken place in developing or preindustrial countries. It is important to note that even China and, especially, Russia are increasingly using the profit motive (a key component of capitalism) as an incentive to work and as a method to stimulate their economies.

In addition, it appears that Marx's theories about the evils of a capitalistic economy are being rejected by many of the societies (such as the former Soviet Union and Poland) that tried to establish economic systems based on Marxist principles. These countries have concluded that, unless they use capitalistic incentives, they cannot motivate their citizens to produce at desired rates. Some authorities are now asserting that Marx's theories about economic production have been tried and tested and have been found to have failed miserably. In terms of productivity, the economies of Eastern Europe that have been based on Marx's theories have fallen far behind those of Western Europe (which have been using capitalistic incentives). In 1990, posters of Karl Marx bearing the caption "Workers of the World! Forgive me" were selling widely in eastern Germany.[16] (Marx had coined the slogan "Workers of the World! Unite.")

PRESENT SOURCES OF ALIENATION

Alienation has many sources. Specialization has led workers to feel that they have meaningless jobs and are contributing insignificantly to the business. It is difficult, for example, for assembly-line workers to take pride in producing an automobile when they only attach an ignition wire.

Working for a large business or corporation and knowing that you can readily be replaced leads to feelings of powerlessness and lowered self-esteem. Not being involved in the decision-making process and being aware that supervisors do not want workers to "make waves" also lead to feelings of powerlessness and meaninglessness.

In some businesses, machines have been developed to do most of the work. This automation (for example, assembly lines in the auto industry) has led workers to feel they are insignificant cogs in the production process. Even the pace at which they work is controlled by the assembly-line machinery. Jobs that offer little opportunity to be creative also contribute to alienation. Such jobs include typist, receptionist, janitor, garbage collector, assembly-line worker, or telephone operator. Most American workers do not hold jobs they had planned for; they are doing what they do for such reasons as "simple chance" or "lack of choice." As a result, many people feel trapped in their jobs.[17]

Alienation also derives from jobs that do not provide opportunities to learn, a sense of accomplishment, or the chance to work with compatible people. Many authorities believe that alienation leads to acts of disruption in the production process—work of poor quality, high rates of absenteeism, and vandalism or theft of company property.

JOB SATISFACTION AND DISSATISFACTION

Dissatisfaction with one's job is a useful indicator of alienation at work. Studies on job satisfaction show wide differences, according to vocation, in worker satisfaction with their jobs.

In research studies, many people state that, if given a choice, they would select a different career.[18] Yet, when public opinion polls (Gallup and other polls) ask people if they are satisfied with their jobs, over 80% consistently answer yes.[19] It is unclear why some approaches to measuring job satisfaction show high levels of satisfaction, whereas others suggest that large numbers of workers are sufficiently dissatisfied that they would choose another occupation if they could.

Although salary is an important factor in worker satisfaction, apparently it is not the most important factor. The *Work in America* report asked workers to rank various job characteristics in order of importance. Respondents gave the following ranking:

1. *Interesting work*
2. *Enough help and equipment to get the job done*
3. *Enough information to get the job done*
4. *Enough authority to get the job done*

Job Dissatisfaction

Mary and Robert Buyze met in college and were married shortly after Mary graduated in 1987. Bob had graduated a year earlier. Bob majored in history and Mary in psychology. Both shared the American dream of having a home in the suburbs, a motorboat, and two cars. Because both had graduated from college, they were optimistic that they were well on their way. They fantasized about taking a yearly trip to such places as Acapulco, Europe, Jamaica, and Hawaii.

It is not six years later. Bob is 29 and Mary is 28. They have yet to take a trip and now have two young children. They are deeply in debt, having tried to buy much of their dream with credit. They purchased a run-down "starter" home with two bedrooms that was advertised as a "fixer's delight." Unexpected repairs to the furnace, the roof, and the plumbing have plunged them even deeper into debt, as have medical expenses, food, and clothing for the family.

What is even sadder is that they both have jobs they dislike. Bob has been a life insurance salesman for a small company for the past three and a half years. Bob states:

I took the job because I couldn't find anything else. There were no job openings for historians when I graduated, so I took a variety of odd jobs, none of which I enjoyed. I was a truck driver, manager of a pizza place, taxicab driver, car salesman—and much of the time I was unemployed.

I hoped when I took this job that I would finally be able to make good money. It just hasn't worked out. I hate selling insurance. Most of the time I go door-to-door and beg people to buy a policy. It's like begging for money for a charity. I absolutely despise having to put myself in a position of peddling policies—and being nice and charming to people who at times end up slamming the door in my face. But I have no choice. I've got so many bills to pay that I can't afford not to work. I also hate to see Mary having

5. *Good pay*

6. *Opportunity to develop special abilities*

7. *Job security*

8. *Opportunity to see the results of one's work*[20]

Morton reviewed a number of studies and identified the following factors as the primary sources of job satisfaction:

■ *Psychological satisfaction.* A satisfactory job provides a sense of accomplishment, an opportunity to learn, is closely matched to a worker's interests and abilities, and provides an opportunity to work with congenial or interesting people.

■ *Monetary compensation.* Workers tend to be satisfied when they feel they are paid fairly.

■ *Physical factors.* Job satisfaction is increased when the setting is pleasant, when the environment is viewed as free of hazards, when commuting time to work is short, and when transportation to work is readily available.

■ *Control.* Workers are more satisfied in jobs in which they feel they have some decision-making responsibilities and some control over their work schedules. They don't like punching a time clock, whereas flextime is appealing. The idea behind flextime is to have most workers present during the busiest time of the day but to leave the re-

to work with the kids being so young. But, again we have no choice. What really hurts is that both of us are slaving away at jobs we don't like. Yet, with all the bills we have to pay, we hardly are able to buy Christmas presents.

Mary is a clothing store clerk. She also was unable to get a job in her field (psychology). After graduating, she worked for two years as a typist, which paid about the same as her present job—slightly above the minimum wage. She quit being a typist shortly before their first child (Rob) was born; she disliked secretarial work even more than her present job. A few months after Rob's birth, she began working part time in the job she now holds full time.

Mary states:

When I was in college, I guess I was too idealistic. I expected to get a challenging job that would help me grow as a person and also pay well. That just hasn't happened. What I earn now is very little, especially after having to pay the babysitter. This job at times is boring, especially during the months when business is slow. November and December are just the opposite—we're running all the time, and I'm exhausted by the end of the day. It's feast or famine. But my day doesn't end when I leave the store. I've got cooking, washing, and cleaning to do—plus trying to find time to spend with the children. The last four years since the kids were born have been a nightmare— changing diapers, getting up in the middle of the night, taking care of sick kids. Don't get me wrong—I wouldn't trade them in, but some days I really wonder where I went wrong. What really hurts is that we have almost nothing to show for our efforts.

I tell you, some mornings I'm so worn out when I get up and so unhappy with work that tears roll out of my eyes when I drive to work. What's just as bad is that I know that Bob hates his job as much as I do. Increasingly, when he has a bad day, he drinks too much—and that is worrying me more and more. I'm in a dead-end job with no chance for advancement, and I can't afford to give it up. Is this all there is to life?

---

maining hours up to the discretion of the workers. Those who want to start earlier, so they can leave earlier, can do so. Those who want to come in later and stay later also have this option. In some places it is possible with flextime to work four days a week (ten hours per day) and thereby have an extra day off.

■ *Institutional aspects.* Workers are more satisfied with jobs that have promotion-from-within policies, training programs, personnel policies that assure equal opportunity for advancement and education, and good physical facilities and conveniences (lounges, cafeterias, gyms, and the like).

■ *Economic, political, and social aspects.* The national mood affects job satisfaction. For example, in the late 1960s and 1970s severe discontent and controversy about the Vietnam War lowered job satisfaction. On the other hand, a feeling of national prosperity increases job satisfaction.[21]

CONFRONTING ALIENATION AND JOB DISSATISFACTION

One of the best-known efforts to increase worker satisfaction and productivity was that of Hawthorne Works, a division of Western Electric Company in Chicago. The results were surprising, as described in Case Example 10.2.

Many employers have become aware that job dissatisfaction reduces efficiency and productivity. There are a number of ways to increase job satisfaction. The first step is to find out precisely what the workers are dissatisfied about. Then changes can be made. In one job setting workers may be the most concerned about safety conditions (as in coal mining); in another they may be most concerned about boring, repetitive work (as on an assembly line); in another it may be wages (as for jobs that pay only the minimum wage); in yet another it may be lack of recognition (as for clerical workers who make their supervisors look good).

A wide variety of changes can be made to improve job satisfaction. The following list is far from exhaustive.

■ Find ways to make the work challenging and interesting.

■ Provide opportunities for career advancement.

■ Provide in-service training on relevant aspects of the work—for example, stress management programs for stressful jobs.

■ Increase wages, salaries, and fringe benefits.

■ Involve workers in the decision-making process.

■ Have social get-togethers to help increase group morale.

■ Improve the physical facilities to make the work experience more pleasant and enjoyable.

■ Give workers more of the profits through a profit-sharing program.

■ Have a reward system to recognize significant contributions made by workers.

■ Institute employee policies that generate a sense of job security.

■ Allow workers to have some control over their schedules—for example, through flextime.

■ Make the work setting as free of hazards as possible.

As noted, adoption of flextime policies has contributed to increased worker satisfaction.

Many government agencies and private companies are now on flextime.[22] Although supervisors have found it is more difficult to coordinate work schedules when using flextime, absenteeism declines and productivity increases under such a program.

A variety of programs involve employees in *participative management.* For example, in *consultive management,* managers consult with their employees (either individually or in small groups) in order to encourage them to think about job-related issues and contribute their own ideas before decisions are made. *Democratic management* goes even further; it systematically allows employee groups to make a number of major decisions. An example of democratic management is the practice of allowing work teams to hire, orient, and train new employees. *Self-managing teams* are a subcategory of democratic management; they are autonomous work groups that are given a high degree of decision-making authority and are expected to control their own behavior and work schedules, with compensation usually being based on the team's overall productivity. *Quality circles* are work-improvement task forces in which managers and employees meet regularly to allow employees to air grievances (which in itself has a ventilating effect in reducing job dissatisfaction), to identify problems that hinder productivity, and to offer suggestions for alleviating these concerns. *Suggestion programs* are formal procedures to encourage employees to recommend work improvements, often in writing; in many companies employees whose suggestions result in cost savings receive monetary awards. *Stock trusts* allow employees to buy or receive stock in the company, thereby becoming partial owners; a benefit of stock trusts is that they act as an incentive for higher productivity among employees. *Employee ownership* occurs when employees provide the capital to purchase control of an existing company; employee ownership generally increases employee interest in the company's financial success and acts as an incentive for workers to remain with the company.[23]

To reduce alienation, General Foods redesigned its work assignments. Extensive efforts were made to make the work challenging and to

CASE EXAMPLE 10.2 The Hawthorne Effect

In 1927 in Chicago, the Hawthorne Works of the Western Electric Company began a series of experiments designed to discover ways to increase worker satisfaction and productivity. Hawthorne Works primarily manufactured telephones, with the plant operating on an assembly-line basis. Workers needed no special skills in this production process and performed simple, repetitive tasks. The employees were not unionized. Management speculated that, if they found ways to increase job satisfaction, the employees would work more efficiently and productivity would increase.

The company tested a number of factors potentially related to productivity. These factors included rest breaks, better lighting, changes in the number of work hours during the day, changes in the wages paid, improved food facilities, and so on.

The results were surprising. Productivity increased, as expected, with improved working conditions. But it also increased when working conditions worsened. (One way that working conditions were worsened was by substantially dimming the lighting.) The finding that productivity increased when working conditions worsened was unexpected and led to additional study to find an explanation.

The investigators discovered that participation in the experiments was extremely attractive to the workers. They felt they had been selected by management for their individual abilities, and so they worked harder, even when working conditions became less favorable. There were additional explanations. The workers' morale and general attitude toward work improved, as they felt they were receiving special attention from management. By participating in this study, they were able to work in smaller groups, and they also became involved in making decisions. Working in smaller groups allowed them to develop a stronger sense of solidarity with their fellow workers. Being involved in decision making decreased feelings of meaninglessness and powerlessness about their work.

The results of this study have become known as the "Hawthorne effect" in sociological and psychological research. The Hawthorne effect holds that, when subjects know they are participants in a study, this awareness may lead them to behave differently and thereby substantially influence the results of the study.

Source: Fritz J. Roethlisberger and William J. Dickson, *Management and the Worker* (Cambridge, MA: Harvard University Press, 1939).

---

eliminate the dull, routine jobs. Those repetitive jobs that could not be eliminated were shared among several workers, so that no one was permanently stuck with a tedious task. In addition, General Foods abolished status symbols (assigned parking stalls, types of office furniture, separate cafeterias) for different ranks of workers. Productivity was found to increase sharply.[24]

Corning Glass improved productivity in the hot-plate division by allowing each worker to perform full assembly of hot plates (instead of the previous system of each worker assembling only a small part) and to initial the finished product. Workers were also encouraged to form their own small groups to conduct quality checks. A six-month review of these changes found that

EXHIBIT 10.2

Theory Y: Improving Productivity and Job Satisfaction

Douglas McGregor developed a theory of management in which he held that management thinking and behavior are based on two different sets of assumptions, which he labeled Theory X and Theory Y.

Theory X managers view employees as being incapable of much growth. Employees are perceived as having an inherent dislike for work, and it is presumed that they will attempt to evade work whenever possible. Therefore, X-type managers believe they must control, direct, force, or threaten employees to make them work. Employees are also viewed as having relatively little ambition, seeking to avoid responsibilities, and preferring to be directed. X-type managers therefore spell out job responsibilities carefully, set work goals without employee input, use external rewards (such as money) to force employees to work, and punish employees who deviate from established rules. Because Theory X managers reduce responsibilities to a level at which few mistakes can be made, work usually becomes so structured that it is monotonous and distasteful. The assumptions of Theory X are, of course, inconsistent with what behavioral scientists assert are effective principles for directing, influencing, and motivating people.

In contrast, *Theory Y managers* view employees as wanting to grow and develop by exerting physical and mental effort to accomplish work objectives to which they are committed. Y-type managers believe that internal rewards, such as self-respect and personal improvement, are stronger motivations than external rewards (money) and punishment. A Y-type manager also believes that, under proper conditions, employees will not only accept responsibility but seek it. Most employees are assumed to have considerable ingenuity, creativity, and imagination for solving the organization's problems. Therefore, employees are given considerable responsibility in order to test the limits of their capabilities. Mistakes and errors are viewed as necessary phases of the learning process, and work is structured so that employees can have a sense of accomplishment and growth.

Employees who work for Y-type managers are generally more creative and productive, experience greater work satisfaction, and are more highly motivated than employees who work for X-type managers. Under both management styles, expectations often become self-fulfilling prophecies.

Source: Douglas McGregor, *The Human Side of Enterprise* (New York: McGraw-Hill, 1960).

productivity had increased by 47%, absenteeism had declined, and hot-plate rejects had dropped from 23% to 1% of output.[25]

Several American companies have increased productivity by conducting "climate surveys," in which workers are asked to vent their concerns and to criticize their jobs. Sometimes such surveys identify problematic situations that can be improved through relatively minor changes. Even when the problems cannot be resolved, work tensions are often temporarily reduced just by allowing workers to let off steam.[26]

Unemployment

THE COSTS OF UNEMPLOYMENT

As illustrated in Case Example 10.3, unemployment can have devastating effects. Most obviously, it reduces (sometimes to below poverty levels) the amount of income that a family or single person receives. Short-term unemployment, especially when one receives unemployment compensation (described in Chapter 3), may have only minor consequences. But long-term unemployment inflicts numerous problems.

Harold Wilensky found that long-term unemployment often leads to extreme personal isolation. Work is a central part of many people's lives. When unemployment occurs, work ties are severed. As a result, many of the unemployed see friends less, cease participating in community life, and become increasingly isolated.[27]

D. D. Braginsky and B. M. Braginsky found that long-term unemployment causes attitude changes that persist even after reemployment.[28] Being laid off (or fired) is often interpreted by the unemployed as a sign of being incompetent and worthless. Self-esteem is lowered, they are likely to experience depression, and they feel alienated from society. Many suffer deep shame and avoid their friends. They feel dehumanized and insignificant and see themselves as an easily replaced statistic. They also tend to lose faith in our political and economic system, with some blaming the political system for their problems. Even when they find new jobs, they do not fully recover their self-esteem.

Harvey Brenner found a strong association between unemployment and emotional problems. During an economic recession, mental hospital admissions increase. The suicide rate also increases, indicating an increase in depression. Also higher during times of high employment are the divorce rate, the incidence of child abuse, and the number of peptic ulcers (a stress-related disease).[29] Just the threat of unemployment can lead to emotional problems.

The National Advisory Commission on Civil Disorders noted in 1967 that unemployment and underemployment are key factors leading to civil disorder.

Employment problems have drastic social impact in the ghetto. Men who are chronically unemployed or employed in the lowest status jobs are often unable or unwilling to remain with their families. The handicap imposed on children growing up without fathers in an atmosphere of poverty and deprivation is increased as mothers are forced to work to provide support.

The culture of poverty that results from unemployment and family breakup generates a system of ruthless exploitative relationships within the ghetto. . . . Children growing up under such conditions are likely participants in civil disorder.[30]

In many cases the long-term unemployed are forced to exhaust their savings, sell their homes, and become public assistance recipients. A few turn to crime, particularly the young. The unemployed no longer enjoy the companionship of their fellow workers. They often experience feelings of embarrassment, anger, despair, depression, anxiety, boredom, hopelessness, and apathy. Such feelings may lead to alcoholism, drug abuse, insomnia, stress-related illnesses, marital unhappiness, and even violence within the family. The work ethic is still prominent in our society: When people lose their jobs, they devalue themselves and also miss the sense of self-worth that comes from doing a job well.

Widespread unemployment also sharply cuts government tax revenues. When tax revenues are reduced, federal departments are forced to cut services at a time when the services are most needed. Such cuts further add to alienation and despair.

High unemployment also leads to high rates of underemployment. Underemployment occurs when people are working at jobs below their level of skill. College graduates, for example, may be forced to take unskilled road construction work or become clerical workers.

WHO ARE THE UNEMPLOYED?

In the past several years the national unemployment rate has ranged from 4% to 11%. Official statistics are compiled by the Bureau of Labor Statistics. The bureau, usually monthly, makes a survey of households randomly selected from the total population.

Virtually all of us will be unemployed at some point during our working years. There is some variation from time to time in the groups that are most vulnerable to unemployment. In the late 1970s and early 1980s, unemployment was particularly high among steel workers and automobile workers. In the late 1970s schoolteachers had

CASE	**American Dream Becomes Economic**
EXAMPLE 10.3	**Nightmare through Unemployment**

Lorraine and Jim Dedrick thought they had it made. They had a five-bedroom, stone-foundation home on a lake, a landscaped yard, two well-behaved children, a car, a van, a motor-powered boat, and a sailboat. The home, the vehicles, and the boats were bought on time payments. Because both were working, they were confident that they could easily make the monthly payments. Mrs. Dedrick describes what happened.

> My husband worked at Dana Corporation (a car and truck-axle manufacturing plant). He was a crew supervisor and was making over $33,000 a year. I was, and still am, a legal secretary.
>
> When the layoffs started in spring 1989, we didn't think it would touch Jim. He had six years of seniority. But by March of 1990 we knew a layoff was inevitable. Neither Dana nor the whole American auto industry was doing well. When the layoff came in June of 1990, we weren't surprised.
>
> At first we weren't worried. Jim thought it would be nice to have a summer off and looked forward to doing some fishing and some fixing up around the house. Because he was 39 years old and had worked steadily since he was 18, I also thought a few months' break would do him good. He was of course able to draw unemployment benefits, and with my salary I was certain we could get by. Surely the auto industry would recover, and he would be called back in the fall.
>
> In late summer, however, a rumor started and quickly spread throughout the plant that Dana was going to close its plant. In September they announced the plant was going to close.
>
> Both of us immediately became alarmed. Jim started looking for other work in earnest. Unfortunately, there were no comparable jobs in the area—and for that matter the whole auto industry was suffering.
>
> Jim applied at many different jobs but had no luck. I know of nothing worse than to see a once-proud, secure person come home each evening with the look on his face that he has once again been rejected. Jim began developing stomach problems from the rejections, and I started having, and still have, tension headaches. We used to go out a lot, laugh, and have a good time. Now, we not only cannot afford it, we no longer have an interest.
>
> Jim grabbed at every straw. He even went to apply for jobs in Milwaukee and Chicago. In the last year he appears to have aged ten years.

high unemployment rates. In the mid-1970s PhDs in the liberal arts and social sciences had high unemployment rates. In the early 1980s the housing industry was in a slump, and there were high unemployment rates among carpenters and construction workers. In the middle and late 1980s there were high rates of unemployment among workers in the petroleum production industry. In the early 1990s businesses and corporations were downsizing their work forces, including administrative positions; as a result, there were high unemployment rates among middle-level managers.

Some groups have chronically high unemployment rates. These groups include African Americans and Latinos, teenagers, women, older workers, the unskilled, and the semiskilled.

In February of 1991 his unemployment benefits ended. Bill collectors began hounding us. We soon depleted all our savings. We got so many calls from bill collectors that we took out an unlisted telephone number. Never before were we unable to pay our bills.

The months since February have been hell. Increasingly we have gotten into arguments. Whenever I bring my check home, Jim has a pained look on his face, as he feels he's not doing his share. I try to tell him that it's not his fault, but whenever we talk about it he appears hurt and becomes angry.

At the end of February he began to advertise by word of mouth that he was an independent carpenter. He's good with his hands. Unfortunately, the few jobs he got have as yet not even paid for the extra tools he's had to buy. It has only gotten us deeper into debt.

When I drive to work, the tears often fall. It's my only time alone. Driving home I often cry as I think about our situation and know I'll have to face Jim's sad look.

We don't associate much with friends now. They either pity us or have that arrogant "I told you so" look in response to our optimism when Jim was first laid off.

It just doesn't look like Jim is going to be able to get a job in this area. Next week he's going to go to Atlanta—we've heard there are a lot of job openings there.

Dennis, our 12-year-old son, is alternately sad and angry about the possibility of leaving this area. He's got a lot of friends and loves to go boating, fishing, and sailing. Having to take your son away from something he really loves is one of the most difficult things I'll probably ever have to do.

Karen, our daughter who's 15, really had a bad year at school. Her grades fell, and, when we asked her why, she said "What's the use in studying—won't help in getting a job." That remark hurt deeply, probably because it may have a ring of truth in it.

It looks like we're going to have to give up our dream house on this lake. (Tears came to Mrs. Dedrick as she spoke.) We've lived here for the past five years and really loved it. This is our first real home. We've added on a patio, a bedroom, and enlarged the living room. We also spend a lot of time in painting and fixing it up. It's really become a part of us. If Jim gets a job in Atlanta, we'll be forced to sell. We checked what market prices are, and there's no way we're going to get what we put into this house.

A few years ago we thought we were starting to live the American dream. This past year and a half has been hell. Here we are broke, unhappy, and about to lose our home. At our age starting life over is almost more than we can take.

High unemployment among African Americans and Latinos is partly due to job discrimination. Unfortunately, there is truth in the cliché that minorities are "last to be hired, first to be fired." Another reason for high unemployment is due to their lower average level of educational achievement, which leaves them unqualified for many of the available jobs. (Lower educational levels and lack of marketable job skills are largely due to *past* discrimination.)

High unemployment among women also stems partly from discrimination. Many employers (most of them men) are still inclined to hire a man before a woman, and many jobs are still erroneously thought to be "a man's job." Women have also been socialized to seek lower-paying jobs, to not be competitive with men, and to believe their place is in the home and not in the work force. (See Chapter 12 for a fuller discussion.)

Myths about older workers—age 40 and over—make it more difficult for them to obtain a new job if they become unemployed. They are *erroneously* thought to be less productive, more difficult to get along with, more difficult to train, clumsier, more accident prone, less healthy, and more prone to absenteeism than younger workers (see Chapter 13 for a further discussion of these myths, along with a review of research studies that refute these stereotypes). An additional problem for unemployed older workers is that younger people are often available at salaries far below what the older applicants were paid at their last job.

Unemployment is high for teenagers and young people. This is partly because many of them have not received the training that would provide them with marketable skills.

Employers are willing to hire unskilled workers when they have simple, repetitive tasks to be performed. But unskilled workers are the first to be laid off when there is a business slump. These workers can readily be replaced if business picks up. Highly skilled workers are more difficult to replace. Also, employers have much more invested in skilled workers, as they have spent more time in training them.

Blue-collar workers are more affected by economic slumps than white-collar workers. Industries that employ large numbers of blue-collar workers—housing, road construction, manufacturers of heavy equipment such as tractors, the auto industry—are quickly and deeply hit by recessions and often forced to lay off workers. As noted earlier, the number of blue-collar jobs is decreasing, whereas white-collar jobs are increasing. A major reason for this decline is *automation,* whereby the system of production is increasingly controlled by means of self-operating machinery. Examples of automation include the automobile assembly line and direct-dial telephone (which displaced thousands of telephone operators). Robots are now replacing workers in a number of

industries, particularly for doing simple, repetitive tasks.

REASONS FOR THE HIGH UNEMPLOYMENT RATE

The reasons for the high unemployment rate in this country are numerous and complex. First, it should be noted that, even when a society has "full employment," there will always be some people capable of working who are temporarily unemployed. Some people will be changing jobs. Some recent graduates or dropouts not yet have found a job. Some people who have had prolonged illness could be starting to look for a job. For these reasons, most countries generally consider that they have full employment when the unemployment rate does not exceed 2–3% of the work force. Unfortunately, the unemployment rate in the United States in recent years has been considerably higher than this figure.

In many areas of the country there are more people in the work force than there are available jobs. Automation in many industries has reduced the number of workers needed and made certain job skills (such as blacksmith) obsolete. Planting and harvesting machines in agriculture, for example, have drastically reduced the number of people needed in producing food. Picking beans, digging potatoes, and picking cotton and corn once required large numbers of workers, but such work is now done by machines.

From the end of World War II until around 1965 there was a "baby boom," when large numbers of children were born. For the past 30 years these baby-boom children have been growing up and entering the labor force in large numbers. The last few decades have also seen women being liberated from the cultural expectation that they should remain at home. Millions of females are now employed or seeking full- or part-time work. This increase in the number of workers seeking employment has added to the unemployment rate.

In the 1970s the oil-producing countries sharply increased the cost of a barrel of oil. Because practically all companies are dependent on oil for energy and in other ways, the price of most products increased. Because consumers were able to buy less, the demand for products slackened. Companies had to reduce production, and layoffs occurred.

Another factor involves foreign trade. A decrease in orders of American products for foreign customers forces U.S. companies to cut back their production and, often, to lay off workers.

Excessively dry summers in our country sharply reduce the amount of food produced. The law of supply and demand therefore drives up the price of available food. Consumers are less able to buy other products, and companies are then forced to cut back production and lay off workers.

High interest rates make it too costly for consumers to buy homes, automobiles, and other expensive items that are normally purchased with a loan. The demand for such items goes down, and again businesses have to cut back production and lay off workers.

Still another major reason for the high unemployment rate in this country is that we have a structural unemployment problem; that is, large numbers of unemployed people are not trained for the positions that are open. In recent years many blue-collar jobs have disappeared (as in the steel industry), while high-skill jobs have opened in other areas (such as in the high-tech field of computers). As people become trained for current positions, the employment needs of our economy will again shift; thus there will continue to be disharmony between skills needed for vacant positions and skills held by unemployed people.

FACTORS THAT REDUCE UNEMPLOYMENT

Many factors increase the number of jobs and thereby reduce the unemployment rate. Lower interest rates encourage consumers to purchase more items through loans and with credit. Consumers buy more, stimulating companies to produce more to meet the demand and thus to hire more people. Lower interest rates have a direct effect on businesses. Companies often borrow money to purchase capital items (for example, additional machinery to produce their goods or buildings to expand the business) in order to increase production. When interest rates are lower, businesses borrow more money to increase production—which usually creates additional jobs.

Wars almost always reduce the unemployment rate. Some workers are drafted to fight as soldiers. Their former jobs are then available for people who are unemployed. In addition, it takes many additional jobs to provide the military with the products needed to fight a war—bullets, bombs, tanks, fighter planes, food, medicine, and so on.

Businesses and governments in many other countries take a much more paternalistic approach to employees and to ensuring that there will be jobs available for those who are unemployed. In the United States when an economic slump occurs, businesses usually lay off workers. By contrast, in Japan businesses are much less likely to lay off workers; indeed, they seek to have their employees spend their entire working lives with the same company. Governments in many other countries attempt, when there is an economic slump, to create jobs for those who are unemployed. Germany, for example, pays the unemployed to receive work training.

The development of new products opens up many new jobs. The invention of the automobile, airplane, television, computer, hair dryer, and refrigerator created jobs not only for factory workers but also for managers, repair personnel, sales personnel, insurance personnel, and so on.

CONFRONTING UNEMPLOYMENT

Economists agree that the ideal way to overcome unemployment is through increased economic growth. They disagree, however, about the causes of a sluggish economy and about the best way to stimulate an economy.

Rapid economic growth, however, is a mixed blessing. It historically has had adverse effects on the natural environment because it leads to more rapid consumption of scarce resources (see Chapter 16). Once again we see that a solution to one problem often creates or aggravates another problem; in sociological terms, the solution has both functional and dysfunctional aspects.

In the early 1960s, the economy was in a

slump, and the unemployment rate was high. President Kennedy stimulated the economy through a tax cut to individuals and to businesses. The tax cut gave individuals more buying power and businesses additional money to reinvest to increase production. Kennedy's plan worked: The economy was stimulated, production increased, more jobs were created, and the unemployment rate went down.

The early 1980s saw another economic slump with high inflation *and* high unemployment rates. The Reagan administration developed and implemented a plan to revitalize the economy that involved tax cuts to individuals and to businesses. The tax cuts achieved the same results as those under Kennedy. Reagan's plan also involved immense cuts in federal spending for social welfare programs and for educational programs. The cuts were designed to reduce the inflation rate. (Big spending by the federal government has often been blamed as a major contributor to inflation.) For the most part, Reagan's plan worked. The economy was again stimulated, and the rates of unemployment and inflation were cut nearly in half. Unfortunately, massive tax cuts (along with sharp increases in military spending) led to other problems: a huge federal deficit that threatens to increase the inflation rate in the future and cuts in social programs that have increased the rates of poverty, homelessness, hunger, and a variety of other social problems.

Economics is a complicated and complex area. Certainly it is a mistake to assume that tax cuts will always stimulate the economy and lead to reductions in unemployment and inflation. For example, a case can be made that high rates of inflation and unemployment in the 1970s were due to rising oil prices, and drops in these rates in the 1980s were due not to tax cuts but to declining oil prices. Petroleum is the major source of energy in producing practically all goods. When the price of petroleum goes up, the cost of production increases, which raises the price of all commodities and results in inflation. With inflation, the public cannot buy as much, which results in an oversupply of goods. Industries then lay off workers, which increases the unemployment rate. When the price of petroleum goes down, the cost of pro-

ducing goods goes down, which reduces prices and thereby reduces the rate of inflation. Also, the public can purchase more goods at lower prices, which reduces the supply of available goods. Industries are then stimulated to produce more goods, which they do by hiring more employees—thus reducing the unemployment rate.

Another proposal to reduce unemployment is for the government to be a "last resort" employer. Those who are unemployed and unable to find jobs in the private sector would be hired by the government. The work to be performed would ideally be useful to society—for example, building and repairing highways, planting trees, and providing services in agencies (such as recreational services to youths in high-delinquency areas). Working for the government in such capacities could also provide workers with job skills that would increase their opportunities in the private sector.

Another proposal is for the government to subsidize private companies to maintain their payrolls (instead of laying people off) during economic recessions. A number of foreign governments do this.

Geographically, there have always been areas of high unemployment and areas that are booming and needing more workers. It has been suggested that the government could take a more active role in identifying peak areas, publicizing what jobs are available in these regions and providing assistance in paying relocation expenses for unemployed workers who are willing to move from areas of high unemployment.

Another proposal is for the government to expand its role in providing job training to the unskilled and semiskilled and to those workers whose skills have become obsolete. Germany, as an example, not only provides such work training but also usually pays workers during the weeks or months they are learning new skills for available jobs.

Critics of the last four proposals argue that extensive government efforts in any of these areas would sharply increase government spending and thereby increase the rate of inflation. They also maintain that government-supplied jobs would merely be a stop-gap measure that would not solve the overall problem of joblessness. According to these critics, government should not be in the business of creating "make-work" jobs.

Occupational Health Hazards

There are a number of occupational health hazards that affect workers. These hazards include on-the-job accidents, work-related illnesses, and job stress.

ON-THE-JOB AND WORK-RELATED HEALTH HAZARDS

Every year over 10,000 workers are killed on the job, and about 2 million suffer disabling injuries from work accidents.[31] Proponents of occupational health have widened their focus to include illnesses as well as accidents, and they have also concentrated on preventing work-related diseases rather than merely treating or compensating workers for them. Over 100,000 Americans die of job-related diseases each year.[32]

Occupations that have high rates of injuries from accidents (some of which are fatal) are shipbuilding and repairing, meat packing, mobile-home construction, timber cutting and logging, aviation, asbestos insulation, structural metal work, electric power line and cable installation and repair, mining, firefighting, roofing, farming, and law enforcement.

Two of the most dangerous worksites are mines and farms. Coal miners, in particular, are exposed to a variety of dangers: underground floods, cave-ins, explosions, and respiratory diseases. Every year we hear about cave-ins in coal mines that trap and kill a number of miners. Statistically, however, incurable lung ailments kill many more miners than cave-ins. Unless a mine is properly ventilated, the air is filled with coal dust. Years of breathing such dust can lead to respiratory diseases. The most publicized miner's disease is black lung, a fatal pneumoconiosis. An estimated 10% of American coal miners have it.[33] An even more common respiratory disease among coal miners is silicosis, a condition of massive fibrosis of the lungs marked by shortness of breath and caused by prolonged inhalation of silica dusts. The 1969 Coal Mine Safety Act set standards for allowable dust levels, and technology is now available to clean the air.

Farming also presents a number of occupational hazards. Farmers, their families, and the workers they employ operate a wide range of heavy equipment. Often they are not carefully trained in the safe operation of that equipment. As a result, we hear frequent reports of people who are fatally injured when a tractor overturns. On-the-job accidents are common on farms. An even graver danger for farmworkers comes from pesticides and herbicides that are misused or overused. More farmworkers are poisoned by chemicals than are injured in farm accidents.[34]

Other industries also have serious health hazards. Cotton dust levels are a threat in the textile and cottonseed-oil industries. Continued inhalation of cotton dust in the mill air causes brown lung, or byssinosis, which is irreversible and fatal. Although brown-lung disease was recognized in the 18th century, it was not until 1968 that it was officially classified as an occupational illness. (Company owners did not want official recognition of the disease, because they did not want to pay compensation for those workers who became ill.) Even after official recognition, it took another eight years of pressure from labor groups (such as the Amalgamated Clothing and Textile Workers Union) to force the government to set standards for allowable levels of cotton dust. Company owners were reluctant to have standards set because of the cost of remodeling buildings and purchasing the necessary equipment to meet these standards. They also argued that it might be more profitable for them to close the plants and relocate in foreign countries where governments are less safety conscious and they could hire workers at much lower wages.

Currently, one of the most controversial occupational hazards is the use of nuclear power for energy purposes. A number of nuclear power plants have already been built. In 1979 an accident at the nuclear plant at Three Mile Island in Pennsylvania caused small amounts of radioactive particles to be released into the air. Although thousands of people in the surrounding area were evacuated, authorities feared a serious threat from the released radioactivity. In 1986 an accident at the nuclear power plant in Chernobyl, Russia, released massive amounts of radioactivity into the atmosphere. More than 20 people died within a few days, and thousands now face the possibility of an early death due to radiation exposure. These accidents have raised a worldwide concern about the dangers of using nuclear energy to produce electricity.

A serious problem involving occupational hazards is that some substances take years before their deadly effects appear. Asbestos is a prime example. Asbestos is a mineral that has multiple uses, from construction to beer brewing. It has been handled by workers in a wide range of industries. Several years ago it was discovered that employees who had worked extensively with asbestos later became high risks to develop cancer. It was not only the workers who were in danger, but also their spouses and children who were being exposed to clinging asbestos particles on the workers' clothes. The government is now advising persons who have been exposed to asbestos to undergo periodic medical examinations for early detection and treatment of cancer.

Asbestos workers die from lung cancer at a rate more than seven times that of the general public.[35] Mesothelioma was once a rare form of cancer; it attacks the abdominal organs and the lining of the lungs and is usually fatal. This type of cancer has now become relatively common among asbestos workers.

Asbestos may be only the tip of the iceberg. There are over 2400 suspected carcinogens (cancer-causing substances). Only a few of them have been so designated and regulated by the government.[36]

Rubber workers are exposed to a variety of carcinogens and are dying of cancer of the prostate, cancer of the stomach, and leukemia and other cancers of the blood and the lymph-forming tissues. These cancer rates for rubber workers range from 50% to 300% higher than those for the general population.[37]

Steelworkers, especially those handling coal, are becoming victims of lung cancer at excessive rates. Workers exposed to benzidine and other aromatic amines (often used in producing dyestuffs) have excessively high rates of bladder cancer. Dry cleaners, painters, printers, and petroleum workers are exposed to benzene, which is a known leukemia-producing agent. Miners of iron ore, uranium, chromium, nickel, and other industrial metals fall victim to a variety of occupationally related cancers. Insecticide workers, farmworkers, and copper and lead smelter workers are exposed to inorganic arsenic, a carcinogen that results in high rates of lymphatic cancer and lung cancer.

One of the gravest health dangers involves the relatively young chemical industry. This industry was born amid the technological innovations of World War II and has been rapidly growing ever since. Chemicals are now involved in the manufacture of practically every product we use—our clothing, the processed food we eat, the soaps we wash with, our televisions, and our automobiles. A number of these chemicals have been found to cause certain diseases, such as cancer, birth defects, heart problems, nervous disorders, weight loss, and sterility. Kepone was described in Chapter 8, and DDT will be described in Chapter 16; both chemicals have been found to be carcinogens. There is some evidence that saccharin (used in the past in diet soft drinks) may be a carcinogen. Because new chemicals are being introduced at the rate of one every 20 minutes,[38] it is extremely difficult to determine the hazards of all the chemicals currently in use, not to mention those that will be discovered and used in the future.

It is extremely difficult to prove that a substance causes cancer. Scientists disagree about how much evidence is needed to document a causal relationship. In addition, cancer, as well as certain other diseases (such as respiratory disorders), can take several years to appear after exposure. When a segment of the population has a high incidence of cancer, it is often difficult to identify the cancer-causing substances they were exposed to years earlier.

Simply documenting that certain chemicals are hazardous does not automatically mean they will be taken off the market. For example, there is

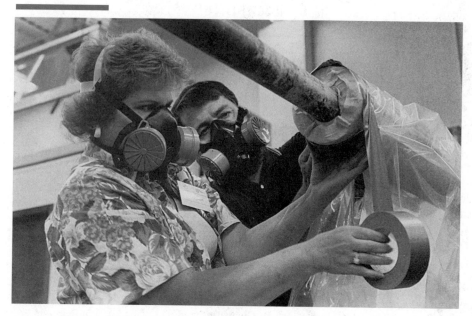

At a training center United Auto Worker health and safety officers learn the proper technique for asbestos removal.

solid evidence that tobacco is a health hazard, yet many Americans continue to smoke.

When given the choice of being unemployed or working in an industry that is a recognized health hazard (such as coal mining or the textile industry) people often elect to work. Because of the high cost of meeting safety standards, businesses commonly drag their feet in complying with government regulations and sometimes threaten to relocate to other countries when the government applies pressure on them. In many occupational areas, such as textile mills, there is considerable controversy regarding what should be considered "safe" levels of exposure to substances.

The federal government has become increasingly concerned about occupational illnesses. In 1970 it passed the Occupational Safety and Health Act, which established two new organizations to combat occupational hazards. The Occupational Safety and Health Administration (OSHA) was created in the Department of Labor to establish

health standards for industry. The National Institute for Occupational Safety and Health (NIOSH) was created in the Department of Health and Human Services to research occupational hazards.

In 1976 the federal government enacted the Toxic Substances Control Act, which established systems and guidelines for screening and controlling dangerous substances. With the rapid development of chemicals and other substances, OSHA and NIOSH face formidable tasks in testing the effects of all of these substances and in setting and enforcing safety limits for substances found to be health hazards.

JOB STRESS

Most standard textbooks in medicine attribute anywhere from 50% to 80% of all diseases to stress-related or psychosomatic origins.[39] One of the main sources of stress is job pressures. Practically any job has stresses. Some of the more stressful jobs are inner-city schoolteacher, police officer, air traffic controller, medical intern, and firefighter (see Exhibit 10.3). (Stress is further described in Chapter 14.) The list of stress-related illnesses includes bronchial asthma, peptic ulcer, ulcerative colitis, mucous colitis, hay fever, arthritis, hyperthyroidism, enuresis, hypertension, alcoholism, insomnia, cancer, migraine headache, impotence, atopic dermatitis, amenorrhea, and chronic constipation. Stress is also one of the causes of emotional disorders.

Employers are become increasingly aware of the cost of stress to employees and to their businesses: absenteeism, low productivity, short- and long-term psychosomatic illnesses, job alienation and job dissatisfaction, marital difficulties, and emotional disorders. Therefore, many companies are sponsoring stress management programs to help their employees learn to reduce stress through such techniques as meditation, relaxation, hypnosis, exercise programs (such as jogging), time management, biofeedback, and hobbies.[40]

SOCIAL WORK IN THE WORKPLACE

Social work in the workplace has had a variety of other titles in recent years, including industrial social work, occupational social work, and employee assistance. No term has yet emerged as "preferred." In this section we will primarily use the terms *social work in the workplace* and *occupational social work*.

Industrial social work is generally viewed as a new and emerging specialization. Social workers in the past decade have been employed in industry in increasing numbers and in a variety of settings and roles. However, the roots of industrial social work go back in time much farther than most people realize.

A Brief History

In the late 1800s there was a welfare movement in American business. Programs and services were developed to help employees in work-related areas, as well as with personal or domestic problems (such as marital conflicts). This movement grew steadily into the 1920s. By 1926, 80% of the 1500 largest companies in the United States had at least one type of welfare program for employees.[41]

The welfare movement emerged at this time for several reasons. Businesses were growing so large that personal contact between personnel and labor was practically nonexistent. In addition, an increasing percentage of the labor force was made up of women and non-English-speaking immigrants whom management did not understand. Employee turnover, employee sabotage, and the development of labor organizations also stimulated management's interest in the welfare movement. The threat of government regulation in the area of employee welfare also influenced businesses to take action.

EXHIBIT 10.3

The 20 Most Stressful Jobs

1. Inner-city schoolteacher
2. Police officer
3. Air traffic controller
4. Medical intern
5. Firefighter
6. Waiter/waitress
7. Assembly-line worker
8. Customer service representative
9. Securities trader
10. Newspaper editor
11. Advertising executive
12. Public relations specialist
13. Middle-level manager
14. Salesperson
15. Attorney
16. Urban bus driver
17. Roofer
18. Real estate agent
19. Politician
20. Banker

Source: "Stressed Out?" *Wisconsin State Journal,* July 1, 1991, p. 1C.

The programs that were developed during this welfare movement required staff to provide the services. The positions that emerged became known as social secretaries, welfare secretaries, or social welfare secretaries. With little previous knowledge on which to draw, these secretaries developed methods and techniques through experimentation. One popular approach was that of group work. It was soon discovered that formation of groups benefited employees in both work- and nonwork-related areas. For example, groups that formed for socialization or recreation fostered employee morale, which was reflected in work production and attitude. In addition to working directly with the employees, these secretaries performed many administrative duties such as handling pension and insurance programs.

The number of positions of welfare secretaries declined sharply in the 1930s, for several reasons.[42] Labor leaders tended to oppose such positions because they felt the secretaries were antiunion. (All too often management urged welfare secretaries to mold employees into loyal workers and to fight unionization.) Laborers came to react negatively to the paternalistic character of the position. With the Great Depression in the 1930s many businesses were forced to cut back on welfare programs.

Aspects of the welfare secretary's role still exist. Many of these functions are now included in what is being called personnel or human relations services, such as handling grievances, linking employees who need help with available resources, and processing health insurance and pensions.

In the 1960s and early 1970s, large corporations developed training programs for inexperienced, long-term unemployed people, including members of minority groups. Directors of these training programs learned that many of the trainees needed help in a variety of areas, such as child care, interpersonal skills, family problems, personal problems, and adequate housing and transportation. In the past two decades industries have increasingly been employing social workers to provide services in these areas.

The development of Employee Assistance Programs (EAPs) has also been a major factor in the emergence of occupational social work. The EAP movement had its roots in the development of alcoholism programs in the 1930s and 1940s. Originally these programs were operated by industrial physicians or were informal programs staffed by recovering alcoholics. Employee Assistance Programs now focus primarily on the restoration of employees' job performance when alcohol or other drug abuse, emotional or personal problems, or changes in the nature of a job have interfered. Occupational social work is now sometimes erroneously considered synonymous with EAP. However, EAP is essentially a specific, performance-focused program, whereas (as we will see) occupational social work is much broader in scope.

There are now thousands of EAPs across the United States. They are staffed by people with a variety of backgrounds: social work, psychology, counseling, medicine, nursing, alcohol and drug abuse counseling, business administration, economics, and management.[43] The professional staff members of EAPs have generally completed some specialized training in alcohol and drug abuse counseling, mental health, and/or employee assistance programming.

The Present Status of Social Work in the Workplace

Businesses and industries perceive occupational social work as an emerging area for social work practice. Schools of social work have begun to modify their curricula for social work students who want a career in industry. Occupational social work has the potential to become one of the higher-paying areas for social work practice because most businesses and industries have considerable financial resources.

Common job titles used to describe the functional positions of occupational social workers in business and industrial settings are employee assistance program coordinator, employee counselor, substance abuse service coordinator, affirmative action officer, employee resources manager, occupational safety and health officer, community relations consultant, corporate relocation officer, training consultant, charitable allocations analyst, human resources policy adviser, career planning and development counselor, urban affairs adviser, outplacement specialist, and coordinator of corporate health and wellness programs. In a newly emerging field there is always considerable confusion over what the specific tasks and functions of the professionals should be. This is particularly true in occupational social work.

Social workers might help employees deal with problems in the following areas: child care, financial problems, family problems, retirement planning, affirmative action, alienation, legal problems, health problems, mental health problems, alcohol and substance abuse, and recreation problems. Social workers might become involved in providing training and staff development programs. They might serve as advocates in developing programs to combat hazardous working conditions. They might design and implement stress management programs. They might provide consultation regarding the physical or social environment within the company. They might help strikers meet basic needs. They might become involved in community relations—for example, acting as a representative of the business in fund raising and/or planning for community services. They might propose new job designs to replace boring, tedious, assembly-line work. Thus, occupational social workers have many more functions than simply being involved in operating direct service programs. Paul Kurzman and Sheila Akabas note:

> Social workers may . . . be called on to consult with management on its human resource policy, donations to tax-exempt activities, collective bargaining demands, or other dimensions of emerging corporate efforts at social responsibility. Professionals may be expected to analyze legislation, administer health and welfare benefit systems, or assist in developing programs designed to attract unorganized workers to trade union membership.[44]

Leo Perlis, longtime community relations director of the American Federation of Labor–Congress of Industrial Organizations, cautions that an occupational social worker needs knowledge of labor/management relations to avoid direct involvement in the adversarial relationship between labor and management.[45] (Occupational social workers should not make the mistake made by many welfare secretaries of becoming identified as being on the side of management.)

A number of other professionals in industry are already providing services similar to those of occupational social work, so questions of turf are arising. Such other professionals include psychiatrists, psychologists, drug and alcohol counselors, nurses, and experts in personnel management. It would seem that the profession of social work needs to develop models of occupational social work that will clarify to management, labor, and other helping professionals what it can realistically provide.

Businesses and industries do not provide social services for humanitarian reasons. Social workers in the workplace are expected to be accountable by demonstrating that their services promote improved productivity and reduced tardiness and absenteeism and make it easier to retain members of the company's work force, many of whom have received expensive training.

There are at least five ways in which social services may be sponsored in business and industry:

1. Sponsorship by management in companies with or without a union.

2. Sponsorship by the union.

3. Sponsorship by both management and labor, with social workers employed by management and dually monitored by both management and labor.

4. Private consultantships by social workers under contract to union or management to provide services to workers and/or the organization.

5. Sponsorship by a community mental health center or family service agency that has a specific contractual arrangement with the company.[46]

Research is needed to identify the merits and shortcomings of each of these approaches to sponsorship.

Employee Assistance Programs

Most social services in the workplace are currently provided by EAPs. As noted earlier, other professionals (such as psychologists and guidance counselors) may also be employed by EAPs.

At present over 12% of workers have access to EAPs, and the number of these programs is growing.[47] It is essential that EAPs operate outside the disciplinary system of an organization. Donald Brieland, Lela Costin, and Charles Atherton describe the importance of employees' feeling free to use EAP services without adverse reactions from management:

> Employees ideally should come for help
> in the early stages of difficulties but are
> understandably reluctant to share information
> that management could use against them.
> Therefore, we have seen that employees tend
> to conceal problems from both management
> and fellow workers. After they are referred by
> management or by a supervisor or union
> steward for help, the employee may feel labeled
> as a problem. If they are confronted by
> management, they fear loss of their job or
> discrimination in promotion. Managers have
> similar fears about revealing their own personal
> problems. Sometimes getting help is specified
> as a condition for retaining a job. Workers have
> to be convinced of the ultimate value of
> getting help.[48]

It is also essential for employees to be aware that what they say to EAP staff will remain confidential; otherwise they will be reluctant to discuss their personal concerns and circumstances openly. Sometimes management finds confidentiality a difficult concession to make because it is paying the bill, but there is no other way to establish trust with employees. Brieland, Costin, and Atherton note:

> Social workers in industry need a written
> agreement to guarantee that the services they
> provide will be confidential and also to spell out
> the guidelines for referral to other community
> resources. . . .

> Management or supervisors who refer to
> the employee should be concerned with job
> performance but not with diagnosis. If they
> detect problems they expect some response. One
> way to handle the issue is to submit a statement
> indicating that the employee was in contact with
> the EAP and to provide a brief statement of
> general progress later.[49]

The primary services provided by EAPs are alcohol and drug abuse counseling, family counseling, career counseling and education, credit counseling, and retirement planning. Each of these areas will be briefly described.

ALCOHOL AND DRUG ABUSE COUNSELING

The major focus of EAPs has been on alcohol and drug abuse. It is well recognized that alcohol and drug abuse costs businesses and industries millions of dollars in productivity each year, through lower-quality work, absenteeism, tardiness, and deterioration of well-trained employees. EAPs tend to view alcoholism and other drug use as a disease and to emphasize total sobriety or total abstinence rather than a reduction in use. Alcoholics Anonymous and Narcotics Anonymous are also promoted in the treatment process. Inpatient hospital treatment is sometimes used, but outpatient efforts are preferred because they cost less and because they do not involve loss of work time. Some EAPs provide treatment to those who are chemically dependent, whereas other EAPs serve as brokers by arranging for treatment with other resources.

Students seeking a career in social work in the workplace are advised to become knowledgeable about drug and alcohol abuse, through coursework and probably a field internship in the treatment of chemical dependency. Employees who have a chemical dependency that is affecting their work are generally offered treatment by EAP staff; such treatment is paid for by the employer (generally through health insurance programs). Employees who refuse treatment encounter the risk of being fired.

EAPs also provide services to employees who have emotional problems, such as depression. As with alcohol and drug abuse treatment, EAP staff either provide treatment services for emotional difficulties or serve as brokers by arranging for treatment with other resources.

FAMILY COUNSELING

Brieland, Costin, and Atherton summarize the primary family problems that EAPs become involved in:

> Stresses involving the spouse and other family members are an important concern. Not only does the employee take family problems to the workplace but he or she brings workplace problems home and displaces them on family members. Marriage counseling and child care are the most common needs. Separation and divorce take their toll in stress on the job. Child abuse and family violence increasingly come to the attention of the assistance program. These behaviors may lead to criminal prosecution. If publicity results, assault may lead to rejection in the workplace, even though no sentence results.[50]

EAPs either provide counseling in these areas or refer employees and their families to other therapists. If the family dispute involves court action, as in the case of spouse abuse, the court may ask the employer to provide an evaluation, which is then often conducted by staff of the EAP.

Financial problems for families are usually created when employees are laid off. EAP staff may help employees to obtain unemployment benefits. Because layoffs may contribute to increased drinking and to child and spouse abuse, EAPs can provide counseling and referral services for such difficulties during layoffs. For employees who need child care, EAPs may play a broker role in helping to link them with child-care services.

CAREER COUNSELING AND EDUCATION

EAPs have become involved in two areas of career counseling: helping employees to set and achieve specific career goals and helping them to learn and use stress management techniques. In the first area, EAPs may administer, or arrange for, aptitude tests. They may also help employees to understand the promotion and advancement opportunities within the company. EAPs help employees to enroll in educational programs that enhance their physical and mental health and increase their skills on the job. Many companies provide or pay for training that will facilitate promotion. Some companies will also pay for courses that increase employees' assertiveness, personal adjustment, self-understanding, and problem-solving capacities. (Many EAPs are reluctant to provide assistance to employees who are seeking a job outside the company.)

EAPs also provide, or arrange for, workshops and seminars on stress management techniques. Such techniques include: using relaxation exercises, hypnosis, time management, or positive thinking; developing hobbies and exercise programs; improving interpersonal relationships; learning to problem solve; and establishing a positive sense of self. Employees who are experiencing burnout or severe job stress may receive counseling by EAP staff or be referred elsewhere for therapy.

CREDIT COUNSELING

Many EAPs have become involved in providing assistance to employees who are having financial difficulties and need credit counseling. One aspect of this involves debt counseling, in which the workers receive assistance in renegotiating their payments to creditors over a longer period of time. They are also encouraged to make a commitment to defer further credit purchases until the financial burden is reduced. Often they also receive financial counseling on developing a budget to meet their financial needs.

In some states creditors can claim part of the debtor's wages through legal garnishment. In such cases the employer must deduct a portion of the employee's wages, which is then paid to the creditor to pay off the debt. This process reveals the credit problems to the employer. (Some employers may view a worker with bad credit as a bad employee and may then discharge her or him.) EAP staff members may get involved in cases of legal garnishment to help employees in trouble to straighten out their financial circumstances.

Some EAPs also provide financial planning assistance to employees who are burdened with alimony and child-support payments.

RETIREMENT PLANNING

In recent years employees have shown increased interest in retirement planning. EAPs can arrange for retirement-planning workshops and seminars for employees. A wide variety of programs can be explained to employees, including Social Security benefits, IRA plans, pension plans, profit-sharing plans, stock option plans, and tax-sheltered annuity plans.

EAP staff should be knowledgeable about the retirement plans available from the firm in order to help individuals in making intelligent decisions. EAP staff may also provide assistance to employees nearing retirement. Such employees need to plan not only for their financial needs but also for what they will do to maintain a high level of positive mental and physical activity.

Occupational social work appears to be a challenging new growth area for social work. But careful planning is needed to avoid the mistakes that led to the demise of welfare secretaries. Because there are over 100 million workers in the United States, employees and their families constitute a massive target population. Business and industry could hire every graduating social worker and hardly dent their payrolls.[51]

SUMMARY

The major social problems involving work are alienation, unemployment, and occupational health hazards. Alienation is the sense of meaninglessness and powerlessness that many people feel about their jobs.

Work is highly esteemed in our society. Under the influence of the Protestant ethic, work has become a moral obligation. It is also a source of self-respect and an opportunity to form friendships, and it may be a source of self-fulfillment and an opportunity to use one's talents. To a large extent our work determines our social status and defines who we are. Before the Protestant Reformation work was denigrated and even considered a curse by some societies.

There have been significant changes or trends in the nature of work and the composition of the work force in the past few decades. The number of white-collar workers has increased, and the number of farmers and blue-collar workers has decreased. Most workers are now employees rather than being self-employed. Work is increasingly becoming specialized, and considerable automation is occurring. More women are entering the labor force, and older male workers are increasingly becoming unemployed. Workers are now seeking intrinsic rewards (rewards that come from the nature of the work itself). Our economy emphasizes high technology. Those who are well educated in high-tech areas have a promising future, whereas the unskilled in our society face increased prospects of being trapped in the lower socioeconomic class.

Alienation appears to be a serious problem for many workers. Sources of alienation include specialization, automation, lack of involvement in the decision-making process, performance of routine and repetitive tasks, and lack of opportunity to be creative or to use one's talents fully. Alienation may lead to poor-quality work, absenteeism, job turnover, and low productivity. Job dissatisfaction is one measure of alienation. Available studies indicate conflicting results about how satisfied American workers are with their jobs. A number of techniques have been proposed for reducing worker alienation and job dissatisfaction.

In recent years the unemployment rate has ranged between 4% and 11%, which is considered high. Long-term unemployment has serious adverse effects: depletion of savings, loss of self-respect, loss of friends, isolation, and feelings of embarrassment, anger, despair, depression, anxiety, boredom, hopelessness, and apathy. It may be a factor leading to emotional problems, suicide, alcoholism, and stress-related illnesses.

Groups that have chronically high rates of unemployment are African Americans and Latinos, teenagers, women, older workers, the unskilled, and the semiskilled. The reasons for high unemployment among these groups, as well as among the total work force, are numerous and complex.

Economists agree that the ideal way to cure unemployment is through rapid economic growth. They disagree, however, about the causes of a sluggish economy and about the best ways to stimulate it.

There are three main occupational health hazards: on-the-job accidents, conditions that lead to work-related physical diseases (for example, breathing coal dust leads to black-lung disease), and job stress. The large number of untested chemicals that are increasingly being used may pose the greatest health danger in the future. Many chemical substances have a delayed reaction in which an illness (such as cancer) first occurs several years after exposure.

Social work in the workplace is an emerging field for social work practice. Most social services in the workplace are currently provided by Employee Assistance Programs (EAPs). EAP services include alcohol and drug abuse counseling, family counseling, career counseling and education, credit counseling, and retirement planning.

NOTES

1. Nancy C. Morse and Robert S. Weiss, "The Function and Meaning of Work," *American Sociological Review* (April 1955), pp. 191–198.
2. Aristotle, *Politics,* Book 3, sec. V, Benjamin Jowett, trans. (Oxford: Clarendon Press, 1945).
3. Quoted in Thomas Sullivan, Kenrick Thompson, Richard Wright, George Gross, and Dale Spady, *Social Problems* (New York: Wiley, 1980), p. 300.
4. Quoted in Ian Robertson, *Social Problems,* 2d ed. (New York: Random House, 1980), p. 87.
5. *Work in America: Report of a Special Task Force to the Secretary of Health, Education and Welfare* (Cambridge, MA: MIT Press, 1973), p. 45.
6. U.S. Bureau of the Census, *Statistical Abstract of the United States, 1993* (Washington, DC: U.S. Government Printing Office, 1993).
7. William Kornblum and Joseph Julian, *Social Problems,* 7th ed. (Englewood Cliffs, NJ: Prentice-Hall, 1992), p. 404.
8. Seymour Wolfbein, *Work in American Society* (Glenview, IL: Scott, Foresman, 1971), p. 45.
9. Robertson, *Social Problems,* p. 89.
10. Charles R. Walker and Robert Guest, *Man on the Assembly Line* (Cambridge, MA: Harvard University Press, 1952), pp. 54–55.
11. Kornblum and Julian, *Social Problems,* p. 402.
12. Ibid.
13. William Glasser, *The Identity Society* (New York: Harper & Row, 1972).
14. Daniel Bell, *The Coming of Post-Industrial Society: A Venture in Social Forecasting* (New York: Basic Books, 1973), pp. 188–195.
15. Karl Marx, *Selected Writings in Sociology and Social Philosophy,* T. B. Bottomore, trans. (New York: McGraw-Hill, 1964), p. 47.
16. Charles Fenyvesi, "Trade Marx," *U.S. News & World Report,* Mar. 12, 1990, p. 23.
17. Karen Ball, "Most Jobs Aren't What We Planned," *Wisconsin State Journal,* Jan. 12, 1990, p. 1A.
18. *Work in America,* p. 19.
19. Robertson, *Social Problems,* p. 108.
20. *Work in America,* p. 16.
21. Herbert C. Morton, "A Look at Factors Affecting the Quality of Working Life," *Monthly Labor Review* (October 1977), p. 64.
22. "The Flextime Concept Gets a Wider Test," *Business Week,* May 24, 1976, p. 38.
23. Keith Davis and John W. Newstrom, *Human Behavior at Work,* 8th ed. (New York: McGraw-Hill, 1989), pp. 232–249.
24. Richard E. Walton, "How to Counter Alienation in the Plant," *Harvard Business Review,* 50 (November–December 1972), pp. 70–82.
25. Robertson, *Social Problems,* p. 115.
26. "A Productive Way to Vent Employee Gripes," *Business Week,* Oct. 16, 1978, pp. 168–171.
27. Harold L. Wilensky, "Work as a Social Problem," in *Social Problems,* Howard Becker, ed. (New York: Wiley, 1966), p. 129.
28. D. D. Braginsky and B. M. Braginsky, "Surplus People: Their Lost Faith in Self and System," *Psychology Today* (August 1975), p. 70.
29. Harvey Brenner, *Mental Illness and the Economy* (Cambridge, MA: Harvard University Press, 1973).
30. *Report of the National Advisory Commission on Civil Disorders* (New York: Bantam Books, 1968), pp. 13–14.
31. Kornblum and Julian, *Social Problems,* p. 410.
32. Ibid.
33. Erik Eckholm, "Unhealthy Jobs," *Environment,* 19 (August–September 1977), p. 29.
34. Joel Schwartz, "Poisoning Farmworkers," *Environment,* 17 (June 1975), pp. 26–33.
35. Larry Agran, "Getting Cancer on the Job," *The Nation,* Apr. 12, 1975, p. 33.
36. Dorothy McGhee, "The Secret Killers," *The Progressive* (August 1977), p. 26.
37. Agran, "Getting Cancer on the Job," p. 39.
38. Joseph Julian, *Social Problems,* 3d ed. (Englewood Cliffs, NJ: Prentice-Hall, 1980), p. 468.

39. K. R. Pelletier, *Mind as Healer, Mind as Slayer* (New York: Delta, 1977).

40. Ibid.

41. Philip R. Popple, "Social Work Practice in Business and Industry, 1875–1930," *Social Service Review,* 55 (June 1981), pp. 257–269.

42. Normal L. Wyers and Malina Kaulukukui, "Social Services in the Workplace: Rhetoric vs. Reality," *Social Work,* 29 (March–April 1984), pp. 167–172.

43. Ibid., p. 168.

44. Paul A. Kurzman and Sheila H. Akabas, "Industrial Social Work as an Arena for Practice," *Social Work,* 26 (January 1981), p. 53.

45. Leo Perlis, "The Human Contract in the Organized Workplace," *Social Thought,* 3 (Winter 1977), p. 49.

46. "Industrial Social Work Movement Expanding," *NASW News,* 23 (February 1978), p. 7.

47. Donald Brieland, Lela B. Costin, and Charles R. Atherton, *Contemporary Social Work,* 3d ed. (New York: McGraw-Hill, 1985), p. 334.

48. Ibid., pp. 342–343.

49. Ibid., p. 343.

50. Ibid., p. 339.

51. Kurzman and Akabas, "Industrial Social Work as an Arena for Practice," p. 52.

11

RACISM, ETHNOCENTRISM, AND STRATEGIES FOR ADVANCING SOCIAL AND ECONOMIC JUSTICE

We see ethnic and racial conflict—riots, beatings, murders, and civil wars—nearly every time we turn on the evening news. In recent years there have been clashes resulting in bloodshed from Northern Ireland to Yugoslavia, from Iraq to Israel, and from the United States to South America. Practically every nation with more than one ethnic group has had to deal with ethnic conflict. The oppression and exploitation of one group by another are particularly ironic in democratic nations because these societies claim to cherish freedom, equality, and justice. In reality, in all societies the dominant group that controls the political and economic institutions rarely agrees to share (equally) its power and wealth with other groups.

Our country was supposedly founded on the principle of human equality. The Declaration of Independence and the Constitution assert equality, justice, and liberty for all. Yet, in practice, our society has always been racist: Inequality, racial prejudice, and discrimination have always existed.

From its earliest days, our society has singled out certain minorities to treat unequally. A *minority* can be defined as a group that has a subordinate status and is being subjected to discrimination.

The categories of people who have been singled out for unequal treatment in our society have changed somewhat over the years. In the late 1800s and early 1900s, people of Irish, Italian, and Polish descent were discriminated against, but that discrimination has been substantially reduced. In the first half of the 19th century, Americans of Chinese and Japanese descent were severely discriminated against, but this bias has also been declining for many decades.

As time passes, new minorities are recognized as being the victims of discrimination. For example, women, persons with a disability, and homosexuals have always been discriminated against, but only in the past 30 years has there been extensive national recognition of this discrimination.

This chapter will:

- Define and describe ethnic groups, ethnocentrism, racial groups, racism, prejudice, discrimination, oppression, and institutional discrimination.

- Outline the sources of prejudice and discrimination.

- Summarize the effects and costs of discrimination and oppression.

- Present background material on racial groups: African Americans, Latinos, Native Americans, and Asian Americans.

- Outline strategies for advancing social and economic justice.

- Describe social work's commitment to ending racial discrimination and oppression.

- Forecast the pattern of race and ethnic relations in the United States in the future.

ETHNIC GROUPS AND ETHNOCENTRISM

An ethnic group has a sense of togetherness, a conviction that its members form a special group, and a sense of common identity or "peoplehood." Milton Gordon defines an ethnic group as:

> any group which is defined or set off by race, religion, or national origin, or some combination of these categories. . . . [A]ll of these categories have a common social-psychological referent, in that all of them serve to create, through historical circumstances, a sense of peoplehood.[1]

Practically every ethnic group has a strong feeling of *ethnocentrism*, which is "the tendency to view the norms and values of one's own culture as absolute and to use them as a standard against which to judge and measure all other cultures."[2] Ethnocentrism leads members of ethnic groups to view their culture as the best, as superior, as the one that other cultures should emulate. It also leads to prejudice against foreigners, who may be viewed as barbarians, heathens, uncultured people, or savages.

Feelings of ethnic superiority within a nation are usually accompanied by the belief that political and economic domination by one's own group is natural, is morally right, is in the best interest of the nation, and perhaps also is "God's will." Ethnocentrism has led to some of the worst human atrocities in history, such as the American colonists' nearly successful attempt to exterminate Native Americans and Adolpf Hitler's mass executions of over 6 million European Jews, gypsies, homosexuals, people with disabilities, and other minority-group members.

In interactions between nations, ethnocentric beliefs sometimes lead to wars and serve as justifications for foreign conquests. At practically any point in the last several centuries there have been at least a few wars being waged in which one society has been seeking to force its culture on another. In the past few decades, the United States and the former Soviet Union engaged in a struggle to extend their influence on other cultures. We hold a number of negative stereotypes about the Russian culture, and their citizens have a number of negative stereotypes about our culture. Israel and the Arab countries have been involved in a bitter struggle in the Middle East. China and Taiwan are in conflict, as are countries in Southeast Asia (such as Cambodia and Vietnam). Yugoslavia is currently in turmoil, and some of the countries that were formerly part of the Soviet Union are now in conflict with one another.

RACE AND RACISM

Although a racial group is often also an ethnic group, the two groups are not necessarily the same. A *race* is believed to have a common set of physical characteristics. But the members of a racial group may or may not share the sense of togetherness or identity that holds an ethnic group together. A group that is both a racial group and an ethnic group is Japanese Americans; they are thought to have some common physical characteristics and also have a sense of "peoplehood." On the other hand, white Americans and white Russians are of the same race, but they hardly have a sense of togetherness. In addition, there are ethnic groups that are composed of a variety

of races. For example, a religious group (such as Roman Catholics) is sometimes considered an ethnic group and is composed of members from diverse racial groups.

In contrast to ethnocentrism, racism is more likely to be based on physical differences than on cultural differences. Racism is ". . . a belief in racial superiority that leads to discrimination and prejudice toward those races considered inferior."[3] Similar to ethnocentric ideologies, most racist ideologies assert that members of other racial groups are inferior.

PREJUDICE, DISCRIMINATION, AND OPPRESSION

To feel *prejudice* means to prejudge, to make a judgment in advance of due examination. The judgment may be favorable or negative. In terms of race and ethnic relations, however, prejudice refers to negative prejudgments. Gordon Allport defines prejudice as thinking negatively of others without sufficient justification.[4] His definition has two elements: an unfounded judgment and a feeling tone of scorn, dislike, fear, and aversion. In regard to race, prejudiced people apply racial stereotypes to all or nearly all members of the group according to preconceived notions of what they believe the group is like and how they think the group behaves. Racial prejudice results from the belief that people who have different skin color and other physical characteristics also have differences in behaviors, values, intellectual functioning, and attitudes.

The term *to discriminate* has two very different meanings. It may have the positive meaning "to be discerning and perceptive." However, in minority-group relations, it means "to make categoric differentiations based on a social group ranked as inferior, rather than judging an individual on his or her own merits." Racial discrimination involves denying to members of minority groups equal access to opportunities, certain residential housing areas, membership in certain religious and social organizations, certain political activities, access to community services, and so on.

Prejudice is a combination of stereotyped beliefs and negative attitudes, so that prejudiced individuals think about people in a predetermined, usually negative, categorical way. Discrimination involves physical actions—unequal treatment of people because they belong to a category. Discriminatory behavior often derives from prejudiced attitudes. Robert Merton, however, notes that prejudice and discrimination can occur independently of each other. Merton describes four different "types" of people:

1. *The unprejudiced nondiscriminator,* in both belief and practice, upholds American ideals of freedom and equality. This person is not prejudiced against other groups and, on principle, will not discriminate against them.

2. *The unprejudiced discriminator* is not personally prejudiced but may sometimes, reluctantly, discriminate against other groups because it seems socially or financially convenient to do so.

3. *The prejudiced nondiscriminator* feels hostile to other groups but recognizes that law and social pressures are opposed to overt discrimination. Reluctantly, this person does not translate prejudice into action.

4. *The prejudiced discriminator* does not believe in the values of freedom and equality and consistently discriminates against other groups in both word and deed.[5]

An example of an unprejudiced discriminator is the owner of a condominium complex in an all-white middle-class suburb who refuses to sell a condominium to an African American family because of fear (founded or unfounded) that the sale would reduce the value of the remaining units. An example of a prejudiced nondiscriminator is a personnel director of a fire department who believes Latinos are unreliable and poor firefighters but complies with affirmative action efforts to hire and train Latinos.

It should be noted that it is very difficult to

keep personal prejudices from eventually leading to some form of discrimination. Strong laws and firm informal social norms are necessary to break the causal relationship between prejudice and discrimination.

Discrimination is of two types: *de jure* and *de facto. De jure* discrimination is legal discrimination. The so-called Jim Crow laws in the South gave force of law to many discriminatory practices against African Americans, including denial of the right to trial, prohibition against voting, and prohibition against interracial marriage. Today, in the United States, there is practically no *de jure* discrimination because such laws have been declared unconstitutional.

De facto discrimination refers to discrimination that actually exists, whether legal or not. Acts of *de facto* discrimination often result from powerful informal norms that are discriminatory. Marlene Cummings gives an example of this type of discrimination and urges victims to confront it assertively:

> *Scene: department store. Incident: Several people are waiting their turn at a counter. The person next to be served is a black woman; however, the clerk waits on several white customers who arrived later. The black woman finally demands service, after several polite gestures to call the clerk's attention to her. The clerk proceeds to wait on her after stating, "I did not see you." The clerk is very discourteous to the black customer; and the lack of courtesy is apparent, because the black customer had the opportunity to observe treatment of the other customers. De facto discrimination is most frustrating . . . ; the customer was served. Most people would rather just forget the whole incident, but it is important to challenge the practice even though it will possibly put you through more agony. One of the best ways to deal with this type of discrimination is to report it to the manager of the business. If it is at all possible, it is important to involve the clerk in the discussion.[6]*

Oppression is the unjust or cruel exercise of authority or power. Members of minority groups in our society are frequently victimized by oppression from segments of the white power structure.

Oppression and discrimination are closely related, because all acts of oppression are also acts of discrimination.

RACIAL AND ETHNIC STEREOTYPES

Racial and ethnic stereotypes involve attributing fixed and usually inaccurate or unfavorable qualities to a racial or ethnic group. Stereotypes may contain some truth but generally are exaggerated, taken out of context, or distorted. Stereotypes are closely related to the way we think, as we seek to perceive and understand things in categories. We need categories to group things that are similar in order to study them and to communicate about them. We hold stereotypes about many categories, including mothers, fathers, teenagers, Communists, Republicans, schoolteachers, farmers, construction workers, miners, politicians, Mormons, and Italians. These stereotypes may contain some useful and accurate information about a member in any category. Yet each member of any category will have many characteristics that are not suggested by the stereotypes and may even have some characteristics that run counter to some of the stereotypes.

Racial stereotypes involve differentiating people in terms of color or other physical characteristics. In our history, for example, many people held the erroneous stereotype that Native Americans would rapidly become intoxicated and irrational when using alcohol. This belief was then translated into laws that existed for a number of years prohibiting Native Americans from buying and consuming alcohol. A more recent stereotype is the belief that African Americans have "natural rhythm" and therefore have greater natural ability to play basketball and certain other sports. Although this stereotype may appear complimentary to African Americans, it has broader, negative implications. The danger is that, if people believe the stereotype, it may well suggest to them that other abilities and capacities (such as intelligence, morals, and work productivity) are also determined by race. In other words, believing this

"positive" stereotype increases the probability that people will also believe negative stereotypes.

RACIAL AND ETHNIC DISCRIMINATION

Gunnar Myrdal points out that minority problems are actually majority problems.[7] The white majority determines the "place" of nonwhites and other ethnic groups in our society. The status of different minority groups varies in our society because whites apply different stereotypes to various groups. For example, African Americans are viewed and treated differently from Japanese Americans. Elmer Johnson notes: "Minority relationships become recognized by the majority as a social problem when the members of the majority disagree as to whether the subjugation of the minority is socially desirable or in the ultimate interest of the majority."[8] Concern about discrimination and segregation has also received increasing national attention because minority groups are demanding (sometimes militantly) equal opportunities and equal rights.

Race as a Social Concept

Ashley Montague considers "race" to be one of the most dangerous and tragic myths in our society.[9] Race is erroneously believed by many to be a biological classification of people. Yet there are no clearly delineating characteristics of any "race," and no "racial" group has unique or distinctive genes. Throughout history the genes of different societies and racial groups have been intermingled. In addition, biological differentiations of racial groups have gradually been diluted through such sociocultural factors as changes in preferences of desirable characteristics in mates, effects of different diets on those who reproduce, and such variables as wars and diseases in selecting those who will live and reproduce.[10]

In spite of definitional problems, it is necessary to use racial categories in the social sciences, because race has important (though not necessarily consistent) social meanings for people. In order to have a basis for racial classifications, a number of social scientists have used a social, rather than a biological, definition. A social definition is based on the way members of a society classify one another by physical characteristics. For example, a frequently used social definition of an African American is anyone who either displays overt black physical characteristics or is known to have a black ancestor.[11] The sociological classification of races is indicated by different definitions of a race among various societies. In the United States, anyone who is not "pure white" and is known to have a black ancestor is considered to be black, whereas in Brazil, anyone who is not "pure black" is classified as white.[12]

Race, according to Montague, becomes a very dangerous myth when people assume that physical traits are linked with mental traits and cultural achievements.[13] Every few years, it seems, some noted scientist stirs the country by making this erroneous assumption. For example, Arthur Jensen[14] asserted several years ago that whites on the average are more intelligent than African Americans, since IQ tests show that whites score 10 to 15 points higher than blacks. Jensen's findings have been sharply criticized by other authorities as falsely assuming that IQ is largely genetically determined.[15] These authorities contend that IQ is substantially influenced by environmental factors, and it is likely that the average achievement of blacks, if given similar opportunities to realize their potential, would be about the same as that of whites. Also, it has been charged that IQ tests are racially slanted; they ask the kinds of questions that whites are more familiar with and thereby more likely to answer correctly. The assumption that blacks are biologically inferior in intelligence is disastrous because it serves to rationalize oppression and rigidly assign African Americans to a second-class, low-income status.

Elmer Johnson summarizes the need for an impartial, objective view of the capacity of different racial groups to achieve:

Race bigots contend that, the cultural achievements of different races being so obviously unlike, it follows that their genetic capacities for achievement must be just as different. Nobody can discover the cultural capacities of any population or race . . . until there is equality of opportunities to demonstrate the capacities.[16]

Most scientists, both physical and social, now believe that, in biological inheritance, all races are alike in every significant way. With the exception of several very small, inbred, isolated primitive tribes, all racial groups appear to show a wide distribution of every kind of ability. All important race differences that have been noted in personality, behavior, and achievement appear to be due to environmental factors.

Causes of Racial Discrimination and Oppression

No single theory provides a complete picture of why racial discrimination and oppression occur. The sources of discrimination are both internal and external to those who are prejudiced. We'll look now, though, at several explanations for this behavior that have been advanced.

PROJECTION

Projection is a psychological defense mechanism in which we attribute to others characteristics that we are unwilling to recognize in ourselves. Many people have personal traits they dislike in themselves. They have an understandable desire to get rid of such traits, but this is not always possible. Such people may then "project" some of these traits onto others (often to some other group in society), thus displacing the negative feelings they would otherwise direct at themselves. In the process, they then reject and condemn those onto whom they have projected the traits.

For example, a minority group may serve as a projection of a prejudiced person's fears and lusts. People who view African Americans as lazy and preoccupied with sex may be projecting their own internal concerns about their industriousness and their sexual fantasies onto another group. It is interesting to note that, although some whites view blacks as being promiscuous, sexually indiscreet, and immoral, historically it has generally been white men who pressured black women (particularly slaves) into sexual encounters. Perhaps these white males felt guilty about their sexual desires and adventures and dealt with their guilt by projecting their own lusts and sexual conduct onto African American males.

FRUSTRATION-AGGRESSION

Another psychic need satisfied by discrimination is the release of tension and frustration. All of us at times become frustrated when we are unable to achieve or obtain something we desire. Sometimes we strike back at the source of our frustration, but many times direct retaliation is not possible. For example, we may be reluctant to tell our employers what we think of them when we feel we are being treated unfairly, because we fear repercussions.

Some frustrated people displace their anger and aggression onto a scapegoat. The scapegoat may not be limited to a particular person but may include a group of people, such as a minority group. Like people who take out their job frustrations on their spouses or family pets, some prejudiced people vent their frustrations on minority groups. (The term *scapegoat* derives from an ancient Hebrew ritual in which a goat was symbolically laden with the sins of the entire community and then chased into the wilderness. It "escaped"—hence the term *scapegoat*. The definition was gradually broadened to apply to anyone who bears the blame for others.)

INSECURITY AND INFERIORITY

Still another psychic need that may be satisfied by discrimination is the desire to counter feelings of insecurity or inferiority. Some insecure people feel better about themselves by putting down another group; they then can tell themselves that they are "better than" these people.

AUTHORITARIANISM

One of the classic works on the causes of prejudice is *The Authoritarian Personality*, by T. W. Adorno et al.[17] Shortly after World War II these researchers studied the psychological causes of the development of European fascism and concluded that there was a distinct type of personality associated with prejudice and intolerance. The *authoritarian personality* is inflexible and rigid and has a low tolerance for uncertainty, has a great respect for authority figures and quickly submits to their will, and highly values conventional behavior while feeling threatened by unconventional behavior in others. In order to reduce this threat, this personality type labels unconventional people as "immature," "inferior," or "degenerate" and thereby avoids any need to question his or her own beliefs and values. The authoritarian personality views members of minority groups as being unconventional, degrades them, and expresses authoritarianism through prejudice and discrimination.

HISTORY

There are also historical explanations for prejudice. Charles F. Marden and Gladys Meyer note that the racial groups now viewed by prejudiced white people as being second class are ones that have been conquered, enslaved, or admitted into our society on a subordinate basis.[18] For example, Africans were imported as slaves during our colonial period and stripped of human dignity. Native Americans were conquered, and their culture was viewed as inferior. Mexicans have been allowed to enter this country primarily to do seasonal, low-paying farmwork.

COMPETITION AND EXPLOITATION

Our society is highly competitive and materialistic. Individuals and groups compete daily to acquire more of the available goods. These attempts to secure economic goods usually result in a struggle for power. In our society, whites have historically sought to exploit nonwhites. As just mentioned, they have conquered, enslaved, or admitted nonwhites into our society on a subordinate basis. They then use their powers to exploit nonwhites through cheap labor—for example, as sweatshop factory laborers, migrant farm hands, maids, janitors, and bellhops.

Members of the dominant group know they are treating the subordinate group as inferior and unequal. To justify such discrimination, they develop an ideology (set of beliefs) that their group is superior and that it is right and proper for them to have more rights, goods, and so on. Often, they assert that God divinely selected their group to be dominant. Furthermore, they assign inferior traits (lazy, immoral, dirty, stupid) to the subordinate group and conclude that the minority need and deserve less because they are biologically inferior.

SOCIALIZATION PATTERNS

Prejudice is also a learned phenomenon, transmitted from generation to generation through socialization processes. Our culture has stereotypes of what different racial group members ''ought to be'' and how they ''ought to behave'' in relationships with members of certain outgroups. These stereotypes provide norms against which a child learns to judge people, things, and ideas. Prejudice, to some extent, is developed through the same processes by which we learn to be religious and patriotic, or to appreciate and enjoy art, or to develop our value system. Racial prejudice, at least in certain segments in our society, is thus a facet of the normative system of our culture.

THE EYE OF THE BEHOLDER

No one of these theories explains all the causes of prejudice, which has many origins. Taken together, however, they identify a number of causative factors. It should be noted that all these theories assert that the causative factors of prejudice are in the personality and experiences of the person holding the prejudice, not in the character of the group against whom the prejudice is directed.

A novel experiment documenting that prejudice does not stem from contact with the people toward whom it is directed was conducted by Eugene Hartley. He gave his subjects a list of prejudiced responses to Jews and African Americans and to three groups that did not even exist: Wallonians, Pireneans, and Danireans. Prejudiced responses included such statements as ''All Wallonians living here should be expelled.'' The respondents were asked to state their agreement or disagreement with these prejudiced assertions. The experiment showed that most of those who were prejudiced against Jews and blacks were also prejudiced against people whom they had never met or heard anything about.[19]

Institutionalized Racism

In the last 30 years, institutionalized racism has become recognized as a major problem. Institutionalized racism refers to discriminatory acts and policies that pervade the major institutions of society, such as the legal system, politics, the economy, and education. Some of these discriminatory acts and policies are illegal; others are not.

Stokely Carmichael and Charles Hamilton make the following distinction between individual racism and institutional racism:

> *When white terrorists bomb a black church and kill five black children, that is an act of individual racism, widely deplored by most segments of society. But when in the same city . . . five hundred black babies dies each year because of the lack of proper food, shelter, and medical facilities, and thousands more are destroyed and maimed physically, emotionally, and intellectually because of conditions of poverty and discrimination in the black community, that is a function of institutional racism.[20]*

Discrimination is built, often unwittingly, into the structure and form of our society. The following examples reflect institutional racism:

- A family counseling agency with branch offices assigns its less skilled counselors and thereby provides lower-quality services to an office located in a minority neighborhood.

- A public welfare department encourages white applicants to request funds for special needs (e.g., clothing) or to use certain services (e.g., day care and homemaker services), whereas nonwhite clients are not informed (or are less enthusiastically informed) of such services.

- A public welfare department takes longer to process the requests of nonwhites for funds and services.

- A police department discriminates against nonwhite staff in terms of work assignments,

Following a speeding incident on the night of March 3, 1991, African American motorist Rodney King was brutally beaten by four white Los Angeles police officers. The event, captured on videotape, shocked viewers around the world. In 1992, a jury that did not include African American members found the police officers not guilty of charges of using excessive force. What followed the verdicts was the worst civil unrest in this country in over a century. Here a Los Angeles business owner reacts as his business burns behind him.

hiring practices, promotion practices, and pay increases.

■ A real estate agency has a pattern of showing white home buyers houses in white neighborhoods, and African American home buyers houses in mixed or predominantly African American areas.

■ A bank and an insurance company engage in redlining, which involves refusing to make loans or issue insurance in areas with large minority populations.

■ A probation and parole agency tends to ignore minor rule violations by white clients but seeks to return nonwhite parolees to prison for similar infractions.

■ A mental health agency tends to label nonwhite clients "psychotic" while ascribing a less serious disorder to white clients.

■ White staff at a family counseling center are encouraged by the executive board to provide intensive services to clients with whom they have a good relationship (often white clients) and are told to give less attention to those clients "they aren't hitting it off well with" who may be disproportionately nonwhite.

And what are the results of institutionalized racism? The unemployment rate for nonwhites has consistently been over twice that for whites. The infant mortality rate for nonwhites is nearly twice as high as for whites. The life expectancy for nonwhites is several years less than for whites. The average number of years of educational achievement for nonwhites is considerably less than for whites.[21]

There are many examples of institutional racism in school systems. Schools in white suburbs generally have better facilities and more highly trained teachers than schools in minority neighborhoods. Minority families are, on the average, less able to provide the hidden costs of "free" education (higher property taxes in the neighborhoods where the best schools are located, transportation, class trips, clothing, and supplies), and therefore their children become less involved in the educational process. Textbooks generally glorify the white race and give scant attention to minorities. Jeannette Henry writes about the effects of history textbooks on Native American children.

What is the effect upon the student, when he learns from his textbooks that one race, and one alone, is the most, the best, the greatest; when he learns that Indians* were mere parts of the landscape and wilderness which had to be cleared out, to make way for the great "movement" of white population across the land; and when he learns that Indians were killed and forcibly removed from their ancient homelands to make way for adventurers (usually called "pioneering goldminers"), for land grabbers (usually called "settlers"), and for illegal squatters on Indian-owned land (usually called "frontiersmen")? What is the effect upon the young Indian child himself, who is also a student in the school system, when he is told that Columbus discovered America, that Coronado "brought civilization" to the Indian people, and that the Spanish missionaries provided havens of refuge for the Indians? Is it reasonable to assume that the student, of whatever race, will not discover at some time in his life that Indians discovered America

thousands of years before Columbus set out upon his voyage; that Coronado brought death and destruction to the native peoples; and that the Spanish missionaries, in all too many cases, forcibly dragged Indians to the missions.[22]

Even in school districts that use busing to attempt to achieve integration, institutional discrimination may occur. One method of discriminating is to use a track system. Primarily white children are placed in an "advanced" track, receiving increased educational attention from teachers, while most nonwhite children are placed in a "slower learner" track, receiving less educational attention.

Our criminal justice system also has elements of institutional racism. The justice system is supposed to be fair and nondiscriminatory. The very name of the system, *justice*, implies fairness and equality. Yet in practice there is evidence of racism. Although African Americans constitute only about 12% of the population, they make up nearly 50% of the prison population.[23] (There is considerable debate about the extent to which this is due to racism as opposed to differential crime rates by race.) The average prison sentence for murder and kidnapping is longer for African Americans than for whites. Nearly half of those sentenced to death are African Americans.[24] Police departments and district attorneys' offices are more likely to vigorously enforce the kinds of crimes committed by lower-income groups and minority groups than those by middle- and upper-class white groups. Poor people (a disproportionate number of nonwhites are poor) are substantially less likely to be able to post bail. As a result, they are forced to remain in jail until their trial, which may take months or sometimes more than a year to come up. Unable to post bail, they are more likely to be found guilty, as Paul Wice notes:

Numerous studies clearly show that detained defendants are far more likely to be found guilty and receive more severe sentences than those released prior to trial. Limited visiting hours, locations remote from the counsel's office, inadequate conference facilities, and censored mail all serve to impede an effective lawyer-client relationship.[25]

---

*The term *Indian* was originally used by early European settlers to describe the native populations of North America. Because of its nonnative derivation and the context of cultural domination surrounding its use, many people, particularly Native Americans, object to the use of the word. The term *Native American* is now generally preferred.

The Effects and Costs of Discrimination and Oppression

Grace Halsell is a white woman who, through chemical treatments, changed the color of her skin to look like a black person for a brief period of time. She was trying to determine what it means to "live black" in a white world. She reports on her experiences in working one day as a maid for a white woman in the South:

> Long before I have one job completed, there are new orders: "Now sweep off the front porch, the side porch, the back porch, and mop the back porch." The tone is unmistakably that of the mistress-slave relationship. . . .
>
> I feel sorry for her. We are two women in a house all day long, and I sense that she desperately wants to talk to me, but it can never be as an equal. She looks on me as less than a wholly dignified and developed person. . . .
>
> My eight hours are up. She asks if I know where to catch the bus. No, I say, should I turn left or right "when I go out the front door?" The front door comes out inadvertently, because I am trying to get an idea of directions. She hands me five dollars and ushers me to the back door, quite pointedly.
>
> Two bus transfers and an hour later, I am back in "nigger-town." Near the Summers Hotel, young, bright-eyed Negro* children I've come to know wave, smile, and say "hi!"
>
> I want to tell each one of them because I feel so degraded, so morally and spiritually depressed, "Don't do what I did! Don't ever sell yourself that cheap! Don't let it happen to you."
>
> And I want to add, ". . . whatever you do, don't do what I did." The assault upon an individual's dignity and self-respect has intolerable limits, and I believe at this moment my limits have been reached.[26]

---

*When this was first written in 1969, the term *Negro* was still widely used. In the 1970s the preferred term changed to *black*, and the term *Negro* now is sometimes used to suggest a black person who interacts submissively with whites. Many authorities now prefer the term *African American* instead of *black*.

Racial discrimination is a handicap. Everyone in our competitive society seeks to obtain the necessary resources to lead a contented and comfortable life. Being a victim of discrimination is another obstacle that has to be overcome. Racial discrimination makes it more difficult to obtain adequate housing, financial resources, a quality education, employment, adequate health care and other services, equal justice in civil and criminal cases, and so on.

Discrimination also has heavy psychological costs. All of us must develop a sense of identity—who we are and how we fit into a complex, swiftly changing world. Ideally, it is important that we form a positive self-concept and strive to obtain worthy goals. Yet, as we have noted before, according to C. H. Cooley's "looking glass self-concept," our idea of who we are and what we are is largely determined by the way others relate to us.[27] When members of a minority group are treated by the majority as if they are inferior, second-class citizens, it is difficult for such members to develop a positive identity. Thus, people who are the objects of discrimination encounter barriers to developing their full potential as human beings.

In 1965, prior to most "black pride" movements, Kenneth Clark described the devastating effects of discrimination on African Americans:

> Human beings who are forced to live under ghetto conditions and whose daily experience tells them that almost nowhere in society are they respected and granted the ordinary dignity and courtesy accorded to others will, as a matter of course, begin to doubt their own worth. Since every human being depends upon his cumulative experiences with others for clues as to how he should view and value himself, children who are consistently rejected understandably begin to question and doubt whether they, their family, and their group really deserve no more respect from the larger society than they receive. These doubts become the seeds of pernicious self- and group-hatred, the Negro's complex and debilitating prejudice against himself. . . . Negroes have come to believe in their own inferiority.[28]

Children in discriminated-against groups develop low self-esteem at an early age. Studies have found that African American children who have been subjected to discrimination have a preference for white dolls and white playmates over black ones[29] (although no comparison was made to those not subjected to discrimination).

Discrimination also has high costs for the majority group. It impairs intergroup cooperation and communication. It has resulted in race riots, particularly in our inner cities, which have caused a number of deaths and cost billions of dollars. Discrimination also contributes to social problems among minorities—for example, higher rates of crime, emotional problems, alcoholism, and drug abuse, all of which have cost billions of dollars in social programs. Albert Szymanski argues that discrimination is a barrier to collective action (for example, unionization) among whites and nonwhites (particularly people in the lower-income classes) and is therefore a factor in perpetuating low-paying jobs and poverty.[30] Of course, this situation increases profits for business owners, but it hurts less affluent whites, who could benefit from collective action.

Finally, discrimination in the United States undermines some of our nation's political goals. Many other countries view us as hypocritical when we advocate human rights and equality. In order to make an effective argument for human rights on a worldwide scale, we must first put our own house in order by eliminating racial and ethnic discrimination. Few Americans realize the extent to which racial discrimination damages our international reputation. Nonwhite foreign diplomats to the United States often complain about being victims of discrimination because they are mistaken for members of American minority groups. With most of the nations of the world being nonwhite, our racist practices severely damage our influence and prestige.

BACKGROUND OF RACIAL GROUPS

The largest racial group in the United States is the white race, which is the majority group, both in numbers (nearly 80% of the population)[31] and in power. African Americans compose about 12% of the population,[32] and Latinos compose about 8% of the population.[33] The other nonwhite groups constitute about 2% of our population and primarily include Native Americans and people of Japanese, Chinese, and Filipino descent. There are also small numbers of the following nonwhite groups: Aleuts, Asian Indians, Eskimo, Hawaiians, Indonesians, Koreans, and Polynesians. In educational attainment, occupational status, and average income, most of these nonwhite groups are clearly at a disadvantage as compared with the white groups. (The two major nonwhite groups that now approach whites in socioeconomic status are Japanese Americans and Chinese Americans.)

African Americans

The United States has always been a racist nation. Although our country's founders talked about freedom, dignity, equality, and human rights, the economy of the United States prior to the Civil War depended heavily on slavery.

Many slaves came from cultures that had well-developed art forms, political systems, family patterns, religious beliefs, and economic systems. However, because their culture was not European, slave owners viewed it as being of "no consequence" and prohibited slaves from practicing and developing their art, language, religion, and family life. For want of practice, their former culture soon died in the United States.

The life of a slave was harsh. Slaves were viewed not as human beings but as chattel to be bought and sold. Long, hard days were spent working in the field, with the profits of their labor going to their white owners. Whippings, mutilations, and hangings were commonly accepted white control practices. The impetus to enslave blacks was not simply racism; many whites believed that it was to their economic advantage to have a cheap supply of labor. Cotton growing, in particular, was thought to require a large labor force that was cheap and docile. Marriages between slaves were not recognized by the law, and slaves were often sold with little regard to marital and family ties. Throughout the slavery period and even afterward, African Americans were discouraged from demonstrating intelligence, initiative, or ambition. For a period of time it was even illegal to teach them to read and write.

Some authorities have noted that the opposition to the spread of slavery preceding the Civil War was due less to moral concern for human rights and equality than to the North's fears of competition from slave labor and the rapidly increasing migration of free blacks to the North and West.[34] Few whites at that time understood or believed in the principle of racial equality—not even Abraham Lincoln, who thought blacks were inferior to whites. In 1858 in a speech in Charleston, Illinois, Lincoln asserted:

> I will say, then, that I am not, nor ever have been in favor of bringing about in any way the social and political equality of the white and black races; that I am not, nor ever have been, in favor of making voters or jurors of Negroes, nor of qualifying them to hold office, nor to inter-marry with White people . . . and inasmuch as they cannot so live, while they do remain together there must be the position of superior and inferior, and I as much as any other man am in favor of having the superior position assigned to the White race.[35]

Following the Civil War, the federal government failed to develop a comprehensive program of economic and educational aid to African Americans. As a result, most of them returned to being economically dependent on the same planters in the South who had held them in bondage. Within a few years, laws were passed in the southern states prohibiting interracial marriages and requiring racial segregation in schools and public places.

A rigid caste system in the South hardened into a system of oppression known as "Jim Crow." The system prescribed how African Americans were supposed to act in the presence of whites, asserted white supremacy, embraced racial segregation, and denied political and legal rights to blacks. Those who opposed Jim Crow were subjected to burnings, beatings, and lynchings. Jim Crow was used to "teach" African

Americans to view themselves as inferior and to be servile and passive in interactions with whites.

World War II opened up new employment opportunities for African Americans, who migrated to the North in large numbers. Greater mobility afforded by wartime conditions led to upheavals in the traditional caste system. Awareness of disparity between the ideal and the real led many people to try to improve race relations, not only for domestic peace and justice, but also to answer criticism from abroad. With each gain in race relations, more African Americans were encouraged to press for their rights.

A major turning point in civil rights history was the 1954 U.S. Supreme Court decision in *Brown* v. *Board of Education,* which ruled that racial segregation in public schools was unconstitutional. Since then there have been a number of organized efforts by both African Americans and certain segments of the white population to secure equal rights and opportunities for minorities. Attempts to change deeply entrenched racist attitudes and practices have produced much turmoil: the burning of our inner cities in the late 1960s,* the assassination of Martin Luther King, Jr., and clashes between militant black groups and the police. There have also been significant advances. Wide-ranging legislation has been passed, protecting civil rights in areas such as housing, voting, employment, and the use of public transportation and facilities. During the riots in 1968 the National Advisory Commission on Civil Disorders warned that our society was careening "toward two societies, one black, one white—separate and unequal."[36] David Gelman summarizes the current atmosphere of black/white relations in our society:

> Twenty years and a social eon have passed. Mercifully, America today is not the bitterly sundered dual society that the riot commission grimly foresaw. Nor is it King's promised land

---

*On April 4, 1968, Martin Luther King, Jr., was killed by a white assassin's bullet. His death helped trigger extensive rioting in 40 cities; in many places whole blocks were burned down.

of racial amity. Rather, it is something uneasily between the two: a society less unequal but also less caring than it was in the '60s. . . .

Blacks and whites now more often work together, lunch together, even live side by side, yet few really count each other as friends.[37]

Four out of five African Americans now live in metropolitan areas, over half of them in our central cities.[38] American cities are still largely segregated, with blacks living primarily in black neighborhoods. In recent years the main thrust of the civil rights movement among African Americans has been economic equality. The economic gap between blacks and whites continues to be immense. Black families are three times as likely as white families to fall below the poverty line.[39] Since the early 1950s the unemployment rate among African Americans has been approximately twice that for whites. This is an especially severe problem for African American teenagers, whose rate of unemployment is substantially higher than that for white youths and has run as high as 50%.[40]

We as a nation have come a long way since the Supreme Court's decision in 1954. But we still have a long way to go before we eliminate poverty and respond to the deep frustrations of the African Americans in our ghettos. Living conditions in ghettos remain as bleak as in the late 1960s, when dissatisfaction led blacks in many inner-city areas to torch and burn down numerous buildings. The buildings were owned largely by white absentee landlords.

Two developments have characterized the socioeconomic circumstances of African Americans in the past 25 years, as Gelman notes:

Two striking developments mark the black situation since the '60s. One is the emergence of an authentic black middle class, better educated, better paid, better housed than any group of blacks that has gone before it. . . .

The second development is, in a way, the reverse side of the first. As comparatively well off blacks move to better neighborhoods, they have left behind a stripped-down, socially disabled nucleus of poor people who have come to be

called (somewhat pejoratively) the "underclass." With a population estimated at 2.5 million—roughly three times what it was in the '70s—this group generates a disproportionate share of the social pathology usually associated with the ghetto, including high crime rates.[41]

It should be noted that the use of terms such as *underclass* may be disparaging and may set in motion a self-fulfilling prophecy. Gans notes:

By the mid-1980's, the term underclass had become so popular in scholarly circles that social scientists, like journalists, began using the term to grab their audiences, for example, by using the term in the titles of journal articles. . . .

Underclass is a particularly nasty label, however. Earlier terms such as pauper, vagrant, and tramp were openly pejorative, but underclass is a technical-sounding word that hides its pejorative meaning. Moreover, once people are labeled as underclass, they are often treated accordingly. Teachers decide that they cannot learn, the police and the courts think that they must be incorrigible, and welfare agencies feel justified in administering harsh policies. Such treatment sets in motion the self-fulfilling prophecy: If the poor are treated like an underclass, their ability to escape poverty is blocked further. In addition, the term is turning into a racial code word, since by now it is increasingly applied solely to blacks. The public expression of racial prejudice being no longer respectable, underclass becomes an acceptable euphemism.[42]

The use of terms like *underclass* by social scientists may contribute to the perpetuation of a social problem.

African Americans who live in inner-city areas tend to be chronically on welfare; often the teenagers drop out of high school, the families are headed by single parents, and the males do not participate in the work force. Around 55% of all African American families are headed by a single female parent. The rate of pregnancy among 15–19-year-old African American women is more than twice that of whites in that age group. African Americans account for about half of all crimes of violence; a shocking statistic is that currently there are more African American males in prison in the United States than in college.[43]

In a study of pregnant teenagers on Chicago's West Side, Orfield's data "showed that most of these girls didn't know anyone who had a job, anyone who went to college, anyone who was married. Within their society, it looks rational to have a baby when you're a teenage girl."[44]

Over half of all African American children are being raised in single-parent families. However, many of these youngsters are living in family structures composed of some variation of the extended family. Many single-parent families move in with relatives during adversity, including economic adversity. In addition, African American families of all socioeconomic levels rely on relatives to care for their children while they work. Notes Norton:

> Many middle-class families pay an aunt or
> cousin or mother to come into their homes
> and babysit, with formal salary arrangements.
> Having reached financial stability themselves,
> they not only share that stability by providing
> economic opportunity for other family members
> but also assure that their children will receive
> responsible, loving and interested family-
> oriented child care. Other, less well off families
> drop their children at the home of relatives,
> making financial arrangements that are
> probably lower in cost. For others, there are no
> financial arrangements, but reciprocity is given
> in returned child care, sharing of food, clothing
> or shelter.[45]

Although it is a reality that many African American families are headed by single mothers, it would be a serious error to view such family structures as inherently pathological. A single parent with good parenting skills, along with a supportive extended family, can provide a functional family environment.

Solomon noted that "black culture contains elements of 'mainstream' white culture, elements from traditional African culture, and elements from slavery, reconstruction and subsequent exposure to racism and discrimination."[46]

Subcultures of African Americans have vocabularies and communication styles that differ from those of dominant white culture. Young children raised in these subcultures often have difficulty understanding the English spoken in schools. African American dialects appear to be the result of a creolized form of English that was at one time spoken on Southern plantations by slaves.[47] (A creolized language is a speaker's native language that is based on two or more other languages.) It has been estimated that approximately 80% of African Americans speak a "radically nonstandard" English.[48] Present-day African American English is a combination of the linguistic remnants of its Southern plantation past and a reflection of the current African American sociocultural situation. As such, it is important to recognize it as a dialect in its own right, not as just a distortion of standard English. Most adult African Americans are bicultural, being fluent in an African American dialect and in standard English.

Religious organizations that are predominantly African American have tended to focus not only on a spirituality but also on social action efforts to combat racial discrimination. Many prominent African American leaders, such as Martin Luther King, Jr., and Jesse Jackson, have been members of the clergy. African American churches have served to develop leadership skills. They have also functioned as social welfare organizations to meet basic needs, such as clothing, food, and shelter. These churches have been natural support systems for troubled black individuals and families.

Many African Americans have had the experience of being negatively evaluated by school systems, social welfare agencies, health care institutions, and the justice system. Because of their past experiences, African Americans are likely to view such institutions with apprehension. Schools, for example, have erroneously perceived African Americans as being less capable of developing cognitive skills. These perceptions often become a self-fulfilling prophecy. If African American children are expected to fail in school, teachers may put forth less effort in challenging them to learn. The children may then also put forth less effort to learn, resulting in a lower level of achievement.

Latinos

Latinos are Americans of Spanish origin. They constitute diverse groups bound somewhat together by their language, culture, and ties to Roman Catholicism. This broad categorization includes Mexican Americans (Chicanos), Puerto Ricans, Cubans, people from Central and South America and the West Indies, and others of Spanish origin (Figure 11.1). The Latino population is growing at five times the rate of the rest of the population.[49] There are three main reasons for this large growth: a tendency to have large families, a continual inflow of immigrants (particularly from Mexico), and the high proportion of Latinos in this country who are of childbearing age.

MEXICAN AMERICANS

The largest Latino group in the United States is Mexican Americans. Although many Americans are unaware of the fact, Mexican Americans have had a long history of settlement and land ownership in what is now the United States. In the 1700s and 1800s there were a number of small Latino communities in what later became the American Southwest—in areas that have since gained statehood (including Texas, Arizona, New Mexico, and California). These early Latinos were generally small landholders. In the 1800s, whites moved into these regions, and competition for good land became fierce. Many Mexican Americans had their land taken away by large white-owned cattle and agricultural interests. Texas was once part of Mexico. In 1836 the settlers (including many of Spanish descent) staged a successful insurrection against the Mexican government and formed an independent republic. In 1845 Texas was annexed to the United States. As a consequence, many of the Mexican settlers became U.S. citizens.

Since the 1850s there has been a steady migration of Mexicans to the United States, with a number of immigrants entering this country illegally. The average income in Mexico is much lower than in the United States, so the quest for higher wages and a better life has lured many Mexicans to this country.

Relations between whites and Mexican Amer-

FIGURE 11.1

Percentage Distribution of Latinos by Land of Origin

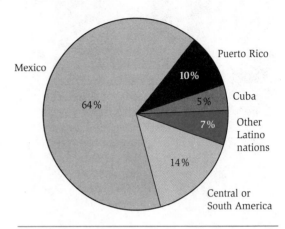

Source: Richard T. Schaefer, *Racial and Ethnic Groups,* 5th ed. (Boston: Little, Brown, 1993), p. 251.

icans have on occasion become vicious and ugly. Similar to black/white confrontations, there have been many riots between whites and Mexican Americans.

Many Mexican Americans live in barrios (Spanish-speaking sections of U.S. cities that have become ghettos) in such cities as Los Angeles, Denver, and Chicago. Although some are moving up in socioeconomic status, most are employed in low-paying occupations.

A smaller number of Mexican Americans are employed in temporary, seasonal work, largely on farms. Some migrate north in the summer to be farm laborers and return to the Southwest in the fall. In rate of acculturation and assimilation, these migrant workers are among the least "Americanized" of all ethnic groups.[50] They are reluctant to seek help from social agencies, partly because of their pride and partly because of language and cultural barriers.

An increasingly large segment of this ethnic group is becoming involved in the "Chicano" movement. Chicanos are Americans of Mexican

César Chávez formed the first successful labor union to represent migrant workers nearly 30 years ago. His nationwide boycotts of table grapes picked by underpaid workers and contaminated with pesticides have inspired other collective action by Chicanos.

origin who resent the stereotypes that demean Mexican Americans—particularly the image of laziness, because many are performing some of the hardest physical labor in our society. The origin of the word *Chicano* is not clear, but until the last generation it was a derogatory term whites used for Mexican Americans. Now the word and the people have come full circle, and *Chicano* has taken on a new, positive meaning. The Chicano movement asserts that social institutions must become more responsive to the needs of Chicanos. There now is a Chicano-oriented college in San Jose, California, and

Chicano-studies programs have been developed at a number of other universities.

The civil rights activities of African Americans have provided encouragement for the Chicanos' militant stance. In addition, second- and third-generation Mexican Americans have fewer ties to Mexico than did their elders, and they are oriented more toward the majority American culture in terms of aspirations and goals. Yet, similar to African Americans, Mexican Americans generally have low-paying jobs, high rates of unemployment, and high levels of poverty. They also have high rates of infant mortality, low levels of educational attainment, and high levels of substandard housing. Their standard of living is no better than that of African Americans.

Studies have found that many employers in the Southwest consistently hire Chicano workers at or below minimum-wage rates—yet another example of institutional racism.[51] One study in the garment industry in California found that only 8% of nearly 1000 companies were paying at or above the minimum wage.[52] Some of these workers are illegal aliens who are unable to file a complaint with authorities for fear of being deported.

In the 1970s and 1980s, César Chávez unionized migrant workers in California, organized several strikes, and led successful nationwide boycotts of fruit and vegetables picked by underpaid workers. Powerful white economic interests made several violent attempts to break these strikes. Chávez's campaigns provided an example and incentive for other collective action by Chicanos. The future is likely to see Chicanos becoming an increasingly powerful political force with which to be reckoned.

PUERTO RICANS

After World War II large numbers of Puerto Ricans migrated to the mainland United States, largely because of population pressure and insufficient job opportunities on the island. Although they are found in all the states, they have settled mainly in New York City, where they are heavily employed in the garment industry and as service workers. Those migrating from Puerto Rico were from the higher socioeconomic classes in their home society. Although their earnings on the mainland are higher than in Puerto Rico, they have experienced lower job status than Anglos in New York and are housed primarily in slum ghettos.

For Puerto Ricans the Spanish culture has been dominant, but they have also been influenced by the Taino, American, African, and European cultures. In Puerto Rico, status is based on culture or class, not skin color, and interracial marriages are common. On entering the mainland United States, many Puerto Ricans, understandably, become puzzled by the greater emphasis given to skin color here.

The island of Puerto Rico is in a commonwealth arrangement with the United States, and citizenship was extended to Puerto Ricans living on the island by the Jones Act of 1917.[53] As a commonwealth, its people have privileges and rights different from those on the mainland. They are subject to military service, selective service registration, and all federal laws. Yet they cannot vote in presidential elections and have no voting representation in Congress. Puerto Ricans pay a local income tax but no federal income tax. There is currently considerable controversy in Puerto Rico as to whether the island should seek independence from the United States, seek statehood, or remain a commonwealth.

Richard Schaefer summarizes the current status of Puerto Ricans:

The Puerto Rican people share many of the same problems of other minority groups—poor housing, inadequate health care, weak political representation, and low incomes. Like Chicanos, they have a language and cultural tradition at variance with that of Anglo society. The dominant society is belatedly removing some of the barriers to Spanish-speaking people in the United States and slowly making education a constructive experience through bilingual, bicultural programs. Chicanos and Puerto Ricans are poorly represented among key decision makers in both corporate offices and governmental agencies. However, both Chicanos and Puerto Ricans, and all Hispanics for that matter, are in close proximity to their home country, which facilitates the maintenance of a rich cultural tradition. The ability of Hispanics to maintain their original identity and solidarity

means they are not as compelled as European immigrants were to assimilate to White American customs and values.

The situation of Puerto Ricans is unique. Those on the island must resolve the issues of its political relationship to the mainland and the proper pace and emphasis of economic development. Those migrating to the mainland must adapt to a social definition of race different from that on the island and adjust to a system that leaves some Puerto Ricans in an ambiguous social position.[54]

CUBANS

Most Cuban Americans are recent migrants to the United States. Many are political refugees, having fled Cuba following the takeover of the government by Fidel Castro in 1959. Many of these Cuban Americans are well educated and have managerial or professional backgrounds. Large numbers have settled in southern Florida, particularly in the Miami area.

In 1980, Castro opened the doors of his socialist island, and over 100,000 more Cubans fled to this country. Many of these latest arrivals were from the lower class, some of whom had been imprisoned in Cuba for a variety of crimes. (Castro apparently sent them to the United States to reduce the costs of the correctional system in Cuba.) Many of these most recent arrivals have also settled in southern Florida, where they have experienced confrontations with Euro-Americans, a high rate of crime, and other adjustment problems.

Native Americans

When Columbus first came to America in 1492, there were about a million Native Americans grouped into more than 600 distinct societies.[55] Tribal wars between groups were common, and there were wide variations among tribes in customs, culture, lifestyles, languages, and religious ceremonies. The whites gradually expanded their settlement, moving westward and slowly usurping native land. Colonists and pioneers adopted a policy that amounted to deliberate extermination of Native Americans. The saying "The only good

Indian is a dead Indian" became popular. Whites took their lands away, depleted the buffalo herds on which many tribes depended for survival, slaughtered tribes, and indirectly killed many others by leading forced marches in freezing weather and bringing diseases and famine.[56] Unable to mobilize a common defense, all native tribes were defeated by 1892.

In 1887, Congress passed the General Allotment Act, which empowered Congress unilaterally to revise treaties made with Native Americans. This action opened the way for land-hungry whites to take productive native land. From 1887 to 1928, the land held by Native Americans decreased from 137 million acres to 50 million acres, with most of the remaining property being some of the least productive real estate in the country.[57]

Contact with the white culture has undermined Native Americans' traditional living patterns. It has been said that "the buffalo are gone"—meaning that Native Americans can no longer sustain themselves through hunting and fishing. Segregation to reservations has further damaged their pride and sense of self-worth. Government programs now attempt to meet subsistence needs, but they also serve to pauperize Native Americans. Native Americans on reservations have high rates of suicide, alcoholism, illiteracy, poverty, homicide, child neglect, and infant mortality.

Earlier in this century, the plight of Native Americans was largely ignored because of their isolation on remote reservations. Through the Bureau of Indian Affairs (BIA) they received the most paternalistic treatment by the government of all minorities. For many years the BIA had programs designed to destroy Native American culture, religion, and language. Today the bureau has become a symbol of frustration and despair.[58]

In the 1960s and 1970s the plight of the Native Americans received national attention, and many whites became actively involved in their problems. In the past, films depicted the "glorious" victories of the whites over "savages." Now we know that early white settlers exploited the Native Americans by taking away their land and destroying their way of life.

During most of the 20th century, Native Americans have not been very active in civil rights activities. However, in the 1960s and 1970s there were some organized efforts to make changes. Like African Americans and Chicanos, Native Americans staged some widely publicized demonstrations, such as one at Wounded Knee, South Dakota, in the 1970s.

In 1978 the U.S. Congress enacted the Indian Child Welfare Act (PL 95-608), which seeks to protect Native American families and tribes. Recognizing that Native American children are the most important resource of the tribes, the act establishes federal standards for involuntary removal of Native American children from their families and provides a legal mechanism for tribes to assume jurisdiction over Native American children who have been involuntarily removed by state and local authorities. The act is therefore designed to promote the security and stability of Native American families and tribes. When a child is removed from a Native American family, the tribe must be notified, and preference must be given to placing the child with relatives, tribal members, or other Native American families. Despite this critical piece of federal legislation, many Native American children continue to be placed in foster care or for adoption with non-Native American families.[59] A significant hindrance to the implementation of PL 95-608 is the lack of awareness of social workers concerning the act's mandates.

High rates of poverty and other social problems continue among Native Americans. Schaefer notes:

> Another enemy of the American Indian people is their disunity—full bloods are pitted against mixed bloods, reservation residents against city dwellers, tribe against tribe, conservative against militant. This disunity reflects the diversity of cultural backgrounds and historical experiences represented by the people collectively referred to as American Indians. It is also counterproductive when it comes to confronting a central government.[60]

Some tribes are taking legal action to recover land that was illegally usurped from them. The

Nonintercourse Act of 1870 stated that any land transaction between Indians and others not approved by Congress is null and void. Many such transactions were not ratified by Congress. Some tribes have brought legal claims for land and for rights to minerals and rivers, and some of these claims have already been upheld. Two tribes in Maine have won their claim to half the land in the state. In Alaska, Native Americans have been awarded $1 billion and 40 million acres of land in compensation for illegal seizures of their territory in the past.[61]

In recent years Native Americans have opened gambling casinos in many states. These casinos have become very popular and highly profitable. (Recent court decisions about federal treaties with Native Americans permit substantial tax breaks on these profits.) Many Native American tribes who are operating casinos are using some of the profits to fund social and educational programs for their tribal members.

Asian Americans

Asian Americans in the United States include the Japanese, Chinese, Filipinos, Koreans, Burmese, Indonesians, Guamanians, Samoans, South Vietnamese, and Thais. A large number of South Vietnamese immigrated to this country in the mid-1970s following the end of the Vietnam War. Contrary to a popular stereotype, Asians are not homogeneous. Each ethnic group has its own history, religion, language, and culture. These Asian American groups also differ in terms of group cohesion, levels of education, and socioeconomic status. Just as it is wrong to view all Europeans as being the same, it is an error to view all Asians as a single entity.

Like other disenfranchised groups, Asian Americans are victimized by discrimination. Immediate problems include housing, education, income maintenance, unemployment and underemployment, health care, and vocational training and retraining. Because of language and cultural barriers, many needy Asians (particularly new immigrants and the elderly) do not seek out services to which they are entitled. The two most

In the 1970s the militant American Indian Movement demanded that government pay attention to their grievances. Some twenty years later, AIM's national director Clyde Bellecourt discussed plans to protest Native American mascots and racism in sports at the 1992 Super Bowl.

prominent Asian groups in this country are Japanese Americans and Chinese Americans.

JAPANESE AMERICANS

Until 1900 few Japanese migrants came to the United States, partly because of legal restrictions against their migration and partly because of the unfriendly reception they received in this country.

After the turn of the century, Japanese migration increased. Immigrants settled primarily on the West Coast. By 1941 (when Pearl Harbor was attacked), there were few distinctive Japanese American settlements outside the West Coast other than in New York City and Chicago. During World War II, Japanese Americans' loyalty was viewed with intense suspicion, and they severely felt the impact of prejudice, war hysteria, and the denial of certain civil rights. On March 2, 1942, the commander of the Western Theater of Operations established "relocation centers" (concentration camps) to which Japanese Americans living on the West Coast were sent. The confused policies of our nation during this war are indicated by the fact that 33,000 Japanese Americans served in the armed forces for the United States while 110,000 Japanese Americans were confined in concentration camps.[62] Not only were their civil rights violated, but they also were forced to sell their property. (In comparison, Americans of German or Italian descent were not similarly persecuted, even though the war was fought against Germany and Italy as well as Japan.) Following the war their return to the West Coast met with some initial opposition, but among whites a counterreaction soon developed that emphasized fair play and acceptance.

Since 1946, Japanese Americans have settled in other parts of the country, and their socioeconomic status is now approaching that of whites. Japanese Americans now have a higher level of educational achievement than white Americans.[63]

An act of Congress in 1988 granted $20,000 to each of the Japanese Americans who were interned during World War II. This act is a hopeful signal of greater intergroup cooperation in the future.

CHINESE AMERICANS

In the 1800s the Chinese were encouraged to immigrate to the United States to do mining, railroad construction, and farm work. These immigrants soon encountered hostility from some whites, particularly in Western states, because of their willingness to work for low wages. Their racial and cultural distinctiveness also made them targets for scapegoating, especially during periods of high unemployment. Charles Henderson et al. describe the extent to which Chinese Americans were subjected to racism during this time period:

> *Racism against Asians is shown in the 1854 decision of the California Supreme Court in* The People *vs.* Hall. *The appellant, a white*

The United States celebrated as Kristi Yamaguchi (above) figure-skated her way to a gold medal in the 1992 Olympics. But, if Kristi had been alive during World War II, she would not have been considered an American. Like the family of Japanese Americans pictured here (right), Kristi's grandparents were deemed a national security risk and interned in government camps, or "relocation centers." Kristi's mother, in fact, was born in the camps. Kristi's presence on the national scene is an ironic reminder that, despite our intolerance of ethnic diversity, one of our country's greatest strengths is its multicultural heritage.

Anglo-American, had been convicted of murder upon the testimony of Chinese witnesses. Was such evidence admissible? The judge ruled that Asians should be ineligible to testify for or against a white man. This ruling opened the floodgate for anti-Chinese abuse, violence, and exploitation. Group murders, lynchings, property damage, and robbery of the Chinese were reported up and down the West Coast.

Because of the harsh treatment of the Chinese, any luckless person was described as not having a "Chinaman's chance."[64]

In the early 1900s, Chinese Americans were concentrated largely on the West Coast, but since the 1920s they have tended to disperse throughout the nation. They have settled in large cities, and many live in Chinatowns in such cities as Los Angeles, San Francisco, New York, Boston, and Chicago.

The struggles of China against Japan before and during World War II brought about a more favorable image of Chinese Americans. Nevertheless, some discrimination continues. They have been subjected to less discrimination in Hawaii than on the mainland, as Hawaii is much closer to being a pluralist society than the rest of the country. Chinese Americans now have a higher level of educational achievement than white Americans.[65] Although Chinese Americans still tend to intra-

marry, they are now more likely to marry a member of another racial group than was true in the past. An increasing number are also moving out of Chinatowns to live in suburbs and in other areas.

STRATEGIES FOR ADVANCING SOCIAL AND ECONOMIC JUSTICE

Social justice is an ideal condition in which all members of a society have the same basic rights, protection, opportunities, obligations, and social benefits.[66] Economic justice is also an ideal condition, in which all members of a society have the same opportunities for attaining material goods, income, and wealth. A wide range of strategies have been developed to reduce racial and ethnic discrimination and oppression, thereby advancing social and economic justice. These strategies include the following: mass media appeals, strategies to increase interaction among the races, civil rights laws, activism, school busing, affirmative action programs, human relations programs, confrontation of racist remarks and actions, and confrontation of the problems in inner-city ghettos.

Mass Media Appeals

Newspapers, magazines, radio, and television at times present information designed to explain the nature and harmful effects of prejudice and to promote harmony among humanity. The mass media are able to reach large numbers of people simultaneously. By expanding public awareness of discrimination and its consequences, the media can counteract the influence of racial extremists. But the mass media have limitations in changing prejudiced attitudes and behaviors; they are primarily providers of information and seldom have a lasting effect in changing deep-seated prejudices through propaganda. Broadcasting such platitudes as "all people are brothers and sisters" and "prejudice is un-American" is not very effective. Highly bigoted people are often unaware of their own prejudices. Even if they are aware of them, they generally dismiss mass media appeals as irrelevant or as propaganda. It should be noted, however, that the mass media probably have had a significant impact in reducing discrimination by showing nonwhites and whites harmoniously interacting in commercials, on news teams, and on other TV fare.

Greater Interaction among the Races

Increased contact among races is not in itself sufficient to alleviate racial prejudice. In fact, increased contact may, in some instances, highlight intergroup differences and increase suspicions and fear. George Simpson and J. Milton Yinger reviewed a number of studies and concluded that prejudice is likely to be increased when contacts are tension-laden or involuntary.[67] Prejudice is likely to subside when individuals are placed in situations in which they share characteristics in nonracial matters (for example, as coworkers, fellow soldiers, or classmates). Equal-status contacts, rather than inferior/superior contacts, also reduce prejudices.[68]

Civil Rights Laws

In the past 25 years, equal rights have been legislated in employment, voting, housing, public accommodation, and education. A key question is "How effective are laws in curbing racial discrimination and reducing racial prejudice?"

Proponents of civil rights legislation make certain assumptions. The first is that new laws will reduce discriminatory behavioral patterns. The laws define what was once "normal" behavior (discrimination) as now being "deviant" behavior. With time, attitudes are expected to change and become more consistent with the forced nondiscriminatory behavior patterns.

A second assumption is that the laws will be enforced. Civil rights laws enacted after the Civil War were seldom enforced and gradually eroded. It is also unfortunately true that some officials will find ways of evading the intent of the law by eliminating only the extreme, overt symbols of discrimination without changing other practices. Thus the enactment of a law is only the first step in the process of changing prejudiced attitudes and practices. However, as Martin Luther King, Jr., noted, "The law may not make a man love me, but it can restrain him from lynching me, and I think that's pretty important."

Activism

The strategy of activism attempts to change the structure of race relations through direct confrontation of discrimination and segregation policies. Activism employs three types of politics: the politics of creative disorder, the politics of disorder, and the politics of escape.[69]

Politics of creative disorder operate on the edge of the dominant social system and include school boycotts, rent strikes, job blockades, sit-ins (for example, at segregated restaurants), public marches, and product boycotts. This type of activism is based on the concept of nonviolent resistance. A dramatic illustration of nonviolent resistance involved Rosa Parks (see Case Example 11.1). The famous Montgomery Bus Boycott that her behavior provoked had an even more important psychological impact: It suggested that minority citizens had rights equal to those of whites and that united nonviolent resistance could overturn discriminatory laws.[70]

Politics of disorder reflect alienation from the dominant culture and disillusionment with the political system. Those being discriminated against resort to mob uprising, riots, and other forms of violence.

In 1969 the National Commission on Causes and Prevention of Violence reported that 200 riots had occurred in our inner cities in the previous five years.[71] In the early 1980s there were riots in Miami and in some other inner cities. In 1992 there were devastating riots in Los Angeles, following the acquittal of four white police officers who had been charged with using excessive force in arresting Rodney King, an African American; the brutal arrest had been videotaped. Most of these riots have involved minority-group aggression against white-owned property.

Politics of escape are characterized by passionate rhetoric about how minorities are being victimized. But, because the focus is not on arriving at solutions, the rhetoric is not productive, except perhaps for providing an emotional release.

The principal value of activism or social protest seems to be the stimulation of public awareness of certain problems. The civil rights protests in the 1960s made practically all Americans aware of the discrimination to which nonwhite groups were being subjected. As a result, at least some of the discrimination has ceased, and race relations have improved. Continued protest beyond a certain (admittedly indeterminate) point, however, appears to have little additional value.[72]

School Busing

Housing patterns in many large metropolitan centers have led to *de facto* segregation; that is, African Americans and certain other racial minorities live in one area, and whites live in another. This segregation has affected educational opportunities for racial minorities. Nonwhite areas have fewer financial resources; as a result, educational quality is often substantially lower than in white areas. In the past two decades courts in a number of metropolitan areas have ordered that a certain proportion of nonwhites be bused to schools in white areas and that a certain proportion of whites be bused to schools in nonwhite areas. The objectives are twofold: to provide equal educational opportunities and to reduce racial prejudice through interaction. In some areas, school busing has become accepted and appears to be meeting the stated objectives. In other areas, however, the approach is highly controversial and has exacerbated racial tensions. Busing in these areas is claimed to (1) be highly expensive; (2) destroy the concept of the "neighborhood school," whereby the facility serves as a recreational, social, and educational center of the community; and (3) result in lower-quality education. A number of parents in these areas feel so strongly about busing that they are sending their children to private schools. In addition, some have argued that busing increases "white flight" from neighborhoods where busing has been ordered.[73] In 1970, William Raspberry, a columnist for the *Washington Post,* commented about the effects of busing in Washington, D.C.: "We find ourselves busing children from all-black neighborhoods all the way across town to schools that are rapidly becoming all-black."[74]

Additional concerns have been expressed about busing. It argued that busing children a long distance is very costly and uses funds that could otherwise be spent to improve the quality of education. Busing lessens local control and interest in schools, and it makes it less practical for parents to become involved in school affairs because the school is less accessible.

In certain communities, busing may also intensify racial tensions. For example, in Boston in 1975 a federal judge ordered school busing in order to counter housing segregation patterns. The Irish and Polish descendants of South Boston (who saw themselves as oppressed ethnic minorities) violently opposed the busing, and racial tensions intensified for several years. Sociologists

<table>
<tr><td>

CASE
EXAMPLE 11.1

</td><td>

Rosa Parks's Act of Courage as a Spark for the Civil Rights Movement

</td></tr>
</table>

O n December 1, 1955, Rosa Parks was waiting for a bus in Montgomery, Alabama. She was in a hurry because she had a lot of things to do. When the bus arrived, she got on without paying attention to the driver. She rode the bus often and was aware of Montgomery's segregated seating law that required African Americans to sit at the back of the bus.

Rosa Parks

In those days in the South, black people were expected to board the front of the bus, pay their fare, and then get off and walk outside the bus to reboard at the back. But she noted that the rear was already crowded, with standing room only. Black passengers were even huddled on the back steps of the bus. It was apparent to Rosa that it would be all but impossible to reboard at the back. Besides, bus drivers sometimes drove off and left black passengers behind, even after accepting their fares. Rosa Parks spontaneously decided to take her chances. She paid her fare in the front of the bus, walked down the aisle, and took a seat in the area reserved for whites. At the second stop, a white man got on and had to stand.

The bus driver saw the white man standing and ordered Rosa Parks to move to the back. She refused, thinking "I want to be treated like a human being." Two police officers were called, and they arrested her. She was taken to city hall, booked, fingerprinted, jailed, and fined. Her arrest—and subsequent appeal all the way to the U.S. Supreme Court—served as a catalyst for a year-long boycott of the city's buses by blacks, who composed 70% of all bus riders. The boycott inspired Martin Luther King, Jr., to become involved. It ended when the Supreme Court declared Montgomery's segregated seating laws unconstitutional. Rosa Parks's unplanned defiance of that law sparked the civil rights movement. This movement not only promoted social and economic justice for African Americans but also inspired other groups to organize to advocate for their civil rights. These groups include other racial and ethnic groups, women, the elderly, persons with a disability, and gays and lesbians.

Source: Marie Ragghianti, "I Wanted to Be Treated Like a Human Being," *Parade*, Jan. 19, 1992, pp. 8–9.

also voice concern that school busing in an atmosphere of hostility may reduce the quality of education and increase racial prejudices and tensions.

School busing to achieve integration was vigorously pursued by the court system and the Justice Department in the 1970s. In 1981 the Reagan administration stated that it would be much less active in advocating busing as a vehicle to achieve integration. The Bush and Clinton administrations have also been fairly inactive in promoting school busing. In the past decade there has been less emphasis in many communities on using busing to achieve integration. In 1991 the U.S. Supreme Court ruled that busing to achieve integration, when ordered, need not be continued indefinitely. The ruling allows communities to end court-ordered busing by convincing a judge they have done everything reasonable to eliminate discrimination against African Americans. School busing for integration purposes is discussed further in Chapter 9.

Affirmative Action Programs

Affirmative action programs provide preferential hiring and admission requirements (for example, admission to medical schools) for minority applicants. The programs apply to all minority groups, including women. They require employers to (1) make active efforts to locate and recruit qualified minority applicants and (2) in certain circumstances, have hard quotas under which specific numbers of minority members must be accepted to fill vacant positions (for example, a university with a high proportion of white, male faculty members may be required to fill half of its faculty vacancies with women and members of other minority groups). Affirmative action programs require that employers demonstrate, according to a checklist of positive measures, that they are not guilty of discrimination.

A major dilemma with affirmative action programs is that preferential hiring and quota programs create reverse discrimination, in which qualified majority-group members are sometimes arbitrarily excluded. There have been several successful lawsuits involving reverse discrimination. The best-known case to date has been that of Alan Bakke, who was initially denied admission to the medical school at the University of California, Davis, in 1973. He alleged reverse discrimination because he had higher grades and higher scores on the Medical College Admissions Test than several minority applicants who were admitted under the university's minorities quota policy. In

1978 his claim was upheld by the U.S. Supreme Court in a precedent-setting decision.[75] The Court ruled that strict racial quotas are unconstitutional, but it did not rule out the use of race as one among many criteria in making admissions decisions.

Charles Henderson et al. summarize some of the views of whites and minority groups about affirmative action:

> The minority worker in white agencies often asks himself: "Why have I been hired?" . . . The worker may meet resistance from white colleagues if he or she is a product of "affirmative action," seen by some white people as simply "reverse discrimination." Whites may be quick to say that competence is what counts. Blacks perceive this as saying that they are not competent. Considering the many ways in which whites have acquired jobs, blacks wonder why competence is now suggested as the only criterion for employment. For every white professional who may dislike affirmative action to compensate for past exclusions and injustices, there is a black professional who feels that it is tragic that organizations have had to be forced to hire minorities.[76]

Supporters of affirmative action programs note that the white majority expressed little concern about discrimination when its members were the beneficiaries instead of the victims. They also assert that there is no other way to make up rapidly for past discrimination against minorities, many of whom may presently score slightly lower on qualification tests simply because they did not have the opportunities and the quality of training that the majority-group members have had.

Affirmative action programs raise delicate and complex questions about achieving equality through preferential hiring and admissions policies for minorities. Yet no other means has been found to end obvious discrimination in hiring and admissions.

Gaining admission to educational programs and securing well-paying jobs are crucial elements in the quest for integration. The history of immigrant groups that have "made it" (such as the Irish, the Japanese, and the Italians) suggests that equality will be achieved only when minority-group members gain middle- and upper-class status and thus become an economic and political force to be reckoned with. The dominant groups then become pressured into modifying their norms, values, and stereotypes. For this reason, a number of authorities have noted that the elimination of economic discrimination is a prerequisite for achieving equality and harmonious race relations.[77] Achieving educational equality among races is also crucial because lower educational attainments lead to less prestigious jobs, lower incomes, lower living standards, and the perpetuation of racial inequalities from one generation to the next.

Human Relations Programs

A number of school systems are developing human relations programs, which are designed to alleviate prejudice and discrimination. The program developed by the public school system in Madison, Wisconsin, will be briefly described for illustrative purposes.[78] Its goal is to help children gain a better awareness of themselves as individuals and a better understanding of, and respect for, individual differences in others.[79]

This program has several components, along with some suggested activities, books, and other helpful hints for parents and teachers to use with their children. Some of the key concepts are as follows:

- Each person is unique, with all people having common needs.

- Each person can do some things better than other things. It is a serious mistake to use yourself as a yardstick to measure others' abilities or to use others as a yardstick to measure yours. Words such as "stupid" or "dumb" hurt deeply, especially when one is doing one's best.

- Each person has different attitudes, ideas, beliefs, and values. Although the beliefs of others may differ from one's own, they are no less important.

- Prejudice differs from a dislike. Prejudice is defined broadly as "when you are against someone you do not know because of some/ one of their differences."[80]

The program teaches children about some of the differences among people and shows that a lack of understanding about these differences can be related to prejudice. For example, the program explains that melanin is the pigment responsible for light and dark skin-color differences. The more melanin we have, the darker we are; but melanin, of course, in no way governs our personality or behavior. Suntanning occurs because the skin produces more melanin to protect it from the hot sun; yet tanning does not change the inner "self"—only the outside wrapping. Students are also given an understanding of other individual differences (retardation, religious differences, epilepsy, hearing impairments, and so on) so they can be more respectful of such variation. The program also assists students in learning about and appreciating cultural and ethnic differences.

Human relation programs have shown considerable promise in reducing discrimination in matters of race, sex, ethnic or cultural differences, religious or political differences, and physical or mental disabilities.

Confrontation of Racist and Ethnic Remarks and Actions

Jokes and sarcastic remarks related to race help shape and perpetuate racist stereotypes and prejudices. It is important that both whites and nonwhites tactfully but assertively indicate that they do not view such remarks as humorous or appropriate. It is also important that people tactfully and assertively point out the inappropriateness of racist actions by others. Such confrontations have a consciousness-raising effect, making explicit the belief that subtle racist remarks and actions are discriminatory and harmful. Gradually these confrontations will reduce racial prejudices and actions.

Noted author, lecturer, and abolitionist Frederick Douglass stated:

> *Power concedes nothing without a demand—it never did, and it never will. Find out just what people will submit to, and you've found out the exact amount of injustice and wrong which will be imposed upon them. This will continue until*

they resist, either with words, blows, or both.
The limits of tyrants are prescribed by the
endurance of those whom they oppress.[81]

Confrontation of the Problems in Inner-City Ghettos

A variety of negative adjectives have been used to describe the dismal living conditions in inner-city ghettos: decaying, inhuman, dreadful, distasteful, shocking, and degrading. Ghettos are inhabited primarily by the poor, by the elderly, and by members of minority groups, particularly African Americans and Latinos. Many ghettos have an ethnic concentration, such as African American, Mexican American, Cuban, or Puerto Rican.

Ghettos have high rates of crime, illiteracy, births out of marriage, single-parent households, mental illness, suicide, drug and alcohol abuse, unemployment, infant mortality, rape, aggravated assault, and delinquency. A large proportion of the residents are on welfare. Many city services are inferior in ghettos: Schools are substandard, streets are narrow and often filled with potholes, and police and fire protection services are inadequate to meet the needs.

The housing is crowded and decaying, and much of it is substandard. Heat in winter is often lacking. Many units lack adequate plumbing. Broken windows, peeling paint, and doors hanging off their hinges are common sights. People of color inhabit much of this substandard housing, because most cannot afford an alternative and because discrimination makes it difficult to relocate even for those whose incomes would enable them to do so.

One of the factors that is leading to the decline of inner cities is the sharp decrease in blue-collar jobs in our society. The employable in inner cities have always held largely blue-collar jobs. For a neighborhood to resist deterioration, a minimal economic base must be maintained. As blue-collar jobs decline and as the quality of municipal services (such as transportation and public schools) deteriorates, faith in community restoration and revitalization fades.

Ghettos are a national disgrace. The United States is the richest and most powerful country in the world, yet we have been unable to improve living conditions in our inner cities.

Our country has tried a variety of approaches to improve ghetto living conditions. Programs and services provided include work training, job placement, financial assistance through public welfare, low-interest loans to start businesses, Head Start, drug and alcohol treatment, crime prevention, housing, rehabilitation, day-care services, health care services, and public health services.

One of the most comprehensive undertakings to assist inner cities was the Model Cities Program, which was part of the War on Poverty in the 1960s. Several inner cities were targeted for this massive intervention. The program involved tearing down dilapidated housing and constructing comfortable living quarters. Salvageable buildings were renovated. In addition, Model City projects included programs that provided job training and placement, health care services, social services, and educational opportunities. The results were more than depressing. The communities have again become slums, and living conditions are as bleak as, or bleaker than, at the start of the Model City interventions.[82]

To date, practically all programs that have been tried have had, at best, only short-term success. No other conclusion can be made. Ghettos continue to have abysmal living conditions. In the 1980s and early 1990s the federal government, at least for the time being, appears to have given up trying to improve living conditions; federal programs for inner cities have been either eliminated or sharply cut back.

Poverty and dependency on welfare are becoming a lifestyle in ghettos, and this lifestyle is being passed on from one generation to another. On January 25, 1986, CBS aired a program entitled "CBS Reports: The Vanishing Black Family." It presented the alarming fact that the single-parent family headed by a mother is becoming the typical family in inner cities. The program suggested that, by the year 2000, unless dramatic changes are made, 70% of African American families will have a female head of household. The program also indicated that many young African American mothers (and the unwed fathers) are using Aid to Families with Dependent Children (AFDC) payments to support their families. For example, one 25-year-old male who had been unemployed for the past two and a half years was interviewed. He was proud that he had fathered six children by four different women and took it for granted that welfare programs would pay the bills for raising his children. The program suggested that AFDC mothers in inner cities are resigned to raising their children on welfare, and such values are being passed on from generation to generation.

Our society, for better or for worse, is a materialistic one. The two main legitimate avenues for acquiring material goods are by getting a good education and obtaining a high-paying job. It appears that many ghetto residents realize their prospects are bleak for either avenue. As a result, many are turning to illegitimate means of getting material goods (shoplifting, drug trafficking, robbery, and con games). Some also turn to immediate gratifications (including sex and drug highs).

One approach that has been suggested to combat the problems of inner cities is to use birth control technology to try to stabilize (and perhaps even slightly reduce) the population in inner cities. Residents of large cities could be encouraged to have only one child. Sex education programs in schools could be expanded to teach responsible sex. Birth control information and services could be provided by the government at no cost to recipients. Increased taxes might be levied on those who have more than one or two children. Health clinics (providing free birth control information and services) could be located in every inner-city high school. Mothers and their teenage daughters who are receiving AFDC benefits might be given higher monthly grants for voluntarily using effective birth control methods. If effective contraceptives (other than condoms, which are frequently not used) are developed for males, young men who are receiving AFDC benefits could also be given higher monthly grants for using these contraceptives.

Such proposals are designed to gradually reduce the number of children on AFDC to stop poverty from being passed from one generation to another, and to strengthen inner-city families. With smaller-sized families on AFDC, the parents should be better able to provide higher-quality care to the children they presently have.

There have been a number of criticisms of these proposals. There is a strong value in our country that every person has a right to be a natural parent to as many children as he or she desires. Some religions, such as the Roman Catholic Church, strongly object to birth control. Encouraging AFDC recipients to use birth control is perceived by many as "nonwhite genocide"; because most AFDC recipients are nonwhites, birth control policies would thereby have the greatest impact on the birth rates of ethnic minorities.

A promising alternative solution to inner-city problems is grass-roots organizations, which can effect positive, long-lasting changes in a variety of settings, including inner cities. Grass-roots organizations are community groups, composed of residents, who work together to improve their surroundings. (It may be that lasting changes can be made only in neighborhoods whose residents are inspired to improve their community.) The following is a description of a successful grass-roots effort in Cochran Gardens in St. Louis, Missouri.[83]

Cochran Gardens was once a low-income housing project typical of many deteriorating housing projects in large urban areas. It was filled with rubbish, graffiti, and broken windows, and its residents were plagued by frequent shootings, crime, and drug trafficking.

Bertha Gilkey grew up in this housing project. Had it not been for her, this neighborhood might have continued to deteriorate. As a youngster, Gilkey believed the neighborhood could improve if residents worked together. As a teenager she attended tenant meetings in a neighborhood church. When she was 20 years old, she was elected to chair this tenants' association. The neighborhood has since undergone gradual, yet dramatically positive, changes.

Gilkey and her group started with small projects. They asked tenants what realistically achievable things they really wanted. There was a consensus that the housing project needed a usable laundromat. The project's previous laundromats had all been vandalized, and the only working laundromat in the project had no locks. In fact, the entry door had been stolen. Bertha and her group requested and received a door from the city housing authority. The organization then held a successful fund raiser for a lock. Next the group held a fund raiser for paint, and that too was a success. The organization then painted the laundromat. The residents were pleased to have an attractive, working facility, and its presence increased their interest in joining and supporting the tenants' association. The group then organized to paint the hallways, floor by floor, of the housing project. Everyone who lived on a floor was responsible for being involved in painting their hallway. Gilkey states:

> Kids who lived on the floor that hadn't been painted would come and look at the painted hallways and then go back and hassle their parents. The elderly who couldn't paint prepared lunch, so they could feel like they were a part of it too.[84]

The organization continued to initiate and successfully complete new projects to spruce up the neighborhood. Each success inspired more and more residents to take pride in their neighborhood and to work toward making improvements. In the process, Gilkey and the tenants' organization also reintroduced a conduct code for the project. A committee formulated rules of behavior and elected monitors on each floor. The rules specified no loud disruptions, no throwing garbage out of the windows, and no fights. Slowly, residents got the message, and living conditions improved, one small step at a time.

The building was renamed Dr. Martin Luther King Jr. Building. (Symbols are important in community development efforts.) The organization also held a party and a celebration for each successfully completed project.

Another focus of Gilkey's efforts was to reach out to children and adolescents. Positive behaviors were highlighted. The young people wrote papers in school on "What I like about living here." In art class they built a cardboard model of the housing project that included the buildings, streets, and playground. Such efforts were designed to build the self-esteem of the young people and to instill a sense of pride in their community.

Today, Cochran Gardens is a public housing project with flower-lined paths, trees, and grass—a beautiful and clean neighborhood filled with trusting people who have a sense of pride in their community. The high-rise buildings have been completely renovated. There is a community center, and there are tennis courts, playgrounds, and townhouse apartments to reduce density in the complex. Cochran Gardens is managed by the tenants. The association (now named Tenant Management Council) has ventured into owning and operating certain businesses: a catering service, day-care centers, health clinics, and a vocational training program.

The Cochran Gardens success story has been based on the principles of self-help, empowerment, responsibility, and dignity. Gilkey states:

> This goes against the grain, doesn't it? Poor people are to be managed. What we've done is cut through all the bullshit and said it doesn't take all that. People with degrees and credentials got us in this mess. All it takes is some basic skills. . . . If we can do it in public housing, it can happen anywhere.[85]

Clearly, it makes sense for our federal, state, and city governments to seek to improve inner-city conditions by encouraging and supporting (including financially) grass-roots efforts.

DISCRIMINATION AND SOCIAL WORK

Social work has an obligation to work vigorously toward ending racial discrimination and advancing social justice. Charles Henderson and Bok-Lim Kim summarize seven recommendations that are consistently advocated in the literature:

1. Clients are entitled to a general understanding of their culture so they are not served inappropriately out of ignorance.

2. All clients should be served without discrimination or prejudice.

3. Minority clients should have a voice in planning and managing services provided for them.

4. Minority staff members are generally best qualified to serve members of their own group and should be hired to do so.

5. Opportunities for promotion and advancement should be made to minority employees on an equitable basis.

6. Minorities should be accorded special opportunities for professional training. This may mean modifications in educational programs.

7. Minority faculty members are essential. Credentials of experience and skill are more important than academic degrees.[86]

Ione Dugger Vargus reports that the following problems arose when African American graduate students in social work were hired in white-dominated social agencies:

1. Some were given all-black caseloads.

2. Students were expected to be authorities on African Americans and were frequently consulted by other workers.

3. Some white workers considered themselves the experts on African Americans and accepted no suggestions or ideas.

4. When African American workers were permitted to develop their own ways of making contact and channeling services, white workers were upset by the departure from the rules.[87]

Most of these students remarked that, although they would prefer to work with African Americans, an all-black caseload implied that both the clients and the worker were inferior.

The students also did not like to be perceived as authorities on African Americans, because they recognized that individual differences make pat answers impossible. They felt some conflicts in giving advice to white practitioners, unless the practitioner had already tried several approaches before seeking advice (in which case the request was just like any other consultation).

The social work professional needs to recognize the reality of practice in a culturally diverse environment. Social workers do have many of the prejudices and misperceptions of the general society, and the tendency to use one's own prejudices and stereotypes poses dangers for the well-meaning practitioner. For example, a social worker assigned to a Native American client might perceive the client's quietness as a sign that the client is being uncooperative or the client is fully agreeing with the worker. It is possible that neither assumption is accurate. As a general rule a Native American will not challenge or correct a worker who is off track because to do so would violate "noninterference." Noninterference is a basic value of Native American culture; it asserts that one should handle unwanted attempts at intervention with withdrawal—emotional, physical, or both.[88]

Another response pattern of white social workers that is counterproductive with Native Americans is the attempt to maintain direct eye contact. Such face-to-face eye contact is considered rude and intimidating by many Native Americans.[89]

A bilingual practitioner working in a Chicano community may not understand all aspects of the language. For example, the special language of the barrio often contains words with a variety of connotations that differ from formal Spanish.[90] As a consequence, the worker who does speak Spanish must be acutely alert to the possibility that words may have very different meanings for clients living in a barrio.

In sum, a worker dealing with diverse cultural groups must (1) acquire a knowledge of self, including one's stereotypes, values, feelings, attitudes, and beliefs; (2) acquire a knowledge of the culture and the characteristics of the people with whom one is working; (3) acquire an understanding of the unique effects that standard counseling and intervention approaches will have on the client group; and (4) learn to challenge and change the stereotypic perceptions that one has of the client group.

You should not form the impression that working effectively with a different cultural group presents insurmountable barriers and obstacles.

In actuality, the similarities between worker and clients almost always outweigh the dissimilarities.[91]

The major professional social work organizations have in the past few decades taken strong positions to work toward ending racial discrimination and oppression. The National Association of Social Workers, for example, has lobbied for the passage of civil rights legislation. The Code of Ethics of NASW (see Appendix) has an explicit statement that every "social worker should act to prevent and eliminate discrimination against any person or group on the basis of race, [or] color. . . ." The Council on Social Work Education (CSWE) requires in its accreditation standards for baccalaureate and master's programs that content on racism be included throughout the social work curriculum. Professional social work education is committed to preparing social work students to understand and appreciate cultural and social diversity. Students are taught to understand the dynamics and consequences of oppression, and they learn to use intervention strategies to combat social injustice, oppression, and their effects. CSWE also has an accreditation standard that prohibits racial discrimination and mandates affirmative action programs in social work educational programs. There is an Association of Black Social Workers, which has been very active in combating racial prejudice and discrimination.

THE FUTURE OF AMERICAN RACE AND ETHNIC RELATIONS

The 1980s turned into a decade of struggle for minorities as they tried to hold onto past gains in the face of reactions against minority rights. Vowing to take "big government" off the back of the American people and to strengthen the economy by giving businesses the incentive to grow and produce, President Reagan and his administration largely removed the federal government from its traditional role as initiator and enforcer of programs to guarantee minority rights. President Bush and his administration continued to follow a similar strategy. The federal government under the Reagan and Bush administrations asserted that private businesses were in the best position to correct the problems of poverty and discrimination. (Because businesses generally profit from paying low wages, most companies in the 1980s and early 1990s did not aggressively seek to improve the financial circumstances and living conditions of minorities.) Perhaps because of the federal government's shift in policies, minorities were less active in the 1980s (as compared to the 1960s and 1970s) in using the strategy of activism. In the 1980s and early 1990s, minority groups were experiencing difficulties in maintaining the gains they had achieved two decades earlier in the job market through affirmative action and Equal Employment Opportunity programs. Bill Clinton, elected president in 1992, ran on a platform that promised a more active role by the federal government in promoting social and economic justice for all racial and ethnic groups in this country.

It is clear that minorities will assertively, and sometimes aggressively, pursue a variety of strategies to change racist attitudes and actions. Counteractions by certain segments of the white dominant society are also likely to occur. (Even in the social sciences, every action elicits a reaction.) For example, in recent years there has been increased membership in organizations that advocate white supremacy, such as the Ku Klux Klan.

In 1988 a report released by the Commission on Minority Participation in Education and American Life asserted:

> *America is moving backward—not forward— in its efforts to achieve the full participation of minority citizens in the life and prosperity of the nation. . . .*
>
> *In education, employment, income, health, longevity, and other basic measures of individual and social well-being, gaps persist—and in some cases are widening—between members of minority groups and the majority population.*
>
> *If we allow these disparities to continue, the United States inevitably will suffer a compromised quality of life and a lower standard of living.*
>
> *In brief, we will find ourselves unable to fulfill the promise of the American dream.*[92]

Minorities have been given the hope of achieving equal opportunity and justice, and it is clear that they will no longer submit to a subordinate status. Obviously we will see continued struggles to achieve racial equality.

What will be the pattern of race relations in the future? Milton Gordon has outlined three possible patterns of intergroup relations: Anglo-conformity, the melting pot, and cultural pluralism:

> Anglo-conformity *assumes the desirability of maintaining modified English institutions, language, and culture as the dominant standard in American life. In practice, "assimilation" in America has always meant Anglo-conformity, and the groups that have been most readily assimilated have been those that are ethnically and culturally most similar to the Anglo-Saxon group.*
>
> The *melting pot is, strictly speaking, a rather different concept, which views the future American society not as a modified England but rather as a totally new blend, both culturally and biologically, of all the various groups that inhabit the United States. In practice, the melting pot has been of only limited significance in the American experience.*
>
> Cultural pluralism *implies a series of coexisting groups, each preserving its own tradition and culture, but each loyal to an overarching American nation. Although the cultural enclaves of some immigrant groups, such as the Germans, have declined in importance in the past, many other groups, such as the Italians, have retained a strong sense of ethnic identity and have resisted both Anglo-conformity and inclusion in the melting pot.*[93]

Members of some European ethnic groups (such as the British, French, and Germans) have assimilated the dominant culture of the United States and are now integrated. Other European ethnic groups (such as the Irish, Italians, Polish, and Hungarians) are now nearly fully assimilated and integrated.

Cultural pluralism appears to be the form that race and ethnic relations are presently taking. There has been a renewed interest on the part of a number of ethnic European Americans in expressing their pride in their own customs, religions, and linguistic and cultural traditions. We see slogans like "Kiss me, I'm Italian," "Irish Power," and "Polish and Proud." African Americans, Native Americans, Latinos, and Asian Americans are demanding entry into mainstream America—but not assimilation. They want to coexist in a plural society while preserving their own traditions and cultures. This pride is indicated by slogans such "Black is beautiful" and "Red power." These groups are finding a source of identity and pride in their own cultural backgrounds and histories.

Some progress has been made toward ending discrimination since the *Brown* v. *Board of Education* Supreme Court decision in 1954. Yet equal opportunity for all people in the United States is still only a dream, as Martin Luther King, Jr., noted in his famous speech in 1963:

> *I say to you today, my friends, though, even though we face the difficulties of today and tomorrow, I still have a dream. It is a dream deeply rooted in the American dream. I have a dream that one day this nation will rise up, live out the true meaning of its creed: "We hold these truths to be self-evident, that all men are created equal."*
>
> *I have a dream that one day on the red hills of Georgia sons of former slaves and the sons of former slave-owners will be able to sit down together at the table of brotherhood. I have a dream that one day even the state of Mississippi, a state sweltering with the heat of injustice, sweltering with the heat of oppression, will be transformed into an oasis of freedom and justice.*
>
> *I have a dream that my four little children will one day live in a nation where they will not be judged by the color of their skin, but by the content of their character.*
>
> *When we allow freedom to ring—when we let it ring from every city and every hamlet, from every state and every city, we will be able to speed up that day when all of God's children, black men and white men, Jews and Gentiles, Protestants and Catholics, will be able to join hands and sing in the words of the old Negro spiritual, "Free at last, Free at last, Great God Almighty, We are free at last."*[94]

This Chicago couple, shown with their teenage children, has been married for nearly twenty years. While the number of interracial marriages has been steadily increasing over the past three decades, the "melting pot" is a concept that is still rarely experienced in America.

SUMMARY

Our country has always been racist and ethnocentric, but there has been progress in the past four decades in alleviating prejudice and discrimination. Yet we cannot relax. Discrimination continues to have tragic consequences for those who are its victims. Individuals who are targets of discrimination are excluded from certain types of employment, educational and recreational opportunities, certain residential housing areas, membership in certain religious and social organizations, certain political activities, access to

some community services, and so on. Discrimination is also a serious obstacle to developing a positive self-concept and has heavy psychological and financial costs. Internationally, racism and ethnocentrism severely damage our credibility in promoting human rights.

Race is primarily a social concept, rather than a biological concept. No "racial" group has any unique or distinctive genes. A social definition is based on the way in which members of a society classify one another by physical characteristics.

Prejudice is an attitude, whereas discrimination involves actions. Discrimination is often based on prejudice, although either may occur independently of the other. Oppression is the unjust or cruel exercise of authority or power.

Racial and ethnic discrimination is largely a social problem of whites who tend to be the primary discriminators in power. (This does not mean, however, that only whites must work to end discrimination; the effort must be an interracial one.)

Theories about the sources of discrimination and oppression involve projection, frustration-aggression, insecurity and inferiority, authoritarianism, historical explanations, competition and exploitation, and socialization processes. Institutionalized racism is pervasive in our society and involves discrimination that is built into the institutions of our society, such as the legal system, politics, employment practices, health care, and education.

There are numerous white and nonwhite groups in our nation, each with a unique culture, language, and history and with special needs. This uniqueness needs to be understood and appreciated if we are to progress toward racial and ethnic equality.

Strategies for advancing social and economic justice include mass media appeals, increased interaction among races, civil rights legislation, protests and activism, school busing, affirmative action programs, human relations programs in school systems, confrontation of racist and ethnic remarks and actions, and confrontation of the problems in inner-city ghettos.

Three possible patterns of intergroup race and ethnic relations in the future are Anglo-

conformity, the melting pot, and cultural pluralism. Cultural pluralism is the form that race and
ethnic relations are presently taking and may well
take in the future. As a profession, social work
has an obligation to work vigorously toward ending racial and ethnic discrimination and oppression and thereby advancing social and economic
justice.

NOTES

1. Milton Gordon, *Assimilation in American Life: The Role of Race, Religion, and National Origins* (New York: Oxford University Press, 1964), pp. 27–28.
2. *Encyclopedia of Sociology* (Guilford, CN: Duskin, 1974), p. 101.
3. Ibid., p. 236.
4. Gordon W. Allport, *The Nature of Prejudice* (Reading, MA: Addison-Wesley, 1954), p. 7.
5. Robert Merton, "Discrimination and the American Creed," in *Discrimination and National Welfare*, Robert M. MacIver, ed. (New York: Harper, 1949).
6. Marlene Cummings, "How to Handle Incidents of Racial Discrimination," in *The Personal Problem Solver*, Charles Zastrow and Dae H. Chang, eds. (Englewood Cliffs, NJ: Prentice-Hall, 1977), p. 200.
7. Gunnar Myrdal, *An American Dilemma* (New York: Harper, 1962), p. 144.
8. Elmer H. Johnson, *Social Problems of Urban Man* (Homewood, IL: Dorsey Press, 1973), p. 344.
9. Ashley Montague, *Man's Most Dangerous Myth: The Fallacy of Race*, 4th ed. (Cleveland: World, 1964).
10. Johnson, *Social Problems of Urban Man*, p. 350.
11. Arnold Rose, *The Negro in America* (New York: Harper & Row, 1964).
12. Paul Ehrlich and Richard Holm, "A Biological View of Race," in *The Concept of Race*, Ashley Montague, ed. (New York: Free Press, 1964), p. 82.
13. Montague, *Man's Most Dangerous Myth*.
14. Arthur Jensen, "How Much Can We Boost I.Q. and Scholastic Achievement?" *Harvard Educational Review*, 39 (1969), pp. 1–123.
15. Ashley Montague, ed., *Race & I.Q.* (London: Oxford University Press, 1975).
16. Johnson, *Social Problems of Urban Man*, p. 50.
17. T. W. Adorno, E. Frenkel-Brunswik, D. J. Devinson, and R. N. Sanford, *The Authoritarian Personality* (New York: Harper & Row, 1950).
18. Charles F. Marden and Gladys Meyer, *Minorities in American Society* (New York: American Book, 1962).
19. Eugene Hartley, *Problems in Prejudice* (New York: King's Crown Press, 1946).
20. Stokely Carmichael and Charles V. Hamilton, *Black Power: The Politics of Liberation in America* (New York: Vintage Books, 1967), p. 4.
21. William Kornblum and Joseph Julian, *Social Problems*, 7th ed. (Englewood Cliffs, NJ: Prentice-Hall, 1992), pp. 262–270.
22. Jeannette Henry, *The Indian Historian*, 1 (December 1967), p. 22.
23. Kornblum and Julian, *Social Problems*, p. 270.
24. Ibid., pp. 174–177.
25. Paul Bernard Wice, *Bail and Its Reform: A National Survey* (Washington, DC: U.S. Government Printing Office, 1973), p. 23.
26. Grace Halsell, *Soul Sister* (New York: Fawcett Crest, 1969), pp. 156–157.
27. C. H. Cooley, *Human Nature and the Social Order* (New York: Scribner's, 1902).
28. Kenneth B. Clark, *Dark Ghetto* (New York: Harper & Row, 1965), p. 32.
29. Judith Porter, *Black Child, White Child: The Development of Racial Attitudes* (Cambridge, MA: Harvard University Press, 1971).
30. Albert Szymanski, "Racial Discrimination and White Gain," *American Sociological Review*, 41 (June 1976), pp. 403–414.
31. Richard T. Schaefer, *Racial and Ethnic Groups*, 5th ed. (New York: HarperCollins, 1993).
32. Ibid.
33. Ibid.
34. Charles H. Henderson and Bok-Lim Kim, "Racism," in *Contemporary Social Work*, Donald Brieland, Lela Costin, and Charles Atherton, eds. (New York: McGraw-Hill, 1975), p. 180.
35. Excerpted from a speech by Abraham Lincoln in Charleston, Illinois, in 1858, as reported in Richard Hofstader, *The American Political Tradition* (New York: Knopf, 1948), p. 116.
36. Quoted in David Gelman, "Black and White in America," *Newsweek*, Mar. 7, 1988, p. 19.
37. Ibid.
38. Schaefer, *Racial and Ethnic Groups*, pp. 237–240.
39. Ibid., pp. 224–227.
40. Ibid.
41. Gelman, "Black and White in America," pp. 19–20.
42. H. J. Gans, "Fighting the Biases Embedded in Social Concepts of the Poor," *Chronicle of Higher Education*, Jan. 8, 1992, p. A56.
43. James W. Coleman and Donald R. Cressey, *Social Problems*, 5th ed. (New York: HarperCollins, 1993), pp. 172–176.

44. Quoted in Gelman, "Black and White in America," p. 20.

45. D. G. Norton, "Black Family Life Patterns, the Development of Self and Cognitive Development of Black Children," in *The Psychosocial Development of Minority Group Children*, G. J. Powell, ed. (New York: Brunner/Mazel, 1983), p. 183.

46. B. B. Solomon, "Social Work with Afro-Americans," in *Social Work: A Profession of Many Faces*, 3rd ed., A. Morales and B. W. Sheafor, eds. (Boston: Allyn & Bacon, 1983), p. 420.

47. J. L. Dillard, *Black English: Its History and Usage in the United States* (New York: Random House, 1972).

48. A. N. Wilson, *The Developmental Psychology of the Black Child* (New York: African Research, 1978).

49. Schaefer, *Racial and Ethnic Groups*, pp. 251–299.

50. Ibid.

51. Ibid., pp. 292–299.

52. Ibid., p. 306.

53. Ibid., p. 323.

54. Ibid.

55. Johnson, *Social Problems of Urban Man*, p. 349.

56. Dee Brown, *Bury My Heart at Wounded Knee* (New York: Holt, Rinehart & Winston, 1971).

57. Helen M. Crampton and Kenneth K. Keiser, *Social Welfare: Institution and Process* (New York: Random House, 1970), p. 104.

58. Brown, *Bury My Heart at Wounded Knee*.

59. Communication with Mace J. Delosme, Arcata, CA.

60. Schaefer, *Racial and Ethnic Groups*, p.182.

61. Ian Robertson, *Social Problems*, 2d ed. (New York: Random House, 1980), p. 218.

62. Johnson, *Social Problems of Urban Man*, p. 349.

63. Schaefer, *Racial and Ethnic Groups*, pp. 387–392.

64. Charles Henderson, Bok-Lim Kim, and Ione D. Vargus, "Racism," in *Contemporary Social Work*, 2d ed., Donald Brieland, Lela Costin, and Charles Atherton, eds. (New York: McGraw-Hill, 1980), p. 403.

65. Schaefer, *Racial and Ethnic Groups*, pp. 354–365.

66. Robert L. Barker, *The Social Work Dictionary*, 2d ed. (Silver Spring, MD: National Association of Social Workers, 1991), p. 219.

67. George E. Simpson and J. Milton Yinger, *Racial and Cultural Minorities*, 3d ed. (New York: Harper & Row, 1965), p. 510.

68. Thomas Sullivan, Kenrick Thompson, Richard Wright, George Gross, and Dale Spady, *Social Problems* (New York: Wiley, 1980), p. 437.

69. Johnson, *Social Problems of Urban Man*, pp. 374–379.

70. Cummings, "How to Handle Incidents," p. 197.

71. Johnson, *Social Problems of Urban Man*, p. 376.

72. Sullivan et al., *Social Problems*, p. 438.

73. Ibid., p. 439.

74. *Washington Post*, Feb. 20, 1970, p. 19.

75. Allan P. Sindler, *Bakke, DeFunis and Minority Admissions: The Quest for Equal Opportunity* (New York: Longmans, Green, 1978).

76. Henderson et al., "Racism," p. 403.

77. David L. Featherman and Robert M. Hauser, "Changes in the Socioeconomic Stratification of the Races, 1962–73," *American Journal of Sociology*, 82 (November 1976), pp. 621–651.

78. Roland L. Buchanan, Jr., and Marlene A. Cummings, *Individual Differences: An Experience in Human Relations for Children* (Madison, WI: Madison Public Schools, 1975).

79. Ibid., p. 1.

80. Ibid., p. 13.

81. Quoted in Cummings, "How to Handle Incidents," p. 201.

82. Kornblum and Julian, *Social Problems*, pp. 419–441.

83. The source for this material is Harry C. Boyte, "People Power Transforms a St. Louis Housing Project," *Occasional Papers* (Chicago: Community Renewable Society, January 1989), pp. 1–5.

84. Quoted in Boyte, "People Power Transforms a St. Louis Housing Project," p. 5.

85. Ibid.

86. Henderson and Kim, "Racism," p. 193.

87. Ione Dugger Vargus, "The Minority Practitioner," in *Contemporary Social Work*, Donald Brieland, Lela Costin, and Charles Atherton, eds. (New York: McGraw-Hill, 1975), p. 421.

88. Jimm G. Good Tracks, "Native American Noninterference," *Social Work*, 18 (November 1973), pp. 30–34.

89. Ronald G. Lewis and Man Keung Ho, "Social Work with Native Americans," *Social Work*, 20 (September 1975), pp. 378–382.

90. Dolores G. Norton, "Incorporating Content on Minority Groups into Social Work Practice Courses," in *The Dual Perspective* (New York: Council on Social Work Education, 1978).

91. Grafton H. Hull, Jr., "Social Work Practice with Diverse Groups," in *The Practice of Social Work*, 5th ed., Charles Zastrow, ed. (Pacific Grove, CA: Brooks/Cole,1995), pp. 347–382.

92. Quoted in Michele Collison, "Neglect of Minorities Seen Jeopardizing Future Prosperity," *Chronicle of Higher Education*, 34, no. 37 (May 25, 1988), p. 1.

93. Milton Gordon, "Assimilation in America: Theory and Reality," *Daedalus*, 90 (Spring 1961), pp. 363–365.

94. Jim Bishop, *The Days of Martin Luther King, Jr.* (New York: Putnam, 1971), pp. 327–328.

12

SEXISM

AND EFFORTS

FOR ACHIEVING

EQUALITY

Women who work full time are paid only about two-thirds as much as men who work full time.[1] The average woman college graduate is paid about the same as the average male high school graduate.[2] The average working white woman is paid less than the average working African American man, and the average working African American woman (subjected to double discrimination) earns least of all.[3] Fully 34% of families headed by women live below the poverty line, compared to 8% of families headed by men.[4]

This chapter will:

- Present a history of sex roles, sexism, and sexual harassment.
- Describe traditional sex-role expectations.
- Examine whether there is a biological basis for sexism.
- Describe traditional sex-role socialization practices.
- Examine the consequences of sexism on males and females.
- Describe the sex-role revolution in our society.
- Present strategies for achieving sexual equality.
- Summarize social work's commitment to combating sexism.

HISTORY OF SEX ROLES AND SEXISM

In almost every known society, women have had a lower status than men.[5] Women have been bound by more social restrictions and have consistently received less recognition for their work than have men. Women have been regarded differently than men, not only biologically but also emotionally, intellectually, and psychologically. Double standards have often existed for dating, for marriage, and for social and sexual conduct.

Most religions (including Judaism, Christianity, Hinduism, and Islam) in their traditional doctrines ascribe an inferior status to women. This tradition continues to exist in most countries, even though women attend religious services more often, hold firmer religious beliefs, pray more often, and are more active in church programs.[6] Many societies have concluded that it is divinely ordained that women should play a secondary and supportive role to men. In many Christian religions, women cannot become ministers or priests. Some orthodox Jewish men offer a daily prayer of thanks to God for not having made them a woman. In almost all houses of worship God is referred to as "He."

Primitive hunting and gathering societies provide insight into the processes that have resulted in women's lower status. Such societies usually lived in small tribes consisting of several mating couples and their dependents. Men generally were the hunters, and women were the gatherers of nuts, plants, and other foods. There are several explanations for this role differentiation. Males were supposedly better suited to hunting because they were physically stronger and could run faster. The infant mortality rate was very high in these tribes, so it was necessary for the women to be pregnant or nursing throughout most of their child-bearing years in order to maintain the size of the tribe. The need to tend to children largely prevented women from leaving the camp for days at a time in order to hunt large game. Even though women often gathered more food than men obtained through hunting, the male's hunting activities were viewed as more prestigious.

Women spent much of their adult lives being pregnant, nursing infants, and raising children. Because they were forced to remain around the home, they were also assigned the "domestic tasks" of cooking, serving, and washing. Once these sex roles became part of tradition, the distinctions were perceived not only as practical but also as "natural."

Gradually, more behavior patterns were added to these sex-role distinctions. Because men were trained at hunting, these skills led them to be recognized as the defenders of their tribe in case of attack from other tribes. Child-rearing patterns were developed to teach boys to value aggression and to be leaders. Women, on the other hand, were taught to be passive and dependent and to provide emotional support to the males.

EXHIBIT 12.1

The Ideal Wife, According to Buddhism

Most traditional religions hold that women should have a submissive and supportive role to men. For example, Buddhism asserts that the ideal wife should be:

> . . . like a maid-servant. She serves her husband well and with fidelity. She respects him, obeys his commands, has no wishes of her own, no ill-feeling, no resentment, and always tries to make him happy.[a]

---

[a]*The Teaching of Buddha* (Tokyo: Kosaido, 1966), p. 448.

Before the Industrial Revolution, practically all societies had come to assign distinct roles to men and women. Females generally performed domestic and child-rearing activities, whereas males were involved in what were then considered to be the productive* (such as hunting and economic support) and protective functions for the family. It should be noted that women in pre-industrial societies also engaged in food producing and economic support, such as making clothes, growing and harvesting garden crops, and helping on the farm. But their specific responsibilities were often viewed as inferior and requiring fewer skills.

The 19th-century Industrial Revolution brought about dramatic changes in sex roles. Men, instead of working on a small farm, left the home to work in a factory or other setting to provide economic support. The economic role of women declined because they were no longer performing economically productive tasks. Women's roles became increasingly defined as child rearing and housework. But the amount of time required to perform these functions declined, for several reasons. Families had fewer children. With compulsory education older children went to school. Gradually, labor-saving devices reduced the need for women to perform time-consuming domestic tasks (baking bread, canning vegetables, and washing). As the traditional roles of women began to change, some females started to pursue activities (for example, outside employment) that had traditionally been reserved for men. With these changes, sex roles began to blur.

The struggle for women's rights in the United States has been going on for nearly two centuries. In the early 19th century women who were working for the abolition of slavery complained that they, too, were denied such rights as voting. (An 1840 antislavery conference even refused to seat women as the male delegates gave impassioned speeches about the moral imperative to end slavery.)

In 1848 two feminists, Susan B. Anthony and Elizabeth Stanton, organized the first women's rights caucus, which was held in the state of New York.[7] These early leaders demanded suffrage (the vote for women) and the reform of many laws that were openly discriminatory toward women. It took over 70 years, until 1920, to pass the Nineteenth Amendment to the Constitution, which gave the vote to women. The suffrage movement was marked by jailings of feminist militants and fierce controversy. Many feminists equated winning the right to vote with achieving sexual equality. As a result, after 1920 the "women's movement" was nearly dormant for the next 40 years.

In the early 1900s some modern birth control techniques became available. This advance gave women greater freedom from the traditional roles of child rearing and housework.

During World War II large numbers of women were employed outside the home for the first time, to fill the jobs of men who had been drafted into the military. At that time over 38% of all women 16 years of age and over were employed, causing a further blurring of traditional sex roles.[8]

The 1960s saw a resurgence of interest in sex-role inequality, for a variety of reasons. The civil

---

*The use of the term *productive* indicates the higher status that was assigned to the role of men. In actuality, the roles of women were as, or even more, "productive" in completing essential tasks.

EXHIBIT 12.2

Female Genital Mutilation: An Extreme Example of Sexism

Female circumcision, or, more accurately, female genital mutilation (FGM), is commonplace in more than half of African countries and in parts of the Middle East. The details of FGM vary somewhat from culture to culture and from region to region, but the basics are the same.

Shannon Brownlee and Jennifer Seter describe FGM as follows:

Sometime between infancy and adulthood, all or part of a girl's external genitalia is cut away with a knife or razor blade, usually with no anesthetic. In most cases, the clitoris and the labia minora are removed. In the most extreme form, known as infibulation, the external labia are also scraped and stitched together with thread or long thorns, leaving only a tiny opening for urine and menstrual blood. The opening must be widened on the woman's wedding night.

The pain lasts far longer than the operation. Many of the 85 million to 110 million women who have endured FGM suffer ill effects ranging from reduced or lost sexual sensation to infections, persistent pain, painful intercourse, infertility, and dangerous childbirth. The purpose is to diminish sexual appetite, in order to maintain a girl's virginity—and thus her marriageability.[a]

Anthropologists believe that the first clitoridectomies, like chastity belts, were a means for husbands to ensure that their children were truly their own; FGM reduces a woman's interest in sex and thus in extramarital affairs. Today, young women in many African countries who have not undergone the procedure are shunned as oversexed, unmarriageable, and unclean. Currently, FGMs are usually performed by select older women, who are held in high esteem in their societies.

Feminist organizations in the United States tend to view FGM as the gender oppression to end all oppressions. Yet most international human rights organizations have been slow to condemn the practice, arguing that it is inappropriate to interfere with other people's cultural practices.

[a]Shannon Brownlee and Jennifer Seter, "In the Name of Ritual," *U.S. News & World Report,* Feb. 7, 1994, pp. 56–58.

---

rights movement had a consciousness-raising effect that made people more aware of and concerned about inequalities. This movement to curb racial discrimination through social action also served as a model, suggesting to a number of concerned women that sexual discrimination also could be alleviated through social action. More women attended college and thereby became more informed about inequalities. As females moved into new occupational positions, they became increasingly aware of discriminatory practices. Moreover, there was an explosion of research suggesting that sex-role differences were not innately determined but were in fact the result of socialization patterns that were discriminatory toward women.

One such study was conducted in 1955 by John Money, J. G. Hampson, and J. L. Hampson on hermaphrodites.[9] A hermaphrodite is a person who is born with both male and female sexual characteristics but is labeled either a male or a female at birth and then related to according to the gender on the birth certificate. These researchers did *not* find a significant correlation between physical characteristics and the hermaphrodites' own feelings about their sexual identities. These people were fulfilling the sex-role expectations of their labeled gender, although their observable anatomical characteristics often tended to place them in the other category. This research raised questions about the biological determination of sex roles.

Other studies have found dramatic differences in socialization patterns between males and females. Boys are given more sports equipment and task-oriented toys (like construction sets) to play with, whereas girls are given dolls and toys relating to marriage and parenthood.[10] During the first few months of life girls receive more distal stimulation (like looking and talking) from their parents, whereas boys receive more proximal stimulation (like rocking and handling).[11] Fathers tend to play more aggressively with sons than with daughters.[12] But American sex-role socialization practices are not universal. In some Middle Eastern societies, males are reared to be more emotional and sensitive than females; females tend to be more impassive and practical.[13] In Sweden most heavy-machine operators are women.[14] In Russia most physicians are women.[15]

Betty Friedan, in her 1963 book *The Feminine Mystique,* provided the ideological base for the resurgence of the women's movement.[16] The term *feminine mystique* referred to the negative self-concept, lack of direction, and low sense of self-worth among women. The book served as a rallying point for women and led Friedan and others to form the National Organization for Women (NOW) in 1966. Today NOW is the largest women's rights group in the country and an influential political force.[17] NOW and other women's groups have been working to end sexual discrimination, to achieve sexual equality, to end sexual double standards, and to improve the self-identity of women.

The Civil Rights Act of 1964, intended primarily to end racial discrimination, also prohibited discrimination on the basis of gender. However, local businesses in some states are exempt from existing sex discrimination laws.[18] A number of states even have laws that discriminate against women and reinforce prejudices against them. For example, some states still have statutes that assign longer sentences to women than men for the same crimes, on the assumption that female offenders require more rehabilitation.[19] (Con-

versely, many states treat women offenders more leniently than men on the assumption that women require the state's protection—which is a form of reverse discrimination.)

In 1972 the Equal Rights Amendment (ERA) received congressional approval but required ratification by three-fourths (38) of the states to become the Twenty-seventh Amendment to the Constitution. The ERA stated: "Equality of rights under the law shall not be denied or abridged by the United States or any state on account of sex." Time ran out on the ERA in 1982, when, after ten years of extensive political action, it narrowly failed to gain the support of enough states to be ratified.

Emotions ran high on both sides of the question of ERA ratification. Proponents asserted that it would be an important legal step toward true gender equality for women.[20] Opponents argued that passage of the ERA would mean that women could be drafted into the armed forces, would lose preferential treatment in divorce actions, and would become equally liable for alimony, child support, and spouse support. They asserted that labor laws giving preferential treatment to women would need to be revised, such as limits on the amount of weight women may lift on the job. Opponents also argued that "maternity leaves" would have to be made available to husbands who want to stay home with a newborn child.[21] A number of women concluded that the ERA would be more detrimental than beneficial to females, and they actively opposed its passage.

A variety of statutes have been passed to prevent sex discrimination. The federal Equal Pay Act of 1963 and a number of similar state laws require equal pay for equal work. As mentioned earlier, the Civil Rights Act of 1964 outlaws discrimination on the basis of race, color, sex, or religion. Executive Order 11246, as amended by Executive Order 11375 on October 13, 1967, forbids sex discrimination by federal suppliers and contractors and provides procedures for enforcement. In addition, numerous court decisions have set precedents establishing the illegality of sex discrimination in hiring, promotions, and rates of pay.[22] Several landmark decisions have required employers to pay female employees millions of

When members of Women's Action Coalition marched in New York in 1992 to draw attention to a variety of women's issues, the primary goal of their foremothers—equal voting rights in national and state elections—had been a reality for over seventy years. But, in spite of affirmative action programs and other important gains of the 1970s and 1980s, full political and economic parity between men and women is yet to come.

dollars in compensation for past wage discriminations.[23] In 1973, for example, American Telephone and Telegraph was required to pay $15 million in back wages to its female employees because the company had been paying them less than males who were doing the same work. In 1988 the State Farm Insurance Company in California agreed (in a multimillion-dollar settlement) to pay damages and back wages to thousands of women who had been refused jobs as insurance agents over a 13-year period. The women had been told that a college degree was required for agents, even though men were hired without degrees.[24]

The Equal Credit Act of 1974 bars discrimination on the basis of marital status or gender in credit transactions. A number of states have passed laws prohibiting discrimination against pregnant women in hiring, training, and promotion.[25] Despite these laws, acts, and precedents, however, substantial illegal sex discrimination still occurs, which women often have to fight on a case-by-case basis. For example, some high schools prohibit pregnant or married girls from attending classes, although unmarried fathers and married boys are allowed to attend.

Affirmative action programs apply to women as well as to certain racial minorities. Women are considered a minority group because for generations they have been subjected to discrimination and have been denied equal opportunities.

The following employers are required to have affirmative action programs: government contractors and suppliers, recipients of government funds, and businesses engaged in interstate commerce. Affirmative action applies primarily to job vacancies. Employers must demonstrate active efforts to locate and recruit minority applicants (defined to include women), must demonstrate positive efforts to increase the pool of qualified applicants (for example, special training programs for minorities), must give hiring preference to minority applicants, and in some cases must set hard quotas that specify numbers of minority members that must be accepted to fill vacant positions. The clout of affirmative action programs is in the threat of loss of government funds if employers do not have such programs effectively in place. (As noted in Chapter 11, the recent active backlash against affirmative action programs could curtail their effectiveness.)

SEXUAL HARASSMENT

Sexual harassment entails repeated and unwanted sexual advances. It has recently become recognized as a form of sex discrimination. Most of the victims are women; men rarely are the objects of unwanted sexual advances.

Paul Horton et al. identify some of the victims of sexual harassment:

> *Sexual harassment is an ancient practice. Attractive female slaves were routinely bought as sex playthings, and domestic servants were often exploited. If the Victorian housemaid denied her bed to a lecherous master, he dismissed her; if she admitted him, she soon became pregnant and disgraced, and his wife dismissed her. Either way, she lost!*
>
> *Sexual harassment can be found anywhere, but is likely to be a problem only where men have supervisory or gatekeeper power over women. The "casting couch" is a well-known feature of show business, and women in many occupations can escape unwelcome attentions only by quitting their jobs, often at a sacrifice. Sexual harassment on the campus has also surfaced, with many female graduate students claiming that senior professors claimed sexual privileges as the price for grades, degrees, and recommendations.*[26]

The definition of what is and what is not sexual harassment is somewhat vague. Repeated, unwanted touching is certainly harassment. A 1986 U.S. Supreme Court decision broadened the definition. Today a hostile work environment in which a woman feels hassled or degraded because of constant unwelcome flirtation, lewd comments, or obscene joking *may* be sufficient grounds for a lawsuit.[27] A number of colleges and universities in recent years have defined sexual harassment to include consenting sexual relationships between faculty and adult students. The rationale is that students are in a low power position

EXHIBIT 12.3

Types of Sexual Harassment

Sexual harassment falls into three categories: verbal, nonverbal, and physical. The following examples may constitute sexual harassment if the behavior is clearly unwelcomed and not reciprocated.

VERBAL

■ sexual innuendo ("So you're majoring in packaging? I love your packaging.")

■ suggestive comments ("Those jeans really fit you well.")

■ sexual remarks about a person's clothing, body, or sexual activities ("I noticed you lost weight. I'm glad you didn't lose your gorgeous chest too.")

■ sexist insults, jokes, or remarks that are stereotypical or derogatory ("Women should be kept barefoot, pregnant, and at the edge of town.")

■ implied or verbal threats concerning one's grades or job ("It's simple. If you want to pass this course, you have to be nice to me, and sex is the nicest thing I can think of.")

■ sexual propositions, invitations, or other pressures for sex ("My office hours are too limited. Why don't you drop by my house tonight? We'll have more privacy and time to get to know each other.")

NONVERBAL

■ visual sexual displays or unwanted displays of pornographic pictures, posters, cartoons, or other materials

■ body language (such as leering at one's body or standing too close)

■ suggestive whistling

■ obscene gestures

PHYSICAL

■ patting, pinching, and any other inappropriate touching or feeling

■ brushing against the body

■ attempted or actual kissing or fondling

■ coerced sexual intercourse

■ sexual assault

---

and may suffer adverse consequences if they refuse.

Those found guilty of sexual harassment are subject to reprimand and other consequences at their place of employment. Unfortunately, even a successful protest sometimes further victimizes the victim. She must endure the unpleasantness of pursuing the complaint, and she may be viewed by some as having invited the advances. Some women who protest eventually are forced to seek a new job because of the discomfort they feel in the old workplace.

In recent years corporate America has received several wake-up calls on sexual harassment. For example, in 1994 a San Francisco jury awarded a legal secretary $7.1 million in punitive damages after finding that her former employer failed to stop an attorney in the firm from harassing her.

TRADITIONAL SEX-ROLE EXPECTATIONS

Sex roles are learned patterns of behavior that are expected of the sexes in a given society. Sex-role expectations, which define how men and women

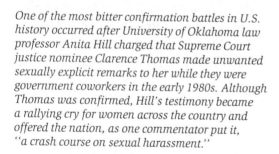

One of the most bitter confirmation battles in U.S. history occurred after University of Oklahoma law professor Anita Hill charged that Supreme Court justice nominee Clarence Thomas made unwanted sexually explicit remarks to her while they were government coworkers in the early 1980s. Although Thomas was confirmed, Hill's testimony became a rallying cry for women across the country and offered the nation, as one commentator put it, "a crash course on sexual harassment."

are to behave and how they are to be treated by others, are based largely on stereotypes. *Stereotyping* involves attributing of fixed and usually inaccurate and unfavorable qualities to a category of people. Stereotyping makes it easier for discrimination (unequal treatment) to occur.

American women traditionally are expected to be affectionate, passive, conforming, sensitive, intuitive, and dependent—"sugar and spice and everything nice." They are supposed to be concerned primarily with domestic life, to be nurturing, to love to care for babies and young children, to fuss over their personal appearance, and to be self-sacrificing for their family. They should not appear to be ambitious, aggressive, competitive, or more intelligent than men. They should be ignorant about and uninterested in sports, economics, and politics. Also, they are not supposed to initiate relationships with men but are expected to be tender, feminine, emotional, and appreciative when in these relationships.

There are also a number of traditional sex-role expectations for males in our society: A male is expected to be tough, fearless, logical, self-reliant, independent, and aggressive. He should have

EXHIBIT 12.4

How to Tell a Businessman from a Businesswoman

- He's aggressive; she's pushy.
- He's good at details; she's picky.
- He loses his temper because he's so involved in his job; she's bitchy.
- When he's depressed (or hung over), everyone tiptoes past his office; she's moody so it must be her "time of the month."
- He follows through; she doesn't know when to quit.
- He's confident; she's conceited.
- He stands firm; she's hard.
- He has judgments; she's prejudiced.
- He's a man of the world; she's "been around."
- He drinks because of excessive job pressure; she's a lush.
- He isn't afraid to say what he thinks; she's mouthy.
- He exercises authority diligently; she's power mad.
- He's close-mouthed; she's secretive.
- He's a stern taskmaster; she's hard to work for.
- He climbed the ladder to success; she slept her way to the top.

Source: Author unknown.

definite opinions on the major issues of the day and make authoritative decisions at work and at home. He is expected to be strong—a sturdy oak—and never to be depressed, vulnerable, or anxious. He is not supposed to be a "sissy"—to cry or openly display emotions that suggest vulnerability. He is expected to be the provider, the breadwinner. He should be competent in all situations, physically strong, athletic, confident, daring, brave, and forceful. He should be in a position to dominate any situation—to be a "Rambo" or a "Clint Eastwood."[28] He is supposed to initiate relationships with women and to be dominant in these relationships. Men who are supported by their wives, or who earn less than their wives, are likely to experience feelings of shame and inadequacy.

Even very young boys are expected to be masculine. Parents and relatives are far more concerned when a boy is a "sissy" than when a girl is a "tomboy." A tomboy is expected to outgrow her "masculine" tendencies, but it is feared that a sissy will never fare well in our competitive society and may even become homosexual. (The right of a boy to wear his hair long had to be won in many court battles in this country, whereas hardly anyone is concerned when a girl wears her hair short.)

IS THERE A BIOLOGICAL BASIS FOR SEXISM?

Let's examine the sexist ideology that assumes the differences between men and women are the result of biology—that anatomy equips men to play an active and dominant role in the world and women to play a passive and secondary role.

There are certain biological differences between men and women. Of course, there are the obvious anatomical, sexual, and reproductive differences. There are also hormonal differences. Each sex has both male and female hormones, but women have higher levels of female hormones and males have higher levels of male hormones. Research on some animal species (which may or may not be applicable to humans) has shown that, if male hormones are injected into females, the females have a heightened sex drive and become more aggressive.[29] Scientists, however, see this hormonal difference as playing only a minor role in humans. This is because human behavior patterns are almost entirely learned, whereas behavior patterns in lower animals are more influenced by hormonal factors.[30]

Men, on the average, are taller and heavier than women and have greater physical strength. Women can tolerate pain better and have greater physical endurance (except in short-term feats of strength).[31] In most respects women are physically healthier.[32] Females are less susceptible to most diseases and on the average live longer. Males have higher rates of fetal and infant mortality. Male fetuses can inherit a greater number of sex-linked weaknesses: Over 30 disorders have been found exclusively among males, including hemophilia, certain types of color blindness, and webbing of the toes.

Soon after birth, female babies tend to be more content and less physically active.[33] As children develop, other differences appear, but it has not yet been determined whether the identified differences are due to inherited or learned factors. Girls learn to talk and read at an earlier age; they also become more docile and dependent and seem more intellectually mature (most remedial education classes have a large majority of boys). Boys are superior in elementary school on tasks requiring spatial, mechanical, and analytic ability, whereas girls are superior at tasks involving verbal capacities and numerical computation.[34] The basis for these differences is uncertain. Girls, for example, may be better at reading and language because they are encouraged to spend more time with adults and to read rather than to engage in competitive sports or similar activities.

There is considerable research supporting the position that sex-role differences are due primarily to socialization patterns. John Money and his associates examined cases in which parents wanted a girl so badly that they raised a male child to be a girl, or vice versa.[35] The study found that children will play the role that they are socialized to learn rather than the gender role outlined by traditional sex-role expectations. Money concluded that children are "psychosexually neuter at birth" and that sex role is independent of physiological sex.

The fact that there are wide variations in sex-role expectations among cultures also suggests that sex roles are learned rather than biologically determined. (If all cultures defined sex-role expectations similarly, this would suggest a biological basis for sex-role distinctions.) Let's consider a few examples. Most cultures expect women to do most of the carrying of heavy objects, whereas in this country and in most European countries men are expected to do most of the lifting and carrying of heavy objects. In some societies, unlike ours, the men do most of the cooking. Not so long ago in Europe it was the males who wore stockings, perfume, and silks. Men in Scotland still wear kilts (skirts). Among the Maoris and the Trobrianders, it is the women who are expected to take the initiative in sexual activity.[36]

Margaret Mead, in a classic study, examined sex-role expectations in three tribes in New Guinea. She found that one tribe required both males and females to behave in a way we would define as "masculine"; a second required both to behave in a "feminine" fashion; and the third had the females act "masculine" and the males act "feminine." Mead concluded that sex-role expectations are determined primarily by cultural learning experiences (see Exhibit 12.5).

SEX-ROLE SOCIALIZATION

In the United States, sex-role socialization starts shortly after birth. Baby girls are dressed in pink, and baby boys are dressed in blue. Babies are given sex-related toys. Boys are bounced on the knee and handled roughly, whereas girls are cooed over. A child becomes aware that he is a "boy" or she is a "girl" long before noticing anatomical differences between the sexes.[37] Lawrence Kohlberg notes that children make basic decisions (based on what others tell them) that they are boys or girls and then select those activities that significant others (people that they view as important to them) define as conforming to this self-concept.[38]

Many parents go to great lengths to socialize their young children according to sex-role expectations. Little boys are given toy trucks to play with, and girls are given dolls. Boys are encouraged to play ball; girls are urged to play house. Ruth Hartley notes:

EXHIBIT 12.5

Sex-Role Expectations Are Culturally Determined

In her classic study *Sex and Temperament in Three Primitive Societies,* Margaret Mead refuted the notion that sex-role expectations are biologically determined. The study was conducted among three tribes in New Guinea in the early 1930s. Mead demonstrated that many characteristics Americans classify as typically female or male are defined differently in these tribes.

Both sexes among the Arapesh would seem feminine to us. Both men and women are gentle, nurturant, and compliant. The personalities of males and females in this society are not sharply differentiated. Both girls and boys learn to be unaggressive, cooperative, and responsive to the needs and wants of others. Relations between husband and wife parallel the traditional mother/child relations in our society, with the Arapesh husband often seeing his role as providing training to his much younger wife.

In contrast, among the Mundugamors, both sexes would seem masculine to us. Both are headhunters and cannibals, are nonnurturant and aggressive, and actively initiate sexual involvement.

The most interesting society studied was the Tchambuli, which virtually reverses our traditional sex-role expectations and stereotypes. The men spend much more time than the women in grooming and decorating themselves and in painting, carving, and practicing dance steps. In contrast, the women are efficient, impersonal, unadorned, managerial, and brisk. They are the traders and have most of the economic power.

Mead concludes:

We no longer have any basis for regarding such aspects of behavior as sex linked. . . . Standardized personality differences between the sexes are . . . cultural creations to which each generation, male or female, is trained to conform.

Source: Margaret Mead, *Sex and Temperament in Three Primitive Societies* (New York: Morrow, 1935).

Girls gain approval . . . by doing the rather undemanding things that are expected of them. . . . A girl need not be bright as long as she is docile and attractive. . . . This kind of treatment is likely to produce rather timid, unventuresome, unoriginal, conformist types.[39]

Young girls in many families are still raised by their parents to be mothers and homemakers and/or are encouraged to seek low-status, low-paid employment. The early socialization of boys, according to Hartley, is quite different:

Almost from birth the boy has more problems to solve autonomously. In addition, he is required to limit his interest at a very early age to sex-appropriate objects and activities, while girls are permitted to amble their way to a similar status at a more gradual and natural pace. . . . He is challenged to discover what he should do by being told what he should not do, as in the most frequently employed negative sanction, "Don't be a sissy!" . . . Interest in girlish things is generally forbidden and anxiety-provoking in American boyhood. . . . The boy is constantly open to a challenge to prove his masculinity. He must perform, adequately and publicly, a variety of physical feats that will have very little utility in most cases in adulthood. He is constantly under pressure to demonstrate mastery over the environment, and, concomitantly, to suppress expression of emotion.[40]

Boys are encouraged to play more competitive games than girls and to be outgoing and aggressive, whereas young girls are encouraged to be passive and reserved.[41] Young children are impressionable. Such sex-role stereotyping often becomes a self-fulfilling prophecy. According to Charles Cooley's "looking glass self-concept," people will come to view themselves as others relate to them.[42]

Research shows that some females are actually taught to fear success and achievement and to "play dumb" in order to "boost the male ego."[43] To be feminine, girls must display softness, helplessness, tenderness, and understanding and be generally nonassertive. Thus, adolescent and adult females are put in a double bind due to *femininity/achievement incompatibility.*[44] There is a traditional view in our society that a woman cannot be both feminine and achievement oriented. (Of course, this traditional view is an arbitrary one that has been a factor in leading women to play a submissive role; there is nothing intrinsically incompatible about femininity and achievement.)

A significant part of the socialization process occurs in school. Girls are often channeled into sewing, typing, and cooking classes, whereas boys are channeled into such classes as woodworking, printing, and mechanics. Although 85% of grade-school teachers are female, close to 90% of principals are male.[45] Thus, children see men in superior, decision-making positions and women in subordinate positions. One study found that grade-school teachers generally hold traditional sex-role stereotypes—that teachers erroneously believe that males are innately more aggressive and more capable of abstract reasoning than females.[46]

Textbooks in preschool, elementary, junior high, and high school portray female characters as being more passive and dependent and less creative than males.[47] Florence Howe, for example, analyzed textbooks in the first three grades and concluded:

Primers used in the first three grades offer children a view of a "typical" American family: a mother who does not work, a father who does, two children—a brother who is always older than a sister—and two pets—a dog and sometimes a cat—whose ages and sexes mirror those of the brother and sister. In these books, boys build or paint things; they also pull girls in wagons and push merry-go-rounds. Girls carry purses when they go shopping; they help mother cook or pretend they are cooking; and they play with their dolls. . . . Plots in which girls are involved usually depend on their inability to do something—to manage their own roller skates or to ride a pony.[48]

Guidance counselors generally advise students to pursue careers not just on the basis of their abilities, but also on the basis of traditional sex-role expectations. For example, a young girl who excels at math may be encouraged to be a teacher, whereas a young boy with equal skills may be urged to consider engineering. Janet Chafetz comments on such counseling practices:

Counselors defend such practices on the basis of what youngsters may "realistically" expect to face in the future: marriage, child care, and a lack of opportunity in a number of career fields for females, and the need to support a family at the highest income and status levels possible for males. "Realism," however, has always been an excuse for maintaining the status quo, and it is no different in the case of sex role stereotypes. If, for instance, females do not prepare to enter previously masculine fields, such fields will remain male-dominated, allowing another generation of counselors to assure girls that females can't work in them. In addition, it is questionable whether counselors' notions of "reality" in fact keep pace with reality. There is undoubtedly a lag between expanding opportunities and changing sex role definitions on the one hand, and counselors' awareness of these phenomena on the other.[49]

Even contemporary theories in psychology describe women as being more passive and emotional, lacking in abstract interests, and as having an instinctive tenderness for babies.[50] Even though masculinity and femininity are largely learned roles, contemporary psychological theories subtly imply (erroneously) that sex-role differences are genetically determined. Sigmund Freud's theory of the development of the female personality is probably the most sexist and outrageous. According to Freud, young girls discover that their genitals differ from boys', which leads them to have "penis envy." Because of this difference, girls conclude that they are biologically inferior to males and then develop a passive, submissive personality as a way to adjust to interactions with males, whom they view as superior.[51]

There are many sexist implications built into the English language. Until several years ago male pronouns (like *he*) automatically referred to a people in general. Additional commonly used words and phrases that subtly (and erroneously) imply the superiority of males include *manmade, mankind, manned, manpower, chairman, congressman, businessman, mailman, salesman, foreman, policeman, the best man for the job,* and *man and wife.* It is customary for women, on marrying, to take the husband's last name, again subtly suggesting the dominance of males.

The mass media, particularly in advertising, also play an important role in sex-role socialization. Women are frequently portrayed in commercials as being wives, mothers, or sex objects or as being obsessed with getting a date. They used to be portrayed as invariably less intelligent and more dependent than men and were hardly ever shown in executive positions. Some TV ads still depict women in traditional sex-role stereotypes such as delighting in waxing their floors or in discovering a new detergent to get their families' white clothes whiter. Fortunately, changes are occurring in the mass media's portrayal of women, reflecting changes in our society. Many commercials are now even reversing traditional roles. Because the mass media are important socialization vehicles, they can assist in changing attitudes about "proper" sex roles in the future.

CONSEQUENCES OF SEXISM

Sexism is prejudice or discrimination against women. Although females represent a numerical majority in our society, they are considered a minority group because they are victims of discrimination on many fronts and have unequal access to valued resources.

Effects on Occupation and Income

Women tend to be concentrated in the lower-paying, lower-status positions: secretaries, child-care workers, receptionists, typists, nurses, hairdressers, bank tellers, cashiers, and file clerks. Men tend to be concentrated in higher-paying positions: lawyers, judges, engineers, college teachers, physicians, and dentists (see Table 12.1).

As noted earlier, full-time working women are paid about two-thirds of what full-time working men are paid.[52] Even though sex discrimination laws have been passed, job discrimination continues to be found in a number of studies.[53]

Women hold fewer than 10% of the nation's elective offices. There has never been a woman president or vice president in the United States. Of the thousands of people who have been U.S. senators, fewer than 30 have been women.[54] It is a rarity when a woman is elected governor in a state. In 1986, Nebraska became the first state in our country's history in which both the Democratic and the Republican nominees for governor were women. Men still control the political processes to nominate candidates and to campaign for their election. The potential political clout of women, however, is immense, because they constitute a majority of the nation's voters.[55]

Women hold less than 1% of the top management positions in American corporations, less than 2% of the directorships of top corporations, and about 5–6% of all middle-management positions in this country.[56] Even successful female executives often complain about an invisible "glass ceiling" that seems to lock them out of the key positions of power. One study, based on interviews with 100 male and female executives from three major U.S. corporations, concluded that there was a clear double standard in promotions and that women had to perform significantly better than their male counterparts to get ahead.[57]

About two-thirds of the women who work outside the home in the United States are employed in the "women's ghetto" positions of housekeepers, secretaries, receptionists, telephone operators, clerks, and so on.[58] And, overall, women earn less income than men in

TABLE 12.1

Employment Positions Held by Women

Position	Percentage Held by Women
Secretaries	99.0
Dental assistants	98.8
Receptionists	97.3
Child-care workers	97.1
Typists	95.1
Cleaners, servants	94.8
Registered nurses	94.3
Teachers' aides	91.9
Hairdressers, cosmetologists	90.8
Bookkeepers	90.7
Telephone operators	89.9
Bank tellers	89.8
Librarians	87.6
Elementary schoolteachers	85.4
General office clerks	82.9
Maids, housemen	82.3
File clerks	81.3
Waiters, waitresses	79.6
Cashiers	79.3
Social workers	68.9
Psychologists	62.5
Food service workers	59.0
Writers, artists, entertainers, athletes	47.2
Financial managers	46.3
College teachers	40.9
Natural scientists	27.2
Lawyers, judges	21.4
Physicians	20.4
Police officers	15.8
Architects	15.3
Dentists	8.5
Engineers	8.5
Firefighters	2.4

Source: U.S. Bureau of the Census, *Statistical Abstract of the United States, 1993* (Washington, DC: U.S. Government Printing Office, 1993), pp. 405–407.

practically every job category.[59] Even in the armed forces, where pay levels are standardized, it is less likely that women will receive additional "flight pay," "combat pay," or "hazardous duty" pay.[60] It is true that differences in income between men and women by job category are due partly to seniority (men earn more because they've held

their jobs longer), but studies taking seniority into account have found that women tend to receive less pay for doing the same job.[61]

There are probably many reasons for these occupational and income differences between men and women. Female children are socialized to seek lower-paying occupations and careers. For example, boys are encouraged to be lawyers and doctors, whereas girls are encouraged to be teachers and secretaries. Men and women are also "sex typed" for various jobs: Males seeking employment are encouraged by prospective employers to apply for higher-status positions, whereas women are encouraged to apply for lower-level positions.[62] Then there is the tendency for our society to assign lower pay to job categories in which women are concentrated: receptionists, secretaries, and typists. Nonetheless, lower pay for women holding the same jobs as men indicates that there are discriminatory practices occurring even after women are hired.

Paul Horton and Gerald Leslie provide additional reasons, stemming from sex-role socialization, for the job and income disparity between men and women:

Motivation for career advancement is difficult to measure, and rash generalization is dangerous. Yet there are good reasons to suspect that intense career ambitions have been less common among women than among men. Beginning in early socialization, most girls are trained to please and charm others; most boys are trained to impress and outdistance others. Boys are trained to dominate and lead; girls, to submit and follow. Boys are taught to make demands upon others; girls learn to serve others' needs. Boys are praised for their strength; girls, for their prettiness and graciousness. As adults, men in our society are evaluated primarily according to their career success ("Meet my son, the doctor"), while women have been evaluated primarily according to their skill in human relationships ("She has a handsome husband and three darling children"). Husbands who knowingly neglected their families to pursue career advancement (moonlighting, night school, weekends working at the office) were praised for their ambition, while wives who allowed their careers to interfere with family life were scolded and scorned. A woman's spectacular success might alienate men, and much has been written about the avoidance-of-success syndrome in women. . . . This all has contributed to a lower level of career expectation among women than among men.[63]

Effects on Human Interactions

The effects of sexism on human interactions are immense. Let's look at some examples.

Parents place more social restrictions on teenage daughters than on teenage sons. Daughters cannot stay out as late, their friends are more closely monitored, they are less likely to be given the family car for going out, and they are discouraged from participating in athletics.

Women are pressured to have the "Miss America" look—to have well-developed busts, shapely figures, and attractive features. Women who are judged to be less attractive, according to current American stereotypes, receive less attention from males, find it more difficult to get dates, and may even have less success at obtaining higher-status employment. The psychological costs are particularly severe when a woman reaches middle age. Socialized into believing her main function is child rearing and her main asset is her physical attractiveness, she often watches with despair as both her children and her youth leave her.

There are many double standards for male and female social interactions. If teenage boys are sexually active, they are viewed as being "studs," whereas sexually active teenage girls may be called derogatory names. To a greater extent, males are allowed to be aggressive and to use vulgar language. There are social restrictions that discourage women from entering certain nightclubs and other places of entertainment. Married women who have an affair are usually subjected to more disapproval than are married men who do.

In interactions between males and females, there is a tendency for the male to seek to be dominant and for the female either to seek an egalitarian relationship or to be manipulated into being submissive. For example, in dating, the male usually is expected to ask the female for a date and to choose what they will do on the date. Also, males often try to be "macho"; some females find that, in order to receive positive reinforcement and social acceptability, they must play along by being submissive, passive, or "feminine." When both husband and wife are working, the wife usually leaves her job and follows her husband to a new geographical area when he gets a job transfer.[64]

Often there are power struggles between males and females related to sex-role expectations. Marriage counselors are now seeing many couples in which the husband wants his wife to play a traditional role: stay at home, raise the children, and do the housework. If a wife does work, the husband often demands that the job not interfere with her doing the domestic tasks. He also perceives her job as a "second income" in contrast to a "career." Wives who want egalitarian relationships and who are becoming increasingly aware of the negative effects of sex-role stereotyping are likely to experience conflict with husbands who want them to fulfill the traditional wife role.

Jessie Bernard has noted that women experience more depression and greater dissatisfaction in marriage than men.[65] Women are expected to make most of the adjustments necessary to keep the marriage intact. Middle-aged women frequently suffer severe depression when many of their tasks as mothers and homemakers are phased out—especially if they do not have outside jobs.[66] Research demonstrates that employed wives are happier than full-time homemakers.[67] Women who are extensively battered by their husbands, yet continue to live in these circumstances for years, sadly document the extent to which some women feel trapped by social arrangements that perpetuate their dependence and submission.

Matina Horner found that many women are motivated to avoid success because they fear that, the more ambitious and successful they are, the less feminine they will appear in their interactions with men.[68]

Sex-role stereotypes also contribute to women's being treated only as sex objects by some men and to women's being sexually harassed at work, at school, and in other settings.

Of course, it is not just female stereotypes that cause difficulties in human interaction. Males also experience problems in living up to the "Clint Eastwood" image (described earlier). It is almost impossible for any male to meet such expectations. Yet there are considerable pressures on males to try—or suffer the consequences. Take the example of Senator Edmund Muskie in the Democratic presidential primary campaign in 1968. Senator Muskie was the leading candidate for the nomination. Then a newspaper in New England made some derogatory accusations about his wife and Muskie reacted by breaking down and crying in public. Very quickly the American public concluded that Muskie did not have the emotional stability to be president, and his popularity plummeted in the polls. Deborah David and Robert Brannon describe another example:

A friend explained to me that he broke down and cried in front of a colleague at the office after some personal tragedies and office frustrations. He explained, "The news of my crying was all over the office in an hour. At first, no one said anything. They just sort of looked. They couldn't handle the situation by talking about it. Before this, only girls had cried. One of the guys did joke, 'Hear you and Sally been crying lately, eh?' I guess that was a jibe at my masculinity, but the 'knowing silence' of the others indicated the same doubts. What really hurt was that two years later, when I was doing very well and being considered for a promotion, it was brought up again. My manager was looking over my evaluations, read a paragraph to himself, and said, 'What do you think about that crying incident?' You can bet that was the last time I let myself cry."[69]

Ruth Hartley notes that sex-role socialization of boys inevitably leads to personal conflicts in later years:

The boy is not adequately socialized for adulthood. . . . The boy is conditioned to live in an all-masculine society, defining his own self-image by rejecting whatever smacks of femininity. In adulthood, he will have to adjust to a heterosexual work world, perhaps even take orders from a female, a species he has been taught to despise as inferior. Finally, the emphasis on repression of the emotions, the high value of stoicism, leaves the boy wholly unprepared for the emotional closeness and intimate personal interaction now more and more expected of a lover and a spouse.[70]

Men frequently feel they must put their careers first and thereby sharply limit the interactions and satisfactions received in being husbands and fathers. In contrast, women are traditionally expected to put their roles as wives and mothers first and thereby limit their growth, capacities, and satisfactions in other areas.

Men in this country are disadvantaged before the law in several areas. In some jurisdictions, husbands are legally required to provide financial support for their families, and failure to do so is grounds for divorce by the wife. If a marriage breaks up, most courts grant custody of the children to the wife. In child custody battles the father bears a heavier burden of proof that he is a fit parent than does the mother, and only in cases in which the mother is demonstrably negligent is the father's claim seriously considered. Alimony is much more frequently awarded to wives, even when both spouses can support themselves. Several men's groups have now formed in various regions of the country to advocate for equal treatment of men in these legal areas.

Sex-role stereotyping probably also plays a key role in the following statistics.[71] Men are three times more likely than women to commit suicide, are three times more likely to have a severe emotional disorder, are substantially more likely to be involved in violence, and commit far more crimes. Alcoholics and drug addicts are primarily men. Males also have higher rates of stress-related illnesses, such as heart disease, ulcers, and hypertension. The life expectancy for men in our society is several years less than for women. This shorter life expectancy stems partly from the pressures they face to succeed financially and from the fact that they are socialized not to vent their emotions. As a result, they experience more psychological stress, which leads to higher rates of stress-related illnesses and thus a shorter life span.

Because of male stereotypes, many men view themselves as failures when they cannot meet the financial needs of their families. Some men are badly beaten in fights because they felt they could not walk away and still be "real men." Many women find it frustrating to interact with men who are unable to be honest and open about their feelings. Not being able to live up to the "model man" image makes many men unhappy, depressed, and unfulfilled. Clearly, sex-role stereotyping has huge costs (financial, social, and personal) not only for women, but also for men.

RECENT DEVELOPMENTS AND A LOOK TO THE FUTURE

There is currently a sex-role revolution occurring in our society. Men as well as women are becoming aware of the negative effects of sex-role distinctions. Increasingly we see courses on this topic in high schools, vocational schools, and colleges. More and more women are entering the labor force. The proportion of employed females to employed males is about 45 to 55.[72]

Women are becoming more involved in athletics than they were in the past, and they are entering certain types of competition previously confined to males. Women are now playing basketball, football, baseball, and volleyball. There are increasing numbers of women in track and field events, swimming, boxing, wrestling, weight lifting, golf, tennis, and stock-car racing.

In 1983 Sandra Day O'Connor became the first woman justice on the United States Supreme Court. In 1984 Geraldine Ferraro was the first woman selected to be a vice-presidential candidate for a major political party.

Women are also pursuing a number of professions and careers that previously were nearly all male: the military, engineers, lawyers, judges, firefighters, physicians, dentists, accountants, administrators, police officers, managers. Entering these new professions often has presented obstacles. Carl Glassman, for example, reports that women police officers receive stares from other citizens and are often viewed with suspicion by male partners.[73] (Male police partners fear that women may break under pressure, may not be able to subdue and handcuff a resisting offender, and may not be able to control disorderly males and several other types of violent situations. Male officers tend to feel both hostile and protective toward female officers, and one woman's failing is often held up as an indictment against all the rest.)

Human interactions are also changing, with more women being assertive and seeking out egalitarian relationships with males. To some extent, men are also (more slowly) beginning to realize that sex-role stereotypes limit the opportunities open to them in terms of emotional expression, interpersonal relationships, occupations, and domestic activities. Jack Sawyer notes:

> If men cannot play freely, neither can they freely cry, be gentle, nor show weakness—because these are "feminine," not "masculine." But a fuller concept of humanity recognizes that all men and women are potentially both strong and weak, both active and passive, and that these and other human characteristics are not the province of one sex.
> The acceptance of sex-role stereotypes not only limits the individual, but also has bad effects on society generally.[74]

Sex-role stereotypes have been costly to society. They have prevented a number of people from assuming more productive roles and have resulted in the expenditure of substantial resources on emotional and physical problems generated by these stereotypes.

Men also are taking on new roles and entering new careers. It is becoming increasingly common for men to accept equal responsibility for domestic tasks and for child rearing. In addition, we are now seeing more male nurses, secretaries, childcare workers, nursery school teachers, telephone operators, and flight attendants.[75]

In the past two decades, millions of Americans have begun to change their ideas about the "naturalness" of sex roles. Traditional discriminations

Women are advancing in areas in which their presence was all but unthinkable just a few years ago. Barbara Harris blesses her congregation after being ordained as the first female bishop in the history of the Episcopal Church.

redefinition of both masculinity and femininity. In the years to come, it is likely that we will see significant shifts in the way children are socialized and revisions of our legal system that affect both men and women. The extent of the change that will occur is something that cannot yet be determined. . . . We are in the midst of a very exciting era of experimentation. We have an opportunity to shape our destiny in this area. If people decide that sexual differences are important, this need not entail a return to the inequality, discrimination, and oppression that were common in the past and still linger today.[76]

If men and women achieve sexual equality in our society, what will be the effects? Kornblum and Julian speculate:

One obvious answer is that society's supply of talent in every segment of the work force would increase. More men would participate in traditionally female fields. . . . Breaking down the occupational barriers that separate women and men would also help them relate to each other as equals. Also, because fewer men would be the sole support for their families, there would be more flexibility in working life: Men and women would be freer to leave their jobs if they were unhappy with them, and in general there would be greater sharing of economic and homemaking responsibilities. This would reduce the pressures that exist for men to "succeed" and for women to remain dependent. The most important result of true sexual equality, then, may be simply that people would be free to be themselves.[77]

are coming to be perceived as an irrational system that threatens women with lifelong inferiority and wasted potential and restricts men to the role of always being competitive, aggressive, and emotionally insensitive.

What will the future be like? Predicting the precise direction that sex-role stereotypes will take is difficult. As Thomas Sullivan et al. note:

It seems likely that any meaningful change in our sex-role structure will involve some degree of

Some feminists and social scientists have urged that men and women be socialized to be flexible in their role playing and to express themselves as human beings rather than in traditional feminine or masculine ways.[78] This idea is called "androgyny," from *andro* (male) and *gyne* (female). The notion is to have people explore a broad range of role-playing possibilities and to choose to express emotions and behaviors without regard to sex-role stereotypes. People thus are encouraged to pursue tasks and careers at which they are most competent and with which they are most comfortable and to express the attitudes and

EXHIBIT 12.6

Strategies for Achieving Sexual Equality

Sexual equality does not imply a "unisex" world. Advocates of sexual equality are not urging that men and women use the same public bathroom facilities, dress the same, or play professional football and hockey together. What they *are* advocating is the equal treatment of the sexes (for example, in employment) and the elimination of traditional sex-role stereotyping. No role, behavior, aptitude, or attitude should be limited to one sex alone. True sexual equality simply means that people would be free to be themselves.

To achieve sexual equality, we must take action in many areas, some of which are summarized as follows:

■ We must put an end to the motherhood myth, which holds that women are most fulfilled as mothers.

■ Fathers must share equally in child rearing and in domestic tasks. This does not mean that men should do exactly half of each domestic task; rather, husband and wife should communicate with each other about how best to allocate family responsibilities. Women cannot compete equally with men in the work world if they also are required to assume all of the traditional child-rearing and homemaker responsibilities.

■ Additional day-care provisions are needed for working mothers and fathers, particularly for one-parent families. Without quality day-care arrangements, many mothers who want to work are prevented from doing so.

■ Laws preventing sex discrimination need to be enforced, and laws in matters in which legal discrimination still exists need to be enacted. (For example, women still sometimes have a more difficult time obtaining a bank loan.) Sex discrimination laws are also needed to protect men in certain matters (such as in alimony and child custody).

■ Dysfunctional sex-role socialization practices should be ended. Children should be reared to take on the roles, attitudes, and behaviors they desire and for which they have aptitudes and interests, rather than having boys raised to be "masculine" and girls to be "feminine." Parents and teachers should learn to relate to each child as an *individual,* not as a *male* or a *female.*

■ Assertiveness-training programs should be used more extensively to help both men and women effectively express themselves and gain skills in countering sex-role stereotypes.

■ Advertisers who still portray women only as homemakers or as sex objects should start to portray the sexes more equally.

■ Consciousness-raising groups need to be expanded to reach more men and women. Such groups are now being held largely with women to help them become more aware of sex-role stereotypes, to help them establish a better self-concept, and to foster contact with others who are working to end sexism.

■ Continued development of such services as shelters for battered women, rape crisis centers, abortion counseling, family planning services, and marriage and sexual counseling is needed if people are to develop their capacities fully.

■ School counselors and teachers should help students to make career decisions based on their abilities, not on their gender.

■ Girls and boys should be encouraged to take vocational courses they desire (cooking, shop, typing, printing) without regard to gender.

■ Publishers should put an end to sex-role stereotyping and portray females and males in a variety of roles—such as males performing domestic tasks and women being pilots and physicians.

Sharing of domestic tasks and child-rearing responsibilities is fundamental to achieving equality between the sexes.

emotions they really feel. If a male wants to be a cook or an elementary school teacher and a female wants to be a soldier or an athlete—and they're good at it—then it is functional for society if both develop their talents and are allowed to achieve everything they're capable of.

SEXISM AND SOCIAL WORK

Females have held, and currently do hold, a number of leadership positions in social work, serving as deans of graduate schools, chairs of undergraduate social work programs, directors of agencies, and presidents of national, state, and local social work organizations. There have also been a vast number of female authors of social work texts and professional journal articles. However,

overall, males predominate in leadership positions in social work.

Because 69% of social workers are female, there is the notion that social work is a female-dominated profession.[79] Some other statistics suggest otherwise. David Fanshel, in a study of NASW members, found that the proportion of men in leadership positions (for example, in administration) was twice that of women.[80] In addition, about half of social work faculty members in the United States are men.[81] Juliana Szakacs compiled statistics on leadership positions by gender in federally funded, private, nonprofit organizations and found that over 80% were held by men.[82]

Salaries of male social workers tend to be substantially higher than those of female social workers.[83] One reason for this discrepancy is that men are more likely to hold administrative positions, which are higher paying, whereas women work predominantly in direct-practice positions. In 1988 Anne Fortune and Lou Hanks conducted a study of 520 recently graduated master's-level social workers.[84] Other relevant factors affecting salary (such as age, experience, and marital status) were controlled. Initial salaries were comparable between men and women at the point of hiring, but the researchers found that men moved into nonclinical positions (supervision and administration) earlier in their careers and within a few years were earning more than women. The authors conclude: "There is little evidence that social work has improved the inequities between men and women in its own ranks."[85]

Social Work's Response to Women's Issues

There is evidence that the profession is responding to women's issues. In 1973 the Delegate Assembly of NASW added sexism to poverty and racism as basic concerns and priorities for the profession. The Council on Social Work Education (CSWE) has required in accreditation standards for baccalaureate and master's programs that content on women's issues be included throughout the curriculum. CSWE also has an accreditation standard that prohibits gender discrimination in social work educational programs and mandates affirmative action programs for women administrators, faculty, students, and staff in social work educational programs.

The NASW Legal Defense Fund has provided financial support in sex discrimination cases. In addition, NASW supported the Equal Rights Amendment and is working on other issues related to sexism.

In practice there is some truth that social work has an emphasis on serving women, because a majority of social work clients are women. About three-fourths of all people receiving public assistance and welfare payments are females.[86] Because women still primarily care for children, they are the main users of child welfare services. They are more likely to seek and receive counseling, and they are the major consumers of services for the aged. In addition, females are the primary consumers of family planning, pregnancy counseling, abortion services, rape crisis services, services from shelters for battered wives, and displaced homemaker services.

There are a number of reasons why more women than men are social work clients. For one thing, women outnumber men in the United States. Julia B. Rauch identifies another reason: "Most women in this country are socialized to accept weakness and dependence with more ease than men. The role of client is compatible with behaviors expected of women but is not congruent with men's expectations of themselves.[87] Women tend to need more services because poverty is a problem that disproportionately affects them; women who work full time are paid substantially less than men who work full time. Women also have higher rates of unemployment and are much more likely to be single heads of households.

Rauch summarizes a number of additional reasons why women are more likely to be social work clients:

> . . . teenage and unwanted pregnancies, postpartum depression, and sexual dysfunction; the need, resulting from the concentration of parenting functions in women's hands, for services for mothers who abuse or neglect their children and for the mothers of emotionally disturbed, learning disabled, mentally retarded, blind, or otherwise handicapped children; women's vulnerability to wife abuse and rape; the limitations of the wife-mother role and the "empty nest" syndrome; the practical and emotional stresses for women of separation or divorce and the difficulties of raising children alone; and the norm that women marry older men, which, in combination with women's longer life expectancy leads to widowhood and the stresses of bereavement, loss of the role of wife, and loneliness.[88]

It is important for social workers to understand that the traditional socialization process and the sex-role stereotypes in our society account for many of the problems that confront female, as well as male, clients. Workers should be skilled in helping clients to actualize themselves and to overcome rigid sex-role stereotypes. As noted earlier, many interaction problems between males and females in our society are consequences of sex-role stereotyping. One therapy approach that is being widely used to help both men and women express themselves more effectively and gain skills in countering sex-role stereotypes is assertiveness training (described later in this chapter). Consciousness-raising groups, largely with women, are helping clients to become more aware of sex-role stereotypes, to establish a better self-concept, and to foster contact with others who are also working to end sexism.

The growing awareness of sexism and women's issues has led to the provision of improved services to groups that had been largely ignored: victims of rape, battered wives, women seeking abortions, husbands and wives with marital concerns, people with sexual dysfunctions, single-parent households headed by women, and displaced homemakers.[89]

The Feminist Perspective on Therapy

Female social work authors have made substantial contributions to developing the feminist perspective on therapy. This perspective has been explored by a number of writers, including Nan Van Den Bergh and L. Cooper.[90]

Feminism is a multifaceted concept that is difficult to accurately define. Barker has defined it as "the social movement and doctrine advocating legal and socioeconomic equality for women."[91] Barker further defines "feminist social work" as "the integration of the *values*, skills, and knowledge of social work with a feminist orientation to help individuals and society overcome the emotional and social problems that result from *sex discrimination*."[92] Barker has also defined "feminist therapy":

> *A psychosocial treatment orientation in which the professional (usually a woman) helps the client (usually a woman) in individual or group settings to overcome the psychological and social problems largely encountered as a result of* sex discrimination *and sex role stereotyping. Feminist therapists help clients maximize potential, especially through* consciousness-raising, *eliminating sex stereotyping, and helping them become aware of the commonalities shared by all women.*[93]

The following nine principles of feminist intervention have been identified.[94]

1. A client's problems should be viewed within a sociopolitical framework. Feminist intervention is concerned with the inequitable power relationships between women and men and is opposed to all "power-over" relationships, regardless of gender, race, class, age, and so on. Such relationships lead to oppression and domination. Feminism seeks to change all social, economic, and political structures based on relationships between "haves" and "have-nots." Another way of stating this principle is that "personal is political." Van Den Bergh comments:

> *This principle maintains that what a woman experiences in her personal life is directly related to societal dynamics that affect other women. In other words, an individual woman's experiences of pejorative comments based on sex and of blocked opportunities are directly related to societal sexism. For ethnic minority women, racism and classism also are factors that affect well being.*[95]

A primary distinguishing characteristic of feminist treatment is helping the client to analyze how her problems are related to systematic difficulties experienced by women in a sexist, classist, and racist society.

2. Traditional sex roles are pathological, and clients need encouragement to free themselves from traditional gender-role bonds. Traditionally, women have been socialized to fill a "learned helplessness" role. Van Den Bergh describes the effects of such sex-role stereotyping:

> *Sex-role stereotypes suggest that women should be submissive, docile, receptive, and dependent. The message is one of helplessness; that women cannot take care of themselves and are dependent upon others for their well being. This sets up a dynamic in which a woman's locus of control is external to her self, preventing her from believing that she can acquire what she needs on her own in order to develop and self-actualize. In other words, oversubscription to sex-role stereotypes engenders a state of powerlessness in which a woman is likely to become involved in situations where she becomes victimized. . . . For example, because young girls are socialized to be helpless, when they become women they tend to have a limited repertoire of responses when under stress; e.g., they respond passively.*[96]

In feminist treatment, clients are helped to see that, by internalizing traditional sex roles, they have set themselves up to play passive, submissive roles and to experience low self-esteem and self-hatred. The feminist approach encourages clients to make their own choices and to pursue the tasks and goals they desire, rather than being constrained by traditional sex roles.

3. Intervention should focus on client empowerment. Van Den Bergh describes the empowerment process:

> *Helping women to acquire a sense of power, or the ability to affect outcomes in their lives, is a crucial component of feminist practice. Empowerment means acquiring knowledge, skills, and resources that enhance an individual's ability to control her own life and*

to influence others. Traditionally women have used indirect, covert techniques to get what they want, such as helplessness, dependency, coyness, and demureness.[97]

Empowerment can be fostered in a variety of ways: (1) by helping the client to define her own needs and clarify her personal goals so that she can then derive a sense of purposefulness; (2) by providing the client with education and access to resources; (3) by helping the client to believe that the ability to change lies within herself—that alterations in her life will result only from her own undertakings; and (4) by focusing on the identification and enhancement of the client's strengths rather than pathologies. Empowered women are ones who have learned to control their environments in order to get what they need.

4. The self-esteem of clients should be enhanced. Self-esteem and self-confidence are essential for empowerment. The worker should seek to be an encouraging person (as described in Chapter 3), helping clients to identify and recognize their unique qualities and strengths. Many clients with low self-esteem tend to blame themselves for everything that is wrong. For example, a battered woman typically blames herself for being battered. Such clients need to look more realistically at those areas in which they are blaming themselves and feeling guilt so they can distinguish where their responsibility for dysfunctional interactions ends and other individuals' begins.

5. Clients should be encouraged to develop their identity (sense of self) based on their own strengths, attributes, interests, and achievements. It is a serious mistake for women to define themselves in terms of their husbands or boyfriends, their children, their friends, or their relatives. Women need an independent identity that is not based on their relationships with others.

6. Clients need to value other women and to develop social support systems with them. In a society that devalues women, it is all too easy for some females to view other females as insignificant. With social support systems, women can vent their concerns and share their experiences and the solutions they've found to similar problems. They can serve as brokers in identifying resources, and they can provide emotional support and nurturance to one another.

7. Clients need to find an effective balance between work and personal relationships. Feminist intervention encourages both women and men to share in the nurturant aspects of their lives and in providing economic resources.

8. The nature of the relationship between practitioner and client should approach equality as much as possible. Feminist practitioners view themselves not as experts in resolving clients' problems but as catalysts in helping clients empower themselves. Feminist practitioners seek to eliminate dominant/submissive relationships. On this topic Van Den Bergh notes:

> *Obviously, there is an innate power differential between practitioner and client because the former has expertise and training as an "authority." However, the feminist admonition is to avoid abusing that status; "abuse" in this sense might be, for example, taking all credit for client change, or using terminology and nomenclature that are difficult for the client to understand.*[98]

9. Clients should be helped to express themselves assertively. (The steps in assertiveness training are described in Exhibit 12.7.) As indicated earlier, many women are socialized to be passive and nonassertive. Through individual and group counseling, clients can become more assertive, which will increase their self-confidence and self-esteem. They will be better able to communicate their thoughts, feelings, and opinions. Also, learning to express oneself is an important component in empowerment.

Many women feel anger over being victimized by sex discrimination and gender stereotyping. Some of these women turn their angry feelings inward, which often results in depression. Assertiveness training can help such women to recognize that they have a right to be angry; it can also help them identify and practice constructive ways of expressing their anger (that is, assertively rather than aggressively).

EXHIBIT 12.7

Assertiveness Training

Do you handle put-downs well? Are you reluctant to express your feelings and opinions openly and honestly in a group? Are you frequently timid in interacting with people in positions of authority? Do you react well to criticism? Do you sometimes explode in anger when things go wrong, or are you able to remain calm? Do you find it difficult to maintain eye contact when talking? If you are uncomfortable with someone smoking near you, do you express your feelings? Are you timid in arranging a date or social event? For anyone who has trouble in any of these situations, there is, fortunately, a useful technique—assertiveness training—that enables people to become more effective in interpersonal interactions.

Assertiveness problems range from extreme shyness, introversion, and withdrawal to inappropriate rage that results in alienating others. A nonassertive person is often acquiescent, fearful, and afraid of expressing his or her real, spontaneous feelings in a variety of situations. Frequently, resentment and anxiety build up, resulting in general discomfort, feelings of low self-esteem, tension headaches, fatigue, and perhaps a destructive explosion of temper, anger, and aggression. Some people are overly shy and timid in nearly all interactions. Most of us, however, encounter occasional problems in isolated matters in which it would be to our benefit to be more assertive. For example, a bachelor may be quite effective and assertive in his job as a store manager but still be awkward and timid while attempting to arrange a date.

There are three basic styles of interacting with others: nonassertive, aggressive, and assertive. Characteristics of these styles have been summarized by Robert Alberti and Michael Emmons:

> *In the* non-assertive style, *you are likely to hesitate, speak softly, look away, avoid the issue, agree regardless of your own feelings, not express opinions, value yourself "below" others, and hurt yourself to avoid any chance of hurting others.*
>
> *In the* aggressive style, *you typically answer before the other person is through talking, speak loudly and abusively, glare at the other person, speak "past" the issue (accusing, blaming, demeaning), vehemently expound your feelings and opinions, value yourself "above" others, and hurt others to avoid hurting yourself.*
>
> *In the* assertive style, *you will answer spontaneously, speak with a conversational tone and volume, look at the other person, speak to the issue, openly express your personal feelings and opinions (anger, love, disagreement, sorrow), value yourself equal to others, and hurt neither yourself nor others.*[a]

EXAMPLES OF BEHAVIOR

You are driving with an acquaintance to another city to attend a conference. The acquaintance lights up a pipe, and you soon find the smoke irritating and the odor somewhat stifling. What are your choices?

1. Nonassertive response: you attempt to carry on a "cheery" conversation for the three-hour trip without commenting about the smoke.

2. Aggressive response: you become increasingly irritated, finally exploding "Either you put out that pipe, or I'll put it out for you—the odor is sickening."

3. Assertive response: you look directly at the acquaintance and in a firm, conversational tone state "The smoke from your pipe is irritating me. I'd appreciate it if you put it away."

---

[a]Robert E. Alberti and Michael L. Emmons, *Stand Up, Speak Out, Talk Back!* (New York: Pocket Books, 1975), p. 24.

(continued)

EXHIBIT 12.7   *(continued)*

At a party with friends, during small-talk conversation, your husband gives you a subtle put-down by stating "Wives always talk too much." What do you do?

1. Nonassertive response: you don't say anything but feel hurt and become quiet.

2. Aggressive response: you glare at him and angrily ask "John, why are you always criticizing me?"

3. Assertive response: you carry on as usual, wait until the drive home, and then calmly look at him and say "When we were at the party tonight, you said that wives always talk too much. I felt you were putting me down when you said that. What did you mean by that comment?"

BEING ASSERTIVE

Simply stated, assertive behavior is expressing yourself without hurting or stepping on others. Assertiveness training is designed to help us realize, feel, and act on the assumption that we have the right to be ourselves and to express our feelings freely. Assertive responses generally are not aggressive responses. The distinction between these two types of interactions is important. If, for example, a wife has an overly critical mother-in-law, aggressive responses by the wife would include ridiculing the mother-in-law, intentionally doing things that she knows will upset the mother-in-law (not visiting, serving the type of food the mother-in-law dislikes, not cleaning the house), urging the husband to tell his mother to "shut up," and getting into loud verbal arguments with the mother-in-law. On the other hand, an effective assertive response would be to counter criticism by saying: "Jane, your criticism of me deeply hurts me. I know you're trying to help me when you give advice, but I feel when you do that you're criticizing me. I know you don't want me to make mistakes. But, to grow, I need to make

my own errors and learn from them. If you want to help me the most, let me do it myself and be responsible for the consequences. The type of relationship that I'd like to have with you is a close, adult relationship and not a mother/child relationship."

The steps for learning to become more assertive are as follows:[b]

1. Examine your interactions. Are there situations that you need to handle more assertively? Do you at times hold opinions and feelings within you for fear of what would happen if you expressed them? Do you occasionally lash out angrily at others? Studying your interactions is facilitated by keeping a diary for a week or longer. Record the situations in which you acted timidly, those in which you were aggressive, and those that you handled assertively.

2. Select those interactions in which it would be to your benefit to be more assertive. They may include situations in which you were overpolite or overly apologetic. Or perhaps you were timid and allowed others to take advantage of you, at the same time harboring feelings of resentment, anger, embarrassment, fear of others, or self-criticism for not having the courage to express yourself. Overly aggressive interactions in which you exploded in anger or walked over others also need to be dealt with. For *each* set of nonassertive or aggressive interactions, you can become more assertive, as shown in the next steps.

3. Concentrate on a specific incident in the past

---

[b]These self-training steps are a modification of assertiveness-training programs developed by Robert E. Alberti and Michael L. Emmons, *Your Perfect Right* (San Luis Obispo, CA: Impact, 1970), and by Herbert Fensterheim and Jean Baer, *Don't Say Yes When You Want to Say No* (New York: Dell, 1975).

(continued)

EXHIBIT 12.7 *(continued)*

in which you were either nonassertive or aggressive. Close your eyes for a few minutes and vividly imagine the details, including what you and the other person said and how you felt at the time and afterward.

4. Write down and review your responses. Ask yourself the following questions to determine how you presented yourself:

   a. Eye contact: Did you look directly at the other person with a relaxed, steady gaze? Looking down or away suggests a lack of self-confidence. Glaring is an aggressive response.

   b. Gestures: Were your gestures appropriate, free-flowing, and relaxed? Did they emphasize your messages effectively? Awkward stiffness suggests nervousness; other gestures (such as an angry fist) signal an aggressive reaction.

   c. Body posture: Did you show the importance of your message by directly facing the other person, by leaning toward that person, by holding your head erect, and by sitting or standing appropriately close?

   d. Facial expressions: Did your facial expressions show a stern, firm pose consistent with an assertive response?

   e. Voice tone and volume: Was your response stated in a firm, conversational tone? Shouting may suggest anger. Speaking softly suggests shyness, and a cracking voice suggests nervousness. By tape recording and listening to your voice, you can practice increasing or decreasing the volume.

   f. Speech fluency: Did your speech flow smoothly, clearly, and slowly? Rapid speech or hesitation in speaking suggests nervousness. Tape recording assertive responses that you want to try out for problem situations is a way to improve fluency.

   g. Timing: Were your verbal reactions to a problem situation stated at the most appropriate time for you and the other person to review the incident? Generally, spontaneous expressions are best, but certain situations should be handled at a later time (for example, challenging some of your boss's erroneous statements in private rather than in front of a group she or he is making a presentation to).

   h. Message content: For a problem situation, which of your responses were nonassertive or aggressive, and which were assertive? Study the content and consider why you responded in a nonassertive or aggressive style.

5. Observe one or more effective models. Watch the verbal and nonverbal approaches that are assertively used to handle the type of interactions with which you are having problems. Compare the consequences of their approach and yours. If possible, discuss their approach and their feelings about using it.

6. Make a list of various alternative approaches for being more assertive.

7. Close your eyes and visualize yourself using each of these alternative approaches. For each approach, think through what the full set of interactions would be, along with the consequences. Select an approach, or combination of approaches, that you believe will be most effective for you to use. Through imagery, practice this approach until you feel comfortable that it will work for you.

8. Role-play the approach with someone else, perhaps a friend or counselor. If certain segments of your approach appear clumsy, awkward, timid, or aggressive, practice modifications until you become comfortable with the approach. Obtain feedback from the other person about the strengths and shortcomings of your approach. Compare your

(continued)

EXHIBIT 12.7 *(continued)*

interactions to the verbal/nonverbal guidelines for assertive behavior in step 4. It may be useful for the other person to model through role playing one or more assertive strategies, which you would then, by reversing roles, practice using.

9. Repeat steps 7 and 8 until you develop an assertive approach that you believe will work best for you and that you are comfortable with.

10. Use your approach in a real-life situation. The previous steps are designed to prepare you for the real event. Expect to be somewhat anxious when first trying to be assertive. If you are still too fearful of attempting to be assertive, repeat steps 5 through 8. For those few individuals who fail to develop the needed confidence to try out being assertive, professional counseling is advised, because expressing yourself effectively in interactions with others is essential for personal happiness.

11. Reflect on the effectiveness of your effort. Did you remain calm? Getting angry at times is a normal human emotion, and it needs to be expressed. However, the anger should be expressed in a constructive, assertive fashion. When expressed in a destructive, lashing-out fashion, it violates the rights of others. Considering the nonverbal/verbal guidelines for assertive behavior discussed in step 4, what components of your responses were assertive, aggressive, and nonassertive? What were the consequences of your effort? How did you feel after trying out this new set of interactions? If possible, discuss how you did in regard to these questions with a friend who may have observed the interactions.

12. Expect some success but not complete personal satisfaction with your initial efforts. Experiencing personal growth and interacting more effectively with others will be a continual learning process. Quite appropriately, "pat yourself on the back" for the strengths of your approach—you earned it. But also note the areas in which you need to improve, and use the above steps for improving your assertiveness efforts.

These steps systematically make sense but are not to be followed rigidly. Each person has to develop a process that works best for himself or herself.

The structure of this technique is relatively simple to understand. Considerable skill (common sense and ingenuity), however, is needed to determine what will be an effective assertive strategy when a real-life situation arises. The joy and pride derived from being able to express oneself assertively are truly life enriching.

Source: From "How to Become More Assertive," by Charles Zastrow, pp. 236–240, in Charles Zastrow and Dae Change (eds.), *The Personal Problem Solver.* Copyright © 1977 Spectrum Books. Reprinted by permission of Prentice-Hall, Englewood Cliffs, New Jersey.

FUTURE DIRECTIONS OF THE WOMEN'S MOVEMENT

Within the women's movement there is currently much debate over policy directions.[99] The conservative trend of the 1980s and early 1990s jeopardized some of the progress that feminists made during the 1960s and 1970s. Both President Ronald and Nancy Reagan, as well as most members of the Reagan cabinet, opposed the Equal Rights Amendment, and it eventually failed to be ratified. The conservative movement and the Reagan and Bush administrations put less emphasis on enforcing affirmative action programs and actively opposed the concept of setting quotas for the percentage of minorities that must be hired by employers. There also were cuts in a number of social programs that the women's movement vigorously supported, such as funding for public day care, sex education, and contraception.

Bill Clinton, who was elected president in 1992, has a more liberal orientation than Reagan and Bush. His wife, Hillary, has been very active in policymaking decisions and is viewed by many as being a role model for contemporary women. President Clinton has appointed a number of feminists to high-level government positions and has supported the feminist position on several social issues, such as the abortion debate and universal health insurance coverage.

The National Organization for Women (NOW) has been united in its determination to fight efforts to prohibit abortions. The women's movement views access to abortions as a basic right of women to decide what happens to their bodies and to their lives.

Women burdened by unwanted children often become dependent on their partners or on welfare and are unable to compete with men in the job market. In a key 1989 abortion decision, *Webster v. Reproductive Health Services,* the U.S. Supreme Court gave indications that it may be backing away from its previous position, passed down in *Roe* v. *Wade* in 1972, which held that women had a right to obtain an abortion in the first trimester of their pregnancy.[100] This 1989 decision gave states the right to pass certain laws regulating abortions. The broader effect of the Court's decision is to throw this hot political issue back to state legislatures. Feminists are hopeful that Clinton will have the opportunity to appoint justices with "pro-choice" views to the Supreme Court, thereby preserving the basic provisions of *Roe* v. *Wade.*

There is also a debate in the women's movement about whether traditional roles held by women should be devalued. Advocates for modern roles emphasize equality and careers, yet some leaders of NOW assert that the role of homemaker should be given equal respect.

One of the directions that the women's movement is taking is to seek help for single-parent families, particularly low-income, female-headed families. There has been a feminization of poverty in this country, and an increasing proportion of

Hillary Rodham Clinton has taken a high-profile role in her husband's administration. Here she testifies before the Senate Labor and Human Resources Committee in 1993 regarding medical costs and lack of insurance among American families.

poor people are women. It is almost impossible for single mothers to be "financially equal" to males in the job market when day care is highly expensive and when women who work full time are paid considerably less than men who work full time. The women's movement is certain to continue to advocate for increased financial support by the federal government for child care.

The women's movement has also been advocating for "comparable worth." Comparable worth involves the concept of "equal pay for comparable work" rather than "equal pay for equal work." Comparable worth asserts that the intrinsic value of different jobs, such as that of a secretary or plumber, can be measured. Those jobs that are evaluated to be of comparable value should receive comparable pay. If implemented, it is believed that the concept will reduce the disparities in pay between women and men who work full time. Goodman found that jobs held mainly by women pay an average of 20% below equivalent jobs held mainly by men.[101] Some states (such as Wisconsin and Washington) have initiated efforts to develop comparable worth programs for state employees.

Another direction that the women's movement is taking is to encourage and support female candidates for public offices at federal, state, and local levels. The women's movement recognizes that achieving social equality depends partly on moving toward political equality.

The women's movement has made important gains in improving the status of women in our society in the past three decades. It is clear that its general thrust toward equality will continue.

SUMMARY

In almost every known society women have had a lower status that men. Women have traditionally been assigned housework and child-rearing responsibilities and have been socialized to be passive, submissive, and feminine. The socialization process and sex-role stereotyping have led to a number of problems. There is sex discrimination in employment, with men who work full time being paid substantially more than women who work full time. There are double standards of conduct for males and females. There are power struggles between males and females because men are socialized to be dominant in interactions with women, whereas women often seek egalitarian relationships. Sex-role stereotyping and the traditional female role have led women to be unhappier in marriages and to be more depressed.

Sex-role stereotyping is pervasive in our society, with aspects being found in child-rearing practices, the educational system, religion, contemporary psychological theories, our language, the mass media, the business world, marriage and family patterns, and our political system.

The women's movement, which had a resurgence in the 1960s, is working to eliminate sex-role stereotypes and is revolutionizing the socialization process. A number of laws forbidding sex discrimination have been enacted. Women as well as men are now pursuing new careers and are taking on roles and tasks that run counter to traditional sex stereotypes. The androgyny notion is gaining strength. Androgynous people explore a broad range of role-playing possibilities and express emotions and behaviors without regard to sex-role stereotypes.

Interestingly, the women's movement also has had many payoffs for males. Men experience extreme difficulties and encounter many problems in trying to fulfill the stereotypes of the model-man role—to always be dominant and strong, to never be depressed or anxious, to hide emotions, to be the provider, to be self-reliant and aggressive, and to never cry. Men are gradually realizing that this stereotypical role limits their opportunities in terms of interpersonal relationships, occupations, emotional expression, and domestic activities. Sex-role stereotyping has huge costs for women, for men, and for society. True sexual equality simply means that people would be free to be themselves.

The social work profession has made commitments to eliminate sexism, both within its own ranks and in the broader society. Although 69% of practicing social workers are female, more males are concentrated in administrative and other leadership positions in social work. Most social work clients are women. Social workers need to become skilled in helping clients to actualize themselves and to stop being negatively influenced by sex-role stereotypes.

NOTES

1. John E. Farley, *American Social Problems,* 2d ed. (Englewood Cliffs, NJ: Prentice-Hall, 1992) p. 140.
2. Ibid.
3. U.S. Bureau of the Census, *Statistical Abstract of the United States, 1992* (Washington, D.C.: U.S. Government Printing Office, 1992), pp. 451–457.
4. Ibid., pp. 447–452.
5. Jean Stockard and Miriam M. Johnson, *Sex Roles*

(Englewood Cliffs, NJ: Prentice-Hall, 1980), pp. 19–42.

6. Joseph H. Fichter and Virginia K. Mills, "The Status of Women in American Churches," *Church and Society* (September-October 1972).

7. Thomas Sullivan, Kenrick Thompson, Richard Wright, George Gross, and Dale Spady, *Social Problems* (New York: Wiley, 1980), p. 452.

8. Francine D. Blair, "Women in the Labor Force: An Overview," in *Women: A Feminist Perspective,* Jo Freeman, ed. (Palo Alto, CA: Mayfield, 1979), p. 272.

9. John Money, J. G. Hampson, and J. L. Hampson, "An Examination of Some Basic Sexual Concepts: The Evidence of Human Hermaphroditism," *Bulletin of the John Hopkins Hospital* (1955), pp. 301–309.

10. H. L. Rheingold and K. V. Cook, "The Contents of Boys' and Girls' Rooms as an Index of Parents' Behavior," *Child Development,* 46 (June 1975), p. 461.

11. Eleanor Maccoby and Carol Jacklin, *The Psychology of Sex Differences* (Stanford, CA: Stanford University Press, 1974).

12. Ibid.

13. Clarice Stasz Stoll, ed., *Sexism: Scientific Debates* (Reading, MA: Addison-Wesley, 1973).

14. Warren Farrell, *The Liberated Man* (New York: Random House, 1975).

15. Sullivan et al., *Social Problems,* p. 455.

16. Betty Friedan, *The Feminine Mystique* (New York: Dell, 1963).

17. Paul R. Horton, Gerald R. Leslie, and Richard F. Larson, *The Sociology of Social Problems,* 9th ed. (Englewood Cliffs, NJ: Prentice-Hall, 1988), p. 252.

18. Ibid., pp. 255–260.

19. William Kornblum and Joseph Julian, *Social Problems,* 6th ed. (Englewood Cliffs, NJ: Prentice-Hall, 1989), p. 312.

20. Horton et al., *The Sociology of Social Problems,* pp. 253–255.

21. Sullivan et al., *Social Problems,* pp. 475–476.

22. Horton et al., *The Sociology of Social Problems,* pp. 253–255.

23. "$2 Million Settlement is Reported in Women's Bias Suit against NBC," New York Times, Feb. 13, 1977.

24. Kornblum and Julian, *Social Problems,* p. 313.

25. "ERA Stalled, But Women Make Piecemeal Gains," *U.S. News & World Report,* Aug. 20, 1979, p. 56.

26. Horton et al., *The Sociology of Social Problems,* p. 261.

27. Amy Saltzman, "Hands Off at the Office," *U.S. News & World Report,* Aug. 1, 1988, pp. 56–58.

28. Deborah S. David and Robert Brannon, eds., *The Forty-Nine Percent Majority: The Male Sex Role* (Reading, MA: Addison-Wesley, 1976).

29. Stockard and Johnson, *Sex Roles,* pp. 133–147.

30. Richard C. Friedman, Ralph M. Richart, and Raymond L. Vande Wiehe, eds., *Sex Differences in Behavior* (New York: Wiley, 1974).

31. See Shirly Weitz, *Sex Roles: Biological, Psychological, and Social Foundations* (New York: Oxford University Press, 1977); Betty Yorburg, *Sexual Identity: Sex Roles and Social Change* (New York: Wiley, 1974); and Michael Teitelbaum, ed., *Sex Roles: Social and Biological Perspectives* (New York: Doubleday Anchor, 1976).

32. Ibid.

33. Maccoby and Jacklin, *The Psychology of Sex Differences.*

34. Ibid.

35. John Money, Joan Hampson, and John Hampson, "Imprinting and the Establishment of Gender Role," *Archives of Neurology and Psychiatry,* 77 (March 1967), pp. 333–336; see also John Money and Anke A. Ehrhardt, *Man and Woman, Boy and Girl* (New York: New American Library, 1974); and Richard Green, *Sexual Identity Conflict in Children and Adults* (Baltimore: Penguin, 1975).

36. Clellan S. Ford and Frank Beach, *Patterns of Sexual Behavior* (New York: Harper & Row, 1951).

37. Allan Katcher, "The Discrimination of Sex Differences by Young Children," *Journal of Genetic Psychology,* 87 (September 1955), pp. 131–143.

38. Lawrence Kohlberg, "A Cognitive-Developmental Analysis of Children's Sex-Role Concepts and Attitudes," in *The Psychology of Sex Differences,* Maccoby and Jacklin, eds., pp. 82–173.

39. Ruth E. Hartley, "American Core Culture: Changes and Continuities," in *Sex Roles in Changing Society,* Georgene H. Seward and Robert C. Williamson, eds. (New York: Random House, 1970), pp. 140–141.

40. Ibid., p. 141.

41. Sullivan et al., *Social Problems,* pp. 460–465.

42. Charles H. Cooley, *Social Organization* (New York: Scribner's, 1909).

43. Matina Horner, "Fail: Bright Women," *Psychology Today* (November 1969), pp. 36–38; and Vivian Gornick, "Why Women Fear Success," *Ms.* (Spring 1972), pp. 50–53.

44. Janet S. Hyde, *Understanding Human Sexuality,* 4th ed. (New York: McGraw-Hill, 1990), p. 372.

45. *Statistical Abstract of the United States, 1992,* pp. 388–389.

46. Pam Maye and Sara McMillan, "Student Project," in *Masculine, Feminine or Human? An Overview of the Sociology of Sex Roles,* Janet Saltzman Chafetz, ed. (Itasca, IL: Peacock, 1974).

47. Lenore Weitzman et al., "Sex Role Socialization in Picture Books for Preschool Children," *American*

Journal of Sociology, 72 (May 1972), pp. 1125–1150; and Sullivan et al., *Social Problems,* p. 463.

48. Florence Howe, "Sexual Stereotypes Start Early," *Saturday Review,* Oct. 16, 1971, p. 82.

49. Chafetz, *Masculine, Feminine, or Human?,* p. 69.

50. Viola Klein, *The Feminine Character: History of an Ideology* (Urbana: University of Illinois Press, 1975).

51. Sigmund Freud, *A General Introduction to Psychoanalysis* (New York: Boni & Liveright, 1924).

52. Farley, *American Social Problems,* p. 140.

53. Horton et al., *Sociology of Social Problems,* p. 258.

54. Farley, *American Social Problems,* pp. 140–145.

55. *Statistical Abstract of the United States, 1992,* pp. 268–275.

56. Farley, *American Social Problems,* pp. 140–145.

57. Ann M. Morrison, "Up against a Glass Ceiling," *Los Angeles Times,* Aug. 23, 1987, sec. 1, p. 3.

58. Kornblum and Julian, *Social Problems,* p. 293.

59. James W. Coleman and Donald R. Cressey, *Social Problems,* 5th ed. (New York: HarperCollins, 1993), pp. 262–265.

60. Sullivan et al., *Social Problems,* p. 468.

61. Coleman and Cressey, *Social Problems,* pp. 262–265.

62. Hyde, *Understanding Human Sexuality,* pp. 366–375.

63. Horton et al., *The Sociology of Social Problems,* p. 258.

64. Ibid.

65. Jessie Bernard, "The Paradox of the Happy Marriage," in *Women in Sexist Society,* Vivian Gonick and Barbara K. Moran, eds. (New York: Basic Books, 1971), pp. 145–162.

66. Hyde, *Understanding Human Sexuality,* pp. 378–382.

67. Carol Tavris and Carole Offir, *The Longest War: Sex Differences in Perspective* (New York: Harcourt Brace Jovanovich, 1976), p. 223.

68. Matina S. Horner, "Femininity and Successful Achievement: A Basic Inconsistency," in *Feminine Personality and Conflict,* Judith M. Bardwich, ed. (Pacific Grove, CA: Brooks/Cole, 1970).

69. David and Brannon, *The Forty-Nine Percent Majority,* pp. 53–54.

70. Hartley, "American Core Culture," p. 142.

71. U.S. Bureau of the Census, *Statistical Abstract of the United States, 1992.*

72. Ibid., pp. 374–384.

73. Carl Glassman, "How Lady Cops Are Doing," *Parade,* July 27, 1980, pp. 4–5.

74. Jack Sawyer, "On Male Liberation," in *Men and Masculinity,* Joseph H. Pleck and Jack Sawyer, eds. (Englewood Cliffs, NJ: Prentice-Hall, 1974), p. 172.

75. *Statistical Abstract of the United States, 1992.*

76. Sullivan et al., *Social Problems,* p. 474.

77. Kornblum and Julian, *Social Problems,* p. 316.

78. Hyde, *Understanding Human Sexuality,* pp. 383–385.

79. *Statistical Abstract of the United States, 1992,* pp. 403–405.

80. David Fanshel, "Status Differentials: Men and Women in Social Work," *Social Work,* 21 (November 1976), pp. 450–451.

81. Julia B. Rauch, "Gender as a Factor in Practice," in *Social Work: A Profession of Many Faces,* Armando Morales and Bradford W. Sheafor, eds. (Boston: Allyn & Bacon, 1989), pp. 335–350.

82. Juliana Szakacs, "Is Social Work a Woman's Profession?" *Womanpower: A Quarterly Newsletter of the Committee on Women in Social Welfare* (February 1977), p. 3.

83. Anne Fortune and Lou Hanks, "Gender Inequities in Early Social Worker Careers," *Social Work,* 33, no. 3 (May–June 1988), pp. 221–225.

84. Ibid.

85. Ibid., p. 225.

86. Rauch, "Gender as a Factor in Practice," pp. 340–342.

87. Ibid., p. 342.

88. Ibid., pp. 343–344.

89. Ketayun H. Gould, "Sexism," in *Contemporary Social Work,* 2d ed., Donald Brieland, Lela Costin, and Charles Atherton, eds. (New York: McGraw-Hill, 1980), pp. 427–428.

90. Nan Van Den Bergh and L. B. Cooper, "Feminist Social Work," in *The Encyclopedia of Social Work* (Washington, DC: NASW, 1987), pp. 610–618.

91. R. L. Barker, *The Social Work Dictionary,* 2d ed. (Silver Spring, MD: NASW, 1991), p. 82.

92. Ibid., p. 83.

93. Ibid.

94. Van Den Bergh and Cooper, "Feminist Social Work," pp. 610–618; Nan Van Den Bergh, "Feminist Treatment for People with Depression," in *Structuring Change,* K. Corcoran, ed. (Chicago: Lyceum, 1992), pp. 95–110; and K. K. Kirst Ashman & G. H. Hull, Jr., *Understanding Generalist Practice,* (Chicago: Nelson-Hall, 1993), pp. 422–463.

95. Van Den Bergh, "Feminist Treatment for People with Depression," p. 103.

96. Ibid., p. 101

97. Ibid., p. 104.

98. Ibid.

99. Kornblum and Julian, *Social Problems,* pp. 315–316.

100. Hyde, *Understanding Human Sexuality,* p. 630.

101. W. Goodman, "Equal Pay for 'Comparable Worth' Growing as Job-Discrimination Issue," *New York Times,* Sept. 4, 1988, p. B9.

13

AGING

AND

GERONTOLOGICAL

SERVICES

The plight of the elderly, so long overlooked, has now become recognized as a major social problem in the United States. The elderly face a number of social and personal problems: high rates of physical illness and emotional difficulties, poverty, malnutrition, lack of access to transportation, low status, lack of a meaningful role in our society, and inadequate housing. To a large extent the elderly are a "recently discovered" minority group. Like other minority groups they are victims of job discrimination, are excluded from the mainstream of American life on the basis of supposed group characteristics, and are subjected to prejudice that is based on erroneous stereotypes.

This chapter will:

- Describe the specific problems faced by the elderly.
- Explore the causes of these problems.
- Discuss current services to meet these problems.
- Note gaps in current services.
- Describe the role of social work in providing services to the elderly.
- Discuss social and political changes needed to improve the status of the elderly.

AN OVERVIEW

Tom Townsend has no serious financial concerns, at least at present (see Case Example 13.1). Gordon and Walter Moss describe the plight of someone who is old and poor.

Some traditional societies have abandoned their elderly because of scarce resources. We can take comfort in the fact that our society is more enlightened, but we've found our own ways of neglecting our older citizens.

An old woman turned quickly away from the dismal scene outside her Florida hotel room window. Listlessly, she mixed her own breakfast: a cup of Sanka and a small glass of Tang. After finishing her breakfast, she looked at her wardrobe. It contained a few unwanted dresses given to her by a relative, and one she had bought herself seven years ago. After choosing one, she made her bed and dusted her dresser, two small tables, and their lamps. She then turned on a small fan in anticipation of a hot
muggy day, wound her clock, straightened her small pile of old books, blew dust from the artificial flowers in a cheap vase, and sat down in her only chair to watch television. Finally, it was noon, time for her to go down to the church for a hot lunch. In the afternoon, she would watch television soap operas, or perhaps spend an hour or two visiting with the many other widows in the hotel.

All the while, uncertainty gnawed at her. Already she was paying over half of her small retirement and welfare income for rent; and if the rent went up any more she would be unable to stay. The hot lunch, sponsored by the federal

CASE EXAMPLE 13.1 The Best Years of Your Life

Tom Townsend had been with the iron works plant for 42 years. Being promoted to foreman 16 years ago had fulfilled his dreams, and there was nothing he wanted more than to be on the job and managing his crew. He has been married to Laura for the past 37 years. At first their marriage had some rough moments, but Laura and Tom grew accustomed to and comfortable with each other over the years. They have a traditional view of the role of women in society. Her main job has always been to maintain the home. They have two grown children who have moved away and now have homes of their own.

Life was at the factory for Tom. He didn't have time to develop other hobbies and interests; nor was he interested in picnics or socials. When he had time off from work, he used it to repair things around the house and to "tool up" for getting back to work. Television replaced talk in his home, and Tom usually spent weekends watching a variety of sports programs.

On May 18, Tom turned 70. The company marked the occasion with a retirement dinner that was well attended. Tom and Laura were there, along with their children and families, the members of Tom's crew and their wives, and the company managers and their wives. At first everyone was a little anxious, because these people did not often get together with one another socially. The dinner, however, went fairly well. Tom was congratulated by everyone, received a gold watch, and made appropriate remarks about his years with the company. After a few more cocktails, everyone went home. Tom was feeling sentimental but also quite good about himself because everyone was acknowledging his contributions.

Tom awoke at 7 o'clock the next morning—the usual time for him to get ready for work. Then it hit him. He was retired, with nowhere to go and no reason to get up. His life at the plant was over. What should he do now? He didn't know.

He spent the next week following Laura around the house, getting on her nerves. At times he complained about feeling useless. Twice he commented that he wished he were dead. He went back to the plant to see his men, but they were too busy to talk. Besides, Bill, who had been promoted to foreman, delighted in showing Tom how the department's productivity had increased and bored Tom with his plans for making changes to increase production further.

Long walks didn't help much, either. As he walked, he thought about his plight and became more depressed. What was he going to do? What could he find to occupy his time meaningfully? He looked into a mirror and saw his receding hairline and numerous wrinkles. More and more, he started to feel a variety of aches and pains. He thought to himself "I guess I'm just a useless old man." He wondered what the future would hold. Would his company pension keep pace with increasing bills? Would he eventually be placed in a nursing home? What was he going to do with the remainder of his life? He just didn't know.

government, cost her only 50 cents and helped a little. Nevertheless, due especially to medical bills, she frequently ran out of money before the end of the month.

Her ulcer was her biggest worry. A few weeks earlier, it had started to bleed, and she had passed out. She had lain helpless for some time before finally managing to crawl to the phone. The desk clerk and some friends had then helped her get to the hospital. She had been more fortunate than some others in the hotel. Their lives had ended in their rooms because they had been too weak from malnutrition to crawl for help.[1]

Do these two stories sound like sentimental fiction? We wish! Sadly, these accounts are typical retirements turned into nightmares.[2]

Throughout time some tribal societies have abandoned their enfeebled old. The Crow, Creek, and Hopi Indians, for example, built special huts away from the tribe where the old were left to die. The Eskimo left their incapacitated elderly in snowbanks or forced them to paddle away in a kayak. The Siriono of the Bolivian forest simply left them behind when they moved on in search of food.[3] Even today the Ik of Uganda leave the elderly and disabled to starve to death.[4] (Generally, the primary reason tribal societies have been forced to abandon the elderly is scarce resources.)

Although we might consider such customs shocking and barbaric, have we not also abandoned the old? We force them to retire when many are still productive. All too often, when a person is forced into retirement, his or her status, power, and self-esteem are lost. Also, in a physical sense we seldom have a place for large numbers of older people. Community facilities—parks, subways, libraries—are oriented to serving children and young people. Most housing is designed and priced for the young couple with one or two children and an annual income in excess of $30,000. If the elderly are not able to care for themselves (and if their families are unable to care for them), we "store" them away from society in nursing homes. Moreover, we do little to relieve the financial problems of the elderly; one-fifth of them have incomes close to or below the poverty line.[5]

(In a sense our abandonment of the elderly is more unethical than that of tribal societies who are motivated by survival pressures—we don't have such serious survival problems.)

A "RECENTLY DISCOVERED" MINORITY GROUP

Our society's treatment of the elderly has only recently come to be viewed as a major social problem. In effect, the elderly are a recently discovered minority group. Like other minority groups, they are subjected to job discrimination. The most striking example of age discrimination has been the practice of mandatory retirement, whereby people are forced to leave their jobs once they reach a certain age.

The legal retirement age used to be 65. In 1978 Congress enacted legislation that raised the age to 70 for most jobs. Then, in 1986, Congress (recognizing that mandatory retirement was overtly discriminatory against the elderly) outlawed most mandatory retirement policies.

The elderly are discriminated against in many ways. Older workers are erroneously believed to be less productive. Unemployed workers in their fifties and sixties have greater difficulty finding new jobs and remain unemployed much longer than younger unemployed workers. The elderly are given no meaningful role in our society.

Ours is a youth-oriented society that devalues old people. We glorify the body beautiful and physical attractiveness and thereby shortchange the elderly. Older persons are viewed as "out of touch with what's happening," and therefore their knowledge is seldom valued or sought. It is also erroneously believed that intellectual ability declines with age. Research shows, however, that intellectual capacity, barring organic problems, remains essentially unchanged until very late in life.[6]

The elderly are misperceived as senile, conservative, resistant to change, inflexible, incompetent and burdensome to the young. Given opportunities, elderly individuals usually prove such prejudicial concepts wrong.

The elderly generally react to prejudice against them in the same way that racial and ethnic minorities react—by displaying self-hatred and by being self-conscious, sensitive, and defensive about their social and cultural status.[7] (Cooley's looking glass self-concept suggests that, if individuals frequently receive negative responses from others, they will eventually come to view themselves negatively.)

DEFINITIONS OF LATER ADULTHOOD

Elizabeth Ferguson describes some of our myths and stereotypes about the elderly:

> Stereotyped notions about aging and the elderly exist in all segments of the population. Many of them are myths, but they are held tenaciously, and sound data to rebut them are scarce. The aging are generally thought to be less intelligent, less able to learn, more rigid, riskier as employees, less ambitious, and therefore more easily satisfied, less able to adapt and cope. How often these stereotypes turn into self-fulfilling prophecies is not known, but the existence of those who refute all the myths should be more widely publicized.[8]

On the other hand, the mass media portray some retired people as always traveling and playing golf, sunning themselves in warm climates in the winter, and being in good health and free of money worries. For the "young aging," particularly those in upper-income groups, there is some validity to this stereotype. But this is not the experience of most of the elderly in our society.

The social and physical needs of the elderly have only recently been recognized. In earlier societies few people survived to advanced ages. Life expectancy has increased dramatically in the United States since the turn of the 20th century— up from 49 years in 1900 to 76 years at present.[9]

EXHIBIT 13.1

Age Need Not Be a Barrier to Making Major Contributions

- At age 77 Ronald Reagan was President of the United States.
- At age 80 George Burns received his first Academy Award for his role in *The Sunshine Boys*.
- At 81 Benjamin Franklin mediated the compromise that led to the adoption of the U.S. Constitution.
- At 82 Winston Churchill finished his four-volume text *A History of the English-Speaking Peoples*.
- At 88 Konrad Adenauer was Chancellor of Germany.
- At 88 Michelangelo designed the Church of Santa Maria degli Angeli.
- At 89 Arthur Rubinstein gave a critically acclaimed recital at Carnegie Hall, in New York City.
- At 89 Albert Schweitzer was directing a hospital in Africa.
- At 90 Pablo Picasso was producing engravings and drawings.
- At 91 Eamon de Valera was President of Ireland.
- At 93 George Bernard Shaw wrote a play entitled *Farfetched Fables*.
- At 100 Grandma Moses was still painting.

Source: *U.S. News & World Report*, September 1, 1980, pp. 52–53.

Also, in most other societies, in contrast to ours, the elderly had some meaningful role to perform—as arbitrators and advisers, as landowners and leaders, as repositories of the wisdom of the tribe, as performers of tasks within their capabilities.

Chronological age is very important to us. Our passage through life is partially governed by our age. Chronological age dictates when we are deemed old enough to go to school, drive a car, marry, or vote. Our society has also generally selected 65 as the beginning of old age.

Members of primitive tribes often do not know how old they are. Old age is determined by physical and mental conditions, not by chronological age. And their definitions of old age are more accurate than ours. Everyone is not in the same mental and physical condition at age 65. Aging is an individual process that occurs at different rates in different people, and social-psychological factors may retard or accelerate the physiological changes.

The process of aging is called *senescence.* Senescence affects different people at different rates. Also, the rates of change in various body processes affected by aging vary among people. Visible signs of aging include the appearance of wrinkled skin, graying and thinning of hair, and stooped or shortened posture from compressed spinal discs.

As a person ages, blood vessels, tendons, the skin, and connective tissue lose their elasticity. Hardening of blood vessels and stiffening of joints occur: bones become brittle and thin; hormonal activity and reflexes slow down. Many of the health problems faced by the elderly result from a general decline of the circulatory system. Reduced blood supply impairs mental sharpness, interferes with balance, and reduces the effectiveness of the muscles and body organs. The probability of strokes and heart attacks also increases.

As a person ages, the muscles lose some of their strength, and coordination and endurance become more difficult. There is also a decline in the functioning of such organs as the lungs, the kidneys, and, to a lesser extent, the brain. As senescence proceeds, hearing and vision capacities decline, food may not taste the same, the sense of touch may become less acute, and there may be a loss of memory of recent and past events. Fortunately, the degree to which one's body loses its vitality can be influenced by one's lifestyle.

People who are mentally and physically active throughout their younger years remain more alert and vigorous in their later years.

A key fact to remember about senescence is that no dramatic decline need take place at one's 65th birthday—or at any other age. We are all slowly aging throughout our lives. The rate at which we age depends on many factors. Most elderly people are physically active and mentally alert. Unfortunately, in reading about the process of aging, you may get the impression that both the physical functioning and the mental functioning of the elderly person are reduced to a minimal level. This is seldom the case. Although functioning may slow somewhat, it remains at a high enough level to enable most elderly persons to be physically active and mentally alert.

There is growing evidence that many of the effects of aging are neither irreversible nor inevitable. Rather, several of the supposed effects of aging are due largely to the inactivity that is often associated with aging. Learning to reduce stress, along with exercising and maintaining a healthful diet, can reverse, or at least hold in abeyance, many of the effects thought to be caused by aging. In one study a group of 70-year-old, inactive men participated in a daily exercise program, and at the end of a year they had regained the physical fitness levels of 40-year-olds.[10]

In defining "old age," the federal government generally uses a chronological cutoff point—age 65—to separate elderly adults from others. There is nothing magical or particularly scientific about 65. In 1883 the Germans set age 65 as the criterion of aging for the world's first modern social security system for the elderly.[11] When the Social Security Act was passed in 1935, the United States also selected 65 as the eligibility age for retirement benefits, based on the German model.

It should be noted that the elderly are an extremely diverse group, spanning a 30- to 35-year age range. This large range, by itself, leads to considerable diversity. Just as there are substantial differences between 20-year-olds and 50-year-olds, there are generally vast differences between those age 65 and those age 95.

An Increasing Elderly Population

There are now over ten times as many people age 65 and older as there were at the turn of the 20th century.[12] (See Table 13.1.)

There are several reasons for the phenomenal growth of the older population. The improved care of expectant mothers and newborn infants has reduced the infant mortality rate, and vaccinations have prevented many life-threatening childhood illnesses, allowing an increased proportion of those born to live to adulthood. New drugs, better sanitation, and other medical advances have increased the life expectancy of Americans. Another reason for the increasing proportion of the aged is that the birthrate is declining; fewer babies are being born.

After World War II there was a baby boom that lasted from about 1947 to 1960. The most rapid rise in birthrates ever recorded in our society occurred during this period. Children born during these years flooded our schools in the 1950s and 1960s. Today these young adults are crowding the labor market. At the turn of the 21st century this generation will reach retirement age. After 1960 there was a ''baby bust''—a sharp decline in birthrates. (The average number of children per woman went down from a high of 3.8 in 1957 to a low of 1.8 in 1976.[13])

The increased life expectancy, the baby boom, and the subsequent baby bust will significantly increase the median age of Americans in future years.

The ''Old Old''—The Fastest-Growing Age Group

As medical science makes strides in treating and preventing heart disease, cancer, strokes, and other killers, an increasing percentage of the elderly are living into their eighties, nineties, and beyond. People age 85 and over constitute, proportionately, the fastest-growing age group in the United States.

Most senior citizens are physically active and mentally alert.

In 1940 only 365,000 Americans were 85 or over, a mere 0.3% of the total population. By the year 2000 this oldest old group will top 5.1 million, almost 2% of all Americans.[14] By the year 2000 more than 100,000 Americans will be age 100 or over.[15]

We are witnessing ''the graying of America,'' also called ''the aging of the aged.'' This population revolution is occurring rather quietly in our society.

Those who are age 85 and over will present a number of problems and difficult decisions for our society. Alan Otten notes:

It is these ''oldest old''—often mentally or physically impaired, alone, depressed—who pose the major problems for the coming decades. It is

TABLE 13.1

Number and Percentage of U.S. Population Age 65 and Older

	Year				
	1900	1950	1970	1980	1990
Number of older people (in millions)	3	12	20	25	31
Percent of total population	4	8	9.5	11	12

Source: United States Bureau of the Census, *Statistical Abstract of the United States, 1993* (Washington, DC: U.S. Government Printing Office, 1993), p. 14.

they who will strain their families with demands for personal care and financial support. It is they who will need more of such community help as Meals on Wheels, homemaker services, special housing. It is they who will require the extra hospital and nursing-home beds that will further burden federal and state budgets.

And it is they whose mounting needs and numbers already spark talk of some sort of rationing of health care. "Can we afford the very old?" is becoming a favorite conference topic for doctors, bioethicists and other specialists.[16]

Many of the old old suffer from a multiplicity of chronic illnesses. Common medical problems include arthritis, heart conditions, hypertension, osteoporosis (brittleness of the bones), Alzheimer's disease, incontinence, hearing and vision problems, and depression.

The older an elderly person becomes, the higher the probability that she or he will become a resident of a nursing home. Although only about 5% of the elderly are currently in a nursing home, nearly one out of three of those age 85 and over are placed in a nursing home at some point.[17] The cost to society for such care is high—over $30,000 a year per person.[18]

Despite the widespread image of families dumping aged parents into nursing homes, most frail elderly still live outside institutional walls, with a spouse, a child, or a relative being the chief caretaker. Some middle-aged people are now encountering simultaneous demands to put children through college and to support an aging parent in a nursing home. (The term *sandwich generation* has recently been coined to refer to middle-aged parents who are caught in the middle of trying to meet the needs of both their aging parents and their children.)

With people retiring at age 65 or 70 and then living to age 85 or 90, the number of years spent in retirement can be considerable. To maintain the same standard of living after retiring will require immense assets.

Rising health care costs and superlongevity have ignited controversy of whether to ration health care to the very old. For example, should people over age 75 be prohibited from receiving liver transplants or kidney dialysis? Discussion of euthanasia (the practice of killing individuals who are hopelessly sick or injured) has also been stirring increased debate. In 1984 Governor Richard Lamm of Colorado made the controversial statement that the terminally ill have a duty to die. Dr. Eisdor Fer stated:

The problem is age-old and across cultures. Whenever society has had marginal economic resources, the oldest went first, and the old people bought that approach. The old Eskimo wasn't put on the ice floe; he just left of his own accord and never came back.[19]

CASE EXAMPLE 13.2 Later Adulthood Is the Age of Recompense

The following case example illustrates that how we live in our younger years largely determines how we will live in our later years.

LeRoy was a muscular, outgoing teenager. He was physically bigger than most of his classmates and starred in basketball, baseball, and football in high school. In football he was chosen all-state linebacker in his senior year. At age 16 he began drinking at least a six-pack of beer each day, and at 17 he began smoking. Because he was an athlete, he had to smoke and drink on the sly. But LeRoy was good at conning others, and he found it fairly easy to smoke, drink, party, and still play sports. That left little time for studying, but LeRoy was not interested in that anyway. He had other priorities. He received a football scholarship and went on to college. He did well in football and majored in partying. His grades suffered, and, when his college eligibility for football was used up, he dropped out. Shortly thereafter he married Rachel Rudow, a college sophomore. She soon became pregnant and dropped out of college.

LeRoy was devastated after leaving college. He had been a jock for ten years, the envy of his classmates. Now he couldn't find a job with status. After a variety of odd jobs, he signed on as a road construction worker. He liked working outdoors and also liked the macho-type guys he worked, smoked, drank, and partied with.

He had three children with Rachel, but he was not a good husband. He was seldom home, and, when he was, he was often drunk. After a stormy seven years of marriage (including numerous incidents of physical and verbal abuse), Rachel moved out and got a divorce. She and the children moved to Florida with her parents so that LeRoy could not continue to harass her and the children. LeRoy's drinking and smoking increased. He was smoking over two packs a day, and he sometimes drank a quart of whiskey also.

A few years later he fathered an out-of-wedlock child for whom he was required to pay child support. At age 39 he married Jane, who was only 20. They had two children together and stayed married for six years. Jane eventually left him, because she became fed up with being belted around when LeRoy was drunk. LeRoy now had a total of six children to help support, and he seldom saw any of them. He continued to drink and also ate to excess. His weight went up to 285 pounds, and by age 48 he was no longer able to keep up with the other road construction workers. He was discharged by the company.

The next several years saw LeRoy taking odd jobs as a carpenter. He didn't earn much, and he spent most of what he earned on alcohol. He was periodically embarrassed by being hauled into court for failure to pay child support. He also was dismayed because he no longer had friends who wanted to get drunk with him. When he was 61, the doctor discovered that he had cirrhosis of the liver and informed LeRoy that he wouldn't live much longer if he continued to drink. Since LeRoy's whole life centered around drinking, he chose to continue. LeRoy also noticed that he had less energy and frequently had trouble breathing. The doctor indicated that he probably had damaged his lungs by smoking and now had a form of emphysema. The doctor lectured LeRoy on the need to stop smoking, but LeRoy didn't heed that advice either.

His health continued to deteriorate, and he lost 57 pounds. At age 64, while drunk, he fell over backward and fractured his skull. He was hospitalized for three and a half months. The injury permanently damaged his ability to walk and talk. He now is confined to a low-quality nursing home. He is no longer allowed to smoke or drink. He is frequently angry, impatient, and frustrated. He has no friends. The staff detests working with him; his grooming habits are atrocious, and he frequently yells obscenities. LeRoy frequently expresses a wish to die to escape his misery.

ElRoy, LeRoy's brother, has lived a vastly different life. ElRoy had a lean, almost puny muscular structure and did not excel at sports. LeRoy was his parents' favorite and had dazzled the young females in school and in the neighborhood. ElRoy had practically no dates in high school and was viewed as a prude. He did well in math and in the natural sciences. He spent much of his time studying and reading. He also liked taking radios and electrical appliances apart. At first he got into trouble because he was not skilled enough to put them back together. However, he soon became known in the neighborhood as someone who could fix radios and electrical appliances.

ElRoy went on to college and studied electrical engineering. He had no social life but graduated with good grades in his major. He went to graduate school and earned a master's degree in electrical engineering. On graduation, he was hired as an engineer by Motorola in Chicago. He did well there and in four years was named manager of a unit. Three years later he was lured to RCA with an attractive salary offer. The group of engineers he worked with at RCA made some significant advances in television technology.

At RCA ElRoy began dating a secretary, Elvira McCann, and they were married when he was 36. Life became much smoother for ElRoy after that. He was paid well and enjoyed annual vacations with Elvira to such places as Hawaii, Paris, and the Bahamas. ElRoy and Elvira wanted to have children but could not. In ElRoy's early forties they adopted two children, both from Korea. They bought a house in the suburbs and also a sailboat. ElRoy and Elvira occasionally had some marital disagreements, but generally they got along well. In their middle adult years, one of their adopted sons, Kim, was tragically killed by a drunk driver. That death was a shock and very difficult for the whole family to come to terms with. But the intense grieving gradually lessened, and after a few years ElRoy and Elvira put their lives back together.

Now, at age 67, ElRoy is still working for RCA and loving it. In a few years he plans to retire and move to the Hawaiian island of Maui. ElRoy and Elvira have already purchased a condominium there. Their surviving son, Dae, has graduated from college and is working for a life insurance company. ElRoy is looking forward to retiring so he can move to Maui and get more involved in his hobbies of photography and model railroads. His health is good, and he has a positive outlook on life. He occasionally thinks about his brother and sends him a card at Christmas and on his birthday. But, since ElRoy never had much in common with LeRoy, he seldom visits him.

PROBLEMS FACED BY THE ELDERLY

We have a personal stake in improving the status and life circumstances of the elderly. They are what we are becoming. If we do not face and solve the problems of the elderly *now,* we will be in dire straits in the future. Let's examine some of these problems.

Low Status

We have generally been unsuccessful in finding anything important or satisfying for the elderly to do. In most primitive and earlier societies, the old were respected and viewed as useful to their people to a much greater degree than is the case in our society. Industrialization and the growth of modern society have robbed the elderly of a high status. Prior to industrialization, older people were the primary owners of property. Land was the most important source of power; therefore the elderly controlled much of the economic and political power. Now people earn their living primarily in the job market. The vast majority of the elderly own little land and are viewed as providing no salable labor.

In earlier societies the elderly were also valued because of the knowledge they possessed. Their experiences enabled them to supervise planting and harvesting and to pass on knowledge about hunting, housing, and craft making. They also played key roles in preserving and transmitting the culture. But the rapid advances of science and technology have tended to limit the value of the elderly's knowledge; books and other "memory-storing" devices have rendered old people less valuable as storehouses of culture and records.

There are other reasons why the status of the elderly has declined over time. Children no longer learn their future profession or trade from their parents; instead, such skills are acquired through institutions, such as the school system. In addition, the children of the elderly are no longer dependent on their parents for their livelihood; they make their living through a trade or profession that is independent of their parents. Finally, the elderly no longer perform tasks that are viewed as essential by society: Often the older workers' skills are viewed as outmoded even before these individuals retire.

The low status of the elderly is closely associated with *ageism,* which refers to discrimination and prejudice against people simply because they are old. Today, many people react negatively to the elderly. Ageism is like sexism or racism because it involves intolerance and unfair treatment of all members of a particular social category.

Ageism is evident in our everyday language, by the use of terms that no racial or ethnic group would ever accept: "old buzzard," "old biddy," "old fogey." From a rational view, ageism makes no sense; those who delight in discriminating against the elderly will one day be old themselves.

Early Retirement

Maintaining a high rate of employment is a major goal in our society. In many occupations the supply of labor is exceeding the demand. An often-used remedy for the oversupply of available employees is the encouragement of ever-earlier retirement. Forced retirements often create financial and psychological burdens that retirees usually face without much assistance or preparation.

Our massive Social Security program supports early retirement, which can come as early as 62. Pension plans of some companies and unions make it financially attractive to retire as early as 55. Perhaps the extreme case is the armed forces, which permit retirement on full benefits after 20 years' service as early as age 38.

Many workers who retire early supplement their pension by taking another job, usually of a lower status. Nearly 90% of Americans 65 years of age and older are retired, even though many are intellectually and physically capable of working.[20]

Early retirement has some advantages to society, such as reducing the labor supply and allowing younger employees to advance faster. But there are also some serious disadvantages. For society the total bill for retirement pensions is already huge and still growing. For the retiree it means facing a new life and status without much preparation or assistance. Although our society has developed formal institutions to prepare the young for the work world, it has not developed comparable avenues for preparing the elderly for retirement. Being without a job in our work-oriented society is often a reality shock for older people.

In our society we still view a person's worth partly by his or her work. People often develop their self-image (their sense of who they are) in terms of their occupation—"I am a teacher," "I am a barber," "I am a doctor." Because the later years generally provide no exciting new roles to replace the occupational roles lost on retirement, a retiree cannot proudly say "I am a . . . ." Instead, she or he must say "I *was* a good . . . ." The more a person's life revolves around work, the more difficult retirement is likely to be.

Retirement often removes people from the mainstream of life. It diminishes their social contacts and their status and places them in a *roleless role*. Individuals who were once valued as salespeople, plumbers, accountants, or secretaries are now considered noncontributors in a roleless role on the fringe of society.

Several myths about the older worker have been widely accepted by both employers and the general public. Older workers are thought to be less healthy, clumsier, more prone to absenteeism, more accident prone, more forgetful, and slower in task performance.[21] Research has shown that these myths are erroneous. Older workers have lower turnover rates, produce at a steadier rate, make fewer mistakes, have lower absenteeism rates, have a more positive attitude toward their work, and have fewer on-the-job injuries than younger employees.[22] However, if the older worker does become ill, she or he usually takes somewhat longer to recover.[23]

Research has shown that at least one-third of retired people have adjustment problems.[24] The two most common problems were adjusting to a reduced income and missing their former jobs. Those who had the most difficulty tended to be either rigid or overly identified with their work, viewing their job as their primary source of satisfaction and self-image. Those who were happiest were able to replace job prestige and financial status with a focus on self-development, personal relationships, and leisure activities.

The "golden age" of leisure following retirement appears to be largely a myth. Lawton found that life in retirement is likely to be sedentary, with TV viewing and sleep outranking such traditional leisure-time activities as gardening, sports, clubs, and other pastimes.[25] Many of the elderly are poorly educated, which makes them less likely to enjoy reading or activities that focus on learning or self-improvement. Gross reduction in income, fear of crime, lack of transportation, and reduced mobility also contribute to the sedentary lifestyle of the elderly.

It would seem far better if workers who are still productive could stay on the job longer on a part- or full-time basis rather than being pensioned off or forced to take another job of a lower status. (This perspective will be expanded on later in this chapter.)

Societal Emphasis on Youth

Our society fears aging and old age more than most other societies do. Our emphasis on youth is indicated both by our dread of getting gray hair and wrinkles or becoming bald and by the pleasure we experience when someone guesses our age to be younger than it actually is. We place a high value on change and newness. European societies, on the other hand, place a higher value on preserving traditional customs and lifestyles. Our society also emphasizes mobility, action, and energy. We like to think we are doers.

But why this emphasis on youth in our society? The reasons are not fully clear. There appear to be several factors. Industrialization has resulted in a demand for laborers who are energetic and agile and have considerable strength. Rapid advances in technology and science have made past knowledge and certain specialized work skills (for example, that of a blacksmith) obsolete. Competition has always been a cornerstone of our society, reinforced by Darwin's notions on evolution and the survival of the fittest. The mass media portray youthfulness and having a beautiful physique as being highly valued in our society, and the advertising industry seeks to sell a variety of diet programs and products, numerous cosmetics, and a variety of exercise equipment and programs that claim to give the consumer a more youthful image.

Health Problems and Costs of Health Care

Old age is a social problem partly because of the high costs of health care. Most of the elderly have at least one chronic condition, and many have multiple conditions. The most frequently occurring health problems are arthritis, hypertension, hearing and visual impairments, heart disease, orthopedic impairments, sinusitis, cataracts, diabetes, and tinnitus (a sensation of hearing ringing or other noises).[26] Older persons visit their doctors more frequently, spend a higher proportion of their income on prescribed drugs, and are hospitalized for longer periods than younger people. As might be expected, the health status of the old old (85 and over) is worse than that of the young old.

The medical expenses of an elderly person average four times those of a young adult.[27] This is partly because the elderly suffer much more from long-term illnesses, such as cancer, heart problems, diabetes, and glaucoma.[28]

Of course, the physical process of aging (senescence) contributes to health problems. However, research in recent years has demonstrated that social and personal stresses also play a major role in causing diseases. The elderly face a wide range of stressful situations: loneliness, death of friends and family members, retirement, changes in living arrangements, loss of social status, reduced income, and a decline in physical energy and physical capacities. Medical conditions may also result from substandard diets, inadequate exercise, cigarette smoking, and excessive alcohol intake. Flynn notes:

Studies of long-living peoples of the world show that neither heredity nor low prevalence of

disease is a significant determinant of longevity. Four other factors are much more likely to predict long-term survival: (1) a clearly defined and valued role in society; (2) a positive self-perception; (3) sustained, moderate physical activity; and (4) abstinence from cigarette smoking. Studies in this country indicate that secure financial status, social relationships, and high education are also important.[29]

(Health care for the elderly is discussed further in Chapter 14.)

Inadequate Income

Many elderly persons live in poverty. A fair number lack adequate food, essential clothes and medicines, and perhaps even a telephone. One-fifth of the elderly have incomes close to or below the poverty line.[30] Only a small minority have substantial savings or investments.

The importance of financial security for the elderly is emphasized by Sullivan et al. as follows:

Financial security affects one's entire lifestyle. It determines one's diet, ability to seek good health care, to visit relatives and friends, to maintain a suitable wardrobe, and to find or maintain adequate housing. One's financial resources, or lack of them, play a great part in finding recreation (going to movies, plays, playing bridge or bingo, etc.) and maintaining morale, feelings of independence, and a sense of self-esteem. In other words, if an older person has the financial resources to remain socially independent (having her own household and access to transportation and medical services), to continue contact with friends and relatives, and to maintain her preferred forms of recreation, she is going to feel a great deal better about herself and others than if she is deprived of her former style of life.[31]

Financial problems among the elderly are compounded by the high cost of health care, as previously discussed. Another factor is inflation, which is especially devastating to those on fixed incomes. Most private pension benefits do not increase after a worker retires. For example, if annual living costs rise at the rate of 7%, a person

EXHIBIT 13.2

Disengagement Theory: Response of Individuals and Society to Aging

In 1961, Elaine Cumming and William E. Henry coined the term *disengagement* to refer to a process whereby people respond to aging by gradually withdrawing from the various roles and social relationships they occupied in middle age.[a] Such disengagement is claimed to be functional for the individual because he or she is thought to gradually lose the energy and vitality to sustain all the roles and social relationships held in younger years.

The term *societal disengagement* has been coined to refer to the process whereby society withdraws from the aging person.[b] It is allegedly functional for our society—which values efficiency, competition, and individual achievement—to disengage from the elderly, who have the least physical stamina and the highest death rate. Societal disengagement occurs in a variety of ways: Older people may not be sought out for leadership positions in organizations, their employers may try to force them to retire, their children may no longer want them involved in making family decisions, and the government may be more responsive to meeting the needs of people who are younger. (Actually, societal disengagement is often unintended and unrecognized by society.) Many elderly persons do not handle forced role losses well. Some even try to escape with alcohol, drugs, or suicide.

With reference to the two terms just explained, *disengagement theory* hypothesizes a mutual disengagement or withdrawal between the individual and society. Disengagement theory has stimulated considerable interest and research.

There is considerable controversy over whether disengagement is functional for the elderly and for our society. Research has found that some people undeniably do voluntarily disengage as they grow older. Yet, disengagement is neither a universal nor an inevitable response to aging. Contrary to disengagement theory, most older people maintain extensive associations with friends. Most also maintain active involvements in organizations (such as church groups, fraternal organizations, and unions). Some elderly persons, after retiring, develop new interests, expand their circle of friends, do volunteer work, and join clubs. Others *rebel* against society's stereotypes and refuse to be treated as if they had little to offer to society. Many of these people are marshaling political resources to force society to adapt to their needs and skills.

A severe criticism of societal disengagement theory is that it can be used to justify both ageism and society's failure to help the elderly maintain meaningful roles. Disengagement theory may, at best, be merely a description of the problems we must confront as we try to combat ageism.

In contrast to the disengagement theory of aging is the activity theory. It asserts that, the more physically and mentally active the elderly are, the more successfully they will age. There is considerable evidence that being physically and mentally active will help to maintain the physiological and psychological functions of the elderly. Whereas disengagement theory expects the elderly to slow down, the activity theory urges them to remain physically and mentally active.

[a]Elaine Cumming and W. E. Henry, *Growing Old: The Process of Disengagement* (New York: Basic Books, 1961), p. 6.
[b]Robert C. Atchley, *Aging: Continuity and Change* (Belmont, CA: Wadsworth, 1983), p. 97.

on a fixed pension would in 20 years be able to buy only one-fourth as many goods and services as she or he could at retirement.[32] Fortunately, in 1974 Congress enacted an "automatic escalator"

clause in Social Security benefits, providing a 3% increase in payments when the Consumer Price Index (CPI) increases a like amount.

Subgroups of the elderly population with high

EXHIBIT 13.3

Alzheimer's Disease

Tony Wiggleworth is 68 years old. Two years ago his memory began to falter. As the months went by, he even forgot what his wedding day to Rose had been like. His grandchildren's visits slipped from his memory in two or three days.

The most familiar surroundings have become strange to him. Even his friends' homes seem like places he has never been before. When he walks down the streets in his neighborhood, he frequently becomes lost.

Tony is now quite confused. He has difficulty speaking and can no longer perform such elementary tasks as balancing his checkbook. At times Rose, who is taking care of him, is uncertain whether he knows who she is. All of this is very baffling for Tony. Until he retired three years ago, he had been an accountant and had excelled at remembering facts and details.

Tony has Alzheimer's disease. This disease now affects about 6–10% of all people over 65 and 20–50% of all people over 85.[a] These statistics indicate that the disease affects the old old to a greater extent than the younger old.

Alzheimer's disease is a degenerative brain disorder that causes gradual deterioration in intelligence, memory, awareness, and ability to control bodily functions. In its final stages, Alzheimer's leads to progressive paralysis and breathing difficulties. The breathing problems often result in pneumonia, the most frequent cause of death for Alzheimer's victims. Other symptoms include irritability, restlessness, agitation, and impairments of judgment. Although most of those affected are over 65, the disease occasionally strikes people in middle age.

Over a period lasting from as few as 5 years to as many as 20, the disease destroys brain cells. The changes in behavior displayed by those afflicted show some variation. Brownlee notes:

> One sufferer refuses to bathe or change clothes, another eats fried eggs without utensils, a third walks naked down the street, a fourth has the family's beloved cats put to sleep, while yet another mistakes paint for juice and drinks it. The outlandish acts committed by Alzheimer's patients take as many forms as there are people who suffer the disease. Yet, in every case, the bizarre behavior serves as a sign that the sufferer is regressing towards unawareness, a second childishness.[b]

---

[a]Diane Papalia and Sally W. Olds, *Human Development*, 5th ed. (New York: McGraw-Hill, 1992), p. 484.

[b]S. Brownlee, "Alzheimer's: Is There Hope?" *U.S. News & World Report*, Aug. 12, 1991, pp. 40–49.

(continued)

---

proportions of members living in poverty include African Americans, Latinos, women, and persons living alone or with nonrelatives (as compared to those living with family).[33]

The Social Security system was never designed to be the main source of income for the elderly. It was originally intended as a form of insurance that would *partially supplement* other assets when retirement, disability, or death of a wage-earning spouse occurred. Yet many elderly do not have investments, pensions, or savings to support them in retirement, and therefore Social Security has become their major or sole source of income.

The U.S. Social Security system was developed in 1935. The system was fairly solvent until recently. During its first few decades, more money was paid into the system from Social Security

EXHIBIT 13.3   *(continued)*

The most prominent early symptom of Alzheimer's is memory loss, particularly for recent events. Other early symptoms (which are often overlooked) are a reduced ability to play a game of cards, reduced performance at sports, and sudden outbreaks of extravagance. More symptoms then develop—irritability, agitation, confusion, restlessness, and impairments of concentration, speech, and orientation. As the disease progresses, the symptoms become more disabling. Caregivers eventually have to provide 24-hour supervision—which is a tremendous burden. As the disease progresses in its final stages, a nursing home placement is often necessary. Near the end, the patient usually cannot recognize family members, cannot understand or use language, and cannot eat without help.

Brownlee describes the mental and physical trauma that caregivers and family members of those afflicted experience:

> They live in a private hell, one that cannot be discussed with neighbors and friends in too much detail because the details are so devastating. They grieve even as their loved ones plunge them into a maelstrom of unreality, where mothers streak through the living room wearing nothing but a shower cap and garter belt and grandfathers try to punch their baby granddaughters.[c]

---

[c]Brownlee, "Alzheimer's: Is There Hope?," p. 48.

In addition, the patient's inability to reciprocate expressions of caring and affection robs relationships of intimacy.

Diagnosing the disease is difficult because the disorder has symptoms that are nearly identical to those of other forms of dementia. The only sure diagnosis at the present time is observation of tissue deep within the brain, which can be done only by autopsy after death. Doctors usually diagnose the disease in a living person by ruling out other conditions that could account for the symptoms.[d]

The cause of Alzheimer's disease continues to be a mystery. Various theories have blamed viral infections, biochemical deficiencies, genetic tendencies, defects of the immune system, and even aluminum poisoning. Genetic tendencies appear to be a contributing factor, because relatives of Alzheimer's patients have an increased risk of developing the disease in the future.[e]

An examination of the brains of victims has found a distinctive tangle of protein filaments in the cortex, the part of the brain responsible for intellectual functions. This research shows that there are biochemical causes for the disease and leads to the conclusion that aging does not automatically involve senility.

---

[d]L. L. Heston and J. A. White, *Dementia* (New York: Freeman, 1983).

[e]Papalia and Olds, *Human Development*, pp. 484–85.

(continued)

---

taxes imposed on employers and employees than was paid out. This was due largely to the fact that life expectancy was only about 60 years of age. The life expectancy rate, however, has gradually increased to 76.[34] There is now a danger that the Social Security system will soon be paying out more than it takes in. Social Security taxes have increased sharply in recent years, but, with the old old being the fastest-growing age group and with the proportion of the elderly increasing in our society, the system may go bankrupt. One projection shows the fund being depleted by the year 2048.[35]

The *dependency ratio* is the ratio between the number of working people and the number of nonworking people in the population. With the

EXHIBIT 13.3   *(continued)*

Scientists are now investigating a number of hypotheses as to what causes Alzheimer's. One intriguing clue comes from the finding that victims of Down's syndrome (a severe form of mental retardation due to a chromosome defect) who survive into their thirties frequently develop symptoms indistinguishable from those of Alzheimer's. Another recent clue is the discovery of fragments of amyloid in brains of persons who died from the disorder. Amyloid is a very tough protein that in normal amounts is necessary for cell growth throughout the body. Some researchers hypothesize that abnormal patches of this protein in the brain set up a chain reaction that progressively destroys brain cells. This amyloid protein is an abnormal product formed from a larger compound called amyloid precursor protein, or APP.

In August 1992 a research team at SIBIA Inc. (located in San Diego) reported initial success in developing a test to diagnose Alzheimer's disease in its early stages.[f] The test detects abnormalities in APP, which appears to be associated with the accumulation of the amyloid protein in the brain.

Further research is needed to confirm the validity of this SIBIA test. If Alzheimer's disease can be detected in its early stages, people will be better able to plan for their future care and make arrangements for their families while they still retain control of their mental faculties. Furthermore, if in fact Alzheimer's disease results from an accumulation of the amyloid protein, and if the early accumulation of this protein can be detected, then it is likely that drugs can be developed to treat the disorder by blocking the formation of amyloid in the brain.[g]

At the present time there is no cure for the disease. Patients with Alzheimer's receive some relief from drugs that reduce depression and agitation and help them sleep. Exercise, physical therapy, proper nourishment, and proper fluid intake are also beneficial. Memory aids assist somewhat in everyday functioning. Especially helpful to patients and their families are emotional and social support provided by groups and professional counseling.

---

[f]T. H. Maugh, "New Test Seems to Detect Early Alzheimer's," *Capital Times*, Aug. 22, 1992, p. 1A.

[g]S. S. Sisodia, E. H. Koo, K. Beyreuthe, A. Unterbeck, and D. L. Price. "Evidence That B-Amyloid Protein in Alzheimer's Disease Is Not Derived by Normal Processing," *Science*, 248 (Apr. 27, 1990), pp. 492–95.

---

elderly proportion of the population increasing, nonworkers will represent a ballooning burden on workers. Authorities predict that by the year 2020 the dependency ratio will decline from the current level of about 3 workers for every nonworking person to a ratio of about 2 to 1.[36]

Clearly, serious problems exist with the system. First, as already noted, the benefits are too small to meet the financial needs of the elderly. With payments from Social Security, an estimated 80% of retirees now live on less than half of their

preretirement annual incomes. The monthly payments from Social Security are generally below the poverty line.[37] Second, it is unlikely that the monthly benefits will be raised much, because the amount of Social Security taxes paid by employees is already quite high (see Table 13.2).

The nation faces some hard choices about how to keep the system solvent in future years. Benefits might be lowered, but this would even further impoverish recipients. Social Security taxes might be raised, but there is little public sup-

TABLE 13.2

▬▬▬▬▬

Taxable Wage Base and Maximum
Social Security Payroll Tax as Set by Legislation

Year	Maximum Tax Rate	Maximum Taxable Earnings	Tax
1971	5.2%	$ 7,800	$ 405.60
1976	5.85%	$15,300	$ 895.05
1981	6.65%	$29,700	$1,975.05
1986	7.15%	$42,000	$3,003.00
1990	7.65%	$51,300	$3,924.50
1994	7.65%	$60,600	$4,635.90

Source: Social Security Administration, Department of Health and Human Services.

port for this. As we see in the table, the maximum rate has already increased more than tenfold since 1971 (from $405.60 to $4635.90).

The future of the Social Security system is unclear. It is likely to continue, but reduced benefits may be inevitable. Young people are well advised to plan for retirement through savings, investment, and pension plans that are independent of the Social Security system.

Loss of Family and Friends

Elderly persons who are single are generally less well off than those who are married. The longer life span of women has left nearly 60% of women over age 65 without a spouse.[38] Gordon Moss and Walter Moss comment about the value of marriage for older persons:

> They now have much more time for and are more dependent upon each other. Some marriages cannot handle this increased togetherness, but those that can become the major source of contentment to both partners. . . . A good marriage, or a remarriage, provides the elderly person with companionship and emotional support, sex, the promise of care if he is sick, a focus for daily activities, and frequently greater financial independence. Sex roles often blur, and the husband actively helps in household chores.[39]

The elderly person's life becomes more isolated and lonely when close friends and relatives move away or die. Of course, later adulthood is a time when close friends are most likely to die.

The needs of aging parents can present some painful dilemmas for their children, especially if the parents are poor or in ill health. The children may have families of their own, with heavy demands on their time and finances. For children on tight budgets, deciding how to divide their resources among their parents, their own children, and themselves can be agonizing. Some face the difficult question of whether to maintain a parent within their home, to leave the parent living alone, to place the parent in a nursing home, or to place the parent in some other type of housing for the elderly (such as a group home).

Substandard Housing

We hear so much about nursing homes that few people realize 95% of the elderly do not live in nursing homes or in any other kind of institution.[40] About 70% of all elderly males are married and live with their wives.[41] Because females tend to outlive their spouses, about 40% of women over age 65 live alone.[42] Nearly 80% of older married couples maintain their own households—in apartments, mobile homes, condominiums, or their own houses.[43] In addition, nearly half of the single elderly (widows, widowers, divorced, never married) live in their own homes.[44] When the elderly do not maintain their own households, they most often live in the homes of relatives, primarily one of their children.

The elderly who live in rural areas generally have a higher status than those in urban areas. People living on farms can retire gradually. Also, people whose income is in land, rather than in a job, can retain importance and esteem to an advanced age.

However, about three-quarters of our population reside in urban areas, where the elderly often live in poor-quality housing.[45] At least 30% of the elderly live in substandard, deteriorating, or dilapidated housing.[46] Often the urban elderly live in inner-city hotels or apartments with inadequate living conditions. Their neighborhoods may be decaying and crime-ridden, which makes them easy prey for thieves and muggers.

Fortunately, many mobile-home parks, retirement villages, and apartment complexes geared to the needs of the elderly have been built throughout the country. Such housing communities provide a social center, security/protection, sometimes a daily hot meal, and perhaps a little help with maintenance.

Transportation

Only the more affluent and physically vigorous elderly can afford the luxury of owning and driving a car. The lack of convenient, inexpensive transportation is a problem faced by most older citizens.

Crime Victimization

Because of their reduced energy, strength, and agility, the elderly are vulnerable to being victimized by crime, particularly robbery, aggravated assault, burglary, larceny, vandalism, and fraud. Many older persons live in constant fear of being victimized, although reported victimization rates for the elderly are actually lower than those for younger people. The true victimization rates for the elderly may be considerably higher than official crime statistics indicate, because many older individuals feel uneasy about becoming involved with the legal and criminal justice systems. Therefore they may fail to report some of these crimes. Also, some elderly people are afraid of retaliation from the offenders if they report the crimes.

Sadly, some of the elderly are hesitant to leave their homes for fear that they will be mugged or that their homes will be burglarized while they are away.

Sexuality in Later Adulthood

There is a common misconception that older people lose their sexual drive. An older male who displays sexual interest is labeled a "dirty old man." When two older people exhibit normal heterosexual behavior, someone may comment "Aren't they cute?" Yet many older people have a strong sexual interest and a satisfying sex life.[47] Sexual capacities, particularly in women, show little evidence of declining with age, and a large percentage of both elderly men and elderly women are capable of sexual relations.[48]

Noted sex researchers William Masters and Virginia Johnson see no reason why sexual activity cannot be enjoyed by the elderly.[49] If sexual behavior does decline, it probably is due more to social reasons than to physical reasons. According to Masters and Johnson, the major deterrents to sexual activity when one is older are the lack of a partner, overindulgence in drinking or eating, boredom with one's partner, attitudes toward sex (such as the erroneous belief that sex is inappropriate for the elderly), poor physical or mental health, attitudes toward menopause, and fear of poor performance.[50]

The attitudes of the younger generations frequently create problems for the elderly. A widow or widower may face strong opposition to remarrying from other family members. Negative attitudes are often strongest when an elderly person becomes interested in someone younger who will become an heir if the older person dies. The elderly are sometimes informed that they should not be interested in members of the opposite sex

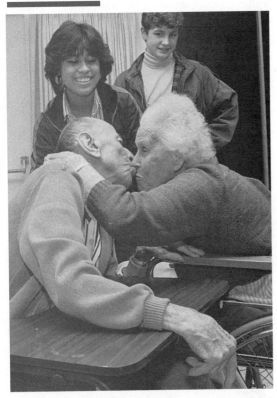

Residents of a private care facility share a kiss. Sexual capacities show little evidence of declining with age.

of the numbers that are involved, but the old as well as the young have new options as societal norms change. The popularity of living together without marriage will probably increase.[51]

Malnutrition

The elderly are the most uniformly undernourished segment of our population.[52] There are a number of reasons for chronic malnutrition among the elderly: transportation difficulties in getting to grocery stores; lack of knowledge about proper nutrition; lack of money to purchase a well-balanced diet; poor teeth or lack of dentures, which can greatly limit one's diet; lack of incentive to prepare an appetizing meal when one is living alone; and inadequate cooking and storage facilities.

Emotional Problems

Depression is the most common emotional problem among the elderly. The suicide rate of white men in their eighties is three times that of men in general.[53] Although the elderly make up about 12% of the population, about 25% of reported suicides occur in this age group.[54] Given the problems of the elderly (many created by our society's making them feel "useless"), the high rate of depression is understandable.

Unless people resolve their emotional problems in earlier life, such problems will persist into the later years. Often these problems will be intensified by the added stresses of aging.

The National Institute of Mental Health, after an 11-year study, identified two major barriers to good mental health in the later years: (1) failure to bounce back from psychosocial losses and (2) failure to have "meaningful" life goals.[55] Later adulthood is a time when drastic changes thrust on the elderly may create emotional problems: loss of a job and its accompanying status, loss of a spouse, loss of friends and relatives through death or moving, poorer health, loss of accustomed income, and changing relationships with one's children and grandchildren.

and that they should not establish new sexual relationships when they have lost a mate.

Fortunately, attitudes toward sexuality in later adulthood are changing. Merlin Taber notes:

> With the changing attitudes of younger people to alternatives to the traditional family, some older people are finding informal arrangements for living together attractive. The couple who do not have a marriage ceremony can share all the companionship and sexual satisfactions without upsetting inheritance rights and retirement benefits. When they become aware of it, their children may accept such a pattern because they find it preferable to remarriage. We have no idea

Unfortunately, it is often erroneously assumed that "senility" and "mental illness" are inevitable and untreatable. Robert Butler has found, on the contrary, that the elderly respond well to both individual and group counseling.[56] In addition, many 90-year-olds show no sign of senility. It is by no means a necessary part of old age.

Death

Preoccupation with death—and particularly with the circumstances surrounding it—is an ongoing concern of the elderly. They see their friends and relatives dying, and they dread the disability, pain, and long periods of suffering that may precede death.[57] They generally hope for a death with dignity; in their own homes, with little suffering, with mental faculties intact, and with families and friends nearby. Old people also worry about the costs of their final illness, the difficulties they may cause others by the manner of their death, and the financial resources to permit a dignified funeral.

In our society we tend to wall off the dying with silence. (Perhaps we do so to avoid having to confront our own mortality.) In hospitals great efforts are made to separate the dying from the living. Often the medical staff attempts to shield the dying person from awareness of his or her impending death. Families, too, begin to treat the patient differently when they know the end is near. (This different treatment often subtly informs the dying that death is imminent.)

A number of authorities have urged our society to treat death more openly.[58] Such openness would enable dying persons to prepare for death better, perhaps by having additional time to reassess their lives. It would also give the dying person more time to become accepting of death and to make financial arrangements, such as drawing up a will. It would give family members time to make necessary arrangements (including financial), as well as time to redress old wrongs and heal misunderstandings. We all need to face, and to come to terms with, our own eventual death. The recent popularity of courses in death and dying on college campuses shows that people feel

a need to become more psychologically comfortable with facing death.

People in primitive societies were generally better prepared for death than we are. Margaret Mead notes:

> *In peasant communities where things didn't change and where people died in the beds they were born in, grandparents taught the young what the end of life was going to be. So you looked at your mother, if you were a girl, and you learned what it was like to be a bride, a young mother. Then you looked at your grandmother and knew what it was like to be old. Children learned what it was to age and die while they were very small. They were prepared for the end of life at the beginning.*[59]

(Unfortunately, in our society many of us seek to deny our own deaths, even though we are all "terminal" from birth.)

In the modern United States most people die in nursing homes or hospitals, surrounded by medical staff.[60] Such deaths often occur without dignity.

Fortunately, the hospice movement that has developed in recent years allows the terminally ill to die with dignity—to live their final weeks in the way they want to. Hospices originated in the Middle Ages among European religious groups who welcomed sick, tired, or hungry travelers.[61] Hospices today are located in a variety of settings—in a separate unit of a hospital, in a building independent of a hospital, or in the dying person's home. Medical services and social services are provided, and extensive efforts are made to allow the terminally ill to spend their remaining days as they choose. Hospices sometimes have educational and entertainment programs, and visitors are common. Pain relievers are used extensively so that the patient can live out his or her final days in relative comfort.

Hospices view the disease as terminal, not the patient. The emphasis is on helping patients to use the time that is left, rather than on trying to keep people alive as long as possible. Many hospice programs are set up to assist patients to live their remaining days in the home of their family. In addition to medical and visiting-nurse services, hospices have volunteers who help the patient and family members with such services as counseling, transportation, insurance forms and other paperwork, and respite care for family members. After patients die, many hospices offer bereavement services for the survivors.

Parent Abuse

Parent abuse refers to abuse of elderly parents by their children. It occurs most often when the parents live with the children or are dependent on them. This problem is described in more depth in Chapter 5.

CURRENT SERVICES

The problems of the elderly are coming into the public spotlight. Many state governments now have an office on aging, and some municipalities and counties have established community councils on aging. A number of universities have established centers for the study of gerontology; and nursing, medicine, sociology, social work, architecture, and other disciplines and professions are establishing fields of study on gerontology. (*Gerontology* is the scientific study of aging and the problems of the elderly.) Government research grants are being given to encourage gerontological study by academicians. Publishers are now producing books and pamphlets to educate the public about the elderly, and a few high schools are offering courses to help teenagers understand the elderly and their circumstances.

Present services and programs for the elderly are principally "maintenance" in nature; that is, they are primarily designed to meet basic physical needs. Nonetheless, there are a number of programs, often federally funded, that provide needed services to the elderly. A few of these are briefly described in Exhibit 13.5.

Older Americans Act of 1965

The Older Americans Act of 1965 created an operating agency (Administration on Aging) within the Department of Health, Education and Welfare.* This law and its amendments are the bases for financial aid by the federal government to assist states and local communities in meeting the needs of the elderly. The act was designed to secure the following for the elderly:

1. An adequate income.
2. Best possible physical and mental health.
3. Suitable housing.
4. Restorative services for those who require institutional care.
5. Opportunity for employment.
6. Retirement in health, honor, dignity.
7. Pursuit of meaningful activity.
8. Efficient community services.
9. Immediate benefit from research knowledge to sustain and improve health and happiness.
10. Freedom, independence, and the free exercise of individual initiative in planning and managing their own lives.[62]

Although these objectives are commendable, the reality is that the goals have not been realized for many of our elderly.

Nursing Homes

Nursing homes were created as an alternative to expensive hospital care and are substantially supported by the federal government through Medicaid and Medicare. Over 1.5 million older people now live in extended-care facilities, making nursing homes a billion-dollar industry.[63] There are more patient beds in nursing homes than in hospitals.[64]

Nursing homes are classified according to the kind of care they provide. At one end of the scale are residential homes that offer primarily room and board, with some nonmedical care (such as help in dressing). At the other end of the scale are nursing-care centers that provide skilled nursing and medical attention 24 hours a day. The more

---

*This department was renamed the Department of Health and Human Services in 1980.

EXHIBIT 13.4

─────

Ethical Issue: Should Assisted Suicide Be Legalized?

The technology of life-support equipment can keep people alive almost indefinitely. Respirators, artificial nutrition, intravenous hydration, and so-called miracle drugs not only sustain life but also trap many of the terminally ill in a degrading mental and physical condition. Such technology has raised a variety of ethical questions. Do people who are terminally ill and in severe pain have a right to die by refusing treatment? Increasingly, through "living wills," patients are able to express their wishes and refuse treatment. However, does someone in a long-term coma who has not signed a living will have a right to die? How should our society decide when to continue and when to stop life-support efforts? Courts and state legislatures are presently working through the legal complexities governing death and euthanasia.

Should assisted death, or assisted suicide, be legalized? As of 1992, only The Netherlands permitted physicians to give qualifying terminally ill patients a lethal dose of drugs. There is considerable controversy about assisted suicide in the United States. Hemlock Society founder Derek Humphry has written a do-it-yourself suicide manual that has become a bestseller. (The Hemlock Society promotes active voluntary euthanasia.) Michigan doctor Jack Kevorkian has made national news by building a machine to help terminally ill people end their lives and by assisting several of them to do so.

People in favor of assisted suicide argue that unnecessary, long-term suffering is without merit and should not have to be endured. They argue that people have a right to a death with dignity, which means a death without excessive emotional and physical pain and without excessive mental, physical, and spiritual degradation. They see assisted suicide as affirming the principle of autonomy—upholding the individual's right to make decisions about his or her dying process. Allowing the option of suicide for the terminally ill is perceived as the ultimate right of self-determination.

Opponents assert that suicide is unethical and is a mortal sin for which the deceased cannot receive forgiveness. They assert that modern health care can provide almost everyone a peaceful, pain-free, comfortable, and dignified end to life. Opponents believe that most terminally ill persons consider suicide not because they fear death but because they fear dying—pain, abandonment, and loss of control—all of which the hospice is designed to alleviate. Horror stories of intense suffering are most often the tragic results of medical mismanagement, they feel. Moreover,

(continued)

─────

skilled and extensive the medical care given, the more expensive the home. The costs per resident average more than $3,000 per month.[65] Although only a small percentage of the elderly live permanently in nursing homes (about 5%), many more spend some time convalescing in them.

Scandals involving nursing-home care are prevalent. A number of years ago in Houston an elderly woman was so neglected in a nursing home that her death was not discovered until rigor mortis had set in; another woman was hospitalized due to rat bites.[66] It has been charged that some doctors are giving needless repeated injections to nursing-home patients in order to make money.[67] In 1980 a nursing home in Madison, Wisconsin, strapped a 37-year-old stroke patient into her wheelchair for over 40 minutes at a time; the patient had no bladder or bowel control, but she was not assisted to the toilet despite her repeated cries for help.[68]

Robert Butler visited a number of nursing homes and found patients lying in their own feces

EXHIBIT 13.4   *(continued)*

assisted-suicide legislation could easily result in the philosophy that the terminally ill have a *duty* to die, in order to avoid being a financial and emotional burden to their families and to society. At their most extreme, the opposition equates assisted suicide with homicide.

Some authorities have sought to make a distinction between active euthanasia (assisting in suicide) and passive euthanasia (withholding or withdrawing treatment). In many states it is legal for physicians and courts to honor a patient's wishes to not receive life-sustaining treatment.

A recent case of passive euthanasia involved Nancy Cruzan. On January 11, 1983, when this Missouri woman was 25, her car overturned. Her brain lost oxygen for 14 minutes following the accident, and for the next several years she was in a "persistent vegetative state," with no hope of recovery. A month after the accident, her parents, Joyce and Joe Cruzan, gave permission for a feeding tube to be inserted. In the months that followed, however, the parents gradually became convinced there was no point in keeping Nancy alive indefinitely in such a hopeless condition.

In 1986 they were shocked when a Missouri state judge informed them that they could be charged with murder for removing the feeding tube. The Cruzans appealed the decision all the way to the U.S. Supreme Court, requesting the Court to overturn a Missouri law that specifically prohibits withdrawal of food and water from hopelessly ill patients. In July 1990 the Supreme Court refused the Cruzans' request that their daughter's tube be removed but ruled that states could sanction the removal if there is "clear and convincing evidence" that the patient would have wished it. Cruzan's family subsequently found other witnesses to testify that Nancy would not have wanted to be kept alive in such a condition.

A Missouri judge decided that the testimony met the Supreme Court's test. The tube was disconnected in December 1990, and Nancy Cruzan died several days later, on December 26.

At the present time, 10,000 Americans are in similar vegetative conditions, unable to communicate. Many of these individuals have virtually no chance to recover. Right-to-die questions will undoubtedly continue to be raised in many of these cases.

Do you believe that the terminally ill have a right to die by refusing treatment? Do you believe that assisted suicide should be legalized? If you had a terminally ill close relative who was in intense pain and asked you to assist her or him in acquiring a lethal dose of drugs, how would you respond? Would you be willing to help? Or would you refuse?

---

or urine.[69] He also reported that the food was so unappetizing that residents at times refused to eat it, that many homes had serious safety hazards, and that boredom and apathy were common among staff as well as residents.

In 1987 investigators for the U.S. Senate Special Committee on Aging found that one-third of nursing homes did not comply with federal regulations and that conditions in 800—almost one in ten—were "shockingly, dangerously bad."[70] The study found neglect, medical maltreatment, and, in a few isolated cases, even beatings and rape. There also was evidence of unnecessary deaths of nursing-home residents; for example, the study found that in California 79 patients died between 1985 and 1986 as a direct result of neglect.[71]

Donald Robinson conducted a nationwide investigation of nursing homes in 1988 and concluded: "I learned that the majority of nursing homes are safe, well-run institutions that take good care of the sick people entrusted to them. Some are superb."[72] Robinson also noted a number of horrors and abuses in some of the homes. The abuses included giving new and unapproved drugs to patients without their consent, giving patients heavy doses of tranquilizers to keep them

EXHIBIT 13.5

Some Programs for the Elderly

- *Medicare:* Helps pay the medical and hospital expenses of the elderly (described in Chapter 14).

- *Old Age, Survivors, and Disability Insurance:* Provides monthly payments to eligible retired workers (described in Chapter 3).

- *Supplemental Security Income:* Provides a minimum income for the indigent elderly (described in Chapter 3).

- *Medicaid:* Pays most medical expenses for low-income people (described in Chapter 14).

- *Food stamps:* Offset some of the food expenses for low-income people who qualify (described in Chapter 3).

- *Nursing Home Ombudsman Program:* Investigates and acts on concerns expressed by residents in nursing homes.

- *Meals on Wheels:* Provides hot and cold meals to housebound recipients who are incapable of obtaining or preparing their own meals but who can feed themselves.

- *Retired Senior Volunteer Program (RSVP):* Seeks to match work and service opportunities with the elderly volunteers seeking them.

- *Foster Grandparent Program:* Pays the elderly for part-time work in which they provide individual care and attention to ill and needy children and youths.

- *Service Corps of Retired Executives (SCORE):* Provides consulting services to small businesses. This program enables retired executives to retain meaningful functions in our society.

- *Senior citizens' centers, golden-age clubs, and similar groups:* Provide leisure-time and recreational activities for the elderly.

- *Special bus rates:* Reduce bus transportation costs for the elderly.

(continued)

---

docile, stealing funds from patients, submitting phony cost reports to Medicare, and charging patients thousands of dollars to gain admission to a home; there were also instances of sexual abuse of patients by staff members.[73]

In spite of the criticism, nursing homes are needed, particularly for the elderly who require medical and nursing care. If nursing homes were abolished, some other institution (such as a hospital) would have to serve older people who can no longer live independently or with their families. Life in nursing homes need not be bad. Where homes are properly administered, residents can expand rather than restrict their life experiences.

At present, people of all ages tend to be prejudiced against nursing homes, even those that are well run. Frank Moss describes the elderly person's view of nursing homes: "The average senior citizen looks at a nursing home as a human junkyard, as a prison—a kind of purgatory, halfway between society and the cemetery—or as the first step of an inevitable slide into oblivion."[74] To some degree there is reality to the notion that nursing homes are places where the elderly wait to die.

Because of limits on reimbursement in nursing homes funded primarily by government sources, a number of other problems may arise. Homes try to keep salaries down and to maintain minimal staffs. A home may postpone repairs and improvements on the facilities. Food is likely to be inexpensive—such as macaroni, which is high in fats and carbohydrates. Congress has provided

EXHIBIT 13.5 *(continued)*

- *Property tax relief:* Available to the elderly in many states.

- *Special federal income-tax deduction:* For people over 65.

- *Housing projects for the elderly:* Built by local sponsors with financial assistance provided by the Department of Housing and Urban Development.

- *Reduced rates at movie theaters and other places of entertainment:* Often offered voluntarily by individual owners.

- *Home health services:* Provide visiting-nurse services, physical therapy, drugs, laboratory services, and sickroom equipment.

- *Nutrition programs:* Provide meals for the elderly at group "eating sites." (These meals are generally provided four or five times a week and usually are lunchtime meals. These programs improve the nutrition of the elderly and offer opportunities for socialization.)

- *Homemaker services:* Provided in some communities to take care of household tasks that the elderly are no longer able to do for themselves.

- *Day-care centers for the elderly:* Provide activities that are determined by the needs of the group. (This service gives the family some relief from 24-hour care. Programs such as home health services, homemaker services, and day-care centers prevent or postpone institutionalization.)

- *Telephone reassurance:* Provided by volunteers, often older people, who telephone elderly people who live alone. (Such calls are a meaningful form of social contact for both parties and also ascertain whether any accidents or other serious problems have arisen that require emergency attention.)

- *Nursing homes:* Provide residential care and skilled nursing care for the elderly who cannot take care of themselves or whose families can no longer take care of them.

---

that every nursing-home patient on Medicaid receive a monthly personal spending allowance. The homes have control over these funds, and some of them keep this money.[75]

Gordon and Walter Moss present additional complaints:

> The quality of care from both particular staff members and from the institution as a whole is another major source of problems and complaints. There may be much delayed or no response to calls for help. Patients may be left sitting for a long time on bedpans. The staff may harass patients they dislike or consider to be insufficiently docile by doing these things, or by withholding services, isolating them in separate rooms in little-used parts of the building, or forcing them to remain bedridden.[76]

There are many complaints about the physical facilities. There may not be enough floor space, or there may be too many people in a room. The call light by the bed may be difficult to reach, or the toilets and showers may not be conveniently located. The building may be decaying. Nursing-home residents also complain about some of the other patients who cause problems by being noisy, by stealing, and by disrupting others' privacy.

Frank Moss, along with a number of other authorities, is critical of our society's response to the problems of the elderly:

> The phenomenon of large numbers of ill elderly is a comparatively recent problem in the United States, as is our solution—nursing homes. The solution reflects today's society: the sick and

EXHIBIT 13.6

Community Options Program: Providing Alternatives to Nursing-Home Placement

Community Options Program (COP) is an innovative program in Wisconsin to provide alternatives to nursing-home placement. COP is funded by the state and by the federal government and is administered by county social services departments.

To qualify for the program, a person must have a long-term or irreversible illness or disability and be a potential or current resident of a nursing home or of a facility for persons with a developmental disability. The person must also have income and assets that are below the poverty line. If these eligibility guidelines are met, a social worker and a nurse assess applicants for their social and physical abilities and disabilities to determine the types of services needed.

If an alternative to nursing-home placement is available, financially feasible, and—most important—preferred by an applicant, a plan for services is drawn up and a start date for in-home or in-community services is determined.

A wide variety of services may be provided as alternatives to placement in nursing homes. Typical services include homemaker services, visiting-nurse services, home-delivered meals, adult foster care, group home care, and case management. COP is a coordinated program that makes use of a number of resources from a variety of agencies. Wisconsin is finding that the program is not only cost effective in comparison to the high cost of nursing-home care but is also preferred over nursing-home care by service recipients. (A number of other states are now offering COP—or programs similar to COP.)

---

the aged are an embarrassment; they remind us of our own mortality and therefore should be removed from view.[77]

At present only 5% of the elderly population reside in nursing homes. However, it is estimated that one out of every five of us who live beyond age 65 will spend part of our life in a nursing home.[78]

SOCIAL WORK AND THE ELDERLY

Social work education is taking a leading role in identifying the problems of the elderly and is developing gerontological specializations within the curricula. Although in the past social workers have not been a significant part of the staff of most agencies serving the aging, this is changing. Some states, for example, are now requiring that each nursing home employ a social worker.

Social workers have a number of skills to help meet the special needs and concerns of the aged. They can function as brokers to link the elderly with available services. In any community there are a wide range of services available, but few people are knowledgeable about the array of services or the eligibility requirements. The elderly are in special need of this "broker" service, because some have difficulty with transportation and communication and others may be reluctant to request needed assistance to which they are entitled.

Counseling is another function social workers can provide to the elderly or to the families of the elderly. Counseling may relate to emotional prob-

The majority of nursing homes are safe and well run. When homes are properly administered, residents can expand rather than restrict their life experiences.

lems, employment, health problems, death and dying, nursing-home placement, or numerous other problems.

Outreach is another role for social workers. This includes identifying and offering services to those aged who need financial assistance, better housing, health care services, recreational and leisure-time services, transportation, companionship, consumer protection services, sex education, and hot-meal programs. Communities are now finding it more cost efficient—and better for most of the elderly—to provide services in people's homes than to use the alternative of a nursing home. Social workers are increasingly becoming involved in providing and coordinating services to the elderly in their home.

Additional roles are opening up for social workers in the field of aging: consultants, community planners, researchers, and administrators of services. The role of advocate may also become crucial. Jordan Kosberg makes the following comments about this role:

Some time in the not-too-distant future there may well be a thundering outcry against the conditions in which the aged live. Call it an eruption of social conscience. Such a phenomenon has occurred in regard to racial prejudice, poverty, the status of women, pollution, and overpopulation. Social workers have the motivation and responsibility to care for the disadvantaged; this care is the raison d'étre of their profession. If they are not in the vanguard of such a movement on behalf of the aged—making sure that it is a long-range effective effort—they will be denying their commitment to their profession and to society.[79]

Because the elderly population is the most rapidly growing age group in our society, it is anticipated that services to the elderly will significantly expand in the next few decades. This expansion will generate a number of new employment opportunities for social workers.

THE EMERGENCE OF THE ELDERLY AS A POWERFUL POLITICAL FORCE

In spite of all the maintenance programs that are now available, the key problems of the elderly remain to be solved. A high proportion of older people do not have meaningful lives, respected status, adequate income, transportation, good living arrangements, a healthy diet, or adequate health care.

Our society has made gains in combating many kinds of prejudice, but ageism is still prevalent. Gordon and Walter Moss comment: "Just as we are learning that black can be beautiful, so we must learn that gray can be beautiful, too. In so learning, we may brighten the prospects of our own age."[80]

In the past, prejudice has been most effectively countered when those being discriminated against joined together for political action. It therefore seems apparent that, if major changes in the elderly's role in our society are to take place, similar action will be needed.

Older people are, in fact, becoming increasingly involved in political activism—and, in some cases, even radical militancy. Two prominent organizations are the American Association of Retired Persons and its affiliated group, the National Retired Teachers Association. These groups, among others, are lobbying for the interests of the elderly at local, state, and federal levels of government.

An action-oriented group that has caught the public's attention is the Gray Panthers. This organization argues that a fundamental flaw in our society is the emphasis on materialism and the consumption of goods and services rather than on improving the quality of life for all citizens (including the elderly). The Gray Panthers are seeking to end ageism and to advance the goals of human freedom, human dignity, and self-development. This organization advocates social action techniques, including getting the elderly to vote as a bloc for their concerns. The founder of the group, Maggie Kuhn, states: "We are not mellow, sweet old people. We have got to effect change, and we have nothing to lose."[81]

There are clear indications that the politics of age have arrived. The elderly are rapidly becoming one of the most politically organized and influential groups in the United States. The past 30 years have seen some significant steps toward securing a better life for the elderly: increased Social Security payments, enactment of Medicare and Medicaid programs, the emergence of hospices, and the expansion of a variety of other programs. With the clout of this powerful political bloc, additional changes to improve the status of the elderly in our society can be expected.

DEVELOPMENT OF SOCIAL ROLES FOR THE ELDERLY

It is essential for our society to find a meaningful, productive role for the elderly. At present, many companies' early retirement programs and society's stereotypic expectations of the elderly often result in older citizens' being unproductive, inactive, dependent, and unfulfilled. There are several steps that can be taken to provide productive roles for older people.

The elderly who want to work and are still performing well should be encouraged to continue working well past age 65 or 70, even if only half time or part time. Two elderly people working half time could be allowed to fill a full-time position. New roles might also be created for the elderly as consultants after they retire in the areas in which they possess special knowledge and expertise. For those who do retire, there should be educational and training programs to help them develop their interests and hobbies (such as photography) into new sources of income.

Working longer would have a number of payoffs for the elderly and for society. Older people would continue to be productive, contributing citizens; they would have a meaningful role; they would continue to be physically and mentally active; they would have higher self-esteem; and they could break down the stereotypes of the elderly being unproductive and a financial burden on society. And, importantly, they would be paying into the Social Security system rather than drawing from it.

Objections to such a system may be raised by those who maintain that some of the elderly are no longer productive. This may be true, but some younger people are also unproductive. What is needed to make the proposed system work is realistic, objective, and behaviorally measurable levels of performance. Individuals at any age who do not meet those standards would be informed about the deficiencies and given training to improve. If the performance levels still were not met, discharge would be used as a last resort. (For example, if a tenured faculty member's performance is inadequate—as measured by students' course evaluations, peer faculty evaluations of teaching, record of public service, record of service to the department and to the campus, and record of publications—she or he would be informed of the deficiencies. Training and other resources to meet standards should be offered. If the performance then does not improve to acceptable levels, dismissal proceedings would be initiated. Some colleges and universities are now moving in this direction.)

Another objection that has been voiced about this new system is that the elderly have worked

Volunteer activities are highly satisfying for many senior citizens.

most of their lives and therefore deserve to retire and live in leisure with a high standard of living. It would be nice if the elderly really had this option. However, that is not realistic. Most older citizens do not have the financial resources, after retiring, to maintain a high standard of living. The only real options in our society are to work and thereby maintain a higher standard of living or to retire and have a lower standard of living.

Some progress is being made in keeping the elderly in productive roles. Most members of the U.S. Supreme Court and many members of Congress are over age 70. In addition, a number of organizations have been formed to promote the productivity of the elderly. Three examples of these organizations are the Retired Senior Volunteer Program, the Service Corps of Retired Executives, and the Foster Grandparent Program.

The *Retired Senior Volunteer Program (RSVP)* offers people over age 60 the opportunity of doing volunteer service to meet community needs. RSVP agencies place volunteers in hospitals, schools, libraries, day-care centers, courts, nursing homes, and a variety of other organizations.

The *Service Corps of Retired Executives (SCORE)* offers retired businessmen and businesswomen an opportunity to help owners of small businesses and managers of community organizations who are having management problems. Volunteers receive no pay but are reimbursed for out-of-pocket expenses.

The *Foster Grandparent Program* employs low-income older people to help provide personal, individual care to children who live in institutions. (Such children include those who have a severe cognitive disability, those who are emotionally disturbed, and those who have a developmental disability.) Foster grandparents are given special assignments in child care, speech therapy, physical therapy or as teacher's aides. This program has been shown to be of considerable benefit to both the children and the foster grandparents.[82] The children served become more outgoing and enjoy improved relationships with peers and staff.

They have increased self-confidence, improved language skills, and decreased fear and insecurity. The foster grandparents have an additional (although small) source of income, increased feelings of vigor and youthfulness, an increased sense of personal worth, a feeling of being productive, and a renewed sense of personal growth and development. For society, foster grandparents provide a vast pool of relatively inexpensive labor that can be used to do needed work in the community.

The success of these programs illustrates that the elderly can be productive in both paid and volunteer positions. In regard to using elderly volunteers in agencies, Robert Atchley makes the following recommendations to increase the opportunities for successful outcomes:

> *First, agencies must be flexible in matching the volunteer's background to assigned tasks. If the agency takes a broad perspective, useful work can be found for almost anyone. Second,* volunteers must be trained. *All too often agency personnel place unprepared volunteers in an unfamiliar setting. Then the volunteer's difficulty confirms the myth that you cannot expect good work from volunteers. Third, a variety of placement options should be offered to the volunteers. Some volunteers prefer to do familiar things; others want to do* anything but *familiar things. Fourth, training of volunteers should not make them feel that they are being tested. This point is particularly sensitive among working-class volunteers. Fifth, volunteers should get personal attention from the placement agency. There should be people (perhaps volunteers) who follow up on absences and who are willing to listen to the compliments, complaints, or experiences of the volunteers. Public recognition from the community is an important reward for voluntary service. Finally, transportation to and from the placement should be provided.*[83]

In a 1990 study a surprisingly large number of recent retirees said they would like to be back at work.[84] Of recent retirees, half are satisfied, a quarter are unable to work because of their health or family situations, and a quarter (about 2 million people) say they would prefer working again over retirement.

PREPARATION FOR LATER ADULTHOOD

Growing old is a lifelong process. Turning 65 does not interrupt the continuities in what a person has been, presently is, and will be. Recognition of this fact should lessen the fear of growing old. For people of modest means who have prepared thoughtfully, later adulthood can be a period, if not of luxury, then at least of reasonable comfort and pleasure.

Our lives depend largely on our goals and our motivations to achieve those goals. How we live prior to retiring will determine whether later adulthood will be a nightmare or a dream. There are a number of areas we should attend to in our younger years:

■ *Health:* A sound exercise plan and periodic health examinations are crucial to the prevention of chronic health problems. Also critically important in maintaining health is learning and using techniques to reduce psychological stress.

■ *Finances:* Saving money for later years is important, as is learning to manage or budget money wisely.

■ *Interests and hobbies:* Psychologically, people who are traumatized most by retirement are those whose self-image and life interests center around their work. Individuals who have meaningful hobbies and interests look forward to retirement so they can devote more of their time to these enjoyable activities.

■ *Self-identity:* People who are comfortable and realistic about who they are and what they want out of life are better prepared, including in later years, to deal with stresses and crises that arise.

■ *A view toward the future:* A person who dwells on the past or rests on past laurels is likely to find the later years depressing. On the other hand, a person who looks to the future is able to find new challenges and new satisfactions in later years. Looking toward the future involves planning for retirement, including deciding where you want to live and what you want to do with your free time.

▪ *Coping with abilities:* If a person learns to cope effectively with crises in younger years, these coping skills will remain when the person is older. Effective coping involves learning to approach problems realistically and constructively.

SUMMARY

Aging is an individual process that occurs at different rates in different people. Chronological age is not an accurate measure of how physically fit or mentally alert an elderly person is.

People 65 and older now compose over one-tenth of our population. The old old are the fastest-growing age group in our society. The elderly encounter a number of problems in our society: low status, lack of a meaningful role, the social emphasis on youth, health problems, inadequate income, loss of family and friends, inadequate housing, transportation problems, restrictive attitudes about expressing their sexuality, malnutrition, crime victimization, and emotional problems such as depression and concern with circumstances surrounding dying. A majority of the elderly depend on the Social Security system as their major source of income. Yet monthly payments are inadequate, and the system is no longer financially sound.

A wide array of services are available to older people, but these are primarily geared to maintaining the elderly, often at or only slightly above a subsistence level of existence. Services provided in many of our nursing homes are inadequate, and the level of care in some of these homes has been sharply criticized. Nursing homes have also been criticized as being "storage centers" for the elderly so that members of our society can avoid coming face to face with their own mortality.

Although the level of care needs to be substantially improved, nursing homes are needed for the elderly who cannot take care of themselves

and/or for those whose families can no longer provide care. Most older persons, however, do not need nursing homes for permanent care or shelter. (It is not generally known that 95% of the elderly live independently or with relatives, not in nursing homes.)

In order to provide the elderly with a productive, meaningful role in our society, it is suggested that they be encouraged to work (either in paid jobs or as volunteers) as long as they are productive and have an interest in working to maintain their standard of living. Empowering the elderly to be productive in their lives would have a number of personal payoffs for them and also be highly beneficial to society.

In many ways the elderly are victims of ageism. Social workers play numerous roles in serving the elderly, including that of an advocate to secure system changes that will better serve the elderly. Increasingly, the elderly are becoming politically active and are organizing to improve their status. Gradually, the composition of the elderly population will change; aging people will become better educated and more powerful politically. In the future there are likely to be a number of social, economic, and political changes that will improve the status of the elderly.

NOTES

1. Gordon Moss and Walter Moss, *Growing Old* (New York: Pocket Books, 1975), pp. 17–18.
2. Eric Sharp, "The 'Retirement in Florida' Dream Can Become a Nightmare for Some," *Detroit Free Press,* Sept. 9, 1973, p. 11.
3. Moss and Moss, *Growing Old,* p. 18.
4. Colin M. Turnbull, *The Mountain People* (New York: Simon and Schuster, 1972).
5. William Kornblum and Joseph Julian, *Social Problems,* 7th ed. (Englewood Cliffs, NJ: Prentice-Hall, 1992), pp. 324–325.
6. Diane E. Papalia and Sally W. Olds, *Human Development,* 5th ed. (New York: McGraw-Hill, 1992), pp. 486–490.
7. Milton L. Barron, "The Aged as a Quasi-Minority Group," in *The Other Minorities,* Edward Sagarin, ed. (Lexington, MA: Ginn, 1971), p. 149.

8. Elizabeth Ferguson, *Social Work: An Introduction,* 3d ed. (Philadelphia: Lippincott, 1975), p. 238.

9. U.S. Bureau of the Census, *Statistical Abstract of the United States, 1993* (Washington, DC: U.S. Government Printing Office, 1993), pp. 68–74.

10. Joan Arehart-Triechel, "It's Never Too Late to Start Living Longer," *New York,* Apr. 11, 1977, p. 38.

11. Thomas Sullivan, Kenrick Thompson, Richard Wright, George Gross, and Dale Spady, *Social Problems* (New York: Wiley, 1980), pp. 335–370.

12. *Statistical Abstract of the United States, 1993.*

13. Ibid.

14. John E. Farley, *American Social Problems,* 2d ed. (Englewood Cliffs, NJ: Prentice-Hall, 1992), pp. 122–123.

15. Ibid.

16. Alan S. Otten, "Ever More Americans Live into 80s and 90s, Causing Big Problems," *The Wall Street Journal,* July 30, 1984, p. 1.

17. Sally Bould, Beverly Sanborn, and Laura Reif, *Eighty-Five Plus: The Oldest Old* (Belmont, CA: Wadsworth, 1989), p. 34.

18. Ibid.

19. Eisdor Fer, quoted in Otten, "Ever More Americans Live into 80s and 90s, Causing Big Problems," p. 10.

20. American Association of Retired Persons, *A Profile of Older Americans: 1990* (Washington, DC: Author, 1990), p. 11.

21. Kornblum and Julian, *Social Problems,* pp. 322–325.

22. Ibid.

23. Robert N. Butler and Myrna I. Lewis, *Aging and Mental Health: Positive Psychosocial Approaches,* 2d ed. (St. Louis: Mosby, 1977).

24. Robert C. Atchley, "Aging as a Social Problem: An Overview," in *Social Problems of the Aging,* M. M. Seltzer, S. L. Corbett, and R. C. Atchley, eds. (Belmont, CA: Wadsworth, 1978).

25. M. P. Lawton, "Leisure Activities for the Aged," *Annals of the American Academy of Political and Social Science,* 438 (1978), pp. 71–79.

26. American Association of Retired Persons, pp. 4–11.

27. Ibid.

28. Ibid., pp. 4–8.

29. Marilyn L. Flynn, "Aging," in *Contemporary Social Work,* 2d ed., Donald Brieland, Lela Costin, and Charles Atherton, eds. (New York: McGraw-Hill, 1980), p. 353.

30. Kornblum and Julian, *Social Problems,* pp. 324–325.

31. Sullivan et al., *Social Problems,* pp. 357–358.

32. "Will Inflation Tarnish Your Golden Years?" *U.S. News & World Report,* Feb. 26, 1979, p. 57.

33. Kornblum and Julian, *Social Problems,* p. 325.

34. *Statistical Abstract of the United States, 1993,* pp. 68–74.

35. A. Saltzman and L. Wiener, "A Boomers' Plan," *U.S. News & World Report,* Aug. 15, 1988, pp. 64–67.

36. Farley, *American Social Problems,* pp. 124–128.

37. Ibid.

38. American Association of Retired Persons, p. 3.

39. Moss and Moss, *Growing Old,* p. 47.

40. American Association of Retired Persons, p. 4.

41. Ibid., pp. 3–4.

42. Ibid.

43. Ibid.

44. Ibid.

45. Ibid., p. 5.

46. Ibid.

47. Janet S. Hyde, *Understanding Human Sexuality* (New York: McGraw-Hill, 1990), pp. 335–341.

48. Ibid.

49. William H. Masters and Virginia E. Johnson, "The Human Sexual Response: The Aging Female and the Aging Male," in *Middle Age and Aging,* L. Neugarten, ed. (Chicago: University of Chicago Press, 1968).

50. Ibid., p. 269.

51. Merlin Taber, "The Aged," in *Contemporary Social Work,* Donald Brieland, Lela Costin, and Charles Atherton, eds. (New York: McGraw-Hill, 1975), p. 359.

52. Bould et al., *Eighty-Five Plus,* pp. 95–96.

53. Kornblum and Julian, *Social Problems,* pp. 317–318.

54. Ibid.

55. Rex A. Skidmore and Milton Thackeray, *Introduction to Social Work,* 2d ed. (Englewood Cliffs, NJ: Prentice-Hall, 1976), p. 225.

56. Robert N. Butler, "Myths and Realities of Aging," address presented at the Governor's Conference on Aging, Columbia, MD, May 28, 1970.

57. Moss and Moss, *Growing Old,* p. 72.

58. See, for example, Elisabeth Kübler-Ross, *On Death and Dying* (New York: Macmillan, 1969); and R. E. Kavanaugh, *Facing Death* (Los Angeles: Nash, 1972).

59. Margaret Mead, "Dealing with the Aged: A New Style of Aging," *Current,* no. 136 (January 1972), p. 44.

60. Carol Staudacher, *Beyond Grief* (Oakland, CA: New Harbinger, 1987).

61. Sullivan et al., *Social Problems,* p. 363.

62. *Older Americans Act of 1965, as Amended, Text and History* (Washington, DC: U.S. Department of Health, Education and Welfare), November 1970.

63. Donald Robinson, "The Crisis in Our Nursing Homes," *Parade,* Aug. 16, 1987, p. 13.

64. Bould et al., *Eighty-Five Plus.*
65. Ibid.
66. Abigail Trafford, "The Tragedy of Care for America's Elderly," *U.S. News & World Report,* Apr. 24, 1978, p. 56.
67. Robert N. Butler, *Why Survive? Being Old in America* (New York: Harper & Row, 1975), p. 264.
68. Dianne Paley, "Nursing Home Is Cited Again," *Wisconsin State Journal,* May 23, 1980, sec. 4, p. 1.
69. Butler, *Why Survive? Being Old in America,* p. 264.
70. Robinson, "The Crisis in Our Nursing Homes," p. 13.
71. Ibid.
72. Ibid.
73. Ibid., pp. 13–14.
74. Frank Moss, "It's Hell to Be Old In the U.S.A.," *Parade,* July 17, 1977, p. 9.
75. Ibid.
76. Moss and Moss, *Growing Old,* p. 61.
77. Moss, "It's Hell to Be Old in the U.S.A.," p. 9.
78. Robinson, "The Crisis in Our Nursing Homes," p. 13.
79. Jordan J. Kosberg, "The Nursing Home: A Social Work Paradox," *Social Work,* 18, no. 2 (March 1973), p. 109.
80. Moss and Moss, *Growing Old,* p. 79.
81. Quoted in Butler, *Why Survive? Being Old In America,* p. 341.
82. Robert C. Atchley, *The Social Forces in Later Life: An Introduction to Social Gerontology,* 2d ed. (Belmont, CA: Wadsworth, 1977), p. 267.
83. Ibid., p. 81.
84. Tamar Lewin, "Many Retirees Tire of Leisurely Lives, Seek New Jobs," *Wisconsin State Journal,* Apr. 22, 1990, p. 1A.

14

MEDICAL

PROBLEMS

AND MEDICAL

SOCIAL

SERVICES

Health and happiness are what we want most in life. Wealthy people who develop a chronic illness often say they would, if given a choice, relinquish their riches for a return to health. Most Americans now consider proper medical care a basic human right for which society should pay if an individual cannot. The view that health care is a basic right rather than a privilege is of relatively recent origin. For example, in 1967 the president of the American Medical Association still asserted that health care should be available only to those who could afford it.[1] The view of health care as a right was expressed by former President Richard Nixon in his Health Message of 1971:

> Just as our National Government has moved to provide equal opportunity in areas such as education, employment, and voting, so we must now work to expand the opportunity for all citizens to obtain a decent standard of medical care. We must do all we can to remove any racial, economic, social, or geographic barriers that now prevent any of our citizens from obtaining adequate health protection. For without good health, no man can fully utilize his other opportunities.[2]

This chapter will:

- Briefly describe the health care system in the United States.

- Summarize problems in health care: profit orientation, limited attention to preventive medicine, unequal access to health services, health care for the elderly, AIDS, unnecessary and harmful medical services, use of life-sustaining equipment, and the high cost of medical care.

- Discuss current efforts to resolve these problems.

- Outline a number of proposed policies and programs to combat these problems.

- Describe medical social work.

PHYSICAL ILLNESSES AND THE HEALTH CARE SYSTEM

There are hundreds of thousands of different medical conditions, ranging in severity from a minor scratch to a terminal illness. The causes are also nearly infinite: accidents, infections, birth defects, viruses, bacteria, the aging process, stress, poor nutrition, and so on.

Medical services in this country are organized into four basic components: physicians in private practice, group outpatient settings, hospital settings, and public health services.[3]

Physicians in individual or solo practice are, proportionately, more often found in rural than in urban areas. Such a physician is usually a general practitioner who is trained to provide treatment for the more common medical ailments. Supervision of general practitioners is minimal or nil; they are primarily accountable only to patients. Except through referrals for consultation and occasional use of laboratories and hospitals, a physician in private practice works in relative isolation from colleagues.

Group outpatient settings can be organized in several ways. A group of general practitioners may share facilities, such as a waiting room, examining rooms, and a laboratory. Or, each physician within a group may have a different specialty and complement the skills of the others. Because medical knowledge and treatment techniques have become so vast and diverse, it is now impossible for a physician to have in-depth knowledge in all areas. Another type of outpatient setting is one in which a third party (a university, union, business, or factory) employs a group of physicians to provide medical care for its constituency. In still another type, a group of doctors with the same specialty (for example, neurological surgery) provide services in the same facility.

A third subsystem of health care is the hospital setting, which has a wide range of laboratory facilities, specialized treatment equipment, inpatient care facilities, and highly skilled technicians. Hospitals employ diverse and numerous medical personnel. A hospital is generally the center of the medical care system in communities. Because of the spiraling costs of hospital care and the lack of sufficient beds, many communities are now building nursing homes and convalescent homes for people who require fairly extensive medical care but not inpatient hospital attention.

Public health services are organized on five levels: local (city or county), regional, state, national, and international. The majority of public health services to a community are provided through local health programs. The priorities in public health keep changing; as success is achieved in dealing with one problem, other problems emerge that demand attention. Public health services have virtually eliminated a number of communicable diseases in this country, such as tuberculosis, polio, and smallpox.

The focus of public health services is primarily preventive in nature. Services provided through local health departments include: (1) health counseling to families regarding family planning, prenatal and postpartum care, child growth and development, nutrition, and medical care; (2) skilled nursing care and treatment to the acute and chronically ill; (3) physical rehabilitation to patients with strokes, arthritis, and similar medical conditions; (4) school health services to public and parochial institutions and liaison services among home, school, and community; (5) disease prevention and control; (6) immunization services; (7) referral of families and individuals in order to make maximum use of available community resources; (8) environmental sanitation, which involves developing and enforcing codes, rules, and regulations designed to maintain and/or improve conditions in the environment that affect health (this activity covers a broad area, including air and water pollution, food protection, waste material disposal, and sanitation of recreation facilities); (9) maintenance of an index of all area births, deaths, marriages, and current communicable diseases; and (10) health education and information services to stimulate the public to recognize existing health problems. In the United States the vast majority of health care services are private

rather than public (that is, administered by the government).

PROBLEMS IN HEALTH CARE

The health care system in the United States faces a number of problems. These include a service orientation versus profit orientation, limited attention to preventive medicine, unequal access to health services, low-quality health care for the elderly, AIDS, unnecessary or harmful care, use of life-sustaining equipment, and the high cost of medical care.

Service Orientation versus Profit Orientation

Most Americans believe that the only focus of health care is to keep people healthy—to prevent diseases, illnesses, and impairments from occurring and to restore to health as rapidly as possible those who do become ill. If this were the only objective, the health care system would not receive very high grades. Our infant mortality rate of 10 per 1000 live births is higher than that of 17 other countries.[4] Thirteen other nations have higher life expectancy rates than ours.[5] The death rate from heart disease in the United States is the highest in the world, and the incidence of and death rate from cancer rank among the highest.[6]

The objectives of health care providers in the United States are not only to restore and maintain health but also to make a profit. There are numerous statistics documenting that the system is prospering. Many of our more than 7000 hospitals are among the most modern in the world. Physicians have the highest median income of any occupational group. They earn several times more than the average wage earner. In 1993 the mean income of American doctors was over $165,000, and their incomes are rising faster than those of any other occupational group.[7] The average daily cost for a hospital bed has gone from $74 in 1970 to $752 in 1991.[8] One of the most profitable small businesses in this country is the private medical practice. Among the most profitable intermediate-sized businesses are nursing homes. The value of nursing-home stocks has risen dramatically in the past two decades on Wall Street. The pharmaceuticals industry, involving the manufacture and sale of drugs, has been one of the most profitable large-sized industries in the country.

The United States spends more money on health care (in both absolute and proportionate terms) than any other country. Medical costs constitute over 10% of our total production of goods and services. The medical system is the third largest industry in the country in terms of money spent, surpassed only by agriculture and construction. Total expenditures on health care have gone from $3.8 billion in 1940 to $900 billion in 1993.[9] Americans spend 171% more per person on health care than the British, 124% more than the Japanese, and 38% more than the Canadians.[10]

Consumers seeking immediate and inexpensive health care in our country are often frustrated and angered over high costs and delays. Access is particularly difficult in urban ghettos, low-income neighborhoods, and smaller rural communities because health care facilities tend to be located in affluent urban and suburban neighborhoods. The late Robert F. Kennedy described the health care system in the United States as "a national failure" that is "providing poor quality care at high costs."[11]

Other industrialized nations regard medical care as a social service, a philosophy based on the premise that the kind of care you receive depends on the kind of illness you have. In contrast, in the United States the kind of medical care you receive depends not only on your illness but also on how much money you are able and willing to spend.

Emphasis on Treatment Rather than on Prevention

Most of the major causes of death today in the United States are chronic diseases: heart disease, cancer, cerebrovascular disease (such as strokes), obstructive pulmonary disease, and the like

TABLE 14.1

Ten Leading Causes of Death in the United States

Rank	Percentage of Total Deaths
1. Heart disease	29.2
2. Cancer	26.0
3. All accidents	6.2
4. Stroke	5.3
5. Chronic obstructive pulmonary disease	3.8
6. Pneumonia and influenza	2.7
7. Diabetes	2.2
8. Suicide	2.2
9. Homicide	2.0
10. Chronic liver disease and cirrhosis	1.7

Source: U.S. Bureau of the Census, *Statistical Abstract of the United States, 1993* (Washington, DC: U.S. Government Printing Office, 1993), p. 90.

(Table 14.1). Chronic diseases progress and persist over a long period of time. They may exist long before we are aware of them, because often there are no symptoms in the early stages and because we tend to ignore early symptoms. Social, psychological, and environmental factors are important influences in the progression of these diseases. Heart disease, for example, is known to be associated with a diet of highly saturated animal fats (beef, butter, and cheese), lack of consistent and vigorous exercise, heavy smoking, and stress.

A major problem is that modern medicine is oriented toward crisis medicine, which is geared to treating people *after they become ill.* The crisis approach is effective in coping with some types of medical conditions, such as acute problems (for example, injuries, influenza, or pneumonia). Unfortunately, with chronic diseases, once the symptoms manifest themselves, much of the damage has already been done, and it is often too late to effect a complete recovery. In order to curb the incapacitating effects of chronic diseases, the

EXHIBIT 14.1

Health and Longevity

N edra Belloc and Lester Breslow, in a study of 6928 adults, found that the following seven health practices are positively related to good health and longevity:

- Eating breakfast.
- Exercising regularly.
- Staying within 10% of your proper weight.
- Not smoking cigarettes.
- Not drinking to excess.
- Not eating between meals.
- Sleeping seven to eight hours a night.

At age 45 a person who follows all seven of these practices will have a life expectancy that is 11 years longer than that of a person who follows fewer than four. A 70-year-old who practices all seven is likely to be as healthy as a 40-year-old who follows only one or two.

Source: A. F. Ehrbar, "A Radical Prescription for Medical Care," *Fortune* (February 1977), p. 169.

health care delivery system needs to emphasize the prevention of illness before extensive damage occurs. To date, preventive medicine has had a lower priority than crisis-oriented medicine in terms of research funding, the allocation of health care personnel, and the construction of medical facilities. (There are more profits to be made in treatment programs than in prevention programs.) This emphasis on treatment violates the common-sense notion that "an ounce of prevention is worth a pound of cure."

The kinds of health problems that we have in this country stem largely from our lifestyles. Millions of Americans smoke, drink, or eat to excess. Our diet is high in starches, sugars, and animal fats, all of which are factors in a wide variety of illnesses, including heart disease and diabetes. A Harris poll found that only 15% of adults are sufficiently active to be physically fit.[12] Environmental factors also pose health risks. Our air and water are filled with thousands of toxic chemicals (caused by emissions from autos and factories) that create health hazards, such as cancer and emphysema. The fatality rate from automobile crashes is staggeringly high. Many such accidents are caused by driving while intoxicated.

Physicians often treat the symptoms of chronic illnesses rather than the underlying causes. Patients who are tense or anxious are prescribed tranquilizers rather than receiving therapy to reduce the psychological stress that is causing the tension. Patients who are depressed are prescribed antidepressant medication rather than being counseled to determine the underlying reasons for the depression. Patients with stress-related disorders (for example, ulcers, migraine headaches, insomnia, diarrhea, digestive problems, hypertension) are often prescribed medication rather than receiving therapy to change certain aspects of their lifestyles that would reduce the underlying psychological stress, which is a major factor in producing such problems.

In recent years, holistic programs, which are preventive in nature, have been established in industry, in hospitals, in school settings, in medical clinics, and elsewhere. Holistic medicine recognizes that our thinking processes function together with our body as an integrated unit, and it focuses on both our physical and psychological functions. K. R. Pelletier documents that the major determinants of most illnesses are our lifestyles (including exercise patterns, diet, sleep, and, particularly, stress reaction patterns).[13] Holistic medicine instructs people in proper exercises, proper diet, and techniques to reduce psychological stress in order to maintain health and curb the development of chronic disorders.

Thomas McKeown emphasized the responsibility that each person has (although it is often not recognized) in maintaining good health:

The role of individual medical care in preventing sickness and premature death is secondary to

EXHIBIT 14.2

Understanding and Reducing Stress

In *Mind as Healer, Mind as Slayer,* K. R. Pelletier documents that rational and positive thinking has a major impact in promoting healing and maintaining health and that irrational and negative thinking is a major determinant of stress-related illnesses. (Thinking is irrational if it is or does one or more of the following: (1) is inconsistent with objective facts, (2) hampers you in protecting your life, (3) hampers you in achieving your short- and long-term goals, (4) causes significant trouble with other people, and (5) leads you to feel unwanted emotions.) Stress-related physiological and psychological disorders have now become our leading health problem.[a]

A simplified description of the effects of our thinking processes in determining stress-related illnesses is as follows:

Stressor {
Events or experiences
↓
Certain kind of self-talk (for example, "This is a very dangerous situation.")
↓
}

Stress {
Emotions (such as tenseness, anxiety, worry, alarm)
↓
Psychological reactions (A general stress reaction will occur. The physiological changes of a general stress reaction have been described by Hans Selye.[b] The symptoms include an accelerated heart and pulse rate, shallow respiration, perspiring hands, tenseness of the neck and upper back, a rise in red blood count for fighting infection, increased metabolism, and secretion of pro-inflammatory hormones. The physiological reactions that most students experience prior to giving a speech before a group are aspects of the general stress reaction.)
}

↓

If the emotional and physiological reactions are intensive and long term, a stress-related disease is likely to develop, such as an ulcer, migraine

---

[a]K. R. Pelletier, *Mind as Healer, Mind as Slayer* (New York: Delta, 1977).

[b]Hans Selye, *The Stress of Life* (New York: McGraw-Hill, 1965).

(continued)

---

that of other influences, yet society's investment in health care is based on the premise that it is the major determinant. It is assumed that we are ill and are made well, but it is nearer the truth to say that we are well and are made ill. Few people think of themselves as having the major responsibility for their own health. . . .

The public believes that health depends primarily on intervention by the doctor and that the essential requirement for health is the early discovery of disease. This concept should be replaced by recognition that disease often cannot be treated effectively, and that health is determined predominately by the way of life individuals choose to follow. Among the important influences on health are the use of tobacco, the misuse of alcohol and drugs, excessive or unbalanced diets, and lack of exercise. With research, the list of significant behavioral influences will undoubtedly increase.[14]

EXHIBIT 14.2   *(continued)*

headache, diarrhea, heart problems, digestive problems, cancer, hypertension, bronchial asthma, hay fever, arthritis, enuresis, certain skin problems, and constipation.

According to the above formula, there are two components of a "stressor": (1) the event and (2) the self-talk that we give ourselves about that event. "Stress" is the emotional and physiological reaction to a "stressor." Self-talk plays a key role in producing stress. The self-talk approach enables us to understand how positive events (as well as negative events) can lead to a stress reaction:

Positive Event: Receiving a promotion.
↓
Self-talk: "I'll have additional responsibilities that I may not be able to handle."

"If I fail at these new responsibilities, I'll be fired and will be a failure. My career plans will never be realized."

"This promotion will make others in the office jealous."

"I'm in big trouble."

Emotion: Worry, tension, anxiety.
↓
Physiological reaction: The general stress reaction will occur. If it is intensive and prolonged, a stress-related illness can develop.

Stress can be reduced in three primary ways. One way is to identify irrational and negative self-talk and then give yourself rational self-challenges (see Chapter 4 for examples of this approach). A second way is to become involved in activities that you enjoy, which will lead you to stop your irrational thinking and instead focus on events you view more positively. For example, if you enjoy golf, playing golf will lead you to stop thinking about your day-to-day problems and instead lead you to think about the enjoyable experiences associated with golfing. Activities that are likely to stop your irrational thinking include hobbies, entertainment events, jogging and other exercise programs, biofeedback programs, muscle relaxation exercises, and meditation.[c] A third way to reduce stress is to change the event that is producing it (for example, taking a job that you view as having less pressure).

---

[c]These stress-reducing techniques are described in Charles Zastrow, *The Practice of Social Work,* 5th ed. (Pacific Grove, CA: Brooks/Cole), 1995.

Unequal Access to Health Services

Aaron Antonovsky has noted that class and race "influence one's chances of staying alive."[15] He has found that the lack of medical care among the poor and racial minorities leads to higher rates of serious illnesses and shortened life expectancies.

The life expectancy for whites is six years longer than for nonwhites.[16] In addition, the infant mortality rate for nonwhites is twice that of whites.[17] Nonwhites have higher rates of practically every illness than whites. Income differences play a part; but, even when income is the same, death rates are still higher for nonwhites.[18]

Membership in a lower social class is also correlated with higher rates of illnesses. The poor are seriously ill more frequently and for longer periods of time. They have higher rates of untreated illnesses and higher mortality rates for almost all illnesses. Contrary to popular belief, the highest rates of heart disease occur among the lowest salaried, not among top-level executives and managers.[19] (Stress levels may in fact be higher among the poor, who continually face psychological stress from financial crises. Differences in diet, exercise, and lifestyle patterns may also be factors.)

Of course, these higher rates of illness among the poor are largely attributable to their inability to afford private, high-quality medical care. Max Seham has noted:

> For the most part, delivery of health care services is geared to the upper- and middle-class culture because these services take on all the qualities of a commodity for sale and the affluent are the preferred and often the only market. This is especially true in the preventive areas.[20]

In addition, because of the profit motive, health care services are located primarily in affluent urban areas and in suburbs. The poor who live in small rural areas or in urban, low-income regions therefore have much more difficulty in gaining access to medical care, especially if they have transportation barriers. In the United States, health care services are provided on a *fee-for-service* basis. As a result, a two-tier system now exists; the upper tier serves the wealthy with high-quality care, and the lower tier serves the poor with inferior care.

When poor people do decide to seek treatment (often they wait until they are seriously ill), they tend to visit a clinic rather than a private or family physician. At the clinic they may feel self-conscious about their appearance. Frequently they must wait for hours in crowded waiting rooms and generally receive impersonal care. A trusting relationship with a physician is seldom developed. Doctors generally come from the middle and upper classes and therefore may face barriers in establishing rapport with low-income and nonwhite patients. Seham notes:

> In general, health professionals have little—if any—understanding of the lifestyle of the poor.

> For a doctor to advise a patient who is living in poverty to increase his intake of protein, without helping him to work out how to do it, is useless. Similarly, to suggest to a working mother that she come to the clinic for weekly treatments, when the clinic hours coincide with her working hours, is tantamount to not providing treatment at all.[21]

Lee Rainwater has noted that being poor promotes poor health. The poor cannot afford to eat properly, so inadequate diet makes them more susceptible to illnesses. They are more likely to live in the most polluted areas, so they are more susceptible to cancer, emphysema, and other respiratory diseases. They cannot afford proper housing, have less heat in the wintertime, and are more exposed to disease-carrying rodents and garbage. Their lives are more stress filled, particularly with respect to financial concerns. They are less likely to know about and use preventive health approaches. They are less likely to seek early treatment that would prevent a serious disorder from developing. Because they are often treated with hostility and contempt by physicians and other medical personnel, they are likely to avoid seeking medical help.[22]

Low-Quality Health Care for the Elderly

As noted in Chapter 13, the proportion of the elderly in our society is increasing dramatically, and the old old (age 85 and over) are our fastest-growing age group. Today there is a crisis in health care for the elderly for a variety of reasons.

The elderly are much more likely to have long-term illnesses. In the 1960s the Medicare and Medicaid programs were created to pay for much of their medical expense. However, in the 1980s the Reagan and Bush administrations decided that the government could no longer pay the full costs of that care. As a result, cuts were made in eligibility for payments and limits were set for what the government will pay for a variety of medical procedures.[23]

Physicians are trained primarily in treating the young and are often less interested in serving

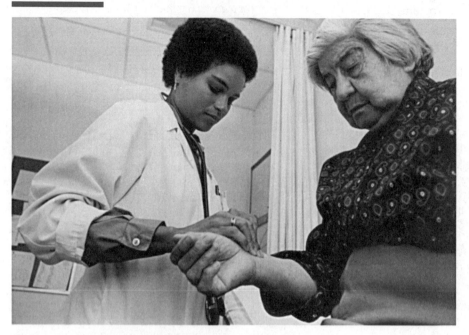

Most physicians today specialize in treating the young. The scarcity of doctors trained in geriatrics has compounded the crisis in health care for the elderly.

the elderly. Accordingly, when the elderly become ill, they may not receive quality medical care. For example, Hugh Downs, in an ABC news report, described the case of an 82-year-old woman who was shuffled from one hospital to another over a three-month period and finally dumped in a county hospital, where she eventually died of a single grossly neglected bedsore. Downs notes:

> *The revolution of longer life has produced a new complex of critical medical needs, needs this nation does not yet seem prepared to meet. For example, there seems little prospect that there will be anything like the numbers of geriatricians needed to care for the elderly. It's a field still avoided by young doctors. Because of the complicated problems of the aging, there is a need for more health evaluation services and more psychiatric and rehabilitation assistance. Even for the limited efforts we now make, funding has always been meager.*
>
> *The new era of the longevity revolution is already bringing with it multiplying health problems to which our society remains largely blind . . . and within this nation's vast medical complex, many old who could be helped are left adrift, trapped, their needs unrecognized.*[24]

Medical conditions of the elderly are often misdiagnosed because doctors lack the specialized training to recognize the unique medical conditions of old people. Many of the elderly who are seriously ill do not get medical attention. One of the reasons physicians are less interested in treating the elderly is that the Medicare program sets reimbursement limits on a variety of procedures. With younger patients the fee-for-service system is much more profitable.

There also are restrictions on hospital payments under Medicare. In the past the payment system covered the full cost of the patient's medical expenses. However, to curtail rampant costs, the federal government in the 1980s set flat payments for each category of illness. These categories are called "diagnostic related groups" (DRGs). With this system, instead of reimbursing hospitals for the actual cost of treating Medicare patients, the government now pays a set fee for each medical condition. If a hospital spends less on a patient than the fixed amount, it makes money; if it spends more, it must absorb the loss. A perverse, unintended consequence of DRGs is that many seriously ill elderly patients are being discharged prematurely.[25] Hospitals that have a social conscience and continue to treat the elderly beyond the length of time allowed by the DRG regulations must cover the expenses themselves and thereby risk bankruptcy.

The elderly who live in the community often have transportation difficulties in getting medical care. Those living in nursing homes sometimes receive inadequate care because health professionals are not interested in providing high-quality medical care for patients who no longer have much time to live. Medical care for our elderly is becoming a national embarrassment.[26]

AIDS

Acquired immune deficiency syndrome (AIDS) is a contagious, presently incurable disease that destroys the body's immune system. AIDS is caused by the human immunodeficiency virus (HIV), which is transmitted from one person to another primarily during sexual contact or through the sharing of intravenous drug needles and syringes.

AIDS made national headlines in 1985 when it was revealed that actor Rock Hudson had contracted the disease. (Hudson died a few months after public release of the story.) National concerns about this disease were spurred again in 1991, when Magic Johnson (a prominent basketball player) announced that he had tested HIV positive. A public hysteria has arisen about AIDS. For example, many parents hesitate to send their children to the same school with a child identified as HIV positive. Exhibit 14.3 describes how people who have AIDS are further victimized by discrimination.

A virus is a protein-coated package of genes that invades a healthy body cell and alters the normal genetic apparatus of the cell, causing the cell to reproduce the virus. In the process the invaded cell is often killed. The HIV virus falls within a special category of viruses called *retroviruses*, so named because they reverse the usual order of reproduction within the cells they infect.

The HIV virus invades cells involved in the body's normal process of protecting itself from disease, and it causes these cells to produce more of the virus. Apparently HIV destroys normal white blood cells, which are supposed to fight off diseases invading the body. As a result, the body is left defenseless and can fall prey to other infections. The virus devastates the body's immune or defense system so that other diseases occur and eventually cause death. Without a functioning immune system to combat germs, the affected person becomes vulnerable to bacteria, fungi, malignancies, and other viruses that may cause life-threatening illnesses, such as cancer, pneumonia, and meningitis.

HIV is a tiny delicate shred of genetic material. As far as scientists know, it can live only in a very limited environment. It prefers one type of cell—the T-helper cell in human blood. Outside of blood and other bodily fluids, the virus apparently dies.

Documented ways in which the AIDS virus can be transmitted are: by having sexual intercourse with someone who has HIV, by using hypodermic needles that were also used by someone who has the virus, and by receiving contaminated blood transfusions or other products derived from contaminated blood. Babies can contract the AIDS virus before or at birth from their infected mothers and through breast milk.

HIV has been isolated in semen, blood, vaginal secretions, saliva, tears, breast milk, and urine. Only blood, semen, vaginal secretions, and to a much lesser extent, breast milk have been identified as capable of transmitting the AIDS virus. Many experts doubt whether there is enough of the virus present in tears and saliva for it to be transmitted in these fluids. Experts rule out casual kissing or swimming in pools as a means of contracting AIDS. Sneezing, coughing, crying, and shaking hands also have not proven to be dangerous. Only the exchange of body fluids (for example, through anal, oral, or genital intercourse) permits infection. The virus is very fragile

EXHIBIT 14.3

AIDS Discrimination

People who test positive to HIV or who have AIDS often are additionally victimized by discrimination. Dr. Robert Huse was a pediatrician who was earning $100,000 annually from his medical practice in Dallas, Texas. In 1985 he went to the public health department for an anonymous HIV antibody test and tested positive. Physicians informed him that he was not a danger to his patients. Two years later, in October 1987, he became involved in a complex civil lawsuit involving his former roommate, and the newspapers in Dallas were allowed by the courts to publish a notice of his positive HIV test. Within a week his patient load dropped from 100 to fewer than 40 people a week. In less than a month he was forced to close his practice. Dr. Huse experienced "utter frustration, bitterness, hurt and mind-numbing depression."[a]

Many Americans have a "them and us" mentality about persons who test positive to HIV or who have AIDS. They want no contact with anyone who has HIV, erroneously believing that casual social contact may put them at risk. As a result, individuals who have the AIDS virus are likely to be shunned, to risk losing their jobs, and often to be abandoned by family, spouse, lovers, and friends. In some communities, when it has become public knowledge that a child has the virus, parents of other children have reacted by not allowing their children to attend the same school and by prohibiting their children from having any contact with the child who has HIV.

Patrick Haney, a social worker who has tested positive to HIV, describes one of the negative aspects of the diagnosis:

Like no other illness since the advent of modern medicine, AIDS carries with it a stigma of shame and pointed finger of blame, suggesting those of us who are sick are at fault for being infected. This is a very negative impact of AIDS, yet it is also illogical. Do we blame Legionnaires for Legionnaires' disease, children for mumps, measles or chicken pox; the elderly for Alzheimer's disease or death, or epileptics for seizures? It makes no sense to blame anyone for AIDS. AIDS is caused by a virus, not by behavior or identity.

Moreover, shame and blame can lead persons with AIDS into denial and hiding, which may cause potential avoidance of medical care, involvement in unsafe sexual activity, and a lack of support from a support system that doesn't know the person is HIV infected. This further isolates the person with AIDS and exacerbates feelings of aloneness and despair.[b]

Social work has traditionally supported and advocated for oppressed and disenfranchised groups in our country—African Americans, Latinos, the poor, the elderly, gays, and women. Social workers have an ethical obligation to combat the numerous injustices connected with AIDS. AIDS is not a gay disease or an intravenous drug users' disease. It is a human disease.

---

[a]Linda Little, "HIV Disclosure Ruins Pediatrician's Practice," *Wisconsin State Journal,* March 18, 1989, sec. 3, p. 1.
[b]Patrick Haney, "Providing Empowerment to the Person with AIDS," *Social Work,* 33, no. 3 (May–June 1988), p. 251.

---

and cannot survive long without a suitable environment; nor is it able to penetrate the skin. In sum, evidence has not shown that AIDS can be spread through any type of casual contact. You cannot get AIDS from doorknobs, toilets, or telephones. Also, it does not appear that HIV can be transmitted by blood-sucking insects such as mosquitos or ticks.

Few lesbians have contracted AIDs. Lesbians are at low risk unless they use intravenous drugs

AIDS has generated a host of highly controversial issues. Some people view Jon Parker (above) as a hero; Parker has given over 50,000 clean hypodermic needles to drug addicts to help combat the spread of AIDS. Other people feel that the distribution of needles to addicts condones and promotes intravenous drug abuse.

or have unsafe sexual contact with people in high-risk groups. Female-to-female transmission is possible, however, through vaginal secretions or blood.

Women who use sperm from an infected donor for artificial insemination are also at risk of infection. Donors should be screened by licensed sperm banks as a preventive measure.

After an individual is exposed to the virus, it usually becomes inactive. Once it is in the body, it apparently needs help to stay active. Such help might include the person's history of infections with certain other viruses, generally poor health, the abuse of certain recreational drugs (such as butyl nitrite), malnutrition, and genetic predisposition. For those who do develop AIDS, the mortality rate is nearly 100%.

In the early 1980s the AIDS virus was transmitted in some cases through blood transfusions. Today blood that is used in transfusions is tested for the presence of antibodies to the AIDS virus, making it unlikely that the virus could be transmitted in this way. Because antibodies do not form immediately after exposure to the virus, a newly infected person may unknowingly donate blood after becoming infected but before his or her antibody test becomes positive. It is estimated that this might occur less than once in 100,000 donations.[27] However, as an added precaution, donated blood is heat treated to inactivate HIV. There is no risk of contracting the AIDS virus by being a blood donor.

Nearly everyone who is infected by HIV will eventually develop AIDS. The length of time between initial infection of HIV and the appearance of AIDS symptoms is called the incubation period for the virus. The average incubation period is estimated to be 7 to 11 years.[28] There has been considerable variation in this incubation period, ranging from a few months (particularly for

The 21,000 panel Names Project AIDS Memorial Quilt was unfolded in Washington in 1992. Each panel is representative of a person who has died of AIDS. Earlier that year activists demonstrating against President Bush's AIDS policies staged a "die-in" on the road to President Bush's vacation home in Maine.

babies who are HIV positive) to 20 years or more. Drugs such as AZT (azidothymidine) and DDI (didanosine) can slow the deterioration of the immune systems in HIV-infected persons and delay the onset of full-blown AIDS, perhaps for years. Once AIDS is evident, median survival times are between 9 and 13 months in developed countries.[29]

Another major health problem involves peo-

ple who are HIV positive but have no symptoms of AIDS. Most of these individuals have not been tested for the AIDS virus and therefore are unaware they have it. They may then infect others, although they experience no life-threatening symptoms themselves. The following is a summary of high-risk factors in contracting AIDS:

■ Having multiple sex partners without using safe sex practices (such as using condoms). The risk of infection increases according to the number of sexual partners, male or female. In considering the risks of acquiring AIDS, a person should heed the assertion "When you have sex with a new partner, you are going to bed not only with this person but also with all this person's previous sexual partners."

■ Sharing intravenous needles. HIV may be transmitted by reusing contaminated needles and syringes.

■ Having anal intercourse with an infected person.

■ Having sex with prostitutes. Prostitutes are at high risk because they have multiple sex partners and often are intravenous drug users.

Sexually active, heterosexual adolescents and young adults are increasingly becoming a high-risk group for contracting HIV. Persons in this age group tend to be sexually active with multiple sex partners. The risk of male-to-female transmission through sexual intercourse is higher than that of female-to-male, but the degrees of risk have not as yet been established. As noted, the risk of woman-to-woman transmission through sexual contact appears to be low but also has as yet not been determined. Although multiple exposures to HIV infection through sexual intercourse are not necessary for transmission, multiple sexual partners increase the likelihood that transmission will occur.

Lloyd describes the ways in which sexual transmission of HIV can be prevented or reduced:

Only two methods of completely preventing sexual transmission have been identified: (1) abstaining from sex or (2) having sexual relations only with a faithful and uninfected partner. The risk of infection through sexual intercourse can be reduced by practicing what has been called "safe sex," which is using a condom for all sexual penetration (vaginal, oral, and anal) whenever there is any doubt about a sexual partner's HIV status; engaging in nonpenetrative sexual activity; limiting the number of sexual partners; and avoiding sexual contact with people such as prostitutes who have had many partners.[30]

Many people believe that any contact with someone who is HIV positive will guarantee illness and death. Such fears are not justified. Body fluids (such as fresh blood, semen, urine, and vaginal secretions) infected with the virus must enter the bloodstream in order for the virus to be transmitted from one person to another. Male homosexuals account for so many AIDS cases because they are likely to engage in anal intercourse. Anal intercourse often results in a tearing of the lining of the rectum, which allows infected semen to get into the bloodstream. Sharing a needle during mainlining a drug with someone who is carrying the virus is also dangerous because it involves transmission of blood. A small amount of the previous user's blood is often drawn into the needle and then injected directly into the bloodstream of the next user.

At the present time there is no evidence that the virus can be spread by "dry" mouth-to-mouth kissing. Although unproven, there is a theoretical risk of transmitting HIV through vigorous "wet" or deep tongue kissing.[31] Nevertheless, the announcement that saliva can contain the virus has led the Screen Actors Guild to inform their members that they have the right to refuse to do kissing scenes if they are afraid of contracting AIDS.

Several tests have been developed to determine if a person has been exposed to the virus. These tests do not directly detect the virus—only the antibodies a person's immune system develops to fight the virus. Two of the most widely used tests are called the ELISA and the Western blot. ELISA stands for Enzyme-Linked Immunosorbent Assay. ELISA can be used in two important ways. First, it can screen donated blood to prevent the AIDS virus from being transmitted by blood trans-

fusions. Second, individuals who fear they may be carriers of the virus can be tested. For a person who has been infected with HIV, it generally takes two to three months before enough antibodies are produced to be detectable by the test.

ELISA is an extremely sensitive test and is therefore highly accurate in detecting the presence of antibodies. It rarely gives a negative result when antibodies are present. However, it has a much higher rate of false positive. That is, it may indicate that antibodies are present when in reality they are not. Therefore, it is recommended that positive results on the ELISA be confirmed by another test called the Western blot or immunoblot. This latter test is much more specific and less likely to give a false positive. Since the Western blot is expensive and difficult to administer, it can't be used for mass blood screening, as can the ELISA.

It must be emphasized that neither test can determine if a person already has AIDS or will actually develop it. The tests establish only the presence of antibodies that indicate exposure to the virus.

The origin of AIDS is unknown, although there have been a variety of speculations. (We probably never will be able to identify the origin, particularly now that AIDS has spread throughout the world.)

Persons with the AIDS virus are now classified as being either HIV asymptomatic (without symptoms of AIDS) or HIV symptomatic (with symptoms of the syndrome). HIV particularly invades a group of white blood cells (lymphocytes) called T-helper cells or T-4 cells. These cells in turn produce other cells, which are critical to the body's immune response in fighting off infections. When HIV attacks T-4 helper cells, it stops them from producing immune cells that fight off disease. Instead, HIV converts T-4 cells so that they begin producing HIV. Eventually the infected person's number of healthy T-4 cells is so reduced that infections cannot be fought off.

Once a person is infected with HIV, several years usually go by before symptoms of AIDS appear. Initial symptoms include dry cough, abdominal discomfort, headaches, oral thrush, loss of appetite, fever, night sweats, weight loss, diarrhea, skin rashes, tiredness, swollen lymph nodes, and lack of resistance to infection. (Many other illnesses have similar symptoms, so it is irrational for persons to conclude they are developing AIDS if they have some of these symptoms.) As AIDS progresses, the immune system is less and less capable of fighting off "opportunist" diseases, making the infected person vulnerable to a variety of cancers, nervous system degeneration, and infections caused by other viruses, bacteria, parasites, and fungi. Ordinarily, opportunistic infections are not life threatening to people with healthy immune systems, but they can be fatal to people with AIDS, whose immunological functioning has been severely compromised.

The serious diseases that afflict persons with AIDS include Kaposi's sarcoma (an otherwise rare form of cancer that accounts for many AIDS deaths), pneumocystic carinii pneumonia (a lung disease that is also a major cause of AIDS deaths), and a variety of other generalized opportunistic infections, such as shingles (herpes zoster), encephalitis, severe fungal infections that cause a type of meningitis, yeast infections of the throat and esophagus, and infections of the lungs, intestines, and central nervous system. The incidence of tuberculosis, a disease once nearly eradicated in the United States, has escalated rapidly in recent years due largely to the epidemic of HIV infection and AIDS.

Until recently, HIV infection was diagnosed as AIDS only when the immune system became so seriously impaired that the infected individual developed one or more severe, debilitating diseases, such as Kaposi's sarcoma or pneumocystic carinii pneumonia. However, on April 1, 1992, the Centers for Disease Control broadened its definition of AIDS; now anyone who is infected with HIV and has a helper T-cell count of 200 cells per cubic millimeter of blood or less is said to have AIDS, regardless of other symptoms that person may or may not have. (Normal helper T-cell counts in healthy people not infected with HIV range from 800 to 900 per cubic millimeter of blood.)

AIDS as a syndrome is not any one specific disease. It simply makes those infected by the virus increasingly more vulnerable to any disease that might come along. The process of AIDS involves a continuum whereby those affected become more and more vulnerable to devastating diseases.

In some patients AIDS may attack the nervous system and cause damage to the brain. This deterioration, called AIDS-dementia complex, occurs gradually over a period of time (sometimes a few years). Several specific intellectual impairments may result from AIDS. These include inability to concentrate, forgetfulness, inability to think quickly and efficiently, visuospatial problems that make it difficult to get from place to place or to perform complex and simultaneous tasks, and slowed motor ability. It is interesting that language capacity and the ability to learn, difficulties that characterize people with Alzheimer's disease, do not seem to be affected.

Contrary to popular belief, people who are HIV positive can live for an indeterminately long time. Gavzer summarizes the characteristics that long-term AIDS survivors tend to have:

■ *They are realistic and accept the AIDS diagnosis but do not take it as a death sentence.*

■ *They have a fighting spirit and refuse to be "helpless-hopeless."*

■ *They are assertive and have the ability to get out of stressful and unproductive situations.*

■ *They are tuned in to their own psychological and physical needs, and they take care of them.*

■ *They are able to talk openly about their illness.*

■ *They have a sense of personal responsibility for their health, and they look at the treating physician as a collaborator.*

■ *They are altruistically involved with other persons with AIDS.*[32]

As noted, at this time there is no cure for AIDS, and there are a multitude of hurdles to overcome in combating the disease. AIDS is caused by a form of virus. Even with modern technology, we don't know how to cure a virus. The common cold is also caused by virus; although pharmaceutical companies have spent millions of dollars on research in the hopes of finding an effective treatment for colds, none has yet been found. Currently, serious research is being undertaken to understand, prevent, and fight AIDS.

Prevention can be pursued in two major ways. First, people can abstain from activities and behaviors that put them at risk for contracting the disease. Second, scientists can work on developing a vaccine to prevent the disease, just as there are vaccines that prevent polio or measles. A vaccine might either block the virus from attacking a person's immune system or bolster the immune systems so that HIV is unable to invade it.

Former Surgeon General C. Everett Koop makes the following recommendations to avoid getting the AIDS virus.

The most certain way to avoid getting the AIDS virus and to control the AIDS epidemic in the United States is for individuals to avoid promiscuous sexual practices, to maintain mutually faithful monogamous sexual relationships and to avoid injecting illicit drugs.[33]

It is advisable to use a condom when having sexual intercourse with a new partner until you are certain the person is not HIV positive. You cannot acquire AIDS from someone who is not infected by HIV.

Unnecessary or Harmful Care

As indicated earlier, one of the objectives of the health care system is to make a profit. All too often this happens by using unnecessary diagnostic and treatment approaches—ordering diagnostic tests that are unnecessary, prescribing drugs and other medications that are unnecessary, and performing unneeded operations.

Nonwhites and women are more likely to be victimized by inferior care. Barbara and John Ehrenreich note:

Since blacks are assumed to be less sensitive than white patients, they get less privacy. Since blacks are assumed to be more ignorant than whites, they get less by way of explanation of what is happening to them. And since they are assumed to be irresponsible and forgetful, they

are more likely to be given a drastic one-shot treatment, instead of a prolonged regimen of drugs, or a restricted diet. . . . Women are assumed to be incapable of understanding complex technological explanations, so they are not given any. Women are assumed to be emotional and "difficult," so they are often classified as neurotic well before physical illness has been ruled out. (Note how many tranquilizer ads in medical journals depict women, rather than men, as likely customers.) And women are assumed to be vain, so they are the special prey of the paramedical dieting, cosmetics, and plastic surgery business.[34]

A more serious problem than unnecessary or inferior care is harmful care. Susan Dentzer notes:

Experts estimate that up to one third of all medical services performed in the U.S. are of questionable value and may even be harmful. In effect, as much as $200 billion spent on health last year could have been poured down a rat hole, and 50,000 Americans may have died from procedures they didn't need.[35]

Thousands of deaths and hundreds of thousands of hospitalizations occur annually from reactions to antibiotics and other prescribed drugs. A large number of people each year become addicted to tranquilizers and to pain-killing drugs prescribed by physicians. Thousands of people die each year from complications after undergoing unnecessary surgery. No surgery is without its risks. Even with such a simple operation as a tonsillectomy, 2 out of every 1000 patients die.[36]

Why does harmful treatment occur? One reason is that physicians make a profit from prescribing unnecessary treatment—and such treatment sometimes leads to complications. Another reason is that it is conservatively estimated that about 10% of the nation's physicians are incompetent and should have their licenses revoked.[37] Unfortunately, most patients are unable to judge the professional competence of their doctors.

Suing has become a national pastime, particularly in the case of malpractice suits in the medical field. The large number of successful suits documents the common existence of harmful treatment. At the same time, the possibility of a malpractice suit arising from failure to make a correct diagnosis because an unlikely procedure was *not* used leads many physicians to routinely order more diagnostic tests than are likely to be needed. Such tests are costly.

Controversy over Use of Life-Sustaining Equipment

Medical technology has made dramatic advances in this century. Today we can keep alive for months, and in many cases years, people who in the past would have died.

Even after a person's brain has stopped functioning, technology can keep the respiratory processes, the heart, the liver, and other vital organs functioning for months. The lives of those who are terminally ill can be prolonged for substantial periods of time, but they may experience considerable pain and will be in a deteriorated condition. Many controversial issues have arisen about the use of life-sustaining technology. How should death now be defined, since vital functions can be kept going even when the brain is dead? Some lawsuits have already been filed in organ donor cases in which organs allegedly were removed before the donor was deceased. Should the lives of the terminally ill be prolonged when there is practically no hope for recovery and the patients are in severe pain? Should society seek to keep alive people who are so severely and profoundly retarded that they cannot (and will never be able to) walk or sit up? Should abortion be mandatory if major genetic defects are detected in the fetus? When should life-prolonging efforts be used, and when should the patient be allowed to die? If terminally ill persons who are in severe pain want to end their life by suicide, should they be legally allowed to—and should others (such as physicians and close relatives) be legally allowed to assist in such suicides?

Because of the adverse consequences of being kept alive indefinitely when there is no hope of recovery, an increasing number of people are signing "living wills." In a living will a person stipulates in writing that, if he or she becomes physically or mentally disabled from a life-threatening illness in which there is no reasonable expectation of recovery, she or he wants to be allowed to die and not be kept alive by artificial means. A living will is not binding, but it conveys a patient's wishes to those (such as relatives and attending physicians) who must make a decision about whether to use life-sustaining equipment. To complement living wills, a number of states have enacted legislation enabling adults to authorize (by filling out a Power of Attorney for Health Care form) other individuals (called health care agents) to make health care decisions on their behalf should they become incapacitated.

The President's Commission for the Study of Ethical Problems in Medicine and Biomedical and Behavioral Research recommended in 1981 that all states define death as occurring when either of the following is judged to have taken place: (1) the irreversible cessation of circulatory and respiratory functions (this is essentially the definition used in the past) or (2) irreversible cessation of all functions of the entire brain, including the brain stem (this is a new definition). In adopting the "whole brain concept," the commission rejected a more controversial argument that death should be deemed to occur when "higher-brain functions" (those controlling consciousness, thought, and emotions) are lost. Patients who have lost higher-brain functions but retain the brain-stem functions can persist for years in a chronic vegetative state. Many of the states have now incorporated this definition of death into their statutes.

The High Cost of Medical Care

Health care costs have risen dramatically in the past 30 years. Expenditures on health care as a percentage of this country's total production of goods and services increased from 5.6% in 1960 to 13.2% in 1991.[38] These high costs are now recognized as a matter of national concern. There are many reasons why health expenses are so high and continue to increase more rapidly than the rate of inflation.

First, as we've seen, one of the objectives of

EXHIBIT 14.4

Should Physician-Assisted Suicide Be Legalized?

As of June 1994, Dr. Jack Kevorkian had assisted 20 terminally ill people end their lives. In 1993, the state of Michigan passed a law to ban assisted suicides—a law aimed expressly at stopping Dr. Kevorkian's actions. Kevorkian was charged with breaking this law in 1994 by helping Thomas Hyde end his life. Hyde had amyotrophic lateral sclerosis, a degenerative disease that left him unable to lift his infant daughter or hold a hammer; he was a 30-year-old ex-construction worker. Dr. Kevorkian admitted providing the carbon monoxide that killed Hyde. Because the jury saw the doctor's behavior as an act of mercy, they found him not guilty. After the verdict, some members of a citizens' committee appointed by the state legislature began urging that Michigan not only repeal the current ban but also become the first place in the world to legalize physician-assisted suicide. Dr. Kevorkian asserts that people who have a terminal illness that is degenerative, and who are in severe pain, should be helped to end their lives if that is what they want.

In the Netherlands an informal, *de facto* arrangement made with prosecutors over 20 years

Dr. Jack Kevorkian

ago allows physicians there to help patients die, as long as certain safeguards are followed. The patient, for example, has to be terminally ill, in considerable pain, and mentally competent; she or he must also repeatedly express a wish to die.

(continued)

the health care system is to make a profit. There are few controls designed to keep fees and prices down. Although the United States uses a marketplace approach to health care, ill consumers are not in a position to shop around for medical treatment. If they are suffering, their priority is to feel better, so they are willing to pay whatever a doctor chooses to charge. Most patients are not even informed before receiving treatment what the physician will charge. Fees for doctors' services are not advertised and therefore are not subjected to the competition that exists elsewhere in marketplace systems. Physicians have successfully established a public image in which they are so

revered that most patients will sit for an hour in a waiting room without complaining and will be reluctant to ask questions about charges before receiving treatment. (The same individuals don't hesitate to voice their frustrations about having to stand in line for five minutes at a checkout counter in a store.)

Another factor in the high cost of health care is dramatic technological advances in life-saving treatment interventions. New equipment, along with the cost of highly skilled personnel to operate it, is expensive. Thirty years ago we did not have cobalt machines, heart pacemakers, artificial heart valves, and microsurgical instruments

EXHIBIT 14.4   *(continued)*

The arguments against physician-assisted suicide are as follows. Some groups see suicide as morally wrong; they thus view assisted suicide as assisted murder. Members of the hospice movement oppose assisted suicide because they believe new painkiller drugs and techniques (including letting patients decide for themselves when to increase dosages) can control practically all the pain associated with most terminal illnesses. Some opponents believe that, once doctors come to think of death as a treatment option, some may encourage and pressure terminally ill people to accept this choice. There is concern

that, if competent people are allowed to seek death, then pressure will grow to use the treatment-by-death option with adults in comas or with others who are mentally incompetent (such as the mentally ill and those who have a severe cognitive disability). Finally, many people worry that, if the "right to die" becomes recognized as a basic right in our society, then it can easily become a "duty to die" for the elderly, the sick, the poor, and others devalued by society. (Americans may find that, the more they consider euthanasia and assisted suicide, the more difficult it becomes to resolve the inherent dangers of these practices.)

---

that enable doctors to perform surgery under a microscope.

Yet another reason is the increased life span of Americans. Now a larger proportion of our population is old, and the elderly require more health care than younger people. Many technically and professionally trained groups (such as nurses and physical therapists) are demanding salaries consistent with their training and responsibilities. These higher salaries are reflected, of course, in the overall costs of medical treatment.

Another contributor is the fact that third-party financing is increasingly paying medical bills. Historically, medical bills were primarily charged to and paid by consumers. Now, most bills are charged to and paid by third parties, including private insurance companies and the public Medicare and Medicaid programs. Physicians are more likely to recommend expensive diagnostic and treatment procedures if they feel such procedures will not be a financial burden to the patient. Third-party payments also tempt some physicians to perform surgeries that may be unnecessary. Spencer Klaw has concluded that "at least one out of every five or six operations in the United States is medically unjustified."[39]

Walter Friedlander and Robert Apte (along with many other authorities) blame the high cost partially on inadequate planning:

> Our health system is a hodge-podge that has grown out of a variety of historical trends rather than out of conscious planning. Care is often fragmented, and is oriented toward treating episodic illnesses rather than toward maintaining the health of the whole person or family. . . . Some of the current high cost of care, in fact, can be attributed to the inefficiency, overlap of effort, and gaps in the system. Consumer groups are beginning to press for a better-organized, comprehensive health system which would give quality care at lower cost. As yet, however, their voice is not strong enough to overcome the opposition of the medical profession and other forces resisting change in the medical care system.[40]

The increase in malpractice suits is also a contributing factor. Juries in many cases have awarded large settlements when malpractice is judged to have occurred. Physicians are required by law to carry malpractice insurance, with annual premiums ranging from $5,000 to over $90,000, depending on a variety of factors—including geographic area and field of practice.[41]

(Neurosurgeons and anesthesiologists are often charged the highest rates, because their fields are considered to be "high risk.") These premium costs are, of course, passed on to consumers.

The tendency toward increased specialization by doctors is another factor. At present 88% of physicians have a specialty.[42] The growth of medical knowledge has encouraged specialization; it is impossible today for a physician to be an expert in all medical areas. However, specialists charge more than general practitioners in order to receive compensation for their additional training and expertise. Specialization also raises costs because patients often are required to consult with (and pay) two or more physicians for each illness that they have. (A serious additional problem caused by specialization is that medical care becomes impersonal, dehumanized, and fragmented because patients now rarely establish a trusting, long-term relationship with one physician.)

Hospital care is extremely expensive. Hospitals compete with one another to offer the most prestigious and expensive equipment, which often leads to a duplication of expensive and seldom-used technology. And hospitals, similar to physicians, are not subjected to fees set by consumers on a supply-and-demand basis. Patients generally are not able to shop around for the hospital they want to go to.

Hospitals, physicians, nursing-home operators, and drug companies are politically powerful. Health care providers are represented by such influential organizations are the American Medical Association, the Pharmaceutical Manufacturers Association, the American Hospital Association, and the American Association of Medical Schools. Health care providers appear, at least at present, to have the political clout to prevent changes in health care that would sharply restrict their profits.

FINANCING MEDICAL CARE

Medical expenses are paid for by private insurance, through governmental programs, and by direct payments from the individual to the health

EXHIBIT 14.5

How Should Financial Resources Be Allocated?

Fiscal conservatives argue that our society cannot afford widespread use of medical technology to prolong the lives of people who will not be productive in the future. They point to cases such as that of Geri D., which they say is proof that too much money is already being spent in some health care situations.

At 5 months of age, Geri D. is in a residential facility for persons with a severe developmental disability. The annual cost there is about $93,000. Geri was born prematurely, with multiple medical problems, including cardiovascular dysfunctions. Lifesaving technology kept her alive. She has a profound cognitive disability—she will never be able to sit up, a developmental milestone that children of average intelligence achieve at 6 months of age. Already, over $250,000 has been spent on this child. By the time she becomes a young adult, more than $2 million will have been spent on keeping her alive.

With medical advances our society will face increasingly difficult issues regarding where financial resources should be used.

care provider. In 1991 private insurance paid 33% of the total costs for health care, the consumer paid 25%, and the government paid 42%.[43]

Most of the 42% of the federal government's health care bill is paid through Medicaid and Medicare. (The government also participates in the health insurance of federal employees, provides medical programs for families of members of the armed forces, and supports Veterans Administration hospitals.)

Medicaid

This program was established in 1965 by an amendment (Title XIX) to the Social Security Act.

Medicaid provides medical care primarily for recipients of public assistance. It enables states to make direct payments to hospitals, doctors, medical societies, and insurance agencies for services provided to those on public assistance. The federal government shares the expense with states, on a 55% to 45% basis, for recipients of Aid to Families with Dependent Children and Supplemental Security Income. Medical expenses that are covered include diagnosis and therapy performed by a surgeon, physician, and dentist; nursing services in the home or elsewhere; and medical supplies, drugs, and laboratory fees.

Under the Medicaid program, benefits vary from state to state. The original legislation encouraged states to include coverage of all self-supporting people whose marginal incomes made them unable to pay for medical care. However, this inclusion was not mandatory, and "medical indigence" has generally been defined by states to provide Medicaid coverage primarily to recipients of public assistance.

Although the stated purpose of Medicaid was to assure adequate health care to the nation's poor and near-poor, the program actually covers less than half of all poor families.[44] This is because the federal government has restricted eligibility in order to cut costs. In the past, hospitals supported the uninsured by charging paying patients more. But, after years of soaring costs, government and private insurers have rebelled against "costshifting" by setting limits on what they will pay for services provided in hospitals. Many hospitals, unable to support the cost of indigent care, are turning these patients away. *A two-tiered system of health care is emerging in this country, based on ability to pay.*[45]

Medicare

The elderly are most afflicted with illnesses yet least able to pay for medical care. People over age 65 now make up 12% of the population, and the percentage is increasing each year. Four times as many dollars are spent per capita on health care for the elderly as for younger people, mostly for hospital or nursing care.[46] Therefore, in 1965

Congress enacted Medicare (Title XVIII of the Social Security Act). Medicare helps the elderly pay the high cost of health care. It has two parts: hospital insurance (Part A) and medical insurance (Part B). Everyone age 65 or older who is entitled to monthly benefits under the Old Age, Survivors, and Disability Insurance program gets Part A automatically, without paying a monthly premium. Practically everyone in the United States age 65 or older is eligible for Part B. Part B is voluntary, and beneficiaries are charged a monthly premium. Disabled people under age 65 who have been getting Social Security benefits for 24 consecutive months or more are also eligible for both Part A and Part B, effective with the 25th month of disability.

Part A—hospital insurance—helps pay for time-limited care in a hospital, in a skilled nursing facility (home), and for home health visits (such as visiting nurses). Coverage is limited to 90 days in a hospital and to 100 days in a nursing facility. If patients are able to be out of a hospital or nursing facility for 60 consecutive days following confinement, they are again eligible for coverage. Covered services in a hospital or skilled nursing facility include the cost of meals and a semi-private room, regular nursing services, drugs, supplies, and appliances.

Part B—supplementary medical services—helps pay for physicians' services, outpatient hospital services in an emergency room, outpatient physical and speech therapy, and a number of other medical and health services prescribed by a doctor, such as diagnostic services, X-ray or other radiation treatments, and some ambulance services.

Private Insurance

All health care costs are rapidly rising, including the costs of health insurance. People who are not covered through group plans at their place of employment are increasingly finding it difficult to purchase private health insurance. Ehrenreich and Ehrenreich have noted:

In the face of rising health care costs, the cost of . . . health insurance has soared, too. As a result, an increasing number of people fall into no man's land—too rich for Medicaid, too young for Medicare, too poor to buy private health insurance, and certainly too poor to pay hospital bills.[47]

An estimated 37 million Americans are without private or government-sponsored health insurance.[48]

IMPROVING THE CURRENT SYSTEM

Practically everyone agrees that the rising costs of medical care are a threat to any family's financial security and, on a broader scale, to the economic stability of our society. Yet there is no consensus on specific measures that should be taken to hold down costs and to resolve the other problems that have been identified in this chapter. Some of the specific suggestions that are being advocated by authorities in the field will be briefly summarized.

Holding Down Costs

A number of proposals to hold down health care costs have been suggested. They include the following:

■ Increase the number of admissions to medical schools in order to train more doctors. Larger numbers of doctors could reduce difficulties in gaining access to health care and encourage competition among physicians in attracting patients, which could lead to reductions in fees.

■ Expand outpatient facilities (such as emergency care facilities that are open not only during the day but also during evening hours and on weekends) so that illnesses can be detected and treated early, thereby preventing the development of more serious and costly medical conditions.

■ Permit doctors to advertise their services and fees. Other professionals, such as attorneys and dentists, are increasingly doing this. Such competition may result in fee reductions.

■ Encourage (through fellowships and scholarships) medical students to become general practitioners rather than specialists.

■ Expand outpatient treatment facilities so that more illnesses can be treated without hospitalization.

■ Train more physician assistants and paramedics to treat routine illnesses (for example, flu and colds), to provide preventive services, and to provide treatment in geographical areas without physicians. China, for example, makes extensive use of laypeople with some training to provide basic health care. These laypersons administer simple diagnostic tests, treat routine illnesses, refer patients with serious symptoms to physicians, and teach nutrition and birth control. This system is considered to be working very successfully.[49]

■ Encourage patients to seek a second opinion before consenting to an operation, in order to reduce unnecessary surgeries. Many insurance programs are now paying the fees for a second opinion.

■ Expand and encourage the use of generic drugs. Generic drugs are nonpatent drugs that have the same chemical composition as patent drugs. The main differences between generic and patent drugs are that the latter carry a trade name and cost considerably more.

Preventive Medicine

Prevention programs usually are cost saving in the long run. Several specific suggestions have been made for expanding the scope of preventive medicine.

Educational programs should be expanded in schools and among the general public to inform people how much our lifestyles (diet, handling of stress, exercise patterns, amount of sleep, hygiene habits) determine when we will become ill and what illnesses we will develop. Educational programs are also needed to help people recognize that, when they become ill, they are important participants in the treatment process; their attitudes, emotions, diet, and hygiene patterns will greatly influence their recoveries. Most Americans, unfortunately, believe that physicians have nearly magical powers and rely on doctors to cure them.

The federal government is encouraging the use of Health Maintenance Organizations (HMOs) as an alternative to other private insurance plans. The present health care system is primarily curative in focus; it concentrates on illness and injury rather than on prevention. At the present time, most private health insurance policies do not cover periodic screening examinations but only provide coverage when a person is actually sick or injured. Such a model rewards providers of health services for treating illnesses but not for preventing them.

HMOs, in contrast, are prepaid health care insurance plans that emphasize prevention. Subscribers pay a fixed annual sum, usually in installments, and in return receive comprehensive care. HMOs vary in size and structure but generally include physicians (both general practitioners and specialists) who provide a wide range of services—diagnostic, treatment, and hospital and home care. An HMO program operates similarly to an insurance program. Subscribers pay a fee (often the fee is paid by the subscriber's employer), and the HMO pays for all medical expenses that arise.

The following is a description of the advantages of HMO:

Because HMO revenues are fixed, their incentives are to keep patients well, for they benefit from patient well-days, not sickness. Their entire cost structure is geared to preventing illness and, failing that, to promoting prompt recovery through the least costly services consistent with maintaining quality. In contrast with prevailing cost-plus insurance plans, the HMO's financial incentives tend to encourage the least utilization of high cost forms of care and also tend to limit unnecessary procedures. . . .

In contrast with more traditional and alternative modes of care, HMOs show lower utilization rates for the most expensive types of care (measured by hospital days in particular); they tend to reduce the consumer's total health care outlay; and—the ultimate test—they appear to deliver services of high quality. Available

research studies show that HMO members are more likely than other population groups to receive such preventive measures as general checkups and prenatal care and to seek care within one day of the onset of symptoms of illness or injuries.[50]

It is crucial that incentives be found throughout the health care system to focus on prevention and cost reduction, as HMOs do. Numerous public and private employers have chosen to provide HMO programs for their employees. HMOs have been successful in reducing overall health care costs per patient, partly because they emphasize prevention. They also have been successful in reducing rates of hospitalization and in limiting the length of hospital stays by providing alternative forms of care and greater use of out-of-hospital surgery.[51]

Additional Health Care Proposals

Several other suggestions for resolving current health care problems have been made. They include the following:

■ Incentives need to be developed to encourage physicians to practice in rural areas and in low-income urban areas. One approach is to give stipends that would help pay the expenses of medical students in exchange for a requirement that recipients practice for a few years in areas currently underserved by physicians.

■ More nonwhite students should be admitted to medical schools. Such students after graduation tend to serve nonwhite communities.

■ Further guidelines need to be established regarding when heroic life-sustaining measures should be used and when "the plug should be pulled." The high cost of keeping alive people who will never again be productive is raising some national concerns about euthanasia—so-called "mercy killing." The issues surrounding assisted suicide also need to be resolved.

■ Colleges and universities need to expand existing programs and develop new programs to

Prevention programs, including health and nutrition counseling, can be cost saving in the long run.

meet the emerging health care needs of the elderly. Physicians and other health care professionals (nurses, social workers, physical therapists, and so on) should receive training in diagnosing and treating the medical conditions of older citizens. Incentives need to be developed to encourage health care professionals to work with the elderly.

■ AIDS task forces, with heavy representation from the field of public health, are needed in every community. These task forces can develop programs to serve people who have HIV, as well as public information programs to inform the community about how AIDS is spread and how it can be prevented and to dispel myths that have led to discrimination against those known to have HIV.

■ Sex education and AIDS education must start at the lowest grade possible as part of any health and hygiene program. People need to be informed of the importance of safer sex (such as using condoms).

■ Offices, factories, and other work sites should develop a plan for educating the work force and accommodating people with AIDS. Employees with AIDS should not be discriminated against but should be dealt with as are any other workers with a chronic illness.

Establishing a National Health Insurance Program in the United States

This country does not as yet have a national health insurance program. Great Britain, Canada, and many other countries do have such a plan (Exhibit 14.6), in which public tax dollars are

EXHIBIT 14.6

The British System: A Comparison

About four decades ago Great Britain created a health care system that has been described as "social medicine." The program illustrates that there are ways of providing health care other than our marketplace, for-profit system.

In the British system, medical care is provided as a public service, similar to the way in which elementary and secondary education is provided here. Most physicians are employed by the British government, which owns and operates the clinics, hospitals, and other facilities.

Every individual selects and registers with a physician. Most doctors are general practitioners who see patients at their office and, when needed, will make house calls. Each physician receives a basic salary paid by the government and an additional small annual fee based on the number of patients on his or her register. (This fee is the same whether a person sees the physician 50 times a year or not at all.) Doctors' incomes, then, depend on the number of people who register with them, not on the amount or kind of treat-

ment they provide. There are some specialists in Great Britain to whom general practitioners may refer cases for consultation and treatment. General practitioners earn, on the average, less than half of what American doctors earn.

Physicians are allowed to take private, fee-paying patients if they desire. (A few doctors serve only private patients.) In addition, some individuals (generally the wealthy) choose to receive private physician and hospital care, which, or course, they pay for. The quality of public care is generally about the same as that of private care, although private patients generally get faster appointments for nonemergency medical care, and private hospital rooms are generally more spacious and pleasant in appearance.

The British system provides free medical care to any person in the country—including visitors who have a medical emergency. Practically all costs (for doctor visits, surgery, hospital rooms and meals, ambulance services, diagnostic tests, and essential medical supplies such as eyeglasses

(continued)

used to pay for medical care for all citizens. In the past three decades a number of congressmen and organizations have pressed for a public health insurance program. Many people subscribe to private insurance plans, which are available primarily to employed persons and their families. Those who are either marginally employed or unemployed are generally not covered by health insurance.

Hospitals cannot survive without assured income when services are provided. Physicians, as well, need to be paid for their services. Alarmingly, 37 million Americans are without private or government-sponsored health insurance.[52]

There are multiple reasons why a national

health insurance plan is needed. The rapid rise in health and insurance costs makes it impossible for the poor, for those of marginal income, and even for middle-class families to pay for insurance or extensive medical bills. The poor who are not covered by Medicaid cannot pay for even moderate medical expenses; as a result, they often forgo early treatment and develop more serious medical conditions. Medicare covers short-term hospitalization expenses for the elderly but not long-term expenses. Extensive medical treatment can wipe out substantial savings and force a family deeply into debt, thereby dramatically changing its standard of living and lifestyle.

Starting with Franklin Roosevelt, every presi-

EXHIBIT 14.6 *(continued)*

and wheelchairs) are paid by the government. There is a small charge for any prescription drug, even though the actual cost may be many times higher. There also is a small charge for each dental visit. (Persons over age 65 and under age 16 are excused from these fees.) Individuals do have to pay for purely cosmetic services such as face lifts or gold fillings.

This health care system is financed through taxes.

British opinion polls show that around 80% of the public approve of the National Health Service. Health care in Great Britain is the most highly rated government service. The system is also supported by the medical profession and by both political parties. In terms of costs, the system appears to be more efficient than ours. The per-person cost of health care in Great Britain is less than half of that in the United States. Britons also appear to be healthier than Americans on a number of indicators: They live longer, have a lower infant mortality rate, and spend less time in hospitals.

The main complaint that Britons have about this public health care system is that there are long waiting lists for treatment of nonemergency medical problems, such as minor illnesses. Patients sometimes must wait days, and in some cases even months, for treatment. Emergency problems such as heart attacks or broken arms receive immediate attention.

Great Britain's historical tradition in health care is different from ours. The primary focus of their system is service, whereas ours has both a service and a profit orientation. It is uncertain whether the British system would work in our country. Our medical profession, which has considerable vested interest in maintaining its high profits, would probably be successful in sabotaging efforts to establish a similar system in this country.

Sources: Judith Randa, "Health Service Is 30 and British Still Love It," New York *Daily News,* July 5, 1978, p. 36; and James W. Coleman and Donald R. Cressey, *Social Problems,* 5th ed. (New York: HarperCollins, 1993), p. 219.

---

dent except Ronald Reagan and George Bush has proposed a national health insurance program— without any being passed. The result is that the United States is the only industrialized nation lacking a comprehensive national medical insurance system.[53] A variety of national programs have in the past been advanced by Democratic and Republican legislators, administration officials, organized labor, representatives of private insurance companies, and the American Medical Association. In January 1991 the National Association of Social Workers proposed a national health care plan that is similar in many respects to the British health care system.[54]

President Clinton in 1993 proposed a national health insurance program that would provide universal coverage for all Americans; he assigned this program the highest priority of his administration. Clinton's proposal was hotly debated by Congress in 1994, and several other alternative plans were proposed in Congress and also intensely debated. At the time of this writing, no proposal has received sufficient support to attain congressional passage.

Proposals for national health insurance have been of three major types. In the public approach, government agencies would collect funds (for example, from employers and employees) and pay the claims. In the mixed public/private approach, health insurance funds would be collected by the federal government and disbursed by private insurance companies. In the private approach, tax credits would be given to individuals for the purchase of private health insurance.

The main objection to national health insurance revolves around the cost to taxpayers and the effect such an expensive new program would have on the economy. There is concern that such a program would escalate the costs of health care in a manner similar to what has happened with Medicare and Medicaid.

MEDICAL SOCIAL WORK

Many public and private social welfare agencies (such as public welfare departments, adoption agencies, family service agencies, neighborhood centers, and probation and parole departments) are perceived as primary settings for social workers. They are *primary* because they are often managed by social workers and because social work is their primary service. Hospitals, medical clinics, and schools are, on the other hand, *secondary* settings, because their primary service is not social work. But this secondary focus does not reduce their importance for social work, because health care and education serve a vital function and expend a substantial proportion of our national resources. Because social workers are not administratively in charge of secondary settings, problems related to status and influence sometimes arise. In such settings it is important for social workers to learn to work with those in control. American doctors are the highest-paid professional group in our society, and they tend to expect a status consistent with their salary. Some allied health professionals who work with physicians state that many doctors expect "Godlike" respect.

The main setting for medical social work is the hospital. Dr. Richard C. Cabot first introduced social services into the Massachusetts General Hospital in Boston in 1905. Now almost every hospital has a social services department. In fact, a social services department is required by the American Hospital Association as a condition for accreditation.[55] Social workers provide not only direct casework with patients and their families but also group work with certain patients, consultation, and training of other professionals. They also are involved in planning and policy development within the hospital and with various health agencies. At times medical social workers teach medical school courses in which they convey their professional knowledge of the sociopsychological components of illnesses and of the treatment process.

It is becoming increasingly recognized that psychological processes are causative factors in nearly every illness—in stress-related illnesses, alcoholism, depression, drug addiction, heart conditions, hypertension, and susceptibility to viruses, bacteria, and other infections. The patient's emotions and motivation for recovery also substantially affect the treatment process. Sexually transmitted diseases (including AIDS) and cirrhosis of the liver, for instance, may evoke feelings of shame and guilt because of the stigma attached to these illnesses. People with heart conditions need to learn how to relax, avoid continued stressful conditions, and follow a prescribed diet. A miscarriage may result in a wide variety of emotional reactions that need to be dealt with. Adjusting to a chronic or permanent disability also evokes a variety of negative psychological reactions. Medical treatment teams depend on social workers to attend to social and psychological factors that are either contributing causes of medical ailments or side effects of a medical condition.

Physicians consider social work an allied medical discipline. Along with doctors, nurses, and other therapists, social workers take part in the study, diagnosis, and treatment-planning processes for patients. A medical social worker frequently obtains important information on the living conditions, environment, habits, personality, and income of patients. Because physicians are no longer as well acquainted with patients, such information is often vital in arriving at a diagnosis and a treatment plan. Through interviews with the patient and members of his or her family, the worker gains a perspective on the social and emotional components of the illness and how such components may affect treatment.

In medical social work (now often referred to

as social work in the health field) a wide variety of problems and situations are encountered. Social workers engage in the following activities:

- Helping terminally ill patients and their families adjust.
- Counseling women who have had a mastectomy.
- Helping a low-income wife from a distant area find lodging in the community while her husband undergoes heart surgery.
- Counseling people who are so depressed they are contemplating suicide.
- Helping an unwed mother plan for the future.
- Providing genetic counseling for a young couple who gave birth to a mentally retarded child.
- Helping an executive of a large company make plans for the future following a severe heart attack.
- Counseling a woman about her emotional reactions following a miscarriage or a stillbirth.
- Being a support person to a hospitalized person with AIDS and to his or her friends and relatives.
- Finding living arrangements that will provide some medical attention for people who no longer need to be hospitalized.
- Counseling alcoholics and drug addicts or making appropriate referrals to other agencies.
- Counseling patients who are apprehensive about undergoing surgery.
- Helping someone suddenly struck with a permanent disability to adjust and make plans for the future.
- Meeting with relatives and friends of patients to help interpret the nature of the medical condition and perhaps to solicit their help in formulating a treatment plan to facilitate recovery.
- Counseling someone with emphysema on how to stop smoking.

- Counseling a rape victim concerning her psychological reactions.
- Informing relatives about the medical condition of someone who has just had a severe automobile accident.

While dealing with such problems and situations, the social worker is almost always a member of a medical team that is headed by a physician.

The job of a social worker in the health field is a dynamic one that requires continued study. With the dramatic expansion of new therapy approaches for medical conditions (for example, organ transplants, new prescription drugs, extensive new surgery techniques), it is essential that medical social workers keep informed about new technological approaches.

Social work in hospitals tends to be short term and crisis oriented because there is generally a fairly rapid turnover of patients. Social workers are often involved in discharge planning (for example, making arrangements for patients to return to their families or to a convalescent home). In recent years there has been a trend throughout the country to reduce the length of hospital stays in order to cut the costs of hospitalization. This trend has increased the importance of discharge planning (and thus of the services of social workers) in hospitals.

At times hospital social workers must act as advocates to ensure that the rights of patients are secured and that their needs are best served. Although social workers in medical settings are involved primarily in direct services to patients and their families, there are occasions when they engage in activity planning, administration of programs (for example, directing a hospice program so that terminal patients can live their final months in dignity), research, and education of other professionals.

The development of specialized clinics and programs—for providing genetics counseling, abortion services, family planning, services to people with AIDS or to people who are HIV positive, services to rape victims, services to the terminally ill, and treatment for alcoholics, drug

CASE
EXAMPLE 14.1   An Illustration of Medical Social Work

Janet Ely was hospitalized to have a hysterectomy because she had a tumor in her uterus. She was an attractive, single, 22-year-old woman.

Before the surgery, the nursing staff noted that she was apprehensive, depressed, and anxious. Following the operation, Ms. Ely became even more agitated and withdrawn. Her physician, again, fully answered her questions related to her hysterectomy. However, Ms. Ely appeared very concerned and confused about her future, making statements such as "No one will ever marry me now," "Life isn't worth living," "My family doesn't care about me—no one does," and "Oh, well, I'm going to die soon anyway." At this point her doctor asked Ms. Ely if she would be willing to discuss her concerns with the social worker at the hospital, Vicki Vogel, and she indicated she would.

Ms. Vogel met with Ms. Ely on five of the remaining seven days of her hospitalization. Ms. Ely had a number of problems, primarily involving planning for her future. She had alienated nearly all her relatives when, at age 17, she quit school in her senior year and began living with her 20-year-old boyfriend. A year and a half later her boyfriend discovered that she was having an affair with another man and demanded that she leave. She went to live with the other man and became rather heavily involved in drinking and experimenting with drugs. A year ago Ms. Ely left this man and moved to this area. She is now living with a divorcé.

Ms. Ely continued to have a number of questions related to her hysterectomy: Would her sex life be changed? Might the cancer reoccur? Would the hysterectomy affect her future as a woman? Can a person be orgasmic following a hysterectomy?

---

abusers, and people with eating disorders—has created new opportunities for social workers in the health field. Sometimes these programs are located in offices away from hospitals. Nursing homes also are increasingly employing social workers.

One of the emerging fields of practice for social workers is combating AIDS. Social workers are getting involved in advocating to end AIDS discrimination in counseling those who test HIV positive, and in providing services in hospitals, nursing homes, and hospices to those who have AIDS. Social workers have become case managers for many people with AIDS. The case manager works with the AIDS patient, her or his loved ones, providers of care, and payers of health care expenses to make certain that pressing medical, financial, social, and other needs are being met and to ensure that the most cost-effective care possible is provided. In serving people with AIDS, the trend is to have more and more of the medical care delivered outside the hospital or nursing home, often at home or in an outpatient clinic.[56]

There is also a trend for group medical clinics, individual practitioners, family practice clinics, and prepaid health clinics to employ social workers to be part of a team in diagnosing and treating patients. Increasingly, social workers in such settings are working with high-risk groups, playing a preventive as well as a therapeutic role. High-risk groups include teenage mothers, women requesting abortions, drug and alcohol abusers, people undergoing organ transplants, severely depressed or highly anxious people, people under stress, people attempting suicide, and amputees.

Ms. Vogel attempted to provide some answers and also arranged for Debra Nass (a 32-year-old woman who had had a hysterectomy three and a half years ago) to talk with Ms. Ely. Although some uncertainty remained (for example, the possible recurrence of a malignancy), Ms. Ely became more comfortable about having undergone the hysterectomy after talking to Ms. Nass.

However, Ms. Ely had a number of questions that she felt she needed to look at. She wondered why, when people were nice to her, she sometimes was "rotten" to them. For instance, she had lived with two different men, and each time she continued to have sexual relationships with other men. She also wondered what the future held for her. She was not skilled at a trade or a profession and did not know what kind of a career, if any, she desired. She was very confused about what she wanted out of life and also admitted that she had occasional blackouts from heavy drinking.

These problems were briefly discussed with Ms. Vogel. The focus of social services at this hospital, however, was limited to short-term, crisis counseling. Because these complicated problems indicated that longer-term counseling was needed, Ms. Vogel suggested, and Ms. Ely agreed to, a referral to the mental health center in the area.

Several months later Ms. Vogel heard from a friend of hers that Ms. Ely had gotten engaged but "on the spur of the moment" moved with another man to live on the West Coast.

In summary, the immediate psychological crisis situations surrounding the hysterectomy appears to have been resolved. However, problems appear to remain in Ms. Ely's relationships with others.

COUNSELING THE TERMINALLY ILL

One of the most difficult tasks of doctors, nurses, social workers, and other allied professionals in the health field is to help a terminally ill patient deal with dying. Death is a frightening event, and the fear of death is felt universally in all cultures.

Most people in our society die in a hospital. This setting, in itself, is one of the primary reasons why dying is so hard. Health professionals are committed to recovery—to healing. When someone is found to have a terminal illness, medical personnel experience a sense of failure. In some cases health professionals may feel guilty that they cannot do more or that they might have made a mistake that contributed to the terminal illness. Many health professionals are not comfortable in counseling the terminally ill. They feel insecure and do not know what to say or do. Often they have not come to terms with their own mortality; that is, they have not come to see death as an integral part of their lives. If a professional person views death as a frightening, horrible, taboo topic, she or he will never be able to face it calmly and helpfully with a patient.

Dr. Elisabeth Kübler-Ross (perhaps the foremost authority on death and dying in our era) has identified five stages that terminally ill patients may go through.[57] (See Exhibit 14.7.) These stages are not absolute; not everyone goes through every stage according to the sequence described. (Some patients never advance beyond the first or second stage, and some patients vacillate back and forth from stage to stage.)

EXHIBIT 14.7

Five Stages of Dying in the Terminally Ill

The following stages identified by Dr. Elisabeth Kübler-Ross have been found to be a valuable paradigm in understanding a terminally ill person's behavior:

Stage 1: Denial. "It can't be." "No, not me." "There must be a mistake." This is generally the first reaction when a person learns she or he has a terminal illness. Dr. Kübler-Ross believes such a reaction is functional because it helps cushion the impact that death will soon be inevitable.

Stage 2: Rage and anger. "Why me?" "Look at the good things I've done and still need to do for the members of my family." "This just isn't fair!" Patients resent the fact that they will soon die while others remain healthy and alive. God is frequently a special target of the anger during this stage, as God is viewed as unfairly imposing a death sentence. Dr. Kübler-Ross believes that such anger is permissible and inevitable. And, she adds, "God can take it."

During this stage, family and hospital staff frequently experience difficulty in coping with the anger, which is displaced in many directions. The patient may charge that the doctor is incompetent, that the hospital surroundings are inhumane, that the nurses are unconcerned about people, that there is too much noise, and so on. The underlying reasons generating the patient's anger need to be remembered during this stage. Reacting personally or angrily to the patient's anger will only feed into that hostile behavior. During this stage, conveying to the patient that she or he is an important person who is worthy of respect, time, and understanding will usually lead to a reduction of angry demands.

Stage 3: Bargaining. "I realize my death is inevitable, but if I could just live six months more I could. . . . " During this stage patients come to accept their terminal illness but try to strike bargains (frequently with God) for more time. They promise to do something worthwhile or to be good in exchange for another month or year of life. Dr. Kübler-Ross indicates that even agnostics and atheists sometimes attempt to bargain with God during this stage.

Stage 4: Depression. "Yes, it will soon be over." "It's really sad, but true." The first phase of this stage is when the patient mourns things not done,

(continued)

The one thing that usually persists through all five stages is hope—hope for a "miracle" cure. Terminally ill patients all seem to have a little bit of it and are supported and nourished by it, especially during their most difficult times. With respect to hope, the desired direction in counseling is to be honest with the patient about the probable outcome while allowing the person to hope for the million-to-one chance of recovery.

To work with the terminally ill requires maturity, which comes only from experience. The most important communication is the "door-opening interview," in which the counselor conveys verbally and nonverbally to the dying patient that she or he is ready and willing to share the dying person's concerns without fear and anxiety. A prerequisite is that the counselors have an attitude toward their own death with which they are comfortable.

Mwalimu Imara views dying as potentially the final stage of growth and gives a number of suggestions on how to come to terms with one's own dying.[58] Having a well-developed sense of identity (that is, a sense of who you are) is an important step. (Chapter 2 in this text discusses ways to develop a positive identity.) This requires arriving at

EXHIBIT 14.7   *(continued)*

past losses, and wrongs committed. This type of depression is frequently exacerbated by guilt or shame about acts of omission or commission. Counseling during this phase generally focuses on helping the patient to resolve feelings of guilt and shame. In some cases this may involve helping family members to make realistic plans for their future and to reassure the patient that vital unfinished situations are being taken care of.

The second phase of this stage is when the patient enters a state of "preparatory grief," in which she or he is getting ready for the inevitable by taking into account impending losses. During this stage the patient should not be encouraged to be cheerful; this would interfere with the necessity for the patient to contemplate his or her impending death. During this phase the patient generally becomes quiet and does not want to see visitors. The patient is in the process of losing everything and everybody she or he loves. If the patient is allowed to express this sorrow, final acceptance of death will be much easier. Also, the patient will be grateful to those who are able to sit quietly nearby, without telling him or her not to be sad. According to Dr. Kübler-Ross, when a dying patient no longer continues to request to see

someone to discuss his or her situation, it is a sign that unfinished business is completed and the patient has reached the final stage.

Stage 5: Acceptance. "I will soon pass on, and it's all right." Dr. Kübler-Ross describes this final stage as "not a happy stage, but neither is it unhappy. It's devoid of feelings but it's not resignation; it's really a victory." During this stage visitors often are not desired because the patient no longer is in a talkative mood. Communications with a counselor may become more nonverbal than verbal. Patients may just want to hold the counselor's hand—to sit together in silence with someone who is comfortable in the presence of a dying person.

Dr. Kübler-Ross notes that some patients continue grieving about their terminal illness without ever reaching the final stage of acceptance. She also notes that not everyone will progress through these stages as presented here. There is often considerable movement back and forth among stages. For example, a patient may go from denial to depression, to rage and anger, back to denial, then to bargaining, then to depression, and so on.

Sources: Elisabeth Kübler-Ross, *On Death and Dying* (New York: Macmillan, 1969); and Elisabeth Kübler-Ross, ed., *Death: The Final Stage of Growth* (Englewood Cliffs, NJ: Prentice-Hall, 1975).

realistic life goals that you will have pride in achieving. Without a blueprint of what will give meaning and direction to our lives, we will experience our lives as fragmented and aimless.

Imara indicates that a dying patient at the fifth stage of acceptance corresponds to a person with a healthy identity. An individual who comes to accept a terminal illness has also arrived at a fairly well-thought-out sense of himself or herself. Death is the final stage of growth in that the patient finally develops a unified sense of self and accepts imminent death. (It is hoped that people will develop a healthy identity long before the fi-

nal crisis and thus be fairly prepared before that crisis arises.)

According to Imara, all of us experience separations and pains throughout life that lead to personal growth—for example, leaving family to attend kindergarten, leaving high school to seek work or attend college, leaving work and friends to seek a better position in a different geographical area, and experiencing romantic and perhaps marital separations. Imara indicates that "abandoning old ways and breaking old patterns is like dying, at least dying to old ways of life for an unknown new life of meaning and relationships. But living without change is not living at all, not growing at all.''[59] Making changes in our lives also creates fears and anxieties in us. But, if such changes lead to personal growth, we will be better prepared to face new challenges and new changes. Through a willingness to risk the unknown, we undertake the search for ourselves. Overcoming fears and anxieties that arise from current challenges (and learning more about ourselves through these experiences) helps prepare us for the fears and anxieties that will arise when we learn that our death is near.

SUMMARY

There are a number of problems with our health care system. In contrast to other industrialized countries in which health care is viewed as having a service orientation, the health care system in the United States has the dual (and sometimes conflicting) objectives of providing service and making a profit. The system is indeed prospering. The United States is now spending substantially more per capita on health care than are other industrialized nations. Yet a number of other countries have lower infant mortality rates and longer life expectancies than ours. Such statistics suggest that other countries are providing health care that is as good as (or better than) ours at a lower cost.

Our health care system is focused on treating people *after* they become ill; little attention is given to preventing illnesses from occurring. It is increasingly being recognized that our lifestyles (including exercise, diet, sleep patterns, and stress-reaction patterns) largely determine whether illness will occur and also influence the recovery process when an illness does occur. People need to realize that they, and not their physicians, have the major responsibility for their own health.

The poor and racial minorities have higher rates of illnesses and shorter life expectancies, for a variety of reasons. Largely because of the profit motive, low-income areas in cities and rural areas are generally underserved by health care services.

The profit motive has also led to the use of unnecessary treatment approaches, including diagnostic tests, medication and drugs, and surgeries. A more devastating problem is receiving harmful care. It is estimated that 10% of practicing physicians are incompetent.

Health care for the elderly is becoming a national disgrace. Many older citizens lack access to quality care. Medical conditions of the elderly are often misdiagnosed, and treatment is often inadequate.

AIDS has emerged as a major health problem. The two primary ways in which it is transmitted from one person to another are through sexual contact and through sharing of intravenous needles. There are many misconceptions about AIDS that have led those who are HIV positive and those who have AIDS to be shunned and discriminated against.

The use of life-sustaining technology has raised a number of questions. Should such equipment be used to prolong the life of someone who is terminally ill and in considerable pain? How should death be defined? Should society seek to keep alive people who have such a profound cognitive disability that they will never be able to walk or even sit? Can society afford to continue to expand the use of such costly life-sustaining equipment? Should physician-assisted suicide for the terminally ill who want to die be legalized?

The high costs of medical care have become an issue of national concern. Illnesses now can threaten a family's financial stability. The high costs are also a threat to the economic stability of our country. There are a variety of reasons why medical expenses are so high, including the profit-making focus, high costs of technological advances, increased life expectancies of people, third-party financing, inadequate health care planning, proliferation of malpractice suits, and increased specialization by doctors.

A number of possibilities are available to resolve each of these problems. Some suggestions include increasing admissions to medical schools, permitting doctors to advertise their services and fees, training more physician assistants and paramedics, expanding use of generic drugs, encouraging patients to seek a second opinion before consenting to an operation, developing more preventive medical programs, expanding the use of health maintenance organizations, and developing a national health insurance program.

Health care is a secondary setting for social work. In such a setting social workers generally function as a member of a team, and they need to learn to work with those in charge. Medical treatment teams are increasingly dependent on social workers to attend to sociopsychological factors that are either contributing causes of illnesses or side effects of a medical condition that must be dealt with to facilitate recovery. As a member of a medical team, social workers have an important role in diagnosing and treating medical conditions.

A social worker in the health field needs skills and knowledge about how to counsel people with a wide variety of medical conditions. Counseling the terminally ill requires a high level of emotional maturity, a well-thought-out identity, and a high level of competence in counseling.

NOTES

1. Joseph Julian, *Social Problems*, 3d ed. (Englewood Cliffs, NJ: Prentice-Hall, 1980), p. 25.
2. Richard Nixon, "Health Message of 1971," Feb. 18, 1971, White House.
3. William Kornblum and Joseph Julian, *Social Problems*, 7th ed. (Englewood Cliffs, NJ: Prentice-Hall, 1992), pp. 28–33.
4. John E. Farley, *American Social Problems*, 2d ed. (Englewood Cliffs, NJ: Prentice-Hall, 1992), pp. 514–515.
5. Ibid.
6. U.S. Bureau of the Census, *Statistical Abstract of the United States, 1993* (Washington, DC: U.S. Government Printing Office, 1993).
7. R. A. Zaldivar, "Health Care Reform," *Wisconsin State Journal*, Jan. 2, 1994, p. 1B.
8. *Statistical Abstract of the United States, 1993*, p. 124.
9. Ibid., p. 107; and Sara Collins, "A Checkup for Health Costs," *U.S. News & World Report*, June 13, 1994, p. 63.
10. James W. Coleman and Donald R. Cressey, *Social Problems*, 5th ed. (New York: HarperCollins, 1993), p. 208.
11. Quoted in John A. Denton, *Medical Sociology* (Boston: Houghton Mifflin, 1978), p. 65.
12. Ian Robertson, *Social Problems*, 2nd ed. (New York: Random House, 1980), p. 318.
13. K. R. Pelletier, *Mind as Healer, Mind as Slayer* (New York: Delta, 1977).
14. Thomas McKeown, "Determinants of Health," *Human Nature*, 1 (April 1978), p. 66.
15. Aaron Antonovsky, "Class and the Chance for Life," in *Social Problems and Public Policy: Inequality and Justice*, Lee Rainwater, ed. (Chicago: Aldine, 1974), p. 177.
16. *Statistical Abstract of the United States, 1993*, p. 87.
17. Ibid., p. 85.
18. Kornblum and Julian, *Social Problems*, p. 38.
19. Ibid., pp. 46–48.
20. Max Seham, *Blacks and American Medical Care* (Minneapolis: University of Minnesota Press, 1973), p. 20.
21. Ibid., pp. 22–23.
22. Rainwater, *Social Problems and Public Policy*.
23. "Growing Old in America," ABC News Program Transcript (New York: Journal Graphics, Dec. 28, 1985).
24. Ibid., p. 11.
25. Ibid.
26. Ibid.
27. C. Everett Koop, *Surgeon General's Report on Acquired Immune Deficiency Syndrome* (Washington, DC: U.S. Department of Health and Human Services, 1987), p. 22.
28. S. Findlay, "AIDS: The Second Decade," *U.S. News & World Report*, June 17, 1991, p. 21.
29. G. A. Lloyd, "AIDS and HIV: The Syndrome and the Virus," *Encyclopedia of Social Work: 1990 Supplement* (Silver Spring, MD: National Association of Social Workers, 1990), p. 25.
30. Ibid., p. 19.
31. Ibid.
32. B. Gavzer, "Why Do Some People Survive AIDS?" *Parade*, Sept. 18, 1988, p. 5.
33. Koop, *Surgeon General's Report on Acquired Immune Deficiency Syndrome*, p. 27.
34. Barbara Ehrenreich and John Ehrenreich, *The American Health Empire: Power Profits and Politics* (New York: Vintage Books, 1971), pp. 14–16.
35. Susan Dentzer, "America's Scandalous Health Care," *U.S. News & World Report*, Mar. 12, 1990, p. 25.
36. Ibid.
37. Paul B. Horton, Gerald R. Leslie, and Richard F. Larson, *The Sociology of Social Problems*, 10th ed. (Englewood Cliffs, NJ: Prentice-Hall, 1991), p. 232.
38. *Statistical Abstract of the United States, 1993*, p. 107.
39. Spencer Klaw, *The Great American Medicine Show* (New York: Viking, 1975).

40. Walter A. Friedlander and Robert Z. Apte, *Introduction to Social Welfare*, 4th ed. (Englewood Cliffs, NJ: Prentice-Hall, 1974), p. 414.

41. Farley, *American Social Problems*, pp. 540–541.

42. *Statistical Abstract of the United States, 1993*, p. 118.

43. Ibid., p. 107.

44. Jennifer B. Hull, "Growing Number in U.S. Lack Health Insurance as Companies, Public Agencies Seek to Cut Costs," *The Wall Street Journal,* June 3, 1986, p. 54.

45. Ibid.

46. American Association of Retired Persons, *A Profile of Older Americans: 1990* (Washington, DC: Author, 1990).

47. Ehrenreich and Ehrenreich, *The American Health Empire*, pp. 130–132.

48. Zaldivar, "Health Care Reform," p. 1B.

49. Victor W. Sidel, "Medical Care in the People's Republic of China: An Example of Rationality," in *Dominant Issues in Medical Sociology*, Howard D. Schwartz and Cary S. Kart, eds. (Reading, MA: Addison-Wesley, 1978), p. 385.

50. *Towards a Comprehensive Health Policy for the 1970's: A White Paper* (Washington, DC: U.S. Department of Health, Education and Welfare, May 1971), pp. 31–32.

51. Kornblum and Julian, *Social Problems*, p. 51.

52. Zaldivar, "Health Care Reform," p. 1B.

53. Kornblum and Julian, *Social Problems*, pp. 50–56.

54. "National Health Care and NASW Plan," *The Wisconsin Social Worker,* 17, no. 2 (March/April 1991), p. 1.

55. Donald Brieland, Lela B. Costin, and Charles R. Atherton, *Contemporary Social Work* (New York: McGraw-Hill, 1975), p. 123.

56. Susan Dentzer, "Why AIDS Won't Bankrupt Us," *U.S. News & World Report,* Jan. 18, 1988, pp. 20–21.

57. Elisabeth Kübler-Ross, *On Death and Dying* (New York: Macmillan, 1969).

58. Mwalimu Imara, "Dying as the Last Stage of Growth," in *Death: The Final Stage of Growth*, Elisabeth Kübler-Ross, ed. (Englewood Cliffs, NJ: Prentice-Hall, 1975), pp. 147–163.

59. Ibid., p. 148.

15

PHYSICAL
AND MENTAL
DISABILITIES
AND
REHABILITATION

There are over 55 million people with a disability in the United States—nearly one out of four people.[1] Persons with a disability include those who:

- Are temporarily injured (from severe burns, injuries to the back or spine, broken limbs).

- Have a chronic physical disability (including people who use canes, crutches, walkers, braces, or wheelchairs; the mobility-impaired elderly; and people with illnesses such as severe cardiovascular disorder, cerebral palsy, chronic arthritis, and AIDS).

- Have a hearing disability.

- Have a visual disability.

- Have a mental disability (including an emotional disorder, a cognitive disability* or a severe learning disability).[2]

This chapter will:

- Provide a brief history of rehabilitation practices and of the ways different cultures have treated persons with a disability.

- Define and describe developmental disabilities.

- Describe different levels of cognitive disability and summarize the causes.

- Discuss our society's reactions to disabilities.

- Identify current services for persons with a disability.

- Summarize the roles of social workers in working with clients who have a disability and their families.

HISTORY OF REHABILITATION PRACTICES

Society's willingness to help persons with a disability has been determined largely by the per-

---

*Because the term *mental retardation* has negative connotations, I use the term *cognitive disability* instead in this text.

ceived causes of the disability, existing medical knowledge, and general economic conditions. Ancient and modern religious faiths (including Christianity) have at times been an aid and at other times a detriment to viewing those with a disability as "people." Attitudes have ranged from perceiving persons with a disability as possessed by demons to viewing them as being saint-like, with the community having a responsibility to care for them.

The early Greeks promoted the philosophy of the unity of body and soul, with a blemish on one signifying a blemish on the other.[3] This philosophy led to a negative attitude toward those with a disability. The extreme implication of this doctrine was found in Sparta, where "the immature, the weak, and the damaged were eliminated purposefully."[4] Centuries later the Romans also put to death some people with a disability who were considered "unproductive."[5] In ancient history there were almost no organized efforts to meet the needs of persons with a cognitive disability. In early Greece and in the Roman Empire, mental illness was seen as stemming from demons entering the body, with exorcism being the primary treatment.[6]

During the Middle Ages, disabilities were seen either as the result of demonic possession or as God's punishment.[7] Modern Judeo-Christian values of charity and humanitarian treatment were generally absent during this period, partly as a result of poor economic conditions. About the only employment provided by feudal lords for persons with a disability was that of court jester, a position considered suitable for those with a cognitive or physical disability.[8] The mentally ill continued to be viewed as being possessed by demons, and cruelty was advocated and used to punish and drive out the demons.

The Elizabethan English Poor Laws of 1601 provided financial support for the involuntarily unemployed (including persons with a disability). These Poor Laws were the first major secular-based relief effort for the poor and persons with a disability.[9]

In early colonial America, conditions were not yet suitable for the development of rehabilitation programs. The colonists were barely able to earn a living from the soil; also, disability was viewed as the result of God's punishment.[10]

In the 19th century gradual recognition was given to the needs of persons with a disability in the United States. The first programs to help these people were developed around that time.

Thomas Gallaudet opened the first school for educating the deaf in this country in 1817 in Hartford, Connecticut.[11] Gallaudet demonstrated that the deaf could be taught to read and speak, which led to the opening of other schools for the deaf. The first school for the blind was opened in 1832 in Massachusetts.[12] The first sheltered-type work situation for the employment of the blind was established in 1850 in Massachusetts.[13]

Cognitive disability, before and during the early part of the 19th century, was thought to be inherited and therefore incurable.[14] In the first half of the 1800s most persons with a cognitive disability "were relegated to lunatic asylums, poorhouses, almshouses, or local jails."[15] Interest in providing services to persons with a cognitive disability began in France, especially after the physician Jean Itard made considerable progress over a five-year period in the early 1800s in educating a 12-year-old "wolf child" found in a forest. The boy was diagnosed as having a severe level of cognitive disability. When found, he was unsocialized and walked on all fours.[16] The philosophy of providing services to persons with a cognitive disability gradually spread to this country. In 1848 the first residential school for persons with a cognitive disability was established in Barge, Massachusetts.[17]

Unfortunately, the orientation toward persons with a cognitive disability in the latter half of the 19th century switched from one of education and training to one of custodial care. A major reason for this change was the popularity of Social Darwinism, which asserted that it was far better for society to allow the poor and the weak to perish than to sustain their existence and encourage their proliferation through government-supported programs.[18] Persons with a cognitive disability were viewed as having defective genetic strains; as a result, sterilization was used extensively at the end of the 19th century.[19]

The first hospitals for the mentally ill were

One of the earliest attempts to meet the needs of people with disabilities occurred in 1817, when Thomas Hopkins Gallaudet founded the first school for deaf children in the United States. Today students with hearing disabilities from around the world attend Gallaudet University in Washington, D.C. (above). In 1988 the board of trustees elected the first deaf president in the college's history.

built in this country in the 1850s and 1860s.[20] Before this time, as Dorothea Dix had documented, the mentally ill were either kept "out of sight" in the homes of their families or confined in almshouses and local jails.[21] It should be noted that the living conditions of almshouses and mental hospitals were deplorable.

Until the latter half of the 19th century, persons with a physical disability were either taken care of by their family or placed in almshouses. Toward the end of the 19th century these persons began to benefit from medical advances: antiseptic surgery, orthopedic surgery, heat and water therapy, use of braces, and exercise programs.[22] Around that same time, public funds began to be used for the education and training of children with a disability.[23]

The charity organization movement during the latter part of the 19th century created a structure not only for future social work practices but also for vocational rehabilitation casework.[24] These early organizations had a rehabilitation rather than a maintenance focus. The movement also advocated extensive investigation of each case and the use of individualized treatment determined by the needs of each client. Unfortunately, the volunteers who provided the services for charity organizations operated from the premise that the causes of poverty and of disabilities had moral roots; thus the primary way to help was through spiritual means.[25]

During the late 19th and early 20th centuries, few precautions were taken by industries to improve worker safety. As a result, a large number of people developed disabilities from poor working conditions and industrial accidents. To meet the tolls being taken by the Industrial Revolution, the first worker's compensation law was passed in 1910 in New York.[26]

In the early 20th century large numbers of unskilled rural youths began flocking to cities seeking employment. There were also increasing numbers of dislocated industrial workers who needed retraining. Therefore, the federal government, in 1917, passed the Smith-Hughes Act, which made federal monies available for vocational education programs and created the Federal Board of Vocational Education.[27] The next year (1918) the Soldier's Rehabilitation Act was passed, which was a program designed to rehabilitate veterans who had a disability.[28]

The federal Social Security Act of 1935 established the permanency of rehabilitation programs and instituted public assistance programs for the blind and for the disabled. The Barden-LaFollette Act of 1943 extended rehabilitation services to the mentally ill and to persons with cognitive disabilities.[29]

During World War II there was a severe labor shortage, which provided work opportunities to people with a disability. These persons were able to demonstrate to thousands of employers that, if placed in an appropriate job, they could perform well. This growing realization led in 1945 to the establishment of the President's Committee on Employment of the Handicapped.[30] After World War II a number of other federal programs underscored society's growing belief that those with a disability could be productive workers and should be given the opportunities and training to demonstrate their work capacities.[31]

Spurred by the civil rights movement of the 1950s and 1960s, a new minority group began to be heard in the late 1960s and 1970s. Persons with a physical disability began speaking out, marching forth, and demanding equal rights. They have been seeking (including through legislation and lawsuits) an end to job discrimination, limited educational opportunities, architectural barriers, and societal discrimination. In 1973 Congress passed the Vocational Rehabilitation Act, one section of which prohibits discrimination against persons with a disability by any program or organization receiving federal funds. Included in this legislation is an affirmative action policy (described in Chapter 11) in which employers who receive federal funds must demonstrate extensive efforts to hire those with a disability.

In 1990 Congress passed, and President Bush signed into law, the Americans with Disabilities Act. This act prohibits discrimination against persons with a disability either in hiring or by limiting access to public accommodations (such as restaurants, stores, museums, and theaters). The law requires that new public buildings be accessible by persons with a disability and that barriers in existing public buildings be removed if the changes can be accomplished without much difficulty or expense. Advocates of the law call it the most significant civil rights legislation since the 1964 act prohibiting discrimination based on race.[32]

The 20th century has seen the development of numerous programs and technological advances to help persons with a disability. Yet, as will be discussed, much remains to be done in changing society's attitudes toward persons with a disability and in helping them to live satisfying and productive lives. Increasingly, people with a disability are receiving improved services that facilitate the development of their capacities.

DEVELOPMENTAL DISABILITIES

Developmental disability is a relatively recent term, and many people erroneously believe it to be synonymous with cognitive disability. How-

Members of Americans Disabled for Attendant Care Today (ADAPT) campaign for a change in funding practices. They believe public money should be transferred from payments for institutional care, particularly nursing home care, to community or home-based care.

ever, it is a broader term that includes not only cognitive disabilities, but also a variety of other conditions that occur before age 22 and hinder development. These conditions include epilepsy, infantile autism, cerebral palsy, and some cases of dyslexia (a learning disability).

The Rehabilitation, Comprehensive Services, and Developmental Disabilities Act (PL 95–602) of 1978 defines developmental disability as follows:

Developmental disability means a severe, chronic disability of a person which is attributable to a mental or physical impairment or combination of mental and physical impairment and

- *is manifest before twenty-two years of age*
- *is likely to continue indefinitely*
- *results in substantial functional limitations in three or more of the following areas of major life activity:*

self-care
receptive and expressive language
learning
mobility
self-direction
capacity for independent living
economic self-sufficiency

- *and reflects the person's need for a combination and sequence of special, interdisciplinary, or generic care, treatment or other services which are of lifelong or extended duration and individually planned and coordinated.*[33]

Autism

Perhaps the most puzzling developmental disability is infantile autism. As yet the causes of this disorder are unknown. David Rosenhan and Martin Seligman define this disorder as follows:

The essential feature of infantile autism is that

the child's ability to respond to others does not develop within the first thirty months of life. That lack of responsiveness is called autism. *Even at this early age, gross impairment of communicative skills is already quite noticeable, as are the bizarre responses these children make to their environments. They lack interest in, and responsiveness to, people and they fail to develop normal attachments. In infancy, these characteristics are manifested by their failure to cuddle, by lack of eye contact, or downright aversion to physical contact and affection. These children may fail entirely to develop language, and if language is acquired, often it will be characterized by* echolalia—*the tendency to repeat or echo immediately or after a brief period precisely what one has just heard—or* pronominal reversals—*the tendency to use "I" where "you" is meant, and vice-versa. Such children also react very poorly to change, either in their routines or in their environments.*[34]

Autism occurs in about 2 to 4 children per 10,000, about the same frequency as deafness and twice that of blindness.[35] With regard to gender differences, boys outnumber girls by about three to one.[36] Surprisingly, the disorder is more common among children from the upper socioeconomic classes.[37] The reason for this class difference is not known. One promising method of treating the disorder is a *direct structured educational approach*, which focuses on improving the specific cognitive, motor, and perceptual disabilities of these children. Long-term follow-up studies of autistic children indicate that the prognosis for them is questionable. Close to 60% are unable to lead an independent life as adults.[38] Only one in six will improve sufficiently to hold a job.[39] A majority of autistic adolescents and young adults are placed in residential facilities.

Cognitive Disability

The largest subcategory of developmental disabilities is cognitive disability. It is a disorder that afflicts 3 out of 100 children, two-thirds of whom are boys.[40] The disorder is somewhat difficult to define precisely or to diagnose accurately. The dif-

ficulty occurs because defining the concept of intelligence (which is at the core of cognitive disability) is problematic. The American Association on Mental Deficiency provides this definition of cognitive disability: ". . . significantly subaverage general intellectual functioning existing concurrently with deficits in adaptive behavior, and manifested during the developmental period."[41] "Subaverage general intellectual functioning" refers to scores on an intelligence test that are minimally two standard deviations below the mean for that test. "Adaptive behavior" refers to the standards of social responsibility and personal independence expected for the person's age and cultural group. "Developmental period" is the period of time between birth and the 18th birthday.

LEVELS OF COGNITIVE DISABILITY

The various levels of cognitive disability, and the percentages of people affected at these levels, are shown in Table 15.1. The IQ scores for this table are based on the Wechsler Intelligence Test. We'll now look at the functioning of people at these various levels.

Mild Cognitive Disability. Persons at this level develop communication and social skills similar to other people's. Their cognitive disability is often not recognized until they are in the third or fourth grade, when they begin to have serious academic difficulties. With help, they can acquire academic skills beyond the sixth-grade level. Other than intellectual functioning, their needs and abilities are indistinguishable from those of others. Special education programs in school often enable these children to acquire the vocational skills that are needed for performing unskilled and semiskilled jobs. As adults, many are able to be employed and to live somewhat independently.

Moderate Cognitive Disability. Children at this level learn to talk and communicate during the preschool years. Unlike other children, however, they have difficulties in learning social customs. They are unlikely to ever perform beyond second-

TABLE 15.1

Levels of Cognitive Disability

Level	Percentage of People with This Level of Cognitive Disability	Wechsler IQ Score
Mild	75.0	55–69
Moderate	20.0	40–54
Severe	3.5	25–39
Profound	1.5	Below 25

Source: David L. Rosenhan and Martin E. P. Seligman, *Abnormal Psychology* (New York: Norton, 1984).

grade level in academic subjects. Some have poor motor coordination. As adults they can learn to contribute to their own support by working at semi-skilled or unskilled tasks in protected settings; many live in group homes and work at sheltered workshops.

Severe Cognitive Disability. People at this level have major difficulties in communicative speech, and before the age of 5 they display considerable evidence of motor coordination problems. At special schools they may learn to talk, and they can be trained in elementary hygiene. As adults they may be able to perform simple and unskilled job tasks under supervision. Some are able to function at a sheltered workshop, and most reside in group homes or in residential institutions.

Profound Cognitive Disability. People at this level display severe disabilities in adaptive behavior. During the preschool years they are able to master only the simplest motor tasks. Later some development of motor skills may occur, and they may learn some elementary self-care skills. This level of cognitive disability is often associated with severe physical deformities and central nervous system difficulties. Health and resistance to diseases are often poor. Life expectancy is substantially shortened. Children and adults at this

level usually need residential housing, often in an institution.

CAUSES OF COGNITIVE DISABILITY

Hundreds of causes of cognitive disability have been identified, and we'll summarize some of the major ones. It should be noted that not everyone who is exposed to some of these factors will automatically experience a cognitive disability. For example, a majority of children whose mothers drank heavily during gestation do not have a cognitive disability.

Cultural/Familial Cognitive Disability. Accounting for about 75% of all cognitive disabilities,[42] this category stems from genetic and environmental influences. The vast majority of people in this category have a mild or moderate level of cognitive disability. Many of them have parents and siblings who also have a cognitive disability, suggesting that at least part of the disability is passed on through the genes.

The second major contributor to this type of cognitive disability is the restricted environment in which the individuals in this category live and develop. People who are raised in poverty have a much higher probability of experiencing this type of cognitive disability. Rosenhan and Seligman note that the types of stimulation children receive play major roles in determining whether cultural/familial cognitive disability will occur.

> *Wealth and social class powerfully determine the kind of stimulation children get. Middle-class mothers, for example, tend to give children more verbal explanations of problem solutions, and more praise when the children have solved the problems, than do lower-class mothers. These explanations increase their children's verbal facility, while the praise augments their interest in such problems and their self-confidence in solving them. Lower-class mothers, on the other hand, tend to be more critical of a child's task performance, and they tend also to be nonverbally intrusive.*[43]

Environmental influences include poor prenatal care, frequent accidents, infections, poor health habits, malnutrition, and lack of stimulation. With cultural/familial cognitive disability, it is nearly impossible to determine for each affected person how much of the cognitive disability is due to genetic variables and how much is due to environmental variables.

Gestational Disorders. Infants born prematurely (before 37 weeks of gestation) are at increased risk of having a cognitive disability. Many metropolitan centers have specialized clinics for pregnant women who are known to be at high risk of premature delivery, and most hospitals have neonatal intensive care units for infants who are born prematurely. Such facilities reduce the risk of neurological damage as a result of gestational problems.

Toxemia. Toxic (poisonous) substances in the blood during the gestation period pose a risk for both the pregnant woman and the fetus. Such substances include prescription drugs, cocaine and other illegal drugs, nicotine (from smoking), and alcohol.

A toxic disorder that has received considerable publicity is fetal alcohol syndrome (FAS). It is associated with heavy drinking (generally considered to be five or six drinks on occasion) during the gestation period. Pregnant women who occasionally have one or two drinks also place their fetus at some risk for FAS, which is characterized by facial and cranial abnormalities, possible heart defects, delayed physical and intellectual development, joint and limb anomalies, decreased weight of the fetus, and increased risk of stillbirth.[44]

The risk of toxemia can be substantially reduced if pregnant women receive early, regular, and specialized care during pregnancy. Pregnant women should follow their physician's advice about which medications to take, and which to avoid, during pregnancy.

Infections during Gestation. Certain infections that pregnant women contract may place the fetus at risk for having a cognitive disability. One of these infections, rubella (also called German measles), can result from the mother's exposure to the virus during the first trimester of pregnancy. The affected fetus is also at higher risk of being born with other congenital abnormalities, such as deafness, blindness, heart anomalies, and microcephalus. Mass immunization programs now provide child-bearing women protection against rubella. Blood tests are also available to determine the level of protection a woman has against the virus; those who are unprotected can then become immunized before pregnancy.

Another infection of pregnant women that can prove devastating for the fetus is syphilis. Syphilis infection, like rubella, is passed on to the fetus through the placenta. The affected fetus is likely to be born with many physical anomalies in addition to a cognitive disability.

A virus that is affecting an increasing number of babies is the AIDS virus. Infants can be infected during gestation, at birth, or after birth from milk from an HIV-positive mother. AIDS infants tend to have a life expectancy of only a few years.

Postnatal Cerebral Infection. A variety of viral and bacterial diseases, such as encephalitis and meningitis, can cause severe and irreversible brain damage, particularly if not treated in the early stages of infection. The AIDS virus may also lead to brain deterioration in older children and adults.

Chromosome Abnormalities. The best-known and most common disorder in this category is Down's syndrome. This condition arises because there are 47 chromosomes, rather than the usual 46, in the cells of those affected. The disorder does not appear to be inherited, although the reason for this chromosome abnormality is not presently known. The disorder occurs in children born to mothers of all ages but with greater frequency in children born to mothers over age 35. The risk of the disorder is about 1 in 1500 for children born to mothers in their twenties; it increases to 1 in 40 when the mother is over 40 when the child is born.[45]

Down's syndrome children and adults generally experience a moderate to severe level of cognitive disability. Their eyes are almond shaped and slanted, and they tend to have a round face.

Many of those affected also have physical anomalies, which may include heart lesions and gastrointestinal difficulties.

There are a variety of other chromosomal abnormalities that may occur. In 1991 scientists discovered the gene that causes fragile X syndrome.[46] This gene was found to be located on the X chromosome. Fragile X syndrome is the most common inherited form of cognitive disability. (Down's syndrome is more common but does not run in families.) Symptoms of fragile X syndrome can range from mild learning disability to a severe level of cognitive disability, with serious behavioral problems. Some carriers are completely normal but can pass the gene that produces the syndrome to later generations. Fragile X syndrome is incurable. It occurs in 1 in 1000 males and 1 in 600 females.[47]

Through a test called amniocentesis, prenatal detection of Down's syndrome, other chromosome defects, and some metabolic disorders is possible. Although some small risk of miscarriage is involved, amniocentesis is a fairly simple procedure. A needle is inserted through the abdomen and into the uterus, and amniotic fluid is extracted for chromosome or chemical studies. The procedure should be performed in the first trimester of pregnancy if the mother is known to be at risk for having a child with a specific chromosome or metabolic condition. The test is recommended if the pregnant woman has a complicated medical or gestational history.

Another test, called chorionic villi sampling (CVS), has recently been developed to help identify certain fetal abnormalities. The test can be performed in a physician's office as early as the fifth week of gestation (which is several weeks earlier than amniocentesis can first be used). CVS is relatively simple to perform and under some conditions is a viable alternative to amniocentesis.

Metabolic Disorders. Phenylketonuria (PKU) is perhaps the best-known metabolic disease. The affected infant cannot metabolize phenylalanine, and essential building block of protein in food. As a result, phenylalanine and its derivative, phenyl

pyruvic acid, build up in the body and rapidly poison the central nervous system, causing irreversible brain damage. About a third of such children cannot walk, about two-thirds never learn to talk, and more than half have a profound level of cognitive disability.[48] PKU results from the action of a recessive gene that is inherited from each parent. At present no test exists to identify the recessive gene in the parents. However, affected babies can be identified by a simple test of the urine about three weeks after birth. Once identified, the infants can be placed on a diet that controls the level of phenylalanine in their system until age 6, at which time the brain is nearly fully developed and their chances of surviving with normal intelligence and health are good.

Lipid storage disorders include Tay-Sachs disease, Hunter's syndrome, and Hurler's syndrome. These disorders involve a progressive degenerative process, due to the accumulation of fatty substances in the cells, that eventually leads to the death of the affected individuals. These conditions are inherited, and as yet effective treatment has not been developed. The incidence, however, has been greatly reduced through genetic counseling programs and prenatal diagnosis.

Disorders of Unknown Prenatal Influence. Of the numerous disorders in this category, two of the better known are hydrocephalus and microcephalus. Hydrocephalus involves a condition in which there is an increased amount of cerebrospinal fluid within the skull that will, unless treated, cause an enlargement of the skull. Neurosurgical techniques are now available that prevent brain damage by decreasing the pressure that causes it.

Microcephalus refers to the condition in which there is a reduced circumference of the head. In some cases this disorder may result from an inherited disorder; in other cases it may result from fetal or neonatal brain damage.

Trauma to the Brain. Injury to the brain can occur at any time during prenatal, perinatal, or postnatal development. During the prenatal period one source of injury is X rays that the pregnant woman may have during gestation. If the fetus's brain is exposed to the X rays, a severe level of cognitive disability may occur.

During the prenatal and perinatal periods, brain injury can result from deprivation of oxygen (anoxia) or from insufficient oxygen (hypoxia) to maintain functioning of the brain tissue. Such conditions destroy brain cells and may result in a cognitive disability. Shortage of oxygen may occur for a variety of reasons, including knotted umbilical cord, premature separation of the placenta, or difficult birth as a result of a breech position.

Postnatal damage can result from an almost infinite number of causes. Brain injury can occur from a blow to the head while boxing or fighting, bicycle and automobile accidents, near-drowning, football injuries, falls from a horse, battering by a parent, or any other damage to the head.

These diverse causes of cognitive disability illustrate how fragile human life is. We are all one accident or one infection away from experiencing a severe cognitive disability. In reviewing the multitude of sources, Maureen Foster addresses the concerns of prospective parents:

The temptation is to think that with all the possibilities of having a retarded child, it is impossible to believe that one could have a baby who is normal and healthy and stays that way through the entire developmental period. The risk of having a retarded child is low, and every prospective parent should approach parenthood with optimism. . . . Although precautions can be taken to decrease the chances of retardation, it can and does occur every day in families in which early and excellent prenatal care was sought, in which the mother stayed away from all agents known or suspected to be toxic, in which no illness occurred during the gestational period, and in which the birth was uncomplicated.[49]

SOCIETY'S REACTIONS TO DISABILITIES

Our culture places a high value on having a beautiful body. We work out at health clubs, and we spend large proportions of our incomes on clothes, cosmetics, hair stylists, and special diets to look more attractive. Beauty is erroneously identified with goodness and ugliness with evil. Movies, television, and books portray heroes and heroines as being physically attractive and villains as being ugly. Snow White, for example, was lovely, whereas the evil witch was horrible looking. Children are erroneously taught that being physically attractive will lead to the good life, whereas having unattractive features is a sign of being inferior. Richardson found that young children rated people with a disability as being "less desirable" than people without a disability.[50]

Unfortunately, this emphasis on the body beautiful has caused persons with a disability to be the objects of cruel jokes and has occasionally led them to be either shunned or treated as inferior. According to C. H. Cooley, if persons with a disability are related to as if they are inferior, second-class citizens, they are likely to come to view themselves as inferior and to have a negative self-concept.[51] Our society needs to reassess its values about the perfect physique. It would seem that other traits ought to be more important: honesty, integrity, a pleasant personality, responsibleness, kindness, and helpfulness.

Wright has noted that the emphasis on beautiful bodies has also led society to believe that persons with a disability "ought" to feel inferior.[52] She has coined the term *the requirement of mourning* for this expectation of society. A person who spends a great deal of time, money, and effort to be physically attractive psychologically wants a person with a disability to mourn the disability because the "body beautiful" person needs feedback that it is worthwhile and important to strive to have an attractive physique.

Another consequence of this misplaced emphasis is that persons with a disability are sometimes pitied as being less fortunate and given sympathy. Many persons with a disability decry receiving pity and being patronized. They seek to be treated as equals.

There is also a tendency in our society to conclude that a person with one kind of disability will also have other kinds of disabilities. Nancy Weinberg has noted that people talk louder in the presence of someone who is blind, erroneously assuming that people who cannot see also have hearing problems.[53] Individuals with a physical disability are also erroneously assumed at times to have a cognitive disability. A 22-year-old college student in a wheelchair describes one example of this tendency:

> I'm in church with my father and my father is standing beside me and I'm in a wheelchair. I'm relatively intelligent, but I'm disabled. I'm sitting there like anyone else. And somebody comes up to my father and they're about as far away from me as from him and they say to my father, "How's he doing?" "Well he's looking pretty good." And I just want to kick him in the stomach.[54]

Such misperceptions may lead those with a physical disability to believe they are less intelligent and less effective in social interactions.

Studies have found that many people cut short their interactions with persons who have a disability.[55] They are uncomfortable when a disabled person is near because they are uncertain about what is appropriate and inappropriate to say and they fear offending the person. Usually they do not want to make any direct remarks about the disability. People show their discomfort in a variety of ways—through abrupt and superficial conversations, fixed stares away from the person with a disability, compulsive talking, or an artificial seriousness. Individuals with a disability are sensitive to such insincere interactions. Fred David describes a few encounters that produce interactional strains:

> I get suspicious when somebody says, "Let's go for a uh, ah [imitates confused and halting speech] push with me down the hall," or something like that. This to me is suspicious because it means that they're aware, really aware, that there's a wheelchair here, and that this is probably uppermost with them. . . . A lot of people in trying to show you that they don't care that you're in a chair will do crazy things. Oh, there's one person I know who constantly kicks my chair, as if to say "I don't care that you're in a wheelchair. I don't even know that it's there." But that is just an indication that he really knows it's there.[56]

Persons with a disability detest being treated as socially different simply because of their disability.

CURRENT SERVICES

A number of programs provide funds and services to persons with a disability. Some of these are federally funded and administered at state or local levels.

Sheltered Workshops

Sheltered workshops provide a variety of services, generally including vocational evaluation, sheltered employment, work adjustment training, counseling services, and placement services.

VOCATIONAL EVALUATION

Clients are assessed on the basis of work behavior, physical capacities, social interaction, psychological functioning, and vocational goals and interests. Emphasis is placed on identifying the client's vocational assets and limitations. (In recent years some sheltered workshops have made a policy change. They now consider their "clients" to be "workers" or "employees." This shift has created a more efficient, work-oriented environment and helped the "employees" maximize their capacities for productive work.)

SHELTERED EMPLOYMENT

These programs provide a work environment for individuals who are unable to secure or maintain jobs in the community. Clients are paid (often below the minimum-wage level) for work produced. Work tasks derive from various subcontract jobs from other industries in the community and allow for long-term vocational development and possible placement into competitive employment. There is periodic evaluation of clients' progress in meeting rehabilitation objectives to ensure maximum vocational and personal development.

WORK ADJUSTMENT TRAINING

Vocational training experiences are provided to clients who are not yet ready for competitive employment following their initial vocational evaluation. The program is conducted in a work setting, using various types of subcontract jobs secured from industries in the community. The employment is designed to train individuals in developing good work skills and appropriate behavior on the job. Counselors are available to discuss problems, to assist learning of new tasks, and to teach better work habits.

COUNSELING SERVICES

Counseling services include individual, group, parent, and vocational guidance. Individual counseling stresses work and intervention goals applied to mutually determined problem areas. Group counseling focuses on peer interaction and development of social skills. Parent counseling acquaints parents with rehabilitation objectives, thus providing support in the home for the total rehabilitation program. Exposure to the work world, development of job-seeking skills, and identification of realistic goals are the major emphases of vocational counseling.

PLACEMENT SERVICES

These programs assist clients in securing competitive employment. First, clients' work habits and skills are assessed. Then they receive training in searching for a job, applying for a job, and holding a job. Counselors then seek, together with clients, to place the clients with local employers. After placement, contact is maintained for a period of time to deal with any adjustment problems that may arise. At many work sites in the community, counselors serve as job coaches (often for a few weeks) to assist the clients in learning and performing the tasks of the positions for which they have been hired.

Educational Programs

Historically, many public schools either refused to serve children with a severe disability or segregated them in special programs. In 1975 Congress enacted the Education for All Handicapped Children Act. This statute mandates that all local school districts provide full and appropriate educational opportunities to all children, including

Special Olympic events foster pride and self-worth for children and adults with developmental disabilities.

those with a disability. An individualized educational program designed to meet the unique needs of each child must be developed to provide instruction in the least restrictive environment that is feasible. The intent is to "mainstream" children with a disability so that they can participate as much as possible in regular educational programs. Most school districts now have "special educational programs" designed to meet the educational needs of children with a cognitive disability, emotionally disturbed children, children

Children with disabilities participate as much as possible in regular educational programs although most school districts have special education programs designed specifically to meet their needs.

with learning disabilities, and children with a physical disability. Most states have schools for children with hearing impairments and for those with visual impairments. Often these specialized schools also provide statewide consultation for young children.

Residential Programs

GROUP HOMES, HALFWAY HOUSES, AND NURSING HOMES

A number of these facilities provide living arrangements for children and adults with a disability who, for a variety of reasons, are unable to live with their families.

RESIDENTIAL TREATMENT CENTERS

Centers that provide residential care and treatment include mental hospitals, residential treatment centers for the emotionally disturbed, and centers for those with a developmental disability.

Average length of stay varies among facilities and may range from several days to permanent care. Some of these residential facilities also serve clients on an outpatient basis, providing diagnostic, evaluative, and planning services.

DAY-CARE CENTERS

These centers provide day-care services to children with a cognitive disability to the emotionally disturbed, and to children with a physical disability. The centers not only give the parents some relief time, but also provide training in self-help, socialization, homemaking, communication, and leisure-time activities.

HOSPITAL SERVICES

Hospitals provide a variety of rehabilitation services for those with a disability, such as medical services, physical therapy, and speech therapy. For individuals who are severely injured or have a serious chronic illness, hospitals are often the entry point into the rehabilitation system.

Home Services

MEALS ON WHEELS

This program provides hot and cold meals to housebound recipients who are incapable of obtaining or preparing their own meals but who can feed themselves.

HOME HEALTH SERVICES

These programs provide visiting nurse services, drugs, physical therapy, laboratory services, and sickroom equipment.

HOMEMAKER SERVICES

In some communities homemakers are available to do household tasks that persons with a disability are unable to do for themselves.

Federal Assistance Programs

VOCATIONAL REHABILITATION FUNDING

Federal funding programs for rehabilitation have developed gradually in this country. Two of the key statutes were the Vocational Rehabilitation Act Amendments of 1954 and the Rehabilitation Act of 1975.[57] At present there are federal matching funds available to states for basic rehabilitation programs at the matching rate of 80% federal and 20% state. Individuals are eligible for vocational rehabilitation services if they have a mental or physical disability that substantially interferes with their capacity to obtain employment and if there is a reasonable expectation that services will enable them to obtain employment. Potential clients receive medical testing free of charge to assess the extent of their disability and to check their overall health. Rehabilitation counselors employed by the state review these results. Applicants found eligible may then receive, at state and federal expense, a variety of services:

■ Special equipment, such as hearing aids, guide dogs, wheelchairs, canes, or prosthetics.

■ Special training in such areas as sign language, vocational training, reading, or social adjustment. This training may take place at a sheltered workshop, at a vocational school, at a public or private college, or on the job.

■ Money for transportation and living expenses during the period of training.

■ Medical, surgical, and other services that will lessen the extent of the client's impairment.

■ Individual counseling and guidance.

■ Assistance in finding a suitable job and essential equipment, licenses, tools, or stock for a small business.

■ Follow-up to smooth the client's entrance into employment.

Under this program states are able to set priorities for categories of eligible clients who will be served when financial resources are limited. For example, states may assign a higher priority to clients who need medical restoration than to those who need psychological counseling. Each state also has the option of deciding whether an economic means test should be used to determine whether the applicant is entitled to certain services.

MEDICAID

This program (described in Chapter 14) covers medical expenses for low-income people.

OLD-AGE, SURVIVORS, AND DISABILITY INSURANCE

This is a social insurance program (described in Chapter 3) for those who are no longer able to work following several years of covered employment.

SUPPLEMENTAL SECURITY INCOME

This is a public assistance program (described in Chapter 3) for low-income persons with a physical or mental disability.

FOOD STAMPS

This program (described in Chapter 3) offsets some of the food expenses for low-income people who qualify.

WORKER'S COMPENSATION PROGRAM

Workers injured or disabled on the job, and surviving dependents of workers who die as a result of such injury, are provided financial assistance to compensate for lost wages and to pay the cost of any required medical or rehabilitative care.

ROLES OF SOCIAL WORKERS

Social workers come in contact with persons with a disability in two general ways.

First, they encounter persons with a disability in settings in which the primary service focus is something other than rehabilitation. For example, workers at family counseling agencies usually see families with marital and interpersonal problems. One or more of these family members may have a disability. The disability may be unrelated to the family problems, or it may be an important contributing factor. In the latter case, the social worker's role is to help the family assess and understand the nature and impact of the disability and then develop effective strategies for handling the difficulties associated with the disability.

Second, social workers may be employed in settings that primarily serve persons with a disability, such as sheltered workshops, nursing homes, general hospitals, day-care centers for persons with a disability, rehabilitation hospitals, and specialized schools (such as schools for persons with a visual impairment).

Rehabilitation for this population can be defined as restoration to the fullest physical, mental, social, vocational, and economic usefulness of which they are capable.[58] Programs focus on vocational training, vocational counseling, psychological adjustment, medical and physical restoration, and job placement. Clients, of course, differ in which of these services are needed. Some clients require help in all of these areas.

A wide range of professionals provide rehabilitation services: physicians, nurses, clinical psychologists, physical therapists, psychiatrists, occupational therapists, recreational therapists, vocational counselors, speech therapists, hearing therapists, industrial arts teachers, social workers, special education teachers, and prosthetists. Most of these therapists focus on the physical functioning of the clients, whereas social workers focus primarily on their social functioning. In most rehabilitation settings a team approach is used.

The major functions of social workers in rehabilitation settings are discussed in the following sections.

Counseling Clients

Counseling in this context involves helping clients adjust to their disability and to the rehabilitation programs at the agency. A wide range of problems may be covered: personal, interpersonal, family, financial, vocational adjustment, and educational adjustment.

Counseling Families

In some rehabilitation settings the social worker is involved primarily in working with the family and not with the client, especially if the client is a young child. Counseling with the family involves helping them to understand the nature of the disability and the prognosis, to make the essential adjustments to help the client, and to deal with personal and interpersonal concerns associated with the disability. In such a role a worker provides information, comfort, understanding, counseling on specific concerns, and sometimes referral services.

Taking Social Histories

A social history contains information about the client's family background and present status. It includes information about what the client's family life was like before contact with the agency, what it is like now, and what it will probably be like in the future. A social history contains a history of the disability, positive and negative reactions of family members to the disability, significant family relationships, summary of strengths and weaknesses within the family for handling the disability, information on social skills of the client, a history of the client's functioning at school and at work, a history of services provided in the past, and a summary of the problems associated with the disability and concerns of family members (see Case Example 15.1). Information for the social history is gathered from the client, from family members, and from case records of other social and medical agencies that the client has had contact with.

Serving as Liaison between the Family and the Agency

Keeping the lines of communication open is essential in any human service setting. In a rehabilitation setting, social workers generally have the responsibility to serve as liaison between the agency staff and the family. At times a worker arranges meetings between the staff and the family to discuss the client's disability, factors affecting rehabilitation, and future plans and services. In a hospital setting it is the physician's responsibility to explain the particular medical condition to the client, but a social worker often discusses the implications of the medical condition with the client and the family. Implications covered include the likely effect the disability will have in the future on the capacity of the affected person to function at work, at school, in social situations, and within the family. To be an effective liaison, a social worker in a rehabilitative setting needs a basic knowledge of a variety of medical conditions and of medical terminology, as well as an awareness of the implications of these medical conditions for emotional, physical, and social functioning.

Being a Broker

Often a social worker functions to link families with other community resources. To be an effective broker, a worker needs a knowledge of other community services, including the programs provided, eligibility requirements, and admission procedures. Clients may need from other community agencies a variety of services, such as

financial assistance, wheelchairs, prosthetic services, day-care services, special job training, visiting nurse services, and transportation.

Doing Discharge Planning

In some rehabilitation settings, such as hospitals, social workers have major responsibility for discharge planning. If a client is unable to return home, arrangements must be made for placement in some other setting, such as a nursing home or a group home. Social workers often help clients and their families prepare for returning to the home or to some other facility. In this capacity the social worker may arrange for financial aid and for such specialized care as visiting nurse services, day care, physical therapy, and job training.

REACTIONS TO HAVING A DISABILITY

To work effectively with persons with a disability and their families, the social worker must understand and deal with the emotional reactions to the disability. Clients and their families experience a variety of reactions on being informed that a disability exists.

The primary response is the realization that a loss has occurred. For example, when parents become aware their young daughter has a cognitive disability, they are likely to mourn the loss of having a "normal" child. When a loss occurs, people go through a grieving process.

Nearly all of us are currently grieving about some loss that we have had. It might be the end of a romantic relationship, or a move away from friends and parents, or the death of a pet, or failure to get a grade we wanted, or the death of someone close. The reactions that a person has when a disability occurs are analogous to these feelings of loss. Examples of disability-related losses include the following: a couple is informed that their 1-year-old daughter has a cognitive disability; a 20-year-old male learns that he will be paralyzed for the rest of his life as the result of an auto accident; a couple is told that their 6-month-old son has cerebral palsy; a 33-year-old business executive has a massive heart attack and is informed that he will have to make major changes in his lifestyle; a husband learns that his wife will have a severe visual disability following an accident at work; a 26-year-old woman is told that she has multiple sclerosis; a 28-year-old farmer is informed that his leg must be amputated following a tractor accident; a couple discovers that their 2-year-old son has a severe hearing disability; a 17-year-old high school student learns that she has rheumatoid arthritis; a 27-year-old actor hears that he has tested HIV positive. This list could go on and on.

The Grieving Process

It is a mistake to believe that grieving over a loss should end in a set amount of time, such as six months, a year, or three years. The "normal" grieving process is often the life span of the griever. When we first become aware of a loss of very high value, we are likely to grieve intensively—to cry, be depressed, be in a state of shock, and so on. Gradually we will have hours, then days, then weeks, then months, when we will not dwell on the loss and will not grieve. However, there will always be something that reminds us of the loss (such as anniversaries of when it occurred), and we will grieve again. The intense grieving periods will, however, gradually become shorter in duration, occur less frequently, and decrease in intensity.

Two important models of the grieving process have been advanced: the Kübler-Ross model and the Westberg model. Some people who are grieving believe the Kübler-Ross model better describes the process, whereas others assert that the Westberg model more accurately describes their feelings. These models help us to understand the grief we feel from *any* loss we experience.

In both of these models, Kübler-Ross and Westberg note the following: (1) Some people continue to grieve and never reach the final stage (acceptance in the Kübler-Ross model and affirming reality in the Westberg model). (2) One should not rigidly believe that everyone will progress through these stages as diagramed. There is often considerable movement back and forth in these stages. For example, in the Kübler-Ross model a person may go from denial to depression, to anger and rage, back to denial, then to bargaining, then to depression, back to anger and rage, and so on.

KÜBLER-ROSS MODEL

In *On Death and Dying*, Kübler-Ross describes five stages of dying that terminally ill people typically proceed through.[59] These five stages (summarized in Chapter 14) include denial, rage and anger, bargaining, depression, and acceptance. In my experience, *all* clients typically display these five stages when confronted with evidence that they have a personal problem—including a disability.

Stage 1: Denial ("No, not me."). During this stage clients tell themselves "No, this can't be," "There must be a mistake," "This just isn't happening." It is difficult for clients (or the families of clients) to admit they have a disability, and they may often (erroneously) perceive themselves as sinful, weak, or irresponsible. In our society, which glorifies "the body beautiful," acknowledging that a disability exists is often erroneously interpreted by clients as indicating that they are less important or worthy. Also, recognizing that a disability exists means acknowledging that one's life will have to change. When such change becomes inevitable, clients often mourn the loss of what used to be. For example, a young, successful businesswoman may need to change her whole life following a heart attack, including pursuing some other career with fewer pressures. Denial is often important and necessary, because it helps cushion the impact of the client's awareness that change is inevitable.

Stage 2: Rage and Anger ("Why me?"). Clients (or their families) resent the fact that others remain the same while they are afflicted with a disability. They feel it is "unfair." Also, they may resent the fact that relatives, old friends, and others are doing the things that they can no longer do. Anyone may be the target of clients' anger, including the social worker who confronts them with the reality of their disability.

<table>
<tr><td>CASE
EXAMPLE 15.1</td><td>

Social History of a Client at a Vocational Testing Division of a Sheltered Workshop

</td></tr>
</table>

Hillside Vocational Training Center
Columbus, Ohio

Name: Jim Frey   Marital Status: Single

Date of Birth: 6-30-75   Height: 5'10"

Address: 550 S. Adams, Columbus   Weight: 180

Telephone: 478-2346

Religion: Lutheran

Occupation: Unemployed

Race: Black

Reason for Testing. On April 30, 1992, Jim Frey was involved in an automobile accident with his older brother, Bob. Bob was killed in the accident, and Jim's spine was severed. Jim was hospitalized for three months, spent five more months convalescing in a nursing home, and since that time has been living with his parents. Jim is paralyzed from the waist down. Following the accident he was also severely depressed. He was referred to this agency by Lakeland Counseling Center, an agency that Jim and his parents have been receiving counseling from. Jim's depression has gradually decreased, and he is now seeking testing and vocational counseling to explore career opportunities.

Family Background and Early History. Jim's father, Donald Frey, has been an insurance salesman for the past 27 years. His mother, Joan Frey, has been a real estate broker for the past 14 years. Both Mr. and Mrs. Frey appear to be very concerned about their son's future, and both stated they are willing to do whatever they can to help. The Freys live in a middle-class neighborhood and have a home that is clean and well kept. The Freys appeared to have considerable respect for each other and a good relationship.

The only children that the Freys had were Jim and Bob, with Bob being two years older. The Freys reported that both their children did well academically in school, and each had a number of friends. The boys were both active in intramural sports, with Bob being a second-string player of the basketball team in his junior and senior years. The most serious trouble that either of the boys had gotten into prior to the accident was Bob being arrested for setting off firecrackers around the 4th of July five years ago.

The automobile accident occurred late one evening after Jim and Bob had left a party in which alcoholic beverages were served. Their car hit a bridge abutment. Bob was killed instantly. The parents reported they were extremely distraught following this accident and felt their whole world had been shattered. They indicated they had few friends they socialized with, as they spent most of their time prior to the accident with their work and their children. They received counseling for grief and depression for 18 months from Lakeland Counseling Center. They indicated they discontinued counseling when the person they were seeing made a job transfer to the West Coast.

For nearly the past two years Mr. and Mrs. Frey have been caring for Jim at home. Mrs. Frey indicated she has taken a leave of absence from her real estate position in order to care for her son. They acknowledged that caring for Jim has been "taxing," as he has been quite depressed and has required considerable physical attention. Only recently has he been able to get into and out of a wheelchair without assistance. The parents still mourn the loss of Bob but are increasingly becoming optimistic with the progress that Jim has been making, including a decrease in his depression, increased physical agility, and now a motivation to receive training for a career.

School Performance. Jim attended Franklin Elementary School, Stevens Junior High, and Randal High School. At the time of his accident, Jim was a senior. He was near graduation but as yet has not completed the course work. School records show that Jim generally received *A*s and *B*s, with a few *C*s. Jim had an intelligence test in his sophomore year in which he achieved a score of 122. Before the accident Jim was planning to attend college. He reportedly had a number of friends, and most continued to visit him for the first several months following the accident. But, as time passed and as Jim's depression continued, his friends gradually stopped coming by to see him. At present he has no close friends.

General Health. Until the accident his health was generally good. He had a hernia operation at age 10 and a broken collarbone at age 12. During the accident Jim suffered a severed spine and is now partially paralyzed. He also had a variety of cuts from glass that required over 80 stitches. Since the accident he at times has experienced considerable pain connected with his injury and has been prone to catch flus and colds. Medical reports indicate Jim received intensive physical therapy while at the hospital and while convalescing in the nursing home. On returning to his home, Jim's parents were instructed on giving him a variety of exercises.

Dating History. Jim indicated he dated a number of young women before the accident. At the time of the accident he was dating someone steadily (during his senior year). At first this person showed considerable interest in Jim and his circumstances. However, Jim stated that after a few months she started dating others, and her interest in continuing their relationship rapidly declined.

Employment History. Jim was a paperboy for a few years. Before the accident he worked part-time as a busboy at a restaurant. He has not worked since the accident.

Prior Contact with Social Agencies. Jim was hospitalized in 1992 for three months at St. Mary's hospital. Records show he received extensive physical therapy and counseling for depression from the social work staff. Following this hospitalization he was transferred to Countryside Nursing Home, where he continued to receive physical therapy and counseling. Jim had fallen asleep on the fateful night when his brother was killed. For months after that, he was depressed and continued to feel guilty

(continued)

CASE EXAMPLE 15.1 *(continued)*

because he felt that, if he had stayed awake, he might have kept his brother awake. (The police concluded that the accident occurred after Bob had fallen asleep.) Jim also has been depressed over the breakup with his girlfriend, over the loss of other friends, and particularly over the shattered hopes and expectations for his future. After Jim returned home, his parents made arrangements with the referring agency (Lakeland Counseling Center) for Jim to receive counseling associated with his depression and also focused on his future. Reports received from Lakeland Counseling Center also indicated that his parents have expressed concerns in the past year that Jim may be drinking beer and other alcoholic beverages to excess.

General Impressions. Jim has made gradual progress in putting his life back together since his auto accident some three years ago. At times he is still somewhat depressed, but he now is making efforts to stop brooding about his past and is motivated to improve his situation. He is looking forward to the test results at the center, since he wants to receive training for a career. At the present time he is uncertain which career he desires to pursue and is uncertain which vocations or professions he is qualified to pursue. He is articulate and personable and appears to possess a high intellect. He has expressed a strong interest in graduating from high school and wonders whether he might have the capacities and financial resources to attend college. His parents appear supportive of his desires to seek a higher education and stated they would be willing and able to provide some financial support.

Jim stated he is also interested in learning to drive and hopes to be able to secure a driver's license and an auto with assistive devices that would enable him to drive.

Jim's drinking was discussed with him. He stated that he may at times drink to excess, but he said this only happens when he is bored or depressed or has nothing to do. It would seem that Jim's drinking is a potential difficulty that should be monitored.

Jim has the support and encouragement of his parents. Jim's present optimism about his future is indeed a positive sign. However, it is important for him to realize that testing is only the first step. Jim hopes to acquire the necessary training, employment, and financial resources to live independently of his parents. Although his parents are supportive, there are occasional conflicts between Jim and his parents, such as over his drinking. Jim may occasionally get discouraged when he encounters obstacles to arriving at the goals that he has set. It is at these times that he may need continued counseling to prevent the return of a long-term depression.

Respectfully submitted,

Frank Lia
Social Worker

Stage 3: Bargaining ("Yes, me, but . . .''). During this stage clients begin to accept the existence of the disability but will bargain for a wide variety of things: getting a second opinion, substituting cigar smoking for cigarette smoking for someone who has emphysema, working two more weeks to organize things at the office before taking an extended period of relaxed recovery for someone who has had a heart attack, and so on. Clients promise to be good or to do something in exchange for another week or month before they accept the alternatives presented to them for change. Or, they hope that there will be scientific breakthroughs that will fully cure their disability.

During the bargaining stage, clients will usually try to change a few circumstances in their lives, hoping that these changes will miraculously eliminate the disability. Parents of a child with a severe cognitive disability may hope, for example, that increased training and education will enable their child, in several years' time, to be of "normal" intelligence.

Stage 4: Depression ("Yes, me."). Clients (and their families) at this stage have stopped denying the existence of their disability. Their anger has subsided, and they no longer try to bargain. They understand the nature of their disability and realize they will need to make changes in their lives. However, they as yet are not ready to put forth the efforts to improve their circumstances. They tend to brood about having a disability and convey an attitude of "Woe is me," "How awful this is," and "Poor me." Often they blame themselves for having the disability. They mourn about how it will affect their future, and they mourn the loss of what they will have to change in their lives.

Stage 5: Acceptance ("I have a problem, but it's all right; I can."). Clients now, for the first time, make a concerted effort to minimize the effects of the disability and to put their lives back together. They have the attitude of "I can do it." There is hope. Fear and apprehension are still present but very much reduced. Only when clients reach this stage are they ready to work on a rehabilitation program.

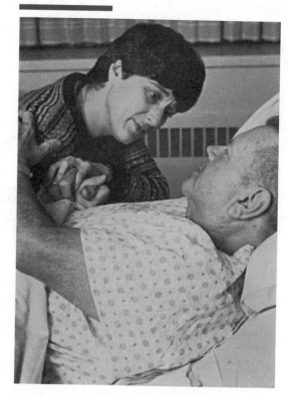

Acceptance is the final phase in Elisabeth Kübler-Ross's model of the grieving process.

WESTBERG MODEL

The Westberg model[60] of the grieving process is diagramed in Figure 15.1.

Shock and Denial. Many people, when informed about a tragic loss, are so numb and in such a state of shock that they are practically devoid of feeling. It could be that, when emotional pain is unusually intense, the system temporarily "blows out." As a result, the person hardly feels anything and thus acts as if nothing has happened. Denial is a way of avoiding the impact of a tragic loss.

Emotions Erupt. As the realization of the loss becomes evident, the person expresses pain through sobs or screams or through gentle tears or deep sighs.

FIGURE 15.1

Westberg Model of the Grieving Process

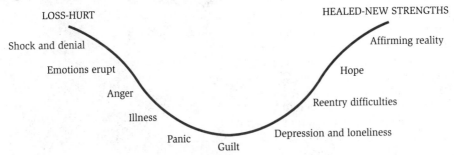

Source: Granger Westberg, Good Grief (Philadelphia: Fortress Press, 1962).

Anger. At some point the person usually experiences anger. It may be directed at God for causing the loss. The anger may stem partly from the unfairness of the loss. If a child is born with a disability, or later develops a disability, it is not uncommon for the parents at times to become angry at the child for having the disability and for complicating their lives.

Illness. Because grief is stress producing, stress-related illnesses are likely to develop, such as colds, flus, ulcers, tension headaches, diarrhea, rashes, insomnia, and so on.

Panic. Realizing that she or he does not feel like the "old self," the grieving person may panic and even worry about going insane. Nightmares, unwanted emotions that appear uncontrollable, and physical illnesses contribute to the panic. A variety of fears may develop. The person with a disability may fear the reactions of others. Parents may fear that their other siblings will suffer from having a brother or sister with a disability, that they will be unable to deal with the burdens of caring for a child with a disability, or that both they and their child will be the target of ridicule.

Guilt. The grieving person may blame himself or herself for having done something that contributed to the loss or disability or may feel guilty for not having done something that might have prevented it. If a child is born with a disability, the mother may wonder "Could this have been caused by my smoking or drinking during pregnancy?" This tendency to blame oneself is reinforced by the questions asked by professionals. For example, the mother may be asked "Did you smoke during the pregnancy? Did you have a serious fall or illness? Did you drink? What pills did you take?" (Although these questions need to be asked, professionals should be careful about how they are phrased because they can have devastating effects.)

Depression and Loneliness. At times the grieving person will feel very sad about the disability or loss and have feelings of isolation and loneliness. She or he may withdraw from others who don't seem supportive or understanding.

Reentry Difficulties. At this point the grieving person makes efforts to put his or her life back together. Reentry problems are likely to arise. The person may resist letting go of attachments to the past, and loyalties to memories may hamper reentry.

Hope. Gradually, hope of putting one's life back together returns and begins to grow.

Affirming Reality. The old feeling of having control of one's life returns. The reconstructed life is not the same as the old, and memories of the loss remain. But the reconstructed life is viewed as "OK."

Facilitating the Grieving Process

The Kübler-Ross and Westberg paradigms can help social workers to better understand why clients are reacting in various ways to their disabilities. It is important that workers help clients identify those emotions that are interfering with a habilitative or rehabilitative program. Strategies can then be developed to counter those emotions that are interfering with progress. For example, a mother of a child born with Down's syndrome may feel guilty because she thinks she caused the problem by lifting too much during her pregnancy. The social worker can arrange for a physician or a genetics counselor to explain the etiology of the disorder and to assure her that her concerns over lifting heavy objects had nothing to do with causing the Down's syndrome.

It should also be noted that Kübler-Ross's and Westberg's paradigms may not always apply to young children. Children born with a disability generally are not initially aware of their condition. Awareness gradually develops through interacting with others over a lengthy period of time. Children with a disability come to learn that they are different and that others often place negative values on their disability. In the following excerpt from an autobiography, Christy Brown, born with cerebral palsy, describes some of his feelings. Christy Brown used to ride in a wagon that was pulled by his brothers and sisters, but when it broke he was unable to get around.

I was now just ten, a boy who couldn't walk, speak, feed, or dress himself. I was helpless, but only now did I begin to realize how helpless I really was. I still didn't know anything about myself: I knew nothing beyond the fact that I was different from others. I didn't understand what made me different or why it should be I. . . .

I couldn't reason this out. I couldn't even think clearly about it. I could only feel it, feel it deep down in the very core of me, like a thin sharp needle. . . .

Up to then I had never thought about myself. True, there had come sometimes a vague feeling that I wasn't like the others, an uneasy sort of stirring in my mind that came and went. But it was just one dark spot in the brightness of things; and I used to soon forget it. . . .

Now it was different. Now I saw everything, not through the eyes of a little boy eager for fun and brimming with curiosity, but through those of a cripple, a cripple who had only just discovered his own affliction.

I looked at Peter's hands. They were brown, steady hands with strong, square fingers, hands that could clasp a hurley firmly or swing a chestnut high into the air. Then I looked down at my own. They were queer, twisted hands, with bent, crooked fingers, hands that were never still, but twitched and shook continually so that they looked more like two wriggling snakes than a pair of human hands.

I began to hate the sight of those hands, the sight of my wobbly head and lopsided mouth.[61]

Christy's awareness of his disability involved four steps: (1) an avoidance of thinking about himself and his disability; (2) a vague sense that he was different from others; (3) a critical incident—not being able to go out—that forced him to acknowledge that he had a disability; and (4) self-deprecation because of his disability.

There is a tendency for parents to overindulge and overprotect a child with a disability. They give the child less responsibility, place fewer limits on unwanted behaviors, indulge personal whims of the child, and are reluctant to punish the child, partly because of their sympathy for the suffering the child is undergoing. Children become aware of this special status and sometimes use this sympathy to manipulate those around them. Louise Baker describes how she manipulated others at age 8, shortly after a leg was amputated following an automobile accident:

Even before I left the hospital my sudden power over people was showing itself. First of all, with completely unconscious brilliance, I chose rather inspired subjects to discuss during my five days of postoperative delirium. I rambled on feverishly but with moving feeling about a doll with real golden hair and blue eyes that opened and closed. I even conveniently mentioned the awesome price and just where such a doll might be purchased, and I sighed over my father's

EXHIBIT 15.1

How to Cope with Grief

If you are grieving, try whichever of the following suggestions you believe will be most useful.

■ Crying is an acceptable and valuable expression of grief. Cry as you feel the need. Crying releases the tension that is part of grieving.

■ Talking about your loss and your plans for the present and the future is very constructive. Sharing your grief with friends, family, the clergy, or a professional counselor is advisable. You may want to become involved with a group of people who are having similar experiences. Talking about your grief eases loneliness, allows you to vent your feelings, and helps you to accept your loss and make constructive plans for the present and the future. Talking with close friends gives you a sense of security and brings you closer to others you love. Talking with others who have similar losses helps put your problems into perspective; you will see that you are not the only one with problems, and you will feel good about yourself when you assist others in handling their losses.

■ Disabilities often cause us to examine and question our faith or philosophy of life. Do not become concerned if you begin questioning your beliefs. Talk about them. For many people a religious faith provides help in accepting the loss.

■ Writing out a rational self-analysis of your grief will help you to identify irrational thinking that is contributing to the grief. (Chapter 4 explains how to write a rational self-analysis.) Once your irrational thinking is identified, you can relieve much of your grief through rational challenges to your irrational thinking.

■ Try not to dwell on how unhappy you feel. Become involved and active in life around you. Do not waste your time and energy on self-pity.

■ If there are certain days of the year when you tend to grieve deeply (such as an anniversary of a disabling automobile accident), spend these days with family and friends who will give you support.

■ You may feel that you have nothing to live for

(continued)

---

attested poverty which prevented him from buying this coveted treasure. . . . The news spread: "The poor little crippled child in the hospital . . . wants a doll. . . ." When I left the hospital it took two cars to transport my loot.

Very soon after I came home from the hospital I realized that all I had to do was mumble the magic words . . . "I'll never be able to run again, will I?" This sad little speech—then the moment was ripe to make almost any demand. . . .

Three months before, I was a reasonably well-mannered child . . . now I was a precocious gold-digger, and anyone was fair game.[62]

When clients or members of their family are reacting (emotionally or behaviorally) in ways that substantially interfere with the rehabilitation process, social workers have a responsibility to confront them about this tactfully. Sometimes a considerable amount of evidence will have to be presented, perhaps over a period of time, before clients and family members will acknowledge that certain reactions are intensifying the negative effects of the disability. Once the acknowledgment occurs, strategies for changing the reaction patterns can be discussed, and one or more ap-

EXHIBIT 15.1   *(continued)*

and may even think about suicide. Understand that many people who encounter severe losses feel this way. Seek to find assurance in the fact that a sense of purpose and meaning will return.

■ Intense grief is very stressful, and stress can lead to a variety of illnesses, such as headaches, colitis, ulcers, colds, and flus. If you become ill, seek a physician's help, and tell the doctor that your illness may be related to grief you are experiencing.

■ Intense grief may also lead to sleeplessness, sexual difficulties, loss of appetite, or overeating. You may find you have little energy and cannot concentrate. All of these reactions are normal. Try the positive view that you will get your life back together—practically everyone does who suffers a loss. Seek during your grief to eat a balanced diet, to get ample rest, and to exercise moderately. Every person's grief is unique. If you are experiencing unusual physical reactions (such as nightmares), try not to become overly alarmed.

■ Medication should be taken sparingly and only under the supervision of a physician. Avoid trying to relieve your grief with alcohol

or other drugs. Many drugs are addictive and may stop or delay the necessary grieving process.

■ Recognize that guilt, real or imagined, is a normal part of grief. Parents who have a child with a disability often feel guilty about things they have done or about things they think they should have done. If you are experiencing intense guilt, share it with friends or with a professional counselor. It might also be helpful to write a rational self-analysis on the guilt (see Chapter 4). Learn to forgive yourself. If you didn't make mistakes, you wouldn't be human.

■ You may find that friends and relatives appear to be shunning you. If this is happening, they are probably uncomfortable around you because they do not know what to say or do. Take the initiative, and talk with them about your loss. Tell them about ways in which you would like them to be supportive to you.

■ If possible, put off making major decisions (changing jobs, moving away, and so on) until you become more emotionally relaxed. When you're highly emotional, you're likely to make unwise decisions.

---

proaches may be selected and implemented in order to eliminate the destructive patterns.

SUMMARY

Persons with a disability include those who are temporarily injured, those with a chronic physical disability, those with a hearing disability or a visual disability, those who have an emotional disorder, those with a cognitive disability, those with a learning disability, and those with degenerative illnesses and chronic health disorders.

Developmental disabilities include cognitive

disability, infantile autism, epilepsy, cerebral palsy, and a variety of other conditions that occur before age 22 and that hinder development. There are hundreds of illnesses and medical conditions that have been identified as contributing causes of cognitive disability.

Throughout history the willingness of societies to care for the needs of those with a disability has always been largely determined by the perceived causes of the disability, the existing medical knowledge, and the general economic conditions. In the past, disability was often viewed as a result of demonic possession or of God's punishment.

In the 20th century our society has made progress in better understanding the needs of persons with a disability and in designing services to meet these needs. Yet there is still a general lack of acceptance of persons with a disability; it is often related to our emphasis on the "body beautiful" in our society. Persons with a disability are still frequently pitied, shunned, or made the brunt of jokes. Our society has yet to learn that persons with a disability are people who want to be treated as peers. (All of us are only an accident away from having a disability.) Until persons with a disability are given an opportunity, not only legally but also socially, to be treated as peers, social services will be only partially effective. Ideally, persons with a disability should be limited only by the physical or mental restrictions of their disability. Sadly, the psychological and social obstacles faced by these persons are often greater than their actual physical or mental limitations. Our society has yet to learn that a person with a disability is a person—a person who happens to have a disability.

Social workers are only one of numerous groups of professionals who provide services to persons with a disability. The roles of social workers in providing rehabilitative services include counseling persons with a disability, counseling family members, gathering information through social histories, serving as liaisons between the family and the agency, being brokers and doing discharge planning.

Another role of the social worker is to help persons with a disability and their family members to change emotional and behavioral reactions that are interfering with the rehabilitative process. Two useful paradigms summarize emotional, behavioral, and physiological reactions to having a disability; the Kübler-Ross model and the Westberg model. Both of these models conceptualize the reactions in terms of loss.

NOTES

1. William Kornblum and Joseph Julian, *Social Problems,* 7th ed. (Englewood Cliffs, NJ: Prentice-Hall, 1992), p. 29.

2. Donald Brieland, Lela B. Costin, and Charles R. Atherton, *Contemporary Social Work,* 3d ed. (New York: McGraw-Hill, 1985), p. 294.

3. G. L. Dickinson, *Greek View of Life* (New York: Collier Books, 1961), p. 95.

4. S. Nichtern, *Helping the Retarded Child* (New York: Grosset & Dunlap, 1974), p. 14.

5. J. F. Garrett, "Historical Background," in *Vocational Rehabilitation of the Disabled,* D. Malikin and H. Rusalem, eds. (New York: New York University Press, 1969), pp. 29–38.

6. J. C. Coleman, *Abnormal Psychology and Modern Life,* 3d ed. (Glenview, IL: Scott, Foresman, 1964).

7. C. E. Obermann, *A History of Vocational Rehabilitation in America* (Minneapolis: Dennison, 1964).

8. L. Kanner, *A History of the Care and Study of the Mentally Retarded* (Springfield, IL: Charles C Thomas, 1964), p. 6.

9. M. Judge, "A Brief History of Social Services," part I, *Social and Rehabilitation Record, 3,* no. 5 (September 1976), pp. 2–8.

10. Stanford Rubin and Richard Roessler, *Foundations of the Vocational Rehabilitation Process* (Baltimore: University Park Press, 1978), p. 4.

11. A. F. Tyler, *Freedom's Ferment* (New York: Harper & Row, 1962), pp. 294–296.

12. J. Lenihan, "Disabled Americans: A History," *Performance, 27,* Bicentennial issue (Washington, DC: The President's Committee on Employment of the Handicapped).

13. Obermann, *A History of Vocational Rehabilitation in America,* p. 333.

14. L. M. Dunn, "A Historical Review of the Retarded," in *Mental Retardation,* J. Rothstein, ed. (New York: Holt, Rinehart & Winston, 1961), pp. 13–17.

15. Obermann, *A History of Vocational Rehabilitation in America,* p. 80.

16. Kanner, *A History of the Care and Study of the Mentally Retarded,* pp. 36–38.

17. Ibid., p. 39.

18. Rubin and Roessler, *Foundations of the Vocational Rehabilitation Process,* pp. 12–13.

19. Ibid., pp. 13–14.

20. Lenihan, "Disabled Americans: A History," pp. 28–37.

21. Tyler, *Freedom's Ferment,* p. 306.

22. Rubin and Roessler, *Foundations of the Vocational Rehabilitation Process,* pp. 8–9.

23. Ibid., pp. 10–11.

24. R. Lubove, *The Professional Altruist* (Cambridge, MA: Harvard University Press, 1965).

25. Ibid.

26. Obermann, *A History of Vocational Rehabilitation in America,* p. 121.

27. Rubin and Roessler, *Foundations of the Vocational Rehabilitation Process,* pp. 22–23.

28. Obermann, *A History of Vocational Rehabilitation in America,* pp. 155–157.

29. R. Thomas, "The Expanding Scope of Service," *Journal of Rehabilitation,* 36, no. 5 (1978), pp. 37–40.

30. Rubin and Roessler, *Foundations of the Vocational Rehabilitation Process,* pp. 30–32.

31. Ibid., pp. 32–45.

32. Gregory Spears, "Bush Inks Disabled Rights Bill," *Wisconsin State Journal,* July 27, 1990, p. 5A.

33. William E. Kiernan and Jack A. Stark, eds. *Pathways to Employment for Adults with Developmental Disabilities* (Baltimore: Brooks, 1986), pp. 12–15.

34. David L. Rosenhan and Martin E. P. Seligman, *Abnormal Psychology* (New York: Norton, 1984), p. 535.

35. Ibid., p. 540.

36. Ibid., p. 541.

37. Ibid., pp. 537–542.

38. Ibid., pp. 543–544.

39. Ibid.

40. Ibid., p. 531.

41. Ibid.

42. Ibid.

43. Ibid.

44. Ruth E. Little, "Drinking during Pregnancy: Implications for Public Health," *Alcohol Health and Research World,* 4, no. 1 (1979), pp. 21–29.

45. Rosenhan and Seligman, *Abnormal Psychology,* pp. 532–533.

46. Daniel Q. Haney, "Retardation Gene Discovered," *Wisconsin State Journal,* May 30, 1991, p. 1A.

47. Ibid.

48. Rosenhan and Seligman, *Abnormal Psychology,* p. 533.

49. Maureen O'Gorman Foster, quoted in Charles Zastrow, *Introduction to Social Welfare,* 4th ed. (Belmont, CA: Wadsworth, 1992), p. 515.

50. S. Richardson et al., "Cultural Uniformity in Reaction to Physical Disabilities," *American Sociological Review,* 26 (April 1961), pp. 241–247.

51. C. H. Cooley, *Human Nature and the Social Order* (New York: Scribner's, 1902).

52. Beatrice A. Wright, *Physical Disability: A Psychological Approach* (New York: Harper & Row, 1960), p. 259.

53. Nancy Weinberg, "Rehabilitation," in *Contemporary Social Work,* 2nd ed., Donald Brieland, Lela Costin, and Charles Atherton, eds. (New York: McGraw-Hill, 1980) p. 310.

54. Ibid.

55. R. Kleck, H. Ono, and A. H. Hastorf, "The Effects of Physical Deviance upon Face-to-Face Interaction," *Human Relations,* 19 (1966), pp. 425–436.

56. Fred David, "Deviance Disavowal: The Management of Strained Interaction by the Visibly Handicapped," in *The Other Side: Perspectives on Deviance,* Howard S. Becker, ed. (New York: Free Press, 1964), p. 123.

57. Rubin and Roessler, *Foundations of the Vocational Rehabilitation Process,* pp. 32–44.

58. *Symposium on the Process of Rehabilitation* (Cleveland: National Council on Rehabilitation, 1944), p. 6.

59. Elisabeth Kübler-Ross, *On Death and Dying* (New York: Macmillan, 1969).

60. Granger Westberg, *Good Grief* (Philadelphia: Fortress Press, 1962).

61. Christy Brown, *The Story of Christy Brown* (New York: Pocket Books, 1971). p. 72.

62. Louise Baker, *Out on a Limb* (New York: Whittlesly House, 1946), pp. 4–5.

16

OVERPOPULATION, MISUSE OF THE ENVIRONMENT, AND FAMILY PLANNING

P roblems associated with overpopulation and despoiling of the environment threaten to reduce the quality of human life throughout the world. The seriousness of these problems is illustrated by the fact that some nations are contemplating the enactment of compulsory sterilization laws. This chapter will:

- Describe the problems associated with rapid population growth throughout the world.
- Discuss pollution and misuse of the environment.
- Summarize current efforts to curtail the growth of the world's population and to preserve the environment.
- Outline proposals that have been advanced for population control and for environmental protection in the future.
- Provide suggestions for what each of us can do to save the earth.
- Describe the role of social work in family planning.

THE POPULATION CRISIS

There are now over 5.5 billion people living on earth.[1] In 1930 there were 2 billion. The world's population is increasing at the rate of 185 people a minute, 11,100 an hour, 266,400 a day, and 97.2 million a year[2] (see Table 16.1).

Assuming a continued doubling rate of 40 years, by 2025 there will be 10 billion people. If this growth continued for 900 years, there would be 60 *million billion* people! This would mean that there would be about 100 people for each square yard of the earth's surface, including both land and water.[3]

Doubling Time and Population Growth

The rate at which the population doubles in a country, and in the world, has immense consequences. Doubling time is based on the extent to which the birthrate exceeds the death rate. Doubling times have a compound effect. Just as interest dollars earn interest, people added to the population produce more people. Table 16.2 shows the relationship between the annual population growth rate and the doubling time of the population. Thus, what seems a small population growth rate of 1.9% per year (the current rate in the world) leads to a dramatic doubling time of 40 years. With an annual growth rate of 1.9% over 95 million people are being added to the world's population annually.[4]

Doubling Time and Developing Countries

The countries experiencing the most severe doubling-time problems are the "developing countries" (also called Third World nations), which are just beginning to industrialize. Sadly, population growth is greatest in the countries that can least afford increases—that is, the countries that need to spend their resources on improving their economic conditions. Developing countries have over two-thirds of the world's population and doubling times of about 20 to 35 years.[5] They tend to have primitive and inefficient agriculture, small gross national products, and high illiteracy rates. Their populations spend most of their time in trying to meet basic subsistence needs, and many people are starving in these countries.

Developing countries are characterized by high birthrates and declining death rates. The trend in the past has been that, when a country begins to industrialize, the death rate drops (people live longer) while the birthrate remains high for a substantial period of time. The result is a rapid population growth rate. Unfortunately, developing countries, where people's living conditions most need improvement, are precisely the nations whose populations are increasing so rapidly that most people are scarcely better off than they were a generation ago. Nine out of every ten people added to the world's population are born in the poorer, developing countries.[6] Third World countries are much more likely than industrial countries to have a population explosion.

TABLE 16.1

Doubling Times of the World's Population

Date	Estimated World Population	Time Required for Population to Double (in years)
8000 B.C.	5 million	
1650 A.D.	500 million	1500
1850	1 billion	200
1930	2 billion	80
1975	4 billion	45
2015	8 billion	40

Sources: Paul R. Ehrlich, *The Population Bomb* (New York: Ballantine Books, 1971); and Werner Fornos, *Gaining People, Losing Ground* (Washington, DC: Population Institute, 1987).

TABLE 16.2

Rate of Population Growth and Doubling Time

Annual Percentage Increase	Doubling Time (in years)
1.0	70
2.0	35
3.0	24
4.0	17

Source: Paul Ehrlich, *The Population Bomb* (New York: Ballantine Books, 1971), p. 10.

The population crisis in the world today is not due to families having more children than they did in the past; family size has not increased. However, more people are living to the age of fertility and beyond. In effect, more babies are growing to maturity to produce babies themselves. This change is due to several factors: advances in medicine, sanitation, and public health, and increased capacity to reduce the effects of famines, floods, droughts, and other natural disasters.

Lee Rainwater has noted that "the poor get children."[7] There is a vicious circle involving rapid population growth and poverty. Rapid population growth places an increasing strain on a nation's ability to feed and clothe its growing masses, which leads to poverty. Poverty, in turn, leads to a high birthrate, which leads to further population growth. Former World Bank President Robert S. McNamara warns: "Short of thermonuclear war itself, rampant population growth is the gravest issue the world faces over the decades ahead."[8]

Developed or industrialized countries have doubling times in the 50- to 200-year range.[9] In the United States in recent years the birthrate has steadily decreased and is nearing a zero-population-growth rate (an average of two children per family). The basic reason the doubling time in developed countries is longer is that people decide to have fewer children (for financial and other reasons). It now costs $140,000 to raise a child from birth to age 18 in this country.[10] Developed nations are characterized by both low birthrates and low death rates.

The slower doubling times in industrialized countries in no way indicate that nations are not part of the problem. If one looks at consumption rates of raw materials, they are the major culprit. The United States, for example, uses about one-third of all the raw materials consumed each year but has less than 1/15 of the world's population.[11] Americans are therefore using five times their "fair share" of raw materials. People in the United States also consume, on the average, four times as much food per person as inhabitants of developing countries.[12]

Werner Fornos noted in 1987 that most of the population growth in the future will occur in the urban centers of the developing (Third World) countries:

The population of the Third World as a whole is increasing by a significant 2.1 percent each year, but the population of the Third World's cities is growing by a swift 3.5 percent annually—fully three times as fast as the industrialized world's urban centers. Africa's cities are growing fastest, at a runaway 5 percent each year. The slum squatter settlements associated with these centers are growing at twice the rate of the cities themselves.[13]

In many developing countries, families average seven or eight children.[14] As a result, these countries are increasingly populated by the young. In Latin America and Asia, nearly 40% of the population is under 15 years old.[15] Figure 16.1 indicates that one result of this younger population is that developing countries are much more likely than industrialized countries to have a population explosion.

An Optimal Population Size

A common question is "What is the capacity of the world to support people?" To say that the population is too large or too small implies there is an optimal size, but no exact figure could accurately be considered the ideal population for the world.

Many variables and values would enter into specifying an optimal world population size, including preservation of a certain standard or quality of life, rate of consumption of nonrenewable raw materials, future technological breakthroughs in finding new energy and food sources, maintenance of "safe" levels of clean air and water, and public acceptance of the government's role (perhaps compulsory) in population control. The industrialized nations, with their high-consumption and high-waste economies, are using up more of the earth's raw materials and generating more pollution than are developing countries. Because of consumption rates, adding 1 million people to industrialized countries is comparable to adding 30 million people to developing countries.[16]

With regard to the question of whether the earth is already overpopulated, Paul Ehrlich and Anne Ehrlich note:

The key to understanding overpopulation is not population density but the numbers of people in an area relative to its resources and the capacity of the environment to sustain human activities; that is, to the area's carrying capacity. When is an area overpopulated? When its population can't be maintained without rapidly depleting

EXHIBIT 16.1

Compulsory Sterilization Laws

Overpopulation is now recognized as one of the severest problems affecting the preservation of the quality of human life. Some countries are now seriously considering enacting compulsory sterilization laws to control rapid population growth. One such country is India. In 1976 Maharashtra (a state in India) passed a compulsory sterilization law to limit family size. The law required all males under age 55, and all females under age 45, to be sterilized within 180 days of the birth of their third living child. Prison terms of up to two years could be assigned to those who failed to comply, although offenders were generally sterilized and then paroled. From April 1976 through December 1976, more than 7 million sterilizations reportedly were performed. This law was rescinded with the fall of Prime Minister Indira Gandhi's government in 1976. Nevertheless, it illustrates the desperation of some countries to alleviate the pressures of unwanted population growth.

Source: "Maharashtra Passes Family Size Limitation Measure," *Intercom*, 9 (September 1976), p. 5; Lynn C. Landman, "Birth Control in India: The Carrot and the Rod?" *Family Planning Perspectives*, 9 (May–June 1977), p. 102.

nonrenewable resources (or converting renewable resources into nonrenewable ones) and without degrading the capacity of the environment to support the population. In short, if the long-term carrying capacity of an area is clearly being degraded by its current human occupants, that area is overpopulated.

By this standard, the entire planet and virtually every nation is already vastly overpopulated.[17]

Problems of Overpopulation

A wide range of problems are associated with overpopulation. These include too little food, too

FIGURE 16.1

Age/Sex Population Pyramids: Industrial and Developing Country Models

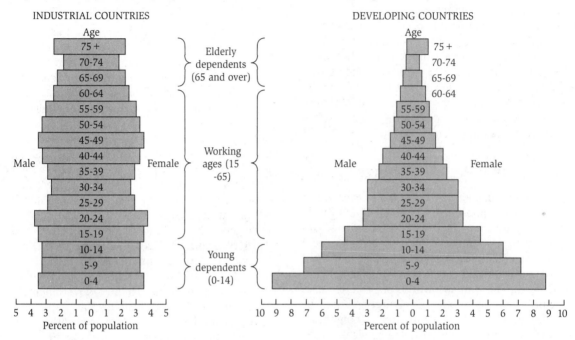

Industrial countries have 3 or 4 adults of economically productive ages for each dependent child. When an industrial country's children grow up and reproduce, the population structure will change only a little.

Developing countries have one (or less) adult of economically productive age for each dependent child. When the developing country's children grow up and reproduce, a population explosion will occur.

little water, economic problems, international terrorism, crowding, immigration issues, too little energy, and shortages of other nonrenewable resources.

TOO LITTLE FOOD

An estimated half-billion people today are under-nourished—that is, slowly starving—and another billion are malnourished.[18] Ehrlich and Ehrlich estimate that 10 to 20 million people, mostly children in developing countries, are dying of starvation each year.[19] Even in the United States many people are undernourished, with some dying of starvation.[20] In approximately the time it takes to

read this sentence, four people will die (three of them children) from malnutrition.[21] Incredible as it may seem, 43% of all deaths in India are of children under the age of 4.[22]

In poor countries, overpopulation leads to malnutrition for many, and often most, of the inhabitants. Malnutrition has severe effects on both the body and the mind. It causes brain damage and cognitive disabilities, stunts physical growth, directly causes a number of diseases, lowers resistance to other diseases, and reduces the life span. The brain of an infant grows to 80% of its adult size within the first three years of life. If supplies of protein are inadequate during this period, the brain stops growing, and the damage is irreversible; such children suffer permanent cognitive disabilities.[23]

Nearly 200 years ago (in 1798), Thomas Malthus asserted that population growth, if left unchecked, would outstrip the food supply.[24] Malthus theorized that uncontrolled population growth increases in powers of 2: 1, 2, 4, 8, 16, 32, 64—that is, in a geometric ratio. In contrast, the food supply cannot possibly increase that fast. At best, the food supply increases in a steady additive fashion: 1, 2, 3, 4, 5, 6, 7—that is, in an arithmetic ratio. Inevitably, according to Malthus, population growth overtakes the growth in food supplies. Therefore, either population has to be controlled by society, or starvation, hunger, and poverty will be the unavoidable fate of most of the world's people. The fact that widespread starvation and poverty are indeed common in many countries today provides some evidence of the validity of the Malthus theory.

There has been an ongoing, heated controversy among scientists over whether technology will be able to substantially increase the world's food supply. Some scientists claim that we have already reached the limit at which technology is no longer able to increase the food supply to meet the needs of even a slowly growing world population. Others are predicting that future technology will provide food for a population ten times as large as our current one.[25]

Which side is right? The verdict is not yet in. Several years ago a technological breakthrough led to a dramatic improvement in the yield of new strains of wheat and rice. This "green revolution," however, requires increased use of fertilizers and water. Fertilizers are becoming scarce and increasingly expensive, and many of the developing countries cannot afford costly irrigation systems. Because of such variables, the beneficial effect of the green revolution is not as yet precisely known.

Research on increasing the food supply is also taking other approaches. One effort is to investigate the feasibility of cultivating the tropical rain forests of Africa, South America, and Indonesia. Such areas have large amounts of sunshine and water but poor soil (requiring large quantities of fertilizer) and severe insect infestations. Another

Ethiopian children are fed at a relief camp. Up to 20 million people, mostly children in developing countries, die of starvation each year.

effort is geared to finding new ways to harvest fish and plant life from the sea. The sea contains huge quantities of food, much of which is currently distasteful. Not only does more food need to be produced, but food distribution systems must be improved. In the United States it is more than ironic that farmers are producing more food than Americans can consume, yet an estimated 30 million people in the country do not have enough to eat.[26]

TOO LITTLE WATER

Somewhat surprisingly, fresh water is also in short supply in the world. Ninety-seven percent of the world's water is salt water; only 3% is fresh water.[27]

Developed nations use substantially more water per person than developing nations. It has been estimated that an African uses 0.8 gallon of water a day, compared to 270 gallons for a New Yorker.[28]

Water is also needed in large quantities to produce food. A pound of wheat requires about 60 gallons of water; a pound of meat requires from 2500 to 6000 gallons.[29] If irrigation efforts are expanded worldwide to grow food, fresh water resources will obviously be depleted at a faster rate. Desalinization (removing salt from water) is now being done on a small scale, but it is so expensive that it is currently being used for drinking only.

ECONOMIC PROBLEMS

In industrialized countries rapid population growth reduces the standard of living and the quality of life by reducing the average per capita income.[30] Because birthrates are consistently higher among the lower-income groups, there are additional social and economic strains. Some authorities openly express alarm that high birthrates among poorer classes may lead to a reduction in average educational achievement and provide a threat to the values espoused by the middle and upper classes. Rapid population growth also leads to other problems: massive unemployment, air and water pollution, traffic jams, inadequate and insufficient housing, and so on.

Economic problems are even more serious in developing nations. Economic progress tends to be canceled out by the increased population. For poor countries to industrialize requires that the inhabitants invest (through either public or private funds) in capital items such as factories, tractors, and industrial equipment. Many developing nations do not even have the funds to provide adequate food for their people. Inability to invest in capital items practically guarantees that they will be unable to improve their people's standard of living.

Lack of funds also creates educational and political problems. Developing countries have a high proportion of school-age children but do not have the resources to provide enough schools. For example, Dr. Benson Morah describes the situation in Nigeria: "You have schools with 70 children in the classrooms, there are children sitting in the windows, children carrying their chairs to school."[31] As a result, in many countries a majority of children do not attend school. Illiteracy and lack of training further lock the inhabitants into poverty.

In addition, people who are poorly housed, hungry, and miserably clothed are likely to view the government as the protector of the rich and the oppressor of the poor. Such conditions often lead to political unrest, revolutions, and civil wars—as have been common in Africa, Asia, and South America.

The gap in living standards between industrialized and developing countries is wide and growing wider. In 1993, for example, the average per capita gross income was over $18,000 in the United States; in some developing nations it was less than $500.[32]

INTERNATIONAL TERRORISM

Rapid population growth is a factor that contributes to civil unrest, violence, and international strife. Overpopulation leads to higher unemployment, rapid urbanization, declining public health, environmental degradation, economic stagnation, and a large youthful population. Young people in Third World countries are in destitute poverty and have little hope for a better future; yet at the same time they have a gnawing awareness that people in industrialized nations are much more affluent. Such conditions create an "Aspiration Bomb." Many young people see violence and terrorism as their only avenue for achieving a better life.

In a 1980 report on population, the U.S. National Security Control noted:

Recent experience, in Iran and other countries, shows that this younger age group, frequently unemployed and crowded into urban slums, is particularly susceptible to extremism, terrorism, and violence as outlets for frustration. On balance, these factors add up to a growing potential for social unrest, political instability, mass migrations, and possible conflicts over control of land and resources.[33]

Werner Fornos makes the following comments about the perils of the "Aspiration Bomb":

Fully 60 percent of the Third World is under 20 years of age; half are 15 years or less. These population pressures create a volatile mixture of youthful aspirations that when coupled with economic and political frustrations help form a large pool of potential terrorists.

The "Aspiration Bomb" may well present a greater threat to U.S. security than the atomic bomb. This is because while there is always the hope that mutual deterrence or common sense will preclude the use of nuclear weapons, there is no such countervailing influence against the violence and frustration embodied in the Aspiration Bomb.[34]

CROWDING

Crowding has been described as a person's subjective judgment that he or she has insufficient space. A number of studies have investigated the effects of crowding on animals. John Calhoun placed rats in laboratory pens and allowed them to breed until their number rose far beyond that found in their natural environment. Several behavioral changes took place. Many females became infertile, others began to abort, and some that bore offspring did not adequately care for their young.[35]

In other studies, overcrowding among animals has led them to become irritable, overly aggressive, nervous, inattentive to grooming, and messy, with some even resorting to cannibalism. In many cases such negative behaviors continued to occur when the animals were returned to a normal environment.[36]

Although animal research is suggestive, it is not necessarily applicable to humans. The effects of crowding on people have not been sufficiently researched. Some authorities believe it is a factor that leads to crime, emotional problems, incest, child abuse, suicide, violence, dirty streets, and polluted air. Other authorities assert that increases in these behaviors are due not to overcrowding but to poverty and to the breakdown in traditional values. Nonetheless, we should remember that *a delicate balance often exists be-*

tween a population and an environment and this balance can be drastically changed by a slight increase in population. For example, adding one or two fish to a fully populated aquarium may result in a shortage of oxygen that kills most of the fish.[37]

IMMIGRATION ISSUES

Overpopulation also intensifies issues related to immigration. *Immigrate* means to enter a country of which one is not a native for permanent residence. Throughout the world people living in poor nations dream of moving to the richer countries. Immigration to the United States has reached levels unmatched since early in the century. Other affluent countries have also experienced an influx of people from poorer nations.

It is often said that the United States is a nation of immigrants. Since the earliest days of European settlement, North America has attracted people from all over the world. Some, like the black slaves from Africa, were brought here against their will. Most other groups came in search of freedom from oppression and economic opportunities. In the past two centuries, millions of immigrants of different religions, races, cultures, and political views have come to the United States. This diversity is one of the attributes and strengths of American culture. The immense variety of dress, diet, and music in our society can be traced to the contributions of immigrants from many different cultures and nations.

Immigration has also contributed to some of the social problems that plague American society. Immigration has resulted in ethnic and racial conflict, exploitation of illegal aliens, competition among different ethnic groups for a "piece of the pie," and the stresses and costs associated with educating and caring for new arrivals.

The presence of illegal aliens (also called undocumented immigrants) is one of the most complex social issues in our country. The number of undocumented immigrants currently in the United States is unknown, as is the number of new arrivals each year. By far, the largest percentage of undocumented immigrants are Mexicans and Central Americans.

The precise effects of illegal residents on the

economy of the United States are unclear. They may take some jobs away from native-born residents. But they also perform distasteful work that U.S. citizens are reluctant to do—such as harvesting garden crops on their knees. They also maintain some industries by accepting lower wages and inferior working conditions. The survival of such industries stimulates growth in associated services, thereby creating more jobs. During economic recessions, undocumented immigrants are generally laid off or discharged more readily than citizens; they thereby help cushion the native-born population from economic uncertainty.

A highly controversial issue related to immigration is whether people who test positive for the HIV virus should be allowed into the United States. As of this writing, individuals who are HIV positive are prohibited from entering the United States.

Undocumented immigrants are easily exploited by ruthless individuals who know that the immigrants cannot complain to authorities when they have been victimized. (If they went to the authorities, their illegal status might be discovered, which would subject them to deportation.) Although many undocumented immigrants are working in the United States, their employment is now illegal. In 1986 Congress passed the Immigration Reform and Control Act, under which employers are subject to civil penalties ranging from $250 to $10,000 for each illegal alien they hire.

The vast majority of the immigrants who arrive in the United States settle in only a few cities and regions, such as the metropolitan areas of New York City, Los Angeles, Miami, and Chicago. The phenomenon of *chain migration* is the primary cause of this urban concentration. The term refers to the tendency of immigrants to migrate to areas where relatives and others from their home communities are already living. These relatives and acquaintances share the immigrants' culture and language (or dialect) and are available to help the immigrants adjust to the new surroundings. The clusters of immigrants in large cities greatly add to the costs of services in these areas, such as education, health care, job training, public housing, and adult English-language classes.

Now, as in the past, much of the opposition to immigration is based on racial and ethnic prejudice, because most of the immigrants to the United States in recent decades have been people of color and non-Europeans. But there is a legitimate question as to whether immigrants raise the unemployment rate by adding to the competition for a limited number of jobs. The costs of public assistance are also affected, because legal immigrants go on welfare when they are unable to find a job.

Sudden surges of political refugees or illegal immigrants may create special problems. For example, in 1980 Fidel Castro released a number of prisoners and residents of mental hospitals in Cuba; many of these individuals fled to southern Florida, particularly Miami. The influx taxed governmental services in southern Florida and also spurred several serious outbreaks of racial violence in the area during the 1980s.

TOO LITTLE ENERGY

The world's consumption of energy has doubled every 12 years in our recent history.[38] Over nine-tenths of all energy is provided by fossil fuel sources: oil, coal, and natural gas. Natural gas sources are rapidly being depleted. The domestic supply of oil in the United States is incapable of meeting our needs, and therefore this country is heavily dependent on foreign sources.

The United States, with less than 5% of the world's people, uses a quarter of all the energy consumed each year; all the industrialized nations combined hold only 25% of the world's people but use an estimated 85–90% of the energy consumed each year.[39]

It has been estimated that the world's petroleum and natural gas reserves will be substantially depleted within a century.[40] New sources of energy that work as well as fossil fuel sources will have to be found.

SHORTAGES OF OTHER NONRENEWABLE RESOURCES

The world's mineral resources also contain elements that are essential for industrial production. These essential elements include copper, lead, zinc, tin, nickel, tungsten, mercury, chromium, manganese, cobalt, molybdenum, aluminum, platinum, iron, and helium. Consumption of these minerals is occurring so rapidly that reserve sources will eventually be depleted, expensive mining of low-quality ores will have to be undertaken, and substitutes will have to be found. As the developing countries continue to industrialize, the demand for these nonrenewable minerals will far exceed the supply.

The Theory of Demographic Transition

As noted, rate of population growth is highest in developing countries. Researchers have observed that growth rates tend to decrease and then stabilize after a fairly high level of industrialization has been achieved. This observation is assumed to be true about population growth in general, and the assumption is called the *theory of demographic transition*. This transition is thought to take place in three stages:

1. *Preindustrial, agricultural societies.* In this stage there is a fairly stable population size. The societies have both high birthrates and high death rates.

2. *Developing societies that are beginning to industrialize.* In such societies the birthrates remain high, but the death rates drop, leading to a rapid increase in the population. The death rates drop because these societies develop the medical capacities to keep people alive and increase the average life span.

3. *Developed industrial societies.* Such societies have both low birthrates and low death rates, resulting in a stable population once again. The low birthrates are thought to be due to people voluntarily limiting the number of children they have. Parents decide to have fewer children in order to maintain a higher standard of living for themselves and their children.

The theory of demographic transition gives hope that, as developing countries continue to industrialize, their high population growth rates will eventually decrease and then stabilize. It should be noted, however, that the concept of demographic transition is merely a theoretical model. It is a summary statement of what happened in the United States and in many other industrialized nations. Because some past societies have had this demographic history does not necessarily mean that current developing nations will repeat the same patterns.

A variety of factors, including religious and cultural values, can affect the rate of population growth. In Japan, for example, certain values rapidly accelerated passage through the second stage in the demographic transition. At the end of World War II, Japan was a developing nation and had a high birthrate. Two variables thrust Japan into the third stage of demographic transition. First, there was a general consensus that population control was needed. Second, abortion was not considered immoral (as it was in Western societies). As a result, in the decade from 1947 to 1957, the birthrate in Japan dropped from 34 children per 1000 to 14 per 1000, one of the sharpest declines on record. During this decade half of all conceptions were terminated by abortion.[41] It is doubtful that such a rapid transition could be achieved in countries with cultural traditions that encourage large families.

In regard to stabilizing population growth, Ian Robertson notes:

> The question is not whether population will stabilize—it will. If the global population exceeds the carrying capacity of the earth, death rates will rise and halt population growth. The issues are whether stability will result from a decrease in birth rates or an increase in death rates, how long it will take before stability occurs, and how many people will be here when this finally happens. The prospect of a demographic transition offers the hope that if certain preconditions are met, population growth rates in the developing world will be reduced by a decline in birth rates rather than the grim alternative.[42]

At present, tragically, most developing countries have become lodged in a "holding pattern" in the middle stage of demographic transition, with high birthrates and lowered death rates.[43] The longer these countries remain in this stage, the more the size of their populations will swell and the more difficult it will become for them to industrialize and complete the "demographic transition."

Problem Attitudes and Values

The Roman Catholic Church still objects to using any birth control approach except the rhythm method. In many countries, widely accepted values encourage parents to have large families. Abortions are still a controversial issue in our society. And many Americans believe that population growth is *not* a major issue requiring immediate attention.[44] With such attitudes and values, it is clear that overpopulation is not being recognized as one of our most serious problems.

With regard to attitudes toward the use of birth control, Ehrlich and Ehrlich note:

We shouldn't delude ourselves: the population explosion will come to an end before very long. The only remaining question is whether it will be halted through the humane method of birth control, or by nature wiping out the surplus. We realize that religious and cultural opposition to birth control exists throughout the world; but we believe that people simply don't understand the choice that such opposition implies. Today, anyone opposing birth control is unknowingly voting to have the human population size controlled by a massive increase in early deaths.[45]

Two Countries with Severe Population Problems

India and China are two countries with immense overpopulation problems. If the population growth rate in the world is not curbed, most countries will face similar conditions in the future.

INDIA

With an area about one-third the size of the United States, India has a population over three times the size of ours; it is approaching 900 mil-

lion people.[46] India is also one of the world's poorest nations, with a per capita income of $250 per year.[47] Many of its citizens are malnourished and starving. The average Indian has a daily food intake of about 2000 calories. (The minimum requirement for staying healthy is about 2300 to 2500 calories.)

In 1952, India became the first country in the world to adopt a public family planning program to reduce the birthrate. At first the program was poorly funded. In 1956, for example, total expenditures amounted to 1¢ per year for every 20 people. The principal contraceptive method that was promoted was the rhythm method—one of the least effective approaches. In the 1960s, vasectomies and the intrauterine device (IUD) were added to the techniques used. At the end of the 1960s oral contraceptives were also added, although vasectomies and IUDs remain the preferred methods.

Although the birthrate has declined somewhat in India, birth control devices have not reduced the rate to the zero-growth level. A major reason is that most people using birth control techniques decide to do so only after they already have a large family.[48]

In 1976 the Indian government under Indira Gandhi decided to promote a more aggressive population control strategy. Public educational programs were developed to try to persuade Indians that their main problem was not too little food but too many people. The federal government threatened to dismiss civil service employees who had more than three children. Individual states were asked to pass bills requiring compulsory sterilization of parents after the birth of their third child. As we saw in Exhibit 16.1, one state, Maharashtra, passed such a law and began compulsory sterilization.

In 1977, however, Mrs. Gandhi received a crushing electoral defeat, partly because of her government's record on civil liberties and partly because of the unpopularity of the population control programs. Following her defeat, the compulsory sterilization law in Maharashtra was rescinded.

At India's current growth rate of over 2% per

Afternoon traffic jams the streets in Calcutta. At its current annual growth rate of about 2%, India will have a population of over 1 billion by the end of the 20th century.

year and a doubling time of 31 years,[49] by the year 2000 India's population will exceed 1 billion.[50] More than 80% of all Indians are Hindus. Hindu husbands frequently will not permit their wives to use contraceptives until they have produced at least two sons.[51] An additional 11% of the population are Muslims. Some Muslim religious leaders denounce birth control of any kind, but especially sterilization, because cutting the body is a violation of religious law.[52] The obsession for sons is so strong in India that, in order to prevent abortions of unwanted female fetuses, national law prohibits physicians from telling a pregnant woman the sex of the unborn child.[53]

Will India continue to race toward starvation and famine, or will it find politically acceptable approaches to controlling its population growth and begin to raise the standard of living for its citizens? Answers to such questions are of vital significance to all developing countries (and will

also have substantial consequences for the rest of the world).

CHINA

In terms of sheer size, China's population dwarfs that of India. China already has over 1 billion people—more than one-fifth the world's entire population.[54]

China's attitude about population growth has varied over the years. For many years the government considered its huge population an important military resource in any conflict with the former Soviet Union or the United States. Furthermore, it urged other developing nations to take the same view. As is common with many developing nations, China's standard of living is low, and much of the farming and factory work is done by hand.

Poor harvests and resulting food shortages (along with changes in the top leadership and a closer relationship with the United States) have convinced the Chinese government that population control is essential. The leaders are now promoting the view that limiting family size will improve the health and living conditions of all its citizens and will also liberate women from traditional restrictions. Propaganda posters advertise that an education and a good career are more easily attained with a small family.

Prior to the present policies on family size, Chinese women averaged three children each.[55] In 1980 China's government established a one-child-per-family policy. It raised the minimum legal age of marriage by two years, to 22 for men and 20 for women. In some higher-density areas, this minimum age is even higher; in Beijing it is 28 for men and 25 for women.[56] (A higher minimum age for marriage is correlated with a smaller average family size.[57]) To have a large family is now regarded as disrespectful to the Communist party and to the country.

Women who become pregnant after the birth of their first child are sometimes pressured to have an abortion. China has also established a number of economic and social incentives for couples to have no more than one child, including income bonuses, priority consideration in urban housing assignments, subsidies in health care, promises of higher pensions, and private vegetable gardens for city residents. For couples who have more than two children, there are also disincentives, such as possible wage deduction to fund welfare programs.

China has greatly slowed its growth rate with these policies. Its doubling time is now 53 years.[58] Yet, amazingly, new problems have emerged. The government has begun to reevaluate its policy of the one-child family. Some fears have surfaced about the possibility of an emerging generation of spoiled and self-centered only children. Also, if the one-child policy were fully achieved, China would become a society without brothers, sisters, uncles, or aunts.[59] Chinese peasants have traditionally placed a high value on having sons, who live with the extended family throughout their lives. Daughters, on the other hand, are expected to move in with their husband's family and are

therefore considered more of a burden than an asset. Having a son is also viewed as vitally important in continuing the family's name and heritage. As a result, the one-child policy has caused a startling increase in female infanticide, because couples then are able, without government opposition, to attempt another pregnancy in the hope of having a male child. The pace of childbearing in China has decelerated faster than in any other large developing county.[60]

In recent years, China has opened it doors to the West, inviting tourists and Western technology and investments. Undoubtedly there will be rapid technological, social, cultural, and lifestyle changes. History suggests that such changes will be accompanied by political turmoil. (For example, in the 1970s the Shah of Iran developed programs to facilitate industrialization, using funds from the sale of its crude oil to foreign countries. These rapid changes led to political unrest, civil war, and the eventual ouster of the shah.) The future changes in China will have immense implications for the rest of the world.

Will coercive population control policies such as those in India and China eventually be needed in the United States? Ehrlich and Ehrlich note:

> We must hope that our government doesn't wait until it too decides that only coercive measures can solve America's population problem. One must always keep in mind that the price of personal freedom in making childbearing decisions may be the destruction of the world in which your children or grandchildren live. How many children a person has now has serious social consequences in all nations, and therefore is a legitimate concern of society as a whole.[61]

ENVIRONMENTAL PROBLEMS

Higher concentrations of people in an area usually intensify environmental problems. In this section, we will examine the following issues: despoilment of the land, waste disposal (including radioactive and solid waste), air pollution, radioactive leaks from nuclear power plants, nuclear war, water pollution, acid rain, and general pollutants.

Despoilment of the Land

The scenic beauty of our land—as well as its long-term economic value—is being spoiled by a variety of short-term human efforts: strip mining of coal, oil drilling, clearing of trees and forests, building of highways, construction of oil pipelines, overgrazing by cattle and sheep, dumping of garbage, littering, and erection of highway billboards. In nature there is often a delicate balance among the elements: Some fertile land needs trees and grass to retain moisture and fertility; grass-eating animals need grass to survive; carnivorous animals need the grass-eating animals; some birds need seed and insects; other birds feed on small animals or larger animals that have died; all are in need of water. Upsetting this balance often leads to destruction. Dinosaurs once ruled the earth, but all died from some as-yet-unknown environmental change. The Sahara Desert, less than 2,000 years ago, was a luxuriant forest. Overgrazing by domesticated sheep and goats and clearing of the forests were major factors in destroying the area.[62]

Currently, 100 acres of rain forest are being destroyed each minute.[63] Every year the world loses an area of tropical forest land that is comparable to the size of England.[64] At this rate, virtually no tropical forests will be left in 30 or 40 years.[65] If the rain forests are destroyed, over a million unique species of animals and planets will die with them.[66]

Paul and Anne Ehrlich describe what happens when forests are cleared:

Numerous animals that depend on the trees for food and shelter disappear. Many of the smaller forest plants depend on the trees for shade; they and the animals they support also disappear. With the removal of trees and plants, the soil is directly exposed to the elements, and it tends to erode faster. Loss of topsoil reduces the water-retaining capacity of an area, diminishes the supply of fresh water, causes silting of dams,

and . . . flooding. . . . Deforestation . . . reduces the amount of water transferred from ground to air by the trees in the process known as "transpiration." This modifies the weather downwind of the area, usually making it more arid and subject to greater extremes of temperature.[67]

Some areas of the world are losing several inches of topsoil each year because of poor management that exposes the land to water and wind erosion. This is particularly alarming in light of the fact that it takes 300 to 1000 years to produce one inch of topsoil under favorable conditions.[68] Each year 25 billion tons of topsoil are lost, primarily by erosion and by being washed into the sea.[69]

Forests, water, and soil are renewable resource systems that have "carrying capacities"—that is, levels at which they can provide maximum yields without injuring their capacity to repeat those yields. We can chop down only a certain number of trees in a forest each year without destroying the forest's capacity to replace those trees. Human populations in many parts of the world have grown so large that they are beginning to exceed the "carrying capacities" of their environments.[70]

Sometimes the environment is despoiled by human accidents. The worst and most expensive oil spill in the United States occurred in March 1989 in Prince William Sound in Alaska. The petroleum tanker Exxon *Valdez* struck rocks, puncturing a huge hole in the vessel. Nearly 11 million gallons of crude oil spilled into the water. Exxon spent $2 billion cleaning up the crude oil but recovered only 5–9% of the oil spilled. Millions of birds, animals, fish, and plants were killed. Local fishing industries, along with many other industries that depended on marine commerce in this area, were ruined.[71]

Sometimes the environment is intentionally despoiled by humans. Prior to being forced out of Kuwait in 1991 during the Gulf War, President Saddam Hussein of Iraq ordered his military forces to set 600 oil wells in Kuwait on fire. Billions of dollars of oil reserves were destroyed, skies were blackened for months, and the persistent smoke and fires had severe adverse effects

A natural disaster can trigger additional environmental concerns. In October 1994 clean-up crews removed oil from the San Jacinto River in Houston where floodwaters caused at least four pipeline breaks and sent more than 1 million gallons of fuel into the river.

on the quality of life for humans and animals in the region.

Waste Disposal

As yet our country does not have a safe way of disposing of radioactive waste material. Solid waste disposal also poses major problems.

RADIOACTIVE WASTES

The United States now has over 100 nuclear power plants and plans to build more in the future.[72] A danger is that nuclear power plants generate radioactive nuclear wastes, and disposing of radioactive wastes is a complex problem. In large doses, radiation from these wastes can cause death; small doses may lead to cancer or birth deformities. These wastes are particularly hazardous because they remain radioactive for huge periods—as long as 300,000 years. The Nuclear Regulatory Commission has considered various proposals for disposing of these wastes: firing

them into space by rockets, burying them at sea, burying them in solid rock formations, and burying them in the deepest abandoned mines that can be found. An ultimate solution has not as yet been found. Such wastes are now generally put in concrete tanks and buried. A serious danger is that these tanks are built to last only for a couple of hundred years, not for the needed thousands of years.

Radioactive wastes remain boiling hot for years. Leakage from some of these waste tanks has already occurred. In 1974 one leak continued for 51 days and raised the radiation count substantially above the minimum acceptable levels.[73] A crucial question is, with our current ways of disposing of nuclear wastes, are we creating a lethal problem for the future?

SOLID WASTE DISPOSAL

So much public concern is focused on radioactive waste disposal that we sometimes overlook another serious disposal problem: good old-

This toxic dumping site in Texas contains 6 million tons of chemical solvents, heavy metals, and radioactive waste. It was operated by Chevron Resources in the 1980s and then sold to General Atomics in 1991. The unlined pond caused contamination of community water wells and environmental activists have demanded monthly air and water sampling.

fashioned trash. Each year, Americans junk billions of tons of wastes: food, glass, paper, plastics, cans, paints, dead animals, abandoned cars, old machinery, and a host of other things. We are often referred to as a "consumer society." More accurately, we are a throw-away society.

Solid wastes are ugly, unpleasant, and odorous. They pollute water that circulates through them and provide breeding grounds for rats and other noxious pests. Today there are an estimated 50,000 toxic dumps and 180,000 toxic pits, ponds, and lagoons in the United States.[74]

The two principal methods of solid waste disposal are landfills (that is, burying in the ground) and incineration. Many garbage-dumping areas, particularly in small towns, do not meet the sanitary standards set by the federal government.[75] In addition, improperly designed municipal incinerators are major contributors to urban air pollution.

Air Pollution

Air pollution is most severe in large, densely populated industrial centers. Some cities (such as Los Angeles) occasionally have such dense smog that, even on clear days, there is a haze over the city. Moreover, it is not only city air that is polluted; the entire atmosphere of the earth is affected to some degree.

HEALTH EFFECTS AND EXTENT OF AIR POLLUTION

Not only does air pollution rot windshield wiper blades and nylon stockings, blacken skies and clothes, damage crops, and corrode paint and steel; it also kills people. Death rates are higher whenever and wherever smog occurs, especially for the very old, the very young, and those with respiratory ailments. Pollution contributes to a higher incidence of pneumonia, emphysema, lung cancer, and bronchitis. A 1952 London smog disaster was directly linked to some 4000 deaths. And such disasters are of substantially less significance than the far-reaching effects of day-to-day living in seriously polluted cities. Every day, New York City residents inhale enough cancer-producing substances to equal two packs of cigarettes.[76] Also, poor visibility caused by smog is recognized as a major factor in both airplane and automobile accidents.

Each year in the United States we release into the air tons of pollutants, including carbon monoxide, hydrocarbons, oxides of nitrogen, oxides of sulfur, soot, and ashes. Cars emit many of these pollutants, industrial centers (particularly pulp and paper mills, petroleum refineries, chemical plants, and iron and steel mills) add a large share, and so do trash incineration and the burning of fuel for heating homes and offices.[77]

Air pollution is believed to contribute to the deaths of at least 53,000 Americans every year.[78] Valleys and closed air basins are more likely to have air pollution than plains and mountains. In the former areas the air can become especially bad when a layer of warmer air moves over a layer of cooler air and seals in pollutants that would ordinarily rise into the upper atmosphere; this condition is known as *temperature inversion.*

AIR POLLUTION AND ENVIRONMENTAL CHANGES

Air pollution may also be breaking down the earth's protective ozone layer. This layer surrounds the earth from an altitude of 8 to 30 miles above sea level and screens out many of the harmful rays from the sun. Some studies suggest that fluorocarbon gases (commonly used in refrigerating systems and aerosol spray cans) may be destroying the ozone layer.[79] If it is breaking down, there reportedly will be sharp increases in skin cancer and crop failure, as well as changes in the world's climate. When these studies became public knowledge, the use of fluorocarbon spray cans by American consumers dropped sharply (demonstrating that individuals acting in concert can and do make a difference). Manufacturers responded to this drop in sales by developing spray cans without fluorocarbons. However, fluoro-

carbons are still being used in coolants in refrigerators and air conditioners, for making plastic foams, and as cleaning solvents for microelectronic circuitry. Under certain conditions these compounds escape into the atmosphere, rise high into the stratosphere, and set off chemical reactions that rapidly destroy ozone.

Air pollutants have the potential to alter the earth's atmosphere and climate in other ways as well. For example, some scientists are concerned that a buildup of carbon dioxide in the atmosphere could produce a "greenhouse" effect; that is, the carbon dioxide could trap heat near the earth's surface, raising the average temperature. Such overheating, even by just a few degrees, could melt polar icecaps and lead to incredible flooding of coastal areas around the world. Other scientists predict that the opposite may occur; that is, air pollutants could reflect sun rays away from the earth. The earth would then become cooler and perhaps enter into a new ice age.[80] The greenhouse effect is largely due to the burning of fossil fuels (such as coal and petroleum), which emit carbon dioxide into the atmosphere. Some evidence that came to light in the 1980s suggests that the world's climate is getting warmer—a finding about which some scientists have expressed grave concerns.[81] Changing temperatures could also change rainfall patterns, which could turn the American Midwest and other major agricultural areas into dust bowls.

Radioactive Leaks from Nuclear Power Plants

We've already discussed one of the problems associated with nuclear energy: radioactive wastes. Another nuclear energy problem is the potential for radioactive leaks into the atmosphere. In the United States there have been numerous malfunctions at nuclear power plants that have resulted in the release of minor amounts of radioactivity into the air.[82] In 1979 over 200,000 residents had to be evacuated from the area surrounding the power plant at Three Mile Island, Pennsylvania. Radioactive leakage from a damaged reactor caused fear that an explosion might occur. In 1986 an explosion did occur at a nuclear power plant in Chernobyl, Ukraine (see Exhibit 16.2).

Nuclear War

On the morning of August 6, 1945, adults in Hiroshima, Japan, were preparing to go to work. An American bomber was spotted overhead. Seconds later it dropped an atomic bomb, which exploded 2000 feet above the center of the city. The destruction was devastating. The heat and force of the blast killed tens of thousands of people almost instantly. It also released radiation, which eventually killed over 100,000 more people.[83] Numerous bombs have since been built that are 1600 times more powerful than the one that destroyed Hiroshima.[84]

One of the greatest dangers to the survival of civilization is nuclear war. A nuclear war would have devastating effects on the environment and, according to many authorities, could end human civilization. Russia and the United States have the nuclear capacity to destroy each other several times over. Many other nations also possess nuclear bombs or are seeking to develop nuclear warheads or purchase them from other countries.[85]

If a nuclear war occurred, life forms located nearby would be killed instantly. Anyone or anything that initially survived would face death from a variety of sources. (Exposure to radiation may cause cancer and a variety of other fatal medical conditions.) Some scientists predict that survivors would face a "nuclear winter," in which a cloud of soot would block the sun over much of the earth, pushing temperatures far below freezing and preventing the growth of most foods. Another worry is that the ozone layer would break down. Clearing of the cloud of soot would cause intense sun rays to penetrate humans and animals, resulting in skin cancer and other disorders. Another danger is that crops would be affected by radioactivity and would be potentially dangerous as food sources. It could well be that the initial survivors would face a slow, painful death. Their quality of life could slip to depths at which they would grub out a brutelike, barely human existence. The social infrastructure would unravel;

EXHIBIT 16.2

Nuclear Power Plant Explosion in Chernobyl, Ukraine

In spring 1986 there was an explosion and fire at a nuclear power plant in Chernobyl, Ukraine. The explosion blew the top off the reactor and sent a radioactive plume across large parts of the former Soviet Union and much of Eastern and Western Europe. The 4000°F fire burned in the reactor's graphite core for over a week before it was extinguished. Within a few weeks after the disaster, over 20 people had died from massive doses of radiation. It is feared that exposure to lesser amounts of radiation will result in early deaths for tens of thousands of other people from cancers of the bone marrow, breast, and thyroid.

The disaster occurred at a highly vulnerable place. Eighty miles from the site is the city of Kiev, which has a population of over 2 million. Chernobyl is also near the bread-basket area of Russia; nearly half of that country's winter wheat is grown there. Much of the grass and animal feed in the area was contaminated with radioactive particles.

Such accidents have alerted the public to the dangers of nuclear power plants and have slowed the growth of nuclear energy use. Whether to expand or curtail the development of nuclear plants is an international issue. It is an issue that illustrates the complexity of trying to choose between energy needs and physical safety, especially when experts are in sharp disagreement about the technological risks. Those exposed to radioactivity in Chernobyl would, if given a choice, undoubtedly opt for less energy over the current reality: that they are now more likely to bear children with birth defects and more likely to die early from cancer.

that is, the industrial, educational, agricultural, transportation, health care, political, and communication systems would cease to function. Those who did survive would also face intense psychological stress from grief, despair, disorientation, hopelessness, and anger.[86]

How can a nuclear war be averted? This is perhaps one of the most important questions facing civilization. Fortunately, the chances of an all-out nuclear war appear to have lessened in recent years, primarily because of the improvement in relationships between Russia and the United States. Prior to the 1990s these two superpowers were unable to agree on a nuclear disarmament plan. As a result, both countries built and stockpiled nuclear weapons that had the capacity to destroy each other several times over.

Only after Russia rejected Communism and started to move toward a democratic form of government around 1990 were the two superpowers willing to trust each other sufficiently to make progress in reducing nuclear warheads. In 1993 Russia and the United States signed the START (Strategic Arms Reduction Treaty) agreement, which reduced U.S. and Russian stockpiles of long-range nuclear missiles to about a third of the levels that existed.[87] A major reason for this more cooperative relationship was the easing of mutually hostile ideologies. Once Russia moved toward democratization and away from a state-controlled economy, it became less ideologically opposed to the United States. At the same time, Russia's move toward democratization led the United States to give up its perception of Russia as "the evil empire." (This term was used by President Reagan in 1984 in referring to the former Soviet Union.)

Water Pollution

Many Americans cities' water supplies are rated by the U.S. Public Heath Service as "potential health hazards" or as "unsatisfactory."[88] Reasons include tap impurities, infrequent testing for bacteria, and impure water sources. About 25% of the U.S. population is not served by sewage treatment facilities.[89] Raw sewage contaminates the water it seeps into. The bacteria in such untreated sewage make the water unfit for swimming, drinking, and many industrial uses.

As the population grows in a particular area, so does industry, which pours into the water a vast array of contaminants: detergents, sulfuric acid, lead, hydrofluoric acid, ammonia, and so on. Increased agricultural production also pollutes water with insecticides, herbicides, and nitrates (from fertilizers). The result is the spread of pollution in creeks, streams, and lakes; along coastlines; and—most seriously—in ground water, where purification is almost impossible. Water pollution poses the threat of epidemics of diseases such as hepatitis and dysentery, as well as poisoning by exotic chemicals. Some rivers and lakes are now so polluted that they cannot support fish and other organisms that require relatively clean, oxygen-rich water. Such lakes and rivers are accurately described as "dead."

The United States has the dubious distinction of being the only country in the world with a river that has been called a fire hazard. So many industrial chemicals, oils, and other combustible pollutants have been dumped into the Cuyahoga River in Ohio that it has twice caught on fire.

Human waste is also a major contributor to water pollution. The sewage from New York City alone produces 5 million cubic yards of sludge a year, which is dumped into the ocean and now covers over 15 square miles of ocean bottom.[90] An even bigger source of pollution is waste from oil refining, food processing, animal feedlots, textile and paper manufacturing, and other industries. Of the world's rural populations, 86%, or more than 2 billion people, lack adequate clean water.[91]

Acid Rain

There is a growing concern over acid rain. Formed from emissions from automobiles and industrial plants, acid rain has become a serious problem in eastern Canada, in the northeastern United States, and in many other countries.[92] It is created when sulfur and nitrogen oxides in emissions combine with moisture in the air to form sulfuric and nitric acids. Acid rain is killing fish in lakes and streams and is reducing the number of plant nutrients in the ground, thereby making soil less fertile. It has also damaged timber and may eventually start affecting synthetic structures, including classic architecture and sculptures. Scientists estimate that

50,000 lakes in the United States and Canada are now so polluted by acid rain that fish populations have been either destroyed or severely damaged.[93]

General Pollutants

Some substances—such as chlorinated hydrocarbons, lead, mercury, and fluorides—reach us in so many ways that they are considered *general pollutants*. Of the chlorinated hydrocarbons, DDT was used the longest but is now banned. DDT is a synthetic insecticide; chemically it breaks down slowly, and it will last for decades in soil. Unhappily, the way DDT circulates in ecosystems leads to a concentration in carnivores (including humans); that is, it becomes increasingly concentrated as it is passed along a food chain. Following World War II, DDT was widely used as an insecticide until research with laboratory animals showed that it affects fertility, causes changes in brain functioning, and increases the incidence of cancer.[94]

The long-term effects of DDT (and of many other general pollutants) are still unknown. The substance is poisonous and may (or may not) lead to subtle physiological changes. An important question is: Among the thousands of chemicals currently being used, which ones will have unknown toxic side effects?

Radioactive wastes and certain poisons such as DDT also pose serious problems because of biological magnification. With this process (mentioned previously), the concentration of the substance increases as it ascends in the food chain. For example, Richard Curtis and Elizabeth Hogan found in a study of the Columbia River in the western United States that, although the radioactivity of the water was at such low levels that it was nonhazardous, the radioactivity of river-related biological life forms was much higher and potentially hazardous:

> . . . the radioactivity of the river plankton was 2,000 times greater; the radioactivity of the fish and ducks feeding on the plankton was 15,000 and 40,000 times greater, respectively; the radioactivity of young swallows fed on insects caught by their parents in the river was 500,000 times greater; the radioactivity of the egg yolks of water birds was more than a million times greater.[95]

The radioactivity was thought to be due to isotopes released into the river from the nuclear power plant at Hanford, Washington.

DDT, many other pesticides, and radioactive material are cumulative poisons; that is, they are retained in the tissues of the organisms that consume them rather than being excreted back into the environment. Thus one never loses the poison of previous exposure, and future exposures compound the potential danger to the individual. In 1984 the National Academy of Sciences released a report stating that little or nothing is known about the effects on humans of 80% of the 48,500 different chemicals in use, because very little research has been conducted in this area.[96]

The use of pesticides by American farmers also has a number of adverse consequences. An article in *Newsweek* noted:

> It's a bit of the devil's bargain. In exchange for using $3 billion worth of pesticides yearly, American farmers reap $12 billion worth of crops that might otherwise be lost to weeds and insects. Without the chemicals, millions of people might face food shortages. On the other hand, less than 1 percent of the poisons reach their target pests; the rest wind up as contaminants in water, residues on produce and poisonous fallout on farm workers. Worldwide, the compounds fatally poison an estimated 10,000 people a year and injure 400,000 more. Uncounted millions more may be at increased risk for cancer, reproductive problems and birth defects due to low-level, chronic exposure. We can't seem to do without pesticides; but can we live with their consequences?[97]

Chronic lead poisoning is also serious; it leads to loss of appetite, weakness, and apathy. It also causes lesions of the neuromuscular system, the circulatory system, the gastrointestinal tract, and the brain. Exposure to lead comes from a variety of sources: combustion of leaded gasoline, pesticides, lead pipes, lead-contaminated food and water. Perhaps the most hazardous instance is when children eat paint containing lead. It should be noted that most household paints today do not contain lead, but the danger still exists with older buildings and furniture that were painted with a lead-based paint. Even when these buildings are painted over with lead-free paint, peeling may expose the original lead-based ones.

Exposure to high concentrations of mercury can cause blindness, deafness, loss of coordination, severe mental disorders, or even death. Mercury is added to the environment in many ways. It may leak into the water from industrial processes that produce chlorine; it is emitted by the pulp and paper industry; it is a primary ingredient of agricultural fungicides. Also, small amounts are released when fossil fuels are burned.

WHAT NEEDS TO BE DONE

Up to now we've merely been describing several national and international problems: overpopulation, food and water shortages, economic problems, international terrorism, crowding, energy shortages, shortages of nonrenewable resources, despoilment of the land, radioactive and solid waste disposal, air pollution, radioactive leaks from nuclear power plants, nuclear war, water pollution, acid rain, and general pollutants. Now we'll look at a number of recommendations for confronting overpopulation and environmental problems.

Confronting Overpopulation

Limiting population growth will have a major positive effect on all of the problems discussed in this chapter. If the world's population growth is reversed to approach a zero growth rate—or even a negative rate—it may give us the necessary time to find solutions to other problems. Limiting population growth is a key factor in maintaining our current quality of life. Ehrlich and Ehrlich note:

> Earth cannot long sustain even 5.3 billion people with foreseeable technologies and patterns of human behavior. If civilization is to survive, population shrinkage below today's size eventually will be necessary.[98]

How can the size of the population be limited? Dr. Paul Ehrlich suggests that, as the most affluent and influential superpower, the United States should become a model for population control by (1) setting a goal of a stable optimum population size for our country and displaying our determination to achieve this goal rapidly and (2) reversing our government's current "reward" system for having children. Specific measures include:

- No longer allowing income-tax deductions for children.
- Placing a luxury tax on layettes, diapers, cribs, expensive toys, and diaper services.
- Rewarding small families by such measures as giving "responsibility prizes" to each man who has a vasectomy after having two children.
- Subsidizing adoptions and simplifying adoption procedures.
- Guaranteeing the right of any woman to have an abortion.
- Enacting a federal law to require sex education in schools—including material on the need for regulating the birthrate and on techniques of birth control.
- Developing new contraceptives that are reliable and easy to use and do not have harmful side effects.[99]

Bernard Berelson compiled a list of other proposals to control population:

- Adding temporary sterilants to water or food supplies, with doses of an antidote being carefully rationed by the government to produce the desired population size (such sterilants are not as yet in existence).
- Making sterilization of men with three or more living children compulsory.
- Raising the minimum age for marriage.
- Providing benefits (money, goods, or services) to couples who do not bear children for extended time periods.
- Requiring that foreign countries establish effective population control programs before *any* foreign aid will be provided.[100]

EXHIBIT 16.3

Tragedy at Love Canal

L ove Canal was once a pleasant neighborhood of tree-lined streets in the city of Niagara Falls, New York. Up until the late 1970s, hardly anyone was concerned that the area had once been a chemical dumping ground. Over a 25-year period ending in 1953, Hooker Chemicals and Plastic Corporation had buried 20,000 tons of toxic substances in leaky drums. Among the chemicals dumped was highly lethal dioxin. In the late 1970s it was noted that the residents of Love Canal had substantially higher rates of birth defects, cancer, miscarriages, chromosome damage, kidney failure, and death.

The neighborhood—home, schools, and parks —had been built above the dump site. Families noted that bluish-black substances sometimes oozed through the ground. The substances were discovered to be toxic. Dumped pesticides and other poisons had polluted the groundwater, seeping up through the earth and into basements, creating hazardous vapors. Tests in certain basements found 80 different toxic chemicals to be present. It was also thought that contamination was occurring from eating home-grown garden vegetables.

In 1980 the Environmental Protection Agency conducted tests in the area and found it to have dangerously high levels of toxic substances. Love Canal has since been evacuated, and the area is now a ghost town.

Environmental experts acknowledge that the Love Canal disaster is not an isolated problem. Of the nearly 50,000 toxic-chemical dumps in the United States, more than 1000 are considered potential health hazards.

Source: "Living with Uncertainty: Saga of Love Canal Families," *U.S. News & World Report,* June 2, 1980, p.32.

Some of these proposals appear too radical for most Americans to accept, and they conflict with the moral and ethical values of many citizens. But will we reach such an overpopulation crisis that they may be necessary in the future? Many developing nations are now instituting sex education and family planning programs, which (at least temporarily) are showing evidence of lowering birthrates. It is hoped that the population control measures recommended by Berelson can be avoided.

A developing country that has had success in reducing the rate of population growth is Mexico. Its government has made progress through a comprehensive "social marketing" campaign to promote the values of smaller-sized families and of delayed childbearing.[101] Mexico has spread these messages through advertisements on radio, television, and billboards. There has even been a popular love song in which a teenage duet agree to delay having sex. Mexico has also produced a television series that promotes the value of smaller-sized families and the view that pure "machismo" is proved by a male fathering only as many children as he can support, rather than by prolific reproduction. This "soap opera" has had considerable success in promoting family planning among young males and females. For use in other countries, Mexico's program must be adapted to each nation's unique culture and values so that viewers can more readily identify with the characters, situations, and dilemmas.[102]

Ehrlich, Ehrlich, and Holdren provide an elegant summary of the need to establish a world-wide vision of the future of the human race:

Perhaps the major necessary ingredient that has been missing from a solution to the problems of both the United States and the rest of the world is a goal, a vision of the kind of Spaceship Earth that ought to be and the kind of crew that should man her. Society has always had its visionaries who talked of love, beauty, peace, and plenty. But sometimes the "practical" men have always been there to praise smog as a sign of progress, to preach "just" wars, and to restrict love while giving hate free rein. It must be one of the greatest ironies of the history of the human species that the only salvation for the practical men now lies in what they think of as the dreams of idealists. The question now is: can the self-proclaimed "realists" be persuaded to face reality in time?[103]

The Abortion Controversy

If the world's population continues to grow at or near its present rate, the current debate over voluntary abortions may pale compared to controversies that will be generated if compulsory population control measures are needed.

The abortion controversy has been going on for two decades, but it was heightened in January 1973, when the U.S. Supreme Court, in a 7–2 decision, overruled state laws that prohibited or restricted a woman's right to obtain an abortion during the first three months of pregnancy. Suing under the assumed name of Jane Roe, a Texas resident argued that her state's law against abortion denied her a constitutional right. The Court agreed that the right of personal privacy includes the right to decide whether to have an abortion. However, the Court held that such a right is not absolute and that states have the authority to impose restrictions after the third month. This decision, known as *Roe* v. *Wade,* also allowed states to prohibit abortions in the last ten weeks of pregnancy (a time when there is a good chance that the fetus will live), except when the life or health of the mother is endangered.

In 1977 Congress passed, and President Carter signed into law, the so-called Hyde Amendment (named for its original sponsor, Representative Henry Hyde from Illinois). This amendment prohibits Medicaid spending for abortions except when a woman's life would be endangered by childbirth or in cases of promptly reported rape or incest. In June 1980 this amendment was upheld as constitutional in a 5–4 vote by the U.S. Supreme Court. The ruling means that the federal government and individual states do not have to pay for most abortions for women on welfare.

The Hyde Amendment is significant because more than one-third of the legal abortions performed in the United States between 1973 and 1977 were for women on welfare.[104] The passage of the amendment illustrates the strength of the anti-abortion forces in this country. Is it fair for middle- and upper-class women to have more access to abortions than lower-income women?

With the election of President Reagan in 1980, there was a move toward conservatism in our society. Certain groups, such as the Catholic Church and right-to-life groups, have been strongly urging that a constitutional amendment be passed to prohibit abortions, except in cases where the woman's life is endangered.

During the Reagan and Bush administrations from 1980 to 1992, some liberal Supreme Court judges retired and were replaced by more conservative judges. As a result, the Supreme Court gradually assumed a more conservative (pro-life) position on the abortion issue. The waning of the Supreme Court majority recognizing a woman's right to an abortion became clear in a 1989 decision, *Webster* v. *Reproductive Health Services.* The case concerned a Missouri law that (1) prohibited state employees from assisting in abortions and prohibited abortions from being performed in state-owned hospitals, and (2) banned abortions of *viable* fetuses. (The Missouri law viewed fetuses as viable if the woman was believed to be 20 weeks or more pregnant and a viability test showed the fetus could live.) The broader effect of the Court's decision was to throw the hot-potato issue of abortion back to state legislatures, many of which debated a variety of abortion bills.

In 1992 Bill Clinton was elected President. He had adhered to a pro-choice position on the abortion issue. President Clinton has had the opportunity to appoint a few liberal judges to the Supreme Court. As of the mid-1990s, it appears that the Court is likely to continue to uphold the basic provisions of *Roe* v. *Wade.*

Pro-life or pro-choice? Abortion is probably the single most divisive public issue today.

The major objection to permitting abortions is based on perceptions of moral principles. The Catholic Church views abortion as one of the most important current moral issues. This church and various "right to life" groups condemn abortions as being synonymous with murder. They assert that life begins at conception—that there is no phase during pregnancy in which there is a distinct, qualitative difference in the development of the fetus. The Catholic Church views abortion as acceptable only when it is done to save the physical life of the mother. This type of abortion is justified on the principle of "double effect," which holds that a morally evil action (performing an abortion) is allowable when it is the side effect of a morally good action (saving the life of the mother).

If abortions were prohibited again, women would seek illegal abortions as they did in the past. Performed in a medical clinic or hospital, an abortion is a relatively safe operation; but, performed under unsanitary conditions, perhaps by an inexperienced or unskilled abortionist , the operation is extremely dangerous and may even imperil the life of the woman. When abortions are illegal, some women attempt to self-abort. Self-induced abortions can be extremely dangerous. Women have tried such techniques as severe exercise, hot baths, and pelvic and intestinal irritants and have even attempted to lacerate the uterus with such sharp object as hat-pins, nail files, and knives.

Opponents of abortion argue that the "right to life" is basic and should in no way be infringed on. Proponents of abortion counter this view by arguing that there may be a more basic right than the right to life: the preservation of the quality of life. Given the overpopulation problem and the fact the abortion is an effective population control technique (in some countries the number of abortions is approaching the number of live births), some authorities are asserting that abortion is a necessary measure (although less desirable than contraception) to preserve the quality of life.[105] Unless life has quality, the right to life is meaningless.

Exhibit 16.4 summarizes the arguments both for and against legal abortion.

Providing Family Planning Services

Family planning services are obviously essential programs for preventing unwanted pregnancies. Such services include birth control information and contraceptives, pregnancy testing, HIV testing and counseling, testing and counseling about other sexually transmitted diseases, sex education, abortion counseling and abortions, counseling on child spacing, sterilization information and operations, infertility counseling, and preparation for parenthood.

GOVERNMENTAL PROGRAMS

National family planning programs involve governmental efforts to lower birthrates by funding programs that provide birth control information and services. With family planning programs, families voluntarily decide whether to limit the number of children they have. Most countries, including both developing and developed nations, now have official family planning programs. This is a remarkable achievement, because 40 years ago no developing country had such a program. (In fact, 40 years ago, several countries had programs with the opposite objective—to increase the birthrate and the rate of immigration.) Concern about world population growth clearly is a recent phenomenon.

Despite these advances, only a few countries have established population control policies. (Population control is the deliberate regulation of the size of the population by society. Family planning, in contrast, is the regulation of births by individual families.) As we noted, India's population control program included a sterilization policy that was soon retracted after the ruling party failed to be reelected. Whether India will attempt to enact another population control policy is unclear; future population growth may be a decisive factor in determining whether such action is necessary.

Until President Lyndon Johnson's 1965 State of the Union Address, family planning was not considered a proper concern for our government. In that address, President Johnson stated that $5 spent on family planning was worth $100 invested in some other area of world economic development. In 1966 the federal government developed regulations that, for the first time, allowed federal funds to provide family planning services to welfare clients on a voluntary basis. The avowed purpose of this policy (which was widely criticized) was not phrased in terms of family planning goals. Rather, the stated objectives were to reduce the welfare burden by lowering the illegitimacy rate and to break the poverty cycle by decreasing the transmission of poverty from one generation to another.

The National Center for Family Planning Services was established by the passage of the Family Planning Services and Population Research Act of 1970. This act recognized that family planning was part of the delivery of comprehensive health services for all. In 1972, Congress mandated that family planning services be provided to all welfare recipients who desired them. At that time, contraceptive policy changes were also made, lifting restrictions on marital status and age for receiving birth control information and devices.

PRIVATE AGENCIES

In the United States, most family planning services in the past were provided by private agencies and organizations. The largest and best-known organization is Planned Parenthood. Founded by Margaret Sanger in 1916 with the opening of the first birth control clinic in Brooklyn, the organization now has clinics throughout the nation. Planned Parenthood offers the following: (1) medical services—physical examinations, Pap-smear tests, urine and blood tests, screening for sexually transmitted diseases, all medically approved methods of contraception, and pregnancy testing; (2) counseling services—infertility, premarital, contraceptive, pregnancy, and sterilization for males and for females; and (3) educational services—sex education, contraceptive information (including effectiveness and side

EXHIBIT 16.4

Legal Abortion: Arguments Pro and Con

Against Legal Abortion	In Favor of Legal Abortion
Human life begins at conception; therefore, abortion is murder. Even scientists have not reached a consensus on any other point in fetal development that can be considered the moment the fetus becomes a person. Life is a matter of fact, not religion or values.	The belief in personhood at conception is a religious belief held by the Roman Catholic Church. Most Protestant and Jewish denominations regard the fetus as a potential human being, not a full-fledged person, and have made position statements in support of legal abortion. When the unborn becomes a person is a matter of religion and values, not absolute fact.
We must pass a constitutional amendment to protect unborn babies from abortion. To say that the law will not be followed and therefore should not be made is like saying laws against murder should be repealed because people still get murdered.	No law has ever stopped abortion, and no law ever will. The issue is not whether abortions will be done, but whether they will be done safely, by doctors, or dangerously, by back-alley butchers or by the women themselves. History has shown that anti-abortion laws are uniquely unenforceable and do not prevent abortions.
Medicaid should not pay for abortion. It is wrong to try to eliminate poverty by killing the unborn children of the poor. Tax money should not be used for the controversial practice of aborting unwanted children. The decision not to have children should be made before one gets pregnant.	The original intent of Medicaid was to equalize medical services between the rich and the poor and to help the poor become independent and self-sufficient. To make them ineligible for abortion defies justice, common sense, and rational policy. Women burdened by unwanted children cannot get job training or go to work and are trapped in the poverty/welfare cycle. Neither abortion nor childbirth should be forced on poor women.
If you believe abortion is morally wrong, you are obligated to work for the passage of a "human life" amendment to the Constitution.	Many people who are personally opposed to abortion, including most Roman Catholics, believe it is wrong to impose their religious or moral beliefs on others.
The right of the unborn to live supersedes any right of a woman to "control her own body."	For women to have equality with men, they must be autonomous and free to make an abortion decision. If women lose the right to have an abortion, their lives and lifestyles would substantially be determined by men and impregnation.
The "abortion mentality" leads to infanticide, euthanasia, and the killing of disabled and elderly people.	In countries where abortion has been legal for years, there is no evidence that respect for life has diminished or that legal abortion leads to the killing of any people. Infanticide, however, is prevalent in countries where the overburdened poor cannot control their childbearing and was also prevalent in Japan before abortion was legalized.
Abortion causes psychological damage to women.	The Institute of Medicine of the National Academy of Sciences has concluded that abortion is not associated with a detectable increase in the incidence of mental illness. The depression and

(continued)

EXHIBIT 16.4　*(continued)*

guilt feelings reported by some women are usually mild, temporary, and outweighed by feelings of relief. Such negative feelings would be substantially lessened if anti-abortion advocates were less vehement in expressing their beliefs. Women choosing abortion should be informed of the risks and benefits to the procedure and should decide for themselves what to do.

Women have abortions for their own convenience or on "whim."

Right-to-life advocates dismiss unwanted pregnancy as a mere annoyance. The urgency of women's need to end unwanted pregnancy is measured by their willingness to risk death and mutilation, to spend huge sums of money, and to endure the indignities of illegal abortion. Women have abortions only when the alternative is unendurable. Women take both abortion and motherhood very seriously.

In a society in which contraceptives are so readily available, there should be no unwanted pregnancies and therefore no need for abortion.

No birth control method is perfectly reliable, and for medical reasons many women cannot, or will not, use the most effective methods. Contraceptive information and services are not available to all women, particularly to teenagers, the poor, and rural women.

Abortion is not the safe and simple procedure we're told it is.

Before the 1973 Supreme Court rulings, illegal abortion was the leading cause of maternal death and mutilation. Having a legal abortion is medically less dangerous than giving birth.

Doctors make large profits from legal abortions.

Legal abortion is less costly and less profitable than illegal abortion was. Many legal abortions are done in nonprofit facilities. If it's not improper to "make money" on childbirth, it is not wrong to earn money by performing legal abortions.

Parents have the right and responsibility to guide their children to important decisions. A law requiring parental notification of a daughter's abortion would strengthen the family unit. (Many states have now passed parental consent laws that are consistent with this argument.)

Many teenagers voluntarily consult their parents, but some simply will not. Forcing the involvement of unsympathetic, authoritarian, or very moralistic parents in a teen's pregnancy (and sexuality) can damage the family unit beyond repair. Some family units are already under so much stress that knowledge of an unwed pregnancy could be disastrous.

Pro-abortionists are antifamily. Abortion destroys the American family.

The unwanted child of a teenage mother has little chance to grow up in a normal, happy American home. Instead, a new family is created: a child and her child, both destined for a life of poverty and hopelessness. Legal abortion helps women limit their families to the number of children they want and can afford, both emotionally and financially, and reduces the number of children born unwanted. Pro-choice is definitely profamily.

TABLE 16.3

Ranking of Effectiveness of Birth Control Methods in Preventing Pregnancies

Method	Number of Pregnancies per 100 Women during One Year of Use
1. Abstinence	0
2. Sterilization	.1
(tie) { 3. Norplant implant	1
3. Depo-Provera	1
5. The Pill	3
6. IUD	4
7. Condom	10
8. Diaphragm	18
(tie) { 8. Vaginal contraceptive sponge	18
8. Cervical cap	18
11. Foam, suppositories, and film	20
(tie) { 11. Withdrawal	20
13. Natural family planning (rhythm)	24

Note: After the first six or seven listed methods, the risk of pregnancy for sexually active users is sharply increased.

Source: Basics of Birth Control (Milwaukee: Planned Parenthood, 1994).

effects of the varied approaches), and breast self-examinations. (Table 16.3 shows a ranking of the effectiveness of various contraceptives in preventing pregnancies.)

Family planning services are now available in practically all areas in the United States from a variety of public and private organizations, including health departments, hospitals, physicians in private practice, Planned Parenthood affiliates, and such other agencies as community action groups and free clinics.

THE FUTURE

A national policy of family planning is needed. Currently there is considerable controversy about a number of issues associated with family planning: sex education in schools, provision of birth control information and devices for teenagers, approaches to prevent HIV and other sexually transmitted diseases, and abortions (including the issue of whether the federal government should

pay for abortions for those who cannot afford them).

In the United States, publicly funded family planning centers have been concentrated in poor communities and in nonwhite communities. Middle-class families receive such services primarily from private agencies and from private physicians. Some leaders of nonwhite communities have charged that public family planning centers have a "genocide" objective—to reduce the size of the nonwhite community.[106] Increased public education programs are needed to understand that family planning is not an antipoverty measure. Our citizens also need to understand that our country's historical treatment of nonwhite groups justifiably makes nonwhites suspicious of outside efforts to limit their number of births. Family planning should be part of a comprehensive approach to health care, not just an attempt to limit births.

If problems associated with overpopulation

EXHIBIT 16.5

RU-486: An Abortion Pill

R U486, a pill that induces abortion early in pregnancy, was developed and introduced in France. This pill is now being widely used in France, Great Britain, Sweden, and China to induce abortions. RU-486 acts by impeding a hormone (progesterone) that is necessary for a fetus to stay implanted in the uterus. The pill, which works only until seven weeks after conception, is effective about 85% of the time. For its effectiveness to reach 96%, it must be followed by a dose of prostaglandin, a substance that induces uterine contractions. Proponents envision a day when a woman who wants to end a suspected pregnancy can merely take a pill in the privacy of her own home, thereby avoiding demonstrators outside abortion clinics.

There are some adverse side effects of RU-486, including heavy bleeding and nausea. (Surgical abortions also pose some risks—from anesthesia, infections, and damage to the cervix and uterus.)

RU-486 is also a highly effective morning-after pill in that it appears to prevent implantation of the fertilized egg in the wall of the uterus. RU-486 may also be effective in treating breast and ovarian cancer (two of the biggest killers of women). It has also been used to treat endometriosis, a leading cause of female infertility.

The right-to-life movement was successful in the late 1980s and early 1990s in keeping RU-486 from being legally distributed in the United States. The Food and Drug Administration banned the pill in 1989 after being pressured by anti-abortion groups. The "pro-life" movement has said it will call for boycotts against any company that seeks to market RU-486 in the United States.

In 1994 the U.S. government announced that an agreement had been reached with France's Roussel Uclaf, the company that originally patented the drug, permitting testing of the pill on 2000 American women. It is anticipated that RU-486 will be licensed for use in the United States by 1996.

Source: Lauran Neergaard, "Agreement Clears Way for Abortion Drug in U.S.," *Wisconsin State Journal,* May 17, 1994, p. 1A.

---

continue to intensify, a national policy of population control may need to be developed. Several authorities are predicting dire consequences for the future of the world unless population control measures are implemented immediately. Other authorities discount overpopulation concerns and predict that technological advance will prevent cataclysmic effects from rapid population growth. If the latter authorities are mistaken, we may be forced in a few years to apply population control measures that now seem unethical and "inhumane."

Werner Fornos strongly urges that the United States fund international programs designed to slow population growth in developing countries:

If Americans now feel anguish over witnessing the recent human suffering and needless deaths in Ethiopia, just imagine a world in which virtually the entire Third World will be wracked by vast poverty and human misery. . . .

And if Americans are now troubled by the specter of instability, revolution, and authoritarianism in the Third World, they have only to imagine the consequences of inaction, because the fragile seed of democracy cannot survive long in societies with escalating misery, crippled economies, and dying environments.

In shaping the federal budget, the U.S. Congress must ask not only how much it will cost to fund population programs, but also what will be the cost of not funding them.[107]

At the Bronx Women's Clinic a social worker takes notes during a patient consultation on her sexual and medical history. Family planning services are now widely available from a variety of public and private organizations.

Confronting Environmental Problems

Although environmental problems are very serious, it would be a mistake to assume that the environment is heading for catastrophe. In the late 1960s the public began to wake up to the environmental problems we face. Dozens of organizations have since been formed (many of them with international memberships) that are working on everything from saving wild animals to recycling aluminum cans to developing new sources of energy.

Since the 1960s there has been progress in a number of areas. Air quality has improved. Less sewage is being dumped into water. Most auto-mobiles have emission control devices. Life expectancy in the United States has been rising, which is an indirect measure that environmental living conditions may be improving. Relationships between the United States and Russia have improved, which reduces the chances for a nuclear war. Obviously, however, much more needs to be done.

Energy development, preservation of the environment, and economic growth are interdependent problems. Programs that advance one of these causes often aggravate the others. For example, the development of nuclear power plants led to the explosion in Chernobyl that may shorten the lives of tens of thousands of people who were exposed. Devices that clean exhaust from automobiles reduce air pollution but also decrease fuel economy and thereby more rapidly deplete oil reserves. Strip mining of coal increases available energy supplies but despoils the scenery. Effective environmental programs in the future will need to strike a balance among our competing objectives.

Environmentalists have been waging a political and educational campaign that has not only increased public awareness of environmental concerns but also prompted passage of significant legislation to protect the nation's air, land, and water. For example, the Clean Air Act of 1970 established the Environmental Protection Agency (EPA) and empowered it to set and enforce standards of environmental quality. However, since the 1980s political opposition to environmental concerns has intensified. For example, some of the largest corporations in the world have sought to drill oil wells and dig mines in fragile wilderness areas or have sought to "get the government off their back" when they spewed pollutants into the air and water.[108] These businesses have spent millions of dollars to persuade the government to let them pursue such activities. Since the 1980s environmentalists have struggled to preserve the gains made in the 1970s. Environmentalists, however, do not have the financial resources that large corporations do. Therefore, it is crucial for those who are concerned about preserving our environment to be aware of political issues in this area and to express their views to government leaders.

It is clear that in the future our environmental problems are not going to disappear on their own. In fact, left alone, existing problems are likely to increase, and new ones will come to the fore. What can be done? Actions needed include changing values from consumption to conservation and developing new sources of energy.

CHANGING VALUES

We must realize that bigger is not necessarily better. We need to focus on preserving and conserving our resources rather than consuming them. George Ritzer notes:

We need a reorientation of American culture, a reorientation that may already be underway. Basically, we need to move away from a system that values things growing constantly bigger and better. We are no longer able to master and subdue all that surrounds us. Rather, we must learn to live more harmoniously with our environment. We need to learn to value and protect our environment rather than seeing it as something to be exploited, raped and despoiled. Most importantly, we need to accept the idea that we are approaching the limits of what the environment can yield to us. At best, we can expect a steady state, at worst a marked decline in our style of life. . . . We need, in other words, to focus on, and invest in, resources that we can renew rather than the current propensity to exploit such nonrenewable resources as coal and oil.[109]

The move toward conserving resources can be put into action in a variety of ways. Garbage can be used as fuel for running mills to make recycled paper. Water in communities can be purified again and again, so that it can continually be reused without being discharged into a river, lake, or ocean. Homes can be better insulated to conserve heat. Smaller cars can be driven at more energy-efficient speeds. People can ride trains and buses instead of cars. Newspapers, aluminum (especially cans), tin, cardboard, magazines, plastic, paper, and glass can be recycled to reduce the amount of solid-waste materials. Recycling a four-foot stack of newspapers saves a 40-foot pine tree.[110] Aluminum recycling saves 95% of the energy needed to make new cans from raw mate-

A radioactive marker placed by the Texas Bureau of Radiation Control indicates that 24.8 acres are contaminated by uranium mining activity that took place in the 1970s. The site is now being remediated under the Uranium Mill Tailings Remediation Act.

rials.[111] Using recycled glass to make new glass reduces the amount of air and water pollution by 50–60% compared to producing glass from silica.[112] Our society needs to use the conservation measures that are already available. Each of us can make a difference in combating the environmental problems on this planet! (See Exhibit 16.6.)

People in this country appear to be increasingly aware that all of us have a responsibility to preserve the environment. There is a growing interest in Earth Day, which was founded on April 22, 1970, and is recognized annually.[113] The pesticide DDT has been banned.[114] The United States has cut sulfur dioxide emissions (from 1970 to 1994) by 28%.[115] Auto emissions have been cleaned up dramatically: catalytic converters cut hydrocarbons by as much as 87%, carbon monoxide by an average of 85%, and nitrogen oxides by 62%.[116] Lead has been removed from gasoline. Emissions of lead into the air dropped by 96%

EXHIBIT 16.6

What *You* Can Do to Help Save Planet Earth

You can make a difference! If everyone takes small steps, major improvements will occur. The following are simple things that you and your family members can do to help the earth:

- Use mugs instead of paper cups, washable cotton towels instead of paper towels, and cloth napkins rather than paper napkins.

- Use both sides of sheets of paper.

- To minimize solid waste, buy products in bulk or products that have the least amount of packaging. Packaging accounts for an amazing 50% of our trash (U.S. output of garbage equals 400,000 tons every day).

- At the market, use paper bags (which you can recycle) instead of plastic bags. Plastics tend to be nonbiodegradable; they do not break down into innocuous materials.

- Buy products that are recyclable, reliable, repairable, refillable, and/or reusable. Avoid disposables. The new buzzword in waste management is "source reduction," which means buying wisely to minimize the consequences of consumption.

- Grow some of your own food, organically when possible. Plant deciduous shade trees (trees whose leaves fall off) that protect south- and west-facing windows from sun in summer but allow it in during winter. Plant and maintain trees, bushes, or shrubbery. Trees and shrubbery consume carbon dioxide and thereby reduce air pollution.

- Avoid use of styrofoam cups, which tend to be nonbiodegradable.

- To save water, install sink faucet aerators and water-efficient showerheads. Such adjustments cut water use up to 80% without a noticeable decrease in performance. Repair leaky faucets.

- Take showers of less than five minutes instead of baths.

- Do not run water continuously when brushing your teeth or shaving.

- Consider ultra-low flush toilets, which use 60–90% less water than conventional models. Conserve water by placing a brick or a jug of water in the toilet's water tank.

- Where possible, use fluorescent bulbs rather than incandescent bulbs. Fluorescent bulbs use considerably less energy.

- Use cloth diapers for babies. Disposable diapers annually account for 18 billion tons of trash that, because of plastic content, will take 500 years to decompose. In addition, disposable diapers in landfills frequently contain fecal matter, which can harbor viruses (such as hepatitis) that may trickle into water supplies.

- Turn down the thermostat at night and when the house is empty. Close off and do not heat or cool unused rooms. Wear a sweater instead of turning up the heat. Keep windows (especially near thermostats) tightly shut.

- Turn the thermostat on the water heater down to 120°F.

- When possible, use a clothesline instead of a dryer.

- Reduce the use of hazardous chemicals in your home. For example, instead of using ammonia-based cleaners, use a mixture of distilled vinegar, salt, and water for surface cleaning, and use baking soda and water for the bathroom.

- Don't buy motorized or electric tools or appliances when hand-powered ones are available. This includes lawn mowers. (Mowing a lawn with an old-fashioned mower is also good exercise.)

(continued)

EXHIBIT 16.6   *(continued)*

- To conserve energy, wash clothes and other materials in warm water and rinse in cold water.

- Open blinds during the day for heat from the sun during cold weather, and close them at night to conserve heat. Close blinds during the day in hot weather to reduce air-conditioning costs.

- Bike, walk, carpool, or use public transit. If at all possible, try to live close to your work and shop close to home.

- Get a low-cost home energy audit from your utility company for suggestions for conserving energy.

- Check caulking around windows and doors, and add it where needed.

- Use latex paints (which are considerably less toxic to the environment) rather than oil-based paints.

- Buy and use cars that are fuel efficient. Keep your car well tuned so that it is fuel efficient. (Burning one gallon of gasoline produces nearly 20 pounds of carbon dioxide, which is a major source of the greenhouse effect that contributes to global warming.)

- Avoid use of aerosols and other products containing chlorofluorocarbons (CFCs). CFCs are depleting the protective ozone layer in the atmosphere. Such depletion has already led to sharp increases in rates of skin cancer caused by the sun's rays.

- Reduce food wastes, which are major contributors to garbage. Whenever possible, compost food wastes.

- Stop the delivery of junk mail. Your local post office will give you the address and instructions for writing to Direct Mail Marketing Association in New York City to request the stoppage of delivery of junk mail.

- Buy products that are made out of recycled paper. Buying recycled paper helps create a market for it.

- Do not litter.

- Cut the grass tall on your lawn. Short grass requires more water. Water lawns at night or early in the morning rather than during direct sunlight. (Watering in direct sunlight is wasteful, because much of the water evaporates.)

- Recycle motor oil. Used oil is highly destructive to the environment when dumped and also is likely to contaminate nearby water supplies.

- Use soap detergents that are low in phosphates. Phosphates are toxic.

- Use dry cleaning sparingly, because it is done with toxic chlorinated solvents.

- Be cautious in using chipboard, plywood, insulation, carpeting, and upholstery; they contain or can create toxic formaldehyde gas.

- Avoid purchasing products made from endangered species—for example, ivory, tortoise shells, and reptile skin.

- Buy eggs in paperboard cartons instead of plastic foam cartons (which tend to be nonbiodegradable).

- Purchase meat, poultry, and other products that are wrapped in paper rather than plastic.

- Buy beverages in aluminum cans or glass bottles, and buy food in glass containers with metal lids instead of plastic. Return the bottles, cans, and glass for recycling.

- Do not put toxic waste products into garbage containers. If deposited into landfills, such products can trickle into nearby water reserves.

- Keep fireplace dampers closed (in order to reduce heat loss) unless there's a fire going.

Source: "A User's Guide to Saving the Planet," CBS television show, broadcast nationally on April 19, 1990; and "What You Can Do to Help Earth," *Wisconsin State Journal,* April 22, 1990, p. 1H.

Learning to live more harmoniously with the environment means changing our attitudes and behavior, usually in simple ways. Recycling is an effective means of putting these new values to a very practical use.

between 1970 and 1994, and overall lead levels in the average American's blood dropped by one-third from 1976 to 1990.[117]

Since the late 1980s, economic and political values have changed significantly in Eastern European countries. These changes have largely been based on former Soviet President Mikhail Gorbachev's concepts of *glasnost* and *perestroika*. Glasnost refers to greater openness and increased freedoms for people in the Eastern Bloc countries. Perestroika involves economic, social, and political reforms in these countries. Based on these principles, a number of these nations have rejected Communism and are moving toward establishing democracies. There is optimism that such restructuring will lead to improved relationships between Western and Eastern nations. If this happens, less money would need to be allocated for defense. Will the savings lead to more funds being available to combat environmental destruction and overpopulation? Will Western and Eastern nations now work cooperatively to overcome the

problems that severely impact all inhabitants of this planet? Slow, but gradual progress is occurring in these areas.

FINDING NEW SOURCES OF ENERGY

Reduction of pollution, population, and energy consumption will not alter the fact that much of our current energy comes from nonrenewable fuel sources. Sooner or later we will have to find new sources of energy. In the meantime it is crucial that all countries set a priority on conserving the earth's nonrenewable fuel sources. Ehrlich and Ehrlich summarize an approach for conserving fuel in the United States:

> *The United States could start by gradually imposing a higher gasoline tax—hiking it by one or two cents per month until gasoline costs $2.50 to $3.00 per gallon, comparable to prices in Europe and Japan. The higher fuel price would create a powerful incentive for people to buy and drive smaller, more fuel-efficient cars and use energy-efficient alternative forms of*

transportation. It would make driving safer once the majority of automobiles were smaller, help preserve crumbling highways and bridges, reduce air pollution and acid precipitation, and slow global warming—among other benefits.[118]

Possible new sources of energy are nuclear energy, synthetic fuel, and solar energy.

Nuclear Energy. Nuclear energy is a potential solution to the energy shortage, but concerns over the safety of nuclear power plants have slowed construction of them. In March 1979 a near-disaster at the nuclear plant at Three Mile Island in Pennsylvania increased these concerns. Radioactive steam escaped, and there was a danger of a meltdown that probably would have killed many people in the area from lethal overdoses of radiation. The April 1986 explosion in Chernobyl was a much more serious accident; tens of thousands of inhabitants were exposed to radioactivity and face the threat of a shortened life span.

Such accidents emphasize that safety in any nuclear power plant cannot be taken for granted. Nuclear energy out of control has the potential for large-scale disaster. A major question is whether future development of nuclear energy is worth the risks.

Synthetic Fuel. In 1980 the federal government passed legislation to create and finance a synthetic-fuel industry. The raw materials for synthetic fuel are in oil shale formations, coal deposits, and gooey-tar sands. The term *synthetic fuel* is actually a misnomer, because its components have the same carbon base as crude oil. Coal, for example, will become gas if it is pulverized and then mixed with oxygen and steam under extreme heat. Shale is a dark-brown, fine-grained rock that contains carbon. Production problems are considerable; it is estimated that it takes 1.7 tons of shale to produce a barrel of oil and that it takes a ton of coal to produce two barrels of oil.[119] Whether synthetic fuel can be cost effective remains a major question. A few years after the initiation of the synthetic-fuel program, a temporary glut of crude oil occurred worldwide. Partly as a result of this glut, synthetic-fuel efforts

have been postponed or discontinued. When another shortage of crude oil occurs, programs to develop synthetic fuel may again be initiated.

On a positive note, it is estimated that the United States has a 600-year supply of the raw materials for synthetic fuel.[120]

Solar Energy. Solar energy is another potential solution to the world's energy crisis. Thousands of U.S. homes and offices are getting all or part of their heating and cooling from the sun.[121] Even the White House has a solar water-heating system on its roof. Another potential use of sunlight is direct conversion to electricity with photovoltaic cells, but at present this process is too expensive to be used widely. A growing number of scientists and concerned citizens are coming to see solar power as the best alternative to solving our energy problems. Such technology is really an imitation of nature, because all energy ultimately comes from the sun.

SOCIAL WORK AND FAMILY PLANNING

Social workers are concerned about overpopulation—about the problems it is creating now and the even greater problems it may create in the future. In almost every social service agency, social workers come in contact with clients who want and need family planning information. Social workers also must respond to controversial issues: dealing with accusations of racism when they provide family planning services for the poor, providing abortion information and making referrals, responding to those who advocate involuntary sterilization of people who have a severe inherited disability, and setting up family planning clinics in high schools so that contraceptive information and devices are more readily accessible to teenagers.

Social workers are increasingly being employed in settings in which the primary service is family planning. Many roles in family planning are well suited for social workers: premarital counseling; pregnancy counseling; provision of contraceptive information including effectiveness and side effects of the varied approaches; sex education services; counseling about sexually transmitted diseases; AIDS education and counseling; abortion counseling; infertility counseling; and community planning efforts to develop family planning services and create a community atmosphere that is accepting of family planning as a legitimate service. Now, family planning counseling is fragmented in many communities: Public health departments provide counseling on sexually transmitted diseases, adoption agencies offer infertility counseling, medical clinics that perform abortions provide abortion counseling, public welfare departments offer contraceptive information for clients, family service agencies provide premarital counseling, and so on.

There are several reasons for anticipating that family planning services will be expanded in future years, thereby creating new career opportunities for social workers. The general public is becoming increasingly aware of the dangers of overpopulation. There has been a growing acceptance in our society of contraceptives. The specter of AIDS has led to greater awareness that AIDS education and sex education are widely needed.

Social workers are being hired in specialized agencies that deal with family planning. These include Planned Parenthood, maternal and child health clinics, and agencies providing abortions and abortion counseling.

School social workers have become increasingly involved in family planning activities in connection with sex education for sexually active teenagers. Social workers in single-parent units of social services departments (also called public welfare or human services departments) also provide family planning services. Other settings in which social workers counsel on family planning include pediatrics and gynecology departments in hospitals and clinics, child welfare agencies, and residential treatment facilitates for teenagers.

Unfortunately, very few undergraduate and graduate social work programs have family planning courses. A number of programs do provide some family planning instructional units in other courses.

SUMMARY

Problems associated with overpopulation and misuse of the environment are very serious and may have an adverse, dramatic effect on the quality of life in the future. The world's population has more than doubled in size since 1930. At current growth rates, the population will again double in size in the next 40 years. Already we are experiencing resource crises. Some of the problems associated with overpopulation and misuse of the environment are:

- Too little food. At present a large proportion of the people in the world are undernourished, and many are starving.

- Too little water. Fresh water is in short supply.

- Economic problems. Overpopulation lowers the average per capita income, reduces the standard of living, and often leads to political turmoil.

- International terrorism. Rapid population growth is a factor that contributes to civil unrest, violence, and international strife.

- Crowding. There is some evidence that the subjective feeling of insufficient space may be a factor in such problems as crime, emotional disturbances, suicide, violence, incest, and child abuse.

- Immigration issues. Immigration has resulted in ethnic and racial conflict, economic competition among different nationality groups, exploitation of undocumented immigrants, and the stresses and costs associated with education and caring for new arrivals.

- Too little energy. We currently have an energy crisis. Fossil fuel resources (oil, coal, and natural gas), which provide over nine-tenths of the world's energy consumption, are rapidly being depleted.

- Depleted mineral resources. Essential elements such as copper, zinc, iron, and manganese are increasingly becoming in short supply.

- Despoiling of the land. Coal strip mining, oil drilling, deforestation, and overgrazing by cattle and sheep not only are unsightly but also cause devastating environmental damage when the delicate balance among nature's elements is interrupted.

- Radioactive wastes. As yet we have not found a safe way to dispose of nuclear wastes, which may create lethal problems in the future.

- Garbage. Increased consumption increases throw-aways, the disposal of which often leads to air pollution, water pollution, and other undesirable environmental effects.

- Air pollution. In large industrial centers, air pollution is a health hazard. There are also growing concerns about the gradual depletion of the ozone layer, about the greenhouse effect, and global warming.

- Water pollution. Water pollution is also a serious health hazard; some rivers and lakes are now so polluted that they cannot support fish and other organisms.

- Acid rain. Acid rain has damaged timber and is killing fish in lakes and streams.

- Radioactive leaks from nuclear power plants. Leaks and accidents at nuclear power plants in the Ukraine and in the United States raise the question of whether nuclear energy is worth the risks.

- Nuclear war. The number of countries that have nuclear warheads is increasing, which makes nuclear war an ever-greater threat to civilization.

- General pollutants. Increasingly, we are becoming aware of the harmful effects of such pollutants as lead, mercury, DDT, and other chlorinated hydrocarbons.

Unless the size of the world's population is brought under control, these problems will intensify. A number of proposals have been advanced to curtail the growth of the world's population, some of which, if implemented, would radically change current lifestyles. Proposals include subsidizing adoptions, expanding sex education in schools, developing safer contraceptives, enforcing compulsory sterilization, raising the minimum age of marriage, no longer allowing tax deductions for children, making birth control information and devices more available, and making abortions more accessible. If nations are not successful in controlling the birthrate through voluntary family planning, pressure will mount for countries to adopt population control programs.

It is essential that we confront our environmental problems. Two primary actions that are needed are changing values toward conserving resources and developing new sources of energy, such as solar energy.

Family planning services are crucial to population control. Social workers are increasingly being employed in settings that offer family planning services. Family planning appears to be an emerging career field for social work, as many roles are well suited for social workers: premarital counseling, pregnancy counseling, provision of contraceptive information, sex education services, abortion counseling, counseling on sexually transmitted diseases, and community planning efforts to further develop family planning services.

All of us can take steps to help save our earth. Whatever happens to the earth will surely affect everyone.

NOTES

1. James W. Coleman and Donald R. Cressey, *Social Problems*, 5th ed. (New York: HarperCollins, 1993), pp. 414–417.
2. Paul B. Horton, Gerald R. Leslie, and Richard F. Larson, *The Sociology of Social Problems*, 10th ed. (Englewood Cliffs, NJ: Prentice-Hall, 1991), p. 245.
3. Paul R. Ehrlich, *The Population Bomb* (New York: Ballantine, 1971), p. 4.
4. John E. Farley, *American Social Problems*, 2d ed. (Englewood Cliffs, NJ: Prentice-Hall, 1992), pp. 342–343.
5. Werner Fornos, *Gaining People, Losing Ground* (Washington, DC: Population Institute, 1987), p. 57.
6. Farley, *American Social Problems*, p. 346.

7. Lee Rainwater, *And the Poor Get Children* (Chicago: Quadrangle Books, 1960).

8. Quoted in Donald C. Bacon, Poor vs. Rich: A Global Struggle,'' *U.S. News & World Report*, July 31, 1978, p. 57.

9. Fornos, *Gaining People, Losing Ground*, pp. 38–61.

10. Beth Brophy, ''Children under Stress,'' *U.S. News & World Report*, Oct. 27, 1986, p. 59.

11. Ehrlich, *The Population Bomb*, p. 129.

12. Paul Ehrlich and Anne Ehrlich, *The Population Explosion* (New York: Simon and Schuster, 1990), pp. 34–36.

13. Fornos, *Gaining People, Losing Ground*, p. 7.

14. Ibid.

15. Ibid., pp. 19–22.

16. Ehrlich and Ehrlich, *The Population Explosion.*

17. Ibid., pp. 38–39.

18. Ibid.

19. Ibid.

20. Sonya Ross, ''Child Poverty Soars,'' *Wisconsin State Journal*, Aug. 12, 1992, p. 1A.

21. Ehrlich and Ehrlich, *The Population Explosion.*

22. Fornos, *Gaining People, Losing Ground*, p. 12.

23. Ian Robertson, *Social Problems*, 2d ed. (New York: Random House, 1980), p. 41.

24. Thomas R. Malthus, *On Population*, Gertrude Himmelfarb, ed. (New York: Modern Library, 1960), pp. 13–14. (Original edition published 1798)

25. Roger Revelle, ''Food and Population,'' in *The Human Population*, ed. *Scientific American* (San Francisco: W. H. Freeman, 1974), pp. 119–130.

26. Jonathan Yenkin, ''Hunger in U.S. Jumps 50% since Mid-'80's,'' *Wisconsin State Journal*, Sept. 10, 1992, p. 1A.

27. Paul R. Ehrlich and Anne H. Ehrlich, *Population, Resources, Environment* (San Francisco: W. H. Freeman, 1970) p. 65.

28. ''Warning: Water Shortages Ahead,'' *Time*, Apr. 4, 1977, p. 48.

29. Ketayun H. Gould, ''Population and Family Planning,'' in *Contemporary Social Work*, Donald Brieland, Lela Costin, and Charles Atherton, eds. (New York: McGraw-Hill, 1975), p. 130.

30. Fornos, *Gaining People, Losing Ground*, pp. 7–23.

31. Quoted in Fornos, *Gaining People, Losing Ground*, p. 10.

32. U.S. Bureau of the Census, *Statistical Abstract of the United States, 1993* (Washington, DC: U.S. Government Printing Office, 1993).

33. Quoted in Fornos, *Gaining People, Losing Ground*, pp. 20–21.

34. Fornos, *Gaining People, Losing Ground*, p. 21.

35. John B. Calhoun, ''Population Density and Social Pathology,'' *Scientific American*, 206 (February 1962), pp. 139–148.

36. Joseph Julian, *Social Problems*, 3d ed. (Englewood Cliffs, NJ: Prentice-Hall, 1980), p. 502.

37. Ibid.

38. Coleman and Cressey, *Social Problems*, p. 447.

39. Ibid.

40. Ibid., pp. 447–450.

41. Irene B. Taeuber, ''Japan's Demographic Transition Reexamined,'' *Population Studies*, 14 (July 1960), p. 39.

42. Robertson, *Social Problems*, p. 43.

43. Fornos, *Gaining People, Losing Ground*, p. 5.

44. Ibid.

45. Ehrlich and Ehrlich, *The Population Explosion*, p. 17.

46. Farley, *American Social Problems*, p. 343.

47. Ehrlich and Ehrlich, *The Population Explosion*, pp. 205–209.

48. Fornos, *Gaining People, Losing Ground*, pp. 45–46.

49. Ibid.

50. Farley, *American Social Problems*, p. 343.

51. ''India's Program Stresses Role of Women,'' *Popline*, vol. 12 (March–April 1990), p. 3.

52. Ibid.

53. Ibid.

54. Farley, *American Social Problems*, p. 343.

55. ''Monster Problems,'' *Parade*, Apr. 19, 1981, p. 14.

56. Fornos, *Gaining People, Losing Ground*, pp. 41–42.

57. Ibid.

58. Ibid., p. 41.

59. Ibid., p. 42.

60. Ehrlich and Ehrlich, *The Population Explosion*, pp. 205–209.

61. Ibid., p. 207.

62. Paul R. Ehrlich, Anne H. Ehrlich, and John P. Holdren, *Human Ecology: Problems and Solutions* (San Francisco: W. H. Freeman, 1973), pp. 159–160.

63. *We Can Blame Billions of People for This* (Washington, DC: Population Institute, 1990), p. 3.

64. Coleman and Cressey, *Social Problems*, p. 443.

65. Ibid.

66. Ibid.

67. Ehrlich and Ehrlich, *Population, Resources, Environment*, p. 202.

68. Ehrlich et al., *Human Ecology*, pp. 80–89.

69. Fornos, *Gaining People, Losing Ground*, p. 14.

70. Ibid., p. 13.

71. David Foster, ''Hidden Oil Soils Alaska's Coast,'' *Wisconsin State Journal*, Mar. 22, 1990, p. 2A.

72. Coleman and Cressey, *Social Problems*, p. 446.

73. Roberston, *Social Problems*, p. 71.

74. Horton et al., *The Sociology of Social Problems*, p. 440.

75. William Kornblum and Joseph Julian, *Social Problems,* 7th ed. (Englewood Cliffs, NJ: Prentice-Hall, 1992), p. 477.
76. Julian, *Social Problems,* p. 528.
77. Coleman and Cressey, *Social Problems,* pp. 437–440.
78. Ibid., p. 438.
79. Ibid., pp. 438–440.
80. Ibid., p. 440.
81. Ibid.
82. Ibid., pp. 445–446.
83. Kornblum and Julian, *Social Problems,* p. 483.
84. Ibid., p. 485.
85. Ibid., pp. 513–517.
86. Orr Kelly, "Nuclear War's Horrors: Reality vs. Fiction," *U.S. News & World Report,* Nov. 28, 1983, pp. 85–86.
87. Barry Schwied, "U.S., Russia Seal Missile Deal," *Wisconsin State Journal,* Jan. 4, 1993, p. 1A.
88. Kornblum and Julian, *Social Problems,* p. 483.
89. Ibid.
90. Ibid., p. 485.
91. Vincent Parrilo, John Stimson, and Ardyth Stimson, *Contemporary Social Problems,* 2d ed. (New York: Macmillan, 1989), p. 501.
92. Erhlich and Erhlich, *The Population Explosion,* pp. 123–124.
93. Farley, *American Social Problems,* p. 317.
94. Ehrlich, *The Population Bomb,* pp. 31–35.
95. Richard Curtis and Elizabeth Hogan, *Perils of the Peaceful Atom* (New York: Ballantine, 1969), p. 194.
96. "Chemical Dangers May Be Unknown," *Wisconsin State Journal,* Mar. 3, 1984, p. 1.
97. "Silent Spring Revisited," *Newsweek,* July 14, 1986, p. 72.
98. Ehrlich and Ehrlich, *The Population Explosion,* p. 238.
99. Ehrlich, *The Population Bomb,* pp. 127–145.
100. Bernard Berelson, "The Present State of Family Planning Programs," *Studies in Family Planning,* 57 (September 1970), p. 2.
101. Fornos, *Gaining People, Losing Ground,* pp. 29–30.
102. Ibid., p. 30.
103. Ehrlich, *Human Ecology,* p. 279.
104. "Abortion Foes Gain Victory," *Wisconsin State Journal,* July 1, 1980, sec. 1, p. 1.
105. Fornos, *Gaining People, Losing Ground,* pp. 78–85.
106. Gould, "Population and Family Planning," p. 138.
107. Fornos, *Gaining People, Losing Ground,* pp. 106–107.
108. Julian, *Social Problems,* p. 502.
109. George Ritzer, *Social Problems,* 2d ed. (New York: Random House, 1986), p. 556.
110. "Don't Throw a Good Thing Away," *Policyholder News,* vol. 23, no. 1 (Spring 1990), p. 3.
111. Ibid.
112. Ibid.
113. Steven Thomma, "Some Problems Solved since Earth Day in '70, But Now We Face New Troubles," *Wisconsin State Journal,* April 22, 1994, p. 1D.
114. Ibid.
115. Ibid.
116. Ibid.
117. Ibid.
118. Ehrlich and Ehrlich, *The Population Explosion,* pp. 219–220.
119. "Fuels for America's Future," *U.S. News & World Report,* Aug. 13, 1979, p. 33.
120. Ibid.
121. Ibid.

SOCIAL

WORK

PRACTICE

17

GENERALIST

SOCIAL

WORK

PRACTICE

The preceding chapters have focused on prominent social problems and current social services to deal with these problems. The focus of this chapter will be on generalist social work practice. This chapter will:

- Define generalist social work practice.
- Summarize the change process in social work practice.
- Describe roles assumed by social workers in social work practice.
- Discuss social work practice with individuals, families, groups, organizations, and the community.
- Summarize the knowledge, skills, and values needed for social work practice.
- Briefly describe educational training for social work practice.

GENERALIST SOCIAL WORK PRACTICE DEFINED

The traditional perception of the social worker has been that of a caseworker, group worker, or community organizer. Practicing social workers know that their roles are more complex than that; every social worker is involved as a change agent (someone who assists in promoting positive changes) in working with individuals, groups, families, organizations, and the larger community. The amount of time spent at these levels varies from worker to worker. But every worker will, at times, be assigned and expected to function effectively at all these levels and therefore needs training in all of them.

The Council on Social Work Education (CSWE) (the national accrediting entity for baccalaureate and master's programs in social work) requires all bachelor's-level and master's-level programs to train their students in generalist social work practice. (MSW programs, in addition, usually require their students to select and study in an area of specialization. These programs generally offer several specializations, such as family therapy, administration, corrections, and clinical social work.)

Anderson has identified three characteristics of a generalist social worker: (1) The generalist is often the first professional to see clients as they enter the social welfare system; (2) the worker must therefore be competent to assess their needs and to identify their stress points and problems; and (3) the worker must draw on a variety of skills and methods in serving clients.[1]

D. Brieland, L. B. Costin, and C. R. Atherton define and describe generalist practice as follows:

The generalist social worker, the equivalent of the general practitioner in medicine, is characterized by a wide repertoire of skills to deal with basic conditions, backed up by specialists to whom referrals are made. This role is a fitting one for the entry-level social worker.

The generalist model involves identifying and analyzing the interventive behaviors appropriate to social work. The worker must perform a wide range of tasks related to the provision and management of direct service, the development of social policy, and the facilitation of social change. The generalist should be well grounded in systems theory that emphasizes interaction and independence. The major system that will be used is the local network of services. . . .

The public welfare worker in a small county may be a classic example of the generalist. He or she knows the resources of the county, is acquainted with the key people, and may have considerable influence to accomplish service goals, including obtaining jobs, different housing, or emergency food and clothing. The activities of the urban generalist are more complex, and more effort must be expended to use the array of resources.[2]

G. Hull defines generalist practice as follows:

The basic principle of generalist practice is that baccalaureate social workers are able to utilize the problem solving process to intervene with various size systems including individuals, families, groups, organizations, and communities. The generalist operates within a systems and person-in-the-environment framework (sometimes referred to as an ecological model). The generalist expects that many problems will require intervention with more than one system (e.g., individual work with a delinquent adolescent plus work with the family or school) and that single explanations of problem situations are frequently unhelpful. The generalist may play several roles simultaneously or sequentially, depending upon the needs of the client (e.g., facilitator, advocate, educator, broker, enabler, case manager, and/or mediator). They may serve as leaders/facilitators of task groups, socialization groups, information groups, and self-help groups. They are capable of conducting needs assessments and evaluating their own practice and the programs with which they are associated. They make referrals when client problems so dictate and know when to utilize supervision from more experienced staff. Generalists operate within the ethical guidelines prescribed by the NASW Code of Ethics and must be able to work with clients, coworkers, and colleagues from different ethnic, cultural, and professional orientations. The knowledge and skills of the generalist are transferable from one setting to another and from one problem to another.[3]

The crux of generalist practice involves (1) viewing a problem situation in terms of the person-in-environment conceptualization (described in Chapter 2) and (2) being willing and able to intervene at several different levels, if necessary, while assuming any number of roles. The next section describes the change process in social work practice and illustrates the approach of responding at different levels in a variety of roles.

THE CHANGE PROCESS

Social workers use the *change process* in working with clients. (Clients include individuals, groups, families, organizations, and communities.) The CSWE, in its Curriculum Policy Statements, identifies the following eight skills that are needed for social work practice:

1. *Defining issues;*

2. *Collecting and assessing data;*

3. *Planning and contracting;*

4. *Identifying alternative interventions;*

5. *Selecting and implementing appropriate courses of action;*

6. *Using appropriate research to monitor and evaluate outcomes;*

7. *Applying appropriate research-based knowledge and technological advances; and*

8. *Termination.*[4]

These eight skills, interestingly, provide an excellent framework for conceptualizing the phases of the change process in social work. I'll use a case example to illustrate this change process.

Carlos Ramirez is a social worker at a high school in a midwestern state. Four teenagers are expelled (consistent with school board policy) for drinking alcoholic beverages at school. The case is referred to Mr. Ramirez for intervention.

Phase 1: Defining Issues

Defining issues, the first step in the change process, often becomes fairly complex. In this case example there are a number of issues (questions/concerns/problems) that the school social worker, Carlos Ramirez, identifies: Do the youths have a drinking problem? Were the boys disenchanted with the school system and displaying their discontent by breaking school rules? What short-term and long-term adverse effects might the expulsions have on the youths? (For example, the expulsions could have a labeling effect, giving these youths a reputation as "troublemakers"; this label could lead them to become further involved in delinquent behavior.) What will be the reactions of the parents to the drinking and to the expulsions? What effects will the expulsions have on other students at the school? (A possible positive effect is that the expulsions may be a deterrent to other students who are considering violating school rules; a possible negative consequence is that the expulsions may encourage other students to violate school rules and get expelled so they can avoid having to attend school.) Will the expulsions create problems for merchants in the community because the expelled youths are now likely to spend their days on the street? Is the school policy of expelling youths for drinking on school grounds a constructive or destructive educational policy? Does the school system have a responsibility to add an educational program on substance abuse to the curriculum? Are there aspects about the school system that encourage youths to rebel? If so, should these aspects be changed?

The issues identified then serve as a guide for the next phase (data collection and assessment). During this initial phase (as well as during the other phases), it is essential that the social worker seek to establish and continue a working relationship with the client(s).

Phase 2: Collecting and Assessing Data

Here the social worker does an in-depth collection and analysis of data in order to find answers to the questions raised in phase 1. For some of the issues, useful information can be obtained directly from the clients (including the youths, in this example). For instance, the question of whether the youths have a drinking problem can perhaps be answered by meeting individually with each boy, forming a trusting relationship, and then asking how often the youth drinks, how much he consumes when drinking, and what problems he has encountered while drinking. For other issues raised in phase 1, useful information will need to be collected from other sources. For example, the short- and long-term adverse effects of the expulsions on the youths might be determined by researching the literature on this topic.

Assessment is the process of analyzing the data to make sense of it. Phase 2 also involves an assessment of the degree of match, or fit, between the client's needs and the agency's eligibility requirements and resources. The service may be terminated for lack of fit. The client may be referred elsewhere for service, perhaps because of the specialization of some other agency's re-

sources. If the fit is deemed appropriate, the social worker and the client then move on to the next phase.

Phase 3: Planning and Contracting

Planning includes formulating initial objectives (goals) and deciding which objectives to pursue. One objective may be to explore with the youths whether they have a drinking problem. Another objective may be to have the youths reinstated in school. Still another might be to change the expulsion policy to in-school suspension. Or perhaps an objective would be to add educational material on substance abuse to the curriculum. Often the social worker will use a technique like cost-benefit analysis (weighing resources expended against estimated potential benefits) to make decisions about which objective(s) to pursue. (In real-life situations, social workers rarely are able to pursue all worthy objectives, because of time and resource constraints.)

Contracting involves making arrangements with the client(s), or with organizations that are providing funding for the client(s), for what services (often with a specification of the objectives) will be offered and at what cost (with a specification of financial arrangements).

Phase 4: Identifying Alternative Interventions

Carlos Ramirez, social worker at the high school the youths were expelled from, selects (in phase 3) as one of his objectives the preventive approach of seeking to add educational material on substance abuse to the curriculum. Numerous questions related to this objective now arise for him. What specific material should be covered in a drug education program? Which drugs should be included? (Mr. Ramirez is aware that certain drugs, such as LSD, are seldom used in the community; some parents may thus question whether educational material about these drugs might actually encourage some youths to experiment with them.) Where should this educational component be added into the curriculum—in large assemblies with all students being required to attend, in health classes, in social science classes, or elsewhere? Will the administration, faculty, school board, students, and parents be supportive of adding this component to the curriculum? What will be the most effective strategy for gaining the support of these various groups?

As a first step in this phase, Mr. Ramirez meets with his immediate supervisor, Dr. Marie Lee, Director of Pupil Services at the high school, to discuss these issues and to generate a list of alternative strategies for how to proceed. Three strategies are considered: (1) Students could be anonymously surveyed to determine the extent of alcohol and other drug use and abuse at the school. Such survey results could document the need for a drug education program. (2) A committee of professional staff in the Pupil Services Department could be appointed to develop a drug education program. (3) The Pupil Services Department could request that the administration and school board appoint a committee—composed of representatives from the school board, school administration, faculty, students, parents, and Pupil Services—to explore the need for and feasibility of a drug education program.

Phase 5: Selecting and Implementing Appropriate Courses of Action

Mr. Ramirez and Dr. Lee decide that the best way to obtain broad support for a drug education program is to pursue the third option listed in phase 4. Dr. Lee meets with the high school principal, Mary Powell. After some contemplation, Ms. Powell agrees that the need for such a program should be explored, and she asks the school board to support the formation of such a committee. The board agrees. A committee is eventually formed, and it begins to hold meetings. Mr. Ramirez is appointed by Dr. Lee to be Pupil Services' representative to this committee.

Phase 6: Using Appropriate Research to Monitor and Evaluate Outcomes

One of the first questions raised by committee members during initial deliberations is which specific drugs should be covered in the program. As a result, the Pupil Services Department is asked to conduct a survey of all the students to identify which drugs are currently being used and to what extent.

A second (related) issue that arises in the committee is the broader question of whether a drug education program really would have preventative value or would have the undesired outcome of promoting illegal drug use. To obtain information on this issue, staff in the Pupil Services Department research the literature on the preventative value of drug education programs nationally, as well as on the most effective formats for such programs.

After 14 months of planning and deliberation, the committee presents a proposal to the school board for a drug education program. The program is designed to become part of the curriculum of health classes in middle schools and high schools throughout the school district. One component of the proposal requires that the Pupil Services Department conduct an annual survey of a random sample of students to obtain (1) information on the extent of drug use/abuse and (2) students' thoughts about the merits and shortcomings of the program. Such a survey provides a way of monitoring and evaluating the outcomes of the drug educational program.

Phase 7: Applying Appropriate Research-Based Knowledge and Technological Advances

The drug education program that is implemented contains the latest research-based knowledge on commonly used drugs by young people in the community. The following topics are covered:

mind-altering effects, physical and psychological dependency, withdrawal, and long-term effects on health. The curriculum also contains research-based information on the most effective treatment approaches, ways of coping when someone in the family is abusing, ways to confront a friend or relative who is abusing, dangers of driving when using drugs, associations between drug use and sexually transmitted diseases (including AIDS), steps to take if one has concerns about his or her own drug use, and ways of saying "no" to peer pressure to use drugs.

Several technological advances are used for this drug education program. Computers search databases for information on effective drug programs in other school systems in the country; they also process data from the surveys on drug use by middle and high school students in the district. Educational films and videotapes are also integrated into the curriculum.

Phase 8: Termination

The committee that developed the drug education program holds its final meeting after the school board approves the proposal. Most members experience mixed emotions—delight that their task is successfully completed but sad that this important and meaningful part of their lives is now ending.

If a close working relationship has formed between the worker and the client, termination is often a painful process—especially for the client but sometimes also for the worker. In the change process, sensitive issues are often addressed, considerable effort is expended on making constructive changes, and dependency may develop. As a result, the client is likely to experience a sense of loss when termination occurs. The client may also feel angry and rejected.

A final evaluation is usually a part of terminating. The final evaluation involves more than the assessment of what occurred during monitoring; it emphasizes the usefulness of the entire change process. The final evaluation is also extremely significant to the agency, because it indicates whether the agency's services have been benefi-

cial. Each agency needs composite evaluations of all their services to all clients in order to provide documentation to funding sources to justify continued funding.

A VARIETY OF ROLES

In working with individuals, groups, families, organizations, and communities, a social worker is expected to be knowledgeable and skillful in a variety of roles. The particular role that is selected should (ideally) be determined by what will be most effective, given the circumstances. The following material identifies some, but certainly not all, of the roles assumed by social workers.

ENABLER

In this role a worker *helps* individuals or groups to articulate their needs, to clarify and identify their problems, to explore resolution strategies, to select and apply a strategy, and to develop their capacities to deal with their own problems more effectively. This is perhaps the most frequently used approach in counseling individuals, groups, and families. The model is also used in community practice—primarily when the objective is to help people organize to help themselves.

It should be noted that this definition of the term *enabler* is very different from the one used in the area of chemical dependency. There the term refers to a family member or friend who facilitates the substance abuser's continued use and abuse of the drug of his or her choice.

BROKER

A broker links individuals and groups who need help (and do not know where it is available) with community services. For example, a wife who is often physically abused by her husband might be referred to a shelter for battered women. Nowadays even moderate-sized communities have 200 or 300 social service agencies/organizations providing community services. Even human services professionals may be only partially aware of the total service network in their community.

ADVOCATE

The role of advocate has been borrowed from the legal profession. It is an active, directive role in which the social worker advocates for a client or for a citizen's group. When a client or a citizen's group is in need of help and existing institutions are uninterested (or even openly negative and hostile) in providing services, then the advocate's role may be appropriate. In such a role the advocate provides leadership for collecting information, for arguing the correctness of the client's need and request, and for challenging the institution's decision not to provide services. The object is not to ridicule or censure a particular institution but to modify or change one or more of its service policies. In this role the advocate is a partisan who is exclusively serving the interests of a client or a citizen's group.

ACTIVIST

An activist seeks institutional change; often the objective involves a shift in power and resources to a disadvantaged group. Activists are concerned about social injustice, inequity, and deprivation, and their tactics include conflict, confrontation, and negotiation. The goal is to change the social environment in order to better meet the recognized needs of individuals. Using assertive and action-oriented methods (for example, organizing welfare recipients to work toward improvements in services and increases in money payments), social workers engage in fact finding, analysis of community needs, research, the dissemination and interpretation of information, mobilization, and other efforts to promote public understanding and support in behalf of existing or proposed social programs. Social action activity can be geared toward a problem that is local, statewide, or national in scope.

MEDIATOR

The mediator role involves intervention in disputes between parties to help them find compromises, reconcile differences, or reach mutually satisfactory agreements. Social workers have used their value orientations and unique skills in many forms of mediation (for example, with divorcing spouses and neighbors in conflict or in landlord/tenant disputes, labor/management disputes, and child custody disputes). A mediator remains neutral, not siding with either party. Mediators make sure they understand the positions of both parties. They may help to clarify positions, identify miscommunication about differences, and help those involved present their cases clearly.

NEGOTIATOR

A negotiator brings together those who are in conflict over one or more issues and seeks to achieve bargaining and compromise in order to arrive at mutually acceptable agreements. Somewhat like mediation, negotiation involves finding a middle ground that all sides can live with. However, unlike a mediator (which is a neutral role), a negotiator usually is allied with one of the sides involved.

EDUCATOR

The educator role involves giving information to clients and teaching them adaptive skills. To be an effective educator, the worker must first be knowledgeable. Additionally, she or he must be a good communicator so that information is clearly conveyed and readily understood by the receiver. Examples include teaching parenting skills to young parents, providing job-hunting strategies to the unemployed, and teaching anger-control techniques to individuals with difficulties in these areas.

INITIATOR

An initiator calls attention to a problem—or even to a potential problem. It is important to realize that some problems can be recognized in advance. For example, a proposal to renovate a low-income neighborhood by building middle-income housing units may result in the current residents' becoming homeless. If the proposal is approved, the low-income families won't be able to afford the costs of the middle-income units. Usually the initiator role must be followed by other functions; merely calling attention to problems usually does not resolve them.

COORDINATOR

Coordinators bring components together in some kind of organized manner. For example, for a multiproblem family it is often necessary for several agencies to work together to meet the complicated financial, emotional, legal, health, social, educational, recreational, and interactional needs of the family members. Someone at an agency needs to assume the role of case manager to coordinate the services from the different agencies in order to avoid duplication of services and to prevent the diverse services from having conflicting objectives.

RESEARCHER

Every social worker is at times a researcher. Research in social work practice includes studying the literature on topics of interest, evaluating the outcomes of one's practice, assessing the merits and shortcomings of programs, and studying community needs.

GROUP FACILITATOR

A group facilitator is one who serves as a leader for group activity. The group may be a therapy group, an educational group, a self-help group, a sensitivity group, a family therapy group, or a group with some other focus.

PUBLIC SPEAKER

Social workers occasionally are recruited to talk to various groups (e.g., high school classes, public service organizations such as Kiwanis, police officers, staff at other agencies) to inform them of available services or to advocate for new services. In recent years a variety of needed services have been identified (for example, runaway centers, services for battered spouses, rape crisis centers, services for persons with AIDS, and group homes for youth). Social workers who have public-speaking skills can explain services to groups of potential clients. Also, if they are paid for these speaking engagements, they have the opportunity to earn a few thousand dollars more each year.

As indicated earlier, a generalist social worker is a change agent (someone who assists in facilitating positive changes) who works with indi-

viduals, groups, families, organizations, and the community. To give you a flavor of social work practice in each of these areas, I'll now present some brief practice-oriented information.

SOCIAL WORK WITH INDIVIDUALS

A majority of social workers spend most of their time working with individuals in public or private agencies or in private practice. Social work with individuals is aimed at helping people, on a one-to-one basis, to resolve personal and social problems. Social work with individuals encompasses a wide variety of activities, such as counseling runaway youths, helping unemployed people secure training or employment, counseling someone who is suicidal, placing a homeless child in an adoptive or foster home, providing protective services to abused children and their families, finding nursing homes for stroke victims who no longer need to be confined in a hospital, counseling individuals with sexual dysfunctions, helping alcoholics to acknowledge that they have a drinking problem, counseling those with a terminal illness, supervising individuals on probation or parole, providing services to single parents, and coordinating services for individuals who have AIDS.

All of us at times face personal problems that we cannot resolve by ourselves. Sometimes other family members, relatives, friends, or acquaintances can help. At other times we need more skilled intervention to help us handle emotional problems, obtain resources in times of crisis, deal with marital or family conflicts, resolve problems at work or school, or cope with a medical emergency. Furnishing skilled, personal help is what social work with individuals is all about.

In their role as change agents in working with individuals, social workers perform many of the functions discussed above: enabler, broker, advocate, educator, and so on. An essential skill and role of a social worker is counseling. (Some authorities assert that counseling and relationship skills are the most important abilities needed by social workers.[5]) As previous examples in this book indicate, social workers counsel people with a wide variety of personal and social problems.

SOCIAL WORK WITH FAMILIES

Often the focus of social work services is on the family. A family is an interacting interdependent system. The problems faced by any individual are usually influenced by the dynamics within a family. Because a family is an interacting system, change in one member affects other members. For example, it has been noted that the abused child is at times a scapegoat on whom the parents vent their anger and hostility. If the abused child is removed from such a home, another child within the family is likely to be selected to be the scapegoat.[6]

Another reason for focusing on the family is that the participation of all members is often needed in the treatment process. For example, other family members can put pressure on an alcoholic to make her or him acknowledge that a problem exists. The family members may all need counseling (or support from a self-help group) to assist them in coping with the alcoholic when she or he is drinking, and these family members may play important roles in providing emotional support for the alcoholic's efforts to stop drinking.

The following is a small listing of some of the infinite number of problems that may occur in families:

■ Divorce
■ Alcohol or drug abuse
■ Unwanted pregnancy
■ Bankruptcy
■ Poverty
■ Terminal illness
■ Chronic illness
■ Death
■ Desertion
■ Empty-shell marriage

■ Emotional problems of one or more members
■ Behavioral problems of one or more members
■ Child abuse
■ Child neglect
■ Sexual abuse
■ Spouse abuse
■ Elder abuse
■ Unemployment of wage earners
■ Money management difficulties
■ Injury from serious automobile accident involving one or more members
■ Cognitive disability in one or more members
■ Incarceration or institutionalization of one or more members
■ Compulsive gambling by one or more members
■ Crime victimization
■ Forced retirement of a wage earner
■ Alzheimer's disease in an elderly relative
■ Involvement of a child in delinquent and criminal activities
■ Illness of a member who acquires AIDS
■ Runaway teenager
■ Sexual dysfunctions of one or more members
■ Infidelity
■ Infertility

When there are problems in a family, social services are often needed. Many types and forms of service are provided by social workers to troubled families. These services require the social worker to perform a variety of roles (broker, educator, advocate, case manager, mediator, and so on). Chapter 5 describes family problems and some of the services to families—including protective services, services to single parents, and marriage counseling.

One important social service provided to families is family therapy (also called family counseling). A substantial amount of literature on family therapy has been developed in social work. Numerous theoretical frameworks for family therapy have been advanced. One of the most prominent frameworks was developed by Virginia Satir, a psychiatric social worker. Satir's approach to family therapy will be briefly summarized.[7]

Satir stresses clarification of family communication patterns. She notes, in particular, that communication patterns among troubled families tend to be vague and indirect. In other words, rather than speaking clearly for themselves, a marital pair may avoid talking with each other about their needs and desires; or perhaps they talk to each other about what they want through their children. The children are thus maneuvered into the stressful position of speaking for, and therefore allying with, one parent or the other, which precipitates fear of loss of the other parent.

In Satir's view, indirect communication in the troubled family begins with courtship of the marital pair (if not before) and is due to the low self-esteem of the individuals involved. Each spouse-to-be feels worthless but hides these feelings by acting confident and strong. Neither person talks about feeling worthless for fear of driving the potential mate away. So each sees in the other a strong person who will take care of him or her. They marry to gain an extension of the self, but a stronger self who will be able to meet all felt needs; in other words, each marries to "get."[8]

Unfortunately, after marriage some of the illusions must fall away. Each spouse is forced to realize at some level that the other spouse is not just an extension of the self. One insists on using a separate toothbrush, for example, while the other wants to share the same one. Such incidents force perceptions of difference, and difference is experienced as bad because it leads to arguments. A desire to fuse and to be cared for conflicts with the other's different felt needs. Facing this difference feels frightening—it might lead to arguments that could result in the other's leaving.

Hence each frightened spouse with low self-esteem and high need for the other tries to mask differences as much as possible. On one level they attempt to please the other to keep him or her; on another level they fear and resent expressed needs from the other that may be experienced as undesirable.

Since both spouses are in the same uncomfortable position of resenting differences yet needing the other, interpersonal communication gradually becomes more and more indirect. Rather than risk a clear statement such as "I'd like to get a dog," the spouse desiring a pet might say something like "Aunt Matilda likes dogs." The hope will be that the other spouse will mind-read the intended message and then spontaneously agree to get a dog for the family. However, the receiver of this particular message will more likely communicate a response dealing with Aunt Matilda, bringing disappointment to the speaker. The speaker isn't able to negotiate the desired dog with this type of communication and is left with angry feelings toward the spouse and a sense of unfulfilled needs. However, this state of affairs is experienced as being preferable to risking a point-blank denial. Meanwhile, the receiver of the message may become aware of the disappointment or anger of the speaker through nonverbal channels but have no idea what caused it. The spouse who is also afraid to deal with conflict will not ask the reason for the apparent upset. So the misunderstanding and tension build.

Satir also notes that communication involves far more than the literal meaning of any words used. First of all, much communication is nonverbal—gestures, facial expressions, voice tone, posture, and the like. Nonverbal communication that matches the meaning of any words used (the words "I am sad" are accompanied by tears and a downturned mouth) is considered *congruent*. The receiver is not likely to misunderstand the meaning of this message because the verbal and nonverbal components agree. However, messages sent are often *incongruent*. For example, the statement "I am sad" may be accompanied by a grin. Which message should the receiver believe—the words or the facial expression? The receiver is likely to make a mistaken interpretation unless he or she explicitly asks the sender to explain.

But the person who feels safe only with indirect communication is not likely to ask. Moreover, the sender who becomes skilled at sending incongruent communication for self-protection may even be unaware of the action and will be unable to explain if asked. Satir believes that incongruent communication can lead to misunderstanding in troubled families. Mother, for example, may say to Father in words "I'm angry with you." However, since she fears rejection if she sends this message too forcefully, she smiles sweetly as she says it. Father may then choose to believe the smile, not take Mother's words seriously, and continue the very behavior that made her use the word *angry*. This is likely to make her angrier, but she may not feel safe enough to express the feeling more congruently. As a result, the communication that is driving the spouses apart goes on.

Another kind of incongruent communication is one that places the receiver in a *double bind*. That is, no matter how one responds, the sender will criticize. Father may say, on the one hand, that all good children should keep their toys picked up; yet on the other hand he tells his son that all "real" boys are messy. The boy who receives both these messages will be unable to please Father whether he keeps his toys neat or messy. He may solve the problem by refusing to listen at all. At the extreme, he may pull away from reality to such a degree that he develops a severe emotional disturbance.

Satir's therapeutic goals and techniques are based on her assumption that people have the inherent ability (even drive) to grow and to mature. She feels that we can choose to take responsibility for our own lives and actions and that the mature person will:

a. *Manifest himself clearly to others.*

b. *Be in touch with signals from his internal self, thus letting himself know openly what he thinks and feels.*

c. *Be able to see and hear what is outside himself as differentiated from himself and as different from anything else.*

d. *Behave toward another person as someone who is separate and unique.*

e. *Treat the presence of differentness as an opportunity to learn and explore rather than as a threat or signal of conflict.*[9]

To help the members of a troubled family differentiate from one another and learn to own their special unique beings, Satir patiently teaches each person to speak for himself or herself and to send "I-messages." "I-messages" are nonblaming messages that communicate only how the sender believes the receiver is adversely affecting him or her. For example, suppose a father becomes frightened while riding in a car with his 17-year-old son who is driving over the speed limit. An I-message that the Father might use is "John, going this fast in a car scares me."

In counseling families, Satir serves as an active, directive, loving role model. She teaches that differentness is normal and should be viewed as a catalyst for growth. She points out incongruent messages and double binds and teaches family members to send clear, congruent messages instead. She uses touch and other nonverbal means, such as family sculpting, to help illustrate to families the unverbalized assumptions they operate by. These techniques take the burden of labeling off the identified client and reveal his or her symptomatic behavior as a product of the family system as a whole.

Family sculpting is used for both assessment and treatment purposes. It involves a physical arrangement of the members of a family, with the placement of each person determined by an individual family member acting as "director." The resulting tableau represents that person's symbolic view of family relationships. Goldenberg and Goldenberg describe family sculpting as follows:

> *The procedure calls for each member to arrange the bodies of all the other family members in a defined space, according to his or her perception of their relationships either at present or at a specific point in the past. Who the sculptor designates as domineering, meek and submissive, loving and touching, belligerent, benevolent, clinging, and so on, and how those people relate to each other becomes apparent to all who witness the tableau. The sculptor is invited to explain the creation, and a lively debate between members may follow. The adolescent boy who places his parents at opposite ends of the family group while he and his brothers and sisters are huddled together in the center conveys a great deal more about his views of the workings of the family system than he would probably be able to state in words. By*

the same token, his father's sculpture—placing himself apart from all others, including his wife—may reveal his sense of loneliness, isolation, and rejection by his family. The mother may present herself as a confidante of her daughter but ignored by the males in the family, and so forth.[10]

Satir also analyzes rules in the family. She helps clarify them in the context that some rules may be bad, but the people setting the rules or bound by them are not. She teaches that bad rules can be changed and has the family members negotiate new ones. She insists that each member be heard in her presence, thus teaching respect for each person and each point of view.

Clearly, then, Satir views the family as a system. Working with the family as a whole is the means of relieving the distress of the identified client, or of the family itself due to the dysfunctional behavior of the identified client. Her major emphasis in intervention with the family as a system is to clarify their communication patterns and to help them become direct and congruent. Basically, Satir's therapeutic goal of improving methods of communication involves three outcomes: (1) Each member should be able to report congruently, completely, and obviously on what he or she sees, hears, feels, and thinks about himself or herself and others. (2) Each person should relate to his or her uniqueness so that decisions are made in terms of exploration and negotiation rather than in terms of power. (3) Differentness should be openly acknowledged and used for growth.[11]

SOCIAL WORK WITH GROUPS

A group may be defined as

a plurality of individuals who are in contact with one another, who take one another into account, and who are aware of some significant commonality—an essential feature of a group is that its members have something in common and that they believe that what they have in common makes a difference.[12]

Group social work had its historical roots in informal recreational organizations—the YWCA and YMCA, scouting, Jewish centers, settlement houses, and 4-H clubs.

George Williams established the Young Men's Christian Association in London in 1844 for the purpose of converting young men to Christian values.[13] Recreational group activities and socialization activities were a large part of the early YMCA's programs. In 1851 YMCAs were founded in this country, in Baltimore and Boston. The Young Women's Christian Association began in Boston in 1866.[14]

Settlement houses, which were established in many large cities of this country in the late 1800s, are largely credited for providing the roots of social group work.[15] Settlement houses sought to use the power of group associations to educate, reform, and organize neighborhoods; to preserve religious and cultural identities; and to give emotional support and assistance to newcomers both from the farm and from abroad.

Today almost every social service agency provides one or more of the following types of groups: recreation-skill, education, socialization, and therapy. Most undergraduate and graduate social work programs offer practice courses to train students to lead groups, particularly socialization and therapy groups. There is a national social work organization, the Association for the Advancement of Social Work with Groups, that holds a yearly symposium and publishes a journal.

The following summary describes a variety of groups in social work: social conversation, recreation, recreation-skill, education, task, problem-solving and decision-making, self-help, socialization, therapy, and sensitivity.

SOCIAL CONVERSATION GROUPS

Conversation is often loose and tends to drift aimlessly. There is no formal agenda. If one topic is dull, the subject is likely to change. Individuals may have some goal (perhaps only to establish an acquaintanceship), but such individual goals may not become the agenda for the entire group. Social conversation is often used for ''testing'' purposes—for example, to determine how deep a re-

Group social work grew out of informal recreational organizations such as 4-H Clubs.

lationship might develop with people we do not know very well. In social work, social conversation with other professionals is frequent, but groups involving clients generally have objectives other than conversation.

RECREATION GROUPS

The objective in this instance is to provide activities for enjoyment and exercise. Often such activities are spontaneous and the groups are practically leaderless. The group service agency (such as YMCA, YWCA, or neighborhood center) may offer little more than physical space and the use of some equipment. Spontaneous playground activities, informal athletic games, and an open game rooms are examples. Some group agencies that provide such physical space claim that recreation and interaction with others help to build "character" and to prevent delinquency among youths by offering an alternative to the street.

RECREATION-SKILL GROUPS

The objective of these groups is to improve a set of skills while at the same time providing enjoyment. In contrast to recreational groups, an adviser, coach, or instructor is generally present and there is more of a task orientation. Examples of activities include golf, basketball, needlework, arts or crafts, and swimming. Competitive team sports and leagues may emerge. Frequently such

groups are led by professionals with recreational training rather than social work training. Social service agencies that provide such services include the YMCA, YWCA, Boy Scouts, Girl Scouts, neighborhood centers, and school recreational departments.

EDUCATION GROUPS

The focus of such groups is for members to acquire knowledge and learn more complex skills. The leader generally is a professional person with considerable training and expertise in the topic area. Examples of topics include child-rearing practices, parent training, preparation for adoption and volunteer training for specialized tasks in a social service agency. These groups may resemble a class, with considerable group interaction and discussion being encouraged.

TASK GROUPS

Task groups exist to achieve a specific set of tasks or objectives. The following are just a few examples of task groups that social workers are likely to interact with or become involved in. A *board of directors* is an administrative group charged with responsibility for setting the policy governing agency programs. A *task force* is a group established for a special purpose; it is usually disbanded after the task is completed. A *committee* of an agency or organization is a group that is formed to deal with specific tasks or matters. An *ad hoc committee*, like a task force, is set up for one purpose and usually ceases functioning after completion of its task.

PROBLEM-SOLVING AND DECISION-MAKING GROUPS

Both providers and consumers of social services may become involved in problem-solving and decision-making groups. (There is considerable overlap between task groups and this category; in fact, problem-solving and decision-making groups could be viewed as a subcategory of task groups.) Providers of services use group meetings for such objectives as developing a treatment plan for a client or a group of clients, deciding how best to allocate scarce resources, deciding how to improve the delivery of services to clients, arriving at policy decisions for the agency, deciding how to improve coordination efforts with other agencies, and so on.

Potential consumers of services may form a group to meet some current community need. Data on the need may be gathered, and the group may be used as a vehicle either to develop a program or to influence existing agencies to provide services. Social workers may function as stimulators and organizers of such group efforts.

In problem-solving and decision-making groups, each participant often has some interest or stake in the process and stands to gain or lose personally by the outcome. Usually there is a formal leader of some sort, and other leaders sometimes emerge during the process.

SELF-HELP GROUPS

Self-help groups are becoming increasingly popular and are often successful in helping individuals with certain social or personal problems. Alfred Katz and Eugene Bender provide a comprehensive definition of self-help groups:

> *Self-help groups are voluntary, small group structures for mutual aid, and the accomplishment of a special purpose. They are usually formed by peers who have come together for mutual assistance in satisfying a common need, overcoming a common handicap or life-*

> *disrupting problem, and bringing about desired social, and/or personal change. The initiators and members of such groups perceive that their needs are not, or cannot be, met by or through existing social institutions. Self-help groups emphasize face-to-face social interactions and the assumption of personal responsibility by members. They often provide material assistance, as well as emotional support. They are frequently "cause"-oriented, and promulgate an ideology or values through which members may attain an enhanced sense of personal identity.*[16]

Alcoholics Anonymous, developed by two former alcoholics, was the first self-help group to demonstrate substantial success. A number of other such groups have since been formed. In a text entitled *Help: A Working Guide to Self-Help Groups,* Alan Gartner and Frank Riessman describe over 200 self-help groups that are now active,[17] some of which are listed in Exhibit 17.1.

Many self-help groups stress (1) a confession to the group by every member that she or he has a problem, (2) a testimony to the group recounting past experiences with the problem and plans for handling it in the future, and (3) phone calls to another member whenever one feels a crisis (for example, an abusive parent having an urge to abuse a child); the person who is called stays with the member until the crisis subsides.

There appear to be several reasons why self-help groups are successful. All members have an internal understanding of the problem, which helps them to help others. Having experienced the misery and consequences of the problem, they are highly motivated and dedicated to find ways to help themselves and others who are fellow sufferers. The participants also benefit from the "helper therapy principle"—that is, the helper also gains psychological rewards.[18] Helping others leads the helper to feel "good" and worthwhile and also to put his or her own problems into perspective by seeing that others have problems that may be as serious, or even more serious.

Some self-help groups, such as the National Organization for Women, focus on social advocacy and attempt to make legislative and policy changes in public and private institutions. Some

EXHIBIT 17.1

Self-Help Groups

Organization	Service Focus
Abused Women's Aid in Crisis	For battered wives and other abused women
Adoptee's Liberty Movement Association	For adoptees searching for their natural parents
Alcoholics Anonymous	For adult alcoholics
American Diabetes Association	Clubs for diabetics, their families, and friends
Brain Tumor Support Group	For people with brain tumors or their loved ones
Burns Recovered	For burn victims
Caesarian Birth Association	For those expecting a cesarian delivery
Candlelighters	For parents of young children with cancer
Checks Anonymous	For people in debt
Concerned United Birthparents	For parents who have surrendered children for adoption
Depressives Anonymous	For depressed people
Divorce Anonymous	For divorced people
Emotions Anonymous	For people with emotional problems
Emphysema Anonymous	For those with emphysema
Fly without Fear	For people who are afraid of flying
Fortune Society	For ex-offenders and their families
Gam-Anon	For families of gamblers
Gray Panthers	An intergenerational group
Make Today Count	For people with cancer and their families
Mensa	For people of high IQs
Naim Conference	For widowed people
National Council of Stutterers	For adult stutterers
National Organization for Women	For advocates of equal rights for women
Overeaters Anonymous	For compulsive overeaters
Parents Anonymous	For parents of abused children
Phobia Self-Help Groups	For people with phobias
Prison Families Anonymous	For family members of prisoners
Resolve	A support group for infertile people
Stroke Clubs	For those who have had strokes and their families
Survivors of Suicide Victims	For the relatives and friends of suicide victims
We Care	Support group for divorced and separated people

A senior citizens' dance illustrates socialization, a primary focus of group work. Motivating the elderly to become more socially active requires a special skill for using groups to foster individual growth.

groups (such as associations of parents of children with a cognitive disability) raise funds and operate community programs. Many people with a personal problem use self-help groups in the same way that others use social agencies. An additional advantage of self-help groups is that they are generally able to operate with a minimal budget.

SOCIALIZATION GROUPS

The objective of such groups generally is to make members' attitudes and behaviors more socially acceptable. Developing social skills, increasing self-confidence, and planning for the future are other focuses. Leaders of such groups might work with predelinquent youths in group activities to curb delinquency, work with youths of diverse ethnic backgrounds to reduce racial tensions,

work with "at-risk" young children in an elementary school to improve their interpersonal and problem-solving skills and to motivate them to succeed in the school setting, work with elderly residents at a nursing home to remotivate them and get them involved in various activities, or work with boys at a correctional school to help them make plans for returning to their home community. Leadership of such groups requires considerable skill and knowledge in using the group to foster individual growth and change. Socialization groups are frequently led by social workers.

THERAPY GROUPS

Therapy groups are generally composed of members with rather severe emotional or personal problems. Leaders must be highly skilled; they

EXHIBIT 17.2

A Socialization Group at a Shelter for Runaways

New Horizons is a private, temporary shelter facility for runaways in a large midwestern city. It is located in a large house that was built 84 years ago. Youths on the run can stay for up to two weeks. State law requires that parents be contacted and parental permission received for New Horizons to provide shelter overnight. Services offered include temporary shelter care, individual and family counseling, and a 24-hour hotline for youths in crisis. The facility is licensed to house up to eight youths. Because the average stay is nine days, the population is continually changing. Intensive counseling is provided for the youths (and often their parents), focusing on reducing family conflicts and on making future living plans. The 14-day limit helps to convey to youths and their families, beginning with day one, that they must work to resolve the reasons for leaving home.

Every evening at 7 P.M. a group meeting is held. All the residents and the two or three staff members on duty are expected to attend. The meetings are convened and led by the staff. This meeting has four main objectives. One is providing a vehicle for residents to express their satisfactions and dissatisfactions with the facilities and program at New Horizons. Sometimes the meeting appears to be primarily a "gripe" session, but the staff members make conscientious efforts to improve those aspects in which the youths' concerns are legitimate. For example, a youth may indicate that the past few days have been "boring," and staff and residents then jointly plan activities for the next few days.

A second objective is to deal with interaction problems that arise between residents or between staff and residents. One resident may be preventing others from sleeping; some youths may refuse to do their "fair share" of domestic tasks; there may be squabbles about which TV program to watch; some residents maybe overly aggressive. Because most of the youths face a variety of crises associated with being on the run, many tend to be anxious and under stress. In such an emotional climate, interaction problems are likely to arise. Staff are sometimes intensely questioned about their actions, decisions, and policies. For example, one policy at New Horizons is that each resident must agree not to use alcohol or illegal drugs while staying at the shelter, with the penalty being expulsion. Occasionally a few youths use some drugs and are caught and expelled. Removing a resident from this facility has an immense impact on the others, and at the following group meetings staff are expected to clarify and explain such decisions.

A third objective is for staff to present material on topics requested by residents. Examples of topics include sex, drugs, homosexuality, physical and sexual abuse (a fair number of residents are abused by family members), ways to avoid being raped, ways to deal with depression and other unwanted emotions, sexually transmitted diseases, legal rights of youths on the run, assertiveness training, ways to make relatives and friends understand why they ran away, and availability of other human services in the community. During such presentations, discussion with residents is encouraged and generally occurs.

The final objective of these group meetings is to convey information about planned daily activities and changes in the overall program at New Horizons.

Example of a Therapy Group

Several years ago, when I was employed as a social worker at a maximum-security hospital for the criminally insane, my supervisor requested that I develop and lead a therapy group. When I asked such questions as "What should the group's objectives be?" and "Who should be selected to join?" my supervisor indicated that those decisions would be mine. No one else was doing any group therapy at this hospital, and the hospital administration thought it would be desirable, for accountability reasons, for group therapy programs to be developed.

Being newly employed at the hospital and wary because I had never led a group before, I asked myself "Who is in the greatest need of group therapy?" and "If the group members do not improve, or even deteriorate, how will I be able to explain this—that is, cover my tracks?" I concluded that I should select those persons identified as being the "sickest" (those labeled as chronic schizophrenics) for the group. Chronic schizophrenics are generally expected to show little improvement. Thus, if they did not improve, I felt I would not be blamed. However, if they did improve, I thought their progress would be viewed as a substantial accomplishment.

My next step was to invite those persons to join the group. I met with each individually and explained the purpose of the group and the probable topics that would be covered. Eight of the 11 I contacted decided to join. Some of the eight stated frankly that they were joining primarily because it would look good on their record and increase their chances for an early release. The approach I used with the group members was based on reality therapy,[a] as described in the following material.

At the first meeting I again presented and described the purpose and the focus of the group. The purpose was not to review the members' past but to help them make their present life more enjoyable and meaningful and to help them to make plans for the future. Topics to be covered included how to convince the hospital staff they no longer needed to be hospitalized, how to prepare themselves for returning to their home community (for example, learning an employable skill while at the institution), what to do when they felt depressed or had some other unwanted emotion, and what actions they should take following their release if they had an urge to do something that would get them into trouble again. I further explained that occasional films covering some of these topics would be shown and then discussed, and I indicated that the group would meet for about an hour each week for the next 12 weeks (until the fall, when I had to return to school).

This focus on improving their current circumstances stimulated their interest, but soon they found it uncomfortable and anxiety producing to examine what the future might hold for them. Being informed that they had some responsibility and some control of that future also created anxiety. Their reaction to this discomfort was to state that, because they were labeled mentally ill, they therefore had an internal condition that was causing their strange behavior. Because they were aware that a cure for schizophrenia had not yet been found, they concluded that they could do little to improve their situation.

The members were told their excuses were "garbage" (stronger terms were used), and we spent a few sessions on getting them to understand that the label "chronic schizophrenic" was meaningless. I spent considerable time explaining (as discussed in Chapter 4) that mental illness is a myth; that is, people do not have a "disease of the mind," even though they may have emotional problems. I went on to explain that what had gotten them locked up was their deviant behavior, and the only way for them to get out was to stop exhibiting their strange behavior and to convince the other staff that they would not exhibit deviant behavior if released. I added that they held the key for getting released—that key was simply to act "sane."

The next set of excuses they tried held that their broken homes, or ghetto schools, or broken romances, or something else in their past had "messed them up" and therefore they could do little about their situation. They were told that such excuses were also "garbage." True, their past experiences were relevant to their being in the hospital. But it was emphasized that what they wanted out of the future, along with their motivation to do something about achieving their goals, was more important than their past experiences in determining what their future would be like.

Finally, after we had worked through a number of excuses, we were able to focus on how they could better handle specific problems: how to handle being depressed, how to stop exhibiting behavior considered "strange," how to present themselves as "sane" to increase their chances of an early release, how they would adjust to returning to their home communities, what kind of work or career they desired on their release, how they could prepare themselves by learning a skill or trade while at this institution, how to examine what they wanted in the future and determine the specific steps they would have to take to achieve their goals, why it was important to continue to take the psychoactive medication that had been prescribed, and so on.

The results of this approach were very encouraging. Instead of idly spending much of the time brooding about their situation, they became motivated to improve their lives. At the end of the 12 weeks the eight members of the group spontaneously stated that the meetings were achieving positive change in their lives. They requested that another social worker from the hospital be assigned to continue the group after my return to college. This was arranged. Three years later, on a return visit to the hospital, I was informed that five of the eight group members had been released to their home communities. Two of the others were considered to have shown improvement. The final group member's condition was described as "unchanged."

[a]William Glasser, *Reality Therapy* (New York: Harper & Row, 1965).

need to be perceptive, to understand human behavior and group dynamics, to have group counseling capacities, and to be able to use the group to bring about behavioral changes, to be aware at all times of how each member is being affected by what is happening, and to develop and maintain a constructive atmosphere within the group. As with one-to-one counseling, the goal of therapy groups is generally to have members explore their problems in depth and then develop one or more strategies for resolving them. The group therapist generally uses one or more of the following psychotherapy approaches as a guide for changing attitudes and behaviors: Gestalt therapy, reality therapy, learning theory, rational therapy, transactional analysis, client-centered therapy, and psychodrama.

Group therapy is being widely used in counseling. It has several advantages over one-to-one therapy. The helper therapy principle generally is operative; members interchange roles and sometimes become the "helper" for someone else's problems. Helping others provides psychological rewards. Groups also help members to put their problems into perspective by realizing that others have problems as serious as their own. Groups help members who are having interaction problems to test out new patterns of interacting. Research has shown that it is generally easier to change an individual's attitude in a group than individually.[19] Group pressure can have a substantial effect on changing attitudes and beliefs.[20] Furthermore, group therapy permits the social worker to treat more than one person at a time and thus maximizes the use of professional staff.

In essence, a group therapist uses the principles of one-to-one counseling (discussed in Chapter 4) and of group dynamics to work with clients to change dysfunctional attitudes and behavior. Often the traditional comprehensive psychotherapy approaches are combined with certain specialized treatment techniques (such as parent effectiveness training and assertiveness training) to help clients resolve personal and emotional problems. The selection of which treatment techniques to use is based on the nature of the problems.

SENSITIVITY GROUPS

Encounter groups, sensitivity training, and T (training)-groups (these terms are used somewhat synonymously) refer to group experiences in which people relate to one another in an intimate manner and self-disclosure is required. The goal is to improve interpersonal awareness. An encounter group may meet for a few hours or for a few days.

The goal of sensitivity groups provides an interesting contrast to those of therapy groups (see Exhibit 17.3). In therapy the goal is to have each member explore personal or emotional problems in depth and then develop a strategy to resolve them. In comparison, sensitivity groups seek to increase their personal and interpersonal awareness and then develop more effective interaction patterns. Sensitivity groups generally do not directly attempt to identify or change specific emotional or personal problems that people have (such as drinking problems, feelings of depression, sexual dysfunctions, and so on). The philosophy behind sensitivity groups is that, with increased personal and interpersonal awareness, people will be better able to avoid, cope with, and/or handle specific personal problems that arise.

Sensitivity groups are being used in our society for a wide variety of purposes: to train professional counselors to be more perceptive and effective in interpersonal interactions with clients and with other professionals, to train people in management positions to be more effective in their business interactions, to help clients with overt relationship problems to become more aware of how they affect others and to develop more effective interaction patterns, and to train interested citizens in becoming more aware and effective in their interactions.

Although encounter, marathon, and sensitivity groups are popular and have received considerable publicity, they remain controversial. In some cases, inadequately trained and incompetent individuals have become self-proclaimed leaders and have enticed people to join through sensational advertising. If mishandled, sensitivity groups can intensify personal problems. Many au-

EXHIBIT 17.3

Contrasting Goals of Therapy versus Sensitivity Groups

Therapy Groups	Sensitivity Groups
Step 1 Examine problem(s) in depth	**Step 1** Help each person become more aware of himself or herself and how he or she affects others in interpersonal interactions
Step 2 Explore and then select (from various resolution approaches) a strategy to resolve the problem	**Step 2** Help a person to then develop more effective interaction patterns

thorities on sensitivity training disclaim the use of encounter groups as a form of psychotherapy and discourage people with serious personal problems from joining such a group.

SOCIAL WORK WITH ORGANIZATIONS

An organization is a collectivity of individuals gathered together to serve a particular purpose. The types of purposes (or goals) that people organize themselves to achieve are infinite in number and can range from obtaining basic necessities to attaining world peace. Organizations exist because people working together can accomplish tasks and achieve goals that cannot be achieved as well (or even at all) by an individual.

The importance of organizations in our lives is described by Etzioni:

> We are born in organizations, educated by organizations, and most of us spend much of our lives working for organizations. We spend much of our leisure time paying, playing, and praying in organizations. Most of us will die in an organization, and when the time comes for burial, the largest organization of all—the state—must grant official permission.[21]

Netting, Kettner, and McMurtry have summarized the importance of organizations for social work practice:

> As social workers, our roles within, interactions with, and attempts to manipulate organizations define much of what we do. Clients often come to us seeking help because they are not able to obtain help from organizations that are critical to their survival or quality of life. In turn, the resources we attempt to gain for these clients usually come from still other organizations: . . . Social workers with little or no idea of how organizations operate, how they interact, or how they can be influenced and changed from both outside and inside are likely to be severely limited in their effectiveness.[22]

Many disciplines (including business, psychology, political science, and sociology) have generated a prodigious amount of theory and research on organizations. However, in spite of the importance of organizations to social work practice, the amount of social work literature devoted to this topic is limited. One significant reference in this area is *Social Work Macro Practice*, by Netting, Kettner, and McMurtry.[23]

Earlier in this chapter, in the section entitled "The Change Process," we saw an example of the processes a social worker used to achieve organizational change. That section described how a new educational component on alcohol and other drug abuse was added to the curriculum in a school district in a midwestern state. The remainder of this section will present material on how social workers can survive and thrive in bureaucratic systems. A bureaucracy is a type of organization or a subcategory of an organization. Distinctive characteristics of a bureaucracy include a vertical hierarchy with power centered at the top; a task-specific division of labor; clearly defined rules; formalized channels of communication; and selection, compensation, promotion,

EXHIBIT 17.4

Analyzing a Human Services Organization

It is essential that a social worker understand and analyze not only the agency/organization that she or he works for but also the other agencies and organizations that she or he interacts with. Some questions that are useful in analyzing an agency or organization are the following:

1. What is the mission statement of the organization?

2. What are the major problems of the organization's clients?

3. What services are provided by the organization?

4. How are client needs determined?

5. What percentage of clients are people of color, women, gays or lesbians, elderly, or members of other at-risk populations?

6. What was the total cost of services of this organization in the past year?

7. How much money is spent on each program?

8. What are the organization's funding sources?

9. How much and what percentage of funds are received from each source?

10. What types of clients does the organization refuse?

11. What other organizations provide the same services in the community?

12. What is the organizational structure? For example, does the organization have a formal chain of command?

13. Is there an informal decision-making process and structure at the organization? (That is, are there people who are quite influential and thus exert more influence than would be expected for their formal positions in the bureaucracy of the organization?)

14. How much input do the direct service providers at the organization have on major policy decisions?

15. Does the organization have a board that oversees its operations? If so, what are the backgrounds of the board members?

16. Do employees at every level feel valued?

17. What is the morale among employees?

18. What are the major unmet needs of the organization?

19. Does the organization have a handbook of personnel policies and procedures?

20. What is the public image of the organization in the community?

21. What has been the rate of turnover in recent years among the staff at the organization? What were departing staff members' major reasons for leaving?

22. Does the organization have a process for evaluating the outcomes of its services? If so, what is the process, and what are the outcome results?

---

and retention of personnel based on technical competence.

There are basic structural conflicts between helping professionals and the bureaucratic systems in which they work. Helping professionals place a high value on creativity and change. Bu-

reaucracies resist change and are most efficient when no one is "rocking the boat." Helping professionals seek to personalize services by conveying to each client "You count as a person." Bureaucracies are highly depersonalized, emotionally detached systems that view every em-

EXHIBIT 17.5

Value Conflicts between a Helping Professional and Bureaucracies

Orientations of a Helping Professional	Orientations of Bureaucratic Systems
Desires democratic system for decision making.	Most decisions are made autocratically.
Desires that power be distributed equally among employees (horizontal structure).	Power is distributed vertically.
Desires that clients have considerable power in the system.	Power is held primarily by top executives.
Desires a flexible, changing system.	System is rigid and stable.
Desires that creativity and growth be emphasized.	Emphasis is on structure and the status quo.
Desires that focus be client oriented.	System is organization centered.
Desires that communication be on a personalized level from person to person.	Communication is from level to level.
Desires shared decision making and shared responsibility structure.	A hierarchical decision-making structure and hierarchical responsibility structure are characteristic.
Desires that decisions be made by those having the most knowledge.	Decisions are made in terms of the decision-making authority assigned to each position in the hierarchy.
Desires shared leadership.	System uses autocratic leadership.
Believes feelings of clients and employees should be highly valued by the system.	Procedures and processes are highly valued.

ployee and every client as being a tiny component of a large system. In a large bureaucracy employees *don't* count as "persons"—only as functional parts of a system. Exhibit 17.5 lists additional conflicting value orientations between a helping professional and bureaucratic systems.

Any of these differences in value orientations can become an arena for conflict between helping professionals and the bureaucracies in which they work. Knopf has concisely summarized the potential areas of conflict:

> The trademarks of a BS (bureaucratic system) are power, hierarchy, and specialization; that is, rules and roles. In essence, the result is depersonalization. The system itself is neither "good" nor "bad"; it is a system. I believe it to be amoral. It is efficient and effective, but in order to be so it must be impersonal in all of its functionings. This then is the location of the

> stress. The hallmark of the helping professional is a highly individualized, democratic, humanized, relationship-oriented service aimed at self-motivation. The hallmark of a bureaucratic system is a highly impersonalized, valueless (amoral), emotionally detached, hierarchical structure of organization. The dilemma of the HP (helping person) is how to give a personalized service to a client through a delivery system that is not set up in any way to do that.[24]

Many helping professionals respond to these orientation conflicts by erroneously projecting a "personality" onto the bureaucracy. They describe it using expressions like "red tape," "officialism," "uncaring," "cruel," "the enemy." Officials of the bureaucracy may be viewed as "paper shufflers," "rigid," "deadwood," "inefficient," and "unproductive." Knopf states:

The HP (helping person) . . . may deal with the impersonal nature of the system by projecting values onto it and thereby give the BS (bureaucratic system) a "personality." In this way, we fool ourselves into thinking that we can deal with it in a personal way. Unfortunately, projection is almost always negative and reflects the dark or negative aspects of ourselves. The BS then becomes a screen onto which we vent our anger, sadness, or fright, and while a lot of energy is generated, very little is accomplished. Since the BS is amoral, it is unproductive to place a personality on it.[25]

A bureaucratic system is neither good nor bad. It has neither a personality nor a value system of its own. It is simply a structure developed to carry out various tasks.

A helping person may experience various emotional reactions to conflicts with bureaucratic systems.* Common reactions are anger at the system, self-blame ("It's all my fault"), sadness and depression ("Poor me"; "Nobody appreciates all I've done"), and fright and paranoia ("They're out to get me"; "If I mess up I'm gone").

Knopf has identified several types of behavior patterns that helping professionals choose in dealing with bureaucracies.[26]

The *warrior* leads open campaigns to destroy and malign the system. A warrior discounts the value of the system and often enters into a win/lose conflict. She or he generally loses and is dismissed.

The *gossip* is a covert warrior who complains to others (including clients, politicians, and the news media) about how terrible the system is. A gossip frequently singles out a few officials to focus criticism upon. Bureaucratic systems often make life very difficult for the gossip by assign-

ing distasteful tasks, refusing to promote, giving very low salary increases, and perhaps even dismissing.

The *complainer* resembles a gossip but confines complaints to other helping persons, to in-house staff, and to family members. A complainer wants people to agree in order to find comfort in shared misery. Complainers want to stay with the system, and generally do.

The *dancer* is skillful at ignoring rules and procedures. Dancers frequently are lonely. They are often reprimanded for incorrectly filling out forms, and they have low investment in the system or in helping clients.

The *defender* is timid, dislikes conflict, and therefore defends the rules, the system, and bureaucratic officials. Defenders often are supervisors and are viewed by others as being "bureaucrats."

The *machine* is a "bureaucrat" who takes on the orientation of the bureaucracy. Often a machine has not been involved in providing direct services for years. Machines are frequently named to head study committees and policy groups and to chair boards.

The *executioner* attacks persons within an organization with enthusiasm and vigor. An executioner usually has a high energy level and is impulsive. He or she abuses power by indiscriminately attacking and dismissing not only employees but also services and programs. Executioners have power and are angry (although the anger is disguised/denied). They are committed neither to the value orientation of helping professionals nor to the bureaucracy.

Knopf has listed 66 tips on how to survive in a bureaucracy.[27] Some of the most useful suggestions are summarized here:

1. Whenever your needs, or the needs of your clients, are not met by the bureaucracy, use the following problem-solving approach:
   (a) Precisely identify which of your needs (or the needs of clients) are in conflict with the bureaucracy; this step is defining the problem.
   (b) Generate a list of possible solutions. Be creative in generating a wide range of ideas.
   (c) Evaluate the merits and shortcomings of

---

*This description highlights a number of the negatives about bureaucratic systems, particularly their impersonalization. In fairness, it should be noted that an advantage of being part of a large bureaucracy is that the potential is there for changing a powerful system to the advantage of clients. In tiny or nonbureaucratic systems the social worker may have lots of freedom but little opportunity or power to influence large systems or mobilize extensive resources on behalf of clients.

the possible solutions. (d) Select a solution. (e) Implement the solution. (f) Evaluate the solution.

2. Learn how your bureaucracy is structured and how it functions. Such knowledge will reduce fear of the unknown, make the system more predictable, and help in identifying rational ways to best meet your needs and those of your clients.

3. Remember that bureaucrats are people, too, and have feelings. Communication gaps are often most effectively reduced if you treat them with as much respect and interest as you treat clients.

4. If you are at war with the bureaucracy, declare a truce. The system will find a way to dismiss you if you remain at war. With a truce, you can identify and use the strengths of the bureaucracy as an ally, rather than having the strengths being used against you as an enemy.

5. Know your work contract and job expectations. If the expectations are unclear, seek clarity.

6. Continue to develop your knowledge and awareness of specific helping skills. Take advantage of continuing-education opportunities (workshops, conferences, courses). Among other advantages, your continued professional development will assist you in being able to contract from a position of competency and skill.

7. Seek to identify your professional strengths and limitations. Knowing your limitations will increase your ability to avoid undertaking responsibilities that are beyond your competencies.

8. Be aware that you can't change everything, so stop trying. In a bureaucracy, focus your change efforts on those aspects that most need change and that you also have a fair chance of changing. Stop thinking and complaining about those aspects you cannot change. It is irrational to complain about things that you cannot change or to complain about those things that you do not intend to make an effort to change.

9. Learn how to control your emotions in your interactions with the bureaucracy. Emotions that are counterproductive (such as most angry outbursts) particularly need to be controlled. Doing a rational self-analysis on your unwanted emotions (see Chapter 4) is one way of gaining control of them. Learning how to respond to stress in your personal life will also prepare you to handle stress better at work.

10. Develop and use a sense of humor. Humor takes the edge off adverse conditions and reduces negative feelings.

11. Learn to accept your mistakes and perhaps even laugh at some of them. No one is perfect.

12. Take time to enjoy and develop a support system with your coworkers.

13. Acknowledge your mistakes, and give in sometimes on minor matters. You may not be right, and giving in allows other people to do the same.

14. Keep yourself physically fit and mentally alert. Learn to use approaches that will reduce stress and prevent burnout. (See Chapter 14 for a description of approaches to reduce stress.)

15. Leave your work at the office. If you have urgent unfinished bureaucratic business, do it before leaving work.

16. Occasionally take your supervisor and other administrators to lunch. Socializing prevents isolation and facilitates your involvement with and understanding of the system.

17. Do not seek self-actualization or ego satisfaction from the bureaucracy. A depersonalized system is incapable of providing these rewards; you must achieve them on your own.

18. In speeches to community groups, accentuate the positives about your agency. Ask after speeches that a thank-you letter be sent to your supervisor or agency director.

19. If you have a problem with the bureaucracy, discuss it with other employees, with the focus being on problem solving rather than on complaining. Groups are much more powerful

and productive than an individual working alone for making changes in a system.

20. No matter how high you rise in a hierarchy, maintain direct service contact. Direct contact keeps you abreast of changing client needs, prevents you from getting stale, and keeps you attuned to the concerns of employees in lower levels of the hierarchy.

21. Do not try to change everything in the system at once. Attacking too much will overextend you and lead to burnout. Start small, and be selective and specific. Double-check your facts to make certain they accurately prove your position before you confront bureaucratic officials.

22. Identify your career goals, and determine whether they can be met within this system. If the answer is no, than (a) change your goals, (b) change the bureaucracy, or (c) seek a position elsewhere in which your goals can be met.

SOCIAL WORK WITH THE COMMUNITY

Most social work students do not consider a career in community practice; they feel that they would rather work directly with people. Many believe that community practice involves skills and techniques that are too complex and too abstract for them to learn. Also, they perceive community practice as having too few rewards and as involving a lot of boring, unenjoyable work. All of these beliefs are erroneous. The realities are that (1) the most basic skill needed in community practice is the ability to work effectively with people; (2) community practice primarily involves working with individuals and with groups; (3) every practicing social worker occasionally becomes involved in community practice projects; (4) seeing a community project developed, approved, and implemented is immensely gratifying; and (5) community practice efforts are often fun.

Workers in direct practice with individuals or groups are likely to become involved in community development activities when gaps in services or unmet needs are identified for clients they are working with. For example, if there is a rapid increase in teenage pregnancy in a community, a school social worker may become involved in efforts to establish a sex education program in the school system. If there are a number of terminally ill patients and their families are complaining about the way they are treated in a hospital, a medical social worker may become involved in efforts to establish a hospice. If a juvenile probation officer notes a sharp increase in juvenile offenses, the officer may become involved in efforts to have young offenders visit a prison and hear from inmates what prison life is like (as depicted in "Scared Straight" programs).

Workers involved in developing needed new services are aware of the human benefits that will result. These payoffs, and the time and effort workers put into community practice projects, often lead them to become highly "ego involved." Success in establishing new services is experienced as a deeply gratifying political victory. On a negative note, a reality is that the development of new services generally involves a number of unanticipated obstacles and requires several times as much time and effort as initially anticipated.

As yet, there is no widely accepted definition of the term *community practice*. The modes of practice performed under this heading have a variety of labels: social planning, community planning, locality development, community action, social action, macropractice, community organization, and community development.

Community practice will be defined here as the process of stimulating and assisting the local community to evaluate, plan, and coordinate its efforts to provide for the community's health, welfare, and recreation needs. In community practice a worker's activities include encouraging and stimulating citizen organization around one or more issues, specifying the nature of the problem, coordinating efforts among concerned groups, fact-finding, formulating realizable goals, becoming involved in public relations and public education, conducting research, planning, identi-

The philosophy of the Peace Corps—that community change is best brought about through the participation of a cross section of people at a local level—has made it a model for many other community development efforts. Here volunteers examine plans for a spillway and reservoir in Thailand.

fying financial resources, developing strategies to achieve a goal, and being a resource person. Agency settings that employ community practice workers include community welfare councils, the United Way, social planning agencies, health planning councils, neighborhood councils, city planning councils, community action groups, and occasionally some other private or public organization.

Community practice workers become involved in a wide variety of social issues, including civil rights, welfare reform, the needs of poor people, education and health issues, housing, improvement of leisure-time services, race relations, minority-group employment, development of services to counteract alienation of youth, urban redevelopment programs, development of services for teenage runaways and drug users, and devel-

opment of services for people who are HIV positive or have AIDS.

A number of other disciplines besides social work provide training in community practice. These include community psychology, urban and regional planning, health planning, corrections planning, recreation, and public administration.

In recent years American citizens have organized around a number of issues. Some that have received national attention include labor/management disputes, women's rights issues, problems of farmers, the abortion question, capital punishment, rights for homosexuals, tax cuts, school closings in many cities, the national defense budget, nuclear energy, decriminalization of marijuana, massage parlors, nude dancing, affirmative action guidelines on hiring, and environmental concerns.

CASE
EXAMPLE 17.2   Case Example of the Locality Development Model

R obert McKearn, a social worker for a juvenile probation department, noticed in
1985 that an increasing number of school-age children were being referred to
his office by the police department, school system, and parents from a small city of
11,000 people in the county served by his agency. The charges included status offenses (such as truancy) and delinquent offenses (such as shoplifting and burglary).
He noted that most of these children were from single-parent families.

Mr. McKearn contacted the community mental health center, the self-help organization Parents Without Partners, the pupil services department of the public school
system, the county social services department, some members of the clergy, and the
community mental health center in the area. Nearly everyone he talked with saw an
emerging need to better serve children in single-parent families. The pupil services
department mentioned that these children were performing less well academically in
school and tended to display more serious disciplinary problems.

Mr. McKearn arranged a meeting of representatives from all the groups and organizations that had been contacted. At the initial meeting a number of concerns were
expressed about the problematic behaviors being displayed by children who had
single parents. The school system considered these children to be "at risk" for high
rates of truancy, dropping out of school, delinquent activities, suicide, emotional
problems, and unwanted pregnancies. Although a number of problems were identified, no one at this initial meeting was able to suggest a viable strategy to better serve

A Brief History of
Community Practice

For centuries people have organized to change social and political conditions. In the 1700s, for example, Americans organized to revolt against the
British and fought what has come to be called the
Revolutionary War.

Community practice in social work began in
the 1800s with the charity organization movement and the settlement house movement.[28]

In the 19th century, private philanthropy bore
the major responsibility for the relief of poverty in
the United States. During the early 1800s a wide
range of private health and welfare agencies were
established to provide funds and services (generally combined with religious conversion efforts)
to those in need. To avoid duplication of services

to the same families, the Charity Organization Society was formed to *coordinate* efforts and to *plan*
for meeting unmet needs.

Reformers associated with the settlement
house movement based many of their programs
on *social action* to promote legislation for providing needed services to neighborhoods. These reformers also encouraged neighborhood residents
to work together to improve living conditions.

Community welfare councils were first organized in 1908.[29] Continuing the efforts begun by
the charity organization movement, these councils served as coordinating organizations for voluntary agencies. The functions of these councils
have continued to the present time and include
planning, coordinating, avoiding duplication of
services, setting standards for services, and improving efficiency and accountability.

single parents and their children. The community was undergoing an economic recession; therefore, funds were unavailable for an expensive new program.

Three more meetings were held. At the first two, several suggestions for providing services were discussed, but all were viewed as either too expensive or impractical. At the fourth meeting of the group, a single mother representing Parents Without Partners mentioned that Big Brothers and Big Sisters programs in some communities reportedly were of substantial benefit to children raised in single-parent families. This idea seemed to energize the group, and suggestions began to "piggyback." However, members determined that no funds were available to hire staff to run a Big Brothers and Big Sisters program. Then, Rhona Quinn, a social worker in the public services department, offered to identify at-risk younger children in single-parent families and to supervise qualified volunteers in a Big Buddy program.

Mr. McKearn mentioned that he was currently supervising a student in an undergraduate field placement from an accredited social work program in a nearby college. He suggested that perhaps undergraduate social work students could be recruited to be Big Buddies to fulfill their required volunteer experience. Rhona Quinn said she would approve the suggestion if she could have the freedom to screen interested applicants. Arrangements were made over the next two months for social work students to be Big Buddies for at-risk younger children from single-parent families. After a two-year experimental period, the school system found the program to be sufficiently successful that it assigned Ms. Quinn to supervise it half-time. Her duties included selecting at-risk children, screening volunteer applicants, matching children with Big Buddies, monitoring the progress of each matched pair, and conducting follow-up to ascertain the outcome of each pairing.

Community Chests (now called United Way) were formed around 1920 to serve as centralized campaigns for raising funds for voluntary agencies.[30] In many communities United Way has been combined with community welfare councils for fund raising and for the allocation of funds to voluntary agencies.

All social welfare agencies and organizations become involved at times in community practice efforts.

Models of Community Practice

A variety of approaches have been developed to bring about community change. In reviewing these approaches, Jack Rothman and John Trop-man categorized them into three models: locality development, social planning, and social action.[31] It should be noted that these models are "ideal types." Actual approaches to community change tend to blend characteristics of all three models. Advocates of the social planning model, for example, may at times use community change techniques (such as extensive discussion and participation by a variety of groups) that are characteristic of the other two models. For analytical purposes, however, we'll view the three models as being "pure" forms. (Examples of these three models are found in Case Examples 17.2, 17.3, and 17.4.)

LOCALITY DEVELOPMENT MODEL
The locality development (also called community development) model asserts that community

Case Example of the Social Planning Model

I n the mid-1960s the U.S. Department of Health, Education and Welfare mandated (for several years) that every community in the nation had to provide information and referral (I&R) services about social programs. If the I&R services met federal guidelines, the government would reimburse local communities for 75% of the cost. In Wisconsin the State Department of Human Services met with local planning agencies and encouraged them to develop I&R services in their local communities. The state agreed to reimburse local communities for an additional 12.5% of their costs. This reimbursement schedule meant that local communities could provide I&R services for only 12.5% of the total cost.

The board of directors of Lincoln County Social Planning Agency authorized its staff to do a feasibility study on establishing a centralized information and referral center. Donald Levi (social planner on the staff) was assigned to direct the study. Mr. Levi collected data showing the following:

■ There were over 350 community service agencies and organizations in this largely metropolitan county. Not only clients but also service providers were confused about what services were available from this array of agencies.

■ There was a confusing array of specialized information and referral services being developed. (Specialized information and referral services provided I&R services in only one or two areas.) Specialized I&R services were developing in suicide prevention, mental health, mental retardation, day care, adoption services, and alcohol and drug treatment.

Mr. Levi then designed a program model for providing a centralized information and referral service. The model described a service that would provide I&R services on *all* human and community services in the county. For example, I&R would provide information not only on what day-care services were available but also on where to find public tennis courts and whom to call to remove a stray cat killed in front of your

change can best be brought about through broad-based participation by a wide spectrum of people at the local community level. The approach seeks to involve a cross section of individuals (including the disadvantaged and the power structure) in identifying and solving problems. Some themes emphasized in this model are democratic procedures, a consensus approach, voluntary cooperation, development of indigenous leadership, and self-help.

The roles of the community practitioner in this approach include enabler, catalyst, coordinator, and teacher of problem-solving skills and ethical values. It is assumed that any conflicts among various interest groups can be creatively and constructively resolved. People are encouraged to

house. The centralized information and referral service number would be widely publicized on television, radio, and billboards and in newspapers and telephone directories. A budget was developed by Mr. Levi for the program costs.

The board of directors of the Lincoln County Social Planning Agency concluded that such a centralized information and referral service would be more efficient and economical than the confusing array that had been developing. The board therefore authorized Mr. Levi to pursue the development of this centralized service.

Mr. Levi conducted a questionnaire survey of all the human service agencies in the county and of all the clergy in the county. The results showed that both groups strongly supported the development of a centralized I&R service. In addition, the Easter Seal Society felt so strongly that such a service was needed that they contacted Mr. Levi to indicate that they were willing to donate funds for the new program. Mr. Levi was delighted, and an arrangement was worked out for the Easter Seal Society to fund the program for a three-year demonstration period.

Only one barrier remained. Federal and state guidelines required that the program be approved by the county welfare board before reimbursement would be made. Mr. Levi and two members of the board of the Lincoln County Social Planning Agency presented the new program proposal to the county's welfare board. The presentation included graphs showing the savings of a centralized I&R service over specialized I&R services and contained written statements of support from a variety of sources, including city council members, the United Way, human service agencies, and members of the clergy. It was also indicated that there would be no cost to the county for a three-year demonstration period. At the end of that time there would be an evaluative study of the merits and shortcomings of the program. Mr. Levi fully expected approval. He was speechless when the county welfare board said no. They turned the proposal down because they felt a centralized I&R would mean that more people would be referred to county social service agencies, which would raise costs to the county, and because they thought there would be pressure on the county to fund the program after the three-year demonstration project ended.

The county continued to be served by less efficient and less effective specialized I&R services. This case example realistically illustrates that some planning efforts are unsuccessful.

---

express their differences freely but to put aside self-interests in order to further the interests of their community. The basic theme of this approach is "Together we can figure out what to do and then do it." The locality development model seeks to use discussion and communication among different factions to reach consensus on which problems to focus on and which strategies or actions to use to resolve these problems. A few examples of such efforts include neighborhood work programs conducted by community-based agencies; Volunteers in Service to America; village-level work in some overseas community development programs, including the Peace Corps; and a variety of activities performed by self-help groups.

Case Example of the Social Action Model

S aul Alinsky, a nationally noted social action strategist, provides an example of a
creative social action effort. The example also shows that social action efforts are
often enjoyable.

> *I was lecturing at a college run by a very conservative, almost fundamentalist
> Protestant denomination. Afterward some of the students came to my motel to talk
> to me. Their problem was that they couldn't have any fun on campus. The weren't
> permitted to dance or smoke or have a can of beer. I had been talking about the
> strategy of effecting change in a society and they wanted to know what tactics they
> could use to change their situation. I reminded them that a tactic is doing what you
> can with what you've got. "Now, what have you got?" I asked. "What do they permit
> you to do?" "Practically nothing," they said, "except—you know—we can chew gum."
> I said, "Fine, Gum becomes the weapon. You get 200 or 300 students to get two packs
> of gum each, which is quite a wad. Then you have them drop it on the campus walks.
> This will cause absolute chaos. Why, with 500 wads of gum I could paralyze Chicago,
> stop all the traffic in the Loop." They looked at me as though I was some kind of nut.
> But about two weeks later I got an ecstatic letter saying, "It worked! It worked!
> Now we can do just about anything so long as we don't chew gum."*

Source: Saul Alinsky, *Rules for Radicals* (New York: Random House, 1972), pp. 145–146.

SOCIAL PLANNING MODEL

The social planning approach emphasizes the
process of problem solving. It assumes that community change in a complex industrial environment requires highly trained and skilled planners
who can guide complex change processes. The
role of the expert is crucial to identifying and resolving social problems. The expert or planner is
generally employed by a segment of the power
structure, such as an area planning agency, city or
county planning department, mental health center, United Way board, Community Welfare Council, and so on. Because the social planner is
employed by the power structure, there is a tendency for him or her to serve the interests of that
structure. Marshaling community resources and
facilitating radical social change are generally not
emphasized in this approach.

The planner's roles in this approach include
gathering facts, analyzing data, and serving as
program designer, implementer, and facilitator.
Community participation may vary from little to
substantial, depending on the community's attitudes toward the problems being addressed. For
example, an effort to design and fund a community center for the elderly may or may not generate a lot of participation by interested community
groups, depending on the politics surrounding
such a center. Much of the focus of the social
planning approach is on identifying needs and on
arranging and delivering goods and services to
people who need them. In effect, the philosophy
is "Let's get the facts and take the next rational
steps."

SOCIAL ACTION MODEL

The social action model assumes that there is a
disadvantaged (often oppressed) segment of the

EXHIBIT 17.6

Three Models of Community Organization Practice According to Selected Practice Variables

	Locality Development	Social Planning	Social Action
1. Goal categories of community action	Self-help; community capacity and integration (process goals)	Problem solving with regard to substantive community problems (task goals)	Shifting of power relationships and resources; basic institutional change (task or process goals)
2. Assumptions concerning community structure and problem conditions	Community eclipsed, anomie; lack of relationships and democratic problem-solving capacities; static traditional community	Substantive social problems; mental and physical health, housing, recreation	Disadvantaged populations, social injustice, deprivation, inequity
3. Basic change strategy	Broad cross section of people involved in determining and solving their own problems	Fact gathering about problems and decisions on the most rational course of action	Crystallization of issues and organization of people to take action against enemy targets
4. Characteristic change tactics and techniques	Consensus: communication among community groups and interests; group discussion	Consensus or conflict	Conflict or contest: confrontation, direct action, negotiation
5. Salient practitioner roles	Enabler/catalyst, coordinator; teacher of problem-solving skills and ethical values	Fact gatherer and analyst, program implementer, facilitator	Activist/advocate; agitator, broker, negotiator, partisan
6. Medium of change	Manipulation of small, task-oriented groups	Manipulation of formal organizations and of data	Manipulation of mass organizations and political processes

(continued)

population that needs to be organized, perhaps in alliance with others, in order to pressure the power structure for increased resources or for social justice. Social action approaches seek basic changes in major institutions or in basic policies of formal organizations. The objective is redistribution of power and resources. Whereas locality developers envision a unified community, social action advocates see the power structure as the opposition—the target of action. Perhaps the best-

known social activist was Saul Alinsky, who advised: "Pick the target, freeze it, personalize it, and polarize it."[32]

The roles of the community practitioner in this approach include advocate, agitator, activist, partisan, broker, and negotiator. Tactics used in social action projects are protests, boycotts, confrontation, and negotiation. The change strategy is one of "Let's organize to overpower our oppressor."[33] The client population is viewed as being

EXHIBIT 17.6   *(continued)*

	Locality Development	Social Planning	Social Action
7. Orientation toward power structure(s)	Members of power structure as collaborators in a common venture	Power structure as employers and sponsors	Power structure as external target of action, oppressors to be coerced or overturned
8. Boundary definition of the community client, system, or constituency	Total geographic community	Total community or community segment (including "functional" community)	Community segment
9. Assumptions regarding interests of community subparts	Common interests or reconcilable differences	Interests reconcilable or in conflict	Conflicting interests that are not easily reconcilable; scarce resources
10. Conception of the public interest	Rationalist/unitary	Idealist/unitary	Realist/individualist
11. Conception of the client population or constituency	Citizens	Consumers	Victims
12. Conception of client role	Participants in an interactional problem-solving process	Consumers or recipients	Employers, constituents, members

Source: Adapted from "Three Models of Community Organization Practice," by J. Rothman, pp. 24–34 in *Social Work Practice,* 1968. Copyright © 1968 Columbia University Press, New York, for the National Conference on Social Welfare. Reprinted by permission.

"victimized" by the oppressive power structure. Examples of the social action approach include boycotts during the civil rights movement of the 1960s, strikes by unions, protests by anti-abortion groups, and protests by African American and Native American groups.

The social action model is not widely used by social workers at present. Involvement in social action activities may lead employing agencies to penalize social workers with unpleasant work assignments, low merit increases, and withholding of promotions. Many agencies will accept minor and moderate changes in their service delivery systems but are threatened by the prospect of such radical changes as are often advocated by the social action approach.

Exhibit 17.6 summarizes the three models that have been discussed.

KNOWLEDGE, SKILLS, AND VALUES FOR SOCIAL WORK PRACTICE

Knowledge Base

The knowledge needed for effective social work practice has been identified by NASW as follows:

■ Knowledge *of casework and group work theory and techniques.*

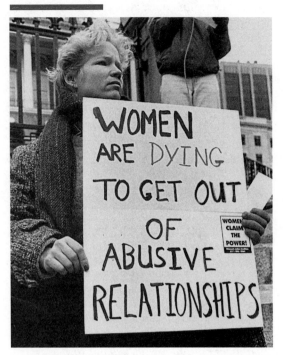

Social activists seek basic institutional change. Their tactics range from negotiation and advocacy to confrontation and protests.

- Knowledge *of community resources and services.*
- Knowledge *of basic federal and state social service programs and their purposes.*
- Knowledge *of community organization theory and the development of health and welfare services.*
- Knowledge *of basic socioeconomic and political theory.*
- Knowledge *of racial, ethnic, and other cultural groups in society—their values and lifestyles and the resultant issues in contemporary life.*
- Knowledge *of sources of professional and scientific research appropriate to practice.*
- Knowledge *of the concepts and techniques of social planning.*

- Knowledge *of the theories and concepts of supervision and the professional supervision of social worker practice.*
- Knowledge *of theories and concepts of personnel management.*
- Knowledge *of common social and psychological statistical and other research methods and techniques.*
- Knowledge *of the theories and concepts of social welfare administration.*
- Knowledge *of social and environmental factors affecting clients to be served.*
- Knowledge *of the theories and methods of psychosocial assessment and intervention and of differential diagnosis.*
- Knowledge *of the theory and behavior of organizational and social systems and of methods for encouraging change.*
- Knowledge *of community organization theory and techniques.*
- Knowledge *of the theories of human growth and development and of family and social interaction.*
- Knowledge *of small-group theory and behavioral dynamics.*
- Knowledge *of the theories of group interaction and therapeutic intervention.*
- Knowledge *of crisis intervention theories and techniques.*
- Knowledge *of advocacy theory and techniques.*
- Knowledge *of the ethical standards and practices of professional social work.*
- Knowledge *of teaching and instructional theories and techniques.*
- Knowledge *of social welfare trends and policies.*
- Knowledge *of local, state, and federal laws and regulations affecting social and health services.* *

---

*Source: From *Standards for the Classification of Social Work Practice*, p. 17. Copyright © 1981 National Association of Social Workers, Inc. Reprinted by permission.

The Council on Social Work Education has categorized the knowledge needed by social workers into ten broad content areas. Every accredited social work educational program is expected to provide the following content, which is excerpted from the 1992 Curriculum Policy Statements.[34]

Liberal Arts Perspective. A liberal arts perspective enriches understanding of the person-environment context of professional social work practice and is integrally related to the mastery of social work content. The baccalaureate professional program in social work is built upon a liberal arts perspective.

A liberal arts perspective provides an understanding of one's cultural heritage in the context of other cultures; the methods and limitations of various systems of inquiry; and the knowledge, attitudes, ways of thinking, and means of communication that are characteristic of a broadly educated person. Students must be capable of thinking critically about society, about people and their problems, and about such expressions of culture as art, literature, science, history, and philosophy. Students must have direct knowledge about social, psychological, and biological determinants of human behavior and of diverse cultures, social conditions, and social problems.

Social Work Values and Ethics. *Programs of social work education must provide specific knowledge about social work values and their ethical implications and must provide opportunities for students to demonstrate their application in professional practice. Students must be assisted to develop an awareness of their personal values and to clarify conflicting values and ethical dilemmas.*

Diversity. Professional social work education is committed to preparing students to understand and appreciate human diversity. Programs must provide curriculum content about differences and similarities in the experiences, needs, and beliefs of people.

The curriculum must include content about differential assessment and intervention skills that will enable practitioners to serve diverse populations.

Each program is required to include content about population groups that are particularly relevant to the program's mission. These include, but are not limited to, groups distinguished by race, ethnicity, culture, class, gender, sexual orientation, religion, physical or mental ability, age, and national origin.

Promotion of Social and Economic Justice. *Programs of social work education must provide an understanding of the dynamics and consequences of social and economic injustice, including all forms of human oppression and discrimination. They must provide students with the skills to promote social change and to implement a wide range of interventions that further the achievement of individual and collective social and economic justice. Theoretical and practice content must be provided about strategies of intervention for achieving social and economic justice and for combating the causes and effects of institutionalized forms of oppression.*

Populations-at-Risk. *Programs of social work education must present theoretical and practice content about patterns, dynamics, and consequences of discrimination, economic deprivation, and oppression. The curriculum must provide content about people of color, women, and gay and lesbian persons. Such content must emphasize the impact of discrimination, economic deprivation, and oppression upon these groups.*

Each program must include content about populations-at-risk that are particularly relevant to its mission. In addition to those mandated above, such groups include, but are not limited to, those distinguished by age, ethnicity, culture, class, religion, and physical or mental ability.

Human Behavior and the Social Environment. *Programs of social work* education must provide content about theories and knowledge of human bio-psycho-social development, including theories and knowledge about the range of social systems in which individuals live (families, groups, organizations, institutions, and communities). The human behavior and the social environment curriculum must provide an understanding of the interactions between and among human biological, social, psychological, and cultural systems as they affect and are affected by human behavior. The impact of social and economic forces on individuals and social systems must be presented. Content must be provided about the ways in which systems promote or deter people in the maintenance or attainment of optimal health and well-being. Content about values and ethical issues related to bio-psycho-social theories must be included. Students must be taught to evaluate theory and apply theory to client situations.

Social Welfare Policy and Services. Social welfare policy and services content must include the history, mission, and philosophy of the social work profession. Content must be presented about the history and current patterns of provision of social welfare services, the role of social policy in helping or deterring people in the maintenance or attainment of optimal health and well-being, and the effect of policy on social work practice. Students must be taught to analyze current social policy within the context of historical and contemporary factors that shape policy. Content must be presented about the political and organizational processes used to influence policy, the process of policy formulation, and the frameworks for analyzing social policies in light of the principles of social and economic justice.

Social Work Practice. At the baccalaureate level, professional social work education prepares students for generalist practice with systems of all sizes. Practice content emphasizes professional relationships that are characterized by mutuality, collaboration, and respect for the client system. Content on practice assessment focuses on the examination of client strengths and problems in the interactions among individuals and between people and their environments.

Social work practice content must include knowledge, values, and skills to enhance the well-being of people and to help ameliorate the environmental conditions that affect people adversely. Practice content must include the following skills: defining issues; collecting and assessing data; planning and contracting; identifying alternative interventions; selecting and implementing appropriate courses of action; using appropriate research to monitor and evaluate outcomes; applying appropriate research-based knowledge and technological advances; and termination. Practice content also includes approaches and skills for practice with clients from differing social, cultural, racial, religious, spiritual, and class backgrounds and with systems of all sizes.

Research. The research curriculum must provide an understanding and appreciation of a scientific, analytic approach to building knowledge for practice and for evaluating service delivery in all areas of practice. Ethical standards of scientific inquiry must be included in the research content.

The research content must include quantitative and qualitative research methodologies; analysis of data, including statistical procedures; systematic evaluation of practice; analysis and evaluation of theoretical bases, research questions, methodologies, statistical procedures, and conclusions of research reports; and relevant technological advances.

Each program must identify how the research curriculum contributes to the student's use of scientific knowledge for practice.

Field Practicum. The field practicum is an integral component of the curriculum in social *work education. It engages the student in supervised social work practice and provides opportunities to apply classroom learning in the field setting.*

The baccalaureate practicum must provide the student with opportunities for:

a. *The development of an awareness of self in the process of intervention.*

b. *Supervised practice experience in the application of knowledge, values and ethics, and practice skills to enhance the well-being of people and to work toward the amelioration of environmental conditions that affect people adversely.*

c. *Use of oral and written professional communications which are consistent with the language of the practicum setting and of the profession.*

d. *Use of professional supervision to enhance learning.*

e. *Critical assessment, implementation, and evaluation of agency policy within ethical guidelines.* *

The curriculum at the master's level in social work also must be based on a liberal arts perspective. The definition of this perspective is very similar to that for the baccalaureate level. The curriculum at the master's level is mandated by the Curriculum Policy Statement of the Council on Social Work Education to be composed of (1) professional foundation content and (2) concentration content in an area. Each of these two components will be briefly described.

The professional foundation includes content on social work values and ethics, diversity, promotion of social and economic justice, populations-at-risk, human behavior and the social environment, social welfare policy and services, social work practice, research, and field practicum. The description of these areas in the mas-

ter's-level Policy Statement is nearly identical to the description in the baccalaureate Curriculum Policy Statement; therefore it will not be repeated here.

Concentration content includes knowledge, values, and skills for advanced practice in an identifiable area. Identifiable areas that are frequently offered by master's programs include fields of practice, problem areas, populations-at-risk, and intervention methods or roles.

Skill Base

Many efforts have been made to articulate the essential skills for entry-level social work positions. We'll look at a few of these conceptualizations in order to illustrate contemporary thinking about core practice skills. Be aware, however, that, despite the similarities among these conceptualizations, there is *not* full agreement on these core skills.

Federico has indirectly described social work skills by outlining roles and activities:

1. Outreach worker—*reaching out into the community to identify need and follow up referrals to service contexts.*

2. Broker—*knowing services available and making sure those in need reach the appropriate services.*

3. Advocate—*helping specific clients obtain services when they might otherwise be rejected, and helping to expand services to cover more needy persons.*

4. Evaluation—*evaluating needs and resources, generating alternatives for meeting needs, and making decisions between alternatives.*

5. Teacher—*teaching facts and skills.*

6. Mobilizer—*helping to develop new services.*

7. Behavior changer—*changing specific parts of a client's behavior.*

8. Consultant—*working with other professionals to help them be more effective in providing services.*

9. Community planner—*helping community groups plan effectively for the community's social welfare needs.*

---

*Reprinted from *Curriculum Policy Statement for Baccalaureate Degree Programs in Social Work Education,* Final Draft July 8, 1992, by permission of the Council on Social Work Education, Alexandria, VA.

10. Care giver—*providing supportive services to those who cannot fully solve their problems and meet their own needs.*

11. Data manager—*collecting and analyzing data for decision-making purposes.*

12. Administrator—*performing the activities necessary to plan and implement a program of services.*[35]

Baer has identified the following ten competencies as being essential for successfully performing the responsibilities of entry-level positions:

1. *Identify and assess situations in which the relationship between people and social institutions needs to be initiated, enhanced, restored, protected, or terminated.*

2. *Develop and implement a plan for improving the well-being of people, based on problem assessment and the exploration of obtainable goals and available options.*

3. *Enhance the problem-solving, coping, and developmental capacities of people.*

4. *Link people with systems that provide them with resources, services, and opportunities.*

5. *Intervene effectively on behalf of populations most vulnerable and discriminated against.*

6. *Promote the effective and humane operation of the systems that provide people with services, resources, and opportunities.*

7. *Actively participate with others in creating new, modified, or improved service, resource, or opportunity systems that are more equitable, just, and responsive to consumers of services; work with others to eliminate unjust systems.*

8. *Evaluate the extent to which the objectives of the intervention plan were achieved.*

9. *Continually evaluate one's professional growth and development through assessment of practice behaviors and skills.*

10. *Contribute to the improvement of service delivery by adding to the knowledge base of the profession as appropriate and supporting and upholding the standards and ethics of the profession.*[36]

These ten competencies were originally developed by Baer and Federico.[37]

NASW has identified the essential skills for social work practice as follows:

■ Skill *in listening to others with understanding and purpose.*

■ Skill *in eliciting information and in assembling relevant facts to prepare a social history, assessment, and report.*

■ Skill *in creating and maintaining professional helping relationships and in using oneself in relationships.*

■ Skill *in observing and interpreting verbal and nonverbal behavior and in using a knowledge of personality theory and diagnostic methods.*

■ Skill *in engaging clients in efforts to resolve their own problems and in gaining trust.*

■ Skill *in discussing sensitive emotional subjects in a nonthreatening, supportive manner.*

■ Skill *in creating innovative solutions to clients' needs.*

■ Skill *in determining the need to end therapeutic relationships and how to do so.*

■ Skill *in interpreting the findings of research studies and professional literature.*

■ Skill *in mediating and negotiating between conflicting parties.*

■ Skill *in providing interorganizational liaison services.*

■ Skill *in interpreting or communicating social needs to funding sources, the public, or legislators.* *

Closely related to the conceptualization of essential skills, NASW has identified the following abilities as being needed for social work practice:

■ Ability *to speak and write clearly.*

■ Ability *to teach others.*

---

*Source: From *Standards for the Classification of Social Work Practice,* p. 17. Copyright © 1981 National Association of Social Workers, Inc. Reprinted by permission.

- Ability *to respond supportively in emotion-laden or crisis situations.*

- Ability *to serve as a role model in a professional relationship.*

- Ability *to interpret complex psychosocial phenomena.*

- Ability *to organize a workload to meet designated responsibilities.*

- Ability *to identify and obtain resources needed to assist others.*

- Ability *to assess one's performance and feelings, and to use help or consultation.*

- Ability *to participate in and lead group activities.*

- Ability *to function under stress.*

- Ability *to deal with conflict situations or contentious personalities.*

- Ability *to relate social and psychological theory to practice situations.*

- Ability *to identify the information necessary to solve a problem.*

- Ability *to conduct research studies of agency services or one's practice.* *

In its 1992 Curriculum Policy Statements for both the baccalaureate and master's programs, the Council on Social Work Education mandated that social work programs provide content on the following skills:

- Defining issues.

- Collecting and assessing data.

- Planning and contracting.

- Identifying alternative interventions.

- Selecting and implementing appropriate courses of action.

- Using appropriate research to monitor and evaluate outcomes.

- Applying appropriate research-based knowledge and technological advances.

- Termination.

---

*Source: From *Standards for the Classification of Social Work Practice*, p. 17. Copyright © 1981 National Association of Social Workers, Inc. Reprinted by permission.

(These skills were elaborated on earlier in this chapter.)

The acquisition of social work skills depends partly on people's innate abilities and partly on learning experiences. Social work educational programs facilitate learning of such skills by presenting theoretical material to students (e.g., material on how to interview) by monitoring and critiquing students who are practicing these skills (e.g., videotaping students in simulated counseling situations), and by extensively supervising students in practicum courses.

Value Base

Should the primary objective of imprisonment be rehabilitation or punishment? Should a father who commits incest be prosecuted, with the likelihood that publicity in the community will lead to family breakup, or should an effort first be made, through counseling, to stop the incest and keep the family intact? Should a wife who is occasionally abused by her husband be encouraged to remain living with him? Should abortion be suggested as one alternative for resolving the problems of someone who is single and pregnant? Should youths who are claimed by their parents to be uncontrollable be placed in correctional schools? If a client informs a social worker that he intends to severely injure some third party, what should the worker do? Suppose a client indicates he is HIV positive but refuses to reveal his condition to his partner, thereby placing the partner in peril through unprotected sexual relations. What action should the social worker take? All of these questions involve making decisions that are based largely on values. Much of social work practice is dependent on making value-based decisions.

Allen Pincus and Anne Minahan concisely define *values* and describe the differences between values and knowledge:

> *Values are beliefs, preferences, or assumptions about what is desirable or good for [humans]. An example is the belief that society has an obligation to help each individual realize his fullest potential. They are not assertions about*

how the world is and what we know about it, but how it should *be. As such, value statements cannot be subjected to scientific investigation; they must be accepted on faith. Thus we can speak of a value as being right or wrong only in relation to the particular belief system or ethical code being used as a standard.*

What we will refer to as knowledge statements, on the other hand, are observations about the world and [humans] which have been verified or are capable of verification. An example is that black people have a shorter life expectancy than white people in the United States. When we speak of a knowledge statement as being right or wrong, we are referring to the extent to which the assertion has been confirmed through objective empirical investigation.[38]

The National Association of Social Workers (NASW) has formulated a Code of Ethics that summarizes important practice ethics for social workers. A summary of the major principles of this code appears in Exhibit 17.7, with the complete code being presented in Appendix A. Appendix B contains the Canadian Association of Social Workers' Code of Ethics.

I'll now summarize some of the values that underlie social work practice.

RESPECT FOR THE DIGNITY AND UNIQUENESS OF THE INDIVIDUAL

This value or principle has also been called *individualization,* which means viewing and treating each person as unique and worthwhile. The social work profession firmly believes that everyone has inherent dignity, which is to be respected.

Every human being is unique in a variety of ways—value system, personality, goals in life, financial resources, emotional and physical strengths, personal concerns, past experiences, peer pressures, emotional reactions, self-identity, family relationships, and behavioral patterns. In working with a client, a social worker needs to perceive and respect the uniqueness of the client's situation.

Individualization is relatively easy for a social worker to achieve when clients have values, goals, behavioral patterns, and personal characteristics that are similar to those of the worker.

It is harder to achieve when clients have values or behavioral patterns that the worker views as unpleasant. For example, a worker holding traditional middle-class values may have difficulty in respecting a client who has killed someone, has raped someone, is filthy, or continually uses vulgar language. A general guideline in such situations is that the worker should seek to accept and respect the client but not the deviant behavior that needs to be changed. If a worker is not able to convey that she or he accepts the client (but not the deviant behavior), a helping relationship will not be established. In that case the worker will have practically no opportunity to help the client make constructive changes. A second guideline is that, if a worker views a client as being unpleasant and is unable to establish a working relationship, then the case should be transferred to another worker. The original social worker need not feel disgrace or embarrassment in having to transfer a case for such reasons; it is irrational to expect to like every client or to be liked by every client.[39]

Social workers occasionally encounter "raw" situations. I have worked with clients who have committed a wide range of asocial and bizarre acts, including incest, rape, murder, sodomy, sexual exhibitionism, and grave robbing. Achieving an attitude of respect for people who commit bizarre actions is difficult at times, but rehabilitation will not occur unless the worker develops respect.

Social psychologists have firmly established that our images of ourselves develop largely out of our interactions and communications with others. A long time ago Charles Cooley labeled this process the "looking glass self-concept."[40] People develop their self-concept in terms of how other people relate to them, as if others were a looking glass or mirror. For example, if you receive respect from others and are praised for your positive qualities, you will feel good about yourself, will gradually develop a positive sense of worth, will be happier, and will seek responsible and socially acceptable ways to continue to maintain the respect of others.

On the other hand, if you are related to by others as if you are irresponsible, you will begin

EXHIBIT 17.7

NASW Code of Ethics

Summary of Major Principles

I. The Social Worker's Conduct and Comportment as a Social Worker

  A. *Propriety.* The social worker should maintain high standards of personal conduct in the capacity or identity as social worker.

  B. *Competence and Professional Development.* The social worker should strive to become and remain proficient in professional practice and the performance of professional functions.

  C. *Service.* The social worker should regard as primary the service obligation of the social work profession.

  D. *Integrity.* The social worker should act in accordance with the highest standards of professional integrity.

  E. *Scholarship and Research.* The social worker engaged in study and research should be guided by the conventions of scholarly inquiry.

II. The Social Worker's Ethical Responsibility to Clients

  F. *Primacy of Clients' Interests.* The social worker's primary responsibility is to clients.

  G. *Rights and Prerogatives of Clients.* The social worker should make every effort to foster maximum self-determination on the part of clients.

  H. *Confidentiality and Privacy.* The social worker should respect the privacy of clients and hold in confidence all information obtained in the course of professional service.

  I. *Fees.* When setting fees, the social worker should ensure that they are fair, reasonable, considerate, and commensurate with the service performed and with due regard for the clients' ability to pay.

III. The Social Worker's Ethical Responsibility to Colleagues

  J. *Respect, Fairness, and Courtesy.* The social worker should treat colleagues with respect, courtesy, fairness, and good faith.

  K. *Dealing with Colleagues' Clients.* The social worker has the responsibility to relate to the clients of colleagues with full professional consideration.

IV. The Social Worker's Ethical Responsibility to Employers and Employing Organizations

  L. *Commitments to Employing Organizations.* The social worker should adhere to commitments made to the employing organizations.

V. The Social Worker's Ethical Responsibility to the Social Work Profession

  M. *Maintaining the Integrity of the Profession.* The social worker should uphold and advance the values, ethics, knowledge, and mission of the profession.

  N. *Community Service.* The social worker should assist the profession in making social services available to the general public.

  O. *Development of Knowledge.* The social worker should take responsibility for identifying, developing, and fully utilizing knowledge for professional practice.

VI. The Social Worker's Ethical Responsibility to Society

  P. *Promoting the General Welfare.* The social worker should promote the general welfare of society.

Source: From *NASW Code of Ethics.* Copyright © 1994 National Association of Social Workers, Inc. Reprinted by permission.

to view yourself as irresponsible and will gradually develop a negative self-concept. With such a view of yourself, you decrease your efforts to act responsibly. In both these examples the ways that others relate to you (positively or negatively) become a self-fulfilling prophecy.[41]

The principle of individualization also plays a key role in social work treatment. Various problems, needs, goals, and values of clients require different patterns of relationships with workers and different methods of helping. For example, a teenage male who is placed in a group home because his parents find him "uncontrollable" may need an understanding but firm counselor who sets and enforces strict limits. At times the youth may need encouragement and guidance in how to perform better at school. If conflicts develop between the youth and other residents at the group home, the counselor may need to play a mediating role. If the boy is shy, assertiveness training may be needed. If his parents are fairly ineffective in their parenting role, the counselor may seek to have them enroll in a Parent Effectiveness Training (PET) program.[42] If the youth is being treated unfairly at school or by the juvenile court, the counselor may play an advocate role for him and attempt to change the system. If the youth has behavior problems, the social worker will need to explore the underlying reasons and develop an intervention program.

CLIENTS' RIGHT TO SELF-DETERMINATION

This principle asserts that clients have the right to hold and express their own opinions and to act on them, as long as doing so does not infringe on the rights of others. This principle is in sharp contrast to the layperson's perception that social workers seek to "remold" clients into a pattern chosen by the workers. Rather, the efforts of social workers are geared to enhancing the capability of clients to help themselves. Client self-determination derives logically from the belief in the inherent dignity of each person. If people have dignity, then it follows that they should be permitted to determine their own lifestyles as far as possible.

Making clients' decisions and doing everything for them are self-defeating; these actions lead to increased dependency rather than to self-reliance and self-sufficiency. For people to grow, to mature, to become responsible, they need to make their own decisions and to take responsibility for the consequences. Mistakes and emotional pain will at times occur. But that is part of life. We learn by our mistakes and by trial and error. Respect for the client's decision-making ability is associated with the principle that social work is a cooperative endeavor between client and worker (client participation). Social work is done *with* a client, not *to* a client. Plans imposed on people without their active involvement have a way of not turning out well.

Self-determination implies that clients should be made aware that there are alternatives for resolving their personal or social problems. They can choose from several courses of action. (If there is only one course of action, there is no choice and therefore no self-determination.) As we've seen, the role of a social worker in helping clients involves (1) building a helping relationship, (2) exploring problems with clients in depth, and (3) exploring alternative solutions, with the clients then choosing a course of action. This third step is the implementation of the principle of self-determination.

Social workers need to recognize that it is the client who *owns* the problem and therefore has the chief responsibility to resolve it. In this respect social work differs markedly from most other professions. Most professionals, such as physicians and attorneys, advise clients about what they ought to do. Doctors, lawyers, and dentists are viewed as experts. Clients' decision making in such situations is generally limited to the professional's advice.

In sharp contrast, social workers seek to establish not an expert/inferior relationship but rather a relationship between equals. The expertise of the social worker does *not* lie in knowing or recommending what is best for the client; it lies in assisting clients to define their problems, to identify and examine alternatives for resolving the problems, to maximize their capacities and opportunities to make decisions for themselves, and to implement the decisions they make. Many students, when they first enter social work or some other helping profession, mistakenly see their role as that of "savior" or "rescuer." Mathew Dumont is highly critical of the rescuer role:

The most destructive thing in psychotherapy is a "rescue fantasy" in the therapist—a feeling that the therapist is the divinely sent agent to pull a tormented soul from the pit of suffering and adversity and put him back on the road to happiness and glory. A major reason this fantasy is so destructive is that it carries the conviction that the patient will be saved only through and by the therapist. When such a conviction is communicated to the patient, verbally or otherwise, he has no choice other than to rebel and leave or become more helpless, dependent, and sick.[43]

The principle of self-determination is complex and has some limitations. If a client decides to take a course of action that the social worker believes will have adverse effects, the social worker must decide whether to intervene. For example, if an elderly female client chooses to live alone in her home when there is serious concern about her physical capacities to live independently, a social worker has the obligation to point out the dangers and to suggest alternative living arrangements. In this situation the social worker may decide not to take further action to force her into a safer living environment. On the other hand, if a client tries to commit suicide, the social worker should do everything possible to prevent another attempt.

Also, if a client discusses an intention to harm another person, a social worker must make a judgment about whether to intervene to prevent the client from carrying out his or her intended actions. For example, if a client indicates that he plans to shoot someone and then bolts out of the social worker's office, the worker may choose (and may well have a legal obligation) to inform the police and the intended victim.

CONFIDENTIALITY

Confidentiality is the implicit or explicit agreement between a professional and a client to maintain the privacy of information about the client. An "absolute" implementation of this principle means that disclosures made to the professional are not shared with anyone else, except when authorized by the client in writing or required by law. Because of the principle of confidentiality, professionals can be sued if they disclose unauthorized information that has a damaging effect on the client.

Confidentiality is important because clients are not likely to share their "hidden secrets," personal concerns, and asocial thoughts and actions with a professional who might reveal that information to others. A basic principle of counseling is that clients must feel comfortable in fully revealing themselves to the professional, without fear that their revelations will be used against them.

Confidentiality is absolute when information revealed to a professional is *never* passed on to anyone in any form. Such information would never be shared with other agency staff, fed into a computer, or written in a case record. A student or beginning practitioner tends to think in absolutes and may even naively promise clients "absolute confidentiality."

In reality, absolute confidentiality is seldom achieved. Social workers today generally function as part of a larger agency. In agencies much of the communication is written into case records and shared orally with other staff as part of the service-delivery process. Social workers share details with supervisors; many work in teams and are expected to share information with other team members. Thus it is more precise to describe confidentiality in social work practice as "relative confidentiality."

Confidentiality is a legal matter, and at present there is a fair amount of uncertainty about what legally constitutes a violation and what does not. There have been few test cases in court to define violations of confidentiality. Let me provide a brief summary of how agencies are now handling issues related to confidentiality.

At agencies it is now generally permissible to discuss a client's circumstances with other professionals at that agency. In some agencies, such as a mental hospital, the input of many professionals (psychiatrists, psychologists, social workers, nurses, physical therapists, and so on) is used in assessing a client and developing a treatment plan.

Many agencies consider it inappropriate to share or discuss the client's case with a secretary. (Yet the secretary does the typing and usually knows as much about each client as the professional staff.)

Most agencies believe it is inappropriate to discuss a client's case with professionals at another agency, unless the client first signs a release form. (However, professionals employed by different agencies do at times informally share information about a client without the client's authorization.)

At the present time nearly all agencies share case information with social work interns. (Whether it is legally permissible to share information with student interns has not yet been determined.)

It is certainly permissible to discuss a case with others for educational purposes if the client is not specifically identified. Yet this is another "gray" area, because the person talking about the case will not be able to determine precisely when identifying information is being given. Take the following example.

Some years ago I was employed at a maximum-security hospital for the criminally insane and had on my caseload a young male who had decapitated his 17-year-old girlfriend. Such a criminal offense is indeed shocking and rare. People in the client's local area will never forget the crime. If I were to discuss this case in a class at a university, I could never be fully certain that no one would be able to identify the offender. There is always the chance that one of the students may be from the client's home community and could recognize the offender.

Another problem area is the thorny question of when a professional should violate confidence and inform others. Again, there are many gray areas surrounding this question.

Most state laws permit or require the professional to inform the appropriate people when a client admits to a past or intended *serious* criminal act. Yet the question of how serious a crime must be before there is an obligation to report it has not been resolved. On the extreme end of the "severity" continuum (for example, when a client threatens to kill someone) it has been established that a professional *must* inform the appropriate people—such as the police and the intended victims.[44]

In regard to the question of how serious a crime must be before it is reported, S. J. Wilson notes:

> How serious must a crime be in order for the professional to take protective measures? Obviously, crimes involving someone's life are sufficiently serious. But what about destruction of personal property, theft, and the hundreds of misdemeanors that are so minor that they are rather easily overlooked? Unfortunately, there seems to be no clear-cut definition of what constitutes a serious crime, and it appears that this will have to be determined by the courts in individual case rulings.[45]

Without guidelines, a professional must use his or her own best judgment about when a client's actions or communications warrant protective measures and about what those measures should be. Student interns and beginning practitioners are advised to consult their supervisors when questions in this area arise.

A few years ago I was the faculty supervisor for a student in a field placement at a public assistance agency. The intern had an unmarried AFDC mother on his caseload. A trusting working relationship between the intern and the mother was developed. The woman then informed the intern that she was dating a man who was sometimes abusive to her when drunk. She further indicated that there was a warrant for this man's arrest in another state for an armed robbery charge. The student contacted me, inquiring whether it was his obligation to inform the police, thereby violating confidentiality. My response was that he should discuss this with his agency supervisor to find out the agency's policy. The student informed the agency supervisor. The supervisor consulted with the attorney for the agency, who advised that the student should inform the woman that the information she revealed would have to be provided to the authorities. Upon being informed, the woman stomped out of the office, presumably to warn her partner. The police were immediately informed and proceeded to arrest him. The woman continued to receive AFDC, but appeared to be very distrusting of all the professional staff at the agency.

Wilson has researched this issue and concludes:

> In summary, a professional whose client confesses an intended or past crime can find himself in a very delicate position, both legally and ethically. There are enough conflicting beliefs on how this should be handled, so that clear guidelines are lacking. Social workers who receive a communication about a serious criminal act by a client would be wise to consult an attorney for a detailed research of appropriate state statutes and a review of recent court rulings that might help determine the desired course of action.[46]

There are a number of other circumstances when a professional is permitted, expected, or required to violate confidentiality.* These include:

- When a client formally (usually in writing) authorizes the professional to release information.

- When a professional is called to testify in a criminal case. (State statutes vary regarding guidelines on what information may be kept confidential in criminal proceedings; practitioners must research their own particular statutes in each instance.)

- When a client files a lawsuit against a professional (e.g., for malpractice).

- When a client threatens suicide. A professional may then be forced to violate confidentiality to save the client's life. Although the treating professional is encouraged to violate confidentiality in such circumstances, there is not necessarily a legal requirement to do so.

- When a client threatens to harm his or her therapist.

- When a professional becomes aware that a minor has committed a crime, when a minor

is used by adults as an accessory in a crime, or when a minor is a victim of criminal actions. In such situations most states require that counselors inform the legal authorities. Again, the question arises of how serious the crime must be before it is reported.

- When there is evidence of child abuse or neglect. Most states require professionals to report the evidence to the designated child protection agency.

- When a client's emotional or physical condition makes his or her employment a clear danger to himself or herself or to others (for example, when a counselor discovers that a client who is an airplane pilot has a serious drinking problem).

All these instances require professional judgment in deciding when the circumstances justify violating confidentiality.

ADVOCACY AND SOCIAL ACTION FOR THE OPPRESSED

Social work recognizes an obligation to advocate for the powerless, oppressed, and the dispossessed. Social work believes that society has a responsibility to all of its members to provide security, acceptance, and satisfaction of basic cultural, social, and biological needs. Only when our basic needs are met can we develop our maximum potentials. Because social work believes in the value of the individual, it has a special responsibility to protect and secure civil rights for all oppressed persons and groups. Social workers have a moral responsibility to work toward eradicating discrimination. Civil rights of clients need to be protected in order to preserve human dignity and self-respect.

ACCOUNTABILITY

Increasingly, federal and state governmental units and private funding sources are requiring that the effectiveness of service programs be measured. Programs found to be ineffective are being phased out. Although some social workers view accountability with trepidation and claim that the paperwork involved interferes with serving clients,

---

*An extended discussion of these circumstances is contained in Suanna J. Wilson, *Confidentiality in Social Work: Issues and Principles* (New York: Free Press, 1978).

social work has an obligation to funding sources to provide the highest-quality services. Accountability studies have yielded some valuable information. For example, they have demonstrated that orphanages are not the best places to serve homeless children, that long-term hospitalization is not the best way to help the emotionally disturbed, that probation generally has higher rehabilitative value than long-term confinement in prison, that the Job Corps program of the 1960s was too expensive for the outcomes achieved, that most children with a cognitive disability can be better served in their home communities through local programs than by confinement in an institution, and that runaways fare better in runaway centers than in detention or in jail.

Social workers need to become skilled at evaluating their effectiveness in providing services. A wide variety of evaluation techniques are now available to assess effectiveness of current services and to identify unmet needs and service gaps. One of the most useful approaches is management by objectives (MBO). This technique involves identifying the objectives of each program, specifying in measurable terms how and when these objectives are to be met, and then periodically measuring the extent to which the objectives are being met.

Management by objectives is also one of the most useful approaches that every social worker can use to assess his or her own effectiveness. Many agencies are now requiring each of their workers, *with the involvement of their clients,* to (1) identify and specify what the goals will be for each client (generally this is done together with clients during the initial interviews), (2) have the client and the worker then write down in detail what each will do to accomplish the goals (deadlines for accomplishing these tasks are also set), and (3) assess the extent to which the goals have been achieved when treatment is terminated (and perhaps periodically during the treatment process).

If goals are not being achieved, the worker needs to examine the underlying reasons. Perhaps unrealistic goals are being set. Perhaps the program or the treatment techniques are ineffective. Perhaps certain components of the treatment program are having an adverse effect. Perhaps other factors account for the low success rate. Depending on the cause, appropriate changes need to be made.

On the other hand, if the goals are being met, the worker can use this information to document to funding sources and to supervisors that high-quality services are being provided.

THE INSTITUTIONAL ORIENTATION

There are currently two conflicting views of the role of social welfare in our society: the residual orientation versus the institutional orientation. These two views were described at length in Chapter 1. Social work believes in the institutional approach and seeks to develop and provide programs with this orientation. Society must provide opportunities for growth and development that will allow each person to realize his or her fullest potential. Social work believes that society has a responsibility to all its members to provide security, acceptance, and satisfaction of basic cultural and biological needs. Social workers reject the views of rugged individualism and Social Darwinism.

VALUES SPECIFIED BY THE COUNCIL ON SOCIAL WORK EDUCATION

The 1992 Curriculum Policy Statements for both the baccalaureate and master's programs in social work education assert:

> Among the values and principles that must be infused throughout every social work curriculum are the following:
>
> 1. Social workers' professional relationships are built on regard for individual worth and dignity and are furthered by mutual participation, acceptance, confidentiality, honesty, and responsible handling of conflict.
>
> 2. Social workers respect people's right to make independent decisions and to participate actively in the helping process.
>
> 3. Social workers are committed to assisting client systems to obtain needed resources.
>
> 4. Social workers strive to make social

*institutions more humane and responsive
to human needs.*

5. *Social workers demonstrate respect for and
acceptance of the unique characteristics of
diverse populations.*

6. *Social workers are responsible for their own
ethical conduct, the quality of their practice,
and seeking continuous growth in the
knowledge and skills of their profession.* *

Because values play a key role in social work
practice, it is essential that social work educational programs (1) help students clarify their values and (2) foster in students the development of
values that are consistent with professional social
work practice.

SOCIAL WORK EDUCATION

Two-Year Associate Programs

During the past two decades a number of community colleges and technical schools have begun
offering two-year associate programs related to
social work education. These programs provide
training for a wide range of associate degrees with
such titles as:

- Social Work Aide/Social Service Associate/
  Social Service Technician
- Probation and Parole Aide
- Mental Health Associate/Mental Health Aide
- Human Services Technician/Human Services
  Aide
- Child-Care Technician/Residential Child-Care
  Aide
- Community Service Assistant/Community
  Services Technician/Community Social Ser-
  vice Worker

All of these degrees are considered preprofessional degrees. The programs seek to achieve two
simultaneous goals: training for employment and
provision of some basic courses that *may* transfer
to four-year educational programs.

As yet, associate degrees are not accredited by
the Council on Social Work Education (CSWE).
(This Council presently reviews social work baccalaureate and master's programs throughout the
United States to determine whether individual
programs meet the standards to warrant accreditation.) Standardization of associate programs in
social work probably will not be achieved unless
CSWE decides to seek to review associate programs for accreditation.

Undergraduate Education

Like graduate programs, undergraduate programs
are accredited by the CSWE, which sets standards
for social work education and promotes and improves the quality of education in social work
programs. Students who attend schools with accredited programs are assured that the quality of
education meets national standards and generally
have an advantage in securing employment
following graduation because social welfare
agencies give hiring preference to graduates from
accredited programs.

Until the early 1970s, undergraduate study in
social work was generally recognized as an academic or preprofessional education; only the master's degree was recognized as the professional
degree in social work. However, because a majority of people employed as social workers did not
(and still do not) have a graduate degree, the need
for professional training at the baccalaureate level
was recognized. Effective July 1, 1974, accreditation requirements for undergraduate programs
were substantially changed to emphasize professional preparation. In fact, the CSWE required
that an accredited baccalaureate program "shall
have as its primary stated educational objective
preparation for beginning professional social
work practice."[47] Secondary objectives for baccalaureate programs include (1) preparation of
students for graduate professional education in

---

*Reprinted from "Curriculum Policy Statement for Bacca-
laureate Degree Programs in Social Work Education, Final
Draft, July 8, 1992 (Alexandria, VA: Council on Social Work
Education, 1992). Reprinted from "Curriculum Policy
Statement for Master's Degree Programs in Social Work Education, Final Draft, July 8, 1992 (Alexandria, VA: Council
on Social Work Education, 1992).

social work and (2) preparation for intelligent, informed citizenship that brings an understanding of a wide range of social problems, intervention techniques on resolving such problems, and an understanding of social welfare concepts.

The 1992 revised Curriculum Policy Statement of CSWE identifies the following specific competencies for graduates of a baccalaureate social work program:

1. *Apply critical thinking skills within the context of professional social work practice.*

2. *Practice within the values and ethics of the social work profession and with an understanding of and respect for the positive value of diversity.*

3. *Demonstrate the professional use of self.*

4. *Understand the forms and mechanisms of oppression and discrimination and the strategies of change that advance social and economic justice.*

5. *Understand the history of the social work profession and its current structures and issues.*

6. *Apply the knowledge and skills of generalist social work to practice with systems of all sizes.*

7. *Apply knowledge of bio-psycho-social variables that affect individual development and behavior, and use theoretical frameworks to understand the interactions among individuals and between individuals and social systems (i.e., families, groups, organizations, and communities).*

8. *Analyze the impact of social policies on client systems, workers, and agencies.*

9. *Evaluate research studies and apply findings to practice, and, under supervision, evaluate their own practice interventions and those of other relevant systems.*

10. *Use communication skills differentially with a variety of client populations, colleagues, and members of the community.*

11. *Use supervision appropriate to generalist practice.*

12. *Function within the structure of organizations and service delivery systems,*

and, under supervision, seek necessary organizational change. *

Graduate Education

MSW (Master of Social Work) programs as a rule require two years of academic study. However, a number of graduate programs are granting advanced standing to students holding an undergraduate major in social work. Advanced standing (up to one academic year of credit) is given on the basis of the number of "core" courses taken as an undergraduate. Core courses are those that are required in both undergraduate and graduate programs and include classes in social welfare policy and services, social work practice, human behavior and the social environment, social research, and field placement.†

Because of the professional preparation focus of graduate programs, field work is an important component of all MSW programs. Students spend an average of two to three days per week at an agency while receiving intensive supervision.

Although there is some variation in the format and structure of master's programs, almost all of them have the following two components: (1) Part of the program has a generic social work practice focus. Courses taken to meet this generic practice focus are similar (and at some schools identical) to the core courses of an undergraduate program. Some schools offer this generic focus during the first year, a few offer it during the first semester, and others have course content in this area for both years. (2) For the second part of the program the student selects a concentration area from several available options and then takes courses in this study area. There is considerable variation among graduate schools in the concentration options that are offered. The CSWE annually publishes *Summary Information on Master*

---

*Reprinted from *Curriculum Policy Statement for Baccalaureate Degree Programs in Social Work Education*, Final Draft July 8, 1992, by permission of the Council on Social Work Education, Alexandria, VA.

†Guidelines for granting advanced standing in MSW programs differ among schools; interested students should therefore consult with the graduate schools they want to attend.

of Social Work Programs, which summarizes the concentration options at each school. Some of the concentration options are policy analysis, planning, research and administration, community organization, direct practice with individuals and small groups, direct practice with large groups, program development, community mental health, family functioning, health care, inner-city neighborhood services, social work in school systems, child welfare, consultation, aging, and crime and delinquency.[48]

Individuals with MSW degrees often, within a year or two following graduation, assume supervisory or administrative responsibilities.

The 1992 revised Curriculum Policy Statement of CSWE specifies the following competencies for graduates of a master's-level program:

> *Graduates of a master's social work program are advanced practitioners who can analyze, intervene, and evaluate in ways that are highly differentiated, discriminating, and self-critical. They must synthesize and apply a broad range of knowledge as well as practice with a high degree of autonomy and skill. They must be able to refine and advance the quality of their practice as well as that of the larger social work profession. These advanced competencies must be appropriately integrated and reflected in all aspects of their social work practice, including their ability to:*
>
> 1. *Apply critical thinking skills within professional contexts, including synthesizing and applying appropriate theories and knowledge to practice interventions.*
> 2. *Practice within the values and ethics of the social work profession and with an understanding of and respect for the positive value of diversity.*
> 3. *Demonstrate the professional use of self.*
> 4. *Understand the forms and mechanisms of oppression and discrimination and the strategies and skills of change that advance social and economic justice.*
> 5. *Understand the history of the social work profession and its current structures and issues.*
> 6. *Apply the knowledge and skills of a generalist social work perspective to practice with client systems of all sizes.*
> 7. *Apply the knowledge and skills of advanced social work practice in an area of concentration.*
> 8. *Critically analyze and apply knowledge of bio-psycho-social variables that affect individual development and behavior, and use theoretical frameworks to understand the interactions among and between individuals and social systems (i.e., families, groups, organizations, and communities).*
> 9. *Analyze the impact of social policies on client systems, workers, and agencies and demonstrate skills for influencing policy formulation and change.*
> 10. *Evaluate relevant research studies and apply findings to practice, and demonstrate skills in quantitative and qualitative research design, data analysis, and knowledge dissemination.*
> 11. *Conduct empirical evaluations of their own practice interventions and those of other relevant systems.*
> 12. *Use complex communication skills differentially with a variety of client populations, colleagues, and members of the community.*
> 13. *Use supervision and consultation appropriate to advanced practice in an area of concentration.*
> 14. *Function within the structure of organizations and service delivery systems and seek necessary organizational change.* *

These outcomes (or competencies) constitute the knowledge, skills, and values needed for beginning-level and advanced-level social work practice.

At the advanced graduate level two additional programs are offered by some schools: (1) a

---

*Reprinted from *Curriculum Policy Statement for Baccalaureate Degree Programs in Social Work Education,* Final Draft July 8, 1992, by permission of the Council on Social Work Education, Alexandria, VA.

"third-year" program aimed at strengthening the professional skills of the student and (2) a Doctor of Social Work (DSW) or Doctor of Philosophy (PhD) degree. The doctoral program requires two or more years of postgraduate studies.

YOUR FUTURE IN COMBATING HUMAN PROBLEMS

This text has described social work and social welfare. A major thrust has been to illustrate the social problems and the diverse fields of practice in which social workers and other human service professionals seek to combat human problems. Through case examples I've tried to show some of the frustrations and gratifications encountered in social work practice. This final chapter has described generalist social work practice. All of this information is designed to help you make a career decision about whether social work is a profession you want to pursue.

Test your interest by answering these questions:

1. Do you enjoy working closely and intensely with people?
2. Do you think you could cope with failure?
3. Do you think you would be willing to acquire the knowledge, skills, and values necessary to make life more meaningful to individuals, groups, families, organizations, and communities?
4. Do you think you would like a profession dedicated to social change and to combating social injustice?

If you honestly can answer yet to each of these questions, you may well have the potential to become an effective social worker.

Whether or not you decide to pursue a career in social work, the material in this text on social problems and social services will give you a framework for making responsible citizenship decisions. As a voter you help decide which political officials will be elected to work for the expansion or the curtailment of social welfare services. You have the opportunity to be a volunteer for a human service agency, to serve on boards and committees of agencies, to participate in fund raisers for human service programs, to become involved in legislative processes that address human issues, and to influence others in daily interactions about controversial social welfare issues. Changes in the structure and functioning of the social welfare system are inevitable. You can work for the improvement of human living conditions. As John F. Kennedy, in his 1961 Presidential Inaugural Address, so eloquently stated, "Ask not what your country can do for you. Ask what you can do for your country."[49]

SUMMARY

A generalist social worker is trained to use the problem-solving process to assess and intervene with the problems confronting individuals, families, groups, organizations, and communities. A social worker uses a change process in working with clients. (Clients include individuals, groups, families, organizations, and communities.) The change process can be conceptualized as involving eight phases: defining issues, collecting and assessing data, planning and contracting, identifying alternative interventions, selecting and implementing appropriate courses of action, using appropriate research to monitor and evaluate outcomes, applying appropriate research-based knowledge and technological advances, and termination.

Social workers are expected to be knowledgeable and skillful in filling a variety of roles, including enabler, broker, advocate, activist, mediator, negotiator, educator, initiator, coordinator, researcher, group facilitator, and public speaker.

Social work with individuals is aimed at helping people on a one-to-one basis to resolve personal and social problems.

When there are problems in a family, social services are often needed. There is extensive variation in the types and forms of services that are provided by social workers to troubled families.

One of the many social services provided to families is family therapy.

Almost every social service agency now provides some group services. The focus of social work groups has considerable variation, including social conversation, recreation, recreation-skill development, education, task, problem solving and decision making, self-help, socialization, therapy, and sensitivity training. The goal in therapy groups is generally to have each member explore, in depth, his or her personal or emotional problems and to develop a strategy to resolve those problems. In contrast, sensitivity groups seek to foster increased personal and interpersonal awareness and to develop more effective interaction patterns.

An organization is a collectivity of individuals gathered together to serve a purpose. The roles of social workers within organizations, and their interactions with organizations (including their attempts to manipulate organizations), define much of what social workers do. There are basic structural conflicts between helping professionals and the bureaucratic systems in which they work. A number of suggestions have been offered on how social workers can survive and thrive in a bureaucracy.

Community practice is the process of stimulating and assisting the local community to evaluate, plan, and coordinate efforts to meet its needs. Social work is one of several disciplines that provides training in community practice. Practically all social workers, in one capacity or another, become involved in community practice efforts. Three models of community practice are: locality development, social planning, and social action. The locality development model asserts that community change can best be brought about through broad participation of a wide spectrum of people at the local community level. The basic theme is "Together we can figure out what to do and then do it." The social planning model emphasizes the process of problem solving. The role of the expert is stressed in this approach to identifying and resolving social problems. The theme of this approach is "Let's get the facts and take the next rational steps." The social action model seeks to organize an oppressed group in order to pressure the power structure for increased resources or for social justice. The basic theme of this approach is "Let's organize to overpower our oppressor."

To provide clients with competent service, social workers must have knowledge, skills, and values that are consistent with effective practice. The value base of social work includes respect for the dignity and uniqueness of each individual, clients' right to self-determination, confidentiality, advocacy and social action to ensure the rights of those who are oppressed, accountability, and an institutional orientation.

The primary educational objective for undergraduate social work programs accredited by the Council on Social Work Education (CSWE) is preparation for beginning professional social work practice. All accredited undergraduate and graduate social work programs are required to train their students for generalist practice. (MSW programs, in addition, usually require their students to select and study in an area of specialization.)

Whether or not you decide to pursue social work as a career, you can get involved in combating human problems.

NOTES

1. Joseph Anderson, *Social Work Methods and Processes* (Belmont, CA: Wadsworth, 1981).
2. Donald Brieland, Lela B. Costin, and Charles R. Atherton, *Contemporary Social Work: An Introduction to Social Work and Social Welfare*, 3d ed. (New York: McGraw-Hill, 1985), pp. 120–121.
3. G. H. Hull, *Social Work Internship Manual* (Eau Claire: University of Wisconsin–Eau Claire, Department of Social Work, 1990), p. 17.
4. *Curriculum Policy Statement for Baccalaureate Degree Programs in Social Work Education* (Alexandria, VA: Council on Social Work Education, 1992); and *Curriculum Policy Statement for Master's Degree Programs in Social Work Education* (Alexandria, VA: Council on Social Work Education, 1992).
5. Felix P. Biestek, *The Casework Relationship* (Chicago: Loyola University Press, 1957).
6. Alfred Kadushin, *Child Welfare Services*, 3d ed. (New York: Macmillan, 1980).
7. Virginia Satir, *Conjoint Family Therapy*, rev. ed. (Palo Alto, CA: Science & Behavior Books, 1967);

and Virginia Satir, *Peoplemaking* (Palo Alto, CA: Science & Behavior Books, 1972).

8. Satir, *Conjoint Family Therapy*, pp. 8–10.

9. Ibid., p. 92.

10. Irene Goldenberg and Herbert Goldenberg, *Family Therapy*, 3d ed. (Pacific Grove, CA: Brooks/Cole, 1991), p. 242.

11. B. Okun and L. Rappaport, *Working with Families: An Introduction to Family Therapy* (North Scituate, MA: Duxbury Press, 1980), p. 93.

12. Michael S. Olmstead, *The Small Group* (New York: Random House, 1959), pp. 21–22.

13. Gerald L. Euster, "Services to Groups," in *Contemporary Social Work*, Donald Brieland, Lela B. Costin, and Charles R. Atherton, eds. (New York: McGraw-Hill, 1975), p. 227.

14. Ibid.

15. Ralph Dolgoff and Donald Feldstein, *Understanding Social Welfare* (New York: Harper & Row, 1980), pp. 27–42.

16. Alfred H. Katz and Eugene I. Bender, *The Strength in Us: Self-Help Groups in the Modern World* (New York: Franklin-Watts, 1976), p. 9.

17. Alan Gartner and Frank Riessman, *Help: A Working Guide to Self-Help Groups* (New York: Franklin-Watts, 1980).

18. Frank Riessman, "The 'Helper Therapy' Principle," *Journal of Social Work* (April 1965), pp. 27–34.

19. Kurt Lewin, "Group Decision and Social Change," in *Readings in Social Psychology*, G. E. Swanson, T. M. Newcomb, and E. L. Hartley, eds. (New York: Holt, 1952). pp. 32–43.

20. S. E. Asch, "Opinions and Social Pressure," *Scientific American*, 193, no. 5 (1955), pp. 31–35.

21. A. Etzioni, *Modern Organizations* (Englewood Cliffs, NJ: Prentice-Hall, 1964), p. 1.

22. F. E. Netting, P. M. Kettner, and S. L. McMurtry, *Social Work Macro Practice* (New York: Longmans, 1993), p. 123.

23. Ibid.

24. R. Knopf, *Surviving the BS (Bureaucratic System)* (Wilmington, NC: Mandala Press, 1979), pp. 21–22.

25. Ibid., p. 25.

26. Ibid.

27. Ibid.

28. A. Panitch, "Community Organization," in *Contemporary Social Work*, 2d ed., Donald Brieland, Lela Costin, and Charles Atherton, eds. (New York: McGraw-Hill, 1980), pp. 124–125.

29. Neil Gilbert and Harry Specht, "Social Planning and Community Organization: Approaches," *Encyclopedia of Social Work*, 17th ed. (Washington, DC: National Association of Social Workers, 1977), pp. 1412–1425.

30. Ibid.

31. Jack Rothman and John E. Tropman, "Models of Community Organization and Macro Practice Perspectives: Their Mixing and Phasing," in *Strategies of Community Organization*, 4th ed., Fred Cox, John Erlich, Jack Rothman, and John E. Tropman, eds. (Itasca, IL: Peacock, 1987), pp. 3–26.

32. Saul Alinsky, *Rules for Radicals* (New York: Random House, 1972), p. 130.

33. Saul Alinsky, *Reveille for Radicals* (New York: Basic Books, 1969), p. 72.

34. *Curriculum Policy Statement for Baccalaureate Degree Programs in Social Work Education*; and *Curriculum Policy Statement for Master's Degree Programs in Social Work Education*.

35. Ronald Federico, *The Social Welfare Institution* (Lexington, MA: Heath, 1973), pp. 146–147.

36. Betty L. Baer, "Developing a New Curriculum for Social Work Education" in *The Pursuit of Competence in Social Work*, Frank Clark and Morton Arkava, eds. (San Francisco: Jossey-Bass, 1979), p. 106.

37. Betty L. Baer and Ronald Federico, *Educating the Baccalaureate Social Worker* (Cambridge, MA: Ballinger, 1978), pp. 92–95.

38. Allen Pincus and Anne Minahan, *Social Work Practice: Model and Method* (Itasca, IL: Peacock, 1973), p. 38.

39. Albert Ellis and R. Harper, *A New Guide to Rational Living* (North Hollywood, CA: Wilshire Books, 1975).

40. C. H. Cooley, *Human Nature and the Social Order* (New York: Scribners, 1902).

41. William Glasser, *The Identity Society* (New York: Harper & Row, 1972).

42. Thomas Gordon, *Parent Effectiveness Training* (New York: Wyden, 1973).

43. Mathew Dumont, *The Absurd Healer* (New York: Viking, 1968), p. 60.

44. "Tarsoff v. Regents of University of California: The Psychotherapist's Peril," *University of Pittsburg Law Review*, 37 (1975), pp. 159–164.

45. Suanna J. Wilson, *Confidentiality in Social Work: Issues and Principles* (New York: Free Press, 1978), pp. 116–117.

46. Ibid., p. 121.

47. "Standards for the Accreditation of Baccalaureate Degree Programs in Social Work" (New York: Council on Social Work Education, 1974), p. 13.

48. *Summary Information on Master of Social Work Programs: 1994* (Alexandria, VA: Council on Social Work Education, 1994).

49. Quoted in James A. Henretta, W. Elliot Brownlee, David Brody, and Susan Ware, *America's History* (Chicago: Dorsey Press, 1987), p. 875.

APPENDIX A

THE NASW

CODE OF

ETHICS*

The National Association of Social Workers, Inc. (NASW), is the professional association that represents the social work profession in the United States. Its Code of Ethics summarizes important practice ethics for social workers and is presented as follows:

Preamble

This code is intended to serve as a guide to the everyday conduct of members of the social work profession and as a basis for the adjudication of issues in ethics when the conduct of social workers is alleged to deviate from the standards expressed or implied in this code. It represents standards of ethical behavior for social workers in professional relationships with those served, with colleagues, with employers, with other individuals and professions, and with the community and society as a whole. It also embodies standards of ethical behavior governing individual conduct to the extent that such conduct is associated with an individual's status and identity as a social worker.

This code is based on the fundamental values of the social work profession that include the worth, dignity, and uniqueness of all persons as well as their rights and opportunities. It is also based on the nature of social work, which fosters conditions that promote these values.

In subscribing to and abiding by this code, the social worker is expected to view ethical responsibility in as inclusive a context as each situation demands and within which ethical judgment is required. The social worker is expected to take into consideration all the principles in this code that have a bearing upon any situation in which ethical judgment is to be exercised and professional intervention or conduct is planned. The course of action that the social worker chooses is expected to be consistent with the spirit as well as the letter of this code.

In itself, this code does not represent a set of rules that will prescribe all the behaviors of social workers in all the complexities of professional life. Rather it offers general principles to guide conduct, and the judicious appraisal of conduct, in situations that have ethical implications. It pro-

*Reprinted by permission of the National Association of Social Workers, Inc.

vides the basis for making judgments about ethical actions before and after they occur. Frequently, the particular situation determines the ethical principles that apply and the manner of their application. In such cases, not only the particular ethical principles are taken into immediate consideration, but also the entire code and its spirit. Specific applications of ethical principles must be judged within the context in which they are being considered. Ethical behavior in a given situation must satisfy not only the judgment of the individual social worker, but also the judgment of an unbiased jury of professional peers.

This code should not be used as an instrument to deprive any social worker of the opportunity or freedom to practice with complete professional integrity; nor should any disciplinary action be taken on the basis of this code without maximum provision for safeguarding the rights of the social worker affected.

The ethical behavior of social workers results not from edict, but from a personal commitment of the individual. This code is offered to affirm the will and zeal of all social workers to be ethical and to act ethically in all that they do as social workers.

The following codified ethical principles should guide social workers in the various roles and relationships and at the various levels of responsibility in which they function professionally. These principles also serve as a basis for the adjudication by the National Association of Social Workers of issues in ethics.

In subscribing to this code, social workers are required to cooperate in its implementation and abide by any disciplinary rulings based on it. They should also take adequate measures to discourage, prevent, expose, and correct the unethical conduct of colleagues. Finally, social workers should be equally ready to defend and assist colleagues unjustly charged with unethical conduct.

I. The social worker's conduct and comportment as a social worker.
   A. Propriety. The social worker should maintain high standards of personal conduct in the capacity or identity as social worker.

1. The private conduct of the social worker is a personal matter to the same degree as is any other person's, except when such conduct compromises the fulfillment of professional responsibilities.
2. The social worker should not participate in, condone, or be associated with dishonesty, fraud, deceit, or misrepresentation.
3. The social worker should distinguish clearly between statements and actions made as a private individual and as a representative of the social work profession or an organization or group.

   B. Competence and professional development. The social worker should strive to become and remain proficient in professional practice and the performance of professional functions.

1. The social worker should accept responsibility or employment only on the basis of existing competence or the intention to acquire the necessary competence.
2. The social worker should not misrepresent professional qualifications, education, experience, or affiliations.
3. The social worker should not allow his or her own personal problems, psychosocial distress, substance abuse, or mental health difficulties to interfere with professional judgment and performance or jeopardize the best interests of those for whom the social worker has a professional responsibility.
4. The social worker whose personal problems, psychosocial distress, substance abuse, or mental health difficulties interfere with professional judgment and performance should immediately seek consultation and take appropriate remedial action by seeking professional help, making adjustments in workload, terminating practice, or taking any other steps

necessary to protect clients and others.

C. Service. The social worker should regard as primary the service obligation of the social work profession.

1. The social worker should retain ultimate responsibility for the quality and extent of the service that individual assumes, assigns, or performs.

2. The social worker should act to prevent practices that are inhumane or discriminatory against any person or group of persons.

D. Integrity. The social worker should act in accordance with the highest standards of professional integrity and impartiality.

1. The social worker should be alert to and resist the influences and pressures that interfere with the exercise of professional discretion and impartial judgment required for the performance of professional functions.

2. The social worker should not exploit professional relationships for personal gain.

E. Scholarship and research. The social worker engaged in study and research should be guided by the conventions of scholarly inquiry.

1. The social worker engaged in research should consider carefully its possible consequences for human beings.

2. The social worker engaged in research should ascertain that the consent of participants in the research is voluntary and informed, without any implied deprivation or penalty for refusal to participate, and with due regard for participants' privacy and dignity.

3. The social worker engaged in research should protect participants from unwarranted physical or mental discomfort, distress, harm, danger, or deprivation.

4. The social worker who engages in the evaluation of services or cases should discuss them only for professional purposes and only with persons directly and professionally concerned with them.

5. Information obtained about participants in research should be treated as confidential.

6. The social worker should take credit only for work actually done in connection with scholarly and research endeavors and credit contributions made by others.

II. The social worker's ethical responsibility to clients.

F. Primacy of clients' interests. The social worker's primary responsibility is to clients.

1. The social worker should serve clients with devotion, loyalty, determination, and the maximum application of professional skill and competence.

2. The social worker should not exploit relationships with clients for personal advantage.

3. The social worker should not practice, condone, facilitate, or collaborate with any form of discrimination on the basis of race, color, sex, sexual orientation, age, religion, national origin, marital status, political belief, mental or physical handicap, or any other preference or personal characteristic, condition, or status.

4. The social worker should not condone or engage in any dual or multiple relationships with clients or former clients in which there is a risk of exploitation of or potential harm to the client. The social worker is responsible for setting clear, appropriate, and culturally sensitive boundaries.

5. The social worker should under no circumstances engage in sexual activities with clients.

6. The social worker should provide clients with accurate and complete information regarding the extent and

nature of the services available to them.

7. The social worker should apprise clients of their risks, rights, opportunities, and obligations associated with social service to them.

8. The social worker should seek advice and counsel of colleagues and supervisors whenever such consultation is in the best interest of clients.

9. The social worker should terminate service to clients, and professional relationships with them, when such service and relationships are no longer required or no longer serve the clients' needs or interests.

10. The social worker should withdraw services precipitously only under unusual circumstances, giving careful consideration to all factors in the situation and taking care to minimize possible adverse effects.

11. The social worker who anticipates the termination or interruption of service to clients should notify clients promptly and seek the transfer, referral, or continuation of service in relation to the clients' needs and preferences.

G. Rights and prerogatives of clients. The social worker should make every effort to foster maximum self-determination on the part of clients.

1. When the social worker must act on behalf of a client who has been adjudged legally incompetent, the social worker should safeguard the interests and rights of that client.

2. When another individual has been legally authorized to act in behalf of a client, the social worker should deal with that person always with the client's best interest in mind.

3. The social worker should not engage in any action that violates or diminishes the civil or legal rights of clients.

H. Confidentiality and privacy. The social worker should respect the privacy of clients and hold in confidence all information obtained in the course of professional service.

1. The social worker should share with others confidences revealed by clients, without their consent, only for compelling professional reasons.

2. The social worker should inform clients fully about the limits of confidentiality in a given situation, the purposes for which information is obtained, and how it may be used.

3. The social worker should afford clients reasonable access to any official social work records concerning them.

4. When providing clients with access to records, the social worker should take due care to protect the confidences of others contained in those records.

5. The social worker should obtain informed consent of clients before taping, recording, or permitting third-party observation of their activities.

I. Fees. When setting fees, the social worker should ensure that they are fair, reasonable, considerate and commensurate with the service performed and with due regard for the clients' ability to pay.

1. The social worker should not divide a fee or accept or give anything of value for receiving or making a referral.

III. The social worker's ethical responsibility to colleagues.

J. Respect, fairness, and courtesy. The social worker should treat colleagues with respect, courtesy, fairness, and good faith.

1. The social worker should cooperate with colleagues to promote professional interests and concerns.

2. The social worker should respect confidences shared by colleagues in the course of their professional relationships and transactions.

3. The social worker should create and maintain conditions of practice that facilitate ethical and competent professional performance by colleagues.

4. The social worker should treat with respect, and represent accurately and fairly, the qualifications, views, and findings of colleagues and use appropriate channels to express judgments on these matters.

5. The social worker who replaces or is replaced by a colleague in professional practice should act with consideration for the interest, character, and reputation of that colleague.

6. The social worker should not exploit a dispute between a colleague and employers to obtain a position or otherwise advance the social worker's interest.

7. The social worker should seek arbitration or mediation when conflicts with colleagues require resolution for compelling professional reasons.

8. The social worker should extend to colleagues of other professions the same respect and cooperation that is extended to social work colleagues.

9. The social worker who serves as an employer, supervisor, or mentor to colleagues should make orderly and explicit arrangements regarding the conditions of their continuing professional relationship.

10. The social worker who has the responsibility for employing and evaluating the performance of other staff members should fulfill such responsibility in a fair, considerate, and equitable manner, on the basis of clearly enunciated criteria.

11. The social worker who has the responsibility for evaluating the performance of employees, supervisees, or students should share evaluations with them.

12. The social worker should not use a professional position vested with power, such as that of employer, supervisor, teacher, or consultant, to his or her advantage or to exploit others.

13. The social worker who has direct knowledge of a social work colleague's impairment due to personal problems, psychosocial distress, substance abuse, or mental health difficulties should consult with that colleague and assist the colleague in taking remedial action.

K. Dealing with colleagues' clients. The social worker has the responsibility to relate to the clients of colleagues with full professional consideration.

1. The social worker should not assume professional responsibility for the clients of another agency or a colleague without appropriate communication with that agency or colleague.

2. The social worker who serves the clients of colleagues, during a temporary absence or emergency, should serve those clients with the same consideration as that afforded any client.

IV. The social worker's ethical responsibility to employers and employing organizations.

L. Commitments to employing organizations. The social worker should adhere to commitments made to the employing organizations.

1. The social worker should work to improve the employing agency's policies and procedures and the efficiency and effectiveness of its services.

2. The social worker should not accept employment or arrange student field placements in an organization which is currently under public sanction by NASW for violating personnel standards or imposing limitations on or penalties for professional actions on behalf of clients.

3. The social worker should act to prevent and eliminate discrimination in the employing organization's work assignments and in its employment policies and practices.

4. The social worker should use with scrupulous regard, and only for the purpose for which they are intended,

the resources of the employing organization.

V. The social worker's ethical responsibility to the social work profession.

M. Maintaining the integrity of the profession. The social worker should uphold and advance the values, ethics, knowledge, and mission of the profession.

1. The social worker should protect and enhance the dignity and integrity of the profession and should be responsible and vigorous in discussion and criticism of the profession.

2. The social worker should take action through appropriate channels against unethical conduct by any other member of the profession.

3. The social worker should act to prevent the unauthorized and unqualified practice of social work.

4. The social worker should make no misrepresentation in advertising as to qualifications, competence, service, or results to be achieved.

N. Community service. The social worker should assist the profession in making social services available to the general public.

1. The social worker should contribute time and professional expertise to activities that promote respect for the utility, the integrity, and the competence of the social work profession.

2. The social worker should support the formulation, development, enactment, and implementation of social policies of concern to the profession.

O. Development of knowledge. The social worker should take responsibility for identifying, developing, and fully utilizing knowledge for professional practice.

1. The social worker should base practice upon recognized knowledge relevant to social work.

2. The social worker should critically examine, and keep current with, emerging knowledge relevant to social work.

3. The social worker should contribute to the knowledge base of social work and share research knowledge and practice wisdom with colleagues.

VI. The social worker's ethical responsibility to society.

P. Promoting the general welfare. The social worker should promote the general welfare of society.

1. The social worker should act to prevent and eliminate discrimination against any person or group on the basis of race, color, sex, sexual orientation, age, religion, national origin, marital status, political belief, mental or physical handicap, or any other preference or personal characteristic, condition, or status.

2. The social worker should act to ensure that all persons have access to the resources, services, and opportunities which they require.

3. The social worker should act to expand choice and opportunity for all persons, with special regard for disadvantaged or oppressed groups and persons.

4. The social worker should promote conditions that encourage respect for the diversity of cultures which constitute American society.

5. The social worker should provide appropriate professional services in public emergencies.

6. The social worker should advocate changes in policy and legislation to improve social conditions and to promote social justice.

7. The social worker should encourage informed participation by the public in shaping social policies and institutions.

APPENDIX B

CANADIAN

ASSOCIATION OF

SOCIAL WORKERS'

CODE OF ETHICS*

DEFINITIONS

In this Code,
Best interest of client means

(a) that the wishes, desires, motivations, and plans of the client are taken by the social worker as the primary consideration in any intervention plan developed by the social worker subject to change only when the client's plans are documented to be unrealistic, unreasonable or potentially harmful to self or others or otherwise determined inappropriate when considered in relation to a mandated requirement,

(b) that all actions and interventions of the social worker are taken subject to the reasonable belief that the client will benefit from the action, and

(c) that the social worker will consider the client as an individual, a member of a family unit, a member of a community, a person with a distinct ancestry or culture and will consider those factors in any decision affecting the client.

Client[1] means

(a) a person, family, group of persons, incorporated body, association or community on whose behalf a social worker provides or agrees to provide a service
  (i) on request or with agreement[2] of the person, family, group of persons, incorporated body, associations or community, or
  (ii) as a result of a legislated responsibility, or

(b) a judge of a court of competent jurisdiction who orders the social worker to provide to the Court an assessment.[3]

Conduct unbecoming means behaviour or conduct that does not meet standard of care requirements and is therefore subject to discipline.[4]

Malpractice and negligence means behaviour that is included as ''conduct unbecoming'' and relates to social work practice behaviour within the parameters of the professional relationship that falls below the standard of practice and results in or aggravates an injury to a client. Without limiting the generality of the above,[5] it includes behaviour which results in assault, deceit, fraudulent misrepresentations, defamation of character, breach of contract, violation of human rights, malicious prosecution, false imprisonment or criminal conviction.

Practice of social work includes the assessment, remediation and prevention of social problems, and the enhancement of social functioning of individuals, families, groups and communities by means of

(a) the provision of direct counselling services within an established relationship between a social worker and client;

(b) the development, promotion and delivery of human service programs, including that done in collaboration with other professionals;

(c) the development and promotion of social policies aimed at improving social conditions and equality; and [6]

(d) any other activities approved by CASW.[7]

Social worker means a person who is duly registered to practice social work in a province or territory or where mandatory registration does not exist, a person practising social work who voluntarily agrees to be subject to this Code.

Standard of practice means the standard of care ordinarily expected of a competent social worker. It means that the public is assured that a social worker has the training, the skill and the diligence to provide them with professional social work services.

PREAMBLE

Philosophy

The profession of social work is founded on humanitarian and egalitarian ideas. Social workers believe in the intrinsic worth and dignity of every human being and are committed to the values of acceptance, self-determination and respect of individuality. They believe in the obligation of all people, individually and collectively, to provide resources, services and opportunities for the overall benefit of humanity. The culture of individuals, families, groups, communities and nations has to be respected without prejudice.[8]

Social workers are dedicated to the welfare and self-realization of human beings; to the development and disciplined use of scientific knowledge regarding human and societal behaviors; to the development of resources to meet individual, group, national and international needs and aspirations; and to the achievement of social justice for all.

Professional Practice Conflicts

If a conflict arises in professional practice, the standards declared in this Code take precedence. Conflicts of interest may occur because of demands from the general public, workplace, organizations or clients. In all cases, if the ethical duties and obligations or ethical responsibilities of this Code would be compromised, the social worker must act in a manner consistent with this Code.

Nature of This Code

The first seven statements in this code establish ethical duties and obligations. These statements provide the basis of a social worker's relationship with a client and are based on the values of social work. A breach of any of these statements forms the basis of a disciplinary action. The remaining three statements are characterized as ethical responsibilities and are seen as being different from the ethical duties and obligations. These ethical responsibilities are not likely to form the basis of any disciplinary action if breached. However these sections may form the basis of inquiry. These ethical responsibilities may be used in conjunction with breaches of other sections of this

Code and may form the basis of necessary background information in any action for discipline. Of equal importance, these ethical responsibilities are desirable goals to be achieved by the social work profession which by its nature is driven by an adherence to the values that form the basis of these desirable ethical behaviours.

SOCIAL WORK CODE OF ETHICS

Ethical Duties and Obligations

1. A social worker shall maintain the best interest of the client as the primary professional obligation.
2. A social worker shall carry out her or his professional duties and obligations with integrity and objectivity.
3. A social worker shall have and maintain competence in the provision of a social work service to a client.
4. A social worker shall not exploit the relationship with a client for personal benefit, gain or gratification.
5. A social worker shall protect the confidentiality of all information acquired from the client or others regarding the client and the client's family during the professional relationship unless
   (a) the client authorizes in writing the release of specified information
   (b) the information is released under the authority of a statute or an order of a court of competent jurisdiction, or
   (c) otherwise authorized by this Code.
6. A social worker who engages in another profession, occupation, affiliation or calling shall not allow these outside interests to affect the social work relationship with the client.
7. A social worker in private practice shall not conduct the business of provision of social work services for a fee in a manner that discredits the profession or diminishes the public's trust in the profession.

Ethical Responsibilities

8. A social worker shall advocate for workplace conditions and policies that are consistent with the Code.
9. A social worker shall promote excellence in the social work profession.
10. A social worker shall advocate change
    (a) in the best interest of the client, and
    (b) for the overall benefit of society, the environment and the global community.

Primary Professional Obligation

1. A social worker shall maintain the best interest of the client as the primary professional obligation.
1.1 The social worker is to be guided primarily by this obligation. Any action which is substantially inconsistent with this obligation is an unethical action.
1.2 A social worker in the practice of social work shall not discriminate against any person on the basis of race, ethnic background, language, religion, marital status, sex, sexual orientation, age, abilities, socio-economic status, political affiliation or national ancestry.[9]
1.3 A social worker shall inform a client of the client's right to consult another professional at any time during the provision of social work services.
1.4 A social worker shall immediately inform the client of any factor, condition[10] or pressure that affects the social worker's ability to perform an acceptable level of service.
1.5 A social worker shall not become involved in a client's personal affairs that are not relevant to the service being provided.
1.6 A social worker shall not state an opinion, judgment or use a clinical diagnosis unless there is a documented assessment, observation or diagnosis to support the opinion, judgment or diagnosis.
1.7 Where possible, a social worker shall provide or secure social work services in the language chosen by the client.

Integrity and Objectivity

2. A social worker shall carry out his or her professional duties and obligations with integrity and objectivity.[11]

2.1 The social worker shall identify and describe education, training, experience, professional affiliations, competence, and nature of service in an honest and accurate manner.

2.2 The social worker shall explain to the client her or his education, experience, training, competence, nature of service and action at the request of the client.

2.3 A social worker shall cite an educational degree only after it has been received from the institution.

2.4 A social worker shall not claim formal social work education in an area of expertise or training solely by attending a lecture, demonstration, conference, panel discussion, workshop, seminar or other similar teaching presentation.[12]

2.5 The social worker shall not make a false, misleading or exaggerated claim of efficacy regarding past or anticipated achievement with respect to clients.

2.6 The social worker shall distinguish between actions and statements made as a private citizen and actions and statements made as a social worker.[13]

Competence in the Provision of Social Work Services

3. A social worker shall have and maintain competence in the provision of a social work service to a client.

3.1 The social worker shall not undertake a social work service unless the social worker has the competence to provide the service or the social worker can reasonably acquire the necessary competence without undue delay, risk or expense to the client.

3.2 Where a social worker cannot reasonably acquire the necessary competence in the provision of a service to a client, the social worker shall decline to provide the service to the client, advising the client of the reason and ensuring that the client is referred to another professional person if the client agrees to the referral.

3.3 The social worker, with the agreement of the client, may obtain advice from other professionals in the provision of service to a client.

3.4 A social worker shall maintain an acceptable level of health and well-being in order to provide a competent level of service to a client.[14]

3.5 Where the social worker has a physical or mental health problem, disability or illness that affects the ability of the social worker to provide competent service or that would threaten the health or well-being of the client, the social worker shall discontinue the provision of social work service to a client
    (a) advising the client of the reason and,[15]
    (b) ensuring that the client is referred to another professional person if the client agrees to the referral.

3.6 The social worker shall have, maintain and endeavor periodically to update an acceptable level of knowledge and skills to meet the standards of practice of the profession.

Limit on Professional Relationship

4. A social worker shall not exploit the relationship with a client for personal benefit, gain or gratification.

4.1 The social worker shall respect the client and act so that the dignity, individuality and rights of the person are protected.

4.2 The social worker shall assess and consider a client's motivation and physical and mental capacity in arranging for the provision of an appropriate service.

4.3 The social worker shall not have a sexual relationship with a client.

4.4 The social worker shall not have a business relationship with a client, borrow money from a client, or loan money to a client.[16]

4.5 The social worker shall not have a sexual relationship with a social work student assigned to the social worker.

4.6 The social worker shall not sexually harass any person.

Confidential Information

5. A social worker shall protect the confidentiality[17] of all information required from the client or others regarding the client and the client's family during the professional relationship[18] unless
   (a) the client authorizes in writing the release of specified information,[19]
   (b) the information is released under the authority of a statute or an order of a court of relevant jurisdiction, or
   (c) otherwise authorized under this Code.
5.1 The requirement of confidentiality also applies to social workers who work as
   (a) supervisors,
   (b) managers,
   (c) educators, or
   (d) administrators.
5.2 A social worker who works as a supervisor, manager or administrator shall establish policies and practices that protect the confidentiality of client information.
5.3 The social worker may disclose confidential information to other persons in the workplace who, by virtue of their responsibilities, have an identified need to know as determined by the social worker.
5.4 Clients shall be the initial or primary source of information about themselves and their problems unless the client is incapable or unwilling to give information or when corroborative reporting is required.
5.5 The social worker has the obligation to ensure that the client understands what is being asked, why and to what purpose the information will be used, and to understand the confidentiality policies and practices of the workplace setting.
5.6 Where information is required by law, the social worker shall explain to the client the consequences of refusing to provide the requested information.
5.7 Where information is required from other sources, the social worker
   (a) shall explain the requirement to the client, and
   (b) shall attempt to involve the client in selecting the sources to be used.
5.8 The social worker shall take reasonable care to safeguard the client's personal papers or property if the social worker agrees to keep the property at the request of the client.

Recording Information
5.9 The social worker shall maintain only one master file on each client.[20]
5.10 The social worker shall record all relevant information, and keep all relevant documents in the file.
5.11 The social worker shall not record in a client's file any characterization that is not based on clinical assessment or fact.

Accessibility of Records
5.12 The social worker who contracts for the delivery of social work services with a client is responsible to the client for maintaining the client record.
5.13 The social worker who is employed by a social agency that delivers social work services to clients is responsible
   (a) to the client for the maintaining of a client record, and
   (b) to the agency to maintain the records to facilitate the objectives of the agency.
5.14 A social worker is obligated to follow the provision of a statute that allows access to records by clients.
5.15 The social worker shall respect the client's right of access to a client record subject to the social worker's right to refuse access for just and reasonable cause.
5.16 Where a social worker refuses a client the right to access a file or part of a file, the social worker shall advise the client of the right to request a review of the decision in accordance with the relevant statute, workplace policy or other relevant procedure.

Disclosure
5.17 The social worker shall not disclose the

identity of persons who have sought a social work service or disclose sources of information about clients unless compelled legally to do so.[21]

5.18 The obligation to maintain confidentiality continues indefinitely after the social worker has ceased contact with the client.

5.19 The social worker shall avoid unnecessary conversation regarding clients.

5.20 The social worker may divulge confidential information with consent of the client, preferably expressed in writing, where this is essential to a plan of care or treatment.

5.21 The social worker shall transfer information to another agency or individual, only with the informed consent of the client or guardian of the client and then only with the reasonable assurance that the receiving agency provides the same guarantee of confidentiality and respect for the right of privileged communication as provided by the sending agency.

5.22 The social worker shall explain to the client the disclosure of information requirements of the law or of the agency before the commencement of the provision of social work services.

5.23 The social worker in practice with groups and communities shall notify the participants of the likelihood that aspects of their private lives may be revealed in the course of their work together, and therefore require a commitment from each member to respect the privileged and confidential nature of the communication between and among members of the client group.

5.24 Subject to section 5.26, the social worker shall not disclose information acquired from one client to a member of the client's family without the informed consent of the client who provided the information.

5.25 A social worker shall disclose information acquired from one client to a member of the client's family where

(a) the information involves a threat of harm to self or others,[22]

(b) the information was acquired from a child of tender years and the social worker determines that its disclosure is in the best interests of the child.[23]

5.26 A social worker shall disclose information acquired from a client to a person or a police officer where the information involves a threat of harm to that person.

5.27 A social worker may release confidential information as part of a discipline hearing of a social worker as directed by the tribunal or disciplinary body.

5.28 When disclosure is required by order of a court, the social worker shall not divulge more information than is reasonably required and shall where possible notify the client of this requirement.

5.29 The social worker shall not use confidential information for the purpose of teaching, public education or research except with the informed consent of the client.

5.30 The social worker may use non-identifying information for the purpose of teaching, public education or research.

Retention and Disposition of Information

5.31 Where the social worker's documentation is stored in a place or computer maintained and operated by an employer, the social worker shall advocate for the responsible retention and disposition of information contained in the file.

Outside Interest

6. A social worker who engages in another profession, occupation, affiliation or calling shall not allow these outside interests to affect the social work relationship with the client.

6.1 A social worker shall declare to the client any outside interests that would affect the social work relationship with the client.

6.2 A social worker shall not allow an outside interest:

(a) to affect the social worker's ability to practise social work;

(b) to present to the client or to the community that the social worker's ability to practise social work is affected; or

(c) to bring the profession of social work into disrepute.[24]

Limit on Private Practice

7. A social worker in private practice shall not conduct the business of provision of social work services for a fee in a manner that discredits the profession or diminishes the public's trust in the profession.

7.1 A social worker shall not use the social work relationship within an agency to obtain clients for his or her private practice.

7.2 Subject to section 7.3, a social worker who enters into a contract for service with a client

(a) shall disclose at the outset of the relationship, the fee schedule for the social work services,

(b) shall not charge a fee that is greater than that agreed to and disclosed to the client, and

(c) shall not charge for hours of service other than the reasonable hours of client services, research, consultation and administrative work directly connected to the case.

7.3 A social worker in private practice may charge differential fees for services except where an increased fee is charged based on race, ethnic background, language, religion, marital status, sex, sexual orientation, age, abilities, socio-economic status, political affiliation or national ancestry.

7.4 A social worker in private practice shall maintain adequate malpractice, defamation and liability insurance.

7.5 A social worker in private practice may charge a rate of interest on delinquent accounts as is allowed by law.[25]

7.6 Notwithstanding section 5.17 a social worker in private practice may pursue civil remedies to ensure payment for services to a client where the social worker has advised the client of this possibility at the outset of the social work service.

Ethical Responsibilities to the Workplace

8. A social worker shall advocate for workplace conditions and policies that are consistent with the Code.

8.1 Where the responsibilities to an employer are in conflict with the social worker's obligations to the client, the social worker shall document the issue in writing and shall bring the situation to the attention of the employer.

8.2 Where a serious ethical conflict continues to exist after the issue has been brought to the attention of the employer, the social worker shall bring the issue to the attention of the Association or regulatory body.[26]

8.3 A social worker shall follow the principles in the Code when dealing with

(a) a social worker under the supervision of the social worker,

(b) an employee under the supervision of the social worker, and

(c) a social work student under the supervision of the social worker.

Ethical Responsibilities to the Profession

9. A social worker shall promote excellence in the social work profession.

9.1 A social worker shall report to the appropriate association or regulatory body any breach of this Code by another social worker which adversely affects or harms a client or prevents the effective delivery of a social service.

9.2 A social worker shall report to the association or regulatory body any unqualified or unlicensed person who is practising social work.

9.3 A social worker shall not intervene in the professional relationship of a social worker and client unless requested to do so by the client and unless convinced that the best interests and well-being of the client require such intervention.

9.4 When a conflict arises between a social worker and other professionals, the social worker shall attempt to resolve the professional differences in ways that uphold the principles of this Code and the honour of the social work profession.

9.5 A social worker engaged in research shall ensure that the involvement of clients in the research is a result of informed consent.

Ethical Responsibilities for Social Change

10. A social worker shall advocate change
   (a) in the best interest of the client, and
   (b) for the overall benefit of society, the environment and the global community.

10.1 A social worker shall identify, document and advocate for the elimination of discrimination.

10.2 A social worker shall advocate for the equal distribution of resources to all persons.

10.3 A social worker shall advocate for the equal access of all persons to resources, services and opportunities.

10.4 A social worker shall advocate for a clean and healthy environment and shall advocate the development of environmental strategies consistent with social work principles.

10.5 A social worker shall provide reasonable professional services in a state of emergency.

10.6 A social worker shall promote social justice.

NOTES

1. A client ceases to be a client 2 years after the termination of a social work service. It is advisable for this termination to be clearly documented on the case file.

2. This sub-paragraph identifies two situations where a person may be considered a voluntary client. The person who requests a social work service is clearly a voluntary client. A person also may originally be receiving services as a result of the actions of a court or other legally mandated entity. This person may receive a service beyond that originally mandated and therefore be able to terminate voluntarily that aspect of the service. A situation where a person is referred by another professional or family member clearly falls into this "voluntary service" relationship when that person agrees with the service to be provided. This type of social work relationship is clearly distinguishable from the relationship in sub-paragraph (ii) where the social worker does not seek or have agreement for the service to be provided.

3. In this situation, the social worker is providing an assessment, information or a professional opinion to a judge of competent jurisdiction to assist the judge in making a ruling or determination. In this situation, the relationship is with the judge and the person on whom the information, assessment or opinion is provided is not the client. The social worker still has some professional obligations towards that person, for example: competence and dignity.

4. In reaching a decision in *Re Matthews and the Board of Directors of Physiotherapy* (1986) 54 O.R. (2d) 375, Saunders J. makes three important statements regarding standards of practice and by implication Code of Ethics:
   (i) Standards of practice are inherent characteristics of any profession.
   (ii) Standards of practice may be written or unwritten.
   (iii) Some conduct is clearly regarded as misconduct and need not be written down whereas other conduct may be the subject of dispute within a profession.

5. The importance of the collective opinion of the profession in establishing and ultimately modifying the Code of Ethics was established in an 1884 case involving the medical profession. Lord Esher, M.R. stated:

> If it is shown that a medical man, in the pursuit of his profession, has done something with regard to it which would be reasonably regarded as disgraceful or dishonourable by his professional brethren of good repute and competency," then it is open to the General Medical Council to say that he has been guilty of "infamous conduct in a professional respect.

6. This definition except paragraph (d) has been taken from *An Act to Incorporate the New Brunswick Association of Social Workers,* chapter 78 of the Statutes of New Brunswick, 1988, section 2.

7. The procedure for adding activities under this paragraph will be established by a bylaw by the CASW Board of Directors.

8. Taken from: *Teaching and Learning about Human Rights; A Manual for School of Social Work and the Social Work Profession*; U.N. Centre for Human Rights, Co-operation with International Federation of Social Workers and International Association of Schools of Social Workers, United Nations, New York, 1992.

9. This obligation goes beyond grounds of discrimination stated in most *Human Rights Legislation* and therefore there is a greater professional obligation than that stated in provincial legislation.

10. The term condition means a physical, mental or psychological condition. There is an implied obligation that the social worker shall actively seek diagnosis and treatment for any signs or warnings of a condition. A disclosure under this section may be of a general nature. See also 3.4.

11. The term objectivity is taken from the Québec Code

of Professional Conduct. See Division 2: Integrity and Objectivity (6.0 Québec) November 5, 1979 Vol. 2 No. 30. The term objectivity is stated in the following: 3.02.01. A social worker must discharge his professional duties with integrity and objectivity.

12. The provincial associations may regulate the areas of expertise to be stated or advertised by a social worker. This will vary in each province according to its enabling legislation. Where there is not sufficient legislative base for this regulation, the claim of an expertise without sufficient training may form the basis of a determination of unprofessional conduct.

13. Even with a distinction made under this section, a social worker's private actions or statements may be of such a nature that the social worker cannot avoid the responsibilities under this Code. See also 6.2(c).

14. This section should be considered in relation to section 1.4 and involves proper maintenance, prevention and treatment of any type of risk to the health or well-being of the social worker.

15. It is not necessary in all circumstances to explain specifically the nature of the problem.

16. Where a social worker does keep money or assets belonging to a client, the social worker should hold this money or asset in a trust account or hold the money or asset in conjunction with an additional professional person.

17. Confidentiality means that information received or observed about a client by a social worker will be held in confidence and disclosed only when the social worker is properly authorized or obligated legally or professionally to do so. This also means that professionally acquired information may be treated as privileged communication and ordinarily only the client has the right to waive privilege.

Privileged communication means statements made within a protected relationship (i.e., husband–wife, professional–client) which the law protects against disclosure. The extent of the privilege is governed by law and not by this Code.

Maintaining confidentiality of privileged communication means that information about clients does not have to be transmitted in any oral, written or recorded form. Such information, for example, does not have to be disclosed to a supervisor, written into a workplace record, stored in a computer or microfilm data base, held on an audio or videotape or discussed orally. The right of privileged communication is respected by the social worker in the practise of social work notwithstanding that this right is not ordinarily granted in law.

The disclosure of confidential information in social work practice involves the obligation to share information professionally with others in the workplace of the social worker as part of a reasonable service to the client. Social workers recognize the need to obtain permission from clients before releasing information about them to sources outside their workplace; and to inform clients at the outset of their relationship that some information acquired may be shared with the officers and personnel of the agency who maintain the case record and who have a reasonable need for the information in the performance of their duties.

18. The social worker's relationship with a client can be characterized as a fiduciary relationship.

In *Fiduciary Duties in Canada* by Ellis, fiduciary duty is described as follows: . . . where one party has placed its "trust and confidence" in another and the latter has accepted—expressly or by operation of law—to act in a manner consistent with the reposing of such "trust and confidence," a fiduciary relationship has been established.

19. The "obligation of secrecy" was discussed by the Supreme Court of Canada in *Halls v. Mitchell*, (1928) S.C.R. 125, an action brought by a disabled CNR worker against a company doctor who had disclosed the employee's medical history, to the latter's detriment. Mr. Justice Duff reviewed the duty of confidentiality:

> We are not required, for the purposes of this appeal, to attempt to state with any sort of precision the limits of the obligation of secrecy which rests upon the medical practitioner in relation to the professional secrets acquired by him in the course of his practice. Nobody would dispute that a secret so acquired is the secret of the patient, and, normally, is under his control, and not under that of the doctor. Prima facie, the patient has the right to require that the secret shall not be divulged; and that right is absolute, unless there is some paramount reason which overrides it.

Thus the right of secrecy/confidentiality rests squarely with the patient; the Court carefully provided that there is an "ownership" extant in the confidentiality of the personal information. Duff J. continued by allowing for "paramount" criteria which vitiates from the right:

> Some reasons may arise, no doubt, from the existence of facts which bring into play overpowering considerations connected with public justice; and there may be cases in which reasons connected with the safety of individuals or of the public, physical or moral, would be sufficiently cogent to supersede or qualify the obligations prima facie imposed by the confidential relation.

Duff J. continued:

> The general duty of medical men to observe secrecy, in relation to information acquired by them confidentially from their patients is subject, no doubt, to some exceptions, which have no operation in the case of solicitors; but the grounds of the legal, social or moral imperatives affecting physicians and surgeons, touching the inviolability of professional confidences, are not, any more than those affecting legal advisers, based exclusively upon the relationships between the parties as individuals.

20. The master file refers to all relevant documents pertaining to the client consisting of such information as demographics, case recordings, court documents, assessments, correspondence, treatment plans, bills, etc. This information is often collected through various means including electronic and computer-driven sources. However the cli-

ent master file exists as one unit, inclusive of all information pertaining to the client, despite the various sources of the recording process. The description and ownership of the master file is most often defined by workplace standards or policies. The client's master file should be prepared keeping in mind that it may have to be revealed to the client or disclosed in legal proceedings.

21. A social worker may be compelled to reveal information under the section when directly ordered by the court to do so. Before disclosing the information, the social worker shall advise the court of the professional obligations that exist under this section of the Code and where reasonably possible inform the client.

22. The case of *Tarasoff* v. *The Regents of the University of California et al.* (1976), 551 p.2d 334 (Cal. Supreme Court) focused on the obligation of a psychiatrist to maintain the confidentiality of his patients' statements in their discussions. In that case the patient told the psychiatrist that the patient had an intention to kill a certain woman. When the patient actually did kill this woman, her parents brought suit alleging that the psychiatrist owed a duty to tell the woman of the danger to her.

It was held that the psychiatrist did have a duty to tell the woman of the threat. The court recognized that the psychiatrist owed a duty to the patient to keep in confidence the statements the patient made in therapy sessions, but held there was also a duty to care to anyone whom the psychiatrist knew might be endangered by the patient. At a certain point the obligation of confidentiality would be overridden by the obligation to this third person. The psychiatrist's knowledge itself gave rise to a duty of care. What conduct would be sufficient to fulfil the duty to this third person would depend on the circumstances, but it might be necessary to give a warning that would reveal what the patient had said about the third party. The court in this case held that the psychiatrist had a duty to warn the woman about the patient's stated intention to kill her, and having failed to warn her the psychiatrist was liable in negligence. Moreover, the court stated that the principle of this duty of care belonged not just to a psychiatrist but also to a psychologist performing therapy. It would follow that the principle would also apply to social workers performing therapy.

23. For the purpose of this Code, a child of tender years shall usually be determined to be a child under the age of seven years subject to a determination by a social worker considering the child's social, physical, intellectual, emotional or psychological development.

24. This section brings the social worker's outside interest and personal actions in line with the professional duties and obligations as set out in this Code.

25. This rate shall be stated on all invoices or bills sent to the client.

26. In this situation the professional obligations outweigh any obligations to a workplace.

PHOTO CREDITS

INDEX

TO THE OWNER OF THIS BOOK:

We hope that you have found *Introduction to Social Work and Social Welfare*, sixth edition, useful. So that this book can be improved in a future edition, would you take the time to complete this sheet and return it? Thank you.

School and address: _____

Department: _____

Instructor's name: _____

1. What I like most about this book is: _____

_____

_____

2. What I like least about this book is: _____

_____

_____

3. My general reaction to this book is: _____

_____

4. The name of the course in which I used this book is: _____

_____

5. Were all of the chapters of the book assigned for you to read? _____

   If not, which ones weren't? _____

 6. In the space below, or on a separate sheet of paper, please write specific suggestions for improving this book and anything else you'd care to share about your experience in using the book.

_____

_____

_____

_____

_____

Optional:

Your name: _____ Date: _____

May Brooks/Cole quote you, either in promotion for *Introduction to Social Work and Social Welfare*, sixth edition, or in future publishing ventures?

Yes: _____ No: _____

Sincerely,

Charles Zastrow

FOLD HERE

FOLD HERE

Brooks/Cole is dedicated to publishing quality publications for education in the human services fields. If you are interested in learning more about our publications, please fill in your name and address and request our latest catalogue, using this prepaid mailer.

Name: ———————————————————————

Street Address: ———————————————————

City, State, and Zip: ————————————————

FOLD HERE

NO POSTAGE
NECESSARY
IF MAILED
IN THE
UNITED STATES

BUSINESS REPLY MAIL

FIRST CLASS   PERMIT NO. 358   PACIFIC GROVE, CA

POSTAGE WILL BE PAID BY ADDRESSEE

ATT: *Human Services Catalogue*

Brooks/Cole Publishing Company
511 Forest Lodge Road
Pacific Grove, California 93950-9968

FOLD HERE